D0903061

# Criminal Law and Procedure: Cases and Materials, Ninth Edition

**Kent Roach**

Faculty of Law, University of Toronto

**Patrick Healy**

Faculty of Law, McGill University

**Gary Trotter**

Faculty of Law, Queen's University

2004
EMOND MONTGOMERY PUBLICATIONS LIMITED
TORONTO, CANADA

Printed in Canada.

Edited, designed, and typeset by WordsWorth Communications, Toronto.

We acknowledge the financial support of the Government of Canada through the Book Publishing Industry Development Program (BPIDP) for our publishing activities.

**Library and Archives Canada Cataloguing in Publication**

Roach, Kent, 1961-
    Criminal law and procedure : cases and materials / Kent Roach, Patrick Healy, Gary Trotter. — 9th ed.

Sixth-8th eds. written by M. L. Friedland and Kent Roach.

ISBN 1-55239-118-3

    1. Criminal law—Canada—Cases. 2. Criminal procedure—Canada—Cases. I. Healy, Patrick. II. Trotter, Gary T., 1961- . III. Friedland, M. L. (Martin Lawrence), 1932- . Criminal law and procedure. IV. Title.

KE8808.5.R62 2004          345.71          C2004-904298-X
KF9220.ZA2R62 2004

# Preface to the Ninth Edition

Much has changed since the last edition of this casebook was published in 1997. Professor Martin L. Friedland has retired from teaching criminal law and procedure and from his editorship of these materials. The first five editions of this book were prepared by him alone and his exceptional contributions both to the teaching of criminal law and to Canadian criminal justice are still very much reflected in these pages.

A constant from the first edition published by Professor Friedland in 1968 to this edition is a common belief that students should be introduced to the criminal law in its procedural and evidentiary contexts. These materials have never been intended to supplant the need for separate courses on criminal procedure, evidence, and sentencing, but they are designed to provide students with a sense of the complexities and context of the criminal law. As before, instructors who wish to focus simply on the general part can do so by omitting the chapters on police powers, the trial process, and sentencing.

This casebook also reflects one of the most important themes of Professor Friedland's scholarship, namely, the recognition of what he describes in *The Trials of Israel Lipski* as "the inherent fallibility of the criminal trial process and the constant danger of error." From the very first edition of this casebook, Professor Friedland included a case study of a possible miscarriage of justice, the prosecution and conviction of Stephen Truscott. This edition continues this tradition with a case study of the wrongful conviction of Donald Marshall Jr.

Two new editors with decades of experience in both the academy and practice join this edition, Professor Patrick Healy of McGill and Professor Gary Trotter of Queen's. Both have collaborated before on teaching materials, in *Sentencing and Penal Policy in Canada* with Professor Allan Manson, published by Emond Montgomery in 2000.

There is some slight reorganization in this edition. The first two chapters deal with sources and limits of the criminal law, topics we believe will be of general interest. Subsequent chapters on police powers and the criminal trial process have been reduced in length and are, we believe, of interest not only to law students but other students of criminal justice. In recognition of the increasingly contextual nature of criminal law principles, we include separate chapters on homicide and sexual assault. As in previous editions, we include participation and inchoate offences at an early stage because of the importance of these extensions of criminal liability. Separate chapters are now included for each defence and the book concludes with a brief examination of sentencing.

This is an opportune time for a new edition of the casebook. The growing complexity of Canadian jurisprudence has allowed us to focus almost exclusively on Canadian case law. Recent developments from the Supreme Court such as the decisions in *Malmo-Levine* on the limits of the criminal law, *Burns and Rafay* on miscarriages of justice, *Cinous* and *Fontaine* on air of reality tests, and *Latimer* and *Ruzic* on excuses have all been incorporated, as have Parliament's significant changes and codification of the principles that govern the criminal liability of organizations.

We are extremely grateful to Professor Friedland for his continued advice and for handing off this important project to us. We are also grateful to everyone at Emond Montgomery for their patience, professionalism, and good cheer in producing this book. Particular thanks are due to Peggy Buchan for her excellent coordination of the production of the book and to Cindy Fujimoto for her excellent copy editing.

KR
PH
GT

June 2004

# Acknowledgments

This book, like many others of its nature, contains extracts from published materials. We have attempted to request permission from, and to acknowledge in the text, all sources of such material. We wish to make specific reference here to the authors, publishers, journals, and institutions that have been generous in giving their permission to reproduce works in this text. If we have inadvertently overlooked any acknowledgment, we offer our sincere apologies and undertake to rectify the omission in any future editions.

**American Law Institute**   Proposed Official Draft *Model Penal Code* (Philadelphia: American Law Institute, 1962). Copyright 1962 by the American Law Institute. Reprinted with permission. All rights reserved.

**Canadian Bar Association**   Alan Mewett, "The Criminal Law, 1867-1967" (1967), 45 *Canadian Bar Review* 1. Reprinted by permission.

**Carswell**   Martin L. Friedland, "Criminal Justice and the Constitutional Division of Power in Canada," in *A Century of Criminal Justice: Perspectives on the Development of Canadian Law* (Scarborough, ON: Carswell, 1984). Reprinted by permission of Carswell, a division of Thomson Canada Limited.

**Her Majesty's Stationery Office**   United Kingdon, English Law Commission, Working Paper No. 31, *The Mental Element in Crime* (London: Kingdom, 1970). Crown copyright is reproduced with the permission of the Controller of Her Majesty's Stationery Office. Reprinted by permission.

**Irwin Law**   Michel Proulx and David Layton, *Ethics and the Canadian Criminal Law* (Toronto: Irwin Law, 2001).

**Public Works and Government Services**   Canadian Sentencing Commission, *Sentencing Reform: A Canadian Approach* (Ottawa: Queen's Printer, 1987).

**Public Works and Government Services**   Law Reform Commission of Canada, Report No. 31 *Recodifying Criminal Law* (Ottawa: Queen's Printer, 1987), at 34-35, 143-44.

**Public Works and Government Services**   Law Reform Commission of Canada, Working Paper 50 *Hate Propaganda* (Ottawa: Queen's Printer, 1986).

**Thomson Sweet Maxwell**   T. Archibald, K. Jull, and K. Roach, "The Changed Face of Corporate Criminal Liability" (2004), 48 *Criminal Law Quarterly* 367. Reprinted by permission.

**University of Toronto Press**   Kent Roach, *Due Process and Victims' Rights: The New Law and Politics of Criminal Justice* (Toronto: University of Toronto Press, 1999).

# Summary Table of Contents

## Part One   Introduction to Criminal Law and Procedure

## Part Two   Principles of Criminal Liability

## Part Three   Extensions of Criminal Liability

## Part Four   The Special Part: Sexual Assault and Homicide

## Part Five   Principles of Exculpation

## Part Six   Disposition

# Detailed Table of Contents

## Part Two    Principles of Criminal Liability

# Part Three   Extensions of Criminal Liability

## Part Four   The Special Part:
## Sexual Assault and Homicide

# Part Six Disposition

# Table of Cases

A page number in boldface type indicates that the text of the case or a portion thereof is reproduced. A page number in lightface type indicates that the case is merely quoted briefly or discussed. Cases within excerpts are not listed.

# PART ONE

# Introduction to Criminal Law and Procedure

# CHAPTER ONE

# Sources of Criminal Law

This chapter provides an introduction to the sources of Canadian criminal law in (1) the constitution as the supreme law; (2) statute law and in particular the *Criminal Code* of Canada, and (3) common law or judge-made decisions of courts including decisions interpreting the constitution and the *Criminal Code*. The first part of the chapter provides an overview of the book. The second part examines the criminal law in the context of the constitutional division of powers between the federal and provincial governments and the constitutional rights provided in the *Canadian Charter of Rights and Freedoms* and mechanisms for justifying limits on those rights. The remaining part of this chapter examines the codification of the criminal law in the *Criminal Code*, the objectives of codification, constitutional prohibitions on vagueness and overbreadth in the criminal law, and the various approaches to the interpretation of the *Criminal Code*.

## I. OVERVIEW OF THE BOOK

The criminal law is the result of a complex process that starts with the decision of a legislature to define something as prohibited. Criminal law in Canada is enacted by the federal Parliament, which under s. 91(27) of the *Constitution Act, 1867*, has exclusive jurisdiction over criminal law and procedure. The *Criminal Code* of Canada contains many offences, ranging from traditional crimes, such as murder, assault, robbery, and theft, to newer crimes, such as operating or having care and control over a vehicle with a blood alcohol level "over 80" and participating in the activities of a criminal organization or a terrorist group. Some offences, such as assault or sexual assault, protect bodily integrity, while others, such as theft, protect property. Crimes such as firearms and drunk driving offences attempt to prevent conduct that presents a significant risk of harm to others. Crimes against the possession and sale of illegal drugs or obscene material may also prevent harm, but they also proclaim standards of socially acceptable behaviour.

The *Canadian Charter of Rights and Freedoms* (being part I of the *Constitution Act, 1982*, as enacted by the *Canada Act, 1982* (U.K.), c. 11), usually referred to simply as the Charter, places limits on the criminal law (chapter 2). For example, criminal offences that prohibit various forms of expression must be justified by the state as demonstrably justified and reasonable limits under s. 1 of the Charter.

Criminal laws are designed primarily to denounce and punish inherently wrongful behaviour and to deter people from committing crimes or engaging in behaviour that presents a serious risk of harm. Courts consider these purposes when sentencing offenders, but they are also concerned with the incapacitation and rehabilitation of the particular offender and providing reparation to the victim and the community for the crime committed.

The *Criminal Code* contains many offences but they constitute only a small number of all the offences in Canada. Most offences are regulatory. Regulatory offences can be enacted by the federal Parliament, provinces, or municipalities. They include traffic offences, such as speeding, polluting, engaging in a regulated activity without a licence or without keeping proper records, and offences relating to harmful commercial practices, such as misleading advertising or not complying with health and safety regulations. The punishment for regulatory offences is usually a fine, but may include imprisonment. In any event, the accused is frequently a corporation that cannot be imprisoned but that can be fined or placed on probation. The primary purpose of regulatory offences is to deter risky behaviour and prevent harm rather than punish intrinsically wrongful and harmful behaviour. Generally, fewer restrictions are placed on the state in the investigation and prosecution of regulatory crimes.

### The Criminal Process

The criminal law assumes concrete meaning when it is administered through the criminal justice system. The bulk of this spending (60 percent) is on the police; 25 percent on corrections, including federal and provincial prisons; 9 percent on courts; and 6 percent on legal aid, to fund the defence of those accused of crime. See "Trends in Justice Spending," 14(6) *Juristat*.

The criminal process has traditionally started with the investigation of crime by the police (chapter 3) and the criminal trial process, which includes pre-trial proceedings, such as the decision whether to grant bail and the selection of the jury (chapter 4). These phases of the criminal process must be procedurally fair or the accused will be able to seek a remedy for the violation of his or her rights under the *Charter of Rights and Freedoms*.

### Principles of Criminal Liability

At the criminal trial, the morally innocent should not be found guilty and punished. As required by the presumption of innocence, the Crown must generally prove beyond a reasonable doubt to the judge or jury that the accused committed the prohibited act or *actus reus* (chapter 5) with the required fault element or *mens rea* (chapter 7). The *actus reus* is usually defined as an overt act, such as the taking of another person's property. The legislature can, however, define the prohibited conduct as an omission or a failure to take action. For example, a parent can be guilty of the criminal offence of failing to provide the necessities of life to his or her child.

A great variety of fault elements are used in criminal and regulatory offences. Sometimes the fault element is specified in the wording of an offence by phrases such as "intentionally," "knowingly," "recklessly," or "negligently." Frequently, however, the courts will have to infer what type of fault element is required. Often a distinction between "subjective" and "objective" fault elements is drawn. A subjective fault or mental element depends on what was in the particular accused's mind at the time that the criminal act was committed. In determining this, the judge or jury must consider all the evidence presented, even if it reveals factors that are peculiar to the accused, such as the accused's diminished intelligence. On the other hand, an objective fault element does not depend on the accused's own state of mind but rather on what a reasonable person in the circumstances would have known or done.

There are special rules for determining liability for non-criminal regulatory offences (chapter 6). Most regulatory offences, known in Canada as strict liability offences, require the accused to establish a defence of due diligence or lack of negligence after the state has proven the prohibited act beyond a reasonable doubt. Other regulatory offences, known as absolute liability offences, only require proof of the prohibited act and do not allow any defence of due diligence or require proof of any fault. When such offences are combined with imprisonment, they can be constitutionally problematic because they can punish individuals and corporations even though they could not have reasonably been expected to have prevented the prohibited act.

Although the simplest form of criminal liability is an individual committing a complete crime with the necessary fault or *mens rea*, there are important extensions of criminal liability examined in part three of this book.

Often a crime is committed by more than one person. A person who assists in the commission of an offence can be convicted of the same offence as the person who actually commits the offence (chapter 8). The parties' provisions in s. 21 of the *Criminal Code* mean that people who have different levels of involvement in a crime may be found guilty of the same offence. The extent of an offender's participation in a crime will be considered by the judge when determining the appropriate sentence.

A person may be guilty of the separate offence of attempting a specified crime even if he or she does not succeed in carrying out the prohibited act, such as an unlawful killing (chapter 9). Section 24 of the *Criminal Code* states that anyone having an intent to commit an offence, who does or omits to do anything beyond mere preparation to commit a criminal offence, is guilty of attempting to commit the offence, regardless of whether it was possible to commit an offence. A person punished for an attempted crime is punished more for his or her intent to commit the crime than the harm caused.

There is a separate regime in the *Criminal Code* for determining the liability of corporations and other organizations, which requires not only that employees or other representatives of the corporation engage in activity that is criminal, but also that some fault be attributed to a "senior officer" in the corporation (chapter 10). A final factor extending criminal liability is the principle found in s. 19 of the *Criminal Code* that ignorance of the criminal law is not an excuse (chapter 11).

Many of the most important principles of criminal law have been developed in the context of a few particular crimes, some of which are examined in part four. The law of sexual assault has been particularly dynamic over the last two decades and is examined in chapter 12. The law of homicide, involving the important distinction between murder and manslaughter, as well as the classification of murder as first and second degree murder, is examined in chapter 13. There is one defence that applies only in homicide cases and reduces what would otherwise be an intentional murder to the less serious offence of manslaughter. It is the defence of provocation which is examined in chapter 14.

## Principles of Exculpation

Even if he or she has committed the prohibited act with the required fault, the accused may still be acquitted if a defence applies. Chapters 15 and 16 examine the related defences of mental disorder and automatism as they relate to the accused's capacity to be at fault and to be held responsible for criminal acts. The mental disorder defence leads to a special disposition in which the accused, although not convicted, may be subject to further detention or treatment. Chapter 17 examines the complex defences of intoxication as they apply to various crimes. Intoxication most often acts as a defence that raises a reasonable doubt about whether the accused had the required fault or intent for a serious crime such as murder but often does not negate a fault for a less serious crime such as manslaughter. As will be seen, it is more controversial when intoxication is used as a defence to a less serious crime. Chapters 18 and 19 examine the related defences of necessity and duress, which excuse crimes committed by people in agonizing circumstances where they have no reasonable choice but to commit the crime. In this chapter and others, we will see that some restrictions on defences may be unconstitutional and violate s. 7 of the Charter because they deprive people of liberty in a manner that is not in accordance with the principles of fundamental justice. Chapter 20 examines self-defence, a defence that is codified in the *Criminal Code*, but subject to continued judicial interpretation.

## Disposition

No examination of criminal justice would be complete without some examination of the sentencing principles that govern the disposition of an accused who has been found guilty (chapter 21). The judge at sentencing has wide discretion to tailor punishment to the offender's degree of responsibility and also to consider what punishment will best deter, rehabilitate, or incapacitate the particular offender; deter others from committing the same crime; and provide reparation to the community and victims for the crime. On sentencing see Allan Manson, Patrick Healy, and Gary Trotter, *Sentencing and Penal Policy in Canada* (Toronto: Emond Montgomery, 2000).

## II. THE CRIMINAL LAW AND THE CONSTITUTION

The supreme source of criminal law in Canada is the constitution, as represented by both the division of powers between federal and provincial governments in ss. 91 and 92 of the *Constitution Act, 1867* and the rights and freedoms in the 1982 *Canadian Charter of Rights and Freedoms*.

### The Canadian Charter of Rights and Freedoms

The Charter pervades the whole of criminal law from the initial decision to criminalize conduct, through the investigation of crime by police, the prosecution of offences, the determination of criminal liability, and even the sentencing of offenders. Almost every chapter in this book will examine some aspect of the Charter. We recognize, however, that the Charter may be unfamiliar to some students and for this reason what follows is a brief introduction to the Charter.

The Charter as part of the supreme law of Canada applies to the activities of Canadian legislatures and governmental officials such as the police. It differs from the *Canadian Bill of Rights* enacted in 1960 both because it is part of the constitution and because it applies to all governments and not just the federal government.

The Charter guarantees a number of rights including freedom of expression and equality rights. The legal rights set out in ss. 7 to 14 of the Charter are designed to protect those subject to criminal investigation, those charged and tried for criminal offences, and those punished for crime. The broadest legal right is contained in s. 7 and it can potentially apply at any of the above stages of the criminal process. It provides as follows:

> Everyone has the right to life, liberty and security of the person and the right not to be deprived thereof except in accordance with the principles of fundamental justice.

Sections 8 to 10 of the Charter protect those subject to investigation by the state. Section 8 provides the right to be secure against unreasonable searches or seizures, while s. 9 provides the right not to be arbitrarily detained or imprisoned. Upon arrest or detention, individuals have a number of rights under s. 10, including the right to retain and instruct counsel without delay and to be informed of that right.

Sections 11 to 14 of the Charter protect those who are charged and tried for offences. For example, before trial, a person who is charged has a right not to be denied reasonable bail without just cause (s. 11(e)) and to be tried within a reasonable time (s. 11(b)). At trial, the accused has among other rights, the right to be presumed innocent until proven guilty in a court of law in a fair and public hearing by an independent and impartial tribunal (s. 11(d)) and the right to a jury trial in certain circumstances (s. 11(f)). When finally acquitted or found guilty and punished for the offence, the accused has the right not to be tried or punished for it again (s. 11(h)).

Everyone has the right not to be 'subjected to any cruel and unusual treatment or punishment (s. 12) and this is the right that is most relevant to sentencing issues.

Another right that has increased relevance to criminal justice is s. 15 of the Charter which provides:

Every individual is equal before and under the law and has the right to the equal protection and equal benefit of the law without discrimination and, in particular, without discrimination based on race, national or ethnic origin, colour, religion, sex, age or mental and physical disability.

Laws and practices can be found to infringe s. 15 of the Charter. At the same time, a concern about equality can be considered as a rationale for some laws such as those prohibiting hate speech or obscenity.

If a law or practice is found to infringe a Charter right, it is open for the state to prove under s. 1 of the Charter that it is a reasonable limit prescribed by law and demonstrably justified in a free and democratic society. If the law or practice is not so justified, then under s. 52 of the *Constitution Act, 1982* any law that is inconsistent with the Charter is to the extent of the inconsistency of no force or effect.

In addition to the remedy of striking laws down, the courts have broad powers to order remedies for Charter violations, including unconstitutional police practices. Section 24(1) of the Charter provides that those whose Charter rights have been infringed may apply to a court of competent jurisdiction to obtain such remedy as the court considers appropriate and just. Section 24(2) governs the remedy of exclusion of evidence obtained in a manner that violates Charter rights by providing that evidence shall be excluded from a criminal trial if it is established that, having regard to all the circumstances, its admission would bring the administration of justice into disrepute.

Finally, it should be noted that in the context of the legal rights discussed above, the state cannot only try to justify laws that violate rights as reasonable limits under s. 1, but it can also provide that an Act or a provision thereof shall operate notwithstanding ss. 2.7-15 of the Charter (s. 33). This power has rarely been used by governments and never used with respect to the criminal law.

For some further readings on the Charter see Peter Hogg, *Constitutional Law of Canada*, 3rd ed. (Toronto: Carswell, 1997); Don Stuart, *Charter Justice in Canadian Criminal Law*, 3rd ed. (Toronto: Carswell, 2001); and Robert Sharpe, Katherine Swinton, and Kent Roach, *The Charter of Rights and Freedoms*, 2nd ed. (Toronto: Irwin Law, 2002).

## The Criminal Law and the Division of Powers

The *Constitution Act, 1867*, s. 91(27) vests in the federal Parliament exclusive jurisdiction to legislate in relation to "the Criminal Law, except the Constitution of Courts of Criminal Jurisdiction, but including the Procedure in Criminal Matters." The federal Parliament also has jurisdiction under s. 91(28) to establish, maintain, and manage penitentiaries, which have been considered to be the place of detention for persons serving terms of imprisonment for two years or more.

The provinces have jurisdiction under s. 92(15) to impose punishment by way of fine, penalty, or imprisonment in order to enforce valid provincial laws. The provinces also have jurisdiction over the administration of justice under s. 92(14), the establishment of "reformatory prisons" (s. 92(6)) (the place of detention for persons serving terms of imprisonment for less than two years), and "asylums" (s. 92(7)).

The federal government appoints the judges of the higher superior trial courts under s. 96 of the *Constitution Act, 1867* while the provinces appoint judges to provincial courts where most criminal trials are held. The federal government also appoints appeal court judges including those on the Supreme Court of Canada.

---

The following excerpt outlines the historical and contemporary importance of federal jurisdiction over criminal law and procedure.

### M.L. Friedland, "Criminal Justice and the Division of Power in Canada"
in *A Century of Criminal Justice* (Toronto: Carswell, 1984), chapter 2 (footnotes omitted)

#### *Confederation*

The discussion and legislative debates leading to Confederation show that there was no controversy over whether legislative power over criminal law and procedure should be given to the federal government. Centralizing the criminal law power was in deliberate contrast to the American Constitution which left control over the criminal law power to the individual states.

Why was the criminal law power given to the federal government? Sir John A. Macdonald, then the Attorney-General, expressed what must have been the consensus at the time when, in the parliamentary debates in 1865, he stated:

> The criminal law too—the determination of what is a crime and what is not and how crime shall be punished—is left to the General Government. This is a matter almost of necessity. It is of great importance that we should have the same criminal law throughout these provinces—that what is a crime in one part of British America, should be a crime in every part—that there should be the same protection of life and property in one as in another.

He then commented on the American division of authority:

> It is one of the defects in the United States system, that each separate state has or may have a criminal code of its own,—that what may be a capital offence in one state, may be a venial offence, punishable slightly, in another. But under our Constitution we shall have one body of criminal law, based on the criminal law of England, and operating equally throughout British America, so that a British American, belonging to what province he may, or going to any other part of the Confederation, knows what his rights are in that respect, and what his punishment will be if an offender against the criminal laws of the land. I think this is one of the most marked instances in which we take advantage of the experience derived from our observations of the defects in the Constitution of the neighboring Republic.

There is no doubt that the Civil War in the United States was a major factor in the desire of many to place some of the more important powers and symbols of nationhood within the legislative authority of the federal government. The criminal law plays an important role in society in stating fundamental values. This can be seen today in the discussions taking place on such criminal law issues as the law of abortion, the law relating to homosexual conduct, the question of the reintroduction of capital punishment, and the activities of the police and the security service. ...

### Scope of the Criminal Law Power

A hundred years ago, the courts gave the criminal law power a very wide meaning. In 1882, in *Russell v. The Queen*, the Privy Council seemed to uphold the validity of the Canada Temperance Act of 1878 under the criminal law power. The Court stated:

> Laws ... designed for the promotion of public order, safety, or morals, and which subject those who contravene them to criminal procedure and punishment, belong to the subject of public wrongs rather than to that of civil rights. They are of a nature which fall within the general authority of Parliament to make laws for the order and good government of Canada, and have direct relation to criminal law, which is one of the enumerated classes of subjects assigned exclusively to the Parliament of Canada.

But doubt was thrown on *Russell* by Lord Watson in 1896 in the *Local Prohibition* case. He explained *Russell* as based on the "peace, order and good government" clause, and went so far as to say, in one example, that "an Act restricting the right to carry weapons of offence, or their sale to young persons, within the province would be within the authority of the provincial legislature" and not of the federal parliament. Lord Watson's enhancement of provincial power over "property and civil rights" at the expense of federal powers such as the criminal law power was also found in Lord Haldane's judgments in the 20th century.

In 1922, in the *Board of Commerce* case, Lord Haldane severely restricted the criminal law power to cases "where the subject matter is one which by its very nature belongs to the domain of criminal jurisprudence." But later decisions have broadened that definition. Lord Atkin in the *P.A.T.A.* case in 1931 gave the following definition: "The criminal quality of an act cannot be discerned by intuition; nor can it be discovered by reference to any standard but one: Is the act prohibited with penal consequences?" But just as Haldane's definition was too narrow, Lord Atkin's has proven to be too wide. The federal government cannot take jurisdiction simply by imposing a criminal penalty. The *Margarine Reference* case in 1951 demonstrated this limitation on the criminal law power. The Supreme Court held that to forbid manufacture and sale of margarine for economic purposes is "to deal directly with the civil rights of individuals in relation to particular trade within the Provinces." A similar approach was taken by the Supreme Court in 1979 with respect to the marketing of apples under the Canada Agricultural Products Standards Act in *Dominion Stores Ltd. v. The Queen* and with respect to the marketing of "light beer" under the federal Food and Drugs Acts in the *Labatt Breweries* case. In both cases the majority of the Supreme Court held that the criminal law power could not justify the legislation and so declared parts of the federal legislation *ultra vires*.

... The recently enacted gun control provisions have been challenged—unsuccessfully—in a number of cases. The Supreme Court of Canada has not yet dealt with the issue. When it does, no doubt it will disregard Lord Watson's statement, quoted earlier, and uphold the federal legislation. Controlling firearms is directly related to the criminal law. One of the reasons why the United States has a gun problem is because of the absence of strong federal legislation which would effectively prevent guns being sent from lax gun control states to other states. …

[The Supreme Court did indeed hold that gun control laws, including those providing that it was a criminal offence to have an unlicensed or unregistered gun, were within the federal jurisdiction. It concluded that "the regulation of guns as dangerous products is a valid purpose within the criminal law power." See *Reference re Firearms Act (Can.)*, [2000] 1 S.C.R. 783, at para. 33. The recent trend seems to be back to an expansive approach to Parliament's criminal law power to include matters such as offences that restrict the advertising of tobacco or the introduction of substances that are toxic to the environment. See *RJR MacDonald Inc. v. Canada (Attorney General)*, [1995] 3 S.C.R. 199; *R. v. Hydro-Quebec*, [1997] 3 S.C.R. 213. See, generally, The Constitutional Law Group, *Canadian Constitutional Law*, 3rd ed. (Toronto: Emond Montgomery, 2003), chapter 11.]

### *Provincial Legislation*

Provincial laws can be struck down either for lack of constitutional power under section 92 or for conflict with federal legislation. Under both heads the Supreme Court of Canada has tended to uphold provincial law. A trio of cases in 1960 showed the reluctance of the Supreme Court of Canada to declare provincial legislation inoperative because of existing federal legislation. Of course it will do so if it *conflicts* with federal legislation. But what is meant by conflicts? In *O'Grady v. Sparling* the Supreme Court upheld provincial careless driving legislation, although the federal Criminal Code makes it an offence to operate a motor vehicle in a criminally negligent manner. In *Stephens v. The Queen* the Supreme Court upheld provincial competence to require a driver involved in an accident to stop, provide particulars, and offer assistance, in spite of a provision in the Criminal Code making the same conduct an offence, though with the added element of "intent to escape civil or criminal liability." Finally, in *Smith v. The Queen* the Supreme Court upheld a section of the Ontario Securities Act making it an offence to furnish false information in any document required to be filed or furnished under the Act, although the Criminal Code makes it an offence for a person to publish a prospectus which he knows is false in a material particular with intent to induce persons to become shareholders in a company. In none of these cases was there held to be a conflict. …

The tendency to uphold provincial legislation can also be seen in a number of recent Supreme Court of Canada cases in which provincial legislation was challenged as not falling within section 92. In 1978 in *Dupont* the majority of the Supreme Court of Canada upheld a Montreal by-law designed to prevent assemblies and passed to cope with occurrences such as the F.L.Q. rallies. The same year the Supreme Court in the *McNeil* case upheld Nova Scotia legislation which permitted the banning of the movie, "Last Tango in Paris," even though there was also federal obscenity legislation in the Criminal Code. In 1982, in the *Schneider* case, the Supreme Court upheld provincial legislation providing for the compulsory treatment of heroin addicts. In the most recent Supreme Court case, *Westendorp v. The Queen*, however, the Court struck down a Calgary by-law which had attempted to deal with prostitution by prohibiting a person from remaining on the street for the purpose of prostitution or approaching another person on the street for the purpose of prostitution. Laskin C.J., for a unanimous Supreme Court, held that the by-law was "a colourable attempt to deal, not with a public nuisance but with the evil of prostitution. ... If a province or municipality may translate a direct attack on prostitution into street control through reliance on public nuisance, it may do the same with respect to trafficking in drugs, and, may it not, on the same view, seek to punish assaults that take place on city streets as an aspect of street control!" Thus, just as there are limits on federal legislation, there are limits on the creation of provincial offences.

[A provincial attempt to prohibit the performance of an abortion other than in a hospital has been held to be an invalid provincial attempt to enact criminal laws. *R. v. Morgentaler*, [1993] 3 S.C.R. 463. Note that five years earlier, the court had struck down a federal *Criminal Code* provision that restricted abortion to those performed in a hospital and approved by a hospital committee on the grounds that it violated s. 7 of the Charter by depriving women of security of the person in a manner that did not accord with the principles of fundamental justice: *R. v. Morgentaler*, [1988] 1 S.C.R. 30.]

*Administering the Criminal Law*

Section 92(14) of the B.N.A. Act gives the provinces authority over "the administration of justice in the province, including the constitution, maintenance, and organization of provincial courts, both of civil and of criminal jurisdiction, and including procedure in civil matters in those courts." Does this give the provinces or the federal government the primary power to prosecute federal offences enacted under the criminal law power? In 1979 in the *Hauser* case the Supreme Court was called on to decide whether the federal government could control prosecutions under the Narcotic Control Act. The Court held that the federal government had this power, although, to the surprise of many, not on the basis that the Narcotic Control Act was criminal law, but rather because it was enacted under the "peace, order and good government" clause. The Court, therefore, left open the question of what would happen when the issue related directly to enforcing the criminal law.

Two important cases decided by the Supreme Court in 1983 dealt with that question. In *A.G. Canada v. Canadian National Transportation Ltd. et al.* the issue was whether the federal government has the power to control prosecutions under the Combines Investigation Act. Section 2 of the Criminal Code gives the power to prosecute federal offences not under the Criminal Code to the Attorney-General of Canada. Chief Justice Laskin gave the judgment for the majority of the seven-member court, holding that the Combines Act is valid under section 91(27), the criminal law power, and that the federal government has exclusive authority to control prosecutions. The majority judgment did not deal with the validity of the legislation under any other head of federal power. Dickson J. upheld federal prosecutorial authority for violations of the Combines Investigation Act under the federal "trade and commerce" power. With respect to the criminal law power, Dickson J. maintained the position he had taken in his dissent in *Hauser* that only the provincial Attorney-General can validly prosecute criminal enactments. ...

In *The Queen v. Wetmore and Kripp*, released the same day as the *Canadian National Transportation* case, the issue was the power to prosecute under the federal Food and Drugs Act. Again, Laskin C.J. held that because the Act fell under the criminal law power the federal government could control who had the power to prosecute. Dickson J., dissenting and characterizing the view of the majority as "blind centralism," held that the legislation was only valid under the criminal law power and thus it was the provincial, not the federal Attorney General who had the power to prosecute. ...

The result of the cases, then, appears to be that the federal government has exclusive power to prosecute federal offences. This power can, however, be delegated to the provincial Attorney General as is done directly in section 2 of the Criminal Code for Criminal Code offences. ...

Thus far the courts have not dealt directly with the question of whether the federal government could, if it wished, control prosecutions under the Criminal Code itself. The issue is not likely to arise because section 2 of the Code now gives this power to the provincial Attorneys General. ...

[Section 2 still generally defines the attorney general in charge of prosecuting *Criminal Code* offences as the provincial attorney general but also now grants the federal attorney general concurrent jurisdiction to prosecute terrorism offences or offences that were committed outside of Canada but can be prosecuted in Canada.]

––––––––––––––––

Do you agree with those, such as Chief Justice Laskin, who support a strong and exclusive federal jurisdiction in matters concerning criminal justice? What would be the advantages and disadvantages of giving the provinces more power in these matters?

Dickson J., as he then was, stated in his dissent in *R. v. Hauser*, [1979] 1 S.C.R. 984, at 1032 that part of the Confederation bargain was that while the criminal law was to be enacted by the federal Parliament, its administration was to be left in the hands of local and provincial authorities "where it could be more flexibly administered":

> The position of decentralized control, which had obtained in England from time immemorial, and in Canada prior to Confederation, with local administration of justice, local police forces, local juries, and local prosecutors, was perpetuated and carried forward into the Constitution through s. 92(14). The administration of justice was to be kept in local hands and out of the control of central government.

––––––––––––––––

Before the enactment of the Charter, exclusive federal jurisdiction over criminal law and procedure was one of the few means to strike down provincial legislation which threatened civil liberties.

Consider the Supreme Court's response to Quebec's "Padlock Act" which was passed in 1937 by the Quebec legislature after a provision in the *Criminal Code* (that made unlawful any associations formed for the purpose of making any governmental, industrial or economic change within Canada by the use of force) was repealed. The constitutionality of the law was challenged by a tenant who had her house "padlocked." How might such a matter be decided today?

## Switzman v. Elbling
Supreme Court of Canada
[1957] S.C.R. 285

KERWIN C.J.C.: Section 1 provides

> 1. This Act may be cited as *Act Respecting Communistic Propaganda.*

Sections 3 and 12 read:

> 3. It shall be illegal for any person, who possesses or occupies a house within the Province, to use it or allow any person to make use of it to propagate communism or bolshevism by any means whatsoever.
> 12. It shall be unlawful to print, to publish in any manner whatsoever or to distribute in the Province any newspaper, periodical, pamphlet, circular, document or writing whatsoever propagating or tending to propagate communism or bolshevism.

Sections 4 to 11 provide that the Attorney-General, upon satisfactory proof that an infringement of s. 3 has been committed, may order the closing of the house; authorize any peace officer to execute such order, and provide a procedure by which the owner may apply by petition to a judge of the Superior Court to have the order revised. Section 13 provides for imprisonment of anyone infringing or participating in the infringement of s. 12. ...

The validity of the statute was attacked upon a number of grounds, but, in cases where constitutional issues are involved, it is important that nothing be said that is unnecessary. In my view it is sufficient to declare that the Act is legislation in relation to the criminal law over which, by virtue of head 27 of s. 91 of the *British North America Act*, the Parliament of Canada has exclusive legislative authority. The decision of this Court in *Bédard v. Dawson et al.* (1923), 40 C.C.C. 404 is clearly distinguishable. As Mr. Justice Barclay points out, the real object of the Act here under consideration is to prevent propagation of communism within the Province and to punish anyone who does so—with provisions authorizing steps for the closing of premises used for such object. The *Bédard* case was concerned with the control and enjoyment of property. ... It is not necessary to refer to other authorities, because, once the conclusion is reached that the pith and substance of the impugned Act is in relation to criminal law, the conclusion is inevitable that the Act is unconstitutional.

[Seven other judges concurred with Kerwin C.J.C. in the result. Taschereau J. dissented and relied on *Bédard v. Dawson* (1923), 40 C.C.C. 404, which had upheld a Quebec law aimed at closing "disorderly houses" after there had been *Criminal Code* convictions for gambling or prostitution offences. Taschereau J. stated that the provinces had the power to legislate to prevent crime such as treason and sedition.]

Even after the enactment of the Charter, the inability of the provinces to enact laws classified as criminal laws was still applied by the courts.

### R. v. Morgentaler
Supreme Court of Canada
[1993] 3 S.C.R. 463

SOPINKA J.: The question in this appeal is whether the *Nova Scotia Medical Services Act*, RSNS 1989, c. 281, and the regulation made under the Act, N.S. Reg. 152/89, are *ultra vires* the province of Nova Scotia on the ground that they are in pith and substance criminal law. The Act and regulation make it an offence to perform an abortion outside a hospital. ...

In January 1988, this Court ruled that the *Criminal Code* provisions relating to abortion were unconstitutional because they violated women's Charter guarantee of security of the person: *R. v. Morgentaler*, [1988] 1 S.C.R. 30 (*Morgentaler* (1988)). At the same time the Court reaffirmed its earlier decision that the provisions were a valid exercise of the federal criminal law power: *Morgentaler v. The Queen*, [1976] 1 S.C.R. 616 (*Morgentaler* (1975)). The 1988 decision meant that abortion was no longer regulated by the criminal law. It was no longer an offence to obtain or perform an abortion in a clinic such as those run by the respondent. ... This legislation deals, by its terms, with a subject historically considered to be part of the criminal law—the prohibition of the performance of abortions with penal consequences. It is thus suspect on its face. Its legal effect partially reproduces that of the now defunct s. 251 of the *Criminal Code*, in so far as both precluded the establishment and operation of free-standing abortion clinics. ... The primary objective of this legislation was to prohibit abortions outside hospitals as socially undesirable conduct and any concern with the safety and security of pregnant women or with health care policy, hospitals or the regulation of the medical profession was merely ancillary. This legislation involves the regulation of the place where an abortion may be obtained, not from the viewpoint of health care policy, but from the viewpoint of public wrongs or crimes. ...

[Lamer C.J.C., La Forest, L'Heureux-Dubé, Gonthier, Cory, McLachlin, Iacobucci, and Major JJ. concurred with Sopinka J. in declaring the impugned law to be an unconstitutional provincial invasion of the federal criminal law power.]

**Reference re Firearms Act (Can.)**
Supreme Court of Canada
[2000] 1 S.C.R. 783

THE COURT:  In 1995, Parliament amended the *Criminal Code*, R.S.C., 1985, c. C-46, by enacting the *Firearms Act*, S.C. 1995, c. 39, commonly referred to as the gun control law, to require the holders of all firearms to obtain licences and register their guns. In 1996, the Province of Alberta challenged Parliament's power to pass the gun control law by a reference to the Alberta Court of Appeal. The Court of Appeal by a 3:2 majority upheld Parliament's power to pass the law. The Province of Alberta now appeals that decision to this Court. ...

The answer to this question lies in the Canadian Constitution. The Constitution assigns some matters to Parliament and others to the provincial legislatures: *Constitution Act, 1867*. The federal government asserts that the gun control law falls under its criminal law power, s. 91(27), and under its general power to legislate for the "Peace, Order and good Government" of Canada. Alberta, on the other hand, says the law falls under its power over property and civil rights, s. 92(13). All agree that to resolve this dispute, the Court must first determine what the gun control law is really about—its "pith and substance"—and then ask which head or heads of power it most naturally falls within.

We conclude that the gun control law comes within Parliament's jurisdiction over criminal law. The law in "pith and substance" is directed to enhancing public safety by controlling access to firearms through prohibitions and penalties. This brings it under the federal criminal law power. While the law has regulatory aspects, they are secondary to its primary criminal law purpose. The intrusion of the law into the provincial jurisdiction over property and civil rights is not so excessive as to upset the balance of federalism. ...

Yet another argument is that the ownership of guns is not criminal law because it is not immoral to own an ordinary firearm. There are two difficulties with this argument. The first is that while the ownership of ordinary firearms is not in itself re-garded by most Canadians as immoral, the problems associated with the misuse of firearms are firmly grounded in morality. Firearms may be misused to take human life and to assist in other immoral acts, like theft and terrorism. Preventing such mis-use can be seen as an attempt to curb immoral acts. Viewed thus, gun control is di-rected at a moral evil.

The second difficulty with the argument is that the criminal law is not confined to prohibiting immoral acts: see *Proprietary Articles Trade Association v. Attorney-General for Canada*, [1931] A.C. 310 (P.C.). While most criminal conduct is also re-garded as immoral, Parliament can use the criminal law to prohibit activities which have little relation to public morality. For instance, the criminal law has been used to prohibit certain restrictions on market competition. ... Therefore, even if gun control did not involve morality, it could still fall under the federal criminal law power.

We recognize the concerns of northern, rural and aboriginal Canadians who fear that this law does not address their particular needs. They argue that it discriminates against them and violates treaty rights, and express concerns about their ability to access the scheme, which may be administered from a great distance. These apprehensions are genuine, but they do not go to the question before us—Parliament's jurisdiction to enact this law. Whether a law could have been designed better or whether the federal government should have engaged in more consultation before enacting the law has no bearing on the division of powers analysis applied by this Court. If the law violates a treaty or a provision of the Charter, those affected can bring their claims to Parliament or the courts in a separate case. The reference questions, and hence this judgment, are restricted to the issue of the division of powers.

We also appreciate the concern of those who oppose this Act on the basis that it may not be effective or it may be too expensive. Criminals will not register their guns, Alberta argued. The only real effect of the law, it is suggested, is to burden law-abiding farmers and hunters with red tape. These concerns were properly directed to and considered by Parliament; they cannot affect the Court's decision. The efficacy of a law, or lack thereof, is not relevant to Parliament's ability to enact it under the division of powers analysis. ... The cost of the program, another criticism of the law, is equally irrelevant to our constitutional analysis.

---

On federalism and the criminal law see P. Hogg, *Constitutional Law of Canada*, 3rd ed. (Toronto: Carswell, 1992), c. 18; E. Colvin, *Principles of Criminal Law*, 2nd ed. (Toronto: Carswell, 1991), 3-15; and P. Monahan, *Constitutional Law*, 2nd ed. (Toronto: Irwin Law, 2002).

## III. CODIFICATION: THE CRIMINAL LAW AS A STATUTE

### History of the Criminal Code

The history of the Canadian *Criminal Code* is briefly stated in the following extract.

### Alan Mewett, "The Criminal Law, 1867-1967"
(1967), 45 *Can. Bar Rev.* 726, at 726-30 (footnotes omitted)

For a large part of the nineteenth century, the idea of codification of the criminal law had been mooted in England and elsewhere in the English-speaking world. In 1838 in England the first Criminal Law Commissioners were appointed to report on and draft such a code and in 1878, largely as a result of the work of Sir James Stephen, the English Draft Code, dealing with indictable offences, was formulated. Although this formed the basis of two Bills presented to the English Parliament, both attempts to introduce a comprehensive criminal code were abortive.

In Canada, the Bill Respecting Criminal Law of 1892 was expressed by Sir John Thompson to be founded on the Draft Code prepared by the Royal Commission in Great Britain in 1880, on Stephen's *Digest of the Criminal Law*, the edition of 1887, Burbidge's *Digest of the Canadian Criminal Law* of 1889 and the Canadian statutory law. He quoted from the *Commission Report* to define the codification as follows:

It is a reduction of the existing law to an orderly written system, freed from needless technicalities, obscurities and other defects which the experience of its administration has disclosed. It aims at the reduction to a system of that kind of substantive law relating to crimes and the law of procedure, both as to indictable offences and as to summary convictions.

A series of amendments resulted in the consolidations of 1906 and 1927, but neither of these could be called revisions. In 1947, a Royal Commission to Revise the Criminal Code was appointed, reported in 1952 and in 1953 the Revised Code was enacted. This revision did not greatly alter the structure or substance of the original Code, no attempt being made to consider or redefine fundamental criminal law concepts. The system of punishments was rationalized, certain procedural reforms were introduced and a relatively small number of specific offences were either redefined or introduced.

One significant change was that enacted by section 8 [now s. 9] stating:

Notwithstanding anything in this Act or any other Act, no person shall be convicted or discharged under section 736
    (a) of an offence at common law,
    (b) of an offence under an Act of the Parliament of England, or of Great Britain, or of the United Kingdom of Great Britain and Ireland, or
    (c) of an offence under an Act or ordinance in force in any province, territory or place before that province, territory or place became a province of Canada,
but nothing in this section affects the power, jurisdiction or authority that a court, judge, justice or provincial court judge had, immediately before April 1, 1955, to impose punishment for contempt of court.

Prior to the enactment of section 8 of the 1953 revision, prosecutions were successful for such common law offences as abuse of office in taking fees wrongfully, public mischief, champerty and maintenance and perhaps barratry.

It was thus not until 1953 that all common law offences were abolished throughout Canada. It is interesting to note that, in contrast, the first English Draft Code proposed the abolition of all common law offences not specifically enacted in the Code. It could not, however, be maintained that prosecution for common law offences was a very frequent occurrence in Canada after 1892, and the Revision Commissioners decided that there was no point in preserving them after 1953. Instead, all those thought applicable to Canada were specifically enacted. ...

On the other hand, faced with the difficulty, if not impossibility of attempting to codify the common law defences, the Commissioners merely recommended, and Parliament enacted, section 7(2) [now s. 8(3)] providing:

Every rule and principle of the common law that renders any circumstance a justification or excuse for an act or a defence to a charge continues in force and applies in respect of proceedings for an offence under this Act or any other Act of the Parliament of Canada, except insofar as they are altered by or are inconsistent with this Act or any other Act of the Parliament of Canada.

For the history of the Code enacted in Canada, see G. Parker, "The Origins of the Canadian Criminal Code," in D. Flaherty, *Essays in the History of Canadian Law* (Toronto: Osgoode Society, 1981), c. 7; D. Brown, *The Genesis of the Canadian Criminal Code* (Toronto: U. of T. Press, 1989); A. Mewett, "The Criminal Code, 1892-1992" (1993), 72 *Can. Bar Rev.* 1. For an alternative code that was not adopted in Canada, see M.L. Friedland, "R.S. Wright's Model Criminal Code: A Forgotten Chapter in the History of the Criminal Law," in M.L. Friedland, *A Century of Criminal Justice* (Toronto: Carswell, 1984), c. 1.

## Common Law Defences

Why should offences at common law (i.e., judge-made law as opposed to legislation) be prohibited under s. 9(a) of the *Criminal Code* but not defences, excuses, or justifications?

### Amato v. The Queen
### Supreme Court of Canada
### (1982), 69 C.C.C. (2d) 31

[In this case, Estey J. interpreted s. 7(3) (now s. 8(3)) of the *Criminal Code* to allow the judicial development of a defence of entrapment. The subsequent development of entrapment will be examined in chapter 3.]

ESTEY J.: If there be a defence of entrapment available to the accused in the circumstances of this appeal it cannot be of statutory origin for it is not to be found in the *Criminal Code*. If a defence arises in the common law it can only find its way into the courts through s. 7(3) of the *Code*:

> 7(3) Every rule and principle of the common law that renders any circumstance a justification or excuse for an act or a defence to a charge continues in force and applies in respect of proceedings for an offence under this Act or any other Act of the Parliament of Canada, except in so far as they are altered by or are inconsistent with this Act or any other Act of the Parliament of Canada.

This provision in turn only supports the application of such a defence if s-s. (3) has a continuing prospective character when properly construed. The Chief Justice assumes this to be the case in *R. v. Kirzner* (1977), 38 C.C.C. (2d) 131 at p. 138, 81 D.L.R. (3d) 229 at p. 236, [1978] 2 S.C.R. 487 at p. 496:

> I do not think that s. 7(3) should be regarded as having frozen the power of the Courts to enlarge the content of the common law by way of recognizing new defences, as they may think proper according to circumstances that they consider may call for further control of prosecutorial behaviour or of judicial proceedings.

… [T]he common law would be allowed to develop defences not inconsistent with the provisions of the Code if the construction adopted was prospective. For this conclusion I find support in the Report of the Imperial Commissioners on the Draft Code of 1879, s. 19 of which is the forerunner of our present s. 7(3). The commissioners explained the inclusion of s. 19 (now s. 7(3)) as follows, at volume I, p. 10, of their report:

> But whilst we exclude from the category of indictable offences any culpable act or omission not provided for by this or some other Act of Parliament, there is another branch of the unwritten law which introduces different considerations; namely, the principles which declare what circumstances amount to a justification or excuse for doing that which would be otherwise a crime, or at least would alter the quality of the crime.
>
> ... At present we desire to state that in our opinion it is, if not absolutely impossible, at least not practicable, to foresee all the various combinations of circumstances which may happen, but which are of so unfrequent occurrence that they have not hitherto been the subject of judicial consideration, although they might constitute a justification or excuse, and to use language at once so precise and clear and comprehensive as to include all cases that ought to be included, and not to include any case that ought to be excluded.
>
> We have already expressed our opinion that it is on the whole expedient that no crimes not specified in the Draft Code should be punished, though in consequence some guilty persons may thus escape punishment. But we do not think it desirable that, if a particular combination of circumstances arises of so unusual a character that the law has never been decided with reference to it, there should be any risk of a Code being so framed as to deprive an accused person of a defence to which the common law entitles him, and that it might become the duty of the judge to direct the jury that they must find him guilty, although the facts proved did show that he had a defence on the merits, and would have an undoubted claim to be pardoned by the Crown. While, therefore, digesting and declaring the law as applicable to the ordinary cases, we think that the common law so far as it affords a defence should be preserved in all cases not expressly provided for. This we have endeavoured to do by Section 19 of the Draft Code.

It might also be noted that in recent years this court has adverted to common law defences of duress (*R. v. Paquette* (1976), 30 C.C.C. (2d) 417, 70 D.L.R. (3d) 129, [1977] 2 S.C.R. 189), necessity (*Morgentaler v. The Queen* (1975), 20 C.C.C. (2d) 449, 53 D.L.R. (3d) 161, [1976] 1 S.C.R. 616), and due diligence (*R. v. City of Sault Ste. Marie* (1978), 40 C.C.C. (2d) 353, 85 D.L.R. (3d) 161, [1978] 2 S.C.R. 1299), without exclusive concern for the state of the law prior to the 1892 introduction of the *Criminal Code*.

Applying the ordinary rule of construction where statutes and common law meet I conclude that s. 7(3) is the authority for the courts of criminal jurisdiction to adopt, if appropriate in the view of the court, defences including the defence of entrapment. The components of such a defence and the criteria for its application raise other issues.

---

The Law Reform Commission of Canada has proposed that all defences be set out in a new Criminal Code "in the interest of comprehensiveness." The commission notes that it would still be "open to the courts to develop other defences insofar as is required by the reference to 'principles of fundamental justice' in s. 7 of the Charter." *Recodifying*

*Criminal Law* Report 31 (1987), at p. 28. Is this a wise departure from s. 8(3) of the present Code as interpreted in *Amato*, *supra*? Note that the sub-committee of the Standing Committee on Justice and the Solicitor-General examining the General Part of the *Criminal Code* recommended in its report of February 1993 that the Code should codify existing defences but continue to allow for the recognition of new defences.

### Common Law Offences

Even before the abolition of common law offences by the 1953 *Criminal Code*, the Supreme Court of Canada in *Frey v. Fedoruk*, [1950] S.C.R. 517 (a civil action for false imprisonment and malicious prosecution) had decided not to increase the number of common law offences and thus refused to declare it to be an offence to be a "peeping tom."

**Frey v. Fedoruk**
Supreme Court of Canada
[1950] S.C.R. 517

CARTWRIGHT J. (speaking for 6 out of 7 members of the Supreme Court sitting on the case stated in part): ... This appeal raises questions as to whether the conduct of the Plaintiff, which is popularly described as that of a "peeping tom," constitutes a criminal offence and if so, whether the Defendants Fedoruk and Stone were justified in arresting the Plaintiff without a warrant.

The majority of the Court of Appeal (O'Halloran, J.A. speaking for the majority) were of opinion that the Plaintiff was guilty of a criminal offence at Common Law, and that the Defendants were justified in the circumstances in arresting him without a warrant.

The only charge laid against the Plaintiff was that he:

> ... unlawfully did act in a manner likely to cause a breach of the peace by peeping at night through the window of the house of S. Fedoruk, there situated, against the peace of our Lord the King, his Crown and dignity; Contrary to the form of Statute in such case made and provided.

On this charge the Plaintiff was convicted by a police magistrate sitting for the summary trial of an indictable offence. The formal conviction concludes with the words:

> and I adjudge the said Bernard Frey for his said offence to keep the Peace and be of good behaviour for the term of one year.

If it should be admitted as a principle that conduct may be treated as criminal because, although not otherwise criminal, it has a natural tendency to provoke violence by way of retribution, it seems to me that great uncertainty would result. I do not think it safe by the application of such a supposed principle to declare an act or acts criminal which have not, up to the present, been held to be criminal in any reported case.

O'Halloran, J.A. does not refer to any reported case in which the conduct of a "peeping tom" has been held to be a criminal offence. As mentioned above, we were referred to no such case by counsel, and I have not been able to find one.

I do not understand O'Halloran, J.A. to suggest in his elaborate reasons that there is precedent for the view that the Plaintiff's conduct in this case was criminal. Rather he appears to support the finding of the trial Judge to that effect on the grounds stated in the following paragraph:

> Criminal responsibility at Common law is primarily not a matter of precedent, but of application of generic principle to the differing facts of each case. It is for the jury to apply to the facts of the case as they find them, the generic principle the Judge gives them. Thus by their general verdict the jury in practical effect decide both the law and the facts in the particular case, and have consistently done so over the centuries, and cf. *Coke on Littleton* (1832 Ed.) vol. 1, note 5, para. 155 (b). The fact finding Judge in this case, as the record shows, had not the slightest doubt on the evidence before him that what the appellant had been accused of was a criminal offence at Common Law.

I am of the opinion that the proposition implicit in the paragraph quoted above ought not to be accepted. I think that if adopted, it would introduce great uncertainty into the administration of the Criminal Law, leaving it to the judicial officer trying any particular charge to decide that the acts proved constituted a crime or otherwise, not by reference to any defined standard to be found in the code or in reported decisions, but according to his individual view as to whether such acts were a disturbance of the tranquillity of people tending to provoke physical reprisal.

---

John Willis saw the Supreme Court's decision in *Frey v. Fedoruk* not to expand the range of common law crimes to cover "peeping toms" as a decision to place "the protection of the individual from the risk of oppression" above "the protection of the state from the risk of disorder." He stated that the decision:

> … enunciates in ringing tones the grand old slogan that Canadians are not at the mercy of the whims of officials, even those officials who are independent of the government in power and called judges. So long as the principle is vindicated, it matters not that the police cannot any longer afford to the householder the protection he has been led to expect.

Willis observed that in England the common law crime of public mischief has been useful in addressing problems such as group libel and "hoaxing the police": "Case Comment" (1950), 28 *Can. Bar Rev.* 1023.

When in 1953 Parliament enacted the present s. 9 of the *Criminal Code* abolishing all but the common law offence of contempt of court, it also introduced an offence of trespassing at night: S.C. 1953-54, c. 51, s. 162 [now s. 177]. The offence provides:

> Every one who, without lawful excuse, the proof of which lies on him, loiters or prowls at night on the property of another person near a dwelling house situated in that property is guilty of an offence punishable on summary conviction.

---

The conspiracy section of the Canadian *Criminal Code* (s. 465) had a provision that was repealed in 1985 [R.S.C. 1985, c. 27, s. 61(3)], which stated:

> Every one who conspires with any one
>   (a) to effect an unlawful purpose, or
>   (b) to effect a lawful purpose by unlawful means,
> is guilty of an indictable offence and is liable to imprisonment for two years.

In *Shaw v. D.P.P.*, [1962] A.C. 220, the House of Lords in England held that the publishers of a directory of prostitutes were guilty of the common law offence of conspiracy to corrupt public morals. There was subsequently considerable controversy as to whether that decision was applicable in Canada to the offence listed above. In *Re Regina and Gralewicz* (1980), 54 C.C.C. (2d) 289 the Supreme Court of Canada clarified the issue by stating that in the conspiracy section: "unlawful purpose means contrary to law, that is prohibited by federal or provincial legislation." See now s. 465 of the *Code*. Subsection (1)(d) provides:

> (d) every one who conspires with any one to commit an offence punishable on summary conviction is guilty of an offence punishable on summary conviction.

## Jobidon v. The Queen
Supreme Court of Canada
[1991] 2 S.C.R. 714

GONTHIER J. (L'Heureux-Dubé, La Forest, Cory, and Iacobucci JJ. concurring):  All criminal offences in Canada are now defined in the Code (s. 9). But that does not mean the common law no longer illuminates these definitions nor gives content to the various principles of criminal responsibility those definitions draw from. As the Law Reform Commission of Canada has noted in its 31st report on recodification, the basic premises of our criminal law—the necessary conditions for criminal liability—are at present left to the common law. (*Recodifying Criminal Law*, at pp. 17, 28 and 34.) … Section 8 expressly indicates that the common law rules and principles continue to apply, but only to the extent that they are not inconsistent with the Code or other Act of Parliament and have not been altered by them.

In light of this communicated understanding of the antecedents and purpose of s. 8(3), it can hardly be said that the common law's developed approach to the role and scope of consent as a defence to assault has no place in our criminal law. If s. 8(3) and its interaction with the common law can be used to develop entirely new defences not inconsistent with the Code, it surely authorizes the courts to look to pre-existing common law rules and principles to give meaning to, and explain the outlines and boundaries of an existing defence or justification, indicating where they will not be recognized as legally effective—provided of course that there is no clear language in the Code which indicates that the Code has displaced the common law. That sort of language cannot be found in the Code. As such, the common law legitimately serves in this appeal as an archive in which one may locate situations or forms of conduct to which the law will not allow a person to consent.

SOPINKA J. (Stevenson J. concurring (in dissent)):  Section 265 states that "[a] person commits an assault when without the consent of another person, he applies force
intentionally to that other person. ..." My colleague Gonthier J. concludes that on the
basis of cases which applied the common law, that section should be interpreted as
excluding the absence of consent as an element of the *actus reus* in respect of an
assault with intent to commit intentional bodily harm. In coming to his conclusion
my colleague relies on a number of English authorities. The issue as not finally resolved in England until the decision of the English Court of Appeal on a reference to
it by the Attorney General in 1980. See *Attorney General's Reference (No. 6 of 1980)*,
[1981] 2 All E.R. 1057. Unconstrained by the expression of legislative policy, the
court moulded the common law to accord with the court's view of what was in the
public interest. On this basis the court discarded the absence of consent as an element
in assaults in which actual bodily harm was either caused or intended. Exceptions
were created for assaults that have some positive social value such as sporting events.
In Canada, the criminal law has been codified and the judiciary is constrained by the
wording of sections defining criminal offences. The courts' application of public
policy is governed by the expression of public policy in the *Criminal Code*. If Parliament intended to adopt the public policy which the English Court of Appeal developed it used singularly inappropriate language. It made the absence of consent a specific requirement and provided that this applied to all assaults without exception. ...
In my opinion the above observations as to the appropriate use of public policy are
sufficient to conclude that the absence of consent cannot be swept away by a robust
application of judge-made policy. This proposition is strengthened and confirmed by
the specific dictates of the Code with reference to the essential elements of a criminal
offence. Section 9(a) of the Code provides that "[n]otwithstanding anything in this
Act or any other Act, no person shall be convicted ... (a) of an offence at common
law." The effect of my colleague's approach is to create an offence where one does
not exist under the terms of the Code by application of the common law. The offence
created is the intentional application of force with the consent of the victim. I appreciate that my colleague's approach is to interpret the section in light of the common
law but, in my view, use of the common law to eliminate an element of the offence
that is required by statute is more than interpretation and is contrary to not only the
spirit but also the letter of s. 9(a). One of the basic reasons for s. 9(a) is the importance of certainty in determining what conduct constitutes a criminal offence. That is
the reason we have codified the offences in the *Criminal Code*. An accused should
not have to search the books to discover the common law in order to determine if the
offence charged is indeed an offence at law.

---

In *United Nurses of Alberta v. A.G. Alberta* (1992), 71 C.C.C. (3d) 225 (S.C.C.), the
accused union was fined $400,000 for contempt of court by disobeying court directives
not to go on strike. McLachlin J. stated for the Supreme Court of Canada:

It is argued that the offence of criminal contempt violates s. 7 of the *Canadian Charter of
Rights and Freedoms* because it is not codified and is vague and arbitrary. ...

The union's first position is that all uncodified common law crimes are unconstitutional. It is a fundamental principle of justice, it submits, that all crimes must be codified. Criminal contempt, although mentioned in s. 9 of the *Code*, is not codified, both its *actus reus* and *mens rea* being defined at common law.

We were referred to no authority in support of the proposition that fundamental justice requires codification of all crimes. The union cites the principle that there must be no crime or punishment except in accordance with fixed, predetermined law. But the absence of codification does not mean that a law violates this principle. For many centuries, most of our crimes were uncodified and were not viewed as violating this fundamental rule. Nor, conversely, is codification a guarantee that all is made manifest in the *Code*. Definition of elements of codified crimes not infrequently requires recourse to common law concepts: see *R. v. Jobidon* (1991), 66 C.C.C. (3d) 454, where the majority of this court, *per* Gonthier J., noted the important role the common law continues to play in the criminal law. The union also relies on the fact that this court has said it is for Parliament, not the courts, to create new offences: *Frey v. Fedoruk* (1950), 97 C.C.C. 1, [1950] 3 D.L.R. 513, [1950] S.C.R. 517; s. 9 of the *Criminal Code*. But this does not mean that the courts should refuse to recognize the common law crime of contempt of court which pre-dated codification and which is expressly preserved by s. 9 of the *Criminal Code*. I conclude that lack of codification in itself does not render the common law crime of criminal contempt of court unconstitutional.

The next argument is that the crime of criminal contempt is so vague and difficult to apply that it violates the fundamental principle of justice that the law should be fixed, predetermined and accessible and understandable by the public. ...

In this case there was ample evidence to support the conclusion that the union chose to defy court orders openly and continuously, with full knowledge that its defiance would be widely publicized and, even putting the union's case at its best, it did not care whether this would bring the court into disrepute.

Criminal contempt, thus defined, does not violate the Charter. It is neither vague nor arbitrary. A person can predict in advance whether his or her conduct will constitute a crime. The trial judges below had no trouble applying the right test, suggesting that the concept is capable of application without difficulty. Thus the case that the crime of contempt violates the principles of fundamental justice has not been made out.

The union's appeal was dismissed and the conviction affirmed.

## Vagueness, Overbreadth, and Certainty in the Criminal Law

Codification is thought to advance some of the most fundamental values of the criminal law. Many of these values are captured in the maxim *nullum crimen sine lege, nulla poena sine lege*: "there must be no crime or punishment except in accordance with fixed, predetermined law." For discussion. see G. Williams, *Criminal Law (The General Part)*, 2nd ed. (London: Stevens and Sons, 1961), c. 12; D. Stuart, *Canadian Criminal Law*, 3rd ed. (Toronto: Carswell, 2001), at 20-42; E. Colvin, "Criminal Law and the Rule of Law," in Fitzgerald, ed., *Crime, Justice and Codification* (Toronto: Carswell, 1986), c. 9.

One aspect of this principle is that crimes not be created or punished on a retroactive basis. This has been protected in ss. 11(g) and (i) of the Charter, which provide that any person charged with an offence has the right:

(g) not to be found guilty on account of any act or omission unless, at the time of the act or omission, it constituted an offence under Canadian or international law or was criminal according to the general principles of law recognized by the community of nations; ...

(i) if found guilty of the offence and if the punishment for the offence has been varied between the time of commission and the time of sentencing, to the benefit of the lesser punishment.

Another value of codification is that the criminal law should be certain.

_____

In *R. v. Nova Scotia Pharmaceutical Society* (1992), 74 C.C.C. (3d) 289, the Supreme Court affirmed the existence of a void for vagueness doctrine under the Charter. Gonthier J. stated:

> Vagueness can be raised under s. 7 of the Charter, since it is a principle of fundamental justice that laws may not be too vague. It can also be raised under s. 1 of the Charter *in limine*, on the basis that an enactment is so vague as not to satisfy the requirement that a limitation on Charter rights be "prescribed by law." ...
>
> The "doctrine of vagueness" is founded on the rule of law, particularly on the principles of fair notice to citizens and limitation of enforcement discretion. ...
>
> *Fair notice to the citizen*
>
> Fair notice to the citizen, as a guide to conduct and a contributing element to a full answer and defence, comprises two aspects.
>
> First of all, there is the more formal aspect of notice, that is acquaintance with the actual text of a statute. In the criminal context, this concern has more or less been set aside by the common law maxim, "Ignorance of the law is no excuse," embodied in s. 19 of the *Criminal Code*.
>
> ... Some authors have expressed the opinion that this maxim contradicts the rule of law, and should be revised in the light of the growing quantity and complexity of penal legislation: see E. Colvin, "Criminal Law and The Rule of Law," in P. Fitzgerald, ed., *Crime, Justice & Codification: Essays in commemoration of Jacques Fortin* (Toronto: Carswell, 1986), p. 125, at p. 151, and J.C. Jeffries, Jr., "Legality, Vagueness, and the Construction of Penal Statutes" (1985), 71 *Va. L. Rev.* 189 at p. 209. Since this argument was not raised in this case, I will refrain from ruling on this issue. In any event, given that, as this court has already recognized, case law applying and interpreting a particular section is relevant in determining whether the section is vague, formal notice is not a central concern in a vagueness analysis. ...
>
> Fair notice may not have been given when enactments are in somewhat general terms, in a way that does not readily permit citizens to be aware of their substance, when they do not relate to any element of the substratum of values held by society. It is no coincidence that these enactments are often found vague. For instance, the vagrancy ordinance invalidated by the United States Supreme Court in *Papachristou v. City of Jacksonville*, 405 U.S. 156 (1972), or the compulsory identification statute struck down in *Kolender v. Lawson*, 461 U.S. 352 (1983), fall in this group.

*Limitation of law enforcement discretion*

Lamer J. in the *Prostitution Reference* (1990), 56 C.C.C. (3d) 65, used the phrase "standardless sweep," first coined by the United States Supreme Court in *Smith v. Goguen*, 415 U.S. 566 (1974) at p. 575, to describe the limitation of enforcement discretion rationale for the doctrine of vagueness. It has become the prime concern in American constitutional law: *Kolender*, at pp. 357-8. Indeed, today it has become paramount, given the considerable expansion in the discretionary powers of enforcement agencies that has followed the creation of the modern welfare state.

A law must not be so devoid of precision in its content that a conviction will automatically flow from the decision to prosecute. Such is the crux of the concern for limitation of enforcement discretion. When the power to decide whether a charge will lead to conviction or acquittal, normally the preserve of the judiciary, becomes fused with the power to prosecute because of the wording of the law, then a law will be unconstitutionally vague.

For instance, the wording of the vagrancy ordinance invalidated by the United States Supreme Court in *Papachristou*, and quoted at length in the *Prostitution Reference* at p. 86, was so general and so lacked precision in its content that a conviction would ensue every time the law enforcer decided to charge someone with the offence of vagrancy. The words of the ordinance had no substance to them, and they indicated no particular legislative purpose. They left the accused completely in the dark, with no possible way of defending himself before the court.

In this case the Supreme Court of Canada unanimously held that s. 32(1)(c) of the then *Combines Investigation Act*, R.S.C. 1970, C-23, which made it an offence to "lessen, unduly, competition" was not impermissibly vague. In most cases, challenges under s. 7 of the Charter to offences on the basis of vagueness have failed with the courts often stressing that courts can still place a limiting interpretation on expansively worded statutes. See Gary Trotter, "*Le Beau*: Towards a Canadian Vagueness Doctrine" (1988), 62 C.R. (3d) 157; Don Stuart, *Charter Justice in Canadian Criminal Law*, 3rd ed. (Toronto: Carswell, 2001), at 102-7. The next case examines one of the few instances where the courts have invalidated a law under s. 7 of the Charter on the grounds that it was vague and overbroad.

## R. v. Heywood
Supreme Court of Canada
[1994] 3 S.C.R. 761

[The case involved s. 179(1)(b) of the *Criminal Code*, which provided that it was an offence for a person with a past sexual violence conviction to be "found loitering in or near a school ground, playground, public park or bathing area." The British Columbia Court of Appeal quashed the conviction of a man with two prior convictions of sexual assault of young girls after he was "found loitering in or near … a playground." He had been found photographing young children at play after a store had alerted the Victoria police that he had brought photos of the crotch area of young girls to be developed. The Crown appealed to the Supreme Court.]

CORY J. (Lamer C.J., Sopinka, Iacobucci, and Major JJ. concurring): ... Overbreadth and vagueness are different concepts, but are sometimes related in particular cases. As the Ontario Court of Appeal observed in *R. v. Zundel* (1987), 58 O.R. (2d) 129, at pp. 157-58, cited with approval by Gonthier J. in *R. v. Nova Scotia Pharmaceutical Society, supra*, the meaning of a law may be unambiguous and thus the law will not be vague; however, it may still be overly broad. Where a law is vague, it may also be overly broad, to the extent that the ambit of its application is difficult to define. Overbreadth and vagueness are related in that both are the result of a lack of sufficient precision by a legislature in the means used to accomplish an objective. In the case of vagueness, the means are not clearly defined. In the case of overbreadth the means are too sweeping in relation to the objective.

Overbreadth analysis looks at the means chosen by the state in relation to its purpose. In considering whether a legislative provision is overbroad, a court must ask the question: are those means necessary to achieve the State objective? If the State, in pursuing a legitimate objective, uses means which are broader than is necessary to accomplish that objective, the principles of fundamental justice will be violated because the individual's rights will have been limited for no reason. The effect of overbreadth is that in some applications the law is arbitrary or disproportionate. ...

In summary, s. 179(1)(b) is overly broad to an extent that it violates the right to liberty proclaimed by s. 7 of the Charter for a number of reasons. First, it is overly broad in its geographical scope embracing as it does all public parks and beaches no matter how remote and devoid of children they may be. Secondly, it is overly broad in its temporal aspect with the prohibition applying for life without any process for review. Thirdly, it is too broad in the number of persons it encompasses. Fourthly, the prohibitions are put in place and may be enforced without any notice to the accused.

I am strengthened in this conclusion by a consideration of the new s. 161 of the *Criminal Code*, S.C. 1993, c. 45, s. 1, which was enacted shortly after the decision of the British Columbia Court of Appeal in this case. ...

It can be seen that this section is limited to clearly defined geographical areas where children are or can reasonably be expected to be present. Further, the prohibition may be for life or a shorter period and a system of review is provided. Additionally, the order of prohibition is made part of the sentencing procedure so that the accused is aware of and notified of the prohibitions. It is thus apparent that overly broad provisions are not essential or necessary in order to achieve the aim of s. 179(1)(b).

GONTHIER J. (La Forest, L'Heureux-Dubé, and McLachlin JJ. concurring (in dissent)): The interpretation I advocate eliminates Cory J.'s concern that the prohibition is overbroad. A lifetime prohibition of activities with a malevolent or ulterior purpose related to reoffending is in no way objectionable or overbroad. Such a prohibition would impose a restriction on the liberty of the affected individuals to which ordinary citizens are not subject, but that restriction is directly related to preventing reoffending. The affected persons' history of offending, the uncertainties prevalent in treating offenders and a desire to disrupt the cycle of reoffending justify what is, in effect, a minor intrusion which does not breach the principles of fundamental justice. ...

In addition to overbreadth, the absence of any notice of the prohibition contained in s. 179(1)(b) was relied upon by Cory J. in concluding that s. 7 of the Charter was violated. The basis for this conclusion was that notice is provided for in the case of certain other prohibitions contained in the *Code* and that the lack of notice in the case of s. 179(1)(b) "is unfair and unnecessarily so." In so concluding, Cory J. would make notice, albeit in limited circumstances, a principle of fundamental justice. With all due respect, I cannot agree. It is a basic tenet of our legal system that ignorance of the law is not an excuse for breaking the law. This fundamental principle has been given legislative expression in s. 19 of the *Criminal Code*: "Ignorance of the law by a person who commits an offence is not an excuse for committing that offence." Though formal notice of the content of s. 179(1)(b) might be preferable, I can see no basis for transforming the legislator's decision to provide notice in respect of certain *Code* prohibitions into a principle of fundamental justice.

---

Might any of the provisions in the new s. 161 be vague or overbroad? See *R. v. Budreo* (2000), 32 C.R. (5th) 127 (Ont. C.A.). Ignorance of the law is examined in chapter 11.

### Canadian Foundation for Children, Youth and the Law v. Canada (Attorney General)
Supreme Court of Canada
2004 SCC 4

[In this case, the Supreme Court considered whether s. 43 of the *Criminal Code* authorizing the use of force "by way of correction toward a pupil or child ... if the force does not exceed what is reasonable under the circumstances" was void because of vagueness or overbreadth. The majority of the court also rejected arguments that it violated ss. 2 and 15 of the Charter.]

McLACHLIN C.J. (Gonthier, Iacobucci, Major, Bastarache, Binnie, and LeBel JJ. concurring): ...

[15] A law is unconstitutionally vague if it "does not provide an adequate basis for legal debate" and "analysis"; "does not sufficiently delineate any area of risk"; or "is not intelligible." The law must offer a "grasp to the judiciary": *R. v. Nova Scotia Pharmaceutical Society*, [1992] 2 S.C.R. 606, at pp. 639-40.

Certainty is not required. As Gonthier J. pointed out in *Nova Scotia Pharmaceutical, supra*, at pp. 638-39,

> ... conduct is guided by approximation. The process of approximation sometimes results in quite a narrow set of options, sometimes in a broader one. *Legal dispositions therefore delineate a risk zone*, and cannot hope to do more, unless they are directed at individual instances. [Emphasis added.]

[16]  A law must set an intelligible standard both for the citizens it governs and the officials who must enforce it. The two are interconnected. A vague law prevents the citizen from realizing when he or she is entering an area of risk for criminal sanction. It similarly makes it difficult for law enforcement officers and judges to determine whether a crime has been committed. This invokes the further concern of putting too much discretion in the hands of law enforcement officials, and violates the precept that individuals should be governed by the rule of law, not the rule of persons. The doctrine of vagueness is directed generally at the evil of leaving "basic policy matters to policemen, judges, and juries for resolution on an ad hoc and subjective basis, with the attendant dangers of arbitrary and discriminatory application": *Grayned v. City of Rockford*, 408 U.S. 104 (1972), at p. 109. ...

[19]  The purpose of s. 43 is to delineate a sphere of non-criminal conduct within the larger realm of common assault. It must, as we have seen, do this in a way that permits people to know when they are entering a zone of risk of criminal sanction and that avoids ad hoc discretionary decision-making by law enforcement officials. People must be able to assess when conduct approaches the boundaries of the sphere that s. 43 provides.

[20]  To ascertain whether s. 43 meets these requirements, we must consider its words and court decisions interpreting those words. The words of the statute must be considered in context, in their grammatical and ordinary sense, and with a view to the legislative scheme's purpose and the intention of Parliament: *Rizzo & Rizzo Shoes Ltd. (Re)*, [1998] 1 S.C.R. 27, at para. 21; *Bell ExpressVu Limited Partnership v. Rex*, [2002] 2 S.C.R. 559, 2002 SCC 42, at para. 26. Since s. 43 withdraws the protection of the criminal law in certain circumstances, it should be strictly construed: see *Ogg-Moss v. The Queen*, [1984] 2 S.C.R. 173, at p. 183.

[21]  Section 43 delineates who may access its sphere with considerable precision. The terms "schoolteacher" and "parent" are clear. The phrase "person standing in the place of a parent" has been held by the courts to indicate an individual who has assumed "all the obligations of parenthood": *Ogg-Moss, supra*, at p. 190. These terms present no difficulty.

[22]  Section 43 identifies less precisely what conduct falls within its sphere. It defines this conduct in two ways. The first is by the requirement that the force be "by way of correction." The second is by the requirement that the force be "reasonable under the circumstances." The question is whether, taken together and construed in accordance with governing principles, these phrases provide sufficient precision to delineate the zone of risk and avoid discretionary law enforcement. ...

[27]  [T]he law has long used reasonableness to delineate areas of risk, without incurring the dangers of vagueness. The law of negligence, which has blossomed in recent decades to govern private actions in nearly all spheres of human activity, is founded upon the presumption that individuals are capable of governing their conduct in accordance with the standard of what is "reasonable." But reasonableness as a guide to conduct is not confined to the law of negligence. The criminal law also relies on it. The *Criminal Code* expects that police officers will know what constitutes "reasonable grounds" for believing that an offence has been committed, such that an arrest can be made (s. 495); that an individual will know what constitutes "reasonable

steps" to obtain consent to sexual contact (s. 273.2(b)); and that surgeons, in order to be exempted from criminal liability, will judge whether performing an operation is "reasonable" in "all the circumstances of the case" (s. 45). These are merely a few examples; the criminal law is thick with the notion of "reasonableness." ...

[30] The first limitation arises from the behaviour for which s. 43 provides an exemption, simple non-consensual application of force. Section 43 does not exempt from criminal sanction conduct that causes harm or raises a reasonable prospect of harm. It can be invoked only in cases of non-consensual application of force that results neither in harm nor in the prospect of bodily harm. This limits its operation to the mildest forms of assault. People must know that if their conduct raises an apprehension of bodily harm they cannot rely on s. 43. Similarly, police officers and judges must know that the defence cannot be raised in such circumstances.

[31] Within this limited area of application, further precision on what is reasonable under the circumstances may be derived from international treaty obligations. Statutes should be construed to comply with Canada's international obligations: *Ordon Estate v. Grail*, [1998] 3 S.C.R. 437, at para. 137. Canada's international commitments confirm that physical correction that either harms or degrades a child is unreasonable. ...

[36] Determining what is "reasonable under the circumstances" in the case of child discipline is also assisted by social consensus and expert evidence on what constitutes reasonable corrective discipline. The criminal law often uses the concept of reasonableness to accommodate evolving mores and avoid successive "fine-tuning" amendments. It is implicit in this technique that current social consensus on what is reasonable may be considered. It is wrong for caregivers or judges to apply their own subjective notions of what is reasonable; s. 43 demands an objective appraisal based on current learning and consensus. Substantial consensus, particularly when supported by expert evidence, can provide guidance and reduce the danger of arbitrary, subjective decision making.

[37] Based on the evidence currently before the Court, there are significant areas of agreement among the experts on both sides of the issue (trial decision, para. 17). Corporal punishment of children under two years is harmful to them, and has no corrective value given the cognitive limitations of children under two years of age. Corporal punishment of teenagers is harmful, because it can induce aggressive or antisocial behaviour. Corporal punishment using objects, such as rulers or belts, is physically and emotionally harmful. Corporal punishment which involves slaps or blows to the head is harmful. These types of punishment, we may conclude, will not be reasonable.

[38] Contemporary social consensus is that, while teachers may sometimes use corrective force to remove children from classrooms or secure compliance with instructions, the use of corporal punishment by teachers is not acceptable. Many school boards forbid the use of corporal punishment, and some provinces and territories have legislatively prohibited its use by teachers: see, e.g., *Schools Act*, 1997, S.N.L. 1997, c. S-12.2, s. 42; *School Act*, R.S.B.C. 1996, c. 412, s. 76(3); *Education Act*, S.N.B. 1997, c. E-1.12, s. 23; *School Act*, R.S.P.E.I. 1988, c. S-2.1, s. 73; *Education Act*, S.N.W.T. 1995, c. 28, s. 34(3); *Education Act*, S.Y. 1989-90, c. 25, s. 36. ...

Section 43 will protect a teacher who uses reasonable, corrective force to restrain or remove a child in appropriate circumstances. Substantial societal consensus, supported by expert evidence and Canada's treaty obligations, indicates that corporal punishment by teachers is unreasonable.

[39] Finally, judicial interpretation may assist in defining "reasonable under the circumstances" under s. 43. It must be conceded at the outset that judicial decisions on s. 43 in the past have sometimes been unclear and inconsistent, sending a muddled message as to what is and is not permitted. In many cases discussed by Arbour J., judges failed to acknowledge the evolutive nature of the standard of reasonableness, and gave undue authority to outdated conceptions of reasonable correction. On occasion, judges erroneously applied their own subjective views on what constitutes reasonable discipline—views as varied as different judges' backgrounds. In addition, charges of assaultive discipline were seldom viewed as sufficiently serious to merit in-depth research and expert evidence or the appeals which might have permitted a unified national standard to emerge. However, "[t]he fact that a particular legislative term is open to varying interpretations by the courts is not fatal": *Reference re ss. 193 and 195.1(1)(c) of the Criminal Code (Man.)*, [1990] 1 S.C.R. 1123, at p. 1157. This case, and those that build on it, may permit a more uniform approach to "reasonable under the circumstances" than has prevailed in the past. Again, the issue is not whether s. 43 has provided enough guidance in the past, but whether it expresses a standard that can be given a core meaning in tune with contemporary consensus.

[40] When these considerations are taken together, a solid core of meaning emerges for "reasonable under the circumstances," sufficient to establish a zone in which discipline risks criminal sanction. Generally, s. 43 exempts from criminal sanction only minor corrective force of a transitory and trifling nature. On the basis of current expert consensus, it does not apply to corporal punishment of children under two or teenagers. Degrading, inhuman or harmful conduct is not protected. Discipline by the use of objects or blows or slaps to the head is unreasonable. Teachers may reasonably apply force to remove a child from a classroom or secure compliance with instructions, but not merely as corporal punishment. Coupled with the requirement that the conduct be corrective, which rules out conduct stemming from the caregiver's frustration, loss of temper or abusive personality, a consistent picture emerges of the area covered by s. 43. It is wrong for law enforcement officers or judges to apply their own subjective views of what is "reasonable under the circumstances"; the test is objective. The question must be considered in context and in light of all the circumstances of the case. The gravity of the precipitating event is not relevant.

[41] The fact that borderline cases may be anticipated is not fatal. As Gonthier J. stated in *Nova Scotia Pharmaceutical*, at p. 639, "... it is inherent to our legal system that some conduct will fall along the boundaries of the area of risk; no definite prediction can then be made. Guidance, not direction, of conduct is a more realistic objective."

[42] Section 43 achieves this objective. It sets real boundaries and delineates a risk zone for criminal sanction. The prudent parent or teacher will refrain from conduct that approaches those boundaries, while law enforcement officers and judges

will proceed with them in mind. It does not violate the principle of fundamental justice that laws must not be vague or arbitrary.

[43] My colleague, Arbour J., by contrast, takes the view that s. 43 is unconstitutionally vague, a point of view also expressed by Deschamps J. Arbour J. argues first that the foregoing analysis amounts to an impermissible reading down of s. 43. This contention is answered by the evidence in this case, which established a solid core of meaning for s. 43; to construe terms like "reasonable under the circumstances" by reference to evidence and argument is a common and accepted function of courts interpreting the criminal law. To interpret "reasonable" in light of the evidence is not judicial amendment, but judicial interpretation. It is a common practice, given the number of criminal offences conditioned by the term "reasonable." If "it is the function of the appellate courts to rein in overly elastic interpretations" (Binnie J., at para. 122), it is equally their function to define the scope of criminal defences.

[44] Arbour J. also argues that unconstitutional vagueness is established by the fact that courts in the past have applied s. 43 inconsistently. Again, the inference does not follow. Vagueness is not argued on the basis of whether a provision has been interpreted consistently in the past, but whether it is capable of providing guidance for the future. Inconsistent and erroneous applications are not uncommon in criminal law, where many provisions admit of difficulty; we do not say that this makes them unconstitutional. Rather, we rely on appellate courts to clarify the meaning so that future application may be more consistent. I agree with Arbour J. that Canadians would find the decisions in many of the past cases on s. 43 to be seriously objectionable. However, the discomfort of Canadians in the face of such unwarranted acts of violence toward children merely demonstrates that it is possible to define what corrective force is reasonable in the circumstances. Finally, Arbour J. argues that parents who face criminal charges as a result of corrective force will be able to rely on the defences of necessity and "*de minimis.*" The defence of necessity, I agree, is available, but only in situations where corrective force is not in issue, like saving a child from imminent danger. As for the defence of *de minimis*, it is equally or more vague and difficult in application than the reasonableness defence offered by s. 43.

*Overbreadth*

[45] Section 43 of the *Criminal Code* refers to corrective force against children generally. The Foundation argues that this is overbroad because children under the age of two are not capable of correction and children over the age of 12 will only be harmed by corrective force. These classes of children, it is argued, should have been excluded.

[46] This concern is addressed by Parliament's decision to confine the exemption to reasonable correction, discussed above. Experts consistently indicate that force applied to a child too young to be capable of learning from physical correction is not corrective force. Similarly, current expert consensus indicates that corporal punishment of teenagers creates a serious risk of psychological harm: employing it would thus be unreasonable. There may however be instances in which a parent or school teacher reasonably uses corrective force to restrain or remove an adolescent from a

particular situation, falling short of corporal punishment. Section 43 does not permit force that cannot correct or is unreasonable. It follows that it is not overbroad. ...

ARBOUR J. (Deschamps J. concurring (in dissent)):
[131] This appeal raises the constitutional validity of s. 43 of the *Criminal Code*, R.S.C. 1985, c. C-46, which justifies the reasonable use of force by way of correction by parents and teachers against children in their care. Although I come to a conclusion which may not be very different from that reached by the Chief Justice, I do so for very different reasons. The Chief Justice significantly curtails the scope of the defence of s. 43 of the *Code*, partly on the basis that s. 43 should be strictly construed since it withdraws the protection of the criminal law in certain circumstances. According to her analysis, s. 43 can only be raised as a defence to a charge of simple (common) assault; it applies only to corrective force, used against children older than two but not against teenagers; it cannot involve the use of objects, and should not consist of blows to the head; and it should not relate to the "gravity" of the conduct attracting correction.
[132] With respect, in my opinion, such a restrictive interpretation of a statutory defence is inconsistent with the role of courts *vis-à-vis* criminal defences, both statutory and common law defences. Furthermore, this restrictive interpretation can only be arrived at if dictated by constitutional imperatives. Canadian courts have not thus far understood the concept of reasonable force to mean the "minor corrective force" advocated by the Chief Justice. In my view, the defence contained in s. 43 of the *Code*, interpreted and applied inconsistently by the courts in Canada, violates the constitutional rights of children to safety and security and must be struck down. Absent action by Parliament, other existing common law defences, such as the defence of necessity and the "*de minimis*" defence, will suffice to ensure that parents and teachers are not branded as criminals for their trivial use of force to restrain children when appropriate.
[133] Section 43 of the *Code* justifies the use of force by parents and teachers by way of correction. The force that is justified is force that is "reasonable under the circumstances." The section does not say that forcible correction is a defence only to common assault. Nor has it been understood to be so restrictive: see *R. v. Pickard*, [1995] B.C.J. No. 2861 (QL) (Prov. Ct.); *R. v. G.C.C.* (2001), 206 Nfld. & P.E.I.R. 231 (Nfld. S.C.T.D.); *R. v. Fritz* (1987), 55 Sask. R. 302 (Q.B.); *R. v. Bell*, [2001] O.J. No. 1820 (QL) (S.C.J.); and *R. v. N.S.*, [1999] O.J. No. 320 (QL) (Ct.J. (Gen. Div.)), where s. 43 was successfully raised as a defence against charges of assault with a weapon and/or assault causing bodily harm.
[134] In the *Code*, the justifiable use of force may be advanced as a defence against a wide range of offences that have at their origin the application of force. These offences range from common assault, to assault causing bodily harm and eventually to manslaughter. ...
[135] In the case at bar, the critical inquiry turns on the meaning of the phrases "force by way of correction" and "reasonable under the circumstances" (s. 43 of the *Code*). To say, as the Chief Justice does, that this defence cannot be used to justify any criminal charge beyond simple assault, that the section cannot justify the use of

corrective force against a child under 2 or against a teenager, and that force is never reasonable if an object is used, is a laudable effort to take the law where it ought to be. However, s. 43 can only be so interpreted if the law, as it stands, offends the Constitution and must therefore be curtailed. Absent such constitutional constraints, it is neither the historic nor the proper role of courts to enlarge criminal responsibility by limiting defences enacted by Parliament. In fact, the role of the courts is precisely the opposite.

[136] Setting aside any constitutional considerations for the moment, courts are expressly prohibited by s. 9 of the *Code* from creating new common law offences. All criminal offences must be enacted by statute. On the other hand, the courts have been and continue to be the guardians of common law defences. This reflects the role of courts as enforcers of fundamental principles of criminal responsibility including, in particular, the fundamental concept of fault which can only be reduced or displaced by statute. ...

[138] In this case, we have been asked to either curtail or abolish altogether a defence created by Parliament. If we are to do this, as I believe we must, it should be for higher constitutional imperatives. Absent a finding of a constitutional violation by Parliament, the reading down of a statutory defence as is done by the Chief Justice amounts to, in my respectful opinion, an abandonment by the courts of their proper role in the criminal process.

[139] Courts, including this Court, have until now properly focussed on what constitutes force that is "reasonable under the circumstances." No pre-emptive barriers have been erected. Nothing in the words of the statute, properly construed, suggests that Parliament intended that some conduct be excluded at the outset from the scope of s. 43's protection. This is the law as we must take it in order to assess its constitutionality. To essentially rewrite it before validating its constitutionality is to hide the constitutional imperative.

[140] The role of the courts when applying defences must be contrasted with the role of courts when they are called upon to examine the constitutional validity of criminal *offences*. In such cases, it is entirely appropriate for the courts to interpret the provisions that proscribe conduct in a manner that least restricts "the liberty of the subject," consistent with the wording of the statute and the intent of Parliament. This is what was done in *R. v. Sharpe*, [2001] 1 S.C.R. 45, 2001 SCC 2, for example. But such a technique cannot be employed to restrict the scope of statutory *defences* without the courts compromising the core of their interplay with Parliament in the orderly development and application of the criminal law.

[141] In the end, I will conclude, not unlike the Chief Justice, that the use of corrective force by parents and teachers against children under their care is only permitted when the force is minimal and insignificant. I so conclude not because this is what the *Code* currently provides but because it is what the Constitution requires. ...

[183] "Reasonableness" with respect to s. 43 is linked to public policy issues and one's own sense of parental authority. "Reasonableness" will always entail an element of subjectivity. As McCombs J. recognized in the case at bar, "[b]ecause the notion of reasonableness varies with the beholder, it is perhaps not surprising that some of the judicial decisions applying s. 43 to excuse otherwise criminal assault

appear to some to be inconsistent and unreasonable" ((2000), 49 O.R. (3d) 662, at para. 4). It is clear, however, that the concept of reasonableness, so widely used in the law generally, and in the criminal law in particular, is not in and of itself unconstitutionally vague. "Reasonableness" functions as an intelligible standard in many other criminal law contexts. ...

[189]  I doubt that it can be said, on the basis of the existing record, that the justification of corporal punishment of children when the force used is "reasonable under the circumstances" gives adequate notice to parents and teachers as to what is and is not permissible in a criminal context. Furthermore, it neither adequately guides the decision-making power of law enforcers nor delineates, in an acceptable fashion, the boundaries of legal debate. The Chief Justice rearticulates the s. 43 defence as the delineation of a "risk zone for criminal sanction" (para. 18). I do not disagree with such a formulation of the vagueness doctrine in this context. Still, on this record, the "risk zone" for victims and offenders alike has been a moving target.

[190]  In the Chief Justice's reasons, it is useful to note how much work must go into making the provision constitutionally sound and sufficiently precise: (1) the word "child" must be construed as including children only over age 2 and younger than teenage years; (2) parts of the body must be excluded; (3) implements must be prohibited; (4) the nature of the offence calling for correction is deemed not a relevant contextual consideration; (5) teachers are prohibited from utilizing corporal punishment; and (6) the use of force that causes injury that is neither transient nor trifling (assault causing bodily harm) is prohibited (it seems even if the force is used by way of restraint). At some point, in an effort to give sufficient precision to provide notice and constrain discretion in enforcement, mere interpretation ends and an entirely new provision is drafted. As this Court concluded in *R. v. Heywood*, [1994] 3 S.C.R. 761, at p. 803:

> The changes which would be required to make s. 179(1)(b) [here, s. 43] constitutional would not constitute reading down or reading in; *rather, they would amount to judicial rewriting of the legislation.* [Emphasis added.]

The restrictions put forth by the Chief Justice with respect to the scope of the defence have not emerged from the existing case law. These restrictions are far from self-evident and would not have been anticipated by many parents, teachers or enforcement officials.

[191]  In my view, we cannot cure vagueness from the top down by declaring that a proper legal debate has taken place and that anything outside its boundaries is simply wrong and must be discarded. Too many people have been engaged in attempting to define the boundaries of that very debate for years in Canadian courtrooms to simply dismiss their conclusions because they do not conform with a norm that was never apparent to anyone until now. As demonstrated earlier, s. 43 has been subject to considerable disparity in application, some courts justifying conduct that other courts have found wholly unreasonable, despite valiant efforts by the lower courts to give intelligible content to the provision. Attempts at judicial interpretation which would structure the discretion in s. 43 have, in my opinion, failed to provide coherent or cogent guidelines that would meet the standard of notice and specificity generally

required in the criminal law. Thus, despite the efforts of judges, some of whom have openly expressed their frustration with what has been described as "no clear test" and a "legal lottery" in the criminal law (McGillivray, "'He'll learn it on his body': Disciplining childhood in Canadian law," [(1997), 5 *Int'l J. Child. Rts* 193], at p. 228; *James, ... per* Weagant Prov. J., at paras. 11-12), the ambit of the justification remains about as unclear as when it was first codified in 1892. As Lamer C.J. stated in *R. v. Morales*, [1992] 3 S.C.R. 711, at p. 729:

> A standardless sweep does not become acceptable simply because it results from the whims of judges and justices of the peace rather than the whims of law enforcement officials. Cloaking whims in judicial robes is not sufficient to satisfy the principles of fundamental justice.

This would not only raise the already high bar set in *Nova Scotia Pharmaceutical*, *supra*; it would essentially make it unreachable.

[192] As a result, I find that the phrase "reasonable under the circumstances" in s. 43 of the *Code* violates children's security of the person interest and that the deprivation is not in accordance with the relevant principle of fundamental justice, in that it is unconstitutionally vague.

### Construction or Interpretation of the Criminal Code

The *Criminal Code* has historically been interpreted in a "strict" manner designed to give the accused the benefit of a doubt concerning any textual ambiguity. Is this a wise policy for the courts to pursue? In recent years, there has been a trend to making resort to the doctrine of strict construction only if there is an ambiguity in a statute after it has been given a purposive interpretation designed to achieve its objectives. What is left of the doctrine of strict construction of the criminal law?

### R. v. Goulis
Ontario Court of Appeal
(1981), 60 C.C.C. (2d) 347

MARTIN J.A. (for the Court):   The Attorney-General for Ontario appeals against the acquittal of the respondent by His Honour Judge Graburn, following a submission by the respondent that there was no case to answer, on a charge:

> ... that he between August 26, 1977 and December 1st, 1977, at the Municipality of Metropolitan Toronto ... with intent to defraud his creditors, concealed property, to wit: shoes to a value of more than $200; contrary to section 350(a)(ii) [now s. 390] of the Criminal Code.

The precise issue in this appeal is whether a bankrupt who deliberately fails to include items of his property in his statement of his affairs to the trustee, required to be submitted under s. 129 of the *Bankruptcy Act*, R.S.C. 1970, c. B-3, and fails to disclose them as assets in his examination by the Official Receiver under s. 132 of the

Act has "concealed" his property with intent to defraud his creditors under s. 350(a)(ii) of the *Code*.

Section 350 of the *Code* reads:

> 350. Every one who,
>
>    (a)  with intent to defraud his creditors,
>
>       (i)  makes or causes to be made a gift, conveyance, assignment, sale, transfer or delivery of his property, or
>
>       (ii)  removes, conceals or disposes of any of his property, or
>
>    (b)  with intent that any one should defraud his creditors, receives any property by means of or in relation to which an offence has been committed under paragraph (a),
>
> is guilty of an indictable offence and is liable to imprisonment for two years. ...

The appeal was argued on the basis of an agreed statement of facts: On August 15, 1977, the respondent, pursuant to s. 31 of the *Bankruptcy Act*, made an assignment for the general benefit of his creditors. On the same date the respondent, pursuant to s. 129(d) of the Act, submitted a statement of his affairs verified by affidavit to the trustee.

Section 129(d) reads:

> 129. The bankrupt shall ...
>
>    (d)  within seven days following his bankruptcy, unless the time is extended by the official receiver, prepare and submit to the trustee in quadruplicate a statement of his affairs in the prescribed form verified by affidavit and showing the particulars of his assets and liabilities, the names and addresses of his creditors, the securities held by them respectively, the dates when the securities were respectively given and such further or other information as may be required, but where the affairs of the bankrupt are so involved or complicated that he cannot himself reasonably prepare a proper statement of his affairs, the official receiver may, as an expense of the administration, authorize the employment of some qualified person to assist in the preparation of the statement. ...

On August 15, 1977, the respondent had assets consisting of 1,173 pairs of assorted ladies' and men's shoes and boots. The respondent in the statement of his affairs did not disclose these assets to his trustee, nor did he disclose them when he was examined, on August 26, 1977, by an Official Receiver pursuant to s. 132(1) of the Act which reads:

> 132(1)  The official receiver shall on the attendance of the bankrupt examine the bankrupt under oath as to his conduct, the causes of his bankruptcy and the disposition of his property and shall put to him the prescribed question or questions to the like effect and such other questions as he may see fit; the official receiver shall make notes of the examination and a report of any facts or circumstances that in his opinion require special consideration or further explanation or investigation and shall forward a copy of his notes and the report to the Superintendent, to the trustee and to the court for deposit therein, and shall communicate the contents thereof to the creditors at their first meeting.

The case for the Crown is that the respondent by failing to disclose to the trustee the existence of the above property, when he was under a duty to do so, concealed his property contrary to s. 350(a)(ii) of the *Code*. The short agreed statement of facts does not disclose where the property in question was at the relevant time.

The learned trial Judge in his reasons for judgment took as his starting point the following statement in Driedger, *The Construction of Statutes* (1974), at p. 153:

> That penal statutes are to be construed "strictly" in the sense described by Lord Radcliffe in *Attorney-General v. Hallet & Carey* [[1952] A.C. 427] is clear from the decisions. In *Tuck & Sons v. Priester* [(1887), 19 Q.B.D. 629 at p. 638] Lord Esher said:
>
> > We must be very careful in construing that section, because it imposes a penalty. If there is a reasonable interpretation which will avoid the penalty in any particular case we must adopt that construction. If there are two reasonable constructions we must give the more lenient one. That is the settled rule for the construction of penal sections.

After referring to the definition of "conceal" in the Oxford English Dictionary the trial Judge stated that "the word 'conceal' can reasonably be construed as meaning either 'refrain from disclosing' or 'remove, put out of sight, or hide.'" The learned trial Judge also pointed out that the word "cache" in the French version, like the word "conceals" in the English version, may connote either a physical act of secreting or refraining from disclosing. He then said:

> Therefore, the word "conceals" must be interpreted in accordance with its ordinary dictionary meaning. I find there are two reasonable interpretations of the word: (1) a positive physical act on the part of the accused; (2) a negative non physical act on the part of the accused in failing to make disclosure.
>
> As there are two reasonable interpretations of the word, this being a penal section I am bound to apply the canon of construction of statutes found in Driedger, to which reference has already been made, and give the word the more lenient interpretation.
>
> Accordingly, I find that "conceals" in s. 350(a), subpara. (ii) means a positive physical act on the part of the accused. Such an interpretation of the word comports with the meaning ascribed to the other words in the section; namely, "removes" and "disposes."
>
> As there is no evidence that on August 26, 1977, the accused did any positive physical act of concealment, the motion for the directed verdict must be allowed.

The learned trial Judge then observed that although the respondent must be acquitted, his conduct fell within certain provisions of s. 169 of the *Bankruptcy Act* which creates a number of specific bankruptcy offences.

Although I am in agreement with the conclusion of the learned trial Judge that the word "conceals" in s. 350(a)(ii) of the *Code* requires a positive act done for the purpose of secreting the debtor's property, as opposed to the mere non-disclosure of assets, I have reached that conclusion for somewhat different reasons.

This Court has on many occasions applied the well-known rule of statutory construction that if a penal provision is reasonably capable of two interpretations, that interpretation which is the more favourable to the accused must be adopted: see, for example, *R. v. Cheetham* (1980), 53 C.C.C. (2d) 109, 17 C.R. (3d) 1; *R. v. Negridge* (1980), 54 C.C.C. (2d) 304, 17 C.R. (3d) 14, 6 M.V.R. 255. I do not think, however, that this principle always requires a word which has two accepted meanings to be given the more restrictive meaning. Where a word used in a statute has two accepted meanings, then either or both meanings may apply. The Court is first required to endeavour to determine the sense in which Parliament used the word from the context in which it appears. It is only in the case of an ambiguity which still exists after the full context is considered, where it is uncertain in which sense Parliament used the word, that the above rule of statutory construction requires the interpretation which is the more favourable to the defendant to be adopted. This is merely another way of stating the principle that the conduct alleged against the accused must be clearly brought within the proscription.

In support of his submission that the word "conceals" includes a failure to disclose the existence of something when under a duty to do so, Mr. Segal relied upon *London Ass'ce v. Mansel* (1879), 11 Ch. D. 363, in which Jessel M.R. said, at p. 370:

> ... because if a man purposely avoids answering a question, and thereby does not state a fact which it is his duty to communicate, that is concealment. Concealment properly so called means non-disclosure of a fact which it is a man's duty to disclose, and it was his duty to disclose the fact if it was a material fact.

It must be borne in mind that the Master of the Rolls was there discussing concealment of a *fact*, not the concealment of property. I have no doubt, however, that the word "conceals" may, depending on the context, include the non-disclosure of the existence of tangible things when there is a duty to disclose their existence. For example, s. 343 [now s. 385] of the *Code* makes it an offence for a vendor or mortgagor of property who is served with a written demand for an abstract of title by or on behalf of the purchaser or mortgagee to conceal from him with intent to defraud any instrument material to the title or any encumbrance on the title. It seems clear that a vendor or mortgagor of property who, in the circumstances mentioned in s. 343, deliberately with intent to defraud fails to disclose the existence of a material instrument, is caught by the section. I share, however, the view of the learned trial Judge that the word "conceals" as used in s. 350(a)(ii) contemplates some positive conduct on the part of the debtor as opposed to a mere failure to disclose the existence of the property, even though under a duty to do so. That section provides that everyone who

> (a)  within intent to defraud his creditors ...
>     (ii)  removes, conceals or disposes of any of his property, or ...
> is guilty of an indictable offence ...

When two or more words which are susceptible of analogous meanings are coupled together they are understood to be used in their cognate sense. They take their colour from each other, the meaning of the more general being restricted to a sense analogous to the less general: see *Maxwell on the Interpretation of Statutes*, 12th ed. (1969), at p. 289. In this case, the words which lend colour to the word "conceals" are, first, the word "removes," which clearly refers to a physical removal of property, and second, the words "disposes of," which, standing in contrast to the kind of disposition which is expressly dealt with in subpara. (i) of the same para. (a), namely, one which is made by "gift, conveyance, assignment, sale, transfer or delivery," strongly suggests the kind of disposition which results from a positive act taken by a person to physically part with his property. In my view the association of "conceals" with the words "removes" or "disposes of" in s. 350(a)(ii) shows that the word "conceals" is there used by Parliament in a sense which contemplates a positive act of concealment. ...

The deliberate failure by a bankrupt to disclose his assets to the trustee, as the learned trial Judge recognized, is an offence under s. 169 of the *Bankruptcy Act*. I do not imply, however, that because such failure is an offence under s. 169 of the *Bankruptcy Act*, a prosecution for an offence under the *Code* is precluded, if the defendant's conduct falls within a section of the *Code*. Although the word "conceals" may, as I have already indicated, include a deliberate failure to disclose assets when under a duty to do so, I am of the opinion, for the reasons given, that it does not have that meaning in s. 350(a)(ii) but is there used in its primary sense of a positive act of secreting.

Accordingly, I would dismiss the appeal.

---

Consider the approach taken by the Supreme Court of Canada to the interpretation of s. 231(5) (formerly s. 214(5)) of the *Criminal Code* in the following case.

### R. v. Paré
Supreme Court of Canada
(1987), 38 C.C.C. (3d) 97

WILSON J. (for the Court):  Section 214(5)(b) of the *Criminal Code*, R.S.C. 1970, c. C-34, as amended by 1974-75-76, c. 105, s. 4, which was in force at the time of the commission of the offence provided that murder is first degree murder when the death is caused by a person while the person is committing indecent assault. The respondent, Marc-André Paré, indecently assaulted and murdered a seven-year-old boy, Steeve Duranleau, the central issue in this appeal is whether the respondent murdered the child "while committing" the indecent assault. ...

### *The Facts*

On July 13, 1982, at about 1:30 in the afternoon the respondent Marc-André Paré, then 17 years old, met Steeve Duranleau, a seven-year-old boy. At Paré's suggestion the two went swimming. After about 15 minutes in the pool Paré offered to take Duranleau to look at some used cars. The offer was only a pretense. Paré's real motive was to get Duranleau alone in order to have sexual relations with him.

After changing, Paré and Duranleau went to a parking-lot where they looked at some used cars. Near the parking-lot was a bridge that crossed the St. Charles River. Paré lured Duranleau under the bridge. Duranleau wanted to leave but Paré told him not to and held him by the arm. Paré sat there for the next 10 minutes holding Duranleau by the arm. Then Paré told Duranleau to lie on his back and keep quiet. Paré pulled Duranleau's shorts down and lowered his own pants and underwear. He then lay on top of Duranleau and indecently assaulted him. After ejaculating beside Duranleau's penis, Paré sat up and got dressed.

At this point Duranleau told Paré that he intended to tell his mother about the incident. Paré told him that he did not want him to tell his mother and that, if he did, he would kill him. After this exchange of words Paré was certain that the boy would tell his mother as soon as he could. Paré made Duranleau lie on his back. He waited for two minutes with his hand on Duranleau's chest. He then killed Duranleau by strangling him with his hands, hitting him on the head several times with an oil filter, and strangling him with a shoe-lace.

The accused was charged as follows (translation):

> That in Quebec City, Quebec, on or around 13 July 1982, he illegally and intentionally killed S.D., thereby committing murder in the first degree contrary to ss. 212—214(5)—218 of the Criminal Code.

At trial the accused admitted all the facts outlined above. On December 7, 1982, the accused was found guilty of first degree murder. The accused's appeal to the Quebec Court of Appeal was dismissed on April 2, 1985 (per L'Heureux-Dubé, Beauregard and LeBel JJ.A.), the court substituting a verdict of second degree murder for the jury's verdict of first degree murder.

*The Courts Below*

*The Court of Appeal for Quebec*

Beauregard and LeBel JJ.A. gave separate reasons; Madame Justice L'Heureux-Dubé agreed with both. Beauregard J.A. examined the case-law and decided that s. 214(5) of the *Criminal Code* should be restrictively interpreted. He concluded that "while committing" must be contrasted with "after having finished committing." A murder committed after the accused had committed the indecent assault was not a first degree murder. Accordingly, when the trial judge said to the jury that a murder committed "on the occasion of" an indecent assault was a first degree murder, he did not invite the jury to consider the really critical question, namely, whether the murder was committed during the commission of the indecent assault or after the indecent assault was over.

Beauregard J.A. was of the opinion that a properly directed jury would not have been convinced beyond a reasonable doubt that the accused murdered his victim while committing the indecent assault. Consequently, he dismissed the appeal and substituted a verdict of second degree murder for the verdict of first degree murder.

LeBel J.A. did not agree with Beauregard J.A.'s conclusion that s. 214(5) required the murder and the indecent assault to be absolutely simultaneous. Even if the section were to be construed restrictively, he stated, it must not be deprived of all effect. By reading s. 214(5) in conjunction with s. 213 LeBel J.A. concluded that the words "while committing" demanded a close temporal connection between the indecent assault and the murder. Moreover, he concluded that the murder must be an immediate consequence of the first offence for s. 214(5) to apply. LeBel J.A. found it difficult to conclude that a jury more completely informed of the nuances of the sections in question would have necessarily returned the same verdict. The charge given to the jury, he stated, effectively prevented the jury from directing its attention to the proper meaning of s. 214(5). Therefore, despite his reservations about Beauregard J.A.'s conclusions of law, LeBel J.A. agreed with his disposition of the case.

*Section 214(5): "While Committing"*

*The Literal Meaning*

Did the respondent murder Duranleau while committing an indecent assault? Counsel for the respondent submit that he did not. The argument here is simple. The murder occurred, it is submitted, after the indecent assault was complete. Thus, by a literal reading of s. 214(5) Paré did not murder Duranleau "while committing" an indecent assault.

This argument is a forceful one but by no means decisive. The literal meaning of words could equally be termed their acontextual meaning. As Professor Dworkin points out, the literal or acontextual meaning of words is "the meaning we would assign them if we had no special information about the context of their use or the intentions of their author": see R. Dworkin, *Law's Empire* (1986), p. 17, Cambridge, Harvard University Press. Thus, the words "while committing" could have one meaning when disembodied from the *Criminal Code* and another entirely when read in the context of the scheme and purpose of the legislation. It is the latter meaning that we must ascertain. …

*The Case-Law*

Further support for the narrow interpretation is found in two subsequent cases: *R. v. Kjeldsen* (1980), 53 C.C.C. (2d) 55, [1980] 3 W.W.R. 411, 20 A.R. 267 (Alta. C.A.) and *R. v. Sargent* (1983), 5 C.C.C. (3d) 429, 22 Sask. R. 230 (Sask. C.A.). In the latter case, the victim was killed after she had been raped by either the appellant or his companion or both. Hall J.A., speaking for the court concluded at p. 436:

> It is manifest that the jury, in returning a verdict of guilty of first degree murder accepted those portions of the evidence which were most unfavourable to the appellant. However, in that event, there is no basis upon which the jury could return the verdict which they did. If the jury found, on the evidence before them, that a rape had occurred, it is clear that the death of the deceased did not occur while that offence was being committed. That is, there was no evidence to support the finding that the actions which resulted in the death of Lenny Lou Cosgrove were perpetrated by the appellant (either alone or with Massong) *while committing the offence of rape*. On the only evidence before the jury, the murder was committed after the actual rape. Therefore the provisions of s. 214(5) do not apply to establish the offence of first degree murder: see *R. v. Kjeldsen*.

*Kjeldsen* took the same approach. In that case the appellant raped his victim and then tied her up. A short time later she freed herself and the appellant then killed her. At trial the appellant was convicted of first degree murder. The Court of Appeal substituted a conviction of second degree murder. The court did not analyze the meaning of the words "while committing" in s. 214(5) but appeared to assume that these words required the underlying offence and the murder to occur simultaneously (p. 85).

The courts, however, have not been unanimous in adopting the narrow interpretation. In *R. v. Stevens* (1984), 11 C.C.C. (3d) 518, another case of rape and murder, Martin J.A. held that there was sufficient evidence on which a jury could conclude that the murder took place during the commission of an indecent assault. He went on, however, to make some interesting comments on the interpretation of the words "while committing" in s. 214(5). At p. 541 he states:

> Thus, it appears clear that where death is caused after the underlying offence is complete and the act causing death is committed for the purpose of facilitating the flight of the offender, the murder is not under ss. 213 and 214(5)(b) first degree murder.
>
> I do not wish, however, to be taken as holding that where the act causing death and the acts constituting the rape, attempted rape, indecent assault or an attempt to commit indecent assault, as the case may be, all form part of one continuous sequence of events forming a single transaction, that death would not be caused during the commission of the offence, even though the underlying offence in s. 213 in a sense could be said to be then complete.

The suggestion here is that the words "while committing" in s. 214(5) do not require an exact coincidence of the murder with the underlying offence. Rather, they require a close temporal and causative link between the two. Which of the competing interpretations should be adopted?

### Strict Construction

Counsel for the respondent argue that the doctrine of strict construction of criminal statutes requires that this court adopt the interpretation most favourable to the accused. According to this argument the words "while committing" must be narrowly construed so as to elevate murder to first degree only when the death and the underlying offence occur simultaneously. In order to assess the validity of this position we must examine the doctrine of strict construction.

The doctrine is one of ancient lineage. It reached its pinnacle of importance in a former age when the death penalty attached to a vast array of offences. As Stephen Kloepfer points out in his article "The Status of Strict Construction in Canadian Criminal Law" (1983), 15 *Ottawa L. Rev.* 553 at pp. 556-60, the doctrine was one of many tools employed by the judiciary to soften the impact of the Draconian penal provisions of the time. Over the past two centuries criminal law penalties have become far less severe. Criminal law remains, however, the most dramatic and important incursion that the state makes into individual liberty. Thus, while the original justification for the doctrine has been substantially eroded, the seriousness of imposing criminal penalties of any sort demands that reasonable doubts be resolved in favour of the accused.

This point was underlined by Dickson J. in *Marcotte v. Deputy Attorney-General of Canada* (1974), 19 C.C.C. (2d) 257 at p. 262, 51 D.L.R. (3d) 259 at p. 264, [1976] 1 S.C.R. 108 at p. 115:

> It is unnecessary to emphasize the importance of clarity and certainty when freedom is at stake. No authority is needed for the proposition that if real ambiguities are found, or doubts of substance arise, in the construction and application of a statute affecting the liberty of a subject, then that statute should be applied in such a manner as to favour the person against whom it is sought to be enforced. If one is to be incarcerated, one should at least know that some Act of Parliament requires it in express terms, and not, at most, by implication. …

### Applying the Doctrine

As we have noted above, it is clearly grammatically possible to construe the words "while committing" in s. 214(5) as requiring murder to be classified as first degree only if it is exactly coincidental with the underlying offence. This, however, does not end the question. We still have to determine whether the narrow interpretation of "while committing" is a reasonable one, given the scheme and purpose of the legislation.

In my view, the construction that counsel for the respondent would have us place on these words is not one that could reasonably be attributed to Parliament. The first problem with the exactly simultaneous approach flows from the difficulty in defining the beginning and end of an indecent assault. In this case, for example, after ejaculation the respondent sat up and put his pants back on. But for the next two minutes he kept his hands on his victim's chest. Was this continued contact part of the assault? It does not seem to me that important issues of criminal law should be allowed to hinge upon this kind of distinction. An approach that depends on this kind of distinction should be avoided if possible.

A second difficulty with the exactly simultaneous approach is that it leads to distinctions that are arbitrary and irrational. In the present case, had the respondent strangled his victim two minutes earlier than he did, his guilt of first degree murder would be beyond dispute. The exactly simultaneous approach would have us conclude that the two minutes he spent contemplating his next move had the effect of reducing his offence to one of second degree murder. This would be a strange result. The crime is no less serious in the latter case than in the former; indeed, if anything, the latter crime is more serious since it involves some element of deliberation. An interpretation of s. 214(5) that runs contrary to common sense is not to be adopted if a reasonable alternative is available.

In my view, such an interpretation has been provided by Martin J.A. in Stevens, *supra*. As noted above, Martin J.A. suggested that "where the act causing death and the acts constituting the rape, attempted rape, indecent assault or an attempt to commit indecent assault, as the case may be, all form part of one continuous sequence of events forming a single transaction" the death was caused "while committing" an offence for the purposes of s. 214(5). This interpretation eliminates the need to draw artificial lines to separate the commission and the aftermath of an indecent assault. Further, it eliminates the arbitrariness inherent in the exactly simultaneous approach.

I would, therefore, respectfully adopt Martin J.A.'s single transaction analysis as the proper construction of s. 214(5).

This approach, it seems to me, best expresses the policy considerations that underlie the provision. Section 214, as we have seen, classifies murder as either first or second degree. All murders are serious crimes. Some murders, however, are so threatening to the public that Parliament has chosen to impose exceptional penalties on the perpetrators. One such class of murders is that found in s. 214(5), murders done while committing a hijacking, a kidnapping and forcible confinement, a rape, or an indecent assault. An understanding of why this class of murder is elevated to murder in the first degree is a helpful guide to the interpretation of the language.

The Law Reform Commission of Canada addressed this issue in its paper on *Homicide* (Working Paper 33, 1984). At p. 79 the paper states:

> ... there is a lack of rationale in the law. Subsection 214(5) provides that, whether planned and deliberate or not, murder is first degree murder when committed in the course of certain listed offences. It is curious that the list there given is considerably shorter than that given in section 213 which makes killing murder if done in the commission of certain specified offences. Inspection and comparison of the two lists, however, reveal no organizing principle in either of them and no rationale for the difference between them.

With respect, I disagree. The offences listed in s. 214(5) are all offences involving the unlawful domination of people by other people. Thus an organizing principle for s. 214(5) can be found. This principle is that where a murder is committed by someone already abusing his power by illegally dominating another, the murder should be treated as an exceptionally serious crime. Parliament has chosen to treat these as murders in the first degree.

Refining then on the concept of the "single transaction" referred to by Martin J.A. in *Stevens, supra,* it is the continuing illegal domination of the victim which gives continuity to the sequence of events culminating in the murder. The murder represents an exploitation of the position of power created by the underlying crime and makes the entire course of conduct a "single transaction." This approach, in my view, best gives effect to the philosophy underlying s. 214(5).

## Conclusion

The respondent murdered Steeve Duranleau two minutes after indecently assaulting him. The killing was motivated by fear that the boy would tell his mother about the indecent assault. The jury found the respondent guilty of first degree murder. They were entitled to do so. The murder was temporally and causally connected to the underlying offence. It formed part of one continuous sequence of events. It was part of the same transaction.

I would allow the appeal and restore the conviction of first degree murder.

In *R. v. Prevost* (1988), 42 C.C.C. (3d) 314 (Ont. C.A.) the accused killed an on-duty police officer while the officer was taking his lunch break. As in *Paré, supra*, the issue was whether the murder was first-degree murder. Section 231(4)(a) provides that irrespective of whether the murder was planned and deliberate, murder is first-degree murder when the victim is a police officer "acting in the course of his duties."

The Ontario Court of Appeal applying *Paré* held that the victim was acting in the course of his duties and suggested that the accused's argument that when the police officer sat down to have lunch the protection of the section was withdrawn "is as offensive to common sense" as the argument, rejected in *Paré*, that the murder be exactly simultaneous with the commission of an underlying offence in s. 231(5).

---

The *Interpretation Act*, R.S.C. 1985, c. I-21 applies to all federal laws. Section 12 provides:

> Every enactment is deemed remedial and shall be given such fair, large and liberal construction and interpretation as best ensures the attainment of its objects.

Can this provision be reconciled with strict construction of the criminal law? In *Bell ExpressVu Limited Partnership v. Rex, et al.* (2002), 212 D.L.R. (4th) 1 (S.C.C.), Justice Iacobucci addressed the issue of how strict and remedial construction should be reconciled, albeit in the context of the interpretation of *Radiocommunication Act*:

(1) Principles of Statutory Interpretation

[26] In Elmer Driedger's definitive formulation, found at p. 87 of his *Construction of Statutes*, 2nd ed. (1983):

> Today there is only one principle or approach, namely, the words of an Act are to be read in their entire context and in their grammatical and ordinary sense harmoniously with the scheme of the Act, the object of the Act, and the intention of Parliament.

Driedger's modern approach has been repeatedly cited by this Court as the preferred approach to statutory interpretation across a wide range of interpretive settings: see, for example, *Canada v. Stubart Investments Ltd.*, [1984] 1 S.C.R. 536 at p. 578, 10 D.L.R. (4th) 1, per Estey J.; *Québec (Communauté urbaine) v. Corp. Notre-Dame de Bon-Secours*, [1994] 3 S.C.R. 3 at p. 17; *Rizzo & Rizzo Shoes Ltd. (Re)*, [1998] 1 S.C.R. 27, 154 D.L.R. (4th) 193, at para. 21; *R. v. Gladue*, [1999] 1 S.C.R. 688, 171 D.L.R. (4th) 385, at para. 25; *R. v. Araujo*, [2000] 2 S.C.R. 992, 193 D.L.R. (4th) 440, 2000 SCC 65, at para. 26; *R. v. Sharpe*, [2001] 1 S.C.R. 45, 194 D.L.R. (4th) 1, 2001 SCC 2, at para. 33, per McLachlin C.J.C.; *Chieu v. Canada (Minister of Citizenship and Immigration)*, 2002 SCC 3, at para. 27 [now reported 208 D.L.R. (4th) 107]. I note as well that, in the federal legislative context, this Court's preferred approach is buttressed by s. 12 of the *Interpretation Act*, R.S.C. 1985, c. I-21, which provides that every enactment "is deemed remedial, and shall be given such fair, large and liberal construction and interpretation as best ensures the attainment of its objects."

[27] The preferred approach recognizes the important role that context must inevitably play when a court construes the written words of a statute: as Professor John Willis

incisively noted in his seminal article "Statute Interpretation in a Nutshell" (1938), 16 *Can. Bar Rev.* 1, at p. 6, "words, like people, take their colour from their surroundings." This being the case, where the provision under consideration is found in an Act that is itself a component of a larger statutory scheme, the surroundings that colour the words and the scheme of the Act are more expansive. In such an instance, the application of Driedger's principle gives rise to what was described in *R. v. Ulybel Enterprises Ltd.*, [2001] 2 S.C.R. 867, 203 D.L.R. (4th) 513, 2001 SCC 56, at para. 52, as "the principle of interpretation that presumes a harmony, coherence, and consistency between statutes dealing with the same subject matter." (See also *Stoddard v. Watson*, [1993] 2 S.C.R. 1069 at p. 1079, 106 D.L.R. (4th) 404 *sub nom. Murphy v. Welsh; Pointe-Claire (City) v. Quebec (Labour Court)*, [1997] 1 S.C.R. 1015, 146 D.L.R. (4th) 1, at para. 61, per Lamer C.J.C.)

[28]  Other principles of interpretation—such as the strict construction of penal statutes and the "Charter values" presumption—only receive application where there is ambiguity as to the meaning of a provision. (On strict construction, see: *Marcotte v. Canada (Deputy Attorney General)*, [1976] 1 S.C.R. 108 at p. 115, 51 D.L.R. (3d) 259, per Dickson J. (as he then was); *R. v. Goulis* (1981), 33 O.R. (2d) 55 at pp. 59-60, 125 D.L.R. (3d) 137 (C.A.); *R. v. Hasselwander*, [1993] 2 S.C.R. 398 at p. 413; *R. v. Russell*, [2001] 2 S.C.R. 804, 203 D.L.R(4th) 1, 2001 SCC 53, at para. 46. ...

[29]  What, then, in law is an ambiguity? To answer, an ambiguity must be "real" (*Marcotte, supra*, at p. 115). The words of the provision must be "reasonably capable of more than one meaning" (*Westminster Bank Ltd. v. Zang*, [1966] A.C. 182 (H.L.) at p. 222, per Lord Reid). By necessity, however, one must consider the "entire context" of a provision before one can determine if it is reasonably capable of multiple interpretations. In this regard, Major J.'s statement in *CanadianOxy Chemicals Ltd. v. Canada (Attorney General)*, [1999] 1 S.C.R. 743, 171 D.L.R. (4th) 733, at para. 14, is apposite: "It is only when genuine ambiguity arises between two or more plausible readings, *each equally in accordance with the intentions of the statute*, that the courts need to resort to external interpretive aids" (emphasis added), to which I would add, "including other principles of interpretation."

[30]  For this reason, ambiguity cannot reside in the mere fact that several courts—or, for that matter, several doctrinal writers—have come to differing conclusions on the interpretation of a given provision. Just as it would be improper for one to engage in a preliminary tallying of the number of decisions supporting competing interpretations and then apply that which receives the "higher score," it is not appropriate to take as one's starting point the premise that differing interpretations reveal an ambiguity. It is necessary, in every case, for the court charged with interpreting a provision to undertake the contextual and purposive approach set out by Driedger, and *thereafter* to determine if "the words are ambiguous enough to induce two people to spend good money in backing two opposing views as to their meaning" (Willis, *supra*, at pp. 4-5).

The court went on to hold that the prohibition on decoding "an encrypted subscription signal" was not ambiguous and included signals from the United States. It was thus not necessary to resort to the principle of strict construction of penal statutes.

CHAPTER TWO

# Limits on Criminal Law

This chapter examines the rationales for the criminal law and continues to explore the limitations that the constitution, and in particular the Charter, places on criminal laws. The first part of this chapter will examine some philosophical perspectives on the role of the criminal law in the context of a debate about whether the criminal law should only respond to harm or whether it also has a role in proclaiming and enforcing the values of the community. Even if the former position is accepted, a related and difficult issue is what constitutes harm. This debate originated in Great Britain and Canada over the issue of whether consensual gay sex ought to be criminalized but also has implications for contemporary debates about prostitution.

The second part of this chapter examines debates about the appropriate role of the criminal law with respect to pornography. This part also continues our examination from the first chapter of the complex interaction between Parliament and the courts over the interpretation of the criminal law and the important role of the Charter in criminal law.

The third part of this chapter examines criminalization of the possession of marijuana and the related question of whether the principle that the criminal law should be used only with respect to proven harms should be recognized as a principle of fundamental justice under s. 7 of the Charter.

The final part of this chapter examines the criminalization of hate speech and various Charter challenges to such crimes. It will also examine the related question of how the particular safeguards of the criminal law, such as the requirement for proof of fault, may affect the question of whether criminal prohibitions are justified under s. 1 of the Charter as reasonable limits on freedom of expression.

## I. PERSPECTIVES ON THE ROLE OF CRIMINAL LAW AND "CONSENSUAL" SEX

The following excerpts are taken from an important debate in Great Britain about the relationship between law and morality at a time when consensual sex between men was a criminal offence. Consider whether the various views expressed in this debate remain relevant today? What other perspectives would be voiced?

49

### The Report of the Committee on Homosexual Offences and
### Prostitution (The Wolfenden Report)
U.K., 1957

… Our primary duty has been to consider the extent to which homosexual behaviour and female prostitution should come under the condemnation of the criminal law, and this has presented us with the difficulty of deciding what are the essential elements of a criminal offence. There appears to be no unquestioned definition of what constitutes or ought to constitute a crime. To define it as "an act which is punished by the State" does not answer the question: What acts ought to be punished by the State? We have therefore worked with our own formulation of the function of the criminal law so far as it concerns the subjects of this enquiry. In this field, its function, as we see it, is to preserve public order and decency, to protect the citizen from what is offensive or injurious, and to provide sufficient safeguards against exploitation and corruption of others, particularly those who are specially vulnerable because they are young, weak in body or mind, inexperienced, or in a state of special physical, official or economic dependence.

It is not, in our view, the function of the law to intervene in the private lives of citizens, or to seek to enforce any particular pattern of behaviour, further than is necessary to carry out the purposes we have outlined. It follows that we do not believe it to be a function of the law to attempt to cover all the fields of sexual behaviour. Certain forms of sexual behaviour are regarded by many as sinful, morally wrong, or objectionable for reasons of conscience, or of religious or cultural tradition; and such actions may be reprobated on these grounds. But the criminal law does not cover all such actions at the present time; for instance, adultery and fornication are not offences for which a person can be punished by the criminal law. Nor indeed is prostitution as such.

We appreciate that opinions will differ as to what is offensive, injurious or inimical to the common good, and also as to what constitutes exploitation or corruption; and that these opinions will be based on moral, social or cultural standards. We have been guided by our estimate of the standards of the community in general, recognising that they will not be accepted by all citizens, and that our estimate of them may be mistaken.

We have had to consider the relationship between the law and public opinion. It seems to us that there are two over-definite views about this. On the one hand, it is held that the law ought to follow behind public opinion, so that the law can count on the support of the community as a whole. On the other hand, it is held that a necessary purpose of the law is to lead or fortify public opinion. Certainly it is clear that if any legal enactment is markedly out of tune with public opinion it will quickly fall into disrepute. Beyond this we should not wish to dogmatise, for on the matters with which we are called upon to deal we have not succeeded in discovering an unequivocal "public opinion," and we have felt bound to try to reach conclusions for ourselves rather than to base them on what is often transient and seldom precisely ascertainable. …

It is against the foregoing background that we have reviewed the existing provisions of the law in relation to homosexual behaviour between male persons. We have found that with the great majority of these provisions we are in complete agreement. We believe that it is part of the function of the law to safeguard those who need protection by reason of their youth or some mental defect, and we do not wish to see any change in the law that would weaken this protection. Men who commit offences against such persons should be treated as criminal offenders. Whatever may be the causes of their disposition or the proper treatment for it, the law must assume that the responsibility for the overt acts remains theirs, except where there are circumstances which it accepts as exempting from accountability. Offences of this kind are particularly reprehensible when the men who commit them are in positions of special responsibility or trust. We have been made aware that where a man is involved in an offence with a boy or youth the invitation to the commission of the act sometimes comes from him rather than from the man. But we believe that even when this is so that fact does not serve to exculpate the man.

It is also part of the function of the law to preserve public order and decency. We therefore hold that when homosexual behaviour between males takes place in public it should continue to be dealt with by the criminal law. ...

Beside the two categories of offence we have just mentioned, namely, offences committed by adults with juveniles and offences committed in public places, there is a third class of offence to which we have had to give long and careful consideration. It is that of homosexual acts committed between adults in private. ...

We have indicated our opinion as to the province of the law and its sanctions, and how far it properly applies to the sexual behaviour of the individual citizen. On the basis of the considerations there advanced we have reached the conclusion that legislation which covers acts in the third category we have mentioned goes beyond the proper sphere of the law's concern. We do not think that it is proper for the law to concern itself with what a man does in private unless it can be shown to be so contrary to the public good that the law ought to intervene in its function as the guardian of that public good. ...

... There remains one additional argument which we believe to be decisive, namely, the importance which society and the law ought to give to individual freedom of choice and action in matters of private morality. Unless a deliberate attempt is to be made by society, acting through the agency of the law, to equate the sphere of crime with that of sin, there must remain a realm of private morality and immorality which is, in brief and crude terms, not the law's business. To say this is not to condone or encourage private immorality. On the contrary, to emphasize the personal and private nature of moral or immoral conduct is to emphasize the personal and private responsibility of the individual for his own actions, and that is a responsibility which a mature agent can properly be expected to carry for himself without the threat of punishment from the law.

We accordingly recommend that homosexual behaviour between consenting adults in private should no longer be a criminal offence. ...

## Devlin, "The Enforcement of Morals"
### Maccabaean Lecture in Jurisprudence of the British Academy, 1959

The criminal law of England has from the very first concerned itself with moral principles. A simple way of testing this point is to consider the attitude which the criminal law adopts towards consent.

Subject to certain exceptions inherent in the nature of particular crimes, the criminal law has never permitted consent of the victim to be used as a defence. In rape, for example, consent negatives an essential element. But consent of the victim is no defence to a charge of murder. It is not a defence to any form of assault that the victim thought his punishment well deserved and submitted to it; to make a good defence the accused must prove that the law gave him the right to chastise and that he exercised it reasonably. Likewise, the victim may not forgive the aggressor and require the prosecution to desist; the right to enter a *nolle prosequi* [stay of proceedings] belongs to the Attorney-General alone.

Now if the law existed for the protection of the individual, there would be no reason why he should avail himself of it if he did not want it. The reason why a man may not consent to the commission of an offence against himself beforehand or forgive it afterwards is because it is an offence against society. It is not that society is physically injured; that would be impossible. Nor need any individual be shocked, corrupted, or exploited; everything may be done in private. Nor can it be explained on the practical ground that a violent man is a potential danger to others in the community who have therefore a direct interest in his apprehension and punishment as being necessary to their own protection. That would be true of a man whom the victim is prepared to forgive but not of one who gets his consent first; a murderer who acts only upon the consent, and maybe the request, of his victim is no menace to others, but he does threaten one of the great moral principles upon which society is based, that is, the sanctity of human life. There is only one explanation of what has hitherto been accepted as the basis of the criminal law and that is that there are certain standards of behaviour or moral principles which society requires to be observed; and the breach of them is an offence not merely against the person who is injured but against society as a whole.

Thus, if the criminal law were to be reformed so as to eliminate from it everything that was not designed to preserve order and decency or to protect citizens (including the protection of youth from corruption), it would overturn a fundamental principle. It would also end a number of specific crimes. Euthanasia or the killing of another at his own request, suicide, attempted suicide and suicide pacts, duelling, abortion, incest between brother and sister, are all acts which can be done in private and without offence to others and need not involve the corruption or exploitation of others. Many people think that the law on some of these subjects is in need of reform, but no one hitherto has gone so far as to suggest that they should all be left outside the criminal law as matters of private morality.

Society means a community of ideas; without shared ideas on politics, morals, and ethics no society can exist. Each one of us has ideas about what is good and what is evil; they cannot be kept private from the society in which we live. If men and women try to create a society in which there is no fundamental agreement about good and evil they will fail; if having based it on common agreement, the agreement goes, the society will disintegrate. For society is not something that is kept together physically; it is held by the invisible bonds of common thought. If the bonds were too far relaxed the members would drift apart. A common morality is part of the bondage. The bondage is part of the price of society; and mankind, which needs society, must pay its price. ...

I think, therefore, that it is not possible to set theoretical limits to the power of the State to legislate against immorality. It is not possible to settle in advance exceptions to the general rule or to define inflexibly areas of morality into which the law is in no circumstances to be allowed to enter. Society is entitled by means of its laws to protect itself from dangers, whether from within or without ...

... You may argue that if a man's sins affect only himself it cannot be the concern of society. If he chooses to get drunk every night in the privacy of his own home, is any one except himself the worse for it? But suppose a quarter or a half of the population got drunk every night, what sort of society would it be? You cannot set a theoretical limit to the number of people who can get drunk before society is entitled to legislate against drunkenness. The same may be said of gambling. ...

How are the moral judgements of society to be ascertained? By leaving it until now, I can ask it in the more limited form that is now sufficient for my purpose. How is the law-maker to ascertain the moral judgements of society? It is surely not enough that they should be reached by the opinion of the majority; it would be too much to require the individual assent of every citizen. English law has evolved and regularly uses a standard which does not depend on the counting of the heads. It is that of the reasonable man. He is not to be confused with the rational man. He is not expected to reason about anything and his judgement may be largely a matter of feeling. It is the viewpoint of the man in the street—to use an archaism familiar to all lawyers—the man in the Clapham omnibus. He might also be called the right-minded man. For my purpose I should like to call him the man in the jury box, for the moral judgement of society must be something about which any twelve men or women drawn at random might after discussion be expected to be unanimous. This was the standard the judges applied in the days before Parliament was as active as it is now and when they laid down rules of public policy. They did not think of themselves as making law but simply as stating principles which every right-minded person would accept as valid. ...

Nothing should be punished by the law that does not lie beyond the limits of tolerance. It is not nearly enough to say that a majority dislike a practice; there must be a real feeling of reprobation. Those who are dissatisfied with the present law on homosexuality often say that the opponents of reform are swayed simply by disgust. If that were so it would be wrong, but I do not think one can ignore disgust if it is deeply felt and not manufactured. Its presence is a good indication that the bounds of toleration are being reached. Not everything is to be tolerated. No society can do without intolerance, indignation, and disgust; they are the forces behind the moral law, and indeed it can be argued that if they or something like them are not present the feelings of society cannot be weighty enough to deprive the individual of freedom of choice. ...

The limits of tolerance shift. This is supplementary to what I have been saying but of sufficient importance in itself to deserve statement as a separate principle which law-makers have to bear in mind. I suppose that moral standards do not shift; so far as they come from divine revelation they do not, and I am willing to assume that the moral judgements made by a society always remain good for that society. But the extent to which society will tolerate—I mean tolerate, not approve—departures from moral standards varies from generation to generation ... It follows as another good working principle that in any new matter of morals the law should be slow to act. By the next generation the swell of indignation may have abated and the law be left without the strong backing which it needs. But it is then difficult to alter the law without giving the impression that moral judgement is being weakened. This is now one of the factors that is strongly militating against any alteration to the law on homosexuality. ...

———————————————

Lord Devlin's ideas are more fully developed in his book, *The Enforcement of Morals* (1965). Criticism of Lord Devlin's views can be found in a number of studies including, Williams, "Authoritarian Morals and the Criminal Law," [1966] *Cr. L. Rev.* 132; H.L.A. Hart, *Law, Liberty and Morality* (1963), *The Morality of the Criminal Law* (1965) and "Social Solidarity and the Enforcement of Morality" (1967), 35 *U. Ch. L. Rev.* 1; Dworkin, "Lord Devlin and the Enforcement of Morals" (1966), 75 *Yale L.J.* 986. For a more contemporary argument that Lord Devlin's approach remains relevant, see J. Paul McCutcheon, "Morality and the Criminal Law: Reflections on Hart-Devlin" (2003), 47 *Crim. L.Q.* 15.

———————————————

The following letter was sent to *The Times* (London) of May 11, 1965, by Lord Devlin and others:

> Sir,—In 1957 the Wolfenden Committee recommended, after three years study of the evidence, that homosexual behaviour between consenting adults in private should no longer be a criminal offence. ...
>
> Seven years ago a distinguished list of signatories wrote in your columns that the existing law clearly no longer represented either Christian or liberal opinion in this country, and that its continued enforcement would do more harm than good to the community as a whole.
>
> We hope that in response to [a motion in the House of Lords] Her Majesty's Government will now recognize the necessity for this reform and will introduce legislation.
>
> Yours faithfully,<br>[other signatories]<br>Devlin: House of Lords

The law was changed in England in 1967 so that homosexual conduct between two consenting adults in private would no longer be an offence: *Sexual Offences Act* 1967, c. 60.

In 1969 the Canadian Parliament passed a proviso that the crimes of bu;gery and gross indecency did not apply to any act committed in private between a husoand and wife or any two consenting persons over 21 years of age. S.C. 1968-69, c. 38, s. 7. Then Justice Minister Pierre Trudeau explained the reform on the basis that the state had no place in the bedrooms of the legislature. In 1988, the offences were replaced with an offence of anal intercourse that did not apply to private acts between a husband and wife or any two persons over the age of 18. See s. 159 of the *Criminal Code*.

The requirement that consenting persons be over the age of 18 was challenged under the Charter as constituting discrimination on the basis of marital status, age, and sexual orientation, given that the age of consent for other sexual activity was 14 years of age. Two courts of appeal have found that s. 159 is unconstitutional. What follows are extracts from the judgment of Abella J.A. in *R. v. M. (C.)* (1995), 98 C.C.C. (3d) 481 (Ont. C.A.):

> In my view, s. 159 arbitrarily disadvantages gay men by denying to them until they are 18 a choice available at the age of 14 to those who are not gay, namely, their choice of sexual expression with a consenting partner to whom they are not married. Anal intercourse is a basic form of sexual expression for gay men. The prohibition of this form of sexual conduct found in s. 159 accordingly has an adverse impact on them. Unmarried, heterosexual adolescents 14 or over can participate in consensual intercourse without criminal penalties; gay adolescents cannot. It perpetuates rather than narrows the gap for an historically disadvantaged group—gay men—it does so arbitrarily and stereotypically and is, therefore, a discriminatory provision which infringes the guarantee of equality.

Abella J.A. than considered whether the violation of s. 15 could be justified as a reasonable limit on the right under s. 1 of the Charter:

> It is not enough for a government to assert an objective for limiting guaranteed rights under s. 1; there must, in my view, also be an underlying evidentiary basis to support the assertion. Since there is no empirical evidence that adolescents are more at risk of HIV transmission than any other group, or that criminalizing their sexual behaviour protects them from this risk, there is, accordingly, no evidentiary foundation to support the government's first articulated objective.
>
> When governments define the ambits of morality, as they do when they enunciate laws, they are obliged to do so in accordance with constitutional guarantees, not with unwarranted assumptions. Sending young people to jail for their own protection when they exercise sexual choices not exercised by the majority, represents, in my view, even if benignly intended, precisely such unwarranted assumptions. The line which has unjustifiably been crossed, therefore, is the one protecting an individual's right under s. 15 to be free from discrimination when the government imposes ambits of morality.
>
> The health risks from unprotected anal intercourse are real and ought to be aggressively addressed. But, in my view, the measures chosen in s. 159 to protect young people from risk are arbitrary and unfair, compared to the measures used to protect against the health risks for individuals who prefer other forms of sexual conduct. There is no evidence that threatening to send an adolescent to jail will protect him (or her) from the risks of anal intercourse. I can see no rational connection between protecting someone from the potential harm of exercising sexual preferences and imprisoning that individual for exercising them.

There is no proportionality between the articulated health objectives and the Draconian criminal means chosen to achieve them.

See also *R. v. Roy* (1998), 125 C.C.C. (3d) 442 (Que. C.A.) much to the same effect.

Another issue that concerns the limits of the criminal law is whether a person can consent to injury.

In *R. v. Brown* (1993), 97 Cr. App. R. 44, the House of Lords in a 3 to 2 decision held that consent was not a defence when men were charged with assault and wounding after private encounters which included branding, blood letting, and other forms of consensual sexual violence. Lord Templeman stated that neither the Wolfenden Committee nor the 1967 reforms provided for such activities and concluded:

> The violence of sado-masochistic encounters involves the indulgence of cruelty by sadists and the degradation of victims. Such violence is injurious to the participants and unpredictably dangerous. I am not prepared to invent a defence of consent of sado-masochistic encounters which breed cruelty ... Society is entitled and bound to protect itself against a cult of violence. Pleasure derived from the infliction of pain is an evil thing. Cruelty is uncivilized.

In dissent, Lord Slynn stated that in the absence of specific legislation to the contrary, "it is not for the courts in the interest of 'paternalism' ... or in order to protect people from themselves, to introduce, into existing statutory crimes relating to offences *against* the person, concepts which do not properly fit there."

In *Jobidon v. The Queen* (1991), 66 C.C.C. (3d) 454 the Supreme Court of Canada in considering a fight held that consent was not a defence to a serious assault. Gonthier J. stated for the majority of the court:

> Foremost among the policy considerations supporting the Crown is the social uselessness of fist fights. As the English Court of Appeal noted in the *Attorney General's Reference*, it is not in the public interest that adults should willingly cause harm to one another without a good reason. There is precious little utility in fist fights or street brawls. These events are motivated by unchecked passion. They so often result in serious injury to the participants. Here it resulted in a tragic death to a young man on his wedding day. ...
>
> Related to a deterrence rationale is the possibility that, by permitting a person to consent to force inflicted by the hand of another, in rare cases the latter may find he derives some form of pleasure from the activity, especially if he is doing so on a regular basis. It is perhaps not inconceivable that this kind of perversion could arise in a domestic or marital setting where one or more of the family members are of frail or unstable mental health. As one criminal law theorist has written:
>
> > [T]he self-destructive individual who induces another person to kill or to mutilate him implicates the latter in the violation of a significant social taboo. The person carrying out the killing or the mutilation crosses the threshold into a realm of conduct that, the second time, might be more easily carried out. And the second time, it might not be particularly significant whether the victim consents or not. Similarly, if someone is encouraged to inflict a sado-masochistic beating on a consenting victim, the experience of inflicting the beating might loosen the actor's inhibitions against sadism in general. (G. Fletcher, *Rethinking Criminal Law* (1978), at 770-71.)

Of course this appeal does not concern sadism or intentional killing. But it comes close to mutilation. In any event, the weight of the argument could hold true for fights. If aggressive individuals are legally permitted to get into consensual fist fights, and they take advantage of that license from time to time, it may come to pass that they eventually lose all understanding that that activity is the subject of a powerful social taboo. They may too readily find their fists raised against a person whose consent they forgot to ascertain with full certitude. It is preferable that these sorts of omissions be strongly discouraged.

Wholly apart from deterrence, it is most unseemly from a moral point of view that the law would countenance, much less provide a backhanded sanction to the sort of interaction displayed by the facts of this appeal. The sanctity of the human body should militate against the validity of consent to bodily harm inflicted in a fight … .

The policy preference that people not be able to consent to intentionally inflicted harms is heard not only in the register of our common law. The *Criminal Code* also contains many examples of this propensity. As noted above, s. 14 of the Code vitiates the legal effectiveness of a person's consent to have death inflicted on him under any circumstances. The same policy appears to underlie ss. 150.1, 159 and 286 in respect of younger people, in the contexts of sexual offences, anal intercourse, and abduction, respectively. All this is to say that the notion of policy-based limits on the effectiveness of consent to some level of inflicted harms is not foreign. Parliament as well as the courts have been mindful of the need for such limits. Autonomy is not the only value which our law seeks to protect.

Some may see limiting the freedom of an adult to consent to applications of force in a fist fight as unduly paternalistic; a violation of individual self-rule. Yet while that view may commend itself to some, those persons cannot reasonably claim that the law does not know such limitations. All criminal law is "paternalistic" to some degree—top-down guidance is inherent in any prohibitive rule. That the common law has developed a strong resistance to recognizing the validity of consent to intentional applications of force in fist fights and brawls is merely one instance of the criminal law's concern that Canadian citizens treat each other humanely and with respect.

In *R. v. Welch* (1995), 101 C.C.C. (3d) 216, the Ontario Court of Appeal indicated that consent would not be a defence to a charge of sexual assault causing bodily harm. The complainant said she did not consent to the acts, but the court reasoned that the accused would still be guilty if there had been consent. Griffiths J.A. stated:

> While the circumstances of this case are not as distasteful as the facts in the House of Lords decision of *Brown*, they are nevertheless disturbing. The sadistic sexual activity here involved bondage (the tying of the victim's hands and feet) and the intentional infliction of injury to the body and rectum of the complainant. The consent of the complainant, assuming it was given, cannot detract from the inherently degrading and dehumanizing nature of the conduct. Although the law must recognize individual freedom and autonomy, when the activity in question involves pursuing sexual gratification by deliberately inflicting pain upon another that gives rise to bodily harm, then the personal interest of the individuals involved must yield to the more compelling societal interests which are challenged by such behaviour.

The author William Wilson, in "Is Hurting People Wrong?," *The Journal of Social Welfare & Family Law* (London: Sweet & Maxwell, 1992), at p. 388, suggests that it is arguable that the House of Lords decision of *Brown* should be treated not as a test case for sexual freedom but for the idea that even a tolerant, pluralistic society must enforce one fundamental residual moral value. Quite simply, it is suggested that hurting people is wrong and this is so whether the victim consents or not, or whether the purpose is to fulfil a sexual need or to satisfy some other desire. At p. 395, the author states:

> How is the balance between freedom and coercion to be drawn? Is the public interest to be secured, in other words, by allowing citizens absolute licence to pursue their own conceptions of the good life, which we take to be the basic moral premise upon which coercion is to be ordered? Or is it to be restricted in order to achieve some more valuable public good, namely societal cohesion and public order? As Fletcher (1978) suggests, a fundamental building block of our moral society is the social taboo against the infliction of injury on another. Remove this building block and not only do sensibilities stand to be damaged but, over time, perhaps our very commitment to the sanctity of life. To reduce this fundamental moral issue to an issue about the presence or absence of consent may be to miss what is really at stake, namely our humanity, as presently conceived. If sadism is allowable, if consented to, then it is consent rather than moral conviction which polices the barrier between a society of would-be sadists and the kind of society most of us would like to inhabit.

> I would dismiss the appeal against conviction.

---

A somewhat more recent take on the rationales and limits of the criminal law can be found in the following report. As you read it, however, question the accuracy of the idea that there is necessary one liberal, conservative, or feminist view on the use of the criminal law.

### Special Committee on Pornography and Prostitution in Canada
### (The Fraser Committee)
(1985)

*The Liberal View*

There is deeply ingrained in the political and philosophical tradition in western societies, the belief that the fundamental value is the freedom of individuals to develop their own view of life, without direction from the state or from the majority. In countries with an Anglo-American legal heritage this view of the world, which penetrates deeply into all aspects of our culture, has its most influential embodiment in the writings of John Stuart Mill. Those who espouse what might be described as the liberal view of the relationship between law and morality, emphasize Mill's dual contention that society benefits from an "open marketplace of ideas" rather than the prescription of majoritarian "wisdom," and that each individual is the best judge of his or her own interests. The necessary corollary of this view of society is that the state is justified in intervening only to punish or control human conduct when it does harm to other people. ...

Apart from children and adults incapable of conducting their own affairs, what people do to themselves or in concert with others, which has no injurious impact on third parties, is the individual's own business, even if it involves the self infliction of either physical or moral harm. ...

Mainstream liberal thought seems to be agreed that harm does embrace both physical harm to others, and the sort of psychic harm involved in people being involuntarily subjected to offensive or objectionable conduct or representations of it. It clearly does not extend to mere feelings of moral distaste that such conduct or depictions of it exist and are being enjoyed by others. Also central to the liberal view of harm is the idea that it is the immediate cause of it which is culpable, not the more remote causes. Thus, for example, it is legitimate to proscribe driving while under the influence of drink because it has been proven to cause accidents. It is not, however, legitimate to proscribe drinking for that reason.

### The Conservative View

This conservative view has two variants. The first states that societies are not simply collections of individuals, but organic units with shared ideas and institutions. The shared moral values of societies are rooted in their cultures, have stood the test of time, and embody the sober wisdom of the majority. Their embodiment in the law is preferable to the easy or uncertain morality of pluralism, which ignores the reality that individual actions, even if directed towards the actor alone, have an impact on the "moral environment" of the community. The second, generally associated with the views of the distinguished British jurist Lord Devlin, adopts the more pessimistic view that, unless the law embodies and enforces traditional moral values, society will lose its "moral cement" and gradually disintegrate. The cohesive power of shared morality is essential to society's welfare, and requires the support of the law.

Both these strains of thinking allow in theory for significant intervention by the law to proscribe immoral conduct, even where it is freely chosen by the individual or individuals concerned, conducted in private and of no direct harm to anyone else. They posit that the state has a right to step in and prevent personal immorality where it clearly offends the sense of propriety and decency of the majority of the community. Moreover, the criminal law, apart from its other functions, has an important symbolic role to play in stating what the common morality will not tolerate. In fact, however, some of the advocates of the "moral environment" and "moral cohesion" approaches admit that these values have to be balanced against others such as liberty and privacy. Furthermore, they accept some pragmatic reservations to these principles, such as those which stem from difficulty of enforcement.

### The Feminist View

It is the feminist position on the rights question which provides a significant challenge to orthodox liberal theorists. According to feminists, the liberal tends to characterize the rights issue in terms of the infringement by the state on the rights of an individual. Little or no attention is paid to the fact that rights issues often develop out of what is, at base, a conflict in the exercise of rights by two individuals. True, the immediate agent of one side may be the state, but that does not alter the fact that a clash of rights between individuals is involved.

If this is correct, then the legal system is not only called upon to protect rights, but also to choose which right is entitled to greater protection. This is unlikely to give the liberal any trouble when it is clear that the exercise of a right by one has caused harm to the other in the exercise of those rights. Much less clear is the liberal reaction when the opposing right has not, in fact, been abridged in the concrete sense but only in the abstract, for example, when a woman claims a pornographic publication infringes her right to equality in that it treats women as degraded or subhuman. Here, the liberal would argue that in the absence of a tangible interference with the "victim's" right, there is no warrant for curtailing the offending activity.

The feminist response to this line of argument is that it demonstrates the bankruptcy of the narrow characterization of the harm principle, and points to the need to redefine the notion of rights in liberal theory. As long as rights in the liberal glossary mean liberty in the sense of being free to act without restraint, they have little value in a society in which fundamental inequalities exist. Thus for women, the fact that on the formal level they enjoy the liberty to do certain things is of little consequence if the social environment prevents the exercise of those rights, and there is no correlative duty on the part of others to see that the rights are exercisable. ...

Feminist writers also join issue with the liberals on the interpretation of the "harm" requirement. As the discussion of the liberal view has demonstrated, the philosophical liberal has a limited perception of harm as a basis for invoking legal proscription of restraint. Either measurable harm, for example, economic, physical or mental to an individual, or statistically verifiable general harm must be established.

Feminists react in two ways to this approach. The first is to challenge the assertion that the "harm" principle is necessarily so limited. Given their perception that sexism in our society is endemic, and their belief that eradication of it requires recognition of the special claims of women, they construct a broader notion of harm which includes a social harm, and in particular, the adverse and potentially divisive effects of a significant segment of the male community developing or reinforcing a thoroughly misogynistic attitude.

Secondly, they will argue that, even if a narrower view of harm is adopted, there is enough data to demonstrate that women are victimized by the sexism inherent in pornography and prostitution. They point to an increasing body of research by social psychologists which, it is claimed, suggest a link between pornography and violence against both women and children. The existence of this link is, they argue, supported by a growing number of reported cases in which battered women report that pornography influenced the conduct of their partners. Finally, they claim, common sense would suggest that frequent exposure to this type of material is likely to have an adverse and brutalizing effect on male perceptions of women as well as male sexuality.

In the same way that feminist writers have difficulty with liberal theory, so they reject acceptance of conservative ideas. On the surface, feminist and conservative theory seem to coincide in that they see "harm" as embracing harm to the community or to society in general. Moreover, insofar as feminist theory views the sexual exploitation of women as subversive of society, it has some similarities to the disintegration theory of Devlin. However, feminist writers are quick to point out that similarities are superficial. They see conservative theory as oppressive and unsatisfactory, because its fundamental assumption is that the ideal society is one in which women have a subordinate and submissive role, and in which sexual expression of all but the most orthodox type is frowned upon. ...

### The Role of the Criminal Law

Each of the philosophical positions discussed above is reflected in attitudes towards the criminal law and its role in society. A wide range of views were put to us during the hearings as to the appropriate role of criminal law in dealing with both pornography and prostitution. These ranged from the extreme conservative position that there should be a complete identification of the criminal law of the state with the "moral law," to the extreme libertarian view that the criminal law should intrude only when physical harm had been caused by one person to another.

It is our view that the role of the criminal law lies mid-way between these extremes. The view that criminal law is somehow the solvent of all social ills is, we believe, naive. History has shown that the enactment of draconian laws has typically had a marginal impact on behaviour patterns. ...

We appreciate fully that law, especially criminal law, has an important and often invisible impact in moulding and influencing peoples' behaviour, and it is clear that some criminal law provisions affect behaviour beneficially without the instrumentation of enforcement. ...

We also disagree with the view that the criminal law should be confined to the tangible harm caused by one individual to another. Although we think that there should be less rather than more intrusion of the criminal law into the lives of citizens, we also think that it has a wider, legitimate ambit than is often claimed for it. Criminal law is, in part, a reflection of the values of society.

### Conclusion

We believe that the development of theory which views pornography as an assault on human rights, will have to be integrated into the conceptual framework of the criminal law on pornography. Our recommendations thus include a complete reworking of the *Criminal Code* prohibitions in this area, to create offences based not on concepts of sexual immorality but rather on the offences to equality, dignity and physical integrity which we believe are involved in pornography. The concern for the vulnerability of young persons has prompted us to devise a number of prohibitions against the use of young persons in sexually explicit material, against the sale, distribution or possession of such material, and the accessibility of such material to young people. ...

With respect to prostitution, our recommendations feature withdrawal of sanctions against simple soliciting: only when the conduct causes actual adverse effect on neighbours and environment is it criminalized. The adult prostitute is accorded by our proposed regime, some leeway to conduct his or her business in privacy and dignity. We would permit one or two prostitutes to receive customers in their own home, hoping thereby to provide people with a safe alternative to the street and parked

cars. In addition, we are recommending that the possibility of allowing small prostitution establishments in non-residential areas be discussed by the federal government
and the provinces and territories.

The idea that adults who engage in prostitution can and should be counted upon to
take responsibility for themselves has led us to recommend cutting back the criminal
prohibitions against procuring and living on the avails of prostitution. Only procuring which is effected by coercion or threats will be criminalized in the case of an
adult. So, too, we stipulate that receiving financial support from an adult prostitute
should be criminal only when that support is exacted by means of coercion or threats.

Where young persons are concerned, the emphasis of our recommendations is to
provide strong protection against exploitation. Procuring children to engage in sexual
activity for reward is made criminal even where no threats are used. So, too, is receiving support from the paid sexual activities of young persons. We have recommended adding to the *Criminal Code* a specific prohibition against engaging, or offering or attempting to engage, in sexual activity with a young person. However, we
do not recommend criminalizing the behaviour of young persons, except to the extent that they come within the general prohibitions because of their own exploitation
of other young persons.

### Reference Re ss. 193 and 195.1(1)(c) of the Criminal Code
Supreme Court of Canada
(1990), 56 C.C.C. (3d) 65

[In this case the Court upheld under the Charter several *Criminal Code* provisions
dealing with prostitution.

The majority of the Court (Dickson C.J.C., Lamer, La Forest and Sopinka JJ.)
held that the prohibition against communicating in any manner in a public place for
the purpose of engaging in prostitution under s. 195.1(1)(c) of the Code [now
s. 213(1)(c)] infringed freedom of expression under s. 2(b) of the Charter but was
justified under s. 1 as reasonable legislation "aimed at the social nuisance of street
solicitation and its eventual elimination."

The majority of the Court also held that the "bawdy house" provisions in s. 193 of
the Code [now s. 210] did not violate s. 7 of the Charter. They were not impermissibly vague given the definitions contained in the case law and the Code. Although
they infringed liberty and security of the person, they did so in accordance with the
principles of fundamental justice.]

DICKSON C.J.C. (La Forest and Sopinka JJ. concurring): The ... argument pertaining to the violation of the principles of fundamental justice rests on the fact that Parliament has chosen to control prostitution indirectly through the criminalization of
certain activities of those involved instead of directly criminalizing prostitution itself. The principle of fundamental justice proffered in this regard is that it is impermissible for Parliament to send out conflicting messages whereby the criminal law
says one thing but means another. Section 193 effectively prohibits the sale of sex in

private settings while s. 195.1(1)(c) makes it impossible to negotiate in public for the sale of sex. It is argued that this legislative scheme attaches the stigma of criminalization to a lawful activity (communication) directed at the achievement of another lawful activity (sale of sex). The question is whether by creating a legal environment indirectly making it, in effect, impossible for a prostitute to sell sex, Parliament has offended the principles of fundamental justice.

While I recognize that Parliament has chosen a circuitous path, I find it difficult to say that Parliament *cannot* take this route. The issue is not whether the legislative scheme is frustrating or unwise but whether the scheme offends the basic tenets of our legal system. The fact that the sale of sex for money is not a criminal act under Canadian law does not mean that Parliament must refrain from using the criminal law to express society's disapprobation of street solicitation. Unless or until this Court is faced with the direct question of Parliament's competence to criminalize prostitution, it is difficult to say that Parliament cannot criminalize and thereby indirectly control some element of prostitution—that is, street solicitation. The principles of fundamental justice are not designed to ensure that the optimal legislation is enacted. I conclude that the legislative scheme embodied by ss. 193 and 195.1(1)(c) of the *Criminal Code* is not so unfair as to violate principles of fundamental justice.

[LAMER J. wrote a separate concurring opinion also holding that s. 195.1(1)(c) was a justified limit on freedom of expression. He concluded that "the legislative objectives of the section go beyond merely preventing the nuisance of traffic congestion and general street disorder. There is the additional objective of minimizing the public exposure of an activity that is degrading to women with the hope that potential entrants in the trade can be deflected at an early stage and of restricting the blight that is associated with public solicitation for the purposes of prostitution." He also dealt with the s. 7 issue as follows:]

In summary then, I conclude that neither s. 193 nor s. 195.1(1)(c) of the *Criminal Code* are in violation of s. 7 of the Charter on account that they are impermissibly vague. In neither case can it be said that fair notice is not given to citizens; courts have been able to give sensible meaning to the terms of the sections and have applied them without difficulty. Further, the discretion of law enforcement officials is sufficiently limited by the explicit legislative standards set out in the sections. Therefore, the appellants' first ground of attack of the impugned provisions under s. 7 of the Charter must fail.

The second ground of attack involves a consideration of whether "liberty" under s. 7 includes within its scope the right to engage in an occupation and to carry on a business, more specifically in this case the trade of prostitution. ... We find ourselves in an anomalous, some would say bizarre, situation where almost everything related to prostitution has been regulated by the criminal law except the transaction itself. The appellants' argument then, more precisely stated, is that in criminalizing so many activities surrounding the act itself, Parliament has made prostitution de facto illegal if not de jure illegal.

The appellants in the case at bar rely on an expansive interpretation of the rights guaranteed by s. 7 to argue that carrying on a lawful occupation is protected by the right to liberty. As a basis for this view the following summary of the position taken by the English philosopher John Stuart Mill is relied upon:

> The only end for which society is warranted in infringing the liberty of action of any individual, he said, is self protection. Power should be exercised to prevent the individual from doing harm to other, but that is the only part of his conduct for which he should be answerable to society. In every other way he should have freedom.

(J. Symons, "Orwell's Prophecies: The Limits of Liberty and the Limits of Law" 9 *Dalhousie L.J.* 115 at p. 116 (1984).) Mill's approach was explicitly adopted by Wilson J. in *Jones v. The Queen* (1986), 28 C.C.C. (3d) 513 at pp. 525-6, 31 D.L.R. (4th) 569, [1986] 2 S.C.R. 284:

> I believe that the framers of the Constitution in guaranteeing "liberty" as a fundamental value in a free and democratic society had in mind the freedom of the individual to develop and realize his potential to the full, to plan his own life to suit his own character, to make his own choices for good or ill, to be non-conformist, idiosyncratic and even eccentric—to be, in today's parlance, "his own person" and accountable as such. John Stuart Mill described it as "pursuing our own good in our own way."

For a further exposition of this view, see the judgment of my colleague Madam Justice Wilson in *R. v. Morgentaler*, supra, at pp. 549-51. [In that case, Justice Wilson struck down a law requiring a hospital committee to approve abortions in part on the basis that "the right to liberty guaranteed by s. 7 of the Charter gives a woman the right to decide for herself whether or not to terminate her pregnancy." The majority of the court struck down the criminal offence on abortions without hospital committee approval on different grounds, emphasizing that the procedural difficulties in obtaining committee approval violated a woman's security of the person in a manner that was not in accord with the principles of fundamental justice.]

This court has until now, save for certain comments of my colleague Wilson J., taken an exclusionary approach to defining liberty and security of the person. … I note that the guarantees of life, liberty and security of the person are placed together with a set of provisions (ss. 8 to 14) which are mainly concerned with criminal and penal proceedings. More specifically, ss. 8 to 14 confer rights related to investigation, detention, adjudication and sanction in relation to offences. It is significant that the rights guaranteed by s. 7 as well as those guaranteed in ss. 8 to 14 are listed under the title "Legal Rights," or in the French version "Garanties juridiques." The use of the term "Legal Rights" suggests a distinctive set of rights different from the rights guaranteed by other sections of the Charter. In this regard I refer to the judgment of this court in *Reference re s. 94(2) of the Motor Vehicle Act* (1985), 23 C.C.C. (3d) 289 at pp. 301-2:

> Sections 8 to 14 … address specific deprivations of the "right" of life, liberty and security of the person in breach of the principles of fundamental justice … They are designed to protect, in a specific manner and setting, the right to life, liberty and security of the person set forth in s. 7.

The common thread that runs throughout s. 7 and ss. 8 to 14, however, is the involvement of the judicial branch as guardian of the justice system. As examples we need only look briefly to ss. 8 to 14. Section 8 protects individuals against unreasonable search or seizure. In that context, it is an independent arbiter, namely, a member of the judiciary, that usually decides whether the state interest in searching outweighs the individual's right of privacy. Sections 9 and 10 involve protections in respect of detention, arrest and imprisonment. One of the central principles to be found in these rights is that of *habeas corpus*, the traditional writ requiring that a person be brought before a judge to investigate and determine the lawfulness of his detention. Sections 11 to 14 involve the proceedings in criminal and penal matters including notice of the offence charged, the actual trial proceedings and protection against cruel or unusual punishment. …

[T]he confinement of individuals against their will, or the restriction of control over their own minds and bodies, are precisely the kinds of activities that fall within the domain of the judiciary as guardian of the justice system. By contrast, once we move beyond the "judicial domain," we are into the realm of general public policy where the principles of fundamental justice, as they have been developed primarily through the common law, are significantly irrelevant. In the area of public policy, what is at issue are political interests, pressures and values that no doubt are of social significance, but which are not "essential elements of a system for the administration of justice," and hence are not principles of fundamental justice within the meaning of s. 7. The courts must not, because of the nature of the institution, be involved in the realm of pure public policy; that is the exclusive role of the properly elected representatives, the legislators. To expand the scope of s. 7 too widely would be to infringe upon that role.

[WILSON J. (L'Heureux-Dubé J. concurring) dissented. Section 195.1(1)(c) infringed freedom of expression but was not a proportionate limit under s. 1. She stated:]

I believe, with respect, that the Attorney General has overlooked a number of significant aspects of the impugned legislation which go directly to the question of its proportionality. The first is that it criminalizes communication or attempted communication for the prohibited purpose in any public place or place open to public view. "Public place" is then expanded in subs. (2) to include any place to which the public have access as of right or by invitation express or implied. In other words, the prohibition is not confined to places where there will necessarily be lots of people to be offended or inconvenienced by it. The prohibited communication may be taking place in a secluded area of a park where there is no-one to see or hear it. It will still be a criminal offence under the section. Such a broad prohibition as to the locale of the communication would seem to go far beyond a genuine concern over the nuisance caused by street solicitation in Canada's major centres of population. It enables the police to arrest citizens who are disturbing no-one solely because they are engaged in communicative acts concerning something not prohibited by the *Code*. It is not reasonable, in my view, to prohibit *all* expressive activity conveying a certain meaning that takes place in public simply because in *some* circumstances and in *some* areas that activity *may* give rise to a public or social nuisance.

I note also the broad scope of the phrase "in any manner communicates or attempts to communicate." It would seem to encompass every conceivable method of human expression. Indeed, it may not be necessary for the prostitute to say anything at all in order to be found to be "communicating" or "attempting to communicate" for the purpose of prostitution. The proverbial nod or wink may be enough. Perhaps more serious, a hapless citizen may be picked up for soliciting when he or she has nothing more pressing in mind than hailing a taxi! While it is true that he or she may subsequently be let go as lacking the necessary intent for the offence, the experience of being arrested is not something the ordinary citizen would welcome. Some definitional limits would appear to be desirable in any activity labelled as criminal. ...

[Wilson J. also held that there was a violation of s. 7 of the Charter. She stated:]

In *R. v. Morgentaler* (1988), 37 C.C.C. (3d) 449, 44 D.L.R. (4th) 385, [1988] 1 S.C.R. 30, the Chief Justice (Lamer J. concurring), made the following remarks at p. 476 about regulation by means of the criminal law as distinct from regulation by other means:

> The criminal law is a very special form of governmental regulation, for it seeks to express our society's collective disapprobation of certain acts and omissions. When a defence is provided, especially a specifically-tailored defence to a particular charge, it is because the legislator has determined that the disapprobation of society is not warranted when the conditions of the defence are met.

In my opinion, it is equally true that where the legislature has *not* criminalized a certain activity it is because the legislator has determined that this uniquely coercive and punitive method of expressing society's collective disapprobation of that activity is not warranted in the circumstances.

While it is an undeniable fact that many people find the idea of exchanging sex for money offensive and immoral, it is also a fact that many types of conduct which are subject to widespread disapproval and allegations of immorality have not been criminalized. Indeed, one can think of a number of reasons why selling sex has not been made a criminal offence. First, as Lamer J. notes in his s. 1 analysis of the legislative objective underlying s. 195.1(1)(c), more often than not the real "victim" of prostitution is the prostitute himself or herself. Sending prostitutes to prison for their conduct may, therefore, have been viewed by legislators as an unsuitable response to the phenomenon. Or the legislators may have realized that they could not send the female prostitute to prison while letting the male customer go, and been reluctant for that reason to make prostitution a criminal offence. Another explanation may be a reluctance on the part of legislators to criminalize a transaction which normally occurs in private between consenting adults. Yet another possibility is that the legislature simply recognized that prostitution is the oldest trade in the world and is clearly meeting a social need. Whatever the reasons may be, the persistent resistance to outright criminalization of the act of prostitution cannot be treated as inconsequential.

I mention these possible reasons for the continuing legality of prostitution not for the purpose of endorsing any particular theory but rather to emphasize that the legality of prostitution must be recognized in any s. 7 analysis and must be respected regardless of one's personal views on the subject. As long as the act of selling sex is lawful, it seems to me that this court cannot impute to it the collective disapprobation reserved for criminal offences. We cannot treat as a crime that which the legislature has deliberately refrained from making a crime.

Nevertheless, the legislature has chosen to place serious constraints on the circumstances in which prostitution may take place and has decided that where someone attempts to engage in prostitution in those prohibited circumstances, the *Criminal Code's* penalties are appropriate. In other words, Parliament has chosen to regulate certain incidents of prostitution by means of the criminal law's power to deprive people of their "physical" liberty. In my view, it is this decision which triggers the application of s. 7 of the Charter.

In the case at bar, conviction under s. 193 or 195.1, may result in a deprivation of the liberty of the person. The convicted prostitute faces a possible prison sentence as well as the stigma of being labelled a criminal. The legislation permitting this result must, therefore, accord with the principles of fundamental justice if it is to survive the constitutional challenge.

[Wilson J. held that because s. 195.1(1)(c) infringed freedom of expression it also infringed liberty and security of the person in a manner not in accordance with the principles of fundamental justice.]

---

In *R. v. Skinner* (1990), 56 C.C.C. (3d) 1, the Supreme Court of Canada held that s. 195.1(1)(c) (now s. 213(1)(c)) prohibiting communicating in a public place for the purpose of engaging in prostitution did not violate freedom of association under s. 2(d) of the Charter.

Wilson J. (L'Heureux-Dubé J. concurring) dissented holding that the impugned provision, by limiting the circumstances in which a prostitute and a potential customer could associate to pursue a lawful objective, violated freedom of association. She stated that the Court "should avoid the temptation to make a moral judgment in deciding whether or not associational activity is protected by s. 2(d)."

## II. PORNOGRAPHY


### R. v. Butler
Supreme Court of Canada
(1992), 70 C.C.C. (3d) 129

[The accused, who operated a shop selling various forms of pornography, was charged with 77 counts of violating s. 163 of the *Criminal Code*. At trial, the judge found that because s. 163 restricted freedom of expression, under s. 1 of the Charter, the state could only prohibit pornography involving violence or cruelty or otherwise dehumanizing material. As a result, Butler was convicted of eight counts. A Crown appeal was allowed and the Manitoba Court of Appeal entered convictions on all counts. The accused's appeal to the Supreme Court was allowed and a new trial was ordered.]

SOPINKA J. (Lamer C.J.C., La Forest, Cory, McLachlin, Stevenson, and Iacobucci JJ.): In order for the work or material to qualify as "obscene," the exploitation of sex must not only be its dominant characteristic, but such exploitation must be "undue." In determining when the exploitation of sex will be considered "undue," the courts have attempted to formulate workable tests. The most important of these is the "community standard of tolerance" test.

Our court was called upon to elaborate the community standards test in *R. v. Towne Cinema Theatres Ltd.* (1985), 18 C.C.C. (3d) 193 at p. 205, 18 D.L.R. (4th) 1, [1985] 1 S.C.R. 494. Dickson C.J.C. reviewed the case-law and found:

> The cases all emphasize that it is a standard of *tolerance*, not taste, that is relevant. What matters is not what Canadians think is right for themselves to see. What matters is what Canadians would not abide other Canadians seeing because it would be beyond the contemporary Canadian standard of tolerance to allow them to see it.
>
> Since the standard is tolerance, I think the audience to which the allegedly obscene material is targeted must be relevant. The operative standards are those of the Canadian community as a whole, but since what matters is what other people may see, it is quite conceivable that the Canadian community would tolerate varying degrees of explicitness depending upon the audience and the circumstances.

There has been a growing recognition in recent cases that material which may be said to exploit sex in a "degrading or dehumanizing" manner will necessarily fail the community standards test. Borins Co. Ct. J. expressed this view in *R. v. Doug Rankine Co. Ltd.* (1983), 9 C.C.C. (3d) 53 at p. 70, 36 C.R. (3d) 154 (Ont. Co. Ct.) ...

Among other things, degrading or dehumanizing materials place women (and sometimes men) in positions of subordination, servile submission or humiliation. They run against the principles of equality and dignity of all human beings. In the appreciation of whether material is degrading or dehumanizing, the appearance of consent is not necessarily determinative. Consent cannot save materials that otherwise contain degrading or dehumanizing scenes. Sometimes the very appearance of consent makes the depicted acts even more degrading or dehumanizing.

Pornography can be usefully divided into three categories: (1) explicit sex with violence, (2) explicit sex without violence but which subjects people to treatment that is degrading or dehumanizing, and (3) explicit sex without violence that is neither degrading nor dehumanizing. Violence in this context includes both actual physical violence and threats of physical violence. Relating these three categories to the terms of s. 163(8) of the *Code*, the first, explicit sex coupled with violence, is expressly mentioned. Sex coupled with crime, horror or cruelty will sometimes involve violence. Cruelty, for instance, will usually do so. But, even in the absence of violence, sex coupled with crime, horror or cruelty may fall within the second category. As for category (3), subject to the exception referred to below, it is not covered.

Some segments of society would consider that all three categories of pornography cause harm to society because they tend to undermine its moral fibre. Others would contend that none of the categories cause harm. Furthermore there is a range of opinion as to what is degrading or dehumanizing: see *Pornography and Prostitution in Canada: Report of the Special Committee on Pornography and Prostitution* (1985) (the Fraser Report), vol. 1, at p. 51. Because this is not a matter that is susceptible of proof in the traditional way and because we do not wish to leave it to the individual tastes of judges, we must have a norm that will serve as an arbiter in determining what amounts to an undue exploitation of sex. That arbiter is the community as a whole.

The courts must determine as best they can what the community would tolerate others being exposed to on the basis of the degree of harm that may flow from such exposure. Harm in this context means that it predisposes persons to act in an antisocial manner as, for example, the physical or mental mistreatment of women by men, or, what is perhaps debatable, the reverse. Antisocial conduct for this purpose is conduct which society formally recognizes as incompatible with its proper functioning. The stronger the inference of a risk of harm the lesser the likelihood of tolerance. The inference may be drawn from the material itself or from the material and other evidence. Similarly evidence as to the community standards is desirable but not essential.

In making this determination with respect to the three categories of pornography referred to above, the portrayal of sex coupled with violence will almost always constitute the undue exploitation of sex. Explicit sex which is degrading or dehumanizing may be undue if the risk of harm is substantial. Finally, explicit sex that is not violent and neither degrading nor dehumanizing is generally tolerated in our society and will not qualify as the undue exploitation of sex unless it employs children in its production.

[Sopinka J. then held that s. 163 violated freedom of expression under s. 2(b) of the Code but could be upheld under s. 1 of the Charter.]

The obscenity legislation and jurisprudence prior to the enactment of s. 163 were evidently concerned with prohibiting the "immoral influences" of obscene publications and safeguarding the morals of individuals into whose hands such works could fall.
... In this sense, its dominant, if not exclusive, purpose was to advance a particular conception of morality. Any deviation from such morality was considered to be inherently undesirable, independently of any harm to society. As Judson J. described the test in *Brodie* (1962), 132 C.C.C. 161 (at p. 181):

[The work under attack] has none of the characteristics that are often described in judgments dealing with obscenity—dirt for dirt's sake, the leer of the sensualist, depravity in the mind of an author with an obsession for dirt, pornography, an appeal to a prurient interest, etc.

I agree with Twaddle J.A. of the Court of Appeal that this particular objective is no longer defensible in view of the Charter. To impose a certain standard of public and sexual morality, solely because it reflects the conventions of a given community, is inimical to the exercise and enjoyment of individual freedoms, which form the basis of our social contract. D. Dyzenhaus, "Obscenity and the Charter: Autonomy and Equality" (1991), 1 C.R. (4th) 367 at p. 370, refers to this as "legal moralism," of a majority deciding what values should inform individual lives and then coercively imposing those values on minorities. The prevention of "dirt for dirt's sake" is not a legitimate objective which would justify the violation of one of the most fundamental freedoms enshrined in the Charter.

On the other hand, I cannot agree with the suggestion of the appellant that Parliament does not have the right to legislate on the basis of some fundamental conception of morality for the purposes of safeguarding the values which are integral to a free and democratic society. As Dyzenhaus, *ibid.*, writes (at p. 376): "Moral disapprobation is recognized as an appropriate response when it has its basis in *Charter* values."

As the respondent and many of the interveners have pointed out, much of the criminal law is based on moral conceptions of right and wrong and the mere fact that a law is grounded in morality does not automatically render it illegitimate. In this regard, criminalizing the proliferation of materials which undermine another basic Charter right may indeed be a legitimate objective.

In my view, however, the overriding objective of s. 163 is not moral disapprobation but the avoidance of harm to society. In *Towne Cinema*, Dickson C.J.C. stated (at p. 204): "It is harm to society from undue exploitation that is aimed at by the section, not simply lapses in propriety or good taste."

I am in agreement with Twaddle J.A. who expressed the view that Parliament was entitled to have a "reasoned apprehension of harm" resulting from the desensitization of individuals exposed to materials which depict violence, cruelty, and dehumanization in sexual relations.

Accordingly, I am of the view that there is a sufficiently rational link between the criminal sanction, which demonstrates our community's disapproval of the dissemination of materials which potentially victimize women and which restricts the negative influence which such materials have on changes in attitudes and behaviour, and the objective.

There are several factors which contribute to the finding that the provision minimally impairs the freedom which is infringed.

First, the impugned provision does not proscribe sexually explicit erotica without violence that is not degrading or dehumanizing. It is designed to catch material that creates a risk of harm to society. It might be suggested that proof of actual harm should be required. It is apparent from what I have said above that it is sufficient in this regard for Parliament to have a reasonable basis for concluding that harm will result and this requirement does not demand actual proof of harm.

The final question to be answered in the proportionality test is whether the effects of the law so severely trench on a protected right that the legislative objective is outweighed by the infringement. The infringement on freedom of expression is confined to a measure designed to prohibit the distribution of sexually explicit materials accompanied by violence, and those without violence that are degrading or dehumanizing. As I have already concluded, this kind of expression lies far from the core of the guarantee of freedom of expression. It appeals only to the most base aspect of individual fulfilment, and it is primarily economically motivated.

The objective of the legislation, on the other hand, is of fundamental importance in a free and democratic society. It is aimed at avoiding harm, which Parliament has reasonably concluded will be caused directly or indirectly, to individuals, groups such as women and children, and consequently to society as a whole, by the distribution of these materials. It thus seeks to enhance respect for all members of society, and nonviolence and equality in their relations with each other.

I therefore conclude that the restriction on freedom of expression does not outweigh the importance of the legislative objective.

[GONTHIER J. (L'Heureux-Dubé J. concurring) wrote a concurring opinion stating that in some circumstances, such as public displays on a billboard, explicit sex that is not violent or dehumanizing could be prohibited under s. 163 and the Charter.]

---

Note that a gay and lesbian bookstore subsequently challenged the *Butler* definition of pornography, and specifically the idea that degrading and dehumanizing pornography could be obscene, as a form of discrimination against gays and lesbians. The Supreme Court, however, rejected this argument, upholding the *Butler* test. See *Little Sisters Books v. Canada*, [2000] 2 S.C.R. 1120.

## R. v. Sharpe
Supreme Court of Canada
[2001] 1 S.C.R. 45

McLACHLIN C.J. (Iacobucci, Major, Arbour, Binnie, and LeBel JJ. concurring):

[1] Is Canada's law banning the possession of child pornography constitutional or, conversely, does it unjustifiably intrude on the constitutional right of Canadians to free expression? That is the central question posed by this appeal.

[2] I conclude that the law is constitutional, except for two peripheral applications relating to expressive material privately created and kept by the accused, for which two exceptions can be read into the legislation. The law otherwise strikes a constitutional balance between freedom of expression and prevention of harm to children. As a consequence, I would uphold the law and remit Mr. Sharpe for trial on all charges. ...

[6] In 1993, Parliament enacted s. 163.1 of the *Criminal Code*, creating a number of offences relating to child pornography. The provision supplemented laws making

it an offence to make, print, publish, distribute, or circulate obscene material (s. 163), and to corrupt children (s. 172). With the enactment of s. 163.1, the *Criminal Code* contains a comprehensive scheme to attack child pornography at every stage—production, publication, importation, distribution, sale and possession. Subsections (2) and (3) of s. 163.1 criminalize possession of child pornography for the purpose of publication and possession for the purpose of distribution or sale. Section 163.1(4) extends the prohibition to possession simpliciter:

> 163.1 ...
>   (4)  Every person who possesses any child pornography is guilty of
>       (a)  an indictable offence and liable to imprisonment for a term not exceeding five years; or
>       (b)  an offence punishable on summary conviction ...

[13]  In the British Columbia Supreme Court, Shaw J. courageously ruled that s. 163.1(4) is unconstitutional. He held that the objective of the law is to combat material that puts children at risk of harm. He reviewed evidence that child pornography arguably creates this risk through its use for grooming or seduction; by the use of children in its manufacture; by confirming or augmenting cognitive distortions of paedophiles; and by inciting paedophiles to commit offences against children. However, although this Court in *R. v. Butler*, [1992] 1 S.C.R. 452, did not require conclusive proof that obscene materials cause harm, Shaw J. apparently required such proof and found little scientific evidence linking the possession of child pornography to these risks. As a result, he considered the salutary effects of the law to be limited. As for the law's deleterious effects, he found that "the invasion of freedom of expression and personal privacy is profound" (para. 49) and held that they were "not outweighed by the limited beneficial effects of the prohibition" (para. 50). Shaw J. concluded that the law was inconsistent with the Charter and could not be justified under s. 1, rendering it invalid under s. 52(1) of the *Constitution Act, 1982*. ...

[29]  These then are the values at stake in this appeal. On the one hand stands the right of free expression—a right fundamental to the liberty of each Canadian and our democratic society. On the other stands the conviction that the possession of child pornography must be forbidden to prevent harm to children. ...

[72]  Section 163.1(4) of the *Criminal Code* evinces a clear and unequivocal intention to protect children from the abuse and exploitation associated with child pornography. It criminalizes the possession of a substantial range of materials posing a risk of harm to children. Written material and visual representations advocating the commission of criminal offences against children is caught. Visual material depicting children engaged in explicit sexual activity is caught, as is material featuring, as a dominant characteristic, the sexual organ or anal region of a child for a sexual purpose. The reach of the proscription is further broadened by extending it to the depiction of both real and imaginary persons. As a result, the law appears to catch a substantial amount of material that endangers the welfare of children. ...

[77]  These examples suggest that s. 163.1(4), at the margins of its application, prohibits deeply private forms of expression, in pursuit of materials that may pose no

more than a nominal risk of harm to children. It is these potential applications that present the most significant concerns at the stage of justification. ...

[110]  I conclude that in broad impact and general application, the limits s. 163.1(4) imposes on free expression are justified by the protection the law affords children from exploitation and abuse. I cannot, however, arrive at the same conclusion in regard to the two problematic categories of materials described above. The legislation prohibits a person from articulating thoughts in writing or visual images, even if the result is intended only for his or her own eyes. It further prohibits a teenager from possessing, again exclusively for personal use, sexually explicit photographs or videotapes of him- or herself alone or engaged with a partner in lawful sexual activity. The inclusion of these peripheral materials in the law's prohibition trenches heavily on freedom of expression while adding little to the protection the law provides children. To this extent, the law cannot be considered proportionate in its effects, and the infringement of s. 2(b) contemplated by the legislation is not demonstrably justifiable under s. 1. ...

[128]  I would summarize my conclusions with respect to s. 163.1(4) in general terms as follows:

1. The offence prohibits the possession of photographs, film, videos and other visual representations that show or depict a person under the age of 18 engaged in explicit sexual activity. Visual representations of any activity that falls short of this threshold are not caught. Thus, representations of casual intimacy, such as depictions of kissing or hugging, are not covered by the offence.

2. The offence prohibits the possession of visual representations that feature, as a dominant characteristic, the depiction of a sexual organ or the anal region of a person under the age of 18 for a sexual purpose. Innocent photographs of a baby in the bath and other representations of non-sexual nudity are not covered by the offence.

3. The offence prohibits the possession of written or visual material that actively induces or encourages unlawful sexual activity with persons under the age of 18. Written description that falls short of this threshold is not covered by the offence.

4. Courts should take an objective approach to determining whether material falls within the definition of child pornography. The question is whether a reasonable person would conclude, for example, that the impugned material portrays "explicit" sexual activity, or that the material "advocates or counsels" sexual offences with persons under 18. Courts should also take an objective approach in determining the availability of any statutory defence.

5. The various statutory defences (i.e., artistic merit; educational, scientific or medical purpose; and public good) must be interpreted liberally to protect freedom of expression, as well as possession for socially redeeming purposes.

6. The guarantees provided in ss. 2(b) and 7 of the Charter require the recognition of two exceptions to s. 163.1(4), where the prohibition's intrusion into free expression and privacy is most pronounced and its benefits most attenuated:

   (a) The first exception protects the possession of expressive material created through the efforts of a single person and held by that person alone, exclusively for his or her own personal use. This exception protects deeply private expression, such as personal journals and drawings, intended solely for the eyes of their creator.

   (b) The second exception protects a person's possession of visual recordings created by or depicting that person, but only where these recordings do not depict unlawful sexual activity, are held only for private use, and were created with the consent of those persons depicted.

7. These two exceptions apply equally to the offence of "making" child pornography under s. 163.1(2).

8. Neither exception affords protection to a person harbouring any other intention than private possession; any intention to distribute, publish, print, share or in any other way disseminate these materials will subject a person to the full force of s. 163.1. ...

[The majority ordered a new trial on the offence as restructured in its decision.]

L'HEUREUX-DUBÉ J. (Gonthier and Bastarache JJ.) (dissenting in part): ...

[186]  The possession of child pornography has no social value; it has only a tenuous connection to the value of self-fulfilment underlying the right to free expression. As such, it warrants only attenuated protection. Hence, increased deference should be accorded to Parliament's decision to prohibit it.

*(d)  Enhancement of Other Charter Values*

[187]  This Court has previously considered the Charter rights of other members of society as a contextual factor relevant to determining the proper level of deference. For example, in *Keegstra*, *supra*, the impugned legislation prohibited the willful promotion of hatred against any identifiable group. Dickson C.J. found that s. 15 and s. 27 of the Charter were relevant to determining the importance of the government's objective of eradicating hate propaganda. At p. 756, he quoted with approval the following statement of one of the interveners in the case:

> Government sponsored hatred on group grounds would violate section 15 of the Charter. Parliament promotes equality and moves against inequality when it prohibits the wilful public promotion of group hatred on these grounds. It follows that government action against group hate, because it promotes social equality as guaranteed by the Charter, deserves special constitutional consideration under section 15.

In *Taylor*, *supra*, Dickson C.J. further emphasized the role of other Charter rights in the application of s. 1, stating that in applying *Oakes*, the Court must "give full recognition to other provisions of the Charter, in particular ss. 15 and 27" (pp. 916-17). In our view, the positive influence of a government measure on other Charter rights, and in turn the negative effect of an expressive activity on the rights of other members of the community, are important factors to be considered in the application of the s. 1 analysis. This approach ensures that the analysis of whether an impugned provision is reasonably justified in a free and democratic society is undertaken in a manner which promotes our democratic values.

[188] In the Fraser Report, ... the Committee described its concerns with child pornography as follows (vol. 2, at p. 571):

> ... we are concerned with depictions that can be seen to undermine the values which we believe are fundamental to our society. It is our view that material which uses and depicts children in a sexual way for the entertainment of adults, undermines the rights of children by diminishing the respect to which they are entitled.

This description of the effects of child pornography on children's rights strikes a sombre chord. The written material and images captured by s. 163.1(1) (which depict children engaged in explicit sexual activity or which depict their sexual organs for a sexual purpose), degrade and dehumanize them. They portray children as mere sexual objects available for the gratification of adults. They play on children's inequality. Hence, this material is in direct conflict with the guarantee of equality in s. 15. In *Butler*, *supra*, Sopinka J. stated as follows, at p. 497:

> ... if true equality between male and female persons is to be achieved, we cannot ignore the threat to equality resulting from exposure to audiences of certain types of violent and degrading material. Materials portraying women as a class as objects for sexual exploitation and abuse have a negative impact on "the individual's sense of self-worth and acceptance."

Similarly, Parliament's attempt to prohibit the possession of child pornography can be seen as promoting children's right to equality.

[189] Child pornography also undermines children's right to life, liberty and security of the person as guaranteed by s. 7. Their psychological and physical security is placed at risk by their use in pornographic representations. Those children who are used in the production of child pornography are physically abused in its production. Moreover, child pornography threatens the physical and psychological security of all children, since it can be encountered by any child. Regardless of its authorship, be it of the child or others, it plays on children's weaknesses and may lead to attitudinal harm; see Fraser Report, ... vol. 2, at pp. 570-71. We recognize that privacy is an important value underlying the right to be free from unreasonable search and seizure and the right to liberty. However, the privacy of those who possess child pornography is not the only interest at stake in this appeal. The privacy interests of those children who pose for child pornography are engaged by the fact that a permanent record of

their sexual exploitation is produced. This privacy interest is also triggered when material which is created by teenagers in a "consensual environment" is disseminated.

[190] In enacting s. 163.1(4) and prohibiting the possession of child pornography, Parliament promulgated a law which seeks to foster and protect the equality rights of children, along with their security of the person and their privacy interests. The importance of these Charter rights cannot be ignored in the analysis of whether the law is demonstrably justified in a free and democratic society and warrants a more deferential application of the criteria set out in *Oakes*.

[191] In enacting s. 163.1(4), Parliament set social policy having regard to moral values, as it is entitled to do. It is accepted that, while the criminal law is not confined to prohibiting immoral acts, Parliament does have the right to make moral judgments in criminalizing certain forms of conduct. In *Butler*, *supra*, Sopinka J. found as follows, at p. 493:

> ... I cannot agree with the suggestion of the appellant that Parliament does not have the right to legislate on the basis of some fundamental conception of morality for the purposes of safeguarding the values which are integral to a free and democratic society.

The Court should be particularly sensitive to the legitimate role of government in legislating with respect to our social values. Like all legislative decisions, however, such moral decisions and judgments must be assessed in light of Charter values. ...

[222] In examining whether the prohibition of the possession of written child pornography minimally impairs the right to free expression, we must bear in mind that only material which advocates or counsels the commission of an offence against a child is included in the definition set out in s. 163.1(1)(b). We disagree with McLachlin C.J. ... where she finds that s. 163.1(1)(b) is overbroad with regard to some materials on the basis of their authorship and the intent of the possessor. The intent of the author or possessor of the material is not relevant to determining whether it advocates or counsels the commission of a crime. Section 163.1(1)(b) covers all written material which seeks to persuade the commission of offences against children. The focus of the inquiry must be on the content of the material itself and not on the circumstances in which it was created, nor on the form of the material, for example whether it be a novel, a poem or a diary. Any material which, upon examining the message which it conveys in the context of the piece as a whole, seeks to persuade the commission of sexual offences against children will be caught by the law. Thus, depending on the context, individual chronicles of sexual activity may well fall within the scope of the definition.

[223] There is evidence to support Parliament's choice to include written material which advocates or counsels the commission of sexual offences against children. Dr. Collins testified that the cognitive distortions of paedophiles were reinforced by written materials which advocate sexual activity with children. Having such views expressed in written form would validate their beliefs about children. In his opinion, written pornography would also fuel the sexual fantasies of paedophiles, and in some cases could incite them to offend. ...

[231] Thus, we cannot agree with the approach to this issue taken by McLachlin C.J. The inclusion of teenage pornography in s. 163.1(4) is consistent with the legislative purpose of providing for the effective protection of children by reducing the potential for harm caused by pornographic material. McLachlin C.J. is not persuaded that auto-depictions of teenage sexual activity are harmful. With respect, Parliament was justified in restricting teenagers from creating a permanent record of their sexual activity. While adolescents between the ages of 14 and 17 may legally engage in sexual activity, the creation of a permanent record of such activity has consequences which children of that age may not have sufficient maturity to understand … .

[232] In considering whether s. 163.1(4), in conjunction with the definition of child pornography, minimally impairs the guarantee of freedom of expression, it is important to bear in mind that the provision does not amount to a total ban on the possession of child pornography. The provision reflects an attempt by Parliament to weigh the competing rights and values at stake and achieve a proper balance. First, the definitional limits act as safeguards to ensure that only material that is antithetical to Parliament's objectives in proscribing child pornography will be targeted. Second, the legislation incorporates defences of artistic merit, educational, scientific or medical purpose, and a defence of the public good. With regard to the defence of artistic merit, McLachlin C.J. writes that "[a]ny objectively established artistic value, however small" (para. 63), provides a complete defence. In our view, the boundaries of the artistic merit defence do not need to be decided in this appeal, especially since the defence also applies to the prohibitions against the publication, distribution and sale of child pornography that are also found in s. 163.1. However, we would consider anomalous interpreting artistic merit to provide a complete defence in a case in which the same material would fail the artistic merit test under the obscenity provisions of the *Criminal Code*. We must give effect to Parliament's deliberate decision to avoid the term artistic "purpose," which it adopted for the educational, scientific and medical defences. Artistic merit must be determined … through careful attention to artistic conventions, expert opinions and modes of production, display and distribution. Simply calling oneself an artist is not an absolute shield to conviction. …

[243] We would allow the appeal and remit the charges for trial.

[At a subsequent trial, Sharpe was convicted of possession of child pornography with respect to photographs but acquitted with respect to written material on the basis that there was a reasonable doubt whether it advocated or counseled sexual activity or alternatively it fell under the artistic merit defence under s. 163.1(6) of the Code.]

## III. MARIJUANA AND THE HARM PRINCIPLE


**R. v. Malmo-Levine; R. v. Caine**
Supreme Court of Canada
2003 SCC 74

GONTHIER and BINNIE JJ. (McLachlin C.J., Iacobucci, Major, and Bastarache JJ. concurring):

[1]  In these appeals, the Court is required to consider whether Parliament has the legislative authority to criminalize simple possession of marihuana and, if so, whether that power has been exercised in a manner that is contrary to the *Canadian Charter of Rights and Freedoms*. The appellant Caine argues in particular that it is a violation of the principles of fundamental justice for Parliament to provide for a term of imprisonment as a sentence for conduct which he says results in little or no harm to other people. ...

[2]  The British Columbia Court of Appeal rejected the appellants' challenges to the relevant provisions of the *Narcotic Control Act* ("NCA"), R.S.C. 1985, c. N-1 [repealed S.C. 1996, c. 19, but see now the *Controlled Drugs and Substances Act*, S.C. 1996, c. 19, s.14], and, in our view, it was right to do so. ...

[The majority of the British Columbia Court of Appeal (2000), 138 B.C.A.C. 218, 2000 BCCA 335... concluded that the "harm principle" was a principle of fundamental justice within the meaning of s. 7. "[The harm principle] is a legal principle and it is concise. Moreover, there is a consensus among reasonable people that it is vital to our system of justice. Indeed, I think that it is common sense that you don't go to jail unless there is a potential that your activities will cause harm to others" (para. 134). Braidwood J.A. however, judged that the deprivation of the appellants' liberty caused by the penal provisions of the NCA was in accordance with the harm principle, and did not violate s. 7. "It is for Parliament to determine what level of risk is acceptable and what level of risk requires action. The Charter only demands ... a 'reasoned apprehension of harm' that is not insignificant or trivial. The appellants have not convinced me that such harm is absent in this case" (para. 158). ... Prowse J.A. disagreed that the threshold of harm justifying parliamentary intervention is harm that is "not insignificant or trivial." In her view, harm must be "serious" and "substantial" to survive a Charter challenge. She concluded that the prohibition of the possession of marijuana breached the appellants' s. 7 Charter rights in a manner inconsistent with a principle of fundamental justice. She would have adjourned the proceedings to permit counsel to make further submissions with respect to the justification of the breach under s. 1 of the Charter.]

[3]  All sides agree that marihuana is a psychoactive drug which "causes alteration of mental function." That, indeed, is the purpose for which the appellants use it. Certain groups in society share a particular vulnerability to its effects. While members of these groups, whose identity cannot in general be distinguished from other

users in advance, are relatively small as a percentage of all marihuana users, their numbers are significant in absolute terms. The trial judge estimated "chronic users" to number about 50,000. A recent Senate Committee report estimated users under 16 (which may overlap to some extent with the chronic user group) also at 50,000 individuals (*Cannabis: Our Position for a Canadian Public Policy* (2002) (the "Senate Committee Report"), vol. I, at pp. 165-66). Pregnant women and schizophrenics are also said to be at particular risk. Advancing the protection of these vulnerable individuals, in our opinion, is a policy choice that falls within the broad legislative scope conferred on Parliament.

[4] A conviction for the possession of marihuana for personal use carries no mandatory minimum sentence. In practice, most first offenders are given a conditional discharge. Imprisonment is generally reserved for situations that also involve trafficking or hard drugs. Except in very exceptional circumstances, imprisonment for simple possession of marihuana would constitute a demonstrably unfit sentence and, if imposed, would rightly be set aside on appeal. Availability of imprisonment in a statute that deals with a wide variety of drugs from opium and heroin to crack and cocaine is not unconstitutional, and its rare imposition for marihuana offences (as a scheduled drug) can and should be dealt with under ordinary sentencing principles. A fit sentence, by definition, complies with s. 7 of the Charter. The mere fact of the availability of imprisonment in a statute dealing with a variety of prohibited drugs does not, in our view, make the criminalization of possession of a psychoactive drug like marihuana contrary to the principles of fundamental justice.

[5] The appellants have assembled much evidence and argument attacking the wisdom of the criminalization of simple possession of marihuana. They say that the line between criminal and non-criminal conduct has been drawn inappropriately and that the evil effects of the law against marihuana outweigh the benefits, if any, associated with its prohibition. These are matters of legitimate controversy, but the outcome of that debate is not for the courts to determine. The Constitution provides no more than a framework. Challenges to the wisdom of a legislative measure within that framework should be addressed to Parliament. Our concern is solely with the issue of constitutionality. We conclude that it is within Parliament's legislative jurisdiction to criminalize the possession of marihuana should it choose to do so. Equally, it is open to Parliament to decriminalize or otherwise modify any aspect of the marihuana laws that it no longer considers to be good public policy. ...

[21] The controversy over the criminalization of the use of marihuana has raged in Canada for at least 30 years. In 1972, the Commission of Inquiry into the Non-Medical Use of Drugs (the "Le Dain Commission"), in its preliminary report entitled Cannabis, recommended that the prohibition against its use be removed from the criminal law. In 1974, the federal government introduced Bill S-19, which would have removed penal sanctions for possession of marihuana for a first offence and substituted a monetary fine in its place. The Bill, however, died on the Order Paper. ...

[22] The trial judge in *Caine* estimated that over 600,000 Canadians now have criminal records for cannabis-related offences, and that widespread use despite the criminal prohibition encourages disrespect for the law. At the time of the hearing of the appeal in this Court, the government announced its intention of introducing a bill

to eliminate the availability of imprisonment for simple possession. Bill C-38, as introduced, states that possession of amounts less than 15 grams of marihuana will render an individual "guilty of an offence punishable on summary conviction and liable to a fine" (s. 4(5.1)). Furthermore, the offence would be designated as a contravention, pursuant to the *Contraventions Act*, S.C. 1992, c. 47, with the effect that an individual convicted for such possession would not receive a criminal record.

[23] These reports and legislative initiatives were directed to crafting what was thought to be the best legislative response to the marihuana controversy. Whether the Bill should proceed, and if so in what form, is a matter of legislative policy for Parliament to decide. The question before us is purely a matter of law. Is the prohibition, including the availability of imprisonment for simple possession, beyond the powers of Parliament, either because it does not properly fall within Parliament's legislative competence, or because the prohibition, and in particular the availability of imprisonment, violate the Charter's guarantees of rights and freedoms? ...

[46] [The trial judge] reviewed the extensive evidence before her court to put in perspective the potential harms associated with the use of marihuana, as presently understood, as follows (at para. 40):

1  The occasional to moderate use of marihuana by a healthy adult is not ordinarily harmful to health, even if used over a long period of time.

2  There is no conclusive evidence demonstrating any irreversible organic or mental damage to the user, except in relation to the lungs and then only to those of a chronic, heavy user such as a person who smokes at least 1 and probably 3-5 marihuana joints per day.

3  There is no evidence demonstrating irreversible, organic or mental damage from the use of marihuana by an ordinary healthy adult who uses occasionally or moderately.

4  Marihuana use causes alteration of mental function and as such should not be used in conjunction with driving, flying or operating complex machinery.

5  There is no evidence that marihuana use induces psychosis in ordinary healthy adults who use [marihuana] occasionally or moderately and, in relation to the heavy user, the evidence of marihuana psychosis appears to arise only in those having a predisposition towards such a mental illness.

6  Marihuana is not addictive.

7  There is a concern over potential dependence in heavy users, but marihuana is not a highly reinforcing type of drug, like heroin or cocaine and consequently physical dependence is not a major problem; psychological dependence may be a problem for the chronic user.

8  There is no causal relationship between marihuana use and criminality.

9  There is no evidence that marihuana is a gateway drug and the vast majority of marihuana users do not go on to try hard drugs. ...

10  Marihuana does not make people aggressive or violent, but on the contrary it tends to make them passive and quiet.

11  There have been no deaths from the use of marihuana.

12  There is no evidence of an amotivational syndrome, although chronic use of marihuana could decrease motivation, especially if such a user smokes so often as to be in a state of chronic intoxication.

13 Assuming current rates of consumption remain stable, the health related costs of marihuana use are very, very small in comparison with those costs associated with tobacco and alcohol consumption.

[47]  Having concluded that the use of marihuana is not as harmful as is sometimes claimed, the trial judge went on to state in *Caine* that marihuana is not "a completely harmless drug for all individual users." She stated:

> The evidence before me demonstrates that there is a reasonable basis for believing that the following health risks exist with [marihuana use]:
>
>> There is a general risk of harm to the users of marihuana from the acute effects of the drug, but these adverse effects are rare and transient. Persons experiencing the acute effects of the drug will be less adept at driving, flying and other activities involving complex machinery. In this regard they represent a risk of harm to others in society. At current rates of use, accidents caused by users under the influence of marihuana cannot be said to be significant.

[48]  Key to [the trial judge's] findings was the identification of perhaps 50,000 chronic users, who cannot be identified in advance, but who pose both a risk to themselves and a potential cost to society:

> There is also a risk that any individual who chooses to become a casual user, may end up being a chronic user of marihuana, or a member of one of the vulnerable persons identified in the materials. *It is not possible to identify these persons in advance.*
>
> As to the chronic users of marihuana, there are health risks for such persons. The health problems are serious ones but they arise primarily from the act of smoking rather than from the active ingredients in marihuana. Approximately 5% of all marihuana users are *chronic users*. At current rates of use, this comes to approximately *50,000 persons*. There is a risk that, upon legalization, rates of use will increase, and with that the absolute number of chronic users will increase.
>
> In addition, there are health risks for those *vulnerable persons* identified in the materials. There is no information before me to suggest how many people might fall into this group. Given that it includes young adolescents who may be more prone to becoming chronic users, I would not estimate this group to be minuscule.
>
> *All of the risks noted above carry with them a cost to society*, both to the health care and welfare systems. At current rates of use, these costs are negligible compared to the costs associated with alcohol and drugs [sic]. There is a risk that, with legalization, user rates will increase and so will these costs. [Emphasis added.] …

[61]  We have been shown no reason to interfere with these findings of fact. It seems clear that the use of marihuana has less serious and permanent effects than was once claimed, but its psychoactive and health effects can be harmful, and in the case of members of vulnerable groups the harm may be serious and substantial. …

[76]  The purpose of the NCA fits within the criminal law power [under s. 91(27) of the *Constitution Act, 1867*], which includes the protection of vulnerable groups: *Rodriguez v. British Columbia (Attorney General)*, [1993] 3 S.C.R. 519, at p. 595. See also *R. v. Morgentaler*, [1988] 1 S.C.R. 30, at pp. 74-75, in which s. 251 of the

*Criminal Code* prohibiting abortions except in therapeutic situations was held to have a valid objective, namely protecting the life and health of pregnant women, although it failed the s. 1 test on other grounds. On somewhat related issues arising under the Charter, the protection of vulnerable groups has also been upheld under s. 1 as a valid federal objective of the exercise of the criminal law power. In *R. v. Sharpe*, [2001] 1 S.C.R. 45, 2001 SCC 2, we upheld s. 163.1(4) of the *Criminal Code* prohibiting the possession of child pornography, noting that the prevention of harm threatening vulnerable members of society is a valid limit on freedom of expression. Similarly in *R. v. Butler*, [1992] 1 S.C.R. 452, at p. 497, we concluded that "legislation proscribing obscenity is a valid objective which justifies some encroachment on the right to freedom of expression." In so doing, we emphasized the impact of the exploitation of women and children, depicted in publications and films, which can in certain circumstances, lead to "abject and servile victimization." In *R. v. Keegstra*, [1995] 2 S.C.R. 381, we held that the restrictions on free speech imposed by the hate speech provision in the *Criminal Code* was a justifiable limit under s. 1 because of potential attacks on minorities.

[77] The protection of vulnerable groups from self-inflicted harms does not ... amount to no more than "legal moralism." Morality has traditionally been identified as a legitimate concern of the criminal law although today this does not include mere "conventional standards of propriety" but must be understood as referring to societal values beyond the simply prurient or prudish: *Butler*, *supra*, at p. 498; The protection of the chronic users identified by the trial judge, and adolescents who may not yet have become chronic users, but who have the potential to do so, is a valid criminal law objective. In *R. v. Hydro-Quebec*, [1997] 3 S.C.R. 213, the Court held at para. 131 that "Parliament has for long exercised extensive control over such matters as food and drugs by prohibitions grounded in the criminal law power." ... In our view, the control of a "psychoactive drug" that "causes alteration of mental function" clearly raises issues of public health and safety, both for the user as well as for those in the broader society affected by his or her conduct.

[78] The use of marihuana is therefore a proper subject matter for the exercise of the criminal law power. *Butler* held, at p. 485, that if there is a reasoned apprehension of harm Parliament is entitled to act, and in our view Parliament is also entitled to act on reasoned apprehension of harm even if on some points "the jury is still out." In light of the concurrent findings of "harm" in the courts below, we therefore confirm that the *Narcotic Control Act* in general, and the scheduling of marihuana in particular, properly fall within Parliament's legislative competence under s. 91(27) of the *Constitution Act, 1867*.

[79] Prior to the enactment of the Charter in 1982, that finding, which validates the exercise of the criminal law power, would have ended the appellants' challenge. Now, of course, Parliament must not only find legislative authority within the *Constitution Act, 1867*, but it must exercise that authority subject to the individual rights and freedoms guaranteed by the Charter. ...

[86] While we accept Malmo-Levine's statement that smoking marihuana is central to his lifestyle, the Constitution cannot be stretched to afford protection to whatever activity an individual chooses to define as central to his or her lifestyle. One individual chooses to smoke marihuana; another has an obsessive interest in golf; a

third is addicted to gambling. The appellant Caine invokes a taste for fatty foods. A society that extended constitutional protection to any and all such lifestyles would be ungovernable. Lifestyle choices of this order are not, we think, "basic choices going to the core of what it means to enjoy individual dignity and independence."

[87]  In our view, with respect, Malmo-Levine's desire to build a lifestyle around the recreational use of marihuana does not attract Charter protection. There is no free-standing constitutional right to smoke "pot" for recreational purposes. ...

[89]  The availability of imprisonment is a different matter. We have no doubt that the risk of being sent to jail engages the appellants' liberty interest. Accordingly, it is necessary to move to the next stage of the s. 7 analysis to determine what are the relevant principles of fundamental justice and whether this risk of deprivation of liberty is in accordance with the principles of fundamental justice. ...

[102]  The appellants contend that unless the state can establish that the use of marihuana is harmful to others, the prohibition against simple possession cannot comply with s. 7. Our colleague Arbour J. accepts this proposition as correct to the extent that "the state resorts to imprisonment" (para. 56). Accordingly, a closer look at the alleged "harm principle" is called for. ...

[106]  What is "the harm principle"? The appellants rely, in particular, on the writings of the liberal theorist, J.S. Mill, who attempted to establish clear boundaries for the permissible intrusion of the state into private life:

> The object of this Essay is to assert one very simple principle, as entitled to govern absolutely the dealings of society with the individual in the way of compulsion and control, whether the means used be physical force in the form of legal penalties, or the moral coercion of public opinion. That principle is, that the sole end for which mankind are warranted, individually or collectively, in interfering with the liberty of action of any of their number, is self-protection. That the only purpose for which power can be rightfully exercised over any member of a civilised community, against his will, is to prevent harm to others. His own good, either physical or moral, is not a sufficient warrant. ... The only part of the conduct of any one, for which he is amenable to society, is that which concerns others. In the part which merely concerns himself, his independence is, of right, absolute. Over himself, over his own body and mind, the individual is sovereign.

(J.S. Mill, *On Liberty and Considerations on Representative Government*, R.B. McCallum, ed. (1946), at pp. 8-9.)

[107]  Thus Mill's principle has two essential features. First, it rejects paternalism—that is, the prohibition of conduct that harms only the actor. Second, it excludes what could be called "moral harm." Mill was of the view that such moral claims are insufficient to justify use of the criminal law. Rather, he required clear and tangible harm to the rights and interests of others.

[108]  At the same time, Mill acknowledged an exception to his requirement of harm "to others" for vulnerable groups. He wrote that "this doctrine is meant to apply to human beings in the maturity of their faculties. ... Those who are still in a state to require being taken care of by others, must be protected against their own actions as well as against external injury" (p. 9).

[109]  Mill's statement has the virtues of insight and clarity but he was advocating certain general philosophic principles, not interpreting a constitutional document. Moreover, even his philosophical supporters have tended to agree that justification for state intervention cannot be reduced to a single factor—harm—but is a much more complex matter. One of Mill's most distinguished supporters, Professor H.L.A. Hart, wrote:

> *Mill's formulation of the liberal point of view may well be too simple. The grounds for interfering with human liberty are more various than the single criterion of "harm to others" suggests*: cruelty to animals or organizing prostitution for gain do not, as Mill himself saw, fall easily under the description of harm to others. Conversely, even where there is harm to others in the most literal sense, there may well be other principles limiting the extent to which harmful activities should be repressed by law. So *there are multiple criteria, not a single criterion, determining when human liberty may be restricted.* [Emphasis added.]

(H.L.A. Hart, "Immorality and Treason," originally appearing in *The Listener* (July 30, 1959), at pp. 162-63, reprinted in *Morality and the Law* (1971), 49, at p. 51.) To the same effect, see Professor J. Feinberg, *The Moral Limits of the Criminal Law*, (1984), vol. 1: *Harm to Others*, at p. 12; also vol. 4: *Harmless Wrongdoing*, at p. 323. …

[112]  In *Re B.C. Motor Vehicle Act*, … Lamer J. (as he then was) explained that the principles of fundamental justice lie in "the basic tenets of our legal system. They do not lie in the realm of general public policy but in the inherent domain of the judiciary as guardian of the justice system" (p. 503). This Court provided further guidance as to what constitutes a principle of fundamental justice for the purposes of s. 7, in *Rodriguez*, … per Sopinka J. (at pp. 590-91 and 607):

> A mere common law rule does not suffice to constitute a principle of fundamental justice, rather, as the term implies, principles upon which there is *some consensus* that they are vital or fundamental to our societal notion of justice are required. Principles of fundamental justice must not, however, be so broad as to be no more than vague generalizations about what our society considers to be ethical or moral. They must be capable of being identified with *some precision* and *applied* to situations in a manner which yields an understandable result. They must also, in my view, be *legal principles*. …
>
>    While the principles of fundamental justice are concerned with more than process, reference must be made to principles which are "fundamental" in the sense that they would have *general acceptance among reasonable people.* [Emphasis added.]

[113]  The requirement of "general acceptance among reasonable people" enhances the legitimacy of judicial review of state action, and ensures that the values against which state action is measured are not just fundamental "in the eye of the beholder *only*": *Rodriguez*, at pp. 607, and 590 (emphasis in original). In short, for a rule or principle to constitute a principle of fundamental justice for the purposes of s. 7, it must be a legal principle about which there is significant societal consensus that it is fundamental to the way in which the legal system ought fairly to operate, and it must be identified with sufficient precision to yield a manageable standard against which to measure deprivations of life, liberty or security of the person.

### a. Is the Harm Principle a Legal Principle?

[114] In our view, the "harm principle" is better characterized as a description of an important state interest rather than a normative "legal" principle. Be that as it may, even if the harm principle could be characterized as a legal principle, we do not think that it meets the other requirements, as explained below.

### b. There Is No Sufficient Consensus that the Harm Principle Is Vital or Fundamental to Our Societal Notion of Criminal Justice

[115] Contrary to the appellants' assertion, we do not think there is a consensus that the harm principle is the sole justification for criminal prohibition. There is no doubt that our case law and academic commentary are full of statements about the criminal law being aimed at conduct that "affects the public," or that constitutes "a wrong against the public welfare," or is "injurious to the public," or that "affects the community." No doubt, as stated, the presence of harm to others may justify legislative action under the criminal law power. However, we do not think that the absence of proven harm creates the unqualified barrier to legislative action that the appellants suggest. On the contrary, the state may sometimes be justified in criminalizing conduct that is either not harmful (in the sense contemplated by the harm principle), or that causes harm only to the accused.

[116] The appellants cite in aid of their position the observation of Sopinka J., writing for the majority in *Butler, supra*, that "[t]he objective of maintaining conventional standards of propriety, independently of any harm to society, is no longer justified in light of the values of individual liberty which underlie the Charter" (p. 498). However, Sopinka J. went on to clarify that it is open to Parliament to legislate "on the basis of some fundamental conception of *morality* for the purposes of safeguarding the values which are integral to a free and democratic society" (p. 493 (emphasis added)).

[117] Several instances of crimes that do not cause harm to others are found in the *Criminal Code*. Cannibalism is an offence (s. 182 of the Code) that does not harm another sentient being, but that is nevertheless prohibited on the basis of fundamental social and ethical considerations. Bestiality (s. 160 of the Code) and cruelty to animals (s. 446 of the Code) are examples of crimes that rest on their offensiveness to deeply held social values rather than on Mill's "harm principle."

[118] A duel fought by consenting adults is an example of a crime where the victim is no less culpable than the perpetrator, and there is no harm that is not consented to, but the prohibition (s. 71 of the Code) is nevertheless integral to our ideas of civilized society. See also *R. v. Jobidon*, [1991] 2 S.C.R. 714. Similarly, in *R. v. F. (R.P.)* (1996), 105 C.C.C. (3d) 435, the Nova Scotia Court of Appeal upheld the prohibition of incest under s. 155 of the *Criminal Code* despite a Charter challenge by five consenting adults. In none of these instances of consenting adults does the criminal law conform to Mill's expression of the harm principle that "[o]ver himself, over his own body and mind, the individual is sovereign," as referenced earlier at para. 106. ...

[124] ... Canada continues to have paternalistic laws. Requirements that people wear seatbelts and motorcycle helmets are designed to "save people from themselves."

There is no consensus that this sort of legislation offends our societal notions of justice. Whether a jail sentence is an appropriate penalty for such an offence is another question. However, the objection in that aspect goes to the validity of an assigned punishment—it does not go to the validity of prohibiting the underlying conduct.

[125]  A recent discussion policy paper from the Law Commission of Canada entitled *What is a Crime? Challenges and Alternatives* (2003) highlights the difficulties in distinguishing between harm to others and harm to self. It notes that "in a society that recognizes the interdependency of its citizens, such as universally contributing to healthcare or educational needs, harm to oneself is often borne collectively" (p. 17).

[126]  In short, there is no consensus that tangible harm to others is a necessary precondition to the creation of a criminal law offence.

### d. The Harm Principle Is Not a Manageable Standard Against Which To Measure Deprivation of Life, Liberty or Security of the Person

[127]  Even those who agree with the "harm principle" as a regulator of the criminal law frequently disagree about what it means and what offences will meet or offend the harm principle. In the absence of any agreed definition of "harm" for this purpose, allegations and counter-allegations of non-trivial harm can be marshalled on every side of virtually every criminal law issue, as one author explains:

> The harm principle is effectively collapsing under the weight of its own success. Claims of harm have become so pervasive that the harm principle has become meaningless: the harm principle no longer serves the function of a critical principle because non-trivial harm arguments permeate the debate. Today, the issue is no longer whether a moral offense causes harm, but rather what type and what amount of harms the challenged conduct causes, and how the harms compare. On those issues, the harm principle is silent.

(B.E. Harcourt, "The Collapse of the Harm Principle" (1999), 90 *J. Crim. L. & Criminology* 109, at p. 113.) Professor Harcourt goes on to point out that "[i]t is the hidden normative dimensions ... [that] do the work in the harm principle, not the abstract, simple notion of harm" (p. 185). In other words, the existence of harm (however defined) does no more than open a gateway to the debate; it does not give any precise guidance about its resolution.

[128]  Harm, as interpreted in the jurisprudence, can take a multitude of forms, including economic, physical and social (e.g., injury and/or offence to fundamental societal values). In the present appeal, for example, the respondents put forward a list of "harms" which they attribute to marihuana use. The appellants put forward a list of "harms" which they attribute to marihuana prohibition. Neither side gives much credence to the "harms" listed by the other. Each claims the "net" result to be in its favour.

[129]  In the result, we do not believe that the content of the "harm" principle as described by Mill and advocated by the appellants provides a manageable standard under which to review criminal or other laws under s. 7 of the Charter. Parliament, we think, is entitled to act under the criminal law power in the protection of legiti-

mate state interests other than the avoidance of harm to others, subject to Charter limits such as the rules against arbitrariness, irrationality and gross disproportionality, discussed below. ...

[133] We do not agree with Prowse J.A. that harm must be shown to the court's satisfaction to be "serious" and "substantial" before Parliament can impose a prohibition. Once it is demonstrated, as it has been here, that the harm is not *de minimis*, or in the words of Braidwood J.A., the harm is "not insignificant or trivial," the precise weighing and calculation of the nature and extent of the harm is Parliament's job. Members of Parliament are elected to make these sorts of decisions, and have access to a broader range of information, more points of view, and a more flexible investigative process than courts do. A "serious and substantial" standard of review would involve the courts in micromanagement of Parliament's agenda. The relevant constitutional control is not micromanagement but the general principle that the parliamentary response must not be grossly disproportionate to the state interest sought to be protected, as will be discussed.

[134] Having said that, our understanding of the view taken of the facts by the courts below is that while the risk of harm to the great majority of users can be characterized at the lower level of "neither trivial nor insignificant," the risk of harm to members of the vulnerable groups reaches the higher level of "serious and substantial." This distinction simply underlines the difficulties of a court attempting to quantify "harm" beyond a *de minimis* standard.

*(iv) In Light of the State Interest Thus Identified, the Prohibition Is Neither Arbitrary Nor Irrational*

[138] The appellants also contend that Parliament's failure to criminalize the consumption of alcohol and tobacco, while criminalizing the use of marihuana (which the appellants say is, if anything, less harmful) shows the arbitrariness of the law. It is clear that the consumption of alcohol and tobacco can be harmful. Moreover in some respects the harm is of a type comparable to that caused by marihuana consumption. Much of the bronchial harm associated with marihuana, for instance, comes from the smoking aspect rather than its intoxicating properties.

[139] However, if Parliament is otherwise acting within its jurisdiction by enacting a prohibition on the use of marihuana, it does not lose that jurisdiction just because there are other substances whose health and safety effects could arguably justify similar legislative treatment. To hold otherwise would involve the courts in not only defining the outer limits of the legislative action allowed by the Constitution but also in ordering Parliament's priorities within those limits. That is not the role of the courts under our constitutional arrangements.

[140] Parliament may, as a matter of constitutional law, determine what is not criminal as well as what is. The choice to use the criminal law in a particular context does not require its use in any other: *RJR Macdonald*, ... at para. 50. Parliament's decision to move in one area of public health and safety without at the same time moving in other areas is not, on that account alone, arbitrary or irrational. ...

[167] We agree with the appellants that imprisonment would ordinarily be an unfit sentence for a conviction on simple possession of marihuana. We disagree, however, that this observation gives rise to a finding of unconstitutionality. Rather, it gives rise, in appropriate circumstances, to an ordinary sentence appeal.

[168] In the result, where there is no minimum mandatory sentence, the mere availability of imprisonment on a charge of marihuana possession does not violate the s. 7 principle against gross disproportionality. There are circumstances, as noted, where imprisonment would constitute a fit sentence. ...

ARBOUR J. (in dissent): ...

[190] We are asked to address, directly for the first time, whether the Charter requires that harm to others or to society be an essential element of an offence punishable by imprisonment. In a landmark 1985 case, Lamer J. (as he then was) said: "A law that has the potential to convict a person who has not really done anything wrong offends the principles of fundamental justice and, if imprisonment is available as a penalty, such a law then violates a person's right to liberty under s. 7 of the Charter ..." (*Re B.C. Motor Vehicle Act*, [1985] 2 S.C.R. 486, at p. 492 ("Motor Vehicle Reference")). In my view, a "person who has not really done anything wrong" is a person whose conduct caused little or no reasoned risk of harm or whose harmful conduct was not his or her fault. Therefore, for the reasons that follow, I am of the view that s. 7 of the Charter requires not only that some minimal mental element be an essential element of any offence punishable by imprisonment, but also that the prohibited act be harmful or pose a risk of harm to others. A law that has the potential to convict a person whose conduct causes little or no reasoned risk of harm to others offends the principles of fundamental justice and, if imprisonment is available as a penalty, such a law then violates a person's right to liberty under s. 7 of the Charter. Imprisonment can only be used to punish blameworthy conduct that is harmful to others. ...

[237] The debate over the harm principle takes place around the traditional confrontation between harm and morality as a basis for restricting an individual's liberty. The liberal view was initially espoused by Victorian philosopher and economist John Stuart Mill. ... Mill's principle was ... "[T]he *only* purpose for which power can be rightfully exercised over any member of a civilized community, against his will, is to prevent harm to others" (p. 52 (emphasis added)).

[238] Mill's assertion was challenged by Sir James Fitzjames Stephen in *Liberty, Equality, Fraternity* (2nd ed. 1967), initially published in 1874, who strongly opposed any limitation on the power of the state to enforce morality. Stephen's argument was best captured in a now-famous passage: "[t]here are acts of wickedness so gross and outrageous that, self-protection apart, they must be prevented as far as possible at any cost to the offender, and punished, if they occur, with exemplary severity" (p. 162). This debate between Mill and Stephen was reignited in England by the recommendation of the Committee on Homosexual Offences and Prostitution (*The Wolfenden Report* (1963)) to decriminalize homosexuality on the basis that "it is not the duty of the law to concern itself with immorality as such" (para. 62). The reac-

tions to the *Wolfenden Report* have been vehement. Lord Patrick Devlin, in his Maccabaean Lecture delivered at the British Academy in 1959 (later published: P. Devlin, *The Enforcement of Morals* (1965)), argued that purportedly immoral activities, like homosexuality and prostitution, should remain criminal offences and he became associated with the principle of legal moralism—the principle that moral offences should be regulated because they are immoral (see on this: B. E. Harcourt, "The Collapse of the Harm Principle" (1999), 90 *J. Crim. L. & Criminology* 109, at pp. 111-12; B. Lauzon, *Les champs légitimes du droit criminel et leur application aux manipulations génétiques transmissibles aux générations futures* (2002), at p. 26).

[239] This position is opposed to the liberal view of Professors Hart and Feinberg who reiterated Mill's harm principle. According to J. Feinberg, who adopts a less exclusive view of the harm principle in *The Moral Limits of the Criminal Law* (1984), in the first volume, entitled *Harm to Others*, at p. 26, "[i]t is always a good reason in support of penal legislation that it would probably be effective in preventing ... harm to persons other than the actor." The debate between legal moralism and the harm principle has stimulated academic discussions and much has been written on this topic (see, *inter alia*, in addition to other sources cited throughout these reasons: "Symposium: The Moral Limits of the Criminal Law" (2001), 5 *Buffalo Crim. L. Rev.*; *Mill's On Liberty: Critical Essays*, edited by Gerald Dworkin (1997)). Braidwood J.A. referred, at paras. 107-12, to various authors who either adopted the harm principle or incorporated it in their writings. One of the most prominent, Herbert L. Packer, in his influential *The Limits of the Criminal Sanction* (1968) said, at p. 267, that "harm to others" must be a "limiting criteri[on] for invocation of the criminal sanction." This debate, which has remained focused, as I said earlier, on what should be criminalized, also permeated the work of the Law Reform Commissions in Canada on possible reforms of the *Criminal Code*. I need not expand on their recommendations for my purposes. Suffice it to say that Braidwood J.A. referred to various reports, all of which basically advocated that the criminal law should only be used, save in exceptional circumstances, where conduct causes or risks causing significant or grave harm to others or society (see paras. 113-16).

[240] This philosophical and theoretical debate is of great interest and is a useful policy tool for law makers. It may also serve as a guide in the characterization of the harm principle as a principle of fundamental justice. However, as guardians of the constitutional principles of fundamental justice, courts are not expected to merely choose from among the competing theories of harm advanced by criminal law theorists. As Doherty J.A. said in *R. v. Murdock* (2003), 11 C.R. (6th) 43 (Ont. C.A.), at para. 31:

> Nor should the harm principle be taken as an invitation to the judiciary to consecrate a particular theory of criminal liability as a principle of fundamental justice. This is so even if that theory has gained the support of law reformers, some of whom also happen to be judges. Judicial review of the substantive content of criminal legislation under s. 7 should not be confused with law reform. Judicial review tests the validity of legislation against the minimum standards set out in the Charter. Law reform tests the legal status quo against the law reformer's opinion of what the law should be. ...

[244] I am of the view that the principles of fundamental justice require that whenever the state resorts to imprisonment, a minimum of harm to others must be an essential part of the offence. The state cannot resort to imprisonment as a punishment for conduct that causes little or no reasoned risk of harm to others. Prohibited conduct punishable by imprisonment cannot be harmless conduct or conduct that only causes harm to the perpetrator. As Braidwood J.A. said in *Caine*, "it is common sense that you do not go to jail unless there is a potential that your activities will cause harm to others" (para. 134).

[245] In *Murdock*, … Doherty J.A. characterized the harm principle as follows, at para. 33:

> The harm principle, as a principle of fundamental justice, goes only so far as to preclude the criminalization of conduct for which there is no "reasoned apprehension of harm" to any legitimate personal or societal interest. If conduct clears that threshold, it cannot be said that criminalization of such conduct raises the spectre of convicting someone who has not done anything wrong. Difficult questions such as whether the harm justifies the imposition of a criminal prohibition or whether the criminal law is the best way to address the harm are policy questions that are beyond the constitutional competence of the judiciary and the institutional competence of the criminal law adversarial process.

… Doherty J.A.'s concern was, by his own words, to draw a distinction "between the harm principle as a principle of fundamental justice and closely related, but distinct policy questions surrounding the application of the criminal law" (para. 34). Indeed, he adds in a footnote at para. 33:

> For example, many argue that the criminal sanction should be a last resort employed only if other forms of governmental action cannot adequately address the harm flowing from the conduct. This minimalist approach to criminal law may well be sound criminal law policy. However, it hardly reflects the historical reality of the scope of the criminal law so as to be properly described as a principle of fundamental justice. Any attempt to apply minimalist doctrine to a specific piece of legislation would raise complex questions of social policy which would defy effective resolution in the context of the adversarial criminal law process.

[246] As I said before, however, the focus must remain on the choice by the state to resort to imprisonment to sanction conduct that it has decided to prohibit through its criminal law power or otherwise. The power of Parliament to use criminal law is broad and any concern as to what should be criminalized remains in the hands of the elected representatives. However, in my view, be it as a criminal sanction or as a sanction to any other prohibition, imprisonment must, as a constitutional minimum standard, be reserved for those whose conduct causes a reasoned risk of harm to others. "Doing nothing wrong" in that sense means acting in a manner which causes little or no reasoned risk of harm to others or to society. The Charter requires that the highest form of restriction of liberty be reserved for those who, at a minimum, infringe on the rights or freedoms of other individuals or otherwise harm society. …

[247]  Where legislation which may deprive individuals of their liberty is aimed at protecting other individuals or society from the risk of harm caused by the prohibited conduct, courts must scrutinize carefully the harm alleged. In victimizing conduct, the attribution of fault is relatively straightforward because of the close links between the actor's culpable conduct and the resulting harm to the victim. This Court has used principles of interpretation aimed at excluding from the criminal ambit conduct that is tenuously related to the alleged harm. Thus, in *R. v. Sharpe*, [2001] 1 S.C.R. 45, 2001 SCC 2, the accused accepted that harm to children justified criminalizing possession of some forms of child pornography. The fundamental question was rather whether the prohibition went too far by criminalizing possession of an unjustifiable range of material. McLachlin C.J., for the majority of this Court, had this to say on whether the causal link between a specific prohibition and the harm to children was sufficient, at paras. 74, 75 and 95:

> These exclusions support the earlier suggestion that Parliament's goal was to prohibit possession of child pornography that poses a reasoned risk of harm to children. The primary definition of "child pornography" does not embrace every kind of material that might conceivably pose a risk of harm to children, but appears rather to target blatantly pornographic material. ...
>
> Yet problems remain. The interpretation of the legislation suggested above reveals that the law may catch some material that particularly engages the value of self-fulfilment and poses little or no risk of harm to children. ... If the law is drafted in a way that unnecessarily catches material that has little or nothing to do with the prevention of harm to children, then the justification for overriding freedom of expression is absent.

While these comments were made under s. 1, they illustrate the threshold to be met to establish a sufficient causal link between prohibited conduct and the harm alleged to be caused by such conduct. Thus, for our purposes, if the prohibition of conduct engages a s. 7 interest, as the threat of imprisonment does, while the conduct poses little or no risk of harm to others, then the law is contrary to s. 7. ...

[249]  Societal interests in prohibiting conduct are evaluated by balancing the harmful effects on society if the conduct in question is not prohibited by law against the effects of prohibiting the conduct in question. It would indeed be misleading to engage in an assessment of the state's interest in prohibiting conduct by evaluating solely the collective harm that the state wishes to prevent without also evaluating the collective costs incurred by preventing such harm (see Packer, *supra*, at p. 267: "[o]ne cannot meaningfully deal with the question of 'harm to others' without weighing benefits against detriments"). The harm or risk of harm to society caused by the prohibited conduct must outweigh any harm that may result from enforcement. ...

[265]  In the cases before us, the societal interests in prohibiting marihuana possession must take into account, on the one hand, the burden that marihuana use imposes on the health care and welfare systems, and, on the other, the costs incurred by society because of the prohibition. [The trial judge] noted that at current rates of use, the costs imposed upon the health care and welfare systems by marihuana are negligible compared to the costs associated with alcohol and drugs. As I mentioned earlier, society's tolerance for the harmful effects that the conduct may entail must be

assessed, where possible, by reference to its tolerance for comparable conduct. I will
thus simply take note of the trial judges' findings that the burden that marihuana use
imposes on society is "negligible" or "very, very small" compared to the costs imposed by comparable conduct that society tolerates (i.e., alcohol and tobacco use).

[266]  If there remained any doubt as to whether the harms associated with marihuana use justified the state in using imprisonment as a sanction against its possession, this doubt disappears when the harms caused by the prohibition are put in the
balance. The record shows and the trial judges found that the prohibition of simple
possession of marihuana attempts to prevent a low quantum of harm to society at a
very high cost. A "negligible" burden on the health care and welfare systems, coupled with the many significant negative effects of the prohibition, cannot be said to
amount to more than little or no reasoned risk of harm to society. I thus conclude that
s. 3(1) and (2) of the *Narcotic Control Act*, as it prohibits the possession of marihuana
for personal use under threat of imprisonment, violates the right of the appellants to
liberty in a manner that is not in accordance with the harm principle, a principle of
fundamental justice, contrary to s. 7 of the Charter.

LEBEL J. (in dissent):

[277]  I have had the opportunity of reading the joint reasons of Justices Gonthier
and Binnie who would dismiss the appeal, and those of Justice Arbour who would
allow it. With respect for the other view, I am in agreement with the disposition suggested by Arbour J. and I would answer the constitutional questions as she proposes.
Nevertheless, I am not yet convinced that we should raise the harm principle "to the
level of a principle of fundamental justice within the meaning of s. 7 of the *Canadian
Charter of Rights and Freedoms*" (the "Charter"). On this question, I share the
skepticism of my colleagues Binnie and Gonthier JJ. I part company with them, however, at the point where they hold that the prohibition of simple possession of marihuana is not an arbitrary or irrational legislative response. On the evidence which is
available to us and which was carefully reviewed by Arbour J., the law, as it stands, is
indeed an arbitrary response to social problems. The Crown has failed to properly
delineate the societal concerns and individual rights at stake, more particularly the
liberty interest involved in this appeal. ...

DESCHAMPS J. (in dissent):

[295]  Although I do not adopt the approach of my colleague Arbour J., who would
limit the sanction of imprisonment to cases where harm is done to others, I agree with
her description of the consequences of marihuana use. The inherent risks of marihuana use, apart from those related to the operation of vehicles and the impact on
public health care and social assistance systems, affect only the users themselves.
These risks can be situated on a spectrum, ranging from no risk for occasional users
to more significant risks for frequent users and vulnerable groups. On the whole,
with a few exceptions, moderate use of marihuana is harmless. Thus, it seems doubtful that it is appropriate to classify marihuana consumption as conduct giving rise to
a legitimate use of the criminal law in light of the Charter. ...

## IV. HATE SPEECH


**R. v. Keegstra**
Supreme Court of Canada
(1990), 61 C.C.C. (3d) 1

[The accused, a high school teacher, was accused of promoting hatred against Jews by teaching students at Eckville High School about "an international Jewish conspiracy" and that Jews were "sadistic," "money-loving," "power hungry," and "child killers." The accused was convicted at trial but the conviction was overturned by the Alberta Court of Appeal on the grounds that ss. 281.2(2) (now s. 319(2)) and 281.2(3)(a) (now s. 319(3)(a)) of the Code violated ss. 2(b) and 11(d) of the Charter and were not justified under s. 1. The Crown appealed. The Supreme Court upheld ss. 281.2(2) (now ss. 319(2)) and 281.2(3)(a) (now s. 319(3)(a)) of the Code in a 4 to 3 decision.]

DICKSON C.J. [Wilson, L'Heureux-Dubé, and Gonthier JJ. held for the Court that s. 319(2) infringed freedom of expression under s. 2(b) of the Charter because it prohibits "communications which convey meaning, namely those communications which are intended to promote hatred against identifiable groups" but was a justified limit under s. 1. He stated]: It is undeniable that media attention has been extensive on those occasions when s. 319(2) has been used. Yet from my perspective, s. 319(2) serves to illustrate to the public the severe reprobation with which society holds messages of hate directed towards racial and religious groups. The existence of a particular criminal law, and the process of holding a trial when that law is used, is thus itself a form of expression, and the message sent out is that hate propaganda is harmful to target group members and threatening to a harmonious society (see Rauf, "Freedom of Expression, the Presumption of Innocence and Reasonable Limits" (1988), 65 C.R. (3d) 356, at p. 359). As I stated in my reasons in *R. v. Morgentaler*, [1988] 1 S.C.R. 30, at p. 70:

> The criminal law is a very special form of governmental regulation, for it seeks to express our society's collective disapprobation of certain acts and omissions.

The many, many Canadians who belong to identifiable groups surely gain a great deal of comfort from the knowledge that the hate-monger is criminally prosecuted and his or her ideas rejected. Equally, the community as a whole is reminded of the importance of diversity and multiculturalism in Canada, the value of equality and the worth and dignity of each human person being particularly emphasized. ... Is s. 319(2) nevertheless overbroad because it captures all public expression intended to promote hatred? ...

[An] important element of s. 319(2) is its requirement that the promotion of hatred be "wilful." The nature of this mental element was explored by Martin J.A. in *R. v. Buzzanga and Durocher* (1979), 49 C.C.C. (2d) 369 (Ont. C.A.) [see chapter 7]. ... Martin J.A. went on to elaborate on the meaning of "wilfully," concluding that this mental element is satisfied only where an accused subjectively desires the promotion of hatred or foresees such a consequence as certain or substantially certain to result from an act done in order to achieve some other purpose (pp. 384-85). On the facts in *Buzzanga*, the trial judge had informed the jury that "wilfully" could be equated with the intention to create "controversy, furor and an uproar" (p. 386). This interpretation was clearly incompatible with Martin J.A.'s requirement that the promotion of hatred be intended or foreseen as substantially certain, and a new trial was therefore ordered.

The interpretation of "wilfully" in *Buzzanga* has great bearing upon the extent to which s. 319(2) limits the freedom of expression. This mental element, requiring more than merely negligence or recklessness as to result, significantly restricts the reach of the provision, and thereby reduces the scope of the targeted expression. Such a reduced scope is recognized and applauded in the Law Reform Commission of Canada's Working Paper on Hate Propaganda, op. cit., it being said that (at p. 36):

> The principle of restraint requires lawmakers to concern themselves not just with whom they want to catch, but also with whom they do not want to catch. For example, removing an intent or purpose requirement could well result in successful prosecutions of cases similar to *Buzzanga*, where members of a minority group publish hate propaganda against their own group in order to create controversy or to agitate for reform. This crime should not be used to prosecute such individuals.

I agree with the interpretation of "wilfully" in *Buzzanga*, and wholeheartedly endorse the view of the Law Reform Commission. ...

While mindful of the dangers identified by Kerans, J.A., I do not find them sufficiently grave to compel striking down s. 319(2). First, to predicate the limitation of free expression upon proof of actual hatred gives insufficient attention to the severe psychological trauma suffered by members of those identifiable groups targeted by hate propaganda. Second, it is clearly difficult to prove a causative link between a specific statement and hatred of an identifiable group. In fact, to require direct proof of hatred in listeners would severely debilitate the effectiveness of s. 319(2) in achieving Parliament's aim. It is well-accepted that Parliament can use the criminal law to prevent the risk of serious harms, a leading example being the drinking and driving provisions in the *Criminal Code*. The conclusions of the Cohen Committee and subsequent study groups show that the risk of hatred caused by hate propaganda is very real, and in view of the grievous harm to be avoided in the context of this appeal, I conclude that proof of actual hatred is not required in order to justify a limit under s. 1.

[Dickson C.J. concluded that s. 319(3)(a) infringed the presumption of innocence under s. 11(d) of the Charter. Note that the presumption of innocence is examined in chapter 4.]

The judgments of the appeal courts in this case and in the accompanying appeal of *Andrews* reveal a divergence of opinion as to whether s. 11(d) of the Charter is infringed by the truth defence. In the Alberta Court of Appeal, Kerans J.A. viewed as crucial the possibility that an accused can be convicted of wilfully promoting hatred though there exists a reasonable doubt that the statements communicated are true. As the defence places an onus on the accused to prove truth on the balance of probabilities, he thus found it to infringe s. 11(d). In contrast to this conclusion, the Ontario

Court of Appeal in *R. v. Andrews*, *supra*, found that s. 319(3)(a) does not place a true reverse onus upon the accused. Relying upon the majority judgment in *R. v. Holmes*, [1988] 1 S.C.R. 914, Grange J.A. felt that s. 319(3)(a) provides a defence which becomes applicable only after all elements of the offence have been proven beyond a reasonable doubt, a circumstance which was said to avoid infringing the presumption of innocence (p. 225). Grange J.A. distinguished this Court's decision in *R. v. Whyte*, [1988] 2 S.C.R. 3, on the grounds that the statutory presumption challenged in that case related to the proof of an essential element of the offence.

It is not overly difficult to settle the disagreement between the Alberta and Ontario Appeal Courts. Though some confusion may have existed after the decision of this Court in *Holmes*, since in *Whyte* it is clear that the presumption of innocence is infringed whenever the accused is liable to be convicted despite the existence of a reasonable doubt as to guilt in the mind of the trier of fact.

[He then held that the violation of s. 11(d) by the reverse onus on the truth defence was justified under s. 1.]

The reverse onus in the truth defence operates so as to make it more difficult to avoid conviction where the wilful promotion of hatred has been proven beyond a reasonable doubt. As the wilful promotion of hatred is hostile to Parliament's aims, placing such a burden upon the accused is rationally connected to a valid s. 1 objective. ...

To include falsity as a component of s. 319(2) for example, or even to require only that the accused raise a reasonable doubt as to the truthfulness of the statements, would excessively compromise the effectiveness of the offence in achieving its purpose. The former option would especially hinder Parliament's objective, for many statements are not susceptible to a true/false categorization. In either instance, however, where a reasonable doubt existed as to the falsity of an accused's statements an acquittal would be entered. To accept such a result it would have to be agreed that this relatively small possibility of truthfulness outweighs the harm caused through the wilful promotion of hatred. Yet to my mind the crucial objective of Parliament in this appeal justifies requiring a more convincing demonstration that a hate-monger's statements may be true, as a successful defence provides an excuse despite the presence of the harm sought to be eradicated (see Rauf, op. cit., at pp. 368-69). Having the accused prove truthfulness on the balance of probabilities is an understandable and valued precaution against too easily justifying such harm, and I hence conclude that the reverse onus provision in s. 319(3)(a) represents a minimal impairment of the presumption of innocence. ...

McLACHLIN J. (Sopinka and La Forest JJ. concurring) dissented finding that s. 319(2) infringed s. 2(b) and was not justified under s. 1. She stated:]

Section 319(2) may well have a chilling effect on defensible expression by law-abiding citizens. At the same time, it is far from clear that it provides an effective way of curbing hatemongers. Indeed, many have suggested it may promote their cause.

Prosecutions under the *Criminal Code* for racist expression have attracted extensive media coverage. Zundel, prosecuted not under s. 319(2) but for the crime of spreading false news (s. 181), claimed that his court battle had given him "a million dollars worth of publicity": Globe and Mail, March 1, 1985, p. 1. There is an unmistakable hint of the joy of martyrdom in some of the literature for which Andrews, in the companion appeal, was prosecuted:

> The Holocaust Hoax has been so ingrained in the minds of the hated "goyim" by now that in some countries ... challenging its validity can land you in jail. *R. v. Andrews* (1988), 65 O.R. (2d) 161, at p. 165 (C.A.). ...

Not only is the category of speech caught by s. 319(2) defined broadly. The application of the definition of offending speech, i.e. the circumstances in which the offending statements are prohibited, is virtually unlimited. Only private conversations are exempt from state scrutiny. Section 319(2) is calculated to prevent absolutely expression of the offending ideas in any and all public forums through any and all mediums. Speeches are caught. The corner soap-box is no longer open. Books, films and works of art—all these fall under the censor's scrutiny because of s. 319(2) of the *Criminal Code*. ...

In summary, s. 319(2) of the *Criminal Code* catches a broad range of speech and prohibits it in a broad manner, allowing only private conversations to escape scrutiny. Moreover, the process by which the prohibition is effected—the criminal law— is the severest our society can impose and is arguably unnecessary given the availability of alternate remedies. I conclude that the criminalization of hate statements does not impair free speech to the minimum extent permitted by its objectives.

Is the limit on free expression effected by s. 319(2) of the *Criminal Code* reasonable and demonstrably justifiable in a free and democratic society? On all three criteria for proportionality laid down in *Oakes*—rational connection between the legislation with its objectives, infringement to the minimum extent possible, and the balance between the importance of the infringement or the right of free speech and the benefit conferred by the legislation—s. 319(2) of the *Criminal Code* emerges wanting. Accepting that the objectives of the legislation are valid and important and potentially capable of overriding the guarantee of freedom of expression, I cannot conclude that the means chosen to achieve them—the criminalization of the potential or foreseeable promotion of hatred—are proportionate to those ends.

[McLACHLIN J. (Sopinka J. concurring) found that s. 319(3)(a) infringed s. 11(d) but was not justified under s. 1. She stated:]

A rational connection between the aims of s. 319(3)(a) and its requirement that the accused prove the truth of his statements is difficult to discern. It is argued that without the reverse onus, it would be difficult if not impossible to obtain convictions for much speech promoting hate. If the objection is that it is merely difficult to prove the statements true or false, the answer is that the burden should be on the state because it has superior resources. If the objection is that it is impossible to know if the statements are true or false (i.e. true opinion), then the answer is that it cannot be ruled out that the statements may be more valuable than harmful, if we accept the ultimate value of the exchange of truthful ideas. The same considerations suggest that s. 319(3)(a)'s infringement of the presumption of innocence is neither minimal nor, given the importance of the infringement in the context of prosecutions under s. 319(2), sufficient to outweigh the dubious benefit of such a provision.

Similar considerations arise on the question of whether s. 319(3)(a) of the *Criminal Code* impairs the presumption of innocence under s. 11(d) as little as possible. It is said that hate promotion against identifiable groups is highly unlikely to be true. But that would be small comfort to a particular accused in the case where such a defence lay but he or she, because of restricted means or for whatever other reason, was unable to prove it. The presumption of innocence should not depend on the percentage of cases in which the defence in question may arise. ...

The final test of proportionality between the effects of the infringement and the objectives it promotes encounters other difficulties. We must start from the proposition that Parliament intended the truth to be a defence and that falsehood is an important element of the offence created by s. 319(2) of the *Criminal Code*. That fact, coupled with the centrality of the presumption of innocence in our criminal law, suggests that only a countervailing state interest of the most compelling kind could justify the infringement. But, as discussed in connection with the infringement of the guarantee of freedom of expression, it is difficult to see what benefits s. 319(2) in fact produces in terms of stemming hate propaganda and promoting social harmony and individual dignity. ... I conclude that s. 319(3)(a) is not saved by s. 1 of the Charter.

[The Crown's appeal in *Keegstra* was allowed. The Alberta Court of Appeal subsequently ordered a new trial because the trial judge had denied the accused an opportunity to challenge the impartiality of jurors, *R. v. Keegstra* (no. 2) (1991), 63 C.C.C. (3d) 110 (Alta. C.A.). In July 1992, Keegstra was convicted and fined $3,000 (1994), 92 C.C.C. (3d) 505. Keegstra successfully appealed this conviction to the Alberta Court of Appeal, but a Crown appeal was unanimously allowed and the conviction restored by the Supreme Court in *R. v. Keegstra* (1996), 105 C.C.C. (3d) 19.]

---

In *R.A.V. v. City of St. Paul*, 112 S. Ct. 2538 (1992), the accused was charged with violating a city ordinance that made it a misdemeanour to display a symbol one knows or has reason to know "arouses anger, alarm or resentment in others on the basis of race, colour, creed, religion or gender." He had burned a cross on the front lawn of a Black family. The United States Supreme Court struck down the ordinance as violating the First Amendment.

Justice Scalia in the opinion of the Court held the ordinance was invalid because it regulated the content of speech. He stated that under the law:

... One could hold up a sign saying, for example, that all "anti-Catholic bigots" are misbegotten; but not that all "papists" are, for that would insult and provoke violence "on the basis of religion." St. Paul has no such authority to license one side of a debate to fight freestyle, while requiring the other to follow Marquis of Queensbury Rules.

... An ordinance not limited to the favored topics, for example, would have precisely the same beneficial effect. In fact the only interest distinctively served by the content limitation is that of displaying the city council's special hostility towards the particular biases thus singled out. That is precisely what the First Amendment forbids. The politicians of St. Paul are entitled to express that hostility—but not through the means of imposing unique limitations upon speakers who (however benightedly) disagree.

... Let there be no mistake about our belief that burning a cross in someone's front yard is reprehensible. But St. Paul has sufficient means at its disposal to prevent such behavior without adding the First Amendment to the fire.

Four other judges disagreed with this basis for striking the law down but said that the law was invalid because it was overbroad. Justice White stated that the law prohibited speech "that causes only hurt feelings, offense, or resentment, and is protected by the First Amendment" unlike "fighting words" that would incite "imminent lawless action."

Keegstra was subject to another trial and after protracted legal procedures and two subsequent appeals to the Supreme Court was convicted and fined $3,000.

### R. v. Zundel
Supreme Court of Canada
(1992), 75 C.C.C. (3d) 449

[The accused was charged under s. 181 of the *Criminal Code* for publishing material denying the Holocaust. He was convicted, but the Ontario Court of Appeal allowed his appeal, (1987), 31 C.C.C. (3d) 97, in part because of concerns about jury selection. Zundel was convicted at his second trial and appealed to the Supreme Court.]

McLACHLIN J. (La Forest, L'Heureux-Dubé, and Sopinka JJ. concurring): Neither the admittedly offensive beliefs of the appellant, Mr. Zundel, nor the specific publication with regard to which he was charged under s. 181 are directly engaged by these constitutional questions. This appeal is not about the dissemination of hate, which was the focus of this court's decision in *R. v. Keegstra* (1990), 61 C.C.C. (3d) 1, and the reasons of my colleagues Cory and Iacobucci JJ. here. In *Keegstra*, this court ruled that the provisions of the *Criminal Code* which prohibit the dissemination of hate violated the guarantee of freedom of expression but were saved under s. 1 of the *Charter*. This case presents the court with the question of whether a much broader and vaguer class of speech—false statements deemed likely to injure or cause mischief to any public interest—can be saved under s. 1 of the *Charter*. In my view, the answer to this question must be in the negative. To permit the imprisonment of people, or even the threat of imprisonment, on the ground that they have made a statement which 12 of their co-citizens deem to be false and mischievous to some undefined public interest, is to stifle a whole range of speech, some of which has long been regarded as legitimate and even beneficial to our society. I do not assert that Parliament cannot criminalize the dissemination of racial slurs and hate propaganda. I do assert, however, that such provisions must be drafted with sufficient particularity

to offer assurance that they cannot be abused so as to stifle a broad range of legitimate and valuable speech.

Before we put a person beyond the pale of the Constitution, before we deny a
person the protection which the most fundamental law of this land, on its face, accords to the person, we should, in my belief, be entirely certain that there can be no
justification for offering protection. The criterion of falsity falls short of this certainty, given that false statements can sometimes have value and given the difficulty
of conclusively determining total falsity. Applying the broad, purposive interpretation of the freedom of expression guaranteed by s. 2(b) hitherto adhered to by this
court, I cannot accede to the argument that those who deliberately publish falsehoods
are for that reason alone precluded from claiming the benefit of the constitutional
guarantees of free speech. I would rather hold that such speech is protected by s. 2(b),
leaving arguments relating to its value in relation to its prejudicial effect to be dealt
with under s. 1.

I turn first to the state's interest in prohibiting the expression here at issue—the
question of whether the Crown has established an overriding public objective, to use
the language of *R. v. Oakes* (1986), 24 C.C.C. (3d) 321.

In determining the objective of a legislative measure for the purposes of s. 1, the
court must look at the intention of Parliament when the section was enacted or
amended. It cannot assign objectives, nor invent new ones according to the perceived
current utility of the impugned provision: see *R. v. Big M Drug Mart Ltd.* (1985), 18
C.C.C. (3d) 385, at p. 344 [S.C.R.], in which this court rejected the United States
doctrine of shifting purposes. Although the application and interpretation of objectives may vary over time (see, e.g., *Butler*, supra, per Sopinka J., at pp. 494-496
[S.C.R.]), new and altogether different purposes should not be invented. The case is
quite different from the anti-obscenity legislation in *Butler* where the goal historically and to the present day is the same—combatting the "detrimental impact" of
obscene materials on individuals and society—even though our understanding or conception of that detrimental impact (a "permissible shift in emphasis") may have
evolved, as Sopinka J. noted. My colleagues say that it is a permissible shift in emphasis that the false news provision was originally focused on the "prevention of
deliberate slanderous statements against the great nobles of the realm" and is now
said to be concerned with "attacks on religious, racial or ethnic minorities." But this
is no shift in emphasis with regard to the purpose of the legislation—this is an outright redefinition not only of the purpose of the prohibition but also of the nature of
the activity prohibited. To convert s. 181 into a provision directed at encouraging
racial harmony is to go beyond any permissible shift in emphasis and effectively
rewrite the section.

It is argued that this interpretation represents a mere shift in emphasis because the
thrust of s. 181 and its predecessors, like the obscenity provisions in *Butler*, disclosed
a single goal: "[t]he protection of the public interest from harm" or from that which
would "threaten the integrity of the social fabric." Yet, all *Criminal Code* provisions—
as well as much statutory regulation in the public and private law spheres—have as
their basic purpose the protection of the public from harm and the maintenance of the
integrity of the social fabric. Indeed, one might argue that such was the goal of the

obscenity provisions under review in *Butler*, yet the court did not adopt that as the legislation's objective. Instead, it relied upon a specific objective concerning the effect of pornographic materials on individuals and the resultant impact on society. If the simple identification of the (content-free) goal of protecting the public from harm constitutes a "pressing and substantial" objective, virtually any law will meet the first part of the onus imposed upon the Crown under s. 1. I cannot believe that the framers of the *Charter* intended s. 1 to be applied in such a manner. Justification under s. 1 requires more than the general goal of protection from harm common to all criminal legislation; it requires a specific purpose so pressing and substantial as to be capable of overriding the *Charter's* guarantees. To apply the language used by Sopinka J. in *Butler* (at p. 496 [S.C.R.]); s. 181 cannot be said to be directed to avoidance of publications which "seriously offend the values fundamental to our society," nor is it directed to a "substantial concern which justifies restricting the otherwise full exercise of the freedom of expression."

All this stands in sharp contrast to the hate propaganda provision of the *Criminal Code* at issue in *Keegstra*—s. 319(2). Both the text of that provision and its long and detailed Parliamentary history, involving Canada's international human rights obligations, the Cohen Committee Report (*Report of the Special Committee on Hate Propaganda in Canada* (Ottawa: Queen's Printer, 1966)) and the Report of the Special Committee on the Participation of Visible Minorities in Canadian Society (*Equality Now!* (Ottawa: Supplies & Services, 1984)), permitted ready identification of the objective Parliament had in mind. Section 319(2), under challenge in *Keegstra*, was part of the amendments to the *Criminal Code* "essentially along the lines suggested by the [Cohen] Committee ..." (per Dickson C.J.C. in *Keegstra*, supra, at p. 725 [S.C.R.]). The evil addressed was hate-mongering, particularly in the racial context. The provision at issue on this appeal is quite different. Parliament had identified no social problem, much less one of pressing concern, justifying s. 181 of the *Criminal Code*. To suggest that the objective of s. 181 is to combat hate propaganda or racism is to go beyond its history and its wording and to adopt the "shifting purpose" analysis this court has rejected. Such an objective, moreover, hardly seems capable of being described as a "nuisance," the rubric under which Parliament has placed s. 181, nor as the offence's target of mere "mischief" to a public interest.

Can it be said in these circumstances that the Crown has discharged the burden upon it of establishing that the objective of the legislation is pressing and substantial, in short, of sufficient importance to justify overriding the constitutional guarantee of freedom of expression? I think not. It may be that s. 181 is capable of serving legitimate purposes. But no objective of pressing and substantial concern has been identified in support of its retention in our *Criminal Code*. Other provisions, such as s. 319(2) of the *Criminal Code*, deal with hate propaganda more fairly and more effectively. Still other provisions seem to deal adequately with matters of sedition and state security. ...

Section 181 can be used to inhibit statements which society considers should be inhibited, like those which denigrate vulnerable groups. Its danger, however, lies in the fact that by its broad reach it criminalizes a vast penumbra of other statements merely because they might be thought to constitute a mischief to some public interest, however successive prosecutors and courts may wish to define these terms. The danger is magnified because the prohibition affects not only those caught and prosecuted, but those who may refrain from saying what they would like to because of the fear that they will be caught. Thus worthy minority groups or individuals may be inhibited from saying what they desire to say for fear that they might be prosecuted. Should an activist be prevented from saying "the rainforest of British Columbia is being destroyed" because she fears criminal prosecution for spreading "false news" in the event that scientists conclude and a jury accepts that the statement is false and that it is likely to cause mischief to the British Columbia forest industry? ...

... All it takes is one judge and 12 jurors who believe that certain "falsehoods" compromise a particular "public" interest, and that such falsehoods "must have been" known to the accused, in order to convict. A jury in Port Alberni, British Columbia, may have a very different view of the overall beneficial impact of false statements of fact impugning the lumber industry than a jury in Toronto. ...

In summary, the broad range of expression caught by s. 181—extending to virtually all controversial statements of apparent fact which might be argued to be false and likely to do some mischief to some public interest—combined with the serious consequences of criminality and imprisonment, makes it impossible to say that s. 181 is appropriately measured and restrained having regard to the evil addressed—that it effects a "minimal impairment" to use the language of *Oakes*, supra. Section 181 is materially different, in this regard, from s. 319(2)—the provision upheld under s. 1 by the majority of this court in *Keegstra*.

To summarize, the restriction on expression effected by s. 181 of the *Criminal Code*, unlike that imposed by the hate propaganda provision at issue in *Keegstra*, cannot be justified under s. 1 of the *Charter* as a "reasonable limit prescribed by law as can be demonstrably justified in a free and democratic society." At virtually every step of the *Oakes* test, one is struck with the substantial difference between s. 181 and the provision at issue in *Keegstra*, s. 319(2) of the Code. In contrast to the hate propaganda provision (*Keegstra*), the false news provision cannot be associated with any existing social problem or legislative objective, much less one of pressing concern. It is, as the Law Reform Commission concluded, "anachronistic." But even if the court were to attribute to s. 181 the objective of promoting racial and social tolerance and conclude that such objective was so pressing and substantial as to be capable of over-riding a fundamental freedom, s. 181 would still fail to meet the criteria of proportionality which prevailed in *Keegstra*. In *Keegstra*, the majority of this court found the objective of the legislation to be compelling and its effect to be appropriately circumscribed. The opposite is the case with s. 181 of the *Criminal Code*. Section 181 catches not only deliberate falsehoods which promote hatred, but sanctions all false assertions which the prosecutor believes "likely to cause injury or mischief to a public interest," regardless of whether they promote the values underlying s. 2(b). At the same time, s. 181's objective, in so far as an objective can be ascribed to the section, ranks much lower in importance than the legislative goal at stake in *Keegstra*. When the objective of s. 181 is balanced against its invasive reach, there can, in my opinion, be only one conclusion: the limitation of freedom of expression is disproportionate to the objective envisaged.

In their laudable effort to send a message condemning the "hate-mongering" of persons such as the appellant by upholding s. 181 as a reasonable limit, it is my respectful opinion that my colleagues Cory and Iacobucci JJ. make three fundamental errors. First, they effectively rewrite s. 181 to supply its text with a particularity which finds no support in the provision's history or in its rare application in the Canadian context. Second, they underrate the expansive breadth of s. 181 and its potential not only for improper prosecution and conviction but for "chilling" the speech of persons who may otherwise have exercised their freedom of expression. Finally, they go far beyond accepted principles of statutory and *Charter* interpretation in their application of s. 1 of the *Charter*. While I share the concerns of my colleagues, I fear that such techniques, taken to their ultimate extreme, might render nugatory the free speech guarantee of the *Charter*. ...

[CORY and IACOBUCCI JJ. (Gonthier J. concurring) in dissent agreed that s. 181 violated s. 2(b) but held that it was justified under s. 1 of the Charter:]

This appeal concerns the wilful publication of deliberate, injurious lies and the legislation which seeks to combat the serious harm to society as a whole caused by these calculated and deceitful falsehoods. Our colleague, McLachlin J., has stated that s. 181 violates s. 2(b) of the *Charter* and is not saved under s. 1. We agree with her conclusion, though not with her reasoning, that s. 181 violates s. 2(b) of the *Charter*. However, with respect, we do not agree that the section cannot be justified under s. 1.

The appellant contends that the term "public interest" is so vague that the section is invalid. It is submitted that the term could be used by an unscrupulous government to render criminal any conduct or opinion opposed by the government of the day.

The fact that the term is undefined by the legislation is of little significance. There are many phrases and words contained in the *Criminal Code* which have been interpreted by the courts. It is impossible for legislators to foresee and provide for every eventuality or to define every term that is used. Enactments must have some flexibility. Courts have in the past played a significant role in the definition of words and phrases used in the Code and other enactments. They should continue to do so in the future.

A survey of federal statutes alone reveals that the term "public interest" is mentioned 224 times in 84 federal statutes. The term appears in comparable numbers in provincial statutes. The term does not and cannot have a uniform meaning in each statute. It must be interpreted in light of the legislative history of the particular provision in which it appears and the legislative and social context in which it is used.

A "public interest" likely to be harmed as a result of contravention of s. 181 is the public interest in a free and democratic society that is subject to the rule of law. A free society is one built upon reasoned debate in which all its members are entitled to participate. Section 181, including its reference to "public interest," should, as this court has emphasized, be interpreted in light of *Charter* values.

As a fundamental document setting out essential features of our vision of democracy, the *Charter* provides us with indications as to which values go to the very core of our political structure. A democratic society capable of giving effect to the *Charter's* guarantees is one which strives toward creating a community committed to equality, liberty and human dignity. The public interest is, therefore, in preserving and promoting these goals.

The term, as it appears in s. 181, should be confined to those rights recognized in the *Charter* as being fundamental to Canadian democracy. It need not be extended beyond that. As an example, the rights enacted in ss. 7, 15 and 27 of the *Charter* should be considered in defining a public interest.

It has been argued that s. 181 is anachronistic and that to attribute to it the purpose of protecting racial and social tolerance is to trigger the invalid shifting purpose doctrine. Those concerns should now be addressed.

It is true the false news provision dates back to 1275. It was submitted that there is really no need at this stage in our history to protect the "great persons of the realm," which was the basis for the section when it was first enacted in the 13th century, and that the provision serves no other purpose. That position cannot be accepted. This section was specifically retained by Parliament in 1955. It has today a very real and pertinent role to play in Canada's multicultural and democratic society.

The tragedy of the Holocaust and the enactment of the *Charter* have served to emphasize the laudable s. 181 aim of preventing the harmful effects of false speech and thereby promoting racial and social tolerance. In fact, it was in part the publication of the evil and invidious statements that were known to be false by those that made them regarding the Jewish people that led the way to the inferno of the Holocaust. The realities of Canada's multicultural society emphasize the vital need to protect minorities and preserve Canada's mosaic of cultures.

Support for the proposition that a shift in emphasis is permissible also stems from the decision in *Butler*, supra. Centuries ago, obscenity laws were enacted to prevent the corruption of the morals of the King's subjects, and therefore to protect the peace of the King and government. ... In *Butler*, however, Sopinka J. found that the objective of the obscenity law is no longer moral disapprobation but rather the avoidance of harm to society.

Sopinka J. concluded by adding that a "permissible shift in emphasis was built into the legislation when, as interpreted by the courts, it adopted the community standards test." ... Similarly, in the present case, the wording of s. 181 includes a permissible shift in emphasis with its test which is based on injury to the public interest.

Just as the community standards test, as applied to the obscenity law, "must necessarily respond to changing mores," ... so too should the test to define "injury to a public interest" take into account the changing values of Canadian society. Those values encompass multiculturalism and equality, precepts specifically included in the provisions of the *Charter*.

At the end of this detailed analysis it is worthwhile to step back and consider what it is that is being placed on the balance.

On one side is s. 181. It infringes to a minimal extent the s. 2(b) right of freedom of expression. In reality, it cannot be said that the prohibition of the wilful publication of false statements that are known to be false is an infringement of the core values of s. 2(b). Rather the infringement is on the extreme periphery of those values. In addition, the section can play an important role in fostering multiculturalism and racial and religious tolerance by demonstrating Canadian society's abhorrence of spreading what are known to be lies that injure and denigrate vulnerable minority groups and individuals.

On the other side, s. 181 provides maximum protection of the accused. It requires the Crown to establish beyond a reasonable doubt that the accused wilfully published false statements of fact presented as truth and that their publication caused or was likely to cause injury to the public interest. Any uncertainty as to the nature of the speech must inure to the benefit of the accused. If ever s. 1 balancing is to be used to demonstrate that a section of the *Criminal Code* is justifiable in a free and democratic society, this is such a case.

Legislation such as this, which is aimed at the protection of society from deceit and aggression, yet provides the widest protection for the accused, should be fostered. Applying the *Charter* to strike s. 181 would be in direct contradiction to the principles established by this court. The section is justifiable in our free and democratic Canadian society.

*Appeal allowed; acquittal entered.*

The Ontario Attorney General subsequently declined to allow a charge against Zundel under s. 319(2) of the *Criminal Code*.

————————————

The Law Reform Commission of Canada in its Working Paper 50 *Hate Propaganda* (1986) summarized previous reform proposals as follows:

The Special Parliamentary Committee Report on Participation of Visible Minorities in Canadian Society, *Equality Now*, recommended: (1) the removal of the "wilfully" requirement from subsection 281.2(2), so that it would no longer be necessary to prove that the accused intended to promote hatred; (2) the removal of the requirement of the consent of the Attorney General to a prosecution under subsection 281.2(2); and (3) clarifying that the burden of proof is on the accused to raise the defences provided for by that subsection. The Special Committee on Racial and Religious Hatred of the Canadian Bar Association differed from the conclusions in *Equality Now* in two respects. First, it believed that requiring the consent of the provincial Attorney General could prevent frivolous prosecutions. Second, it believed that two of the existing defences to a charge under subsection 281.2(2) should be abolished. These were: (1) a good faith opinion on a religious subject; and (2) a reasonable belief in the truth of the statements if they were relevant to the public interest and were discussed for the public benefit. The Fraser Committee also recommended the removal of the "wilfully" requirement and the consent of the Attorney General. But, unlike the other reports, it advocated enlarging the definition of "identifiable group" to include the categories of sex, age, and mental or physical disability, at least insofar as the definition applies to section 281.2 of the *Code*.

While these laws and these proposals are useful to us in some degree, those who have either passed laws or have proposed reforms in this area have not adequately considered the fundamental principle of restraint which must shape our criminal law.

The Commission examined the offence created under s. 319(2) of the Code:

> The crucial issue involving *mens rea* is whether the crime should retain the word "wilfully" or an equivalent phrase which makes the crime effectively one of specific intent, or whether "wilfully" should be dropped altogether to create a crime of recklessness. The preferred view of many persons, as reflected in *Equality Now* and the Fraser Committee report, is that the "wilfully" requirement must be dropped.
>
> With respect, we do not share this view. The principle of restraint requires lawmakers to concern themselves not just with whom they want to catch, but also with whom they do not want to catch. For example, removing an intent or purpose requirement could well result in successful prosecutions of cases similar to *Buzzanga*, where members of a minority group publish hate propaganda against their own group in order to create controversy or to agitate for reform. This crime should not be used to prosecute such individuals.
>
> In effect, this crime should be used only to catch the most extreme cases of fomenting hatred, when the accused is motivated by enmity. Accordingly, we recommend that this crime should continue to be one of intent or purpose. This is best achieved by removing the "wilfully" requirement and substituting in its place an "intentionally" or "purposely" requirement. This change in wording would not result in any change to the *mens rea* requirement for this crime as set out in *Buzzanga and Durocher*, but it would avoid the problems inherent in the word "wilfully," which has been defined inconsistently in criminal law.

The Commission proposed that the definition of identifiable group should be expanded to protect groups identifiable on the basis of race, national or ethnic origin, colour, religion, sex, age or mental and physical disability.

The Commission concluded the prohibition against the spreading of false news in s. 181 of the Code should be abolished.

> It is too wide, because it is too vague. It is too vague because it catches any statement which the publisher knows is false, if likely to cause "mischief to a public interest." But what is "mischief to a public interest?" While this phrase may appear to catch only harmful conduct, the appearance is deceptive. Unfortunately, the reported prosecutions under this offence, save for the *Zundel* case, seem unwarranted: for example, a conviction of an angry store owner for saying that Americans were not wanted in Canada; a trial conviction (later overturned on appeal) of an underground newspaper printing a false story that the mayor of Montréal was killed by a dope-crazed hippie.
>
> On the other hand, does section 177 [now s. 181] serve a useful purpose when used to prosecute persons like Zundel? Surely not. Using section 177 for this purpose is inappropriate for two reasons. First, denials of the Holocaust should be dealt with for what they are—a form of hate propaganda. Second, on principle, if Parliament intends that promoting hatred be dealt with in a certain way and creates safeguards such as the requirement of the Attorney General's consent to avoid an abusive application of the criminal law, a private prosecutor should not be able to avoid these safeguards by offence shopping elsewhere.

# CHAPTER THREE

# Police Powers

This chapter is designed to present an introduction and overview of some common law, statutory and constitutional constraints on the investigation of crime. The focus will be on the competing values and goals at stake when the state investigates crime and the priority that has and should be accorded to these values. Thought should also be given to how decisions about the limits of the criminal law discussed in chapter 2 affect the role of the police, for example, with respect to drug- and prostitution-based crimes.

The first part of the chapter examines various models of the criminal process, with an emphasis on competing values such as crime control and due process and the role of the Charter with respect to those values. The second part examines common law and constitutional requirements for the taking of statements from suspects and the question of whether Canada has moved toward the due process model under the Charter and adopted its own *Miranda* rule. The third part examines the defence of entrapment first recognized by the Supreme Court of Canada in 1988. The fourth part examines search issues with an emphasis on the distinction that the court often draws between the criminal and regulatory context. The fifth part examines detention and arrest issues with a focus on the interaction between the Charter, the common law, and statutory powers. The final part provides a case study of the effects of various Charter rights on the investigation of drunk driving.

## I. MODELS OF THE CRIMINAL PROCESS

### Kent Roach, *Due Process and Victims' Rights:*
### *The New Law and Politics of Criminal Justice*
(Toronto: U. of T. Press, 1999) (references omitted)

The most successful attempt to construct models of the criminal process was achieved by the American legal scholar Herbert Packer. ... The essence of each of Packer's two models is captured by an evocative metaphor. The criminal process in the crime-control model resembles a high-speed "assembly-line conveyor belt" operated by the police and prosecutors. The end product of the assembly-line is a guilty plea. In contrast, the due-process model is an "obstacle course" in which defence lawyers argue before judges that the prosecution should be rejected because the accused's rights have been violated. The assembly line of the crime-control model is primarily concerned with efficiency, while the due-process model is concerned with fairness to the accused and "quality control" ... .

Prior to the enactment of the Charter and the "due-process revolution" of the 1980s, the formal law of the Canadian criminal justice system embraced crime-control values. The few due-process initiatives that occurred were undertaken by Parliament, not the Supreme Court. This runs contrary to Packer's predictions that courts, not legislatures, would be the champions of due process. It also illustrates the dynamic nature of legal and political culture. In the 1980s, the Supreme Court and Parliament switched roles, with the former taking a proactive due-process lead and Parliament being concerned with crime control and victims' rights, frequently in reaction to due-process court decisions.

Before the Charter, Canadian courts had limited grounds to intervene in the criminal process. ... Canadian courts traditionally placed discovering the truth about the factually guilty before the fair treatment of the accused. Justice Ivan Rand rejected the notion that suspects' statements would be inadmissible because the police failed to read the proper warnings. "It would be a serious error to place the ordinary modes of investigation of crime in a strait-jacket of artificial rules. ... Rigid formulas can be both meaningless to the weakling and absurd to the sophisticated or hardened criminal; and to introduce a new rite as an inflexible preliminary condition would serve no genuine interest of the accused and but add an unreal formalism to that vital branch of the administration of justice." Thus, *Miranda*-type warnings were dismissed by even the most liberal of Canadian judges before the Charter. Consistent with crime-control concerns about truth and reliability, Canadian courts were concerned only about the propriety of police conduct when doubt was "cast on the truth of the statement." Truth, not fairness, mattered.

Commitment to crime control meant a reluctance to exclude relevant evidence even if unfairly obtained. In *Wray* (1970), the Supreme Court admitted into evidence a gun and an involuntary confession taken from a suspect subjected to a coercive ten-hour interrogation during which the police deliberately kept his lawyer at bay. The gun was admissible as reliable evidence, and the confession was admissible to the extent that its reliability was confirmed when the suspect led the police to the murder weapon. The admission of this relevant and truthful evidence was "unfortunate" for the accused, but not "unfair." There was no "judicial authority in this country or in England which supports the proposition that a trial judge has a discretion to exclude admissible evidence because, in his opinion, its admission would be calculated to bring the administration of justice into disrepute." As will be seen, *Wray* would be decided very differently under section 24(2) of the Charter.

Consistent with their general lack of concern about what happened beyond the courtroom door, the Supreme Court limited the right against self-incrimination to not being compelled to testify in one's own trial. A refusal by an accused to participate in an identification line-up could be used as incriminating evidence. The accused's blood and other "incriminating conditions of the body" could be admitted into evidence even though involuntarily and illegally obtained. Under the Charter, the Court would extend the right against self-incrimination from the courthouse to the police station and exclude reliable evidence, including incriminating bodily material, because it was unfairly conscripted from the accused.

The crime-control model did not necessarily condone police misconduct, but insisted that it be addressed outside of the accused's trial through civil suits, disciplinary hearings, and criminal prosecutions against the police. During the 1950s, the Supreme Court upheld damage awards stemming from police abuses in Quebec, and the right to seek damages was celebrated as the accused's most viable remedy. The damage remedy, however, was illusory, except for the most persistent and ultimately consistent with crime-control values because it required the accused's rights to be vindicated outside of the criminal process. Americans discontent with the Warren Court's reliance on the exclusionary rule looked longingly north of the border. One critic of the Warren Court invoked the Canadian example of crime control by quoting a commissioner of the Royal Canadian Mounted Police (RCMP) who argued that "when the policeman exceeds his authority, bring him up short, but when he is doing, as most of them are doing, a tough, thankless and frequently dangerous job for you and for all you hold dear, for God's sake get off his back."

Canadian acceptance of broad police powers is best symbolized by writs of assistance which gave members of the RCMP open-ended powers to conduct drug or Customs searches. Consistent with crime-control values, the writs relied on the expertise of police officers to decide when a search was warranted. As late as 1976, there were 935 writs held by RCMP officers which were used to authorize more than 4,000 searches. As one American commentator noted with some disgust, the writs empowered a police officer "without prior authorization or subsequent judicial review, to dismantle a house [in a search for narcotics] on their own decision." The use of the writs by English Customs officials had been one of the leading grievances in the American Revolution, and such general warrants were specifically prohibited in the American Bill of Rights. In Canada, however, even the reformist 1969 Ouimet Commission refused to recommend their abolition, and the writs were upheld under the Canadian Bill of Rights because that statutory bill of rights did not grant Canadians rights against unreasonable searches and seizures, and the writs did not interfere with the accused's right to a fair trial in the courtroom. Again, judicial concerns about fairness did not extend beyond the courtroom door. ...

Under the 1960 Canadian Bill of Rights, Canadian courts defined the accused's right in a minimal fashion and refused to grant effective remedies. The right to consult counsel did not include the right to talk to a lawyer in private. A drunk-driving suspect required upon pain of criminal conviction to provide a breath sample at the side of the road was not detained and entitled to consult counsel. Although a denial of the right to counsel could qualify as a reasonable excuse for not providing a breathalyser, the Court would not exclude a breath sample given by a less assertive accused who was also denied counsel. As Laskin J. accurately noted in his dissent, the Court's choice was "to favour the social interest in the repression of crime despite the unlawful invasion of individual interests ... by public officers. ..." ... In short, both the law and the practice of criminal justice before the Charter closely resembled Packer's crime-control model. As will be seen in the next section, the values of crime control almost survived the enactment of the Charter.

*The Development of Due Process*

Although they are the most frequently litigated part of the Charter, the legal rights and remedies of the accused were never at the heart of Pierre Trudeau's patriation project. Support for due process was at the mercy of the intergovernmental bargaining that defined constitutional politics until the late 1980s. The precarious place of due process in the drafting of the Charter, like other messy facts of history, embarrasses claims that due process was an inevitable development necessary to legitimate and distract a criminal justice system that was losing credibility. ...

[T]he federal government ... diluted the legal rights and remedies in an attempt to obtain provincial support. By October 1980, the right against unreasonable search and seizure had been watered down to the right "not to be subjected to search or seizure except on grounds, and in accordance with procedures, established by law." The writs of assistance, however Draconian, were still established by law. Similarly, detainees had rights against detention, imprisonment, and the denial of bail only if the deprivations of liberty were not "in accordance with procedures established by law." Those subject to detention or arrest had the right to counsel, but not the right to be informed of that right. As under the CBR, only the most knowledgeable and aggressive of accused would benefit from their rights.

The October draft did contain more robust rights such as the presumption of innocence and the right to be tried in a reasonable time, but these rights only ensured fairness in the courtroom. Like all other Charter rights, they were subject to "reasonable limits as are generally accepted in a free and democratic society with a parliamentary system of government." The reference to a parliamentary system of government would encourage courts to defer to the ability of Parliament to enact criminal laws and procedures and was criticized as a "Mack Truck" exception to the guaranteed rights. The October draft also inhibited the development of remedies by providing that all Charter rights (except the traditional right against being called as a witness in one's own trial) did not affect existing laws allowing unfairly obtained but relevant evidence to be admitted in criminal trials or the ability of legislatures to provide their own standards of admissibility.

The October draft preserved, behind a thin façade of rights and due process, the unfettered discretion of police, prosecutors, and legislatures fundamental to the crime-control model. It affirmed due process in the abstract while enabling substantial crime-control limitations on these rights. ...

After the collapse of intergovernmental bargaining, the federal government referred the Charter to a special Joint Committee of the House of Commons and Senate. ... Legal rights and remedies were fundamentally strengthened in the Joint Committee process The Canadian Civil Liberties Association (CCLA), which claimed a membership of only 5,000 individuals was probably the most influential group in beefing up the rights that would be the foundation of Canada's due-process revolution. ... Alan Borovoy of the CCLA argued that the October prohibition could have upheld an infamous drug raid in Fort Erie where more than 100 patrons of a bar were searched under the expansive legal powers of the Narcotics Control Act and a writ of assistance possessed by one of the officers. The section was a "verbal illusion in the sense that it may pretend to give us something, but in fact, gives us nothing more than we already have." The B.C. Civil Liberties Association claimed that the provision was worse than nothing and would justify some of the warrantless searches uncovered by the McDonald Commission into RCMP wrongdoing. Despite their small membership, the civil-liberties groups effectively invoked well-publicized police abuses. The Canadian Bar Association (CBA) stressed the danger of a standard that could "be altered by the arbitrary action of a legislature, as well as by the arbitrary action of a public official." The lawyers wanted judges, not Parliament, to have the last word. ...

The October draft provided the accused with the right to retain and instruct counsel without delay, but did not require the police to inform detainees of this right. Borovoy successfully proposed that the right be amended so that "nervous, frightened, bewildered" detainees not be interrogated until informed of the right to counsel. ... This gave the Supreme Court of Canada a textual basis to require the police to provide *Miranda*-style warnings to those they detained or arrested. Civil-liberties groups and the New Democratic Party failed, however, to entrench the right to legal aid, and this omission was later used by the Court as a reason not to require all provinces to provide 1-800 numbers to ensure that detainees could speak to lawyers.

Section 26 of the October draft of the Charter would have preserved legislative supremacy for laws governing the admissibility of evidence. It was strongly criticized by civil-liberties groups and defence lawyers, but vigorously defended by police and prosecutors. The CBA argued that it preserved parliamentary supremacy when the Charter would give courts "an entrenched right to construe every other specified legal right." In contrast, an association of prosecutors defended section 26 for leaving "the law of evidence to the type of evolution that we have been used to in this country, that is a combination of parliament and the courts." The CBA favoured the judicial supremacy that was fundamental to the due-process model, while the prosecutors wished to conserve legislative supremacy and the crime-control values of the common law. ...

The government agreed to delete section 26 in early January 1981 and add a "general remedies" section allowing courts to order whatever remedy they considered to be appropriate and just in the circumstances. [Later, s. 24(2) was finalized.] ... The only note of caution came from Coline Campbell of the Liberals, who inquired whether the amendment introduced the American "tainted fruit doctrine" and wondered why section 24(2) did not specify the factors to be considered when deciding whether the admission of evidence would bring the administration of justice into disrepute. E.G. Ewaschuk of the Department of Justice reassured her that a judge would consider "the seriousness of the case, the seriousness of the breach by the police, the manner in which the evidence was obtained" before deciding whether to exclude the evidence. Moreover, he argued that the remedy would be triggered only by "very blameworthy, repugnant and very reprehensible" conduct; in short, when "the admission of this evidence would make me vomit, it was obtained in such a reprehensible manner" ... the vomit test did not win judicial favour. In its desire to protect an expanded right against self-incrimination, the Supreme Court developed a quasi-absolutist exclusionary rule which precluded judges from considering the seriousness of the offence charged or the seriousness of the violation.

The provinces eventually obtained the ability to enact legislation, notwithstanding the legal rights. This power has never been used in the criminal justice field despite the political appeal of crime control and victims' rights. It has proven unnecessary because Parliament has used ordinary legislation to respond to, and even overturn, unpopular due-process Charter decisions. This contrasts with the American experience of courts ignoring legislative attempts to overrule *Miranda*, but it is facilitated by the structure of the Charter, which allows government to justify legislation that violates Charter rights as "reasonable limits prescribed by law as can be demonstrably justified in a free and democratic society" (Charter, s. 1).

---

Are the values of due process and crime control exhaustive of the relevant values in the investigation of crime. What about the question of community standards examined in the last chapter? What about the interests or rights of victims or groups that may be disproportionately subject to some crimes?

## II. QUESTIONING SUSPECTS

### The Common Law Governing Confessions

Long before the 1982 enactment of the Charter, the courts excluded or kept out involuntary confessions as part of a judge-made or common law rule.

Consider, as you read this material, whether the purpose of the confession rule is because of the danger that the statement may be untrue, or obtained in a manner offensive to community standards, or to control improper police practices, or to protect the accused against self-incrimination.

---

In *Boudreau v. The King* (1949), 94 C.C.C. 1, the Supreme Court of Canada held that the fundamental question relating to the admissibility of a confession made to a person in authority is whether it is *voluntary*. The court in *Boudreau* affirmed the conviction (Estey J., dissenting) holding that a warning that the accused is not obliged to say anything but that anything that he or she says may be recorded and given in evidence is not absolutely necessary. Only part of the judgments of Kellock and Rand JJ. are reproduced here. Kellock J. stated:

> The governing principle is stated by Lord Sumner in *Ibrahim v. The King*, [1914] A.C. 599 at pp. 609-10, as follows: "It has long been established as a positive rule of English criminal law, that no statement by an accused is admissible in evidence against him unless it is shewn by the prosecution to have been a voluntary statement, in the sense that it has not been obtained from him either by fear of prejudice or hope of advantage exercised or held out by a person in authority. The principle is as old as Lord Hale. The burden of proof in the matter has been decided by high authority in recent times in *Reg. v. Thompson*, [1893] 2 Q.B. 12."

Rand J. stated:

The cases of *Ibrahim v. The King*, [1914] A.C. 599, *R. v. Voisin*, [1918] 1 K.B. 531, and *Prosko v. The King*, 66 D.L.R. 340, 37 Can. C.C. 199, 63 S.C.R. 226, lay it down that the fundamental question is whether the statement is voluntary. No doubt arrest and the presence of officers tend to arouse apprehension which a warning may or may not suffice to remove, and the rule is directed against the danger of improperly instigated or induced or coerced admissions. It is the doubt cast on the truth of the statement arising from the circumstances in which it is made that gives rise to the rule. What the statement should be is that of a man free in volition from the compulsions or inducements of authority and what is sought is assurance that that is the case. The underlying and controlling question then remains: Is the statement freely and voluntarily made? Here the trial Judge found that it was. It would be a serious error to place the ordinary modes of investigation of crime in a strait-jacket of artificial rules; and the true protection against improper interrogation or any kind of pressure or inducement is to leave the broad question to the Court. Rigid formulas can be both meaningless to the weakling and absurd to the sophisticated or hardened criminal; and to introduce a new rite as an inflexible preliminary condition would serve no genuine interest of the accused and but add an unreal formalism to that vital branch of the administration of justice.

## Confessions and the Right to Counsel

The next case deals both with the development of the common law governing the admissibility of confessions and s. 10(b) of the Charter, which provides as follows:

> 10.  Everyone has the right on arrest or detention ...
>      (b)  to retain and instruct counsel without delay and to be informed of that right ...

### Clarkson v. The Queen
Supreme Court of Canada
(1986), 25 C.C.C. (3d) 207

WILSON J.:  This case raises an issue as to the admissibility of a confession made by an accused while in an intoxicated state and without the benefit of counsel.

### *The Facts*

The appellant, in an apparently intoxicated state, telephoned her sister in the early morning hours of December 8, 1982, to tell her that her (the appellant's) husband had been shot. The sister initially quoted the appellant as having said "I did it. I shot him" but upon cross-examination acknowledged that the appellant had been in a rather inarticulate state and could have said something like "Somebody shot him" or "James has been shot." In any event, several of the appellant's family members arrived at her house soon after the telephone call and from there they called the police. The appellant was found crying and screaming in a hysterical condition. Her husband, James

Clarkson, lay sprawled out on a living-room chair with a bullet hole in his head at the right temple. A rifle, on which no fingerprints could be found, was located near the deceased's body.

The police arrived on the scene and after some initial investigation charged the appellant with murder. She was given the customary police warning and duly informed of her right to retain and instruct counsel before being driven to a Fredericton hospital accompanied by her aunt, Lorna Estey. While *en route* to the hospital the police overheard a conversation between the appellant and Mrs. Estey which, according to the police, contained admissions of guilt on the appellant's part. These conversations, along with a number of other casual remarks made by the appellant to Mrs. Estey and others and overheard by the police, were ruled inadmissible at trial. Upon arrival at the hospital the appellant was physically examined and, upon consent, provided a blood sample which showed her to have a blood-alcohol level of 210 mg. per 100 ml. of blood notwithstanding that nearly four and a half hours had passed since the initial telephone call. Again, a number of comments made by the appellant during the medical examination were held inadmissible at trial.

The police proceeded to take the appellant to the police station where, in the presence of Mrs. Estey, an interrogation was conducted. Once again she was instructed of her right to counsel and apparently nodded in the affirmative when asked if she understood the question. She responded in a similar fashion when asked by the police if it was all right to use a tape recorder during the interview. At this point Mrs. Estey made the first of her interjections, asking whether it was proper for the appellant to be questioned without her lawyer being present. The police responded by pointing out that the appellant had been read those rights of which she was required to be informed and then proceeded with the interrogation. At several points during the questioning Mrs. Estey attempted to have the interrogation halted and to convince the appellant to stop answering questions until she had a lawyer present. It would seem, however, that the appellant waved off Mrs. Estey's suggestion, stating that there was "no point" and that she did not need the help of a lawyer. The police questioning continued and the over-all effect of the appellant's responses was to provide the police and the Crown with a statement that was highly inadequate. ...

*Admissibility of the Intoxicated Confession*

The debate over the test of admissibility of (for want of a better phrase) an intoxicated confession may be succinctly stated as being between a standard in which an accused must be capable of comprehending what he or she is saying and a standard in which an accused must comprehend the consequences of saying it.

... One explanation for the rejection of the statement of an incapacitated person is that, like the statement of a person acting involuntarily or under some compulsion, it would be so unreliable as to be unsafe to admit it: *Cross on Evidence* 5th ed. (1979), p. 545. Indeed, the identity of the concerns underlying the general rule in *Ibrahim v. The King*, [1914] A.C. 599 with those underlying the rule for intoxicated confessions has been recognized in express terms by the Supreme Court of New Zealand in *R. v. Williams*, [1959] N.Z.L.R. 502. In that case, Hardie Boys J. quoted with approval

(p. 505) the following passage from the earlier judgment of Finlay J. in *R. v. Phillips*, [1949] N.Z.L.R. 316 at p. 356 (C.A.):

> In broad terms, any circumstance which robs a confession of the quality described by the word "voluntary" will render the confession inadmissible. It may be deprived of that quality by a variety of circumstances. Those circumstances may well cover the whole field of motivation, and are not limited to threats or promises. They may comprehend a defect in consciousness or comprehension.

The test emerging from this line of reasoning focuses therefore on whether the accused was coherent enough to understand his or her own words, but does not go beyond this since the question of comprehension is the only one that goes to the probative value of the confession. Any further consideration of the accused's state of mind at the time of the confession, such as an assessment as to whether or not he or she appreciated the consequences of making the statement, is not directed to the reliability of the statement as evidence probative of the truth. Indeed, one might say that the likelihood of truthfulness is increased where the accused is unaware that the statement will ultimately be utilized by the Crown at his or her trial.

This approach to the problem may be readily contrasted with the reasoning of Beetz J. in *Horvath v. The Queen* (1979), 44 C.C.C. (2d) 385, 93 D.L.R. (3d) 1, [1979] 2 S.C.R. 376. In that case the issue was the admissibility of a confession made by the accused while under hypnosis. Mr. Justice Beetz stated (p. 424 C.C.C., p. 40 D.L.R., p. 425 S.C.R.):

> Horvath was in control of his faculties when Sergeant Proke cautioned him at the beginning of the interview but, under hypnosis, he ceased to be in a state of full consciousness and awareness. His awareness of what was at stake in making any statement is very much a matter of doubt.

There was little doubt in this case that the accused was capable of comprehending what he was saying under the influence of what was described as "light hypnosis" so that the broad New Zealand test of a "defect in consciousness or comprehension" did not apply. Indeed, the probative value of the statements may be viewed as having been enhanced by the fact that hypnosis made it unlikely that the accused could consciously lie. Accordingly, the concern expressed by Beetz J. in determining that the evidence was inadmissible was not that the accused did not understand his own statement but rather that he did not understand "what was at stake" in making the statement. This focus reveals a concern not so much for the probative value of the statement as for adjudicative fairness in the criminal process and for control of police conduct in interrogating accused persons. ...

It seems to me that if it is the concern over fair treatment of an accused which must prevail, then the test of awareness of the consequences as espoused by Beetz J. in *Horvath*, *supra*, must displace the more restrictive "operating mind" test as the appropriate standard against which to measure the admissibility of intoxicated confessions. The continued interrogation of an accused who, although not so incapacitated as to be incoherent and uncomprehending of her own words, incriminates herself without being aware that that is what she is doing, is incompatible with the view that the adjudicative process must arrive at the truth in a way which does not reflect an abuse by the police or the Crown of its dominant position vis-à-vis the individual. In order to avoid the problem of a person unwittingly inculpating herself in a criminal offence, the police must necessarily hold off their interrogation until their suspect has become sober enough to appreciate the consequences of making a statement.

On the other hand, if the paramount concern underlying the admissibility of evidence is perceived as being to probe the truth of the facts in issue without too much regard for the fairness of the adjudicative process, then the "operating mind" test adopted by Angers J.A. in the court below might be viewed as acceptable. As already indicated, the relevant case-law has produced two conflicting lines of reasoning which reflect these two underlying concerns and it is difficult, if not impossible, to reconcile them. It is perhaps entirely appropriate then that the common law has left the task of balancing these two concerns to the discretion of the trial judge who has the unique advantage of hearing the entire body of evidence and who can consequently best assess both the probative value and the prejudice to the accused in the over-all context of the case. The tension between the concern over the probative value of evidence and the concern over police conduct and fairness in obtaining the evidence may not, however, have to be resolved in this case as the issue may be effectively pre-empted by the second issue raised by the appellant, namely, the alleged violation of her constitutional right to counsel.

The question whether the appellant's right to counsel has been violated may well provide an acceptable alternative approach to the problem posed by the police extraction of an intoxicated confession. This right, as entrenched in s. 10(b) of the *Canadian Charter of Rights and Freedoms* is clearly aimed at fostering the principles of adjudicative fairness. As Lamer J. indicated in *R. v. Therens* (1985), 18 C.C.C. (3d) 481 at p. 490, 18 D.L.R. (4th) 655 at p. 665, [1985] 1 S.C.R. 613 at p. 624:

> where a detainee is required to provide evidence which may be incriminating ... s. 10(b) also imposes a duty not to call upon the detainee to provide that evidence without first informing him of his s. 10(b) rights and providing him with a reasonable opportunity and time to retain and instruct counsel.

This constitutional provision is clearly unconcerned with the probative value of any evidence obtained by the police but rather, in the words of Le Dain J. in *Therens*, *supra*, pp. 503-4 C.C.C., p. 678 D.L.R., pp. 641-2 S.C.R., its aim is "to ensure that in certain situations a person is made aware of the right to counsel" where he or she is detained by the police in a situation which may give rise to a "significant legal consequence."

Given the concern for fair treatment of an accused person which underlies such constitutional civil liberties as the right to counsel in s. 10(b) of the Charter, it is evident that any alleged waiver of this right by an accused must be carefully considered and that the accused's awareness of the consequences of what he or she was saying is crucial. Indeed, this Court stated with respect to the waiver of statutory procedural guarantees in *Korponey v. A.G. Can.* (1982), 65 C.C.C. (2d) 65 at p. 74, 132 D.L.R. (3d) 354 at p. 363, [1982] 1 S.C.R. 41 at p. 49, that any waiver

... is dependent upon it being *clear and unequivocal that the person is waiving the procedural safeguard and is doing so with full knowledge of the rights the procedure was enacted to protect and of the effect the waiver will have on those rights in the process.*

(Emphasis in original.) ...

[Wilson J. concluded that the accused had not voluntarily waived her right to counsel with a full awareness of the consequences.]

... At the very minimum it was incumbent upon the police to delay their questioning and the taking of the appellant's statement until she was in a sufficiently sober state to properly exercise her right to retain and instruct counsel or to be fully aware of the consequences of waiving this right. Accordingly, regardless of the view one takes of the admissibility of the intoxicated confession *per se*, the conclusion that the appellant's confession was improperly obtained is inescapable.

Having come to the conclusion that the constitutional rights of the appellant were infringed by the police in their obtaining of her confession, it remains to be decided whether exclusion of the confession from the evidence is the appropriate remedy. Section 24(2) of the Charter provides:

> 24(2)  Where, in proceedings under subsection (1), a court concludes that evidence was obtained in a manner that infringed or denied any rights or freedoms guaranteed by this Charter, the evidence shall be excluded if it is established that, having regard to all the circumstances, the admission of it in the proceedings would bring the administration of justice into disrepute.

In the case at bar, the court is confronted with a blatant violation by the police of the appellant's rights under s. 10(b) of the Charter. The appellant's drunken assertion that there was "no point" in retaining counsel in face of a murder charge could not possibly have been taken seriously by the police as a true waiver of her constitutional right, especially when viewed in conjunction with the efforts of Mrs. Estey to convince the police to postpone their interrogation until defence counsel could be retained. This was not a situation in which the police were for some urgent reason compelled to act immediately in gathering evidence. Rather, the actions of the police in interrogating the intoxicated appellant seem clearly to have been aimed at extracting a confession which they feared they might not be able to get later when she sobered up and appreciated the need for counsel. In other words, this seems to be a clear case of deliberate exploitation by the police of the opportunity to violate the appellant's rights. In this context the words of Estey J. writing for the majority of this Court in *Therens*, *supra*, become highly relevant (p. 488 C.C.C., pp. 662-3 D.L.R., pp. 621-2 S.C.R.):

> Here the police authority has flagrantly violated a Charter right without any statutory authority for so doing. Such an overt violation as occurred here must, in my view, result

in the rejection of the evidence thereby obtained. ... To do otherwise than reject this
evidence on the facts and circumstances in this appeal would be to invite police officers
to disregard Charter rights of the citizens and to do so with an assurance of impunity.

As Estey J. went on to point out, such action on the part of the police in blatantly
violating the right to counsel must result in the inadmissibility of evidence thereby
directly obtained, otherwise s. 10(b) would cease to have any meaningful content
whatsoever. Accordingly, allowing the appellant's confession to be admitted into evidence would necessarily "bring the administration of justice into disrepute." Whatever the scope of the s. 24(2) test for admissibility of evidence obtained in violation
of the Charter, the flagrant exploitation by the police of the fact that to their knowledge the appellant was in no condition to insist on her rights has to be the kind of
violation that gives rise to the exclusionary remedy. The decision of the trial judge to
exclude this evidence was therefore correct and the jury verdict, based as it was solely
on evidence admissible at trial, must be restored.

I would accordingly allow the appeal, set aside the order of the New Brunswick
Court of Appeal and restore the verdict of acquittal rendered by the jury.


McINTYRE J.:  I have read the reasons for judgment of my colleague, Wilson J. ...

I am in agreement with the result she has reached. I do not find it necessary to
consider the Charter in reaching this conclusion. In my view, the two tests described
above overlap. A non-operative mind would not only be unaware of its utterances but
also of the consequences of those utterances. It would be for either of these reasons
that those utterances would be inadmissible. Thus, if the mind operated sufficiently
to make a conscious statement but could not have the knowledge of the consequences
of making the statement, the evidence should as well be excluded.

The two tests in reality collapse into one when approached in the manner chosen
by the trial judge where he said:

> Was the accused so intoxicated that the words she uttered were not her statement in the
> sense that she did not comprehend her statement and was not capable of making a
> rational judgment as to whether she ought, under the circumstances, to answer ques-
> tions, the answers to which would ultimately be used at her trial on a charge of murder?

There is no real difference between the two tests and under either the result in this
case would be the exclusion of the evidence.

The test to be applied then in determining whether a statement made to a police
officer or other person in authority by an accused person may be rendered inadmissible because of intoxication of the accused involves two questions:

1. Was the accused aware of what she was saying? and

2. Was she aware of the consequences of making the statement on the particular
   occasion in question?

To be aware of the consequences in this context simply means to be capable of understanding that her statement could be used in evidence in proceedings to be taken against her. There is no novelty in this approach. It is consistent with the familiar and customary warning derived from the English judges' rules which was to the effect that "you may remain silent but anything you say will be taken down in writing and may be given in evidence." This warning was designed to ensure knowledge of the consequences of the statement, that is, its possible use in proceedings against the accused. It must be observed that common sense would dictate that a very high degree of intoxication would be required to render such a statement inadmissible.

The trial judge found that, because of drunkenness, the appellant lacked the knowledge of the consequences of making the statement and he excluded the statement. I would not disturb this finding, and would accordingly allow the appeal.

[Estey, Lamer, Le Dain, and La Forest JJ. concurred with Wilson J. in allowing the appeal and restoring the verdict of acquittal. Chouinard J. joined the concurring opinion of McIntyre J.]

*Appeal allowed.*

### R. v. Manninen
Supreme Court of Canada
(1987), 34 C.C.C. (3d) 385

LAMER J.: On October 26, 1982, there was a robbery at a Mac's Milk store in Toronto …

On October 28th, two days after the robbery, police officers MacIver and Train, acting on information received, attended at E & R Simonizing on Caledonia Rd. in Toronto at around 1:30 p.m. Both officers were in plain clothes. At approximately 2:33 p.m., the respondent drove up to the premises in a car which answered the description of the stolen car used in the armed robbery.

The respondent left the car and proceeded to the office premises where Train was waiting. MacIver, who had been waiting in the parking-lot, investigated the car. He saw a gun butt protruding from under the driver's seat. He put the gun into his hip pocket, and he then followed the respondent into the office. When the respondent entered the office, Train greeted him with "Hi Ron." The respondent asked "Do I know you?" At that stage both officers identified themselves as police officers and showed the respondent their badges. They searched and handcuffed the respondent.

At 2:40 p.m. Train arrested the respondent for theft and possession of the stolen car and for the armed robbery of the Mac's Milk store. He read him his rights from a card which was issued to all police officers when the Charter was proclaimed. The card from which the constable read stated as follows:

**Charter of Rights**

1. Notice Upon Arrest

   I am arresting you for _____ (briefly describe reasons for arrest).

2. Right to Counsel

   It is my duty to inform you that you have the right to retain and instruct counsel without delay.

   Do you understand?

   Caution to Charged Person

   You (are charged, will be charged) with _____. Do you wish to say anything in answer to the charge? You are not obliged to say anything unless you wish to do so, but whatever you say may be given in evidence.

   Secondary Caution to Charged Person

   If you have spoken to any police officer or to anyone with authority or if any such person has spoken to you in connection with this case, I want it clearly understood that I do not want it to influence you in making any statement.

The respondent made a flippant remark at the reading of the caution and the right to counsel to the effect that "it sounds like an American T.V. programme." Train reread the whole card to the respondent and, at that time, the respondent said: "Prove it. I ain't saying anything until I see my lawyer. I want to see my lawyer."

MacIver then questioned the respondent as follows:

Q. What is your full name?

A. Ronald Charles Manninen.

Q. Where is your address?

A. Ain't got one.

Q. Where is the knife that you had along with this (showing the respondent the $CO_2$ gun found in the car) when you ripped of the Mac's Milk on Wilson Avenue?

A. He's lying. When I was in the store I only had the gun. The knife was in the tool box in the car.

This last answer was relied on by the trial judge in convicting the respondent on the charge of armed robbery. ...

There was an operating telephone in the small office where the respondent was arrested and the police officers used it in the course of the afternoon. The respondent did not make a direct request to use the telephone and the police officers did not volunteer the use of the telephone to the respondent. The trial judge made the following finding: "I find the police had no desire to have him call a lawyer, and intended to call a lawyer back at the station when the arrest was completed. The respondent did not speak to his lawyer until the lawyer called him at the police station at 8:35 p.m. ...

*Violation of the Right to Counsel*

Section 10(b) of the Charter provides:

> 10.  Everyone has the right on arrest or detention
>    (b)  to retain and instruct counsel without delay and to be informed of that right ...

It is not disputed that the respondent was informed of his right to retain and instruct counsel without delay. Further, the sufficiency of the communication is not challenged. ...

In my view, s. 10(b) imposes at least two duties on the police in addition to the duty to inform the detainee of his rights. First, the police must provide the detainee with a reasonable opportunity to exercise the right to retain and instruct counsel without delay. The detainee is in the control of the police and he cannot exercise his right to counsel unless the police provide him with a reasonable opportunity to do so. ...

In my view, this aspect of the right to counsel was clearly infringed in this case. The respondent clearly asserted his right to remain silent and his desire to consult his lawyer. There was a telephone immediately at hand in the office, which the officers used for their own purposes. It was not necessary for the respondent to make an express request to use the telephone. The duty to facilitate contact with counsel included the duty to offer the respondent the use of the telephone. Of course, there may be circumstances in which it is particularly urgent that the police continue with an investigation before it is possible to facilitate a detainee's communication with counsel. There was no urgency in the circumstances surrounding the offences in this case.

Further, s. 10(b) imposes on the police the duty to cease questioning or otherwise attempting to elicit evidence from the detainee until he has had a reasonable opportunity to retain and instruct counsel. The purpose of the right to counsel is to allow the detainee not only to be informed of his rights and obligations under the law but, equally if not more important, to obtain advice as to how to exercise those rights. In this case, the police officers correctly informed the respondent of his right to remain silent and the main function of counsel would be to confirm the existence of that right and then to advise him as to how to exercise it. For the right to counsel to be effective, the detainee must have access to this advice before he is questioned or otherwise required to provide evidence.

This aspect of the respondent's right to counsel was clearly infringed in the circumstances of this case. Immediately after the respondent's clear assertion of his right to remain silent and his desire to consult his lawyer, the police officer commenced his questioning as if the respondent had expressed no such desire. Again, there may be circumstances in which it is particularly urgent that the police proceed with their questioning of the detainee before providing him with a reasonable opportunity to retain and instruct counsel, but there was no such urgency in this case.

The Crown contends that there was no infringement of the right to counsel because the respondent had waived his right by answering the police officer's questions. While a person may implicitly waive his rights under s. 10(b), the standard will be very high (*Clarkson*, *supra*, at pp. 217-8 C.C.C., pp. 504-5 D.L.R., pp. 394-5 S.C.R.). In my view, the respondent's conduct did not constitute an implied waiver of his right to counsel. It seems that he did not intend to waive his right, as he clearly asserted it at the beginning and at the end of the questioning. Rather, the form of the questioning was such as to elicit involuntary answers. The police officer asked two innocuous questions followed by a baiting question which led the respondent to incriminate himself. In addition, where a detainee has positively asserted his desire to exercise his right to counsel and the police have ignored his request and have proceeded to question him, he is likely to feel that his right has no effect and that he must answer. Finally, the respondent had the right not to be asked questions, and he must not be held to have implicitly waived that right simply because he answered the questions. Otherwise, the right not to be asked questions would only exist where the detainee refused to answer and thus where there is no need for any remedy or exclusionary rule.

For these reasons, I would conclude that the respondent's rights under s. 10(b) were infringed.

### Bringing the Administration of Justice into Disrepute

The first point that must be made is that the violation of the respondent's rights to counsel was very serious. The respondent clearly asserted his right to remain silent and to consult his lawyer. There was a telephone at hand. There was no urgency which would justify the immediate questioning or the denial of the opportunity to contact his lawyer. In effect, the police officers simply ignored the rights they had read to him and his assertion of the right to silence and the right to counsel. The Ontario Court of Appeal characterized this violation as "wilful and deliberate" and as an "open and flagrant disregard of the [respondent's] rights," and I fully agree.

Further, the evidence obtained was self-incriminatory. As I stated in *Collins* (1987), 33 C.C.C. (3d) 1, *supra*, the use of self-incriminatory evidence obtained following a denial of the right to counsel will generally go to the very fairness of the trial and thus, will generally bring the administration of justice into disrepute.

It is true that the offence was a serious one and that the respondent's guilt is clearly established by the statement sought to be excluded, but that cannot justify the admission of the evidence in light of the seriousness of the violation and the effect of the evidence on the fairness of the trial.

[The statement had been admitted at trial and the accused was convicted. The Supreme Court affirmed the Ontario Court of Appeal's decision to quash the conviction, exclude the statement and order a new trial. Dickson C.J.C., Beetz, McIntyre, Wilson, Le Dain and La Forest JJ. concurred with Lamer J.]

**R. v. Brydges**
Supreme Court of Canada
(1990), 53 C.C.C. (3d) 330

[The accused, a resident of Edmonton, was arrested in Strathclair, Manitoba on a charge of second degree murder and advised of his right to retain and instruct counsel without delay. When taken to Brandon for interrogation he asked a detective if "they have any free Legal Aid or anything like that up here" and stated "won't be able to afford anyone, heh? That's the main thing." The detective asked if there was a reason for wanting to talk to a lawyer and the accused replied "not right now no." The accused proceeded to answer questions and gave prejudicial statements until he eventually asked to see a lawyer and was provided with one.

The trial judge found that the accused was requesting counsel when he inquired about Legal Aid and excluded subsequent statements made to the police under s. 24(2) of the Charter. As a result the accused was acquitted. The Alberta Court of Appeal reversed and held that the accused had "elected to go it alone. ..."]

LAMER J.: A detainee may, either explicitly or implicitly, waive his right to retain and instruct counsel, although the standard will be very high where the alleged waiver is implicit. A majority of this Court in *Clarkson*, *supra*, concluded as follows in respect of a waiver of the right to counsel at pp. 394-95, a passage that has been cited with approval in subsequent cases dealing with s. 10(b):

> ... it is evident that any alleged waiver of this right by an accused must be carefully considered and that the accused's awareness of the consequences of what he or she is saying is crucial. Indeed, this Court stated with respect to the waiver of statutory procedural guarantees in *Korponey v. Attorney General of Canada*, [1982] 1 S.C.R. 41, at p. 49, that any waiver: "... is dependent upon it being *clear and unequivocal that the person is waiving the procedural safeguard and is doing so with full knowledge of the rights the procedure was enacted to protect and of the effect the waiver will have on those rights in the process.*" [Emphasis in original.]

... the appellant specifically stated that "the main thing" was that he was unable to afford counsel. The trial judge found that this amounted to a request for counsel. The appellant, however, was left with the mistaken impression that his inability to afford a lawyer prevented him from exercising his right to counsel. I agree with Harradence J.A. in dissent that in this context the appellant did not understand the full meaning of his right to counsel. In this respect, it can hardly be said that the appellant was in a position to carefully consider the consequences of waiving that which he did not understand. I am therefore of the view that the appellant, given the standard for waiver set out by this Court in *Clarkson* and in subsequent cases, did not waive his right to retain and instruct counsel. ...

The failure of the police to inform the appellant of the existence of Legal Aid or duty counsel at the time that he first indicated a concern about his ability to pay a lawyer, was a restriction on the appellant's right to counsel, insofar as the appellant was left with an erroneous impression of the nature and extent of his s. 10(b) rights.

As a result, I would conclude, along with the trial judge and Harradence J.A. in dissent at the Court of Appeal, that the appellant's s. 10(b) rights were violated. ...

... As regards the test set out to determine whether the admission of the evidence obtained in violation of the *Charter* would bring the administration of justice into disrepute, I note the following. First, the nature of the evidence obtained was conscripted or self-incriminatory evidence whose admission would normally render a trial unfair. The fairness of the trial would be adversely affected since, in the words of Wilson J. in *R. v. Black*, [1989] 2 S.C.R. 138, at p. 160, "the admission of the statement would infringe on the appellant's right against self-incrimination, a right which could have been protected had the appellant had an opportunity to consult counsel." Second, in terms of the seriousness of the violation, although it cannot be said that the conduct of the officer was flagrant or blatant, it was a serious error not to inform the appellant of the existence of Legal Aid or duty counsel especially when the appellant explicitly raised the issue, and in light of the fact that such information was readily at hand. Finally, in balancing the admission of the evidence against the exclusion of the evidence, I note that the Crown concedes that the statements at most represent evidence of consciousness of guilt and admissions of recent possession of property stolen from the home of the victim. In addition, this Court has repeatedly held that the mere fact that an accused is charged with a serious offence provides no justification for admitting the evidence where there has been a serious *Charter* violation and the admission of the evidence would affect the fundamental fairness of the trial: see *Black*, *supra*, at p. 160, and also *Manninen*, *supra*, at p. 1246. I would conclude, therefore, that the evidence obtained as a result of the s. 10(b) violation was properly excluded by the trial judge.

... the view that the right to retain and instruct counsel, in modern Canadian society, has come to mean more than the right to retain a lawyer privately. It now also means the right to have access to counsel free of charge where the accused meets certain financial criteria set up by the provincial Legal Aid plan, and the right to have access to immediate, although temporary, advice from duty counsel irrespective of financial status. These considerations, therefore, lead me to the conclusion that as part of the information component of s. 10(b) of the *Charter*, a detainee should be informed of the existence and availability of the applicable systems of duty counsel and Legal Aid in the jurisdiction, in order to give the detainee a full understanding of the right to retain and instruct counsel.

[Lamer J. concluded that a transition period of 30 days from the delivery of the judgment was "sufficient time for the police forces to react, and to prepare new cautions."

Lamer J. allowed the appeal and restored the acquittal. Wilson, Gonthier, and Cory JJ. concurred with Lamer J.; La Forest J. (L'Heureux-Dubé and McLachlin JJ. concurring) agreed with Lamer J. on the facts of the case, allowing the appeal and restoring the acquittal. They, however, found it "unnecessary to consider the broader issues raised by [Lamer J.] in the latter part of his reasons."]

---

After the Supreme Court's decision in *Brydges*, Ontario set up a toll-free 1-800 number so that arrested and detained people throughout the province could at all hours contact a duty counsel paid by legal aid. Nova Scotia did not.

## R. v. Prosper
Supreme Court of Canada
(1994), 92 C.C.C. (3d) 353

[The accused was arrested in Nova Scotia on a Saturday afternoon for drunk driving and advised of his right to counsel and his right to apply to legal aid. He was given a list of legal aid lawyers and made 15 calls but was unsuccessful in reaching a lawyer, in part because the legal aid lawyers had decided not to take calls outside regular working hours. Then, after informing the police officer that he could not afford a private lawyer, the accused provided a breath sample over the legal limit.]

LAMER C.J.C. (Sopinka, Cory, Iacobucci, and Major JJ. concurring): In *Brydges*, the issue of whether s. 10(b) imposes, either alone or in conjunction with other provisions of the Charter, a positive obligation on governments to ensure that duty counsel is available to detainees did not arise for consideration ...

In sum, then, I am satisfied that various systems of duty counsel are widely available to detainees in this country and that they need not be costly to set up and maintain. As well, I would note that an effective duty counsel service does not have to be an elaborate one. For instance, it need not consist of anything more than a basic service accessed by dialling a 1-800 (toll-free) number which provides free preliminary advice over the telephone, or the police providing up-to-date lists of lawyers, either from Legal Aid offices or from the private bar, who are prepared to serve as duty counsel at specific times: *e.g.*, once the local Legal Aid office closes down for the day or the weekend ...

I am of the view that it is neither appropriate nor necessary for this court to find that s. 10(b) of the Charter imposes on governments a substantive obligation to ensure that "*Brydges* duty counsel" is available to detainees, or likewise, that it provides all detainees with a corresponding right to such counsel. Several factors lead me to this conclusion ...

In light of the language of s. 10 of the Charter, which on its face does not guarantee any substantive right to legal advice, and the legislative history of s. 10, which reveals that the framers of the Charter decided not to incorporate into s. 10 even a relatively limited substantive right to legal assistance (*i.e.*, for those "without sufficient means" and "if the interests of justice so require"), it would be a very big step for this court to interpret the Charter in a manner which imposes a positive *constitutional* obligation on governments. The fact that such an obligation would almost certainly interfere with governments' allocation of limited resources by requiring them to expend public funds on the provision of a service is, I might add, a further consideration which weighs against this interpretation.

Secondly, if this court were to hold that there is, under the Charter, an obligation on governments to make available "*Brydges* duty counsel" to all detainees, and that any provincial or territorial government (the level of government in charge of the administration of legal aid and duty counsel services) which fails to do so violates the s. 10(b) rights of detainees, the implications would be far-reaching. In effect, this court would be saying that in order to have the power of arrest and detention, a province must have a duty counsel system in place. In provinces and territories where no duty counsel system exists, the logical implication would be that all arrests and detentions are *prima facie* unconstitutional. Moreover, devising an appropriate remedy under circumstances in which a government was found to be in breach of its constitutional obligation for failure to provide duty counsel would prove very difficult. Unless absolutely necessary to protect the Charter rights of individuals, I believe that a holding with implications of this magnitude should be avoided.

Fortunately, there is an alternative solution which avoids the problems and complications associated with finding that s. 10(b) imposes a substantive constitutional obligation on governments to make available "*Brydges* duty counsel" to all detainees, and which sufficiently protects the Charter rights and freedoms of detainees. This alternative, which I shall refer to as the obligation on police to "hold off" until a detainee has been given a reasonable opportunity to contact counsel, is fully consistent with the existing s. 10(b) jurisprudence of this court. While this alternative may not be ideal from the Crown's perspective, and especially in terms of concerns it may have for administrative and evidentiary expediency, this is a trade-off that governments which persist in refusing to implement a "*Brydges* duty counsel" system, for whatever reason, will have to endure and accept …

Once a detainee has indicated a desire to exercise his or her right to counsel, the state is required to provide him or her with a reasonable opportunity in which to do so. In addition, state agents must refrain from eliciting incriminatory evidence from the detainee until he or she has had a reasonable opportunity to reach counsel. As the majority indicated in *R. v. Ross* (1989), 46 C.C.C. (3d) 129 at p. 136 (S.C.C.), once a detainee asserts his or her right to counsel, the police cannot in any way compel him or her to make a decision or participate in a process which could ultimately have an adverse effect in the conduct of an eventual trial until that person has had a reasonable opportunity to exercise that right. In other words, the police are obliged to "hold off" from attempting to elicit incriminatory evidence from the detainee until he or she has had a reasonable opportunity to reach counsel …

In a situation such as the one in this case, where duty counsel services are available during regular office hours (although only to those eligible for legal aid) and a detainee expresses a desire to contact counsel and is duly diligent in exercising that right, but is prevented from doing so due to institutional factors beyond his or her control, s. 10(b) requires that the police hold off from trying to elicit incriminatory evidence from the detainee until he or she has had a reasonable opportunity to reach counsel. Similarly, the "reasonable opportunity" provided to detainees in jurisdictions lacking duty counsel might extend to when the local Legal Aid office opens, when a private lawyer willing to provide free summary advice can be reached, or when the detainee is brought before a justice of the peace for bail purposes and his or her needs can be properly assessed and accommodated. In determining what is a reasonable opportunity, the fact that the evidence may cease to be available as a result of a long delay is a factor to be considered.

[On the facts of the case, Lamer C.J.C. held the police must hold off even if this meant losing the benefit of the presumption in s. 258(1)(c)(iii) of the *Criminal Code*.]

A detainee's Charter-guaranteed right to counsel must take precedence over the statutory right afforded to the Crown which allows it to rely on an evidentiary presumption about what a breathalyzer reading would have been at the time of care and control of a vehicle. Loss of the benefit of this presumption is simply one of the prices which has to be paid by governments which refuse to ensure that a system of "*Brydges* duty counsel" is available to give detainees free, preliminary legal advice on an on-call, 24-hour basis ...

In my view, among the five s. 10(b) appeals heard together by this court, the facts of this case present the most compelling basis for exclusion of evidence under s. 24(2). The breath samples were conscripted evidence which might not have been obtained had the appellant's s. 10(b) rights not been infringed. In other words, the breach of the appellant's right to counsel goes directly to his privilege against self-incrimination, and receipt of the breathalyzer evidence resulting from this breach would undermine this privilege, thereby rendering the trial process unfair. Neither the undeniable good faith of the police, nor the relative seriousness of the drinking and driving offence with which the appellant was charged can compensate for the adjudicative unfairness which I find admission of the evidence would produce.

To conclude, I am fully satisfied that admission of the evidence in this case would adversely affect the fairness of the trial and bring the administration of justice into disrepute. The evidence was obtained by conscripting the appellant against himself and infringing his right against self-incrimination, a right which might have been protected had he been provided with a reasonable opportunity to consult a Legal Aid lawyer.

L'HEUREUX-DUBÉ J. (La Forest and Gonthier JJ. concurring): ... [T]he Chief Justice's "hold off" proposal effectively rings the death knell of the breathalyzer as a device to help take drunk drivers off the roads in provinces that do not have 24-hour duty counsel service programs or their equivalent. If police have to "hold off" from requiring detainees to take breathalyzer tests in such provinces, one can foresee that drivers, from 5 p.m. to 9 a.m. on weekdays and on weekends, would be free to drink and drive at leisure, with the inevitable consequences of deaths and serious injuries on the roads (a carnage that the breathalyzer device was designed to reduce substantially), all on the premise that they did not have access to 24-hour duty counsel, which, as I have already noted, is not even required by s. 10(b) of the Charter. In my view, the Charter was not enacted to produce such an aberrant result. To suggest that provinces which do not provide services which they are not constitutionally required to provide will be penalized in their means of promoting safety on their roads is to me unacceptable.

*Appeal allowed; acquittal restored.*

---

In the companion Ontario case of *R. v. Bartle* (1994), 92 C.C.C. (3d) 289 (S.C.C.), the accused was arrested for drunk driving and informed of his right to counsel and the availability of legal aid, but not the toll-free 1-800 number that Ontario had established shortly after the court's decision in *Brydges*. The Supreme Court held that Bartle's s. 10(b) rights had been violated and excluded the breathalyzer sample under s. 24(2) of the Charter.

---

Based on the above cases, to what extent does Canada have a constitutional standard equivalent to that in *Miranda v. Arizona*, 384 U.S. 436 (1966). In *Miranda*, Chief Justice Warren stated:

> Our holding will be spelled out with some specificity in the pages which follow but briefly stated it is this: the prosecution many not use statements, whether exculpatory or inculpatory, stemming from custodial interrogation of the defendant unless it demonstrates the use of procedural safeguards effective to secure the privilege against self-incrimination. By custodial interrogation, we mean questioning initiated by law enforcement officers after a person has been taken into custody or otherwise deprived of his freedom of action in any significant way. As for the procedural safeguards to be employed, unless other fully effective means are devised to inform accused persons of their right of silence and to assure a continuous opportunity to exercise it, the following measures are required. Prior to any questioning, the person must be warned that he has a right to remain silent, that any statement he does make may be used as evidence against him, and that he has a right to the presence of an attorney, either retained or appointed. The defendant may waive effectuation of these rights, provided the waiver is made voluntarily, knowingly and intelligently. If, however, he indicates in any manner and at any stage of the process that he wishes to consult with an attorney before speaking there can be no questioning. Likewise, if the individual is alone and indicates in any manner that he does not wish to be interrogated, the police may not question him. The mere fact that he may have answered some questions or volunteered some statements on his own does not deprive him of the right to refrain from answering any further inquiries until he has consulted with an attorney and thereafter consents to be questioned.

> The constitutional issue we decide in each of these cases is the admissibility of statements obtained from a defendant questioned while in custody or otherwise deprived of his freedom of action in any significant way. In each, the defendant was questioned by police officers, detectives, or a prosecuting attorney in a room in which he was cut off from the outside world. In none of these cases was the defendant given a full and effective warning of his rights at the outset of the interrogation process. In all the cases, the questioning elicited oral admissions, and in three of them, signed statements as well were admitted at their trials. They all thus share salient features—incommunicado interrogation of individuals in a police-dominated atmosphere, resulting in self-incriminating statements without full warnings of constitutional rights.

> In these cases, we might not find the defendants' statements to have been involuntary in traditional terms. Our concern for adequate safeguards to protect precious Fifth Amendment rights is, of course, not lessened in the slightest. In each of the cases, the defendant was thrust into an unfamiliar atmosphere and run through menacing police interrogation procedures. The potentiality for compulsion is forcefully apparent, for example, in *Miranda*, where the indigent Mexican defendant was a seriously disturbed individual with pronounced sexual fantasies, and in *Stewart*, in which the defendant was an indigent Los Angeles Negro who had dropped out of school in the sixth grade. To be sure, the records do not evince overt physical coercion or patent psychological ploys. The fact remains that in none of these cases did the officers undertake to afford appropriate safeguards at the outset of the interrogation to insure that the statements were truly the product of free choice.

> It is obvious that such an interrogation environment is created for no purpose other than to subjugate the individual to the will of his examiner. This atmosphere carries its own

badge of intimidation. To be sure, this is not physical intimidation, but it is equally destructive of human dignity. The current practice of incommunicado interrogation is at odds with one of our Nation's most cherished principles—that the individual may not be compelled to incriminate himself. Unless adequate protective devices are employed to dispel the compulsion inherent in custodial surroundings, no statement obtained from the defendant can truly be the product of his free choice.

---

See K. Roach and M.L. Friedland, "Borderline Justice: Policing in the Two Niagaras" (1996), 23 *Am J. of Crim. L.* 241; D. Paciocco, "The Development of Miranda-Like Doctrines Under the Charter" (1987), 19 *Ottawa L. Rev.* 49; Paciocco, "More on Recent *Miranda* Developments Under Subsection 10(b) of the Charter" (1987), 19 *Ottawa L. Rev.* 573; Paciocco, "The Judicial Repeal of s. 24(2) and the Development of the Canadian Exclusionary Rule" (1990), 32 *Crim. L.Q.* 326; R. Harvie and H. Foster, "Different Drummers, Different Drums: The Supreme Court of Canada, American Jurisprudence and the Continuing Revision of Criminal Law under the Charter" (1992), 24 *Ottawa L. Rev.* 39; H. Foster and R. Harvie, "Ties that Bind?: The Supreme Court of Canada, American Jurisprudence and the Revision of Canadian Criminal Law under the Charter" (1990), 28 *Osgoode Hall L.J.* 729; D. McDonald, *Legal Rights in the Canadian Charter of Rights and Freedoms*, 2nd ed. (Toronto: Carswell, 1989) chapter 9, 28; L. Baker, *Miranda: Crime, Law and Politics* (New York: Antheneum, 1983); R. Ericson and P. Baranek, *The Ordering of Justice* (Toronto: U. of T. Press, 1982) chapter 2; E. Ratushny, *Self-Incrimination in the Canadian Criminal Process* (Toronto: Carswell, 1979); K. Moore, "Police Implementation of Charter Decisions: An Empirical Study" (1992), 30 *Osgoode Hall L.J.* 547.

## III. ENTRAPMENT

Entrapment issues generally arise in the investigation of certain types of crime which require the police to participate in some way in the crime. In *Kirzner v. The Queen*, [1978] 2 S.C.R. 487, Chief Justice Laskin stated that entrapment issues often arose in the area of the investigation of "consensual crimes." He stated:

> Methods of detection of offences and of suspected offences and offenders necessarily differ according to the class of crime. Where, for example, violence or breaking, entering and theft are concerned, there will generally be external evidence of an offence upon which the police can act in tracking down the offenders; the victim or his family or the property owner, as the case may be, may be expected to call in the police and provide some clues for the police to pursue. When "consensual" crimes are committed, involving willing persons, as is the case in prostitution, illegal gambling and drug offences, ordinary methods of detection will not generally do. The participants, be they deemed victims or not, do not usually complain or seek police aid; that is what they wish to avoid. The police, if they are to respond to the public disapprobation of such offences as reflected in existing law, must take some initiatives.
>
> They may, for example, use a spy, either a policeman or another person, to obtain information about a consensual offence by infiltration; they may make arrangements with

informers who may be parties to offences on which they report to the police to enable the other parties to be apprehended; or the police may use decoys or themselves act under cover to provide others with the opportunity to commit a consensual offence or to encourage its commission. Going one step farther, the police may use members of their force or other persons to instigate the commission of an offence, planning and designing it *ab initio* to ensnare others.

In *R. v. Mack*, [1988] 2 S.C.R. 903, Justice Lamer adopted the above and added:

I would note that in addition to so-called "victimless" or "consensual" crimes, active law enforcement techniques may be used to combat crimes where there are victims, but those victims are reluctant to go to the police because of intimidation or blackmail, as may be the case with the offence of extortion. Further, some criminal conduct may go unobserved for a long time if the victims are not immediately aware of the fact that they have been the subject of criminal activity, in the case, for example, of commercial fraud and also bribery of public officials. In general it may be said that many crimes are committed in secret and it is difficult to obtain evidence of their commission after the fact.

---

What is an appropriate test for entrapment? How is this related to the purposes the doctrine is meant to serve?

The proposed American Law Institute test is as follows:

Section 2.13. Entrapment.

(1) A public law enforcement official or a person acting in cooperation with such an official perpetrates an entrapment if for the purpose of obtaining evidence of the commission of an offense, he induces or encourages another person to engage in conduct constituting such offense by either:

(a) making knowingly false representations designed to induce the belief that such conduct is not prohibited: or

(b) employing methods of persuasion or inducement which create a substantial risk that such an offense will be committed by persons other than those who are ready to commit it.

(2) Except as provided in Subsection (3) of this Section, a person prosecuted for an offense shall be acquitted if he proves by a preponderance of evidence that his conduct occurred in response to an entrapment. This issue of entrapment shall be tried by the Court in the absence of the jury.

(3) The defense afforded by this Section is unavailable when causing or threatening bodily injury is an element of the offense charged and the prosecution is based on conduct causing or threatening such injury to a person other than the person perpetrating the entrapment.

Compare the *Ouimet Report* (1969) at pp. 79-80:

For the reasons previously stated, the Committee recommends the enactment of legislation to provide:

1. That a person is not guilty of an offence if his conduct is instigated by a law enforcement officer or agent of a law enforcement officer, for the purpose of obtaining evidence for the prosecution of such person, if such person did not have a pre-existing intention to commit the offence.

2. Conduct amounting to an offence shall be deemed not to have been instigated where the defendant had a pre-existing intention to commit the offence when the opportunity arose and the conduct which is alleged to have induced the defendant to commit the offence did not go beyond affording him an opportunity to commit it.

3. The defence that the offence has been instigated by a law enforcement officer or his agent should not apply to the commission of those offences which involve the infliction of bodily harm or which endanger life.

Compare Commission of Inquiry Concerning Certain Activities of the Royal Canadian Mounted Police *Freedom and Security Under the Law* (1981) at p. 1053:

> WE RECOMMEND THAT the Criminal Code be amended to include a defence of entrapment embodying the following principle:
>
> > The accused should be acquitted if it is established that the conduct of a member or agent of a police force in instigating the crime has gone substantially beyond what is justifiable having regard to all the circumstances, including the nature of the crime, whether the accused had a pre-existing intent, and the nature and extent of the involvement of the police.

---

What should the remedy for entrapment be? In *R. v. Jewitt*, [1985] 2 S.C.R. 128, a stay of proceedings was entered at trial because of entrapment on a charge of trafficking in narcotics. A majority of the British Columbia Court of Appeal held that a stay was not the equivalent of an acquittal and so no appeal by the Crown was possible.

The Supreme Court of Canada reversed, holding that the Crown was entitled to appeal from a stay because the stay was the equivalent of an acquittal, at least for purposes of appeal. More importantly, the Court in a judgment delivered by Chief Justice Dickson affirmed the courts' inherent jurisdiction to issue a stay of proceedings to protect their own processes from abuse.

> ... It seems to me desirable and timely to end the uncertainty which surrounds the availability of a stay of proceedings to remedy abuse of process. Clearly, there is a need for this Court to clarify its position on such a fundamental and wide-reaching doctrine.
>
> Lord Devlin has expressed the rationale supporting the existence of a judicial discretion to enter a stay of proceedings to control prosecutorial behaviour prejudicial to accused persons in *Connelly v. Director of Public Prosecutions*, [1964] A.C. 1254 at p. 1354 (H.L.):
>
> > Are the courts to rely on the Executive to protect their process from abuse? Have they not themselves an inescapable duty to secure fair treatment for those who come or who are brought before them? To questions of this sort there is only one possible answer. The courts cannot contemplate for a moment the transference to the Executive of the responsibility for seeing that the process of law is not abused.

I would adopt the conclusion of the Ontario Court of Appeal in *R. v. Young* (1984), 40 C.R. (3d) 289, and affirm that [p. 31]:

> ... there is a residual discretion in a trial court judge to stay proceedings where compelling an accused to stand trial would violate those fundamental principles of justice which underlie the community's sense of fair play and decency and to prevent the abuse of a court's process through oppressive or vexatious proceedings.

I would also adopt the caveat added by the court in *Young* that this is a power which can be exercised only in the "clearest of cases." ...

The court did not deal with the entrapment issues, sending the case back to the Court of Appeal to hear the Crown's appeal on the merits.

## Amato v. The Queen
Supreme Court of Canada
(1982), 69 C.C.C. (2d) 31

[A paid police informer repeatedly asked Amato to supply him with a small amount of cocaine. After numerous phone calls and visits, Amato supplied the informer with a small amount of cocaine. The informer continued to call Amato. Amato then supplied the informer with a half ounce of cocaine and at this time Amato was introduced to an undercover R.C.M.P. officer who made subsequent phone calls to Amato asking him to get more cocaine. At one point the undercover officer told Amato not to be frightened because the officer had experience with guns, that he "did not screw around" and that he needed cocaine "to answer to these people, if not these people will be coming to see you in the morning." The next day Amato participated in a sale of 2½ ounces of cocaine and was charged and convicted of trafficking in narcotics. The British Columbia Court of Appeal affirmed his conviction and he appealed to the Supreme Court of Canada.]

DICKSON J. (Martland, Beetz, and Chouinard JJ. concurring): ... the trial judge concluded:

> I am satisfied that the evidence in this case falls far short of the evidence required at law to establish the defence of entrapment. The evidence amounts no more than to persistent solicitation by the informer and the undercover officer to persuade the accused Amato to engage in trafficking in cocaine.

When the matter reached the Court of Appeal, Taggart J.A. referred to the passage from the judgment at trial which I have just quoted and said [51 C.C.C. (2d) 401 at p. 404, 12 C.R. (3d) 386]: "I am not persuaded that the evidence to which we have been referred by counsel for the appellant does other than support the conclusion reached by the trial Judge." Seaton J.A., in the course of his judgment, said [at p. 405]:

> In the case at bar the police are not blamed, it is the informer who it is said importuned the appellant. The police, according to counsel for the appellant, did not have any rea-

son to go after the appellant and were not after him. It seems to me to follow that they did not entrap him. What the appellant is saying is "I did commit the offence, I was importuned by another, and fortunately for me that other had some relationship with the police and as a result I should be found not guilty." I do not accept that. I think that entrapment as such is not a general defence.

Carrothers J.A. agreed with each Mr. Justice Taggart and Mr. Justice Seaton.

The four British Columbia judges before whom the matter has come have been unanimous in concluding that, on the facts, the defence of entrapment does not arise. It does not seem to me to fall to this court to retry the case and arrive at different findings.

I would therefore dismiss this appeal.

RITCHIE J. (concurring): As will hereafter appear the defence of entrapment has been recognized in a number of cases in the Supreme Court of the United States, but it is categorically denied by the courts in the United Kingdom as going to the guilt or innocence of the accused, although some consideration may be given to it in regard to sentence. This is made plain in the following passage from a judgment of Lord Chief Justice Widgery in *R. v. Mealey and Sheridan* (1974), 60 Cr. App. R. 59 at p. 62, where he says that it is

> … quite clearly established that the so-called defence of entrapment, which finds some place in the law of the United States of America, finds no place in our law here. It is abundantly clear on the authorities, which are uncontradicted on this point, that if a crime is brought about by the activities of someone who can be described as an agent provocateur, although that may be an important matter in regard to sentence, it does not affect the question of guilty or not guilty. …

In my view, it is only where police tactics are such as to leave no room for the formation of independent criminal intent by the accused that the question of entrapment can enter into the determination of his guilt or innocence. …

ESTEY J. dissenting (Laskin C.J., McIntyre, and Lamer JJ. concurring): If there be a defence of entrapment available to the accused in the circumstances of this appeal it cannot be of statutory origin for it is not to be found in the *Criminal Code*. If a defence arises in the common law it can only find its way into the courts through s. 7(3) of the Code [now s. 8(3)].

Applying the ordinary rule of construction where statutes and common law meet I conclude that s. 7(3) is the authority for the courts of criminal jurisdiction to adopt, if appropriate in the view of the court, defences including the defence of entrapment. The components of such a defence and the criteria for its application raise other issues.

Having found the way open for the development of defences not contrary to the provisions of the *Code* or other statutes of Canada, consideration must be given to the juristic nature of the doctrine of entrapment. While it is frequently referred to in legal writings and sometimes in the courts as the "defence of entrapment" it is not a defence in the traditional sense of that term. A successful defence leads to an acquittal on the charge, a determination that the offence has not been committed by the accused. Here, axiomatically, the crime from a physical point of view at least has been committed. Indeed, it may be that the necessary intent and act have been combined to form a complete crime. The successful application of the doctrine of entrapment, if it be a defence in the ordinary sense, would support an acquittal. The *Criminal Code* authorizes acquittals in somewhat similar circumstances as in the case of the defence of duress. However, as will be seen later, the successful application of the concept of entrapment leads to a stay of prosecution, the court withholding its processes from the prosecution on the basis that such would bring the administration of justice into disrepute. This is an exercise of the inherent powers of the courts.

Entrapment is not in a traditional sense a defence. For convenience and ease of reference as well as to conform to the present vocabulary of the law, I sometimes refer to the doctrine as the "defence of entrapment" although in strict law it is not a defence. Therefore, for this technical reason, it may not be necessary to invoke s. 7(3) other than to illustrate by analogy the continuing flexibility of the criminal law within and without the *Criminal Code*.

The availability of this defence in law and the proper constituent elements of the offence are closely entwined. Assuming the defence to be known to the common law and available in Canadian criminal law, in a proper case what are the component elements, the criteria to be met for its invocation? It is, of course, impossible to cast *in futuro* a set of guides, principles, rules or yardsticks with satisfactory precision and detail. This defence perhaps more than any other will succeed only in an unusual and delicately balanced set of circumstances. Case-law will have to paint in the variants. The principal elements or characteristics of the defence are that an offence must be instigated, originated or brought about by the police and the accused must be ensnared into the commission of that offence by the police conduct; the purpose of the scheme must be to gain evidence for the prosecution of the accused for the very crime which has been so instigated, and the inducement may be but is not limited to deceit, fraud, trickery or reward, and ordinarily but not necessarily will consist of calculated inveigling and persistent importuning. The character of the initiative taken by the police is unaffected by the fact that the law enforcement agency is represented by a member of a police force or an undercover or other agent, paid or unpaid, but operating under the control of the police. In the result, the scheme so perpetrated must in all the circumstances be so shocking and outrageous *as to bring the administration of justice into disrepute*.

At least one relevant circumstance in examining the character in law of the police conduct (such as persistent importuning) is whether the law enforcement agency had a reasonable suspicion that the accused would commit the offence without inducement. By itself and without more the predisposition in fact of the accused is not relevant to the availability of the defence. On the other hand, where the true purpose of the police initiative is to put the enforcement officers in a position to obtain evidence of an offence when committed, absent other circumstances already noted, the concept of entrapment does not arise.

… The overriding need in the field which we have been examining on this appeal is for a device in the criminal justice system which will not expose the community to the spectacle of a person being convicted of a crime, the commission of which in substance was the work of the State itself ...

... I would ... apply a stay of prosecution where the defence of entrapment is operative ... The stay of proceedings in the presence of entrapment finds its way into the law or fails to do so as a matter of judicial view of the proper policy of the law in these circumstances.

... I am of the view that it is open to this court and consistent with authority to recognize a defence of entrapment and to give effect to it in proper cases.

The conduct of the investigatory authority here in my view clearly gives rise to entrapment. In a period of two and one-half months the accused received 15 to 20 telephone calls, together with visits to the accused by the police or their agent at work or at home. These importunings were accompanied by successful efforts by the agent to gain the confidence and friendship of the accused. All this occurred after he had told the police informer that the accused could not be counted upon to provide the cocaine. In the second period of contact requests for drugs were made on a daily basis and accompanied by frequent visits by the undercover policeman at the accused's place of employment. In this second period there were also numerous urgent telephone calls requesting drugs, sometimes accompanied by implied threats of physical violence. That there was persistent inveigling and importuning is clear. It is also clear that the purpose of the programme initiated by the police was to obtain evidence for the prosecution of the accused. It is the plain fact that the drug trafficking which occurred was promoted by the police at a time when the police had no reason to suspect, let alone believe, that the accused was in any way related to such activity. The cumulative effect of such a deliberately launched enterprise by the police would in my view "in all the circumstances" be viewed in the community as shocking and outrageous, and such conduct is clearly contrary to the proper principles upon which justice must be done by the courts.

For all the reasons advanced and discussed above, I would recognize the defence of entrapment and would apply that defence to the facts and circumstances of this case; and therefore would allow the appeal, set aside the conviction and direct a stay of prosecution.

## R. v. Mack
Supreme Court of Canada
(1988), 44 C.C.C. (3d) 513

[The accused was a former drug user with several drug convictions. Over a 6 month period he was repeatedly asked by a police informer to supply drugs. The accused repeatedly said no, stating at one point he was interested only in real estate deals. On one occasion the informer took the accused into the woods to shoot a hand-gun and told the accused: "a person could get lost" in the woods. The accused interpreted this as a threat. On another occasion the informer took the accused to see a purchaser for the drugs (an undercover police officer) who showed the accused $50,000 in cash. The accused was arrested and charged with unlawful possession of narcotics for the purpose of trafficking when he delivered 12 ounces of cocaine (bought on credit for $27,000) to the informer.

He was convicted at trial with the trial judge refusing to enter a stay of proceedings because "it is far more probable that the accused became involved in this transaction for profit, rather than through persistent inducement or fear." The trial judge added that in fairness to the accused if the issue was that the Crown had to negate entrapment beyond a reasonable doubt the trial judge would have such a doubt. The British Columbia Court of Appeal confirmed the accused's conviction and he appealed to the Supreme Court of Canada.]

LAMER J.:  There is a crucial distinction, one which is not easy to draw, however, between the police or their agents—acting on reasonable suspicion or in the course of a bona fide inquiry—providing an opportunity to a person to commit a crime, and the state actually creating a crime for the purpose of prosecution. The former is completely acceptable as is police conduct that is directed only at obtaining evidence of an offence when committed: see *Amato*, *supra*, per Estey J., at p. 62 C.C.C., p. 446 S.C.R. The concern is rather with law enforcement techniques that involve conduct that the citizenry cannot tolerate. In many cases the particular facts may constitute a classic example of what may be referred to as "entrapment" which has been described by an American judge as "the conception and planning of an offense by an officer, and his procurement of its commission by one who would not have perpetrated it except for the trickery, persuasion, or fraud of the officer": *Sorrells v. United States*, 287 U.S. 435 at p. 454 (1932), per Roberts J. ...

### The Rationale

#### The Regulation of the Administration of Justice

It is critical in an analysis of the doctrine of entrapment to be very clear on the rationale for its recognition in Canadian criminal law. Much of what is contained in the opinion of Justice Estey in *Amato*, *supra*, provides this rationale. As was explained by Estey J., central to our judicial system is the belief that the integrity of the court must be maintained. This is a basic principle upon which many other principles and rules depend. If the court is unable to preserve its own dignity by upholding values that our society views as essential, we will not long have a legal system which can pride itself on its commitment to justice and truth and which commands the respect of the community it serves. It is a deeply ingrained value in our democratic system that the ends do not justify the means. In particular, evidence or convictions may, at times, be obtained at too high a price. This proposition explains why as a society we insist on respect for individual rights and procedural guarantees in the criminal justice system. All of these values are reflected in specific provisions of the Charter such as the right to counsel, the right to remain silent, the presumption of innocence and in the global concept of fundamental justice. Obviously, many of the rights in ss. 7 and 14 of the Charter relate to norms for the proper conduct of criminal investigations and trials, and the courts are called on to ensure that these standards are observed. ...

It is the belief that the administration of justice must be kept free from disrepute that compels recognition of the doctrine of entrapment. In the context of the Charter, this court has stated that disrepute may arise from "judicial condonation of unacceptable conduct by the investigatory and prosecutional agencies": *Collins v. The Queen* (1987), 33 C.C.C. (3d) 1 at pp. 16-7. ...

It must be stressed, however, that the central issue is not the power of a court to *discipline* police or prosecutorial conduct but, as stated by Estey J. in *Amato, supra* (at p. 73 C.C.C., p. 461 S.C.R.): "the avoidance of the improper invocation by the State of the judicial process and its powers." In the entrapment context, the court's sense of justice is offended by the spectacle of an accused being convicted of an offence which is the work of the state (*Amato, supra*, at p. 62 C.C.C., p. 447 S.C.R.). The court is, in effect, saying it cannot condone or be seen to lend a stamp of approval to behaviour which transcends what our society perceives to be acceptable on the part of the state. The stay of the prosecution of the accused is the manifestation of the court's disapproval of the state's conduct. The issuance of the stay obviously benefits the accused but the court is primarily concerned with a larger issue: the maintenance of the public confidence in the legal and judicial process. In this way, the benefit to the accused is really a derivative one. We should affirm the decision of Estey J., in *Amato, supra*, that *the basis upon which entrapment is recognized lies in the need to preserve the purity of administration of justice.*

### The Guilt of the Accused

It is not fruitful, in my view, to deal with impermissible police conduct through the vehicle of substantive criminal law doctrine. There are three problems with the appellant's proposition. First, the conduct of the police or their agents in most cases will not have the effect of negating *mens rea* or, for that matter, *actus reus*. There may be exceptional cases however; see, for example, the decision of this court in *Lemieux v. The Queen*, [1968] 1 C.C.C. 187, 63 D.L.R. (2d) 75, [1967] S.C.R. 492 (S.C.C.).

[In *Lemieux* a police informant solicited the accused to participate in a burglary. The police arranged with the owner of the house to let them have the key to the house. The Supreme Court quashed the burglary conviction on the grounds that no burglary had in fact been committed since the owner had consented to the break-in for the purpose of entrapping the accused.]

The physical act of the accused is a voluntary one and the accused will have an aware state of mind. The prohibited act will have been committed intentionally and with knowledge of the facts which constitute the offence and the consequences which flow from them. ...

... Secondly, the circumstances in which an accused is placed in an entrapment situation are not agonizing in the sense acknowledged by the defences of duress or necessity. Where the police conduct does amount to duress, that defence can be pleaded in conjunction with an abuse of process allegation. I would note, however, that any "threats" by the police, even if insufficient to support the defence of duress, will be highly relevant in the assessment of police conduct for the purpose of an abuse of process claim. The third reason why I am unwilling to view entrapment as relating to culpability is that if it did, there would not be a valid basis on which to limit the defence to entrapment by the state. The lack of support for an extension of the defence to provide against entrapment by private citizens demonstrates that the real problem is with the propriety of the *state* employing such law enforcement techniques for the purpose of obtaining convictions. If this is accepted, then it follows that the focus must be on the police conduct. ...

In conclusion, and to summarize, the proper approach to the doctrine of entrapment is that which was articulated by Estey J. in *Amato, supra*, and elaborated upon in these reasons. As mentioned and explained earlier there is entrapment when,

(a) the authorities provide a person with an opportunity to commit an offence without acting on a reasonable suspicion that this person is already engaged in criminal activity or pursuant to a *bona fide* inquiry;

(b) although having such a reasonable suspicion or acting in the course of a *bona fide* inquiry, they go beyond providing an opportunity and induce the commission of an offence.

It is neither useful nor wise to state in the abstract what elements are necessary to prove an entrapment allegation. It is, however, essential that the factors relied on by a court relate to the underlying reasons for the recognition of the doctrine in the first place.

Since I am of the view that the doctrine of entrapment is not dependent upon culpability, the focus should not be on the effect of the police conduct on the accused's state of mind. Instead, it is my opinion that as far as possible an objective assessment of the conduct of the police and their agents is required. The predisposition, or the past, present or suspected criminal activity of the accused, is relevant only as a part of the determination of whether the provision of an opportunity by the authorities to the accused to commit the offence was justifiable. Further, there must be sufficient connection between the past conduct of the accused and the provision of an opportunity, since otherwise the police suspicion will not be reasonable. While predisposition of the accused is, though not conclusive, of some relevance in assessing the initial approach by the police of a person with the offer of an opportunity to commit an offence, *it is never relevant* as regards whether they went beyond an offer, since that is to be assessed with regard to what the average non-predisposed person would have done.

The absence of a reasonable suspicion or a *bona fide* inquiry is significant in assessing the police conduct because of the risk that the police will attract people who would not otherwise have any involvement in a crime and because it is not a proper use of the police power to simply go out and test the virtue of people on a random basis. The presence of reasonable suspicion or the mere existence of a *bona fide* inquiry will, however, never justify entrapment techniques: the police may not go beyond providing an opportunity regardless of their perception of the accused's character and regardless of the existence of an honest inquiry. To determine whether the police have employed means which go further than providing an opportunity, it is useful to consider any or all of the following factors:

- the type of crime being investigated and the availability of other techniques for the police detection of its commission;
- whether an average person, with both strengths and weaknesses, in the position of the accused would be induced into the commission of a crime;
- the persistence and number of attempts made by the police before the accused agreed to committing the offence;
- the type of inducement used by the police including: deceit, fraud, trickery or reward;
- the timing of the police conduct, in particular whether the police have instigated the offence or became involved in ongoing criminal activity;
- whether the police conduct involves an exploitation of human characteristics such as the emotions of compassion, sympathy and friendship;
- whether the police appear to have exploited a particular vulnerability of a person such as a mental handicap or a substance addiction;
- the proportionality between the police involvement, as compared to the accused, including an assessment of the degree of harm caused or risked by the police, as compared to the accused, and the commission of any illegal acts by the police themselves;
- the existence of any threats, implied or express, made to the accused by the police or their agents;
- whether the police conduct is directed at undermining other constitutional values.

This list is not exhaustive, but I hope it contributes to the elaboration of a structure for the application of the entrapment doctrine. …

*Procedural Issues*

*Who Decides: Judge or Jury?*

Both the appellant and respondent agree that objective entrapment, involving police misconduct and not the accused's state of mind, is a question to be decided by the trial judge, and that the proper remedy is a stay of proceedings. I too am of this view. …

This court has held that the determination of whether the admission of evidence obtained in violation of a Charter right would bring the administration of justice into disrepute is one which should be made by a trial judge: *R. v. Therens* (1985), 18 C.C.C. (3d) 481 at p. 513, 18 D.L.R. (4th) 655, [1985] 1 S.C.R. 613 at p. 653, *per* Le Dain J. In articulating how a trial judge should engage him or herself in that analysis, I stated in *Collins, supra*, that a judge should consider the question from the perspective of a reasonable person, "dispassionate and fully apprised of [all] the circumstances," and I commented that "The reasonable person is usually the average person in the community but only when that community's current mood is reasonable": *supra*, at p. 18 C.C.C., p. 282 S.C.R. The issue there, as here, is maintaining respect for the values which, over the long term, hold the community together. One of those very fundamental values is the preservation of the purity of the administration of justice. In my opinion, a judge is particularly well suited to make this determination. …

Finally, I am of the view that before a judge considers whether a stay of proceedings lies because of entrapment, it must be absolutely clear that the Crown had discharged its burden of proving beyond a reasonable doubt that the accused had committed all the essential elements of the offence. If this is not clear and there is a jury, the guilt or innocence of the accused must be determined apart from evidence which is relevant only to the issue of entrapment. This protects the right of an accused to an acquittal where the circumstances so warrant. If the jury decides the accused has committed all of the elements of the crime, it is then open to the judge to stay the proceedings because of entrapment by refusing to register a conviction. …

*Who Bears the Burden of Proof and on What Standard?*

I have come to the conclusion that it is not inconsistent with the requirement that the Crown prove the guilt of the accused beyond a reasonable doubt to place the onus on the accused to prove on a balance of probabilities that the conduct of the state is an abuse of process because of entrapment. I repeat: the guilt or innocence of the accused is not in issue. The accused has done nothing that entitles him or her to an acquittal; the Crown has engaged in conduct, however, that disentitles it to a conviction. …

*Disposition*

From the facts it appears that the police had reasonable suspicion that the appellant was involved in criminal conduct. The issue is whether the police went too far in their efforts to attract the appellant into the commission of the offence.

Returning to the list of factors I outlined earlier, this crime is obviously one for which the state must be given substantial leeway. The drug trafficking business is not one which lends itself to the traditional devices of police investigation. It is absolutely essential, therefore, for police or their agents to get involved and gain the trust and confidence of the people who do the trafficking or who supply the drugs. It is also a crime of enormous social consequence which causes a great deal of harm in society generally. This factor alone is very critical and makes this case somewhat difficult.

The police do not appear, however, to have been interrupting an ongoing criminal enterprise, and the offence was clearly brought about by their conduct and would not have occurred absent their involvement. The police do not appear to have exploited a narcotics addiction of the appellant since he testified that he had already given up his use of narcotics. Therefore, he was not, at the time, trying to recover from an addiction. None the less, he also testified that he was no longer involved in drugs and, if this is true, it suggests that the police were indeed trying to make the appellant take up his former life-style. The persistence of the police requests, as a result of the equally persistent refusals by the appellant, supports the appellant's version of events on this point. The length of time, approximately six months, and the repetition of requests it took before the appellant agreed to commit the offence also demonstrate that the police had to go further than merely providing the appellant with the opportunity once it became evident that he was unwilling to join the alleged drug syndicate.

Perhaps the most important and determinative factor, in my opinion, is the appellant's testimony that the informer acted in a threatening manner when they went for a walk in the woods, and the further testimony that he was told to get his act together after he did not provide the supply of drugs he was asked for. I believe this conduct was unacceptable. If the police must go this far, they have gone beyond providing the appellant with an opportunity. I do not, therefore, place much significance on the fact that the appellant eventually committed the offence when shown the money. Obviously, the appellant knew much earlier that he could make a profit by getting involved in the drug enterprise and he still refused. I have come to the conclusion that the average person in the position of the appellant might also have committed the offence, if only to finally satisfy this threatening informer and end all further contact. As a result I would, on the evidence, have to find that the police conduct in this case was unacceptable. Thus, the doctrine of entrapment applies to preclude the prosecution of the appellant. In my opinion, the appellant has met the burden of proof and the trial judge should have entered a stay of proceedings for abuse of process.

I would, accordingly, allow the appeal, set aside the conviction of the appellant, order a new trial and enter a stay of proceedings.

[Dickson C.J., Beetz, McIntyre, Wilson, La Forest, and L'Heureux-Dubé JJ. concurred with Lamer J.]

---

In *R. v. Showman*, [1988] 2 S.C.R. 893, the Supreme Court, applying *Mack*, held there was no entrapment when a police informer (a former friend of the accused) made several telephone calls to arrange for the accused to sell drugs to an undercover police officer. Lamer J. stated: "the police acted on reasonable suspicion and they were fully entitled to provide [the accused] with an opportunity to commit the offence." The police had not gone beyond providing this opportunity in part because "the average narcotics supplier is not going to respond to the very first call" and the appeal to friendship "was not unduly exploitative." Lamer J. concluded: "I have no doubt that the average person would not be induced into the commission of an offence as a result of this contact."

## R. v. Barnes
Supreme Court of Canada
(1991), 63 C.C.C. (3d) 1

[This case involved a "buy and bust" operation by the police near the Granville Mall in Vancouver.]

LAMER C.J.C. (Wilson, La Forest, Sopinka, Gonthier, Cory, and Stevenson JJ. concurring): The officer testified at trial that she approached the accused and his friend because she had "a hunch, a feeling that they'd—possibly might be in possession." She believed that he and his friend fit the description of persons who possibly had drugs in their possession and who would be willing to sell to her: "I had a feeling.

They fit my general criteria. I look for males hanging around, dressed scruffy and in jeans, wearing a jean jacket or leather jacket, runners or black boots, that tend to look at people a lot." The officer indicated that there was nothing else that aroused her suspicions.

The officer approached the accused and asked him if he had any "weed." He said "no," but his friend repeated to him: "She wants some weed." The accused again responded negatively. The officer persisted and the accused then agreed to sell a small amount of *cannabis* resin to the officer for $15. Shortly afterwards, the accused was arrested by another officer and small amounts of *cannabis* resin and marijuana were seized from his person. ...

The trial judge held that the police officer had engaged in "random virtue testing," which was unacceptable according to the judgment of this court in *Mack, supra*, and therefore ordered a judicial stay of the proceedings.

As I summarized in *Mack*, at pp. 559-60, there are two principal branches of the test for entrapment. The defence is available when:

> (a)  the authorities provide a person with an opportunity to commit an offence without acting on a reasonable suspicion that this person is already engaged in criminal activity or pursuant to a *bona fide* inquiry;
>
> (b)  although having such a reasonable suspicion or acting in the course of a *bona fide* inquiry, they go beyond providing an opportunity and induce the commission of an offence ...

The absence of a reasonable suspicion or a *bona fide* inquiry is significant in assessing the police conduct because of the risk that the police will attract people who would not otherwise have any involvement in a crime and because it is not a proper use of the police power to simply go out and test the virtue of people on a random basis.

It is apparent that the police officer involved in this case did not have a "reasonable suspicion" that the accused was already engaged in unlawful drug-related activity. The factors that drew the officer's attention to this particular accused—his manner of dress, the length of his hair—were not sufficient to give rise to a reasonable suspicion that criminal acts were being committed. Furthermore, the subjectiveness of the officer's decision to approach the accused, based on a "hunch" or "feeling" rather than extrinsic evidence, also indicates that the accused did not, as an individual, arouse a reasonable suspicion.

Consequently, the police conduct in this case will amount to entrapment *unless* the officer presented the accused with the opportunity to sell drugs *in the course of a bona fide inquiry*. In my opinion, the police officer involved in this case was engaged in such a *bona fide* investigation. First, there is no question that the officer's conduct was motivated by the genuine purpose of investigating and repressing criminal activity. The police department had reasonable grounds for believing that drug-related crimes were occurring throughout the Granville Mall area. The accused was not, therefore, approached for questionable motives unrelated to the investigation and repression of crime.

Secondly, the police department directed its investigation at a suitable area within the City of Vancouver. …

Random virtue testing, conversely, only arises when a police officer presents a person with the opportunity to commit an offence *without* a reasonable suspicion that:

(a) the person is already engaged in the particular criminal activity, or

(b) the physical location with which the person is associated is a place where the particular criminal activity is likely occurring.

In this case, the accused was approached by the officer when he was walking near the Granville Mall. The notion of being "associated" with a particular area for these purposes does not require more than being *present* in the area. As a result, the accused was associated with a location where it was reasonably believed that drug-related crimes were occurring. The officer's conduct was therefore justified under the first branch of the test for entrapment set out in *Mack*.

McLACHLIN J. (in dissent):  In advocating a more refined test for *bona fide* inquiry than does Lamer C.J.C., I am motivated by concern for the implications of the test he proposes. That test would permit the police to extend their Granville Mall operation to all of Vancouver if statistics could be found to suggest that drug offences were occurring throughout Vancouver generally. The example is extreme. Yet it indicates the deficiency I see in the test proposed by Lamer C.J.C. In my view, a more sensitive test than that proposed by Lamer C.J.C.—one which permits appreciation of all relevant factors—is required.

I conclude that determination that the police were operating in the course of a *bona fide* inquiry within the meaning of *Mack* requires the court to consider not only the motive of the police and whether there is crime in the general area, but also other factors relevant to the balancing process, such as the likelihood of crime at the particular location targeted, the seriousness of the crime in question, the number of legitimate activities and persons who might be affected, and the availability of other less intrusive investigative techniques. In the final analysis, the question is whether the interception at the particular location where it took place was reasonable, having regard to the conflicting interests of private citizens in being left alone from state interference and of the state in suppressing crime. If the answer to this question is yes, then the inquiry is *bona fide*. …

I arrive then at the conclusion that in the case at bar the individual interest in being left alone and free to pursue one's daily business without being confronted by undercover police operatives vastly outweighs the state interest in the repression of crime. It follows that the police officer in this case cannot be said to have been acting pursuant to a *bona fide* inquiry. Any other conclusion would be, in my respectful opinion, unfitting in a society which heralds the constitutional protection of individual liberties and places a premium on "being left alone."

The June 1993 *Federal Proposals to Amend the General Principles of the Criminal Code* propose to codify *Mack* subject to the following:

> Entrapment is not a basis for a stay of proceedings in respect of an offence the commission of which requires the intentional or reckless causing of death or serious bodily harm.

———————————

On entrapment see S. France, "Problems in the Defence of Entrapment" (1988), 22 *U.B.C.L. Rev.* 1; R. Park, "The Entrapment Controversy" (1976), 60 *Minn. L.R.* 163; M.L. Friedland, "Controlling the Administrators of Criminal Justice" (1988-89), 31 *Crim. L.Q.* 280; M. Stober, "The Limits of Police Provocation in Canada" (1992), 34 *Crim. L.Q.* 290; B. Fisse, "Entrapment as a Defence" (1988), 12 *Crim. L.J.* 367; D. Camp, "Out of the Quagmire After *Jacobson v. United States*: Towards a More Balanced Entrapment Standard" (1993), 83 *J. of Crim. Law and Criminology* 1055; and E. Colvin, *Principles of Criminal Law*, 2nd ed. (Toronto: Thomson Professional Publishing Canada, 1991), pp. 275-79.

## IV.  SEARCH AND SEIZURE

Section 8 of the Charter provides as follows:

> 8.  Everyone has the right to be secure against unreasonable search or seizure.

In the following case the court considered s. 10(1) of *Combines Investigation Act*, R.S.C. 1970, c. C-23, which allowed the director of investigations to enter premises, and examine or take away materials on the basis of the director's belief that the evidence was relevant to an investigation. Section 10(3) of that Act provided that before exercising the power under s. 10(1) the director should obtain a certificate of authorization from a member of the Restrictive Trades Practices Commission.

### Hunter v. Southam Inc.
Supreme Court of Canada
(1984), 14 C.C.C. (3d) 97

DICKSON J.:  At the outset it is important to note that the issue in this appeal concerns the constitutional validity of a statute authorizing a search and seizure. It does not concern the reasonableness or otherwise of the manner in which the appellants carried out their statutory authority. It is not the conduct of the appellants, but rather the legislation under which they acted, to which attention must be directed. …

I begin with the obvious. The *Canadian Charter of Rights and Freedoms* is a purposive document. Its purpose is to guarantee and to protect, within the limits of reason, the enjoyment of the rights and freedoms it enshrines. It is intended to constrain governmental action inconsistent with those rights and freedoms; it is not in itself an authorization for governmental action. In the present case this means, as Prowse J.A. pointed out, that in guaranteeing the right to be secure from unreasonable searches and seizures, s. 8 acts as a limitation on whatever powers of search and seizure the federal or provincial governments already and otherwise possess. It does not in itself confer any powers, even of "reasonable" search and seizure, on these governments. This leads, in my view, to the further conclusion that an assessment of the constitutionality of a search and seizure, or of a statute authorizing a search or seizure, must focus on its "reasonable" or "unreasonable" impact on the subject of the search or the seizure, and not simply on its rationality in furthering some valid government objective.

Since the proper approach to the interpretation of the *Canadian Charter of Rights and Freedoms* is a purposive one, before it is possible to assess the reasonableness or unreasonableness of the impact of a search or of a statute authorizing a search, it is first necessary to specify the purpose underlying s. 8: in other words, to delineate the nature of the interests it is meant to protect.

Historically, the common law protections with regard to governmental searches and seizures were based on the right to enjoy property and were linked to the law of trespass. It was on this basis that in the great case of *Entick v. Carrington* (1765), 19 State Tr. 1029, the court refused to countenance a search purportedly authorized by the Executive, to discover evidence that might link the plaintiff to certain seditious libels. Lord Camden prefaced his discussion of the rights in question by saying, at p. 1066:

> The great end, for which men entered into society, was to preserve their property. That right is preserved sacred and incommunicable in all instances where it has not been taken away or abridged by some public law for the good of the whole.

The defendants argued that their oaths as King's messengers required them to conduct the search in question and ought to prevail over the plaintiff's property rights. Lord Camden rejected this contention, at p. 1067:

> Our law holds the property of every man so sacred, that no man can set his foot upon his neighbour's close without his leave: if he does he is a trespasser though he does no damage at all; if he will tread upon his neighbour's ground, he must justify it by law.

Lord Camden could find no exception from this principle for the benefit of King's messengers. He held that neither the intrusions nor the purported authorizations were supportable on the basis of the existing law. That law would only have countenanced such an entry if the search were for stolen goods and if authorized by a justice on the basis of evidence upon oath that there was "strong cause" to believe the goods were concealed in the place sought to be searched. In view of the lack of proper legal authorization for the governmental intrusion, the plaintiff was protected from the intended search and seizure by the ordinary law of trespass.

In my view, the interests protected by s. 8 are of a wider ambit than those enunciated in *Entick v. Carrington*. Section 8 is an entrenched constitutional provision. It is not therefore vulnerable to encroachment by legislative enactments in the same way as common law protections. There is, further, nothing in the language of the section to restrict it to the protection of property or to associate it with the law of trespass. It guarantees a broad and general right to be secure from unreasonable search and seizure.

The Fourth Amendment, of the United States Constitution, also guarantees a broad right. It provides:

Amendment IV

> The right of the people to be secure in their persons, houses, papers, and effects, against unreasonable searches and seizures, shall not be violated, and no warrants shall issue but upon probable cause, supported by oath or affirmation, and particularly describing the place to be searched, and the persons or things to be seized.

Construing this provision in *Katz v. United States* (1967), 389 U.S. 347, Stewart J., delivering the majority opinion of the United States Supreme Court, declared at p. 351 that "the Fourth Amendment protects people, not places." Justice Stewart rejected any necessary connection between that Amendment and the notion of trespass. With respect, I believe this approach is equally appropriate in construing the protections in s. 8 of the *Canadian Charter of Rights and Freedoms*.

In *Katz*, Stewart J. discussed the notion of a right to privacy, which he described at p. 350 as "the right to be let alone by other people." Although Stewart J. was careful not to identify the Fourth Amendment exclusively with the protection of this right, nor to see the Amendment as the only provision in the *Bill of Rights* relevant to its interpretation, it is clear that this notion played a prominent role in his construction of the nature and the limits of the American constitutional protection against unreasonable search and seizure. In the Alberta Court of Appeal, Prowse J.A. took a similar approach to s. 8, which he described as dealing "with one aspect of what has been referred to as a right of privacy which is the right to be secure against encroachment upon the citizens' reasonable expectation of privacy in a free and democratic society."

Like the Supreme Court of the United States, I would be wary of foreclosing the possibility that the right to be secure against unreasonable search and seizure might protect interests beyond the right of privacy, but for the purposes of the present appeal I am satisfied that its protections go at least that far. The guarantee of security from *unreasonable* search and seizure only protects a *reasonable* expectation. This limitation on the right guaranteed by s. 8, whether it is expressed negatively as freedom from "unreasonable" search and seizure, or positively as an entitlement to a "reasonable" expectation of privacy, indicates that an assessment must be made as to whether in a particular situation the public's interest in being left alone by government must give way to the government's interest in intruding on the individual's privacy in order to advance its goals, notably those of law enforcement.

### (A)  When Is the Balance of Interests To Be Assessed?

If the issue to be resolved in assessing the constitutionality of searches under s. 10 were whether *in fact* the governmental interest in carrying out a given search outweighed that of the individual in resisting the governmental intrusion upon his privacy, then it would be appropriate to determine the balance of the competing interests *after* the search had been conducted. Such a *post facto* analysis would, however, be seriously at odds with the purpose of s. 8. That purpose is, as I have said, to protect individuals from unjustified State intrusions upon their privacy. That purpose requires a means of *preventing* unjustified searches before they happen, not simply of determining, after the fact, whether they ought to have occurred in the first place. This, in my view, can only be accomplished by a system of *prior authorization*, not one of subsequent validation.

A requirement of prior authorization, usually in the form of a valid warrant, has been a consistent prerequisite for a valid search and seizure both at common law and under most statutes. Such a requirement puts the onus on the State to demonstrate the superiority of its interests to that of the individual. As such it accords with the apparent intention of the Charter to prefer, where feasible, the right of the individual to be free from State interference to the interests of the State in advancing its purposes through such interference.

I recognize that it may not be reasonable in every instance to insist on prior authorization in order to validate governmental intrusions upon individuals' expectations of privacy. Nevertheless, where it is feasible to obtain prior authorization, I would hold that such authorization is a pre-condition for a valid search and seizure. ...

### (B)  Who Must Grant the Authorization?

The purpose of a requirement of prior authorization is to provide an opportunity, before the event, for the conflicting interests of the State and the individual to be assessed, so that the individual's right to privacy will be breached only where the appropriate standard has been met, and the interests of the State are thus demonstrably superior. For such an authorization procedure to be meaningful it is necessary for the person authorizing the search to be able to assess the evidence as to whether that standard has been met, in an entirely neutral and impartial manner. ...

[Dickson J. then examined the functions of the Restrictive Trades Practices Commission and concluded:]

In my view, investing the commission or its members with significant investigatory functions has the result of vitiating the ability of a member of the commission to act in a judicial capacity when authorizing a search or seizure under s. 10(3). ...

### (C)  On What Basis Must the Balance of Interests Be Assessed?

... The purpose of an objective criterion for granting prior authorization to conduct a search or seizure is to provide a consistent standard for identifying the point at which the interests of the State in such intrusions come to prevail over the interests of the individual in resisting them. To associate it with an applicant's reasonable belief that relevant evidence *may* be uncovered by the search, would be to define the proper standard as the *possibility* of finding evidence. This is a very low standard which would validate intrusion on the basis of suspicion, and authorize fishing expeditions of considerable latitude. It would tip the balance strongly in favour of the State and limit the right of the individual to resist to only the most egregious intrusions. I do not believe that this is a proper standard for securing the right to be free from unreasonable search and seizure.

Anglo-Canadian legal and political traditions point to a higher standard. The common law required evidence on oath which gave "strong reason to believe" that stolen goods were concealed in the place to be searched before a warrant would issue. Section 443 of the *Criminal Code* [now s. 487] authorizes a warrant only where there has been information upon oath that there is "reasonable ground to believe" that there is evidence of an offence in the place to be searched. The American *Bill of Rights* provides that "no warrants shall issue but upon probable cause, supported by oath or affirmation. ..." The phrasing is slightly different but the standard in each of these formulations is identical. The State's interest in detecting and preventing crime begins to prevail over the individual's interest in being left alone at the point where credibly-based probability replaces suspicion. History has confirmed the appropriateness of this requirement as the threshold for subordinating the expectation of privacy to the needs of law enforcement. Where the State's interest is not simply law enforcement as, for instance, where State security is involved, or where the individual's interest is not simply his expectation of privacy as, for instance, when the search threatens his bodily integrity, the relevant standard might well be a different one. That is not the situation in the present case. In cases like the present, reasonable and probable grounds, established upon oath, to believe that an offence has been committed and that there is evidence to be found at the place of the search, constitutes the minimum standard, consistent with s. 8 of the Charter, for authorizing search and seizure. In so far as s. 10(1) and (3) of the *Combines Investigation Act* do not embody such a requirement, I would hold them to be further inconsistent with s. 8.

[Ritchie, Beetz, Estey, McIntyre, Chouinard, Lamer, and Wilson JJ. concurred in the judgment of Dickson J.]

### Thomson Newspapers Ltd. v. Canada (Director of Investigations, Restrictive Trade Practices Commission)
Supreme Court of Canada
(1990), 54 C.C.C. (3d) 417

[The Supreme Court held in a 3 to 2 decision that the powers of the director of investigations to demand the production of books, papers, records, or other documents under s. 17 of the *Combines Investigation Act*, R.S.C. 1970, c. C-23 did not violate s. 8 of the Charter, although it amounted to a seizure under the section.]

La FOREST J.:  The foregoing conclusion is in no way inconsistent with this Court's decision in *Hunter v. Southam Inc.*, *supra*, notwithstanding that it also concerned the constitutionality of investigative powers under the *Combines Investigation Act*, specifically those provided by s. 10. ...

... To hold that anti-combines investigators must always obtain a warrant by showing reasonable and probable grounds as to the commission of an offence and the existence of relevant evidence before they exercise *any* power of investigation that falls within the ambit of s. 8 of the *Charter* would, in these circumstances, immunize perpetrators of anti-competitive offences from discovery and prosecution.

I see no reason to interpret *Hunter v. Southam Inc.* in this rigid fashion. It must be remembered that that case was concerned with the constitutionality of s. 10 of the Act, and that that provision, unlike s. 17, conferred on the Director of Investigations a power of *search* as well as seizure. It must surely be obvious that a power to search premises and take away documents is far more intrusive than a mere power to order the production of documents. Accordingly, the fact that the power there was held to be an unreasonable violation of reasonable expectations of privacy in no way determines that a power to order the production of documents must also be held to be an unreasonable intrusion on privacy. ...

WILSON J. (in dissent):   There is no doubt that an individual's expectation of privacy goes beyond a concern for the inviolability of his body and extends to his possessions including his books, records and other documents. Matters of the utmost confidence are often recorded in retrievable form, be they business strategies, trade secrets or personal reflections noted in a diary. An individual's interest in having these confidences respected can be significant—not something with which governmental agencies should lightly interfere. ...

... Section 17 of the *Combines Investigation Act* contemplates an investigation one of the purposes of which is to collect evidence with a view to the laying of a "criminal" charge. Section 17 is contained in the same part of the Act as s. 10, the section in relation to which the criteria in *Hunter* were imposed. In my view, it is important to look past the "form" of the information gathering, i.e. by *subpoena duces tecum*, and look at the effect the information gathering has on the individual, i.e. the compulsory production of evidence which can be used in a criminal prosecution.

For the above reasons I would conclude that the criteria set forth in *Hunter* must be substantially if not completely met by s. 17 of the *Combines Investigation Act*. The question then is whether s. 17 does meet these criteria or at least responds to the policy concerns underlying these criteria in a meaningful way.

The criteria, once again, are as follows:

(a)  a system of prior authorization, by an entirely neutral and impartial arbiter who is capable of acting judicially in balancing the interests of the State against those of the individual;

(b)  a requirement that the impartial arbiter must satisfy himself that the person seeking the authorization has reasonable grounds, established under oath, to believe that an offence has been committed;

(c)  a requirement that the impartial arbiter must satisfy himself that the person seeking the authorization has reasonable grounds to believe that something which will afford evidence of the particular offence under investigation will be recovered; and

(d)  a requirement that the only documents which are authorized to be seized are those which are strictly relevant to the offence under investigation.

[Wilson J. concluded that these requirements were not satisfied and that s. 17 of the *Combines Investigation Act* could not be justified under s. 1 of the Charter.

L'Heureux-Dubé and Sopinka JJ. wrote separate concurring opinions holding that there was no violation of s. 8 of the Charter. Lamer J. concurred with Wilson J. that there was a violation of s. 8.]

---

The Supreme Court has subsequently indicated "the greater the departure from the realm of criminal law, the more flexible will be the approach to the standard of reasonableness." It upheld warrantless inspections of business records and warrantless demands for business records. See *B.C. Securities Commission v. Branch* (1995), 38 C.R. (4th) 133, at p. 158; *Potash* (1994), 91 C.C.C. (3d) 315 as well as warrantless search of school lockers: *M (M.R.)* (1998), 20 C.R. (5th) 197 (S.C.C.). See also chapter 6 on regulatory offences.

## Reasonable Expectation of Privacy

### R. v. LeBeau and Lofthouse
Ontario Court of Appeal
(1988), 41 C.C.C. (3d) 163

[In this case the police videotaped sexual activities in a public washroom in Silvercreek Park in Guelph. They obtained permission from the Chief of Police but no prior judicial authorization. Over two days, 18 charges were laid. The appellants were charged with and convicted of acts of gross indecency (since repealed S.C. 1987, c. 24, s. 3 see now s.173 of the *Criminal Code*). On appeal they argued that the videotaping violated s. 8 of the Charter and should be excluded under s. 24(2) of the Charter. The Ontario Court of Appeal stated:]

BY THE COURT: It has been decided by this court that electronic surveillance by way of video recording may amount to a search within the meaning of s. 8 of the Charter if carried out while the person observed by the camera had a reasonable expectation of privacy: *R. v. Wong* (1987), 34 C.C.C. (3d) 51, 56 C.R. (3d) 352. After considering the provisions of s. 8 of the Charter and decisions of our courts, the 14th Amendment to the Constitution of the United States of America and related decisions of their courts, Cory J.A. said for this court at p. 59:

> Thus, in the United States, which has a constitutional provision similar to that of s. 8 of the Charter, it has been determined that surreptitious video surveillance can constitute a search.
>
> The same conclusion should be reached in Ontario. The direction the court should follow has been set out in *Hunter et al. v. Southam Inc.* (1984), 14 C.C.C. (3d) 97 at p. 107, 11 D.L.R. (4th) 641, 2 C.P.R. (3d) 1, where Dickson C.J.C., after quoting with approval from *Katz v. U.S.*, *supra*, [(1967), 389 U.S. 347] stated:

There is, further, nothing in the language of the section to restrict it to the protection of property or to associate it with the law of trespass. It guarantees a broad
and general right to be secure from unreasonable search and seizures.

It is thus clear that surreptitious video surveillance must constitute a search in circumstances where the person observed by the camera had a reasonable expectation of
privacy. ...

### *Was There a Reasonable Expectation of Privacy?*

Relying on the references to the judgment of Stewart J. in *Katz v. The United States*,
*supra*, and Dickson J. in *Hunter v. Southam*, *supra*, the appellants contend that the
video surveillance constituted an invasion of their private acts which occurred when
they had a reasonable expectation of privacy. They submit that the appellants sought
to preserve the privacy of their actions: in the case of LeBeau by closing the wash-
room cubicle door and in the case of Lofthouse by posting two look-outs at the
washroom door to ensure that no one could approach and enter. To do this, they contend, meets the two-fold test adopted by this court in *Wong*. Reference was made to a
number of cases in courts of the United States dealing with the reasonable expectation of privacy and public wash-room cubicles. ...

An examination of these cases reveals that each turns on its own facts. Many of
them are considered in *Search and Seizure: A Treatise on the Fourth Amendment*,
2nd ed., by Wayne R. La Fave. At p. 437 the author says:

(c) *Private areas in public places: rest rooms and fitting rooms.* Police sometimes
engage in clandestine surveillance of public rest rooms in an attempt to detect criminal
conduct—typically use of drugs or homosexual conduct—occurring therein. Often this
is accomplished by an officer taking a position on the roof or in a compartment above
an enclosed stall and looking therein through a hole or vent. At least since the *Katz*
decision, it is clear beyond question that such surveillance into a closed rest room stall
constitutes a Fourth Amendment search.

After considering a number of cases the author concludes, at p. 440:

It does not follow, of course, that every instance of police observation in a public rest
room constitutes a Fourth Amendment search. There is no justified expectation of privacy as to incriminating conduct which occurs in the public area of a rest room rather
than inside one of the stalls.

In our opinion, the appellants had no reasonable expectation of privacy. The police surveillance established that this public washroom had become the meeting-place
for this group of men, to which both of the appellants appear to have adhered, for the
practice of homosexual acts. The conduct probably offended s. 157 of the *Criminal
Code*. That others would observe and recognize what was going on from the persistent use that these men made of the place was a risk that they undoubtedly understood.
In the circumstances, by reason of their look-outs and precautions, perhaps they had
an expectation that they would escape detection by the police or interference by the
public. But that is not an expectation of privacy. This is not a case of persons resorting

to the privacy of a closed cubicle in a public wash-room for its expected use or for some personal indulgence that would be considered objectionable if carried on in public. On the contrary, the evidence, in the case of the appellant Mr. Lofthouse, allows no conclusion other than that the group intended to take over the public wash-room as their meeting-place so that they could engage in their activities without seeking the privacy of the closed toilet cubicles and, by reason of look-outs, without concern for interruption by others not members of their group. Mr. Lofthouse was very frank when he spoke of the privacy he expected as privacy "in the washroom" (not the closed cubicle) and "in the sense of privacy to a family"—the group. …

We think that there is no real basis to distinguish the case against Mr. LeBeau. This was group activity. It seems clear that Mr. LeBeau went to the public wash-room to meet another man who was waiting, indeed, had been waiting in the wash-room for nearly two hours. The other's conduct alone would attract attention and make intervention likely. This was the same sort of activity which had been observed by the police during their investigation: some men would visit the place for short intervals of five to fifteen minutes while some would stay there much longer. In any event, having regard to the jury's verdict, it appears that they found that Mr. LeBeau's actions in kneeling on the floor of the wash-room clearly facing a cubicle partition so as to engage in the conduct described would have been visible to persons entering the wash-room. We are sure he understood this and also that to see his conduct would have been very alarming to most people. In the circumstances, he cannot say that he had a reasonable expectation of privacy.

Accordingly, there being no reasonable expectation of privacy on the part of either of the appellants, the electronic surveillance by video camera carried out by the police did not violate their rights under s. 8 of the Charter.

*Appeal dismissed.*

### R. v. Wong
Supreme Court of Canada
(1990), 60 C.C.C. (3d) 460

[The accused was charged with keeping a common gaming house and the Crown sought to introduce a video tape of gambling conducted in a Toronto hotel room. The trial judge held that the video tape was obtained in violation of s. 8 and should be excluded under s. 24(2) of the Charter. The Ontario Court of Appeal reversed on the grounds that the accused had no reasonable expectation of privacy. The accused appealed to the Supreme Court.]

La FOREST J. (Dickson C.J.C., L'Heureux-Dubé, and Sopinka JJ. concurring): … The Court of Appeal, after stating, by way of an initial premise, that a person attending a function to which the general public has received an open invitation can have no interest in "being left alone," went on to draw the following conclusions from the facts of this case (at pp. 63-4):

None of the respondents testified that they had a subjective expectation of privacy and it is difficult to believe that they could give such evidence. It may well be that they were in the same room with strangers. The occupants' only common interest was to gamble illegally for high stakes. All but Santiago Wong were no more than casual visitors to the rooms with no basis for challenging the legality of the search. Neither is it possible that Santiago Wong had any reasonable expectation of privacy. He was booking the room regularly and it was clear from police observation that the room had been used for gambling on other occasions. Wong had invited and accepted so many people into the room that there could not have been any reasonable expectation of privacy by anyone in the room, least of all Santiago Wong who benefited by the presence of the others.

Video surveillance of persons in a hotel room could in certain circumstances constitute a search of the most intrusive kind. However, in this case, as there was no reasonable expectation of privacy, s. 8 of the Charter cannot have any application.

The Court of Appeal has, in effect, applied a variant of the risk analysis rejected by this court, for it has chosen to rest its conclusion on the notion that the appellant, by courting observation by the other persons in the room, has effectively relinquished any right to maintain a reasonable expectation of freedom from the much more intrusive invasion of privacy constituted by surreptitious video surveillance on the part of the state.

Moreover, it is clear from the excerpt cited above that the Court of Appeal, in assessing the constitutionality of the search, has allowed itself to be influenced by the fact that the appellant was carrying on illegal activities.

… If reliance were to be placed on such *ex post facto* reasoning, and the courts to conclude that persons who were the subject of an electronic search could not have had a reasonable expectation of privacy because the search revealed that they were in fact performing a criminal act, the result would inevitably be to adopt a system of subsequent validation for searches. Yet it was precisely to guard against this possibility that this court in *Hunter v. Southam Inc.*, *supra*, at p. 109, stressed that prior authorization, wherever feasible, was a necessary pre-condition for a valid search and seizure.

[La Forest J. concluded that the accused's s. 8 rights had been violated because the police had not obtained a warrant for the video taping. He held, however, that the admission of the video tape would not bring the administration of justice into disrepute under s. 24(2) because the police acted in good faith and there was no *Criminal Code* provision at the time that would have allowed them to obtain a warrant. (See now *Criminal Code*, s. 487.01.) Wilson J. agreed with La Forest J. that the accused's s. 8 rights had been violated but would have excluded the video tape under s. 24(2).]

LAMER J. (McLachlin J. concurring (in dissent)): I agree with La Forest J. that a person who retires to a hotel room and closes the door behind him or her will normally have a reasonable expectation of privacy. The nature of the place in which the surveillance occurs will always be an important factor to consider in determining whether the target has a reasonable expectation of privacy in the circumstances. It is not, however, determinative. A person who is situated in what would normally be characterized as a public place (a restaurant, for example) may well have a reasonable expectation of privacy. For example, he or she would not reasonably expect that the police will surreptitiously monitor and record the private conversation taking place at his or her table. By the same token, that which would normally be characterized as a private place (a personal residence, for example) may well, by the manner in which it is utilized, become a place in which one does not have a reasonable expectation of privacy.

The expectation of privacy which normally exists with respect to a hotel room will not be circumscribed by the fact that illegal activity may be taking place in the room, nor will it necessarily be waived by the mere fact that others have been invited to the room. However, in some cases, additional facts may be present which will indicate that the target does not have a reasonable expectation of privacy.

In the case at bar, the appellant was situated in a hotel room. In most cases, a hotel room is a location in which one has a reasonable expectation of privacy. However, in this case the appellant had, indiscriminately, extended invitations to the gaming session which was to take place in the hotel room. He had passed out numerous notices in public restaurants and bars, thereby inviting the public into the hotel room. It is impossible to conclude that a reasonable person, in the position of the appellant, would expect privacy in these circumstances. A reasonable person would know that when such an invitation is extended to the public at large, one can no longer expect that strangers, including the police, will not be present in the room. In this case, the police effected their presence in the room via the video camera which was installed in the drapery valence.

I do not wish to be taken as adopting the "risk analysis" which this court rejected in *Duarte*, *supra*. I am not equating the risk that strangers will be in the hotel room with the risk that the police will be electronically recording the activity in the hotel room. The issue is not so much concerned with risk as it is with reasonable expectations. Here it was not reasonable for the appellant to expect that strangers, including the police, would not be present in the room.

The appellant may well have had a reasonable expectation of privacy in the hotel room had he extended a few invitations to particular individuals. However, that was not the case here. In my view, and with respect for other views, the appellant had no reasonable expectation of privacy in these circumstances; as a result, no search took place within the meaning of s. 8.

*Appeal dismissed.*

At the time of *Wong*, the *Criminal Code* did not authorize the use of video cameras. See now s. 487.01 providing general warrants for any investigative technique that might constitute an unreasonable search or seizure.

Does a man have a reasonable expectation of privacy in his girlfriend's apartment? In *R. v. Edwards* (1996), 104 C.C.C. (3d) 136, the Supreme Court held that the accused did not have a reasonable expectation of privacy in his girlfriend's apartment even though he had a key to the apartment and occasionally stayed overnight.

Does a passenger have a reasonable expectation of privacy in the search of a car in which they are travelling? In *R. v. Belnavis*, [1997] 3 S.C.R. 341, the Supreme Court held that a passenger had no reasonable expectation of privacy with respect to the search of bags and the trunk of a car in which she was travelling.

## Prior Judicial Authorization of Search and Seizure

Search warrants to search buildings, receptacles, or places are issued by a justice of the peace under s. 487 of the *Criminal Code*. The justice of the peace is a judicial official who hears evidence under oath to determine if there are reasonable grounds to believe that an offence has been committed and that a search will reveal evidence of the offence. Despite these safeguards, a number of studies of randomly drawn search warrants have revealed that about 40 percent of warrants were invalidly issued with most legal errors being insufficient establishment of reasonable and probable grounds including a lack of sourcing, belief based on uncorroborated informants of unknown reliability, and a lack of nexus between the offence and the items to be searched and seized. See Casey Hill, "The Role of Fault in Section 24(2) of the Charter," in J. Cameron, *The Charter's Impact on the Criminal Justice System* (Toronto: Carswell, 1996), at 57ff. A more recent study demonstrated an even higher error rate. See Casey Hill, Scott Hutchinson, and Leslie Pringle, "Search Warrants: Protection or Illusion?" (2000), 28 C.R. (5th) 89.

The United States Supreme Court has held in *U.S. v. Leon*, 468 U.S. 897 (1984) that evidence seized unreasonably but in reasonable reliance on a judicial warrant should not be excluded. Justice White stated for the court:

> Because a search warrant provides the detached scrutiny of a neutral magistrate, which is a more reliable safeguard against improper searches than the hurried judgment of a law enforcement officer engaged in the often competitive enterprise of ferreting out crime ... we have expressed a strong preference for warrants. ...

He concluded that the exclusionary rule need not be applied to those judicial officers who issue search warrants. He elaborated:

> The exclusionary rule is designed to deter police misconduct rather than to punish the errors of judges and magistrates. Second, there exists no evidence suggesting that judges and magistrates are inclined to ignore or subvert the Fourth Amendment or that lawlessness among these actors requires application of the extreme sanction of exclusion. Third, and most important, we discern no basis and are offered none, for believing that exclusion of evidence seized pursuant to a warrant will have a significant deterrent effect on the issuing judge or magistrate.

Justice Brennan in dissent argued that the long-run effect of the majority's ruling "will be to undermine the integrity of the warrant process." He stated that creation of the exception implicitly tells magistrates that they need not take much care in reviewing warrant applications because their mistakes will have virtually no consequence and that the ruling will encourage police to provide the bare minimum of information to obtain a warrant and in doing so insulate themselves from the exclusionary sanction.

What effect should reliance on a search warrant have in deciding whether evidence should be excluded under s. 24(2) of the Charter? See *R. v. Harris et al.* (1987), 35 C.C.C. (3d) 1 (Ont. C.A.). In that case, the Court of Appeal admitted evidence under s. 24(2) on the basis that the police had acted in good faith in obtaining a warrant even though the warrant was defective and demonstrated, in the trial judge's findings, police negligence. In *R. v. Hosie* (1996), 107 C.C.C. (3d) 385, however, the same Court of Appeal excluded drugs seized under a warrant because the information supplied by the police to obtain the warrant was "careless." Rosenberg J.A. stated: "The Courts should not be seen as condoning the use of language in search warrants which masks the true state of affairs and deprives a judicial officer of the opportunity to fairly assess whether the state's interest in detecting crime outweighs the individual's privacy interest in his or her own home."

### Electronic Surveillance and the Charter

### R. v. Duarte
Supreme Court of Canada
(1990), 53 C.C.C. (3d) 1

[The accused was charged with trafficking in narcotics. The trial judge held that the surreptitious tape recording of the accused's conversations with an informer (with the informer's consent) violated the accused's rights under s. 8 of the Charter and should be excluded.

The Ontario Court of Appeal allowed the appeal, holding that there was no violation of s. 8 because the accused risked that his conversations with an informer both might be revealed by the informer's testimony at a trial and through electronic recording. The accused appealed.]

La FOREST J.:  This appeal is concerned with the protection accorded by s. 8 of the *Canadian Charter of Rights and Freedoms* against electronic recording of the conversations of individuals with the police and informers in the absence of judicial authorization. ...

The importance of the issues can hardly be gainsaid. James Carr, *The Law of Electronic Surveillance* (New York: Clark Boardman, 1977), points out, at pp. 3-61, that in the United States this mode of surveillance is without question "the most widely used and most frequently practiced [sic] mode of eavesdropping." Though I have found no data on the relative frequency of this practice in Canada, the cases would indicate that it is also widespread here. The extensive use of electronic surveillance in this country is documented. The Law Reform Commission of Canada's Working Paper 47 on "Electronic Surveillance" (Ottawa: Law Reform Commission, 1986), reports that on a relative basis, Canadian law enforcement authorities request *20* times more authorizations to conduct electronic surveillance than their American counterparts (p. 10).

Canada, in common with the United States, has taken important steps to ensure judicial supervision of electronic surveillance by Part IV.1 [now Part VI] of the *Criminal Code*. Section 178.11(1) [now s. 184(1)] makes it an offence to engage in this activity. It reads:

> 178.11(1) Every one who, by means of an electromagnetic, acoustic, mechanical or other device, wilfully intercepts a private communication is guilty of an indictable offence and liable to imprisonment for five years.

Under Part IV.1, the police generally may only conduct electronic surveillance once in possession of an authorization issued by a superior court judge and are bound to conduct such surveillance in strict accordance with the terms and conditions of the authorization. By contrast, participant surveillance is left entirely to the discretion of the police. Section 178.11(2)(a) of the *Code* provides the following exception to s. 178.11(1):

> 178.11(2) Subsection (1) does not apply to
>
> (a) a person who has the consent to intercept, express or implied, of the originator of the private communication or of the person intended by the originator thereof to receive it;

The police are thus free to make the decision to conduct this type of surveillance on whom they wish, where they wish, and for as long as they wish (in the present case, for example, the operation lasted some two years).

I begin by stating what seems to me to be obvious: that, as a general proposition, surreptitious electronic surveillance of the individual by an agency of the state constitutes an unreasonable search or seizure under s. 8 of the Charter. ...

The reason for this protection is the realization that if the state were free, at its sole discretion, to make permanent electronic recordings of our private communications, there would be no meaningful residuum to our right to live our lives free from surveillance. The very efficacy of electronic surveillance is such that it has the potential, if left unregulated, to annihilate any expectation that our communications will remain private. A society which exposed us, at the whim of the state, to the risk of having a permanent electronic recording made of our words every time we opened our mouths might be superbly equipped to fight crime, but would be one in which privacy no longer had any meaning. As Douglas J., dissenting in *United States v. White*, *supra*, put it, at p. 756: "Electronic surveillance is the greatest leveler of human privacy ever known." If the state may arbitrarily record and transmit our private communications, it is no longer possible to strike an appropriate balance between the right of the individual to be left alone and the right of the state to intrude on privacy in the furtherance of its goals, notably the need to investigate and combat crime.

This is not to deny that it is of vital importance that law enforcement agencies be able to employ electronic surveillance in their investigation of crime. Electronic surveillance plays an indispensable role in the detection of sophisticated criminal enterprises. Its utility in the investigation of drug related crimes, for example, has been proven time and again. But, for the reasons I have touched on, it is unacceptable in a free society that the agencies of the state be free to use this technology at their sole discretion. The threat this would pose to privacy is wholly unacceptable.

It thus becomes necessary to strike a reasonable balance between the right of individuals to be left alone and the right of the state to intrude on privacy in the furtherance of its responsibilities for law enforcement. Parliament has attempted to do this by enacting Part IV.1 of the *Code*. An examination of Part IV.1 reveals that Parliament has sought to reconcile these competing interests by providing that the police must always seek prior judicial authorization before using electronic surveillance. Only a superior court judge can authorize electronic surveillance, and the legislative scheme sets a high standard for obtaining these authorizations. A judge must be satisfied that other investigative methods would fail, or have little likelihood of success, and that the granting of the authorization is in the best interest of the administration of justice. I share the approach of Martin J.A. in *R. v. Finlay* (1985), 23 C.C.C. (3d) 48 at 70, that this latter prerequisite imports as a minimum requirement that the issuing judge must be satisfied that there are reasonable and probable grounds to believe that an offence has been, or is being, committed and that the authorization sought will afford evidence of that offence. It can, I think, be seen that the provisions and safeguards of Part IV.1 of the *Code* have been designed to prevent the agencies of the state from intercepting private communications on the basis of mere suspicion.

In proceeding in this fashion, Parliament has, in my view, succeeded in striking an appropriate balance. It meets the high standard of the Charter which guarantees the right to be secure against unreasonable search and seizure by subjecting the power of the state to record our private communications to external restraint and requiring it to be justified by application of an objective criterion. The reason this represents an acceptable balance is that the imposition of an external and objective criterion affords a measure of protection to the citizen whose private communications have been intercepted. It becomes possible for any individual to call the state to account if he can establish that a given interception was not authorized in accordance with the requisite standard. If privacy may be defined as the right of the individual to determine for himself when, how, and to what extent he will release personal information about himself, a reasonable expectation of privacy would seem to demand that an individual may proceed on the assumption that the state may only violate this right by recording private communications on a clandestine basis when it has established to the satisfaction of a detached judicial officer that an offence has been or is being committed and that interception of private communications stands to afford evidence of the offence.

This, it seems to me, flows inexorably from the principles enunciated in *Hunter v. Southam Inc.*, *supra*. In that case, this court (p. 106 C.C.C., p. 650 D.L.R.) made the important point that the "assessment of the constitutionality of a search and seizure … must focus on its 'reasonable' or 'unreasonable' impact on the subject of the search or the seizure, and not simply on its rationality in furthering some valid government objective." Applying this standard, it is fair to conclude that if the surreptitious recording of private communications is a search and seizure within the meaning of s. 8 of the Charter, it is because the law recognizes that a person's privacy is intruded on in an unreasonable manner whenever the state, without a prior showing of reasonable cause before a neutral judicial officer, arrogates to itself the right surreptitiously to record communications that the originator expects will not be intercepted by anyone other than the person intended by its originator to receive them, to use the language of the *Code*.

By contrast to the general provisions on electronic surveillance, the *Code* places no restriction on participant surveillance. The police may employ this practice in their absolute discretion, against whom they wish and for whatever reasons they wish, without any limit as to place or duration. There is a total absence of prior judicial supervision of this practice. …

The appellant raises the additional point that dispensing the police from the requirement to seek a warrant for conducting participant surveillance effectively allows the police to do indirectly what Part IV.1 [now Part VI] of the *Code* prohibits them from doing directly. Faced with the choice of having to seek a warrant, and being able to proceed without one, it can reasonably be expected that they will, circumstances permitting, elect to proceed without one. …

To conclude, the Charter is not meant to protect us against a poor choice of friends. If our "friend" turns out to be an informer, and we are convicted on the strength of his testimony, that may be unfortunate for us. But the Charter is meant to guarantee the right to be secure against unreasonable search and seizure. A conversation with an informer does not amount to a search and seizure within the meaning of the Charter. Surreptitious electronic interception and recording of a private communication does. Such recording, moreover, should be viewed as a search and seizure in all circumstances save where *all* parties to the conversation have expressly consented to its being recorded. Accordingly the constitutionality of "participant surveillance" should fall to be determined by application of the same standard as that employed in third party surveillance, *i.e.*, by application of the standard of reasonableness enunciated in *Hunter v. Southam Inc.*, *supra*. By application of that standard, the warrantless participant surveillance engaged in by the police here was clearly unconstitutional. …

That being so, one must consider the question of the admissibility of the communication under s. 24(2) of the Charter. That provision provides that evidence that was obtained in a manner that infringed or denied any right or freedom guaranteed under the Charter shall be excluded if it is established that, having regard to all the circumstances, its admission would bring the administration of justice into disrepute.

In *R. v. Collins* (1987), 33 C.C.C. (3d) 1, 38 D.L.R. (4th) 508, [1987] 1 S.C.R. 265, Lamer J. dealt with the manner in which s. 24(2) must be approached. The first point to observe is that the onus is on the person who seeks the exclusion of evidence to establish that its admission would bring the administration of justice into disrepute. Lamer J., at pp. 18-9 C.C.C., p. 525 D.L.R., set forth many of the factors to be considered, namely:

- what kind of evidence was obtained?
- what Charter right was infringed?
- was the Charter violation serious or was it of a merely technical nature?
- was it deliberate, wilful or flagrant, or was it inadvertent or committed in good faith?
- did it occur in circumstances of urgency or necessity?
- were there other investigatory techniques available?
- would the evidence have been obtained in any event?
- is the offence serious?

- is the evidence essential to substantiate the charge?
- are other remedies available?

Of cardinal importance in assessing these factors is the fairness of the process, and, in particular, its impact on the fairness of the trial. Undoubtedly, the breach infringed upon an important Charter right, and the evidence could have been obtained without breaching the Charter. But what strikes one here is that the breach was in no way deliberate, wilful or flagrant. The police officers acted entirely in good faith. They were acting in accordance with what they had good reason to believe was the law—as it had been for many years before the advent of the Charter. The reasonableness of their action is underscored by the seriousness of the offence. They had reasonable and probable cause to believe the offence had been committed, and had they properly understood the law, they could have obtained an authorization under the *Code* to intercept the communication. Indeed, they could have proceeded without resorting to electronic surveillance and relied solely on the evidence of the undercover officer or the informer. In short, the Charter breach stemmed from an entirely reasonable misunderstanding of the law by the police officers who would otherwise have obtained the necessary evidence to convict the accused in any event. Under these circumstances, I hold that the appellant has not established that the admission of the evidence would bring the administration of justice into disrepute.

[The appeal was dismissed and a new trial ordered. (Dickson C.J., L'Heureux-Dubé, Sopinka, Gonthier, and McLachlin JJ. concurred.) Lamer J. wrote a separate concurring opinion agreeing with the Ontario Court of Appeal that there was no violation of s. 8.

See now ss. 184.1 to 184.6 of the *Criminal Code* enacted in part in response to the above case.]

## V.  ARREST AND DETENTION

### The Deaths of Helen Betty Osborne and John Joseph Harper
Report of the Aboriginal Justice Inquiry of Manitoba (1991)

… At approximately 2:37 a.m., Cross left his patrol car and one minute later, while he was still in the back lane, he heard that the suspect had been arrested. Heading toward the place where the suspect had been arrested, he walked from the lane and then across Logan Avenue. He encountered J.J. Harper on Logan, adjacent to Stanley Knowles Park.

Upon seeing Harper, he approached him and asked for identification. According to Cross, Harper replied that he did not have to tell Cross anything. Cross said Harper then started to walk past him. Cross reached out, placed his hand on Harper's arm and turned him around. At that point, Cross said, Harper pushed him, causing him to fall backward onto the sidewalk. As he fell, he grabbed Harper, pulling him down on top of him. Cross testified that while he was on his back, he struggled with Harper and felt a tugging at his holster. He said that he thought Harper was trying to pull his gun from its holster and, therefore, he reached down to grab his revolver. He said the gun came out of the holster with his and Harper's hands on it. He testified that he and Harper both were tugging at the gun when it went off. The blast hit Harper in the middle of the chest. …

It is clear from all the evidence that he did not confront Harper until *after* Pruden (the suspect) had been arrested. Cross' evidence was that within a minute of hearing of Pruden's arrest he confronted Harper.

It was obvious that Harper didn't fit major elements of the description of the suspect. Cross and Hodgins described the man whom they had seen fleeing from the stolen car as a "native male, 22 years of age, wearing dark clothing." Harper was a native male wearing dark clothing, but he was 37 years of age, considerably heavier than Pruden and of much stockier build. Pruden had outrun the police, while Harper was walking and apparently not breathing heavily. …

In an encounter between an officer and a citizen, the officer legitimately may exercise his or her right to ask questions and request identification, and generally the citizen will comply, but also legitimately may exercise his or her right to refuse to do so. Up to this point, both are within their respective legal rights and powers. But, if an officer does not place the citizen under arrest, or if the officer is not making a lawful detention and has no intention of doing so, the officer exceeds his or her authority by grabbing and detaining the citizen forcibly. While the use of force to detain individuals falls within the general scope of a police officer's rights, an officer's actions may amount to an unjustifiable use of police power if he or she uses force without making a lawful arrest or detention. Beyond those parameters the officer's use of force is not authorized or justified. …

Cross, we believe, got caught up in the excitement of the chase. We believe that he decided to stop and question Harper simply because Harper was a male Aboriginal person in his path. We are unable to find any other reasonable explanation for his being stopped. We do not accept Cross' explanation. It was clearly a retroactive attempt to justify stopping Harper. We believe that Cross had no basis to connect him to any crime in the area and that his refusal or unwillingness to permit Harper to pass freely was, for reasons which we discuss later, racially motivated.

As disclosed by the facts, Cross had neither reasonable nor probable grounds to believe that Harper was the suspect the police were after. He had been informed that the person chased from the very lane he had been watching had been apprehended, and he had no reason to believe that his fellow officers were mistaken. If Cross had doubts or suspicions about the suspect in custody, he erred in not seeking further information by radio from those who had arrested Pruden. Harper was walking, not running, and it is highly unlikely that he would have gone far had Cross decided to radio quickly for further information. Also, according to Cross' own account of the incident, Harper was not behaving or walking in a suspicious manner. It would appear, then, that Harper simply had the misfortune of being an Aboriginal man in dark clothing, in that area late at night. In our opinion, Cross exercised poor judgment in pursuing the matter forcibly as he did after Harper legitimately had refused to identify himself.

The *Report of the Commission on Systemic Racism in the Ontario Criminal Justice System* (1996), chapter 10 reported that black respondents were more frequently stopped by police than white and Chinese respondents. Black respondents also reported higher levels of dissatisfaction with their investigative encounters with the police. The commission recommended the development of provincial guidelines for the exercise of police discretion to stop and question people.

## Detention Powers

In *R. v. Simpson* (1993), 79 C.C.C. (3d) 482 (Ont. C.A.), the police observed the accused emerge from a house described in a police memorandum as a "crack house" and get into a car. The car was then pulled over and the accused questioned. The police officer noticed a bulge in the accused's pocket, touched it, and felt a hard lump. The officer then asked Simpson to remove the object. The object was cocaine and the accused was convicted at trial of possession of narcotics for the purpose of trafficking. His appeal was allowed by the Ontario Court of Appeal and an acquittal entered. Doherty J.A. stated:

> In my opinion, where an individual is detained by the police in the course of efforts to determine whether that individual is involved in criminal activity being investigated by the police, that detention can only be justified if the detaining officer has some "articulable cause" for the detention.
>
> The phrase "articulable cause" appears in American jurisprudence concerned with the constitutionality of investigative detentions. In *Terry v. Ohio*, 392 U.S. 1, 88 S. Ct. 1868 (1968), the court considered whether a police officer could "stop and frisk" a suspect whom he did not have reasonable cause to arrest. ... The court held at pp. 20-1, that no interference with the individual's right to move about could be justified absent articulable cause for that interference. Chief Justice Warren for the majority said:
>
>> And in justifying the particular intrusion the police officer must be able to point to specific and articulable facts which, taken together with rational inferences from those facts, reasonably warrant that intrusion. The scheme of the Fourth Amendment becomes meaningful only when it is assured that at some point the conduct of those charged with enforcing the laws can be subjected to the more detached, neutral scrutiny of a judge who must evaluate the reasonableness of a particular search or seizure in light of the particular circumstances. And in making that assessment it is imperative that the facts be judged against an objective standard: would the facts available to the officer at the moment of the seizure or the search "warrant a man of reasonable caution in the belief" that the action taken was appropriate? *Cf. Carroll v. United States*, 267 U.S. 132 (1925); *Beck v. Ohio*, 379 U.S. 89, 96-97 (1964). Anything less would invite intrusions upon constitutionally guaranteed rights based on nothing more substantial than inarticulate hunches, a result this Court has consistently refused to sanction. See, *e.g.*, *Beck v. Ohio*, *supra*; *Rios v. United States*, 364 U.S. 253 (1960); *Henry v. United States*, 361 U.S. 98 (1959). And simple "'good faith on the part of the arresting officer is not enough.' ... If subjective good faith alone were the test, the protections of the Fourth Amendment would evaporate, and

the people would be 'secure in their persons, houses, papers and effects,' only in the discretion of the police." *Beck v. Ohio, supra*, at 97.

The requirement that the facts must meet an objectively discernible standard is recognized in connection with the arrest power (*R. v. Storrey* (1990), 53 C.C.C. (3d) 316 at p. 324 [see infra]), and serves to avoid indiscriminate and discriminatory exercises of the police power. A "hunch" based entirely on intuition gained by experience cannot suffice, no matter how accurate that "hunch" might prove to be.

Such subjectively based assessments can too easily mask discriminatory conduct based on such irrelevant factors as the detainee's sex, colour, age, ethnic origin or sexual orientation. Equally, without objective criteria, detentions could be based on mere speculation. A guess which proves accurate becomes in hindsight a "hunch." In this regard, I must disagree with *R. v. Nelson* (1987), 35 C.C.C. (3d) 347 at p. 355, 29 C.R.R. 80, 46 M.V.R. 145 (Man. C.A.), where it is said that detention may be justified if the officer "intuitively senses that his intervention may be required in the public interest." Rather, I agree with Professor Young in "All Along the Watch Tower" (1991), 28 *Osgoode Hall L.J.* 328, at p. 375:

> In order to avoid an attribution of arbitrary conduct, the state official must be operating under a set of criteria that at minimum, bears some relationship to a reasonable suspicion of crime but not necessarily to a credibly-based probability of crime.

I also find some support for the fixing of the limits of police interference with an individual's right to move about to instances where the police can demonstrate articulable cause in *R. v. Mack* (1988), 44 C.C.C. (3d) 513, [1988] 2 S.C.R. 903, 67 C.R. (3d) 1. In setting the contours of the defence of entrapment, Lamer J. said at p. 552, after referring to *R. v. Amato* (1982), 69 C.C.C. (2d) 31, 140 D.L.R. (3d) 405, [1982] 2 S.C.R. 418:

> I take this statement to mean that the police are entitled to provide opportunities for the commission of offences where they have reasonable suspicion to believe that the individuals in question are already engaged in criminal conduct. The absence of a reasonable suspicion *may* establish a defence of entrapment for two reasons: first, it may indicate the police are engaged in random virtue-testing or, worse, are carrying on in that way for dubious motives unrelated to the investigation and repression of crimes and are as such *mala fides*.

Turning to this case, I can find no articulable cause justifying the detention. Constable Wilkin had information of unknown age that another police officer had been told that the residence was believed to be a "crack house." Constable Wilkin did not know the primary source of the information and he had no reason to believe that the source in general, or this particular piece of information, was reliable. It is doubtful that this information standing alone could provide a reasonable suspicion that the suspect residence was the scene of criminal activity.

Any glimmer of an articulable cause disappears, however, when one considers whether Constable Wilkin had reason to suspect that the appellant or the driver of the car was involved in criminal activity. He knew nothing about either person and he did not suggest that anything either had done, apart from being at the house, aroused his suspicion or suggested criminal activity. Attendance at a location believed to be the site of ongoing criminal activity is a factor which may contribute to the existence of "articulable cause." Where that is the sole factor, however, and the information concerning the location is itself of unknown age and reliability, no articulable cause exists. Were it otherwise, the police would have a general warrant to stop anyone who happened to attend at any place which the police had a reason to believe could be the site of ongoing criminal activity.

The Court of Appeal concluded that the accused's rights under s. 9 and s. 8 of the Charter had been violated and that the evidence should be excluded under s. 24(2) in part because:

> The seriousness of these constitutional violations is also clear. Constable Wilkin obviously considered that any and all individuals who attended at a residence that the police had any reason to believe might be the site of ongoing criminal activity were subject to detention and questioning by the police. This dangerous and erroneous perception of the reach of police powers must be emphatically rejected. Judicial acquiescence in such conduct by the reception of evidence obtained through that conduct would bring the administration of justice into disrepute.
>
> The evidence should have been excluded.

Note that the detention powers contemplated in *Simpson* have been widely accepted by other courts. What is the source of law for this arguable expansion of police powers? How clear are the limits to this power? Does s. 10 of the Charter apply to a *Simpson* detention? What about powers of search incident to arrest discussed below? On *Simpson* see J. Stribopoulos, "Unchecked Power: The Constitutional Regulation of Arrest Reconsidered" (2003), 48 *McGill L.J.* 225; T. Quigley, "Brief Investigatory Detentions: A Critique of R. v. Simpson" (2004), 41 *Alta. L. Rev.* 935.

### Arrest Powers

Section 494 of the *Criminal Code* sets out the arrest powers that anyone has without a judicial warrant and s. 495 sets out the wider arrest powers of a peace officer without a warrant. Note that under s. 495(2), the general rule is that a peace officer shall not arrest a person without warrant for less serious offences under the Code where the public interest in establishing the identity and securing the attendance of the person in court, securing evidence of the offence, and preventing the repetition of the offence or the commission of another offence can be satisfied by issuing an appearance notice.

A judicial warrant for an arrest can also be obtained. Under s. 507(4) of the *Criminal Code*, if the justice of the peace considers that a case has been made out on oath for compelling an accused to answer the charge of the offence, then he or she will issue a summons unless the evidence presented discloses reasonable grounds to believe that it is necessary in the public interest to issue an arrest warrant. In this, as in many other of the arrest provisions in the *Criminal Code*, there is a distinct preference for the procedure that constitutes the least drastic interference with the accused's liberty.

In *R. v. Storrey* (1990), 53 C.C.C. (3d) 316 the Supreme Court examined s. 495(1). Cory J. stated that the section

makes it clear that the police were required to have reasonable and probable grounds that the appellant had committed the offence of aggravated assault before they could arrest him. Without such an important protection, even the most democratic society could all too easily fall prey to the abuses and excesses of a police state. In order to safeguard the liberty of citizens, the *Criminal Code* requires the police, when attempting to obtain a warrant for an arrest, to demonstrate to a judicial officer that they have reasonable and probable grounds to believe that the person to be arrested has committed the offence. In the case of an arrest made without a warrant, it is even more important for the police to demonstrate that they have those same reasonable and probable grounds upon which they base the arrest.

There is an additional safeguard against arbitrary arrest. It is not sufficient for the police officer to personally believe that he or she has reasonable and probable grounds to make an arrest. Rather, it must be objectively established that those reasonable and probable grounds did in fact exist. That is to say a reasonable person, standing in the shoes of the police officer, would have believed that reasonable and probable grounds existed to make the arrest.

In summary then, the *Criminal Code* requires that an arresting officer must subjectively have reasonable and probable grounds on which to base the arrest. Those grounds must, in addition, be justifiable from an objective point of view. That is to say, a reasonable person placed in the position of the officer must be able to conclude that there were indeed reasonable and probable grounds for the arrest. On the other hand, the police need not demonstrate anything more than reasonable and probable grounds. Specifically they are not required to establish a *prima facie* case for conviction before making the arrest.

In the case at bar, the trial judge specifically stated that "Larkin had reasonable and probable grounds" to make the arrest. In my view there was ample evidence on which the trial judge could very properly make that finding. The reasonable grounds could be based subjectively on the testimony of Larkin and objectively upon the cumulative effect of the following items; (a) the possession and ownership by Storrey of a 1973 blue Thunderbird, which was a relatively unusual and uncommon car and was the type of car used in the infraction; (b) the fact that he had been stopped by the police on several occasions driving that car; (c) his past record of violence; (d) the fact that two of the victims picked out a picture of Cameron as someone who looked like their assailant; and (e) the remarkable resemblance of Storrey to Cameron. These factors taken together clearly were sufficient in their cumulative effect to constitute reasonable and probable grounds for Larkin to arrest the appellant.

It should be noted, as well, that there is nothing to indicate that there was anything in the circumstances of the arrest which would make it suspect on any other ground. That is to say, there is no indication that the arrest was made because a police officer was biased towards a person of a different race, nationality or colour, or that there was a personal enmity between a police officer directed towards the person arrested. These factors, if established, might have the effect of rendering invalid an otherwise lawful arrest. However, the arrest of the appellant was in every respect lawful and proper.

**Powers Incident to Arrest**

### Cloutier v. Langlois
Supreme Court of Canada
(1990), 53 C.C.C. (3d) 257

[In this case, a lawyer charged two police officers with assault after he was frisk searched before he was placed in a police car while being arrested for unpaid parking tickets. The court held that the search of the lawyer, who was being verbally abusive, was justified for the police officer's safety and not conducted with excessive force or constraint. They dismissed the assault charges in the following opinion for the court:]

L'HEUREUX-DUBÉ: A "frisk" search incidental to a lawful arrest reconciles the public's interest in the effective and safe enforcement of the law on the one hand, and on the other its interest in ensuring the freedom and dignity of individuals. The minimal intrusion involved in the search is necessary to ensure that criminal justice is properly administered. I agree with the opinion of the Ontario Court of Appeal as stated in … *R. v. Morrison* [(1987), 35 C.C.C. (3d) 437 (Ont. C.A.)] … that the existence of reasonable and probable grounds is not a prerequisite to the existence of a police power to search. The exercise of this power is not, however, unlimited. Three propositions can be derived from the authorities and a consideration of the underlying interests.

1.   This power does not impose a duty. The police have some discretion in conducting the search. Where they are satisfied that the law can be effectively and safely applied without a search, the police may see fit not to conduct a search. They must be in a position to assess the circumstances of each case so as to determine whether a search meets the underlying objectives.

2.   The search must be for a valid objective in pursuit of the ends of criminal justice, such as the discovery of an object that may be a threat to the safety of the police, the accused or the public, or that may facilitate escape or act as evidence against the accused. The purpose of the search must not be unrelated to the objectives of the proper administration of justice, which would be the case, for example, if the purpose of the search was to intimidate, ridicule or pressure the accused in order to obtain admissions.

3.   The search must not be conducted in an abusive fashion and, in particular, the use of physical or psychological constraint should be proportionate to the objectives sought and the other circumstances of the situation.

A search which does not meet these objectives could be characterized as unreasonable and unjustified at common law.

Should the police be able to seize hair or cheek swab samples for DNA testing as part of their search powers incident to arrest?

In *R. v. Stillman* (1997), 113 C.C.C. (3d) 321, a majority of the Supreme Court held that the taking of bodily samples for DNA testing without the accused's consent and without a warrant infringed ss. 7 and 8 of the Charter and that the samples should be excluded under s. 24(2). Cory J. for the majority (Lamer C.J., La Forest, Sopinka, Iacobucci, and Major JJ.) stated:

> The power to search and seize incidental to arrest was a pragmatic extension to the power of arrest. Obviously the police must be able to protect themselves from attack by the accused who has weapons concealed on his person or close at hand. The police must be able to collect and preserve evidence located at the site of the arrest or in a nearby motor vehicle. ...
>
> The common law power cannot be so broad as to empower police officers to seize bodily samples. They are usually in no danger of disappearing. Here, there was no likelihood that the appellant's teeth impressions would change, nor that his hair follicles would present a different DNA profile with the passage of time. There was simply no possibility of the evidence sought being destroyed if it was not seized immediately. It should be remembered that one of the limitations to the common law power articulated in *Cloutier v. Langlois*, [*supra*], was the discretionary aspect of the power and that it should not be abusive. The common law power of search incidental to arrest cannot be so broad as to encompass the seizure without valid statutory authority of bodily samples in the face of a refusal to provide them. If it is, then the common law rule itself is unreasonable, since it is too broad and fails to properly balance the competing rights involved. ...
>
> The taking of the dental impressions, hair samples and buccal swabs from the accused also contravened the appellant's s. 7 Charter right to security of the person. The taking of the bodily samples was highly intrusive. It violated the sanctity of the body which is essential to the maintenance of human dignity. It was the ultimate invasion of the appellant's privacy. See *Pohoretsky* (1987), 33 C.C.C. (3d) 398 ... . In *Dyment* (1988), 45 C.C.C. (3d) 244 ... , La Forest J. emphasized that "the use of a person's body without his consent to obtain information about him, invades an area of personal privacy essential to the maintenance of his human dignity." Quite simply, the taking of the samples without authorization violated the appellant's right to security of his person and contravened the principles of fundamental justice.

See now *Criminal Code*, ss. 487.04 to 487.09 for warrants to secure hair and blood for DNA testing.

L'Heureux-Dubé J. (Gonthier J. concurring) dissented and held that the seizures of the bodily samples were authorized by the common law powers of search incident to arrest because there was a minimal invasion of the accused's bodily integrity and no search warrant procedure for seizing samples for DNA analysis existed at the time.

*R. v. Stillman* is also the leading case on the proper test for excluding evidence under s. 24(2) of the Charter. Cory J. excluded the seized bodily samples under s. 24(2) as conscriptive evidence that would affect the fairness of the trial. He stressed that they were obtained by compelling the accused to participate in providing the evidence and were not otherwise discoverable "by the state without the conscription of the accused in violation of the Charter." He stated:

If the evidence, obtained in a manner which violates the Charter, involved the accused being compelled to incriminate himself either by a statement or the use as evidence of the body or of bodily substances it will be classified as conscriptive evidence. See *Manninen*, ...; *Ross*, ... and *Bartle* ... . On the other hand, if the evidence, obtained in a manner which violates the Charter, did not involve the accused being compelled to incriminate himself either by a statement or the use as evidence of the body or of bodily substances it will be classified as non-conscriptive evidence. ...

Where evidence is determined to be non-conscriptive, its admission generally will not render the trial unfair and the court should proceed to consider the seriousness of the violation. However, where evidence is found to be of a conscriptive nature the court must proceed to the second step, which involves an assessment of whether the evidence would have been discovered in the absence of (but for) the Charter violation.

... [W]here the conscriptive evidence would not have been discovered in the absence of the unlawful conscription of the accused, its admission would generally tend to render the trial unfair. In those circumstances it is not necessary to consider the seriousness of the violation, or the repute of the administration of justice, as a finding that the admission of the evidence would render the trial unfair means that the administration of justice would necessarily be brought into disrepute if the evidence were not excluded under s. 24(2). ...

The summary itself can be reduced to this short form:

1. Classify the evidence as conscriptive or non-conscriptive based upon the manner in which the evidence was obtained. If the evidence is non-conscriptive, its admission will not render the trial unfair and the court will proceed to consider the seriousness of the breach and the effect of exclusion on the repute of the administration of justice.

2. If the evidence is conscriptive and the Crown fails to demonstrate on a balance of probabilities that the evidence would have been discovered by alternative non-conscriptive means, then its admission will render the trial unfair. The Court, as a general rule, will exclude the evidence without considering the seriousness of the breach or the effect of exclusion on the repute of the administration of justice. This must be the result since an unfair trial would necessarily bring the administration of justice into disrepute.

3. If the evidence is found to be conscriptive and the Crown demonstrates on a balance of probabilities that it would have been discovered by alternative non-conscriptive means, then its admission will generally not render the trial unfair. However, the seriousness of the Charter breach and the effect of exclusion on the repute of the administration of justice will have to be considered.

Cory J. admitted a tissue discarded in the police station containing mucous because the accused had not been forced to provide that bodily sample and the unreasonable seizure of the tissue against the accused's wishes was not a serious violation because it did not interfere with the accused's "bodily integrity, nor cause him any loss of dignity."

McLachlin J. (L'Heureux-Dubé and Gonthier JJ. concurring) would not have excluded the bodily samples and stated that excluding evidence under s. 24(2) simply because it was conscriptive evidence that would affect the fairness of the trial

runs counter to the spirit and wording of s. 24(2), which requires that judges in all cases balance all factors which may affect the repute of the administration of justice, and elevates the factor of trial unfairness to a dominant and in many cases conclusive status. Second, it rests on an expanded and, with respect, erroneous concept of self-incrimination or conscription which equates any non-consensual participation by or use of the accused's body in evidence gathering with trial unfairness. Third, it erroneously assumes that anything that affects trial fairness automatically renders the trial so fundamentally unfair that other factors can never outweigh the unfairness, with the result that it becomes unnecessary to consider other factors.

---

When should the police be able to conduct a strip search as part of a search incident to arrest?

## R. v. Golden
Supreme Court of Canada
(2001), 159 C.C.C. (3d) 449

IACOBUCCI and ARBOUR JJ. (Major, Binnie, and LeBel JJ. concurring): Since *Cloutier*, this Court has addressed the constitutionality of the seizure of bodily samples at common law in *Stillman*, supra. Cory J., speaking for the majority, held that the seizure of bodily samples, namely hair samples, buccal swabs and dental impressions, was not authorized by the common law power to search incident to arrest. Such a serious interference with a person's bodily integrity required statutory authorization and could not be justified under the common law power to search incident to arrest. Cory J. distinguished the situation in *Stillman* from other cases, such as *Cloutier*, supra, where searches incident to arrest had been found not to infringe the Charter on the basis that "completely different concerns arise where the search and seizure infringes upon a person's bodily integrity, which may constitute the ultimate affront to human dignity" (*Stillman*, supra, at para. 39). …

Strip searches are thus inherently humiliating and degrading for detainees regardless of the manner in which they are carried out and for this reason they cannot be carried out simply as a matter of routine policy. The adjectives used by individuals to describe their experience of being strip searched give some sense of how a strip search, even one that is carried out in a reasonable manner, can affect detainees: "humiliating," "degrading," "demeaning," "upsetting," and "devastating." … Some commentators have gone as far as to describe strip searches as "visual rape" (P.R. Shuldiner, "Visual Rape: A Look at the Dubious Legality of Strip Searches" (1979), 13 *J. Marshall L. Rev.* 273). Women and minorities in particular may have a real fear of strip searches and may experience such a search as equivalent to a sexual assault. … The psychological effects of strip searches may also be particularly traumatic for individuals who have previously been subject to abuse (Commission of Inquiry into Certain Events at the Prison for Women in Kingston, *The Prison for Women in Kingston* (1996), at pp. 86-89). Routine strip searches may also be distasteful and difficult for the police officers conducting them. …

The fact that the police have reasonable and probable grounds to carry out an arrest does not confer upon them the automatic authority to carry out a strip search, even where the strip search meets the definition of being "incident to lawful arrest" as discussed above. Rather, additional grounds pertaining to the purpose of the strip search are required. In *Cloutier*, supra, this Court concluded that a common law search incident to arrest does not require additional grounds beyond the reasonable and probable grounds necessary to justify the lawfulness of the arrest itself: *Cloutier*, supra, at pp. 185-86. However, this conclusion was reached in the context of a "frisk" search, which involved a minimal invasion of the detainee's privacy and personal integrity. In contrast, a strip search is a much more intrusive search and, accordingly, a higher degree of justification is required in order to support the higher degree of interference with individual freedom and dignity. In order to meet the constitutional standard of reasonableness that will justify a strip search, the police must establish that they have reasonable and probable grounds for concluding that a strip search is necessary in the particular circumstances of the arrest.

In light of the serious infringement of privacy and personal dignity that is an inevitable consequence of a strip search, such searches are only constitutionally valid at common law where they are conducted as an incident to a lawful arrest for the purpose of discovering weapons in the detainee's possession or evidence related to the reason for the arrest. In addition, the police must establish reasonable and probable grounds justifying the strip search in addition to reasonable and probable grounds justifying the arrest. Where these preconditions to conducting a strip search incident to arrest are met, it is also necessary that the strip search be conducted in a manner that does not infringe s. 8 of the Charter.

Parliament could require that strip searches be authorized by warrants or telewarrants, which would heighten compliance with the Charter. At a minimum, if there is no prior judicial authorization for the strip search, several factors should be considered by the authorities in deciding whether, and if so how, to conduct such a procedure.

In this connection, we find the guidelines contained in the English legislation, P.A.C.E. concerning the conduct of strip searches to be in accordance with the constitutional requirements of s. 8 of the Charter. The following questions, which draw upon the common law principles as well as the statutory requirements set out in the English legislation, provide a framework for the police in deciding how best to conduct a strip search incident to arrest in compliance with the Charter:

1. Can the strip search be conducted at the police station and, if not, why not?

2. Will the strip search be conducted in a manner that ensures the health and safety of all involved?

3. Will the strip search be authorized by a police officer acting in a supervisory capacity?

4. Has it been ensured that the police officer(s) carrying out the strip search are of the same gender as the individual being searched?

5.  Will the number of police officers involved in the search be no more than is reasonably necessary in the circumstances?

6.  What is the minimum of force necessary to conduct the strip search?

7.  Will the strip search be carried out in a private area such that no one other than the individuals engaged in the search can observe the search?

8.  Will the strip search be conducted as quickly as possible and in a way that ensures that the person is not completely undressed at any one time?

9.  Will the strip search involve only a visual inspection of the arrestee's genital and anal areas without any physical contact?

10. If the visual inspection reveals the presence of a weapon or evidence in a body cavity (not including the mouth), will the detainee be given the option of removing the object himself or of having the object removed by a trained medical professional?

11. Will a proper record be kept of the reasons for and the manner in which the strip search was conducted?

Strip searches should generally only be conducted at the police station except where there are exigent circumstances requiring that the detainee be searched prior to being transported to the police station. Such exigent circumstances will only be established where the police have reasonable and probable grounds to believe that it is necessary to conduct the search in the field rather than at the police station. Strip searches conducted in the field could only be justified where there is a demonstrated necessity and urgency to search for weapons or objects that could be used to threaten the safety of the accused, the arresting officers or other individuals. The police would also have to show why it would have been unsafe to wait and conduct the strip search at the police station rather than in the field. Strip searches conducted in the field represent a much greater invasion of privacy and pose a greater threat to the detainee's bodily integrity and, for this reason, field strip searches can only be justified in exigent circumstances.

Having said all this, we believe that legislative intervention could be an important addition to the guidance set out in these reasons concerning the conduct of strip searches incident to arrest. Clear legislative prescription as to when and how strip searches should be conducted would be of assistance to the police and to the courts. …

BASTARACHE J. (McLachlin C.J., Gonthier and L'Heureux-Dubé JJ. concurring) dissented: The same requirements justifying the conduct of a search incident to arrest apply regardless of whether the accused is subjected to a "frisk," a fingerprinting, the taking of a bodily sample or a strip search. These requirements … include that the search be carried out for a valid objective in pursuit of the ends of criminal justice, such as the discovery of a weapon or evidence, and that it not be conducted in an abusive fashion. In addition, the power to search incident to arrest is a discretionary one and need not be exercised where police are satisfied that the law can be effectively and safely applied in its absence; see *Cloutier*, supra, at p. 186.

The unworkability of an approach that would create distinct categories of searches rests in the fact that all of the types of searches listed above may take many forms ranging from a low degree of intrusiveness to a high degree of intrusiveness, depending on the circumstances of the case. For example, on the facts of this case, the strip search of the accused which occurred in the stairwell was possibly not more intrusive than "pat-down" or frisk searches. By contrast, the search in the restaurant impacted more severely on the privacy and dignity of the accused. [The stairwell search involved looking down the suspect's pants while the restaurant search involved pulling drugs from his buttocks.] The standard of justification to which police will be held depends on the circumstances of the specific search in question, not upon the category into which it is placed.

An approach which would categorize searches according to the degree of intrusiveness also risks confusion. The taking of a hair or other easily obtainable bodily sample may seem no more intrusive than a full strip search. The taking of a hair sample in the absence of a warrant may nonetheless be found to violate s. 8 if police are not able to justify the search on the basis that it was for the purpose of discovering and preserving evidence or seizing weapons incident to arrest; see *R. v. Stillman*, [1997] 1 S.C.R. 607. By contrast, a strip search conducted in the absence of prior authorization may be lawful if it meets the common law requirements of a search incident to arrest even if the search was very intrusive.

In all cases, providing the arrest is lawful and the object of the search is related to the crime, the sole issue is the reasonability of the search. My colleagues assert that the fact that police have reasonable and probable grounds to carry out an arrest does not confer on them the authority to carry out a strip search, even where the strip search is related to the purpose of the arrest. They add an additional requirement in the case of strip searches that the police must establish reasonable and probable grounds justifying the conduct of the strip search itself. By placing strip searches in a category distinct from other types of searches, my colleagues have bypassed this Court's decision in *Cloutier*, supra, at pp. 185-86, that the existence of reasonable and probable grounds is not a prerequisite to the existence of a police power to search. I agree with my colleagues that the more intrusive the search and the higher the degree of infringement of personal privacy, the higher degree of justification; however, I disagree that the common law requires police to prove that they had reasonable and probable grounds to justify the strip search. Interpreting the common law in a manner consistent with Charter principles does not require the Court to redefine the common law right by adding this additional requirement. The existing common law rule that police demonstrate an objectively valid reason for the arrest rather than for the search is consistent with s. 8 of the Charter, provided that the strip search is for a valid objective and is not conducted in an abusive fashion.

---

Should the common law power of warrantless searches incident to arrest extend to a search of the accused's car? A search conducted six hours after the arrest? See *R. v. Caslake* (1998), 121 C.C.C. (3d) 97, where the Supreme Court answers "yes" to both questions.

## VI. A CASE STUDY OF THE INVESTIGATION OF DRUNK DRIVING

Drunk driving offences are a commonly prosecuted *Criminal Code* offence. Under s. 253, it is an offence to operate or have the care and control of a motor vehicle if a person's ability to operate the vehicle is impaired by alcohol or a drug or that person has a blood alcohol concentration in excess of 80 milligrams of alcohol/100 millilitres of blood.

The police have developed spot check campaigns that involve the random stopping of vehicles in order to detect whether a driver has been drinking. If the police officer "reasonably suspects" that a driver has alcohol in his or her body, then the police officer under s. 254(2) of the *Criminal Code* may demand that the driver supply forthwith a breath sample.

If by failure of a roadside breath test or other evidence, the police officer believes on reasonable and probable grounds that the driver has committed a drinking driving offence under s. 253, then he or she may under s. 254(3) demand that the driver supply forthwith or as soon as practicable a breath sample into an evidentiary breathalyzer at the police station or, if the provision of the breath sample is not possible or impracticable, a blood sample. Warrants can be obtained for the taking of blood samples under s. 256 of the Code.

Under s. 254(5), everyone commits a criminal offence "who, without reasonable excuse, fails or refuses to comply with a demand made by a police officer under this section." This offence applies to refusal to provide either roadside or police station breath samples.

### R. v. Therens
Supreme Court of Canada
(1985), 18 C.C.C. (3d) 481

[The accused in this case lost control of his vehicle and collided with a tree. The investigating officer demanded under what is now s. 254(3) that the accused accompany him to the police station to provide breath samples. The accused was cooperative and complied. A certificate that his blood alcohol level was over the legal limit was obtained as a result of the breath test. At no time was the accused informed of his right under s. 10(b) of the Charter to retain and instruct counsel.]

Le DAIN J.: In determining the meaning that should be given to the word "detention" in s. 10 of the Charter it is necessary to consider the purpose of the section. This is the approach to the interpretation and application of the Charter that was affirmed by this Court in *Hunter v. Southam Inc.*, *supra*, in which Dickson J. (as he then was) said at p. 106 C.C.C., pp. 650-1 D.L.R., p. 157 S.C.R.:

> Since the proper approach to the interpretation of the *Canadian Charter of Rights and Freedoms* is a purposive one, before it is possible to assess the reasonableness or unreasonableness of the impact of a search or of a statute authorizing a search, it is first necessary to specify the purpose underlying s. 8: in other words, to delineate the nature of the interests it is meant to protect.

The purpose of s. 10 of the Charter is to ensure that in certain situations a person is made aware of the right to counsel and is permitted to retain and instruct counsel without delay. The situations specified by s. 10—arrest and detention—are obviously not the only ones in which a person may reasonably require the assistance of counsel, but they are situations in which the restraint of liberty might otherwise effectively prevent access to counsel or induce a person to assume that he or she is unable to retain and instruct counsel. In its use of the word "detention," s. 10 of the Charter is directed to a restraint of liberty other than arrest in which a person may reasonably require the assistance of counsel but might be prevented or impeded from retaining and instructing counsel without delay but for the constitutional guarantee.

In addition to the case of deprivation of liberty by physical constraint, there is, in my opinion, a detention within s. 10 of the Charter when a police officer or other agent of the State assumes control over the movement of a person by a demand or direction which may have significant legal consequences and which prevents or impedes access to counsel. ...

[Le Dain J. then held that the criminal liability under s. 254(5) of the Code for refusal to provide the breath sample constitutes psychological compulsion or coercion sufficient to make the accused's compliance involuntary.]

Although it is not strictly necessary for purposes of this case, I would go further. In my opinion, it is not realistic, as a general rule, to regard compliance with a demand or direction by a police officer as truly voluntary, in the sense that the citizen feels that he or she has the choice to obey or not, even where there is in fact a lack of statutory or common law authority for the demand or direction and therefore an absence of criminal liability for failure to comply with it. Most citizens are not aware of the precise legal limits of police authority. Rather than risk the application of physical force or prosecution for wilful obstruction, the reasonable person is likely to err on the side of caution, assume lawful authority and comply with the demand. The element of psychological compulsion, in the form of a reasonable perception of suspension of freedom of choice, is enough to make the restraint of liberty involuntary. Detention may be effected without the application or threat of application of physical restraint if the person concerned submits or acquiesces in the deprivation of liberty and reasonably believes that the choice to do otherwise does not exist.

[ESTEY J. agreed with Le Dain J. that s. 10(b) of the Charter had been violated and held that the evidence of the breathalyzer certificate should be excluded under s. 24(2) of the Charter because it was obtained as a result of a "flagrant" and "overt" Charter violation. He concluded:]

... If s. 10(b) of the Charter of Rights can be offended without any statutory authority for the police conduct here in question and without the loss of admissibility of evidence obtained by such a breach then s. 10(b) would be stripped of any meaning and would have no place in the catalogue of "legal rights" found in the Charter.

[Dickson C.J.C., Beetz, Lamer, Chouinard, and Wilson JJ. concurred with Estey J. on this point. Le Dain and McIntyre JJ. dissented on the s. 24(2) issue and held that the admission of the breath certificate would not bring the administration of justice into disrepute largely because the police had acted in good faith in relying on a Supreme Court decision under the *Canadian Bill of Rights* that the accused was not detained in the circumstances.]

---

In *R. v. Mohl* (1989), 47 C.C.C. (3d) 575, the Supreme Court held that the admission of breathalyzer results would not bring the administration of justice into disrepute even if the accused's rights under s. 10(b) were violated because he was too drunk to understand his right to counsel.

---

The next cases deal with the legality and constitutionality of roadside spot checks for drunk driving and roadside breath tests. In each case, the accused had been charged with refusing to provide a roadside breath sample and challenged the legal validity of the request and detention.

### R. v. Dedman
Supreme Court of Canada
(1985) 20 C.C.C.(3d) 97

[A motorist was stopped by a RIDE (Reduce Impaired Driving Everywhere) spot check in 1980 and refused to provide a breath sample. He challenged the legality of the random stop.]

Le DAIN J. (McIntyre, Lamer, and Wilson JJ. concurring): Reliance was also placed on the general duties of police officers as the foundation for a common law authority to stop a motor vehicle for the purpose contemplated by the R.I.D.E. programme. ... It has been held that at common law the principal duties of police officers are the preservation of the peace, the prevention of crime, and the protection of life and property, from which is derived the duty to control traffic on the public roads.

The common law basis of police power has been derived from the nature and scope of police duty. Referring to the "powers associated with the duty," Ashworth J. in *R. v. Waterfield*, [[1964] 1 Q.B. 164], at pp. 170-1, laid down the test for the existence of police powers at common law, as a reflection of police duties. ...

The test laid down in *Waterfield*, while generally invoked in cases in which the issue is whether a police officer was acting in the execution of his duties, has been recognized as being a test for whether the officer had common law authority for what he did. ...

The first question, then, under the *Waterfield* test is whether the random stop fell within the general scope of the duties of a police officer under statute or common law. I do not think there can be any doubt that it fell within the general scope of the duties of a police officer to prevent crime and to protect life and property by the control of traffic. These are the very objects of the R.I.D.E. programme, which is a measure to improve the deterrence and detection of impaired driving, a notorious cause of injury and death.

Turning to the second branch of the *Waterfield* test, it must be said respectfully that neither *Waterfield* itself nor most of the cases which have applied it throw much light on the criteria for determining whether a particular interference with liberty is an unjustifiable use of a power associated with a police duty. There is a suggestion of the correct test, I think, in the use of the words "reasonably necessary." … The interference with liberty must be necessary for the carrying out of the particular police duty and it must be reasonable, having regard to the nature of the liberty interfered with and the importance of the public purpose served by the interference. Because of the seriousness of the problem of impaired driving, there can be no doubt about the importance and necessity of a programme to improve the deterrence of it. The right to circulate on the highway free from unreasonable interference is an important one, but it is, as I have said, a licensed activity subject to regulation and control in the interest of safety. The objectionable nature of a random stop is chiefly that it is made on a purely arbitrary basis, without any grounds for suspicion or belief that the particular driver has committed or is committing an offence. It is this aspect of the random stop that makes it capable of producing unpleasant psychological effects for the innocent driver. These effects, however, would tend to be minimized by the well-publicized nature of the programme, which is a necessary feature of its deterrent purpose. Moreover, the stop would be of relatively short duration and of slight inconvenience. Weighing these factors, I am of the opinion that having regard to the importance of the public purpose served, the random stop, as a police action necessary to the carrying out of that purpose, was not an unreasonable interference with the right to circulate on the public highway. It was not, therefore, an unjustifiable use of a power associated with the police duty, within the *Waterfield* test. I would accordingly hold that there was common law authority for the random vehicle stop for the purpose contemplated by the R.I.D.E. programme.

DICKSON C.J. (Beetz and Chouinard JJ. concurring (in dissent)): The R.I.D.E. programme was not, at the time the appellant was stopped, expressly authorized by statute, either federal or provincial. I agree with Mr. Justice Le Dain that none of the provincial statutory provisions relied upon can be interpreted to grant police officers authority to request a motorist stop for the purposes of the R.I.D.E. programme. In particular, s. 14 of the *Highway Traffic Act*, R.S.O. 1970, c. 202, as amended by 1979, c. 57, s. 2 (now R.S.O. 1980, c. 198, s. 19), does not provide statutory authority for the signal to stop. It is unnecessary to express any opinion as to the constitutional validity of s. 14. …

With respect, I am unable to agree with Mr. Justice Le Dain that the general duties of police officers provide the foundation for common law authority to stop a motor vehicle for the purpose and in the manner contemplated by the R.I.D.E. programme. It has always been a fundamental tenet of the rule of law in this country that the police, in carrying out their general duties as law enforcement officers of the State, have limited powers and are only entitled to interfere with the liberty or property of the citizen to the extent authorized by law. ... Short of arrest, the police have never possessed legal authority at common law to detain anyone against his or her will for questioning, or to pursue an investigation. ...

I conclude that, without validly enacted legislation to support them, the random stops by the police under the R.I.D.E. programme are unlawful. In striving to achieve one desirable objective, the reduction of the death and injury that occurs each year from impaired driving, we must ensure that other, equally important, social values are not sacrificed. Individual freedom from interference by the State, no matter how laudable the motive of the police, must be guarded zealously against intrusion. Ultimately, this freedom is the measure of everyone's liberty and one of the cornerstones of the quality of life in our democratic society.

### R. v. Thomsen
Supreme Court of Canada
(1988), 40 C.C.C. (3d) 411

Le DAIN J.:  The first issue in the appeal is whether the demand made by the police officer to the appellant, pursuant to s. 234.1(1) of the *Criminal Code* [see now s. 254(2)], to accompany the officer to his car and to provide a sample of breath for a roadside screening device resulted in a detention of the appellant within the meaning of s. 10 of the Charter. ...

I venture to restate what I perceive to be the essentials of those reasons, as they appear in my judgment in *Therens*, as follows:

1.  In its use of the word "detention," s. 10 of the Charter is directed to a restraint of liberty other than arrest in which a person may reasonably require the assistance of counsel but might be prevented or impeded from retaining and instructing counsel without delay but for the constitutional guarantee.

2.  In addition to the case of deprivation of liberty by physical constraint, there is a detention within s. 10 of the Charter, when a police officer or other agent of the state assumes control over the movement of a person by a demand or direction which may have significant legal consequence and which prevents or impedes access to counsel.

3.  The necessary element of compulsion or coercion to constitute a detention may arise from criminal liability for refusal to comply with a demand or direction, or from a reasonable belief that one does not have a choice as to whether or not to comply.

4.  Section 10 of the Charter applies to a great variety of detentions of varying duration and is not confined to those of such duration as to make the effective use of *habeas corpus* possible.

In my opinion, the s. 234.1(1) demand by the police officer to the appellant to accompany him to his car and to provide a sample of breath into a roadside screening device fell within the above criteria. The demand by which the officer assumed control over the movement of the appellant was one which might have significant legal consequences because, although the evidence provided by the roadside screening could not be introduced against the appellant, it might provide the basis for a s. 235(1) breathalyzer demand [see now s. 254(3)]. For this reason, and given the criminal liability under s. 234.1(2) for refusal [see now s. 254(5)], without reasonable excuse, to comply with the demand, the situation was one in which a person might reasonably require the assistance of counsel. The criminal liability for refusal also constituted the necessary compulsion or coercion to make the restraint of liberty a detention. The difference in duration of the restraint of liberty resulting from a s. 234.1(1) demand and that resulting from a s. 235(1) demand is not such as to prevent the former from constituting a detention within the meaning of s. 10 of the Charter. For these reasons I am of the opinion that as a result of the s. 234.1(1) demand the appellant was detained within the meaning of s. 10 of the Charter. ...

[Le Dain J. stated that the appellant had a right, upon being asked for a roadside breath sample and before providing it, to obtain and instruct counsel without delay. He then found that a denial of that right was implicit in the use of the words "forthwith" and "roadside" in s. 234.1(1) of the Code. He concluded that this denial of s. 10(b) rights was justified under s. 1 of the Charter, which provides as follows:]

> 1. The Canadian Charter of Rights and Freedoms guarantees the rights and freedoms set out in it subject only to such reasonable limits prescribed by law as can be demonstrably justified in a free and democratic society.

The important role played by roadside breath testing is not only to increase the detection of impaired driving, but to increase the perceived risk of its detection, which is essential to its effective deterrence. In my opinion the importance of this role makes the necessary limitation on the right to retain and instruct counsel at the roadside testing stage a reasonable one that is demonstrably justified in a free and democratic society, having regard to the fact that the right to counsel will be available, if necessary, at the more serious breathalyzer stage.

[Dickson C.J.C., Beetz, Estey, McIntyre, Wilson, and La Forest JJ. concurred with Le Dain J.]

---

In *R. v. Grant* (1991), 67 C.C.C. (3d) 268 the Supreme Court held that s. 252(2) of the Code did not authorize a demand for a roadside breath test when the police could not make the demand forthwith but rather had to wait 30 minutes until another officer could bring an approved roadside screening device. The court also held that the accused's right to counsel had been violated during this time and that, in the circumstances, s. 252(2) did not provide a justification under s. 1 for limiting the accused's right to counsel. In the result, the court restored the accused's acquittal of failing to provide a breath sample.

In *R. v. Bernshaw* (1995), 95 C.C.C. (3d) 193, the Supreme Court indicated that the requirement to provide a sample forthwith did not require an immediate demand if a 15-minute wait was necessary to ensure an accurate test. For example, the test would not be accurate if it was administered immediately after the accused had consumed alcohol. The court also indicated that the accused was not entitled to contact counsel during this time and any limit on the s. 10(b) right was justified under s. 1 of the Charter.

## R. v. Hufsky
### Supreme Court of Canada
### (1988), 40 C.C.C. (3d) 398

Le DAIN J.: The ... issue in the appeal is whether the random stop of the appellant's motor vehicle resulted in the appellant's being arbitrarily detained within the meaning of s. 9 of the *Canadian Charter of Rights and Freedoms*, which provides:

> 9. Everyone has the right not to be arbitrarily detained or imprisoned.

The first issue with respect to the appellant's contention based on s. 9 of the Charter is whether the random stop of the appellant for the purposes of the spot check procedure—in this case, to check the driver's licence and proof of insurance and to observe his condition or "sobriety"—resulted in a detention of the appellant within the meaning of s. 9. I refer to the period during which the appellant was stopped for the purposes of the spot check procedure, as distinct from the period following the s. 234.1(1) demand. In my opinion the random stop of the appellant for the purposes of the spot check procedure, although of relatively brief duration, resulted in a detention of the appellant within the meaning of s. 9 of the Charter. It fell within the general concept of detention that was applied in *R. v. Therens* (1985), 18 C.C.C. (3d) 481, 18 D.L.R. (4th) 655, [1985] 1 S.C.R. 613, and reaffirmed by the court in *R. v. Thomsen, post*, p. 411, which was heard at the same time as this appeal and in which judgment has been rendered today. By the random stop for the purposes of the spot check procedure the police officer assumed control over the movement of the appellant by a demand or direction that might have significant legal consequence, and there was penal liability for refusal to comply with the demand or direction. Although *Therens* and *Thomsen* were concerned with the meaning of "detention" in s. 10 of the Charter, there is, in my opinion, no reason in principle why the general approach to the meaning of detention reflected in those cases should not be applied to the meaning of "detained" in s. 9. The further restraint of liberty as a result of the s. 234.1(1) demand was also a detention, as was held in *Thomsen*, but that demand was not based directly on random choice, as was the stop for purposes of the spot check procedure, but on a reasonable suspicion, formed as a result of the observation of the appellant in the course of the spot check procedure, that the appellant had alcohol in his blood.

The next issue with respect to the appellant's contention based on s. 9 of the Charter is whether the detention resulting from the random stop for the purposes of the spot check procedure was arbitrary within the meaning of s. 9. Section 189a(1) of the

Ontario *Highway Traffic Act*, R.S.O. 1980, c. 198 empowers a police officer who is in the lawful execution of his duties and responsibilities to require the driver of a motor vehicle to stop. It does not specify that there must be some grounds or cause for stopping a particular driver but on its face leaves the choice of the drivers to be stopped to the discretion of the officer. In carrying out the purposes of the spot check procedure, including the observation of the condition or "sobriety" of the driver, the officer was clearly in the lawful execution of his duties and responsibilities. Although authorized by statute and carried out for lawful purposes, the random stop for the purposes of the spot check procedure nevertheless resulted, in my opinion, in an arbitrary detention because there were no criteria for the selection of the drivers to be stopped and subjected to the spot check procedure. The selection was in the absolute discretion of the police officer. A discretion is arbitrary if there are no criteria, express or implied, which govern its exercise. The appellant was therefore arbitrarily detained, within the meaning of s. 9 of the Charter, as a result of the random stop for the purposes of the spot check procedure, and the second constitutional question should accordingly be answered in the affirmative. ...

In view of the importance of highway safety and the role to be played in relation to it by a random stop authority for the purpose of increasing both the detection and the perceived risk of detection of motor vehicle offences, many of which cannot be detected by mere observation of driving, I am of the opinion that the limit imposed by s. 189a(1) of the *Highway Traffic Act* on the right not to be arbitrarily detained guaranteed by s. 9 of the Charter is a reasonable one that is demonstrably justified in a free and democratic society. The nature and degree of the intrusion of a random stop for the purposes of the spot check procedure in the present case, remembering that the driving of a motor vehicle is a licensed activity subject to regulation and control in the interests of safety, is proportionate to the purpose to be served. ...

The final issue in the appeal is whether, as contended by the appellant, the demand by the police officer that the appellant surrender his driver's license and insurance care for inspection, as required by s. 19(1) of the *Highway Traffic Act* and s. 3(1) of the *Compulsory Automobile Insurance Act*, infringed the right to be secure against unreasonable search or seizure guaranteed by s. 8 of the Charter, which is as follows:

> 8.   Everyone has the right to be secure against unreasonable search or seizure.

The appellant contended that the compelled production of his driver's licence and insurance card constituted a search within the meaning of s. 8 and that it was an unreasonable search because there were no criteria or guidelines for determining when a driver should be required to surrender these documents for inspection. In my opinion, the demand by the police officer, pursuant to the above legislative provision, that the appellant surrender his driver's licence and insurance card for inspection did not constitute a search within the meaning of s. 8 because it did not constitute an intrusion on a reasonable expectation of privacy: *cf. Hunter v. Southam Inc.* (1984), 14 C.C.C. (3d) 97, 11 D.L.R. (4th) 641, [1984] 2 S.C.R. 145. There is no such intrusion where a person is required to produce a licence or permit or other documentary evidence of a status or compliance with some legal requirement that is a lawful condition of the exercise of a right or privilege. There was therefore no infringement of the right to be secure against unreasonable search or seizure.

[Dickson C.J.C., Beetz, Estey, McIntyre, Wilson, and La Forest JJ. concurred with Le Dain J.]

## R. v. Ladouceur
### Supreme Court of Canada
### (1990), 56 C.C.C. (3d) 22

[In this case, the same provision as was upheld in *Hufsky*, *supra* (s. 189(a)(1) of the *Highway Traffic Act*, R.S.O. 1980, c. 198 as amended S.O. 1981, c. 72, s. 2), was again challenged under s. 9 of the Charter after a driver was randomly stopped and discovered to be driving with a suspended licence. The Supreme Court, following *Hufsky*, *supra*, agreed that the legislation violated s. 9 of the Charter but disagreed on the application of s. 1.]

CORY J. (Lamer, L'Heureux-Dubé, Gonthier, and McLachlin JJ. concurring): It might be sought to distinguish the *Hufsky* decision on the ground that it applied to an organized program of roadside spot checks, whereas this case concerns the constitutionality of completely random stops conducted by police as part of a routine check which was not part of any organized program. It might well be that since these stops lack any organized structure, they should be treated as constitutionally more suspect than stops conducted under an organized program. Nonetheless, so long as the police officer making the stop is acting lawfully within the scope of a statute, the random stops can, in my view, be justifiably conducted in accordance with the *Charter*.

In my view the random stop is rationally connected and carefully designed to achieve safety on the highways. The stops impair as little as possible the rights of the driver. In addition, the stops do not so severely trench on individual rights that the legislative objective is outweighed by the abridgement of the individual's rights. ...

Officers can stop persons only for legal reasons, in this case reasons related to driving a car such as checking the driver's licence and insurance, the sobriety of the driver and the mechanical fitness of the vehicle. Once stopped the only questions that may justifiably be asked are those related to driving offences. Any further, more intrusive procedures could only be undertaken based upon reasonable and probable grounds. Where a stop is found to be unlawful, the evidence from the stop could well be excluded under s. 24(2) of the *Charter*.

[Sopinka J. (Dickson C.J.C., Wilson, and La Forest JJ. concurring):]

This case may be viewed as the last straw. If sanctioned, we will be agreeing that a police officer can stop any vehicle at any time, in any place, without having any reason to do so. For the motorist, this means a total negation of the freedom from arbitrary detention guaranteed by s. 9 of the *Charter*. This is something that would not be tolerated with respect to pedestrians in their use of the public streets and walk-ways. ...

... Random checking at a stationary, predetermined location infringes the right much less than the unlimited right contended for. The decision to locate the check point will be made either by a superior officer or by the decision of several officers. While the decision as to which automobile will be stopped will be made by an individual officer, his conduct can be observed by other officers. Since he has limited time to observe a vehicle, his decision will be either truly random or based on some objective basis.

By contrast, the roving random stop would permit any individual officer to stop any vehicle, at any time, at any place. The decision may be based on any whim. Individual officers will have different reasons. Some may tend to stop younger drivers, others older cars, and so on. Indeed, as pointed out by Tarnopolsky J.A., racial considerations may be a factor too. ...

... Any perfectly law-abiding citizen travelling late at night on a lonely country road must be prepared to have a police car approach, perhaps, from the rear, siren blaring, lights flashing, and must then and there come to a stop to prove his or her legitimacy on the roadway. How many innocent people will be stopped to catch one unlicensed driver? We have no information on this, but the statistics show that, in 1984, 1 in 37 drivers in Ontario was serving a licence suspension. The ratio, therefore, of licensed drivers to those driving while their licenses were under suspension will be 37 to some fraction of 1. The probability is that in excess of 37 innocent motorists will be stopped for each offender.

[Cory J. dismissed the accused's appeal from his conviction. Sopinka J. would also have dismissed the accused's appeal on the basis that the evidence that the accused was driving while under suspension should not be excluded under s. 24(2) of the Charter because its admission would not bring the administration of justice into disrepute in large part because of the absence of "high-handed" police behaviour.]


### R. v. Mellenthin
Supreme Court of Canada
(1992), 76 C.C.C. (3d) 481

[The Supreme Court held that an accused's s. 8 rights had been violated when a police officer had asked what was in a gym bag on the front seat of the car during a random traffic spot check. When the accused opened the gym bag, narcotics were discovered.]

CORY J. (Sopinka, Gonthier, McLachlin, and Iacobucci JJ. concurring) stated: ... Check-stop programs result in the arbitrary detention of motorists. The programs are justified as a means aimed at reducing the terrible toll of death and injury so often occasioned by impaired drivers or by dangerous vehicles. The primary aim of the program is thus to check for sobriety, licences, ownership, insurance and the mechanical fitness of cars. The police use of check stops should not be extended beyond these aims. Random stop programs must not be turned into a means of conducting either an unfounded general inquisition or an unreasonable search.

... The rights granted to police to conduct check-stop programs or random stops of motorists should not be extended. This indeed was emphasized in *R. v. Ladouceur*, *supra*, where the following appears in the reasons of the majority at p. 44:

> Finally, it must be shown that the routine check does not so severely trench upon the s. 9 right so as to outweigh the legislative objective. The concern at this stage is the perceived potential for abuse of this power by law enforcement officials. In my opinion, these fears are unfounded. There are mechanisms already in place which prevent abuse. Officers can stop persons only for legal reasons, in this case related to driving a car such as checking the driver's licence and insurance, the sobriety of the driver and the mechanical fitness of the vehicle. *Once stopped the only questions that may justifiably be asked are those related to driving offences. Any further, more intrusive procedures could only be undertaken based upon reasonable and probable grounds.* Where a stop is found to be unlawful, the evidence from the stop could well be excluded under s. 24(2) of the Charter.

(Emphasis added.)

[He then considered whether the evidence should be excluded under s. 24(2) of the Charter.]

### (1) Factors Affecting the Fairness of the Trial

*Collins*, *supra*, made it apparent that the admission of real evidence which was obtained in a manner that violated the Charter will rarely operate unfairly in the conduct of the trial. There can be no doubt that in this case the *cannabis* which was discovered constituted real evidence. However, it must also be remembered that in *R. v. Ross* (1989), 46 C.C.C. (3d) 129 at p. 139, [1989] 1 S.C.R. 3, 67 C.R. (3d) 209, it was said that: "... the use of any evidence that could not have been obtained but for the participation of the accused in the construction of the evidence for the purposes of the trial would tend to render the trial process unfair."

The unreasonable search carried out in this case is the very kind which the court wished to make clear is unacceptable. A check stop does not and cannot constitute a general search warrant for searching every vehicle, driver and passenger that is pulled over. Unless there are reasonable and probable grounds for conducting the search, or drugs, alcohol or weapons are in plain view in the interior of the vehicle, the evidence flowing from such a search should not be admitted.

It would surely affect the fairness of the trial should check stops be accepted as a basis for warrantless searches and the evidence derived from them was to be automatically admitted. To admit evidence obtained in an unreasonable and unjustified search carried out while a motorist was detained in a check stop would adversely and unfairly affect the trial process and most surely bring the administration of justice into disrepute.

It follows that the conclusions of the trial judge in this regard are neither unreasonable nor an error in law. It is clear that the admission of the evidence would render the trial unfair and there is no need to consider the other factors referred to in *Collins*, *supra*: see *R. v. Hebert* (1990), 57 C.C.C. (3d) 1 at p. 20, [1990] 2 S.C.R. 151, 77 C.R. (3d) 145. That is really a sufficient basis for dealing with the issue.

Yet in light of the extent of the argument that was submitted with regard to the seriousness of the Charter violation some brief comments on that subject might be appropriate.

### *(2)  Seriousness of the Violation*

The trial judge was not unreasonable in her conclusion that the breach was a serious one. It is true that there was not, in this case, any bad faith on the part of the police. They conducted the search, before the reasons of this court in *Ladouceur* had been released. None the less, the violation must be considered a serious one. It was conducted as an adjunct to the check stop and was not grounded on any suspicion, let alone a reasonable and probable cause. It is the attempt to extend the random stop programs to include a right to search without warrant or without reasonable grounds that constitutes the serious Charter violation.

### *Conclusion*

The appellant was detained at a check stop. While he was so detained, he was subjected to an unreasonable search. To admit the evidence obtained as a result of an unreasonable search of a motorist in a check stop would render the trial of the appellant unfair. Admitting such evidence would thus bring the administration of justice into disrepute. The evidence derived from the unreasonable search cannot be admitted.

### ADDITIONAL READING

On drinking and driving and the Charter, see:

- R. Solomon and S. Usprich, "Drinking/Driving Legislation and the Charter: An Overview" (1989), 1 *J.M.V.L.* 225;
- S. Bradley, "*R. v. Hufsky*: The Roadblock to Charter Rights" (1990), 2 *J.M.V.L.* 23;
- R. Pomerance, "'Over 80' and Under Scrutiny: Selected Charter Issues in Drinking and Driving Cases" (1992), 4 *J.M.V.L.* 121.

On racial profiling and the Charter, see:

- D. Tanovich, "Using the Charter to Stop Racial Profiling" (2002), 40 *Osgoode Hall L.J.* 145;
- S. Choudhry and K. Roach, "Racial and Ethnic Profiling: Statutory Discretion, Constitutional Remedies and Democratic Accountability" (2003), 41 *Osgoode Hall L.J.* 1.

# CHAPTER FOUR

# The Trial Process

This chapter is designed to present an overview of the criminal trial process with special attention to the constitutional and structural safeguards that are afforded the accused. The Donald Marshall Jr. case has been chosen as a case study because it provides an example of the frailty of the criminal process to neglect and improper motive and because it raises serious questions about the adequacy of our adversarial system of criminal justice, its treatment of the disadvantaged and the recurring problem of miscarriages of justice. As M.L. Friedland stated in *The Trials of Israel Lipski* (London: Macmillan, 1984), at 204:

> A trial may in theory be an objective pursuit of truth, but in practice there are many subjective factors which influence the course of events. Justice may in theory be blind, but in practice she has altogether too human a perspective ... . The case shows the inherent fallibility of the trial process and the constant danger of error. Society should think twice before shifting the balance too far in favour of the prosecution. Further, the case strengthens the arguments against capital punishment.

The first part of the chapter presents the Marshall case in its various aspects in some detail. Extracts from the royal commission that examined the wrongful conviction are examined as well as an important Supreme Court of Canada decision that holds in large part that because of the possibility of wrongful convictions, it will generally violate the Charter to extradite a fugitive to another country without obtaining assurances from that country that the death penalty will not be applied. The second part examines legal and ethical issues concerning the distinctive role of the prosecutor and defence counsel in a criminal trial including the constitutional obligation on the prosecutor to disclose relevant evidence to the accused. The third part examines the important issue of pre-trial detention or bail. The fourth part examines the issue of pre-trial publicity and change of venue, and the fifth part examines how jurors are chosen in the minority of cases tried by jury. The final part examines the important issue of the presumption of innocence and the burden and quantum of proof.

## I. THE WRONGFUL CONVICTION OF DONALD MARSHALL JR.

Donald Marshall was convicted of murder by a judge and jury in 1971. He appealed his conviction to the Nova Scotia Supreme Court, Appellate Division in 1972 where his conviction was upheld. In 1983, his conviction was overturned by the same appeal court after a new appeal was ordered by the minister of justice when Marshall applied under a procedure then known as applying for the mercy of the Crown. (For the present procedure of applying to the minister of justice when a person's appeals have been exhausted and the ability of the minister of justice to order a new trial or appeal if "there is a reasonable basis to conclude that a miscarriage of justice likely occurred," see ss. 696.1 to 696.6 of the *Criminal Code*.)

## Marshall's Appeals

### R. v. Marshall
Nova Scotia Supreme Court, Appellate Division
(1972), 8 C.C.C. (2d) 329

McKINNON C.J.N.S. (for the Court):  The appellant Donald Marshall Jr. was charged in an indictment, that he, on or about the 28th day of May, 1971, at Sydney, in the County of Cape Breton, Province of Nova Scotia, did murder Sanford William (Sandy) Seale. ...

After a trial by jury, presided over by Dubinsky, J., the appellant was found guilty and sentenced to serve a term of life imprisonment in Dorchester Penitentiary.

The grounds of appeal relied on by the appellant may be summarized as follows:

(1)  that the learned trial judge erred in law in not adequately instructing the jury on the defence evidence, and in expressing opinions which were highly prejudicial to the accused;

(2)  that the learned trial judge misdirected the jury on the meaning of reasonable doubt; that the evidence did not establish guilt beyond a reasonable doubt, the conviction was against the weight of evidence and was perverse;

(3)  ground 3 relates to the evidence of the witnesses Pratico and Chant; also that the trial judge did not make proper inquiry as to whether or not they understood the nature of an oath;

(4)  that the learned trial judge permitted the prosecuting officer to cross-examine the witness, Maynard Chant, before ruling that he was adverse; that the trial judge permitted the prosecuting officer, in the absence of the jury, while the witness Chant was on the witness stand, to read the evidence he gave at the preliminary hearing, thereby conditioning him for the evidence he would give before the jury;

(5)  that the trial judge erred in instructing the jury they did not have to consider the question of manslaughter.

Briefly, the facts are that one, John Pratico, aged 16, was in the company of the deceased Seale and the appellant Marshall a very short time before Seale was stabbed. Pratico left the two men and stationed himself behind a bush in Wentworth Park, which is adjacent to Crescent Street, in Sydney, where he proceeded to consume a bottle of beer; while behind this bush, he observed Marshall and Seale.

Maynard Chant, aged 15, was in Wentworth Park at the same time, but not in the company of Pratico. Chant had attended church in Sydney and was attempting to get home to Louisbourg after having missed his bus. He was taking a shortcut through Wentworth Park when he noticed Pratico behind the bush. Pratico appeared to be watching something, and Chant decided to see what had drawn Pratico's attention.

They saw two men standing together and arguing in loud tones. One of the men, whom Pratico identified as the appellant Marshall, reached in his pocket and pulled out a "long shiny object" which he plunged into the "stomach" of the other, whom Pratico identified as Seale. Seale then collapsed.

Both Pratico and Chant fled the scene, but not together. In a nearby area, Chant was approached by the appellant Marshall who said, "look what they did to me" and displayed a cut on the inner part of his left forearm. M.D. Mattson, who lives at 103 Byng Avenue, overheard the conversation referred to, and called the police.

The appellant Marshall flagged down a car, and he and Chant had the operator drive to the spot where Seale was lying on the pavement of Crescent Street. Seale was taken to the Sydney City Hospital where he died as a result of his injuries on the following day, despite two surgical operations and massive blood transfusions.

According to the evidence of the appellant Marshall, he and Seale, who was a friend, were standing on the footbridge which spans two creeks in the park, when they were called to by two men who were on Crescent Street, and who wanted cigarettes or matches. The appellant and Seale walked up to the street and were met by two men dressed in long blue coats who identified themselves as priests from Manitoba. The strangers wanted to know if there were girls in the park and asked where they could find a bootlegger. According to the appellant, the older of the two men then made an unprovoked attack with a knife on Seale and the appellant, which resulted in Seale's fatal injury and the appellant being slashed on the arm.

According to the appellant Marshall, at the time of the attack, the man with the knife said he did not like niggers or Indians. The appellant is an Indian while the deceased was a negro. The appellant said that he then fled, being in fear of his life. …

The only issue before the Court at trial in relation to the charge against the appellant was whether or not he had committed the murder with which he was charged. His sole defence was a denial of that act, and the theory of the defence was based on his own evidence that the murder was committed by one of two strangers, who claimed to be priests from Manitoba.

In reviewing the evidence for the defence, the learned trial judge read fairly extensively from the testimony of the appellant, and commented on that evidence as follows:

> Now, gentlemen, you have to give very careful consideration to the story of the accused. I'm sure you will. As was his absolute right, he has gone on the stand and has given his version of the events that took place on that fateful night. Now contrary to what Pratico said, he said he was not in the vicinity of St. Joseph's Hall. And although he was with Mr. Seale, he had no dispute with him—those are the words I think—and he did not lay a hand on him. I repeat, he had no dispute with him and he did not lay a hand on him. And he told you how Seale came to get the injuries that he did receive.

And I remind you, Mr. Foreman, that although the accused was subjected to a very vigorous and rigorous cross-examination, he adhered to his story that he told throughout. Now if you believe the version of the events that was told by Donald Marshall Jr., then it goes without saying that you must acquit him of this charge. Having gone on the stand he has become another witness in this case. You have the right to determine the credibility of him as a witness as you have the right to determine the credibility of any other witness. But you will bear in mind, Mr. Foreman—and I repeat, you will bear in mind—that Donald Marshall does not have to convince you of his innocence. He does not have to convince you of his innocence. It is the Crown, as I said over and over again, that must prove his guilt beyond a reasonable doubt. He does not have to convince you of his innocence!

The Crown, of course, understandably, has attacked this story. There was some considerable discussion among counsel as to the nature of the wound that he had on his left arm, the depth of it, whether there was bleeding. Mrs. Davis said there was no bleeding, it's true. You saw the mark on his arm there. It's a pretty prominent mark even today after a number of months.

[When Marshall's arm was shown to the jury, it also revealed a tattoo that read "I hate cops."]

You will bear in mind that he at the time showed Maynard Chant, "Look what they did to me." It was then and there at the that time he told Chant what was done to him. At that time he managed to stop a car and got into a car and went back to Crescent Street. I think it was Maynard Chant—your recollection would be better—who said that it was he, Donald Marshall, the accused, who flagged down a police car. And it was Donald Marshall who went to the hospital and to the police station with the police. I think you have to ask yourselves on the one hand, is that the action of a man who has just committed a crime, who will flag down a police car, who will go with the police, who will do the things that he did and who maintains the consistency of his story. Keep in mind, as I said, that he does not have to prove his innocence.

On the other hand, Mr. Foreman, gentlemen on the other hand—in my opinion, you will have to assess very carefully the story that he told—two strangers who he says looked like priests, because they wore long coats and blue. He asked them, he said, whether they were priests and one of them said they were and said they were from Manitoba. They asked for cigarettes, smokes; they gave him the smokes. He and Seale gave smokes to these people, or he did. Then the man, one of these men asked him if there were any women and they said yes, there were lots of them in the park. And out of the blue comes this denunciation against blacks and Indians: "I don't like niggers and I don't like Indians." …

In my opinion, the foregoing passages afford an adequate answer to the ground of objection that the learned trial judge did not adequately instruct the jury on the defence evidence and the theory of the defence. I am satisfied that he did so adequately, fairly and in a manner that was not capable of being understood by the jury as prejudicial to the accused.

… As to ground No. 2, counsel for the appellant contends that while the trial judge stated a number of times that the charge must be proved beyond a reasonable doubt, in other parts of his address, he used the words "satisfied" and "to your satisfaction" and this was misdirection. Further that he did not instruct the jury that if the evidence created a reasonable doubt, this would entitle them to acquit the accused.

This part of his charge reads as follows:

> I said before that I would deal with the question of onus or burden of proof. The onus or burden of proving the guilt of an accused person beyond a reasonable doubt rests upon the Crown and never shifts. There is no burden on an accused person to prove his innocence. I repeat, there is no burden on an accused person to prove his innocence. Let me make that abundantly clear. If during the course of this trial, from beginning to end, during anything that may have been said by counsel during their speeches, that might in the slightest way be considered as suggestive of any burden on the accused to prove anything, let me tell you that there is no burden on the accused. The Crown must prove beyond a reasonable doubt that an accused is guilty of the offence with which he is charged before he can be convicted. If you have a reasonable doubt as to whether the accused committed the offence of non-capital murder, the offence with which he is charged, then it is your duty to give the accused the benefit of that doubt and to find him not guilty. In other words, if after considering all the evidence, the addresses of counsel and my charge to you, you come to the conclusion that the Crown has failed to prove to your satisfaction beyond a reasonable doubt that the accused, Marshall, committed the offence of non-capital murder, it is your duty to give this accused the benefit of the doubt and to find him not guilty.

The learned trial judge then proceeded to define "reasonable doubt" as an "honest doubt," a doubt which causes you to "say to yourselves, or any of you, 'I am not morally certain that he committed the offence,' then that would indicate to you—that would indicate there is a doubt in your mind and it would be a *reasonable* doubt which prevents you from arriving at the state of mind which would require you to find a verdict of guilty against this man."

Placing the instructions of the trial judge in their proper context, the jury could not, and were not, misled as to the proper application of the law regarding the "burden of proof." …

Ground three relates to the evidence of the witnesses Pratico and Chant, counsel for the appellant contending that the trial judge did not make proper inquiry as to whether either witness understood the nature of an oath.

The record indicates that the trial judge declared himself satisfied that both Pratico, aged 16, and Chant, aged 15, understood the nature of an oath, and they were sworn without objection by the defence. This was a question of fact to be decided by the trial judge and I can see no good reason, under the circumstances, to interfere with that finding.

Counsel for the appellant also objects to the quality and sufficiency of the evidence given by Pratico and Chant.

Pratico testified that he saw the deceased Seale and the appellant Marshall at the scene of the crime and he gave direct evidence that he saw Marshall stab Seale. He was acquainted with both men. Under a rigorous cross-examination, he admitted to drinking on the night of the stabbing. The learned trial judge in his address to the jury reviewed this evidence and in clear language related Pratico's drinking to his credibility and left it for the jury to decide.

Regarding a conflict in his statements before and during trial, this is explained by the record which discloses that Pratico's life was threatened if he testified that the appellant stabbed Seale.

[The day before his testimony at Marshall's trial, Pratico told several people outside the courtroom, including Marshall's lawyer, the Crown prosecutor, and the investigating police officer, that Marshall did not stab Seale. Pratico had previously testified at the preliminary hearing that he had seen Marshall stab Seale. When Pratico testified, the trial judge prevented Marshall's defence lawyers from asking Pratico to explain why he had made these inconsistent statements. The Royal Commission examining the Marshall Prosecution subsequently concluded:

> We believe a full and complete cross-examination of John Pratico at this stage by Khattar [Marshall's lawyer] almost certainly would have resulted in his recanting evidence given during his examination-in-chief that he had seen Marshall stab Seale. In those circumstances, no jury would have convicted Donald Marshall Jr. (at 79)

On re-examination, the Crown prosecutor tried to introduce evidence that third parties had threatened Pratico [if he "squealed on Junior"] shortly after Marshall was charged. The trial judge disallowed evidence of the alleged threats because the third parties were not before the court, but allowed the Crown prosecutor to ask Pratico why he had said outside the courtroom that Marshall did not stab Seale, when he had given testimony to the opposite effect. Pratico replied that he was "scared for his life." The trial judge then asked:

Q. Now your being scared of your life, is that because of anything the accused said to you at the time?

A. No.

(at 174 of the trial transcript).]

Chant's evidence corroborated in every material particular that of the witness Pratico. He testified that he saw a person crouched in the bushes at the place where Pratico said he witnessed the stabbing.

Chant, at first, declined to swear that the man who did the stabbing was the appellant Marshall, but this was inconsistent with a previous statement under oath made by him at the preliminary hearing. ...

Under ground No. 4, counsel for the appellant contends that when the jury was absent, the Crown prosecutor was permitted, while Chant was on the witness stand, to read the evidence he gave at the preliminary hearing, thereby conditioning him for the evidence he would give when the jury would return, this being highly improper and prejudicial to the appellant. ...

[The prosecutor read the transcript of Chant's testimony at the preliminary hearing in which Chant testified that he saw Marshall stab Seale. This was done in an attempt to have Chant, a Crown witness, declared an adverse witness who could be impeached with statements inconsistent with his previous testimony. After this, Chant was then questioned by both the prosecutor and the judge. The prosecutor asked (at 99-100):

Q. Who was the man that hauled out the object and drove it—

A. Donald Marshall.

After this the judge asked:

Q. But more, what do you say about the man that you recognized as Donald Marshall and the person who you saw doing something hauling out something and putting it into the stomach of the other person: what do you say about that?

A. The only thing I know is—

Q. Never mind—tell me, do you or don't you—what do you say as to who that person was?

A. I don't know who that person was.

Q. You say you don't know who the person was who pulled out the knife and stuck it in Seale's body?

A. No, I didn't.

Chant was read his testimony given at the preliminary hearing on two more occasions. After both readings Chant testified that he had seen Marshall stab Seale.

The Court of Appeal approved of this procedure, stating it was allowed because the prosecutor was alleging that his witness, Chant, had made a prior statement inconsistent with his original testimony under s. 9(2) of the *Canada Evidence Act* R.S.C. 1970, c. E-10 [now R.S.C. 1985, c. C-5, s. 9(2)]. McKinnon C.J.N.S. stated: "[i]t does not appear to me that the appellant suffered any prejudice through Chant hearing the evidence he had previously given, for when the jury returned, the same evidence was read to him question by question." The Court of Appeal concluded "if there was an error in the application of the section, no substantial wrong or miscarriage of justice resulted, and I would apply the provisions of s. 613(1)(b)(iii) [now s. 686(1)(b)(iii)]. This provision allows an appeal court to sustain a conviction despite an error of law committed by the trial judge, but only if the appeal court concludes no substantial wrong or miscarriage of justice has occurred.]

The final ground of appeal is that the trial judge advised the jury their verdict was limited to "guilty" or "not guilty" of murder, and that they did not have to consider a verdict of manslaughter, although there was evidence that the deceased Seale had put up his fists.

In his instructions to the jury, the trial judge included the following:

My opinion is that whoever caused these wounds committed non-capital murder ... the facts in this case as they came before you, gentlemen of the jury, from beginning of the case to the end, do *not* give rise to your having to consider the crime of manslaughter ...

Now Mr. Foreman, the defence in this case is not self-defence. This is not a case of self-defence. This is a complete denial. The defence is, I didn't do it—complete denial! Not self-defence but even if it were self-defence, I would have to instruct you that if that were the evidence, the late Mr. Seale put up his fists, then to strike him with an instrument and stab him was something that would go far, far beyond the right of self-defence. That sort of defence would not be commensurate with the other man's act. That issue does not arise here because as I said, the defence here is a complete denial.

There was no suggestion at any time during trial by counsel for the appellant that the verdict of manslaughter should be left with the jury. I accept the Crown's contention that what the appellant now seeks is to completely discard the line of defence followed at the trial and argue that the trial judge should have told the jury that they might disbelieve substantially the whole of the evidence tendered by the Crown; that they might also disbelieve the appellant's evidence and find that the appellant stabbed Seale, but did so, in self-defence or as a result of provocation.

I am satisfied that the instruction of the learned trial judge excluding manslaughter from consideration by the jury was, on the evidence, a proper direction to place before them.

It is my opinion that the appeal should be dismissed.

*Appeal dismissed.*

### R. v. Marshall
Nova Scotia Supreme Court, Appellate Division
(1983), 57 N.S.R. (2d) 286

BY THE COURT:  On June 16, 1982 the Honourable Jean Chrétien, Minister of Justice of Canada referred the following matter to the Supreme Court of Nova Scotia, Appeal Division:

WHEREAS Donald Marshall Jr. was convicted on 5 November, 1971 by a court composed of Mr. Justice J.L. Dubinsky and a jury that he, on or about 29 May, 1971 at Sydney, in the County of Cape Breton, Province of Nova Scotia, murdered Sandford William (Sandy) Seale and was on the same date sentenced to a term of life imprisonment.

AND WHEREAS an appeal from that conviction to this Honourable Court was dismissed on 8 September, 1972.

AND WHEREAS evidence was subsequently gathered and placed before the undersigned which appears to be relevant to the issue whether Donald Marshall Jr. is guilty of the crime of which he stands convicted.

AND WHEREAS application for the mercy of the Crown has been made on behalf of Donald Marshall Jr. pursuant to section 617 of the *Criminal Code*.

> AND WHEREAS the Attorney General of Nova Scotia and counsel acting on behalf of Donald Marshall Jr. agree with the undersigned that this new evidence is of sufficient importance to be considered by this Honourable Court.
>
> NOW THEREFORE, the undersigned pursuant to paragraph 617(b) of the *Criminal Code*, hereby refers the said conviction to this Honourable Court for hearing and determination in the light of the existing judicial record and any other evidence which the court, in its discretion, receives and considers, as if it were an appeal by Donald Marshall Jr.

The powers of this court on this reference, in our opinion, are those possessed by the court when hearing an ordinary appeal. They are set forth in s. 613 of the *Criminal Code* [now s. 686], the applicable parts of which are as follows:

> 613.(1) On the hearing of an appeal against a conviction or against a verdict that the appellant is unfit, on account of insanity, to stand his trial, or against a special verdict of not guilty on account of insanity, the court of appeal
>> (a) may allow the appeal where it is of the opinion that
>>> (i) the verdict should be set aside on the ground that it is unreasonable or cannot be supported by the evidence ...
>>> (iii) on any ground there was a miscarriage of justice;
>> (b) may dismiss the appeal where ...
>>> (ii) the appeal is not decided in favour of the appellant on any ground mentioned in paragraph (a),
> (2) Where a court of appeal allows an appeal under paragraph (1)(a), it shall quash the conviction and
>> (a) direct a judgment or verdict of acquittal to be entered, or
>> (b) order a new trial.

The role of an appellate court when exercising its powers under s. 613 of the *Criminal Code* has been considered by the Supreme Court of Canada in *Corbett v. The Queen* (1974), 1 N.R. 258; 14 C.C.C. (2d) 385, where Pigeon J., said at p. 386:

> Of course, if the judges of the majority had held that their function was only to decide whether there was evidence, this would be reversible error. The *Criminal Code* expressly provides that the appeal may be allowed, not only when the verdict cannot be supported by the evidence but also when it is unreasonable. In other words, the Court of Appeal must satisfy itself not only that there was evidence requiring the case to be submitted to the jury, but also that the weight of such evidence is not so weak that a verdict of guilty is unreasonable. This cannot be taken to mean that the Court of Appeal is to substitute its opinion for that of the jury. The word of the enactment is "unreasonable," not "unjustified." The jurors are the triers of the facts and their finding is not to be set aside because the judges in appeal do not think they would have made the same finding if sitting as jurors. This is only to be done if they come to the conclusion that the verdict is such that no 12 reasonable men could possibly have reached it acting judicially.

... The defence theory was that the killing happened as Donald Marshall Jr., said and that his evidence was supported by the fact that immediately after the killing he had related the entire facts not only to Maynard Chant but also to the police, who he called to the scene. Further confirmation could be found in the fact that the doctor at the hospital thought it necessary to place ten or more stitches in the left arm of the appellant to close an actual wound that he had recently received.

Counsel for the defence attacked, very strongly, the evidence of the two witnesses, Maynard Chant and John L. Pratico, showing that neither of them had reported seeing Donald Marshall Jr., commit the crime when they were first in contact with the police. Furthermore, Pratico had admitted to being drunk at the time and had told other civilians that Marshall did not commit the act. He even told the sheriff and counsel in the courthouse during the trial that Marshall had not stabbed Seale.

After full instructions by the trial judge, who related the principles of law to the evidence before the court, the jury reached the conclusion that Donald Marshall Jr., was guilty of the offence charged and had in fact murdered Sandy Seale. In order to reach this conclusion they had to disbelieve the evidence of the appellant and accept the eyewitness evidence of at least one of the two witnesses, Maynard Chant and John L. Pratico. They must have also, in our opinion, drawn an inference that the uncertainties of the accounts of the eyewitnesses and their failure to immediately inform the police of what they had seen had been caused by some pressures brought to bear upon them on behalf of the accused.

The trial had lasted from November 2 to 5, 1971, and after the guilty verdict the court pronounced the sentence of life imprisonment prescribed for the offence of non-capital murder by the *Criminal Code of Canada*. ...

Donald Marshall Jr., commenced serving his life sentence in prison November 5, 1971, having been confined to jail since June 20, 1971. He was paroled from penitentiary on August 29, 1981, and the Minister of Justice referred this matter to this court on June 16, 1982. The appellant contends that he never was guilty of the offence of murdering Sandy Seale, and that the fresh evidence taken before this court on December 1 and 2, 1982, when considered along with the prior record of the case, is of sufficient force to require the Appeal Division at this time to set aside the original conviction of the appellant and enter a verdict of acquittal.

We turn now to a consideration of the fresh evidence.

James W. MacNeil is a thirty-seven-year-old labourer, who was born in Sydney and lived there all his life. He testified that on the evening of May 28, 1971, he was at the State Tavern on George Street, in the city of Sydney, where he met by accident an older man by the name of Roy Ebsary, whom he had known for a period of months. He had visited Mr. Ebsary's home on Argyle Street several times, and when they had finished drinking together for the evening, near eleven o'clock, they were returning there once again. The two of them cut through Wentworth Park, crossed the bridge and arrived on Crescent Street on their way home.

Mr. MacNeil describes Mr. Ebsary as about sixty years of age, kind of stocky, not real tall, about 5' 7", with a little hunch back. He was wearing a kind of black shawl and a sports coat. Mr. MacNeil's testimony then continues:

> A. Then we went up and we went up to like the top of the hill. Like I said we were crossing over the street and we were—we were approached by this coloured youth and

this Mr. Marshall. At that time I remember I recall that Mr. Marshall put my hand up behind my back like that, eh, and I remember I kinda like panicked because I—in a situation like that, you get "stensafied" or something like that but I remember the coloured fellow asking Roy Ebsary for money. He said, like, "Dig, man, dig." and he said, "I got something for you." and then he—I just heard the coloured fellow screaming and everything was so you know, like, "tensafied" and every darn thing and I seen him running and flopping. I seen him running and flopping.

His testimony continued:

A. ... The next day I went to Ebsary's house and I told him that that fellow died, I said. I said: "You didn't have to kill him." You know, "You should have give him the money." You know, and I told—I told his son that so his son just said, well, he said: "Well, if you say anything," well, he said—

Mr. MacNeil was then asked if he had ever communicated his story to the police, and in response he said:

A. Yeh, I told the police in Sydney.

Q. Sir?

A. I told the police in Sydney after I—after I heard that this fellow was in gaol, Mr. Marshall, for something he didn't do so I went and I told the police this and it bothered me because I wouldn't like to be in gaol for something I didn't do.

Q. When can you recall having spoken to Sergeant MacIntyre concerning that event?

A. It was about a week after you were sentenced.

Q. Are you able to explain why you waited that length of time before going to the police?

A. Well because like, ah, Roy's son told me, he said: "The whole family would be in trouble there." ...

Mr. Marshall was asked for an explanation of the difference between his testimony at the original trial and his recent testimony, and he said:

Q. Well in what way does your testimony differ in 1971 to today?

A. In 1971 I did not mention anything about hitting somebody or robbing somebody or something like that. I did not mention that.

Q. Why didn't you speak of that?

A. The robbery didn't happen. It wasn't even an attempt of a robbery. I wasn't dealing with a robbery and I was afraid that one way or the other they would put the finger at me saying—one way or the other they would have found a way—in my opinion, they would have found a way to put it on me whether I told them or not.

Q. To put what on you?

A. Attempted robbery. Maybe the murder probably—the robbery would have probably tried to cover up for the murder.

Q. Do you recall who the solicitors were who or the lawyers who acted for you at the
1971 trial?

A. C.M. Rosenblum and Simon Khattar.

Q. And were they aware of what—at the time in 1971, were they aware of what you
said in court today?

A. No. ...

There was also evidence before us to the effect that counsel for Marshall at the
time of his trial had no knowledge of the prior inconsistent statements given to the
police by Chant, Pratico and Harris ... .

Although Mr. Marshall now puts forward Mr. MacNeil as his chief witness, their
evidence in the main is in conflict. The only material particular on which they agree
is that Ebsary stabbed Seale ... .

Mr. Marshall categorically denies jumping Mr. MacNeil from behind and putting
his arm behind his back. He is obviously not prepared to admit at this stage that he
was engaged in a robbery.

How two people could describe the same incident in such a conflicting manner
has caused us great concern and casts doubt on the credibility of both men. However,
the fact remains that Marshall's new evidence, despite his evasions, prevarications
and outright lies, supports the essence of James MacNeil's story—namely, that Seale
was *not* killed by Marshall but died at the hands of Roy Ebsary in the course of a
struggle during the attempted robbery of Ebsary and MacNeil by Marshall and Seale.
In our opinion, Marshall's evidence, old and new, if it stood alone, would hardly be
capable of belief.

Even though the various members of this court may have varying degrees of belief as to some aspects of that evidence, we have no doubt that in the light of all the
evidence now before this court no reasonable jury could, on that evidence, find Donald
Marshall Jr. guilty of the murder of Sandy Seale. That evidence, even if much is not
believed makes it impossible for a jury to avoid having a reasonable doubt as to
whether the appellant had been proved to have killed Seale.

Putting it another way, the new evidence "causes us to doubt the correctness of the
judgment at the trial."—Reference *Re Regina v. Truscott* (1967), 1 C.R.N.S. 1 (S.C.C.)

We must accordingly conclude that the verdict of guilt is not now supported by the
evidence and is unreasonable and must order the conviction quashed. In such a case a
new trial should ordinarily be required under s. 613(2)(b) of the *Criminal Code*. Here,
however, no purpose would be served in so doing. The evidence now available, with
the denials by Pratico and Chant that they saw anything, could not support a conviction of Marshall. Accordingly we must take the alternative course directed by
s. 613(2)(a) and direct that a judgment of acquittal be entered in favour of the
appellant.

This course accords with the following submission of counsel for the Crown as set forth in his factum:

> It is respectfully submitted that the appeal should be allowed, that the conviction should be quashed, and a direction made that a verdict of acquittal be entered.
>
> It is also submitted that the basis of the above disposition should be that, in light of the evidence now available, the conviction of the appellant cannot be supported by the evidence.

Donald Marshall Jr. was convicted of murder and served a lengthy period of incarceration. That conviction is now to be set aside. Any miscarriage of justice is, however, more apparent than real.

In attempting to defend himself against the charge of murder Mr. Marshall admittedly committed perjury for which he still could be charged.

By lying he helped secure his own conviction. He misled his lawyers and presented to the jury a version of the facts he now says is false, a version that was so far-fetched as to be incapable of belief.

By planning a robbery with the aid of Mr. Seale he triggered a series of events which unfortunately ended in the death of Mr. Seale.

By hiding the facts from his lawyers and the police Mr. Marshall effectively prevented development of the only defence available to him, namely, that during a robbery Seale was stabbed by one of the intended victims. He now says that he knew approximately where the man lived who stabbed Seale and had a pretty good description of him. With this information the truth of the matter might well have been uncovered by the police.

Even at the time of taking the fresh evidence, although he had little more to lose and much to gain if he could obtain his acquittal, Mr. Marshall was far from being straightforward on the stand. He continued to be evasive about the robbery and assault and even refused to answer questions until the court ordered him to do so. There can be no doubt but that Donald Marshall's untruthfulness through this whole affair contributed in large measure to his conviction.

We accordingly allow the appeal, quash the conviction and direct that a verdict of acquittal be entered.

---

The concluding passages of the Appellate Division's judgment created considerable controversy. The Royal Commission appointed to inquire into the causes of Marshall's wrongful conviction attempted to compel the judges who sat on the 1983 appeal to testify as to their reasons for making these comments. One of the judges on the 1983 Panel, Justice Leonard Pace, had served as Attorney General of Nova Scotia at the time of Marshall's conviction.

The Supreme Court of Canada decided that the principle of judicial independence gave the judges absolute immunity from testifying about the evidence before them and the meaning of their reasons. A majority also ruled that the Chief Justice of Nova Scotia could not be questioned as to why Justice Pace sat on the Marshall case. A minority would have allowed such questions, distinguishing them as concerning the administrative as opposed to the judicial function of the courts. See *Mackeigan v. Hickman*, [1989] 2 S.C.R. 796.

An inquiry committee appointed by the Canadian Judicial Council decided in 1990 not to recommend that the judges who sat on the 1983 Reference should be removed from office. Four members stated: "[w]hile their remarks in *obiter* were, in our view, in error, and inappropriate in failing to give recognition to manifest injustice, we do not feel that they are reflective of conduct so destructive that it renders the judges incapable of executing their office impartially and independently with continued public confidence." One member, McEachern C.J.B.C., agreed but also stated that most of the criticisms of the judges in the 1983 reference by the *Royal Commission on the Donald Marshall Jr. Prosecution* "are not valid" because the appeal court had enough evidence before them to support their opinions about Marshall's conduct.

––––––––––––––––––––

Roy Ebsary was subsequently charged with the murder of Sandy Seale. A judge at a preliminary hearing determined there was insufficient evidence of Ebsary's intent to commit him for a trial for murder, so he was committed for trial for manslaughter. Ebsary's first trial ended in a hung jury because the jury apparently could not decide if he had acted in self-defence. He was convicted of manslaughter at a second trial. An appeal was allowed and a new trial ordered. At the third trial, Ebsary was again convicted of manslaughter. He was sentenced to three years imprisonment but, on appeal, this sentence was reduced to a year imprisonment.

### Royal Commission on the Donald Marshall Jr. Prosecution
(1989)

[In 1986, the Nova Scotia government appointed a public inquiry into the prosecution of Donald Marshall Jr. The commission was chaired by Chief Justice Alexander Hickman and included Associate Chief Justice Poitras and Justice Gregory Evans.

After extensive hearings, consultation, and research, it issued a seven-volume report in 1989. What follows are its main factual findings and policy recommendations.]

*Factual Findings*

Late in the evening of May 28, 1971, Donald Marshall Jr. and Sandy Seale met by chance shortly after Seale left St. Joseph's Church Hall on George Street in Sydney. The two were walking through Wentworth Park when they met two other men, Roy Ebsary and James (Jimmy) MacNeil. Following a brief conversation initiated when Ebsary or MacNeil asked for a cigarette, Marshall and/or Seale asked Ebsary and MacNeil for money.

[The commission found that Seale said "Dig man, dig" to Ebsary and "this represented, at most, an expression of impatience or frustration by Seale, who wanted Ebsary to check more quickly to find out whether he had any money, and that the request was not accompanied by any verbal or physical threats from Mar' hall or Seale."]

This was a low-key, non-violent, non-criminal request, similar to the solicitations many of us routinely experience while walking the streets of any Canadian city. But this simple request triggered in the drunken and dangerous Ebsary a deadly over-reaction. Ebsary's intoxicated and irrational state likely made him believe he was under threat of attack when no such threat existed. Before their encounter that night, in fact, Ebsary had already decided—as he described it later—that "the next man that struck me would die in his tracks." (Exhibit 19, Page 145)

It has been suggested in some previous proceedings that the stabbing may have occurred in the course of an actual or attempted robbery, rolling or mugging, but these terms all imply some degree of criminality and we conclude Seale was not killed as a result of any such incident.

This is not merely an academic distinction. In its 1983 decision acquitting Marshall of Seale's murder, the Court of Appeal of Nova Scotia concluded Marshall and Seale had been involved in an attempted robbery at the time the stabbing took place and that Marshall, by failing to disclose this fact, had contributed in large measure to his own conviction. This conclusion adversely affected Marshall's later attempt to win compensation for his wrongful imprisonment.

Given Ebsary's history, it is conceivable that Ebsary's attack was totally unpro-voked. But our view is that his volatility and his desire to be a heroic man of action led him to misinterpret a simple "panhandling" request, and then to overreact to an imagined threat of attack—with tragic consequences. ...

The criminal justice system failed Donald Marshall Jr. at virtually every turn, from his arrest and wrongful conviction in 1971 up to—and even beyond—his acquittal by the Court of Appeal in 1983. The tragedy of this failure is compounded by the evi-dence that this miscarriage of justice could have—and should have—been prevented, or at least corrected quickly, if those involved in the system had carried out their duties in a professional and/or competent manner.

If, for example, the Sergeant of Detectives of the Sydney City Police Department had not prematurely concluded—on the basis of no supporting evidence and in the face of compelling contradictory evidence—that Donald Marshall Jr. was responsi-ble for the death of Sandy Seale, Marshall would almost certainly never have been charged with the crime. If the Crown prosecutor had provided full disclosure to Marshall's lawyers of the conflicting statements provided by alleged eyewitnesses; if Marshall's lawyers had conducted a more thorough defence, including pressing for such disclosure and conducting their own investigations into the killing; if the judge in the case had not made critical errors in law; Marshall would almost certainly not have been convicted.

When Marshall's wrongful conviction was finally discovered in the early 1980s, the Court of Appeal compounded the miscarriage of justice by describing Marshall as having contributed in large measure to his own conviction and by stating that any miscarriage of justice in the case was more apparent than real.

This Commission has concluded that Donald Marshall Jr. was not to blame for his own conviction and that the miscarriage of justice against him was real. ...

## The Police Investigation

The four Sydney police officers who initially responded to the report of the stabbing—Constables Leo Mroz, Howard Dean, Richard Walsh and Martin MacDonald—did not do a professional job. They did not cordon off the crime scene, search the area or question witnesses. In fact, none of the four officers dispatched to the scene even remained there to protect the area after Seale had been taken to the hospital. We found their conduct entirely inadequate, incompetent and unprofessional.

The same can be said of the subsequent police investigation directed by then Sergeant of Detectives John MacIntyre. MacIntyre very quickly decided that Marshall had stabbed Seale in the course of an argument, even though there was no evidence to support such a conclusion. MacIntyre discounted Marshall's version of events partly because he considered Marshall a troublemaker and partly because, in our view, he shared what we believe was a general sense in Sydney's White community at the time that Indians were not "worth" as much as Whites.

Regardless of the reasons for his conclusions, MacIntyre's investigation seemed designed to seek out only evidence to support his theory about the killing and to discount all evidence that challenged it.

The most damning evidence against Marshall came from two teenaged "eyewitnesses," Maynard Chant, a 14-year-old who was on probation in connection with a minor criminal offence, and John Pratico, a mentally unstable 16-year-old whose psychiatrist later testified that he was known to fantasize and invent stories to make himself the centre of attention.

Shortly after Seale died, both youths gave statements to MacIntyre. Chant, although he had seen nothing, generally corroborated Marshall's version of events, while Pratico claimed to have seen two men running away from the stabbing scene. A few days later, however, they both gave contradictory second statements to MacIntyre. Pratico claimed he had seen Marshall stab Seale during an argument. Chant said he had also heard the argument and seen the stabbing. He placed a "dark-haired fellow"—presumably Pratico—in the bushes near where the stabbing took place.

None of this, as we now know, was true. The information in these second statements came from Pratico and Chant accepting suggestions John MacIntyre made to them. His attempt to build a case against Marshall that conformed to his theory about what had happened went far beyond the bounds of acceptable police behaviour. MacIntyre took Pratico, an impressionable, unstable teenager, to a murder scene, offered the youth his own version of events and then persuaded Pratico to accept that version as the basis for what became Pratico's detailed and incriminating statement. MacIntyre then pressured Chant, who was on probation and frightened about being sent to jail, into not only corroborating Pratico's statement, but also into putting Pratico at the scene of the crime. MacIntyre's oppressive tactics in questioning these and other juvenile witnesses were totally unacceptable.

Largely because of the untrue statements MacIntyre had obtained, Donald Marshall Jr. was charged on June 4, 1971 with murdering Sandy Seale.

## The Trial Process

In order for an accused to be committed for trial following a preliminary inquiry, the judge must be satisfied on the basis of what he or she has heard that there is admissible evidence which could, if it were believed, result in a conviction. Not surprisingly, Marshall was committed for trial before judge and jury on a charge of murder.

Trials are conducted under an adversarial system in which the interest of the State is represented by a Crown prosecutor and the interest of the accused is represented by defence counsel. In order for a person to be convicted of murder, a jury of the accused's peers must decide unanimously that the evidence establishes the person's guilt beyond reasonable doubt. The role of the defence counsel is to satisfy the jury that the Crown has failed to prove its case beyond a reasonable doubt. Defence counsel has a responsibility to the court not to mislead, but otherwise is responsible only to the accused.

The interest of the State, on the other hand, is to see that justice is done. The objectives of Crown counsel were put succinctly by Justice Rand in his judgment in the 1954 Supreme Court of Canada case of *Boucher v. The Queen*, [1955] S.C.R. 16:

> It cannot be over-emphasized that the purpose of a criminal prosecution is not to obtain a conviction, it is to lay before a jury what the Crown considers to be credible evidence relevant to what is alleged to be a crime. Counsel have a duty to see that all available legal proof of the facts is presented; it should be done fairly. The role of prosecutor excludes any notion of winning or losing; his function is a matter of public duty than which in civil life there can be none charged with greater personal responsibility. It is to be efficiently performed with an ingrained sense of the dignity, the seriousness and the justness of judicial proceedings.

If Crown counsel is aware of evidence that could be helpful to the accused, they must disclose its existence to the accused, or the accused's counsel, before the trial takes place. In certain circumstances, it may even be incumbent upon Crown counsel to make such disclosures directly to the court. ...

## The Crown Prosecutor

Donald MacNeil was the chief Crown prosecutor in charge of this case. He presented the Crown's case at the preliminary inquiry and during the trial. ...

[The commission found that MacNeil knew that Chant and Pratico had given inconsistent statements.]

Given the importance of these witnesses to the Crown's case, we believe he should have interviewed each of them separately in depth as part of what should be standard pre-trial preparation. That the witnesses were juveniles who had given conflicting statements made these interviews even more critical. MacNeil should have used these sessions to find out why they had made earlier, conflicting statements, and to satisfy himself that their later statements were truthful. We believe that if MacNeil had interviewed Chant [and] Pratico ... separately, he might very well have learned that neither Chant nor Pratico had actually witnessed Marshall stabbing Sandy Seale.

MacNeil not only did not make the necessary effort to find out the reasons for those conflicting statements but he also—and just as importantly—did not disclose the existence of those earlier statements to Marshall's defence counsel.

According to the evidence before us, MacNeil generally did disclose the contents of statements of various witnesses to defence counsel if they asked for such information. If they did not, however, he would not make any disclosure. ...

The evidence the Crown had in its possession in this particular case illustrates why the Crown must discharge this obligation to disclose. If defence counsel had been armed with the prior inconsistent statements by Chant [and] Pratico ... , we believe they could have used them to raise at least a reasonable doubt about Marshall's guilt in the minds of the jury.

We believe MacNeil had an obligation prior to the preliminary inquiry to disclose to defence counsel the contents of the inconsistent statements given by Chant [and] Pratico ... , and at least the names of George and Sandy MacNeil. His failure to discharge this obligation was a contributing factor leading to Donald Marshall Jr.'s wrongful conviction.

### *The Defence Counsel*

Donald Marshall's defence was in the hands of counsel who were considered to be among the most experienced and competent in Cape Breton County. All the evidence indicates that C.M. Rosenblum, now deceased, was a skilled criminal defence lawyer and that Simon Khattar had a long and distinguished career at the Bar. Rosenblum and Khattar were retained by the Union of Nova Scotia Indians and the Department of Indian Affairs, and were paid substantial fees. They also had access to any funds they needed to do whatever they decided was necessary in order to provide for Marshall's defence. ...

Marshall was a young Native with no personal resources. He was in jail continuously from June 4 through the time of his preliminary inquiry and trial. He therefore had to depend exclusively on the efforts of Rosenblum and Khattar to meet the charges against him. They let him down. We consider their actions, or lack thereof, to be the antithesis of what one would expect from competent, skilled counsel.

Rosenblum and Khattar did not carry out or arrange for any independent investigation. They did not interview any of the witnesses for the Crown. ...

Defence counsel also did not ask the Crown to disclose the existence of statements or the details of the case against their client. ...

We conclude that Rosenblum and Khattar were aware Chant [and] Pratico ... had given statements to the police, although they likely did not know the details contained in such statements. For their own reasons, defence counsel elected not to attempt to obtain those statements. Eleven years later, in affidavits filed with the Court of Appeal in connection with the Reference hearing, they stated that "if evidence of the contents of the Statements ... had been adduced at trial, then the jury might reasonably have been induced to change its views regarding the guilt of Donald Marshall Jr." (Exhibit 134, Page 130) These statements, in their own words, faithfully describe the consequence of their failure to obtain copies of these crucial statements.

Why did they not obtain them? It is one of many questions we have concerning the role played by Marshall's defence counsel. Why, for example, did they not have an independent investigation conducted? Why did they not contact the Crown to learn the case to be met? Why did they not find out that Pratico, a key witness for the Crown, spent the time between the preliminary inquiry and the trial in the Nova Scotia Hospital being treated for mental illness?

Bernard Francis, a court worker in Sydney in 1971, testified that in his opinion Rosenblum did not work as hard for Native clients. We also heard evidence to suggest that Rosenblum and Khattar believed Marshall was guilty. Did those feelings influence the effort they put into mounting Marshall's defence?

We conclude that the fact that Marshall was a Native did indeed influence Rosenblum and Khattar. Given the reputation for competence they enjoyed in the Cape Breton legal community and the totally inadequate defence they provided to Marshall, the irresistible conclusion is that Marshall's race did influence the defence provided to him.

For whatever reason, Donald Marshall Jr. did not get the professional services to which any accused is entitled. Had defence counsel taken even the most rudimentary steps an accused should be entitled to expect from his or her counsel, it is difficult to believe Marshall would have been convicted.

[The commission found that Marshall's lawyer failed to bring fundamental errors of law to the Appellate Division's attention in 1972 and that his conduct amounted to a "serious breach of the standard of professional conduct expected and required of defence counsel."]

### The Trial Judge

During the course of Donald Marshall Jr.'s trial, the trial judge, Mr. Justice Louis Dubinsky, made various incorrect rulings on evidence. While many of those errors may not have influenced the outcome of the trial when considered individually, some were indeed serious and may have had an effect on the verdict. In any case, the cumulative effect of the errors is such that we must conclude that Marshall did not receive a fair trial.

Professor Bruce Archibald, who teaches criminal law and criminal procedure at Dalhousie University Law School, provided us with a comprehensive opinion (Exhibit 83) that reviewed various incorrect rulings on evidence by the trial judge.

In summary, his criticism of the rulings of the trial judge included Mr. Justice Dubinsky's rulings on the use of hearsay evidence, or what the judge and counsel incorrectly considered to be hearsay; his ruling in allowing an improper reference to a tattoo on Marshall's arm that read "I Hate Cops" (an irrelevant aside in the evidence that was extremely prejudicial to Marshall); his ruling allowing the parents of Sandy

Seale to be called as witnesses (ostensibly to establish continuity of exhibits, but which was also likely to obtain sympathy from the jurors); and his rulings improperly limiting the cross-examination of important witnesses. We accept Archibald's opinion on all of these issues.

There is one particular error by the judge that Archibald considers in detail and on which we wish to comment as well. This concerns Mr. Justice Dubinsky's handling of John Pratico's attempt to recant his statement that Donald Marshall Jr. had killed Seale and that he had witnessed the stabbing. ...

In the corridor while he was waiting to testify, Pratico, of his own volition, approached Donald Marshall Sr. He told him that Donald Marshall Jr. did not kill Sandy Seale and that Pratico had lied when he testified at the preliminary inquiry that he had witnessed the stabbing.

When Pratico was sworn, MacNeil immediately attempted to introduce the evidence of what had been said outside the courtroom. The judge refused to permit it to be heard at that time. (Exhibit 1, Page 156) Subsequently, Khattar did bring out what Pratico said outside the courtroom during his cross-examination of Pratico, but MacNeil objected and the trial judge refused to permit a thorough and searching cross-examination about why Pratico had said what he did, why he had lied at the Preliminary and other matters. (Exhibit 1, Page 182). ...

We believe a full and complete cross-examination of John Pratico at this stage by Khattar almost certainly would have resulted in his recanting the evidence given during his examination-in-chief that he had seen Marshall stab Seale. In those circumstances, no jury would have convicted Donald Marshall Jr.

But that, unfortunately, is not what happened. Marshall was convicted and sentenced to life in prison. During the course of the trial, Justice Dubinsky made a comment that, in retrospect, now seems ironic in the extreme:

> Whether I am right—who is there in this world who can say that he never made mistakes, is a matter which may, may, if necessary, be looked into at some future time.

## The 1972 Appeal

For our part, we believe a court of appeal has a duty to review the record of a criminal case placed before it. If the court becomes aware during this review of a significant error, which has not been raised by counsel, we believe the court has an obligation to raise the issue with counsel and to ensure that it is properly argued. If necessary, counsel should be recalled to deal with the issue. In this case, the Court of Appeal did not comment on the serious issues which were readily apparent on a reading of the trial transcript. These errors were so serious that a new trial should have been the inevitable result of any appeal.

We recognize that a duty such as we have outlined imposes a heavy burden on an appellate court, but it is important to remember that a provincial Court of Appeal is for all practical purposes the court of last resort for a convicted appellant. Since the possibility of a "routine" criminal matter being heard by the Supreme Court of Canada is virtually non-existent, provincial Courts of Appeal represent the final opportunity to make sure the law is properly applied according to accepted principles.

Our criminal justice system functions as an adversarial process, which is supposed to ensure that only the guilty are convicted. The overriding principle is the search for justice. There can be no justice if a conviction is sustained because of the inadequacy of counsel. The Appeal Courts must ensure that justice is done. When counsel fails, the courts must step in. ...

### The Correctional System

On July 29, 1982, the Court of Appeal granted an application for bail for Donald Marshall Jr. By that time, Marshall had been incarcerated, either in the Cape Breton County Jail, Dorchester Penitentiary, the Medium Security Facility at Springhill, Nova Scotia, or at the Carlton Centre halfway house in Halifax, Nova Scotia for approximately 11 years and one month. ...

Having entered prison as a 17-year-old boy in 1971 and then having spent 11 years there for a crime he did not commit, Donald Marshall Jr., 28, was out on the street again in July 1982. Because he had been released on bail, however, he received none of the institutional assistance he would have been entitled to if he, in fact, had committed the crime for which he had been imprisoned and been released on parole. The bitter irony is that the system, which had failed Donald Marshall Jr. on so many occasions in the past, failed him again even as it sent him back into society.

This is not the fault of the corrections system, which is geared to assist offenders reintegrate into society but cannot logically exercise control over those who are not guilty of any crime. The system is simply not set up to deal with the unique situation in which Marshall found himself. While that is understandable, it is nonetheless difficult to imagine a more tragic circumstance. ...

### The 1983 Reference

[The commission concluded that the 1983 *Reference* should have been established by the minister of justice as a broad-ranging inquiry into the miscarriage of justice under s. 690(c) (see now s. 696.3(2)) rather than as an appeal by Marshall from his conviction under s. 690(b) (formerly s. 617(b)) (see now s. 696.3(3)(a)(ii)).]

As a practical matter, this decision to refer under Section 617(b) left Marshall with the burden of preparing and presenting the case to prove his own innocence. This reinforced the adversarial nature of an appeal, and it served to limit the issues canvassed before the Court. Although both governments felt that a full public airing was essential, the Section 617(b) appeal effectively confined the public hearing to the facts of the incident, and precluded a complete examination of why the wrongful conviction occurred. ...

By using Section 617(b), the possibility of a new trial was raised, an outcome which no one wanted; of perhaps more importance, the evidence would be directed solely at guilt or innocence, and not to the factors leading to the wrongful conviction.

[The commission strongly criticized parts of the 1983 *Reference* decision.]

This Commission has carefully examined the Court's judgment in the light of the record before the Court. We believe the Court made a serious and fundamental error when it placed the blame on Donald Marshall Jr. The Court reached conclusions unsupported by evidence and either ignored or refused to hear evidence that would have been critical of anyone other than Marshall. In so doing, the Court not only appeared to be acquitting Marshall with the greatest of reluctance, but it also absolved the criminal justice system of any responsibility for his wrongful conviction and imprisonment. ...

The Court of Appeal concluded that Donald Marshall Jr. had been engaged in an attempted robbery at the time Sandy Seale was murdered. From that initial finding, the Court drew a number of conclusions. The first was that Marshall was therefore guilty of "evasions, prevarications and outright lies." (Exhibit 4, Page 143) The Court did not indicate what Marshall's "outright lies" were, but presumably the Court accepted Jimmy MacNeil's evidence that the murder was the result of a struggle that occurred during an attempted robbery and rejected Marshall's evidence that no robbery or attempted robbery took place. If this, in fact, is the case, the Court took it upon itself to "convict" Marshall of an offence—committing a robbery—with which he was never charged. ...

Having concluded that Marshall was involved in a robbery attempt, the Court then took it upon itself to blame him for not confessing to this criminal offence—one with which he had not been charged—in order to win his freedom on another charge, of which he was not guilty.

> By hiding the facts from his lawyers and the police Mr. Marshall effectively prevented development of the only defence available to him, namely, that during a robbery Seale was stabbed by one of the intended victims. He now says that he knew approximately where the man lived who stabbed Seale and had a pretty good description of him. With this information the truth of the matter might well have been uncovered by the police.

The Court's characterization of the "robbery" as being the "only defence available" to Marshall is curious in the extreme. Surely in our criminal justice system there is no onus on an accused to develop a defence. Surely the onus and obligation on the part of the Crown is to bring forward truthful evidence which, if accepted, will support the conviction. How can an accused be blamed if he is convicted on the basis of perjured testimony? ...

We find it incomprehensible that the Court of Appeal failed to identify the perjured testimony and its source and the non-disclosure by the Crown of inconsistent statements as the key contributing factors to Donald Marshall Jr.'s conviction, and then suggested Marshall contributed "in large measure" to his own conviction. The thrust of the Court of Appeal's gratuitous comments in the last two pages of the judgment is to pin the blame on Marshall for his conviction and to ignore any evidence which would suggest fault on the part of the criminal justice system. The decision amounted to a defence of the system at Marshall's expense, notwithstanding overwhelming evidence to the contrary.

*Righting the Wrong: Dealing with the Wrongfully Convicted*

How should society deal with situations in which people are convicted and jailed for crimes they did not commit? How do we make sure we find out about such situations and, once we have learned about them, how do we determine a fair method to compensate those who have been the victims of such injustices?

We believe an independent review mechanism needs to be established to deal with allegations of wrongful conviction. Its existence must be well publicized so that both those who claim to have been wrongfully convicted and those who have knowledge about a wrongful conviction will know who to approach with their concerns. The review mechanism must be independent so that those with information will be willing to come forward. Finally, if it is to be effective, this body will need to have investigative powers to look into the allegations and obtain access to all relevant information and interview all witnesses.

We recommend that the Attorney General take up the matter of establishing a review mechanism with his Federal and Provincial counterparts.

If it is determined that someone has been wrongfully convicted and imprisoned, we recommend that a judicial inquiry be constituted to consider any claim for compensation. Such an inquiry would also have the power to look into the factors that led to the wrongful conviction. We do not believe there should be any pre-set limit on the amount of appropriate compensation, nor do we believe that the person wrongfully convicted should be required to pay his or her legal fees out of whatever compensation they receive. Such expenses should be regarded as part of the expenses of the inquiry.

*Visible Minorities and the Criminal Justice System*

Having found that racism played a part in Donald Marshall Jr.'s wrongful conviction and imprisonment, we believed it was important to ensure that our justice system will not—and cannot—be influenced by the colour of a person's skin.

While we recognize that many of the causes of discrimination are rooted in institutions and social structures outside the criminal justice system, we believe there are specific steps that can—and should—be taken to reduce discrimination in the justice system itself.

In order to make sure that visible minorities are better represented at all levels of the criminal justice system, we recommend that the Department of Attorney General and Solicitor General adopt and publicize a Policy on Race Relations—with goals and timetables for implementation—based on a commitment to employment equity and the elimination of inequalities based on race. We also recommend that a Cabinet Committee on Race Relations, including both the Attorney General and the Solicitor General, be established, and that it meet regularly with representatives of minority groups to obtain their input on criminal justice matters.

To ensure that more minority group members have the opportunity to participate in the justice system as Crown prosecutors, defence counsel and judges, we recommend that the Governments of Canada and Nova Scotia, as well as the Nova Scotia

Bar, financially support Dalhousie Law School's new special minority admissions program for Micmacs and indigenous Blacks.

We also recommend that the Government appoint qualified visible minority judges and administrative board members wherever possible.

In order to ensure that those involved in the criminal justice system are aware of—and sensitive to—the concerns of visible minorities, we recommend that the Dalhousie Law School, the Nova Scotia Barristers Society and the Judicial Councils support courses and programs dealing with legal issues facing visible minorities. We also recommend that the Attorney General establish continuing education programs for Crown prosecutors that will familiarize them with the problem of systemic discrimination and suggest ways in which they can reduce its impact. Similarly, we recommend that training for police officers include discussion of minority issues and encourage sensitivity to minority concerns.

To assist visible minority group members themselves to better understand their rights, we recommend that the Public Legal Education Society work with Native and Black groups to develop and provide appropriate materials and services. This activity should be financially supported by the Government.

In order that visible minority members, many of whom are also poor, are treated fairly by the criminal justice system, we recommend that the Government immediately proclaim the *Alternative Penalty Act* so that individuals will not have to go to jail simply because they are too poor to pay a fine. We also recommend that the Government, in cooperation with Black and Native groups, formulate appropriate diversion programs specifically geared to Blacks and Natives.

Because of the lack of visible minority members now employed as guards or administrative staff in the corrections system, we urge the Government of Nova Scotia to press federal corrections officials to implement programs to recruit and hire more minority group members, as well as to implement programs and/or sensitize other employees to the particular needs of Black and Native offenders.

### *Nova Scotia Micmac and the Criminal Justice System*

Although we have dealt in the foregoing section with recommendations that would affect both Blacks and Natives, we recognize that, on a number of issues, Blacks and Natives regard the criminal justice system in different ways. There are historic, cultural and constitutional factors, for example, that have placed Natives in a special position in Canada. In the following two sections, we will address ourselves to recommendations relating more specifically to each of these groups.

In our view, Native Canadians have a right to a justice system that they respect and which has respect for them, and which dispenses justice in a manner consistent with and sensitive to their history, culture and language. To help achieve this, we recommend that a community controlled Native Criminal Court be established in Nova Scotia, initially as a five-year pilot project. This would involve, on one or more reserves, Native Justices of the Peace hearing summary conviction cases, the development of community diversion and mediation services and community work projects as alternatives to fines and imprisonment, the establishment of aftercare services and the provision of court worker services. Native communities would be entitled to choose to opt in or out of this pilot project model.

In order to facilitate this, as well as to deal with the questions of incorporating traditional Native customary law into the criminal and civil law as it applies to Native people and other important Native justice issues in Nova Scotia, we recommend that a Native Justice Institute be established with funding from the Federal and Provincial Governments. We also recommend that a tripartite forum involving Micmacs and federal and provincial governments be established to mediate and resolve outstanding issues between the Micmac and governments.

To improve the treatment of those Native accused who will continue to appear in our regular criminal courts, we recommend that Micmac interpreters be hired to work in all courts in the province; that the Provincial and Federal Governments, in consultation with Native communities, establish a Native court worker program in Nova Scotia; that the Chief Judge of the Provincial Court take steps to establish regular sittings of the Provincial Court on reserves; and that Judges seek the advice of Native Justice Committees composed of community leaders when sentencing Natives.

We also endorse a recommendation by counsel to the Attorney General that a study be done concerning proportional representation of visible minorities on juries.

To improve relations between Native accused and lawyers, we recommend that Nova Scotia Legal Aid be funded to assign sensitized lawyers to work specifically with Native clients and to hire a Native social worker/counsellor to act as a liaison between the Legal Aid service and Native people. At the same time, we recommend that the Nova Scotia Barristers Society develop a continuing liaison program with Native people and educate its members regarding the special needs of Native clients.

To enhance the policing function in Native communities, we recommend that the RCMP and municipal police forces, where applicable, take immediate steps to recruit and hire Native Constables.

### Blacks and the Criminal Justice System

The only legislation in Nova Scotia that specifically protects the rights of Blacks and other visible minorities is the Nova Scotia *Human Rights Act*. We believe it has not been as effective as it should be, so we recommend that the Act be amended to establish a Race Relations Division within the Commission, with at least one full time member who will be designated as Race Relations Commissioner.

We also recommend that the amended Act specifically state that those aspects of the criminal justice system that come under provincial jurisdiction are covered by the Act; that the Minister will (rather than may) appoint a Board of Inquiry if the Commission recommends it; and that the Commission be given the funds necessary to hire independent legal counsel rather than depending on the advice of the Department of Attorney General.

We also believe that in order to fulfill its education mandate, the Commission should be provided with the necessary funds to engage in an active public awareness program and that the Commission should produce an annual report of its activities.

In order to ensure that Blacks are more equitably treated in the courts, we recommend that the Province re-examine its funding of legal aid to ensure there are enough lawyers available to serve the needs of minority clients and, as well, that the Chief Justices and the Chief Judges of each court in the province exercise leadership to ensure fair treatment of minorities in the system.

### Administration of Criminal Justice

As an important first step, we are recommending that a statutory office of Director of Public Prosecutions be established. He or she should have at least 10 years experience and would be appointed for a 10-year term by the Governor in Council, after consultation with the Nova Scotia Barristers Society and the two Chief Justices of the Supreme Court. The Director of Public Prosecutions would have the status of a Deputy Department head and would exercise all the functions of the Attorney General in relation to the administration of criminal justice, filing an annual report with the Attorney General.

To ensure equitable treatment before the courts, we recommend that the Attorney General—after consultation with the Director of Public Prosecutions—issue and then table in the legislature guidelines for the exercise of prosecutorial discretion.

Although the Attorney General would still be able to intervene in a prosecution, he or she would have to issue written instructions to that effect, which instructions would then be published at the appropriate time in the Royal Gazette.

To reinforce the police's unfettered right to lay charges, we recommend that the Solicitor General issue general instructions to the police informing them of their ultimate right and duty to determine the form and content of charges to be laid in a particular case, subject to the Crown's right to withdraw or stay charges after they have been laid.

Based on our findings concerning the lack of disclosure in the Marshall case, we recommend that the Attorney General urge the Federal Government to amend the *Criminal Code* to provide for full and timely disclosure of the evidence in possession of the Crown, including information that might mitigate or negate guilt. Judges would be required not to proceed with a case until they are satisfied such disclosure has taken place. Until such amendments are passed, we recommend that the Attorney General adopt and enforce similar provisions as policy. ...

### Conclusion

Our purpose as Commissioners has been to review and assess the system of administration of criminal justice in Nova Scotia in the context of the wrongful conviction of Donald Marshall Jr.

Based on our review and assessment we have found that there were, and are, serious shortcomings in that system which must be addressed. Our recommendations are intended to remedy those shortcomings and to promote a system of administration of justice which responds appropriately and fairly in all cases.

While it is impossible to guarantee that there will never be another miscarriage of justice such as befell Donald Marshall Jr., it is imperative that those in authority act responsibly to reduce or eliminate such a possibility. It is to that end that we submit this Report.

---

See, generally, H.A. Kaiser, "The Aftermath of the Marshall Commission: A Preliminary Opinion" (1990), 13 *Dal. L.J.* 364; B. Wildsmith, "Getting at Racism: the Marshall Inquiry" (1990), 55 *Sask. L. Rev.* 97; Forum, "Report of the Canadian Judicial Council" (1991), 40 *U.N.B.L.J.* 209; J. Mannette, ed., *Elusive Justice: Beyond the Marshall Inquiry* (Halifax: Fernwood, 1992); K. Roach, "Canadian Public Inquiries and Accountability," in P. Stenning, ed., *Accountability for Criminal Justice* (Toronto: U. of T. Press, 1995); K. Roach, *Due Process and Victims' Rights: The New Law and Politics of Criminal Justice* (Toronto: U. of T. Press, 1999), at 251-56; and K. Roach, "Wrongful Convictions and Criminal Procedure" (2003), 42 *Brandeis L.J.* 349.

What would have happened if the death penalty had been available in Marshall's case?

## United States of America v. Burns and Rafay
### Supreme Court of Canada
### [2001] 1 S.C.R. 283

THE COURT—

[1] Legal systems have to live with the possibility of error. The unique feature of capital punishment is that it puts beyond recall the possibility of correction. In recent years, aided by the advances in the forensic sciences, including DNA testing, the courts and governments in this country and elsewhere have come to acknowledge a number of instances of wrongful convictions for murder despite all of the careful safeguards put in place for the protection of the innocent. The instances in Canada are few, but if capital punishment had been carried out, the result could have been the killing by the government of innocent individuals. The names of Marshall, Milgaard, Morin, Sophonow and Parsons signal prudence and caution in a murder case. Other countries have also experienced revelations of wrongful convictions, including states of the United States where the death penalty is still imposed and carried into execution.

[2] The possibility of a miscarriage of justice is but one of many factors in the balancing process which governs the decision by the Minister of Justice to extradite two Canadian citizens, Glen Sebastian Burns and Atif Ahmad Rafay, to the United States. A competing principle of fundamental justice is that Canadians who are accused of crimes in the United States can ordinarily expect to be dealt with under the law which the citizens of that jurisdiction have collectively determined to apply to offences committed within their territory, including the set punishment.

[3] Awareness of the potential for miscarriages of justice, together with broader public concerns about the taking of life by the state, as well as doubts about the effectiveness of the death penalty as a deterrent to murder in comparison with life in prison without parole for 25 years, led Canada to abolish the death penalty for all but a handful of military offences in 1976, and subsequently to abolish the death penalty for all offences in 1998. ...

### 7  The Principles of Fundamental Justice Are To Be Found
### in "The Basic Tenets of Our Legal System"

[70]  The content of the "principles of fundamental justice" was initially explored by Lamer J. (as he then was) in *Re B.C. Motor Vehicle Act* [see chapter 6], at p. 503:

> ... *the principles of fundamental justice are to be found in the basic tenets of our legal system.* They do not lie in the realm of general public policy but in the inherent domain of the judiciary as guardian of the justice system. Such an approach to the interpretation of "principles of fundamental justice" is consistent with the wording and structure of s. 7, the context of the section, i.e., ss. 8 to 14, and the character and larger objects of the Charter itself. It provides meaningful content for the s. 7 guarantee all the while avoiding adjudication of policy matters. [Emphasis added.]

[71]  The distinction between "general public policy" on the one hand and "the inherent domain of the judiciary as guardian of the justice system" is of particular importance in a death penalty case. The broader aspects of the death penalty controversy, including the role of retribution and deterrence in society, and the view that capital punishment is inconsistent with the sanctity of human life, are embedded in the basic tenets of our legal system, but they also reflect philosophic positions informed by beliefs and social science evidence outside "the inherent domain of the judiciary." The narrower aspects of the controversy are concerned with the investigation, prosecution, defence, appeal and sentencing of a person within the framework of the criminal law. They bear on the protection of the innocent, the avoidance of miscarriages of justice, and the rectification of miscarriages of justice where they are found to exist. These considerations are central to the preoccupation of the courts, and directly engage the responsibility of judges "as guardian[s] of the justice system." We regard the present controversy in Canada and the United States over possible miscarriages of justice in murder convictions (discussed more fully below) as falling within the second category, and therefore as engaging the special responsibility of the judiciary for the protection of the innocent. ...

[95]  The avoidance of conviction and punishment of the innocent has long been in the forefront of "the basic tenets of our legal system." It is reflected in the presumption of innocence under s. 11(d) of the Charter and in the elaborate rules governing the collection and presentation of evidence, fair trial procedures, and the availability of appeals. The possibility of miscarriages of justice in murder cases has long been recognized as a legitimate objection to the death penalty, but our state of knowledge of the scope of this potential problem has grown to unanticipated and unprecedented proportions in the years since *Kindler* [[1991] 2 S.C.R. 779] and *Ng* [[1991] 2 S.C.R. 858] were decided. [These cases decided that it did not violate the Charter to extradite a fugitive to face the death penalty.] This expanding awareness compels increased recognition of the fact that the extradition decision of a Canadian Minister could pave the way, however unintentionally, to sending an innocent individual to his or her death in a foreign jurisdiction.

*(a) The Canadian Experience*

[96] Our concern begins at home. There have been well-publicized recent instances of miscarriages of justice in murder cases in Canada. Fortunately, because of the abolition of the death penalty, meaningful remedies for wrongful conviction are still possible in this country.

[97] The first of a disturbing Canadian series of wrongful murder convictions, whose ramifications were still being worked out when *Kindler* and *Ng* were decided, involved Donald Marshall, Jr. He was convicted in 1971 of murder by a Nova Scotia jury. He served 11 years of his sentence. He was eventually acquitted by the courts on the basis of new evidence. In 1989 he was exonerated by a Royal Commission which stated that:

> The criminal justice system failed Donald Marshall, Jr. at virtually every turn from his arrest and wrongful conviction for murder in 1971 up to, and even beyond, his acquittal by the Court of Appeal in 1983. The tragedy of the failure is compounded by evidence that this miscarriage of justice could—and should—have been prevented, or at least corrected quickly, if those involved in the system had carried out their duties in a professional and/or competent manner. That they did not is due, in part at least, to the fact that Donald Marshall, Jr. is a Native.

(Royal Commission on the Donald Marshall, Jr. Prosecution, *Digest of Findings and Recommendations* (1989), at p. 1)

In June 1990, a further commission of inquiry recommended that Marshall receive a compensation package consisting, among other things, of a payment for pain and suffering and monthly annuity payments guaranteed over a minimum period of 30 years, at the end of which he will have received in excess of $1 million. The miscarriage of justice in his case was known at the time *Kindler* and *Ng* were decided. What was not known was the number of other instances of miscarriages of justice in murder cases that would surface in subsequent years in both Canada and the United States.

[98] In 1970, David Milgaard was convicted of murder by a Saskatchewan jury and sentenced to life imprisonment. He served almost 23 years in jail. On two occasions separated by almost 22 years, it was held by Canadian courts that Milgaard was given the benefit of a fair trial, initially by the Saskatchewan Court of Appeal in January 1971 in *R. v. Milgaard* (1971), 2 C.C.C. (2d) 206, leave to appeal refused (1971), 4 C.C.C. (2d) 566n, and subsequently by this Court in *Reference re Milgaard (Can.)*, [1992] 1 S.C.R. 866. There was no probative evidence that the police had acted improperly in the investigation or in their interviews with any of the witnesses, and no evidence that there had been inadequate disclosure in accordance with the practice prevailing at the time. Milgaard was represented by able and experienced counsel. No serious error in law or procedure occurred at the trial. Notwithstanding the fact that the conviction for murder followed a fair trial, new evidence surfaced years later. This Court, on a special reference, considered that "[t]he continued conviction of Milgaard would amount to a miscarriage of justice if an opportunity was not provided for a jury to consider the fresh evidence" (p. 873). In 1994, Milgaard commenced proceedings against the Government of Saskatchewan for wrongful conviction and in 1995 he sued the provincial Attorney General personally after the

latter had told the media he believed Milgaard was guilty of the murder. DNA testing in 1997 ultimately satisfied the Saskatchewan government that Milgaard had been wrongfully convicted. In May 2000 another individual was prosecuted and convicted for the same murder. His appeal is pending before the Saskatchewan Court of Appeal. Compensation in the sum of $10 million was paid to Milgaard. The history of the wrongful conviction of David Milgaard shows that in Canada, as in the United States, a fair trial does not always guarantee a safe verdict.

[99] Of equal concern is the wrongful conviction for murder of Guy Paul Morin who was only 25 years old when he was arrested on April 22, 1985, and charged with the first degree murder of a child named Christine Jessop who was his next door neighbour. While initially acquitted by an Ontario jury, he was found guilty at a second jury trial in 1992. DNA testing carried out while the second appeal was pending before the Ontario Court of Appeal, more than 10 years after his initial arrest, exonerated him. His appeal was then uncontested, and he received an apology from the Attorney General of Ontario, compensation of $1.25 million, and the establishment of a commission (the Kaufman Inquiry) to look into the causes of the wrongful conviction. In his 1998 Report, the Commissioner, a former judge of the Quebec Court of Appeal, concluded:

> The case of Guy Paul Morin is not an aberration. By that, I do not mean that I can quantify the number of similar cases in Ontario or elsewhere, or that I can pass upon the frequency with which innocent persons are convicted in this province. We do not know. What I mean is that the causes of Mr. Morin's conviction are rooted in systemic problems, as well as the failings of individuals. It is no coincidence that the same systemic problems are those identified in wrongful convictions in other jurisdictions worldwide.

(Commission on Proceedings Involving Guy Paul Morin, *Report* (1998), vol. 2, at p. 1243)

[100] Thomas Sophonow was tried three times for the murder of Barbara Stoppel. He served 45 months in jail before his conviction was overturned in 1985 by the Manitoba Court of Appeal. It was not until June 2000 that the Winnipeg police exonerated Sophonow of the killing, almost 20 years after his original conviction. The Attorney General of Manitoba recently issued an apology to Mr. Sophonow and mandated the Honourable Peter Cory, recently retired from this Court, to head a commission of inquiry which is currently looking into the conduct of the investigation and the circumstances surrounding the criminal proceedings, both to understand the past and to prevent future miscarriages of justice. The commission will also examine the issue of compensation.

[101] In 1994, Gregory Parsons was convicted by a Newfoundland jury for the murder of his mother. He was sentenced to life imprisonment with no eligibility for parole for 15 years. Subsequently, the Newfoundland Court of Appeal overturned his conviction and ordered a new trial. Before that trial could be held, Parsons was cleared by DNA testing. The provincial Minister of Justice apologized to Parsons and his family and asked Nathaniel Noel, a retired judge, to conduct a review of the investigation and prosecution of the case and to make recommendations concerning the payment of compensation.

[102] These miscarriages of justice of course represent a tiny and wholly exceptional fraction of the workload of Canadian courts in murder cases. Still, where capital punishment is sought, the state's execution of even one innocent person is one too many.

[103] In all of these cases, had capital punishment been imposed, there would have been no one to whom an apology and compensation could be paid in respect of the miscarriage of justice (apart, possibly, from surviving family members), and no way in which Canadian society with the benefit of hindsight could have justified to itself the deprivation of human life in violation of the principles of fundamental justice.

[104] Accordingly, when Canada looks south to the present controversies in the United States associated with the investigation, defence, conviction, appeal and punishment in murder cases, it is with a sense of appreciation that many of the underlying criminal justice problems are similar. The difference is that imposition of the death penalty in the retentionist states inevitably deprives the legal system of the possibility of redress to wrongfully convicted individuals.

*(b) The U.S. Experience*

[105] Concerns in the United States have been raised by such authoritative bodies as the American Bar Association which in 1997 recommended a moratorium on the death penalty throughout the United States because, as stated in an ABA press release in October 2000:

> The adequacy of legal representation of those charged with capital crimes is a major concern. Many death penalty states have no working public defender systems, and many simply assign lawyers at random from a general list. The defendant's life ends up entrusted to an often underqualified and overburdened lawyer who may have no experience with criminal law at all, let alone with death penalty cases.
>
> The U.S. Supreme Court and the Congress have dramatically restricted the ability of our federal courts to review petitions of inmates who claim their state death sentences were imposed in violation of the Constitution or federal law.
>
> Studies show racial bias and poverty continue to play too great a role in determining who is sentenced to death.

[106] The ABA takes no position on the death penalty as such (except to oppose it in the case of juveniles and the mentally retarded). Its call for a moratorium has been echoed by local or state bars in California, Connecticut, Ohio, Virginia, Illinois, Louisiana, Massachusetts, New Jersey and Pennsylvania. The ABA reports that state or local bars in Florida, Kentucky, Missouri, Nebraska, North Carolina and Tennessee are also examining aspects of the death penalty controversy.

[107] On August 4, 2000, the Board of Governors of the Washington State Bar Association, being the state seeking the extradition of the respondents, unanimously adopted a resolution to review the death penalty process. The Governor was urged to obtain a comprehensive report addressing the concerns of the American Bar Association as they apply to the imposition of the death penalty in the State of Washington. In particular, the Governor was asked to determine "[w]hether the reversal of capital cases from our state by the federal courts indicates any systemic problems regarding how the death penalty is being implemented in Washington State."

[108]  Other retentionist jurisdictions in the United States have also expressed recent disquiet about the conduct of capital cases, and the imposition and the carrying
out of the death penalty. These include:

(i)  Early last year Governor George Ryan of Illinois, a known retentionist, declared
a moratorium on executions in that state. The Governor noted that more than half the
people sentenced to die there in the last 23 years were eventually exonerated of murder.
Specifically, Illinois exonerated 13 death row inmates since 1977, one more than it
actually executed. Governor Ryan said "I have grave concerns about our state's shame-
ful record of convicting innocent people and putting them on death row." He remarked
that he could not support a system that has come "so close to the ultimate nightmare,
the state's taking of innocent life" (Governor Ryan Press Release, January 31, 2000).

(ii)  The Illinois moratorium followed closely in the wake of a major study on wrongful convictions in death penalty cases by the Chicago Tribune newspaper, and a confer-
ence held at Northwestern University School of Law: see L.B. Bienen, "The Quality of
Justice in Capital Cases: Illinois as a Case Study" (1998) 61 *Law & Contemp. Probs.*
193, at p. 213, fn. 103. The study examined the 285 death penalty cases that had occurred in Illinois since capital punishment was restored there. "The findings reveal a
system so plagued by unprofessionalism, imprecision and bias that they have rendered
the state's ultimate form of punishment its least credible" (*Chicago Tribune*, November
14, 1999, at p. C1).

(iii)  One of the more significant exonerations in Illinois was the case of Anthony
Porter who came within 48 hours of being executed for a crime he did not commit
(*Chicago Tribune*, December 29, 2000, at p. 22N). …

(vii)  On September 12, 2000, the United States Justice Department released a study
of the death penalty under federal law. It was the first comprehensive review of the
federal death penalty since it was reinstated in 1988. The data shows that federal prosecutors were almost twice as likely to recommend the death penalty for black defendants when the victim was non-black than when he or she was black. Moreover, a white
defendant was almost twice as likely to be given a plea agreement whereby the prosecution agreed not to seek the death penalty. The study also revealed that 43 percent of
the 183 cases in which the death penalty was sought came from 9 of the 94 federal
judicial districts. This has led to concerns about racial and geographical disparity. The
then Attorney General Janet Reno said that she was "sorely troubled" by the data and
requested further studies (*New York Times*, September 12, 2000, at p. 17).

[109]  Foremost among the concerns of the American Bar Association, the Washington State Bar Association and other bodies who possess "hands-on" knowledge of
the criminal justice system, is the possibility of wrongful convictions and the potential state killing of the innocent. It has been reported that 43 wrongfully convicted
people have been freed in the United States as a result of work undertaken by The
Innocence Project, a clinical law program started in 1992 at the Cardozo School of
Law in New York. See, generally, B. Scheck, P. Neufeld, and J. Dwyer, *Actual Innocence: Five Days to Execution and Other Dispatches from the Wrongly Convicted*
(2000). One of the authors, Peter Neufeld testified to the House of Representatives
Committee on the Judiciary that "DNA testing only helps correct conviction of the

innocent in a narrow class of cases; most homicides do not involve biological evidence that can be determinative of guilt or innocence."

[110] Finally, we should note the recent Columbia University study by Professor James Liebman and others which concludes that 2 out of 3 death penalty sentences in the United States were reversed on appeal: *A Broken System: Error Rates in Capital Cases*, 1973-1995 (June 12, 2000). The authors gathered and analyzed all of the available cases from the period of 1973 to 1995, the former being the year that states began to enact new death penalty statutes following the United States Supreme Court's decision in *Furman*, ... , invalidating the existing regimes. Collection of the data for the study began in 1991, the year *Kindler* and *Ng* were decided. In their executive summary, the authors report that "the overall rate of prejudicial error in the American capital punishment system was 68%." These errors were detected at one of three stages of appeal in the American legal system. The authors say that with "so many mistakes that it takes three judicial inspections to catch them" there must be "grave doubt about whether we *do* catch them all" (emphasis in original). The authors point out in footnote 81 that "[b]etween 1972 and the beginning of 1998, 68 people were released from death row on the grounds that their convictions were faulty, and there was too little evidence to retry the prisoner" and as of May 2000 "the number of inmates released from death row as factually or legally innocent apparently has risen to 87, including nine released in 1999 alone." For an abridged version of the Liebman study, see "Capital Attrition: Error Rates in Capital Cases, 1973-1995" (2000), 78 *Tex. L. Rev.* 1839.

[111] It will of course be for the United States to sort out the present controversy surrounding death penalty cases in that country. We have referred to some of the reports and some of the data, but there is much more that has been said on all sides of the issue. Much of the evidence of wrongful convictions relates to individuals who were saved prior to execution, and can thus be presented as evidence of the system's capacity to correct errors. The widespread expressions of concern suggest there are significant problems, but they also demonstrate a determination to address the problems that do exist. Our purpose is not to draw conclusions on the merits of the various criticisms, but simply to note the scale and recent escalation of the controversy, particularly in some of the retentionist states, including the State of Washington.

*(c)  The Experience in the United Kingdom*

[112] Countries other than Canada and the United States have also experienced their share of disclosure of wrongful convictions in recent years. In the United Kingdom, in 1991, the then Home Secretary announced the establishment of a Royal Commission on Criminal Justice (the Runciman Commission) to examine the effectiveness of the criminal justice system in securing the conviction of the guilty and the acquittal of the innocent. In making the announcement, the Home Secretary referred to such cases as the "Birmingham Six" which had seriously undermined public confidence in the administration of criminal justice. The report of the Commission, pointing to potential sources of miscarriage of justice, was presented to the British Parliament in 1993. The new *Criminal Appeal Act*, adopted in 1995, created the Criminal Cases Review Commission, an independent body responsible for investigating

suspected miscarriages of criminal justice in England, Wales and Northern Ireland and referring appropriate cases to the Court of Appeal.

[113] The Criminal Cases Review Commission started its casework in April 1997. As of November 30, 2000, it had referred 106 cases to the Court of Appeal. Of these, 51 had been heard, 39 convictions quashed, 11 upheld and one remained under reserve. The convictions overturned by the court as unsafe included 10 convictions for murder. In two of the overturned murder convictions, the prisoners had long since been hanged.

[114] In *R. v. Bentley (Deceased)*, [1998] E.W.J. No. 1165 (QL) (C.A.), the court posthumously quashed the murder conviction of Derek Bentley who was executed on January 28, 1953. The Crown had alleged that Bentley and an accomplice had embarked upon "a warehouse-breaking expedition" during which a police officer was killed. It was argued that the trial judge had erred in summing up to the jury. It was also argued that fresh evidence made the conviction unsafe. The Lord Chief Justice, Lord Bingham, said about the summing up in this case (at para. 78):

> It is with genuine diffidence that the members of this court direct criticism towards a trial judge widely recognised as one of the outstanding criminal judges of this century [Lord Goddard C.J.]. But we cannot escape the duty of decision. In our judgment the summing up on this case was such as to deny the appellant that fair trial which is the birthright of every British citizen.

After quashing the conviction on this basis, Lord Bingham C.J. said (at para. 95):

> It must be a matter of profound and continuing regret that this mistrial occurred and that the defects we have found were not recognised at the time.
>
> It does not appear that the Court of Appeal gave much weight to the fresh evidence, though one component of this evidence (dealing with the taking of the appellant's statement) was said to provide "additional support" (para. 130) for the conclusion that the conviction was unsafe.

[115] Another recent case is *R. v. Mattan*, [1998] E.W.J. No. 4668 (QL) (C.A.). Mahmoud Hussein Mattan was convicted of murdering a Cardiff shopkeeper in 1952. The shopkeeper's throat had been cut. On August 19, 1952, the Court of Criminal Appeal refused his application for leave to appeal. He was hanged in Cardiff Prison on September 8, 1952. Fresh evidence came to light in 1969 but the Home Secretary declined in February 1970 to have the case re-opened. The Commission, however, referred the matter to the Court of Appeal, which found that the Crown had failed to disclose highly relevant evidence to the defence. In the result, the conviction was quashed. Near the end of its judgment, the Court of Appeal stated that "[i]t is, of course, a matter of very profound regret that in 1952 Mahmoud Mattan was convicted and hanged and it has taken 46 years for that conviction to be shown to be unsafe." It also observed that the case demonstrates that "capital punishment was not perhaps a prudent culmination for a criminal justice system which is human and therefore fallible" (para. 39).

[116] The U.K. experience is relevant for the obvious reason that these men might be free today if the state had not taken their lives. But there is more. These convictions were quashed not on the basis of sophisticated DNA evidence but on the basis

of frailties that perhaps may never be eliminated from our system of criminal justice. It is true, as the English Court of Appeal noted in *Mattan*, that the present rules require far more disclosure on the part of the Crown. And it is true that there was some blood on the shoes of Mattan that could now be shown by DNA testing not to have belonged to the victim. But there is always the potential that eyewitnesses will get it wrong, either innocently or, as it appears in the case of *Mattan*, purposefully in order to shift the blame onto another. And there is always the chance that the judicial system will fail an accused, as it apparently did in *Bentley*. These cases demonstrate that the concern about wrongful ~onvictions is unlikely to be resolved by advances in the forensic sciences, welcome as those advances are from the perspective of protecting the innocent and punishing the guilty.

*(d)  Conclusion*

[117]  The recent and continuing disclosures of wrongful convictions for murder in Canada, the United States and the United Kingdom provide tragic testimony to the fallibility of the legal system, despite its elaborate safeguards for the protection of the innocent. When fugitives are sought to be tried for murder by a retentionist state, however similar in other respects to our own legal system, this history weighs powerfully in the balance against extradition without assurances.

## II.  THE ROLE OF THE PROSECUTOR AND DEFENCE COUNSEL

In the *Donald Marshall Jr.* case the prosecutor's failure to make full disclosure and the defence counsel's failure to press the case as hard as possible played important roles in the wrongful conviction.

As you read the following material, think about whether the criminal justice system is or should be based on an adversarial system of justice? If all the lawyers in the *Marshall* case had acted as competent and aggressive adversaries, could the miscarriage of justice have been prevented? Are there other problems?

### Crown Counsel

The following case is a leading authority on the role of Crown counsel in a criminal trial.

### Boucher v. The Queen
Supreme Court of Canada
(1954), 110 C.C.C. 263

RAND J.:  There are finally the statements of counsel, which I confine to those dealing with the investigation by the Crown of the circumstances of a crime:

> (Translation) It is the duty of the Crown, when an affair like that happens, no matter what affair, and still more in a serious affair, to make every possible investigation, and if in the course of these investigations with our experts, the conclusion is come to that

the accused is not guilty or that there is a reasonable doubt, it is the duty of the Crown, gentlemen, to say so, or if the conclusion is come to that he is not guilty, not to make an arrest. That is what was done here.

When the Crown put in that evidence, it is not with the intention of bearing down on the accused, it was with the intention of rendering justice to him.

Many, if not the majority of, jurors acting, it may be, for the first time, unacquainted with the language and proceedings of Courts, and with no precise appreciation of the role of the prosecution other than as being associated with Government, would be extremely susceptible to the implications of such remarks. So to emphasize a neutral attitude on the part of Crown representatives in the investigation of the facts of a crime is to put the matter to unsophisticated minds as if there had already been an impartial determination of guilt by persons in authority. Little more likely to colour the consideration of the evidence by jurors could be suggested. It is the antithesis of the impression that should be given to them: they only are to pass on the issue and to do so only on what has been properly exhibited to them in the course of the proceedings. ...

It cannot be over-emphasized that the purpose of a criminal prosecution is not to obtain a conviction; it is to lay before a jury what the Crown considers to be credible evidence relevant to what is alleged to be a crime. Counsel have a duty to see that all available legal proof of the facts is presented: it should be done firmly and pressed to its legitimate strength, but it must also be done fairly. The role of prosecutor excludes any notion of winning or losing; his function is a matter of public duty than which in civil life there can be none charged with greater personal responsibility. It is to be efficiently performed with an ingrained sense of the dignity, the seriousness and the justness of judicial proceedings. ...

The conviction, therefore, must be set aside and a new trial directed.

[Four other judges wrote separate concurring opinions.]

---

Both the *Royal Commission on the Donald Marshall Jr. Prosecution* (1989) and the Law Reform Commission of Canada in Working Paper 62, *Controlling Criminal Prosecutions: The Attorney General and the Crown Prosecutor* (1990) recommended that prosecutions be conducted under the supervision of a director of public prosecutions subject only to public directives from the attorney general. The Law Reform Commission explained that such a reform was "[t]o ensure the independence of the prosecution service from partisan political influences, and reduce potential conflicts of interests within the Office of the Attorney General." Nova Scotia introduced such a system in 1990. See *Public Prosecutions Act*, S.N.S. 1990, c. 21.

An important element of prosecutorial discretion is the number of charges laid and proceeded with in relation to any particular incident. The Manitoba Aboriginal Justice Inquiry reported:

According to our analysis of the Provincial Court study statistics, 22% of Aboriginal persons appearing in Provincial Court faced four or more charges, compared to only 13% of non-Aboriginal persons. At the other end of the scale, while 50% of non-Aboriginal charged persons faced only one charge, this was true for only 37% of the Aboriginal persons.

The data showed that Aboriginal persons who were charged faced 2.72 charges per person, compared to 2.19 for non-Aboriginal persons (almost 25% more charges per Aboriginal person).

On the role of Crown counsel and the attorney general, see J.Ll.J. Edwards, *The Law Officers of the Crown* (London: Sweet & Maxwell, 1964); J.Ll.J. Edwards, *The Attorney-General, Politics and the Public Interest* (London: Sweet & Maxwell, 1984); P. Stenning, *Appearing for the Crown* (Cowansville, PQ: Brown Legal Publications, 1986); I. Scott, "Law, Policy, and the Role of the Attorney-General: Constancy and Change" (1989), 39 *U.T.L.J.* 104; K. Roach, "The Attorney General and the Charter Re-visited" (2002), 50 *U.T.L.J.* 1; and D. Mullan and G. Trotter, eds., *The Attorney General in the 21st Century: Essays in Honour of Ian Scott* (forthcoming).

## Disclosure

Marshall's defence at his trial and his 1972 appeal were severely prejudiced by the fact that inconsistent statements that the "eyewitnesses" Pratico and Chant had made to the police and MacNeil's original 1971 statement to the police identifying Ebsary as the killer were not disclosed to the defence. If the same events occurred today, would there be disclosure?

Rule 9(9) of the Canadian Bar Association *Code of Professional Conduct* (1987) outlines the ethical duties of the prosecutor:

> When engaged as a prosecutor, the lawyer's prime duty is not to seek a conviction, but to present before the trial court all available credible evidence relevant to the alleged crime in order that justice may be done through a fair trial upon the merits. The prosecutor exercises a public function involving much discretion and power and must act fairly and dispassionately. The prosecutor should not do anything that might prevent the accused from being represented by counsel or communicating with counsel and, to the extent required by law and accepted practice, should make timely disclosure to the accused or defence counsel (or to the court if the accused is not represented) of all relevant facts and known witnesses, whether tending to show guilt or innocence, or that would affect the punishment of the accused.

The Royal Commission on the Donald Marshall Jr. Prosecution recommended the enactment of *Criminal Code* provisions requiring disclosure. They stated:

> This decision of most American States to codify disclosure requirements is a good one. The approach reflected in current case law involves assessing each individual case of real or alleged non-disclosure to determine if it actually impairs the accused's constitutional right to make full answer and defence. We believe that such an *ad hoc* approach to disclosure means uncertainty and possible unfairness. The inability of an accused to adequately prepare a defence threatens the fairness of the criminal justice system, and it is desirable that as much discretion and subjectivity as possible be removed from decisions concerning disclosure.

The fundamental interest in a fair trial of the accused requires that the accused receive from the Crown all information known to the Crown that might reasonably be considered useful to the accused. The Crown should have a positive and continuing duty to provide this information to the defence. It is immaterial whether or not defence counsel fails to request disclosure of the information in possession of the Crown, or indeed whether defence counsel is negligent in failing to do so. The circumstances of non-disclosure should not be permitted to affect adversely the fairness of the trial received by the accused. The focal point of the issue of fairness is the fact of disclosure of material evidence.

We recommend that the Department of Attorney General of Nova Scotia urge the Federal Government to implement amendments to the *Criminal Code* of Canada as follows:

1. A justice shall not proceed with a criminal prosecution unless he is satisfied:

(a) that the accused has been given a copy of the information or indictment reciting the charge or charges against him in that prosecution; and

(b) that the accused has been advised of his right to disclosure.

2.(1) Without request, the accused is entitled, before being called upon to elect the mode of trial or to plead to the charge of an indictable offence, whichever comes first, and thereafter:

(a) to receive a copy of his criminal record;

(b) to receive a copy of any statement made by him to a person in authority and recorded in writing or to inspect such a statement if it has been recorded by electronic means; and to be informed of the nature and content of any verbal statement alleged to have been made by the accused to a person in authority and to be supplied with any memoranda in existence pertaining thereto;

(c) to inspect anything that the prosecutor proposes to introduce as an exhibit and, where practicable, receive copies thereof;

(d) to receive a copy of any statement made by a person whom the prosecutor proposes to call as a witness or anyone who may be called as a witness, and recorded in writing or, in the absence of a statement, a written summary of the anticipated testimony of the proposed witness, or anyone who may be called as a witness;

(e) to receive any other material or information known to the Crown and which tends to mitigate or negate the defendant's guilt as to the offence charged, or which would tend to reduce his punishment therefore, notwithstanding that the Crown does not intend to introduce such material or information as evidence;

(f) to inspect the electronic recording of any statement made by a person whom the prosecutor proposes to call as a witness;

(g) to receive a copy of the criminal record of any proposed witness; and

(h) to receive, where not protected from disclosure by the law, the name and address of any other person who may have information useful to the accused, or other details enabling that person to be identified.

2.(2) The disclosure contemplated in subsection (1), paragraphs (d), (e) and (h) shall be provided by the Crown and may be limited only where, upon an *inter partes* application by the prosecutor, supported by evidence showing a likelihood that such disclosure will endanger the life or safety of such person or interfere with the administration of justice, a justice having jurisdiction in the matter deems it just and proper.

2.(3) Subsection (1) imposes a continuing obligation on the prosecutor to disclose the items as above provided.

3. Where a justice having jurisdiction in the matter is satisfied that there has not been compliance with the provisions of subsections 2(1) and 2(2) above, he shall, at the accused's request, adjourn the proceedings until, in his opinion, there has been compliance, and he may make such other order as he considers appropriate in the circumstances.

We recommend that until the proposed statutory amendments to the *Criminal Code* are effected, the Attorney General adopt and implement as a matter of policy the duties of disclosure reflected in the preceding recommendation.

The above recommendations have not been enacted in the *Criminal Code*. The Supreme Court of Canada, however, has constitutionalized a broad right to disclosure under s. 7 of the Charter in the following case.

### R. v. Stinchcombe
Supreme Court of Canada
(1991), 68 C.C.C. (3d) 1

SOPINKA J. (La Forest, L'Heureux-Dubé, Gonthier, Cory, McLachlin, and Iacobucci JJ. concurring): This appeal raises the issue of the Crown's obligation to make disclosure to the defence. A witness who gave evidence at the preliminary inquiry favourable to the accused was subsequently interviewed by agents for the Crown. Crown counsel decided not to call the witness and would not produce the statements obtained at the interview. The trial judge refused an application by the defence for disclosure on the ground that there was no obligation on the Crown to disclose the statements. The Court of Appeal affirmed the judgment at trial and the case is here with leave of this court.

It is difficult to justify the position which clings to the notion that the Crown has no legal duty to disclose all relevant information. The arguments against the existence of such a duty are groundless while those in favour, are, in my view, overwhelming. The suggestion that the duty should be reciprocal may deserve consideration by this court in the future but is not a valid reason for absolving the Crown of its duty. The contrary contention fails to take account of the fundamental difference in the respective roles of the prosecution and the defence. In *Boucher v. The Queen* (1955), 110 C.C.C. 263, [1955] S.C.R. 16, 20 C.R. 1, Rand J. states (at p. 270):

It cannot be over-emphasized that the purpose of a criminal prosecution is not to obtain a conviction; it is to lay before a jury what the Crown considers to be credible evidence relevant to what is alleged to be a crime. Counsel have a duty to see that all available legal proof of the facts is presented: it should be done firmly and pressed to its legitimate strength, but it must also be done fairly. The role of prosecutor excludes any notion of winning or losing; his function is a matter of public duty than which in civil life there can be none charged with greater personal responsibility. It is to be efficiently performed with an ingrained sense of the dignity, the seriousness and the justness of judicial proceedings.

I would add that the fruits of the investigation which are in the possession of counsel for the Crown are not the property of the Crown for use in securing a conviction but the property of the public to be used to ensure that justice is done. In contrast, the defence has no obligation to assist the prosecution and is entitled to assume a purely adversarial role toward the prosecution. The absence of a duty to disclose can, therefore, be justified as being consistent with this role.

Other grounds advanced by advocates of the absence of a general duty to disclose all relevant information are that it would impose onerous new obligations on the Crown prosecutors resulting in increased delays in bringing accused persons to trial. This ground is not supported by the material in the record. As I have already observed, disclosure is presently being made on a voluntary basis. The extent of disclosure varies from province to province, from jurisdiction to jurisdiction and from prosecutor to prosecutor. The adoption of uniform, comprehensive rules for disclosure by the Crown would add to the work-load of some Crown counsel but this would be offset by the time saved which is now spent resolving disputes such as this one surrounding the extent of the Crown's obligation and dealing with matters that take the defence by surprise. In the latter case an adjournment is frequently the result of non-disclosure or more time is taken by a defence counsel who is not prepared. There is also compelling evidence that much time would be saved and, therefore, delays reduced by reason of the increase in guilty pleas, withdrawal of charges and shortening or waiver of preliminary hearings. ...

This review of the pros and cons with respect to disclosure by the Crown shows that there is no valid practical reason to support the position of the opponents of a broad duty of disclosure. Apart from the practical advantages to which I have referred, there is the overriding concern that failure to disclose impedes the ability of the accused to make full answer and defence. This common law right has acquired new vigour by virtue of its inclusion in s. 7 of the Canadian Charter of Rights and Freedoms as one of the principles of fundamental justice. ... The right to make full answer and defence is one of the pillars of criminal justice on which we heavily depend to ensure that the innocent are not convicted. Recent events have demonstrated that the erosion of this right due to non-disclosure was an important factor in the conviction and incarceration of an innocent person. In the Royal Commission on the Donald Marshall, Jr., Prosecution, Vol. 1: Findings and Recommendations (1989) (the "Marshall Commission Report"), the Commissioners found that prior inconsistent statements were not disclosed to the defence. This was an important contributing factor in the miscarriage of justice which occurred and led the Commission to state that "anything less than complete disclosure by the Crown falls short of decency and fair play" (Vol. 1 at p. 238). ...

With respect to what should be disclosed, the general principle to which I have referred is that all relevant information must be disclosed subject to the reviewable discretion of the Crown. The material must include not only that which the Crown intends to introduce into evidence but also that which it does not. No distinction should be made between inculpatory and exculpatory evidence. … This obligation to disclose is not absolute. It is subject to the discretion of counsel for the Crown. This discretion extends both to the withholding of information and to the timing of disclosure. For example, counsel for the Crown has a duty to respect the rules of privilege. In the case of informers the Crown has a duty to protect their identity. In some cases serious prejudice or even harm may result to a person who has supplied evidence or information to the investigation. While it is a harsh reality of justice that ultimately any person with relevant evidence must appear to testify, the discretion extends to the timing and manner of disclosure in such circumstances. A discretion must also be exercised with respect to the relevance of information. While the Crown must err on the side of inclusion, it need not produce what is clearly irrelevant.

I am of the opinion that, subject to the discretion to which I have referred above, all statements obtained from persons who have provided relevant information to the authorities should be produced notwithstanding that they are not proposed as Crown witnesses. Where statements are not in existence, other information such as notes should be produced, and, if there are no notes, then in addition to the name, address and occupation of the witness, all information in the possession of the prosecution relating to any relevant evidence that the person could give should be supplied. …

In this case, we are told that the witness gave evidence at the preliminary hearing favourable to the defence. The subsequent statements were not produced and, therefore, we have no indication from the trial judge as to whether they were favourable or unfavourable. Examination of the statements, which were tendered as fresh evidence in this court, should be carried out at trial so that counsel for the defence, in the context of the issues in the case and the other evidence, can explain what use might be made of them by the defence. In the circumstances, we must assume that non-production of the statements was an important factor in the decision not to call the witness. The absence of this evidence might very well have affected the outcome.

Accordingly, I would allow the appeal and direct a new trial at which the statements should be produced.

## Plea Bargaining

Because of Donald Marshall Jr.'s insistence on his innocence, plea bargaining was not a factor in the *Marshall* case. In many cases, however, an agreement between the prosecutor and the defence to a plea is an important and even determinative factor.

Would it have been proper in the face of Marshall's claims of innocence for the prosecutor to have offered him a plea bargain to a charge of manslaughter? Would it have been proper for defence counsel to have recommended that Marshall accept such a plea?

In *North Carolina v. Alford*, 400 U.S. 25 (1970), the United States Supreme Court held it was constitutionally permissible to accept a guilty plea from an accused who claimed to be innocent if there was a strong factual basis for the plea and it represented a voluntary and intelligent choice among the alternatives open to him or her. Should this sort of plea bargaining be allowed in Canada?

## Defence Counsel

Consider the role of the defence counsel. If Donald Marshall had told his lawyers that he and Seale were asking Ebsary and MacNeil for money, what should they have done? What if Marshall had told his lawyer (contrary to the Royal Commission's findings) that they planned to rob Ebsary and MacNeil?

The Manitoba Aboriginal Justice Inquiry concluded:

> Our survey of inmates revealed that Aboriginal inmates spend considerably less time with their lawyers. In fact, Aboriginal accused are more likely than non-Aboriginal accused to appear in court without a lawyer. While 61% of Aboriginal respondents saw their lawyers three or fewer times, 63% of non-Aboriginal respondents saw their lawyers four or more times. Forty-eight per cent of the Aboriginal respondents spent less than an hour in total with their lawyers, compared to 46% of non-Aboriginal inmates who saw their lawyers for three or more hours. The lack of time spent with a lawyer can have significant consequences for how an accused is dealt with in the system, because the lawyer may be less informed about the circumstances of the offence, the potential defences and the resources available as alternatives to detention.

Do you think the chances for effective representation are better under the "judicare" system used in some provinces in which a qualified accused obtains a certificate to pay for the lawyer he or she prefers or a "public defender" system with full-time salaried defence lawyers? Another alternative is publicly funded legal aid clinics designed to service particular communities.

Rules 9(10) and (11) of the Canadian Bar Association's *Code of Professional Conduct* (1987) provides as follows:

Duties of Defence Counsel

10.  When defending an accused person, the lawyer's duty is to protect the client as far as possible from being convicted except by a court of competent jurisdiction and upon legal evidence sufficient to support a conviction for the offence charged. Accordingly, and not-withstanding the lawyer's private opinion as to credibility or merits, the lawyer may properly rely upon all available evidence or defences including so-called technicalities not known to be false or fraudulent.

11.  Admissions made by the accused to the lawyer may impose strict limitations on the conduct of the defence and the accused should be made aware of this. For example, if the accused clearly admits to the lawyer the factual and mental elements necessary to constitute the offence, the lawyer, if convinced that the admissions are true and voluntary, may properly take objection to the jurisdiction of the court, or to the form of the indictment, or to the admissibility or sufficiency of the evidence, but must not suggest that some other person committed the offence, or call any evidence that, by reason of the admissions, the lawyer believes to be false. Nor may the lawyer set up an affirmative case inconsistent with such admissions, for example, by calling evidence in support of an alibi intended to show that the accused could not have done, or in fact had not done, the act. Such admissions will also impose a limit upon the extent to which the lawyer may attack the evidence for the prosecution. The lawyer is entitled to test the evidence given by each individual witness for the prosecution and argue that the evidence taken as a whole is insufficient to amount to proof that the accused is guilty of the offence charged, but the lawyer should go no further than that.

## Law Society of Upper Canada, "Defending a Criminal Case"
(1969)

CHIEF JUSTICE GALE: … What is the position of counsel when defending a client who has admitted his guilt?

1.  What restrictions does this place upon the conduct of the trial by counsel?

2.  Assume that counsel has explained the limitations which the client's admission imposes on counsel and the client agrees to permit counsel to defend him in accordance with these limitations but during the trial he insists upon giving evidence and gets into the witness box.

Mr. Sedgwick, would you take this on?

MR. SEDGWICK: Yes sir.

The question is, as to a client who has admitted his guilt. Guilt is a question of mixed law and fact. …

The client who admits his guilt may only be saying that he did something and in law he may not be guilty of any offence, or at least he may not be guilty of the offence with which he is charged. However, assuming that the guilt of the accused seems reasonably clear, counsel is still entitled to put forward any defence available. As for instance such legal or technical defences as may go to the form of the indictment, limitations, etc. He may not, however, put forward a lying defence, such as an alibi, nor *a fortiori* may he put forward any defence that goes to prove that some person other than the accused is the guilty party. This he must explain to his client so that he will not misunderstand the ethical limitations to which counsel is subject, and he should get the client's concurrence to the proposed course of conduct.

As to the second part of the question, … . The accused has the right to give evidence and counsel has no right to prevent him although he may and, of course, should give his opinion as to the wisdom of that course. The case of *Tuckiar v. The King* (1934), 52 C.L.R. 335 is an illuminating one and in that case—it was a murder case—the defence called no evidence, and following a verdict of Guilty, counsel said in open court, and before sentence:

> I would like to state publicly that I have had an interview with the convicted prisoner, Tuckiar, in the presence of an interpreter. I asked him to tell the interpreter which was the true story. I asked him why he told the other story. He told me he was too much worried so he told a different story and that story was a lie. As an advocate, I did not deem it advisable to put the accused in the box.

That, I think, was bad enough but the trial judge made matters worse by following with this. He said:

> It did not occur to me at the time but I think I should have stated publicly that immediately on that confession being made to you, you and the protector of the Aborigines consulted me and asked my opinion as to the proper course for you, as counsel, to take and I then told you that if your client had been a white man—he was by the way an Aborigine—and had made a confession of guilt to you, I thought your proper course

would have been to withdraw from the case; but as your client was an Aborigine and there might be some remnant of doubt as to whether his confession to you was any more reliable than any other confession he had made, the better course would be for you to continue to appear for him because if you had retired from the case it would have left it open to ignorant, malicious and irresponsible persons to say that this native had been abandoned and left without any proper defence.

It was an amazing performance. You will be pleased to know that the High Court of Australia quashed the conviction and discharged the accused and in doing so they made some very sensible comments about the duties and obligations of counsel. What that Court said was this:

Counsel seems to have taken the course calculated to transfer to the judge the embarrassment which he appears to have so much felt. Why he should have conceived himself to have been in so grave a predicament, it is not easy for those experienced in advocacy to understand. Counsel had a plain duty both to his client and the court to press such rational considerations that the evidence fairly gave rise to in favour of complete acquittal or conviction of manslaughter only. Whether he be in fact guilty or not, a prisoner is, in point of law, entitled to acquittal from any charge which the evidence fails to establish he committed and it is not incumbent on his counsel by abandoning his defence to deprive him of the benefit of such rational arguments that fairly arise on the proofs submitted.

And then as to the subsequent disclosure of the communication made to him, the Court said:

The subsequent action of the prisoner's counsel in openly disclosing the privileged communication of his client and acknowledging the correctness of more serious testimony against him is wholly indefensible. It was his paramount duty to respect the privilege attaching to the communication made to him as counsel, a duty the obligation of which was by no means weakened by the character of his client or the moment which he chose to make the disclosure. He was not entitled to divulge what he had learnt from the prisoner as his counsel. Our system of administering justice fairly imposes on those who practise advocacy duties which have no analogies and the system cannot dispense with their strict observance.

A situation in point arose in Canada as recently as 1965 in the *Colpitts* case [1965] S.C.R. 739, and I quote very briefly from what Mr. Justice Spence said there. He said:

It must be remembered that counsel for the appellant before calling the appellant as the only witness for the defence stated to the Learned Trial Judge in the presence of the jury ... "My Lord, yes, I am going to call one witness for the defence and that will be Reginald Colpitts, the accused. And Sir, I must, as a matter of professional ethics, do assert that this is going to happen against my better judgment and counsel. But Mr. Colpitts has decided to take the stand and I, of course, will act as examiner."

Of this Mr. Justice Spence said:

As I have pointed out above, the learned trial judge in his charge gave to the jury two conclusions suggesting that they choose the more logical and one of them was framed in the words "and that after two months of deliberation he would have *concocted* the story that he insisted on telling you yesterday."

Mr. Justice Spence went on:

I am of the opinion that that portion of the charge, when considered in the light of the remarks of the then counsel for the appellant which I have quoted could only suggest, and strongly suggest to the jury that they could place no reliance upon the evidence given by the appellant in his defence.

Reverting to my own voice, it is my view that counsel was ill-advised to make any such statement. He should merely have said the accused wishes to give evidence. Any reference to his own better judgment or to the advice that he had given his client was, in my view, improper and it was a breach of his obligations as counsel; and lastly, of course, what the client tells counsel may or may not be true. I have had clients tell me things and I have said, "For all I know, somebody may believe it—I can't." And you know, he may be merely trying it on for effect. But certainly he is not when talking to his counsel in any sense under oath and so if he elects to take the box and be sworn, you have no right to assume that he will commit perjury. I took longer than I should have done, Chief Justice, but that is at least my longest answer.

---

A recent book by Michel Proulx and David Layton, *Ethics and Canadian Criminal Law* (Toronto: Irwin Law, 2001), deals with the case of *Colpitts* as follows:

Frequently, counsel's knowledge concerning the guilt of the client comes from confidential information, most often in the form of a client confession. In such a case, counsel is bound by the duty of confidentiality owed to the client and is prohibited from sharing the information with anyone. Sadly, this duty has not always been followed. The lawyers in ... *Tuckiar* acted improperly by sharing information of their client's guilt with the presiding judge and others. Taking such actions not only violates the client's confidence but may compromise the judge's ability to try the case fairly.

It is equally unacceptable to reveal a client's incriminating confidences by way of a cryptic comment, or to make statements that imply impropriety on the part of the client. The resulting harm to the client can be seen in *R. v. Colpitts* ... The accused's testimony was likely sabotaged in advance, however, by defence counsel's damning pronouncement to the judge and jury, made just prior to calling his client to the stand:

My Lord, yes, I am going to call one witness for the defence, and that will be Reginald Colpitts, the accused. And sir, I must—as a matter of professional ethics— do assert that this is going to happen against my better judgment and counsel. ...

This pronouncement was ill-advised, intimating the real possibility that the client had admitted guilt to counsel but was nonetheless insistent on taking the stand and committing perjury. ... The trial judge followed counsel's suit, making no reference to the accused's

potentially perjurious testimony in his charge. But the Supreme Court of Canada ruled that
the judge erred in not doing and granted the appellant a new trial.

The authors go on to make recommendations about how lawyers should react to both
anticipated and completed client perjury. They recommend that counsel should first
attempt to convince the client not to engage in perjury and inform the client of the serious
adverse consequences that can flow from perjury including the lawyer's remedies, which
in their view, may include withdrawal of the lawyer from the case and even disclosure by
the lawyer if the client actually commits perjury and does not retract the false testimony.
They conclude:

> In our view, disclosure is mandated when the perjury has occurred and the client refuses to
> correct the falsehood. However, some Canadian governing bodies arguably forbid disclo-
> sure absent the client's consent or are at least unclear on this point.

How should the competing interests in preserving confidentiality and solicitor and
client privilege and in ensuring that the court is not misled by false testimony be
balanced?

For a further discussion of the ethical problems involved in defending a guilty person,
see M. Orkin, "Defence of One Known To Be Guilty" (1958), 1 *Crim. L.Q.* 170; W. Simon,
"The Ethics of Criminal Defence" (1993), 91 *Mich. L. Rev.* 1703; M. Freedman, "Professional Responsibility of the Criminal Defense Lawyer: The Three Hardest Questions"
(1966), 64 *Mich. L. Rev.* 1469; M. Freedman, *Lawyers' Ethics in an Adversary System*
(Indianapolis: Bobbs Merrill, 1975), critically reviewed by Rotunda in (1976), 89 *Harv.
L. Rev.* 622; and M. Freedman, "Client Confidences and Client Perjury: Some Unan-
swered Questions" (1988), 136 *U. Penn. L. Rev.* 1939.

## III.  PRE-TRIAL RELEASE AND BAIL

Sandy Seale died May 29, 1971. Donald Marshall was arrested and charged with his
murder on Friday June 4, 1971. He was denied bail and held in jail during his preliminary
hearing and trial. How might this have affected his trial? Marshall's pretrial detention
occurred before the introduction of the *Bail Reform Act*, R.S.C. 1970 (2nd Supp.), c. 2
proclaimed in 1972 and now found in part XVI of the *Criminal Code*. In addition to the
1972 reforms, s. 11(e) of the Charter now provides that those charged with an offence
have the right not to be denied reasonable bail without just cause.

Would Marshall be released under the current law? Because he was charged with
murder, Marshall, not the Crown, would have to show cause why his detention was not
justified on either the primary ground of ensuring his attendance in court or on the
secondary ground of "the protection or safety of the public, having regard to all the
circumstances including any substantial likelihood that the accused will, if he is released
from custody, commit a criminal offence or interfere with the administration of justice":
*Criminal Code*, s. 515(10). What conditions short of cash bail could have been designed
to secure these goals? Could his release on bail have helped prevent his wrongful
conviction?

The Manitoba Aboriginal Justice Inquiry stated:

Studies of Provincial Court data reveal that:

- Aboriginal charged persons were 1.34 times more likely (55% versus 41% of non-Aboriginal charged persons) to be held in pre-trial detention.
- Of adult males between the ages of 18 and 34, Aboriginal persons spent approximately 1.5 times longer in pre-trial detention.
- Aboriginal charged women aged 18–34 were 2.4 times (48% compared to 20% of non-Aboriginal charged women) more likely to be held in pre-trial detention.
- In Winnipeg, Aboriginal detained persons spent more than twice as long in pre-trial detention as non-Aboriginal persons. Of persons held in pre-trial detention but subsequently released on bail, Aboriginal persons spent more time in custody before release.
- Aboriginal youth in pre-trial detention were detained an average of 29.3 days, compared to 10.8 days for non-Aboriginal youth.

The *Report of the Commission on Systemic Racism in the Ontario Criminal Justice System* (1996) found that

while white people were imprisoned before trial at about the same rate as after sentence (approximately 329 per 100,000 persons in the population before trial, and 334 after sentence), the pre-trial admission rate of black people was twice their sentenced admission rate (approximately 2,136 per 100,000 before trial, and 1,051 after sentence) … .

Excessive detention of untried accused was documented in Martin Friedland's 1965 study of Toronto courts [*Detention Before Trial* (Toronto: U. of T. Press, 1965)], and subsequent *Criminal Code* amendments were intended to reduce imprisonment of untried persons. Nevertheless, every year in Ontario tens of thousands of untried accused spend time behind bars. In 1992/93, for example, 41,195 (49%) of a total of 83,405 admissions to Ontario prisons were unsentenced prisoners, of whom the vast majority had not been tried. By 1993/94, these remand admissions (46,151) amounted to 54% of total admissions (86,022) to provincial prisons … .

In effect, these findings are evidence of the state exercising discretion as if it has more compelling reasons to imprison black adult males before their trials than white adult males charged with the same offences. This bias may reflect explicit beliefs that black men cannot be trusted to appear for trial, or are more dangerous or criminal than white men. But it could also arise from more implicit and subtle assumptions, since important characteristics of the release process are likely to promote stereotypical decision-making.

As presently organized, the bail system demands fast decisions, sometimes made within minutes, and it expects both the police and bail justices to make predictions based on vague criteria and information that is often inadequate. These features obviously do not compel decision-makers to rely on racial or other stereotypes, nor in any way excuse such reliance. But they establish conditions in which reliance on stereotypes, perhaps subconsciously, may make decisions easier. For example, a justice who assumes that police testimony about drug charges is seldom mistaken and that most black males charged with drug offences sell drugs for profit may quickly conclude at a bail hearing that a specific black male accused is likely to offend before trial. By drawing on such assumptions, the justice avoids the more difficult task of attempting to predict the likely behaviour of that individual.

The Commission's research suggests that in practice, the exception for charges laid under the *Narcotic Control Act* [see now *Controlled Drugs and Substances Act*] may be contributing significantly to disproportionate imprisonment of untried black accused. This exception arose out of a perceived need to strengthen law enforcement to combat the drug trade at the top of the drug distribution pyramid. In practice, however, the vast majority of trafficking and importing charges under the *Narcotic Control Act* are laid against minor actors in the drug trade. Most people charged with trafficking offences are petty "street traders" whose activities are a nuisance to local residents and business. A large proportion of persons charged with importing are small-scale couriers, often women, whose participation in the drug trade is likely limited. Because such people are easily replaced by those who control drug supplies, imprisonment of minor dealers and couriers has a negligible impact on the availability of illegal drugs to users.

The commission's recommendations concerning pre-trial detention included the following:

- require police officers and officers in charge to explain in writing why the accused was not released;
- require the relevance of any reference to the accused's immigration status, nationality, race, ethnicity, religion, place of origin or birth to be explained to a Crown attorney;
- bail interview officers be funded by legal aid to help accused prepare for bail hearings;
- the reverse onus for those charged with importing, trafficking, and related offences be repealed;
- direct Crown attorneys to eliminate irrelevant references to immigration and citizenship status and be aware of the dangers of inadvertent discrimination in relying on factors such as residence and employment history to predict whether the accused will appear in court. Also do not consider roots in the community with respect to the secondary ground for detention;
- direct Crown attorneys to ensure that cash bail is not set too high and unnecessary and intrusive conditions such as "carry bail papers" are not imposed;
- increased training for justices of peace and judges regarding bail and how to avoid assumptions that may subtly discriminate against racialized people;
- better use of interpreters at bail hearings and for the accused's meetings with counsel; and
- development of bail supervision programs.

---

Because Donald Marshall was charged with murder, an offence listed under s. 469, he could not be released under the present s. 522(2) (formerly s. 457.7(2)) unless he was able to show cause why his continued detention was not justified. Section 522(2) provides:

(2) Where an accused is charged with an offence listed in section 469, a judge of or a judge presiding in a superior court of criminal jurisdiction for the province in which the

accused is charged shall order that the accused be detained in custody unless the accused, having been given a reasonable opportunity to do so, shows cause why his detention in custody is not justified within the meaning of subsection 515(10).

In the following cases, two Courts of Appeal reached opposite conclusions on whether this onus on the accused in s. 522(2) violated s. 11(e) of the Charter.

### R. v. Bray
Ontario Court of Appeal
(1983), 2 C.C.C. (3d) 325

MARTIN J.A.: The *Bail Reform Act*, 1970-71-72 (Can.), c. 37, introduced a liberal and enlightened system of pre-trial release. The object of the legislation clearly was to reduce pre-trial detention consistent with securing the attendance of the accused at his trial and the protection of the public interest. Counsel for the appellant stated that he was not challenging in this review that the primary and secondary grounds for detention specified in s. 457(7) [now s. 515(10)] constitute "just cause" for the detention of an accused within s. 11(e) of the Charter.

In general, under the *Code*, the onus is on the prosecution to justify the detention of the accused on either the primary or secondary ground specified in s. 457(7). However, after some four years of experience with the new legislation, Parliament, in response to concern by some segments of the public, by the *Criminal Law Amendment Act*, 1974-75-76 (Can.), c. 93, modified the original legislation by placing the onus on the accused in a limited number of offences, including murder, to show that his detention is not justified: see *R. v. Quinn* (1977), 34 C.C.C. (2d) 473 at p. 476, 34 N.S.R. (2d) 481.

In our view, the reverse onus provision in s. 457.7(2)(f) does not contravene the provisions of s. 11(e) of the Charter. Section 11(e) provides that a person charged with a criminal offence shall not be denied bail without "just cause." The primary and secondary grounds specified in s. 457(7) clearly constitute "just cause." Section 11(e) does not address the issue of onus and says nothing about onus. Further, the legal rights guaranteed by the Charter are not absolute and under s. 1 are subject to:

> … such reasonable limits prescribed by law as can be demonstrably justified in a free and democratic society.

The reverse onus provision in s. 457.7(2)(f) is a reasonable limitation even if, *prima facie*, it conflicts with s. 11(e); and we think that it does not. The reverse onus provision requires only that the accused satisfy the judge on a balance of probabilities that his detention is not justified on either the primary or secondary ground, a burden which it is rationally in his power to discharge. There is no burden cast upon him to disprove the offence or his implication in it, the onus is on the Crown to adduce evidence of the accused's implication in the offence.

**R. v. Pugsley**
Nova Scotia Court of Appeal
(1982), 2 C.C.C. (3d) 266

PACE J.A.: Section 457.7(2)(f) places a very substantial burden on an accused person to show on a balance of probabilities that if he is released his attendance in court is ensured and his detention is not necessary in the public interest or for the protection and safety of the public.

Section 11 of the *Canadian Charter of Rights and Freedoms* reads in part as follows:

> 11.  Any person charged with an offence has the right ...
>
> > (e)  not to be denied reasonable bail without just cause;

Under the Charter it seems clear to me that a person who is charged with an offence is entitled to reasonable bail unless the Crown can show just cause for a continuance of his detention. When one compares s. 457.7(2)(f) of the *Code* with s. 11(e) of the Charter it becomes obvious that there exists a glaring inconsistency which by the application of s. 52 of the *Constitution Act, 1982* renders the provision contained in the *Code* of no force or effect. However, this does not end the matter.

On the application before Grant J. the Crown, in opposing the release, showed facts which we considered relevant to this review. Those facts were that the accused was 42 years of age at the time of the alleged offence, unmarried and was self-employed on the family farm where he resided with his deceased father and stepmother. The offence was allegedly carried out by striking the father on the head with a stove poker and setting fire to the house in which both parents perished. The record reveals that the accused had a serious drinking problem and that he had at least two previous criminal convictions related to his addiction. However, both convictions were for driving offences and did not reveal any propensity for violence. There is evidence that at the time the present incident occurred the accused was drinking and that in the past he spent approximately $300 to $400 a week on alcoholic beverage. There is no evidence that his problem has been cured or that the accused is or was receiving active medical treatment for his illness. There is also evidence that the community in which the offence occurred would have a feeling of insecurity if the accused was released.

*The denial of bail was affirmed.*

---

In large part because of the next case, the Nova Scotia Court of Appeal in *R. v. Sanchez* (1999), 136 C.C.C. (3d) 31 reversed *Pugsley* and held that the onus under s. 522(2) on those charged with murder to show cause why they should not be subject to pre-trial detention is constitutional.

## R. v. Pearson
### Supreme Court of Canada
### (1992), 77 C.C.C. (3d) 124

LAMER C.J.C. (L'Heureux-Dubé, Sopinka, Gonthier, and Iacobucci JJ. concurring):  The respondent Edwin Pearson was arrested in September, 1989, and charged with five counts of trafficking in narcotics, contrary to s. 4 of the *Narcotic Control Act*, R.S.C. 1985, c. N-1. A bail hearing was held shortly after his arrest. Pearson was denied bail and ordered detained in custody until trial.

Section 11(e) guarantees the right of any person charged with an offence "not to be denied reasonable bail without just cause." In my opinion, s. 11(e) contains two distinct elements, namely, the right to "reasonable bail" and the right not to be denied bail without "just cause." ...

Most of the current bail provisions in the *Criminal Code* were enacted in the *Bail Reform Act*, S.C. 1970-71-72, c. 37. The *Bail Reform Act* established a basic entitlement to bail. Bail must be granted unless pre-trial detention is justified by the prosecution. In *R. v. Bray* (1983), 2 C.C.C. (3d) 325 at p. 328, 144 D.L.R. (3d) 305, 32 C.R. (3d) 316, (Ont. C.A.), Martin J.A. described the *Bail Reform Act* as "a liberal and enlightened system of pre-trial release." In my view, s. 11(e) transforms the basic entitlement of this liberal and enlightened system into a constitutional right. Section 11(e) creates a basic entitlement to be granted reasonable bail unless there is just cause to do otherwise.

Section 515(6)(d) must be placed in context. In general, a person charged with an offence and produced before a justice, unless he or she pleads guilty, is to be released on an undertaking without conditions. However, the Crown is to be given a reasonable opportunity to show cause why either detention or some other order should be made: s. 515(1). Detention may be justified on the primary ground that "his detention is necessary to ensure his attendance in court" or, on the secondary ground that "detention is necessary in the public interest or for the protection or safety of the public ...": s. 515(10)(a) and (b).

Under s. 515(6)(d), where the accused is charged with an offence under the *Narcotic Control Act*, ss. 4 (trafficking or possession for the purpose of trafficking) or 5 (importing or exporting), or with conspiracy to commit any of these offences, the justice is to order the accused's detention. The accused, however, is to be afforded a reasonable opportunity to show cause why detention is not justified having regard to the primary and secondary grounds noted above. [The present s. 515(6)(d) has a similar provision relating to the *Controlled Drugs and Substances Act*.]

The very specific characteristics of the offences subject to s. 515(6)(d) suggest that the special bail rules created by s. 515(6)(d) are necessary to create a bail system which will not be subverted by continuing criminal activity and by absconding accused. The offences subject to s. 515(6)(d) are undertaken in contexts in which criminal activity will tend to continue after arrest and bail, and they create the circumstances under which offenders are able to abscond rather than face trial. The special bail rules in s. 515(6)(d) combat these problems by requiring the accused to demonstrate that these problems will not arise.

The special bail rules in s. 515(6)(d) do not have any purpose extraneous to the bail system, but rather merely establish an effective bail system for specific offences for which the normal bail system would allow continuing criminal behaviour and an intolerable risk of absconding. The scope of these special rules is narrow and carefully tailored to achieve a properly functioning bail system. I therefore conclude that there is just cause for s. 515(6)(d) to depart from the basic entitlement of s. 11(e) and to deny bail in certain circumstances. Accordingly, I conclude that s. 515(6)(d) does not violate s. 11(e).

McLACHLIN J. (La Forest J. concurring (in dissent)):  I have had the advantage of reading the reasons of the Chief Justice. I agree with them, save for his conclusion that s. 515(6)(d) of the *Criminal Code*, R.S.C. 1985, c. C-46, does not violate the constitutional right "not to be denied reasonable bail without just cause" guaranteed by s. 11(e) of the *Canadian Charter of Rights and Freedoms*. I share the Court of Appeal's concern that s. 515(6)(d) fails to distinguish between the large-scale commercial drug trafficker and the "small-time" drug trafficker. Were s. 515(6)(d) confined to the large-scale organized trafficker, there might be just cause for denying bail to people in this group. As the section stands, however, it can be used to deny bail to people when there is no reason or "just cause" for denying them bail. And where bail is denied without just cause, s. 11(e) of the Charter is infringed on its plain words.

[McLachlin J. also found that s. 515(6)(d) could not be justified under s. 1 because it was not proportionate.]

### R. v. Morales
Supreme Court of Canada
(1992), 77 C.C.C. (3d) 91

LAMER C.J.C. (La Forest, Sopinka, McLachlin, and Iacobucci JJ. concurring):  The respondent Maximo Morales was arrested in December, 1990. He was charged with trafficking in narcotics, possession of narcotics for the purpose of trafficking, importing narcotics and conspiracy to import narcotics, contrary to ss. 4 and 5 of the *Narcotic Control Act*, R.S.C. 1985, c. N-1, and s. 465(1)(c) of the *Criminal Code*. He is alleged to have participated in a major network to import cocaine into Canada. At the time of his arrest, Morales was awaiting trial for assault with a weapon, an indictable offence. He has subsequently been convicted of that offence.

A bail hearing was held shortly after Morales was arrested. Bail was denied and Morales was ordered detained in custody until trial.

[The accused appealed and challenged the constitutionality of the secondary grounds of detention under s. 515(10)(b).]

As the appellant submits, the secondary ground contains two separate components. Detention can be justified either in the "public interest" or for the "protection or safety of the public." In my view each of these components entails very different constitutional considerations. As a result, the following analysis considers the public interest and public safety components of s. 515(10)(b) separately.

In my view, the criterion of "public interest" as a basis for pre-trial detention under s. 515(10)(b) violates s. 11(e) of the Charter because it authorizes detention in terms which are vague and imprecise. D. Kiselbach, "Pre-trial Criminal Procedure: Preventive Detention and the Presumption of Innocence," 31 C.L.Q. 168 (1988-89), at p. 186, describes "public interest" as "the most nebulous basis for detention." I agree with this characterization of the public interest component of s. 515(10)(b) and view it as a fatal flaw in the provision.

… Since pre-trial detention is extraordinary in our system of criminal justice, vagueness in defining the terms of pre-trial detention may be even more invidious than is vagueness in defining an offence.

I am also unable to accept the submission of the intervener, the Attorney-General for Ontario, that the doctrine of vagueness should not apply to s. 515(10)(b) because it does not authorize arbitrary practices by law enforcement officials but rather merely authorizes judicial discretion. A standardless sweep does not become acceptable simply because it results from the whims of judges and justices of the peace rather than the whims of law enforcement officials. Cloaking whims in judicial robes is not sufficient to satisfy the principles of fundamental justice.

Nor would it be possible in my view to give the term "public interest" a constant or settled meaning. The term gives the courts unrestricted latitude to define any circumstances as sufficient to justify pre-trial detention. The term creates no criteria to define these circumstances. No amount of judicial interpretation of the term "public interest" would be capable of rendering it a provision which gives any guidance for legal debate.

As a result, the public interest component of s. 515(10)(b) violates … s. 11(e) of the Charter because it authorizes a denial of bail without just cause.

[Chief Justice Lamer held that the public interest ground was not justified under s. 1 of the Charter.]

… The vague and overbroad concept of public interest permits far more pre-trial detention than is required to meet the limited objectives of preventing crime and preventing interference with the administration of justice by those who are on bail. Accordingly, it does not constitute a minimal impairment of rights.

[He then held that the public safety ground did not violate s. 11(e) of the Charter.]

In *Pearson*, I identified two factors which in my view are vital to a determination that there is just cause under s. 11(e). First, the denial of bail must occur only in a narrow set of circumstances. Secondly, the denial of bail must be necessary to promote the proper functioning of the bail system and must not be undertaken for any purpose extraneous to the bail system. In my opinion, the public safety component of s. 515(10)(b) provides just cause to deny bail within these criteria.

I am satisfied that the scope of the public safety component of s. 515(10)(b) is sufficiently narrow to satisfy the first requirement under s. 11(e). Bail is not denied for all individuals who pose a risk of committing an offence or interfering with the administration of justice while on bail. Bail is denied only for those who pose a "substantial likelihood" of committing an offence or interfering with the administration of justice, and only where this "substantial likelihood" endangers "the protection or safety of the public." Moreover, detention is justified only when it is "necessary" for public safety. It is not justified where detention would merely be convenient or advantageous. Such grounds are sufficiently narrow to fulfil the first requirement of just cause under s. 11(e).

I am also satisfied that the public safety component of s. 515(10)(b) is necessary to promote the proper functioning of the bail system and is not undertaken for any purpose extraneous to the bail system. In my view, the bail system does not function properly if an accused interferes with the administration of justice while on bail. The entire criminal justice system is subverted if an accused interferes with the administration of justice. If an accused is released on bail, it must be on condition that he or she will refrain from tampering with the administration of justice. If there is a substantial likelihood that the accused will not give this co-operation, it furthers the objectives of the bail system to deny bail.

In my view, the bail system also does not function properly if individuals commit crimes while on bail. One objective of the entire system of criminal justice is to stop criminal behaviour. The bail system releases individuals who have been accused but not convicted of criminal conduct, but in order to achieve the objective of stopping criminal behaviour, such release must be on condition that the accused will not engage in criminal activity pending trial. In *Pearson*, the reality that persons engaged in drug trafficking tend to continue their criminal behaviour even after an arrest was one basis for concluding that there is just cause to require persons charged with certain narcotics offences to justify bail. Similarly, if there is a substantial likelihood that the accused will engage in criminal activity pending trial, it furthers the objectives of the bail system to deny bail.

[GONTHIER J. (L'Heureux-Dubé J. concurring) in dissent held that the public interest ground was not inconsistent with the requirement of just cause under s. 11(e). He stated:]

... the concept of public interest is broader than that of protection or safety of the public, and includes interests which may not be properly included within the categories of public health or safety. The aim of avoiding interference with the administration of justice is one such example. Other examples of a public interest which have been mentioned as having been actually experienced are the protection of the accused himself from suicide or from the actions of others, the prevention of activities which involve the possession of or dealing in small quantities of illegal narcotics, or the preparation of reports for the court which require the presence of the accused. Also important is the consideration that the criterion of necessity in the public interest is capable of encompassing circumstances which have not been foreseen or, indeed, which may be unforeseeable, yet when they occur, albeit rarely, they obviously make the detention necessary and undoubtedly provide just cause for denying bail within the meaning of s. 11(e) of the Charter. The courts must be able to deal with such circumstances. The good governance of society and the rule of law itself require that Parliament be allowed to provide for social peace and order even in unforeseen circumstances. The appropriate instrument for doing this is through the administration of justice by the courts and allowing them a measure of discretion which they are bound to exercise judicially, that is, for reasons that are relevant, within the limits provided by law and in accordance with the Charter.

### R. v. Hall
Supreme Court of Canada
[2002] 3 S.C.R. 309; 2002 SCC 64

[In this case, the court dealt with the constitutionality of s. 515(10)(c) added to the *Criminal Code* in 1997 and in response to the invalidation of the tertiary "public interest" ground for denial of bail in *R. v. Morales*.]

McLACHLIN C.J. (L'Heureux-Dubé, Gonthier, Bastarache, and Binnie JJ. concurring):
   [1]  On May 3, 1999, Peggy Jo Barkley-Dube's body was found on the kitchen floor of her home in the city of Sault Ste. Marie. The cause of death was massive hemorrhage from approximately 37 separate slash wounds to her hands, forearms, shoulder, neck and face. Her neck had been cut to the vertebrae and medical evidence indicated that the assailant intended to cut her head off.
   [2]  On June 4, 1999, the appellant, the victim's husband's second cousin, was charged with first degree murder. Compelling evidence linked him to the crime. Areas in the victim's home contained traces of the appellant's blood. Footprint impressions containing the victim's blood and matching the type of running shoes worn by the appellant were found in her dining room and kitchen. The same footprint impressions had been left by the appellant in his parents' home. A surveillance video from a convenience store showed the appellant on the night of the homicide wearing shoes matching those seized from his parents' home. The appellant admitted to police that he had been in the convenience store that night but denied that he had been wearing the shoes.
   [3]  The murder received much media attention and caused significant public concern. A police officer testified that there was a general sense of fear that there was a killer at large, and the victim's father testified that his wife and three other daughters were very fearful.
   [4]  The appellant applied for bail. The *Criminal Code*, R.S.C. 1985, c. C-46, s. 515(10) provides that bail may be denied in three situations:

   (a)   Where the detention is necessary to ensure [the accused's] attendance in court in order to be dealt with according to law;

(b) Where the detention is necessary for the protection or safety of the public ... including any substantial likelihood that the accused will, if released from custody, commit a criminal offence or interfere with the administration of justice; and

(c) on any other just cause being shown and, without limiting the generality of the foregoing, *where the detention is necessary in order to maintain confidence in the administration of justice, having regard to all the circumstances, including the apparent strength of the prosecution's case, the gravity of the nature of the offence, the circumstances surrounding its commission and the potential for a lengthy term of imprisonment.* [Emphasis added.]

[5] Bolan J. held that the evidence did not support denying bail on the first two grounds. He was satisfied that the accused's community and family ties, plus the ample security proposed, would ensure that the accused would appear for his trial should he be released on bail. He was also satisfied that there was no reason to think the accused would commit an offence while on release and that bail conditions could be imposed which would eliminate this risk. He found, however, that the accused's detention was necessary to maintain confidence in the administration of justice in view of the highly charged aftermath of the murder, the strong evidence implicating the accused, and the other factors referred to in s. 515(10)(c). ...

[22] The first phrase of s. 515(10)(c) which permits denial of bail "on any other just cause being shown" is unconstitutional. Parliament cannot confer a broad discretion on judges to deny bail, but must lay out narrow and precise circumstances in which bail can be denied: *Pearson* and *Morales*, supra. This phrase does not specify any particular basis upon which bail could be denied. The denial of bail "on any other just cause" violates the requirements enunciated in *Morales*, supra, and therefore is inconsistent with the presumption of innocence and s. 11(e) of the Charter. Even assuming a pressing and substantial legislative objective for the phrase "on any other just cause being shown," the generality of the phrase impels its failure on the proportionality branch of the *Oakes* test (*R. v. Oakes*, [1986] 1 S.C.R. 103). Section 52 of the *Constitution Act, 1982*, provides that a law is void to the extent it is inconsistent with the Charter. It follows that this phrase fails. The next phrase in the provision, "without limiting the generality of the foregoing," is also void, since it serves only to confirm the generality of the phrase permitting a judge to deny bail "on any other just cause."

[23] However, this does not mean that all of s. 515(10)(c) is unconstitutional. The loss of the above phrases leaves intact the balance of s. 515(10)(c), which is capable of standing alone grammatically and in terms of Parliament's intention. Whatever the fate of the broad initial discretion para. (c) seems to convey, Parliament clearly intended to permit bail to be denied where necessary to maintain confidence in the administration of justice, having regard to the four specified factors. This leaves the question of whether this latter part of s. 515(10)(c), considered on its own, is unconstitutional. ...

[30] Bail denial to maintain confidence in the administration of justice is not a mere "catch-all" for cases where the first two grounds have failed. It represents a

separate and distinct basis for bail denial not covered by the other two categories. The same facts may be relevant to all three heads. For example, an accused's implication in a terrorist ring or organized drug trafficking might be relevant to whether he is likely to appear at trial, whether he is likely to commit further offences or interfere with the administration of justice, and whether his detention is necessary to maintain confidence in the justice system. But that does not negate the distinctiveness of the three grounds. ...

IACOBUCCI J. (Major, Arbour, and LeBel JJ. concurring) in dissent: ...

[81] After the "public interest" component of s. 515(10)(b) was struck down by this Court in *Morales*, pre-trial detention could be justified only under one of the two traditional grounds, namely, ensuring the accused's attendance in court or protecting the safety of the public. As already mentioned, s. 515(10) was eventually amended to add the tertiary ground in dispute here. The other major change was the removal of the primary/secondary structure of the provision. As a result, bail can now be denied under any one of paras. (a), (b), or (c) of s. 515(10) without consideration of the other paragraphs.

[82] As noted above, Parliament waited five years before reacting to *Morales* by amending s. 515(10), and it is significant that the respondent was unable to point to any evidence that during these five years the pre-trial detention scheme was lacking in any way. Indeed, the only justification for the creation of the tertiary ground that the respondent was able to suggest was that "courts should have the exceptional power to deny bail in limited circumstances not covered by the existing legislation" (respondent's factum, at para. 21). However, in the absence of evidence of any deficiencies in the bail system during the five years after the *Morales* decision, the argument that bail judges require this residual category loses much of its force. Although the lack of an empirical foundation for the provision says nothing, in and of itself, as to its validity under s. 11(e) of the Charter (but it does arise in the s. 1 analysis), it is important to bear in mind the context underlying this appeal, namely, that for five years there was no indication that the bail system was in need of a tertiary ground in addition to the two traditional grounds for denying bail. ...

[99] The factors listed under s. 515(10)(c) are: "the apparent strength of the prosecution's case, the gravity of the nature of the offence, the circumstances surrounding its commission and the potential for a lengthy term of imprisonment." On their face, these factors seem relevant to a determination of whether bail should be granted or denied; however, one must assume here that the bail decision is not being made in order to ensure the accused attends court or to protect the public, otherwise the decision would be made under either s. 515(10)(a) or (b) which deal specifically with those grounds. As such, I find it difficult to see how these factors could promote the proper administration of justice when it has already been concluded that it is not necessary to detain the accused in order to ensure the attendance of the accused at trial or to protect the safety of the public. ...

[106] Given this underpinning in public perceptions, s. 515(10)(c) is ripe for misuse, allowing for irrational public fears to be elevated above the Charter rights of the accused. In the face of a highly publicized serious crime and a strong *prima facie*

case, the importance of the presumption of innocence or the right to bail will not be at the forefront of the minds of most members of the public. Many individuals will instead accept the factors listed in the provision to be a proxy for the accused's guilt, and the release of the accused may very well provoke outrage among certain members of the community. However, this outrage cannot be used by the bail judge as a justification for denying bail, whether or not it is dressed up in administration of justice language. Indeed, the case at bar aptly illustrates this very pitfall. Bolan J. said:

> This City, like any other small cities, looks to its courts for protection. The feelings of the community have been expressed by certain witnesses. Some people are afraid, and some people have voiced their concerns. This is a factor which I will accordingly take into consideration when I assess the third ground.

[107]  With respect, the bail judge erred in considering the subjective fears of members of the public when he had already determined that the accused should not be denied bail for fear of flight or threat to the public. Although it may well be that the reaction of the public can play a role in determining the threat posed by the accused's release under the public safety ground, that is not what the bail judge decided in this case. It is the role of courts to guard the Charter rights of the accused when they conflict with irrational and subjective public views, even when sincerely held. The problem with s. 515(10)(c) is that, stripped to its essence, its very purpose is to allow these subjective fears to form the sole basis by which bail is denied. ...

[128]  Finally, I emphasize that the role of this Court, and indeed of every court in our country, to staunchly uphold constitutional standards is of particular importance when the public mood is one which encourages increased punishment of those accused of criminal acts and where mounting pressure is placed on the liberty interest of these individuals. Courts must be bulwarks against the tides of public opinion that threaten to invade these cherished values. Although this may well cost courts popularity in some quarters, that can hardly justify a failure to uphold fundamental freedoms and liberty. ...

---

On pre-trial release, see G. Trotter, "*Pearson* and *Morales*: Distilling the Right to Bail" (1993), 17 C.R. (4th) 150; G. Trotter, *The Law of Bail in Canada*, 2nd ed. (Toronto: Carswell, 1999); and D. Stuart, *Charter Justice in Canadian Criminal Law*, 3rd ed. (Toronto: Carswell, 2001), at 360-68.

## IV.  PRE-TRIAL PUBLICITY AND CHANGE OF VENUE

The killing of Sandy Seale and the subsequent trial of Donald Marshall raised much emotion and controversy in Sydney, Nova Scotia. It was Sydney's first murder case in five years. (The last one involved the killing of a person from a minority group and had not been solved.) If you were the defence counsel in the *Marshall* case would you have moved for a change of venue under s. 599 (formerly s. 527) of the Code? If you decided to do so, do you think the trial judge would have granted your request? Consider the following case.

### R. v. Bryant
Ontario High Court
(1980), 54 C.C.C. (2d) 54

HENRY J. (orally):  The accused is charged on the indictment with rape which is alleged to have occurred at the City of Kitchener in the Judicial District of Waterloo on August 9, 1979. He applies before the commencement of the trial, which is to take place at the sittings over which I am now presiding to change the venue from Kitchener to Toronto. ...

The ground of the application is that the accused is a member of a motorcycle club known as Satan's Choice; that this group with certain other such clubs, particularly the Henchmen, have received wide-spread publicity in the local press over many years for the activities of their members which are said to be characterized by deeds of violent crime in the community; that there is wide-spread and local antipathy towards members of these clubs in the community fed by persistent media coverage of their alleged and actual association with violent crime, and intimidation of citizens; and that because of his association with the Satan's Choice Motorcycle Club there is a fair and reasonable probability of partiality or prejudice in this jurisdiction against the accused so that a full and impartial trial cannot be held in this jurisdiction. ...

Whether or not all of the alleged facts and rumours published are true is not my concern; what is relevant is that the press reports I have been shown indicate that the public perceives the members of these clubs as evil, antisocial and dangerous while the members regard the public and authorities with contempt. Such is the public perception as I derive it from the material.

I think it is fair to say that it is unlikely that a jury could be chosen in this jurisdiction that did not have some awareness, and indeed some strong feeling, about the perceived conduct of members of the clubs generally. At the same time I consider, on the basis of common knowledge as to media coverage in other parts of Ontario, that it would be unrealistic to assume that the situation is likely to be very different (except perhaps in degree) in Toronto or any other community in Ontario. The Toronto press, for example, carries reports of the activities and philosophy of these and similar clubs in Canada and the United States, including their internecine wars but as the affidavit of a press crime reporter who has reported both for the Kitchener-Waterloo Record and the Toronto Star sets out, the ratio in Metropolitan Toronto of reporting of crime by motorcycle club members to crime reporting generally, is much less than in the Kitchener-Waterloo area.

A change of venue which is the subject of this application under s. 527(1)(a) of the *Criminal Code* [now s. 599] is a matter for the exercise of judicial discretion. The relevant provision is:

> 527(1)  A court before which an accused is or may be indicted, at any term or sittings thereof, or a judge who may hold or sit in that court, may at any time before or after an indictment is found, upon the application of the prosecutor or the accused, order the trial to be held in a territorial division in the same province other than that in which the offence would otherwise be tried if
>
>    (a)  it appears expedient to the ends of justice. ...

There is a very fundamental principle at common law (of which this section is a codification) that an accused should be tried in the territorial jurisdiction within which the offence alleged was committed. The authorities are consistent that that venue should not lightly be changed and the trial moved elsewhere; the Court's discretion should be exercised with great caution and only on strong grounds. The onus is on the applicant to satisfy the Court that this principle should be displaced by the exercise of the Court's discretion. ...

An examination of the jurisprudence shows that the case law as developed recognizes two criteria for a change of venue—first, where it is clearly made out that there is a fair and reasonable probability of partiality or prejudice in the jurisdiction; secondly, that the place of trial ought not be altered unless the Court is satisfied that a full and impartial trial cannot be held in the particular county in which the venue has been properly laid. ...

In *R. v. Adams*, 86 C.C.C. 425, McRuer, C.J.H.C., has set down the criteria in the following language which has been consistently followed in the jurisprudence at pp. 427-8:

> The provisions of this section appear only to codify the common law.
>
>    As early as 1762 it was said: "There was no rule better established than, 'that all causes shall be tried in the county, and by the neighbourhood of the place, where the fact is committed.' And therefore that rule ought never to be infringed, unless it plainly appears that a fair and impartial trial cannot be had in that county": *R. v. Harris*, 3 Burr. 1330 at p. 1334, 97 E.R. 858. ...
>
>    In *Reg. v. Ponton* (1898), 2 Can. C.C. 192, Robertson J. at pg. 200-1 quotes from a judgment of Sir Adam Wilson in *Reg. v. Carroll* (unreported) in which he says: "And the Court will refuse or grant the motion as it may see fit. But it will be granted when there is a reasonable probability that a fair and impartial trial cannot be had in the place where the cause would otherwise be tried. ... But to justify me in making the change asked for, I must be satisfied that it is expedient to the ends of justice that it should be so changed, and I cannot say that I am satisfied that it is clearly made out that there is a fair and reasonable probability of partiality or prejudice in the jurisdiction within which the indictment would otherwise be tried." ...
>
>    I have come to the conclusion that the most satisfactory statement of the law is contained in Short and Mellor's Crown Practice, 2nd. ed., p. 106. The author deduces from the cases that the Courts will permit a change of venue only in cases where they are satisfied that a *full and impartial trial* cannot be had in the particular county in which the

venue has been properly laid. The words "*full and impartial trial*," in my view, comprehend the considerations involved in an application of this character. There may be cases where the inconvenience to a party may be so great that without a change in the place of trial there may be a denial of justice. In such cases a "full" trial cannot be had. ...

The real issue in the case before me is that it, in effect, raises the question of what is generally called "guilt by association." That is that his very membership in the motorcycle club will automatically place in the mind of prospective jurors a prejudice against him at his trial. In my opinion, that is a matter that ought properly to be left to the trial Judge to lay to rest by a firm instruction to the jury, and by the invoking of the safeguards available in a criminal trial to achieve to the extent possible the empanelling of an impartial jury. ...

The strength of the jury system is the ability of jurors under proper instructions from the trial Judge to rise to the occasion and consciously to assume the role of Judges and to put aside their knowledge and prejudices, if any, and try the charge on the evidence presented to them at trial.

I am confident that in this case a jury may be empanelled that will conduct themselves accordingly, given the usual safeguards of challenges in the process of their selection and the instructions of the trial Judge. These safeguards are supplemented by the rule of unanimity and the oath which is taken by each juror at the outset of trial. In this respect the author of the "Royal Commission Report on Inquiry into Civil Rights," the Honourable J.C. McRuer (Report No. 1, vol. 2) says at p. 764:

> When jurors are selected they are required to take an oath "to give a true verdict according to the evidence." Judges in charging juries invariably caution them to put out of their mind anything they have learned about the case, except that which is revealed in the evidence. Nothing has been brought to the attention of this Commission to suggest that jurors do not take their oaths seriously. If jurors cannot be depended upon to adhere to their oaths as jurymen, the whole jury system loses its fundamental strength as a protection of the rights of the individual.
>
> The requirement that the verdict of a jury must be unanimous constitutes a very real safeguard against bias or prejudice. There may be some risk that one or two jurors may allow their preconceived notions to deflect them from the requirements of their oaths as jurymen, but that twelve jurors will all be derelict to the sanctity of their oaths is very remote. ...

The application will, accordingly, be dismissed.

### R. v. Ebsary
Nova Scotia Supreme Court, Appellate Division
(1984), 15 C.C.C. (3d) 38

[The accused was charged with manslaughter for the stabbing death of Sandy Seale in 1971. On May 10, 1983 Donald Marshall's conviction for Seale's death was overturned. The accused was convicted of manslaughter for Seale's death on November 8, 1983 and subsequently argued on appeal that his trial violated s. 11(d) of the Charter providing that the accused has the right "to be presumed innocent until proven guilty in a fair and public hearing by an independent and impartial tribunal."]

MacKEIGAN C.J.N.S.: On this trial we should be concerned about the rights of Ebsary. Ebsary had a basic right to be fairly tried. ... The objection under s. 11(d) of the Charter is based mainly on the extensive local and even national publicity which made Marshall's name a household word as a man who spent over eleven years in prison "for a crime he did not commit" or words to that effect. He has been pictured as a completely innocent victim of maladministration of justice. Ebsary has been frequently referred to as the "killer." His counsel claims that the presumption of innocence was violated and that a fair trial was not held and indeed cannot be held. He argues that Crown counsel at the trial (who was not the Crown counsel on this appeal) violated the principle of fairness which should govern the conduct of Crown prosecutors by overemphasizing the innocence of Marshall and exaggerating the lies of Ebsary.

Defence counsel claims that the trial judge failed to counter the prejudice and failed to correct the Crown prosecutor.

In my opinion the jury was adequately instructed by the trial judge to disregard anything heard outside the courtroom and to base their verdict solely on the evidence. The usual jury selection process was properly followed. I am not prepared to say that a jury properly instructed, after a trial properly conducted on evidence properly admitted, would have been unable to give Ebsary a fair trial. The trial judge thus did not err in refusing to quash the indictment for violation of the Charter.

## V. THE JURY

The jury is composed of 12 people from the community in which the crime was alleged to have been committed, unless there has been a change of venue. The judge instructs the jury as to the relevant law; the jury's duty is to make determinations of fact, apply the law, and render the verdict. In *R. v. Turpin and Siddiqui* (1989), 48 C.C.C. (3d) 8 (S.C.C.), Wilson J. stated for the court (Dickson C.J.C., Beetz, Lamer, La Forest, and L'Heureux-Dubé JJ. concurring):

The right of the accused to receive a trial before a judge and jury of his or her peers is an important right which individuals have historically enjoyed in the common law world. The jury has often been praised as a bulwark of individual liberty. Sir William Blackstone, for example, called the jury "the glory of English law" and "the most transcendent privilege which any subject can enjoy": W. Blackstone, *Three Commentaries on the Law of England* (8th ed.) 1778, 379.

The jury serves collective or social interest in addition to protecting the individual. The jury advances social purposes primarily by acting as a vehicle of public education and lending the weight of community standards to trial verdicts. Sir James Stephen underlined the collective interests served by trial by jury when he stated:

... trial by jury interests large numbers of people in the administration of justice and makes them responsible for it. It is difficult to overestimate the importance of this. It gives a degree of power and of popularity to the administration of justice which could hardly be derived from any other source. [J. Stephen, *A History of the Criminal Law of England*, pp. 572-73.]

Section 11(f) of the Charter provides as follows:

11. Any person charged with an offence has the right …

(f) except in the case of an offence under military law tried before a military tribunal, to the benefit of trial by jury where the maximum punishment for the offence is imprisonment for five years or a more severe punishment; …

### Requiring Trial by Jury

Donald Marshall Jr. was convicted by a judge and jury. Because he was charged with murder, he did not have a choice under the *Criminal Code* provisions then in force to elect a trial by judge alone. In *R. v. Turpin and Siddiqui*, supra the accused were charged with the murder of the accused Turpin's husband. Under the same *Criminal Code* provisions that applied to Donald Marshall, they were required to be tried by a judge and jury. They argued that their rights under s. 11(f) of the Charter should be interpreted to give them a right to choose not to be tried by a jury. The Court rejected this argument, Wilson J. stating:

There is no constitutional right to a non-jury trial. There is a constitutional right to a jury trial and there may be a "right," using that term loosely, in an accused to waive the right to a jury trial. An accused may repudiate his or her s. 11(f) right but such repudiation does not, in my view, transform the constitutional right to a jury trial into a constitutional right to a non-jury trial so as to overcome the mandatory jury trial provisions of the *Criminal Code*. …

The mandatory jury trial provisions that applied in the murder trials of both Donald Marshall Jr. and Sharon Turpin have been replaced by s. 473 of the Code which allows a person accused of murder to obtain a non jury trial if both the accused and the Attorney General consent. What considerations should govern the Attorney General in the exercise of his or her veto over an accused's request for a non-jury trial?

### Selecting the Jury

There are three main factors determining who sits on a jury. The first is the procedure used to summon a cross-section of the population for jury service. The second is the use of a limited number of peremptory challenges that can be used by both the accused and the prosecutor to challenge jurors without the need for any stated reason. The third is the availability of the challenge for cause procedure, which allows both the accused and the prosecutor to challenge an unlimited number of potential jurors on various grounds, the most important being that they are not indifferent between the Crown and the accused.

The jury that tried Donald Marshall was composed of 12 white men. At the time, the jury pool was selected from those who paid taxes on property. The Royal Commission on the Donald Marshall Jr. prosecution commented as follows:

The lack of Natives on juries in Nova Scotia concerns members of the Native community. We know of no evidence that suggests Natives are deliberately excluded from jury duty in Nova Scotia. Nor can we argue definitively that the presence of a Native person on a jury in a case involving a Native accused will result in fairer treatment for the Native. Still, Native concerns are not unreasonable: Would a White person facing a Native prosecutor, defence lawyer, judge and jury, have some apprehension whether he would get as fair a hearing as if everyone were White?

... It has been indicated to us that, in fact, no Native has ever been on a jury in Nova Scotia. We were given no explanation for this. We do, however, urge those involved in selecting juries for trials involving Native people—both prosecutors and defence counsel— not to automatically exclude Natives simply because they are of the same race as the accused.

---

In *R. v. Johnstone* (1985), 68 N.S.R. (2d) 302 (S.C.), aff'd. 26 C.C.C. (3d) 401 (C.A.), an accused was denied standing to challenge the constitutionality of a Nova Scotia law that required jurors to be between 19 and 65 years of age and have been assessed for property taxes. The court concluded the accused's own right to be a juror was not affected. Is this persuasive? What rights of the accused might be violated by this provision? Does this case help explain the above finding by the Marshall commission?

---

The Manitoba Aboriginal Justice Inquiry stated:

The purpose of the jury is to bring together 12 fair-minded representatives of the community to make a determination on the facts of a case. Counsel, however, see their role during jury selection as requiring them to try to select jurors likely to be supportive of their position. This attitude can distort the jury selection process. The ability, which both Crown and defence counsel have, to dismiss jurors without stating any reason makes this distortion of the process almost inevitable. We believe that any 12 people not otherwise disqualified by the Act, who direct their minds to the evidence and apply the law given to them by the judge, and have heard the arguments and submissions of the lawyers, will bring in a reasonable verdict.

We have concerns about the manner in which peremptory challenges and stand-asides are used. While some defence lawyers and Crown attorneys make no distinction on the basis of race, we believe it is common practice for some Crown attorneys and defence counsel to exclude Aboriginal jurors through the use of stand-asides and peremptory challenges.

One example of such exclusion is the Helen Betty Osborne case in The Pas. There, the jury had no Aboriginal members. The six Aboriginal people who were called forward were peremptorily challenged by counsel for the defence. The lack of Aboriginal people on a jury in a case of that kind, in an area of the province where Aboriginal people make up at least 50% of the population, raises valid concerns about the manner in which our jury selection process operates.

The commission recommended that the *Criminal Code* be amended so that the only challenges to prospective jurors could be challenges for an articulated cause, not stand asides or peremptory challenges. It also recommended steps to ensure greater local and aboriginal participation on juries:

> We believe it is necessary to provide local communities with greater input into the legal system. Currently, the Manitoba Court of Queen's Bench is the only court in Manitoba with the authority to hold jury trials. That court only holds jury trials in six communities—none of which is Aboriginal. In our chapter on court reform, we recommend that jury trials be held in the community where the offence was alleged to have been committed. Recent changes in the Northwest Territories could serve as a model for what we are proposing.
>
> The *Jury Act* of the Northwest Territories provides that no person who resides more than 20 miles from the place fixed for the sitting of the court shall be included in the jury list. The Act was amended in 1986 to add the following section:
>
> > 5.2. An Aboriginal person who does not speak and understand either the French language or the English language, but who speaks and understands an Aboriginal language as defined in the *Official Languages Act* ... and is otherwise qualified under this Act, may serve as a juror in any action or proceeding that may be tried by a jury in the Territories.
>
> This has made it possible for an Aboriginal person to be tried by an all-Aboriginal jury and for all Aboriginal people to serve on juries. We are impressed by the Northwest Territories' method of limiting the area from which a jury is drawn. It has a number of advantages, the most important of which is that it involves the community in the trial of one of its members.

See C. Peterson, "Institutionalized Racism: The Need for Reform of the Criminal Jury Selection Process" (1993), 38 *McGill L.J.* 147.

## Challenging the Array

### R. v. Kent et al.
Manitoba Court of Appeal
(1986), 27 C.C.C. (3d) 405

[In this case, one of the accused, a member of the Mathias Columb Band whose first language was Cree, challenged the racial composition of a jury. Of 148 prospective jurors, two identified themselves as Indian and one of these persons sat on the 12-person jury.]

MATAS J.A.: In this Court, Mr. Prober argued that ss. 15 and 25 of the Charter had been infringed and invited us to review the pre-Charter decision of this Court in *R. v. LaForte* (1975), 25 C.C.C. (2d) 75, 62 D.L.R. (3d) 86. Mr. Prober equated a jury of peers to a jury of "equals, that is, those that are of the same race, same culture who speak the same language." Relying on the presence of only two Indians on the jurors' list and one Indian on the panel to prove discrimination, Mr. Prober said at the trial, "We do not need more evidence than that." Mr. Prober said that the petit jury should have included six Indians, or at least a number greater than one, and preferably persons who spoke Cree. To make possible a proportionate representation of Indians on a jury panel, Mr. Prober submitted that the jurors' list for a trial in Winnipeg should not be confined to names of persons living in the Eastern Judicial District, but should include names from the whole province. Counsel also argued that Indians are discriminated against because the *Code* does not guarantee a right to a mixed jury in the same way that s. 555 of the *Code* [now s. 627] provides for a mixed jury of English and French-speaking jurors. ...

I respectfully agree with Esson J.A., speaking for the court, in *R. v. Butler*, [1985] 2 C.N.L.R. 107, who, after reviewing *R. v. Bradley and Martin* (No. 1) (1973), 23 C.R.N.S. 33 (Ont. H.C.J.), *R. v. Diabo* (1974), 27 C.C.C. (2d) 411, 30 C.R.N.S. 75 (Que. C.A.), and *R. v. LaForte*, *supra*, noted that

> ... [I]t is implicit in the reasoning of each that, if there had been deliberate exclusion of persons of a particular race or origin, that would be contrary to the Bill of Rights and would require the dismissal of the array.

In my view, this principle would be equally applicable to a challenge to a jury array based on the Charter.

The equality provisions of s. 15 do not require a jury composed entirely or proportionately of persons belonging to the same race as the accused. An accused has no right to demand that members of his race be included on the jury. To so interpret the Charter would run counter to Canada's multicultural and multiracial heritage and the right of every person to serve as a juror (unless otherwise disqualified). It would mean the imposition of inequality. See the comment of Galligan J. in *R. v. Bradley and Martin (No. 2)* (1973), 23 C.R.N.S. 39 at pp. 40-1:

> In my view it would be as much discrimination to insist that a particular number of persons be of a particular race or colour as it would be to say that such persons cannot participate as jurors in the trial process. ...

In any event, it is not enough to point to the absence of a member of a particular race on a particular jurors' list as proof of discrimination. Mere assertion is not proof. The jurors' list in the case at bar is racially neutral and must be presumed to provide a fair cross-section of the community and to be reasonably representative. And to suggest bringing in jurors from around the province for a trial in Winnipeg is completely impractical and without merit.

Sinclair has not been deprived of a jury of his peers.

Section 25 of the Charter does not assist the appellant. That section provides that the guarantee in the Charter of certain rights and freedoms shall not be construed so as to abrogate or derogate from any aboriginal treaties or other rights or freedoms that pertain to the aboriginal peoples of Canada. The right of Indians to serve on a jury in any particular proportion is not a right encompassed under s. 25. Nor does s. 27, providing for interpretation of the Charter in a manner consistent with the preservation and enhancement of the multicultural heritage of Canadians, assist the appellant. On the contrary, it supports the position of the Crown that every qualified citizen is entitled to be called for jury duty.

I do not accept the argument that because of the provision in the *Code* for mixed juries based on language, the appellant has been deprived of his right to equality under the law. The provision for use of the French and English language is based on the entrenchment of rights to language in the *Constitution Act, 1982*. Language, because of its special place in the constitutional history of Canada, is given a special categorization in the Charter consistent with our constitutional history. Indians are treated the same as all other races. No other race, speaking a particular language, is guaranteed a special right to sit on a jury. As I pointed out above, if it were otherwise, considering the multiracial character of Canada, the jury system would be subject to unreasonable constraints. Accepting that aboriginals have a special place in Canadian constitutional development, it is impossible to transpose the right given to the English and French languages to the rights given to a racial group, whether aboriginal or other.

In my view, Sinclair has not shown that he has been deprived of any Charter rights under ss. 7, 15, 25 and 27.

---

For an example of a successful challenge to the array when the Sheriff admitted he did not call aboriginal people to serve as jurors, see *R. v. Butler* (1984), 63 C.C.C. (3d) 243 (B.C.C.A.). For a decision holding that only allowing citizens to sit on juries was not an unjustified violation of s. 15 of the Charter, see *R. v. Laws* (1998), 128 C.C.C. (3d) 516 (Ont. C.A).

## Peremptory Challenges

Under s. 634 of the *Criminal Code*, the accused and the prosecutor can make peremptory challenges of 4 to 20 jurors depending on the seriousness of the charge.

The Manitoba Aboriginal Justice Inquiry found that in the trial of James Houghton and Dwayne Johnston in The Pas for the death of Helen Betty Osborne, six potential aboriginal jurors had been subject to peremptory challenges by the accused. They concluded: "The jury was not representative of the community from which it was drawn and in which the crime was committed. As well, we believe that Aboriginal people were excluded because of their race. Unfortunately, the jury selection process designed in our *Criminal Code* allows such practices to occur."

In *Batson v. Kentucky*, 476 U.S. 79 (1986), the United States Supreme Court held that when a prosecutor used peremptory challenges to remove four African Americans from a jury in a trial of an African American accused, there was a *prima facie* violation of the right to equal protection of the law. It was also held that a prosecutor could not rebut this *prima facie* showing by simply affirming his or her good faith or arguing that the jurors would be partial because of their shared race with the accused. Justice Marshall concurred and stated: "The decision today will not end the racial discrimination that peremptories inject into the jury-selection process. That goal can be accomplished only by eliminating peremptory challenges entirely."

In *Georgia v. McCollum*, 112 S.Ct. 2348 (1992), the court extended the same restrictions to the accused's use of peremptory challenges. The case involved white accused who wished to use their peremptory challenges to challenge potential African-American jurors. Justice Thomas stated that if it had not been for precedent, he would have dissented. He added: "I am certain that black criminal defendants will rue the day that this court ventured down this road that inexorably will lead to the elimination of peremptory challenges."

In *JEB v. Allaway*, 114 S.Ct. 1419 (1994), the United States Supreme Court extended the above rules to peremptory challenges that may be motivated by gender discrimination.

**R. v. Pizzacalla**
Ontario Court of Appeal
(1992), 69 C.C.C. (3d) 115

MORDEN A.C.J.O. (orally):  The appellant was convicted on each of three counts in an indictment which alleged that he had committed sexual assault. He was sentenced to a total custodial term of five months. He appeals against his convictions and, alternatively, against the sentence imposed.

The appellant is a barber and each of the alleged victims was a young woman employed in his barbershop. The prosecution's evidence was to the effect that the assaults took the form of the appellant's improper touching of these employees. The appellant in his evidence denied any improper touching.

The ground of appeal from conviction is based on the manner in which the jury selection procedure was used. Crown counsel employed 23 stand-asides during the selection process, 20 of which he frankly admitted were used to exclude men from the jury. The result was that the jury which was selected and which tried the appellant was composed entirely of women. …

Crown counsel then put his position clearly on the record before the judge. In the course of his submissions he said:

> Yes, Your Honour, the selection process is obviously weighted in favour of the Crown, inasmuch as, if the Crown chooses to employ its stand-asides, it can outlast the number of challenges … I will concede that most of the challenges I used were directed at keeping men from this jury, and preferring to have women try this particular case. I have tried, in my experience, probably 50 or 100 jury trials involving sexual assaults. I have never before used the option that I used in this case, of attempting to get a jury of all women. This is a case involving sexual harassment in the workplace. In my experience, I was of the view that I might encounter a man or more than one man who felt that, somehow, a person in the workplace has the right to fondle, touch, make passes at, or otherwise touch people in the workplace.

Counsel for the respondent before us agrees with the appellant's submission that the manner in which Crown counsel exercised the right to stand aside jurors gave "the appearance that the prosecutor secured a favourable jury, rather than simply an impartial one."

... On the particular facts of this case, which include Crown counsel's candid statement of his purpose, we agree with this concession. In giving effect to the concession we are not, of course, saying that a jury composed entirely of women, or of men, cannot render an impartial verdict in a case involving an accused person of the opposite sex or in any other case. Our decision is based upon the way in which the jury selection process was used.

*Appeal allowed; new trial ordered.*

In *R. v. Biddle* (1995), 96 C.C.C. (3d) 321 (S.C.C.), an all-female jury was selected to hear a case involving a male accused who was alleged to have attacked two women in an underground parking lot. The Crown used 28 stand asides to exclude potential male jurors and the accused used 10 peremptory challenges to exclude potential female jurors. Gonthier J. would have ordered a new trial because of the Crown's use of stand asides. He stated:

> In my view, if there is conduct which is not to be condoned, it is the attempt by the Crown to fashion a jury which may seem favourable to it. The *actual* effect of such a prosecutorial practice on the fundamental characteristics of the jury, namely impartiality, representativeness, and to a lesser extent, competence, does not seem to me to be a determining element. It is rather a matter of gauging the anticipated effect of the conduct of the Crown in its selection of the jury on the *perception* of a reasonable observer as to the quality of the jury ... .
>
> While representativeness is not an essential quality of a jury, it is one to be sought after. The surest guarantee of jury impartiality consists in the combination of the representativeness with the requirement of a unanimous verdict. Consequently, an apparent attempt by the prosecution to modify the composition of the jury so as to exclude representativeness, as occurred in this case, in itself undermines the impartiality of a jury.

McLachlin J. (L'Heureux-Dubé J. concurring) disagreed:

> Gonthier J. suggests that a jury must be "impartial, representative and competent." I agree that a jury must be impartial and competent. But, with respect, the law has never suggested that a jury must be representative. For hundreds of years, juries in this country were composed entirely of men. Are we to say that all these juries were for that reason partial and incompetent?
>
> To say that a jury must be representative is to confuse the means with the end. I agree that representativeness may provide extra assurance of impartiality and competence. I would even go so far as to say that it is generally a good thing. But I cannot accept that it is essential in every case, nor that its absence automatically entitles an accused person to a new trial. ...
>
> I see no reason to suppose that an all-woman jury cannot be as impartial as all-male juries have been presumed to be for centuries. Nor can I see any reason to suppose that an all-woman jury would be seen by a reasonable member of the public as favouring the Crown. The question is not whether people, or even a number of people, might for irrational

reasons object to an all-woman jury. The question is rather whether such people could *reasonably* object to an all-woman jury, each member of which has been judged to be impartial and competent and, apart from gender, fit to judge the issues in the case. That question must, in my view, be answered in the negative. Therefore, I agree with the Court of Appeal below that no error was demonstrated in the selection of the jury.

This issue was not addressed by the other members of the court.

## Challenges for Cause

Under s. 638 the prosecutor and the accused are entitled to any number of challenges for cause. The most common ground of a challenge for cause is that a juror is not indifferent between the Queen and the accused. The challenge for cause is decided by the last two members of the jury sworn or if two jurors have not been selected, by other members of the public present in the courtroom.

In *R. v. Hubbert* (1975), 29 C.C.C. (2d) 279 the Ontario Court of Appeal stated in a unanimous judgment of five members of the court (the judgment was delivered "By the Court"):

> The challenge for cause should not be used deliberately as an aid to counsel in deciding whether to exercise the right of peremptory challenge, although indirectly a proper challenge and the trial of its truth may have that effect. ...
>
> The next principle requiring enunciation is that the trial Judge has a wide discretion and must be firmly in control of the challenge process. We believe that from time to time, and in various parts of the Province, the process has been abused by counsel. The influence of American practices in some States has crossed the border—and sometimes not in the actual form of the prescribed practices, but as they are thought to be by Canadian imitators. The challenge process must be fair to prospective jurors as well as to the accused. Concern over undue prolongation of criminal trials has recently been voiced in England and the United States, particularly where long *voir dires* occupy substantial portions of the trial. Trials should not be unnecessarily prolonged by speculative and sometimes suspect challenges for cause. ...
>
> In this era of rapid dissemination of news by the various media, it would be naive to think that in the case of a crime involving considerable notoriety, it would be possible to select 12 jurors who had not heard anything about the case. Prior information about a case, and even the holding of a tentative opinion about it, does not make partial a juror sworn to render a true verdict according to the evidence. ...
>
> Furthermore, the trial Judge has to know what the reason is, in more than general words; otherwise he cannot properly direct and control the trial of the truth of the challenge. Counsel must be prepared to state the reason for his challenge, and if he refuses to do so, the trial Judge may refuse to permit the trial of its truth, because that trial cannot properly be had without some definition of the issue.
>
> The contested challenges will nearly always be on the ground that the prospective juror is "not indifferent." If the alleged basis of non-indifference appears far-fetched to the Judge, he may in his discretion require some further elucidation by counsel or the tendering of some evidence, oral or by affidavit, before permitting the trial of the issue to proceed. ...

With great respect to those in England and Canada who have expressed a contrary view, we hold that once the Judge has ruled that the trial of the challenge may proceed, the party making the challenge may call the proposed juror as a witness without first calling other evidence to establish a *prima facie* case.

An appeal to the Supreme Court of Canada was dismissed (1977), 33 C.C.C. (2d) 207.

**R. v. Parks**
Ontario Court of Appeal
(1993), 84 C.C.C. (3d) 353

[The accused was convicted by judge and jury of second degree murder for killing a person during a cocaine deal. The accused wished to ask prospective jurors whether their ability to judge witnesses without bias, prejudice, or partiality would be affected by (1) the fact that the accused and the deceased were involved with drugs and (2) by the fact that the accused is a black Jamaican immigrant and the deceased is a white man. The trial judge disallowed both questions and after conviction, the accused appealed.]

DOHERTY J.A.: On appeal, counsel for the appellant argued that both questions should have been allowed. I see no merit in the argument as it relates to the first question. The question implies that a witness's involvement in the drug trade and his or her personal use of illicit drugs should have no relevance in "judging witnesses." To the contrary, those factors could properly be considered by the jury in its assessment of the credibility and reliability of witnesses.

The propriety of the second question does require detailed consideration. The appellant does not challenge the proscription against challenges based on race, or the beliefs, opinions or prejudices of potential jurors set down in *Hubbert*, and reiterated in *R. v. Zundel*. Counsel did not seek to inquire into individual jurors' lifestyles, antecedents, or personal experiences with a view to exposing underlying racial prejudices. He did not propose the kind of wide-ranging personalized disclosure involved in *voir dire* inquiries into potential racial prejudice permitted in some American jurisdictions. Canadian courts have resisted that approach to jury selection. ...

A question directed at revealing those whose bias renders them partial does not "inject" racism into the trial, but seeks to prevent that bias from destroying the impartiality of the jury's deliberations.

In this case, the issue to be determined on a challenge for cause was not whether a particular potential juror was biased against blacks, but whether if that prejudice existed, it would cause that juror to discriminate against the black accused in arriving at his or her verdict. ...

In other words, the presumption that jurors will perform their duty according to their oath must be balanced against the threat of a verdict tainted by racial bias.

Racism, and in particular anti-black racism, is a part of our community's psyche. A significant segment of our community holds overtly racist views. A much larger segment subconsciously operates on the basis of negative racial stereotypes. Furthermore, our institutions, including the criminal justice system, reflect and perpetuate those negative stereotypes. These elements combine to infect our society as a whole with the evil of racism. Blacks are among the primary victims of that evil.

The criminal trial milieu may also accentuate the role of racial bias in the decision making process. Anti-black attitudes may connect blacks with crime and acts of violence. A juror with such attitudes who hears evidence describing a black accused as a drug dealer involved in an act of violence may regard his attitudes as having been validated by the evidence. That juror may then readily give effect to his or her preconceived negative attitudes towards blacks without regard to the evidence and legal principles essential to a determination of the specific accused's liability for the crime charged.

I am satisfied that in at least some cases involving a black accused there is a realistic possibility that one or more jurors will discriminate against that accused because of his or her colour. In my view, a trial judge, in the proper exercise of his or her discretion, could permit counsel to put the question posed in this case, in any trial held in Metropolitan Toronto involving a black accused. I would go further and hold that it would be the better course to permit that question in all such cases where the accused requests the inquiry.

The interracial nature of the violence involved in this case, and the fact that the alleged crime occurred in the course of the black accused's involvement in a criminal drug transaction, combined to provide circumstances in which it was essential to the conduct of a fair trial that counsel be permitted to put the question. With respect, I must conclude that the trial judge erred in refusing to allow counsel to ask the question.

*Appeal was allowed; new trial ordered.*

### R. v. Williams
Supreme Court of Canada
[1998] 1 S.C.R. 1128

[The accused was an aboriginal man charged with robbery. Relying on *Parks*, he sought to ask prospective jurors whether their ability to judge the case impartially would be affected by the fact that he was aboriginal and that the complainant was white. The trial judge did not allow the question and the British Columbia Court of Appeal dismissed his appeal. An unanimous Supreme Court reversed.]

McLACHLIN J. stated:

[14] A judge exercising the discretion to permit or refuse challenges for cause must act on the evidence and in a way that fulfills the purpose of s. 638(1)(b)—to prevent persons who are not indifferent between the Crown and the accused from serving on the jury. Stated otherwise, a trial judge, in the exercise of the discretion, cannot "effectively curtail the statutory right to challenge for cause": see *R. v. Zundel (No. 1)* (1987), 31 C.C.C. (3d) 97, at p. 135 (leave to appeal refused [1987] 1 S.C.R.

xii). To guide judges in the exercise of their discretion, this Court formulated a rule in *Sherratt*, *supra*:

> the judge should permit challenges for cause where there is a "realistic potential" of the existence of partiality. *Sherratt* was concerned with the possibility of partiality arising from pre-trial publicity. However, as the courts in this case accepted, it applies to all requests for challenges based on bias, regardless of the origin of the apprehension of partiality.

[15] Applying *Sherratt* to the case at bar, the enquiry becomes whether in this case, the evidence of widespread bias against aboriginal people in the community raises a realistic potential of partiality. ...

[21] To suggest that all persons who possess racial prejudices will erase those prejudices from the mind when serving as jurors is to underestimate the insidious nature of racial prejudice and the stereotyping that underlies it ... racial prejudice interfering with jurors' impartiality is a form of discrimination. It involves making distinctions on the basis of class or category without regard to individual merit. It rests on preconceptions and unchallenged assumptions that unconsciously shape the daily behaviour of individuals. Buried deep in the human psyche, these preconceptions cannot be easily and effectively identified and set aside, even if one wishes to do so. For this reason, it cannot be assumed that judicial directions to act impartially will always effectively counter racial prejudice: see Johnson, *supra*. Doherty J.A. recognized this in *Parks, supra*, at p. 371:

> In deciding whether the post-jury selection safeguards against partiality provide a reliable antidote to racial bias, the nature of that bias must be emphasized. For some people, anti-black biases rest on unstated and unchallenged assumptions learned over a lifetime. Those assumptions shape the daily behaviour of individuals, often without any conscious reference to them. In my opinion, attitudes which are engrained in an individual's subconscious, and reflected in both individual and institutional conduct within the community, will prove more resistant to judicial cleansing than will opinions based on yesterday's news and referable to a specific person or event.

[22] Racial prejudice and its effects are as invasive and elusive as they are corrosive. We should not assume that instructions from the judge or other safeguards will eliminate biases that may be deeply ingrained in the subconscious psyches of jurors. Rather, we should acknowledge the destructive potential of subconscious racial prejudice by recognizing that the post-jury selection safeguards may not suffice. Where doubts are raised, the better policy is to err on the side of caution and permit prejudices to be examined. Only then can we know with any certainty whether they exist and whether they can be set aside or not. It is better to risk allowing what are in fact unnecessary challenges, than to risk prohibiting challenges which are necessary. ...

[28] Racial prejudice against the accused may be detrimental to an accused in a variety of ways. The link between prejudice and verdict is clearest where there is an "interracial element" to the crime or a perceived link between those of the accused's race and the particular crime. But racial prejudice may play a role in other, less obvious ways. Racist stereotypes may affect how jurors assess the credibility of the

accused. Bias can shape the information received during the course of the trial to conform with the bias: see *Parks*, *supra*, at p. 372. Jurors harbouring racial prejudices may consider those of the accused's race less worthy or perceive a link between those of the accused's race and crime in general. In this manner, subconscious racism may make it easier to conclude that a black or aboriginal accused engaged in the crime regardless of the race of the complainant: see Kent Roach, "Challenges for Cause and Racial Discrimination" (1995), 37 *Crim. L.Q.* 410, at p. 421. ...

[30]   Ultimately, it is within the discretion of the trial judge to determine whether widespread racial prejudice in the community, absent specific "links" to the trial, is sufficient to give an "air of reality" to the challenge in the particular circumstances of each case. The following excerpt from *Parks*, *supra*, at pp. 379-80, per Doherty J.A., states the law correctly:

> I am satisfied that in at least some cases involving a black accused there is a realistic possibility that one or more jurors will discriminate against that accused because of his or her colour. In my view, a trial judge, in the proper exercise of his or her discretion, could permit counsel to put the question posed in this case, in any trial held in Metropolitan Toronto involving a black accused. I would go further and hold that it would be the better course to permit that question in all such cases where the accused requests the inquiry.
>
> There will be circumstances in addition to the colour of the accused which will increase the possibility of racially prejudiced verdicts. It is impossible to provide an exhaustive catalogue of those circumstances. Where they exist, the trial judge must allow counsel to put the question suggested in this case. ...

[32]   Section 638(2) requires two inquiries and entails two different decisions with two different tests. The first stage is the inquiry before the judge to determine whether challenges for cause should be permitted. The test at this stage is whether there is a realistic potential or possibility for partiality. The question is whether there is reason to suppose that the jury pool may contain people who are prejudiced and whose prejudice might not be capable of being set aside on directions from the judge. The operative verbs at the first stage are "may" and "might." Since this is a preliminary inquiry which may affect the accused's *Charter* rights (see below), a reasonably generous approach is appropriate.

[33]   If the judge permits challenges for cause, a second inquiry occurs on the challenge itself. The defence may question potential jurors as to whether they harbour prejudices against people of the accused's race, and if so, whether they are able to set those prejudices aside and act as impartial jurors. The question at this stage is whether the candidate in question will be able to act impartially. To demand, at the preliminary stage of determining whether a challenge for cause should be permitted, proof that the jurors in the jury pool will not be able to set aside any prejudices they may harbour and act impartially, is to ask the question more appropriate for the second stage. ...

[41]   A rule that accords an automatic right to challenge for cause on the basis that the accused is an aboriginal or member of a group that encounters discrimination conflicts from a methodological point of view with the approach in *Sherratt*, *supra*,

that an accused may challenge for cause only upon establishing that there is a realistic potential for juror partiality. For example, it is difficult to see why women should have an automatic right to challenge for cause merely because they have been held to constitute a disadvantaged group under s. 15 of the *Charter*. Moreover, it is not correct to assume that membership in an aboriginal or minority group always implies a realistic potential for partiality. The relevant community for purposes of the rule is the community from which the jury pool is drawn. That community may or may not harbour prejudices against aboriginals. It likely would not, for example, in a community where aboriginals are in a majority position. That said, absent evidence to the contrary, where widespread prejudice against people of the accused's race is demonstrated at a national or provincial level, it will often be reasonable to infer that such prejudice is replicated at the community level.

[42] On the understanding that the jury pool is representative, one may safely insist that the accused demonstrate widespread or general prejudice against his or her race in the community as a condition of bringing a challenge for cause. It is at this point that bigoted or prejudiced people have the capacity to affect the impartiality of the jury.

[43] I add this. To say that widespread racial prejudice in the community can suffice to establish the right to challenge for cause in many cases is not to rule out the possibility that prejudice less than widespread might in some circumstances meet the *Sherratt* test. The ultimate question in each case is whether the *Sherratt* standard of a realistic potential for partiality is established. ...

[49] Section s. 638(1)(b) should be read in light of the fundamental rights to a fair trial by an impartial jury and to equality before and under the law. A principled exercise of discretion in accordance with *Charter* values is required: see *Sherratt, supra*.

[50] Although allowing challenges for cause in the face of widespread racial prejudice in the community will not eliminate the possibility of jury verdicts being affected by racial prejudice, it will have important benefits. Jurors who are honest or transparent about their racist views will be removed. All remaining jurors will be sensitized from the outset of the proceedings regarding the need to confront racial prejudice and will help ensure that it does not impact on the jury verdict. Finally, allowing such challenges will enhance the appearance of trial fairness in the eyes of the accused and other members of minority groups facing discrimination: see *Parks, supra*. ...

[57] There is a presumption that a jury pool is composed of persons who can serve impartially. However, where the accused establishes that there is a realistic potential for partiality, the accused should be permitted to challenge prospective jurors for cause under s. 638(1)(b) of the Code: see *Sherratt, supra*. Applying this rule to applications based on prejudice against persons of the accused's race, the judge should exercise his or her discretion to permit challenges for cause if the accused establishes widespread racial prejudice in the community.

[58] Although they acknowledged the existence of widespread bias against aboriginals, both Esson C.J. and the British Columbia Court of Appeal held that the evidence did not demonstrate a reasonable possibility that prospective jurors would be partial. In my view, there was ample evidence that this widespread prejudice included

elements that could have affected the impartiality of jurors. Racism against aboriginals includes stereotypes that relate to credibility, worthiness and criminal propensity. As the Canadian Bar Association stated in Locking up Natives in Canada: A Report of the Committee of the Canadian Bar Association on Imprisonment and Release (1988), at p. 5:

> Put at its baldest, there is an equation of being drunk, Indian and in prison. Like many stereotypes, this one has a dark underside. It reflects a view of native people as uncivilized and without a coherent social or moral order. The stereotype prevents us from seeing native people as equals.

There is evidence that this widespread racism has translated into systemic discrimination in the criminal justice system: see *Royal Commission on Aboriginal Peoples, Bridging the Cultural Divide: A Report on Aboriginal People and Criminal Justice in Canada*, at p. 33; *Royal Commission on the Donald Marshall Jr. Prosecution, Volume 1: Findings and Recommendations* (1989), at p. 162; *Report on the Cariboo-Chilcotin Justice Inquiry* (1993), at p. 11. Finally, as Esson C.J. noted, tensions between aboriginals and non-aboriginals have increased in recent years as a result of developments in such areas as land claims and fishing rights. These tensions increase the potential of racist jurors siding with the Crown as the perceived representative of the majority's interests.

[59] In these circumstances, the trial judge should have allowed the accused to challenge prospective jurors for cause. Notwithstanding the accused's defence that another aboriginal person committed the robbery, juror prejudice could have affected the trial in many other ways. Consequently, there was a realistic potential that some of the jurors might not have been indifferent between the Crown and the accused. The potential for prejudice was increased by the failure of the trial judge to instruct the jury to set aside any racial prejudices that they might have against aboriginals. It cannot be said that the accused had the fair trial by an impartial jury to which he was entitled.

[60] I would allow the appeal and direct a new trial.

---

If jurors can be asked about the possibility of racial prejudice and stereotypes influencing their deliberations, what about their attitudes toward specific crimes such as sexual abuse of young children? See *R. v. Find*, [2001] 1 S.C.R. 863.

## Jury Unanimity

The jury deliberates in secret. Section 649 of the Code makes it a summary conviction offence for a juror to disclose any information relating to the proceedings of the jury unless in connection to the investigation and trial of the offence of obstruction of justice in relation to a juror. In the United States, jurors are routinely interviewed as to jury deliberations. One of the jurors who wrongfully convicted Donald Marshall Jr. in 1971 was reported in the press as giving an explanation for the verdict based on racist stereotypes (*Toronto Star*, June 8, 1986, A8). This issue was not examined in the Royal Commission. In its report to Parliament, *The Jury* (1982), the Law Reform Commission of Canada recommended retaining this offence but making an exemption for "the further-ance of scientific research about juries which is approved by the Chief Justice of the Province." For a case affirming the constitutionality of the secrecy of the jury's delibera-tions and the constitutionality of s. 649 of the Code in the face of an allegation that a juror made racist remarks, see *R. v. Pan; R. v. Sawyer*, [2001] 1 S.C.R. 344.

## VI. QUANTUM AND BURDEN OF PROOF

### Burden of Proof

The burden on the Crown to prove the guilt of an accused beyond a reasonable doubt is one of the most important safeguards in the criminal justice system. Re-read the trial judge's instructions to the jury in the *Marshall* case concerning the quantum and burden of proof. Were they correct in the light of the following cases?

### Woolmington v. D.P.P.
House of Lords
[1935] A.C. 462

VISCOUNT SANKEY L.C. (for the Court): My Lords, the appellant, Reginald Woolmington, after a trial at the Somerset Assizes at Taunton on January 23, at which, after an absence of one hour and twenty-five minutes, the jury disagreed, was con-victed at the Bristol Assizes on February 14 of the wilful murder of his wife on De-cember 10, 1934, and was sentenced to death. He appealed to the Court of Criminal Appeal, substantially upon the ground that the learned judge had misdirected the jury by telling them that in the circumstances of the case he was presumed in law to be guilty of the murder unless he could satisfy the jury that his wife's death was due to an accident.

The appeal came before the Court of Criminal Appeal upon March 18 and was dismissed. The Court said "it may be that it might have been better" had the learned judge who tried the case said to the jury that if they entertained reasonable doubt whether they could accept his explanation they should either acquit him altogether or convict him of manslaughter only; but, relying upon s. 4, sub-s. 1, of the Criminal Appeal Act, 1907, which provides "that the court may, notwithstanding that they are of opinion that the point raised in the appeal might be decided in favour of the appel-lant, dismiss the appeal if they consider that no substantial miscarriage of justice has actually occurred," they dismissed the appeal.

Thereupon the Attorney-General gave his fiat certifying that the appeal of Reginald Woolmington involved a point of law of exceptional public importance and that in his opinion it was desirable in the public interest that a further appeal should be brought. The matter now comes before your Lordships' House.

The facts are as follows. Reginald Woolmington is 21½ years old. His wife, who was killed, was 17½ years old last December. They had known each other for some

time and upon August 25 they were married. Upon October 14 she gave birth to a
child. Shortly after that there appears to have been some quarrelling between them
and she left him upon November 22 and went to live with her mother. Woolmington
apparently was anxious to get her to come back, but she did not come. The prosecution proved that at about 9:15 in the morning of the 10th Mrs. Daisy Brine was hanging out her washing at the back of her house at 25 Newtown, Milborne Port. While
she was engaged in that occupation, she heard voices from the next door house, No.
24. She knew that in that house her niece, Reginald Woolmington's wife, was living.
She heard and could recognize the voice of Reginald Woolmington saying something
to the effect "are you going to come back home?" She could not hear the answer.
Then the back door in No. 24 was slammed. She heard a voice in the kitchen but
could not tell what it said. Then she heard the sound of a gun. Upon that she looked
out of the front window and she saw Reginald Woolmington, whose voice she had
heard just before speaking in the kitchen, go out and get upon his bicycle, which had
been left or was standing against the wall of her house, No. 25. She called out to him
but he gave no reply. He looked at her hard and then he rode away.

According to Reginald Woolmington's own story, having brooded over and deliberated upon the position all through the night of December 9, he went on the morning
of the 10th in the usual way to the milking at his employer's farm, and while milking
conceived this idea that he would take the old gun which was in the barn and he
would take it up that morning to his wife's mother's house where she was living, and
that he would show her that gun and tell her that he was going to commit suicide if
she did not come back. He would take the gun up for the purpose of frightening her
into coming back to him by causing her to think that he was going to commit suicide.
He finished his milking, went back to his father's house, had breakfast and then left,
taking with him a hack saw. He returned to the farm, went into the barn, got the gun,
which had been used for rook shooting, sawed off the barrels of it, then took the only
two cartridges which were there and put them into the gun. He took the two pieces of
the barrel which he had sawn off and the hack saw, crossed a field about 60 yards
wide and dropped them into the brook. Having done that, he returned on his bicycle,
with the gun in his overcoat pocket, to his father's house and changed his clothes.
Then he got a piece of wire flex which he attached to the gun so that he could suspend
it from his shoulder underneath his coat, and so went off to the house where his wife
was living. He knocked at the door, went into the kitchen and asked her: "Are you
coming back?" She made no answer. She came into the parlour, and on his asking her
whether she would come back she replied she was going into service. He then, so he
says, threatened he would shoot himself, and went on to show her the gun and brought
it across his waist, when it somehow went off and his wife fell down and he went out
of the house. He told the jury that it was an accident, that it was a pure accident; that
whilst he was getting the gun from under his shoulder and was drawing it across his
breast it accidentally went off and he was doing nothing unlawful, nothing wrong,
and this was a pure accident. There was considerable controversy as to whether a
letter in which he set out his grievances was written before or after the above events.
But when he was arrested at 7:30 on the evening of the 10th and charged with having
committed murder he said: "I want to say nothing, except I done it, and they can do

what they like with me. It was jealousy I suppose. Her mother enticed her away from me. I done all I could to get her back. That's all."

The learned judge in summing-up the case to the jury said:

> If you accept his evidence, you will have little doubt that she died in consequence of a gunshot wound which was inflicted by a gun which he had taken to this house, and which was in his hands, or in his possession, at the time that it exploded. If you come to the conclusion that she died in consequence of injuries from the gun which he was carrying, you are put by the law of this country into this position: The killing of a human being is homicide, however he may be killed, and all homicide is presumed to be malicious and murder, unless the contrary appears from circumstances of alleviation, excuse, or justification. "In every charge of murder, the fact of killing being first proved, all the circumstances of accident, necessity, or infirmity are to be satisfactorily proved by the prisoner, unless they arise out of the evidence produced against him: for the law will presume the fact to have been founded in malice until the contrary appeareth." That has been the law of this country for all time since we had law. Once it is shown to a jury that somebody has died through the act of another, that is presumed to be murder, unless the person who has been guilty of the act which causes the death can satisfy a jury that what happened was something less, something which might be alleviated, something which might be reduced to a charge of manslaughter, or was something which was accidental, or was something which could be justified.

At the end of his summing-up he added:

> The Crown has got to satisfy you that this woman, Violet Woolmington, died at the prisoner's hands. They must satisfy you of that beyond any reasonable doubt. If they satisfy you of that, then he has to show that there are circumstances to be found in the evidence which has been given from the witness-box in this case which alleviate the crime so that it is only manslaughter or which excuse the homicide altogether by showing that it was a pure accident.

In the argument before the Court of Criminal Appeal cases were cited by the learned counsel on either side and text-books of authority were referred to, but the learned judges contented themselves with saying "there can be no question to start with that the learned judge laid down the law applicable to a case of murder in the way in which it is to be found in the old authorities." They repeated the learned judge's words and said: "No doubt there is ample authority for that statement of the law." They then relied, as I have already mentioned, upon the proviso to s. 4 of the Criminal Appeal Act, 1907, and dismissed the appeal.

It is true as stated by the Court of Appeal that there is apparent authority for the law as laid down by the learned judge. But your Lordships' House has had the advantage of a prolonged and exhaustive inquiry dealing with the matter in debate from the earliest times, an advantage which was not shared by either of the Courts below. Indeed your Lordships were referred to legal propositions dating as far back as the reign of King Canute (994-1035). But I do not think it is necessary for the purpose of this opinion to go as far back as that. Rather would I invite your Lordships to begin by considering the proposition of law which is contained in Foster's Crown Law, written in 1762, and which appears to be the foundation for the law as laid down by the learned judge in this case. It must be remembered that Sir Michael Foster, although a distinguished judge, is for this purpose to be regarded as a text-book writer, for he did not lay down the doctrine in any case before him, but in an article which is described as the "Introduction to the Discourse of Homicide." In the folio edition, published at Oxford at the Clarendon Press in 1762, at p. 255, he states: "In every charge of murder, the fact of killing being first proved, all the circumstances of accident, necessity, or infirmity are to be satisfactorily proved by the prisoner, unless they arise out of the evidence produced against him; for the law presumeth the fact to have been founded in malice, until the contrary appeareth. And very right it is, that the law should so presume. The defendant in this instance standeth upon just the same foot that every other defendant doth: the matters tending to justify, excuse, or alleviate, must appear in evidence before he can avail himself of them."

Now the first part of this passage appears in nearly every text-book or abridgment which has been since written. To come down to modern times, the passage appears in Stephen's Digest of the Criminal Law (7th ed., 1926); also in the well known treatise of Archbold, Criminal Pleading, Evidence and Practice (29th ed., 1934), which is the companion of lawyers who practise in the criminal courts. It also appears almost textually in Russell on Crimes (8th ed., 1923), and in the second edition of Halsbury's Laws of England (1933, vol. 9), which purports to state the law as on May 1, 1933, where it is said: "When it has been proved that one person's death has been caused by another, there is a prima facie presumption of law that the act of the person causing the death is murder, unless the contrary appears from the evidence either for the prosecution or for the defence. The onus is upon such person when accused to show that his act did not amount to murder." The authority for that proposition is given as Foster, pp. 255, 290, and also the case of *Rex v. Greenacre* (1837), 8 C. & P. 35.

The question arises, Is that statement correct law? Is it correct to say, and does Sir Michael Foster mean to lay down, that there may arise in the course of a criminal trial a situation at which it is incumbent upon the accused to prove his innocence? To begin with, if that is what Sir Michael Foster meant, there is no previous authority for his proposition, and I am confirmed in this opinion by the fact that in all the text-books no earlier authority is cited for it. ...

The case of *Rex v. Greenacre* ((1837) 8 C. & P. 35) was certainly heard by a very distinguished judge, Tindal, C.J. But it is to be observed that the dictum relied upon by the prosecution in this case—namely: "that where it appears that one person's death has been occasioned by the hand of another, it behoves that other to show from evidence, or by inference from the circumstances of the case, that the offence is of a mitigated character, and does not amount to the crime of murder," was contained in the summing-up of the learned judge to the jury. It is the passage in Sir Michael Foster and this summing-up which are usually relied on as the authority for the proposition that at some particular time of a criminal case the burden of proof lies on the prisoner to prove his innocence. The presumption of innocence in a criminal case is strong, and it is doubtful whether either of these passages means any such thing. Rather do I think they simply refer to stages in the trial of a case. All that is meant is that if it is proved that the conscious act of the prisoner killed a man and nothing else appears in the case, there is evidence upon which the jury may, not must, find him guilty of murder. It is difficult to conceive so bare and meagre a case, but that does not mean that the onus is not still on the prosecution.

If at any period of a trial it was permissible for the judge to rule that the prosecution had established its case and that the onus was shifted on the prisoner to prove that he was not guilty and that unless he discharged that onus the prosecution was entitled to succeed, it would be enabling the judge in such a case to say that the jury must in law find the prisoner guilty and so make the judge decide the case and not the jury, which is not the common law. It would be an entirely different case from those exceptional instances of special verdicts where a judge asks the jury to find certain facts and directs them that on such facts the prosecution is entitled to succeed. Indeed, a consideration of such special verdict shows that it is not till the end of the evidence that a verdict can properly be found and that at the end of the evidence it is not for the prisoner to establish his innocence, but for the prosecution to establish his guilt. Just as there is evidence on behalf of the prosecution so there may be evidence on behalf of the prisoner which may cause a doubt as to his guilt. In either case, he is entitled to the benefit of the doubt. But while the prosecution must prove the guilt of the prisoner, there is no such burden laid on the prisoner to prove his innocence and it is sufficient for him to raise a doubt as to his guilt; he is not bound to satisfy the jury of his innocence.

This is the real result of the perplexing case of *Rex v. Abramovitch* ((1914) 11 Cr. App. R. 45), which lays down the same proposition, although perhaps in somewhat involved language. Juries are always told that, if conviction there is to be, the prosecution must prove the case beyond reasonable doubt. This statement cannot mean that in order to be acquitted the prisoner must "satisfy" the jury. This is the law as laid down in the Court of Criminal Appeal in *Rex v. Davies* ((1913) 8 Cr. App. R. 211), the headnote of which correctly states that where intent is an ingredient of a crime there is no onus on the defendant to prove that the act alleged was accidental. Throughout the web of the English Criminal Law one golden thread is always to be seen, that it is the duty of the prosecution to prove the prisoner's guilt subject to what I have already said as to the defence of insanity and subject also to any statutory exception. If, at the end of and on the whole of the case, there is a reasonable doubt, created by the evidence given by either the prosecution or the prisoner, as to whether the prisoner killed the deceased with a malicious intention, the prosecution has not made out the case and the prisoner is entitled to an acquittal. No matter what the charge or where the trial, the principle that the prosecution must prove the guilt of the prisoner is part of the common law of England and no attempt to whittle it down can be entertained. When dealing with a murder case the Crown must prove (a) death as a result of a voluntary act of the accused and (b) malice of the accused. It may prove malice either expressly or by implication. For malice may be implied where death occurs as the result of a voluntary act of the accused which is (i) intentional and (ii) unprovoked. When evidence of death and malice has been given (this is a question for the jury) the accused is entitled to show, by evidence or by examination of the circumstances adduced by the Crown that the act on his part which caused death was either unintentional or provoked. If the jury are either satisfied with his explanation or, upon a review of all the evidence, are left in reasonable doubt whether, even if his explanation be not accepted, the act was unintentional or provoked, the prisoner is entitled to be acquitted. It is not the law of England to say, as was said in the summing-up in the present case: "if the Crown satisfy you that this woman died at the prisoner's hands then he has to show that there are circumstances to be found in the evidence which has been given from the witness-box in this case which alleviate the crime so that it is only manslaughter or which excuse the homicide altogether by showing it was a pure accident." If the proposition laid down by Sir Michael Foster or the summing-up in *Rex v. Greenacre* means this, those authorities are wrong.

We were then asked to follow the Court of Criminal Appeal and to apply the proviso of s. 4 of the Criminal Appeal Act, 1907, which says: "the Court may, notwithstanding that they are of opinion that the point raised in the appeal might be decided in favour of the appellant, dismiss the appeal if they consider that no substantial miscarriage of justice has actually occurred." There is no doubt that there is ample jurisdiction to apply that proviso in a case of murder. The Act makes no distinction between a capital case and any other case, but we think it impossible to apply it in the present case. We cannot say that if the jury had been properly directed they would have inevitably come to the same conclusion.

In the result we decline to apply the proviso and, as already stated, we order that the appeal should be allowed and the conviction quashed.

*Appeal allowed; conviction quashed.*

### R. v. Oakes
Supreme Court of Canada
(1986), 24 C.C.C. (3d) 321

DICKSON C.J.C.: This appeal concerns the constitutionality of s. 8 of the *Narcotic Control Act*, R.S.C. 1970, c. N-1. The section provides, in brief, that if the court finds the accused in possession of a narcotic, he is presumed to be in possession for the purpose of trafficking. Unless the accused can establish the contrary, he must be convicted of trafficking. ...

The respondent, David Edwin Oakes, was charged with unlawful possession of a narcotic for the purpose of trafficking, contrary to s. 4(2) of the *Narcotic Control Act*. ... At trial, the Crown adduced evidence to establish that Mr. Oakes was found in possession of eight one gram vials of cannabis resin in the form of hashish oil. Upon a further search conducted at the police station, $619.45 was located. Mr. Oakes told the police that he had bought ten vials of hashish oil for $150 for his own use, and that the $619.45 was from a workers' compensation cheque. He elected not to call evidence as to possession of the narcotic. Pursuant to the procedural provisions of s. 8 of the *Narcotic Control Act*, the trial judge proceeded to make a finding that it was beyond a reasonable doubt that Mr. Oakes was in possession of the narcotic. Following this finding, Mr. Oakes brought a motion to challenge the constitutional validity of s. 8 of the *Narcotic Control Act*, which he maintained imposes a burden on an accused to prove that he or she was not in possession for the purpose of trafficking. He argued that s. 8 violates the presumption of innocence contained in s. 11(d) of the Charter. ... The relevant portions of s. 8 read:

> 8. ... if the court finds that the accused was in possession of the narcotic ... he shall be given an opportunity of establishing that he was not in possession of the narcotic for the purpose of trafficking ... if the accused fails to establish that he was not in possession of the narcotic for the purpose of trafficking, he shall be convicted of the offence as charged. ...

In determining the meaning of these words, it is helpful to consider in a general sense the nature of presumptions. ...

A permissive presumption leaves it optional as to whether the inference of the presumed fact is drawn following proof of the basic fact. A mandatory presumption requires that the inference be made.

Presumptions may also be either rebuttable or irrebuttable. If a presumption is rebuttable, there are three potential ways the presumed fact can be rebutted. First, the accused may be required merely to raise a reasonable doubt as to its existence. Secondly, the accused may have an evidentiary burden to adduce sufficient evidence to bring into question the truth of the presumed fact. Thirdly, the accused may have a legal or persuasive burden to prove on a balance of probabilities the non-existence of the presumed fact.

Finally, presumptions are often referred to as either presumptions of law or presumptions of fact. The latter entail "frequently recurring examples of circumstantial evidence" (*Cross on Evidence*, at p. 124) while the former involve actual legal rules. ...

I conclude that s. 8 of the *Narcotic Control Act* contains a reverse onus provision imposing a legal burden on an accused to prove on a balance of probabilities that he or she was not in possession of a narcotic for the purpose of trafficking. It is therefore necessary to determine whether s. 8 of the *Narcotic Control Act* offends the right to be "presumed innocent until proven guilty" as guaranteed by s. 11(d) of the Charter.

Section 11(d) of the Charter constitutionally entrenches the presumption of innocence as part of the supreme law of Canada. For ease of reference, I set out this provision again:

> 11. Any person charged with an offence has the right ...
>
> (d) to be presumed innocent until proven guilty according to law in a fair and public hearing by an independent and impartial tribunal. ...

The presumption of innocence is a hallowed principle lying at the very heart of criminal law. Although protected expressly in s. 11(d) of the Charter, the presumption of innocence is referable and integral to the general protection of life, liberty and security of the person contained in s. 7 of the Charter (see *Re B.C. Motor Vehicle Act*, [1985] 2 S.C.R. 486, per Lamer J.). The presumption of innocence protects the fundamental liberty and human dignity of any and every person accused by the State of criminal conduct. An individual charged with a criminal offence faces grave social and personal consequences, including potential loss of physical liberty, subjection to social stigma and ostracism from the community as well as other social, psychological and economic harms. In light of the gravity of these consequences, the presumption of innocence is crucial. It ensures that until the State proves an accused's guilt beyond all reasonable doubt, he or she is innocent. This is essential in a society committed to fairness and social justice. The presumption of innocence confirms our faith in humankind; it reflects our belief that individuals are decent and law-abiding members of the community until proven otherwise. ...

To return to s. 8 of the *Narcotic Control Act*, it is my view that, upon a finding beyond a reasonable doubt of possession of a narcotic, the accused has the legal burden of proving on a balance of probabilities that he or she was not in possession of the narcotic for the purpose of trafficking. Once the basic fact of possession is proven, a mandatory presumption of law arises against the accused that he or she had the intention to traffic. Moreover, the accused will be found guilty of the offence of trafficking unless he or she can rebut this presumption on a balance of probabilities. ...

The Legislature, by using the word "establish" in s. 8 of the *Narcotic Control Act*, intended to impose a legal burden on the accused. This is most apparent in the words "if the accused fails to establish that he was not in possession of the narcotic for the purpose of trafficking, he shall be convicted of the offence as charged." ...

In general one must, I think, conclude that a provision which requires an accused to disprove on a balance of probabilities the existence of a presumed fact, which is an important element of the offence in question, violates the presumption of innocence in s. 11(d). If an accused bears the burden of disproving on a balance of probabilities an essential element of an offence, it would be possible for a conviction to occur despite the existence of a reasonable doubt. This would arise if the accused adduced sufficient evidence to raise a reasonable doubt as to his or her innocence but did not convince the jury on a balance of probabilities that the presumed fact was untrue.

The fact that the standard is only the civil one does not render a reverse onus clause constitutional. As Sir Rupert Cross commented in the [Wright Lecture], "The Golden Thread of the English Criminal Law: The Burden of Proof," delivered in 1976 at the University of Toronto, at pp. 11-3:

> It is sometimes said that exceptions to the Woolmington rule are acceptable because, whenever the burden of proof on any issue in a criminal case is borne by the accused, he only has to satisfy the jury on the balance of probabilities, whereas on issues on which the Crown bears the burden of proof the jury must be satisfied beyond a reasonable doubt. ... The fact that the standard is lower when the accused bears the burden of proof than it is when the burden of proof is borne by the prosecution is no answer to my objection to the existence of exceptions to the Woolmington rule as it does not alter the fact that a jury or bench of magistrates may have to convict the accused although they are far from sure of his guilt.

As we have seen, the potential for a rational connection between the basic fact and the presumed fact to justify a reverse onus provision has been elaborated in some of the cases discussed above and is now known as the "rational connection test." ... A basic fact may rationally tend to prove a presumed fact, but not prove its existence beyond a reasonable doubt. An accused person could thereby be convicted despite the presence of a reasonable doubt. This would violate the presumption of innocence. ...

I should add that this questioning of the constitutionality of the "rational connection test" as a guide to interpreting s. 11(d) does not minimize its importance. The appropriate stage for invoking the rational connection test, however, is under s. 1 of the Charter. This consideration did not arise under the Canadian Bill of Rights because of the absence of an equivalent to s. 1. ... To my mind, it is highly desirable to keep s. 1 and s. 11(d) analytically distinct. ...

To return to s. 8 of the *Narcotic Control Act*, I am in no doubt whatsoever that it violates s. 11(d) of the Charter by requiring the accused to prove on a balance of probabilities that he was not in possession of the narcotic for the purpose of trafficking. Mr. Oakes is compelled by s. 8 to prove he is *not* guilty of the offence of trafficking. He is thus denied his right to be presumed innocent and subjected to the potential penalty of life imprisonment unless he can rebut the presumption. This is radically and fundamentally inconsistent with the societal values of human dignity and liberty which we espouse, and is directly contrary to the presumption of innocence enshrined in s. 11(d). Let us turn now to s. 1 of the Charter. ...

The Crown submits that even if s. 8 of the *Narcotic Control Act* violates s. 11(d) of the Charter, it can still be upheld as a reasonable limit under s. 1 which, as has been mentioned, provides:

> 1. The Canadian Charter of Rights and Freedoms guarantees the rights and freedoms set out in it subject only to such reasonable limits prescribed by law as can be demonstrably justified in a free and democratic society.

The question whether the limit is "prescribed by law" is not contentious in the present case since s. 8 of the *Narcotic Control Act* is a duly enacted legislative provision. It is, however, necessary to determine if the limit on Mr. Oakes' right, as guaranteed by s. 11(d) of the Charter, is "reasonable" and "demonstrably justified in a free and democratic society" for the purpose of s. 1 of the Charter, and thereby saved from inconsistency with the Constitution.

It is important to observe at the outset that s. 1 has two functions: first, it constitutionally guarantees the rights and freedoms set out in the provisions which follow; and, second, it states explicitly the exclusive justificatory criteria (outside of s. 33 of the *Constitution Act, 1982*) against which limitations on those rights and freedoms must be measured. Accordingly, any s. 1 inquiry must be premised on an understanding that the impugned limit violates constitutional rights and freedoms—rights and freedoms which are part of the supreme law of Canada. As Wilson J. stated in *Singh v. Minister of Employment and Immigration*, supra, at p. 218: "... it is important to remember that the courts are conducting this inquiry in light of a commitment to uphold the rights and freedoms set out in the other sections of the Charter."

A second contextual element of interpretation of s. 1 is provided by the words "free and democratic society." Inclusion of these words as the final standard of justification for limits on rights and freedoms refers the Court to the very purpose for which the Charter was originally entrenched in the Constitution: Canadian society is to be free and democratic. The Court must be guided by the values and principles essential to a free and democratic society which I believe embody, to name but a few, respect for the inherent dignity of the human person, commitment to social justice and equality, accommodation of a wide variety of beliefs, respect or cultural and group identity, and faith in social and political institutions which enhance the participation of individuals and groups in society. The underlying values and principles of a free and democratic society are the genesis of the rights and freedoms guaranteed by the Charter and the ultimate standard against which a limit on a right or freedom must be shown, despite its effect, to be reasonable and demonstrably justified.

The rights and freedoms guaranteed by the Charter are not, however, absolute. It may become necessary to limit rights and freedoms in circumstances where their exercise would be inimical to the realization of collective goals of fundamental importance. For this reason, s. 1 provides criteria of justification for limits on the rights and freedoms guaranteed by the Charter. These criteria impose a stringent standard of justification, especially when understood in terms of the two contextual considerations discussed above, namely, the violation of a constitutionally guaranteed right or freedom and the fundamental principles of a free and democratic society.

The onus of proving that a limit on a right or freedom guaranteed by the Charter is reasonable and demonstrably justified in a free and democratic society rests upon the party seeking to uphold the limitation. It is clear from the text of s. 1 that limits on the rights and freedoms enumerated in the Charter are exceptions to their general guarantee.

The presumption is that the rights and freedoms are guaranteed unless the party invoking s. 1 can bring itself within the exceptional criteria which justify their being limited. This is further substantiated by the use of the word "demonstrably" which clearly indicates that the onus of justification is on the party seeking to justify the limit.

The standard of proof under s. 1 is the civil standard, namely, proof by a preponderance of probability. The alternative criminal standard, proof beyond a reasonable doubt, would, in my view, be unduly onerous on the party seeking to limit. Concepts such as "reasonableness," "justifiability" and "free and democratic society" are simply not amenable to such a standard. Nevertheless, the preponderance of probability test must be applied rigorously. Indeed, the phrase "demonstrably justified" in s. 1 of the Charter supports this conclusion. …

To establish that a limit is reasonable and demonstrably justified in a free and democratic society, two central criteria must be satisfied. First, the objective, which the measures responsible for a limit on a Charter right or freedom are designed to serve, must be "of sufficient importance to warrant overriding a constitutionally protected right or freedom." … The standard must be high in order to ensure that objectives which are trivial or discordant with the principles integral to a free and democratic society do not gain s. 1 protection. It is necessary, at a minimum, that an objective relate to concerns which are pressing and substantial in a free and democratic society before it can be characterized as sufficiently important.

Second, once a sufficiently significant objective is recognized, then the party invoking s. 1 must show that the means chosen are reasonable and demonstrably justified. This involves "a form of proportionality test" Although the nature of the proportionality test will vary depending on the circumstances, in each case courts will be required to balance the interests of society with those of individuals and groups. There are, in my view, three important components of a proportionality test. First, the measures adopted must be carefully designed to achieve the objective in question. They must not be arbitrary, unfair or based on irrational considerations. In short, they must be rationally connected to the objective. Second, the means, even if rationally connected to the objective in this first sense, should impair "as little as possible" the right or freedom in question. Third, there must be a proportionality between the effects of the measures which are responsible for limiting the Charter right or freedom, and the objective which has been identified as of "sufficient importance.".…

Having outlined the general principles of a s. 1 inquiry, we must apply them to s. 8 of the *Narcotic Control Act*. Is the reverse onus provision in s. 8 a reasonable limit on the right to be presumed innocent until proven guilty beyond a reasonable doubt as can be demonstrably justified in a free and democratic society?

[The Chief Justice then concluded that the legislative objective of "curbing drug trafficking by facilitating the conviction of drug traffickers" was a substantial and pressing concern of sufficient importance to warrant overriding a constitutional right.]

As outlined above, this proportionality test should begin with a consideration of the rationality of the provision: is the reverse onus clause in s. 8 rationally related to the objective of curbing drug trafficking? At a minimum, this requires that s. 8 be internally rational; there must be a rational connection between the basic fact of possession and the presumed fact of possession for the purpose of trafficking. Otherwise, the reverse onus clause could give rise to unjustified and erroneous convictions for drug trafficking of persons guilty only of possession of narcotics.

In my view, s. 8 does not survive this rational connection test. As Martin J.A. of the Ontario Court of Appeal concluded, possession of a small or negligible quantity of narcotics does not support the inference of trafficking. In other words, it would be irrational to infer that a person had an intent to traffic on the basis of his or her possession of a very small quantity of narcotics. The presumption required under s. 8 of the *Narcotic Control Act* is overinclusive and could lead to results in certain cases which would defy both rationality and fairness. In light of the seriousness of the offence in question, which carries with it the possibility of imprisonment for life, I am further convinced that the first component of the proportionality test has not been satisfied by the Crown.

Having concluded that s. 8 does not satisfy this first component of proportionality, it is unnecessary to consider the other two components.

[Chouinard, Lamer, Wilson, and Le Dain JJ. concurred with Dickson C.J.C. Estey and McIntyre JJ. agreed with the result, stressing in their s. 11(d) analysis the lack of a rational connection between the proved fact of possession and the presumed fact of an intention to traffic.]

**R. v. Whyte**
Supreme Court of Canada
(1988), 42 C.C.C. (3d) 97

[The present s. 258(1) of the *Criminal Code* provides that when a person is charged
under s. 253 (that is, operating or having the care or control of a motor vehicle whether
it is in motion or not while impaired or with a blood alcohol content over 80 mg/100
ml), if it is proved that the accused occupied the driver's seat, "the accused shall be
deemed to have had the care and control of the vehicle ... unless the accused establishes that he did not occupy that seat or position for the purpose of setting the vehicle ... in motion. ..." This case examines the constitutionality of a former s. 237(1)(a)
of the Code, which was substantially the same as s. 258(1).]

DICKSON C.J.C. (with whom Beetz, McIntyre, Lamer, La Forest, and L'Heureux-
Dubé JJ. concurred):  The evidence disclosed that when the investigating constables
came upon the appellant's vehicle, it was in a parked position along the roadside, its
hood was warm, the dashboard ignition light was on, keys were in the ignition, but
the engine was not running. The appellant was seated in the driver's seat with his
body slumped over the steering-wheel. Counsel for the defence concedes that the
appellant's ability to operate a motor vehicle was impaired by alcohol when he was
found by the police. ...

[Dickson C.J.C. examined the Court's decision in *Appleby* (1971), 3 C.C.C. (2d) 354
(S.C.C.).]

Writing for the majority on this point, Ritchie J. observed that s. 2(f) gave statutory
approval to the principle enunciated by Viscount Sankey L.C. in *Woolmington v. Director of Public Prosecutions*, [1935] A.C. 462 at p. 481:

> Throughout the web of the English Criminal Law one golden thread is always to be
> seen, that it is the duty of the prosecution to prove the prisoner's guilt subject to what I
> have already said as to the defence of insanity *and subject also to any statutory excep-
> tion*. (Emphasis was added by Ritchie J.)

Ritchie J. went on to hold as follows (at pp. 363-4 C.C.C.):

> the words "presumed innocent until proved guilty according to law" as they appear in
> s. 2(f) of the *Canadian Bill of Rights*, must be taken to envisage a law which recognizes
> the existence of statutory exceptions reversing the onus of proof with respect to one or
> more ingredients of an offence in cases where certain specific facts have been proved
> by the Crown in relation to such ingredients.

In my view, the reasoning of the court in *Appleby* was manifestly influenced by
the limited extent to which the court considered the *Canadian Bill of Rights* could
override otherwise valid legislation which conflicted with its terms. ...

   I conclude, therefore, that despite the holding in *Appleby* that s. 237(1)(a) does not
infringe the presumption of innocence, the question of the validity of s. 237(1)(a) in
the face of s. 11(d) of the Charter is still an open one. ...

In *Vaillancourt* (1987), 39 C.C.C. (3d) 118, Lamer J., for the majority on that point, again considered s. 11(d). He confirmed that the presumption of innocence requires that the trier of fact be convinced beyond a reasonable doubt of the existence of all the essential elements of the offence. A provision that permits or requires a conviction in spite of a reasonable doubt as to the existence of one or more of the elements of the offence violates the presumption of innocence. Lamer J. recognized that Parliament can in some cases permit proof of a substituted fact to be taken as proof of an essential element of the offence, but that there are limitations on the scope of such substitutions (at p. 136 C.C.C.):

> Finally, the legislature, rather than simply eliminating any need to prove the essential element, may substitute proof of a different element. In my view, this will be constitutionally valid only if upon proof beyond reasonable doubt of the substituted element it would be unreasonable for the trier of fact not to be satisfied beyond reasonable doubt of the existence of the essential element. If the trier of fact may have a reasonable doubt as to the essential element notwithstanding proof beyond a reasonable doubt of the substituted element, the substitution infringes ss. 7 and 11(d).

The next stage in the development of these principles occurred in *Holmes*, which raised the question whether a requirement that the accused prove a lawful excuse, rather than disprove an essential element of the offence, violated the presumption of innocence. Two members of the court held that a requirement of this sort would offend s. 11(d) [at p. 512]:

> Any burden on an accused which has the effect of dictating a conviction despite the presence of reasonable doubt, whether that burden relates to proof of an essential element of the offence or some element extraneous to the offence but none the less essential to verdict, contravenes s. 11(d) of the Charter. An accused must not be placed in the position of being required to do more than raise a reasonable doubt as to his or her guilt, regardless of whether that doubt arises from uncertainty as to the sufficiency of Crown evidence supporting the constituent elements of the offence or from uncertainty as to criminal culpability in general.

Is s. 237(1)(a) consistent with these principles? The basic fact which the Crown must prove to invoke the section is that the accused occupied the seat normally occupied by the driver of the motor vehicle. The presumed fact is that the accused had the care or control of the vehicle. ...

The exact relationship between s. 237(1)(a) and the *mens rea* requirement of s. 234 was the subject of uncertainty for some time. Is the intention to set the vehicle in motion an ingredient of the offence of having care or control of a motor vehicle while impaired, or is the absence of such intention simply a way for an accused to rebut the presumption of care or control? This court settled the question in *Ford v. The Queen* (1982), 65 C.C.C. (2d) 392, 133 D.L.R. (3d) 567, [1982] 1 S.C.R. 231, when Ritchie J. for the majority held that the intention to set the vehicle in motion is not an element of the offence. Proof of lack of intention is simply an evidentiary point that rebuts the presumption of care or control of the vehicle established by s. 237(1)(a). The court recently reaffirmed *Ford* in *R. v. Toews* (1985), 21 C.C.C. (3d) 24, 20 D.L.R. (4th) 758, [1985] 2 S.C.R. 119.

In the case at bar, the Attorney-General of Canada argued that since the intention to set the vehicle in motion is not an element of the offence, s. 237(1)(a) does not infringe the presumption of innocence. Counsel relied on the passage from *Oakes* quoted above, with its reference to an "essential element," to support this argument. The accused here is required to disprove a fact collateral to the substantive offence, unlike *Oakes* where the accused was required to disprove an element of the offence.

The short answer to this argument is that the distinction between elements of the offence and other aspects of the charge is irrelevant to the s. 11(d) inquiry. The real concern is not whether the accused must disprove an element or prove an excuse, but that an accused may be convicted while a reasonable doubt exists. When that possibility exists, there is a breach of the presumption of innocence.

The exact characterization of a factor as an essential element, a collateral factor, an excuse, or a defence should not affect the analysis of the presumption of innocence. It is the final effect of a provision on the verdict that is decisive. If an accused is required to prove some fact on the balance of probabilities to avoid conviction, the provision violates the presumption of innocence because it permits a conviction in spite of a reasonable doubt in the mind of the trier of fact as to the guilt of the accused. The trial of an accused in a criminal matter cannot be divided neatly into stages, with the onus of proof on the accused at an intermediate stage and the ultimate onus on the Crown. Section 237(1)(a) requires the accused to prove lack of intent on a balance of probabilities. If an accused does not meet this requirement the trier of fact is required by law to accept that the accused had care or control and to convict. But of course it does not follow that the trier of fact is convinced beyond a reasonable doubt that the accused had care or control of the vehicle. Indeed, in this case, as in *Appleby*, the trier of fact stated that he convicted the accused despite the existence of a reasonable doubt as to care or control, an element of the offence.

In the passage from *Vaillancourt* quoted earlier, Lamer J. recognized that in some cases substituting proof of one element for proof of an essential element will not infringe the presumption of innocence if, upon proof of the substituted element, it would be unreasonable for the trier of fact not to be satisfied beyond a reasonable doubt of the existence of the essential element. This is another way of saying that a statutory presumption infringes the presumption of innocence if it requires the trier of fact to convict in spite of a reasonable doubt. Only if the existence of the substituted fact leads inexorably to the conclusion that the essential element exists, with no other reasonable possibilities, will the statutory presumption be constitutionally valid.

The presumption in s. 237(1)(a) does not have this inexorable character, as the section itself recognizes. A person can be seated in the driver's seat without an intention to assume care or control of the vehicle within the meaning of s. 234. *Appleby* provides an illustration: the accused in that case explained that he sat in the driver's seat of a taxi to use the radio to report an accident, and for no other purpose. The accused failed to convince the trial judge on a balance of probabilities, but the judge admitted that he had a reasonable doubt about the explanation. Other reasonable explanations for sitting in the driver's seat can readily be imagined. It cannot be said that proof of occupancy of the driver's seat leads inexorably to the conclusion that the essential element of care or control exists, and therefore, s. 237(1)(a) does not meet the test set out by Lamer J. in *Vaillancourt*.

Section 237(1)(a) requires the trier of fact to accept as proven that an accused had care or control of a vehicle, an essential element of the offence, in spite of a reasonable doubt about the existence of that element. The section therefore breaches the presumption of innocence guaranteed by s. 11(d) of the Charter. ...

[Dickson C.J.C. then held that the presumption was justified under s. 1 of the Charter. The deterrence of drinking and driving was an objective of sufficient importance to warrant overriding a constitutional right. He concluded that there was a rational connection between the proved fact and the fact to be presumed: "There is every reason to believe the person in the driver's seat has the care or control of the vehicle." After examining the legislative history of the offence and the presumption and noting the minimal *mens rea* requirement for the offence of care and control he stated:]

It is important for the purposes of the s. 1 analysis to view s. 237(1)(a) in the context of its over-all statutory setting. Parliament has attempted to strike a balance. On the one hand, the Crown need only prove a minimal level of intent on account of the fact that consumption of alcohol is itself an ingredient of the offence. On the other hand, where an accused can show that he or she had some reason for entering the vehicle and occupying the driver's seat other than to drive the vehicle, the accused will escape conviction. Viewed in this light, s. 237(1)(a) constitutes a minimal interference with the presumption of innocence guaranteed by s. 11(d) of the Charter.

The final stage of the *Oakes* test is to ask whether there is proportionality between the effects of the impugned measure and the objective being advanced. In my view, s. 237(1)(a) satisfies this final element in s. 1 analysis. The threat to public safety posed by drinking and driving has been established by evidence in this case and recognized by this court in others. While s. 237(1)(a) does infringe the right guaranteed by s. 11(d) of the Charter, it does so in the context of a statutory setting which makes it impracticable to require the Crown to prove an intention to drive. The reverse onus provision, in effect, affords a defence to an accused which could not otherwise be made available.

*Appeal dismissed.*

---

In *R. v. Laba* (1994), 34 C.R. (4th) 360, the Supreme Court held that the requirement in s. 394(1) of the *Criminal Code* that a person who sells or purchases precious metals establish ownership of the metals was an unjustified violation of s. 11(d) of the Charter. Sopinka J. stated for the court:

There is a wide range of innocent people who could be caught within the ambit of s. 394(1)(b) and could conceivably be unable to prove that their purchase or sale of ore was legitimate. For example, a tourist who purchases a souvenir containing precious metal ore from a gift shop in a city such as Timmins where such products are available might not be able to meet the burden of proof unless at the time of purchase she demanded and obtained admissible evidence from the seller establishing that he was the owner etc. or was in a position to call the seller as a witness. Section 394(1)(b) strikes at the heart of the protection afforded by s. 11(d) by increasing the likelihood that the innocent will be convicted.

He then held that the reverse onus was not justified under s. 1 of the Charter, but then read the burden down under s. 52 of the *Constitution Act* so that it imposed only an evidential burden on the accused:

> In drafting s. 394(1)(b) Parliament could have chosen merely to place an evidentiary burden rather than a full legal burden of proving ownership, agency or lawful authority upon the accused. Under such a provision the accused would simply be required to adduce or point to evidence which, if accepted, would be capable of raising a reasonable doubt as to whether he was the owner or agent of the owner or was acting under lawful authority. If he or she succeeded in raising such a doubt the burden would shift to the Crown to prove the contrary beyond a reasonable doubt. If the Crown failed to dispel a reasonable doubt, the accused would be acquitted. Knowledge of the availability of this option must be imputed to Parliament since evidentiary burdens of this kind are and were commonly used to relieve the Crown of the burden of proving that an accused did not legitimately acquire possession of property.

See now the new s. 394(4) of the *Criminal Code* enacting an evidential burden that applies "in the absence of evidence raising a reasonable doubt to the contrary." Based on the next case, would this legislative reply to *Laba* still violate s. 11(d) of the Charter? Would it be justified as a reasonable limit on the presumption of innocence under s. 1 of the Charter?

## R. v. Downey
### Supreme Court of Canada
### (1992), 72 C.C.C. (3d) 1

[The accused, who assisted in the operation of an escort agency, was convicted of living off the avails of prostitution. He argued that s. 195(2) (now s. 212(3)) of the Code, which provides that evidence that a person lives with or is habitually in the company of prostitutes, is, in the absence of evidence to the contrary, proof that the person lives off the avails of prostitution violated s. 11(d) of the Charter. He was convicted with the trial judge ruling that the impugned provision did not violate s. 11(d) because it created an evidential presumption that could be rebutted by raising a reasonable doubt as to its validity.]

CORY J. (L'Heureux-Dubé, Sopinka, and Gonthier JJ. concurring): Perhaps it may be helpful to summarize the principles to be derived from the authorities.

I.  The presumption of innocence is infringed whenever the accused is liable to be convicted despite the existence of a reasonable doubt.

II.  If by the provisions of a statutory presumption, an accused is required to establish, that is to say to prove or disprove, on a balance of probabilities either an element of an offence or an excuse, then it contravenes s. 11(d). Such a provision would permit a conviction in spite of a reasonable doubt.

III. Even if a rational connection exists between the established fact and the fact to be presumed, this would be insufficient to make valid a presumption requiring the accused to disprove an element of the offence.

IV. Legislation which substitutes proof of one element for proof of an essential element will not infringe the presumption of innocence if as a result of the proof of the substituted element, it would be unreasonable for the trier of fact not to be satisfied beyond a reasonable doubt of the existence of the other element. To put it another way, the statutory presumption will be valid if the proof of the substituted fact leads inexorably to the proof of the other. However, the statutory presumption will infringe s. 11(d) if it requires the trier of fact to convict in spite of a reasonable doubt.

V. A permissive assumption from which a trier of fact may but not must draw an inference of guilt will not infringe s. 11(d).

VI. A provision that might have been intended to play a minor role in providing relief from conviction will none the less contravene the Charter if the provision (such as the truth of a statement) must be established by the accused: see *Keegstra*, *supra*.

VII. It must of course be remembered that statutory presumptions which infringe s. 11(d) may still be justified pursuant to s. 1 of the Charter. (As, for example, in *Keegstra*, *supra*.)

It is now necessary to apply these principles to the presumption set out in s. 195(2) to determine whether it contravenes s. 11(d) of the Charter.

The presumption contained in s. 195 infringes s. 11(d) of the Charter since it can result in the conviction of an accused despite the existence of a reasonable doubt. For example, consider the situation of a spouse or companion of a prostitute, who is working, self-supporting and not dependent or relying upon the income garnered by the spouse or companion from prostitution. There is nothing parasitical about such a relationship. Neither being a prostitute nor being a spouse of a prostitute constitutes a crime. Yet as a result of the presumption, the spouse could be found guilty despite the existence of a reasonable doubt. The fact that someone lives with a prostitute does not lead inexorably to the conclusion that the person is living on avails. The presumption therefore infringes s. 11(d). …

The procedure which should be followed in order to determine whether a statutory provision which infringes a Charter right is nevertheless justified under s. 1 has been stated in *R. v. Oakes*, *supra*, and restated many times since.

When the presumption set out in s. 195(2) is reviewed in the context of s. 195 itself, it is apparent that the objective of the impugned provision is of sufficient importance to warrant overriding s. 11(d). … The section is attempting to deal with a cruel and pervasive social evil. The pimp personifies abusive and exploitative malevolence.

In order to be valid the measures taken must be carefully designed to respond to the objective. Yet the proportionality test can and must vary with the circumstances. Parliament is limited in the options which it has at hand to meet or address the problem. Rigid and inflexible standards should not be imposed on legislators attempting to resolve a difficult and intransigent problem. Here, Parliament has sought, by the presumption, to focus on those circumstances in which maintaining close ties to prostitutes gives rise to a reasonable inference of living on the avails of prostitutes. This is not an unreasonable inference for Parliament to legislatively presume, as it cannot be denied that there is often a connection between maintaining close ties to prostitutes and living on the avails of prostitution. Evidence of pimps living on avails would ordinarily be expected to come from prostitutes, yet the reluctance of prostitutes to testify against pimps is well documented. By enacting this section, Parliament has recognized that evidence of this type was difficult if not impossible to obtain without the cooperation of prostitutes which is seldom forthcoming. The section recognizes both the social evil of pimps and prostitutes' fear of violence at their pimps' hands. I have no concern that the section will result in innocent persons who have non parasitic legitimate living arrangements with prostitutes being inculpated. A description sufficient to constitute evidence to the contrary will generally be included in the Crown's case. If not, such evidence can easily be led. In either event, the presumption will be displaced.

It has been determined that Parliament is not required to choose the absolutely least intrusive alternative in order to satisfy this branch of the analysis. Rather the issue is "whether Parliament could reasonably have chosen an alternative means which would have achieved the identified objective as effectively." (See Chaulk, *supra*, at p. 1341.)

Prostitutes are a particularly vulnerable segment of society. The cruel abuse they suffer inflicted by their parasitic pimps has been well documented. The impugned section is aimed not only at remedying a social problem but also at providing some measure of protection for the prostitute by eliminating the necessity of testifying. It would be unfortunate if the Charter were used to deprive a vulnerable segment of society of a measure of protection. The nature of the infringement of s. 11(d) by s. 195(2) is minimal. All that is required of the accused is to point to evidence capable of raising a reasonable doubt. That can often be achieved as a result of cross-examination of Crown witnesses. The section does not necessarily force the accused to testify. In my view, s. 195(2) is justified under s. 1 of the Charter and is valid.

In the result the appeal must be dismissed.

McLACHLIN J. dissenting (La Forest and Iacobucci JJ. concurring): ... In *Oakes*, this court held that there was insufficient rational connection between the substituted fact of being in possession of a narcotic, and the presumed fact of being in possession for the purposes of trafficking. The reverse onus clause in issue there was held to be irrational despite the obvious fact that in some cases an inference could be made from proof of possession that that possession was for the purposes of trafficking. The fact that there would be some cases, for example, where the possession was of only a small quantity of narcotics, where the inference would be unreasonable, was sufficient to render the reverse onus clause irrational and therefore incapable of being saved with reference to s. 1 of the Charter.

This holding in *Oakes* suggests that s. 1 requires a very high degree of internal rational connection between the substituted and presumed facts. The fact that the existence of the presumed fact would be a rational inference in some cases is not enough—the connection between the substituted and presumed facts must be more certain than that in order to pass constitutional muster. An example of a sufficiently close connection can be found in the decision of this court in *R. v. Whyte* (1988), 42 C.C.C. (3d) 97 at pp. 111-2, 51 D.L.R. (4th) 481, [1988] 2 S.C.R. 3. In that case, it was held that the connection between the substituted fact of a person being in the driver's seat and the presumed fact that that person was in care or control of the vehicle was sufficiently close to meet the rational connection test. As Dickson C.J.C. said at p. 112:

> … there is plainly a rational connection between the proved fact and the fact to be presumed. There is every reason to believe the person in the driver's seat has the care or control of the vehicle. … It is true that a vehicle can be occupied by one who does not assume care or control, but a person in this state of mind is likely to assume a position in the vehicle intended for a passenger rather than the driver. In my view, the relationship between the proved fact and the presumed fact under s. 237(1)(a) is direct and self-evident, quite unlike that which confronted the court in *Oakes*. …

The rationality test from *Oakes* also has a fairness aspect. An irrational presumption operates unfairly in that it unduly enmeshes the innocent in the criminal process by arbitrarily catching within its ambit those who are not guilty of the offence. Of course, any presumption may occasionally catch an innocent person, leaving it to him or her to establish or raise a reasonable doubt with respect to innocence. But where the presumption is so broadly cast that it catches persons whom it is unlikely were engaged in the prohibited crime, it goes too far.

In the case of s. 195(2) the required logical link is lacking, rendering it both irrational and unfair. It cannot be said that it is likely that one who lives with or is habitually in the company of a prostitute is parasitically living on the avails of prostitution. It is a possible inference, reasonable in some cases, but not in all or even in most. Spouses, lovers, friends, children, parents, room-mates, business associates, providers of goods and services—all of these may live with or be habitually in the company of a prostitute. …

The unfairness caused by this irrational presumption is arguably much worse than it was in *Oakes*. There, at least, the onus to establish that one was not in possession of narcotics for the purposes of trafficking was placed only on those who had already been proven to be guilty of a criminal offence, namely, possession of a narcotic. In the case of s. 195(2), the evidential burden of raising a reasonable doubt with respect to whether one is living on the avails of prostitution is placed on those who have been proven only to be habitually in the company of a prostitute, which is not a criminal offence. Yet the presumption applies to these innocent people, placing on them the burden of raising a reasonable doubt as to whether they have been living on the avails of prostitution. Any presumption which has the potential to catch such a wide variety of innocent people in its wake can only be said to be arbitrary, unfair and based on irrational considerations.

*Appeal dismissed.*

## Quantum of Proof

### R. v. Lifchus
Supreme Court of Canada
[1997] 3 S.C.R. 320

[The trial judge told the jury to use the phrase "reasonable doubt" in its "ordinary, natural every day sense." The Supreme Court held this was an error.]

CORY J. stated:

[36] Perhaps a brief summary of what the definition should and should not contain may be helpful. It should be explained that:

- the standard of proof beyond a reasonable doubt is inextricably intertwined with that principle fundamental to all criminal trials, the presumption of innocence;
- the burden of proof rests on the prosecution throughout the trial and never shifts to the accused;
- a reasonable doubt is not a doubt based upon sympathy or prejudice;
- rather, it is based upon reason and common sense;
- it is logically connected to the evidence or absence of evidence;
- it does not involve proof to an absolute certainty; it is not proof beyond any doubt nor is it an imaginary or frivolous doubt; and
- more is required than proof that the accused is probably guilty
- a jury which concludes only that the accused is probably guilty must acquit.

[37] On the other hand, certain references to the required standard of proof should be avoided. For example:

- describing the term "reasonable doubt" as an ordinary expression which has no special meaning in the criminal law context;
- inviting jurors to apply to the task before them the same standard of proof that they apply to important, or even the most important, decisions in their own lives;
- equating proof "beyond a reasonable doubt" to proof "to a moral certainty";
- qualifying the word "doubt" with adjectives other than "reasonable," such as "serious," "substantial" or "haunting," which may mislead the jury; and
- instructing jurors that they may convict if they are "sure" that the accused is guilty, before providing them with a proper definition as to the meaning of the words "beyond a reasonable doubt."

[38] A charge which is consistent with the principles set out in these reasons will suffice regardless of the particular words used by the trial judge. Nevertheless, it may, as suggested in *Girard, supra*, at p. 556, be useful to set out a "model charge" which could provide the necessary instructions as to the meaning of the phrase beyond a reasonable doubt.

[39]  Instructions pertaining to the requisite standard of proof in a criminal trial of proof beyond a reasonable doubt might be given along these lines:

> The accused enters these proceedings presumed to be innocent. That presumption of innocence remains throughout the case until such time as the Crown has on the evidence put before you satisfied you beyond a reasonable doubt that the accused is guilty.
>
> What does the expression "beyond a reasonable doubt" mean?
>
> The term "beyond a reasonable doubt" has been used for a very long time and is a part of our history and traditions of justice. It is so engrained in our criminal law that some think it needs no explanation, yet something must be said regarding its meaning.
>
> A reasonable doubt is not an imaginary or frivolous doubt. It must not be based upon sympathy or prejudice. Rather, it is based on reason and common sense. It is logically derived from the evidence or absence of evidence.
>
> Even if you believe the accused is probably guilty or likely guilty, that is not sufficient. In those circumstances you must give the benefit of the doubt to the accused and acquit because the Crown has failed to satisfy you of the guilt of the accused beyond a reasonable doubt.
>
> On the other hand you must remember that it is virtually impossible to prove anything to an absolute certainty and the Crown is not required to do so. Such a standard of proof is impossibly high.
>
> In short if, based upon the evidence before the court, you are sure that the accused committed the offence you should convict since this demonstrates that you are satisfied of his guilt beyond a reasonable doubt.

[40]  This is not a magic incantation that needs to be repeated word for word. It is nothing more than a suggested form that would not be faulted if it were used. For example, in cases where a reverse onus provision must be considered, it would be helpful to bring to the attention of the jury either the evidence which might satisfy that onus or the absence of evidence applicable to it. Any form of instruction that complied with the applicable principles and avoided the pitfalls referred to would be satisfactory.

### R. v. Starr
Supreme Court of Canada
[2000] 2 S.C.R. 144

[The trial judge told the jury that the phrase "reasonable doubt" had no special connotation and it did not require proof of an absolute certainty. The Supreme Court held this was an error.]

IACOBUCCI J. (Major, Binnie, Arbour, and LeBel JJ. concurring): …
[107]  With respect to the jury instructions on the phrase "beyond a reasonable doubt," as set out in *Lifchus*, supra, an instruction like the one in this case, which fails

to explain that the beyond a reasonable doubt standard has special legal significance and requires a significantly higher quantum of proof than the balance of probabilities, will not satisfy the *Lifchus* standard. ...

[239]  The key difficulty with this instruction is that it was not made clear to the jury that the Crown was required to do more than prove the appellant's guilt on a balance of probabilities. The trial judge told the jury that they could convict on the basis of something less than absolute certainty of guilt, but did not explain, in essence, how much less. In addition, rather than telling the jury that the words "reasonable doubt" have a specific meaning in the legal context, the trial judge expressly instructed the jury that the words have no "special connotation" and "no magic meaning that is peculiar to the law." By asserting that absolute certainty was not required, and then linking the standard of proof to the "ordinary everyday" meaning of the words "reasonable doubt," the trial judge could easily have been understood by the jury as asserting a probability standard as the applicable standard of proof.

[240]  The trial judge did comply with some of the requirements discussed in *Lifchus*, supra. He explained that a reasonable doubt is not an imaginary or frivolous doubt resting on speculation or guess, and that a reasonable doubt is a real doubt based on reason and common sense upon a review of the evidence. He also explained, as mentioned, that the standard of proof beyond a reasonable doubt does not involve proof to an absolute certainty. However, the trial judge's adherence to these requirements would have benefited primarily the Crown, not the appellant.

[241]  In the present case, the trial judge did refer to the Crown's onus and to the presumption of innocence, and he stated that the appellant should receive the benefit of any reasonable doubt. The error in the charge is that the jury was not told how a reasonable doubt is to be defined. As was emphasized repeatedly in *Lifchus* ... , a jury must be instructed that the standard of proof in a criminal trial is higher than the probability standard used in making everyday decisions and in civil trials. Indeed, it is this very requirement to go beyond probability that meshes the standard of proof in criminal cases with the presumption of innocence and the Crown's onus. However, as Cory J. explained in these earlier decisions, it is generally inappropriate to define the meaning of the term "reasonable doubt" through examples from daily life, through the use of synonyms, or through analogy to moral choices. The criminal standard of proof has a special significance unique to the legal process. It is an exacting standard of proof rarely encountered in everyday life, and there is no universally intelligible illustration of the concept, such as the scales of justice with respect to the balance of probabilities standard. Unlike absolute certainty or the balance of probabilities, reasonable doubt is not an easily quantifiable standard. It cannot be measured or described by analogy. It must be explained. However, precisely because it is not quantifiable, it is difficult to explain.

[242]  In my view, an effective way to define the reasonable doubt standard for a jury is to explain that it falls much closer to absolute certainty than to proof on a balance of probabilities. As stated in *Lifchus*, a trial judge is required to explain that something less than absolute certainty is required, and that something more than probable guilt is required, in order for the jury to convict. Both of these alternative standards are fairly and easily comprehensible. It will be of great assistance for a jury if the

trial judge situates the reasonable doubt standard appropriately between these two standards. The additional instructions to the jury set out in *Lifchus* as to the meaning and appropriate manner of determining the existence of a reasonable doubt serve to define the space between absolute certainty and proof beyond a reasonable doubt. In this regard, I am in agreement with Twaddle J.A. in the court below, when he said, at p. 177:

> If standards of proof were marked on a measure, proof "beyond reasonable doubt" would lie much closer to "absolute certainty" than to "a balance of probabilities." Just as a judge has a duty to instruct the jury that absolute certainty is not required, he or she has a duty, in my view, to instruct the jury that the criminal standard is more than a probability. The words he or she uses to convey this idea are of no significance, but the idea itself must be conveyed. …

[243]  In the appellant's case, with respect, the trial judge did not give instructions that could be construed as having located the reasonable doubt standard above the probability standard. Not only was the jury not told that something more than probability was required in order to convict, but nearly all of the instructions they were given (i.e., less than absolute certainty required, ordinary everyday words, no special meaning, more than a frivolous doubt required) weakened the content of the reasonable doubt standard in such a manner as to suggest that probability was indeed the requisite standard of proof. … While obviously a mistake in the charge will not always be fatal, at no point did the instructions in this case cure the mistake. The fact that the trial judge repeatedly stated that the prosecution must prove guilt beyond a reasonable doubt is no cure given his failure to ever define reasonable doubt correctly. … I reach this finding notwithstanding the fact that, like the jury charge in *Lifchus* when read as a whole, the jury charge in the present case was largely a model of fairness to the accused. The fact that other elements of the charge were fair to the accused cannot eliminate the prejudice caused by the improper instructions. Thus I conclude that there was not substantial compliance with the *Lifchus* principles. I would therefore allow the appeal on this ground. …

L'HEUREUX-DUBÉ J. (McLachlin C.J., Gonthier, and Bastarache JJ. concurring) in dissent:

[23]  On the issue of the jury charge on reasonable doubt, the *Lifchus* standard provides guidelines for trial judges rather than an iron-clad roster of proscriptions and prohibitions. I do not read *Lifchus* as providing that the inclusion or exclusion of certain phrases automatically vitiates a jury charge. Instead, I read *Lifchus* as mandating that a charge be examined in its entirety to determine whether the jury properly understood the concept of proof beyond a reasonable doubt. I am of the opinion that the jury charge in this case properly communicated this concept to the jury. …

[94]  The trial judge's charge, however, was not flawless. Specifically, we must examine the effect of the trial judge's misstatement that the words "reasonable doubt" are used in their everyday, ordinary sense and have no special legal meaning. It is asserted that this flaw in the charge, together with the failure of the trial judge to state

expressly that the Crown was required to do more than prove the appellant's guilt on a balance of probabilities, constitutes reversible error. With respect, I cannot agree.

[95] The verdict ought not to be disturbed because the charge, "when read as a whole, makes it clear that the jury could not have been under any misapprehension as to the correct burden and standard of proof to apply": *Lifchus*, at para. 41. While the judge told the jury that the words "reasonable doubt" had no special meaning, this was harmless error because he proceeded to give them all the legal information they required. The jury knew the accused was presumed innocent, they knew the standard of proof was very high—a standard just below absolute certainty—and they knew that they could not convict on a balance of probabilities. ...

[97] Moreover, the charge complied with *Lifchus*'s first principle that it must be made clear to the jury that the standard of proof beyond a reasonable doubt is inextricably linked to the presumption of innocence and that this burden never shifts to the accused: *Lifchus*, at para. 27. The relevant portion of the trial judge's charge on this point is:

> Let me first emphasize the presumption of innocence. Simply put, the accused is pre-sumed to be innocent and he continues to be and remain innocent unless and until the Crown has satisfied you beyond reasonable doubt of his guilt. This presumption re-mains with the accused and for his benefit from the beginning of the case until the end of the case. The onus of proving guilt rests upon the Crown from the beginning to the end of the case and it never shifts. There is no burden whatsoever on the accused to prove his innocence. The Crown must prove beyond a reasonable doubt that an accused person is guilty of the offence or offences with which he is charged before he can be convicted.

[98] In light of the trial judge's compliance with the bulk of the principles enunci-ated in *Lifchus*, I am loath to find that the charge was automatically vitiated by the failure to include a specific item mentioned in *Lifchus* or by the inclusion of an im-proper item. To do so would contravene our holding that "an error in the instructions as to the standard of proof may not constitute a reversible error": *Lifchus*, at para. 41.

[99] Jurors are sophisticated persons who are instructed to listen to and follow the entirety of the judge's charge to them. We must assume that they do so. It would ill behoove a reviewing court to do exactly what the jury is commanded not to do and isolate a phrase or a small section of the charge, ignoring the whole of it. I do not believe that is what Cory J. intended in *Lifchus*. Rather, he was attempting to provide guidance to trial judges in the extremely difficult task of articulating what is proof beyond a reasonable doubt and communicating this standard to the jury.

[100] *Lifchus* should be viewed as a broad template for trial judges to assist them in their difficult task. Cory J.'s suggestions provide a touchstone for comparison for courts in reviewing jury charges. However, reviewing courts must resist the tempta-tion to use the *Lifchus* suggestions as a mandatory checklist. The tendency to do so is natural and understandable as it would make the task of reviewing a jury charge far easier. However, a jury charge is not a multiple choice exam that can be marked by a computer. Rather, it is akin to a work of literature that must be studied in its entirety in order to evaluate it as a whole.

[101] Examining the charge in its entirety, I do not find that a reasonable likelihood existed that the jury misapprehended the correct standard of proof. Accordingly, I would dismiss this ground of appeal.

*New trial ordered.*

# PART TWO

# Principles of Criminal Liability

# CHAPTER FIVE

# Conduct or Actus Reus

Criminal liability can only exist where there is a valid definition in law of criminal wrongdoing. This affirmation may be justified, at least in part, by reference to the principle of legality. That principle excludes retroactive application of the criminal law and, according to Canadian constitutional jurisprudence examined in chapter 1, it excludes the enforcement of offences that are impermissibly vague or overly broad. But what else is implied in the requirement for a valid definition of criminal wrongdoing? This chapter looks at the requirement for some form of prohibited conduct.

One of the foundational principles of criminal liability is found in the maxim *actus non facit reum nisi mens sit rea*. It conveys the idea that there can be no culpable act unless it is performed with a culpable mental state. The same might be said in reverse: there can be no criminal liability unless a guilty mind expresses itself in the performance of a prohibited act. The requirement for a criminal act is an important limitation on the ambit and the legitimacy of the criminal sanction. Without it, there would be no bar to the imposition of criminal liability for prohibited thoughts, which in itself would be intolerable in a free and democratic society, and not least because there is no principle of harm or utility that could justify this extension of the criminal law. Lord Mansfield said as much in 1784: "So long as an act rests in bare intention, it is not punishable by our laws." *Scofield* Cald. 397. Liability for thoughts alone would also raise intractable problems of definition and proof.

The first two sections of this chapter are concerned with the basic principles of voluntariness and contemporaneity that apply in the assessment of all forms of criminal conduct. The third section provides illustrations of different types of conduct, notably acts of commission, omissions, and status. The fourth section emphasizes the need to examine particular circumstances that might be included in the definition of an offence. The fifth section is concerned with prohibited consequences and thus with issues of causation.

It is self-evident that people do not always act alone in the commission of criminal offences and that they are not always successful in the completion of a crime. In chapter 8 attention is given to extensions of criminal liability to cover various modes of participation in criminal conduct. In chapter 9 attention is given to liability for inchoate offences, notably attempt, incitement, and conspiracy. These are offences in which a criminal offence is undertaken in some way but not completed and yet the law treats the commencement of the offence as a sufficient basis for criminal liability.

289

## I. VOLUNTARINESS

The requirement for prohibited conduct among the elements of an offence expresses the principle that criminal liability cannot be attributed to a person unless that person is responsible for his or her acts. Responsible agency requires not only that a person performed a prohibited act but, as will be seen in the extracts below, that the person voluntarily performed that act. The distinction between the voluntary and involuntary performance of an act may be seen in illustrations. For example, if you fall on a slippery surface and in the course of falling strike the person next to you, is the application of force a voluntary act? If you have a statutory duty to maintain safe storage of dangerous products, does the destruction of your precautions by a third person or a natural force mean that you have voluntarily breached your duty? If you lose consciousness while driving due to a heart attack, is your dangerous driving a voluntary act?

### R. v. Ruzic
#### Supreme Court of Canada
#### [2001] 1 S.C.R. 687

LEBEL J.: ...

[34]  Even before the advent of the *Charter*, it became a basic concern of the criminal law that criminal responsibility be ascribed only to acts that resulted from the choice of a conscious mind and an autonomous will. In other words, only those persons acting in the knowledge of what they were doing, with the freedom to choose, would bear the burden and stigma of criminal responsibility. Although the element of voluntariness may sometimes overlap both *actus reus* and *mens rea* (see *R. v. Daviault*, [1994] 3 S.C.R. 63 (S.C.C.), at pp. 73-75, *per* Cory J.), the importance of *mens rea* and of the quality of voluntariness in it underscores the fact that criminal liability is founded on the premise that it will be borne only by those persons who knew what they were doing and willed it. ...

[43]  Let us examine the notion of "voluntariness" and its interplay with duress more closely. As Dickson J. stated in *R. v. Rabey*, [1980] 2 S.C.R. 513 (S.C.C.), at p. 522, "it is a basic principle that absence of volition in respect of the act involved is always a defence to a crime. A defence that the act is involuntary entitles the accused to a complete and unqualified acquittal." Dickson J.'s pronouncement was endorsed by the Court in *R. v. Parks*, [1992] 2 S.C.R. 871 (S.C.C.). The principle of voluntariness was given constitutional status in *Daviault, supra*, at pp. 102-3, where Cory J. held for the majority that it would infringe s. 7 of the *Charter* to convict an accused who was not acting voluntarily, as a fundamental aspect of the *actus reus* would be absent. More recently, in *R. v. Stone*, [1999] 2 S.C.R. 290 (S.C.C.), the crucial role of voluntariness as a condition of the attribution of criminal liability was again confirmed (at para. 1, *per* Binnie J., and paras. 155-58, *per* Bastarache J.) in an appeal concerning the defence of automatism. ...

[45]  What underpins ... these conceptions of voluntariness is the critical importance of autonomy in the attribution of criminal liability: *Perka* ... at pp. 250-51;

Fletcher ... at p. 805. The treatment of criminal offenders as rational, autonomous and choosing agents is a fundamental organizing principle of our criminal law. Its importance is reflected not only in the requirement that an act must be voluntary, but also in the condition that a wrongful act must be intentional to ground a conviction. *Sault Ste. Marie (City)*, *Reference re s. 94(2) of the Motor Vehicle Act (British Columbia)*, and *Vaillancourt* all stand for the proposition that a guilty verdict requires intentional conduct or conduct equated to it like recklessness or gross negligence. Like voluntariness, the requirement of a guilty mind is rooted in respect for individual autonomy and free will and acknowledges the importance of those values to a free and democratic society: *Martineau* ... at pp. 645-46. Criminal liability also depends on the capacity to choose—the ability to reason right from wrong. As McLachlin J. observed in *Chaulk* ... at p. 1396, in the context of the insanity provisions of the *Criminal Code*, this assumption of the rationality and autonomy of human beings forms part of the essential premises of Canadian criminal law: ...

[46] Punishing a person whose actions are involuntary in the physical sense is unjust because it conflicts with the assumption in criminal law that individuals are autonomous and freely choosing agents: see Shaffer ... at pp. 449-50. It is similarly unjust to penalize an individual who acted in a morally involuntary fashion. This is so because his acts cannot realistically be attributed to him, as his will was constrained by some external force.

[47] Although moral involuntariness does not negate the *actus reus* or *mens rea* of an offence, it is a principle which, similarly to physical involuntariness, deserves protection under s. 7 of the *Charter*. It is a principle of fundamental justice that only voluntary conduct—behaviour that is the product of a free will and controlled body, unhindered by external constraints—should attract the penalty and stigma of criminal liability. Depriving a person of liberty and branding her with the stigma of criminal liability would infringe the principles of fundamental justice if the accused did not have any realistic choice. The ensuing deprivation of liberty and stigma would have been imposed in violation of the tenets of fundamental justice and would thus infringe s. 7 of the *Charter*.

---

The concept of moral involuntariness will be considered later in relation to specific defences. Physical involuntariness can cover a wide range of conduct, including reflexive action, sleepwalking, or accident. The essential characteristic of voluntariness is the conscious control of action. Consciousness alone, however, is not enough to establish voluntariness because a person might be conscious and yet still incapable of controlling his or her conduct. The element of control is necessary in order to attribute responsibility for conduct. In sum, the voluntariness of a person's conduct will be established if his or her conduct is the product of conscious choice.

This implies that there is some mental element in the *actus reus* of a crime, although this minimal mental element is distinguishable from elements of fault such as intention, knowledge, or recklessness. As opposed to defences that are concerned with the absence of voluntariness, such as automatism or accident, it is rare that a case will turn on proving affirmatively what that element conscious control in voluntary conduct actually is. Nevertheless, as can be seen in the extracts from *Ruzic*, the concept of voluntary conduct is central to the coherence and legitimacy of the criminal law. Involuntariness, for example, is practically important in cases of absolute liability, where the absence of voluntary conduct is virtually the only defence open to the accused.

## II. CONTEMPORANEITY

With regard to all offences that require proof of fault, the offence cannot be proved unless the element of fault and the *actus reus* coincide. In 1798, the Court of King's Bench made this pronouncement on the principle of contemporaneity in *Fowler v. Padget*, 101 E.R. 1103, at 1106; 7 Term Rep. 509:

> It is a principle of natural justice, and of our law, that *actus non facit reum nisi mens sit rea*. The intent and the act must concur to constitute the crime.

The principle of contemporaneity requires proof that the prohibited conduct was committed with the measure of fault in the definition of the offence. For the most part, this might seem straightforward but, as the following cases show, there can be some difficulty in determining whether or when fault coincides with conduct.

### Fagan v. Commissioner of Metropolitan Police
#### Court of Appeal, Criminal Division
#### [1969] 1 Q.B. 439

JAMES J. (with whom Lord Parker agreed): The appellant, Vincent Martel Fagan, was convicted by the Willesden magistrates of assaulting David Morris, a police constable, in the execution of his duty on August 31, 1967. He appealed to quarter sessions. On October 25, 1967, his appeal was heard by Middlesex Quarter Sessions and was dismissed. This matter now comes before the court on appeal by way of case stated from that decision of quarter sessions.

The sole question is whether the prosecution proved facts which in law amounted to an assault.

On August 31, 1967, the appellant was reversing a motor car in Fortunegate Road, London, N.W. 10, when Police Constable Morris directed him to drive the car forwards to the kerbside so that he could ask the appellant to produce documents relating to the appellant's driving, and standing in front of the car pointed out a suitable place in which to park. At first the appellant stopped the car too far from the kerb for the officer's liking. Morris asked him to park closer and indicated a precise spot. The appellant drove forward towards him and stopped it with the offside wheel on Morris's left foot. "Get off, you are on my foot," said the officer. "Fuck you, you can wait," said the appellant. The engine of the car stopped running. Morris repeated several times "Get off my foot." The appellant said reluctantly "Okay man, okay," and then slowly turned on the ignition of the vehicle and reversed it off the officer's foot. The appellant had either turned the ignition off to stop the engine or turned it off after the engine had stopped running.

The justices at quarter sessions on those facts were left in doubt as to whether the mounting of the wheel on to the officer's foot was deliberate or accidental. They were satisfied, however, beyond all reasonable doubt that the appellant "knowingly, provocatively and unnecessarily allowed the wheel to remain on the foot after the officer said 'Get off, you are on my foot.' " They found that on those facts an assault was proved.

Mr. Abbas for the appellant relied upon the passage in Stone's Justices' Manual (1968), Vol. 1, p. 651, where assault is defined. He contends that on the finding of the justices the initial mounting of the wheel could not be an assault and that the act of the wheel mounting the foot came to an end without there being any *mens rea*. It is argued that thereafter there was no act on the part of the appellant which could constitute an *actus reus* but only the omission or failure to remove the wheel as soon as he was asked. That failure, it is said, could not in law be an assault, nor could it in law provide the necessary *mens rea* to convert the original act of mounting the foot into an assault.

Mr. Rant for the respondent argues that the first mounting of the foot was an *actus reus* which act continued until the moment of time at which the wheel was removed. During that continuing act, it is said, the appellant formed the necessary intention to constitute the element of *mens rea* and once that element was added to the continuing act, an assault took place. In the alternative, Mr. Rant argues that there can be situations in which there is a duty to act and that in such situations an omission to act in breach of duty would in law amount to an assault. It is unnecessary to formulate any concluded views on this alternative.

In our judgment the question arising, which has been argued on general principles, falls to be decided on the facts of the particular case. An assault is any act which intentionally—or possibly recklessly—causes another person to apprehend immediate and unlawful personal violence. Although "assault" is an independent crime and is to be treated as such, for practical purposes today "assault" is generally synonymous with the term "battery" and is a term used to mean the actual intended use of unlawful force to another person without his consent. On the facts of the present case the "assault" alleged involved a "battery." Where an assault involves a battery, it matters not, in our judgment, whether the battery is inflicted directly by the body of the offender or through the medium of some weapon or instrument controlled by the action of the offender. An assault may be committed by the laying of a hand upon another, and the action does not cease to be an assault if it is a stick held in the hand and not the hand itself which is laid on the person of the victim. So for our part we see no difference in principle between the action of stepping on to a person's toe and maintaining that position and the action of driving a car on to a person's foot and sitting in the car whilst its position on the foot is maintained.

To constitute the offence of assault some intentional act must have been performed: a mere omission to act cannot amount to an assault. Without going into the question whether words alone can constitute an assault, it is clear that the words spoken by the appellant could not alone amount to an assault: they can only shed a light on the appellant's action. For our part we think the crucial question is whether in this case the act of the appellant can be said to be complete and spent at the moment of time when the car wheel came to rest on the foot or whether his act is to be regarded as a continuing act operating until the wheel was removed. In our judgment a distinction is to be drawn between acts which are complete—though results may continue to flow—and those acts which are continuing. Once the act is complete it cannot thereafter be said to be a threat to inflict unlawful force upon the victim. If the act, as distinct from the results thereof, is a continuing act there is a continuing threat to inflict unlawful force. If the assault involves a battery and that battery continues there is a continuing act of assault.

For an assault to be committed both the elements of *actus reus* and *mens rea* must be present at the same time. The "*actus reus*" is the action causing the effect on the victim's mind (see the observations of Park B. in *Regina v. St. George* (1840), 9 C. & P. 483, 490, 493). The "*mens rea*" is the intention to cause that effect. It is not necessary that *mens rea* should be present at the inception of the *actus reus*; it can be superimposed upon an existing act. On the other hand the subsequent inception of *mens rea* cannot convert an act which has been completed without *mens rea* into an assault.

In our judgment the Willesden magistrates and quarter sessions were right in law. On the facts found the action of the appellant may have been initially unintentional, but the time came when knowing that the wheel was on the officer's foot the appellant (1) remained seated in the car so that his body through the medium of the car was in contact with the officer, (2) switched off the ignition of the car, (3) maintained the wheel of the car on the foot and (4) used words indicating the intention of keeping the wheel in that position. For our part we cannot regard such conduct as mere omission or inactivity.

There was an act constituting a battery which at its inception was not criminal because there was no element of intention but which became criminal from the moment the intention was formed to produce the apprehension which was flowing from the continuing act. The fallacy of the appellant's argument is that it seeks to equate the facts of this case with such a case as where a motorist has accidentally run over a person and, that action having been completed, fails to assist the victim with the intent that the victim should suffer.

We would dismiss this appeal.

BRIDGE J. (dissenting): I fully agree with my Lords as to the relevant principles to be applied. No mere omission to act can amount to an assault. Both the elements of *actus reus* and *mens rea* must be present at the same time, but the one may be superimposed on the other. It is in the application of these principles to the highly unusual facts of this case that I have, with regret, reached a different conclusion from the majority of the court. I have no sympathy at all for the appellant, who behaved disgracefully. But I have been unable to find any way of regarding the facts which satisfies me that they amounted to the crime of assault. This has not been for want of trying. But at every attempt I have encountered the inescapable question: after the wheel of the appellant's car had accidentally come to rest on the constable's foot, what was it that the appellant did which constituted the act of assault? However the question is approached, the answer I feel obliged to give is: precisely nothing. The car rested on the foot by its own weight and remained stationary by its own inertia. The appellant's fault was that he omitted to manipulate the controls to set it in motion again.

Neither the fact that the appellant remained in the driver's seat nor that he switched off the ignition seem to me to be of any relevance. The constable's plight would have been no better, but might well have been worse, if the appellant had alighted from the car leaving the ignition switched on. Similarly I can get no help from the suggested analogies. If one man accidentally treads on another's toe or touches him with a stick, but deliberately maintains pressure with foot or stick after the victim protests, there is clearly an assault. But there is no true parallel between such cases and the present case. It is not, to my mind, a legitimate use of language to speak of the appellant "holding" or "maintaining" the car wheel on the constable's foot. The expression which corresponds to the reality is that used by the justices in the case stated. They say, quite rightly, that he "allowed" the wheel to remain.

With a reluctantly dissenting voice I would allow this appeal and quash the appellant's conviction.

*Appeal dismissed.*

## R. v. Miller
Court of Appeal, Criminal Division
[1982] 2 All E.R. 386

[One night, while squatting in someone else's house, the appellant lit a cigarette and then lay down on a mattress in one of the rooms. He fell asleep before he had finished smoking the cigarette and it dropped onto the mattress. Later he woke up and saw that the mattress was smouldering. He did nothing about it; he merely moved to another room and went to sleep again. The house caught fire. The appellant was rescued and subsequently charged with arson, contrary to the *Criminal Damage Act* 1971.]

MAY L.J., for the Court: … In both *Fagan*'s case and the present, justice and good sense required that the defendant should not escape liability merely because the last thing that happened in the relevant story was an omission on his part. With respect to the Divisional Court in *Fagan*'s case, we agree with Professor Glanville Williams's criticism of the reasoning of the majority of the court. In reality, driving the car wheel onto the policeman's foot was an act, was something which the driver did: the latter's failure thereafter to drive it off, despite the officer's request, was something which the driver did not do, it was an omission, and we think that it is unreal to describe it as any more than that.

On the other hand, in the driver's failure to release the officer's foot in the knowledge that he had just driven onto it, we think that there was clearly a substantial element of adoption by the driver, at the later stage, of what he had done a little earlier. We think that the conduct of the driver in that case can and should have been looked at as a whole and as the whole contained both the actus reus and the mens rea

they were sufficiently coincident to render the driver guilty of an assault, without
having to resort to the somewhat artificial reasoning of the majority of the Divisional
Court. In our opinion, an unintentional act followed by an intentional omission to
rectify that act or its consequences can be regarded in toto as an intentional act. We
do not seek to define the rule, if rule it be, any more precisely because each case must
depend on its own facts and we prefer to leave it to the trial judge to give the jury
what he considers to be the appropriate direction in any given case. We would only
say that an unintentional act followed by an intentional omission to rectify it or its
consequences, or a reckless omission to do so when recklessness is a sufficient mens
rea for the particular case, should only be regarded in toto as an intentional or reckless act when reality and common sense so require; this may well be a matter to be
left to the jury. Further, in the relevant analysis we think that whether or no there is on
the facts an element of adoption on the part of the alleged offender of what he has
done earlier by what he deliberately or recklessly fails to do later is an important
consideration.

In these circumstances, although we doubt whether the learned recorder was correct in holding that when the appellant in the present case woke up there was any
duty on him at criminal law to extinguish the smouldering mattress, nevertheless we
do think that the whole of the appellant's conduct in relation to the mattress from the
moment he lay on it with a lighted cigarette until the time he left it smouldering and
moved to the adjoining room can and should be regarded as one act. Clearly his
failure with knowledge to extinguish the incipient fire had in it a substantial element
of adoption on his part of what he had unintentionally done earlier, namely set it on
fire. …

*Appeal dismissed.*

[A further appeal to the House of Lords was dismissed: [1983] 2 A.C. 161.]

LORD DIPLOCK: I see no rational ground for excluding from conduct capable of
giving rise to criminal liability, conduct which consists of failing to take measures
that lie within one's power to counteract a danger that one has oneself created, if at
the time of such conduct one's state of mind is such as constitutes a necessary ingredient of the offence. I venture to think that the habit of lawyers to talk of "actus reus,"
suggestive as it is of action rather than inaction, is responsible for any erroneous
notion that failure to act cannot give rise to criminal liability in English law.

I cannot see any good reason why, so far as liability under criminal law is concerned, it should matter at what point of time before the resultant damage is complete
a person becomes aware that he has done a physical act which, whether or not he
appreciated that it would at the time when he did it, does in fact create a risk that
property of another will be damaged; provided that, at the moment of awareness, it
lies within his power to take steps, either himself or by calling for the assistance of
the fire brigade if this be necessary, to prevent or minimise the damage to the property at risk.

The recorder, in his lucid summing up to the jury (they took 22 minutes only to reach their verdict) told them that the accused having by his own act started a fire in the mattress which, when he became aware of its existence, presented an obvious risk of damaging the house, became under a duty to take some action to put it out. The Court of Appeal upheld the conviction, but their *ratio decidendi* appears to be somewhat different from that of the recorder. As I understand the judgment, in effect it treats the whole course of conduct of the accused, from the moment at which he fell asleep and dropped the cigarette on to the mattress until the time the damage to the house by fire was complete, as a continuous act of the accused, and holds that it is sufficient to constitute the statutory offence of arson if at any stage in that course of conduct the state of mind of the accused, when he fails to try to prevent or minimise the damage which will result from his initial act, although it lies within his power to do so, is that of being reckless as to whether property belonging to another would be damaged.

My Lords, these alternative ways of analysing the legal theory that justifies a decision which has received nothing but commendation for its accord with commonsense and justice, have, since the publication of the judgment of the Court of Appeal in the instant case, provoked academic controversy. Each theory has distinguished support. Professor J.C. Smith espouses the "duty theory"; Professor Glanville Williams who, after the decision of the Divisional Court in *Fagan v. Metropolitan Police Commissioner*, [1969] 1 Q.B. 439 appears to have been attracted by the duty theory, now prefers that of the continuous act. When applied to cases where a person has unknowingly done an act which sets in train events that, when he becomes aware of them, present an obvious risk that property belonging to another will be damaged, both theories lead to an identical result; and since what your Lordships are concerned with is to give guidance to trial judges in their task of summing up to juries, I would for this purpose adopt the duty theory as being the easier to explain to a jury; though I would commend the use of the word "responsibility," rather than "duty" which is more appropriate to civil than to criminal law since it suggests an obligation owed to another person, i.e., the person to whom the endangered property belongs, whereas a criminal statute defines combinations of conduct and state of mind which render a person liable to punishment by the state itself.

---

In *R. v. Cooper* (1993), 78 C.C.C. (3d) 289 (S.C.C.), the accused was charged with murder by manual strangulation and was convicted. The accused testified that he became angry with the deceased and grabbed her by the throat with both hands and shook her. He then said that he could recall nothing else until he awoke in his car and found the body of the deceased beside him. The accused had no recollection of causing her death. There was evidence that the accused had consumed a considerable amount of alcohol. In directing the jury as to the accused's liability for murder under s. 212(a)(ii) of the *Criminal Code*, the trial judge directed to the jury that once the accused had formed the intent to cause the deceased bodily harm, which he knew was likely to cause her death, he need not be aware of what he was doing at the moment she actually died. The

Newfoundland Court of Appeal ordered a new trial, but the Supreme Court of Canada restored the conviction, Lamer C.J.C. dissenting. Cory J. stated for the court:

> Not only must the guilty mind, intent or *mens rea* be present, it must also be concurrent with the impugned act. ...
>
> Yet, it is not always necessary for the guilty act and the intent to be completely concurrent: see, for example, *Fagan v. Metropolitan Police Commissioner*, [1968] 3 All E.R. 442 (Q.B.). In that case a motorist stopped his car on the foot of a police office. This was apparently done by accident. When the officer, not unreasonably, asked the accused to move the car, he at first refused but eventually did move on. It was determined that while the first action of stopping was innocent of criminal intent, it acquired the necessary *mens rea* when the accused was made aware that the car was resting on the officer's foot and still refused to move. James J., concurring in the result, stated at p. 445: "It is not necessary that *mens rea* should be present at the inception of the actus reus; it can be superimposed on an existing act."
>
> There is, then, the classic rule that at some point the *actus reus* and the *mens rea* or intent must coincide. Further, I would agree with the conclusion of James J. that an act (*actus reus*) which may be innocent or no more than careless at the outset can become criminal at a later stage when the accused acquires knowledge of the nature of the act and still refuses to change his course of action.
>
> The determination of whether the guilty mind or *mens rea* coincides with the wrongful act will depend to a large extent upon the nature of the act. For example, if the accused shot the victim in the head or stabbed the victim in the chest with death ensuing a few minutes after the shooting or stabbing, then it would be relatively easy to infer that the requisite intent or *mens rea* coincided with the wrongful act (*actus reus*) of shooting or stabbing. As well, a series of acts may form part of the same transaction. For example the repeated blows of the baseball bat continuing over several minutes are all part of the same transaction. In those circumstances if the requisite intent coincides at any time with the sequence of blows then that could be sufficient to found a conviction.
>
> An example of a series of acts that might be termed a continuous transaction appears in *Meli v. The Queen*, [1954] 1 W.L.R. 228 (P.C.). There the accused intended to kill the deceased, and to this end struck a number of blows. The effect of the blows was such that the accused thought the victim was dead and threw the body over a cliff. However, it was not the blows but rather the exposure suffered by the victim while he lay at the base of the cliff that resulted in the death. It was argued on behalf of the accused that when there was the requisite *mens rea* (during the beating) death did not ensue and when death did ensue there was no longer any intention to kill. The judicial committee of the Privy Council concluded that the entire episode was one continuing transaction that could not be subdivided in that way. At some point, the requisite *mens rea* coincided with the continuing series of wrongful acts that constituted the transaction. As a result, the conviction for murder was sustained. I agree with that conclusion.
>
> Did the accused possess such a mental state after he started strangling the victim? Here death occurred between 30 seconds and two minutes after he grabbed her by the neck. It could be reasonably inferred by the jury, that when the accused grabbed the victim by the neck and shook her that there was, at that moment, the necessary coincidence of the

wrongful act of strangulation and the requisite intent to do bodily harm that the accused knew was likely to cause her death. Cooper was aware of these acts before he "blacked out." Thus although the jury was under no compulsion to do so, it was none the less open to them to infer that he knew that he was causing bodily harm and knew that it was so dangerous to the victim that it was likely to cause her death. It was sufficient that the intent and the act of strangulation coincided at some point. It was not necessary that the requisite intent continue throughout the entire two minutes required to cause the death of the victim.

Lamer C.J.C., dissenting, stated:

> The intention to cause bodily harm by no means leads inexorably to the conclusion that the accused knew that the bodily harm was likely to cause death. It is, of course, this aspect which is essential to a finding of guilt of murder under s. 212(a)(ii). Particularly with respect to an action such as grabbing by the neck, there may be a point at the outset when there is no intention to cause death and no knowledge that the action is likely to cause death. But there comes a point in time when the wrongful conduct becomes likely to cause death. It is, in my view, at that moment or thereafter, that the accused must have a conscious awareness of the likelihood of death. This awareness need not, however, continue until death ensures.

On several occasions the Supreme Court has asserted that the principle of voluntariness is a principle of fundamental justice within the meaning of s. 7 of the Charter. No statement of comparable clarity has been made concerning the principle of contemporaneity but a strong argument can be advanced for this conclusion. To the extent that the Charter requires proof of fault for criminal liability, it is implicit that such fault must coincide with the element of voluntary conduct.

## III.  ACTION, INACTION, AND STATUS

The three subsections that follow are concerned in turn with acts of commission, acts of omission, and conduct relating to status. It is already clear that the principles of voluntariness and contemporaneity apply to each. It is imperative in the interpretation of criminal offences to ascertain as precisely as possible the conduct that is prohibited. Sometimes there are uncertainties or ambiguities about the nature or the scope of prohibited conduct that demand judicial resolution.

### Action

Most offences require proof of some positive act, such as stealing, driving, trespassing, or killing. This is positive action in the same way that walking or running, as opposed to standing still, is positive action. Positive action is thus the "verb" in the definition of criminal liability. There are circumstances in which doing nothing can constitute prohibited conduct but that is understood as an omission. In some instances Parliament has provided definitions in an attempt to clarify what is meant by specific terms used in the definition of prohibited conduct. See, for example, the definitions for "break" (s. 321), "communicating" (s. 319(7)), "operate" (s. 214), "sell" (ss. 183 and 462.1), or "transfer"

(s. 84). See also s. 2, the general section for definitions (consider the definition of cattle). Note that definitions are often provided a limited meaning in relation to specific offences. This means that words can mean different things by express definition. Trafficking is given a specific definition in s. 342(4) of the Code and another in s. 2(1) of the *Controlled Drugs and Substances Act*, S.C. 1996, c. 19. Other provisions perform the same function as conventional definitions but in a somewhat different form. For example, publication of a defamatory libel is an offence under s. 301 of the Code but ss. 303 and following provide a long list of exceptions that restricts the *actus reus* of publication.

### Inaction (Omissions)

A failure to act can also constitute the *actus reus* of criminal offences but, at the outset, it is important to underscore that liability for omissions is an issue that raises broad and complex problems of policy. As a general proposition, doing nothing is not criminal conduct. Under what conditions, then, can it be said sensibly that inaction is criminal conduct? The answer is that the legislature has identified specific circumstances in which doing nothing is sufficiently harmful in itself to merit criminalization or the law otherwise imposes a duty of positive action and criminal sanction for failure to fulfill that duty. On this account, liability for omissions is exceptional and reflects the sound policy that liability for inaction should not be generalized. Nevertheless, even within this restrictive view, there is considerable scope for liability based upon omissions. Most notable in this regard are the definitions of "criminal negligence" and "duty" in s. 219 of the Code.

> (1)  Every one is criminally negligent who
>      (a)  in doing anything, or
>      (b)  in omitting to do anything that it is his duty to do,
> shows wanton or reckless disregard for the lives or safety of other persons.
>      (2)  For the purposes of this section, "duty" means a duty imposed by law.

This definition applies, for example, in offences of criminal negligence causing death or bodily harm. The outer limits of liability for omissions is marked only by the principles of primary and secondary participation in criminal offences and by principles of causation.

The reasons given in *Fagan* and *Miller* show how easily the element of conduct allows a matter of positive action to be reformulated as a culpable omission (or *vice versa*). In *Fagan* the majority concluded that even if the accused did not at first know that he had driven onto the officer's foot, his failure to get off the foot became voluntary as soon as he realized the situation. Lord Diplock in *Miller* said that the failure of the accused to attend to the burning mattress was the equivalent of setting the fire. These are, obviously, controversial issues. If you borrow your friend's umbrella with consent, but knowingly fail to return it, is that sufficient for theft?

Much of the controversy about liability for omissions relates to the extent to which the criminal law should create positive duties and sanction non-compliance with them. To what extent should the criminal law enforce a duty to prevent the commission or continuation of an offence? Should the law punish the failure to report the commission of an offence? These questions have been staunchly debated for centuries. For a very long time there was an offence at common law, known as misprision of felony, consisting of a failure to report the commission of a serious offence. This offence was eventually abolished in favour of the position that inaction should only exceptionally be criminalized. It flows from this position that being a spectator to crime is not an offence. It means that there is no duty to intervene, prevent, or offer assistance unless the legislature specifically says so.

Article 2 of the *Charter of Human Rights and Freedoms* in Quebec, R.S.Q., c. C-12, not only declares that every person in peril has the right to assistance but imposes a duty upon others to assist a person in peril. This raises the interesting question whether noncompliance with the duty of assistance under this provincial enactment could support a prosecution for manslaughter.

There is a further question concerning the scope of liability for omissions that constitute a breach of legal duty. Legal duties can be statutory or recognized at common law. If they are statutory, they can be found in provincial or federal legislation. In federal legislation the duty might lie in an enactment that is in substance criminal law or is derived from another head of legislative jurisdiction. (See, for example, ss. 215-217 of the *Criminal Code*.) At common law, duties can be found in the law relating to extra-contractual liability (tort) and elsewhere. The question is whether any or only some of these duties will provide a sufficient basis for criminal liability.

## Moore v. The Queen
### Supreme Court of Canada
### [1979] 1 S.C.R. 195

SPENCE J. (Martland, Ritchie, Pigeon, and Beetz JJ. concurring):

[1] This is an appeal from the judgment of the Court of Appeal for British Columbia, pronounced on 7th June 1977 [[1977] 5 W.W.R. 241, 40 C.R.N.S. 93, 36 C.C.C. (2d) 481].

[2] The appellant had been acquitted after his trial before Millward Co. Ct. J. and a jury upon an indictment charging him:

> That at the City of Victoria, County of Victoria, Province of British Columbia, on the 19th day of April, 1976, he did unlawfully and wilfully obstruct a Peace Officer, to wit, Constable Sutherland, in the execution of his duty as such Peace Officer, contrary to the Criminal Code of Canada.

[3] The appellant was acquitted by a verdict directed by the learned trial judge at the close of the Crown's case. The facts are outlined in an admission by counsel for Moore, which I quote:

> If it please, your Honour, I have certain admissions of fact to make to expedite matters. Firstly, I am instructed to admit that on or about the 19th of April 1976, at or about 9:10 a.m., the Accused, Richard Harvey Moore, was southbound on Government Street at Pandora and at that intersection proceeded through a light which had not yet turned

green and was, in fact red when he proceeded through on his ten-speed bicycle. That is the extent of my admission of fact.

The facts are further dealt with by Carrothers J.A. in his reasons for judgment as follows [p. 250]:

> Constable Sutherland, a peace officer with the Victoria City Police, in uniform and on a motorcycle, observed this infraction on the part of Moore and set about to "ticket" Moore. The constable and Moore proceeded side by side on their respective cycles, with Moore sometimes taking elusive action by riding his bicycle on the sidewalk, with the constable repeatedly requesting Moore to "pull over and stop" and Moore lewdly rebuffing each such request with an obscene demand to leave him alone as he was in a hurry. I attach no importance to the particular salacious vulgarity used by Moore in rejecting the policeman's request to stop as it has been used by the unimaginative so excessively and indiscriminately as to have lost its literal quality, but there is no doubt that it constituted flat refusals on the part of Moore to stop as requested by the policeman.

[4] As a result of this occurrence, Moore was charged upon an indictment, as I have said above, but he was not charged with failing to stop at a stop light, only with obstructing a peace officer in the performance of his duty. The obstruction which the Crown put forward as constituting the offence was the failure of the appellant to give his name when requested to do so by the police constable.

[5] The relevant sections of the provincial statutes with which I shall deal hereafter are as follows: Firstly, the Motor-vehicle Act, R.S.B.C. 1960, c. 253. Section 2 contains definitions of "motor-vehicle" and "vehicle," as follows:

> "motor-vehicle" means a vehicle, not run upon rails, that is designed to be self-propelled or propelled by electric power obtained from overhead trolley-wires; ...

> "vehicle" means a device in, upon, or by which a person or thing is or may be transported or drawn upon a highway, except a device designed to be moved by human power or used exclusively upon stationary rails or tracks [en. 1963, c. 27, s. 2].

Section 58 of the said Motor-vehicle Act provides:

> 58. Every person driving or operating or in charge of a motor-vehicle on any highway who refuses or fails
>
> (a) to stop his motor-vehicle when signalled or requested to stop by any police officer or constable who is in uniform or who displays his police badge conspicuously on the outside of his outer coat; or
>
> (b) to state correctly his name and address and the name and address of the owner of the motor-vehicle when requested by any peace officer or constable to state same is guilty of an offence.

[6] It will be seen plainly that a bicycle is neither a "motor-vehicle" nor a "vehicle" of any kind under the provisions of the aforesaid definitions. A bicycle is plainly not self-propelled and therefore cannot be a "motor-vehicle," and it is a device designed to be moved by human power and therefore cannot be a "vehicle" at all. ...

[7]  I turn next to the question of whether the appellant was guilty of an offence when he proceeded into the intersection of Government Street and Pandora when facing a red traffic light. Section 121 [am. 1975, c. 46, s. 6] of the Motor-vehicle Act provides as follows:

> "cycle" means a device having any number of wheels that is propelled by human power and on which a person may ride.

And s. 173(1) of the Motor-vehicle Act provides:

> 173.(1)  In addition to the duties imposed by this section, a person operating a bicycle upon a highway has the same rights and duties as a driver of a vehicle.

[8]  The appellant, Moore, was riding a bicycle. A bicycle is a device having any number of wheels—to wit, two—and is propelled by human power, and a person may ride on it, as Moore was riding. Therefore it is a "cycle" within the definition and, therefore, by the provision of s. 173(1) Moore was under the same duties as the driver of a vehicle. ...

[18]  I am of the opinion that the Court of Appeal of British Columbia was correct in finding that when the appellant, Moore, refused to accede to the constable's request for his identification he was obstructing that constable in the performance of his duties. As did the members of the Court of Appeal, I am confining my consideration of this matter to the actual circumstances which occurred, that is, that a constable on duty observed the appellant in the act of committing an infraction of the statute and that that constable had no power to arrest the accused for such offence unless and until he had attempted to identify the accused so that he might be the subject of summary conviction proceedings. ...

[20]  Therefore, for the reasons which I have outlined above, I am of the opinion that the officer was under a duty to attempt to identify the wrongdoer, and the failure to identify himself by the wrongdoer did constitute an obstruction of the police officer in the performance of his duties.

[21]  I add that in coming to this conclusion I have not forgotten the provisions of the Bill of Rights, R.S.C. 1970, App. III, or the topic of individual freedom generally, but I am of the opinion that there is not even minimal interference with any freedom of a citizen who is seen committing an infraction by a police constable in the police constable's simply requesting his name and address without any attempt to obtain from that person any admission of fault or any comment whatsoever. On the other hand, the refusal of a citizen to identify himself under such circumstances causes a major inconvenience and obstruction to the police in carrying out their proper duties, so that if anyone were engaged in any balancing of interest, there could be no doubt that the conclusion to which I have come would be that supported by the overwhelming public interest.

[22]  I would dismiss the appeal.

DICKSON J. (Estey J. concurring) (dissenting): ...

[24]  The appellant went through an intersection against a red light on his bicycle. A motorcycle policeman, observing the infraction, stopped the appellant and, with

the intention of giving him a traffic ticket, asked for identification. The appellant refused to give his name and address. As a result, he was charged with unlawfully and wilfully obstructing a peace officer in the execution of his duty. The point is whether the failure of the accused to identify himself when requested to do so by the constable was evidence to go to the jury of the offence of wilfully obstructing a police officer in the execution of his duty, contrary to s. 118 [am. 1972, c. 13, s. 7] of the Criminal Code, R.S.C. 1970, c. C-34 [now s. 129 of the *Criminal Code*, R.S.C. 1985, c. C-46].

## *The General Principle*

[25]  Any duty to identify oneself must be found in either common law or statute, quite apart from the duties of the police. A person is not guilty of the offence of obstructing a police officer merely by doing nothing, unless there is a legal duty to act. Omission to act in a particular way will give rise to criminal liability only where a duty to act arises at common law or is imposed by statute: 11 Hals. (4th) 15. This idea was expressed by Schroeder J.A. in *R. v. Patrick*, [1960] O.W.N. 206, 32 C.R. 338 at 343, 128 C.C.C. 263 (C.A.):

> Counsel for the appellant submitted that to sustain a charge of obstructing a peace officer in the execution of his duty, it was necessary for the Crown to prove either a positive act of interference, or a refusal to perform some act required to be done by a statute … It not having been shown that the appellant was under any duty or obligation to communicate to the peace officer the information required of him under the provisions of either s. 221(2) of The Criminal Code [1953-54 (Can.), c. 51], or s. 110(1) of The Highway Traffic Act [R.S.O. 1950, c. 167], the Crown has failed to bring home to the appellant the commission of a criminal offence. This is sufficient to dispose of the appeal.

[26]  The point under discussion is dealt with at some length by Dr. Glanville Williams in an article entitled "Demanding Name and Address" (1950), 66 Law Quarterly Rev. 465. The general principle of the common law is stated [at p. 465]:

> … neither a private person nor a constable has any effective power to demand the name and address of a person on the ground that he has committed an offence or is under a civil liability. …

## *No Statutory Duty*

[27]  It appears to me impossible to extract from the statutory provisions of the British Columbia Motor-vehicle Act, R.S.B.C. 1960, c. 253, a duty on a cyclist caught riding through a red light to identify himself. Section 58 of the Act specifically places a duty on a person driving a "motor-vehicle" to state correctly his name and address when requested to do so by a peace officer. This in itself appears to recognize the absence of any such duty where there is no statutory requirement. Section 58 does not apply to persons operating either "vehicles" (as defined in s. 2) or bicycles, and there is no other provision in the Motor-vehicle Act or any other relevant statute

placing such a duty on a cyclist caught committing a summary conviction offence under the Motor-vehicle Act.

[28]  I have had the advantage of reading the reasons of Spence J. and I am in full agreement, for the reasons stated by him and by the Court of Appeal of British Columbia, that the accused was not in breach of s. 58 of the Motor-vehicle Act when he refused to give his name and address to the constable.

[29]  At trial, the Crown took the position that the obligation on the part of the accused to respond to the police officer's questions lay within the confines of the Motor-vehicle Act. That argument was pursued unsuccessfully in the British Columbia Court of Appeal and in this court. There is simply no statutory duty on a cyclist committing a traffic infraction to divulge his name and address. ...

### No Common Law Duty

[31]  There is no duty at common law to identify oneself to police. As was stated by Lord Parker C.J. in *Rice v. Connolly*, [1966] 2 Q.B. 414, [1966] 2 All E.R. 649 at 652 (D.C.):

> It seems to me quite clear that though every citizen has a moral duty or, if you like, a social duty to assist the police, there is no legal duty to that effect, and indeed the whole basis of the common law is the right of the individual to refuse to answer questions put to him by persons in authority, and a refusal to accompany those in authority to any particular place, short, of course, of arrest.

The case stands for the proposition that refusal to identify oneself to the police could not constitute obstruction of the police. The court distinguished a refusal to answer, which is legal, from a "cock and bull" story to the police, which might constitute obstruction. No other distinction was made. Lord Parker C.J. said, p. 652:

> In my judgment there is all the difference in the world between deliberately telling a false story, something which on no view a citizen has a right to do, and preserving silence or refusing to answer, something which he has every right to do. ...

[35]  ... Where does one find the legal compulsion to answer? A person cannot "obstruct" by refusing to answer a question unless he is under a legal duty to answer.

### An "Implied" or "Reciprocal" Duty?

[36]  It was strongly urged in argument before us that, because a duty rested upon constables to investigate crime and enforce provincial laws, an "implied" or "reciprocal" duty rested upon a person suspected of an infraction to give his name and address and that refusal to do so amounted to such frustration as to constitute the offence of obstructing the police in the execution of their duty.

[37]  The Crown perforce had to fall back upon the proposition that, because there was duty upon the police officer to inquire before exercising the power to arrest under s. 450 [re-en. 1970, c. 2 (2nd Supp.), s. 5] of the Code, there was a reciprocal duty upon the alleged culprit to respond. The alleged duty, as I understand the argument, is

to be limited to divulging name and address prior to arrest when caught in the commission of an offence.

[38]  The notion of "found committing" or "within his view" is not unknown. The
concept has been resorted to on occasion to give a power of arrest where the offence
is committed in the presence of the arrester. But even here the application of the
concept is not without problems. In an article by D.A. Thomas, "Arrest: a General
View," [1966] Crim. L.R. 639 at 645, the following appears:

> The difficulty with this formula is two fold—first, there has been no consistency in the
> judicial approach to the interpretation of the section, courts holding variously that rea-
> sonable suspicion that an offence has been committed is sufficient, or that in fact the
> arrested person must be guilty to justify the arrest. The second problem is that to con-
> fine the power in this way deprives the officer of a power in many situations where it is
> necessary to arrest, for no apparent reason. Thus a person who, having caused an acci-
> dent by his dangerous driving, refuses to stop, cannot be arrested unless the accident
> has actually been witnessed by the officer. It seems equally absurd that a person who
> throws a brick through a shop window can be arrested if the officer sees him do it, but
> not if the officer is around the corner and hearing the crash of the glass, sees the of-
> fender, perhaps the only possible culprit, or if the offence is witnessed by a private
> person who calls the police.

Although the idea of "within his view" has been applied to arrests, its application in
relation to a duty to disclose identity is novel and bizarre. It runs counter to all authority. The right to remain silent, enunciated in *Rice v. Connolly*, supra, does not
admit of such erosion. There is nothing in the language or in the facts of that case to
suggest that the broad principle ceased to have application in the event of a police
officer witnessing an infraction.

[39]  A limited obligation to respond, effective only when the policeman is an
eye-witness, introduces into the criminal law, which should rest upon "broad, plain,
intelligible" principles, a qualification unsound in principle and unworkable in
practice.

[40]  The fact that a police officer has a duty to identify a person suspected of or
seen committing an offence says nothing about whether the person has the duty to
identify himself on being asked. Each duty is entirely independent. Only if the police
have a lawful claim to demand that a person identify himself does the person have a
corresponding duty to do so. As McFarlane J.A. said in *R. v. Bonnycastle*, 68 W.W.R.
407 at 409, 7 C.R.N.S. 37, [1969] 4 C.C.C. 198 (B.C. C.A.):

> The duty of a peace officer to make inquiries must not be confused with the right of a
> person to refuse to answer questions in circumstances where the law does not require
> him to answer.

[41]  The legislature deliberately imposed a duty to identify upon the drivers of
motor vehicles—perhaps because of their more lethal nature—but chose not to impose such a duty on the drivers of other vehicles, such as bicycles. The legislature
must be taken to have intended to relieve bicycle riders of the duty. To require the
riders of bicycles to give their names and addresses would be tantamount to amend-

ing the Motor-vehicle Act. It would also appear that Parliament, in providing in ss. 450(2) and 452(1)(f)(i) [re-en. 1970, c. 2 (2nd Supp.), s. 5] of the Criminal Code for arrest and detention for the purpose of establishing identity, did not recognize a duty to identify oneself existing apart from statute, breach of which would expose the offender to a charge of "obstructing." Examples from English legislation of statutory obligation to disclose identity to police constables, unnecessary if the obligation existed otherwise, are to be found in the Protection of Birds Act, 1954 (U.K.), c. 30, s. 12(1)(a); the Dangerous Drugs Act, 1965 (U.K.), c. 15, s. 15; the Representation of the People Act, 1949 (U.K.), c. 68, s. 84(3); the Road Traffic Act, 1960 (U.K.), c. 16, s. 228; and the Prevention of Crime Act, 1953 (U.K.), c. 14, s. 1(3).

[42] The criminal law is no place within which to introduce implied duties, unknown to statute and common law, breach of which subjects a person to arrest and imprisonment. ...

[45] I would allow the appeal, set aside the judgment of the Court of Appeal and restore the judgment at trial.

## R. v. Thornton
### Ontario Court of Appeal
### (1991) 3 C.R. (4th) 381

GALLIGAN J.A.:

[1] The presence in a person's blood of antibodies to Human Immunodeficiency Virus ("HIV") indicates that the person is probably infected with Acquired Immune Deficiency Syndrome ("AIDS"). AIDS is a grave illness which is usually fatal. It is infectious and particularly contagious through the blood.

[2] All of this is now well known. The appellant knew it in November 1987. In fact, he was well-informed about AIDS and its means of transmission. He knew as well that he was a member of a group which was highly at risk of contracting AIDS. Moreover, he knew that he had twice tested positive for HIV antibodies and that he was therefore infectious. He knew that the Canadian Red Cross collected blood for transfusion to persons in need of it, and that AIDS is transmitted by blood. He also knew that the Red Cross would not knowingly accept donations of blood from persons who had tested positive to HIV antibodies or who were members of his high-risk group. Nevertheless, on November 16, 1987, he donated blood to the Red Cross at a clinic in Ottawa. Fortunately, the Red Cross's screening process detected the contaminated blood and it was put aside.

[3] The appellant was charged with an offence contrary to s. 176(a) of the *Criminal Code* of Canada, R.S.C., c. C-34. That provision is now s. 180 and in these reasons for judgment reference will be made to the present provision. It was charged that he:

> [O]n or about the 16th day of November, 1987, at the City of Ottawa in the said Judicial District did commit a common nuisance endangering the lives or health of the public by donating to the Canadian Red Cross Society a quantity of his blood knowing that his

blood had previously been found to contain antibodies to Human Immunodeficiency
Virus and intentionally withholding the information from the Canadian Red Cross Society, contrary to Section 176(a) of the Criminal Code of Canada.

He was convicted of the charge by Flanigan J., sitting without a jury, and sentenced
to a term of 15 months' imprisonment. He appeals both his conviction and his
sentence.

[4] Counsel for the appellant attacked the conviction on three grounds:

1. That reprehensible as the appellant's conduct may have been, it did not amount
   to an offence known to the law.

2. That it was not proved that his conduct endangered the lives or health of the
   public or any member of it.

3. That the appellant did not have the necessary mens rea.

[5] The provisions of s. 180 of the Code are:

> 180.(1) Every one who commits a common nuisance and thereby
>    (a) endangers the lives, safety or health of the public, or
>    (b) causes physical injury to any person,
> is guilty of an indictable offence and liable to imprisonment for a term not exceeding
> two years.
>    (2) For the purposes of this section, every one commits a common nuisance who
> does an unlawful act or fails to discharge a legal duty and thereby
>    (a) endangers the lives, safety, health, property or comfort of the public; or
>    (b) obstructs the public in the exercise or enjoyment of any right that is common
> to all the subjects of Her Majesty in Canada.

[6] I will deal first with the argument that the appellant's conduct did not amount
to an offence known to law. If, in the circumstances, the appellant's act of donating
blood which he knew was HIV contaminated to the Red Cross was neither an unlawful act nor a failure to discharge a legal duty, then the indictment does not allege an
offence known to law.

[7] Section 180(2)(a) provides that a common nuisance is committed by either
the doing of an unlawful act, or the failure to discharge a legal duty which endangers
the lives or health of the public. For the purposes of this appeal, I am prepared to
assume the correctness of Mr. Greenspon's cogent argument that the words "unlawful act" must be taken to mean conduct which is specifically proscribed by legislation. The Code does not make it an offence to donate contaminated blood. Counsel
were unable to refer the Court to any other statutory provision, federal or provincial,
which does so. On the assumption, therefore, that the appellant's conduct could not
constitute an "unlawful act," I will examine whether it amounted to a failure to discharge a "legal duty."

[8] I am unable to find any provision in the Code, or any other statute which I can
read, as specifically imposing a legal duty upon a person to refrain from donating
contaminated blood. The immediate issue therefore is two-fold. Can a "legal duty"

within the meaning of s. 180(2) be one which arises at common law, or must it be one found in a statute? Is there a "legal duty" arising at common law the breach of which, assuming the other essential elements of the offence were proved, could be the basis of an offence under s. 180?

[9] There are no cases deciding whether the "legal duty" in s. 180(2) must be a duty imposed by statute or whether it can be a duty according to common law. However, the "duty imposed by law" which forms part of the definition of criminal negligence set out in s. 219 of the Code has been held to be either a duty imposed by statute or a duty arising at common law. The provisions of s. 219 are as follows:

> 219.(1) Every one is criminally negligent who
>> (a) in doing anything, or
>> (b) in omitting to do anything that it is his duty to do,
> shows wanton or reckless disregard for the lives or safety of other persons.
>> (2) For the purposes of this section, "duty" means a duty imposed by law.

[10] In *R. v. Coyne* (1958), 31 C.R. 335, 124 C.C.C. 176, the New Brunswick Supreme Court, Appeal Division, considered the criminal negligence provisions of the Code in relation to a hunting accident. Speaking for that Court, Ritchie J.A. held at pp. 179-180 [C.C.C., p. 338 C.R.]:

> The "duty imposed by law" may be a duty arising by virtue of either the common law or by statute. Use of a firearm, in the absence of proper caution, may readily endanger the lives or safety of others. Under the common law anyone carrying such a dangerous weapon as a rifle is under the duty to take such precaution in its use as, in the circumstances, would be observed by a reasonably careful man. If he fails in that duty and his behaviour is of such a character as to show or display a wanton or reckless disregard for the lives or safety of other persons, then, by virtue of s. 191, his conduct amounts to criminal negligence.

[11] In *R. v. Popen* (1981), 60 C.C.C. (2d) 232, this Court also had occasion to consider the nature of the "duty imposed by law" contained in the definition of criminal negligence. It was a child abuse case. In giving the judgment of the Court, Martin J.A. said at p. 240:

> [A] parent is under a legal duty at common law to take reasonable steps to protect his or her child from illegal violence used by the other parent or by a third person towards the child which the parent foresees or ought to foresee.

The effect of that judgment is to hold that the common law duty, which was there described, was a "duty imposed by law" within the meaning of s. 219 because the Court held that its breach could amount to criminal negligence.

[12] These decisions lead me to the opinion that it is well settled that, for the purpose of defining criminal negligence, a "duty imposed by law" includes a duty which arises at common law.

[13] While the words "legal duty" in s. 180(2) are not the same as a "duty imposed by law" used in s. 219, they have exactly the same meaning. It follows therefore that the meaning given to a "duty imposed by law" in s. 219 should also be given

to the "legal duty" contained in s. 180(2). Thus, I am of the opinion that the legal duty referred to in s. 180(2) is a duty which is imposed by statute or which arises at common law. It becomes necessary, then, to decide whether at common law there is a duty which would prohibit the donating of blood known to be HIV contaminated to the Red Cross.

[14]   While this is not a civil case and the principles of tort law are not directly applicable to it, the jurisprudence on that subject is replete with discussions about the legal duties of one person to another which arise at common law. The jurisprudence is constant that those duties are legal ones: that is, they are ones which are imposed by law. Throughout this century and indeed since much earlier times, the common law has recognized a very fundamental duty, which while it has many qualifications, can be summed up as being a duty to refrain from conduct which could cause injury to another person.

[15]   This is not the place to make a detailed examination of the jurisprudence on the subject of tort law but a few references to authority are in order. In *La Lievre and Dennes v. Gould*, [1893] 1 Q.B. 491 (C.A.), after a reference to *Heaven v. Pender* (1883), 11 Q.B.D. 503, [1881-5] All E.R. Rep. 35 (C.A.), Lord Esher M.R. said at p. 497:

> That case established that, under certain circumstances, one man may owe a duty to another, even though there is no contract between them. If one man is near to another, or is near to the property of another, *a duty lies upon him not to do that which may cause a person injury to that other*, or may injure his property. [Emphasis added.]

[16]   In the course of his oft-quoted speech in the famous case of *M'Alister (or Donoghue) v. Stevenson*, [1932] A.C. 562, (sub nom. *Donoghue (or M'Alister v. Stevenson)*, [1932] All E.R. Rep. 1 (H.L.) Lord Atkin said at p. 580:

The rule that you are to love your neighbour becomes in law, you must not injure your neighbour.

[17]   The editors of *Bevan on Negligence*, 4th ed., vol. 1 at p. 8, have described the fundamental common law duty of one person toward another and the rationale for it:

> Before the law every man is entitled to the enjoyment of unfettered freedom so long as his conduct does not interfere with the equal liberty of all others. Where one man's sphere of activity impinges on another man's, a conflict of interests arises. The debateable land where these collisions may occur is taken possession of by the law, which lays down the rules of mutual intercourse. A liberty of action which is allowed therein is called a right, the obligation of restraint a duty, and these terms are purely relative, each implying the other. Duty, then, as a legal term indicates the obligation to limit freedom of action and to conform to a prescribed course of conduct. *The widest generalisation of duty is that each citizen "must do no act to injury another."* [Emphasis added.]

The authority which the editors give for their quoted statement of the duty is the judgment of Bramwell L.J. in *Foulkes v. Metropolitan District Ry. Co.* (1880), 5 C.P.D. 157 (C.A.).

[18] That brief reference to jurisprudence in civil matters shows that there is deeply embedded in the common law a broad fundamental duty which, although subject to many qualifications, requires everyone to refrain from conduct which could injure another. It is not necessary to decide in this case how far that duty extends. At the very least, however, it requires everyone to refrain from conduct which it is reasonably foreseeable could cause serious harm to other persons. Accepting, as I have, that a "legal duty" within the meaning of that term in s. 180(2) includes a duty arising at common law, I think that the common law duty to refrain from conduct which it is reasonably foreseeable could cause serious harm to other persons is a "legal duty" within the meaning of that term in s. 180(2).

[19] Donating blood which one knows to be HIV contaminated, to an organization whose purpose is to make the blood available for transfusion to other persons, clearly constitutes a breach of the common law duty to refrain from conduct which one foresees could cause serious harm to another person. It is thus a failure to discharge a "legal duty" within the contemplation of s. 180(2). It is therefore my conclusion that the indictment which alleges the commission of a nuisance by the donation of blood which the appellant knew to be HIV contaminated does allege an offence known to law. The first argument made by counsel for the appellant cannot be accepted.

[20] Counsel for the Crown referred to a number of cases where, at common law, the courts held that the exposing of others to the risk of becoming infected by a contagious disease constituted a common nuisance. Those cases are: *R. v. Vantandillo* (1815), 4 M. & S. 73, *R. v. Burnett* (1815), 4 M. & S. 272 and *R. v. Henson* (1852), Dears. 24. I have not cited them as authority in this case because s. 9(a) of the Code abolishes common law offences. They are, however, very helpful for two reasons. The first is they seem to be based upon the fundamental duty recognized by the common law to refrain from conduct which one can foresee could cause injury to others. The second reason is perhaps a stronger one. It has been said by the editor of *Tremeear's Annotated Criminal Code*, 6th ed. (Toronto: Carswell 1964) at p. 241 that the statutory definition of a common nuisance contained in the Code "does not differ from a criminal common nuisance at common law." Those cases show that the conduct of donating blood known to be HIV contaminated, if it exposed others to the risk of infection, is conduct very similar to that which the law has recognized to be a criminal common nuisance for almost 200 years. Finding that conduct to constitute a common nuisance under s. 180 is consistent with the common law position and does not extend it.

[21] In turn now, consider the appellant's second argument, namely that it was not proved that the donation by the appellant of HIV contaminated blood endangered the lives or health of the public.

[22] In the course of his comprehensive reasons for judgment, Flanigan J. held:

> In the Court's view, upon the facts of this case as set out earlier, the public was in danger from the moment the accused donated his blood on the 16th day of November, 1987. The public, in general, was at risk and the fact that the effective screening by the

Red Cross Society prevented injury or death, is of no assistance in the Court's view to this accused.

[23] There was ample evidence to support that finding. In order to show the magnitude of the risk to which the public was subjected by the conduct of the appellant, I will make brief reference to the evidence. Had it not been detected as contaminated by the screening process, the appellant's blood was destined for what is called "fractionation." That is a process whereby the blood from many individual donors is mixed together in order to produce blood products which then go out to hundreds or thousands of recipients. According to Dr. Gail Rock, the medical director of the Red Cross at Ottawa, the potential consequences of the unit of blood infected with the HIV virus getting into the fractionation process "are quite catastrophic."

[24] Fortunately, the Red Cross screening process is very good. But it is not perfect. The evidence is that the test is 99.3 per cent accurate. There are three reasons why the screening is not perfect. One of the reasons is not applicable in this case. The other two reasons are human error in the laboratory, and failure of the material used in the screening process.

[25] In addition to the risk of infection by recipients of the blood, there is another group of persons who are at risk of infection. They are health-care workers who are called upon to handle contaminated blood. The following question and answer are found in the transcript of Dr. Rock's evidence:

Q. Apart from your concerns, as you expressed about infecting the blood pool, do you have any concerns with respect to staff at the Red Cross Centre who are actually involved in dealing with a donor, or dealing with any blood?

A. Well of course we do have concerns and they are very real concerns because there are reported cases, well documented, of the transmission of AIDS to health care workers through handling blood samples. So any time that the nursing staff and the technologists are required to handle the blood samples which are contaminated, they run the risk of exposure.

[26] Section 180 requires that the conduct of a person "endanger" the lives or health of the public. It does not require actual injury or damage. The word "endanger" does not have any special technical meaning. Among the ordinary meanings of that word are the concepts of exposing someone to danger, harm or risk, or putting someone in danger of something untoward occurring (See Webster's *New World Dictionary*, 2d College ed., p. 461 and the *Shorter Oxford English Dictionary*, 3d ed., vol. 1 (Oxford: Clarendon Press), p. 654). The conduct of the appellant in donating his blood to the Red Cross obviously put potential recipients and health-care workers at risk, or in danger of an untoward happening when he donated his blood.

[27] When the gravity of the potential harm is great—in this case "catastrophic"— the public is endangered even where the risk of harm actually occurring is slight, indeed even if it is minimal. I am therefore of the opinion that Flanigan J. was correct when he held that the public was in danger from the moment the appellant donated his blood. The second argument advanced by the appellant's counsel must fail.

[28]  I now turn to consider his argument that the appellant did not have the mens rea necessary to have found a conviction. It was contended that the offence requires proof that the appellant actually knew of the danger created by his action, and that the trial Judge erroneously applied an objective standard when he decided that the appellant had mens rea.

[29]  I am not convinced that Flanigan J. applied an objective test in this case. His finding respecting mens rea is as follows:

> In my view, by his actions, the accused has shown a rash want of care for the lives of others. *He did this knowing the full consequences of his blood being passed, in any form, to others.* [Emphasis added.]

[30]  He clearly found that the appellant had personal knowledge of the consequences of his blood being passed to others. There was ample evidence to justify this finding. In his evidence, the appellant admitted that he had the following personal knowledge:

1.  That prior to donating his blood on November 16, 1987, he had twice tested positive to HIV antibodies.

2.  That his blood contained antibodies to the HIV virus.

3.  That he was infectious at the time and that his blood must not be transferred to another person by any means.

4.  That the reason the Red Cross collected blood was to give it to other persons.

5.  That, according to Red Cross policies and procedures, he was not permitted to give blood.

6.  That signs and a pamphlet which he had read made it clear that he was not permitted to give blood.

7.  That there was no doubt in his mind that he was not to donate blood.

8.  That he was well informed about AIDS, how it affected a person through the blood and that there was no known cure for it.

[31]  He also admitted that he deliberately withheld from the Red Cross the information that he had tested positive for HIV antibodies and that he was in a high-risk group because he knew that, if he did so, his blood would not be accepted.

[32]  The appellant testified that he donated his blood as a form of blood-letting to get rid of some of the contaminated blood, hoping that it would lessen the odds of his developing the fatal disease. He also said that he thought that the Red Cross screening system was foolproof and that his blood would not get through the system.

[33]  Athena Munroe, a friend of the appellant, testified that in late November or early December 1987, she and the appellant discussed his giving of blood to the Red Cross. During her evidence in-chief, she said:

> Then I discussed with him the seriousness of what would happen if the blood got into the general population and he didn't seem all that concerned about that very much. He

said: "I just wanted to see if I could get away with it. See if I get caught." That was pretty well it. I think we changed the subject after that.

In cross-examination, she gave the following evidence:

Q. At least as far as you were concerned, his understanding was that it, to use your words, more than likely would be screened and he would be caught.

A. More than likely, yes, but not absolutely.

In his evidence the appellant testified that, while that conversation did occur, he was just kidding in what he said to Ms. Munroe.

[34] Ms. Munroe testified that the appellant never told her that he gave blood as a form of blood-letting to help himself. She said that he made this up as a story after the event. The appellant testified that it was true and not made up.

[35] After a careful review of the evidence and of the appropriate factors to be taken into account in assessing the credibility of witnesses, Flanigan J. accepted the evidence of Ms. Munroe over that of the appellant where they were at variance. He also found that the appellant's evidence about blood-letting was concocted and that his explanation was neither true nor could it have reasonably been true.

[36] In the light of the findings of the trial Judge on the issue of credibility, and in the light of all of the other evidence, there can be no doubt that this appellant had personal knowledge that he should not donate his blood, that it was possible for it to get through the testing screen, and that it could cause serious damage to the life and health of members of the public. It follows that he knew that, by giving his blood to the Red Cross, he was endangering the lives and health of other members of the public. It therefore becomes unnecessary to decide whether some lesser form of mens rea could satisfy the requirements of s. 180. This appellant knew personally the danger to which the public was subjected by his donation of blood. He clearly had mens rea. Mr. Greenspon's third argument fails.

[37] It is my opinion that the appellant was properly convicted of the offence under s. 180. Accordingly, I would dismiss the appeal from conviction.

[38] With respect to sentence, the trial Judge did not impose the maximum sentence prescribed by law. The maximum sentence must be reserved for the worst offender committing the worst category of the offence. The sentence imposed took into account that, because of his prior good record, the appellant would not fall into the category of the worst offender. The offence, however, can certainly be categorized as among the worst offences. The appellant's conduct verges on the unspeakable. It cried out for a sentence which would act as a deterrent to others and which would express society's repudiation of what he did. One must have great compassion for this man. He faces a terrible future. Nevertheless, the sentence demonstrates no error in principle and is one that is eminently fit.

[39] While I would allow the application for leave to appeal sentence, I would dismiss the appeal from sentence.

*Appeal dismissed.*

[This case was appealed further to the Supreme Court and dismissed summarily.]

LAMER C.J.C.:

[1] We are all of the view that this appeal fails. Section 216 imposed upon the appellant a duty of care in giving his blood to the Red Cross. This duty of care was breached by not disclosing that his blood contained HIV antibodies. This common nuisance obviously endangered the life, safety and health of the public.

[2] The appeal is dismissed.

---

In *Thornton* the Supreme Court said nothing of common law duties and ruled that the conviction could be sustained on the basis of s. 216 of the Code. Reliance on this provision appears to distort the scope and content of that duty. In *R. v. Cuerrier*, [1998] 2 S.C.R. 371, however, the court created and imposed a duty of disclosure in a manner that resembles the creation of a common law duty. In effect, the court decided that non-disclosure by the accused of his HIV-positive status foreclosed any possibility of a valid consent, thus enforcing a duty of disclosure in some circumstances. There is no doubt room for judicial clarification of legislative uncertainty. It can be argued—and was by McLachlin J.—that the result in *Cuerrier* exceeds that function and is only judicial legislation of a rule concerning valid consent.

Canadian criminal law remains surprisingly unsettled on the duties that might be invoked to establish liability for omissions. As a matter of principle, it seems that such liability should be limited to instances where Parliament, acting under its authority to enact criminal law, has created a statutory duty. Only this is consistent with the abolition of common law crimes and the principle of legality, including the protection against vagueness or overbreadth. Statutory duties enacted by Parliament without reliance on its power over criminal law, and *a fortiori* duties enacted by provincial legislatures, are created for a purpose other than marking the boundary between criminal and non-criminal conduct. A breach of such duties in no way entails criminal sanction and there is no principled basis to say that it should. The only argument would be that breach of a civil (i.e., non-criminal) duty is an unlawful act and as such merits criminal sanction when it causes a result that is prohibited by the criminal law. This might have been acceptable in a unified jurisdiction that allowed for common law crimes but today the case is weak. It would, in theory, allow a prosecution for manslaughter where a tort of civil negligence leads to death.

In our view, criminal liability for non-compliance with legal duties should be restricted to statutory duties enacted by Parliament in reliance on s. 91(27) of the *Constitution Act, 1867*.

### Status

In some offences, the *actus reus* consists essentially of status or some specific state of affairs. Such offences are rare, thankfully, because they come close to punishing a person for what he or she is, rather than for voluntary acts of commission or omission. Nevertheless, there are some status offences in the Code. Vagrancy was one such crime until s. 179(1)(b) was declared void for overbreadth in *R. v. Heywood*, [1994] 3 S.C.R. 761.

*Heywood* is reproduced in chapter 1. Other status offences include being a keeper of a gaming house or bawdy house, being a found-in in such establishment (see ss. 202 and 210), and living off the avails of prostitution (s. 212). Another, nearly the ultimate, would be the offence of being nude in a public place (s. 174).

For an interesting illustration of a status offence, and the difficulties associated with such offences, see *Larsonneur* (1933), 24 Cr. App. R. 74 (C.C.A.). The accused was a French national who was given leave to enter the United Kingdom. Her visa was subsequently revoked, whereupon she went to the Irish Free State. She was ordered deported from the Irish Free State and forcibly returned to England. There she was arrested and charged as being an alien to whom leave to remain had been refused. She was convicted by a jury and that verdict was upheld on appeal. Lord Hewart L.C.J. said that "[s]he was found here and was, therefore, deemed to be in the class of persons whose landing had been prohibited by the Secretary of State, by reason of the fact that she had violated the condition on her passport." That she did not voluntarily enter England from the Irish Free State, and was detained upon her arrival, was no defence. In effect, it might be argued that the accused was convicted in the absence of an *actus reus*. See Clark, "Overmastering Physical Force: R. v. Larsonneur Revisited" (1971-72), 14 *Crim. L.Q.* 413 and Lanham, "Larsonneur Revisited," [1976] *Crim. L.R.* 276.

Parliament considered but rejected the option to create offences of being a member of a criminal organization or a terrorist organization. Instead Parliament created offences of participation in the activities of such organizations.

83.18(1)  Participation in activity of terrorist group

(1)  Every one who knowingly participates in or contributes to, directly or indirectly, any activity of a terrorist group for the purpose of enhancing the ability of any terrorist group to facilitate or carry out a terrorist activity is guilty of an indictable offence and liable to imprisonment for a term not exceeding ten years.

83.18(2)  Prosecution

(2)  An offence may be committed under subsection (1) whether or not

(a)  a terrorist group actually facilitates or carries out a terrorist activity;

(b)  the participation or contribution of the accused actually enhances the ability of a terrorist group to facilitate or carry out a terrorist activity; or

(c)  the accused knows the specific nature of any terrorist activity that may be facilitated or carried out by a terrorist group.

83.18(3)  Meaning of participating or contributing

(3)  Participating in or contributing to an activity of a terrorist group includes

(a)  providing, receiving or recruiting a person to receive training;

(b)  providing or offering to provide a skill or an expertise for the benefit of, at the direction of or in association with a terrorist group;

(c)  recruiting a person in order to facilitate or commit

(i)  a terrorism offence, or

(ii)  an act or omission outside Canada that, if committed in Canada, would be a terrorism offence;

(d) entering or remaining in any country for the benefit of, at the direction of or in association with a terrorist group; and

(e) making oneself, in response to instructions from any of the persons who constitute a terrorist group, available to facilitate or commit

(i) a terrorism offence, or

(ii) an act or omission outside Canada that, if committed in Canada, would be a terrorism offence.

83.18(4) Factors

(4) In determining whether an accused participates in or contributes to any activity of a terrorist group, the court may consider, among other factors, whether the accused

(a) uses a name, word, symbol or other representation that identifies, or is associated with, the terrorist group;

(b) frequently associates with any of the persons who constitute the terrorist group;

(c) receives any benefit from the terrorist group; or

(d) repeatedly engages in activities at the instruction of any of the persons who constitute the terrorist group.

467.11(1) Participation in activities of criminal organization

(1) Every person who, for the purpose of enhancing the ability of a criminal organization to facilitate or commit an indictable offence under this or any other Act of Parliament, knowingly, by act or omission, participates in or contributes to any activity of the criminal organization is guilty of an indictable offence and liable to imprisonment for a term not exceeding five years.

The remaining subsections of s. 467.11 are the same in principle as ss. 83.18(2) to (4). Are these offences sufficiently different from status offences to alleviate concerns about excessive discretion and possible unfairness?

Another category of offence that can be viewed as a form of liability for status or states of affairs are offences of possession because they are concerned essentially with the relationship between people and things around them. Actual possession rarely raises conceptual difficulties but constructive possession requires attention.

**R. v. Terrence**
Supreme Court of Canada
[1983] 1 S.C.R. 357

RITCHIE J. (for the Court):

[1] This is an appeal brought with leave of this court at the instance of the Attorney General of Ontario, pursuant to s. 621(1)(b) of the Criminal Code, R.S.C. 1970, c. C-34, from a judgment of the Court of Appeal for Ontario [17 C.R. (3d) 390, 47 N.R. 13] whereby that court allowed the appeal and quashed the conviction of the accused entered at trial before Megginson Prov. J. in the Ontario Provincial Court (Criminal Division) for the county of Frontenac, Ontario, on a charge that he:

... on or about the 30th day of January, 1980 at the Township of Kingston and elsewhere in the County of Frontenac, unlawfully did have in his possession one 1980
Chevrolet automobile, of a value exceeding $200.00, the property of Trudeau Motors,
Belleville, Ontario which had been theretofore obtained by a person unknown by an
offence committed in Canada punishable on indictment, to wit: theft, the said Kelly
Brett Terrence, then knowing the said automobile to have been so obtained and did
thereby commit an indictable offence, contrary to section 313(a) [re-en. 1974-75-76,
c. 93, s. 30] of the Criminal Code of Canada.

[2]  The important question raised by this appeal relates to the true meaning to be
attached to the word "possession" as the same occurs in the context of s. 3(4)(b) of
the Criminal Code and more particularly whether "possession" as there employed
imports control as an essential element. Section 3(4)(b) reads as follows:

(4)  For the purposes of this Act ...
    (b)  where one of two or more persons, with the knowledge and consent of the
    rest, has anything in his custody or possession, it shall be deemed to be in the cus-
    tody and possession of each and all of them.

[3]  The only evidence in the record of this appeal which is in any way descriptive
of the manner in which the respondent first became aware of the existence of the
automobile in question is the evidence of the respondent himself, which is, in my
view, accurately summarized in the judgment of MacKinnon A.C.J.O. at pp. 391-92
of the case on appeal herein as follows:

The 17-year-old appellant testified at his trial. His evidence was that Bill Rorback,
Rorback's brother and one Rick Hayes lived across the street from him in Belleville.
He often went across to visit after dinner and he had done so on the evening of 29th
January 1980. When he arrived, Rick Hayes was not present, and the appellant and the
two Rorbacks watched television. At about midnight Hayes drove up to the front of the
house in a new Camaro automobile and asked if anybody wanted to go for a ride in his
"brother-in-law's new car." The appellant said, "Sure!" and went with Hayes.

According to the appellant's evidence, Hayes and the appellant drove around town
for three-quarters of an hour or so and then started east along Highway 401 towards
Kingston. It was established that the Camaro had in fact been recently stolen and the
licence plates it carried had recently been stolen from another Camaro in Belleville.
The appellant knew that Hayes did not own his own motor vehicle, but Hayes had on
previous occasions borrowed his brother-in-law's car, which the appellant described as
"an old junker." He thought that it was probably time for Hayes' brother-in-law to acquire a new car and, as Hayes had the keys to the car, he had no suspicion at the time
that the car was stolen.

Hayes turned onto Highway 2 around Napanee and shortly thereafter an Ontario
Provincial Police ("O.P.P.") cruiser gave chase. Constable Mallock testified that the
stolen vehicle, on being pursued, increased its speed to 150 kilometres per hour, although the appellant's evidence was that the vehicle did not speed up but rather continued at a constant pace. The car was finally stopped by an O.P.P. roadblock some time
shortly after 2:30 a.m. The Camaro pulled over to the shoulder and was apparently

slowing down to a stop when the appellant jumped from the moving vehicle, rolled onto the shoulder and ran into the adjoining field. The Camaro collided with a cruiser and then came to a stop ...

[4] As I have indicated, this was the account given by the respondent, and it remains uncontradicted by any direct evidence; it accordingly appears to me that the only basis for doubting the accuracy of this account was the repeated assertion by the trial judge that he "utterly" disbelieved it.

[5] There is no doubt about the fact that the vehicle had been stolen from a garage in Belleville and indeed there was evidence to the effect that the theft occurred on the very night when the respondent accepted the invitation from Hayes to go for a ride "in his brother-in-law's car." It was this latter circumstance which permitted the trial judge to say:

> ... this car was as hot as a car could be, having been taken by someone during the same night ...

[6] There was, as I have said, no direct evidence to contradict the respondent's version of what occurred, but it is evident from his somewhat acid comments that the judge's finding of his "possession" is in great measure based on his disbelief of the respondent and it is apparent that the judge proceeded on the assumption that the respondent's knowledge of the stolen character of the vehicle was a proven fact.

[7] Based on the assumption that the respondent knew the car to be stolen property, the trial judge went on [quoted at p. 393] to find that:

> Even if the accused was not the operator of the vehicle and in that sense had the control of it, if the person who had control of the vehicle had it with his knowledge and consent and he was in the vehicle as well, in my view that is sufficient to found the necessary conditions to constitute constructive possession under s. 3(4)(b) of the Criminal Code as defined.

[8] In allowing the appeal and quashing the conviction entered at trial, the Court of Appeal for Ontario declined to follow the reasoning of the trial judge, and it is their disagreement as to "the constituent and essential elements of 'possession'" [p. 391] under s. 3(4)(b) that has given rise to this appeal, as can be seen from the grounds upon which application was made to this court for leave to appeal:

(1) That the Court of Appeal for the Province of Ontario erred in law in holding that a constituent and essential element of possession under section 3(4)(b) of the Criminal Code is a measure of control on the part of the person deemed to be in possession by that provision of the Criminal Code.

(2) That the Court of Appeal for the Province of Ontario erred in law in holding that a passenger in a stolen automobile which he knows to be stolen is not pursuant to section 3(4)(b) of the Criminal Code in possession of that vehicle where the Crown proves:

(a) possession of an object by another person;

(b)  the accused's knowledge of this other person's possession of the object; and

(c)  the accused's consent to the other person's possession of the object.

[9]  It will be seen that the second ground of appeal is predicated on it having been proved that the "passenger" knew the automobile to have been stolen and in this connection I think it well to reiterate the fact that there is absolutely no direct evidence to support such an assumption, which is denied by the respondent, who also states that he first knew of the theft when the O.P.P. chase began on the highway and the stolen car was finally being brought to a halt, although the respondent had jumped to the highway while it was still moving.

[10]  The ratio decidendi of the trial judge's decision is to be found in the following excerpt:

> I utterly disbelieved the explanation for recent possession of stolen goods, having found the accused in possession in the other case. I utterly disbelieve the explanation tendered and on the authority of the *Proudlock* case [*R. v. Proudlock*, [1979] 1 S.C.R. 525, 5 C.R. (3d) 21, [1978] 6 W.W.R. 357, 43 C.C.C. (2d) 321, 91 D.L.R. (3d) 449, 24 N.R. 199] that leaves me in the position where there simply is no evidence before me to explain the possession. That leaves you with the doctrine of recent possession, which says that from the fact of the accused's possession of recently stolen goods the court may infer at the lower level that he was in possession with the knowledge of their stolen origin; at the higher level, where the recency of possession in the circumstances warrant, that he was the thief or one of the thieves. In this case, on all of the evidence, and utterly having disbelieved the defence evidence adduced, I am left with the operation of the fact of possession of recently stolen goods and the inferences fairly to be drawn therefrom, and I infer beyond any reasonable doubt in my mind that Mr. Terrence was a knowing participant in the events of that night relating to the vehicle and its licence plates from the beginning. There will be a finding of guilt.

[11]  The *Proudlock* case is authority for the proposition that evidence which is disbelieved by the trier of fact is not "evidence to the contrary" within the meaning of subs. (2)(a) of s. 306 of the Criminal Code and it has little bearing on the central question raised by this appeal, namely, whether the Crown has proved beyond a reasonable doubt that the respondent was in fact in "possession" of the car within the meaning of s. 3(4)(b).

[12]  In the course of his reasons for judgment rendered on behalf of the Court of Appeal, MacKinnon A.C.J.O. reviewed the relevant cases concerning the ingredients of possession under s. 3(4)(b) of the Criminal Code and concluded that in order to establish "possession" under that section it was necessary that there should be evidence of control on the part of the accused. In the course of these reasons he said [p. 399]:

> In my view, on the proven facts the necessary measure of control was not established beyond a reasonable doubt by the Crown, nor do those facts allow for the invocation of s. 21. If, by way of example only, it were established that the appellant had directed Hayes to drive to Kingston, that, in light of all the other proven facts, would, in my

view, satisfy the requirement of some measure of control over the car. If, by way of further example, he had been seen handing the stolen licence plates to Hayes for them to be placed on the motor vehicle, that, once again in my view, would be sufficient to warrant the application of s. 21 and to establish constructive possession of the car by the appellant.

[13]  Section 21 of the Criminal Code defines the meaning of "parties" to an of-fence and involves the question of common intention. It will be remembered that in the present case there is no suggestion that the respondent participated in any way in the actual theft of the car by an unknown person, which took place some time before he was invited to drive in it, and there is nothing to support a finding of common intention in relation to the offence of "possession" with which the respondent is here charged.

[14]  The Court of Appeal had reference to the case of *R. v. Lou Hay Hung*, [1946] O.R. 187, 1 C.R. 274, 85 C.C.C. 308, [1946] 3 D.L.R. 111, which was a decision of its own court concerned with a charge under the Opium and Narcotic Drug Act, 1929 (Can.), c. 49, and in which Roach J.A. in the course of his reasons for judgment referred to and quoted s. 5(2) of the Criminal Code, R.S.C. 1927, c. 36, the predeces-sor of s. 3(4)(b), in the following terms at p. 321:

> Under s. 5(2), both "knowledge" and "consent" are necessary. I have already stated that, in my opinion, there is no doubt that the appellant knew that the accused Watson had opium in the premises. I have been more than a little concerned with the question whether or not, on the evidence, it should be held that he also consented.

[15]  In the same set of reasons, Roach J.A. referred to the judgment of O'Halloran J.A. in *R. v. Colvin*, 58 B.C.R. 204, [1942] 3 W.W.R. 465, 78 C.C.C. 282, [1943] 1 D.L.R. 20 (C.A.), where he said at p. 25:

> The "knowledge and consent" which is an integral element of joint possession in s. 5(2) must be related to and read with the definition of "possession" in the previous s. 5(1)(b). It follows that "knowledge and consent" cannot exist without the co-existence of some measure of control over the subject-matter. If there is the power to consent there is equally the power to refuse and vice versa. They each signify the existence of some power or authority which is here called control, without which the need for their exer-cise could not arise or be invoked.

[16]  In the course of the reasons for judgment rendered by MacKinnon A.C.J.O. on behalf of the Court of Appeal in the present case, he had occasion to say [p. 396] of the above passage from O'Halloran J.A.'s judgment:

> The judgment of O'Halloran J.A. in *Colvin*, supra, the relevant passage of which for our purposes being the one quoted by Roach J.A. to the effect that "'knowledge and consent' cannot exist without the co-existence of some measure of control over the subject-matter," has been followed by British Columbia courts in subsequent decisions: *R. v. Sherman*, 62 B.C.R. 241, 1 C.R. 153, [1946] 1 W.W.R. 479 (C.A.); *R. v. Bunyon* (1954), 110 C.C.C. 119 (C.A.); *R. v. Dick* (1969), 7 C.R.N.S. 75, 68 W.W.R. 437 (C.A.); *R. v. Baker*, [1976] W.W.D. 132 (C.A.).

[17]  The courts in Quebec have adopted the same reasoning, as will be seen by reference to *Sigouin v. R.*, 43 C.R. 211, [1966] 1 C.C.C. 235 (C.A.), and *R. v. Fournier* (1978), 43 C.C.C. (2d) 468 (C.A.).

[18]  As I have indicated, I agree with the Court of Appeal that a constituent and essential element of possession under s. 3(4)(b) of the Criminal Code is a measure of control on the part of the person deemed to be in possession by that provision of the Criminal Code, and accordingly I do not consider that the Court of Appeal for the province of Ontario erred in this regard.

[19]  As to the second ground of appeal, it appears to me to be implicit in the manner in which it is stated that the respondent knew the automobile to be stolen and, as I do not find any evidence to justify this conclusion, I do not think that the question arises in the present case.

[20]  For all these reasons, I would dismiss this appeal.

*Appeal dismissed.*

## IV. CIRCUMSTANCES

It was said earlier that the *actus reus* is in large measure the "verb" in the definition of criminal conduct. This is true of the central element of conduct but there is more to the definition of the *actus reus*. It is commonplace for the legislature to include specific circumstances among the elements of an offence. Wherever there are such elements, they are as much part of the *actus reus* as the element of voluntary conduct and failure by the Crown to prove such circumstances will lead to acquittal on the charge.

Examples can be found almost at random, but a critical point in the interpretation of offences is to identify what circumstances, if any, are essential elements. In a case of abduction in violation of a valid custody order, the existence of a valid order must be proved. Where the charge is sexual interference with a person under fourteen years, the age of the complainant must be proved. Assault of a police officer requires proof that the person assaulted was a police officer. Impaired operation of a motor vehicle requires proof that the accused had care and control of the vehicle. And so on. Often the circumstances in question present little difficulty, while others can be more challenging. A common issue, arising in all forms of assault, is the absence of consent.

Statutory definitions are sometimes provided to assist in clarifying relevant circumstances that might otherwise be ambiguous in large or small measure. Several of these can be found in the general section on definitions (s. 2 of the Code) and others can be found elsewhere. Some circumstantial aspects of the *actus reus* might be clarified only through judicial interpretation.

For purposes of illustration, consider the following provisions of the Code and identify the relevant circumstances that form part of the *actus reus*.

249(1)  Dangerous operation of motor vehicles, vessels and aircraft

    (1)  Every one commits an offence who operates

        (a)  a motor vehicle in a manner that is dangerous to the public, having regard to all the circumstances, including the nature, condition and use of the place at which the motor vehicle is being operated and the amount of traffic that at the time is or might reasonably be expected to be at that place;

(b) a vessel or any water skis, surf-board, water sled or other towed object on or over any of the internal waters of Canada or the territorial sea of Canada, in a manner that is dangerous to the public, having regard to all the circumstances, including the nature and condition of those waters or sea and the use that at the time is or might reasonably be expected to be made of those waters or sea;

(c) an aircraft in a manner that is dangerous to the public, having regard to all the circumstances, including the nature and condition of that aircraft or the place or air space in or through which the aircraft is operated; or

(d) railway equipment in a manner that is dangerous to the public, having regard to all the circumstances, including the nature and condition of the equipment or the place in or through which the equipment is operated.

249(2)  Punishment

(2)  Every one who commits an offence under subsection (1)

(a) is guilty of an indictable offence and liable to imprisonment for a term not exceeding five years; or

(b) is guilty of an offence punishable on summary conviction.

249(3)  Dangerous operation causing bodily harm

(3)  Every one who commits an offence under subsection (1) and thereby causes bodily harm to any other person is guilty of an indictable offence and liable to imprisonment for a term not exceeding ten years.

249(4)  Dangerous operation causing death

(4)  Every one who commits an offence under subsection (1) and thereby causes the death of any other person is guilty of an indictable offence and liable to imprisonment for a term not exceeding fourteen years.

249.1(1)  Flight

(1)  Every one commits an offence who, operating a motor vehicle while being pursued by a peace officer operating a motor vehicle, fails, without reasonable excuse and in order to evade the peace officer, to stop the vehicle as soon as is reasonable in the circumstances.

249.1(2)  Punishment

(2)  Every one who commits an offence under subsection (1)

(a) is guilty of an indictable offence and liable to imprisonment for a term not exceeding five years; or

(b) is guilty of an offence punishable on summary conviction.

249.1(3)  Flight causing bodily harm or death

(3)  Every one commits an offence who causes bodily harm to or the death of another person by operating a motor vehicle in a manner described in paragraph 249(1)(a), if the person operating the motor vehicle was being pursued by a peace officer operating a motor vehicle and failed, without reasonable excuse and in order to evade the police officer, to stop the vehicle as soon as is reasonable in the circumstances.

249.1(4)  Punishment

(4)  Every person who commits an offence under subsection (3)

(a)  if bodily harm was caused, is guilty of an indictable offence and liable to imprisonment for a term not exceeding 14 years; and

(b)  if death was caused, is guilty of an indictable offence and liable to imprisonment for life.

265(1)  Assault

(1)  A person commits an assault when

(a)  without the consent of another person, he applies force intentionally to that other person, directly or indirectly;

(b)  he attempts or threatens, by an act or a gesture, to apply force to another person, if he has, or causes that other person to believe on reasonable grounds that he has, present ability to effect his purpose; or

(c)  while openly wearing or carrying a weapon or an imitation thereof, he accosts or impedes another person or begs.

265(2)  Application

(2)  This section applies to all forms of assault, including sexual assault, sexual assault with a weapon, threats to a third party or causing bodily harm and aggravated sexual assault.

265(3)  Consent

(3)  For the purposes of this section, no consent is obtained where the complainant submits or does not resist by reason of

(a)  the application of force to the complainant or to a person other than the complainant;

(b)  threats or fear of the application of force to the complainant or to a person other than the complainant;

(c)  fraud; or

(d)  the exercise of authority.

265(4)  Accused's belief as to consent

(4)  Where an accused alleges that he believed that the complainant consented to the conduct that is the subject-matter of the charge, a judge, if satisfied that there is sufficient evidence and that, if believed by the jury, the evidence would constitute a defence, shall instruct the jury, when reviewing all the evidence relating to the determination of the honesty of the accused's belief, to consider the presence or absence of reasonable grounds for that belief.

267.  Assault with a weapon or causing bodily harm

Every one who, in committing an assault,

(a)  carries, uses or threatens to use a weapon or an imitation thereof, or

(b)  causes bodily harm to the complainant,

is guilty of an indictable offence and liable to imprisonment for a term not exceeding ten years or an offence punishable on summary conviction and liable to imprisonment for a term not exceeding eighteen months.

268(1) Aggravated assault

(1) Every one commits an aggravated assault who wounds, maims, disfigures or endangers the life of the complainant.

268(2) Punishment

(2) Every one who commits an aggravated assault is guilty of an indictable offence and liable to imprisonment for a term not exceeding fourteen years.

268(3) Excision

(3) For greater certainty, in this section, "wounds" or "maims" includes to excise, infibulate or mutilate, in whole or in part, the labia majora, labia minora or clitoris of a person, except where

(a) a surgical procedure is performed, by a person duly qualified by provincial law to practise medicine, for the benefit of the physical health of the person or for the purpose of that person having normal reproductive functions or normal sexual appearance or function; or

(b) the person is at least eighteen years of age and there is no resulting bodily harm.

268(4) Consent

(4) For the purposes of this section and section 265, no consent to the excision, infibulation or mutilation, in whole or in part, of the labia majora, labia minora or clitoris of a person is valid, except in the cases described in paragraphs (3)(a) and (b).

433. Arson—disregard for human life

Every person who intentionally or recklessly causes damage by fire or explosion to property, whether or not that person owns the property, is guilty of an indictable offence and liable to imprisonment for life where

(a) the person knows that or is reckless with respect to whether the property is inhabited or occupied; or

(b) the fire or explosion causes bodily harm to another person.

434. Arson—damage to property

Every person who intentionally or recklessly causes damage by fire or explosion to property that is not wholly owned by that person is guilty of an indictable offence and liable to imprisonment for a term not exceeding fourteen years.

434.1 Arson—own property

Every person who intentionally or recklessly causes damage by fire or explosion to property that is owned, in whole or in part, by that person is guilty of an indictable offence and liable to imprisonment for a term not exceeding fourteen years, where the fire or explosion seriously threatens the health, safety or property of another person.

435(1) Arson for fraudulent purpose

(1) Every person who, with intent to defraud any other person, causes damage by fire or explosion to property, whether or not that person owns, in whole or in part, the property, is guilty of an indictable offence and liable to imprisonment for a term not exceeding ten years.

435(2)  Holder or beneficiary of fire insurance policy

(2)  Where a person is charged with an offence under subsection (1), the fact that the person was the holder of or was named as a beneficiary under a policy of fire insurance relating to the property in respect of which the offence is alleged to have been committed is a fact from which intent to defraud may be inferred by the court.

436(1)  Arson by negligence

(1)  Every person who owns, in whole or in part, or controls property is guilty of an indictable offence and liable to imprisonment for a term not exceeding five years where, as a result of a marked departure from the standard of care that a reasonably prudent person would use to prevent or control the spread of fires or to prevent explosions, that person is a cause of a fire or explosion in that property that causes bodily harm to another person or damage to property.

436(2)  Non-compliance with prevention laws

(2)  Where a person is charged with an offence under subsection (1), the fact that the person has failed to comply with any law respecting the prevention or control of fires or explosions in the property is a fact from which a marked departure from the standard of care referred to in that subsection may be inferred by the court.

## V. CONSEQUENCES AND CAUSATION

Many offences are defined in a way that they are complete on completion of the act or omission without regard for any specific consequence of the act or omission. Many others include a specific element of causation, such as causing death or bodily harm. Consider, for example, the offence of dangerous driving, which is complete where the manner of driving shows a marked departure from the standard that might be expected in the circumstances. This is distinguishable from dangerous driving causing death or bodily harm, which obviously require proof of those specific results.

As with specific circumstances that might be required by the definition of the offence, offences must be closely scrutinized to ascertain whether they include an element of causation that requires proof of a particular consequence or result. This is usually not difficult to see but some instances are less obvious than others. Homicide requires proof that the act of the accused caused death. An unlawful act causing bodily harm requires proof of some harm that violates bodily integrity that is not trifling. Frightening the sovereign would appear to require proof that Her Majesty, and nobody else (including the governor general), was frightened. Sometimes the result that is prohibited is not a concrete event. It might be a risk, as in fraud, where the actions of the accused jeopardize the pecuniary interests of the victim.

What will suffice to establish a causal connection between conduct and a prohibited consequence?

**Smithers v. The Queen**
Supreme Court of Canada
[1978] 1 S.C.R. 506

DICKSON J.:

[1]  This is an appeal from a judgment of the Court of Appeal for Ontario [9 O.R. (2d) 127, 24 C.C.C. (2d) 344] dismissing an appeal brought by the appellant from his conviction by judge and jury on a charge of manslaughter. The indictment alleges that the appellant did unlawfully kill Barrie Ross Cobby by kicking him.

[2]  On 18th February 1973 a hockey game was played between the Applewood Midget Team and the Cooksville Midget Team at the Cawthra Park Arena in the town of Mississauga. The leading player on the Applewood team was the deceased, Barrie Cobby, 16 years of age; the leading player on the Cooksville team was the appellant. The game was rough, the players were aggressive and feelings ran high. The appellant, who is black, was subject to racial insults by Cobby and other members of the Applewood team. Following a heated and abusive exchange of profanities, both the appellant and Cobby were ejected from the game. The appellant made repeated threats that he was going to "get" Cobby. Cobby was very apprehensive and left the arena at the end of the game, some 45 minutes later, accompanied by eight or ten persons including friends, players, his coach and the team's manager. The appellant repeated his threats and challenges to fight as the group departed. Cobby did not take up the challenge. Instead, he hurried toward a waiting car. The appellant caught up with him at the bottom of the outside steps and directed one or two punches to Cobby's head. Several of Cobby's teammates grabbed the appellant and held him. Cobby, who had taken no steps to defend himself, was observed to double up and stand back while the appellant struggled to free himself from those holding him. While Cobby was thus bent over, and approximately two to four feet from the appellant, the appellant delivered what was described as a hard, fast kick to Cobby's stomach area. Only seconds elapsed between the punching and the kick. Following the kick, Cobby groaned, staggered towards his car, fell to the ground on his back, and gasped for air. Within five minutes he appeared to stop breathing. He was dead upon arrival at the Mississauga General Hospital.

[3]  Dr. David Brunsdon, who performed an autopsy, testified that in his opinion death was due to the aspiration of foreign materials present from vomiting. He defined aspiration as the breathing, or taking in, of foreign material through the windpipe into the lungs. It appears from the medical evidence that aspiration is generally due to barbiturate overdosage, alcohol intoxication, motor vehicle accidents or epilepsy. One medical witness testified as to the possibility of spontaneous aspiration, whereby foreign material may be aspirated without any precipitating cause. This witness had seen three such cases out of the 900 to 1,000 cases of aspiration which he had experienced. In none of the three cases was the aspiration preceded by a blow. The consensus among the doctors was that spontaneous aspiration was a rare and unusual cause of death in the case of a healthy teenager such as Cobby. Normally, when a person vomits the epiglottis folds over to prevent the regurgitated stomach

contents from entering the air passage. In the instant case this protective mechanism failed.

[4] In the Court of Appeal for Ontario three points were raised: (i) whether there was evidence of a causal connection between the kick and the death, upon which the jury was entitled to convict; (ii) whether the verdict was unreasonable; and (iii) whether the charge of the trial judge adequately delineated the essential issues and related the evidence to them. The majority of the court (Evans and Martin JJ.A.) concluded that the issue of causation fell to be determined by the jury on the whole of the evidence, not the medical evidence alone. It was held that the charge, viewed in its totality, was adequate and contained no error in law. Houlden J.A., dissenting, noted that three doctors gave expert medical evidence for the prosecution as to the kick and the vomiting and all three doctors agreed that the kick probably caused the vomiting though they could not positively state that it did. He agreed that there was evidence upon which the jury could find beyond a reasonable doubt that the kick caused Cobby's death, but, in his opinion, the trial judge erred in failing to make clear to the jury that the Crown had to prove beyond a reasonable doubt that the kick caused the vomiting. In his view, by dealing generally with the law concerning man-slaughter, assault and self-defence and then setting out at length the Crown and de-fence theories, the trial judge confused the jury. The judgment of the Ontario Court of Appeal dismissing the appeal specified the point of dissent in these terms: the trial judge failed to [p. 349] "sufficiently delineate the issue as to the cause of death [of the deceased Cobby] and to relate the evidence to that issue."

[5] The ground of dissent in the Ontario Court of Appeal forms the first ground of appeal in this court. Counsel for the appellant submits that the trial judge, in empha-sizing the act of assault as a constituent element in the crime of manslaughter, did not make it clear to the jury that the act of assault must also cause the death of the de-ceased and, secondly, that in giving his summation of the Crown and defence theo-ries, the trial judge referred to the issue of causation as defence counsel's argument that the cause of death had not been proven beyond a reasonable doubt. It is con-tended that the effect of these remarks was to minimize this issue in the minds of the jury. The jury was never instructed, it is said, that as a matter of law one of the issues on which it had to be satisfied beyond a reasonable doubt was that the kick caused the vomiting.

[6] The trial judge commenced the general part of his charge with instruction as to onus of proof, presumption of innocence and reasonable doubt. He moved then to a discussion of circumstantial evidence and related that subject to what he referred to as "an important area, the cause of death," adding, "here no one saw inside Barry Cobby's throat, or stomach or his lungs and here the evidence is circumstantial and indirect." Later in the charge, while discussing intent in relation to manslaughter, the trial judge said:

> Therefore, in this case, if you find the accused acted unlawfully in kicking Cobby and that death resulted therefrom, it is immaterial whether the accused intended, or did not intend, to cause death.

In giving his general directions on the law of manslaughter the trial judge stated:

> ... manslaughter is the causing of death of a human being by an unlawful act, but not an intentional act.

Later he added:

> ... any improper use of force, which is unlawful, if death results, is manslaughter.

The following passage of the charge is attacked by the appellant on the ground that it failed to emphasize that the act of assault must also cause the death of the accused:

> So that one difference between manslaughter and the act of assault is that in manslaughter the intent to kill is not necessary, whereas in assault the intent to apply force is necessary. Because a person commits assault without consent when he applies force intentional to the person of the other, directly or indirectly. So once you have an assault—the unlawful application of force—and a person dies as a result thereof, whether it is intended that he die or not, then you have the crime of manslaughter.

[7] It seems to me that this criticism is unwarranted because the judge stated plainly that in order to constitute the crime of manslaughter there must not only be an assault but a person must die as a result thereof. ...

[21] It is important in considering the issue of causation in homicide to distinguish between causation as a question of fact and causation as a question of law. The factual determination is whether A caused B. The answer to the factual question can only come from the evidence of witnesses. It has nothing to do with intention, foresight or risk. In certain types of homicide jurors need little help from medical experts. Thus if D shoots P or stabs him and death follows within moments, there being no intervening cause, jurors would have little difficulty in resolving the issue of causality from their own experience and knowledge.

[22] Expert evidence is admissible, of course, to establish factual cause. The work of expert witnesses in an issue of this sort, as Glanville Williams has pointed out ("Causation in Homicide," [1957] Crim. L.R. 429 at 431), is "purely diagnostic and does not involve them in metaphysical subtleties"; it does not require them to distinguish between what is a "cause," i.e., a real and contributing cause of death, and what is merely a "condition," i.e., part of the background of the death. Nor should they be expected to say, where two or more causes combine to produce a result, which of these causes contributes the more.

[23] In the case at bar the Crown had the burden of showing factual causation— that beyond a reasonable doubt the kick caused the death. In my view, the trial judge did not err in failing to instruct the jury that in determining that issue they could consider only the medical evidence. The issue of causation is for the jury and not the experts. The weight to be given to the evidence of the experts was entirely for the jury. In the search for truth, the jury was entitled to consider all of the evidence, expert and lay, and accept or reject any part of it. Non-medical testimony is available to both the Crown and the accused, and in the instant case lay evidence was vital to the defence raised by the appellant. That evidence tended to show that all the

circumstances preceding the kick were such as to create in the deceased boy a highly emotional state which might well have given rise to spontaneous vomiting, unassociated with the kick.

[24] The second sub-question raised is whether there was evidence on the basis of which the jury was entitled to find that it had been established beyond a reasonable doubt that the kick caused the death. In answer to this question it may shortly be said that there was a very substantial body of evidence, both expert and lay, before the jury indicating that the kick was at least a contributing cause of death, outside the de minimis range, and that is all that the Crown was required to establish. It is immaterial that the death was in part caused by a malfunctioning epiglottis, to which malfunction the appellant may, or may not, have contributed. No question of remoteness or of incorrect treatment arises in this case.

[25] I should like to adopt two short passages from a case note on *Rex v. Larkin* (1942), 29 Cr. App. R. 18, by G.A. Martin, as he then was, which appeared in (1943), 21 Can. Bar. Rev. 503 at 504-505:

> There are many unlawful acts which are not dangerous in themselves and are not likely to cause injury which, nevertheless, if they cause death, render the actor guilty of culpable homicide, *e.g.*, the most trivial assault, if it should, through some unforeseen weakness in the deceased, cause death, will render the actor guilty of culpable homicide …

> In the case of so-called intentional crimes where death is an unintended consequence the actor is always guilty of manslaughter at least. The act of the accused in *Rex v. Larkin* fell within the class of intentional crimes because he was engaged committing an assault upon Nielsen, and the fact that he caused a different type of harm to that which he intended did not free him from criminal responsibility.

The Crown was under no burden of proving intention to cause death or injury. The only intention necessary was that of delivering the kick to Cobby. Nor was foreseeability in issue. It is no defence to a manslaughter charge that the fatality was not anticipated or that death ordinarily would not result from the unlawful act.

[26] In *Regina v. Cato* (1975), 62 Cr. App. R. 41, the act supporting the manslaughter conviction was the injection by the accused into another person of morphine which the accused had unlawfully taken into his possession. Attention was directed to causation and the link alleged to exist between the injection of morphine and the death. The appellant's argument based on the medical evidence of causation and the rejection of that argument by the Court of Appeal are to be found in the following passage, pp. 44-45:

> First of all, he invited us to look at the evidence of causation, and he pointed out that the medical evidence did not at any point say "This morphine killed Farmer"; the actual link of that kind was not present. The witnesses were hesitant to express such a view and often recoiled from it, saying it was not for them to state the cause of death. It is perfectly true, as Mr. Blom-Cooper says, that the expert evidence did not in positive terms provide a link, but it was never intended to do so. The expert witnesses here spoke to factual situations, and the conclusions and deductions therefrom were for the

jury. The first question was: was there sufficient evidence upon which the jury could
conclude, as they must have concluded, that adequate causation was present?

[27] The third sub-question is whether there was evidence from which the jury
was entitled to find that it had been established beyond a reasonable doubt that the
kick caused the aspiration. It is contended that the burden on the Crown was to prove
beyond a reasonable doubt that the kick caused both the vomiting and the aggravated
condition of aspiration. I do not agree. A person commits homicide, according to
s. 205(1) of the Code, when directly or indirectly, by any means, he causes the death
of a human being. Once evidence had been led concerning the relationship between
the kick and the vomiting, leading to aspiration of stomach contents and asphyxia,
the contributing condition of a malfunctioning epiglottis would not prevent conviction for manslaughter. Death may have been unexpected and the physical reactions of
the victim unforeseen, but that does not relieve the appellant.

[28] In *Regina v. Garforth*, [1954] Crim. L.R. 936, a decision of the Court of
Criminal Appeal of England, the accused, aged 16, and another young man, S., quar-
relled with the deceased, aged 18, outside a dance hall. S. kicked the deceased and
when he doubled up stabbed him in the neck and heart, then the accused kicked him
on the body and legs and S. kicked him on the head. S. was found guilty of murder
and the accused was found guilty of manslaughter. The accused appealed against his
conviction on the grounds that there was no evidence that what he did was a cause of
death. It was held, dismissing the appeal, that there was clear evidence that the accused unlawfully assaulted the deceased and inflicted minor injuries which contributed to the death. Had the jury found that the accused intended to do grievous bodily
harm, he would have been guilty of murder.

[29] It is a well-recognized principle that one who assaults another must take his
victim as he finds him. An extreme example of the application of the principle will be
found in the English case of *Regina v. Blaue*, [1975] 1 W.L.R. 1411, [1975] 3 All E.R.
446, in which the court upheld a conviction for manslaughter where the victim's
wounds were only fatal because of her refusal, on religious grounds, to accept a blood
transfusion. The court rejected the argument that the victim's refusal had broken the
chain of causation between the stabbing and the death.

[30] Although causation in civil cases differs from that in a criminal case, the
"thin skulled man" may appear in the criminal law as in the civil law. The case of *Rex
v. Nicholson* (1926), 47 C.C.C. 113, 59 N.S.R. 323 (C.A.), will serve as an illustration. In that case, the accused dealt the deceased man two heavy blows. The man who
was struck was in poor physical condition. His heart was abnormally small and he
was suffering from Bright's disease. An eminent medical specialist was asked if the
blow or blows could cause death, given the condition of the body which was described, and he said it was possible. The blow might be one of the causes. Overindulgence in alcohol, bad health, and the blow and tussle combined, in his opinion,
to account for the result. The appeal from conviction was dismissed. Even if the unlawful act, alone, would not have caused the death, it was still a legal cause so long as
it contributed in some way to the death. I myself presided at a jury trial in which the
accused, one Alan Canada, following an argument, struck his brother lightly on the

head with a piece of firewood as a result of which the brother died some time later without regaining consciousness. The medical evidence showed that the bony structure of his skull was unusually thin and fragile. The accused, on the advice of counsel, pleaded guilty to a charge of manslaughter and I have never considered that he was wrong in doing so.

[31] I would conclude this point by saying that although Dr. Hillsdon Smith thought that once vomiting had been induced, aspiration in these circumstances was no more than an accident; both Dr. Brunsdon and Dr. Butt acknowledged that the kick may have contributed to the epiglottal malfunction.

[32] That brings me to the third and final ground of appeal, namely, whether the trial judge's charge to the jury on the issue of self-defence amounted to misdirection. Although undoubtedly much upset by the actions and language of Cobby during the first ten minutes of play, thereafter the appellant alone was the aggressor. He relentlessly pursued Cobby some 45 minutes later for the purpose of carrying out his threat to "get" Cobby. Despite the frail factual underpinning for such a defence, the trial judge charged fully on self-defence and in a manner which, in my opinion, was not open to criticism.

[33] I would dismiss the appeal.

### R. v. Cribbin
Ontario Court of Appeal
(1994), 89 C.C.C. (3d) 67

ARBOUR J.A. (for the Court):

[1] The appellant, along with his co-accused Charles Reid, was charged with second degree murder in the death of Dominic Ginell. In the course of the trial, Reid pleaded guilty to second degree murder. The appellant was convicted of manslaughter and he was sentenced to eight years' imprisonment and a ten-year firearm prohibition. He appeals his conviction and alternatively, seeks leave to appeal his sentence.

[2] Counsel for the appellant raised several issues in his factum, some of which he abandoned at the hearing of the appeal. The principal issues raised in the conviction appeal relate to the trial judge's instructions to the jury with respect to party liability and to his instructions on the law of causation. As well, the appellant challenges the constitutionality of the causation test for manslaughter articulated by the Supreme Court of Canada in *R. v. Smithers* (1977), 34 C.C.C. (2d) 427 [40 C.R.N.S. 79].

### *I. Overview of the Facts*

[3] In the early morning hours of July 19, 1989, Dominic Ginell suffered a serious beating to his face, head and body. The beating led to unconsciousness, which was likely deepened by Ginell's consumption of cocaine and alcohol. Although the injuries themselves were not life-threatening, Ginell was abandoned unconscious and

he drowned in his own blood. I will briefly summarize the salient facts which led to the assault, as they relate to the issues raised in this appeal.

[4]  According to his evidence, the appellant met the deceased Ginell at a bar called "My Place." The appellant was there with Pauline Gamarra and Betty Gates. When he went to the washroom, he was approached by a man, Ginell, who offered him what the appellant assumed was cocaine. The appellant declined and, as he was proceeding to leave, the man grabbed him in the genital area. The appellant pushed the man's hand away and told him that he was not homosexual. Ginell subsequently bought the appellant a beer, which the appellant accepted as an apology. Ginell joined the appellant and his friends Gamarra and Gates at their table and eventually the four left the bar together after last call. They went looking for David Simms, a friend of Gates. He wasn't home, but Gates returned a few minutes later with Charles Reid.

[5]  There are some discrepancies in the evidence as to the subsequent events. All five, the appellant, Ginell, Gamarra, Gates and Reid drove to a bootlegger's and bought some beer. A fight erupted between Pauline Gamarra and Betty Gates, and Gamarra went home. The remaining four drove away, with Reid and Ginell in the front and Gates and the appellant in the back of the car. The appellant testified that he thought that they were going to a party and that he had heard nothing about a plan to rob Ginell. The appellant also testified that he had a lot to drink all day and that he and Pauline Gamarra drank approximately 36 beers between mid-morning and four in the afternoon. He continued to drink all evening and considered himself very drunk at that point, although he could remember the subsequent events.

[6]  The car stopped on a deserted road. Everyone got out and took some beer. The appellant testified that Ginell leaned forward and touched him on the shoulder and asked him if he wanted to go for a walk alone in the woods. The appellant said that, as a reflex to this unwanted proposition, he punched Ginell in the cheek and kicked him in the leg. According to the appellant, at this point Reid hit Ginell over the head with a beer bottle. Ginell fell to the ground and Reid punched and kicked Ginell repeatedly, while Gates was screaming for him to stop. The appellant said that he tried to stop Reid but that Reid had just "gone nuts on him." Eventually, Reid pulled something out of Ginell's pocket and ran for the car. Gates and the appellant followed and the three drove away in Ginell's car, with the appellant driving. The appellant admitted that he knew that Ginell was not moving, but said that he did not know that he was bleeding or unconscious. The three went shopping in London and Kitchener, using Ginell's credit cards. They were stopped by the police for a driving offence and after identifying themselves, were allowed to go. The appellant found out about Ginell's death through the newspaper and, after consulting with counsel, he turned himself in.

[7]  In her evidence at trial, Betty Gates said that all she could remember of the assault was Ginell's head hitting the ground. She could remember nothing else, including who hit him. Gates had given both a videotaped statement and a signed written unsworn statement to the police, on the basis of which she was declared to be an adverse witness and was cross-examined by the Crown. Under cross-examination, Gates maintained that she did not remember giving the statements, that they did not refresh her memory, and that they could contain the truth or some lies. In her

videotaped statement, Gates stated that she saw Ginell being beaten by both Reid and Cribbin and that Reid hit the victim first. Although her statements in part confirmed the appellant's testimony, they also, in many respects, implicated him beyond what he admitted in his own testimony. I will return later to the issues related to the use of these prior inconsistent statements. …

### III. Issues Relating to Causation

#### (1) The Sufficiency of the Judge's Instructions

[30] Mr. Nakatsuru, for the appellant, submits that, as the present law stands, the charge to the jury was inadequate in that it failed to provide meaningful assistance to the jury in the determination of whether the appellant's acts could be said to have caused the death of the victim. As indicated earlier, the appellant also challenges the constitutionality of the present law and I will return to this point shortly.

[31] In his reasons for sentence, the trial judge indicted that he interpreted the jury's verdict to mean that they accepted that the appellant had not been involved in the robbery aspect of Ginell's death, and that the jury did take into account the amount of alcohol and drugs that the appellant had consumed that day. The trial judge stated that, based on the pathology evidence, Cribbin was not the person who landed the fatal blows. However, the trial judge remarked that Cribbin gave the first blow, that he was the catalyst for Reid's actions, and that he later tried to intervene to stop Reid.

[32] Counsel for the appellant points to these remarks in support of his contention that there is a real issue as to whether it could be said that Cribbin, by his own actions, caused Ginell's death. The only reference to causation in the judge's instructions to the jury is as follows:

> If the Crown has failed to satisfy you beyond a reasonable doubt *that the assault by the accused contributed to the death of the deceased*, the accused committed culpable homicide, you must find the accused not guilty for he has committed no crime. If the Crown has failed to prove beyond a reasonable doubt *that Cribbin did anything which contributed to the death of Ginell*, then the accused is to be found not guilty and the homicide has not been proved. (Emphasis added.)

[33] Appellant's counsel submits that the jury should have been told that the Crown must prove beyond a reasonable doubt that the assault by the appellant was an operative cause of the deceased's death, and not merely one of the circumstances in which the killing took place. Moreover, counsel contends that the jury should have been instructed that they could only convict if they found that the appellant's assault *substantially* contributed to the death, and that no intervening cause, such as Reid's actions, interrupted the chain of causation linking the appellant's assault to the victim's death.

[34] Mr. Naster, for the Crown, relies on s. 222 of the *Criminal Code* which provides that a person commits homicide if, directly or indirectly, by any means, that person causes the death of a human being. Mr. Naster maintains that the judge's instructions were sufficient to convey to the jury the applicable standard of causation established by the Supreme Court of Canada in *R. v. Smithers*, supra, at pp. 435-36

[C.C.C., pp. 89-90 C.R.]. In that case the court held that any unlawful act that was at least a contributing cause of death outside the *de minimis* range was sufficient to engage criminal responsibility for manslaughter.

[35] Leaving aside for the moment the appellant's contention as to the constitutional inadequacy of the *Smithers* test, I agree with counsel for the Crown that the trial judge was not required to instruct the jury that they could convict only if they found that the appellant's assault substantially contributed to the victim's death. The requirement of "substantial causation," necessary to establish liability for first degree murder under s. 231(5) of the Code, was recently contrasted with the *Smithers* test in *R. v. Harbottle*, supra, where Cory J. said at pp. 323-24:

> Accordingly, I suggest a restrictive test of *substantial* cause should be applied under s. 214(5). That test will take into account the consequences of a conviction, the present wording of the section, its history and its aim to protect society from the most heinous murderers.
>
> The consequences of a conviction for first degree murder and the wording of the section are such that the test of causation for s. 214(5) must be a strict one. In my view, an accused may only be convicted under the subsection if the Crown establishes that the accused has committed an act or series of acts which are of such a nature that they must be regarded as a substantial and integral cause of the death. A case which considered and applied a substantial cause test from Australia is *R. v. Hallett*, [1969] S.A.S.R. 141 (S.C. *in Banco*). In that case, the victim was left beaten and unconscious by the sea and was drowned by the incoming tide. The court formulated the following test of causation, at p. 149, which I find apposite:

> > The question to be asked is whether an act or series of acts (in exceptional cases an omission or series of omissions) consciously performed by the accused is or are so connected with the event that it or they must be regarded as having a sufficiently substantial causal effect which subsisted up to the happening of the event, without being spent or without being in the eyes of the law sufficiently interrupted by some other act or event.

> The substantial causation test requires that the accused play a very active role— usually a physical role—in the killing. Under s. 214(5), the actions of the accused must form an essential, substantial and integral part of the killing of the victim. Obviously, this requirement is much higher than that described in *Smithers v. The Queen*, [1978] 1 S.C.R. 506, which dealt with the offence of manslaughter. There it was held at p. 519 that sufficient causation existed where the actions of the accused were "a contributing cause of death, outside the *de minimis* range." That case demonstrates the distinctions in the degree of causation required for the different homicide offences.

[36] Had the trial judge properly distinguished between Cribbin's potential liability for the homicide as a principal offender, on the basis of his own assault on the deceased, and his potential liability as an accessory to Reid's murder, it would have been unnecessary to burden the jury with distinctions between intervening and supervening causes capable or not, in law, of interrupting the chain of causation. The question of intervening cause would only arise if the jury were to conclude that the

appellant and Reid were truly independent actors, which was a somewhat remote possibility despite the jury's apparent rejection of the robbery theory in so far as Cribbin was concerned. On any realistic view of the facts, Reid and Cribbin were either co-perpetrators or accomplices. If the jury were to reject the appellant's contention that he struck Ginell in self-defence, as this jury obviously did, the appellant's unlawful assault on the victim could hardly be said to be merely part of the history of the setting in which Reid inflicted the fatal blows to Ginell (see *R. v. Smith* (1959), 43 Cr. App. R. 121 (C.A.), at p. 131). The appellant admitted in cross-examination that he had hit the victim with sufficient force that he thought afterwards that his hand was broken. He struck the deceased on the cheek with a closed fist and his hand was still swollen and sore a few days later. He left with the others, abandoning the victim after having witnessed, if not participated in, the vicious attack inflicted by Reid on the deceased immediately after he, Cribbin, had initiated the assault.

[37]  Cribbin's own assaultive acts need not have been the medical cause of death. They were not, and neither were Reid's. The medical cause of death was anoxia. On the facts of this case, it cannot be said that the acts of Reid, which may have been the more immediate and the more severe factor in causing the unconsciousness from which the victim did not recover, operated as a supervening cause such as to insulate the appellant from the legal consequences flowing from Ginell's death. No useful purpose would have been served in instructing the jury further on that point. In my opinion, the charge was sufficient even though it did not invite the jury to examine whether Cribbin's contribution to Ginell's death was beyond the *de minimis* range.

*(2)  The Constitutionality of the Smithers Test*

(a)  Introduction

[38]  The respondent correctly points out that the proper time for raising a constitutional issue of this kind is at trial. If the trial judge had been asked to consider the constitutionality of the *Smithers* test, and had considered it an infringement of s. 7 of the *Charter*, he could have instructed the jury in accordance with the causation standard that the appellant submits is the correct one. However, since this case must be sent back for a new trial, and in light of the helpful and thorough submissions presented to us by both counsel on this appeal, I think it is appropriate to dispose of the appellant's constitutional challenge.

[39]  The appellant submits that the test in *Smithers* sets the causation threshold in homicide so low as to infringe upon the principles of fundamental justice in s. 7 of the *Charter*. In *Smithers*, Dickson J. held that on a charge of manslaughter, all the Crown has to establish is that the assault inflicted upon the victim "was at least a contributing cause of death, outside the *de minimis* range" (p. 435 [C.C.C., p. 90 C.R.N.S.]). Dickson J. added, at p. 436 [C.C.C., p. 90 C.R.N.S.]:

> I should like to adopt two short passages from a case note on *R. v. Larkin* (1942), 29 Cr. App. R. 18, by G.A. Martin, as he then was, which appeared in 21 *Can. Bar. Rev.* 503 at pp. 504-5 (1943):

> There are many unlawful acts which are not dangerous in themselves and are not likely to cause injury which, nevertheless if they cause death, render the actor guilty of culpable homicide, e.g., the most trivial assault, if it should, through some unforeseen weakness in the deceased, cause death, will render the actor guilty of culpable homicide.

In the case of so-called intentional crimes where death is an unintended consequence the actor is always guilty of manslaughter at least. The act of the accused in *R. v. Larkin* fell within the class of intentional crimes because he was engaged in committing an assault upon Nielsen, and the fact that he caused a different type of harm to that which he intended did not free him from criminal responsibility.

[40]  It seems to me that the adoption by the Supreme Court of this passage in a case comment is to be taken as stating only the legal definition of causation and, limited to that, is still valid. The fault element in the crime of manslaughter has now been authoritatively stated to require objective foreseeability of bodily harm which is neither trivial nor transitory, in the context of a dangerous act, such that the most trivial assault, not dangerous in itself and not likely to cause injury would not give rise to a conviction for manslaughter if it did somehow cause death (*R. v. Creighton*, supra). In my opinion, the test articulated in *Smithers* must now be understood in combination with the degree of fault expressed in the requirement of objective foreseeability of death. I will return to this point later when I consider the relation between causation and fault as a basis for the intervention of the criminal law.

[41]  As I understand it, the constitutional argument advanced by the appellant is a two-pronged proposition. First, it is argued that the articulation of a legal causation rule involves a moral judgment as to blameworthiness, rather than a scientific inquiry, and that the principles of fundamental justice require that the rule triggering criminal responsibility, in this case the causation rule, be commensurate with the moral blameworthiness of the conduct that it prohibits. Under this argument, it is said to be unfair to punish for manslaughter one whose moral blameworthiness, reflected by both his conduct and his intention, never went beyond a simple assault. In short, the *de minimis* test is said to be too remote to satisfy the requirements of s. 7. Second, it is argued that the present law defining causation is void for vagueness.

(b)  Is the De Minimis Test Too Vague?

[42]  In my opinion, the vagueness point can be summarily dismissed as the appellant has not demonstrated in what way a different causation test, such as the substantial connection test, the "but-for," or the "*causa causans*" test, to refer only to a few that are well known in the legal literature, would add any precision to the rule such as to give better guidance to citizens as to how to conduct their affairs in order to avoid criminal liability, and so as to properly curtail the discretionary powers of law enforcement officials. Even though analytical rules have evolved which are as rigorous as the methodologies commonly employed in many of the social sciences, whichever test is adopted, one has to recognize that causation in criminal law, as in other branches of the law, cannot be articulated with mathematical precision. The

constitutional standard of precision which defeats the doctrine of vagueness was expressed by the Supreme Court as one which provides guidance to legal debate
(*Canada v. Pharmaceutical Society (Nova Scotia)* (1992), 74 C.C.C. (3d) 289 [15
C.R. (4th) 1]). The criminal law of causation, both in Canada and throughout the
Anglo-American system, has a long and reputable history of doctrinal debate, the
aim of which is to bring that concept within the boundaries that delineate criminal
responsibility. The *de minimis* test, under attack as unduly vague, is indistinguishable, on a vagueness standard alone, from the more stringent test of substantial cause
which the appellant says should be substituted for it.

(c)  Is the De Minimis Test Too Remote?

   (i)  The meaning of the de minimis test

[43]  The remaining constitutional argument suggests that the *de minimis* test is
too remote to engage criminal responsibility for homicide. In *R. v. Harbottle*, supra,
the Supreme Court considered the causation requirements which had to be met before a person guilty of murder could be found guilty of first degree murder under
s. 231(5) of the *Criminal Code*, which provides that murder is first degree in respect
of a person *when death is caused by that person* in the commission of certain enumerated offences. In light of the language of the section, its legislative history and its
purpose, Cory J. concluded that a narrower test of substantial cause should be applied.

[44]  Cory J. specifically contrasted that test with the *de minimis* test applicable in
the case of manslaughter, remarking that there were distinctions in the degree of causation required for the different homicide offences.

[45]  The *de minimis* test was enunciated in *Smithers*, supra, in the context of a
charge of manslaughter. However, it must be taken to apply to murder in the same
way. The *actus reus* of murder is indistinguishable from that of manslaughter. What
distinguishes the two forms of culpable homicide is the different degree of fault represented by the constitutional requirement of subjective foresight in the case of murder, in contrast to the objective foreseeability of serious bodily harm which suffices
for a conviction for manslaughter. Causation is a legal concept that addresses an aspect of the prohibited conduct and, as such, has significance only in crimes where
consequences must flow from acts or omissions.

[46]  Specific causation rules are contained in various provisions of the Code dealing with homicide, such as ss. 222(1) and (6), and ss. 223 to 228. The common law
provides the guiding principles. Issues of causation rarely arise in murder cases, probably because the requirement that the Crown prove beyond a reasonable doubt the
mental element related to the bringing about of the consequence, i.e. the death of the
victim, overshadows any concern that the consequence may not have been caused by
the accused. In other words, if the jury is satisfied that the accused, in assaulting the
deceased, intended to kill or intended to cause bodily harm that he knew was likely to
cause death and was reckless as to that consequence, it will be rare for the jury to
have a doubt as to whether the accused actually caused the death that he intended. In
such a rare case, of course, a proper verdict could be attempted murder, assuming

that the acts of the accused were not too remote. (See Hart and Honoré, *Causation in the Law*, 2nd ed. Oxford Univ. Press, Oxford, 1985, pp. 390-91.)

[47] Causation, on the other hand, is central to the law of manslaughter. It is essentially the vehicle by which the same act or omission of the accused will be defined as an assault, or some other appropriate offence depending on the circumstances, or as a homicide.

[48] Before embarking upon an analysis of the constitutional argument as such, it is useful to examine more closely the meaning of the *Smithers* test. The appellant contends that the case of *Smithers* has set a causation requirement in manslaughter lower than its equivalent in England or Australia. For example, counsel points out that in *R. v. Harbottle*, supra, Cory J. adopted the definition of substantial cause from the Australian case of *R. v. Hallett*, [1969] S.A.S.R. 141 (S.C. in Banco) as the applicable causation test for first degree murder only, while *Hallett* was a murder case setting out the basic principle of causation applicable in homicide generally (see also *R. v. Hodgetts* (sub nom. *R. v. Jackson*) (1989), 44 A. Crim. R. 320 (Qd. C.A.) at p. 327, where the court followed the English case of *R. v. Pagett* (1983), 76 Cr. App. R. 279 (C.A.)).

[49] In *Pagett*, the Court of Appeal noted that it is rarely necessary in homicide cases to give any direction to the jury on causation. Goff L.J., speaking for the court added, at p. 288:

> Even where it is necessary to direct the jury's minds to the question of causation, it is usually enough to direct them simply that in law the accused's act need not be the sole cause, or even the main cause, of the victim's death, it being enough that his act contributed significantly to that result.

[50] More recently, in *R. v. Cheshire*, [1991] 3 All E.R. 670 (C.A.), the court, per Beldam L.J., reiterated that test of "significant contribution" in the following terms, at p. 677:

> It is not the function of the jury to evaluate competing causes or to choose which is dominant provided they are satisfied that the accused's acts can fairly be said to have made a significant contribution to the victim's death. We think the word "significant" conveys the necessary substance of a contribution made to the death which is more than negligible.

[51] This is consistent with the articulation of the substantial cause test in *R. v. Hennigan*, [1971] 3 All E.R. 133 (C.A.), which does not appear to mean anything different than the *Smithers* test of "beyond *de minimis*." In *Hennigan*, when dealing with the offence of dangerous driving causing death, Lord Chief Justice Parker said, at p. 135:

> The court would like to emphasise this, that there is of course nothing in s. 1 of the Road Traffic Act 1960 which requires the manner of the driving to be a substantial cause, or a major cause, or any other description of cause, of the accident. So long as the dangerous driving is a cause and something more than *de minimis*, the statute operates. What has happened in the past is that judges have found it convenient to direct the jury in the form that it must be, as in one case it was put, the substantial cause. That was

the case in which Finnemore J. gave a direction to the jury, in *R. v. Curphey*. That, in the opinion of this court, clearly went too far, and Brabin J. in a later case of *R. v. Gould*, left it to the jury in the form of "a substantial cause."

Although the word does not appear in the statute, it is clearly a convenient word to use to indicate to the jury that it must be something more than *de minimis*, and also to avoid possibly having to go into details of legal causation, remoteness and the like. [Footnotes omitted.]

[52] I am not persuaded that, even when the terminology used is slightly different, the Canadian standard by which causation is established in homicide differs from the English or Australian standard such as to present an anomaly which might suggest that it is set too low. *Harbottle* is clear in holding that s. 231(5) of the *Criminal Code* imposes a higher degree of causation for first degree murder than is required merely to establish the homicide. Cory J. referred to a substantial and integral cause of death, requiring that the accused play a very active role—usually a physical role— in the killing. He used the expression "the actions of the accused must form an essential, substantial and integral part of the killing." This test is not the same as the sometimes called "substantial cause test" referred to in the English authorities dealing with causation in homicide, where the standard contemplated, in my view, is akin to the one in *Smithers*.

[53] Finally, I add that the *Smithers* test is not an exhaustive statement of all the criminal causation rules which have a bearing on liability for homicide. Other rules, some provided for in the Code, some at common law, complement the general test of attributable cause which is at issue in this appeal (see, for example, the legislative choice to curtail liability expressed in s. 227 which restricts the applicability of the law of homicide to cases where death occurred within a year and a day).

(ii)  The constitutionality of the de minimis test

[54] As I see it, the appellant's argument raises two issues: Whether the criminal law of causation amounts to a principle of fundamental justice within the meaning of s. 7 of the *Charter*, and, if so, whether the *de minimis* standard applicable in homicides infringes upon that principle of fundamental justice. Causation as a constitutional standard has not been addressed directly by the Supreme Court of Canada. However, in *R. v. Creighton*, supra, the court held that the offence of unlawful act manslaughter requires objective foreseeability of bodily harm which is neither trivial nor transitory, arising from a dangerous act. The Crown relies on the following statement by McLachlin J., at pp. 40-41:

In my view, the offence of unlawful act manslaughter, as defined by our courts and those in other jurisdictions for many centuries, is entirely consistent with the principles of fundamental justice. There is no need to read up its requirements; as it stands, it conforms to the *Charter*.

[55] Although the constitutionality of the *de minimis* test was not at issue in *Creighton*, supra, the entire focus of the analysis in that case was on the required element of fault with respect to death having ensued from the unlawful act of the

accused. McLachlin J. expressed the view that, in light of the "thin-skull" rule, the distinction between foreseeability of death and foreseeability of bodily harm in man-slaughter largely disappears. In expanding on that idea, she referred to *R. v. Smithers*, supra, in the following terms (p. 52):

> In *Smithers v. The Queen*, [[1978] 1 S.C.R. 506] at pp. 521-22, Dickson J., writing for a unanimous Court, confirmed this principle:
>
> > It is a well-recognized principle that one who assaults another must take his victim as he finds him. ...
> >
> > Although causation in civil cases differs from that in a criminal case, the "thin skulled man" may appear in the criminal law as in the civil law. ... Even if the unlawful act, alone, would not have caused the death, it was still a legal cause so long as it contributed in some way to the death.
> >
> > The thin-skull rule is a good and useful principle. It requires aggressors, once embarked on their dangerous course of conduct which may foreseeably injure others, to take responsibility for all the consequences that ensue, even to death. That is not, in my view, contrary to fundamental justice.

[56] The idea of taking responsibility for the consequences of one's actions expresses a link between causation and fault. Cory J. noted in *R. v. Harbottle*, supra, at pp. 320-21, the tendency of the courts to elevate the causation requirement when the *mens rea* for a form of murder was statutorily reduced. He referred to *R. v. Black*, [1966] 3 C.C.C. 187 [49 C.R. 357] (Ont. C.A.); *R. v. Gourgon* (sub nom. *R. v. Gourgon (No. 1)*) (1979), 9 C.R. (3d) 313 (B.C. S.C.), affirmed (1979), 19 C.R. (3d) 272 (B.C. C.A.); *R. v. Dollan* (1980), 53 C.C.C. (2d) 146 (Ont. H.C.), affirmed (1982), 65 C.C.C. (2d) 240 [25 C.R. (3d) 308] (Ont. C.A.); and *R. v. Woods* (1980), 57 C.C.C. (2d) 220 [19 C.R. (3d) 136] (Ont. C.A.) as examples of courts requiring a high level of causation for first degree murder at a time when it was possible to convict for murder on the basis of objective foresight alone. The fact that a more stringent causation requirement was used in these first degree murder cases demonstrated, in Cory J.'s opinion, an understandable attempt by the courts to impose an appropriate limitation to the reach of the first degree murder section because of the possibility of convicting of murder persons who had no intention to kill. Cory J. then noted that many of the concerns previously expressed by the courts have disappeared in light of the Supreme Court constitutional jurisprudence imposing a subjective *mens rea* for murder.

[57] I refer to the link between causation and the fault element in crime, represented in homicide by foresight of death or bodily harm, whether subjective or objective, because it serves to confirm that the law of causation must be considered to be a principle of fundamental justice akin to the doctrine of *mens rea*. The principle of fundamental justice which is at stake in the jurisprudence dealing with the fault element in crime is the rule that the morally innocent should not be punished. This was the premise acceptable to all the judges in *Creighton*. McLachlin J. said, at pp. 60-61:

> I agree with the Chief Justice that the rule that the morally innocent not be punished in the context of the objective test requires that the law refrain from holding a person criminally responsible if he or she is not capable of appreciating the risk.

[58] In my opinion, causation is embodied in the same principle of fundamental justice and it requires that the law should refrain from holding a person criminally responsible for consequences that should not be attributed to him or her. This is so because criminal causation as a legal rule is based on concepts of moral responsibility, rather than on demonstrable mechanical or scientific formulas. This is expressed by Glanville Williams in the following terms:

> When one has settled the question of but-for causation, the further test to be applied to the but-for cause in order to qualify it for legal recognition is not a test of causation but a moral reaction. The question is whether the result can fairly be said to be imputable to the defendant ... If the term "cause" must be used, it can best be distinguished in this meaning as the "imputable" or "responsible" or "blamable" cause, to indicate the value-judgment involved. The word "imputable" is here chosen as best representing the idea. Whereas the but-for cause can generally be demonstrated scientifically, no experiment can be devised to show that one of a number of concurring but-for causes is more substantial or important than another, or that one person who is involved in the causal chain is more blameworthy than another. Williams, *Textbook of Criminal Law*, 2nd Ed. (1983) at pp. 381-382

[59] This finds support in Hart and Honoré, supra, in the chapters dealing with causation and responsibility, and causation and the principles of punishment. Moral judgment is engaged when causation is used not merely as an explanation for the unfolding of events, but as a way of making people account for their contribution to a result. The morally innocent could be wrongly punished if criminal causation was reduced to a simple *sine qua non* requirement.

[60] This link between causation and the fault element, both being based on the same notion of moral responsibility, leads me to conclude that the appellant's argument cannot succeed in light of *Creighton*. Not only must I consider that the approval of *Smithers* by McLachlin J., although obiter, disposes of the issue; more importantly, I think that the articulation of the fault element in unlawful act manslaughter in *Creighton* removes any danger that the *de minimis* causation test casts the net so broadly as to risk punishing the morally innocent. As the law of manslaughter stands, if a person commits an unlawful dangerous act, in circumstances where a reasonable person would have foreseen the risk of bodily harm which is neither trivial nor transitory, and the unlawful act is at least a contributing cause of the victim's death, outside the *de minimis* range, then the person is guilty of manslaughter. Both causation and the fault element must be proved beyond a reasonable doubt before the prosecution can succeed. Combined in that fashion, both requirements satisfy the principles of fundamental justice in that any risk that the *de minimis* test could engage the criminal responsibility of the morally innocent is removed by the additional requirement of objective foresight.

[61] Therefore, in my opinion, the appellant's constitutional challenge fails on the basis of the Supreme Court decision in *R. v. Creighton*, supra, and the application of s. 1 of the *Charter* does not arise.

*Appeal allowed; conviction quashed; new trial ordered.*

In *Cribbin* the Court held that the test of causation stated in *Smithers* not only remains good law but is constitutionally sound. In the following case the Supreme Court appears to be unanimous in its reassertion that *Smithers* remains good law but divided on what a judge should say to a jury about causation in a case of second-degree murder. This division raises some doubt about whether indeed *Smithers* remains intact.

### R. v. Nette
Supreme Court of Canada
(2001), 158 C.C.C. (3d) 486

L'HEUREUX-DUBÉ J. (concurring in the result) (McLachlin C.J.C., Gonthier, and Bastarache JJ. concurring):

[1] I had the benefit of reading my colleague Madam Justice Arbour's reasons and while I concur in the result she reaches, I do not agree with her suggestion to rephrase the standard of causation for culpable homicide set out by this Court in *R. v. Smithers* (1977), [1978] 1 S.C.R. 506 (S.C.C.). Writing for the Court, Dickson J. (as he then was) articulated the causation test in the following manner (at p. 519):

> The second sub-question raised is whether there was evidence on the basis of which the jury was entitled to find that it had been established beyond a reasonable doubt that the kick caused the death. In answer to this question it may shortly be said that there was a very substantial body of evidence, both expert and lay, before the jury indicating that the kick was at least *a contributing cause of death, outside the* de minimis *range*, and that is all that the Crown was required to establish. [Emphasis added.]

[2] To avoid resorting to the Latin expression, Lambert J.A., in the Court of Appeal's ruling in this case ((1999), 141 C.C.C. (3d) 130 (B.C. C.A.)), suggested an English version that I believe adequately reflects *Smithers'* beyond *de minimis* standard (at para. 29):

> In the *Smithers* case the relevant causal standard is described in the words "a contributing cause beyond *de minimis*." If one were to avoid the Latin, which a jury may find confusing, the *Smithers* standard is "*a contributing cause that is not trivial or insignificant*." See *Crimji* 6.45, para.17. [Emphasis added.]

[3] In her reasons, my colleague also refers to the English translation of the *Smithers* test when she writes (at para. 54): "Since *Smithers*, the terminology of 'beyond *de minimis*' or 'more than a trivial cause' has been used interchangeably with 'outside the *de minimis* range' to charge juries as to the relevant standard of causation for all homicide offences, be it manslaughter or murder."

[4] The terms "not trivial" and "not insignificant" are accurate and do not alter the *Smithers* standard which, it is worth noting, has withstood the test of time. As one author points out, *Smithers* is "the generally authoritative test of causation for all criminal offences" (J. Presser, "All For a Good Cause: The Need for Overhaul of the *Smithers* Test of Causation" (1994), 28 C.R. (4th) 178, at p. 178). In that regard, my

colleague also recognizes that the *Smithers* causation standard is valid and applicable to all forms of homicide (at paras. 85 and 88):

> As discussed above, I conclude that the test of causation is the same for all homicide offences and that it is not appropriate to apply a different standard of causation to the offences of manslaughter and murder. *The applicable standard of causation has traditionally been articulated in this country on the basis of the language used in* Smithers *that the accused must be a cause of the death beyond* de minimis. *This standard has not been overruled in any subsequent decisions of this Court, including* Harbottle. ...
>
> There is only one standard of causation for homicide offences, including second degree murder. That standard may be expressed using different terminology, *but it remains the standard expressed by this Court in the case of* Smithers, *supra*. [Emphasis added.]

[5]  Having said so, my colleague suggests reformulating the *Smithers* beyond *de minimis* test, i.e., "a contributing cause [of death] that is not trivial or insignificant" in the language of a "significant contributing cause." She asserts that (at para. 70):

> There is a semantic debate as to whether "not insignificant" expresses a degree of causation lower than "significant." This illustrates the difficulty in attempting to articulate nuances in this particular legal standard that are essentially meaningless.

[6]  Evidently, my colleague considers that this rephrasing is merely a matter of semantics and, in her view, it does not alter the current test. I respectfully disagree. In my opinion, this issue is a matter of substance, not semantics. There is a meaningful difference between expressing the standard as "a contributing cause that is not trivial or insignificant" and expressing it as a "significant contributing cause." Changing the terminology of the *Smithers* test in this manner would drastically change its substance. ...

[7]  To claim that something not unimportant is important would be a sophism. Likewise, to consider things that are not dissimilar to be similar would amount to an erroneous interpretation. In the same vein, a substantial difference exists between the terms "not insignificant" and "significant," and there is no doubt in my mind that to remove the double negative formulation from the *Smithers* causation test would effect a radical change to the law. I therefore agree with the position of both the respondent and the intervener that a "significant contributing cause" calls for a more direct causal relationship than the existing "not insignificant" or "non trivial" test, thus raising the standard from where it currently stands. ...

[9]  Accordingly, I find that recasting the *Smithers* "beyond *de minimis*" test in the language of a "significant contributing cause" is unwarranted because it raises the threshold of causation for culpable homicide without any reasons for doing so and none, of course, is given since my colleague indicates that the proposed reformulation does not modify the *Smithers* standard.

[10]  Words have a meaning that should be given to them and different words often convey very different standards to the jury. In my view, describing a contributing cause as having a "significant" impact attaches a greater degree of influence or importance to it than do the words "not insignificant." ...

[14] In conclusion, I reiterate that the causation test in *Smithers* remains the law and to rephrase it in the language of a "significant contributing cause," as my colleague suggests, would draw the line at a different place, thus drastically changing the law. I have found no legitimate reason to reformulate the *Smithers* test, rather it is my opinion that such alteration should be strenuously proscribed since it will elevate the threshold of causation. As a result, I consider the current language of "a contributing cause [of death] that is not trivial or insignificant" to be the correct formulation that trial judges should use when expressing to the jury the standard of causation for all homicide offences.

[15] I would dismiss the appeal.

ARBOUR J. (Iacobucci, Major, Binnie, and LeBel JJ. concurring):

### 1. Introduction

[16] The present appeal raises the issue of causation in second degree murder. It requires a determination of the threshold test of causation that must be met before an accused may be held legally responsible for causing a victim's death in a charge of second degree murder. We must also examine how the applicable standard of causation should be conveyed to the jury.

### 2. Factual Background

[17] On Monday, August 21, 1995, Mrs. Clara Loski, a 95-year-old widow who lived alone in her house in Kelowna, British Columbia, was found dead in her bedroom. Her house had been robbed. Mrs. Loski was bound with electrical wire in a way that is referred to colloquially as "hog-tying." Her hands were bound behind her back, her legs were brought upwards behind her back and tied, and her hands and feet were bound together. A red garment was tied around her head and neck and entrapped her chin. This garment formed a moderately tight ligature around her neck, but did not obstruct her nose or mouth.

[18] One of Mrs. Loski's neighbours, Deanna Taylor, testified that she was standing in her backyard smoking on the afternoon of Friday, August 18, 1995 when she heard Mrs. Loski's door close and saw two male Caucasian youths leave through Mrs. Loski's back gate and run down the alley.

[19] Some 24 to 48 hours after Mrs. Loski was robbed and left hog-tied on her bed, she died. At some point she had fallen from the bed to the floor. The Crown's medical expert, Dr. Roy, was of the opinion that the cause of death was asphyxiation due to upper airway obstruction.

[20] The RCMP mounted an undercover operation with the appellant Nette as a target. In the course of this investigation, the appellant was induced to tell an undercover police officer, who was posing as a member of a criminal organization, about his involvement in the robbery and death of Mrs. Loski. This admission was recorded by the undercover officer and was put in evidence at trial.

[21] At trial, the appellant testified in his own defence. He stated that he went to Mrs. Loski's house alone on Saturday, August 19, 1995 just after midnight with the

intention of breaking and entering her house. He testified that he knocked on the back door and it swung open on its own. He stated that it looked as if someone had already broken into the home. He testified that he found Mrs. Loski already dead in her bedroom and then left the home. With respect to the intercepted conversations obtained through the undercover operation, the appellant testified that he had made up the story about robbing and tying up Mrs. Loski in order to impress the undercover officer.

[22] The only medical evidence at trial on the issue of cause of death was the evidence of Dr. Roy, the forensic pathologist who investigated Mrs. Loski's death and who testified for the Crown. Dr. Roy concluded that Mrs. Loski died as a result of asphyxiation due to an upper airway obstruction. Dr. Roy could not isolate one factor from among the circumstances of Mrs. Loski's death and state that it alone caused her death by asphyxiation. In his view, a number of factors contributed to the asphyxial process, in particular, her hog-tied position, the ligature around her neck, as well as her age and corresponding lack of muscle tone. In cross-examination, Dr. Roy agreed that other factors, including Mrs. Loski's congestive heart failure and asthma may possibly have speeded up the process of asphyxiation.

[23] The appellant was charged with first degree murder on the basis that he had committed murder while committing the offence of unlawfully confining Mrs. Loski. The Crown's position at trial was that the act of causing death and the acts comprising the offence of unlawful confinement all formed part of one continuous sequence of events making up a single transaction, and that the appellant was therefore guilty of first degree murder pursuant to s. 231(5) of the *Criminal Code*. The appellant was tried before a judge and jury. The jury returned a verdict of second degree murder and the Court of Appeal dismissed the appellant's appeal from that verdict. The only ground of appeal both before the Court of Appeal and before us concerns the test of causation applicable to second degree murder. ...

## 5. *Issues*

[39] The only issue on this appeal is the standard of causation for second degree murder and how the applicable standard should be explained to the jury.

## 6. *Analysis*

### A. *Introduction*

[40] There is no issue raised in this appeal with respect to the charge on first degree murder or manslaughter. The appellant's only ground of appeal is the propriety of the charge on second degree murder and, specifically, the applicable standard of causation for second degree murder. The appellant's position is that there is one standard of causation applicable to all forms of homicide and that the standard should be conveyed to the jury by using the words "substantial cause" that this Court said applied to the offence of first degree murder under s. 231(5) of the *Criminal Code* in *Harbottle*. The appellant says that the trial judge erred in effectively instructing the jury that the *Smithers* standard of "beyond *de minimis*" applied to the offence of second degree murder. Had the jurors been properly instructed on the standard of

causation applicable to second degree murder, says the appellant, they might have acquitted the appellant on the second degree murder charge. The appellant therefore submits that the appeal should be allowed and a new trial ordered on the ground that the trial judge misdirected the jury on the standard of causation applicable to second degree murder.

[41] The respondent and the intervener Attorney General of Ontario submit that the applicable standard for second degree murder is the standard of "beyond *de minimis*" articulated in *Smithers, supra*. Their position is that the "substantial cause" test of causation is a higher standard of causation that only applies to the offence of first degree murder under s. 231(5) of the *Criminal Code*. As well, the Attorney General of Ontario submits that the higher *Harbottle* standard also applies to first degree murder under s. 231(6) of the *Criminal Code*, which uses the same terminology of "caused by that person" found in s. 231(5) in relation to murder committed in the course of criminal harassment. The respondent and intervener therefore say that the trial judge properly charged the jury on the applicable standard of causation in relation to second degree murder and that the appeal should accordingly be dismissed.

[42] While the standard of causation for second degree murder has not been raised squarely before this Court until now, it was before the Ontario Court of Appeal in *Cribbin, supra*, and *Meiler, supra*. In both of these cases, the *Smithers* standard of "beyond *de minimis*" was expressly approved of in relation to a charge of second degree murder.

## B. The Standard of Causation for Homicide Offences

[43] The parties and intervener on this appeal characterize the decision required of this Court in the present case as a choice between the terminology of "beyond *de minimis*" on the one hand and "substantial cause" on the other in describing the standard of causation for second degree murder to the jury. In my view, this characterization does not properly reflect the decision that is required in this case. It confuses the question of what the standard of causation for second degree murder *is* with the question of how the standard of causation for second degree murder should be *expressed* in charging the jury. In my view, these two separate questions are best dealt with sequentially.

[44] In determining whether a person can be held responsible for causing a particular result, in this case death, it must be determined whether the person caused that result both in fact and in law. Factual causation, as the term implies, is concerned with an inquiry about how the victim came to his or her death, in a medical, mechanical, or physical sense, and with the contribution of the accused to that result. Where factual causation is established, the remaining issue is legal causation.

[45] Legal causation, which is also referred to as imputable causation, is concerned with the question of whether the accused person should be held responsible in law for the death that occurred. It is informed by legal considerations such as the wording of the section creating the offence and principles of interpretation. These legal considerations, in turn, reflect fundamental principles of criminal justice such as the principle that the morally innocent should not be punished: see *Reference re*

*s. 94(2) of the Motor Vehicle Act (British Columbia)*, [1985] 2 S.C.R. 486 (S.C.C.), at
p. 513; *R. v. Vaillancourt*, [1987] 2 S.C.R. 636 (S.C.C.), at p. 652-53; *R. v.
Stinchcombe*, [1991] 3 S.C.R. 326 (S.C.C.), at p. 336; *R. v. Creighton*, [1993] 3 S.C.R.
3 (S.C.C.), at pp. 22-23; *Cribbin, supra*, at p. 568. In determining whether legal causation is established, the inquiry is directed at the question of whether the accused
person should be held criminally responsible for the consequences that occurred. The
nature of the inquiry at the stage of determining legal causation is expressed by G.
Williams as follows in his *Textbook of Criminal Law* (2nd ed. 1983), at pp. 381-82,
quoted in *Cribbin* at p. 568:

> When one has settled the question of but-for causation, the further test to be applied to
> the but-for cause in order to qualify it for legal recognition is not a test of causation but
> a moral reaction. The question is whether the result can fairly be said to be imputable to
> the defendant. ... If the term "cause" must be used, it can best be distinguished in this
> meaning as the "imputable" or "responsible" or "blamable" cause, to indicate the value-
> judgment involved. The word "imputable" is here chosen as best representing the idea.
> Whereas the but-for cause can generally be demonstrated scientifically, no experiment
> can be devised to show that one of a number of concurring but-for causes is more
> substantial or important than another, or that one person who is involved in the causal
> chain is more blameworthy than another.

[46]  In a given case, the jury does not engage in a two-part analysis of whether
both factual and legal causation have been established. Rather, in the charge to the
jury, the trial judge seeks to convey the requisite degree of factual and legal causation
that must be found before the accused can be held criminally responsible for the
victim's death.

[47]  While causation is a distinct issue from *mens rea*, the proper standard of
causation expresses an element of fault that is in law sufficient, in addition to the
requisite mental element, to base criminal responsibility. The starting point in the
chain of causation which seeks to attribute the prohibited consequences to an act of
the accused is usually an unlawful act in itself. When that unlawful act is combined
with the requisite mental element for the offence charged, causation is generally not
an issue. For example, in the case of murder, where an accused intends to kill a person and performs an act which causes or contributes to that person's death, it is rare
for an issue to arise as to whether the accused caused the victim's death. As I discussed in *Cribbin, supra*, where the jury is faced with a charge of murder and is
satisfied that the accused intended to kill or intended to cause bodily harm that he
knew was likely to cause death and was reckless as to whether death occurred, it will
rarely be necessary for the trial judge to charge the jury on the standard of causation.
In such a case, the *mens rea* requirement generally resolves any concerns about causation. It would be rare in a murder case where the intention to kill or to cause bodily
harm likely to cause death is proven for the accused to be able to raise a doubt that,
while he intended the result that occurred, he did not cause the intended result. Where
it is established that the accused had the subjective foresight of death or serious bodily harm likely to cause death required to sustain a murder conviction, as opposed to
the lower manslaughter requirement of objective foreseeability of serious bodily harm,

it would be unusual for an issue of causation to arise. Assuming a case arose where intention was established but causation was not proven, a proper verdict might be attempted murder: *Cribbin*, at p. 564.

[48] The law of causation is in large part judicially developed, but is also expressed, directly or indirectly, in provisions of the *Criminal Code*. For example, s. 225 of the *Code* provides that where a person causes bodily injury that is in itself dangerous and from which death results, that person causes the death notwithstanding that the immediate cause of death is proper or improper treatment. Similarly, ss. 222(5)(c) and 222(5)(d) provide that a person commits culpable homicide where he causes the death of a person by causing that person, by threats, fear of violence or by deception, to do anything that causes his death or by wilfully frightening a child or sick person. These statutory provisions and others like them in the *Code* preempt any speculation as to whether the act of the accused would be seen as too remote to have caused the result alleged, or whether the triggering of a chain of events was then interrupted by an intervening cause which serves to distance and exonerate the accused from any responsibility for the consequences. Where the factual situation does not fall within one of the statutory rules of causation in the *Code*, the common law general principles of criminal law apply to resolve any causation issues that may arise.

[49] In light of the statutory rules mentioned above, and in light of general principles of criminal responsibility, the civil law of causation is of limited assistance. The criminal law does not recognise contributory negligence, nor does it have any mechanism to apportion responsibility for the harm occasioned by criminal conduct, except as part of sentencing after sufficient causation has been found. In the same way it provides for the possibility of attributing responsibility through the law of attempt, which has no equivalent in the civil context. As a result, I do not find the appellant's submissions relating to the civil standard of causation to be helpful in elucidating the applicable criminal standard.

[50] In determining whether an accused is guilty of first or second degree murder, the first step for the trier of fact is to determine whether murder has been committed, pursuant to ss. 229 or 230 of the *Criminal Code*: *Farrant*, *supra*, at p. 141. Once this has been established, the remaining question is whether the offence should be classified as first or second degree murder in accordance with the criteria set out in s. 231 of the *Code*, which is, in essence, a sentencing provision: *Farrant*, *supra*; *R. v. Droste*, [1984] 1 S.C.R. 208 (S.C.C.); *R. v. Paré*, [1987] 2 S.C.R. 618 (S.C.C.); *R. v. Arkell*, [1990] 2 S.C.R. 695 (S.C.C.); *R. v. Luxton*, [1990] 2 S.C.R. 711 (S.C.C.), and *Harbottle*, *supra*. Where, as here, the Crown relies on s. 231(5) of the *Code*, the jury must first find that the accused is guilty of murder before moving on to a consideration of whether the accused's participation in the underlying offence and in the killing of the victim was so direct and substantial that a conviction for first degree murder is appropriate.

*C. Did Harbottle Raise the Standard of Causation?*

[51] This Court has previously examined the issue of causation in the homicide context in relation to manslaughter in *Smithers, supra*, and in relation to first degree murder under s. 231(5) of the *Code* in *Harbottle, supra*. In considering causation in relation to second degree murder in the present cause, it is helpful to first discuss the facts and legal principles set out in *Smithers* and *Harbottle*, before moving on to a consideration of whether *Harbottle* raised the standard of causation for first degree murder under s. 231(5) of the *Code* only or for homicide offences generally.

[52] In *Smithers*, the appellant and victim became engaged in a physical altercation following a heated and rough junior hockey game. The appellant gave the victim one or two punches to the head and then, while the victim was doubled over, gave the victim one hard, fast kick in the stomach. Within a few minutes of the kick, the victim was dead. An autopsy revealed that death had occurred from aspiration of vomit, which was an extremely rare occurrence resulting from the malfunctioning of the victim's epiglottis. The Crown's theory was that the kick had precipitated the vomiting and the aspiration of the vomit, and that the appellant had accordingly caused the victim's death. The jury convicted the appellant of manslaughter and the Ontario Court of Appeal dismissed the appellant's appeal.

[53] Two grounds of appeal were raised by the appellant before this Court in *Smithers*. On the first ground, the appellant argued that the trial judge had not made it clear to the jury that the act of assault must also have caused the death of the deceased. Dickson J., as he then was, writing for the Court, concluded that the issue as to the cause of death was properly and sufficiently delineated by the trial judge in charging the jury. On the second ground of appeal, the appellant argued that the Court of Appeal had erred in holding that there was evidence on which the jury could find that the kick had caused the death. This ground of appeal was also rejected by Dickson J. as follows (at p. 519):

> In answer to this question it may shortly be said that there was a very substantial body of evidence, both expert and lay, before the jury indicating that the kick was at least a contributing cause of death, outside the *de minimis* range, and that is all that the Crown was required to establish. It is immaterial that the death was in part caused by a malfunctioning epiglottis to which malfunction the appellant may, or may not, have contributed.

[54] Since *Smithers*, the terminology of "beyond *de minimis*" or "more than a trivial cause" has been used interchangeably with "outside the *de minimis* range" to charge juries as to the relevant standard of causation for all homicide offences, be it manslaughter or murder. The standard of causation was more recently revisited by this Court in *Harbottle, supra*, in relation to a conviction of first degree murder under s. 214(5) (now s. 231(5)) of the *Criminal Code*. *Harbottle* involved the rape, forcible confinement and killing of a young woman. The appellant and his accomplice forcibly confined the victim and the appellant watched as his accomplice brutally sexually assaulted her and mutilated her with a knife. His accomplice then proceeded to kill the victim, first trying to slash her wrists and, when that proved unsuccessful, strangling

her with her brassiere. To stop the victim from kicking to defend herself, the appellant held down her legs so that his accomplice could succeed in strangling her.

[55] The trial judge in *Harbottle* charged the jury on first degree murder on the basis of planning and premeditation and also on the basis of the murder having been committed while the victim was being sexually assaulted or forcibly confined pursuant to s. 214(5) of the *Code*. The issue before this Court was whether the trial judge had properly charged the jury with respect to s. 214(5). The appellant conceded that he was a party to the murder of the victim while participating in her forcible confinement or sexual assault, but he argued that the words "caused by that person" in s. 214(5) of the *Code* meant that he could only be found guilty of first degree murder if his actions in holding down the victim's legs were the diagnostic cause of death. The medical evidence revealed that the diagnostic cause of death was asphyxia. Clearly the asphyxia was not directly caused by the holding of her legs but rather by the actions of the appellant's accomplice in strangling her. The Crown argued that the words "caused by that person" in s. 214(5) did not create a causation requirement distinct from the causation required for murder generally.

[56] Cory J., writing for the Court in *Harbottle*, rejected the interpretations of both the Crown and defence as to the correct interpretation of the words "caused by that person" in s. 214(5) of the *Code*. He noted that s. 214(5) is in essence a sentencing provision, and only comes into play once the jury has found the accused guilty of murder for having caused the death of the victim. Once the jury has found the accused guilty of murder, the next step is to determine whether the accused is guilty of first degree murder under s. 214(5). In order for the accused to be found guilty under s. 214(5), with the increased stigma and sentence a conviction of first degree murder entails, Cory J. concluded that the accused must play a very active role—usually a physical role—in the killing and his actions must form an essential, substantial and integral part of the killing of the victim. Cory J. expressly stated that this substantial causation test under s. 214(5) is much higher than the *Smithers* standard of "a contributing cause of death, outside the *de minimis* range": *Harbottle*, *supra*, at p. 324.

[57] The appellant submits that *Harbottle* was a parties case and not a causation case and that it should not be interpreted as having adopted a more stringent legal test of causation for multiple cause cases. The appellant says that there was no debate as to what caused the victim's death in *Harbottle*: she was strangled by the co-accused Ross. *Harbottle* was therefore not a multiple cause case, in the appellant's submission. The real issue in *Harbottle*, says the appellant, was whether the accused had played an active enough role in the killing that he could be liable for first degree murder. What *Harbottle* did, according to the appellant, was to clarify the law on parties in the context of first degree murder under s. 231(5) of the *Code*, not create a higher standard of causation for offences under s. 231(5). The appellant's position is that the terminology of "substantial cause" used in *Harbottle* should be used in charging the jury for all homicide offences and that it does not represent a more stringent standard of causation than the "beyond *de minimis*" standard set out in *Smithers*.

[58] In oral argument, the appellant submitted that the *Smithers* test applies to all culpable homicide but that the *Smithers* test should be reformulated and "crystallized" to the specific standard of "significant" or "substantial" rather than using the

*Smithers* terminology of "beyond *de minimis*" or "more than trivial." The "crystal-lized" test of "significant" or "substantial" cause simply clarifies the language of causation so that the jury can properly focus on the correct standard, in the appel-lant's submission, and does not raise the threshold of causation required. The alleged errors made by the trial judge are first that the jury was instructed on the *Smithers* standard of "more than a trivial cause" rather than the "crystallized" test of "signifi-cant" or "substantial" and, second, that the trial judge twice erred in expressing the *Smithers* standard of "more than a trivial cause" by describing it instead as a "slight or trivial cause." The appellant submits that, as a result of these errors, the trial judge incorrectly explained the standard of causation for second degree murder to the jury and the jury may therefore have failed to understand the correct standard of causation.

[59]  The position of the respondent and the intervener Attorney General of On-tario is that *Harbottle* did establish an elevated causation threshold with the use of the terminology of "substantial cause" but that this elevated standard only applies to the offence of first degree murder pursuant to s. 231(5) of the *Criminal Code* and possibly also s. 231(6) of the *Code*. With respect to second degree murder and man-slaughter, the respondent and intervener submit that the *Smithers* standard continues to apply.

[60]  There appears to be an inconsistency in the appellant's argument in the present case. On the one hand, he is arguing that the "substantial cause" terminology of *Harbottle* does not represent a higher standard of causation than the *Smithers* stand-ard and that using the terminology of "substantial cause" in relation to all homicide offences would not raise the causation threshold. On the other hand, however, he is arguing that Wilkinson J.'s use of the *Smithers* terminology instead of the *Harbottle* terminology in charging the jury on second degree murder was an error of law so serious that it justifies overturning the conviction for second degree murder and or-dering a new trial. If, as the appellant submits, "substantial cause" is not a higher standard of causation than the *Smithers* formulation of "beyond *de minimis*," it would seem to follow that using the *Smithers* terminology instead of the *Harbottle* termi-nology could not be an error of law, much less an error so serious that it should result in a new trial.

[61]  I agree with the appellant that what *Harbottle* really stresses is not solely or even primarily a higher causation requirement to raise murder to first degree murder under s. 231(5) of the *Code*, but rather the increased degree of participation required before the accused may be convicted of first degree murder under s. 231(5). How-ever, I do not agree that the terminology of "substantial cause" should be used to describe the requisite degree of causation for all homicide offences.

[62]  Harbottle caused the victim's death within the requirements of s. 231(5) of the *Code* because he was a co-principal in the murder. The degree of participation in the killing by a party whose liability for murder is based on aiding or abetting under s. 21(1)(b) or (c) of the *Criminal Code* or common intention under s. 21(2) of the *Code*, may, under the *Harbottle* formulation, be insufficient to permit a finding that the murder amounts to first degree under s. 231(5), which requires that the murder be committed "by that person" in the course of committing the underlying offence. In the present case, the underlying offence was the unlawful confinement of Mrs. Loski.

The underlying offences listed in s. 231(5) of the *Code* all involve the unlawful domination of victims. Where an accused exploits this position of power and commits murder, such an egregious crime warrants the increased stigma and sentence attached to first degree murder: see *Paré, supra*. As explained by Cory J. in *Harbottle*, in order to raise culpability to first degree murder under s. 231(5), something more is required. The "something more" is not that the accused *caused more* the death of the victim. What is required is that his participation in the killing be sufficiently immediate, direct and substantial to warrant the greater stigma and sentence attached to first degree murder.

[63] As *Harbottle, Cribbin* and the present case illustrate, causation issues tend to arise in homicides involving multiple parties. Absent s. 21 of the *Criminal Code*, the attribution of criminal responsibility to an individual who aided or abetted another in the commission of the offence would indeed be problematic. However, the law of parties provides that individuals may bear criminal responsibility for the acts of another, and in that way speaks conclusively on some issues of causation. By virtue of s. 21 of the *Code*, Cory J. in *Harbottle* found it unnecessary to engage in fine distinctions as to the degree of participation of the two perpetrators in the killing. Rather, he focused on the meaning of the words "when the death is caused by that person" in s. 214(5) (now s. 231(5)) in deciding whether the appellant could be found guilty of first degree murder. Cory J. concluded that the use of the word "caused" in s. 214(5) imposed an additional causation requirement separate from the causation required for the offence of murder, which comes into play once the jury has already concluded that the accused is guilty of murder for having caused the death of the victim: *Harbottle, supra*, at pp. 316-17. Although not relevant to the present appeal, I note that s. 231(6) of the *Code* also uses the wording "when the death is caused by that person" found in s. 231(5) to elevate murder to first degree murder where the murder is committed in the course of the offence of criminal harassment under s. 264 of the *Code*. Such wording is not found in s. 231(6.1) of the *Code*, which raises murder to first degree where the murder is caused while committing an offence involving the use of explosives under s. 81 of the *Code* for the benefit of a criminal organization.

[64] Once the jury concludes that the accused has committed murder, *Harbottle* indicates that the jury should then move on to consider whether aggravating circumstances exist that justify the increased sentence and stigma of a first degree murder conviction under s. 231(5). The additional "causation" requirement under s. 231(5) does not refer to factual causation but rather to an increased degree of legal causation. In other words, once the jury has determined that the accused committed murder, which entails a finding that the accused caused the victim's death in both factual and legal terms, it is then necessary to consider whether the moral culpability of the accused, as evidenced by his role in the killing, justifies a verdict of first degree murder. As Cory J. states in *Harbottle*, "[t]he gravity of the crime and the severity of the sentence both indicate that a substantial and high degree of blameworthiness, above and beyond that of murder, must be established in order to convict an accused of first degree murder"(p. 323 (emphasis deleted)). Such a high degree of blameworthiness would only be established where the actions of the accused were found to be

"an essential, substantial and integral part of the killing of the victim" (*Harbottle*, at p. 324). The terminology of "substantial cause" is used to indicate a higher degree of legal causation but it is a standard that only comes into play at the stage of deciding whether the accused's degree of blameworthiness warrants the increased penalty and stigma of first degree murder.

[65] It is clear from a reading of *Harbottle* that the "substantial cause" test expresses the increased degree of moral culpability, as evidenced by the accused person's degree of participation in the killing, that is required before an accused can be found guilty under s. 231(5) of the *Criminal Code* of first degree murder. The increased degree of participation in the killing, coupled with a finding that the accused had the requisite *mens rea* for murder, justifies a verdict of guilty under s. 231(5) of the *Code*.

### D. Explaining the Standard of Causation to the Jury

[66] As I discussed earlier, it is important to distinguish between what the legal standard of causation is and how that standard is conveyed to the jury. The difference between these two concepts has been obscured somewhat in the present case by the parties' focus on the terminology used to describe the standard of causation. I agree with the appellant's submission that there is only one standard of causation for all homicide offences, whether manslaughter or murder. However, I do not agree with the appellant that the standard must be expressed for all homicide offences, including second degree murder, as one of "substantial cause" as stated in *Harbottle*. Nor must the applicable standard be expressed with the terminology of "beyond *de minimis*" used in the *Smithers* standard.

[67] At para. 28, Lambert J.A. took note of the various terms used to describe the relevant standard of causation for homicide offences and emphasized the need to distinguish between the concept of causation and the terminology used to express it:

> As can readily be seen, there is a diversity of terminology available to describe the relevant causal connection. It is important to be guided by the concepts relevant to causality rather than by the terminology.

[68] In his text *Canadian Criminal Law: A Treatise* (3rd ed. 1995), Professor D. Stuart quotes at p. 130 from the English case of *Loach v. British Columbia Electric Railway* (1915), [1916] 1 A.C. 719 (British Columbia P.C.), in which the court expressed scepticism that special terminology could lead to an adequate approach to the issue of causation. While made in the context of a civil action, I find the comments in that case to be applicable to the present context (at p. 727):

> It is surprising how many epithets eminent judges have applied to the cause, which has to be ascertained for this judicial purpose of determining liability, and how many more to other acts and incidents, which for this purpose are not the cause at all. "Efficient or effective cause," "real cause," "proximate cause," "direct cause," "decisive cause," "immediate cause," "causa causans," on the one hand, as against, on the other, "cause sine qua non," "occasional cause," "remote cause," "contributory cause," "inducing cause," "condition," and so on. No doubt in the particular cases in which they occur they were

thought to be useful or they would not have been used, but the repetition of terms without examination in other cases has often led to confusion, and it might be better, after pointing out that the inquiry is an investigation into responsibility, to be content with speaking of the cause of the injury simply and without qualification.

[69] In describing the *Smithers* standard of causation, Lambert J.A. concluded that the phrase "a contributing cause that is not trivial or insignificant" reflected the applicable standard without the need to resort to the use of the Latin expression "beyond *de minimis*." He further found that a cause that is "not insignificant" can be expressed positively as a cause that is "significant" and that it would therefore be correct to describe the *Smithers* standard as a "significant contributing cause" (para. 29).

[70] There is a semantic debate as to whether "not insignificant" expresses a degree of causation lower than "significant." This illustrates the difficulty in attempting to articulate nuances in this particular legal standard that are essentially meaningless. I agree with Lambert J.A. that even if it were desirable to formulate a causation test for second degree murder that is higher than the *Smithers* standard for manslaughter but less strict than the *Harbottle* standard for first degree murder under s. 231(5), which I conclude it is not, it would be difficult to formulate such a test in a meaningful way and even more difficult for a jury to grasp the subtle nuances and apply three different standards of causation.

[71] The causation standard expressed in *Smithers* is still valid and applicable to all forms of homicide. In addition, in the case of first degree murder under s. 231(5) of the Code, *Harbottle* requires additional instructions, to which I will return. The only potential shortcoming with the *Smithers* test is not in its substance, but in its articulation. Even though it causes little difficulty for lawyers and judges, the use of Latin expressions and the formulation of the test in the negative are not particularly useful means of conveying an abstract idea to a jury. In order to explain the standard as clearly as possible to the jury, it may be preferable to phrase the standard of causation in positive terms using a phrase such as "significant contributing cause" rather than using expressions phrased in the negative such as "not a trivial cause" or "not insignificant." Latin terms such as "*de minimis*" are rarely helpful.

[72] In deciding how the applicable standard of causation should be articulated to the jury, trial judges have a discretion in choosing the terminology they wish to use to explain the standard. Causation issues are case-specific and fact-driven. For that reason, it is important to afford a trial judge with the flexibility to put issues of causation to the jury in an intelligible fashion that is relevant to the circumstances of the case, including whether or not there are multiple accused persons or parties. As I discussed in *Cribbin*, *supra*, at pp. 565-66, while different terminology has been used to explain the applicable standard in Canada, Australia and England, whether the terminology used is "beyond *de minimis*," "significant contribution" or "substantial cause," the standard of causation which this terminology seeks to articulate, within the context of causation in homicide, is essentially the same: see *R. v. Pagett* (1983), 76 Cr. App. R. 279 (Eng. C.A.); *R. v. Hallett*, [1969] S.A.S.R. 141 (Australia S.C.); *R. v. Royall* (1991), 100 A.L.R. 669 (Australia H.C.); *R. v. Smith* (1959), 43 Cr. App. R.

121 (Eng. C.A.); *R. v. Cheshire*, [1991] 3 All E.R. 670 (Eng. C.A.), and *R. v. Hennigan*, [1971] 3 All E.R. 133 (Eng. C.A.). For example, in *Cheshire*, the court stated that (at p. 677):

> It is not the function of the jury to evaluate competing causes or to choose which is dominant provided they are satisfied that the accused's acts can fairly be said to have made a significant contribution to the victim's death. We think the word 'significant' conveys the necessary substance of a contribution made to the death which is more than negligible.

Similarly, in *Hennigan*, the court described the standard of causation on a charge of causing death by dangerous driving as follows at p. 135:

> The court would like to emphasise this, that there is of course nothing in s. 1 of the Road Traffic Act 1960 which requires the manner of the driving to be a substantial cause, or a major cause, or any other description of cause, of the accident. So long as the dangerous driving is a cause and something more than de minimis, the statute operates. What has happened in the past is that judges have found it convenient to direct the jury in the form that it must be, as in one case it was put, the substantial cause.

To the extent that trial judges may find it more useful to express the standard of causation in *Smithers* in a more direct and affirmative fashion, they may find it preferable to express the standard positively as a "significant contributing cause," to use the terminology of Lambert J.A. in the present appeal.

[73]  In light of *Harbottle*, where the jury must be instructed on first degree murder under s. 231(5) of the *Code* in addition to manslaughter or second degree murder, the terminology of "substantial cause" should be used to describe the applicable standard for first degree murder so that the jury understands that something different is being conveyed by the instructions concerning s. 231(5) of the *Code* with respect to the requisite degree of participation of the accused in the offence. In such cases, it would make sense to instruct the jury that the acts of the accused have to have made a "significant" contribution to the victim's death to trigger culpability for the homicide while, to be guilty of first degree murder under s. 231(5), the accused's actions must have been an essential, substantial and integral part of the killing of the victim.

### E.  Is Causation an Issue on the Facts of the Present Appeal?

[74]  As I mentioned earlier, causation issues rarely arise in murder offences. Thus, in the usual case, it will be unnecessary for the trial judge to explain the applicable standard of causation to the jury in relation to either second degree murder or first degree murder. Causation issues arise more frequently in manslaughter cases, in which the fault element resides in a combination of causing death by an unlawful act, or by criminal negligence, and mere objective foreseeability of death. As the cases illustrate, causation issues tend to arise in factual situations involving multiple parties (e.g. *Harbottle*), thin skull victims (e.g. *Smithers*), intervening events (e.g. *Hallett*) or some combination of these factors.

[75] The appellant submits that the present appeal is a case involving multiple causation in which the trier of fact must decide whether the acts of the accused were a "beyond *de minimis*" contribution that triggers criminal liability. The respondent and intervener do not take issue with the appellant's characterization of this appeal as a case involving multiple causes.

[76] The appellant submits that in this case several causes contributed to Mrs. Loski's death. The appellant submits that the Crown's medical expert, Dr. Roy, agreed that there were probably multiple factors contributing to Mrs. Loski's asphyxia, namely, being hog-tied, the ligature around her neck, her congestive heart failure, her cardiac abnormality, her asthma and the old-fashioned corset girdle that she was wearing. In the appellant's submission, the acts of the appellant and the victim's pre-existing medical conditions may both have contributed to her death. The appellant submits that the medical evidence in the present case is equivocal as to what caused asphyxiation. The appellant submits that in a case involving only one cause of death, the "but for" test usually resolves the causation issue. However, in a case such as the present one involving two or more causes of death, the appellant submits that the trier of fact must decide whether the accused's act contributed to the victim's death sufficiently to attract criminal liability.

[77] The difficulty in establishing a single, conclusive medical cause of death does not lead to the legal conclusion that there were multiple operative causes of death. In a homicide trial, the question is not what caused the death or who caused the death of the victim but rather did the accused cause the victim's death. The fact that other persons or factors may have contributed to the result may or may not be legally significant in the trial of the one accused charged with the offence. It will be significant, and exculpatory, if independent factors, occurring before or after the acts or omissions of the accused, legally sever the link that ties him to the prohibited result.

[78] In my view, this case does not involve truly multiple independant causes, as for instance, when improper treatment can also be responsible for the victim's death. An example of a case that involves multiple causes is *Hallett, supra*. In that case, the victim was beaten and left unconscious by the sea and was drowned by the incoming tide. The question in that case was whether the accused's actions were such that he should be held responsible for the death despite the intervening cause of the incoming tide. The court expressed the test of causation as follows at p. 149:

> The question to be asked is whether an act or series of acts (in exceptional cases an omission or series of omissions) consciously performed by the accused is or are so connected with the event that it or they must be regarded as having a sufficiently substantial causal effect which subsisted up to the happening of the event, without being spent or without being in the eyes of the law sufficiently interrupted by some other act or event.

Unlike *Hallett*, no intervening causes arose in the present case between the appellant's action and the victim's death.

[79] Nor does this case present an illustration of the operation of the thin-skull rule in the criminal context. The thin-skull rule, which is a long-standing principle of

tort law, provides that a wrongdoer must take his victim as he finds him: *Dulieu v. White & Sons*, [1901] 2 K.B. 669 (Eng. K.B.); *Athey v. Leonati*, [1996] 3 S.C.R. 458 (S.C.C.). Thus, the fact that a victim's head injuries are aggravated beyond what would normally be expected because of the victim's unusually thin skull does not relieve a tortfeasor of liability for the full extent of the harm that resulted from his wrongdoing. That principle applies equally in the criminal context and is reflected, in part, in ss. 222(5)(d) and 226 of the *Criminal Code*. As expressed by McLachlin J., as she then was, in *Creighton, supra*, at p. 52:

> The thin-skull rule is a good and useful principle. It requires aggressors, once embarked on their dangerous course of conduct which may foreseeably injure others, to take responsibility for all the consequences that ensue, even to death.
>
>   The potential harshness of the application of the thin-skull rule in the criminal context is mitigated by the requirement that the accused have the requisite *mens rea* for the offence charged, which consists of "objective foreseeability of the risk of bodily harm which is neither trivial nor transitory, in the context of a dangerous act": *Creighton, supra*, at p. 45.

[80]  The present appeal does not present the classic thin-skull scenario where the victim's death occurred unexpectedly as a result of the victim's unusual and unforeseeable susceptibility to injury. It is clear on the medical evidence that the victim's physical conditions related to her advanced age may have hastened her demise. However, there was no evidence to indicate that Mrs. Loski's death would have occurred without the actions of the appellant and his accomplice. Nor is there any evidence that she was a thin-skull victim whose physical characteristics were unusual for a woman of her age. By all accounts, she was healthy and active. A much younger victim, subjected to the same treatment, may also have failed to survive. An example of a true thin-skull situation is *Smithers*, the facts of which are discussed earlier. There is also no evidence of any intervening cause which resulted in Mrs. Loski's death. The various potential causes of death that are advanced by the appellant in the present case would all be caught by the statutory or common law principles that preclude an interruption of the chain of causation such as to eliminate the criminal responsibility of the accused.

[81]  In the appellant's own submission, it is only in cases involving multiple causes that the jury need be charged on the applicable standard of causation. In my view, this is not such a case. The fact that the appellant's actions might not have caused death in a different person, or that death might have taken longer to occur in the case of a younger victim, does not transform this case into one involving multiple causes. Clearly, where an accused person hog ties an elderly woman, places a ligature of clothing around her neck and abandons her, in the knowledge that she lives alone, without notifying anyone of her plight, it is not unexpected that death will result if no one rescues the victim in time.

[82]  In my view, it was unnecessary in this case to instruct the jury on the law of causation for homicide, beyond stating the need to find that the accused caused the death of the victim. I agree with Braidwood J.A. and McEachern C.J. in the Court of Appeal that there was no plausibility to the appellant's submission that telling the

jury that the standard of causation was "substantial cause" instead of "more than a trivial cause" could possibly have made any difference to the verdict of second degree murder. There was no evidence that anything other than the actions of the appellant and his accomplice caused Mrs. Loski's death. Mrs. Loski's death resulted from being left alone hog-tied in her bedroom with a ligature around her neck. Nothing that occurred following the actions of the appellant and his accomplice in tying her up and leaving her alone can be said to have broken the chain of causation linking them with her death. However, in relation to the charge of first degree murder, it was necessary for the trial judge to instruct the jury in accordance with *Harbottle* under s. 231(5) of the *Code*, given the requirement that the Crown establish that the physical actions of the accused form an essential, substantial and integral part of the killing of the victim.

[83]  As I stated in *Cribbin*, causation is a legal rule based on concepts of moral responsibility and is not a mechanical or mathematical exercise. On the facts of the present appeal, the jury properly found that the appellant caused Mrs. Loski's death and must bear legal responsibility for having done so. The central issue at trial was whether there was sufficient evidence of the necessary intent to put the charge of murder to the jury. The defence made an application at trial to withdraw murder from the jury. The question before Wilkinson J. on this application was whether there was some evidence on which the jury could conclude that the appellant meant to cause bodily harm to Mrs. Loski that he knew was likely to cause death within the meaning of s. 229(a) (ii) of the *Criminal Code*. Wilkinson J. denied the defence application to withdraw the charge of murder from the jury.

[84]  In my view, the real issue of concern in this case with respect to the charge of murder was not whether or not the appellant caused the victim's death, but whether or not he knew that his actions were likely to cause her death. Did he know that the actions taken by him and by his accomplice were likely to cause Mrs. Loski's death? Did he know that someone of Mrs. Loski's age would likely die from the effects of being hog-tied? Did he anticipate that the gag might slip? Did he foresee that no one might come by her house and rescue her before she died?

*F.  The Charge to the Jury and the Verdict*

[85]  As discussed above, I conclude that the test of causation is the same for all homicide offences and that it is not appropriate to apply a different standard of causation to the offences of manslaughter and murder. The applicable standard of causation has traditionally been articulated in this country on the basis of the language used in *Smithers* that the accused must be a cause of the death beyond *de minimis*. This standard has not been overruled in any subsequent decisions of this Court, including *Harbottle*.

[86]  In this case, the charge to the jury was entirely satisfactory. The trial judge charged the jury on the elements of manslaughter, second degree murder and first degree murder under s. 231(5) of the *Criminal Code*. With respect to manslaughter and second degree murder, the trial judge told the jurors that they must find that the accused was "more than a trivial cause" of death in order to conclude that the accused

caused Mrs. Loski's death. In essence, this reflects the test of causation set out in *Smithers*, and accurately states the correct standard of causation for second degree murder. On two occasions, once in the main charge and once in responding to a question from the jurors, Wilkinson J. misspoke in describing the appropriate test of causation for second degree murder, by contrasting the high standard of causation for first degree murder with the "slight or trivial cause necessary to find second degree murder." In my view, these errors, which reflect the difficulty of expressing a standard in the negative, would not have caused the jury to believe that the applicable standard of causation for second degree murder was lower than the *Smithers* standard of "more than a trivial cause." What the slips in the jury charge do illustrate is the fact that it is easier to express the standard of causation in positive terms, by referring to a "significant" contribution or cause, instead of using the negative phraseology of "beyond *de minimis*" or "more than a slight or trivial cause" in explaining causation to the jury.

[87]  Given that the jury found the accused guilty of second degree murder, we must conclude that the jury found that the appellant had the requisite intent for the offence of murder, namely subjective foresight of death. In light of the jury's conclusion with respect to intent, which in my view could not have been affected by the instructions on causation, it is clear that no reasonable jury could have had any doubt about whether the appellant's actions constituted a significant, operative cause of the victim's death. What is not clear from the verdict is the basis for the acquittal on the charge of first degree murder. The appellant suggests that the jury acquitted on first degree murder because it had a reasonable doubt as to whether the accused caused the victim's death on the *Harbottle* standard of causation, but convicted of second degree murder because it was satisfied the accused caused death on the lower *Smithers* standard. In my view, the conviction for second degree murder was amply supported on the evidence and the jury was correctly charged on the applicable legal requirements of causation. The jury was entitled to have a doubt as to whether the degree of participation of the accused in the underlying offence of unlawful confinement, combined with the need for his substantial contribution to the death of the victim, was sufficient to elevate the murder to first degree. Whatever the jury's reasons for acquitting the appellant of first degree murder, the jury's verdict of second degree murder is unimpeachable.

## VII.  Conclusion and Disposition

[88]  For these reasons, I conclude that the trial judge correctly charged the jury on the applicable standard of causation for second degree murder in expressing the standard as one in which the accused must have been more than an insignificant or trivial cause of the victim's death. There is only one standard of causation for homicide offences, including second degree murder. That standard may be expressed using different terminology, but it remains the standard expressed by this Court in the case of *Smithers*, *supra*. The terminology of substantial cause in *Harbottle* is used to indicate the increased degree of participation in the killing that is required to raise the accused's culpability to first degree murder under s. 231(5) of the *Code*. *Harbottle*

did not raise the standard of causation that applies to all homicide offences from the standard expressed in *Smithers*.

[89]  As is clear from the above, I also agree with Braidwood J.A. and McEachern C.J. in the Court of Appeal that telling the jury that the standard of causation for second degree murder was one of "substantial cause" instead of "more than a trivial cause" would not have altered the result in the present case. I would dismiss the appeal and uphold the jury's verdict of second degree murder.

*Appeal dismissed.*

───────────────────

The cases in this chapter are concerned with basic principles of causation. For the most part issues of causation do not typically raise problems of great difficulty. Conceptually, however, the subject of causation is rich and complex. Where an offence prohibits a specified result, proof of causation is plainly an essential element, without which the prosecution must fail. Where there are multiple causes, the prosecution must prove that the conduct of the accused contributed to the result within the defined standard. The standard set in *Smithers* is comparatively low. Even so, in a case of homicide in which the victim was attacked by more than one aggressor, the prosecution cannot succeed unless it proves conduct by the accused that specifically links him or her with the cause of death. See, for example, *Lucas* (2001), 45 C.R. (5th) 74 (Que. C.A.).

───────────────────

The following two cases are concerned with intervening causes.

**R. v. Menezes**
Ontario Superior Court of Justice
(2002), 50 C.R. (5th) 343

HILL J.:

*Introduction*

[1]  The accused pleaded not guilty to causing the death of Jacob Meuszynski by criminal negligence while operating a motor vehicle.

[2]  Christopher Menezes and the deceased were friends. On January 17th, 2000, late in the evening, each young man was driving his car along a stretch of roadway in north Mississauga. Neither had consumed alcohol. The vehicles travelled at a high rate of speed. At a point, Mr. Meuszynski's car left the road and struck a utility pole. Tragically, the driver was killed instantly.

[3]  The prosecution theory of criminal liability rests on establishing the accused engaged in a dangerous race with the deceased as a result of which Jacob Meuszynski lost control of his car and died.

[4]  The case is perhaps one of first impression in this jurisdiction insofar as determining whether a person who survived a street race in which the second participating

party lost his life can be held criminally accountable for that death solely on the basis of his co-participation in the dangerous racing activity. ...

### Applicable Legal Principles

[71] Where criminal negligence causing death is charged, the court's first task is to determine whether the accused drove his or her motor vehicle in a manner which constituted negligence or dangerous driving—only then is an inquiry to be made as to whether it was by reason of criminal negligence or dangerous driving that death ensued: *R. v. R. (R.L.)* (1988), 8 M.V.R. (2d) 116 (Ont. C.A.) at 122 *per curiam.* ...

### Causation

[87] While evidence of an unusual or dangerous driving pattern before an accident is admissible, it must be probative of that accident and its cause: *R. v. Galloway, supra; R. v. Ewart* (1989), 53 C.C.C. (3d) 153 (Alta. C.A.) (leave to appeal refused *R. v. Ewart*, [1990] 1 S.C.R. x (S.C.C.)) at 158 *per* McClung J.A. If, in prosecution of a criminal driving charge alleging death as a consequence, a real connection between the driving misconduct and the death is not established, as required by law, the Crown may be left simply with discharge of proof for a lesser offence, i.e. dangerous driving *simpliciter.*

[88] A determination of causation requires a finding that the accused caused the death of another both in fact and in law.

[89] Factual causation is concerned with an inquiry as to how the victim came to his or her death, in a medical, mechanical, or physical sense, *and* with the contribution of the accused to that result: *R. v. Nette, supra* at 505. Was the conduct of the accused a significant contributing cause of the prohibited consequence? In other words, were the actions of the accused beyond negligible? Where there are multiple operative, independent, and significant contributing causes, competing causes need not be sorted out by the trier of fact in an effort to identify a predominant cause. As there can be more than one cause of death, the causation test is not restricted to a search for the most proximate, the primary, or the only cause of death: *R. v. Meiler* (1999), 136 C.C.C. (3d) 11 (Ont. C.A.) at 20 *per* O'Connor J.A. Regardless of whether the accused's conduct is the sole cause, was it a material cause?

[90] The legal or imputable causation inquiry concerns itself with the question of whether the accused should be held criminally responsible in law for the death that occurred—a moral reaction, a value-judgment as to moral responsibility—whether, in the circumstances, a "blamable" cause ought to be identified: *R. v. Nette, supra* at 505-6. Causation expresses an element of fault. That, together with the requisite mental element, is in law sufficient to base criminal responsibility.

[91] The starting point in the chain of causation which seeks to attribute the prohibited consequence to an act of the accused is usually an unlawful act in itself. When the commission of the unlawful act is with the relevant mental element for the crime charged, causation is generally not an issue.

[92] The causation inquiry, other than in sentencing, is generally unconcerned with contributory negligence. As well, a wrongdoer cannot escape the thinskull rule—

a wrongdoer must take the victim as found: *R. v. Nette*, *supra* at 518; *R. v. Creighton*, *supra* at 377-8. In examining the traceable origin of the chain of events causing death, remoteness may become an issue. If the act of the accused is too remote to have caused the result alleged, causation is not established. If the accused's actions are fairly viewed as only part of the history of the setting in which the prohibited result unfolded, without more, causation is not proven: *R. v. Cribbin* (1994), 89 C.C.C. (3d) 67 (Ont. C.A.) at 80 *per* Arbour J.A. (as she then was). However, where the unlawful driving can be said to "still demonstrably influence the actual injury accident beyond serving as its backdrop," causation is established: *R. v. F. (D.L.)*, *supra* at 364.

[93]  Likewise, if the triggering of a chain of events is interrupted by an intervening cause, it can serve to distance and exonerate the accused from any responsibility for the consequence: *R. v. Nette*, *supra* at 507. Put differently, do independent factors exist which might reasonably be said to sever the link that ties the accused to the prohibited result? Or is the chain unbroken with the effect of the accused's actions subsisting up to the happening of the event or consequence? Is there a *supervening* cause such as to insulate the accused from the legal consequences flowing from the death? (*R. v. Cribbin*, *supra* at 80).

[94]  An intervening act terminating the causal chain of events may be the withdrawal or abandonment by the accused of involvement in the dangerous enterprise. Ordinarily, as a matter of law, abandonment requires communication or timely notice of intention to abandon the common pursuit: *R. v. Miller* (1976), 38 C.R.N.S. 139 (S.C.C.), at 146 *per* Ritchie J.; *R. v. Henderson* (1948), 91 C.C.C. 97 (S.C.C.), at 107-9 *per* Taschereau J. (as he then was) (dissenting in part). In other words, as a general rule, "in the absence of exceptional circumstances," something more is necessary than a mere mental change of intention and physical change of place by the person wishing to disassociate from the joint venture and the consequences attendant upon participation up to the point of the crime: *R. v. Kirkness* (1990), 60 C.C.C. (3d) 97 (S.C.C.), at 128 *per* Cory J. and at 114-7 *per* Wilson J. (in dissent in the result). The standard of positive action required of the accused for legal abandonment will often depend on the nature of the offence and his or her degree of participation in the unlawful enterprise. ...

[103]  We recognize, from mere participation in the dangerous racing endeavour, causative responsibility in *both* racers for the death of a passenger in one racer's vehicle when control is lost or that car is otherwise involved in an accident during the course of the race: *R. v. Elphick*, *supra*. The English authorities accord with this view: *R. v. Morley*, [2001] E.W.J. No. 4940 (Eng. C.A.); *R. v. Burke*, [2001] E.W.J. No. 1096 (Eng. C.A.); *R. v. Padley*, [2000] E.W.J. No. 431 (Eng. C.A.).

[104]  In my view, there is no reason rooted in law or policy not to identify the same degree of moral blameworthiness in the surviving racer when it is the driver of the second vehicle, and not the passenger therein, who loses his or her life or is injured. ...

[105]  Those at risk from the unreasonable and unjustified danger of an escapade of competitive driving, whether a spontaneous or planned event, include the occupants of other vehicles, cyclists, pedestrians, passengers in the racers' autos, and the co-participants themselves. There is one danger. Each driver bears equal responsibility

for its continued lifespan subject to withdrawal or intervening event. As each driver in effect induces the other to drive in an unlawfully unsafe manner, each is taken to assume any consequential risk objectively within the ambit of the danger created. This surely includes a risk of bodily harm or death to a co-principal arising out of miscalculation or other judgment error by that individual in the course of, and related to, pursuing the jointly maintained, and unlawfully conducted, dangerous activity. So, for example, where one of the race participants over-corrects in a curve at the excessive speed of the venture and loses control resulting in his own death, that consequence is a reasonably foreseeable result in the context of the hazardous course of conduct jointly undertaken and not simply an unconnected fortuitous or coincidental event. The consequence was, in legal contemplation, as a result of the act of both. ...

### Did the Accused Cause Mr. Meuszynski's Death?

[115]  The Crown quite properly points to evidence capable of supporting its submission that the accused and the deceased were still in a competitive show of speed when Mr. Meuszynski lost control of his car. Doris Waddell saw the two Hondas fan out ahead of her going neck-and-neck and accelerating away at increasing speed. Heather Waddell recalled the vehicles parallel to one another. Although I do not accept that Mr. Mann was able to see the Hondas as far to the west of Argentia Road as he maintained, I accept his testimony that the two cars were side-by-side at the Argentia intersection. While Ms. Doan saw the blue Honda ahead of the red Civic, she did not see Mr. Meuszynski's vehicle shoot ahead of the accused's car after the Hondas passed through the Argentia Road intersection. Ms. Khan was scared throughout her journey on Derry Road in Mr. Menezes' car.

[116]  On the accused's statement to the police, he hedged on his commitment to a position that he caught up to his friend at Argentia Road. At first he claimed he had. Subsequently, he retreated from that statement it seemed, from my review of the videotaped statement, under the recognition that to so acknowledge would suggest the race was still on.

[117]  The racing behaviour had lasted for a number of blocks. The more prolonged the course of racing, the greater the burden on the individual quitting the venture to alert his or her co-participant of that decision in order to escape continued liability for any reasonably foreseeable consequence of the second racer's ongoing conduct.

[118]  In terms of a rough time and distance reference point, both the accused and Ms. Khan actually saw the Meuszynski vehicle lose control and crash, and Ms. Khan saw the utility pole fall.

[119]  It is apparent from the accused's statement to the police he was in the race at least to the point of exiting from under the Highway #401 overpass. In the face of the accused's claim to have then slowed to a degree, confirmed somewhat in Tina Khan's testimony, the prosecution nevertheless argues that Mr. Menezes did not act within a time and distance sufficient in fact and law to communicate his posture of withdrawal to his co-racer. If he slowed, for example, to 100 k./hr. out of the Highway #401 overpass tunnel, and Mr. Meuszynski sped on at 139 k./hr., there would be

only about eight seconds' difference in the time it would take the Hondas to cover the last 736 to 805 metres to the point of the beginning of the tire marks where Mr. Meuszynski lost control. On this view of the case, and accepting that Jacob Meuszynski overcorrected in steering out of the West Credit Ave. curve of Derry Road, it could reasonably be said that his loss of control was simply a miscalculation within the stimulus and ambit of the ongoing dangerous race—the accused would be criminally responsible for Mr. Meuszynski's death.

[120] The defence, however, points to evidence in the record said to support its argument that there must be a doubt as to whether Christopher Menezes caused his friend's demise.

[121] The accused maintained in his statement to the police that he slowed to perhaps 50 k./hr. at a point he described as "under that bridge" and as "once I hit that bridge." This is a clear reference to the Highway #401 overpass. The accused told the officer he raced at the beginning and tried to catch his friend but abandoned the race at the point of the first curve after a long straight-away of travel on Derry Road. Mr. Menezes related to Constable Carty that he knew he would lose control of his car as his two front tires were bald and couldn't handle such a curve and his alignment was "off." These features of the accused's car are confirmed by the mechanic's inspection. …

[125] Mr. Menezes's view, expressed in the police interview, was that his friend would clearly have seen, in his rear-view mirror, that he was backing away and had given up the race. It seems to me that with the competitive nature of the street race conducted here along Derry Road, it is not at all unreasonable to believe the participants were at all times keeping an eye on one another. In these circumstances, if the accused slowed his speed to the range of 60% of that of the deceased nearly half a mile from the point of control loss, there must be a reasonable doubt, although nothing more, that his withdrawal from the race amounted to a sufficiently dramatic lack of commitment to keeping pace for it to be known to Jacob Meuszynski. The deceased, as an independent agent, as he had done before January 17th, then chose to maintain excessive speed for motives unrelated to Christopher Menezes' presence on Derry Road. His death was a result of his independent actions.

## Conclusion

[126] The accused is found not guilty of criminal negligence causing the death of Jacob Meuszynski.

[127] Mr. Menezes is found guilty of dangerous driving.

*Order accordingly.*

**R. v. Reid & Stratton**
Nova Scotia Court of Appeal
(2003), 180 C.C.C. (3d) 151

SAUNDERS J.A.:

*Introduction*

[1] A few minutes of stupidity after a reckless night of drinking left a young man dead and two others convicted of manslaughter for killing him. This appeal raises a most serious point concerning the requirement in law that in order for a culpable homicide to have been committed, the person accused of the crime must be shown to have *caused the death of* a human being.

[2] I have concluded that in the unique and tragic circumstances of this case the incompleteness of the trial judge's directions to the jury concerning this essential element of the offence, amounted to a serious error of law and that it cannot be said with any confidence that the error occasioned no substantial wrong or miscarriage of justice.

[3] Accordingly I would set aside the verdict and order a new trial for both Joey Robert Reid ("Reid") and Michael Gene Stratton ("Stratton").

[4] In light of my conclusion and disposition it will not be necessary for me to comment further on the several other grounds advanced by Reid and Stratton in their appeals from conviction, nor express any opinion on the separate appeal taken by the Crown against their sentences. ...

[13] An argument developed between Joey Reid and Jason Boudreau. Evidently upon hearing that Rachel was going to use her car to find a source of cocaine, Joey Reid told his cousin that she was in no condition to be operating a motor vehicle. This prompted Jason Boudreau to tell Joey Reid to "mind his own business." For reasons that are not entirely clear from the evidence the argument between Reid and Boudreau somehow escalated into a physical altercation between the victim MacKay, Reid and Stratton. Stratton and MacKay exchanged punches. At some point both men slipped to the ground. Stratton was able to grab MacKay around the neck in a headlock. While MacKay was on the ground Reid administered some kicks. After noticing that MacKay was no longer resisting or struggling, Stratton let go and got to his feet. It soon became apparent that MacKay was unconscious.

[14] Some in the group attempted resuscitation, to no avail. A telephone call to 911 sought an ambulance. Rather than wait and seeing that their efforts to resuscitate MacKay were ineffective, Pace, Rachael Reid and DeCoste carried MacKay to a vehicle and drove to the hospital while Pace continued CPR. MacKay was pronounced dead at the hospital. Reid and Stratton who had remained at the scene were apprehended by police and taken in for questioning. On January 28 they were charged with manslaughter. ...

[23] The uncontroverted evidence at trial, the view shared by all of the doctors whose reports and testimony were before the jury, was that Joey MacKay's death was due to asphyxia after he aspirated on his stomach contents. Put simply he choked to death on his own vomit. The botched attempts to resuscitate him tragically brought

on his death, when the pressure of physical resuscitation efforts forced large quantities of vomitus into his lungs. ...

[34] In light of this uncontroverted medical evidence it therefore became an essential inquiry for the jury to determine what in fact *caused* the victim's death. In order for the jury to convict Reid and Stratton, they had to be satisfied beyond a reasonable doubt that their actions in fact and in law caused MacKay's death. That determination obliged them to consider not just the facts as they found them relating to the physical contact among MacKay and Stratton and Reid, but also to carefully reflect upon the activities of those who attempted to revive Mr. MacKay with various attempts at CPR. This complete analysis was made all the more important in view of the medical experts' shared opinion as to how and why he died. ...

[35] In my respectful opinion, in light of this unique set of circumstances surrounding Mr. MacKay's death, it obliged the trial judge to instruct the jury with far greater precision and clarity than occurred here. ...

[38] Regrettably, although he spoke of the ill-administered CPR attempts, among other causes, for the aspiration of stomach contents, and later spoke of a chain of events, the trial judge did not provide any instructions to the jury on the issue of intervening act and intervening cause as it related to the CPR resuscitation efforts which, on the unanimous view of all of the medical experts, was the cause of MacKay's death. ...

[58] In her reasons Justice Arbour went to considerable lengths to emphasize that cause of death cases are fact specific and that *Nette*, and *Harbottle*, and *Smithers* were all to be distinguished from cases where the unlawful act may have been *interrupted* by an *intervening event*. ...

[62] I take from these repeated and cautionary statements, that intervening causes do constitute a unique category of case such that in circumstances like these where, upon the evidence, the failed attempts at CPR clearly *interrupted* and therefore separated the acts of Stratton and Reid from MacKay's ultimate death, the trial judge was obliged to give the jury a clear and specific instruction with respect to intervening events. It was critical that the jury understood their obligation to consider whether or not any independent, intervening and therefore exculpatory factors occurred after the two accused's acts, thereby severing the link in the chain which tied them to MacKay's death. ...

[77] I found little help in the reported cases that have considered the application of s. 225 (or its predecessors) of the *Criminal Code*. Cases like *R. v. Kitching* (1976), 32 C.C.C. (2d) 159 (Man. C.A.), *R. v. Torbiak* (1978), 40 C.C.C. (2d) 193 (Ont. C.A.), and *R. v. McCallum*, [1990] O.J. No. 3158 (Ont. Dist. Ct.) and other similar cases all address the conduct of doctors whose subsequent medical treatment or surgical intervention is said, by the accused, to have been the true cause of death. The matters and principles considered in those cases have little application here where the rescue efforts were attempted by young bystanders, many of whom were intoxicated and where, according to the uncontroverted medical evidence, the botched and lethal attempt to resuscitate him was the sole cause of MacKay's death.

[78] Before the hearing we referred counsel to the recent decision of the British Columbia Court of Appeal in *R. v. Pangowish*, 2003 BCCA 62 (B.C. C.A.), judgment

released January 20, 2003, which had not been cited in their written facta. (Leave to appeal to the Supreme Court of Canada dismissed, September 11, 2003 [2003] S.C.C.A. No. 126 (S.C.C.).) We invited and received their oral representations at the hearing. After carefully considering their submissions I conclude that the matters addressed in *Pangowish* have little application to this case. There the female victim had been savagely assaulted and left in circumstances suggesting that she had been bludgeoned to death while a rolled up sock had been stuffed in her mouth. The medical evidence established that the victim's death was not instantaneous and that *both* blunt head trauma and asphyxiation were the principal contributing causes of death. In other words, it was a case of *competing* causes as contrasted with this case where the uncontroverted medical evidence points, arguably, to an independent intervening cause of Mr. MacKay's death.

[79]  The most recent 2002 update of *Crimji*, Canadian Criminal Jury Instructions (3rd Edition by Ferguson & Bouck), contains a brief paragraph as a suggested instruction in a case when there is some evidence of an intervening cause. It reads:

> 20A.  In this case, _____ [THE ACCUSED] alleges that the death was caused by an independent intervening cause, namely _____ [SPECIFY THE INTERVENING CAUSE]. However, the existence of an independent, intervening cause does not mean the _____ [THE UNLAWFUL ACT] by _____ [THE ACCUSED] is not also a cause of the death since there can be more than one cause for an event. However, _____ [THE ACCUSED] does not, in law, cause the death if the independent intervening cause so overwhelms _____ [THE UNLAWFUL ACT] by _____ [THE ACCUSED] as a cause that _____ [THE UNLAWFUL ACT] becomes merely the background or the setting for the independent intervening cause to take effect. In that case, the _____ [THE UNLAWFUL ACT] is too trivial (or insignificant) to be a legal (i.e. significant) cause of the death.

[80]  With great respect to the authors of this important work, I am not convinced that this single paragraph is sufficient to explain what is essential to the jury's deliberations. Neither am I persuaded that the authors' characterization of the "independent" intervening cause having to be such that it "overwhelms" the original unlawful act as a cause, necessarily or accurately captures the jury's inquiry into causation.

[81]  I have also had the privilege of reviewing the results of Justice David Watts' remarkable efforts in preparing the Ontario Specimen Jury Instructions (Criminal) published recently by Carswell. In the section dealing with Final Instructions on a charge of unlawful act manslaughter the specimen jury charge naturally includes a reminder that the Crown is obliged to prove each of several essential elements beyond a reasonable doubt, among them, that the accused *caused* the victim's death by an unlawful act. Using plain language to explain the point the text provides:

> For an act (or omission) to cause someone's death, it must be at least a contributing cause, one that is beyond something that is trifling or minor in nature. There must *not* be anything that somebody else does later that results in (NOA)'s act or omission no longer being a contributing cause of (NOC)'s death. (Italics in original)

This extract provides a footnoted reference to the Supreme Court of Canada's decision in *Nette*, supra, together with the advice that:

> Where it is preferable to phrase the standard of causation in positive terms, and in a more direct and affirmative way, the phrase "significant contributing cause" may be used. (Referencing Justice Arbour's reasons for the majority in *Nette*.)

[82]  With great respect, while undoubtedly sound as far as they go, I am not persuaded that this brief instruction, without considerably more, would be sufficient in circumstances such as these to provide an adequate and meaningful direction to the jury on intervening acts.

[83]  Before setting out what I would consider to be appropriate instructions I suggest that it would have been prudent to *separately* relate for the jury the evidence surrounding the actions of Stratton, and the actions of Reid. This would avoid confusing the jury in their subsequent deliberations.

[84]  Various terms or expressions were used by witnesses to describe the maneuver of placing one's arm around someone else's neck so as to momentarily restrain or incapacitate them. Descriptions included "cardiac sleeper," "choke hold," "sleeper," "purposeful hold," among others. In these reasons I will simply describe the move as a form of headlock.

[85]  Dr. Bowes gave evidence as to the manner of applying it. He said it is often used by law enforcement personnel as a less than lethal means of force to subdue someone who may be violent or resisting arrest, but that "it can also be rendered by anyone." He said it did not require a great deal of strength as long as sufficient pressure were applied around the neck to decrease blood flow in the carotid artery. A reduction in blood flow of 85% will be enough to produce unconsciousness. Studies have shown that six seconds' worth of compression is all it takes to reduce blood flow in the neck by 85%. According to Dr. Bowes if compression is released at the six second mark at a point when one is just on the verge of losing consciousness, it will take fourteen seconds for blood pressure and blood flow to return to normal. If the hold were administered for thirty seconds Dr. Bowes testified that it "may be a couple of minutes before consciousness may return." He said it was "a dangerous hold" that "does result in a fair number of deaths as have been reported in the literature recently."

[86]  From this evidence, together with evidence of witnesses at the scene and Stratton's own description of the way and very brief amount of time in which he applied the hold, it was open to the jury to conclude that if MacKay had simply been left unattended, he may well have "come to" and returned to consciousness on his own.

[87]  This was an important feature of the case that ought to have been identified by the trial judge when reviewing the evidence as to cause of death. The trial judge then ought to have provided the jury with examples of situations that the law would recognize as legitimate, intervening and exculpatory events, ones that would absolve an accused charged with causing the death of someone, from criminal liability. ... He might have explained that if A assaults B, leaving him unconscious on the floor of a building in which the assault occurred and before B regains consciousness he is killed

when the building collapses in a sudden earthquake, A cannot be held criminally responsible for the homicide. The law would attribute B's death to another intervening cause and not to A's assault even though B would not have been in the building but for the force of A's blow that rendered him unconscious. The assault was the reason that B was there but the blow was not the cause of the man's death.

[88]  Similarly, consider the situation where A strikes B and leaves him unconscious under a tree where later a branch falls killing the man by its own weight. Or A strikes B and the blow renders B unconscious. Other people carry B to a nearby clinic but on route they tumble down an open well where B drowns; or they are waylaid by a gang of thieves and in the ensuing robbery B is stabbed to death; or upon arrival at the hospital for treatment B contracts streptococcus, flesh eating disease from which he dies within days. These are all examples where the law would recognize a supervening cause, an interrupting exculpatory event. The intervening acts break the chain of causation. They interrupt the original infliction of injury. Some other act or event has intervened before death. The question for the jury is whether the initial injury can still be viewed as a significant contributing cause of the victim's death. Such situations ought to have been mentioned to illustrate for the jury the notion of intervening cause in law so that the jury might then go on to decide as a matter of fact whether such had occurred in this case.

[89]  After providing such illustrations to explain the point and after then reviewing the evidence concerning the separate conduct of the two accused, the trial judge ought to have directed the jury in words to the following effect:

> In order to be satisfied beyond a reasonable doubt that Stratton or Reid caused the death of MacKay, you are required to consider the whole of the evidence and decide:
>
>> 1. whether the accused's unlawful acts (specifically, as I have reviewed with you, in the case of Stratton the so-called headlock and in the case of Reid the alleged kicks) in fact amounted to a significant contributing cause of MacKay's death?
>
> If you are satisfied as to the first question, you should then go on to ask yourselves:
>
>> 2. Whether any intervening cause which resulted in MacKay's death occurred between the accused's acts and the victim's death? Put another way, are you satisfied beyond a reasonable doubt that the actions of either Stratton or Reid are so connected to the death of MacKay that they can be said to have had a significant causal effect which continued up to the time of his death, without having been interrupted by some other act or event, in this case the failed attempts at CPR?
>
> As I have already explained to you, in order for you to convict either Stratton or Reid, you must find that the Crown has proved each of the essential elements of the offence beyond a reasonable doubt. Here of course we have been considering the requirement that the Crown prove that the accused's unlawful acts caused MacKay's death. Remember that to meet that burden the Crown does not have to show that either Reid's kicking or Stratton's headlock was the sole cause of MacKay's death. It is enough

for the Crown to prove to your satisfaction that in the case of Reid, his kicking; or in the case of Stratton, his having a hold of MacKay's neck, was a significant contributing cause of MacKay's death.

The question you will now want to consider during your deliberations is this. Were the actions by those at the scene to resuscitate MacKay—which all of the doctors said was what caused his death—in your opinion an intervening event which broke the chain of causation between what Reid and Stratton are said to have done, and MacKay's death, such that the actions of either of them are no longer seen by you as being a significant contributing cause of his death?

If you were satisfied that the chain of causation was unbroken, or you were not left with a reasonable doubt about it, you would then conclude that this element of the offence of manslaughter was made out. If on the other hand you decided that the CPR efforts had severed the chain of causation linking either of the accused to MacKay's death, or were left with a reasonable doubt about it, then the Crown would have failed to establish this essential element of the charge and would therefore be unable to convict that accused of manslaughter. Your deliberations at that point would be over.

[90] It is regrettable that counsel were not of greater assistance to the trial judge in either helping to formulate this part of his charge or in correcting this critical omission with a pointed recharge of the jury. Neither counsel raised the notion of intervening cause in their closing addresses to the jury. Rather their theory seemed to be that the medical evidence alone as to the failed CPR efforts being the cause of MacKay's asphyxiation, was enough to raise a reasonable doubt whether the actions of Stratton or Reid caused his death. Further, in Reid's defence, it was argued by his counsel that there was no evidence whatsoever that the kicks said to have been administered by Reid (if any were at all) caused or contributed in any way to MacKay's death. That said, neither counsel mentioned or sought from the trial judge any special directions as to the consequence in law—in this unique set of circumstances—of an interruption in the causal chain by an *intervening act* or an *intervening cause*.

[91] Counsel for both Stratton and Reid are senior, skilled and very experienced criminal lawyers. During argument in this court defence counsel suggested that they and most everyone else present at the trial were surprised by the verdict, believing that on the strength of the medical testimony and lay evidence from witnesses at the scene, their clients' acquittals were practically assured. Counsel felt the doctors' uncontroverted evidence alone was enough to establish a reasonable doubt as to either accused's actions having brought about MacKay's death. The idea that causation in fact and in law ought to have been better explained to the jury or that they required specific instruction on the issue of intervening act and intervening cause as it related to the failed CPR procedures "just wasn't on counsel's radar," we were told.

[92] It is unfortunate that these issues were not brought to the trial judge's attention at a time when counsel's advice would have been most profitable.

*Appeal allowed; new trial ordered.*

## ADDITIONAL READING

- D. Stuart, *Canadian Criminal Law*, 4th ed. (Toronto: Carswell, 2001), chapter 2;
- K. Roach, *Criminal Law*, 3rd ed. (Toronto: Irwin Law, 2004), chapter 2;
- I.H.E. Patient, "Some Remarks About the Element of Voluntariness in Offences of Absolute Liability" [1968] *Crim. L.R.* 23;
- A.C.E. Lynch, "The Mental Element in the Actus Reus" (1982), 98 *Law Quarterly Review* 109;
- M.S. Moore, *Act and Crime: The Philosophy of Action and Its Implications for Criminal Law* (Oxford: Oxford University Press, 1993);
- H. Hart and T. Honoré, *Causation in the Law*, 2nd ed. (Oxford: Clarendon Press, 1985);
- D. Galloway, "Causation in Criminal Law: Interventions, Thin Skulls and Lost Chances" (1989), 14 *Queen's L.J.* 71;
- A. Manson, "Rethinking Causation: The Implications of Harbottle" (1994), 24 C.R. (4th) 153;
- J. Presser, "All for a Good Cause: The Need for Overhaul of the Smithers Test of Causation" (1994), 28 C.R. (4th) 178;
- A.W. Mewett, "Causation and the Charter" (1994), 37 *Crim. L.Q.* 1;
- D.M. Tanovich and J. Lockyer, "Revisiting Harbottle: Does the Substantial Cause Test Apply to All Murder Offences?" (1996), 38 *Crim. L.Q.* 322;
- D. Stuart, "*Nette*: Confusing Cause in Reformulating the Smithers Test" (2002), 46 C.R. (5th) 230.

# CHAPTER SIX

# Absolute and Strict Responsibility

This chapter and chapter 7 address pre-conditions for liability beyond the requirement of a cognizable act, discussed in chapter 5. The issue is whether the criminal law should require proof of something more than a voluntary act or omission on the part of the accused in order to establish liability, or is mere proof of the act or omission sufficient for the purposes of censure and punishment. This confronts fundamental issues of moral philosophy—is it justifiable for the state to impose punishment on someone who was morally blameless (at least in the sense of the person having committed the guilty act, but without any intention, knowledge, foresight, or carelessness in having done so)? See, generally, the classic book by H.L.A. Hart, *Punishment and Responsibility: Essays in the Philosophy of Law* (Oxford: Oxford University Press, 1968).

The criminal law, especially since the entrenchment of the Charter, has required something more than proof of the criminal act in order to justify punishment. In other words, there must usually be proof of some guilty state of mind. The law presumes the requirement of some mental state with respect to "true criminal offences." This is a concept that is discussed below. However, with respect to other types of offences, often referred to as regulatory or public welfare offences, the state is not held to such a high standard. Subject to certain restraints imposed by the Charter, liability for regulatory or public welfare offences may be satisfied by proof of the act requirement, accompanied by no further fault requirement ("absolute liability") or a much reduced fault requirement (referred to as "strict liability").

The cases in the next section of this chapter were decided when offences were classified as either "true criminal offences" (requiring a presumption of full *mens rea*) or "public welfare offences" (permitting no additional fault requirement at all). As revealed later in *R. v. Sault Ste. Marie* (1978), 40 C.C.C. (2d) 353 (S.C.C.), all offences enacted by a provincial or territorial government fall into the category of "public welfare" or "regulatory offences." But the distinction made by the cases in the next section is important for determining whether federal offences (other than those in the *Criminal Code* and the *Controlled Drugs and Substances Act*) are "true criminal offences" or "regulatory offences." In other words, the cases in the following section are still important for classificatory purposes. Section II of this chapter addresses the emergence of a new category of offences, called "strict liability offences." These are offences with a reduced fault element requiring the prosecution to prove the prohibited act, with the burden then shifting to the accused to establish due diligence (or lack of negligence) on a balance of probabilities. Like absolute liability, strict liability is particular to regulatory or public

welfare offences. Section III considers the constitutional challenges that have been made
to absolute liability and strict liability offences.

## I. PUBLIC WELFARE OR TRUE CRIMINAL OFFENCES

### Beaver v. The Queen
Supreme Court of Canada
(1957), 118 C.C.C. 129

CARTWRIGHT J. (with whom Rand and Locke JJ. concurred): The appellant was
tried jointly with one Max Beaver before His Honour Judge Forsyth and a jury in the
Court of General Sessions of the Peace for the County of York on an indictment
reading as follows:

> The jurors for our Lady the Queen present that
>
> LOUIS BEAVER and MAX BEAVER, at the City of Toronto, in the County of York, on
> or about the 12th day of March, in the year 1954, unlawfully did sell a drug, to wit,
> diacetylmorphine, without the authority of a licence from the Minister of National Health
> and Welfare or other lawful authority, contrary to Section 4(1)(f) of the Opium and Nar-
> cotic Drug Act, Revised Statutes of Canada, 1952, Chapter 201 and amendments thereto.
>
> The said jurors further present that the said LOUIS BEAVER and MAX BEAVER, at
> the City of Toronto, in the County of York, on or about the 12th day of March, in the
> year 1954, unlawfully did have in their possession a drug, to wit, diacetylmorphine,
> without the authority of a licence from the Minister of National Health and Welfare or
> other lawful authority, contrary to Section 4(1)(d) of the Opium and Narcotic Drug Act,
> Revised Statutes of Canada 1952, Chapter 201, and amendments thereto ...

On September 19, 1955, the accused were found guilty on both counts and on the
same day the learned trial Judge found them to be habitual criminals. On October 17,
1955, the learned Judge sentenced them to 7 years' imprisonment on each count, the
sentences to run concurrently, and also imposed sentences of preventive detention.

Max Beaver has since died and we are concerned only with the case of the appellant.

The appellant appealed to the Court of Appeal for Ontario against both convictions and against the finding that he was an habitual criminal. These appeals were
dismissed.

On February 19, 1957, the appellant was given leave to appeal to this Court [117
Can. C.C. 340, [1957] S.C.R. 119] from the convictions on the two counts.

It is not necessary to set out the facts in detail. There was evidence on which it was
open to the jury to find (i) that Max Beaver sold to a police officer, who was working
under cover, a package which in fact contained diacetylmorphine, (ii) that the appellant was a party to the sale of the package, (iii) that while the appellant did not have
the package on his person or in his physical possession he and Max Beaver were
acting jointly in such circumstances that the possession which the latter had of the
package was the possession of both of the accused, and (iv) that the appellant had no

knowledge that the substance contained in the package was diacetylmorphine and believed it to be sugar of milk.

I do not mean to suggest that the jury would necessarily have made the fourth finding but there was evidence on which they might have done so, or which might have left them in a state of doubt as to whether or not the appellant knew that the package contained anything other than sugar of milk.

The learned trial Judge, against the protest of the appellant, charged the jury, in effect, that if they were satisfied that the appellant had in his possession a package and sold it, then, if in fact the substance contained in the package was diacetylmorphine, the appellant was guilty on both counts, and that the questions (i) whether he had any knowledge of what the substance was, or (ii) whether he entertained the honest but mistaken belief that it was a harmless substance were irrelevant and must not be considered. Laidlaw J.A. who delivered the unanimous judgment of the Court of Appeal, [116 Can. C.C. 231], was of opinion that this charge was right in law and that the learned trial Judge was bound by the decision in *R. v. Lawrence*, 102 Can. C.C. 121, [1952] O.R. 149, to direct the jury as he did. The main question on this appeal is whether this view of the law is correct.

The problem is one of construction of the *Opium and Narcotic Drug Act*, R.S.C. 1952, c. 201, and particularly the following sections, which at the date of the offences charged read as follows:

4.(1)  Every person who …

(d)  has in his possession any drug save and except under the authority of a licence from the Minister first had and obtained, or other lawful authority; …

(f)  manufactures, sells, gives away, delivers or distributes or makes any offer in respect of any drug, or any substance represented or held out by such person to be a drug, to any person without first obtaining a licence from the Minister, or without other lawful authority; …

is guilty of an offence, and is liable

(i)  upon indictment, to imprisonment for any term not exceeding seven years and not less than six months, and to a fine not exceeding one thousand dollars and not less than two hundred dollars, and, in addition, at the discretion of the judge, to be whipped; or

(ii)  upon summary conviction, to imprisonment with or without hard labour for any term not exceeding eighteen months and not less than six months, and to a fine not exceeding one thousand dollars and not less than two hundred dollars.

(2)  Notwithstanding the provisions of the *Criminal Code*, or of any other statute or law, the court has no power to impose less than the minimum penalties herein prescribed, and shall, in all cases of conviction, impose both fine and imprisonment.

11.(1)  No person shall, without lawful authority or without a permit signed by the Minister or some person authorized by him in that behalf, import or have in his possession any opium pipe, opium lamp, or other device or apparatus designed or generally used for the purpose of preparing opium for smoking, or smoking or inhaling opium, or any article capable of being used as or as part of any such pipe, lamp or other device or apparatus.

(2) Any person violating the provisions of this section is liable, upon summary conviction, to a fine not exceeding one hundred dollars, and not less than fifty dollars, or to imprisonment for a term not exceeding three months, or to both fine and imprisonment.

15. Where any person is charged with an offence under paragraph (a), (d), (e), (f), or (g) of subsection (1) of section 4, it is not necessary for the prosecuting authority to establish that the accused had not a licence from the Minister or was not otherwise authorized to commit the act complained of, and if the accused pleads or alleges that he had such licence or other authority the burden of proof thereof shall be upon the person so charged.

17. Without limiting the generality of paragraph (d) of subsection (1) of section 4, any person who occupies, controls, or is in possession of any building, room, vessel, vehicle, enclosure or place, in or upon which any drug or any article mentioned in section 11 is found, shall, if charged with having such drug or article in possession without lawful authority, be deemed to have been so in possession unless he prove that the drug or article was there without his authority, knowledge or consent, or that he was lawfully entitled to the possession thereof.

The judgment in appeal is supported by earlier decisions of Appellate Courts in Ontario, Quebec and Nova Scotia, but a directly contrary view has been expressed by the Court of Appeal for British Columbia. While this conflict has existed since 1948, this is the first occasion on which the question has been brought before this Court.

It may be of assistance in examining the problem to use a simple illustration. Suppose X goes to the shop of Y, a druggist, and asks Y to sell him some baking soda. Y hands him a sealed packet which he tells him contains baking soda and charges him a few cents. X honestly believes that the packet contains baking soda, but in fact it contains heroin. X puts the package in his pocket, takes it home and later puts it in a cupboard in his bathroom. There would seem to be no doubt that X has had actual manual and physical possession of the package and that he continues to have possession of the package while it is in his cupboard. The main question raised on this appeal is whether, in the supposed circumstances, X would be guilty of the crime of having heroin in his possession?

[A number of cases are then examined.]

When the decisions as to the construction of the *Opium and Narcotic Drug Act* on which the respondent relies are examined it appears that two main reasons are assigned for holding that *mens rea* is not an essential ingredient of the offence created by s. 4(1)(d), these being (i) the assumption that the subject-matter with which the Act deals is of the kind dealt with in the cases of which *Hobbs v. Winchester Corp.*, [1910] 2 K.B. 471, is typical and which are sometimes referred to as "public welfare offence cases," and (ii) by implication from the wording of s. 17 of the Act.

As to the first of these reasons, I can discern little similarity between a statute designed, by forbidding the sale of unsound meat, to ensure that the supply available to the public shall be wholesome, and a statute making it a serious crime to possess or deal in narcotics; the one is to ensure that a lawful and necessary trade shall be carried on in a manner not to endanger the public health, the other to forbid altogether conduct regarded as harmful in itself. As a necessary feature of his trade, the butcher holds himself out as selling meat fit for consumption; he warrants that quality; and it is part of his duty as trader to see that the merchandise is wholesome. The statute simply converts that civil personal duty into a public duty.

As to the second reason, the argument is put as follows. Using again the illustration I have taken above, it is said (i) that the words of s. 17 would require the conviction of X if the package was found in his bathroom cupboard "unless he prove that [it] was there without his authority, knowledge or consent," that is, he is *prima facie* presumed to be guilty but can exculpate himself by proving lack of knowledge, and (ii) that since no such words as "unless he prove that the drug was in his possession without his knowledge" are found in s. 4(1)(d) it must be held that Parliament intended that lack of knowledge should be no defence.

[Cartwright J. then held that the wording of s. 17 does not compel the court to construe s. 4 as not requiring *mens rea*.]

If the matter were otherwise doubtful I would be drawn to the conclusion that Parliament did not intend to enact that *mens rea* should not be an essential ingredient of the offence created by s. 4(1)(d) by the circumstance that on conviction a minimum sentence of 6 months' imprisonment plus a fine of $200 must be imposed. Counsel informed us that they have found no other statutory provision which has been held to create a crime of strict responsibility, that is to say, one in which the necessity for *mens rea* is excluded, on conviction for which a sentence of imprisonment is mandatory. The legislation dealt with in *Hobbs v. Winchester*, *supra*, provided that a sentence of imprisonment might, not must, be imposed on a convicted person.

It would, of course, be within the power of Parliament to enact that a person who, without any guilty knowledge, had in his physical possession a package which he honestly believed to contain a harmless substance such as baking soda but which in fact contained heroin, must on proof of such facts be convicted of a crime and sentenced to at least 6 months' imprisonment; but I would refuse to impute such an intention to Parliament unless the words of the statute were clear and admitted of no other interpretation. To borrow the words of Lord Kenyon in *Fowler v. Padget* (1798), 7 Term R. 509 at p. 514, 101 E.R. 1103: "I would adopt any construction of the statute that the words will bear, in order to avoid such monstrous consequences as would manifestly ensue from the construction contended for by the defendant."

For the above reasons I would quash the conviction on the charge of having possession of a drug.

As to the charge of selling, as is pointed out by my brother Fauteux, the appellant's version of the facts brings his actions within the provisions of s. 4(1)(f) since he and his brother jointly sold a substance represented or held out by them to be heroin; and I agree with the conclusion of my brother Fauteux that the conviction on the charge of selling must be affirmed.

For the above reasons, I would dismiss the appeal as to the first count (that is, of selling) but would direct that the time during which the appellant has been confined pending the determination of the appeal shall count as part of the term of imprisonment imposed pursuant to that conviction. As to the second count (that is, of having possession) I would allow the appeal, quash the conviction and direct a new trial. As leave to appeal from the finding that the appellant is an habitual criminal was granted conditionally upon the appeal from the convictions being successful, and as the appeal as to one conviction has failed, we are without jurisdiction to review the finding that the appellant is an habitual criminal and in the result that finding stands.

FAUTEUX J. (with whom Abbott J. concurred), dissenting in part: … The plain and apparent object of the Act is to prevent, by a rigid control of the possession of drugs, the danger to public health, and to guard society against the social evils which an uncontrolled traffic in drugs is bound to generate. The scheme of the Act is this: The importation, exportation, sale, manufacture, production and distribution of drugs are subject to the obtention of a licence which the Minister of National Health and Welfare may issue, with the approval of the Governor-General in Council, and in which the place where such operations may be carried on is stated. Under the same authority are indicated ports and places in Canada where drugs may be exported or imported, the manner in which they are to be packed and marked for export, the records to be kept for such export, import, receipt, sale, disposal and distribution. The Act also provides for the establishment of all other convenient and necessary regulations with respect to duration, terms and forms of the several licences therein provided. Without a licence, it is an offence to import or export from Canada and an offence for anyone who, not being a common carrier, takes or carries, or causes to be taken or carried from any place in Canada to any other place in Canada, any drug. Druggists, physicians, dentists and veterinary surgeons stand, of course, in a privileged class; but even their dealings in drugs for medicinal purposes are the object of a particular control. Under penalties of the law, some of them have to keep records of their operations, while others have the obligation to answer inquiries in respect thereto. Having in one's possession drugs without a licence or other lawful authority, is an offence. In brief, the principle underlying the Act is that possession of drugs covered by it is unlawful; and where any exception is made to the principle, the exceptions themselves are attended with particular controlling provisions and conditions.

The enforcement sections of the Act manifest the exceptional vigilance and firmness which Parliament thought of the essence to forestall the unlawful traffic in narcotic drugs and cope effectively with the unusual difficulties standing in the way of the realization of the object of the statute. Substantive and procedural principles generally prevailing under the *Criminal Code* in favour of the subject are being restricted or excepted. The power to search by day or by night, either premises or the person, is largely extended under s. 19. Special writs of assistance are provided for under s. 22. The consideration of the provisions of ss. 4 and 17 being deferred for the moment, the burden of proof is either alleviated or shifted to persons charged with violations under ss. 6, 11, 13, 16 and 18. Minimum sentences are provided or are made mandatory, under ss. 4 and 6. Deportation of aliens found guilty is also mandatory and this notwithstanding the provisions of the *Immigration Act* [R.S.C. 1952, c. 325] or any other Act, under s. 26. And the application of the *Identification of Criminals Act* [R.S.C. 1952, c. 144], ordinarily limited to the case of indictable offences, is, by s. 27, extended to any offence under the Act.

All of these provisions are indicative of the will of Parliament to give the most efficient protection to public health against the danger attending the uncontrolled use of drugs as well as against the social evils incidental thereto, by measures generally centred and directed to possession itself of the drugs covered by the Act. The subject-matter, the purpose and the scope of the Act are such that to subject its provisions to the narrow construction suggested on behalf of appellant would defeat the very object of the Act.

The main provisions to consider are those of s. 4(1)(d), reading as follows:

> 4.(1) Every person who ...
>
> (d) has in his possession any drug save and except under the authority of a licence from the Minister first had and obtained, or other lawful authority; ... is guilty of an offence, and is liable.

On the plain, literal and grammatical meaning of the words of this section, there is an absolute prohibition to be in possession of drugs, whatever be the various meanings of which the word possession may be susceptible, unless the possession is under the authority of a licence from the Minister, first had and obtained, or under other lawful authority.

... Furthermore, and if it is argued that knowledge is of the essence of unlawful possession under both s. 4(1)(d) and s. 17, then one is at a loss to understand why Parliament should have, in the latter section, provided for a defence resting on the proof of lack of knowledge. A like interpretation of s. 17 strips this exculpatory provision of any meaning and effect. The language of the two sections can only be rationalized, I think, by interpreting s. 4(1)(d) as meaning what it says, i.e., as creating an absolute prohibition, and by interpreting s. 17 as extending the meaning of s. 4(1)(d), i.e., this absolute prohibition, to the circumstances described in s. 17, with however, and only in such circumstances, a defence resting on the proof of lack of knowledge.

As interpreted by most of the members of the Canadian Courts of Appeal since 1932, the provisions of s. 4(1)(d) are, like many other provisions of the Act, undoubtedly severe. The duty of the Courts is to give effect to the language of Parliament. And notwithstanding that the views expressed in *Morelli* and *Lawrence*, in particular, had been prevailing ever since 1932 and are still prevailing, Parliament has not seen fit to intervene. For all these reasons, I find it impossible to accede to the proposition that knowledge of the nature of the substance is of the essence of the offence of unlawful possession under the Act.

As to sale: Though the substance delivered to and paid for by Tassie was a drug, as admittedly it was represented and held out to be by appellant, it is said that the latter could not be guilty of the offence of sale under s. 4(1)(f) because, on his story, he intended and thought the substance sold to be sugar of milk. To this submission, the provisions of s. 4(1)(f) afford, I think, a complete answer:

> 4.(1) Every person who ...
>
> (f) ... sells, ... any drug, *or any substance represented or held out by such person to be a drug*, to any person without first obtaining a licence from the Minister, or without other lawful authority ... .

That the enforcement of the provisions of the Act may, in exceptional cases, lead to some injustice, is not an impossibility. But, to forestall this result as to such possible cases, there are remedies under the law, such as a stay of proceedings by the Attorney-General or a free pardon under the Royal Prerogative.

I would dismiss the appeal against the unanimous judgment of the Court of Appeal for Ontario affirming the conviction on the primary charges and, in view of this result, the unanimous judgment of the Court of Appeal, affirming the decision that appellant is an habitual criminal, remains undisturbed.

*Appeal from conviction for possession of drug allowed;*
*appeals from conviction for sale of a drug and*
*finding of being an habitual criminal dismissed.*

### R. v. Pierce Fisheries Ltd.
Supreme Court of Canada
[1970] 5 C.C.C. 193

[The accused was charged with having undersized lobsters in its possession contrary to the Lobster Fishery Regulations made pursuant to the *Fisheries Act*, R.S.C. 1952, c. 119. The evidence showed that on the day in question the company would have bought or brought to its plant by truck and by boat 50,000 to 60,000 lbs. of lobsters, and among these a fishery officer found 26 undersized lobsters. The Supreme Court of Canada allowed an appeal from an acquittal.]

RITCHIE J. (for the majority): I agree with the submission made on behalf of the appellant, which appears to have received qualified approval in the reasons for judgment rendered on behalf of the Appeal Division by the Chief Justice of Nova Scotia, that the *Lobster Fishery Regulations* are obviously intended for the purpose of protecting lobster beds from depletion and thus conserving the source of supply for an important fishing industry which is of general public interest.

I do not think that a new crime was added to our criminal law by making regulations which prohibit persons from having undersized lobsters in their possession, nor do I think that the stigma of having been convicted of a criminal offence would attach to a person found to have been in breach of these regulations. The case of *Beaver v. The Queen*, ... affords an example of provisions of a federal statute other than the *Criminal Code* which were found to have created a truly criminal offence, but in the present case, to paraphrase the language used by the majority of this Court in the *Beaver* case, I can discern little similarity between a statute designed, by forbidding the possession of undersized lobsters to protect the lobster industry, and a statute making it a serious crime to possess or deal in narcotics.

In view of the above, it will be seen that I am of opinion that the offence created by s. 3(1)(b) of the Regulations falls within the first class of exceptions referred to by Wright, J., in *Sherras v. De Rutzen*, ... and that it should be construed in accordance with the language in which it was enacted, free from any presumption as to the requirement of *mens rea*.

In considering the language of the Regulation, s. 3(1)(b), it is significant, though not conclusive, that it contains no such words as "knowingly," "wilfully," "with intent" or "without lawful excuse," whereas such words occur in a number of sections of the *Fisheries Act* itself which create offences for which *mens rea* is made an essential ingredient.

CARTWRIGHT C.J.C. (dissenting): … In my view a principle of construction of a statute which makes possession of a forbidden substance an offence was laid down by this Court in *Beaver v. The Queen*, 118 C.C.C. 129, [1957] S.C.R. 531, 26 C.R. 193, where it was said by the majority at p. 140:

> The essence of the crime is the possession of the forbidden substance and in a criminal case there is in law no possession without knowledge of the character of the forbidden substance.

Applying this principle to the words of the charge against the respondent in the case at bar, it appears to me that the express finding of fact that the respondent had no knowledge, factually or inferentially, that any of the lobsters on its premises and under its control were undersized necessarily leads to a finding of not guilty.

Parliament could, of course, provide by apt words that anyone having in fact an undersized lobster on his premises and under his control should be guilty of an offence although he had no knowledge that such lobster was undersized but, in my opinion, no such words have been used, and no such intention can be implied from the words which have been used considered in the light of all relevant circumstances.

---

In the decision of *R. v. Wholesale Travel Group Inc.* (1991), 67 C.C.C. (3d) 193 (S.C.C.), parts of which are reproduced later in this chapter, the court grappled again with the distinction between "true criminal offences" and "regulatory offences," in the context of a charging provision under the *Competition Act*. Justice Cory said the following in attempting to make this distinction:

## I. Regulatory Offences and Strict Liability

### A. The Distinction Between Crimes and Regulatory Offences

The common law has long acknowledged a distinction between truly criminal conduct and conduct, otherwise lawful, which is prohibited in the public interest. Earlier, the designations *mala in se* and *mala prohibita* were utilized; today prohibited acts are generally classified as either crimes or regulatory offences.

While some regulatory legislation such as that pertaining to the content of food and drink dates back to the Middle Ages, the number and significance of regulatory offences increased greatly with the onset of the Industrial Revolution. Unfettered industrialization had led to abuses. Regulations were, therefore, enacted to protect the vulnerable—particularly the children, men and women who laboured long hours in dangerous and unhealthy surroundings. Without these regulations many would have died. It later became necessary to regulate the manufactured products themselves and, still later, the discharge of effluent resulting from the manufacturing process. There is no doubt that regulatory offences were originally and still are designed to protect those who are unable to protect themselves.

English courts have for many years supported and given effect to the policy objectives animating regulatory legislation. In *Sherras v. De Rutzen*, [1895] 1 Q.B. 918 at p. 922, it was held that, while the *mens rea* presumption applied to true crimes because of the fault and moral culpability which they imply, that same presumption did not apply to offences "which ... are not criminal in any real sense, but are acts which in the public interest are prohibited under a penalty." This case illustrates the essential distinction in the legal treatment of regulatory as opposed to criminal offences—namely, the removal of the *mens rea* requirement.

The distinction between true crimes and regulatory offences was recognized in Canadian law prior to the adoption of the Charter. In *R. v. Pierce Fisheries Ltd.*, [1970] 5 C.C.C. 193 at p. 199, Ritchie J. referred to "a wide category of offences created by statutes enacted for the regulation of individual conduct in the interests of health, convenience, safety and the general welfare of the public" which are not subject to the common law presumption of *mens rea* as an essential element to be proven by the Crown.

*Regina v. Sault Ste. Marie*, [1978] 2 S.C.R. 1299, affirmed the distinction between regulatory offences and true crimes. There, on behalf of a unanimous court, Justice Dickson (as he then was) recognized public welfare offences as a distinct class. He held (at pp. 357-8 C.C.C., pp. 165-6 D.L.R.) that such offences, although enforced as penal laws through the machinery of the criminal law, "are in substance of a civil nature and might well be regarded as a branch of administrative law to which traditional principles of criminal law have but limited application."

The *Sault Ste. Marie* case recognized strict liability as a middle ground between full *mens rea* and absolute liability. Where the offence is one of strict liability, the Crown is required to prove neither *mens rea* nor negligence; conviction may follow merely upon proof beyond a reasonable doubt of the proscribed act. However, it is open to the defendant to avoid liability by proving on a balance of probabilities that all due care was taken. This is the hallmark of the strict liability offence: the defence of due diligence.

Thus, *Sault Ste. Marie* not only affirmed the distinction between regulatory and criminal offences, but also subdivided regulatory offences into categories of strict and absolute liability. The new category of strict liability represented a compromise which acknowledged the importance and essential objectives of regulatory offences but at the same time sought to mitigate the harshness of absolute liability which was found, at p. 363 C.C.C., p. 171 D.L.R., to "violate" fundamental principles of penal liability.

The Rationale for the Distinction

It has always been thought that there is a rational basis for distinguishing between crimes and regulatory offences. Acts or actions are criminal when they constitute conduct that is, in itself, so abhorrent to the basic values of human society that it ought to be prohibited completely. Murder, sexual assault, fraud, robbery and theft are all so repugnant to society that they are universally recognized as crimes. At the same time, some conduct is prohibited, not because it is inherently wrongful, but because unregulated activity would result in dangerous conditions being imposed upon members of society, especially those who are particularly vulnerable.

The objective of regulatory legislation is to protect the public or broad segments of the public (such as employees, consumers and motorists, to name but a few) from the potentially adverse effects of otherwise lawful activity. Regulatory legislation involves a shift of emphasis from the protection of individual interests and the deterrence and punishment of acts involving moral fault to the protection of public and societal interests. While criminal offences are usually designed to condemn and punish past, inherently wrongful conduct, regulatory measures are generally directed to the prevention of future harm through the enforcement of minimum standards of conduct and care.

It follows that regulatory offences and crimes embody different concepts of fault. Since regulatory offences are directed primarily not to conduct itself but to the consequences of conduct, conviction of a regulatory offence may be thought to import a significantly lesser degree of culpability than conviction of a true crime. The concept of fault in regulatory offences is based upon a reasonable care standard and, as such, does not imply moral blameworthiness in the same manner as criminal fault. Conviction for breach of a regulatory offence suggests nothing more than that the defendant has failed to meet a prescribed standard of care.

That is the theory but, like all theories, its application is difficult. For example, is the single mother who steals a loaf of bread to sustain her family more blameworthy than the employer who, through negligence, breaches regulations and thereby exposes his employees to dangerous working conditions, or the manufacturer who, as a result of negligence, sells dangerous products or pollutes the air and waters by its plant? At this stage it is sufficient to bear in mind that those who breach regulations may inflict serious harm on large segments of society. Therefore, the characterization of an offence as regulatory should not be thought to make light of either the potential harm to the vulnerable or the responsibility of those subject to regulation to ensure that the proscribed harm does not occur. It should also be remembered that, as social values change, the degree of moral blameworthiness attaching to certain conduct may change as well.

Nevertheless there remains, in my view, a sound basis for distinguishing between regulatory and criminal offences. The distinction has concrete theoretical and practical underpinnings and has proven to be a necessary and workable concept in our law. Since *Sault Ste. Marie*, this court has reaffirmed the distinction. Most recently, in *Thomson Newspapers Ltd. v. Canada (Director of Investigation and Research, Restrictive Trade Practices Commission)* (1990), 54 C.C.C. (3d) 417 at p. 479 Justice La Forest adopted the following statement of the Law Reform Commission of Canada (Criminal Responsibility for Group Action, Working Paper No. 16, 1976, at p. 12):

> [The regulatory offence] is not primarily concerned with values, but with results. While values necessarily underlie all legal prescriptions, the regulatory offence really gives expression to the view that it is expedient for the protection of society and for the orderly use and sharing of society's resources that people act in a prescribed manner in prescribed situations, or that people take prescribed standards of care to avoid risks of injury. The object is to induce compliance with rules for the overall benefit of society.

*B. The Fundamental Importance of Regulatory Offences in Canadian Society*
Regulatory measures are the primary mechanisms employed by governments in Canada to implement public policy objectives. What is ultimately at stake in this appeal is the ability

of federal and provincial governments to pursue social ends through the enactment and enforcement of public welfare legislation.

Some indication of the prevalence of regulatory offences in Canada is provided by a 1974 estimate by the Law Reform Commission of Canada. The commission estimated that there were, at that time, approximately 20,000 regulatory offences in an average province, plus an additional 20,000 regulatory offences at the federal level. By 1983, the commission's estimate of the federal total had reached 97,000. There is every reason to believe that the number of public welfare offences at both levels of government has continued to increase.

Statistics such as these make it obvious that government policy in Canada is pursued principally through regulation. It is through regulatory legislation that the community seeks to implement its larger objectives and to govern itself and the conduct of its members. The ability of the government effectively to regulate potentially harmful conduct must be maintained.

It is difficult to think of an aspect of our lives that is not regulated for our benefit and for the protection of society as a whole. From cradle to grave, we are protected by regulations; they apply to the doctors attending our entry into this world and to the morticians present at our departure. Every day, from waking to sleeping, we profit from regulatory measures which we often take for granted. On rising, we use various forms of energy whose safe distribution and use are governed by regulation. The trains, buses and other vehicles that get us to work are regulated for our safety. The food we eat and the beverages we drink are subject to regulation for the protection of our health.

In short, regulation is absolutely essential for our protection and well being as individuals, and for the effective functioning of society. It is properly present throughout our lives. The more complex the activity, the greater the need for and the greater our reliance upon regulation and its enforcement. For example, most people would have no idea what regulations are required for air transport or how they should be enforced. Of necessity, society relies on government regulation for its safety.

## II.  THE EMERGENCE OF STRICT LIABILITY

### R. v. City of Sault Ste. Marie
Supreme Court of Canada
(1978), 40 C.C.C. (2d) 353

DICKSON J. (for the Court):  In the present appeal the Court is concerned with offences variously referred to as "statutory," "public welfare," "regulatory," "absolute liability," or "strict responsibility," which are not criminal in any real sense, but are prohibited in the public interest: *Sherras v. De Rutzen*, [1895] 1 Q.B. 918. Although enforced as penal laws through the utilization of the machinery of the criminal law, the offences are in substance of a civil nature and might well be regarded as a branch of administrative law to which traditional principles of criminal law have but limited application. They relate to such everyday matters as traffic infractions, sales of impure food, violations of liquor laws, and the like. In this appeal we are concerned with pollution.

The City of Sault Ste. Marie was charged that it did discharge, or cause to be discharged, or permitted to be discharged, or deposited materials into Cannon Creek and Root River, or on the shore or bank thereof, or in such place along the side that might impair the quality of the water in Cannon Creek and Root River, between March 13, 1972 and September 11, 1972. The charge was laid under s. 32(1) of the *Ontario Water Resources Act*, R.S.O. 1970, c. 332, [formerly *Ontario Water Resources Commission Act*, renamed by 1972, c. 1, s. 70(1)] which provides, so far as relevant, that every municipality or person that discharges, or deposits, or causes, or permits the discharge or deposit of any material of any kind into any water course, or on any shore or bank thereof, or in any place that may impair the quality of water, is guilty of an offence and, on summary conviction, is liable on first conviction to a fine of not more than $5,000 and on each subsequent conviction to a fine of not more than $10,000, or to imprisonment for a term of not more than one year, or to both fine and imprisonment.

Public welfare offences involve a shift of emphasis from the protection of individual interests to the protection of public and social interests: see F.B. Sayre, "Public Welfare Offenses," 33 *Columbia Law Rev.* 55 (1933); Hall, *General Principles of Criminal Law* (1947), c. 13, p. 427; R.M. Perkins, "Civil Offense," 100 *U. of Pa. L. Rev.* 832 (1952); Jobson, "Far From Clear," 18 *Crim. L.Q.* 294 (1975-76). The unfortunate tendency in many past cases has been to see the choice as between two stark alternatives: (i) full *mens rea*; or (ii) absolute liability. In respect of public welfare offences (within which category pollution offences fall) where full *mens rea* is not required, absolute liability has often been imposed. English jurisprudence has consistently maintained this dichotomy: see "Criminal Law, Evidence and Procedure," 11 Hals., 4th ed., pp. 20-22, para. 18. There has, however, been an attempt in Australia, in many Canadian Courts, and indeed in England, to seek a middle position, fulfilling the goals of public welfare offences while still not punishing the entirely blameless. There is an increasing and impressive stream of authority which holds that where an offence does not require full *mens rea*, it is nevertheless a good defence for the defendant to prove that he was not negligent.

Dr. Glanville Williams has written: "There is a half-way house between *mens rea* and strict responsibility which has not yet been properly utilized, and that is responsibility for negligence" (*Criminal Law: General Part*, 2nd ed. (1961), p. 262). Morris and Howard, in *Studies in Criminal Law* (1964), p. 200, suggest that strict responsibility might with advantage be replaced by a doctrine of responsibility for negligence strengthened by a shift in the burden of proof. The defendant would be allowed to exculpate himself by proving affirmatively that he was not negligent.

In the House of Lords case of *Sweet v. Parsley*, [1970] A.C. 132, Lord Reid noted the difficulty presented by the simplistic choice between *mens rea* in the full sense and an absolute offence. He looked approvingly at attempts to find a middle ground. Lord Pearce, in the same case, referred to the "sensible half-way house" which he thought the Courts should take in some so-called absolute offences. The difficulty, as Lord Pearce saw it, lay in the opinion of Viscount Sankey, L.C., in *Woolmington v. Director of Public Prosecutions*, [1935] A.C. 462, if the full width of that opinion were maintained. Lord Diplock, however, took a different and, in my opinion, a preferable view, at p. 164:

> *Woolmington*'s case did not decide anything so irrational as that the prosecution must
> call evidence to prove the absence of any mistaken belief by the accused in the exist-
> ence of facts which, if true, would make the act innocent, any more than it decided that
> the prosecution must call evidence to prove the absence of any claim of right in a charge
> of larceny. The jury is entitled to presume that the accused acted with knowledge of the
> facts, unless there is some evidence to the contrary originating from the accused who
> alone can know on what belief he acted and on what ground the belief, if mistaken, was
> held.

In *Woolmington*'s case the question was whether the trial Judge was correct in directing the jury that the accused was required to prove his innocence. Viscount Sankey,
L.C., referred to the strength of the presumption of innocence in a criminal case and
then made the statement, universally accepted in this country, that there is no burden
on the prisoner to prove his innocence; it is sufficient for him to raise a doubt as to his
guilt. I do not understand the case as standing for anything more than that. It is to be
noted that the case is concerned with criminal offences in the true sense; it is not
concerned with public welfare offences. It is somewhat ironic that *Woolmington*'s
case, which embodies a principle for the benefit of the accused, should be used to
justify the rejection of a defence of reasonable care for public welfare offences and
the retention of absolute liability, which affords the accused no defence at all. There
is nothing in *Woolmington*'s case, as I comprehend it, which stands in the way of
adoption, in respect of regulatory offences, of a defence of due care, with burden of
proof resting on the accused to establish the defence on the balance of probabilities.

There have been several cases in Ontario which open the way to acceptance of a
defence of due diligence.

[A number of Ontario cases are then discussed.]

It is interesting to note the recommendations made by the Law Reform Commission
to the Minister of Justice (*Our Criminal Law*) in March, 1976. The Commission ad-
vises (p. 32) that (i) every offence outside the *Criminal Code* be recognized as admitting of a defence of due diligence; (ii) in the case of any such offence for which intent
or recklessness is not specifically required the onus of proof should lie on the defendant to establish such defence; (iii) the defendant would have to prove this on the
preponderance or balance of probabilities. The recommendation endorsed a working
paper (*Meaning of Guilt: Strict Liability*, June 20, 1974), in which it was stated that
negligence should be the minimum standard of liability in regulatory offences, that
such offences were (p. 32):

> ... to promote higher standards of care in business, trade and industry, higher standards
> of honesty in commerce and advertising, higher standards of respect for the ... environ-
> ment and [therefore] the ... offence is basically and typically an offence of negligence;

that an accused should never be convicted of a regulatory offence if he establishes
that he acted with due diligence, that is, that he was not negligent. In the working
paper, the Commission further stated (p. 33), "... let us recognize the regulatory of-

fence for what it is—an offence of negligence—and frame the law to ensure that guilt depends upon lack of reasonable care." The view is expressed that in regulatory law, to make the defendant disprove negligence—prove due diligence—would be both justifiable and desirable.

The decision of this Court in *The Queen v. Pierce Fisheries Ltd.*, [1970] 5 C.C.C. 193, 12 D.L.R. (3d) 591, [1971] S.C.R. 5, is not inconsistent with the concept of a "half-way house" between *mens rea* and absolute liability. In *Pierce Fisheries* the charge was that of having possession of undersized lobsters contrary to the Regulations under the *Fisheries Act*, R.S.C. 1952, c. 119. Two points arise in connection with the judgment of Ritchie, J., who wrote for the majority of the Court. First, the adoption of what had been said by the Ontario Court of Appeal in *R. v. Pee-Kay Smallwares Ltd.* (1947), 90 C.C.C. 129 at p. 137, [1948] 1 D.L.R. 235 at p. 243, 6 C.R. 28:

> If on a prosecution for the offences created by the Act, the Crown had to prove the evil intent of the accused, or if the accused could escape by denying such evil intent, the statute, by which it was obviously intended that there should be complete control without the possibility of any leaks, would have too many holes in it that in truth it would be nothing more than a legislative sieve.

Ritchie, J., held that the offence was one in which the Crown, for the reason indicated in the *Pee-Kay Smallwares* case, did not have to prove *mens rea* in order to obtain a conviction. This, in my opinion, is the *ratio decidendi* of the case. Secondly, Ritchie, J., did not, however, foreclose the possibility of a defence. The following passage from the judgment (at p. 205 C.C.C., p. 603 D.L.R., p. 21 S.C.R.) suggests that a defence of reasonable care might have been open to the accused, but that in that case care had not been taken to acquire the knowledge of the facts constituting the offence:

> As employees of the company working on the premises in the shed "where fish is weighed and packed" were taking lobsters from boxes "preparatory for packing" in crates, and as some of the undersized lobsters were found "in crates ready for shipment," it would not appear to have been a difficult matter for some "officer or responsible employee" to acquire knowledge of their presence on the premises.

In a later passage Ritchie, J., added (at pp. 205-6 C.C.C., p. 604 D.L.R., p. 22 S.C.R.):

> In this case the respondent knew that it had upwards of 60,000 lbs. of lobsters on its premises; it only lacked knowledge as to the small size of some of them, and I do not think that the failure of any of its responsible employees to acquire this knowledge affords any defence to a charge of violating the provisions of s. 3(1)(b) of the *Lobster Fishery Regulations*.

I do not read *Pierce Fisheries* as denying the accused all defences, in particular the defence that the company had done everything possible to acquire knowledge of the undersized lobsters. Ritchie, J., concluded merely that the Crown did not have to prove knowledge.

We have the situation therefore in which many Courts of this country, at all levels, dealing with public welfare offences favour (i) *not* requiring the Crown to prove *mens rea*, (ii) rejecting the notion that liability inexorably follows upon mere proof of the *actus reus*, excluding any possible defence. The Courts are following the lead set in Australia many years ago and tentatively broached by several English Courts in recent years.

It may be suggested that the introduction of a defence based on due diligence and the shifting of the burden of proof might better be implemented by legislative act. In answer, it should be recalled that the concept of absolute liability and the creation of a jural category of public welfare offences are both the product of the judiciary and not of the Legislature. The development to date of this defence, in the numerous decisions I have referred to, of Courts in this country as well as in Australia and New Zealand, has also been the work of Judges. The present case offers the opportunity of consolidating and clarifying the doctrine.

The correct approach, in my opinion, is to relieve the Crown of the burden of proving *mens rea*, having regard to *Pierce Fisheries* and to the virtual impossibility in most regulatory cases of proving wrongful intention. In a normal case, the accused alone will have knowledge of what he has done to avoid the breach and it is not improper to expect him to come forward with the evidence of due diligence. This is particularly so when it is alleged, for example, that pollution was caused by the activities of a large and complex corporation. Equally, there is nothing wrong with rejecting absolute liability and admitting the defence of reasonable care.

In this doctrine it is not up to the prosecution to prove negligence. Instead, it is open to the defendant to prove that all due care has been taken. This burden falls upon the defendant as he is the only one who will generally have the means of proof. This would not seem unfair as the alternative is absolute liability which denies an accused any defence whatsoever. While the prosecution must prove beyond a reasonable doubt that the defendant committed the prohibited act, the defendant must only establish on the balance of probabilities that he has a defence of reasonable care.

I conclude, for the reasons which I have sought to express, that there are compelling grounds for the recognition of three categories of offences rather than the traditional two:

1.  Offences in which *mens rea*, consisting of some positive state of mind such as intent, knowledge, or recklessness, must be proved by the prosecution either as an inference from the nature of the act committed, or by additional evidence.

2.  Offences in which there is no necessity for the prosecution to prove the existence of *mens rea*; the doing of the prohibited act *prima facie* imports the offence, leaving it open to the accused to avoid liability by proving that he took all reasonable care. This involves consideration of what a reasonable man would have done in the circumstances. The defence will be available if the accused reasonably believed in a mistaken set of facts which, if true, would render the act or omission innocent, or if he took all reasonable steps to avoid the particular event. These offences may properly be called offences of strict liability. Mr. Justice Estey so referred to them in *Hickey*'s case.

3.  Offences of absolute liability where it is not open to the accused to exculpate
    himself by showing that he was free of fault.

Offences which are criminal in the true sense fall in the first category. Public welfare offences would, *prima facie*, be in the second category. They are not subject to
the presumption of full *mens rea*. An offence of this type would fall in the first category only if such words as "wilfully," "with intent," "knowingly," or "intentionally"
are contained in the statutory provision creating the offence. On the other hand, the
principle that punishment should in general not be inflicted on those without fault
applies. Offences of absolute liability would be those in respect of which the Legislature had made it clear that guilt would follow proof merely of the proscribed act. The
over-all regulatory pattern adopted by the Legislature, the subject-matter of the legislation, the importance of the penalty, and the precision of the language used will be
primary considerations in determining whether the offence falls into the third category.

Turning to the subject-matter of s. 32(1)—the prevention of pollution of lakes,
rivers and streams—it is patent that this is of great public concern. Pollution has
always been unlawful and, in itself, a nuisance: *Groat v. City of Edmonton*, [1928] 3
D.L.R. 725, [1928] S.C.R. 522. A riparian owner has an inherent right to have a stream
of water "come to him in its natural state, in flow, quantity and quality": *Chasemore
v. Richards* (1859), 7 H.L. Cas. 349 at p. 382. Natural streams which formerly afforded "pure and healthy" water for drinking or swimming purposes become little
more than cesspools when riparian factory owners and municipal corporations discharge into them filth of all descriptions. Pollution offences are undoubtedly public
welfare offences enacted in the interests of public health. There is thus no presumption of a full *mens rea*.

There is another reason, however, why this offence is not subject to a presumption
of *mens rea*. The presumption applies only to offences which are "criminal in the true
sense," as Ritchie J., said in *The Queen v. Pierce Fisheries, supra*, at p. 199 C.C.C.,
p. 597 D.L.R., p. 13 S.C.R. The Ontario *Water Resources Act* is a provincial statute.
If it is valid provincial legislation (and no suggestion was made to the contrary), then
it cannot possibly create an offence which is criminal in the true sense.

The present case concerns the interpretation of two troublesome words frequently
found in public welfare statutes: "cause" and "permit." These two words are troublesome because neither denotes clearly either full *mens rea* nor absolute liability.

[A number of authorities are then cited.]

The Divisional Court of Ontario relied on these latter authorities in concluding that
s. 32(1) created a *mens rea* offence.

The conflict in the above authorities, however, shows that in themselves the words
"cause" and "permit" fit much better into an offence of strict liability than either full
*mens rea* or absolute liability. Since s. 32(1) creates a public welfare offence, without
a clear indication that liability is absolute, and without any words such as "knowingly" or "wilfully" expressly to import *mens rea*, application of the criteria which I
have outlined above undoubtedly places the offence in the category of strict liability.

As I am of the view that a new trial is necessary, it would be inappropriate to discuss at this time the facts of the present case … .

*Appeal dismissed; cross-appeal dismissed.*

## III. CONSTITUTIONAL CONSIDERATIONS

**Reference re Section 94(2) of the B.C. Motor Vehicle Act**
Supreme Court of Canada
(1985), 23 C.C.C. (3d) 289

[The lieutenant-governor in council of British Columbia referred the following question to the British Columbia Court of Appeal: "Is s. 94(2) of the *Motor Vehicle Act*, R.S.B.C. 1979, as amended by the *Motor Vehicle Amendment Act*, 1982, consistent with the *Canadian Charter of Rights and Freedoms*?" Section 94(2) provides that the offence created by s. 94(1) "creates an absolute liability offence in which guilt is established by proof of driving, whether or not the defendant knew of the prohibition or suspension." Section 94(1) provides that a person who drives a motor vehicle while he or she is prohibited from driving or while his or her driver's licence is suspended commits an offence and is liable on first conviction to a fine and to imprisonment for not less than seven days and not more than six months. The British Columbia Court of Appeal answered the question in the negative.

The attorney-general for British Columbia appealed to the Supreme Court of Canada. Lamer J. delivered the judgment of the court.]

LAMER J. (with whom Dickson C.J.C., Beetz, Chouinard, and Le Dain JJ. concurred): A law that has the potential to convict a person who has not really done anything wrong offends the principles of fundamental justice and, if imprisonment is available as a penalty, such a law then violates a person's right to liberty under s. 7 of the *Canadian Charter of Rights and Freedoms* (Part I of the *Constitution Act, 1982*, as enacted by the *Canada Act*, 1982 (U.K.), c. 11).

In other words, absolute liability and imprisonment cannot be combined. …

In the framework of a purposive analysis, designed to ascertain the purpose of the s. 7 guarantee and "the interests it was meant to protect" (*R. v. Big M Drug Mart Ltd.*, …), it is clear to me that the interests which are meant to be protected by the words "and the right not to be deprived thereof except in accordance with the principles of fundamental justice" of s. 7 are the life, liberty and security of the person. The principles of fundamental justice, on the other hand, are not a protected interest, but rather a qualifier of the right not to be deprived of life, liberty and security of the person.

Given that, as the Attorney-General for Ontario has acknowledged, "when one reads the phrase 'principles of fundamental justice,' a single incontrovertible meaning is not apparent," its meaning must, in my view, be determined by reference to the interests which those words of the section are designed to protect and the particular role of the phrase within the section. As a qualifier, the phrase serves to estab ish the parameters of the interests but it cannot be interpreted so narrowly as to frustrate or stultify them. For the narrower the meaning given to "principles of fundamental justice" the greater will be the possibility that individuals may be deprived of these most basic rights.

Sections 8 to 14, in other words, address specific deprivations of the "right" of life, liberty and security of the person in breach of the principles of fundamental justice, and as such, violations of s. 7. They are designed to protect, in a specific manner and setting, the right to life, liberty and security of the person set forth in s. 7. It would be incongruous to interpret s. 7 more narrowly than the rights in ss. 8 to 14. The alternative, which is to interpret all of ss. 8 to 14 in a "[n]arrow and technical" manner for the sake of congruity, is out of the question: *Law Society of Upper Canada v. Skapinker*, ... at p. 488 C.C.C., p. 168 D.L.R., p. 366 S.C.R.

Sections 8 to 14 are illustrative of deprivations of those rights to life, liberty and security of the person in breach of the principles of fundamental justice. For they, in effect, illustrate some of the parameters of the "right" to life, liberty and security of the person; they are examples of instances in which the "right" to life, liberty and security of the person would be violated in a manner which is not in accordance with the principles of fundamental justice. ...

Thus, ss. 8 to 14 provide an invaluable key to the meaning of "principles of fundamental justice." Many have been developed over time as presumptions of the common law, others have found expression in the international conventions on human rights. All have been recognized as essential elements of a system for the administration of justice which is founded upon a belief in "the dignity and worth of the human person" (preamble to the *Canadian Bill of Rights*, R.S.C. 1970, App. III), and on "the rule of law" (preamble to the *Canadian Charter of Rights and Freedoms*).

It is this common thread which, in my view, must guide us in determining the scope and content of "principles of fundamental justice." In other words, the principles of fundamental justice are to be found in the basic tenets of our legal system. They do not lie in the realm of general public policy but in the inherent domain of the judiciary as guardian of the justice system. Such an approach to the interpretation of "principles of fundamental justice" is consistent with the wording and structure of s. 7, the context of the section, *i.e.*, ss. 8 to 14, and the character and larger objects of the Charter itself. It provides meaningful content for the s. 7 guarantee all the while avoiding adjudication of policy matters. ...

A number of courts have placed emphasis upon the Minutes of the Proceedings and Evidence of the Special Joint Committee of the Senate and of the House of Commons on the Constitution in the interpretation of "principles of fundamental justice." ...

In particular, the following passages, dealing with the testimony of federal civil servants from the Department of Justice, have been relied upon:

Mr. Strayer (Assistant Deputy Minister, Public Law):

> Mr. Chairman, it was our belief that the words "fundamental justice" would cover the same thing as what is called procedural due process, that is the meaning of due process in relation to requiring fair procedure. However, it in our view does not cover the concept

of what is called substantive due process, which would impose substantive requirements as to policy of the law in question.

[The admissibility and weight of such statements are then examined.]

Moreover, the simple fact remains that the Charter is not the product of a few
individual public servants, however distinguished, but of a multiplicity of individuals who played major roles in the negotiating, drafting and adoption of the Charter.
How can one say with any confidence that within this enormous multiplicity of actors, without forgetting the role of the provinces, the comments of a few federal civil
servants in any way be determinative?

Were this Court to accord any significant weight to this testimony, it would in
effect be assuming a fact which is nearly impossible of proof, *i.e.*, the intention of the
legislative bodies which adopted the Charter. In view of the indeterminate nature of
the data, it would in my view be erroneous to give these materials anything but minimal weight.

Another danger with casting the interpretation of s. 7 in terms of the comments
made by those heard at the joint committee proceedings is that, in so doing, the rights,
freedoms and values embodied in the Charter in effect become frozen in time to the
moment of adoption with little or no possibility of growth, development and adjustment to changing societal needs. ...

Whether any given principle may be said to be a principle of fundamental justice
within the meaning of s. 7 will rest upon an analysis of the nature, sources, *rationale*
and essential role of that principle within the judicial process and in our legal system,
as it evolves.

Consequently, those words cannot be given any exhaustive content or simple
enumerative definition, but will take on concrete meaning as the courts address alleged violations of s. 7. ...

This Court's decision in the latter case [*Regina v. City of Sault Ste. Marie* (1978),
40 C.C.C. (2d) 353 (S.C.C.)] is predicated upon a certain number of postulates one of
which, given the nature of the rules it elaborates, has to be to the effect that absolute
liability in penal law offends the principles of fundamental justice. Those principles
are, to use the words of Dickson J., to the effect that "there is a generally held revulsion against punishment of the morally innocent" [at p. 363 C.C.C., p. 170 D.L.R.,
p. 1310 S.C.R.]. He also stated at [at p. 363 C.C.C., p. 171 D.L.R., p. 1311 S.C.R.]
that the argument that absolute liability "violates fundamental principles of penal
liability" was the most telling argument against absolute liability and one of greater
force than those advanced in support thereof. ...

A law enacting an absolute liability offence will violate s. 7 of the Charter only if
and to the extent that it has the potential of depriving of life, liberty or security of the
person.

Obviously, imprisonment (including probation orders) deprives persons of their
liberty. An offence has that potential as of the moment it is open to the judge to
impose imprisonment. There is no need that imprisonment, as in s. 94(2), be made
mandatory.

I am therefore of the view that the combination of imprisonment and of absolute liability violates s. 7 of the Charter and can only be salvaged if the authorities demonstrate under s. 1 that such a deprivation of liberty in breach of those principles of fundamental justice is, in a free and democratic society, under the circumstances, a justified reasonable limit to one's rights under s. 7. ...

Of course, I understand the concern of many as regards corporate offences, specially, as was mentioned by the Court of Appeal, in certain sensitive areas such as the preservation of our vital environment and our natural resources. This concern might well be dispelled were it to be decided, given the proper case, that s. 7 affords protection to human persons only and does not extend to corporations. ...

I do not take issue with the fact that it is highly desirable that "bad drivers" be kept off the road. I do not take issue either with the desirability of punishing severely bad drivers who are in contempt of prohibitions against driving. The bottom line of the question to be addressed here is: whether the Government of British Columbia has demonstrated as justifiable that the risk of imprisonment of a few innocent is, given the desirability of ridding the roads of British Columbia of bad drivers, a reasonable limit in a free and democratic society. That result is to be measured against the offence being one of strict liability open to a defence of due diligence, the success of which does nothing more than let those few who did nothing wrong remain free.

As did the Court of Appeal, I find that this demonstration has not been satisfied, indeed, not in the least.

In the result, I would dismiss the appeal and answer the question in the negative, as did the Court of Appeal, albeit for somewhat different reasons, and declare s. 94(2) of the *Motor Vehicle Act*, as amended by the *Motor Vehicle Amendment Act, 1982*, inconsistent with s. 7 of the *Canadian Charter of Rights and Freedoms*.

[McIntyre and Wilson JJ. delivered separate concurring judgments, limiting their decision to a case in which absolute liability is combined with a minimum term of imprisonment.]

*Appeal dismissed.*

### R. v. Pontes
Supreme Court of Canada
(1995), 100 C.C.C. (3d) 353

[After the Supreme Court's decision in the *B.C. Motor Vehicle Act* case, British Columbia repealed s. 94(2), which had stated: "subsection (1) creates an absolute liability offence in which guilt is established by proof of driving, whether or not the defendant knew of the prohibition or suspension." Section 4.1 of the B.C. *Offence Act* was amended to provide that "no person is liable to imprisonment with respect to an absolute liability offence." Further, s. 72 of the *Offence Act* provides that failure to pay a fine will not result in a jail term.]

CORY J. (with whom four other members of the Court concurred) held that section 94 was still an absolute liability offence, stating in part: From the cases which followed the passage of the Charter, the following can be derived: first, generally speaking, an offence of absolute liability is not likely to offend s. 7 of the Charter unless a prison sanction is provided; secondly, an accused charged with an absolute liability offence cannot avoid liability by demonstrating that he exercised due diligence; thirdly, one of the prime bases for distinguishing a strict liability offence from an absolute liability offence is the availability of the defence of due diligence; fourthly, any provincial regulatory offence providing for a term of imprisonment must make a defence of due diligence available to the accused. I would leave open for future consideration the situation presented by an absolute liability offence punishable by fine with the possibility of imprisonment for its non-payment in those circumstances where the legislation provides that the imposition and collection of any fine is subject to a means test.

In *Reference re: Section 94(2) of the Motor Vehicle Act*, *supra*, it was found that s. 94, as it was then worded, created an absolute liability offence. At the time of that decision, s. 94 contained a s-s. (2) which read:

> (2) Subsection (1) creates an absolute liability offence in which guilt is established by proof of driving, whether or not the defendant knew of the prohibition or suspension.

That provision was found to contravene the Charter and was deleted from the Act in 1986. However, I am of the view that the removal of that subsection does not change the offence into one of strict liability. As all the judges in the courts below have found, the situation has not been changed in any significant manner by the deletion of that subsection. The deleted subsection did no more than emphasize and reiterate that this was an absolute liability offence. Yet, the same conclusion can be reached from a consideration of the remaining wording of s. 94. Section 94(1)(a) still refers to s. 92 which, in turn, provides that a driver will "automatically and without notice" be prohibited from driving for a period of 12 months. In effect, the combination of s. 92 and s. 94 provides for the conviction of the prohibited driver whether or not he knows that he is prohibited from driving.

Section 94 goes further. Because the prohibition to drive in s. 92 is automatic and without notice, s. 94 effectively prevents an accused who is unaware of the prohibition from raising a defence of due diligence.

The defence of due diligence must be available to defend a strict liability offence. If that defence is removed, the offence can no longer be classified as one of strict liability. When, as a result of the wording of the section, the only possible defence an accused can put forward is his ignorance of the fact that his licence had been suspended by the provisions of the provincial statute, which constitutes a mistake of law and therefore is not available as a defence, the accused is effectively denied the defence of due diligence. In those circumstances, the offence ought to be characterized as one of absolute liability.

In summary, it is my opinion that ss. 92 and 94 of the B.C. *Motor Vehicle Act* create an absolute liability offence since they effectively eliminate the defence of due diligence. Nevertheless, the absolute liability offence does not contravene the Charter. This conclusion flows from the application of s. 4.1 and of s. 72(1) of the *Offence*

*Act*. These sections respectively indicate that, notwithstanding the provisions of any other Act, no person is liable to imprisonment for an absolute liability offence, and that the non-payment of a fine will not result in imprisonment. Thus, an accused convicted under ss. 92 and 94 of the B.C. *Motor Vehicle Act* faces no risk of imprisonment and there is, accordingly, no violation of the right to life, liberty and security of the person under s. 7 of the Charter.

GONTHIER J. (with whom La Forest, L'Heureux-Dubé, and McLachlin JJ. concurred) held that section 94 was now a strict liability offence, stating in part: I have had the benefit of the reasons of my colleague Justice Cory. I respectfully disagree with his conclusion that the combined effect of ss. 92 and 94(1) of the *Motor Vehicle Act*, R.S.B.C. 1979, c. 288, is to create an offence of absolute liability. In my view, these provisions create an offence of strict liability where the fact of driving while prohibited by statute *prima facie* imports the offence, but where it is nevertheless possible for an accused to avoid conviction by demonstrating that he reasonably believed that he had not been convicted of one of the underlying offences to which the 12-month statutory prohibition attaches, or that he exercised due diligence in seeking to acquire knowledge of the underlying conviction. As a result, the impugned provisions adequately provide for the constitutionally minimum *mens rea* of negligence in order to ground a conviction and thus imprisonment for the regulatory or public welfare offence of driving while prohibited by statute. I would therefore answer the constitutional question posed by Lamer C.J.C. in the negative, allow the appeal and order a new trial.

It is my view, then, that the British Columbia legislature has not used language of sufficient precision to make it clear that the offence created by the combined effect of ss. 92 and 94 is to be of absolute liability. In this respect, the language in the impugned provision falls far short of the express language employed in the now repealed s. 94(2) of the *Motor Vehicle Act*, which read:

> 94(2) *Subsection (1) creates an absolute liability offence* in which guilt is established by proof of driving, whether or not the defendant knew of the prohibition or suspension.

(Emphasis added.) Speaking for a majority of the court on the constitutionality of this provision in *Reference re: Section 94(2) of the Motor Vehicle Act, supra*, Lamer J. (as he then was) stated at p. 314:

> No doubt s. 94(2) enacts in the clearest of terms an absolute liability offence, the conviction for which a person will be deprived of his or her liberty, and little more, if anything, need to be added.

Notwithstanding this ruling, my colleague Cory J. suggests that s. 94(2) "did no more than emphasize and reiterate that this was an absolute liability offence" (para. 30). In other words, s. 94(1) created an absolute liability offence regardless of s. 94(2). This conclusion effectively equates "automatically and without notice" in s. 94(1) with "absolute liability" in s. 94(2). I have some difficulty with this conclusion. If the legislature of British Columbia was simply emphasizing and reiterating in s. 94(2) the legal effect of s. 94(1), it is curious indeed that in obeying this court's decision in *Reference re: Section 94(2) of the Motor Vehicle Act* on the unconstitutionality of combining absolute liability with the possibility of imprisonment, that same legislature would choose to repeal only s. 94(2) and not also s. 94(1) (*Motor Vehicle Amendments Act, 1986*, S.B.C. 1986, c. 19, s. 5, assented to June 17, 1986). With respect, Cory J.'s interpretation impliedly imputes to that sovereign body ignorance, indifference, or worse, possibly even contempt for this court's ruling.

[Gonthier J. went on to argue that the majority was extending the due diligence defence to include ignorance of the law contrary to s. 19 of the *Criminal Code* and that this "would eviscerate the ignorance of the law rule and render many of our law unenforceable." This rule and *Pontes* will be discussed again in chapter 10.]

*Appeal dismissed.*

---

In *Irwin Toy Ltd. v. Quebec (Attorney-General)* (1989), 58 D.L.R. (4th) 577, the Supreme Court held that corporations do not come within s. 7 of the Charter. Dickson C.J.C. and Lamer and Wilson JJ. stated (with the other members of the court, McIntyre and Beetz JJ. concurring):

> In order to put forward a s. 7 argument in a case of this kind where the officers of the corporation are not named as parties to the proceedings, the corporation would have to urge that its own life, liberty or security of the person was being deprived in a manner not in accordance with the principles of fundamental justice. In our opinion, a corporation cannot avail itself of the protection offered by s. 7 of the Charter. First, we would have to conceive of a manner in which a corporation could be deprived of its "life, liberty, or security of the person." We have already noted that it is nonsensical to speak of a corporation being put in jail. To say that bankruptcy and winding-up proceedings engage s. 7 would stretch the meaning of the right to life beyond recognition. The only remaining argument is that corporations are protected against deprivations of some sort of "economic liberty."
>
> There are several reasons why we are of the view that this argument can not succeed. It is useful to reproduce s. 7, which reads as follows:
>
> > 7. Everyone has the right to life, liberty and security of the person and the right not to be deprived thereof except in accordance with the principles of fundamental justice.
>
> What is immediately striking about this section is the inclusion of "security of the person" as opposed to "property." This stands in contrast to the classic liberal formulation, adopted, for example, in the Fifth and Fourteenth Amendments in the American Bill of Rights, which provide that no person shall be deprived "of life, liberty or property, without due process of law." The intentional exclusion of property from s. 7, and the substitution therefor of "security of the person" has, in our estimation, a dual effect. First, it leads to a general inference that economic rights as generally encompassed by the term "property" are not within the perimeters of the s. 7 guarantee. This is not to declare, however, that no right with an economic component can fall within "security of the person." Lower courts have

found that the rubric of "economic rights" embraces a broad spectrum of interests, ranging from such rights, included in various international covenants, as rights to social security, equal pay for equal work, adequate food, clothing and shelter, to traditional property—contract rights. To exclude all of these at this early moment in the history of Charter interpretation seems to us to be precipitous. We do not, at this moment, choose to pronounce upon whether those economic rights fundamental to human life or survival are to be treated as though they are of the same ilk as corporate-commercial economic rights. In so stating, we find the second effect of the inclusion of "security of the *person*" to be that a *corporation's* economic rights find no constitutional protection in that section.

That is, read as a whole, it appears to us that this section was intended to confer protection on a singularly human level. A plain, common sense reading of the phrase "Everyone has the right to life, liberty and security of the person" serves to underline the human element involved; only human beings can enjoy these rights. "Everyone" then, must be read in light of the rest of the section and defined to exclude corporations and other artificial entities incapable of enjoying life, liberty or security of the person, and include only human beings.

## R. v. 1260448 Ontario Inc. (c.o.b. William Cameron Trucking); R. v. Transport Robert (1973) Ltée
### Ontario Court of Appeal
### (2003), 180 C.C.C. (3d) 254

THE COURT: The issue in these two appeals is whether it is open to the Legislature to create an absolute liability offence where there is no possibility of imprisonment or probation if the defendant is convicted. Section 84.1(1) of the *Highway Traffic Act*, R.S.O. 1990, c. H.8 provides that the owner and operator of a commercial motor vehicle are guilty of an offence where a wheel becomes detached from the vehicle while it is on a highway. Subsection (5) provides that it is no defence to the charge that the defendant exercised due diligence to avoid or prevent the detaching of the wheel. The penalty for the offence is a fine of not less than $2,000 and not more than $50,000, but the defendant is not liable to imprisonment or probation as a result of the conviction or for default in payment of the fine resulting from the conviction (subsection (4)).

The defendants submit that notwithstanding the only possible penalty for this offence is a monetary one, the creation of this absolute liability offence violates the guarantee to security of the person in s. 7 of the *Canadian Charter of Rights and Freedoms* and the presumption of innocence in s. 11(d) of the Charter. For the following reasons we have concluded that there is no violation of s. 7 or s. 11(d). We therefore allow the Crown appeal in the *Transport Robert* case and dismiss the appeal by William Cameron Trucking.

### *History of the Proceedings*

In separate incidents, 1260448 Ontario Inc., operating as William Cameron Trucking, and Transport Robert (1973) Ltée, were charged with being the owner of commercial motor vehicles from which a wheel separated while on a public highway, contrary to s. 84.1(1) of the HTA. At their separate trials, the defendants argued that creation of an absolute liability offence violated s. 7 and 11(d) of the Charter and that it should be open to them to defend the charge on the basis that they exercised due diligence. The defendants adduced evidence to explain the loss of the wheel from the commercial vehicle and to show that they acted with due diligence.

In the *Transport Robert* prosecution Justice of the Peace McNish found that there was a violation of s. 11(d). He also accepted that the defendant had exercised due diligence and dismissed the charge. An appeal by the Crown to Knazan J. of the Provincial Offences Appeal Court was successful in part. Knazan J. found that there was a violation of s. 7 of the Charter but allowed the Crown appeal and ordered a new trial because Justice of the Peace McNish erred in excluding certain expert evidence that the Crown sought to call on the due diligence issue.

In the *William Cameron Trucking* case, Justice of the Peace Leaman at trial and Baig J. on appeal found that there was no violation of either s. 7 or 11(d) of the Charter. William Cameron Trucking was accordingly convicted and fined $2,500.

## The Facts

In view of our conclusion on the constitutional issue, it is unnecessary to review the facts of either prosecution in any great deal. Most of the evidence adduced at the trials was led in an attempt to explain how the wheels became detached and why the defendants nevertheless acted with due diligence.

### Transport Robert

On May 29, 1999, a truck operated by Transport Robert was travelling westbound on Highway 401 at Leslie Street in the City of Toronto, when a wheel separated from the attached trailer. The wheel fasteners had backed off of the studs.

The wheel that separated from the trailer was newly installed to replace an older wheel. The theory of the Crown was that the newly installed wheel probably came loose because, contrary to manufacturers' recommendations, the defendant had not had the wheel retorqued within 80 to 160 km after the installation. The defendants disputed this explanation and also led extensive evidence to justify their standard practice for retorquing.

### William Cameron Trucking

On December 5, 1998, a truck owned by William Cameron Trucking was found on the eastbound shoulder of Hwy 11/17. The right front wheel was missing from the tractor unit. The missing wheel was found in a nearby ditch.

William Cameron Trucking suggested that the wheel separation occurred because of the breaking of a stud, which caused the clamp to fall off. At trial, William Cameron Trucking's expert, Dr. A.G. Gillies, testified that while he could not determine the exact cause of the stud failure, it could be attributed to "hydrogen embrittlement," a corrosion process, that could have been caused at the manufacturing stage, or, as a result of exposure to environmental elements.

The theory of the Crown was that a wheel clamp, which was fastened by a nut, had worn lose. The Crown submitted that the principal causes of wheel stud breakage are factors that are within the control of the truck owner, including improper maintenance. The Crown evidence suggested that hydrogen embrittlement was an unlikely cause.

*Analysis*

### Section 11(d)

The argument based on s. 11(d) of the Charter can be dealt with quickly. As Professor Hogg points out in *Constitutional Law of Canada*, (Carswell, Toronto, 1997) vol. 2, p. 48-17, while s. 11(d) prohibits the reversal of the burden of proof of a fact that is an element of the offence, that subsection says nothing about elimination of an element. If the offence as drafted includes certain elements or if s. 7 mandates proof of a certain element as a matter of fundamental justice, placing the burden of proof of such elements on the defence may be an unconstitutional violation of s. 11(d) subject to the Crown establishing that the reversal is a reasonable limit under s. 1. However, there is no violation of s. 11(d) because the legislature has defined an offence so as to eliminate an element, or as here, a possible common law defence.

The real and only constitutional issue in this case then is whether, despite the wording of s. 84.1 of the HTA, s. 7 mandates that the defendants be able to defend the case on the basis of due diligence. We therefore turn to that issue.

### Section 7

Although the rights guaranteed by s. 7 can only be enjoyed by human beings, a corporation has standing to challenge the constitutionality of a penal provision on the basis that the provision violates the s. 7 rights of a human being: *R. v. Wholesale Travel Group Inc.*, [1991] 3 S.C.R. 154. Thus, it is open to these corporate defendants to challenge the constitutionality of s. 84.1 of the HTA.

As the law now stands, a defendant alleging a violation of s. 7 must establish both a violation of the right to life, liberty or security of the person and that the deprivation of that right does not accord with the principles of fundamental justice. The defendants properly concede that since there is no possibility that an individual convicted of the offence can be either imprisoned or placed on probation, s. 84.1 of the HTA does not violate any liberty interest protected by s. 7. They do submit, however, that the provision infringes the security of the person of an individual because it allows for the conviction of a person who is without fault. Their submission of an infringement of the security of the person is primarily based on the effect of the stigma attached to a conviction together with the large possible monetary penalty, the highest in the HTA.

### R. v. Pontes

The Crown's principal submission is that the Supreme Court of Canada has already dealt with the issue of whether an absolute liability offence, with no risk of imprisonment or probation, violates s. 7 of the Charter in *R. v. Pontes*, [1995] 3 S.C.R. 44. In

Pontes, the defendant was charged under s. 94(1) of the British Columbia *Motor Vehicle Act*, R.S.B.C. 1979, c. 288, with driving a motor vehicle at a time when he was "automatically and without notice" prohibited from doing so under s. 92 of that Act. A violation of s. 94 can result in a fine and potential imprisonment. The Supreme Court of Canada held that the wording "automatically and without notice" created an absolute liability offence. However, the majority held that the offence did not violate s. 7 of the Charter because s. 4.1 and s. 72(1) of the British Columbia *Offence Act*, R.S.B.C. 1979, c. 305, s. 4.1 provide that, notwithstanding the provisions of any other Act, there can be no sanction of imprisonment attached to absolute liability offences. Thus, at para. 9 of *Pontes*, Cory J. held as follows:

> Obviously, if the offence is one of absolute liability, but there is no risk of imprisonment, then the provision will not offend s. 7 of the *Canadian Charter of Rights and Freedoms*.

The defendants submit that in *Pontes*, the Supreme Court dealt only with the liberty interest of s. 7 and not security of the person. It is not clear that *Pontes* can be limited in that way. Thus, at para. 47, Cory J. held that where the accused faces no risk of imprisonment, "there is, accordingly, no violation of the right to life, liberty and *security of the person* under s. 7 of the Charter" [emphasis added].

On the other hand, at para. 26 Cory J. deals with the issue in less absolute terms: "*Generally speaking*, an offence of absolute liability *is not likely* to offend s. 7 of the Charter unless a prison sanction is provided" [emphasis added]. The Crown explains this language on the basis that the court has simply left open the question of whether an absolute liability offence would infringe s. 7 where the only possibility of imprisonment was as a result of the defendant's failure to pay a fine. See *Pontes* at para. 16. That issue did not arise in *Pontes* and does not arise in this case because of the terms of s. 84.1(4) of the HTA.

For the purposes of this appeal, we are nevertheless prepared to proceed on the basis that *Pontes* has not fully resolved the question of whether absolute liability violates the guarantee to security of the person under s. 7. We will therefore deal with the submissions of the defendants that s. 84.1 of the HTA does violate the security of the person guarantee in s. 7.

*Security of the Person and Absolute Liability*

As indicated, the defendants submit that as a result of the combination of the high maximum fine and the stigma attached to the s. 84.1 of the HTA offence, a conviction for that offence results in the deprivation of security of the person. They point out that s. 84.1 was enacted in response to a number of highly publicized incidents and recommendations from inquests following the deaths of motorists when wheels came loose from commercial vehicles. They argue that a person convicted of this offence is stigmatized as someone who has exposed innocent motorists or pedestrians to the risk of serious injury or death. They also point out that the offence should be considered, not from the point of view of a large trucking company, but that of an individual, possibly an owner/operator with one commercial vehicle.

In considering the constitutionality of s. 84.1, it is necessary to take into account certain contextual factors. The section applies only to owners and operators of commercial vehicles. These persons operate for profit in a highly regulated industry. In *R. v. Ladouceur* (1990), 56 C.C.C. (3d) 22 at 39 (S.C.C.), Cory J. for the majority of the Supreme Court explained that driving is a privilege and not a right: "[I]t is fitting that governmental action be taken to prevent or at least to lessen this carnage on our highways. Proper laws and regulations are necessary to regulate the privilege of driving a motor vehicle on public thoroughfares."

Although s. 84.1 provides for a maximum fine of $50,000 and a minimum fine of $2,000, under s. 59(2) of the *Provincial Offences Act*, R.S.O. 1990, c. P.33, in exceptional circumstances, the court may impose a fine that is less than the minimum or suspend the sentence. The Crown points out that s. 84.1 has received a narrow interpretation from this court in *Ontario (Minister of Transport) v. Ryder Truck Rental Canada Ltd.* (2000), 47 O.R. (3d) 171 at para. 16 (C.A.), where it was held that the offence only applies if a wheel becomes detached and does not apply where the entire axle, hub, wheel and tire assembly comes off in one piece. The Crown also concedes that although due diligence is not available as a defence, certain other *actus reus* "defences" would be available as where the wheel became detached in a collision caused by a third party.

While the courts have not fully defined the limits of security of the person in s. 7, there are certain propositions established by the cases. In *Blencoe v. British Columbia (Human Rights Commission)*, [2000] 2 S.C.R. 307 at para. 57, Bastarache J. speaking for the majority held that, "[N]ot all state interference with an individual's psychological integrity will engage s. 7. Where the psychological integrity of a person is at issue, security of the person is restricted to 'serious state-imposed psychological stress.'" Thus, "[N]ot all forms of psychological prejudice caused by government will lead to automatic s. 7 violations." Further, there is no "generalized right to dignity, or more specifically, a right to free from stigma" (para. 57) and, "[d]ignity and reputation are not self-standing rights. Neither is freedom from stigma" (para. 80).

In *Blencoe*, the concern was with the lengthy delay in dealing with a human rights complaint, a proceeding that according to the respondent Blencoe, had ruined his reputation. Bastarache J. held at para. 83 that it would only be in "exceptional cases where the state interferes in profoundly intimate and personal choices of an individual that state-caused delay in human rights proceedings could trigger the s. 7 security of the person interest … they would not easily include the type of stress, anxiety and stigma that result from administrative or civil proceedings."

There are admittedly distinctions between the *Blencoe* context and the context of these cases. In particular, the defendants here are charged with quasi-criminal offences and required to appear in open court to face the charges. We also take the point that this offence was enacted in response to a serious public safety issue "in the wake of several serious incidents of 'flying truck wheels.'" See *Ryder Truck Rental*, supra, at para. 1.

However, we are not convinced that a prosecution for the s. 84.1 offence engages the kind of exceptional state-induced psychological stress, even for an individual, that would trigger the security of the person guarantee in s. 7. The offence does not

create a true crime, and like most regulatory offences, it focuses on the harmful consequences of otherwise lawful conduct rather than any moral turpitude. Thus, in
*Wholesale Travel*, supra, at p. 224, Cory J. rejected the accused's claim that conviction for false advertising carried the stigma of dishonesty. In that case, where due
diligence was available, the court characterized the fault element as one of "negligence rather than one involving moral turpitude" and thus, "any stigma that might
flow from a conviction is very considerably diminished." The same can be said in
this case. The s. 84.1 offence focuses on the unintended but harmful consequences of
the commercial trucking industry. We reject the proposition that a defendant charged
with this offence is stigmatized as a person operating in a wanton manner, heedless of
the extreme dangers to life and limb posed by his or her operation. Conviction for the
offence at most implies negligence and like the misleading advertising offence considered in *Wholesale Travel*, any stigma is very considerably diminished.

The diminished stigma attached to the s. 84.1 offence is not sufficient to trigger
the security interest in s. 7 even when coupled with the possibility of a significant
fine. This is simply not the kind of serious state-imposed psychological stress that is
intended to be covered by security of the person. It is qualitatively different than the
kinds of stresses that have been recognized in the cases. A review of those cases
demonstrates a concern with state action that intrudes in an intimate and profound
way as in *New Brunswick (Minister of Health and Community Services) v. G.(J.)*,
[1999] 3 S.C.R. 46 (attempt to take a child away from its parents); *Rodriguez v. British Columbia (Attorney General)*, [1993] 3 S.C.R. 519 (criminal prohibition on assisting suicide for a desperately ill patient) and *R. v. Morgentaler*, [1988] 1 S.C.R. 30
(regulating abortion).

The right to security of the person does not protect the individual operating in the
highly regulated context of commercial trucking for profit from the ordinary stress
and anxieties that a reasonable person would suffer as a result of government regulation of that industry. As Lamer C.J.C. said in *G.(J.)* at para. 59, "[I]f the right were
interpreted with such broad sweep, countless government initiatives could be challenged on the ground that they infringe the right to security of the person, massively
expanding the scope of judicial review, and, in the process, trivializing what it means
for a right to be constitutionally protected."

Accordingly, s. 84.1 of the HTA does not violate s. 7. It is therefore unnecessary to
consider whether any violation could be saved by s. 1.

### Disposition

The appeal by the defendant William Cameron Trucking is dismissed. The appeal by
the Crown in *Transport Robert* is allowed, the order for a new trial set aside and a
conviction entered.

## R. v. Wholesale Travel Group Inc.
Supreme Court of Canada
(1991), 67 C.C.C. (3d) 193

[The accused corporation was charged with several counts of false or misleading advertising, contrary to s. 36(1)(a) of the *Competition Act*, R.S.C. 1970, c. C-23. At trial, the court held that s. 36 of the *Competition Act* and s. 37.3, which creates a statutory due diligence defence, were inconsistent with ss. 7 and 11(d) of the *Canadian Charter of Rights and Freedoms*, and therefore of no force and effect. The judge accordingly dismissed the charges against the accused. The Crown appealed by way of summary appeal to a Supreme Court judge who allowed the appeal, finding that the provisions were not unconstitutional. He then remitted the case to the Provincial Court judge for trial. The Ontario Court of Appeal held (Zuber J.A. dissenting) that s. 37.3(2) of the *Competition Act* imposed a persuasive burden that the accused establish that he or she exercised due diligence and thus violated s. 11(d) of the Charter.
Section 37.3(2) of the *Competition Act* provides:

> 37.3(2) No person shall be convicted of an offence under section 36 or 36.1, if he establishes that,
>
> (a) the act or omission giving rise to the offence with which he is charged was the result of error;
>
> (b) he took reasonable precautions and exercised due diligence to prevent the occurrence of such error;

The Crown appealed from the judgment of the Ontario Court of Appeal. (An appeal by the accused is not dealt with in this extract.)
The Supreme Court unanimously held that it is not an infringement of s. 7 of the Charter to create an offence for which the mental element is negligence.]

LAMER C.J. (with whom six other members of the Supreme Court, including La Forest J., agreed on this point) stated: Counsel for Wholesale Travel has argued that the offence of false/misleading advertising is one of those offences, contemplated by this Court in *Vaillancourt*, [1987] 2 S.C.R. 636, for which the special nature of the stigma attaching to a conviction and/or the severity of the available punishment is such that *subjective mens rea* is constitutionally required by s. 7.

Counsel for Wholesale Travel argued that the stigma attaching to a conviction of false/misleading advertising is akin to the stigma of dishonesty which attaches to a conviction of theft. Given that the stigma attaching to theft was explicitly contemplated in *Vaillancourt* as one which may well necessitate a subjective *mens rea*, it was argued that the offence of false/misleading advertising also requires an element of subjective *mens rea* in order to comply with the principles of fundamental justice. In my view, while a conviction for false/misleading advertising carries some stigma, in the sense that it is not morally-neutral behaviour, it cannot be said that the stigma associated with this offence is analogous to the stigma of dishonesty which attaches to a conviction for theft. A conviction for false/misleading advertising will rest on a variety of facts, many of which will not reveal any dishonesty but, rather, carelessness and the conviction of same does not brand the accused as being dishonest. In my opinion, the same cannot be said for a conviction for theft.

While an aware state of mind may well be the most appropriate minimum standard of fault for imprisonment or for any offence included in the *Criminal Code*, a matter upon which I refrain from expressing any view, it does not follow that this standard of fault is entrenched in the *Charter*. As I stated in *Lippé v. Québec (Procureur général)*, (1991), 128 N.R. 1, at p. 34, "the *Constitution* does not always guarantee the ideal." As this Court stated in *Vaillancourt, supra*, the principles of fundamental justice dictate that negligence is the minimum fault requirement where an accused faces possible imprisonment upon conviction except for certain offences such as murder. For the reasons given above, it is my view that s. 7 of the *Charter* does not dictate the higher fault requirement contemplated by the Ontario Law Reform Commission for the offence of false/misleading advertising. Whether a fault requirement higher than this constitutional minimum ought to be adopted where an accused faces possible imprisonment or conviction of any offence under the *Criminal Code* is a question of public policy which must be determined by Parliament, and for the courts to pronounce upon this would be contrary to what this Court has said in *Re B.C. Motor Vehicle Act*, [1985] 2 S.C.R. 486, at p. 498-99: that we refrain from "adjudicating upon the merits or wisdom of enactments." It is not the role of this Court to "second guess" the policy decisions made by elected officials.

La FOREST J. added the following in his concurring judgment: For my part, I am prepared to accept the requirement of due diligence as sufficient for *Charter* purposes in the case of regulatory offences and some criminal offences having a significant regulatory base (e.g., gun control *R. v. Schwartz*, [1988] 2 S.C.R. 443). However, for most criminal offences I would be reluctant to accept a lower level of *mens rea* than criminal negligence.

CORY J. (with whom L'Heureux-Dubé concurred) stated: Those who argue against differential treatment for regulatory offences assert that there is no valid reason to distinguish between the criminal and regulatory accused. Each, it is said, is entitled in law to the same procedural and substantive protections. This view assumes equality of position between criminal and regulatory defendants; that is to say, it assumes that each starts out from a position of equal knowledge, volition and "innocence." The argument against differential treatment further suggests that differentiating between the regulatory and criminal defendants implies the subordination and sacrifice of the regulatory accused to the interests of the community at large. Such a position, it is argued, contravenes our basic concern for individual dignity and our fundamental belief in the importance of the individual. It is these assumptions which the licensing justification challenges.

The licensing concept rests on the view that those who choose to participate in regulated activities have, in doing so, placed themselves in a responsible relationship to the public generally and must accept the consequences of that responsibility. Therefore, it is said, those who engage in regulated activity should, as part of the burden of responsible conduct attending participation in the regulated field, be deemed to have accepted certain terms and conditions applicable to those who act within the regulated sphere. Foremost among these implied terms is an undertaking that the conduct of the regulated actor will comply with and maintain a certain minimum standard of care.

The licensing justification is based not only on the idea of a conscious choice being made to enter a regulated field but also on the concept of control. The concept is that those persons who enter a regulated field are in the best position to control the harm which may result, and that they should therefore be held responsible for it.

Does section 7 require in all cases that the Crown prove *mens rea* as an essential element of the offence? The resolution of this question requires that a contextual approach be taken to the meaning and scope of the s. 7 right. Certainly, there can be no doubt that s. 7 requires proof of some degree of fault. That fault may be demonstrated by proof of intent, whether subjective or objective, or by proof of negligent conduct, depending on the nature of the offence. While it is not necessary in this case to determine the requisite degree of fault necessary to prove the commission of particular crimes, I am of the view that with respect to regulatory offences, proof of negligence satisfies the requirement of fault demanded by s. 7. Although the element of fault may not be removed completely, the demands of s. 7 will be met in the regulatory context where liability is imposed for conduct which breaches the standard of reasonable care required of those operating in the regulated field.

Regulatory schemes can only be effective if they provide for significant penalties in the event of their breach. Indeed, although it may be rare that imprisonment is sought, it must be available as a sanction if there is to be effective enforcement of the regulatory measure. Nor is the imposition of imprisonment unreasonable in light of the danger that can accrue to the public from breaches of regulatory statutes. The spectre of tragedy evoked by such names as Thalidomide, Bhopal, Chernobyl and the *Exxon Valdez* can leave no doubt as to the potential human and environmental devastation which can result from the violation of regulatory measures. Strong sanctions including imprisonment are vital to the prevention of similar catastrophes. The potential for serious harm flowing from the breach of regulatory measures is too great for it to be said that imprisonment can never be imposed as a sanction.

[The Supreme Court was divided on the question whether the shifting of the onus violated s. 11(d) of the Charter.]

LAMER C.J. (with whom three other members of the Court concurred) stated that the provision violated section s. 11(d) and could not be upheld under s. 1: In *Vaillancourt, supra*, this Court held that s. 11(d) is offended when an accused may be convicted despite the existence of a reasonable doubt on an essential element of the offence (including those elements required by s. 7 of the *Charter*).

In *Whyte*, [1988] 2 S.C.R. 3, a majority of this Court held that the distinction between elements of the offence and other aspects of the charge is irrelevant to the s. 11(d) inquiry. Thus, the real concern is not whether the accused must disprove an element or prove an excuse, but that an accused may be convicted while a reasonable doubt exists.

Again, both the Crown and a number of interveners have argued that this interpretation of s. 11(d) should not apply in a regulatory setting. I can only reiterate my earlier comment that it is the fact that the state has resorted to the restriction of liberty through imprisonment for enforcement purposes which is determinative of the *Charter* analysis. A person whose liberty has been restricted by way of imprisonment has lost no *less* liberty because he or she is being punished for the commission of a regulatory offence as opposed to a criminal offence. A person whose liberty interest is imperilled is entitled to have the principles of fundamental justice fully observed. The presumption of innocence, guaranteed by s. 11(d), is clearly a principle of fundamental justice.

IACOBUCCI J. (with whom Gonthier and Stevenson JJ. concurred) agreed that the section violated s. 11(d), but held that it was valid under s. 1:  At the outset, I would like to point out that it is now clear that a rigid or formalistic approach must be avoided when applying the various criteria of the *Oakes*, [1986] 1 S.C.R. 103, analysis, and that proper consideration must be given to the circumstances and context of a particular case: *R. v. Keegstra*, [1990] 3 S.C.R. 697, at pp. 737-38, *per* Chief Justice Dickson speaking for the majority. In the present case, the special nature of the legislation and offence in question must be kept in mind when applying s. 1 of the *Charter*. In this respect, I agree with Cory J. that what is ultimately involved in this appeal is the ability of federal and provincial governments to pursue social ends through the enactment and enforcement of public welfare legislation. While I abstain from commenting on the dichotomy articulated by Cory J. between "true crimes" and "regulatory offences," I agree with my colleague that the offence of false or misleading advertisement may properly be characterized as a public welfare offence and that the prohibition of such offences is of fundamental importance in Canadian society.

However, it is with respect to the third requirement of the *Oakes* analysis, that I respectfully disagree with the conclusions of Lamer C.J. This step requires a consideration of whether the means chosen impair the right or freedom in question *no more than is necessary to accomplish the desired objective*. Lamer C.J. is of the opinion that the use of a persuasive burden in s. 37.3(2) of the *Competition Act* cannot pass this third step of the *Oakes* analysis because of the presence of an alternative means open to Parliament that would be less intrusive on s. 11(d) of the *Charter* and would "go a long way" in achieving the objective. The alternative in question is the use of a "mandatory presumption of negligence" (following from the proof of the *actus reus*) which could be rebutted by something less than an accused establishing due diligence on a balance of probabilities, i.e., by raising a reasonable doubt as to due diligence. With respect, I cannot agree that such a means would achieve the stated objective as effectively nor would it go a long way in achieving it. Such a means would shift to the accused the burden of simply raising a reasonable doubt as to due diligence and would not thereby allow the effective pursuit of the regulatory objective. It would leave the Crown the legal burden of proving facts largely within the peculiar knowledge of the accused.

CORY J. (with whom L'Heureux-Dubé J. concurred) held that the provision did not violate s. 11(d):  Wholesale Travel argues that the placing of a persuasive burden on the accused to establish due diligence on a balance of probabilities violates the presumption of innocence as guaranteed by s. 11(d) of the *Charter*. As the due diligence defence is the essential characteristic of strict liability offences as defined in *Sault Ste. Marie*, [1978] 2 S.C.R. 1299, the appellant's s. 11(d) claim represents a fundamental challenge to the entire regime of regulatory offences in Canada.

In *Sault Ste. Marie*, Dickson J. carefully considered the basic principles of criminal liability, including the presumption of innocence, and balanced them against the public goals sought to be achieved through regulatory measures. He determined that strict liability represented an appropriate compromise between the competing interests involved. This conclusion is no less valid today. The *Charter* was not enacted in a vacuum. The presumption of innocence which it guarantees had long been established and was well recognized at common law. The due diligence defence recognized in *Sault Ste. Marie* which is the target of the present challenge was itself a function of the presumption of innocence.

The reasons for ascribing a different content to the presumption of innocence in the regulatory context are persuasive and compelling. As with the *mens rea* issue, if regulatory mechanisms are to operate effectively, the Crown cannot be required to disprove due diligence beyond a reasonable doubt. Such a requirement would make it virtually impossible for the Crown to prove regulatory offences and would effectively prevent governments from seeking to implement public policy through regulatory means.

Quite simply, the enforcement of regulatory offences would be rendered virtually impossible if the Crown were required to prove negligence beyond a reasonable doubt. The means of proof of reasonable care will be peculiarly within the knowledge and ability of the regulated accused. Only the accused will be in a position to bring forward evidence relevant to the question of due diligence.

The conclusion that strict liability does not violate either s. 7 or s. 11(d) of the *Charter* is supported by the American approach to regulatory offences. Generally speaking, American courts have not recognized an intermediate category of strict liability. Rather, the U.S. Supreme Court has held that, where the person charged is aware of the regulated nature of the impugned conduct, it is constitutionally permissible to enact absolute liability offences, even where imprisonment is available as a penalty: see, for example, *United States v. Balint*, 258 U.S. 250 (1922); *United States v. Dotterweich*, 320 U.S. 277 (1943); *Morissette v. United States*, 342 U.S. 246 (1952); *Lambert v. California*, 355 U.S. 225 (1957). Furthermore, even in the case of serious criminal offences, it has been held that placing a persuasive burden on the accused to establish a defence does not violate the presumption of innocence: see *Patterson v. New York*, 432 U.S. 197 (1977); *Martin v. Ohio*, 480 U.S. 228 (1987). The constitutional validity of regulatory legislation which imposes strict liability would, under the American approach, seem to be beyond question.

[The majority of the court also held that the accused company had standing to challenge the provision under ss. 7 and 11(d).]

LAMER C.J. (with whom six other members of the Court agreed) stated: In *Irwin Toy Ltd. v. Quebec (Attorney General)*, [1989] 1 S.C.R. 927, this Court held that only human beings can enjoy the right to life, liberty and security of the person guaranteed by s. 7 of the *Charter*, and that a corporation was therefore unable to seek a declaration that certain provisions of the *Consumer Protection Act* infringed s. 7 of the *Charter* and could not be upheld under s. 1 of the *Charter*. However, the majority was careful to note that there were no penal proceedings pending in the case and that the principle enunciated in *R. v. Big M Drug Mart Ltd.*, [1985] 1 S.C.R. 295, was therefore not involved.

A number of parties contended, in oral argument, that while this Court has held that a corporation which has been charged with a penal provision has standing to challenge the constitutionality of that provision, this does not necessarily mean that the corporation can *benefit* from a finding that the provision violates a *human being's* constitutional rights. In other words, when a corporation's constitutional challenge gives rise to a finding that a statutory provision violates a *human being's Charter* rights, the appropriate remedy under s. 52(1) of the *Constitution Act, 1982* is that the provision is of no force or effect with respect to human beings (because this is the extent of the inconsistency between the Constitution and the law), but the provision remains of force and effect with respect to corporations (because the provision as applied to corporations is *not* inconsistent with the Constitution).

Such an interpretation of the words "to the extent of the inconsistency" contained in s. 52(1) would be inconsistent with this Court's holding in *R. v. Big M Drug Mart Ltd.*, *supra*, and would not accord with this Court's general approach to s. 52(1). For example, in *R. v. Morgentaler*, [1988] 1 S.C.R. 30, this Court restored Dr. Morgentaler's acquittal on the basis that s. 251 (the abortion provision) of the *Criminal Code*, R.S.C. 1970, c. C-34, limited women's rights under s. 7 of the *Charter*, could not be upheld under s. 1 and was therefore of no force or effect. Dr. Morgentaler, as an accused person, was entitled to challenge the constitutionality of s. 251 on the basis that it violated women's *Charter* rights. Moreover, he was entitled to *benefit* from the finding that the provision was inconsistent with the Constitution and was, therefore, of no force or effect. I am not prepared to depart from this approach to s. 52(1).

Thus, it is my view that Wholesale Travel does have standing to challenge the constitutionality of the false/misleading advertising provisions under ss. 7 and 11(d) of the *Charter* and may benefit from a finding that these provisions are unconstitutional. However, this is *not* to say that if the same provisions were enacted so as to apply *exclusively* to corporations, a corporation would be entitled to raise the *Charter* arguments which have been raised in the case at bar. The problem with ss. 36(1) and 37.3(2) of the *Competition Act* is that they are worded so as to encompass *both* individual and corporate accused; in this sense, they are "over-inclusive." Therefore, if the provisions violate an individual's *Charter* rights they must be struck down (to the extent of the inconsistency) under s. 52(1). Once the provisions are held to be of no force or effect, they cannot apply to *any* accused, whether corporate or individual.

[The result was (5 to 4) that the reverse onus provision be upheld. The Crown's appeal was therefore allowed.]

---

In *R. v. Ellis-Don Ltd.* (1992), 71 C.C.C. (3d) 63, the Supreme Court of Canada followed *Wholesale Travel* and allowed an appeal from an Ontario Court of Appeal decision that had held that s. 37(2) of the *Occupational Health and Safety Act* as well as the reverse onus under *Sault Ste. Marie* violated s. 11(d) of the Charter. The majority of the Court of Appeal had held that the reversal could not be justified under s. 1 of the Charter. Galligan J.A. stated:

> It is now settled that s. 11(d) of the *Charter* implies proof of guilt beyond reasonable doubt. The effect of the onus, created by s. 37(2) of the Act and by the common law in *Sault Ste. Marie*, to prove the defence of due diligence on the balance of probabilities means that a court is required to convict an accused if it is not satisfied on the balance of probabilities that the accused has exercised due diligence even though it may have a reasonable doubt on the issue. It is a commonplace that it is unacceptable for someone to be convicted of an offence when there is a reasonable doubt about guilt. The constitutional issue is thus whether the statutory objective, significantly important as it is, justifies the imposition of that unsatisfactory situation. I am seriously troubled about how it could be said that the objective of this Act is so pressingly important that a risk should be taken of convicting someone who might be innocent. Important as the protection of workers' health and safety in the workplace may be I am unable to say that it is more important than protecting innocent citizens from homicide. Yet the law does not permit the conviction of a person charged with murder if the court has a doubt about his guilt. ...
>
> I do not think that it is necessary to strike out the words in s. 37(2) or in the common law defence which impose upon the accused the burden of proving the defence of due diligence. It is sufficient that they be interpreted as imposing upon the accused only the evidential burden of showing some evidence which could raise a reasonable doubt on the issue of due diligence. The defence of due diligence both under s. 37(2) of the Act and at common law remains a viable defence. The defence of due diligence must be given effect to if at the end of all of the evidence the court is left in a state of reasonable doubt about whether in the particular circumstances the accused did in fact act with due diligence.

Houlden J.A. took the same approach:

> When a person can be convicted and subjected to a heavy fine or imprisonment, even though the trier of fact has a reasonable doubt about whether the accused exercised due diligence, I believe there is a lack of proportionality between the effects and the objective. With respect, I would adopt the view of the Ontario Law Reform Commission in its "Report on the Basis of Liability for Provincial Offences," 1990, at pp. 47-48 on the necessity for preserving the presumption of innocence in strict liability offences.

Carthy J.A. dissented, stating:

> Freedoms must live side by side with structure and order. Section 1 is where the balance is assessed. In my judgment the balance of probabilities test is a necessary, proper, fair and justified means of maintaining a structure that protects the safety of working persons and at the same time impinges modestly and to little account in practical application upon the employer. All rights and freedoms, once declared, tend to appear absolute. Section 1 provides a means of restraint and balance against that extreme to meet society's greater needs. Safety in the workplace is such a need.

Lamer C.J.C. stated orally for the Supreme Court:

We are all of the view that this appeal must succeed. The existence of a restriction to s. 11(d) is governed by this court's decision in *R. v. Wholesale Travel Group Inc.* (1991), 67 C.C.C. (3d) 193, 84 D.L.R. (4th) 161, [1991] 3 S.C.R. 154. The s. 1 analysis in *Wholesale* is applicable here, as there is no difference of substance between the nature of the legislation in that case and this one.

Accordingly, the appeal is allowed and the case is remitted to the Court of Appeal for disposal of the other grounds of appeal raised below and not dealt with by the Court of Appeal.

For a comment on the 1990 Ontario Law Reform Commission Report on Liability for Provincial Offences, see K. Roach (1990), 69 *Can. Bar Rev.* 802. For a contrasting view see T. Archibald, "Liability for Provincial Offences: Fault, Penalty and the Principles of Fundamental Justice in Canada" (1991), 14 *Dalhousie L.J.* 65. See also A. Brudner, "Imprisonment and Strict Liability" (1990), 40 *U.T.L.J.* 738; C. Ruby and K. Jull, "The Charter and Regulatory Offences: A Wholesale Revision" (1992), 14 C.R. (4th) 226; C. Tollefson, "*R. v. Wholesale Travel Group Inc.*" (1992), 71 *Can. Bar Rev.* 369; D. Stuart, "The Supreme Court Drastically Reduces the Constitutional Requirement of Fault: A Triumph of Pragmatism and Law Enforcement Expediency" (1993), 15 C.R. (4th) 88; and J. Keefe, "The Due Diligence Defence: A Wholesale Review" (1993), 35 *Crim. L.Q.* 480.

### ADDITIONAL READING

- K. Roach, *Criminal Law*, 3rd ed. (Toronto: Irwin Law, 2004), chapter 5;
- A. Mewett and M. Manning, *Criminal Law*, 3rd ed. (Toronto: Butterworths, 1994), at 223-50;
- D. Stuart, *Canadian Criminal Law*, 4th ed. (Toronto: Carswell, 2001), at 163-96;
- J.C. Smith and B. Hogan, *Criminal Law*, 6th ed. (London: Butterworths, 1988), at 98-119;
- G. Williams, *Criminal Law*, 2nd ed. (London: Stevens and Sons, 1961), at 215-65;
- G. Williams, *Textbook of Criminal Law*, 2nd ed. (London: Stevens and Sons, 1983), at 927-50;
- W. LaFave and A. Scott, *Criminal Law*, 2nd ed. (St. Paul, MN: West, 1986), at 242-50;
- Law Reform Commission of Canada, *Studies on Strict Liability* (1974);
- R. Sharpe, "Strict Liability and Due Diligence in Public Welfare Offences: *R. v. City of Sault Ste. Marie*" (1979), 3 *Can. Bus. L.J.* 453.

# CHAPTER SEVEN

# Fault or Mens Rea

This chapter builds on the previous chapter by discussing the additional pre-conditions for liability that are required by the law, beyond those inherent in a voluntary "act." This notion of culpability, goes by various names, including "*mens rea*," "mental state," the "mental element," "guilty mind," "fault element," and others. Indeed, each of these labels carries with it a number of different concepts, as discussed below.

In *R. v. Tolson* (1889), 23 Q.B.D. 168 (Ct. for Cr. Cases Reserved), Stephen J. stated, with respect to the phrase "*non est reus, nisi mens sit rea*":

> Though this phrase is in common use, I think it most unfortunate, and not only likely to mislead, but actually misleading, on the following grounds. It naturally suggests that, apart from all particular definitions of crimes, such a thing exists as a "mens rea," or "guilty mind," which is always expressly or by implication involved in every definition. This is obviously not the case, for the mental elements of different crimes differ widely. "Mens rea" means in the case of murder, malice aforethought; in the case of theft, an intention to steal; in the case of rape, an intention to have forcible connection with a woman without her consent; and in the case of receiving stolen goods, knowledge that the goods were stolen. In some cases it denotes mere inattention. For instance, in the case of manslaughter by negligence it may mean forgetting to notice a signal. It appears confusing to call so many dissimilar states of mind by one name. It seems contradictory indeed to describe a mere absence of mind as "mens rea," or guilty mind. The expression again is likely to and often does mislead. To an unlegal mind it suggests that by the law of England no act is a crime which is done from laudable motives, in other words, that immorality is essential to crime.
>
> Like most legal Latin maxims, the maxim on mens rea appears to me to be too short and antithetical to be of much practical value. It is, indeed, more like the title of a treatise than a practical rule. …
>
> The principle involved appears to me, when fully considered, to amount to no more than this. The full definition of every crime contains expressly or by implication a proposition as to a state of mind. Therefore, if the mental element of any conduct alleged to be a crime is proved to have been absent in any given case, the crime so defined is not committed; or, again, if a crime is fully defined, nothing amounts to that crime which does not satisfy that definition. Crimes are in the present day much more accurately defined by statute or otherwise than they formerly were. The mental element of most crimes is marked by one of the words "maliciously," "fraudulently," "negligently," or "knowingly," but it is the general—I might, I think, say the invariable—practice of the legislature to leave unexpressed

some of the mental elements of crime. In all cases whatever, competent age, sanity, and some degree of freedom from some kinds of coercion are assumed to be essential to criminality, but I do not believe they are ever introduced into any statute by which any particular crime is defined.

The meanings of the words "malice," "negligence," and "fraud" in relation to particular crimes has been ascertained by numerous cases. Malice means one thing in relation to murder, another in relation to the Malicious Mischief Act, and a third in relation to libel, and so of fraud and negligence.

The English Law Commission Working Paper No. 31, *The Mental Element in Crime* (1970) states:

> One of the major stumbling blocks to the orderly development of English criminal law has been the confusion that has existed for the past 100 years or so over the question whether the language used in the creation of a statutory offence imports full *mens rea* (intention, knowledge or recklessness), some fault element short of *mens rea*, i.e., negligence, or some form of "absolute" or "strict" liability.

The Government of Canada document, *The Criminal Law in Canadian Society* (1982) states at p. 48:

> To summarize, it is vital to retain the standard of responsibility and fault for a finding of criminal liability, because of the significant meaning and impact of the criminal process and criminal sanctions. Second, it is important to clarify the ambiguities which currently exist as to the precise standard of culpability required for each criminal offence. Third, it is not necessary or desirable to confine the criminal law to acts committed by individuals against other individuals; rather, it is advisable to clarify and give greater consideration to the liability of organizations, and individuals acting within organizations, where serious harm to an individual or to the general good is caused or threatened.

These excerpts remind us that it is important to approach the issue of fault with some care. There is no singular type of fault, applicable to crime in general. To determine the fault requirement for a particular offence, the wording of the statute must be consulted, along with common law definitions. It is also important to remember that many offences have more than one mental element and different types of fault might be applicable. A good example of this is the offence of criminal harassment (or "stalking"), which is found in s. 264.1 of the *Criminal Code*. For a discussion of the complex fault require-ments of this offence, see *R. v. Krushel* (2000), 142 C.C.C. (3d) 1 (Ont. C.A.). It is also necessary not only to identify the appropriate level of fault (that is, intent, knowledge, recklessness, negligence, etc.), but also to describe the relation of the particular fault element to the prohibited act.

The rest of this chapter focuses on "true" criminal offences. As discussed in the previous chapter (Absolute and Strict Liability), the common law generally presumes that a positive fault requirement attaches to these offences. Indeed, as discussed below, the *Canadian Charter of Rights and Freedoms* requires that there be a level of fault in certain circumstances.

In section I, various legislative attempts to provide comprehensive fault definitions are considered. Section II considers subjective states of fault. In section III, we examine objective fault requirements, those that do not require an inquiry into what went on in the accused's mind at the time of the offence. Finally, in section IV, constitutional considerations are raised once again.

# I. LEGISLATIVE DEFINITIONS OF FAULT

In Canada, there is no uniform definition of the fault requirements that apply to offences. For example, the *Criminal Code* does not include a comprehensive part (referred to by academics and law reformers as a "general part") that provides definitions of commonly used fault-related terms, like "intention," "knowledge," "willfull," "purpose," or "criminal negligence." The definitional enterprise is left largely to the courts to interpret terms on an offence-by-offence, term-by-term basis. This gives rise to a lack of clarity and inconsistency between offences. This state of the law has led law reformers and others to call for the creation of a "general part." Many respectable attempts have been made by law reformers in Canada, the United Kingdom, and the United States. Despite a very respectable attempt at this endeavour by the now defunct Law Reform Commission of Canada (see *Recodifying Criminal Law*, below), Parliament has shown little interest in reshaping the *Criminal Code* in this way. The following excerpts explore this issue and provide some examples of attempts to codify general concepts.

### American Law Institute, *Model Penal Code*
Proposed Official Draft, 1962

[The institute's *Model Penal Code* provides in the part on general principles of liability as follows:]

*Section 2.02.  General Requirements of Culpability.*

*(1)  Minimum Requirements of Culpability.*

Except as provided in Section 2.05, a person is not guilty of an offense unless he acted purposely, knowingly, recklessly or negligently, as the law may require, with respect to each material element of the offense.

*(2)  Kinds of Culpability Defined.*

(a)  Purposely.

A person acts purposely with respect to a material element of an offense when:
    (i)  if the element involves the nature of his conduct or a result thereof, it is his conscious object to engage in conduct of that nature or to cause such a result; and
    (ii)  if the element involves the attendant circumstances, he is aware of the existence of such circumstances or he believes or hopes that they exist.

(b) Knowingly.

A person acts knowingly with respect to a material element of an offense when:

(i) if the element involves the nature of his conduct or the attendant circumstances, he is aware that his conduct is of that nature or that such circumstances exist; and

(ii) if the element involves a result of his conduct, he is aware that it is practically certain that his conduct will cause such a result.

(c) Recklessly.

A person acts recklessly with respect to a material element of an offense when he consciously disregards a substantial and unjustifiable risk that the material element exists or will result from his conduct. The risk must be of such a nature and degree that, considering the nature and purpose of the actor's conduct and the circumstances known to him, its disregard involves a gross deviation from the standard of conduct that a law-abiding person would observe in the actor's situation.

(d) Negligently.

A person acts negligently with respect to a material element of an offense when he should be aware of a substantial and unjustifiable risk that the material element exists or will result from his conduct. The risk must be of such a nature and degree that the actor's failure to perceive it, considering the nature and purpose of his conduct and the circumstances known to him, involves a gross deviation from the standard of care that a reasonable person would observe in the actor's situation.

*(3) Culpability Required Unless Otherwise Provided.*

When the culpability sufficient to establish a material element of an offense is not prescribed by law, such element is established if a person acts purposely, knowingly or recklessly with respect thereto.

*(4) Prescribed Culpability Requirement Applies to All Material Elements.*

When the law defining an offense prescribes the kind of culpability that is sufficient for the commission of an offense, without distinguishing among the material elements thereof, such provisions shall apply to all the material elements of the offense, unless a contrary purpose plainly appears.

*(5) Substitutes for Negligence, Recklessness and Knowledge.*

When the law provides that negligence suffices to establish an element of an offense, such element also is established if a person acts purposely, knowingly or recklessly. When recklessness suffices to establish an element, such element also is established if a person acts purposely or knowingly. When acting knowingly suffices to establish an element, such element also is established if a person acts purposely.

*(6) Requirement of Purpose Satisfied if Purpose Is Conditional.*

When a particular purpose is an element of an offense, the element is established although such purpose is conditional, unless the condition negatives the harm or evil sought to be prevented by the law defining the offense.

*(7) Requirement of Knowledge Satisfied by Knowledge of High Probability.*

When knowledge of the existence of a particular fact is an element of an offense, such knowledge is established if a person is aware of a high probability of its existence, unless he actually believes that it does not exist.

*(8) Requirement of Wilfulness Satisfied by Acting Knowingly.*

A requirement that an offense be committed wilfully is satisfied if a person acts knowingly with respect to the material elements of the offense, unless a purpose to impose further requirements appears.

*(9) Culpability as to Illegality of Conduct.*

Neither knowledge nor recklessness or negligence as to whether conduct constitutes an offense or as to the existence, meaning or application of the law determining the elements of an offense is an element of such offense, unless the definition of the offense or the Code so provides.

*(10) Culpability as Determinant of Grade of Offense.*

When the grade or degree of an offense depends on whether the offense is committed purposely, knowingly, recklessly or negligently, its grade or degree shall be the lowest for which the determinative kind of culpability is established with respect to any material element of the offense.

**English Law Commission,** *The Mental Element in Crime*
Working Paper No. 31 (1970)

[The commission suggests the following legislative definitions for existing and future offences:]

*Intention and knowledge*

7.A.(1)  a person intends an event not only
    (a)  when his purpose is to cause that event but also
    (b)  when he has no substantial doubt that that event will result from his conduct. (First alternative)
    (c) when he foresees that that event will probably result from his conduct. (Second alternative)

(2) a person is not by reason only of proposition 7A(1)(b) to be taken to intend the wrongdoing of others.

(3) a person knows of circumstances not only when he knows that they exist but also when he has no substantial doubt that they exist. (First alternative) he knows that they probably exist. (Second alternative)

### Recklessness

B. a person is reckless if,

(a) knowing that there is a risk that an event may result from his conduct or that a circumstance may exist, he takes that risk, and

(b) it is unreasonable for him to take it having regard to the degree and nature of the risk which he knows to be present.

### Negligence

C. a person is negligent if he fails to exercise such care, skill or foresight as a reasonable man in his situation would exercise.

**Law Reform Commission of Canada,** *Recodifying Criminal Law*
Report 31 (1987), at 143-44

### 2(4)  Requirements for Culpability.

*(a)  General Requirements as to Level of Culpability.*

Unless otherwise provided:

(i) where the definition of a crime requires purpose, no one is liable unless as concerns its elements he acts

(A) purposely as to the conduct specified by that definition,

(B) purposely as to the consequences, if any, so specified, and

(C) knowingly or recklessly as to the circumstances, if any, so specified;

(ii) where the definition of a crime requires recklessness, no one is liable unless as concerns its elements he acts

(A) purposely as to the conduct specified by that definition,

(B) recklessly as to the consequences, if any, so specified, and

(C) recklessly as to the circumstances, whether specified or not;

(iii) where the definition of a crime requires negligence, no one is liable unless as concerns its elements he acts

(A) negligently as to the conduct specified by that definition,

(B) negligently as to the consequences, if any, so specified, and

(C) negligently as to the circumstances, whether specified or not.

*(b)  Definitions.*

"Purposely."

(i)  A person acts purposely as to conduct if he means to engage in such conduct, and, in the case of an omission, if he also knows the circumstances giving rise to the duty to act or is reckless as to their existence.

(ii)  A person acts purposely as to a consequence if he acts in order to effect:

(A)  that consequence; or

(B) another consequence which he knows involves that consequence.

"Recklessly."

A person is reckless as to consequences or circumstances if, in acting as he does, he is conscious that such consequences will probably result or that such circumstances probably obtain.

[Alternative:]

"Recklessly."

A person is reckless as to consequences or circumstances if, in acting as he does, he consciously takes a risk, which in the circumstances known to him is highly unreasonable to take, that such consequences may result or that such circumstances may obtain.

"Negligently."

A person is negligent as to conduct, circumstances or consequences if it is a marked departure from the ordinary standard of reasonable care to engage in such conduct, to take the risk (conscious or otherwise) that such consequences will result, or to take the risk (conscious or otherwise) that such circumstances obtain.

*(c)  Greater Culpability Requirement Satisfies Lesser.*

(i)  Where the definition of a crime requires negligence, a person may be liable if he acts, or omits to act, purposely or recklessly as to one or more of the elements in that definition.

(ii)  Where the definition of a crime requires recklessness, a person may be liable if he acts, or omits to act, purposely as to one or more of the elements in that definition.

*(d)  Residual Rule.*

Where the definition of a crime does not explicitly specify the requisite level of culpability, it shall be interpreted as requiring purpose.

## II. SUBJECTIVE STATES OF FAULT

There are different ways of classifying fault for particular crimes. One fundamental distinction is between those aspects of fault that focus on what passed through the mind of the accused person at the relevant time, and fault that is not concerned with what the accused subjectively intended or thought, but whether the accused measured up to some normative of objective standard. This is one of the most important distinctions to be made in substantive criminal law. However, merely because subjective fault is a *formal* requirement for an offence, this does not mean that objective considerations are irrelevant. What a reasonable person would have realized or known may be of some value in the determination of what the accused person actually thought. This point is made in the two excerpts below.

### R. v. Buzzanga and Durocher
Ontario Court of Appeal
(1979), 49 C.C.C. (2d) 369

MARTIN J.A.:  Since people are usually able to foresee the consequences of their acts, if a person does an act likely to produce certain consequences it is, in general, reasonable to assume that the accused also foresaw the probable consequences of his act and if he, nevertheless, acted so as to produce those consequences, that he intended them. The greater the likelihood of the relevant consequences ensuing from the accused's act, the easier it is to draw the inference that he intended those consequences. The purpose of this process, however, is to determine what the particular accused intended, not to fix him with the intention that a reasonable person might be assumed to have in the circumstances, where doubt exists as to the actual intention of the accused. The accused's testimony, if he gives evidence as to what was in his mind, is important material to be weighed with the other evidence in determining whether the necessary intent has been established. Indeed, Mr. Justice Devlin, in his charge to the jury in *R. v. Adams* (*The Times*, April 10, 1957), said that where the accused testified as to what was in his mind and the jury "thought he might be telling the truth," they would "have the best evidence available on what was in his own mind."

---

We return to *Buzzanga* below in exploring the definitions of "intention" and "wilfully."

### R. v. Tennant and Naccarato
Ontario Court of Appeal
(1975), 23 C.C.C. (2d) 80

THE COURT ...  Where liability is imposed on a subjective basis, what a reasonable man ought to have anticipated is merely evidence from which a conclusion may be drawn that the accused anticipated the same consequences. On the other hand, where the test is objective, what a reasonable man should have anticipated constitutes the basis of liability.

## Intention and Knowledge

This part of the chapter examines the two basic subjective fault requirements of intention and knowledge. They are at the core of subjective states of liability. Before looking at how the courts have analyzed these concepts, it is important to understand the difference between intention and the concept of motive.

### R. v. Lewis
Supreme Court of Canada
(1979), 47 C.C.C. (2d) 24

[The accused was charged with murder of T.'s daughter and son-in-law. The victims received an electric kettle in which there was a bomb, which exploded and killed them. The theory of the Crown was that the accused, L., either made the bomb and mailed it, or at the very least mailed the package, knowing that it contained a bomb. In the passage below, Chief Justice Dickson addresses the importance and place of motive in the criminal trial.]

DICKSON C.J.: …

#### *Motive in Law*

In ordinary parlance, the words "intent" and "motive" are frequently used interchangeably, but in the criminal law they are distinct. In most criminal trials, the mental element, the *mens rea* with which the Court is concerned, relates to "intent," i.e., the exercise of a free will to use particular means to produce a particular result, rather than with "motive," i.e., that which precedes and induces the exercise of the will. The mental element of a crime ordinarily involves no reference to motive: 11 Hals., 4th ed. (1976), p. 17, para. 11.

Difficulty arises, however, from the vagueness in law of the notion of "motive." There would appear to be substantial agreement amongst textwriters that there are two possible meanings to be ascribed to the term. Glanville Williams in his Criminal Law: The General Part, 2nd ed. (1961), p. 48, Section 21, distinguishes between these meanings:

(1) It sometimes refers to the emotion prompting an act, e.g., "D killed P, his wife's lover, from a motive of jealousy." (2) It sometimes means a kind of intention, e.g., "D killed P with the motive (intention, desire) of stopping him from paying attentions to D's wife."

It is this second sense, according to Williams, which is employed in criminal law:

… motive is ulterior intention—the intention with which an intentional act is done (or, more clearly, the intention with which an intentional consequence is brought about). Intention, when distinguished from motive, relates to the means, motive to the end …

Smith and Hogan in their *Criminal Law*, 4th ed. (1978), p. 63, put the matter in slightly sharper perspective. Dealing with the first of the above meanings:

> If D causes an actus reus with mens rea, he is guilty of the crime and it is entirely
> irrelevant to his guilt that he had a good motive. The mother who kills her imbecile and
> suffering child out of motives of compassion is just as guilty of murder as is the man
> who kills for gain.

The authors discuss also the species of intention implicit in the second meaning above
(pp. 63-4):

> For example, D intends (a) to put poison in his uncle's tea, (b) to cause his uncle's death
> and (c) to inherit his money. We would normally say that (c) is his motive. Applying
> our test of "desired consequence" (c) is certainly also intended. The reason why it is
> considered merely a motive is that it is a consequence ulterior to the mens rea and the
> actus reus; it is no part of the crime. If this criterion as to the nature of motive be
> adopted then it follows that motive, by definition, is irrelevant to criminal responsibil-
> ity—that is, a man may be lawfully convicted of a crime whatever his motive may be,
> or even if he had no motive.

Both of these texts were drawn upon in a brief discussion of motive by Lord
Hailsham of St. Marylebone in *Hyam v. Director of Public Prosecutions*, [1975] A.C.
55 at pp. 73-4 (H.L.). The appellant in that case had had a relationship with a man
who became engaged to another woman B. The appellant had gone to B's house at
night and set fire to the house. While B escaped, her two daughters did not and the
two died of suffocation. The appellant's defence was that she had only intended to
frighten B. If one were to use the first sense of motive as emotion, the appellant's
admitted motive was jealousy of B; if the second sense of motive as ulterior intention, her motive was to frighten B so that she would leave the neighbourhood. In the
former sense, states Lord Hailsham (p. 73):

> It is the emotion which gives rise to the intention and it is the latter, and not the former,
> which converts an actus reus into a criminal act …
>
>     It is, however, important to realise that in the second sense too motive, which in that
> sense is to be equated with the ultimate "end" of a course of action, often described as
> its "purpose" or "object," although "a kind of intention," is not co-extensive with inten-
> tion, which embraces, in addition to the end, all the necessary consequences of an ac-
> tion including the means to the end and any consequences intended along with the end.

In the case at bar, the parties have employed the notion of "motive" in the second
of Williams' senses.

Accepting the term "motive" in a criminal law sense as meaning "ulterior intention," it is possible, I think, upon the authorities, to formulate a number of propositions.

(1)  As evidence, motive is always relevant and hence evidence of motive is
     admissible.

This statement is drawn from Smith and Hogan where the authors state (p. 64):

> This means simply that, if the prosecution can prove that D had a motive for commit-
> ting the crime, they may do so since the existence of a motive makes it more likely that
> D in fact did commit it. Men do not usually act without a motive. …

While evidence of motive is always relevant on the issue of intent or identity, motive must be evidenced by human acts and there are limits to the extent to which such acts may be introduced as motive: see *R. v. Barbour* (1938), 71 C.C.C. 1.

(2)  Motive is no part of the crime and is legally irrelevant to criminal responsibility. It is not an essential element of the prosecution's case as a matter of law.

In language reminiscent of Smith and Hogan, Schroeder, J.A., puts the matter this way in *R. v. Imrich* (1974), 21 C.C.C. (2d) 99:

> When a defendant is indisputably shown to be the criminal, evidence of motive is immaterial. Motive relates to a consequence ulterior to the *mens rea* and the *actus reus* and, adopting this criterion, motive is irrelevant to criminal responsibility, viz., a man may be lawfully convicted of a crime whatever his motive may be or even if he has no motive. It is, of course, relevant as evidence for if the prosecution can prove that the defendant had a motive for committing the crime it may do so, since the existence of a motive makes it more likely that the defendant did in fact commit it ... All matters of motive are for the jury and are not to be dealt with as matters of law. Motive is never to be confused with intent and it is wholly inaccurate to say that without motive there can be no intent.

This majority view of the case was upheld upon subsequent appeal to this Court. ...

(3)  Proved absence of motive is always an important fact in favour of the accused and ordinarily worthy of note in a charge to the jury.

In support of this proposition is the judgment of Davis, J., in *Markadonis v. The King* (1935), 64 C.C.C. 41 at p. 45, [1935] 3 D.L.R. 424 at p. 428, [1935] S.C.R. 657 at p. 665, who, prefacing his remarks with these words:

> Moreover, I cannot escape from the view that the charge of the learned trial Judge did not present certain aspects of the case in favour of the accused that should have been dealt with and considered. ...

(4)  Conversely, proved presence of motive may be an important factual ingredient in the Crown's case, notably on the issues of identity and intention, when the evidence is purely circumstantial.

This is, in effect, merely a restatement of Davis, J.'s comments in *Markadonis*, supra. In *Barbour*, Mr. Justice Kerwin in dissent pointed out: "While the Crown is not obliged to adduce evidence of motive, the presence or absence of motive may be of very considerable importance." McWilliams, at pp. 299-300, refers to the opening statement of the Attorney-General in Palmer's Case (1856) [see Stephen, *A History of the Criminal Law of England* (1883), vol. 3, p. 389] that "if we find strong motives, the more readily shall we be led to believe in the probability of the crime having been committed; but if we find an absence of motive, the probability is the other way."

(5)  Motive is therefore always a question of fact and evidence and the necessity of referring to motive in the charge to the jury falls within the general duty of the trial Judge "to not only outline the theories of the prosecution and defence but to give the jury matters of evidence essential in arriving at a just conclusion."

The latter portion of this proposition is drawn from the judgment of Mr. Justice Spence in *Colpitts v. The Queen*, [1966] 1 C.C.C. 146 at p. 752, referred to by both Ritchie, J., in Imrich, supra, at p. 146 C.C.C., p. 247 D.L.R., p. 626 S.C.R., and by Dubin, J.A., at p. 112 C.C.C., p. 509 O.R., in support of their differing views of that case. I think this latter conflict is instructive—in each case, there will clearly be differences of opinion as to whether certain matters of evidence are essential to the case for either party. A good deal of latitude should be allowed to the judgment of the trial Judge as to which matters of evidence are essential or not.

(6)  Each case will turn on its own unique set of circumstances. The issue of motive is always a matter of degree.

The necessity of charging a jury on motive may be looked upon as a continuum, at one end of which are cases where the evidence as to identity of the murderer is purely circumstantial and proof of motive on the part of the Crown so essential that reference must be made to motive in charging the jury. The Crown's case against Tatlay was just such a situation. It was essential to establish motive and the trial Judge properly referred to motive in charging the jury in relation to Tatlay. At the other end of the continuum, and requiring a charge on motive, is the case where there is proved absence of motive and this may become of great significance as a matter in favour of the accused. Between these two end points in the continuum there are cases where the necessity to charge on motive depends upon the course of the trial and the nature and probative value of the evidence adduced. In these cases, a substantial discretion must be left to the trial Judge. In Imrich, for example, the evidence of exclusive opportunity was such that motive receded into the background.

---

The following cases demonstrate how the issue of intent can become easily confused with motive in specific contexts.

**R. v. Steane**
Court of Criminal Appeal, England
[1947] 1 K.B. 997

[Appeal from a conviction at the Central Criminal Court before Henn-Collins J. on an indictment charging the appellant with doing acts likely to assist the enemy with intent to assist the enemy contrary to reg. 2A of the Defence (General) Regulations, 1939. He was charged with entering the service of the German Broadcasting System on a date in January 1940.

Regulation 2A provided: "If with intent to assist the enemy, any person does any act which is likely to assist the enemy ... then, without prejudice to the law relating to treason, he shall be guilty of an offence against this regulation and shall, on conviction on indictment, be liable to penal servitude for life."

The appellant, a British subject, entered the service of the German broadcasting system, and on several occasions broadcast through that system. The evidence called by the prosecution was that of one witness who proved that the appellant did, in fact, so broadcast and said that he had seen a telegram, in the appellant's possession, signed Emmie Goering, which stated that he could expect to be released and be home very shortly. The principal evidence against him was a statement taken from him by an officer of the British Intelligence Service in October 1945, purporting to give an account of his activities in the German broadcasting service. Before the war, the appellant was employed in Germany as a film actor and was so engaged when the war broke out. His wife and two sons were living in Germany. On the outbreak of war the appellant was at once arrested, but his wife and two sons remained in Oberammergau.

The only other evidence was that of the appellant. He said that on his arrest he was questioned and that the interview ended with the order: "Say Heil Hitler, you dirty swine." He refused and was thereupon knocked down losing several teeth, and he was interned on September 11, 1939. Just before Christmas of that year he was sent for by Goebbels, who asked him to broadcast. He refused. He was thereupon warned that he was in an enemy country and that they had methods of making people do things. A week later an official named von Brockman saw him and dropped hints as to German methods of persuasion. A professor named Kossuth also warned him that these people could be dangerous to those who gave trouble. In consequence, he submitted to a voice test, trying to perform as badly as he could. The next day he was ordered to read news three times a day, and did so until April 1940. In that month he refused to do any more broadcasting. Two Gestapo men called on him. They said: "If you don't obey, your wife and children will be put in a concentration camp." In May three Gestapo men saw him and he was badly beaten up, one ear being partly torn off. He agreed to work for his old employers, helping to produce films. There was no evidence that the films he helped to produce were or could be of any assistance to the Germans or at all harmful to this country. He swore that he was in continual fear for his wife and children. He asserted, and said he had asserted, in his report of July 5, 1945, that he never had the slightest idea or intention of assisting the enemy, and that what he did was done to save his wife and children.

The appellant was convicted and sentenced to three years penal servitude, but appealed.

*Roberts* K.C. and *E. Clarke* for appellant. The summing-up of the trial judge to the jury was inadequate. The jury were never specifically asked whether the act which the appellant admittedly did—entering the service of the German broadcasting system—was due to the intent to assist the enemy. The appellant's case was that his act was done with the intent that his wife and children should not be sent to a concentration camp. If the evidence was consistent with that being the appellant's intent, he was entitled to be acquitted. Once that intention had been put forward, the jury could not act on any presumption that the appellant must be taken to have intended the natural consequence of his acts. The judge said that if what the accused did was to help the enemy, then unless he was without any intent at all by reason of some duress, he must have intended by that act to assist the enemy. This was misdirection. Before any question of duress, which is a matter of defence, could arise, the prosecution had to prove an intent to assist the enemy, and, in face of the evidence given by the appellant, there was no presumption that the appellant intended to help the enemy. Whether there was that intent was a question of fact and the trial judge did not remind the jury of the threats to which the appellant had been exposed or of the atmosphere of terror to which he was subjected.

*Gerald Howard* and *J.S. Bass* for Crown.  On the evidence it was clear that the appellant did an act likely to assist the enemy, and so, as a natural consequence, in the absence of accident, with an intent to assist the enemy. He must have intended the natural consequence of his act. His motives for doing the act are irrelevant, except perhaps, on the issue of duress. The fact that the appellant did the act for this or that reason, for money or to avoid calamity to himself or his family, shows his motive or motives—not his intention. The question on this issue was not: Why did the appellant broadcast? But what was his intention at the moment when he entered the German broadcasting system?]

LORD GODDARD C.J. (for the Court): The difficult question that arises is in connexion with the direction to the jury with regard to whether these acts were done with the intention of assisting the enemy. The case as opened, and indeed, as put by the learned judge appears to this court to be this: A man is taken to intend the natural consequences of his acts; if, therefore, he does an act which is likely to assist the enemy, it must be assumed that he did it with the intention of assisting the enemy. Now, the first thing which the court would observe is that, where the essence of an offence or a necessary constituent of an offence is a particular intent, that intent must be proved by the Crown just as much as any other fact necessary to constitute the offence. The wording of the regulation itself shows that it is not enough merely to charge a prisoner with doing an act likely to assist the enemy; he must do it with the particular intent specified in the regulation. While no doubt the motive of a man's act and his intention in doing the act are, in law, different things, it is, none the less, true that in many offences a specific intention is a necessary ingredient and the jury have to be satisfied that a particular act was done with that specific intent, although the natural consequences of the act might, if nothing else were proved, be said to show the intent for which it was done.

We repeat that where a particular intent must be laid and charged, that intent has to be proved. An illustration given by the learned judge in the course of his rather brief summing-up, related to what are commonly called the black-out regulations. He pointed out to the jury that if a person accidentally omitted to put up his black-out curtains or left some gap in them, although he was doing an act likely to assist the enemy, as it was accidental, he would not be committing the offence with intent to assist the enemy. Matters which involve accidental acts are perhaps not altogether a happy illustration. A nearer case would be if a person deliberately took down his black-out curtains or shutters with the result that light appeared on the outside of his house, perhaps during an air raid; it might well be that if no evidence or explanation were given, and if all that was proved was that, during that raid the prisoner exposed lights by a deliberate act, a jury could infer that he intended to signal or assist the enemy. But, if the evidence in the case showed, for instance, that he or someone was overcome by heat and that he tore down the black-out to ventilate the room, the jury would certainly have to consider whether his act was done with intent to assist the enemy or with some other intent, so that, while he would be guilty of an offence against the black-out regulations, he would not be guilty of an offence with intent to assist the enemy.

In this case the court cannot but feel that some confusion arose with regard to the question of intent by so much being said in the case with regard to the subject of duress. Duress is a matter of defence where a prisoner is forced by fear of violence or imprisonment to do an act which in itself is criminal. If the act is a criminal act, the prisoner may be able to show that he was forced into doing it by violence, actual or threatened, and to save himself from the consequences of that violence. There is very little learning to be found in any of the books or cases on the subject of duress and it is by no means certain how far the doctrine extends, though we have the authority both of Hale and of Fitzjames Stephen, that while it does not apply to treason, murder and some other felonies, it does apply to misdemeanors; and offences against these regulations are misdemeanors. But here again, before any question of duress arises, a jury must be satisfied that the prisoner had the intention which is laid in the indictment. Duress is a matter of defence and the onus of proving it is on the accused. As we have already said, where an intent is charged on the indictment, it is for the prosecution to prove it, so the onus is the other way.

Now, another matter which is of considerable importance in this case, but does not seem to have been brought directly to the attention of the jury, is that very different considerations may apply where the accused at the time he did the acts is in subjection to an enemy power and where he is not. British soldiers who were set to work on the Burma road, or if invasion had unhappily taken place, British subjects who might have been set to work by the enemy digging trenches would undoubtedly be doing acts likely to assist the enemy. It would be unnecessary surely in their cases to consider any of the niceties of the law relating to duress, because no jury would find that merely by doing this work they were intending to assist the enemy. In our opinion it is impossible to say that where an act was done by a person in subjection to the power of others, especially if that other be a brutal enemy, an inference that he intended the natural consequences of his act must be drawn merely from the fact that he did it. The guilty intent cannot be presumed and must be proved. The proper direction to the jury in this case would have been that it was for the prosecution to prove the criminal intent, and that while the jury would be entitled to presume that intent if they thought that the act was done as a result of the free uncontrolled action of the accused, they would not be entitled to presume it, if the circumstances showed that the act was done in subjection to the power of the enemy, or was as consistent with an innocent intent as with a criminal intent, for example, the innocent intent of a desire to save his wife and children from a concentration camp. They should only convict if satisfied by the evidence that the act complained of was in fact done to assist the enemy, and if there was doubt about the matter, the prisoner was entitled to be acquitted.

It is to be observed also in this case that in summing-up the learned judge did not remind the jury of the various threats to which the prisoner swore he had been exposed. The jury might, of course, have disbelieved his evidence. The matters of these threats depended upon his evidence alone, and while it is fair to say that he does not appear to have been in any way shaken in cross-examination on these matters, the jury were not necessarily bound to believe it. But we do not think that the summing-up contained anything like a full enough direction as to the prisoner's defence. The defence must be fully put to the jury and we think they ought to have been reminded of various matters upon which the accused relied as negativing the intent. The jury may well have been left under the impression that, as they were told that a man must be taken to intend the natural consequences of his acts, these matters, as to which he had given evidence, were of no moment.

*Appeal allowed; conviction quashed.*

## Hibbert v. The Queen
Supreme Court of Canada
(1995), 99 C.C.C. (3d) 193

[At his trial for attempted murder, the accused relied on the defence of duress. The victim of the offence was the accused's friend. The accused testified that he was forced by the principal offender to accompany him to the victim's apartment building and to lure the victim down to the lobby. The accused stood by while the principal offender then shot the victim. In the charge to the jury, the trial judge instructed the jury that if the accused joined in the common plot to shoot the victim under threats of death or grievous bodily harm, that would negative his having a common intention with the principal offender to shoot the victim and he must be found not guilty. The trial judge also instructed the jury that the accused could not rely on the common law defence of duress if a safe avenue of escape existed. The accused was acquitted of attempted murder, but convicted of the included offence of aggravated assault. The accused's appeal to the Ontario Court of Appeal was dismissed, but his further appeal to the Supreme Court of Canada was allowed and a new trial was ordered. The aspects of the case dealing with duress are set out in chapter 19 of this casebook.]

LAMER C.J.C. stated for the Court: ... That threats of death or serious bodily harm can have an effect on a person's state of mind is indisputable. However, it is also readily apparent that a person who carries out the *actus reus* of a criminal offence in response to such threats will not necessarily lack the *mens rea* for that offence. Whether he or she does or not will depend both on what the mental element of the offence in question happens to be, and on the facts of the particular case. As a practical matter, though, situations where duress will operate to "negate" *mens rea* will be exceptional, for the simple reason that the types of mental states that are capable of being "negated" by duress are not often found in the definitions of criminal offences.

In general, a person who performs an action in response to a threat will *know* what he or she is doing, and will be aware of the probable consequences of his or her actions. Whether or not he or she *desires* the occurrence of these consequences will depend on the particular circumstances. For example, a person who is forced at gunpoint to drive a group of armed ruffians to a bank will usually know that the likely result of his or her actions will be that an attempt will be made to rob the bank, but he or she may not desire this result—indeed, he or she may strongly wish that the robbers' plans are ultimately foiled, if this could occur without risk to his or her own safety. In contrast, a person who is told that his or her child is being held hostage at another location and will be killed unless the robbery is successful will almost certainly have an active subjective desire that the robbery succeed. While the existence of threats clearly has a bearing on the *motive* underlying each actor's respective decision to assist in the robbery, only the first actor can be said not to *desire* that the robbery take place, and neither actor can be said not to have knowledge of the consequences of their actions.

[Lamer C.J.C. first dealt with the meaning of the word "purpose" in s. 21(1)(b) of the Code, which creates liability for a person who "does or omits to do anything for the purpose of aiding any person to commit" an offence. Lamer C.J.C. then went on to discuss s. 21(2) "in the interests of avoiding undue confusion in the law that applies to duress cases."]

It is impossible to ascribe a single fixed meaning to the term "purpose." In ordinary usage, the word is employed in two distinct senses. One can speak of an actor doing something "on purpose" (as opposed to by accident), thereby equating purpose with "immediate intention." The term is also used, however, to indicate the ultimate ends an actor seeks to achieve, which imports the idea of "desire" into the definition. This dual sense is apparent in the word's dictionary definition.

… Our task in the present case is to consider the meaning of "purpose" as it is employed in s. 21(1)(b) of the *Code* in light of the parliamentary objective underlying the subsection. It must be emphasized, however, that the word "purpose" is employed in many different sections of the *Criminal Code*, in a number of distinct contexts. My conclusions in the present case on the proper interpretation of the word "purpose" as it is employed in s. 21(1)(b) of the *Code* are thus restricted to this particular subsection. It may well be that in the context of some other statutory provision a different interpretation of the term will prove to be the most appropriate.

The problems associated with the "purpose equals desire" interpretation are several. First, incorporating the accused's feelings about the desirability of the commission of an offence by the principal into the definition of the *mens rea* for "aiding" can result in distinctions being made which appear arbitrary and unreasonable in light of the policy underlying s. 21(1)(b). As Professor Colvin notes, under the "purpose equals desire" interpretation, a person would not be guilty of aiding in the commission of an offence if he or she were "genuinely opposed or indifferent to it" (p. 123). The reason for the aider's indifference or opposition would be immaterial. The perverse consequences that flow from this are clearly illustrated by the following hypothetical situation described by Mewett and Manning:

> If a man is approached by a friend who tells him that he is going to rob a bank and would like to use his car as a getaway vehicle for which he will pay him $100, when that person is … charged under s. 21 for doing something for the purpose of aiding his friend to commit the offence, can he say "My purpose was not to aid the robbery but to

make $100"? His argument would be that while he knew that he was helping the rob-
bery, his desire was to obtain the $100 and he did not care one way or the other whether
the robbery was successful or not.

(*Criminal Law*, *supra*, at p. 112.) I agree with the authors' conclusion that "[t]hat would
seem an absurd result" (p. 112).

The leading English case on the issue of whether duress negates the *mens rea* of
parties to offences (under the common law governing party liability) is the House of
Lords' decision in *Lynch*, *supra*. As Professor G. Williams observes in his *Textbook
of Criminal Law*, 2nd ed. (London: Stevens & Sons, 1983), at p. 624: "The view
taken by the majority of the House of Lords in *Lynch* was that duress is a defence on
its own, and does not negative either the doing of the act charged or the *mens rea*.
This is plainly right."

The position at common law, of course, does not in and of itself determine the
meaning to be ascribed to the word "purpose" in the context of s. 21(1)(b) of the
*Code*. It can, however, provide useful guidance when it comes to choosing between
the two interpretations of the term that are available—one that accords with the common law position and the other that contradicts it. In the absence of reason to believe
that Parliament intended its enactment of s. 21(1)(b) to radically alter the common
law principles governing party liability, the interpretation that accords with the common law would seem to also be the most likely to accurately embody Parliament's
intentions. This observation strengthens my conclusion that Parliament's use of the
term "purpose" in s. 21(1)(b) should not be seen as incorporating the notion of "desire" into the mental state for party liability, and that the word should instead be
understood as being essentially synonymous with "intention" …

For these reasons, I conclude that the expression "for the purpose of aiding" in
s. 21(1)(b), properly understood, does not require that the accused actively view the
commission of the offence he or she is aiding as desirable in and of itself. As a result,
the *mens rea* for aiding under s. 21(1)(b) is not susceptible of being "negated" by duress.

As was the case with the term "purpose" in s. 21(1)(b), the phrase "intention in
common" [in s. 21(2)] is capable of being understood in more than one sense. One
possible interpretation is that "intention in common" means no more than that the two
persons must have in mind the same unlawful purpose. Alternatively, however, it might
be argued that the requirement of "commonality" requires that the two persons' intentions match in greater detail—in particular, that their motives or subjective views as to
the desirability of the commission of the "unlawful purpose" match up. If this latter
interpretation were adopted, it could be argued that although persons who assist others
to commit criminal acts as a result of threats made by the others would "intend" to
provide such assistance, their intention would not be "in common" with the intentions
of the threatener, due to the different motives and, possibly, views as to the immediate
desirability of the criminal activity at issue. In contrast, under the former interpretation
a person would fall within the ambit of s. 21(2) if they intended to assist in the commission of the same offence envisioned by the principal, regardless of the fact that their
intention might be due solely to the principal's threats. Of course, it would be open to
such a person to avoid criminal liability through the common law defence of duress.

As noted earlier in *Paquette*, *supra*, Martland J. took the position that "intention in common" meant something more than "intention to commit or aid in the same offence," arguing (at p. 423) that:

> A person whose actions have been dictated by fear of death or of grievous bodily injury cannot be said to have formed a genuine common intention to carry out an unlawful purpose with the person who has threatened him with those consequences if he fails to co-operate.

The phrase "intention in common" is certainly open to being interpreted in this manner. However, notwithstanding the considerable weight I place on and the respect I have for the opinion of Martland J., I have come to the conclusion that, in the context of s. 21(2), the first interpretation discussed above is more consistent both with Parliament's intention and with the interpretation of s. 21(1)(b) I have adopted in these reasons. Many of the factors I considered earlier in the course of determining the meaning to be ascribed to the term "purpose" in s. 21(1)(b) apply with similar force to the problem of interpreting s. 21(2).

The conclusions that can be extracted from the discussion in the previous sections may be summarized as follows:

1. The fact that a person who commits a criminal act does so as a result of threats of death or bodily harm can in some instances be relevant to the question of whether he or she possessed the *mens rea* necessary to commit an offence. Whether or not this is so will depend, among other things, on the structure of the particular offence in question—that is, on whether or not the mental state specified by Parliament in its definition of the offence is such that the presence of coercion can, as a matter of logic, have a bearing on the existence of *mens rea*. If the offence is one where the presence of duress is of potential relevance to the existence of *mens rea*, the accused is entitled to point to the presence of threats when arguing that the Crown has not proven beyond a reasonable doubt that he or she possessed the mental state required for liability.

2. A person who commits a criminal act under threats of death or bodily harm may also be able to invoke an excuse-based defence (either the statutory defence set out in s. 17 or the common law defence of duress, depending on whether the accused is charged as a principal or as a party). This is so regardless of whether or not the offence at issue is one where the presence of coercion also has a bearing on the existence of *mens rea*.

3. The mental states specified in s. 21(1)(b) and (2) of the *Criminal Code* are not susceptible to being "negated" by duress. Consequently, it is not open to persons charged under these sections to argue that because their acts were coerced by threats they lacked the requisite *mens rea*. Such persons may, however, seek to have their conduct *excused* through the operation of the common law defence of duress.

It should be reiterated, however, that the holding in the present case is based on an interpretation of the particular terms of two specific offence-creating statutory provisions, s. 21(1)(b) and (2) of the *Criminal Code*. The question of whether other offences can be found, either in the *Code* or in some other statute, that are defined in such a way that the presence of coercion *is* relevant to the existence of *mens rea*, remains open.

*Appeal allowed; new trial ordered.*

———————————

Materials on duress are set out in chapter 19.

### R. v. Buzzanga and Durocher
Ontario Court of Appeal
(1979), 49 C.C.C. (2d) 369

[The accused were charged with wilfully promoting hatred against Francophones. The accused were both sympathetic with the French community in which they lived. They published the pamphlet reproduced below. They said they did so to combat apathy in the French-speaking community in relation to the building of a French-language school.]

MARTIN J.A.: ... At about the same time, the appellants began preparing for dissemination the following document, the distribution of which is the subject of the charge:

WAKE UP CANADIANS
YOUR FUTURE IS AT STAKE!

IT IS YOUR TAX DOLLARS THAT SUBSIDIZE THE ACTIVITIES OF THE FRENCH MINORITY OF ESSEX COUNTY,

DID YOU KNOW THAT THE ASSOCIATION CANADIAN FRANCAIS DE L'ONTARIO HAS INVESTED SEVERAL HUNDREDS OF THOUSANDS OF DOLLARS OF YOUR TAX MONEY IN QUEBEC?

AND THAT NOW THEY ARE STILL DEMANDING 5 MILLION MORE OF YOUR TAX DOLLARS TO BUILD A FRENCH LANGUAGE HIGH SCHOOL?

YOU ARE SUBSIDIZING SEPARATISM WHETHER IN QUEBEC OR ESSEX COUNTY.

DID YOU KNOW THAT THOSE OF THE FRENCH MINORITY WHO SUPPORT THE BUILDING OF THE FRENCH LANGUAGE HIGH SCHOOL ARE IN FACT A SUBVERSIVE GROUP AND THAT MOST FRENCH CANADIANS OF ESSEX COUNTY ARE OPPOSED TO THE BUILDING OF THAT SCHOOL?

WHO WILL RID US OF THIS SUBVERSIVE GROUP IF NOT OURSELVES?

IF WE GIVE THEM A SCHOOL, WHAT WILL THEY DEMAND NEXT ... INDEPENDENT CITY STATES? CONSIDER THE ETHNIC PROBLEM OF THE UNITED STATES AND TAKE HEED.

WE MUST STAMP OUT THE SUBVERSIVE ELEMENT WHICH USES HISTORY TO
JUSTIFY ITS FREELOADING ON THE TAXPAYERS OF CANADA, NOW.

THE BRITISH SOLVED THIS PROBLEM ONCE BEFORE WITH THE ACADIANS,
WHAT ARE WE WAITING FOR ... ?

. . .

Both appellants testified as to their purpose in preparing and distributing the pamphlet. The appellant Durocher testified that his purpose was to show the prejudice directed towards French Canadians and expose the truth about the real problem that existed with respect to the French-language school. He said that the statement was largely composed from written material he had seen and from experiences he had had, although the paragraph: "WHO WILL RID US OF THIS SUBVERSIVE GROUP, IF NOT OURSELVES?" was pure theatrics and has its origin in the quotation "Who will rid me of this meddlesome priest," attributed to Henry II. He testified in some detail as to the origin of various parts of the document and endeavoured to show that it reflected statements contained in such sources as letters to the editor of the *Windsor Star*, a document alleged to have been circulated by a member of the Essex County Ratepayers Association, a paid advertisement published in several newspapers, a book entitled "Bilingual Today, French Tomorrow," and the like. He said that he thought the pamphlet would be a catalyst that would bring a quick solution to the problem of the French-language school by provoking a Government reaction and thereby put pressure on the school board. He thought that by stating these things people would say: "This is ridiculous." A fair reading of his evidence is that he did not want to promote hatred against the "French people," for to do so would be to promote hatred against himself.

The appellant Buzzanga, too, said that he wanted to expose the situation, to show the things that were being said so that intelligent people could see how ridiculous they were. The pamphlet was intended as a satire. He wanted to create a furor that would reach the "House of Commons" and compel the Government to do something that would compel the opposing factions on the school question to reopen communications. He said it was not his intention "to raise hatred towards anyone." ...

### Grounds of Appeal

Although additional grounds of appeal were advanced, only the following grounds of appeal require discussion. The first and principal ground of appeal was that the learned trial Judge misdirected himself with respect to the meaning of the word "wilfully" in the expression "wilfully promotes hatred" in s. 281.2(2) of the Code by holding that "wilfully" meant intentionally as opposed to accidentally.

#### "Wilfully promotes hatred"

The following are the relevant provisions of the Code:

281.1(1) Every one who advocates or promotes genocide is guilty of an indictable offence and is liable to imprisonment for five years.

(2) In this section "genocide" means any of the following acts committed with intent to destroy in whole or in part any identifiable group, namely:

(a) killing members of the group, or

(b) deliberately inflicting on the group conditions of life calculated to bring about its physical destruction.

(3) No proceeding for an offence under this section shall be instituted without the consent of the Attorney General.

(4) In this section "identifiable group" means any section of the public distinguished by colour, race, religion or ethnic origin. [enacted idem]

281.2(1) Every one who, by communicating statements in any public place, incites hatred against any identifiable group where such incitement is likely to lead to a breach of the peace, is guilty of

(a) an indictable offence and is liable to imprisonment for two years; or

(b) an offence punishable on summary conviction.

(2) Every one who, by communicating statements, other than in private conversation, wilfully promotes hatred against any identifiable group is guilty of

(a) an indictable offence and is liable to imprisonment for two years; or

(b) an offence punishable on summary conviction.

(3) No person shall be convicted of an offence under subsection (2)

(a) if he establishes that the statements communicated were true;

(b) if, in good faith, he expressed or attempted to establish by argument an opinion upon a religious subject;

(c) if the statements were relevant to any subject of public interest, the discussion of which was for the public benefit, and if on reasonable grounds he believed them to be true; or

(d) if, in good faith, he intended to point out, for the purpose of removal, matters producing or tending to produce feelings of hatred towards an identifiable group in Canada.

(4) Where a person is convicted of an offence under section 281.1 or subsection (1) or (2) of this section, anything by means of or in relation to which the offence was committed, upon such conviction, may, in addition to any other punishment imposed, be ordered by the presiding magistrate or judge to be forfeited to Her Majesty in right of the province in which that person is convicted, for disposal as the Attorney General may direct.

(5) Subsections 181(6) and (7) apply mutatis mutandis to section 281.1 or subsection (1) or (2) of this section.

(6) No proceeding for an offence under subsection (2) shall be instituted without the consent of the Attorney General.

(7) In this section

"communicating" includes communicating by telephone, broadcasting or other audible or visible means;

"identifiable group" has the same meaning as it has in section 281.1;

"public place" includes any place to which the public have access as of right or by invitation, express or implied;

"statements" includes words spoken or written or recorded electronically or electro-magnetically or otherwise, and gestures, signs or other visible representations.

The threshold question to be determined is the meaning of "wilfully" in the term "wilfully promotes hatred" in s. 281.2(2) of the *Criminal Code*. It will, of course, be observed that the word "wilfully" modifies the words "promotes hatred," rather than the words "communicating statements."

The word "wilfully" has not been uniformly interpreted and its meaning to some extent depends upon the context in which it is used. Its primary meaning is "intentionally," but it is also used to mean "recklessly": see Glanville Williams, Criminal Law, The General Part, 2nd ed. (1961), pp. 51-2; Glanville Williams, Textbook of Criminal Law (1978), p. 87; Smith and Hogan, Criminal Law, 4th ed. (1978), pp. 104-5. The term "recklessly" is here used to denote the subjective state of mind of a person who foresees that his conduct may cause the prohibited result but, nevertheless, takes a deliberate and unjustifiable risk of bringing it about: see Glanville Williams, Textbook of Criminal Law, pp. 70 and 76; Smith and Hogan, Criminal Law, 4th ed., pp. 52-3.

The word "wilfully" has, however, also been held to mean no more than that the accused's act is done intentionally and not accidentally. In *R. v. Senior*, [1899] 1 Q.B. 283, Lord Russell of Killowen, C.J., in interpreting the meaning of the words "wilfully neglects" in s. 1 of the *Prevention of Cruelty to Children Act*, 1894 (U.K.), c. 41, said at pp. 290-1: "'Wilfully' means that the act is done deliberately and intentionally, not by accident or inadvertence, but so that the mind of the person who does the act goes with it."

On the other hand, in *Rice v. Connolly*, [1966] 2 Q.B. 414, where the accused was charged with wilfully obstructing a con stable in the execution of his duty, Lord Parker, L.C.J., said at p. 419: "'Wilful' in this context not only in my judgment means 'intentional' but something which is done without lawful excuse ... ."

In *Willmott v. Atack*, [1976] 3 All E.R. 794, the appellant was convicted on a charge of wilfully obstructing a peace officer in the execution of his duty. A police officer, acting in the execution of his duty, arrested a motorist who struggled and resisted. The appellant, who knew the motorist, intervened with the intention of assisting the officer but, in fact, his conduct obstructed the officer. The Queen's Bench Divisional Court quashed the conviction and held that it was not sufficient to prove the appellant intended to do what he did, and which resulted in an obstruction, but that the prosecution must prove that the appellant intended to obstruct the officer.

The judgment of the Court of Criminal Appeal of Queensland in *R. v. Burnell*, [1966] Qd. R. 348, also illustrates that, depending on its context, the word "wilfully" may connote an intention to bring about a proscribed consequence. In that case the appellant was charged with arson in having set fire to a shed. Section 461 of the Queensland Criminal Code provides that "... any person who wilfully and unlawfully sets fire to ... any building or structure is guilty of a crime ... ." The accused had deliberately set fire to some mattresses in a shed whereby the shed was set on fire. The trial Judge instructed the jury that "wilfully" connoted no more than a willed and voluntary act as distinguished from the result of an accident or mere negligence. The Queensland Court of Criminal Appeal, in setting aside the conviction, held that in the context of the section "wilfully" required proof that the accused did an act which resulted in setting fire to the building with the intention of bringing about that result. Gibbs, J. (with whom Douglas, J., concurred), said at p. 356:

> Under s. 461 it is not enough that the accused did the act which resulted in setting fire to the building foreseeing that his act might have that effect but recklessly taking the risk; it is necessary that the accused did the act which resulted in setting fire to the building with the intention of bringing about that result.

Mr. Manning conceded that in some cases the element of wilfulness is supplied by recklessness but he contended that in its context in s. 281.2(2) of the *Criminal Code* "wilfully" means with the intention of promoting hatred. In the course of his argument, Mr. Manning stressed the definition of "wilfully" contained in s. 386(1) of the Code, which reads:

> 386(1) Every one who causes the occurrence of an event by doing an act or by omitting to do an act that it is his duty to do, knowing that the act or omission will probably cause the occurrence of the event and being reckless whether the event occurs or not, shall be deemed, for the purposes of this Part, willfully to have caused the occurrence of the event.

Mr. Manning emphasized that s. 386(1) provides that wilfully is to have the meaning specified in that section for the purposes of Part IX of the Code. He argued with much force that the state of mind specified in s. 386(1) is recklessness and that where Parliament intends to extend the meaning of wilfully to include recklessness it does so expressly. In *R. v. Rese*, [1968] 1 C.C.C. 363 at p. 366, Laskin J.A. (as he then was), referred to the definition now contained in s. 386(1) as an extended meaning of "wilfully."

As previously indicated, the word "wilfully" does not have a fixed meaning, but I am satisfied that in the context of s. 281.2(2) it means with the intention of promoting hatred, and does not include recklessness. The arrangement of the legislation proscribing the incitement of hatred, in my view, leads to that conclusion.

Section 281.2(1), unlike s. 281.2(2), is restricted to the incitement of hatred by communicating statements in a public place where such incitement is likely to lead to a breach of the peace. Although no mental element is expressly mentioned in s. 281.2(1), where the communication poses an immediate threat to public order, *mens rea* is, none the less, required since the inclusion of an offence in the *Criminal Code* must be taken to import *mens rea* in the absence of a clear intention to dispense with it: see *R. v. Prue; R. v. Baril* (1979), 46 C.C.C. (2d) 257 at pp. 260-1. The general *mens rea* which is required and which suffices for most crimes where no mental element is mentioned in the definition of the crime, is either the intentional or reckless bringing about of the result which the law, in creating the offence, seeks to prevent and, hence, under s. 281.2(1) is either the intentional or reckless inciting of hatred in the specified circumstances.

The insertion of the word "wilfully" in s. 281.2(2) was not necessary to import *mens rea* since that requirement would be implied in any event because of the serious nature of the offence: see *R. v. Prue*, supra. The statements, the communication of which are proscribed by s. 281.2(2), are not confined to statements communicated in a public place in circumstances likely to lead to a breach of the peace and they, consequently, do not pose such an immediate threat to public order as those falling under s. 281.2(1); it is reasonable to assume, therefore, that Parliament intended to limit the offence under s. 281.2(2) to the intentional promotion of hatred. It is evident that the use of the word "wilfully" in s. 281.2(2), and not in s. 281.2(1), reflects Parliament's policy to strike a balance in protecting the competing social interests of freedom of expression on the one hand, and public order and group reputation on the other hand. ...

Having concluded that proof of an intention to promote hatred is essential to constitute the offence under s. 281.2(2), it is necessary to consider the mental attitude which must be established to constitute an intention to promote hatred. The state of mind connoted by "intention," where an intention to bring about a certain result is an element of the offence, has been the subject of much discussion, and writers on jurisprudence, as well as Judges, have not always been in agreement as to its meaning. Some eminent legal scholars hold the view that a consequence is not intended unless it is desired, recognizing that a consequence may be desired not as an end in itself but desired in order to accomplish some other purpose: see Salmond on Jurisprudence, 8th ed. (1930), pp. 393-6 (but cf., the view of P. J. Fitzgerald, the editor of the 12th edition, pp. 367-9; Holmes, The Common Law, pp. 52-3; Glanville Williams, Textbook of Criminal Law, p. 51). Other eminent legal scholars hold that the test of intention is not whether the actor desired the relevant consequence, but whether he decided or resolved to bring it about, even though it may have been distasteful to him: see Jerome Hall, General Principles of Criminal Law, 2nd ed. (1960), p. 112; Russell on Crime, 12th ed. (1964), vol. 1, p. 41. The latter description of intention is in accord with the views expressed by Lord Hailsham as to the meaning of intention in *Hyam v. Director of Public Prosecutions*, [1975] A.C. 55 at p. 74, and with those of the Court of Appeal (Criminal Division) in *R. v. Mohan* (1975), 60 Cr. App. R. 272 at pp. 276 and 278.

There are cases which appear to provide support for the proposition that where an intention to produce a particular consequence is essential to constitute the offence, an act is not done with intent to produce the prohibited consequence unless it is the actor's conscious purpose to bring it about, and that the actor's foresight of the certainty of the consequence is not synonymous with an intention to produce it: see *R. v. Miller* (1959), 125 C.C.C. 8 at p. 30; *R. v. Ahlers*, [1915] 1 K.B. 616; *Sinnasamy Selvanayagam v. The King*, [1951] A.C. 83; *R. v. Steane*, [1947] 1 K.B. 997. Most of these cases are subjected to critical examination by Dr. Glanville Williams in Criminal Law, The General Part, 2nd ed. (1961), pp. 40-2.

There is, however, substantial support for the proposition that in the criminal law a person intends a particular consequence not only when his conscious purpose is to bring it about, but also when he foresees that the consequence is certain or substantially certain to result from his conduct: see Glanville Williams, Criminal Law, The General Part, 2nd ed. (1961), p. 38; Walter Wheeler Cook, Act, Intention, and Motive in the Criminal Law (1916-17), 26 Yale L.J. 645 at pp. 654-8; Rollin Perkins, A Rationale of Mens Rea, 52 Harv. L. Rev. 905 at pp. 910-1 (1938-39).

Smith and Hogan, the learned authors of Criminal Law, 4th ed., state at p. 51, that the authorities referred to by them:

... suggest that in the criminal law generally, though not universally, a person intends a consequence if it is his purpose to achieve it or if he knows that the achievement of some other purpose is certain, or "morally" certain, to produce the consequence in question.

In *R. v. Lemon; R. v. Gay News Ltd.*, ... Lord Diplock, however, defined intention in much wider terms. He said that where intention to produce a particular result is a necessary element of an offence, no distinction is to be drawn in law between the state of mind of one who does an act because he desires to produce that particular result, and the state of mind of one who, when he does the act, is aware that it is likely to produce that result but is prepared to take the risk that it may do so in order to achieve some other purpose. He considered that the law has been settled by *Hyam v. Director of Public Prosecutions*, supra, "that both states of mind constitute 'intention' in the sense in which that expression is used in the definition of a crime whether at common law or in a statute" (at p. 905).

*Hyam v. Director of Public Prosecutions*, supra, was concerned with the mental element required to constitute "malice aforethought." It may well be that either an intention to kill or cause serious bodily harm, or foresight that death or serious bodily harm is a highly probable consequence of an act done for some other purpose, is a sufficient *mens rea* for murder at common law. I do not consider, however, that the actor's foresight that a consequence is highly probable, as opposed to substantially certain, is the same thing as an intention to bring it about: see *Hyam v. Director of Public Prosecutions*, supra, per Lord Hailsham at p. 75; *R. v. Belfon*, [1976] 3 All E.R. 46; Smith and Hogan, Criminal Law, 4th ed., pp. 47-51; Commentary on *R. v. Lemon et al.*, [1979] Crim. L.R. 311 at p. 314. In my view, the mental attitude described by Lord Diplock is a form of recklessness.

I agree, however (assuming without deciding that there may be cases in which intended consequences are confined to those which it is the actor's conscious purpose to bring about), that, as a general rule, a person who foresees that a consequence is certain or substantially certain to result from an act which he does in order to achieve some other purpose, intends that consequence. The actor's foresight of the certainty or moral certainty of the consequence resulting from his conduct compels a conclusion that if he, none the less, acted so as to produce it, then he decided to bring it about (albeit regretfully), in order to achieve his ultimate purpose. His intention encompasses the means as well as to his ultimate objective.

I conclude, therefore, that the appellants "wilfully" (intentionally) promoted hatred against the French Canadian community of Essex County only if: (a) their conscious purpose in distributing the document was to promote hatred against that group, or (b) they foresaw that the promotion of hatred against that group was certain or morally certain to result from the distribution of the pamphlet, but distributed it as a means of achieving their purpose of obtaining the French-language high school.

*Whether the trial Judge misdirected himself as to the meaning of wilfully?*

Mr. Manning contended before us that the learned trial Judge erred in his interpretation of the meaning of "wilfully." He said that the trial Judge, in concluding that the document, viewed objectively, promoted hatred, separated the word "wilfully" from the words "promotes hatred" and, consequently, fell into error in only considering the question whether the document was distributed intentionally as opposed to accidentally, when the offence charged was committed only if the appellants' purpose in distributing the document was to promote hatred. Mr. Manning said that the trial Judge was concerned only with the effect of the document, whereas if he had "looked for" an intention to promote hatred, he would have come to a different conclusion with respect to the appellants' guilt. Mr. Hunt for the Crown did not dispute that the central issue in the case is whether the appellants, when they distributed the pamphlet, intended to promote hatred. He contended, however, that the trial Judge found that the appellants intended to promote hatred as a means of accomplishing their purpose.

Despite Mr. Manning's able argument I am not persuaded that the learned trial Judge fell into the error of detaching the word "wilfully" from the words "promotes hatred" and applied it only to the distribution of the pamphlet. I am of the view, however, that the learned trial Judge erred in holding that "wilfully" means only "intentional as opposed to accidental." Although, as previously indicated, "wilfully" has sometimes been used to mean that the accused's act, as distinct from its consequences, must be intended and not accidental (as in *R. v. Senior*, [1899] 1 Q.B. 283), it does not have that meaning in the provisions under consideration.

The learned trial Judge's view of the meaning of "wilfully" inevitably caused him to focus attention on the intentional nature of the appellants' conduct, rather than on the question whether they actually intended to produce the consequence of promoting hatred. I observe that even if, contrary to the view which I have expressed, recklessness satisfies the mental element denoted by the word "wilfully," recklessness when used to denote the mental element attitude which suffices for the ordinary *mens rea*, requires actual foresight on the part of the accused that his conduct may bring about the prohibited consequence, although I am not unmindful that for some purposes recklessness may denote only a marked departure from objective standards. Where the prosecution, in order to establish the accused's guilt of the offence charged, is required to prove that he intended to bring about a particular consequence or foresaw a particular consequence, the question to be determined is what was in the mind of this particular accused, and the necessary intent or foresight must be brought home to him subjectively: see *R. v. Mulligan* (1974), 18 C.C.C. (2d) 270 at pp. 274-5. …

I am, with deference to the learned trial Judge, of the view that an intention to create "controversy, furor and an uproar" is not the same thing as an intention to promote hatred, and it was an error to equate them. I would, of course, agree that if the appellants intentionally promoted hatred against the French-speaking community of Essex County as a means of obtaining the French-language high school, they committed the offence charged. The appellants' evidence, if believed, does not, however, as the learned trial Judge appears to have thought, inevitably lead to that conclusion. The learned trial Judge, not having disbelieved the appellants' evidence, failed to give appropriate consideration to their evidence on the issue of intent and, in the circumstances, his failure so to do constituted self-misdirection. …

*Conclusion*

I have concluded that the self-misdirection with respect to the meaning of the word "wilfully," and the failure to appreciate the significance of the appellants' evidence on the issue of intent requires a new trial. The outrageous conduct of the appellants in preparing and distributing this deplorable document was evidence to be weighed in determining their intent, but in the peculiar circumstances of this case I am not satisfied that the inferences to be drawn from it are such as to inevitably lead to a conclusion that they had the requisite intent or that the trial Judge would inevitably have reached that conclusion but for his self-misdirection.

In the result, I would allow the appeal, set aside the convictions and order new trials.

*Appeal allowed; new trial ordered.*

---

The following case looks at the definition of "actual knowledge," a slightly lesser form of subjective fault than intentional or wilful conduct.

## R. v. Theroux
### Supreme Court of Canada
### (1993), 79 C.C.C. (3d) 449

[The accused was convicted of fraud for accepting deposits from investors in a building project having told them that he had purchased deposit insurance when he in fact had not. The general fraud provision in the *Criminal Code* provides:

380(1) Every one who, by deceit, falsehood or other fraudulent means, whether or not it is a false pretence within the meaning of this Act, defrauds the public or any person, whether ascertained or not, of any property, money or valuable security,

(a) is guilty of an indictable offence and liable to a term of imprisonment not exceeding ten years, where the subject-matter of the offence is a testamentary instrument or where the value of the subject-matter of the offence exceeds one thousand dollars; or

(b) is guilty

(i) of an indictable offence and is liable to imprisonment for a term not exceeding two years, or

(ii) of an offence punishable on summary conviction,

where the value of the subject-matter of the offence does not exceed one thousand dollars.]

McLACHLIN J. (as she then was): ...

### 3. The Mens Rea of Fraud

*(i) Doctrinal Considerations*

This brings us to the *mens rea* of fraud. What is the guilty mind of fraud? At this point, certain confusions inherent in the concept of *mens rea* itself become apparent. It is useful initially to distinguish between the mental element or elements of a cri re and the *mens rea*. The term *mens rea*, properly understood, does not encompass all of the mental elements of a crime. The *actus reus* has its own mental element; the act must be the voluntary act of the accused for the *actus reus* to exist. *Mens rea*, on the other hand, refers to the guilty mind, the wrongful intention, of the accused. Its function in criminal law is to prevent the conviction of the morally innocent—those who do not understand or intend the consequences of their acts. Typically, *mens rea* is concerned with the consequences of the prohibited *actus reus*. Thus in the crimes of homicide, we speak of the consequences of the voluntary act—intention to cause death, or reckless and wilfully blind persistence in conduct which one knows is likely to cause death. In other offences, such as dangerous driving, the *mens rea* may relate to the failure to consider the consequences of inadvertence.

This brings me to the question of whether the test for *mens rea* is subjective or objective. Most scholars and jurists agree that, leaving aside offences where the *actus reus* is negligence or inadvertence and offences of absolute liability, the test for *mens rea* is subjective. The test is not whether a reasonable person would have foreseen the consequences of the prohibited act, but whether the accused subjectively appreciated those consequences at least as a possibility. In applying the subjective test, the court looks to the accused's intention and the facts as the accused believed them to be: G. Williams, Textbook of Criminal Law, 2nd ed. (1983), pp. 727-8.

Two collateral points must be made at this juncture. First, as Williams underlines, this inquiry has nothing to do with the accused's system of values. A person is not saved from conviction because he or she believes there is nothing wrong with what he or she is doing. The question is whether the accused subjectively appreciated that certain consequences would follow from his or her acts, not whether the accused believed the acts or their consequences to be moral. Just as the pathological killer would not be acquitted on the mere ground that he failed to see his act as morally reprehensible, so the defrauder will not be acquitted because he believed that what he was doing was honest.

The second collateral point is the oft-made observation that the Crown need not, in every case, show precisely what thought was in the accused's mind at the time of the criminal act. In certain cases, subjective awareness of the consequences can be inferred from the act itself, barring some explanation casting doubt on such inference. The fact that such an inference is made does not detract from the subjectivity of the test.

Having ventured these general comments on *mens rea*, I return to the offence of fraud. The prohibited act is deceit, falsehood, or some other dishonest act. The prohibited consequence is depriving another of what is or should be his, which may, as we have seen, consist in merely placing another's property at risk. The *mens rea* would then consist in the subjective awareness that one was undertaking a prohibited act (the deceit, falsehood or other dishonest act) which could cause deprivation in the sense of depriving another of property or putting that property at risk. If this is shown, the crime is complete. The fact that the accused may have hoped the deprivation would not take place, or may have felt there was nothing wrong with what he or she was doing, provides no defence. To put it another way, following the traditional criminal law principle that the mental state necessary to the offence must be determined by reference to the external acts which constitute the *actus* [*reus*] of the offence (see Williams, ibid., c. 3), the proper focus in determining the *mens rea* of fraud is to ask whether the accused intentionally committed the prohibited acts (deceit, falsehood, or other dishonest act) knowing or desiring the consequences proscribed by the offence (deprivation, including the risk of deprivation). The personal feeling of the accused about the morality or honesty of the act or its consequences is no more relevant to the analysis than is the accused's awareness that the particular acts undertaken constitute a criminal offence.

This applies as much to the third head of fraud, "other fraudulent means," as to lies and acts of deceit. Although other fraudulent means have been broadly defined as means which are "dishonest," it is not necessary that an accused personally consider these means to be dishonest in order that he or she be convicted of fraud for having undertaken them. The "dishonesty" of the means is relevant to the determination whether the conduct falls within the type of conduct caught by the offence of fraud; what reasonable people consider dishonest assists in the determination whether the *actus reus* of the offence can be made out on particular facts. That established, it need only be determined that an accused knowingly undertook the acts in question, aware that deprivation, or risk of deprivation, could follow as a likely consequence.

I have spoken of knowledge of the consequences of the fraudulent act. There appears to be no reason, however, why recklessness as to consequences might not also attract criminal responsibility. Recklessness presupposes knowledge of the likelihood of the prohibited consequences. It is established when it is shown that the accused, with such knowledge, commits acts which may bring about these prohibited consequences, while being reckless as to whether or not they ensue.

These doctrinal observations suggest that the *actus reus* of the offence of fraud will be established by proof of:

1. the prohibited act, be it an act of deceit, a falsehood or some other fraudulent means; and

2. deprivation caused by the prohibited act, which may consist in actual loss or the placing of the victim's pecuniary interests at risk.

Correspondingly, the *mens rea* of fraud is established by proof of:

1. Subjective knowledge of the prohibited act; and

2. Subjective knowledge that the prohibited act could have as a consequence the deprivation of another (which deprivation may consist in knowledge that the victim's pecuniary interests are put at risk).

Where the conduct and knowledge required by these definitions are established, the accused is guilty whether he actually intended the prohibited consequence or was reckless as to whether it would occur.

The inclusion of risk of deprivation in the concept of deprivation in *Olan* requires specific comment. The accused must have subjective awareness, at the very least, that his or her conduct will put the property or economic expectations of others at risk. As noted above, this does not mean that the Crown must provide the trier of fact with a mental snapshot proving exactly what was in the accused's mind at the moment the dishonest act was committed. Normally, the inference of subjective knowledge of the risk may be drawn from the facts as the accused believed them to be. The accused may introduce evidence negating that inference, such as evidence that his deceit was part of an innocent prank, or evidence of circumstances which led him to believe that no one would act on his lie or deceitful or dishonest act. But in cases like the present one, where the accused tells a lie knowing others will act on it and thereby puts their property at risk, the inference of subjective knowledge that the property of another would be put at risk is clear.

### (ii) Jurisprudential Considerations

The view of *mens rea* suggested above accords with earlier rulings of this Court which rejected the notion that the accused's subjective appreciation of his or her dishonesty is relevant to the *mens rea* of fraud. In *Lafrance v. The Queen* (1975), 13 C.C.C. (2d) 289, the accused had taken a car with the intention of returning it later. This court was faced with the issue of whether this amounted to theft. Martland J. (for the majority) held that it did and that the taking was fraudulent, at p. 298: "The taking was intentional, under no mistake and with knowledge that the motor vehicle was the property of another. In my opinion this made the taking fraudulent … ."

In *R. v. Lemire*, [1965] 4 C.C.C. 11, this court held that the accused's belief that his actions would subsequently be ratified afforded no defence. The accused, the Chief of the Quebec Liquor Police, had been told by the Premier of Quebec to submit fictitious expense accounts in order to receive a salary increase which had been agreed to but which could not be officially paid until a government-wide salary review, then underway, had been completed. In submitting the expense accounts Lemire no doubt felt that his actions, if unorthodox, were not dishonest. Nevertheless, Lemire was convicted. Reversing the decision in the Court of Appeal, Martland J. (for the majority) held, at p. 32:

> In other words [the court below held that], there is no intent to defraud within the require-
> ment of s. 323(1) [now s. 380(1)] if the accused person, while deliberately committing an
> act which is clearly fraudulent, expects that that which he is doing may, at a later date, be
> validated. To me the very statement of this proposition establishes its error in law.

I do not, of course, overlook the fact that a variety of rulings can be found in lower courts, some of which adopt the position that unless the Crown establishes that the accused subjectively intended to act dishonestly, the *mens rea* of fraud is not proven and the accused is entitled to be acquitted: see *R. v. Bobbie* (1988), 43 C.C.C. (3d) 187 (Ont. C.A.); *R. v. Lacroix* (1989), 22 Q.A.C. 264 (C.A.); *R. v. Daigle* (1987), 39 C.C.C. (3d) 542, [1987] 9 Q.A.C. 140 R.J.Q. 2374; *R. v. Sebe* (1987), 35 C.C.C. (3d) 97 (Sask. C.A.), and *R. v. Mugford* (1990), 58 C.C.C. (3d) 172 (Nfld. C.A.). This was the position adopted by Proulx J.A. in the appeal now before this court.

These decisions are largely predicated on the English approach in *R. v. Landy*, [1981] 1 All E.R. 1172 (C.A.), which held that the accused must subjectively believe his or her actions to be dishonest to support conviction, or upon the modification of that approach in *R. v. Ghosh*, [1982] 2 All E.R. 689 (C.A.), where it was held that the accused must subjectively realize that his or her conduct falls below the ordinary standard of reasonable and honest people. There are two problems with applying the English authorities to the Canadian offence of fraud. First, the relevant English offence rests on language different from that of the Canadian offence. Specifically, the English offence (ss. 1 and 15(1) of the *Theft Act*, 1968 (U.K.), c. 60) expressly refers to "dishonest appropriation" and "dishonestly" obtaining by deception, respectively. This wording, absent in Canada, has been interpreted in England to show Parliament's intention to require subjective awareness of dishonesty. The second problem is, as I see it, that the English authorities cannot be reconciled with the basic principles of criminal law relating to *mens rea*.

The British Columbia Court of Appeal for these reasons rejected the English approach in *R. v. Long* (1990), 61 C.C.C. (3d) 156. Taggart J.A. held at p. 169 that *Landy* was not the law in Canada. With respect to *Ghosh*, he stated, at p. 170: "I agree with Ewart's [ibid.] opinion that the *Ghosh* approach is predicated upon assumptions which have no relevance to the Canadian law of fraud." Taggart J.A. summarized the mental element of fraud as follows, at p. 174:

> ... the mental element of the offence of fraud must not be based on what the accused thought about the honesty or otherwise of his conduct and its consequences. Rather, it must be based on what the accused knew were the facts of the transaction, the circumstances in which it was undertaken and what the consequences might be of carrying it to a conclusion.

In my opinion, Taggart J.A. was correct in rejecting the English approach. While the authorities are far from consistent, the better view is that the accused's belief that the conduct is not wrong or that no one will in the end be hurt affords no defence to a charge of fraud.

### (iii)  Pragmatic Considerations

Pragmatic considerations support the view of *mens rea* proposed above. A person who deprives another person of what the latter has should not escape criminal responsibility merely because, according to his moral or her personal code, he or she was doing nothing wrong or because of a sanguine belief that all will come out right in the end. Many frauds are perpetrated by people who think there is nothing wrong in what they are doing or who sincerely believe that their act of placing other people's property at risk will not ultimately result in actual loss to those persons. If the offence of fraud is to catch those who actually practise fraud, its *mens rea* cannot be cast so narrowly as this. As stated in *R. v. Allsop*, ... approved by this court in *Olan*, at p. 150:

> Generally the primary objective of fraudsmen is to advantage themselves. The detriment that results to their victims is secondary to that purpose and incidental. It is "intended" only in the sense that it is a contemplated outcome of the fraud that is perpetrated.

The law of fraud must be sufficiently broad to catch this secondary incident of the defrauder's purpose or it will be of little avail.

This approach conforms to the conception of the offence of fraud which imbues this court's decision in *Olan*. *Olan* points the way to a conception of fraud broad enough in scope to encompass the entire panoply of dishonest commercial dealings. It defines the *actus reus* accordingly; the offence is committed whenever a person deceives, lies or otherwise acts dishonestly, and that act causes deprivation (including risk of deprivation) to another. To adopt a definition of *mens rea* which requires subjective awareness of dishonesty and a belief that actual deprivation (as opposed to risk of deprivation) will result, is inconsistent with *Olan*'s definition of the *actus reus*. The effect of such a test would be to negate the broad thrust of *Olan* and confine the offence of fraud to a narrow ambit, capable of catching only a small portion of the dishonest commercial dealing which *Olan* took as the target of the offence of fraud.

The question arises whether the definition of *mens rea* for fraud which I have proposed may catch conduct which does not warrant criminalization. I refer to the fear, reflected in the appellate decisions adopting a narrower definition of the required *mens rea*, that the reach of the offence of fraud may be extended beyond criminal dishonesty to catch sharp or improvident business practices which, although not to be encouraged, do not merit the stigma and loss of liberty that attends the criminal sanction. The concern is that any misrepresentation or practice which induces an incorrect understanding or belief in the minds of customers, or which causes deprivation, will become criminal. As Marshall J.A. put it in *Mugford*, supra, at pp. 175-6:

> ... it is not sufficient to base fraud merely upon a finding that the appellant induced a state of mind in his customers which was not correct. Any misrepresentation may have that effect. Criminal dishonesty extends further ...
>
> It would be a startling extension of criminal liability if every statement urging the public to purchase one's wares because only a limited supply remain were by itself to be visited with criminal sanction.

This poses starkly the critical question: does a view of the offence of fraud which catches a broad range of dishonest commercial dealing also catch conduct which should not be regarded as criminal, but rather left to the civil sanction?

In my view, the approach to the offence of fraud adopted in *Olan* and perused in these reasons does not take us out of the proper domain of the criminal sanction. To establish the *actus reus* of fraud, the Crown must establish beyond a reasonable doubt that the accused practised deceit, lied, or committed some other fraudulent act. Under the third head of the offence it will be necessary to show that the impugned act is one which a reasonable person would see as dishonest. Deprivation or the risk of deprivation must then be shown to have occurred as a matter of fact. To establish the *mens rea* of fraud the Crown must prove that the accused knowingly undertook the acts which constitute the falsehood, deceit or other fraudulent means, and that the accused was aware that deprivation could result from such conduct.

The requirement of intentional fraudulent action excludes mere negligent misrepresentation. It also excludes improvident business conduct or conduct which is sharp in the sense of taking advantage of a business opportunity to the detriment of someone less astute. The accused must intentionally deceive, lie or commit some other fraudulent act for the offence to be established. Neither a negligent misstatement, nor a sharp business practice, will suffice, because in neither case will the required intent to deprive by fraudulent means be present. A statement made carelessly, even if it is untrue, will not amount to an intentional falsehood, subjectively appreciated. Nor will any seizing of a business opportunity which is not motivated by a person's subjective intent to deprive by cheating or misleading others amount to an instance of fraud. Again, an act of deceit which is made carelessly without any expectation of consequences, as for example, an innocent prank or a statement made in debate which is not intended to be acted upon, would not amount to fraud because the accused would have no knowledge that the prank would put the property of those who heard it at risk. We are left then with deliberately practised fraudulent acts which, in the knowledge of the accused, actually put the property of others at risk. Such conduct may be appropriately criminalized, in my view.

### Recklessness and Wilful Blindness

There are two forms of subjective *mens rea* or fault that are thought to be extensions of the core standards of intention and knowledge. Recklessness is often seen as an extension of intention, whereas wilful blindness is seen as an extension of knowledge.

**R. v. Sansregret**
Supreme Court of Canada
(1985), 18 C.C.C. (3d) 223

[The accused was charged under s. 143(b)(i) of the *Criminal Code* with sexually violating the victim after breaking into her home and assaulting and terrorizing her. The victim became compliant with the accused in order to ensure her own safety. At trial, the accused raised the defence of mistake of fact in consent. This issue is dealt with more extensively in chapter 12 (Sexual Assault). In the excerpt below, the court provides an authoritative account of the concepts of recklessness and wilful blindness.]

McINTYRE J.: ... The concept of recklessness as a basis for criminal liability has been the subject of much discussion. Negligence, the failure to take reasonable care, is a creature of the civil law and is not generally a concept having a place in determining criminal liability. Nevertheless, it is frequently confused with recklessness in the criminal sense and care should be taken to separate the two concepts. Negligence is tested by the objective standard of the reasonable man. A departure from his accustomed sober behaviour by an act or omission which reveals less than reasonable care will involve liability at civil law but forms no basis for the imposition of criminal penalties. In accordance with well-established principles for the determination of criminal liability, recklessness, to form a part of the criminal *mens rea*, must have an element of the subjective. It is found in the attitude of one who, aware that there is danger that his conduct could bring about the result prohibited by the criminal law, nevertheless persists, despite the risk. It is, in other words, the conduct of one who sees the risk and who takes the chance. It is in this sense that the term "recklessness" is used in the criminal law and it is clearly distinct from the concept of civil negligence. ...

The idea of wilful blindness in circumstances such as this has been said to be an aspect of recklessness. While this may well be true, it is wise to keep the two concepts separate because they result from different mental attitudes and lead to different legal results. A finding of recklessness in this case could not override the defence of mistake of fact. The appellant asserts an honest belief that the consent of the complainant was not caused by fear and threats. The trial judge found that such an honest belief existed. In the facts of this case, because of the reckless conduct of the appellant, it could not be said that such a belief was reasonable but, as held in *Pappajohn*, the mere honesty of the belief will support the "mistake of fact" defence, even where it is unreasonable. On the other hand, a finding of wilful blindness as to the very facts about which the honest belief is now asserted would leave no room for the application of the defence because, where wilful blindness is shown, the law presumes knowledge on the part of the accused, in this case knowledge that the consent had been induced by threats.

Wilful blindness is distinct from recklessness because, while recklessness involves knowledge of a danger or risk and persistence in a course of conduct which creates a risk that the prohibited result will occur, wilful blindness arises where a person who has become aware of the need for some inquiry declines to make the inquiry because he does not wish to know the truth. He would prefer to remain ignorant. The culpability in recklessness is justified by consciousness of the risk and by proceeding in the face of it, while in wilful blindness it is justified by the accused's fault in deliberately failing to inquire when he knows there is reason for inquiry. Cases such as *R. v. Wretham* (1971), 16 C.R.N.S. 124 (Ont. C.A.); *R. v. Blondin* (1970), 2 C.C.C. (2d) 118 (B.C.C.A.); appeal dismissed in this Court in 4 C.C.C. (2d) 566n; *R. v. Currie* (1975), 24 C.C.C. (2d) 292 (Ont. C.A.); *R. v. McFall et al.* (1975), 26 C.C.C. (2d) 181 (B.C.C.A.); *R. v. Aiello* (1978), 38 C.C.C. (2d) 485 (Ont. C.A.); *Roper v. Taylor's Central Garages (Exeter), Ltd.*, [1951] 2 T.L.R. 284, among others illustrate these principles. The text-writers have also dealt with the subject, particularly Glanville Williams (Criminal Law: The General Part, 2nd ed. (1961), pp. 157-60). He says, at p. 157:

> Knowledge, then, means either personal knowledge or (in the licence cases) imputed knowledge. In either event there is someone with actual knowledge. To the requirement of actual knowledge there is one strictly limited exception. Men readily regard their suspicions as unworthy of them when it is to their advantage to do so. To meet this, the rule is that if a party has his suspicion aroused but then deliberately omits to make further enquiries, because he wishes to remain in ignorance, he is deemed to have knowledge.

He then referred to the words of Lord Sumner in *Zamora No. 2*, [1921] 1 A.C. 801 at pp. 811-2, which was a case wherein a ship and cargo were condemned in the Prize Court as contraband. The managing director of the shipping company denied knowledge of the contraband carried by the ship, and on this subject Lord Sumner said, at pp. 811-2:

> Lord Sterndale [the president of the Prize Court] thus expressed his final conclusion: "I think the true inference is that, if Mr. Banck did not know this was a transaction in contraband, it was because he did not want to know, and that he has not rebutted the presumption arising from the fact of the whole cargo being contraband."
>
> Their Lordships have been invited to read this as saying that Mr. Banck is not proved to have known the contraband character of the adventure; that if he did not know, because he did not want to know, he was within his rights and owed no duty to the belligerents to inform himself; and that the Zamora is condemned contrary to the passage above cited

from *The Hakan* [[1918] A.C. 148] upon a legal presumption arising solely and arbitrarily from the fact that the whole cargo was contraband. It may be that in his anxiety not to
state more than he found against Mr. Banck, the learned President appeared to state something less, but there are two senses in which a man is said not to know something because
he does not want to know it. A thing may be troublesome to learn, and the knowledge of
it, when acquired, may be uninteresting or distasteful. To refuse to know any more about
the subject or anything at all is then a wilful but a real ignorance. On the other hand, a
man is said not to know because he does not want to know, where the substance of the
thing is borne in upon his mind with a conviction that full details or precise proofs may be
dangerous, because they may embarrass his denials or compromise his protests. In such a
case he flatters himself that where ignorance is safe, 'tis folly to be wise, but there he is
wrong, for he has been put upon notice and his further ignorance, even though actual and
complete, is a mere affectation and disguise.

Glanville Williams, however, warns that the rule of deliberate blindness has its dangers and is of narrow application. He says, at p. 159:

> The rule that wilful blindness is equivalent to knowledge is essential, and is found through-
> out the criminal law. It is, at the same time, an unstable rule, because judges are apt to
> forget its very limited scope. A court can properly find wilful blindness only where it can
> almost be said that the defendant actually knew. He suspected the fact; he realised its
> probability; but he refrained from obtaining the final confirmation because he wanted in
> the event to be able to deny knowledge. This, and this alone, is wilful blindness. It re-
> quires in effect a finding that the defendant intended to cheat the administration of justice.
> Any wider definition would make the doctrine of wilful blindness indistinguishable from
> the civil doctrine of negligence in not obtaining knowledge.

This subject is also dealt with by Professor Stuart in Canadian Criminal Law (1982), p.
130 et seq., where its relationship to recklessness is discussed.

The case reveals, in my view, an appropriate set of circumstances for the application of the "wilful blindness" rule. I have outlined the circumstances which form the
background. I have referred to the findings of the trial judge that the appellant blinded
himself to the obvious and made no inquiry as to the nature of the consent which was
given. If the evidence before the court was limited to the events of October 15th, it
would be difficult indeed to infer wilful blindness. To attribute criminal liability on the
basis of this one incident would come close to applying a constructive test to the effect
that he should have known she was consenting out of fear. The position, however, is
changed when the evidence reveals the earlier episode and the complaint of rape which
it caused, knowledge of which, as I have said, had clearly reached the accused. Considering the whole of the evidence then, no constructive test of knowledge is required. The
appellant was aware of the likelihood of the complainant's reaction to his threats. To
proceed with intercourse in such circumstances constitutes, in my view, self-deception
to the point of wilful blindness. ...

I would dismiss the appeal.

*Appeal dismissed.*

**R. v. Duong**
Ontario Court of Appeal
(1998), 124 C.C.C. (3d) 392

[The accused was charged with being an accessory after the fact to murder. The accused allowed another individual, L., wanted for murder, to stay in his apartment. The accused had heard about the killing through the media and L. told the accused that he was "in trouble for murder."]

DOHERTY J.A.: …

### The Wilful Blindness Issue

[10] At trial, the Crown and defence agreed that the appellant could only be convicted if he knew that Lam had been a party to murder. They agreed that wilful blindness of that fact would suffice. On appeal, both the Crown and the defence retreated somewhat from the positions taken at trial. The Crown argues that it was only necessary to show that the appellant knew or was wilfully blind to the fact that Lam had committed "a criminal offence." The appellant argues that the appellant could only be convicted if he knew that Lam had been a party to murder and that wilful blindness has no application to this case.

[11] The Crown's submission that it need only show that the appellant had knowledge that Lam had committed "a criminal offence" runs aground on the language of s. 23(1) of the *Criminal Code*:

> 23(1) *An accessory after the fact to an offence is one who, knowing that a person has been a party to the offence*, receives, comforts or assists that person for the purpose of enabling that person to escape. [Emphasis added.]

[12] Section 23(1) contemplates aid given to someone who has committed an offence (the principal) by a person who knew that principal had committed that offence when the assistance was provided. This indictment reflects the language of s. 23(1) and charges that the appellant "knowing that Chinh Lam was a party to the offence of murder, did assist Chinh Lam."

[13] It is also significant that the crime of being an accessory after the fact to murder has its own penalty provision (s. 240) which is more severe than the penalty provision applicable to those who are accessories to other crimes (s. 463). This is a further indication that where the Crown chooses to charge someone with being an accessory after the fact to murder, it cannot gain a conviction based on a more generalized knowledge that the principal had committed some crime.

[14] There is little Canadian case law dealing with the knowledge requirement in s. 23(1), perhaps because the language of s. 23(1) is unambiguous. In *R. v. Vinette* (1974), 19 C.C.C. (2d) 1 (S.C.C.), the accused was charged with being an accessory after the fact to manslaughter. Both the majority (per Pigeon J. at p. 7) and the dissent (per Laskin C.J.C. at pp. 2-3) accepted that the Crown had to prove that an accused charged with being an accessory after the fact to a homicide had knowledge of "the

unlawful killing." Similarly, in *R. v. A. (M.)*, released March 22, 1996, this court proceeded on the basis that knowledge of the offence committed by the person aided was an essential element of the charge of being an accessory after the fact. See, also, D. Watt, Accessoryship After the Fact: Substantive Procedural and Evidentiary Considerations (1981), 21 C.R. (3d) 307 at 308, 318-19; V. Rose, Parties to an Offence (1982) at pp. 164-66, 194.

[15] In other jurisdictions where provisions like s. 23(1) were in effect, or the common law prevailed, courts required that the Crown prove that the accessory after the fact knew of the specific offence committed by the person assisted: *R. v. Levy*, [1912] 1 K.B. 158 (C.C.A.) at 160; *R. v. Tevendale*, [1955] V.L.R. 95 (Vict. S.C.); *R. v. Carter and Savage* (1990), 47 A. Crim. R. 55 (Queensland C.A.) at 63; P. Gillies, Criminal Law (1990) at 765-66. For example, in *R. v. Carter and Savage*, supra, Carter J. said at p. 63:

> It follows that in this case it was incumbent upon the Crown to establish the fact that the principal offender had done the acts said to constitute the offence of murder, that the accused knew that and, with that knowledge, received or assisted Carter in order to enable him to escape punishment.

[16] The authorities referred to by Crown counsel rely on statutory language which is very different from that found in s. 23(1). These statutes create a more generic offence involving the hindering of an investigation, or interference with the apprehension or conviction of a person. For example, in *R. v. Morgan*, [1972] 1 Q.B. 436 (C.A.) at 438, the relevant statutory provision provided:

> Where a person has committed an arrestable offence, any other person who, *knowing or believing him to be guilty of the offence or of some other arrestable offence*, does without lawful authority or reasonable excuse any act with intent to impede his apprehension or prosecution shall be guilty of an offence. [Emphasis added.]

[17] Parliament could have enacted similar legislation. It has not, however, done so and it is beyond the authority of the courts to enact such legislation by judicial fiat. I am not moved by the Crown's further contention that the requirement that the Crown prove that the accessory had knowledge of the offence committed by the person aided will allow individuals to escape justice when they aid someone believing that person has committed crime "x" when in fact the person has committed crime "y." If that is the effect of the present legislation, it is for Parliament to decide whether the statutory prohibition should be expanded. Moreover, it seems to me that the circumstances posited by the Crown would give rise to a charge of obstructing justice under s. 139(2) of the *Criminal Code*.

[18] A charge a laid under s. 23(1) must allege the commission of a specific offence (or offences) and the Crown must prove that the alleged accessory knew that the person assisted was a party to that offence. The Crown will meet its burden if it proves that the accused had actual knowledge of the offence committed. Whether wilful blindness will suffice is addressed below. The further question of whether recklessness as to the offence committed by the principal would be sufficient need not be decided in this case.

[19]  The appellant argues that wilful blindness can only be relied on by the Crown if the Crown proves that an accused whose suspicions were aroused had the means available to verify the accuracy of those suspicions. The appellant goes on to contend that he could have turned only to Lam to verify his suspicions and that the record does not suggest that Lam would have admitted his culpability in the murders. It follows, says the appellant, that he did not have the means available to him to verify his suspicions and should not, therefore, be held culpable on the basis of wilful blindness. The appellant cites no authority for this proposition.

[20]  Wilful blindness is explained in *R. v. Sansregret* (1985), 18 C.C.C. (3d) 223 (S.C.C.) at 235:

> … wilful blindness arises where a person who has become aware of the need for some inquiry declines to make the inquiry because he does not wish to know the truth. He would prefer to remain ignorant. The culpability in recklessness is justified by consciousness of the risk and by proceeding in the face of it, *while in wilful blindness it is justified by the accused's fault in deliberately failing to inquire when he knows there is reason for inquiry.* [Emphasis added.]

[21]  More recently, in *R. v. Jorgensen* (1995), 102 C.C.C. (3d) 97 (S.C.C.) at 135, Sopinka J. described wilful blindness in these terms in reference to a charge of selling obscene material:

> *It is well established in criminal law that wilful blindness will also fulfil a* mens rea *requirement.* If the retailer becomes aware of the need to make further inquiries about the nature of the videos he was selling yet deliberately chooses to ignore these indications and does not make any further inquiries, then the retailer can be nonetheless charged under s. 163(2)(a) for "knowingly" selling obscene materials. *Deliberately choosing not to know something when given reason to believe further inquiry is necessary can satisfy the mental element of the offence.* …
>
> A finding of wilful blindness involves an affirmative answer to the question: Did the accused shut his eyes because he knew or strongly suspected that looking would fix him with knowledge? [Emphasis added.]

[22]  These authorities make it clear that where the Crown proves the existence of a fact in issue and knowledge of that fact is a component of the fault requirement of the crime charged, wilful blindness as to the existence of that fact is sufficient to establish a culpable state of mind. Liability based on wilful blindness is subjective. Wilful blindness refers to a state of mind which is aptly described as "deliberate ignorance" (D. Stuart, Canadian Criminal Law, 3rd ed. (1995) at p. 209). Actual suspicion, combined with a conscious decision not to make inquiries which could confirm that suspicion, is equated in the eyes of the criminal law with actual knowledge. Both are subjective and both are sufficiently blameworthy to justify the imposition of criminal liability.

[23]  The appellants submission misunderstands the basis upon which liability is imposed where wilful blindness exists. Liability turns on the decision not to inquire once real suspicions arise and not on the hypothetical result of inquiries which were

never made. Where an accused chooses to make no inquiries, preferring to remain "deliberately ignorant," speculation as to what the accused would have learned had he chosen to make the necessary inquiries is irrelevant to the determination of the blameworthiness of that accused's state of mind.

[24] The appellant also submits that even if wilful blindness has application in the circumstances of this case, the trial judge erred in finding that the appellant was wilfully blind to the fact that Lam was a party to murder. This is in essence an argument that the trial judge's finding is unreasonable. It was urged that the appellant's statements to the police suggested only that he suspected that Lam had some connection, perhaps as a witness, to the homicides. The appellant submits that a finding of knowledge that Lam was a party to murder based on those statements was more speculation than reasonable inference.

[25] It was certainly open to trial counsel to advance the argument now urged upon this court. I cannot say, however, that the trial judge's rejection of that argument and his conclusion that the appellant's suspicions extended to a suspicion that Lam had been a party to murder was unreasonable. It was open to him to infer that the appellant's statements revealed a state of mind which encompassed the suspicion that Lam was in trouble because he had been a party to murder. The fact that the appellant may have contemplated other possible connections between Lam and the murders afforded no bar to a finding that he was wilfully blind to the fact that Lam was a party to murder.

---

In the following case, the Supreme Court interprets the statutory use of the term "reckless" in what is now s. 229(a)(ii) (then s. 212(a)(ii)), the charging provision for murder. Notice how closely the court aligns recklessness in this context with an actual intention to cause death.

### R. v. Cooper
Supreme Court of Canada
(1993), 78 C.C.C. (3d) 289

CORY J.: ... Section 212(a)(ii) provides:

> s. 212.  Culpable homicide is murder
>
>> (a)  where the person who causes the death of a human being ...
>>
>>> (ii)  means to cause him bodily harm that he knows is likely to cause his death,
>>
>> and is reckless whether death ensues or not;

This section was considered in *R. v. Nygaard*. On the issue of the requisite intent the court was unanimous. At p. 435, it was said: "The essential element is that of intending to cause bodily harm of such a grave and serious nature that the accused knew that it was likely to result in the death of the victim. The aspect of recklessness is almost an afterthought ..."

The aspect of recklessness can be considered an afterthought since to secure a conviction under this section it must be established that the accused had the intent to cause such grievous bodily harm that he knew it was likely to cause death. One who causes bodily harm that he knows is likely to cause death must, in those circumstances, have a deliberate disregard for the fatal consequences which are known to be likely to occur. That is to say he must, of necessity, be reckless whether death ensues or not.

The concept of recklessness was considered by this court in *R. v. Sansregret* (1985), 18 C.C.C. (3d) 223. At p. 233 it was said:

> [Recklessness] is found in the attitude of one who, aware that there is danger that his conduct could bring about the result prohibited by the criminal law, nevertheless persists, despite the risk. It is, in other words, the conduct of one who sees the risk and who takes the chance.

The same words can apply to s. 212(a)(ii) with this important addition: it is not sufficient that the accused foresee simply a danger of death; the accused must foresee a likelihood of death flowing from the bodily harm that he is occasioning the victim.

It is for this reason that it was said in *Nygaard* that there is only a "slight relaxation" in the *mens rea* required for a conviction for murder under s. 212(a)(ii) as compared to s. 212(a)(i). The position was put in this way at p. 436:

> … [where] two accused form the intent to repeatedly and viciously strike a person in the head with a baseball bat realizing full well that the victim will probably die as a result. None the less they continue with the bone-splintering, skull-shattering assault. The accused … must have committed as grave a crime as the accused who specifically intends to kill … I would conclude that the crime defined in s. 212(a)(ii) [now s. 229(a)(ii)] can properly be described as murder and on a "culpability scale" it varies so little from s. 212(a)(i) as to be indistinguishable.

The intent that must be demonstrated in order to convict under s. 212(a)(ii) has two aspects. There must be (a) subjective intent to cause bodily harm; (b) subjective knowledge that the bodily harm is of such a nature that it is likely to result in death. It is only when those two elements of intent are established that a conviction can properly follow.

---

Historically, the difficulty with recklessness has been in keeping it analytically distinct from the concept of negligence, which is discussed below. In *R. v. Caldwell* (1981), 73 Cr. App. R. 13 (H.L.), the accused was convicted of recklessly endangering life by setting fire to a hotel. Lord Diplock for the majority of the House of Lords stated that the word "reckless" had not

> become a term of legal art with some more limited esoteric meaning than that which it bore in ordinary speech—a meaning which surely includes not only deciding to ignore a risk of harmful consequences resulting from one's acts that one has recognised as existing, but also failing to give any thought to whether or not there is any such risk in circumstances where, if any thought were given to the matter, it would be obvious that there was.

Lord Edmund-Davies, with whom Lord Wilberforce concurred, dissented, stating:

> So if a defendant says of a particular risk, "It never crossed my mind," a jury could not on those words alone properly convict him of recklessness simply because they considered that the risk *ought* to have crossed his mind, though his words might well lead to a finding of negligence. But a defendant's admission that he "closed his mind" to a particular risk could prove fatal, for "A person cannot, in any intelligible meaning of the words, close his mind to a risk unless he first realises that there is a risk; and if he realises that there is a risk that is the end of the matter."

(Glanville Williams, *Textbook of Criminal Law* (London: Stevens & Sons, 1978), at 79.)

In *R. v. Lawrence* (1981), 73 Cr. App. R. 1 (H.L.) the accused was convicted of reckless driving by driving his motorcycle at a high rate of speed. There was no evidence of drinking. Lord Diplock stated:

> In my view, an appropriate instruction to the jury on what is meant by driving recklessly would be that they must be satisfied of two things. First, that the defendant was in fact driving the vehicle in such a manner as to create an obvious and serious risk of causing physical injury to some other person who might happen to be using the road or of doing substantial damage to property; and secondly, that in driving in that manner the defendant did so without having given any thought to the possibility of there being any such risk or, having recognised that there was some risk involved had nonetheless gone on to take it.

Both *Caldwell* and *Lawrence* are controversial decisions that received intense criticism from academics. The two decisions have not been followed in Canada. However, over 20 years later, and after rejecting previous invitations to reconsider these decisions, the House of Lords reversed *Caldwell* in *R. v. G.*, [2003] All E.R. 765. Writing the lead judgment, Lord Bingham gave the following reasons for not following the previous decisions:

> First, it is a salutary principle that conviction of serious crime should depend on proof not simply that the defendant caused (by act or omission) an injurious result to another but that his state of mind when so acting was culpable. This, after all, is the meaning of the familiar rule *actus non facit reum nisi mens sit rea*. The most obviously culpable state of mind is no doubt an intention to cause the injurious result, but knowing disregard of an appreciated and unacceptable risk of causing an injurious result or a deliberate closing of the mind to such risk would be readily accepted as culpable also. It is clearly blameworthy to take an obvious and significant risk of causing injury to another. But it is not clearly blameworthy to do something involving a risk of injury to another if (for reasons other than self-induced intoxication: *R. v. Majewski*, [1977] A.C. 443) one genuinely does not perceive the risk. Such a person may fairly be accused of stupidity or lack of imagination, but neither of those failings should expose him to conviction of serious crime or the risk of punishment.
>
> Secondly, the present case shows, more clearly than any other reported case since *R. v. Caldwell*, that the model direction formulated by Lord Diplock … is capable of leading to obvious unfairness. As the excerpts … reveal, the trial judge regretted the direction he (quite rightly) felt compelled to give, and it is evident that this direction offended the jury's sense of fairness. The sense of fairness of 12 representative citizens sitting as a jury (or of a

smaller group of lay justices sitting as a bench of magistrates) is the bedrock on which the administration of criminal justice in this country is built. A law which runs counter to that sense must cause concern. Here, the appellants could have been charged under section 1(1) with recklessly damaging one or both of the wheelie-bins, and they would have had little defence. As it was, jury might have inferred that boys of the appellants' age would have appreciated the risk to the building of what they did, but it seems clear that such was not their conclusion (nor, it would appear, the judge's either). On that basis the jury thought it unfair to convict them. I share their sense of unease. It is neither moral nor just to convict a defendant (least of all a child) on the strength of what someone else would have apprehended if the defendant himself had no such apprehension. Nor, the defendant having been convicted, is the problem cured by imposition of a nominal penalty.

Thirdly, I do not think the criticism of *R. v. Caldwell* expressed by academics, judges and practitioners should be ignored. A decision is not, of course, to be overruled or departed from simply because it meets with disfavour in the learned journals. But a decision which attracts reasoned and outspoken criticism by the leading scholars of the day, respected as authorities in the field, must command attention. One need only cite (among many other examples) the observations of Professor John Smith ([1981] Crim. L.R. 392, 393-396) and Professor Glanville Williams ("Recklessness Redefined" (1981), 40 C.L.J. 252). This criticism carries greater weight when voiced also by judges as authoritative as Lord Edmund-Davies and Lord Wilberforce in *R. v. Caldwell* itself, Robert Goff L.J. in *Elliott v. C.*, [1983] 1 W.L.R. 939 and Ackner L.J. in *R. v. Stephen Malcolm R.* (1984), 79 Cr. App. R. 334. The reservations expressed by the trial judge in the present case are widely shared. The shopfloor response to *R. v. Caldwell* may be gauged from the editors' commentary, to be found in the 41st edition of *Archbold* (1982): paragraph 17-25, pages 1009-1010. The editors suggested that remedial legislation was urgently required.

Fourthly, the majority's interpretation of "reckless" in section 1 of the 1971 Act was, as already shown, a misinterpretation. If it were a misinterpretation that offended no principle and gave rise to no injustice there would be strong grounds for adhering to the misinterpretation and leaving Parliament to correct it if it chose. But this misinterpretation is offensive to principle and is apt to cause injustice. That being so, the need to correct the misinterpretation is compelling. ...

I cannot accept that restoration of the law as understood before *R. v. Caldwell* would lead to the acquittal of those whom public policy would require to be convicted. There is nothing to suggest that this was seen as a problem before *R. v. Caldwell*, or ... before the 1971 Act. There is no reason to doubt the common sense which tribunals of fact bring to their task. In a contested case based on intention, the defendant rarely admits intending the injurious result in question, but the tribunal of fact will readily infer such an intention, in a proper case, from all the circumstances and probabilities and evidence of what the defendant did and said at the time. Similarly with recklessness: it is not to be supposed that the tribunal of fact will accept a defendant's assertion that he never thought of a certain risk when all the circumstances and probabilities and evidence of what he did and said at the time show that he did or must have done.

## III. OBJECTIVE STATES OF FAULT

This section examines fault requirements that fall short of a purely subjective inquiry into what passed through the mind of the accused person. We look at standards of fault that focus on holding accused persons to an objective standard of conduct. Objective standards focus on what the accused ought to have thought or contemplated about his or her actions, as opposed to what he or she did actually think about.

An inquiry into objective standards of fault is often preoccupied with criminal negligence. Negligence as a standard for criminal liability is controversial. The courts have gone to great lengths to distinguish criminal negligence from civil negligence. Also, as discussed below in *Tutton* and *Creighton*, the courts have debated the extent to which subjective factors ought to be relevant.

### R. v. Tutton and Tutton
Supreme Court of Canada
(1989), 48 C.C.C. (3d) 129

[The accused were convicted of manslaughter under s. 205 of the Code (the present s. 222) through criminal negligence (s. 202, now s. 219) causing the death of their five-year-old son by omitting to provide the necessaries of life (s. 197, now. s. 215). Because of religious views and their belief in faith-healing, they refused to administer insulin injections to their diabetic son; the jury convicted after the trial judge had said: "The standard to be applied in determining whether the failure to do so shows wanton or reckless disregard for the life or safety of the child is the standard of reasonable parents." A new trial was ordered by the Ontario Court of Appeal on the basis that, although an objective test is required for criminal negligence, a subjective test is necessary for acts of omission. Dubin J.A. stated for the court: "I think a distinction should be made between acts of commission and acts of omission and, in the latter case, a subjective test should be used." The Crown appealed to the Supreme Court of Canada, which unanimously held that a new trial should be ordered. No member of the court, however, accepted the distinction between omissions and commissions. The issue was whether the test for criminal negligence was subjective or objective. Three members of the court (Beetz, Estey, and Le Dain JJ.) heard the appeal, but took no part in the judgment.]

McINTYRE J. (with whom L'Heureux-Dubé J. concurred):  In reaching a conclusion as to whether the conduct of an accused person has shown, within the meaning of s. 202 of the *Criminal Code*, wanton or reckless disregard for the lives or safety of other persons, the authorities dictate an objective test: see the review of the authorities on this subject by Cory J.A. for the Court of Appeal in *R. v. Waite* (1986), 28 C.C.C. (3d) 327, approved in this Court (judgment given concurrently). Indeed, in the Court of Appeal, Dubin J.A. accepted the objective test as one of general application, but made an exception in cases where the conduct complained of consisted of an act or acts of omission, as opposed to those of commission. In such cases, it was his view that occasions would arise where a subjective test would be required where acts of omission were under consideration. He considered this was such a case. It is my view, however, that no such distinction as Dubin J.A. would adopt may be made. I am wholly unable to see any difference in principle between cases arising from an omission to act and those involving acts of commission. Indeed, the words of s. 202 of the *Criminal Code* make it clear that one is criminally negligent who, *in doing anything* or *in omitting to do anything* that it is his duty to do, shows wanton or reckless disregard for the lives or safety of other persons. The objective test must, therefore, be employed where criminal negligence is considered for it is the conduct of the accused, as opposed to his intention or mental state, which is examined in this inquiry.

Our concept of criminal culpability relies primarily upon a consideration of the mental state which accompanies or initiates the wrongful act, and the attribution of criminal liability without proof of such a blameworthy mental state raises serious concerns. Nonetheless, negligence has become accepted as a factor which may lead to criminal liability and strong arguments can be raised in its favour. Section 202 of the *Criminal Code* affords an example of its adoption. In choosing the test to be applied in assessing conduct under s. 202 of the *Criminal Code*, it must be observed at once that what is made criminal is negligence. Negligence connotes the opposite of thought-directed action. In other words, its existence precludes the element of positive intent to achieve a given result. This leads to the conclusion that what is sought to be restrained by punishment under s. 202 of the *Code* is conduct, and its results. What is punished, in other words, is not the state of mind but the consequence of mindless action. This is apparent, I suggest, from the words of the section, which make criminal, conduct which *shows* wanton or reckless disregard. It may be observed as well that the words "wanton or reckless" support this construction, denying as they do the existence of a directing mental state. Nor can it be said that criminal negligence, as defined in s. 202, imports in its terms some element of malice or intention. This point was made in the Crown's factum in para. 41, which provided, in part:

> The plain and ordinary meaning of the terms "wanton" and "reckless" when used in connection with the concept of negligence would seem to include a state of being heedless of apparent danger. Section 202(1) does not use the term "reckless" as an extended definition of intention or malice, but rather employs the term as part of a definition of conduct which amounts to "negligence" in a criminal context.

In my view, then, an objective standard must be applied in determining this question because of the difference between the ordinary criminal offence, which requires proof of a subjective state of mind, and that of criminal negligence. In criminal cases, generally, the act coupled with the mental state or intent is punished. In criminal negligence, the act which exhibits the requisite degree of negligence is punished. If this distinction is not kept clear, the dividing line between the traditional *mens rea* offence and the offence of criminal negligence becomes blurred. The difference, for example, between murder and manslaughter, both unlawful killings, is merely one of intent. If the question of an accused's intent had to be considered and separately proved in offences under s. 202, of the *Criminal Code*, the purpose of the section would be defeated because intentional conduct would perforce be considered under other sections of the *Code* and

s. 202, aimed at mindless but socially dangerous conduct, would have no function. For these reasons, the objective test should be employed and, in my view, the Court of Appeal was in error in concluding in this case that a subjective test would be required. The test is that of reasonableness, and proof of conduct which reveals a marked and significant departure from the standard which could be expected of a reasonably prudent person in the circumstances will justify a conviction of criminal negligence.

In reaching this conclusion, I am not overlooking the comments I made in *Sansregret v. The Queen*, [1985] 1 S.C.R. 570, at pp. 581-82, which were cited by counsel for the appellant. In *Sansregret*, I expressed the view that "recklessness, to form a part of the criminal *mens rea*, must have an element of the subjective." I then went on to say that "[I]t is in this sense that the term 'recklessness' is used in the criminal law and it is clearly distinct from the concept of civil negligence." It was argued upon the basis of these words and later comments on the nature of negligence in relation to the criminal law that a subjective test should therefore be applied in considering the existence of criminal negligence under s. 202 of the *Code*. I would reject that argument on the basis that the concept of recklessness there described is not applicable in a case under s. 202 of the *Code*. Sansregret was charged with rape, a crime which involves positive mind-directed conduct on the part of the accused which aims at the accomplishment of a specific result. It is a traditional *mens rea* offence and a mental state must be proved, in that case an intention to persist with his purpose despite the fact that the complainant's consent has been extorted by threats and fear. Recklessness on his part forms a part of the *mens rea* (the blameworthy state of mind) and has to be proved on a subjective basis as part of the mental element of the offence. In this sense, the words in *Sansregret* are apposite. Section 202, on the other hand, has created a separate offence; an offence which makes negligence—the exhibition of wanton or reckless behaviour—a crime in itself and has thus defined its own terms. As noted by Cory J.A. in *R. v. Waite*, s. 202 of the *Criminal Code* was enacted in its present form as a codification of the offence which had emerged in Canadian jurisprudence, and in respect of which the necessary *mens rea* may be inferred on an objective basis from the acts of the accused.

The application of an objective test under s. 202 of the *Criminal Code*, however, may not be made in a vacuum. Events occur within the framework of other events and actions and when deciding on the nature of the questioned conduct surrounding circumstances must be considered. The decision must be made on a consideration of the facts existing at the time and in relation to the accused's perception of those facts. Since the test is objective, the accused's perception of the facts is not to be considered for the purpose of assessing malice or intention on the accused's part but only to form a basis for a conclusion as to whether or not the accused's conduct, in view of his perception of the facts, was reasonable.

[McIntyre J. upheld the order for a new trial, however, because of an error with respect to the burden of proof.]

LAMER J. concurred: I have read the reasons of my colleague, Mr. Justice McIntyre, and I am in agreement with them, subject to the following remarks. I am of the view that, when applying the objective norm set out by Parliament in s. 202 of the *Criminal*

*Code*, must be made "a generous allowance" for factors which are particular to the accused, such as youth, mental development, education (see Don Stuart, *Canadian Criminal Law: A Treatise*, 2nd ed., Toronto: Carswell, 1987, p. 194; see also Toni Pickard, "Culpable Mistakes and Rape: Relating *Mens Rea* to the Crime" (1980), 30 *U.T.L.J.* 75). When this is done, as we are considering conduct which is likely to cause death, that is high risk conduct, the adoption of a subjective or of an objective test will, in practice, nearly if not always produce the same result (see Eric Colvin, "Recklessness and Criminal Negligence" (1982), 32 *U.T.L.J.* 345).

I should note that Parliament, when enacting s. 202, did not purport to determine the nature of the negligence which is required when grounding criminal liability thereupon. My understanding of s. 202 is that Parliament has in that section simply defined the expression "criminal negligence" whenever used in the *Criminal Code*.

I should finally mention that in this case the constitutionality of s. 205(5)(b) was not in issue. Indeed, assuming without now deciding that it is a principle of fundamental justice that knowledge of a likely risk or deliberate ignorance thereof (foresight or wilful blindness) is an essential element of the offense of manslaughter, the issue as to whether proof of the substituted element of "criminal negligence" as defined by Parliament and interpreted by this Court satisfies the test set out in *R. v. Vaillancourt*, [1987] 2. S.C.R. 636, does not arise. I therefore do not by my concurrence feel precluded or limited when addressing such a constitutional challenge, of course, if and when called upon to do so.


WILSON J. (with whom Dickson C.J.C. and La Forest J. concurred): I have had the benefit of the reasons of my colleagues McIntyre and Lamer JJ. and I agree with them that the appeal should be dismissed and a new trial ordered because the trial judge's charge failed to make clear to the jury that the Crown had the burden to prove all the elements of the offence of manslaughter by criminal negligence. I do not, however, agree with my colleagues' conclusion that criminal negligence under s. 202 of the *Criminal Code*, R.S.C. 1970, c. C-34, consists only of conduct in breach of an objective standard and does not require the Crown to prove that the accused had any degree of guilty knowledge. I also have reservations concerning the approach my colleagues suggest is available in order to relieve against the harshness of the objective standard of liability which they find in s. 202 and to ensure that the morally innocent are not punished for the commission of serious criminal offences committed through criminal negligence. ...

Section 202 of the *Criminal Code* is, in my view, notorious in its ambiguity. Since its enactment in its present form in the 1955 Amendments to the *Criminal Code* it has bedevilled both courts and commentators who have sought out its meaning. The interpretation put upon it usually depends upon which words are emphasized. On the one hand, my colleague's judgment demonstrates that emphasizing the use of the words "shows" and "negligence" can lead to the conclusion that an objective standard of liability was intended and that proof of unreasonable conduct alone will suffice. On the other hand, if the words "wanton or reckless disregard for the lives or safety of other persons" are stressed along with the fact that what is prohibited is not negligence simpliciter but "criminal" negligence, one might conclude that Parliament intended some

degree of advertence to the risk to the lives or safety of others to be an essential element
of the offence. When faced with such fundamental ambiguity, it would be my view that
the court should give the provision the interpretation most consonant, not only with the
text and purpose of the provision, but also, where possible, with the broader concepts
and principles of the law: see also *R. v. Paré*, [1987] 2 S.C.R. 618. ...

It is my view that the phrase "reckless disregard for the lives or safety of other
persons" found in s. 202, when read in the context of Canadian criminal law jurisprudence, requires the Crown to prove advertence or awareness of the risk that the prohibited consequences will come to pass. This Court has adopted a subjective approach to
recklessness in *Pappajohn* (1980), 52 C.C.C. (3d) 481, and has reaffirmed this in the
recent case of *Sansregret, supra*. In doing so the Court has, I believe, implicitly rejected
the view that failure to give any thought to whether or not there is a risk can be substituted for the mental state of recklessness as that view is articulated in the majority
decisions in *Commissioner of Police of the Metropolis v. Caldwell*, [1982] A.C. 341
(H.L.), and *R. v. Lawrence*, [1982] A.C. 510 (H.L.). ...

I would add that the importance of what the reasonable person would have foreseen to the determination of whether a particular accused would have become aware
or wilfully blind to the prohibited risk will vary with the context. For example, in the
case of a licensed driver engaging in high risk motoring, I am in general agreement
with Morden J.A. in *R. v. Sharp* (1984), 12 C.C.C. (3d) 428 (Ont. C.A.), at pp. 434-
35, that it is open to the jury to find the accused's blameworthy state of mind from
driving which shows wanton or reckless disregard for the lives or safety of others
subject to an explanation in the evidence which would account for the deviant conduct such as a sudden mechanical malfunction or a bee sting or other accident beyond the accused's control. I would think that in the driving context where risks to
the lives and safety of others present themselves in a habitual and obvious fashion the
accused's claim that he or she gave no thought to the risk or had simply a negative
state of mind would in most, if not all, cases amount to the culpable positive mental
state of wilful blindness to the prohibited risk.

The minimal nature of the requirement of a blameworthy state of mind and the relevance of the objective standard as a rebuttable mode of proof suggests to me that a
holding that s. 202 requires proof of the mental element of advertence to the risk or
wilful blindness to the risk will not undermine the policy objectives of the provision.
The loss in terms of deterrence and social protection would seem to be negligible when
the retention of a subjective standard would at most offer protection for those who due
to some peculiarity or unexpected accident commit conduct which, although it shows a
reckless or wanton disregard for the lives or safety of others, can be explained as inconsistent with any degree of awareness of or wilful blindness to such a risk. Should social
protection require the adoption of an objective standard it is open to Parliament to enact
a law which clearly adopts such a standard. In my respectful view this Court should not
do it for them. ...

I am in complete agreement with what my colleague Justice Lamer has to say concerning the issue of constitutionality. I would only add that in light of this Court's decision in *R. v. Stevens*, [1988] 1 S.C.R. 1153, the *Charter* could not have been applied to
the tragic events culminating in Christopher Tutton's death on October 17, 1981.

To sum up, although I agree with my colleagues as to the proper disposition of this appeal, I am unable to agree with their conclusion that the offence of manslaughter by criminal negligence consists of conduct in breach of an objective standard.

---

In *R. v. Waite* (1989), 48 C.C.C. (3d) 1, the Supreme Court of Canada allowed the Crown's appeal from acquittals of the accused on four counts of causing death by criminal negligence. The accused was driving his car at high speeds while intoxicated and killed four people running on the roadside alongside slow-moving vehicles taking part in a church hayride. The trial judge instructed the jury as follows as to the difference between dangerous driving and criminal negligence:

> The position is that in dangerous driving the intention or the state of mind, if you wish, of the driver is not important. You look objectively at the manner of driving. You just look at the manner of driving.
>
> Now when you go over to criminal negligence, you have to look at two things, the objective driving, as you do for dangerous driving, and you also have to look at the subjective element, that is the attitude, or what is in the mind of the accused. That is whether there is a deliberate and wilful assumption of the risk involved in driving in the manner in which he was driving. So that you have in one, the dangerous driving, there is simply an objective standard, as compared to what the prudent driver would do. In the criminal negligence you have that, plus the subjective element of assumption and deliberate assumption of the risk.

McIntyre, L'Heureux-Dubé, and Lamer JJ. held that this was an error in law in not setting forth the objective tests that they had articulated in their judgments in *Tutton* and ordered a new trial. Wilson J., Dickson C.J.C., and La Forest J. concurred in the result and stated:

> In my view the trial judge's final instruction to the jury was in error as to the degree of *mens rea* required under s. 202 of the *Criminal Code*, R.S.C. 1970, c. C-34. When the jury asked the trial judge to explain the moral difference between dangerous driving and causing death by criminal negligence, the trial judge instructed the jury that the subjective element in criminal negligence was "a deliberate and wilful assumption of the risk involved in driving in the manner in which he was driving." Later in his reply to the jury he repeated that the subjective element in criminal negligence was "assumption and deliberate assumption of the risk." Although I believe there is a subjective element to criminal negligence, the judge in this case placed much too high an onus on the Crown to prove elements of deliberation and wilfulness. For the reasons I gave in *Tutton*, I am of the view that the mental element in criminal negligence is the minimal intent of awareness of the prohibited risk or wilful blindness to the risk.

---

In *R. v. Gingrich and McLean* (1991), 65 C.C.C. (3d) 188 (Ont. C.A.), McLean, the president of a trucking company, and Gingrich, the driver of a truck, were charged with criminal negligence causing death after a fatal motor vehicle accident when the truck's brakes failed. Gingrich had experienced increasing problems with the brakes over several days. Both were convicted and appealed to the Ontario Court of Appeal. Gingrich's conviction was upheld. McLean's conviction was quashed. Finlayson J.A. stated for the court:

This court has held in two recent decisions (see *R. v. Cabral* (1990), 54 C.C.C. (3d) 317, 21 M.V.R. (2d) 252, 38 O.A.C. 67, and *R. v. Nelson* (1990), 54 C.C.C. (3d) 285, 75 C.R. (3d) 70, 44 C.R.R. 193), that the *mens rea* for criminal negligence in the operation of a motor vehicle involves an objective assessment of the accused's conduct notwithstanding the decisions of the Supreme Court of Canada delivered in *Tutton* and *R. v. Waite* (1989), 48 C.C.C. (3d) 1, [1989] 1 S.C.R. 1436, 69 C.R. (3d) 323, released concurrently with *Tutton*. In *Nelson, supra,* this court said of those decisions at p. 287:

> In *R. v. Waite* and *R. v. Tutton, supra,* the judges of the Supreme Court of Canada divided equally. Three judges adopted an objective test and three others adopted a subjective test. All six judges did agree that no distinction should be made in relation to acts of omission as opposed to acts of commission.

and at p. 289:

> First, the decisions of the Supreme Court of Canada in *Waite* and *Tutton* do not stand for the proposition that the objective test as enunciated by this court in *Waite,* and *Sharp* is incorrect. Until the Supreme Court of Canada holds that to be the case, this court ought not to depart from the objective standard: *Rider v. Snow* (1891), 20 S.C.R. 12.

Counsel for the appellants argued that the decisions of this court in *Nelson* and *Cabral* ought to be reassessed in view of the recent decisions of the Supreme Court of Canada in *R. v. Logan* (1990), 58 C.C.C. (3d) 391, 73 D.L.R. (4th) 40, [1990] 2 S.C.R. 731; *R. v. Martineau* (1990), 58 C.C.C. (3d) 353, [1990] 2 S.C.R. 633, 79 C.R. (3d) 129.

With great respect, I do not think that the cases of *Logan* or *Martineau* have anything to do with the proper standard of care to apply in cases involving criminal negligence.

In my opinion, much of the argument as to the requirement of a subjective intent when dealing with the offence of criminal negligence is misdirected. The crime of criminal negligence is negligence. There is no need to import the concept of a subjective intent in order to obtain a conviction. The crime is the well recognized tort of civil negligence; the sins of omission and commission that cause injury to one's neighbour, elevated to a crime by their magnitude of wanton and reckless disregard for the lives and safety of others.

However, having accepted that the court is still bound by the objective approach, it is clear to me that the charge to the jury under appeal with respect to MacLean was deficient. ... Before McLean can be held jointly culpable with Gingrich on the facts of this case, the Crown must prove beyond a reasonable doubt, that at the time of the accident, McLean had the same or similar knowledge as Gingrich had as to the condition of the braking system on the tractor and trailer making up the defective unit.

Most courts follow *Gingrich and McLean* as interpreting criminal negligence as an objective form of fault, especially in light of the next two cases.

---

In *R. v. Hundal* (1993), 79 C.C.C. (3d) 97, the accused was charged with dangerous driving causing death. The accused, while driving an overloaded dump truck, proceeded into an intersection against a red light and killed the driver of a car which had moved into the intersection on a green light. The trial judge rejected the accused's explanation that he was only a short distance from the intersection when the light turned amber and because it was dangerous to try and stop he made a decision to go through the amber light. The accused's appeal to the Supreme Court of Canada was dismissed, Cory J. stating for the court:

> The appellant contends that the prison sentence which may be imposed for a breach of s. 233 (now s. 249) makes it evident that an accused cannot be convicted without proof beyond a reasonable doubt of a subjective mental element of an intention to drive dangerously. Certainly every crime requires proof of an act or failure to act, coupled with an element of fault which is termed the *mens rea*.
>
> In my view, to insist on a subjective mental element in connection with driving offences would be to deny reality. It cannot be forgotten that the operation of a motor vehicle is, as I have said so very often, automatic and with little conscious thought. It is simply inappropriate to apply a subjective test in determining whether an accused is guilty of dangerous driving.
>
> Although an objective test must be applied to the offence of dangerous driving, it will remain open to the accused to raise a reasonable doubt that a reasonable person would have been aware of the risks in the accused's conduct. The test must be applied with some measure of flexibility. That is to say the objective test should not be applied in a vacuum but rather in the context of the events surrounding the incident.
>
> ... In summary, the *mens rea* for the offence of dangerous driving should be assessed objectively but in the context of all the events surrounding the incident. That approach will satisfy the dictates both of common sense and fairness. As a general rule, personal factors need not be taken into account. This flows from the licensing requirement for driving which assures that all who drive have a reasonable standard of physical health and capability, mental health and a knowledge of the reasonable standard required of all licensed drivers.
>
> In light of the licensing requirement and the nature of driving offences, a modified objective test satisfies the constitutional minimum fault requirement for s. 233 (now s. 249) of the *Criminal Code* and is eminently well suited to that offence.
>
> It follows then that a trier of fact may convict if satisfied beyond a reasonable doubt that, viewed objectively, the accused was, in the words of the section, driving in a manner that was "dangerous to the public, having regard to all the circumstances, including the nature, condition and use of such place and the amount of traffic that at the time is or might reasonably be expected to be on such place." In making the assessment, the trier of fact should be satisfied that the conduct amounted to a marked departure from the standard of care that a reasonable person would observe in the accused's situation.
>
> Next, if an explanation is offered by the accused, such as a sudden and unexpected onset of illness, then in order to convict, the trier of fact must be satisfied that a reasonable person in similar circumstances ought to have been aware of the risk and of the danger involved in the conduct manifested by the accused. If a jury is determining the facts, they may be instructed with regard to dangerous driving along the lines set out above. There is no necessity for a long or complex charge. Neither the section nor the offence requires it. Certainly the instructions should not be unnecessarily confused by any references to advertent or inadvertent negligence. The offence can be readily assessed by jurors who can arrive at a conclusion based on common sense and their own everyday experiences.

Let us now consider whether the modified objective test was properly applied in this case. The trial judge carefully examined the circumstances of the accident. He took into account the busy downtown traffic, the weather conditions, and the mechanical conditions of the accused vehicle. He concluded, in my view very properly, that the appellant's manner of driving represented a gross departure from the standard of a reasonably prudent driver. No explanation was offered by the accused that could excuse his conduct. There is no reason for interfering with the trial judge's finding of fact and application of the law.

In the result the appeal must be dismissed.

La Forest J. concurred, adding:

I would simply add that both in its wording and object (it is a *quasi*-regulatory offence), this provision differs from the general offence of criminal negligence which, concurring with Wilson J. (in *Tutton v. Tutton*,) I concluded required subjective *mens rea*.

In *R. v. Creighton*, the Supreme Court of Canada considered the constitutionality of the offence of the unlawful act of manslaughter. This aspect of the case is explored below. The court also spoke about the objective test for the unlawful act of manslaughter and for criminal negligence.

### R. v. Creighton
Supreme Court of Canada
(1993), 83 C.C.C. (3d) 346

McLACHLIN J.: … I respectfully differ from the Chief Justice on the nature of the objective test used to determine the *mens rea* for crimes of negligence. In my view, the approach advocated by the Chief Justice personalizes the objective test to the point where it devolves into a subjective test, thus eroding the minimum standard of care which Parliament has laid down by the enactment of offences of manslaughter and penal negligence.

By way of background, it may be useful to restate what I understand the jurisprudence to date to have established regarding crimes of negligence and the objective test. The *mens rea* of a criminal offence may be either subjective or objective, subject to the principle of fundamental justice that the moral fault of the offence must be proportionate to its gravity and penalty. Subjective *mens rea* requires that the accused have intended the consequences of his or her acts, or that, knowing of the probable consequences of those acts, the accused have proceeded recklessly in the face of the risk. The requisite intent or knowledge may be inferred directly from what the accused said or says about his or her mental state, or indirectly from the act and its circumstances. Even in the latter case, however, it is concerned with "what was actually going on in the mind of this particular accused at the time in question": L'Heureux-Dubé J. in *R. v. Martineau*, … at p. 367, quoting Stuart, Canadian Criminal Law, 2nd ed. (1987), p. 121.

Objective *mens rea*, on the other hand, is not concerned with what the accused intended or knew. Rather, the mental fault lies in failure to direct the mind to a risk which the reasonable person would have appreciated. Objective *mens rea* is not concerned with what was actually in the accused's mind, but with what should have been there, had the accused proceeded reasonably.

It is now established that a person may be held criminally responsible for negligent conduct on the objective test, and that this alone does not violate the principle of fundamental justice that the moral fault of the accused must be commensurate with the gravity of the offence and its penalty: *R. v. Hundal* (1993), 79 C.C.C. (3d) 97.

However, as stated in *Martineau*, it is appropriate that those who cause harm intentionally should be punished more severely than those who cause harm inadvertently. Moreover, the constitutionality of crimes of negligence is also subject to the caveat that acts of ordinary negligence may not suffice to justify imprisonment: *R. v. Sault Ste Marie (City)* (1978), 40 C.C.C. (2d) 353; *R. v. Sansregret* (1985), 18 C.C.C. (3d) 223. To put it in the terms used in *Hundal*: The negligence must constitute a "marked departure" from the standard of the reasonable person. The law does not lightly brand a person as a criminal. For this reason, I am in agreement with the Chief Justice in *R. v. Finlay*, ... that the word "careless" in an underlying firearms offence must be read as requiring a marked departure from the constitutional norm.

It follows from this requirement, affirmed in *Hundal*, that in an offence based on unlawful conduct, a predicate offence involving carelessness or negligence must also be read as requiring a "marked departure" from the standard of the reasonable person. As pointed out in *DeSousa*, the underlying offence must be constitutionally sound.

To this point, the Chief Justice and I are not, as I perceive it, in disagreement. The difference between our approaches turns on the extent to which personal characteristics of the accused may affect liability under the objective test. Here we enter territory in large part uncharted. To date, debate has focused on whether an objective test for *mens rea* is ever available in the criminal law; little has been said about how, assuming it is applicable, it is to be applied. In *R. v. Hundal*, supra, it was said that the *mens rea* of dangerous driving should be assessed objectively in the context of all the events surrounding the incident. But the extent to which those circumstances include personal mental or psychological frailties of the accused was not explored in depth. In these circumstances, we must begin with the fundamental principles of criminal law.

### Underlying Principles

The debate about the degree to which personal characteristics should be reflected in the objective test for fault in offences of penal negligence engages two fundamental concepts of criminal law.

The first concept is the notion that the criminal law may properly hold people who engage in risky activities to a minimum standard of care, judged by what a reasonable person in all the circumstances would have done. This notion posits a uniform standard for all persons engaging in the activity, regardless of their background, education or psychological disposition.

The second concept is the principle that the morally innocent not be punished *Reference re: s. 94(2) of Motor Vehicle Act* (1985), 23 C.C.C. (3d) 289; *R. v. Gosset*, S.C.C., No. 22523, September 9, 1993, reasons of Lamer C.J.C. at p. 20. This principle is the foundation of the requirement of criminal law that the accused must have a guilty mind, or *mens rea*.

I agree with the Chief Justice that the rule that the morally innocent not be punished in the context of the objective test requires that the law refrain from holding a person criminally responsible if he or she is not capable of appreciating the risk. Where I differ from the Chief Justice is in his designation of the sort of educational, experiential and so-called "habitual" factors personal to the accused which can be taken into account. The Chief Justice, while in principle advocating a uniform standard of care for all, in the result seems to contemplate a standard of care which varies with the background and predisposition of each accused. Thus an inexperienced, uneducated, young person, like the accused in *R. v. Naglik*, S.C.C. Nos. 22490 and 22636, September 9, 1993, could be acquitted, even though she does not meet the standard of the reasonable person: reasons of the Chief Justice, at p. 24. On the other hand, a person with special experience, like Mr. Creighton in this case, or the appellant police officer in *R. v. Gosset*, supra, will be held to a higher standard than the ordinary reasonable person.

I must respectfully dissent from this extension of the objective test for criminal fault. In my view, considerations of principle and policy dictate the maintenance of a single, uniform legal standard of care for such offences, subject to one exception: incapacity to appreciate the nature of the risk which the activity in question entails.

This principle that the criminal law will not convict the morally innocent does not, in my view, require consideration of personal factors short of incapacity. The criminal law, while requiring mental fault as an element of a conviction, has steadfastly rejected the idea that a person's personal characteristics can (short of incapacity) excuse the person from meeting the standard of conduct imposed by the law.

In summary, I can find no support in criminal theory for the conclusion that protection of the morally innocent requires a general consideration of individual excusing conditions. The principle comes into play only at the point where the person is shown to lack the capacity to appreciate the nature and quality or the consequences of his or her acts. Apart from this, we are all, rich and poor, wise and naive, held to the minimum standards of conduct prescribed by the criminal law. This conclusion is dictated by a fundamental proposition of social organization. As Justice Oliver Wendell Holmes wrote in The Common Law (1881), p. 108: "… when men live in society, a certain average of conduct, a sacrifice of individual peculiarities going beyond a certain point, is necessary to the general welfare."

The ambit of the principle that the morally innocent shall not be convicted has developed in large part in the context of crimes of subjective fault—crimes where the accused must be shown to have actually intended or foreseen the consequences of his or her conduct. In crimes of this type, personal characteristics of the accused have been held to be relevant only to the extent that they tend to prove or disprove an element of the offence. Since intention or knowledge of the risk is an element of such offences, personal factors can come into play. But beyond this, personal characteristics going to lack of capacity are considered under the introductory sections of the Code defining the conditions of criminal responsibility and have generally been regarded as irrelevant.

What then is the situation for crimes of inadvertence? Here actual intention or knowledge is not a factor; hence personal characteristics are not admissible on that ground. Nor, in my view, can a case be made for considering them on any other basis, except in so far as they may show that the accused lacked the capacity to appreciate the risk. This appears to be the settled policy of the law, applied for centuries to offences involving manslaughter or penal negligence based on objectively assessed fault. Here, as in crimes of subjective intent, the courts have rejected the contention that the standard prescribed by the law should take into account the individual peculiarities of the accused, short of incapacity.

LAMER C.J. (Sopinka, Iacobucci, and Major JJ. concurring): Since the decision of this court in *Reference re: s. 94(2) of Motor Vehicle Act* (1985), 23 C.C.C. (3d) 289 at p. 297, 24 D.L.R. (4th) 536, [1985] 2 S.C.R. 486, courts have been "empowered, indeed required, to measure the content of legislation" against the principles of fundamental justice contained in s. 7 of the Charter, and specifically, to ensure that the morally innocent not be punished. In *R. v. Vaillancourt* (1987), 39 C.C.C. (3d) 118, 47 D.L.R. (4th) 399, [1987] 2 S.C.R. 636, I emphasized that the guiding principle underlying the constitutional analysis of fault in criminal law is that the state cannot punish a person as morally blameworthy unless such blameworthiness has been established. For example, as I stated in *Vaillancourt*, at p. 134, if the purpose of a crime is to punish a person for theft, the elements of that crime must include proof beyond a reasonable doubt of dishonesty.

In *Vaillancourt*, I emphasized that the hallmark of murder is that there must be some special mental element with respect to death which gives rise to the moral blameworthiness which justifies the stigma and sentence attached to a murder conviction. As I said:

> … murder is distinguished from manslaughter only by the mental element with respect to the death. *It is thus clear that there must be some special mental element with respect to the death before a culpable homicide can be treated as a murder.* That special mental element gives rise to the moral blameworthiness which justifies the stigma and sentence attached to a murder conviction. I am presently of the view that it is a principle of fundamental justice that a conviction for murder cannot rest on anything less than proof beyond a reasonable doubt of subjective foresight.

It is now well established that there is a group of offences, albeit a small group, that requires a subjectively determined culpable mental state in relation to the prohibited result. As I said in *Vaillancourt*, *supra*, at p. 134:

> But, whatever the minimum *mens rea* for the act or the result may be, there are, though very few in number, certain crimes where, because of the special nature of the stigma attached to a conviction therefor or the available penalties, the principles of fundamental justice require a *mens rea* reflecting the particular nature of that crime.

Subsequent decisions of this court, notably *R. v. Hundal* (1993), 79 C.C.C. (3d) 97, [1993] 1 S.C.R. 867, 19 C.R. (4th) 169, and *R. v. DeSousa* (1992), 76 C.C.C. (3d) 124, 95 D.L.R. (4th) 595, [1992] 2 S.C.R. 944, make it clear that there is no general constitutional principle requiring subjective foresight for criminal offences. In other words, an objective fault requirement is constitutionally sufficient for a broad range of offences other than those falling within the relatively small group of offences alluded to in *Vaillancourt*. [*Hundal* and *DeSousa* are set out in this chapter.]

The only basis upon which subjective foresight of death or the risk of death could be found to be constitutionally required in the case of unlawful act manslaughter, therefore, would be to find that the offence is one of those crimes which "because of the special nature of the stigma attached to a conviction therefor or the available penalties, the principles of fundamental justice require a *mens rea* reflecting the particular nature of that crime": see *R. v. Vaillancourt, per* Lamer J., at p. 134.

In my view, the stigma which attaches to a conviction for unlawful act manslaughter is significant, but does not approach the opprobrium reserved in our society for those who *knowingly* or *intentionally* take the life of another. It is for this reason that manslaughter developed as a separate offence from murder at common law.

What then is the constitutionally required fault element with respect to unlawful act manslaughter? In this regard, the recent decision of this court in *DeSousa* is instructive. At issue in that case was the constitutional sufficiency of the offence of unlawfully causing bodily harm (s. 269 of the *Code*). The unanimous court (Sopinka, Gonthier, Cory, McLachlin and Iacobucci JJ.), speaking through Sopinka J., found that a fault requirement based on objective foreseeability of the risk of bodily harm, coupled with the fault requirement of the predicate unlawful act (which itself must be constitutionally sufficient), satisfies the principles of fundamental justice under s. 7 of the Charter.

I am of the view that while there is a general constitutional requirement that a mental element must relate to the consequences of an underlying act where an offence is structured in that fashion, the existence of that mental element may be established in one of two ways. First, for offences where a consequence forms the essence of an offence, such that it can be said that the pith and substance of the offence includes a particular consequence, as is the case with death in the offence of unlawful act manslaughter and with bodily harm in the offence of unlawfully causing bodily harm, a fault element must be demonstrated beyond a reasonable doubt in relation to that consequence. Secondly, for offences where a consequence forms part of the *actus reus* of an offence, but where the essence of the offence is conduct which is inherently risky to life or limb, such offences are therefore presumed to involve objective foresight of the risk. In other words, proof of the accused having engaged in prohibited conduct which is such that any reasonable person would inevitably have foreseen the risk involved, will serve as a substitute for objective foresight, relieving the prosecution from having to introduce additional evidence to prove the existence of such foresight. The possibility of satisfying a constitutional requirement by means of such a substituted element was discussed in *Vaillancourt, supra*, at p. 136, where I stated the following:

> Finally, the legislature, rather than simply eliminating any need to prove the essential element, may substitute proof of a different element. In my view, this will be constitutionally valid only if upon proof beyond a reasonable doubt of the substituted element it would be unreasonable for the trier of fact not to be satisfied beyond reasonable doubt of the existence of the essential element.

Examples of the class of offences where a substituted element for proof of foreseeability will satisfy s. 7 of the Charter are few, but would include offences such as impaired driving causing bodily harm (s. 255(2)), impaired driving causing death (s. 255(3)), dangerous operation causing bodily harm (s. 249(3)) and dangerous operation causing death (s. 249(4)). What these offences have in common is that the moral blameworthiness of the offence stems from the conduct of driving a car in a fashion which creates a high risk of injury. Whether such an injury leads to bodily harm or death will increase the seriousness of the punishment that will flow from a conviction, but the result does not alter the essence of the moral blameworthiness being punished.

Thus, as I stated, unlawful act manslaughter falls into the class of offences where a mental element in relation to the consequence must be established, but in any event, I find the stigma attached to a conviction for culpable homicide, albeit culpable homicide which is not murder, to be significant enough to require, at a minimum, objective foresight of the risk of death in order for the offence to comply with s. 7 of the Charter.

[Lamer C.J. then articulated the objective standard of fault he would require.]

An accused can only be held to the standard of a reasonable person if the accused was capable, in the circumstances of the offence, of attaining that standard. Consequently, in determining whether a reasonable person in the circumstances of the accused would have foreseen the risk of death arising from the unlawful act, the trier of fact must pay particular attention to any human frailties which might have rendered the accused incapable of having foreseen what the reasonable person would have foreseen. If the criminal law were to judge every accused by the inflexible standard of the monolithic "reasonable person," even where the accused could not possibly have attained that standard, the result, as Stuart notes, would be "absolute responsibility" for such persons: *Canadian Criminal Law: A Treatise*, 2nd ed. (1987), p. 192. H.L.A. Hart advanced a similar argument in "Negligence, *Mens Rea* and Criminal Responsibility" in *Punishment and Responsibility* (1968), p. 154:

> If our conditions of liability are invariant and not flexible, i.e. if they are not adjusted to the capacities of the accused, then some individuals will be held liable for negligence though they could not have helped their failure to comply with the standard.

The reasonable person will be invested with any *enhanced* foresight the accused may have enjoyed by virtue of his or her membership in a group with special experience or knowledge related to the conduct giving rise to the offence. For example, in *Gosset* the accused police officer's experience and training in the handling of firearms is relevant to the standard of care under s. 86(2) of the *Criminal Code* concerning the careless use of firearms. In the present case, the reasonable person should be deemed to possess Mr. Creighton's considerable experience in drug use.

It must be emphasized that this is *not* a subjective test: if a reasonable person with the frailties of the accused would nevertheless have appreciated the risk, and the accused did not in fact appreciate the risk, the accused must be convicted.

The rationale of incorporating capacity into the objective determination of fault is analogous to the rationale underlying the defence of mistake of fact in criminal law, where an accused who has an honest and reasonably held belief in an incorrect set of facts, and acts on the basis of those facts, is excused from punishment for the resulting harm. Human frailties which may affect the capacity of an accused to recognize the risks of unlawful conduct must be considered, however, not because they result in the accused believing in an incorrect set of facts, but rather because they render the accused incapable of perceiving the correct set of facts. It is, however, only those human frailties which relate to an accused's capacity to appreciate the risk in question that may be considered in this inquiry.

I shall now turn to elaborating what "human frailties" may factor into the objective test. It is perhaps best to begin by stating clearly what is not included. Intoxication or impairment through drug use which occurs as a result of voluntary consumption cannot serve to vitiate liability for the risks created by the negligent conduct of an accused. Additionally, a sudden and temporary incapacity to appreciate risk due to exigent circumstances (an emergency which diverts one's attention from an activity, for example) is not properly considered under the third part of the test, but may well result in an acquittal under the first part of the test, that is, would a reasonable person's attention in the same circumstances of the accused have been diverted from that activity.

Human frailties encompass personal characteristics habitually affecting an accused's awareness of the circumstances which create risk. Such characteristics must be relevant to the ability to perceive the particular risk. For example, while illiteracy may excuse the failure to take care with a hazardous substance identifiable only by a label, as the accused may be unable, in this case, to apprehend the relevant facts, illiteracy may not be relevant to the failure to take care with a firearm. This attention to the context of the offence and the nature of the activity is explored in greater detail below.

It should be emphasized that the relevant characteristics must be traits which the accused could not control or otherwise manage in the circumstances. For example, while a person with cataracts cannot be faulted for having reduced vision, he or she may be expected to avoid activity in which that limitation will either create risk or render him or her unable to manage risk which is inherent in an activity (driving, for example). The reasonable person is expected to compensate for his or her frailties, to the extent he or she is conscious of them and able to do so.

Applied to the facts of this case, therefore, one must ask whether the reasonable individual in the circumstances of the offence and with Mr. Creighton's experience in drug use would have been aware of the risk of death arising from the injection of the deceased with the cocaine. In reviewing the evidence against Mr. Creighton, the trial judge stated the following:

> The accused's evidence [is] that he would permit no one but himself to measure the dose of cocaine that he would accept by injection into his own body. That is evidence capable of the inference which I draw, that Mr. Creighton on October 27, 1989, was

knowledgeable of the dangerous prospensity of that narcotic to cause death or serious bodily harm.

Subsequently, the trial judge summarized his findings as follows:

> Mr. Creighton swore, in effect, that he was and is an experienced cocaine user. He said that he insisted on measuring out his own quantity of cocaine intake. From that evidence alone, I draw the inference that at the time he gave part of that narcotic he had purchased to Miss Martin, he knew she was going to ingest it immediately. *He also knew that he was giving her a very dangerous, volatile, lawfully prohibited narcotic, capable of causing death or serious bodily harm.*

In instructing himself on the law with respect to unlawful act manslaughter, the trial judge, with respect, erred in adopting the standard of objective foreseeability contained in the earlier line of cases which referred to "the risk of some harm … albeit not serious harm": *R. v. Church*, *supra*, at p. 213, and *R. v. Tennant*, *supra*, at p. 96. However, whether or not a reasonable person in the circumstances of the appellant would have foreseen a risk of death as opposed to merely a risk of harm arising from the unlawful act is an inquiry that is made unnecessary given the finding above that the appellant actually did appreciate the risk of death resulting from his injection of the cocaine into the deceased.

Therefore, with respect to the test for determining if a new trial is required under s. 686(1)(b)(iii) of the *Code*, I conclude that, although the learned trial judge erred in law in not expressly considering the capacity of the appellant to appreciate the risk resulting from his conduct, and in instructing himself on the proper test for assessing foreseeability under s. 222(5)(a) of the *Code*, it is clear from his findings that had he instructed himself properly, he would have necessarily arrived at the same verdict: see *Colpitts v. The Queen*, [1966] 1 C.C.C. 146 at p. 149, 52 D.L.R. (2d) 416, [1965] S.C.R. 739. Therefore, I find that, despite the trial judge's error, there is no substantial wrong or miscarriage of justice which would require a new trial.

McLACHLIN J. (La Forest, L'Heureux-Dubé, Gonthier, and Cory JJ. concurring): I respectfully disagree with the Chief Justice on two points. The first is his conclusion that the common law offence of manslaughter is unconstitutional because it does not require foreseeability of death. The Chief Justice concludes that the offence of manslaughter must be "read up" to include this requirement in order to bring it into line with the principles of fundamental justice enshrined in s. 7 of the *Canadian Charter of Rights and Freedoms*, and in particular with the principle that the moral fault required for conviction be commensurate with the gravity and the stigma of the offence. In my view, the offence of unlawful act manslaughter, as defined by our courts and those in other jurisdictions for many centuries, is entirely consistent with the principles of fundamental justice. There is no need to read up its requirements; as it stands, it conforms to the Charter.

The second point on which I respectfully diverge is the Chief Justice's conclusion that the standard of care on the objective test in manslaughter and in crimes of negligence varies with the degree of experience, education, and other personal characteristics of the accused. This leads the Chief Justice to hold Mr. Creighton to a higher standard of care than that of the reasonable person in determining if he would have foreseen the risk in question, because of Creighton's long experience as a drug user. For the reasons set out below I believe the appropriate standard to be that of the reasonable person in all the circumstances of the case. The criminal law is concerned with setting minimum standards of conduct; the standards are not to be altered because the accused possesses more or less experience than the hypothetical average reasonable person.

Before venturing on analysis, I think it appropriate to introduce a note of caution. We are here concerned with a common law offence virtually as old as our system of criminal law. It has been applied in innumerable cases around the world. And it has been honed and refined over the centuries. Because of its residual nature, it may lack the logical symmetry of more modern statutory offences, but it has stood the practical test of time. Could all this be the case, one asks, if the law violates our fundamental notions of justice, themselves grounded in the history of the common law? Perhaps. Nevertheless, it must be with considerable caution that a twentieth century court approaches the invitation which has been put before us: to strike out, or alternatively, rewrite, the offence of manslaughter on the ground that this is necessary to bring the law into conformity with the principles of fundamental justice.

To the extent that stigma is relied on as requiring foreseeability of the risk of death in the offence of manslaughter, I find it unconvincing. The most important feature of the stigma of manslaughter is the stigma which is *not* attached to it. The *Criminal Code* confines manslaughter to non-intentional homicide. A person convicted of manslaughter is *not* a murderer. He or she did *not* intend to kill someone. A person has been killed through the fault of another, and that is always serious. But by the very act of calling the killing *manslaughter* the law indicates that the killing is less blameworthy than murder. It may arise from negligence, or it may arise as the unintended result of a lesser unlawful act. The conduct is blameworthy and must be punished, but its stigma does not approach that of murder.

I conclude that the standard of *mens rea* required for manslaughter is appropriately tailored to the seriousness of the offence.

The Chief Justice correctly observes that the criminal law has traditionally aimed at symmetry between the *mens rea* and the prohibited consequences of the offence. The *actus reus* generally consists of an act bringing about a prohibited consequence, *e.g.*, death. Criminal law theory suggests that the accompanying *mens rea* must go to the prohibited consequence. The moral fault of the accused lies in the act of bringing about that consequence. The Chief Justice reasons from this proposition that since manslaughter is an offence involving the prohibited act of killing another, a *mens rea* of foreseeability of harm is insufficient; what is required is foreseeability of death.

I turn first to the distinction between appreciation of the risk of bodily harm and the risk of death in the context of manslaughter. In my view, when the risk of bodily harm is combined with the established rule that a wrongdoer must take his victim as he finds him and the fact that death did in fact occur, the distinction disappears. The accused who asserts that the risk of death was not foreseeable is in effect asserting that a normal person would not have died in these circumstances, and that he could not foresee the peculiar vulnerability of the victim. Therefore, he says, he should be convicted only of assault causing bodily harm or some lesser offence. This is to abrogate the thin-skull rule that requires that the wrongdoer take his victim as he finds him. Conversely, to combine the test of reasonable foreseeability of bodily harm with the thin-skull rule is to mandate that in some cases, foreseeability of the risk of bodily harm alone will properly result in a conviction for manslaughter.

What the appellant asks us to do, then, is to abandon the "thin-skull" rule. It is this rule which, on analysis, is alleged to be unjust. Such a conclusion I cannot accept. The law has consistently set its face against such a policy. It decrees that the aggressor must take his victim as he finds him.

In *R. v. Smithers*, at p. 437, Dickson J., writing for a unanimous court, confirmed this principle:

> It is a well-recognized principle that one who assaults another must take his victim as he finds him. ...
>
> Although causation in civil cases differs from that in a criminal case, the "thin skulled man" may appear in the criminal law as in the civil law. ... Even if the unlawful act, alone, would not have caused the death, it was still a legal cause so long as it contributed in some way to the death.

The thin-skull rule is a good and useful principle. It requires aggressors, once embarked on their dangerous course of conduct which may foreseeably injure others, to take responsibility for all the consequences that ensue, even to death. That is not, in my view, contrary to fundamental justice. Yet the consequence of adopting the amendment proposed by the Chief Justice would be to abrogate this principle in cases of manslaughter.

In fact, when manslaughter is viewed in the context of the thin-skull principle, the disparity diminishes between the *mens rea* of the offence and its consequence. The law does not posit the average victim. It says the aggressor must take the victim as he finds him. Wherever there is a risk of harm, there is also a practical risk that some victims may die as a result of the harm. At this point, the test of harm and death merge.

It is important to distinguish between criminal law theory, which seeks the ideal of absolute symmetry between *actus reus* and *mens rea*, and the constitutional requirements of the Charter. As the Chief Justice has stated several times, "the Constitution does not always guarantee the 'ideal'": *R. v. Lippé* (1991), 64 C.C.C. (3d) 513 at p. 532, [1991] 2 S.C.R. 114, 5 C.R.R. (2d) 31; *R. v. Wholesale Travel Group Inc.* (1991), 67 C.C.C. (3d) 193 at p. 213, 84 D.L.R. (4th) 161, [1991] 3 S.C.R. 154; *R. v. Finlay*, S.C.C., No. 22596, released concurrently, at p. 12.

I know of no authority for the proposition that the *mens rea* of an offence must always attach to the precise consequence which is prohibited as a matter of constitutional necessity. The relevant constitutional principles have been cast more broadly. No person can be sent to prison without *mens rea*, or a guilty mind, and the seriousness of the offence must not be disproportionate to the degree of moral fault. Provided an element of mental fault or moral culpability is present, and provided that it is proportionate to the seriousness and consequences of the offence charged, the principles of fundamental justice are satisfied.

The need to deter dangerous conduct which may injure others and in fact may kill the peculiarly vulnerable supports the view that death need not be objectively foreseeable, only bodily injury. To tell people that if they embark on dangerous conduct which foreseeably may cause bodily harm which is neither trivial nor transient, and which in fact results in death, that they will not be held responsible for the death but only for aggravated assault, is less likely to deter such conduct than a message that they will be held responsible for the death, albeit under manslaughter not murder. Given the finality of death and the absolute unacceptability of killing another human being, it is not amiss to preserve the test which promises the greatest measure of deterrence, provided the penal consequences of the offence are not disproportionate. This is achieved by retaining the test of foreseeability of bodily harm in the offence of manslaughter.

[McLachlin J. then articulated the objective standard of fault she would require.]

I respectfully differ from the Chief Justice on the nature of the objective test used to determine the *mens rea* for crimes of negligence. In my view, the approach advocated by the Chief Justice personalizes the objective test to the point where it devolves into a subjective test, thus eroding the minimum standard of care which Parliament has laid down by the enactment of offences of manslaughter and penal negligence.

I agree with the Chief Justice that the rule that the morally innocent not be punished in the context of the objective test requires that the law refrain from holding a person criminally responsible if he or she is not capable of appreciating the risk. Where I differ from the Chief Justice is in his designation of the sort of educational, experiential and so-called "habitual" factors personal to the accused which can be taken into account. The Chief Justice, while in principle advocating a uniform standard of care for all, in the result seems to contemplate a standard of care which varies with the background and predisposition of each accused. Thus an inexperienced, uneducated, young person, like the accused in *R. v. Naglik*, S.C.C. Nos. 22490 and 22636, September 9, 1993, could be acquitted, even though she does not meet the standard of the reasonable person: reasons of the Chief Justice, at p. 24. On the other hand, a person with special experience, like Mr. Creighton in this case, or the appellant police officer in *R. v. Gosset*, *supra*, will be held to a higher standard than the ordinary reasonable person.

I must respectfully dissent from this extension of the objective test for criminal fault. In my view, considerations of principle and policy dictate the maintenance of a single, uniform legal standard of care for such offences, subject to one exception: incapacity to appreciate the nature of the risk which the activity in question entails.

In summary, I can find no support in criminal theory for the conclusion that protection of the morally innocent requires a general consideration of individual excusing conditions. The principle comes into play only at the point where the person is shown to lack the capacity to appreciate the nature and quality or the consequences of his or her acts. Apart from this, we are all, rich and poor, wise and naïve, held to the minimum standards of conduct prescribed by the criminal law. This conclusion is dictated by a fundamental proposition of social organization. As Justice Oliver Wendell Holmes wrote in *The Common Law* (1881), p. 108: "... when men live in society, a certain average of conduct, a sacrifice of individual peculiarities going beyond a certain point, is necessary to the general welfare."

To the principle of a uniform minimum standard for crimes having an objective test there is but one exception—incapacity to appreciate the risk. Justice Holmes, speaking of the failure to take reasonable care, put it this way (*ibid.*, p. 109):

> There are exceptions to the principle that every man is presumed to possess ordinary capacity to avoid harm to his neighbours, which illustrate the rule, and also the moral basis of liability in general. When a man has a distinct defect of such a nature that all can recognize it *as making certain precautions impossible*, he will not be held answerable for not taking them.

(Emphasis added.)

Consistent with these principles, this court has rejected experiential, educational and psychological defences falling short of incapacity. Thus it has excluded personal characteristics short of incapacity in considering the characteristics of the "ordinary person" for the defence of provocation for the offence of murder: *Salamon v. The Queen* (1959), 123 C.C.C. 1, 17 D.L.R. (2d) 685, [1959] S.C.R. 404; *R. v. Hill, supra*, at pp. 338-9. One commentator sums up the non-exculpatory characteristics as follows: "Thus, the temperament, peculiar psychological make-up, unusual excitability or pugnaciousness of an accused person cannot be taken into account by the jury for the purpose of determining the level of self-control the accused should have shown. The ordinary person is none of these things": M. Naeem Rauf, "The Reasonable Man Test in the Defence of Provocation: What Are the Reasonable Man's Attributes and Should the Test Be Abolished?", 30 C.L.Q. 73 (1987-88), at p. 79.

To summarize, the fundamental premises upon which our criminal law rests mandate that personal characteristics not directly relevant to an element of the offence serve as excuses only at the point where they establish incapacity, where the incapacity be the ability to appreciate the nature and quality of one's conduct in the context of intentional crimes, or the incapacity to appreciate the risk involved in one's conduct in the context of crimes of manslaughter or penal negligence. The principle that we eschew conviction of the morally innocent requires no more.

Mental disabilities short of incapacity generally do not suffice to negative criminal liability for criminal negligence. The explanations for why a person fails to advert to the risk inherent in the activity he or she is undertaking are legion. They range from simple absent-mindedness to attributes related to age, education and culture. To permit such a subjective assessment would be "co-extensive with the judgment of each individual, which would be as variable as the length of the foot of each individual" leaving "so vague a line as to afford no rule at all, the degree of judgment belonging to each individual being infinitely various": *Vaughan v. Menlove* (1837), 3 Bing. (N.C.) 468 at p. 475, 132 E.R. 490; see A.M. Linden, *Canadian Tort Law*, 4th ed. (1988), pp. 116-7. Provided the capacity to appreciate the risk is present, lack of education and psychological predispositions serve as no excuse for criminal conduct, although they may be important factors to consider in sentencing.

The trial judge properly found that Mr. Creighton committed the unlawful act of trafficking in cocaine. He also found that he was guilty of the criminal negligence, using the standard which I view as correct, the standard of the reasonable person. The only remaining question, on the view I take of the law, was whether the reasonable person in all the circumstances would have foreseen the risk of bodily harm. I am satisfied that the answer to this question must be affirmative. At the very least, a person administering a dangerous drug like cocaine to another has a duty to inform himself as to the precise risk the injection entails and to refrain from administering it unless reasonably satisfied that there is no risk of harm. That was not the case here, as the trial judge found.

The conviction was properly entered and should not be disturbed. Like the Chief Justice, I find it unnecessary to consider the alternative ground of manslaughter by criminal negligence.

*Appeal dismissed.*

---

For discussion of *Creighton*, see I. Grant and C. Boyle, "Equality, Harm and Vulnerability: Homicide and Sexual Assault Post-Creighton" (1993), 23 C.R. (4th) 252; P. Healy, "The Creighton Quartet: Enigma Variations in a Lower Key" (1993), 23 C.R. (4th) 265; and A. Brudner, "Proportionality, Stigma and Discretion" (1996), 38 *Crim. L.Q.* 302.

## IV. CONSTITUTIONAL CONSIDERATIONS

As discussed at the end of the previous chapter, s. 7 of the Charter has had a significant impact on minimal levels of fault for both criminal and quasi-criminal offences. *Reference re s. 94(2) of the Motor Vehicle Act (B.C.)* (1985), 23 C.C.C. (3d) 289 (S.C.C.) and *R. v. Pontes* (1995), 100 C.C.C. (3d) 353 (S.C.C.) established the proposition that some level of fault is required prior to the loss (or potential loss) of liberty by an accused person.

Section 7 of the Charter has also helped shape the fault requirement for true criminal offences. The cases of *R. v. Vaillancourt* (1987), 39 C.C.C. (3d) 118 (S.C.C.) and *R. v. Martineau* (1990), 58 C.C.C. (3d) 353 (S.C.C.) have held that nothing less than subjective foresight is required before an accused person can be convicted of murder. *R. v. Logan* (1990), 58 C.C.C. (3d) 391 (S.C.C.) has held that the phrase "ought to have known" in s. 21(2) of the *Criminal Code* is of no force and effect when applied to the crimes of murder or attempted murder. These fault requirements for murder are addressed in chapter 13. But short of murder, attempted murder, and crimes against humanity (discussed below), something less than subjective fault will suffice for most criminal offences. As long as there is a meaningful fault requirement, s. 7 of the Charter may be satisfied by objective fault components.

For example, in *R. v. Durham* (1992), 76 C.C.C. (3d) 219, the Ontario Court of Appeal held that Parliament could use the civil standard of negligence for the offence of using a firearm in a careless manner or without reasonable precautions for the safety of others (s. 86(2) of the Code). Arbour J.A. stated for the court:

> Generally speaking, there is likely to be more stigma attached to a criminal conviction than to the violation of a non-criminally related statute. Yet not all criminal offences carry the same amount of stigma. The stigma is proportional not only to the gravity of the conduct and of its consequences, but to the level of fault, represented by the mental element, with which the act or omission was performed.
>
> It is constitutionally impermissible for Parliament to treat as murder a conduct devoid of the essential characteristic upon which the stigmatization of murderers came to be based, the moral turpitude represented by the intention to kill. In the same way, if it is his dishonesty that stigmatizes the convicted thief, Parliament will not be permitted, absent justification under s. 1 of the Charter, to brandish as a thief someone who has not been shown to be dishonest. In my opinion, this is the extent to which cases such as *Vaillancourt* … and *Reference re: s. 94(2) of Motor Vehicle Act* … compel the consideration of stigma as a factor from which compliance with s. 7 may be determined. Even though a person convicted of an offence under s. 86(2) of the *Code* will carry the stigma of having a criminal conviction, that is not sufficient to dictate that the offence must contain a subjective mental element.

The Supreme Court of Canada in *R. v. Finlay* (1993), 83 C.C.C. (3d) 513, agreed with Arbour J.A.'s decision and held that an objective test satisfies the *mens rea* requirement for the offence of careless storage of firearms (s. 86(2)). Lamer C.J.C. stated for the Court: "there is not sufficient stigma arising from a conviction under s. 86(2) to require subjective *mens rea*."

In *R. v. Peters* (1991), 69 C.C.C. (3d) 461, the B.C. Court of Appeal held that subjective foresight of consequences was not required for s. 434(a) of the Code, which makes it an offence to wilfully set fire to certain objects. McEachern C.J.B.C. stated:

> It is also apparent that the level of social stigma attaching to a conviction for some offences is a more important consideration than the range of sentence prescribed for that offence. The Supreme Court of Canada has particularized murder, and attempted murder which require an intent to cause death, and theft which requires a measure of dishonesty, as offences which require subjective *mens rea*. It has not provided a schedule of such offences, but it has frequently mentioned that this requirement applies "for only a very few offences" (*Logan*, p. 399). From time to time trial and appellate judges will have to categorize those few offences which require subjective foreseeability.
>
> While I confess I have some difficulty distinguishing levels of social stigma attached to theft as compared with other offences frequently committed for financial gain, I am content, for the purposes of this appeal, to conclude that subjective *mens rea* is not constitutionally required with respect to consequences resulting from a wilful act other than murder or theft caused by a lack of care on the part of the accused.

In *R. v. DeSousa* (1992), 76 C.C.C. (3d) 124, the Supreme Court of Canada held that s. 269 of the Code (unlawfully causing bodily harm) requiring an objective foresight of bodily harm was constitutionally valid under s. 7 of the Charter. Sopinka J. stated for the court:

Although I have concluded by means of statutory interpretation that s. 269 requires objective foresight of the consequences of an accused's unlawful act, the appellant argues that s. 7 of the Charter requires subjective foresight of all consequences which comprise part of the *actus reus* of an offence. The appellant notes that in *R. v. Martineau* (1990), 58 C.C.C. (3d) 353, [1990] 2 S.C.R. 633, 79 C.R. (3d) 129, Lamer C.J.C., speaking for the majority of the court, discussed (at p. 360) a: "… general principle that criminal liability for a particular result is not justified except where the actor possesses a culpable mental state in respect of that result … ." The appellant also relies on *R. v. Metro News Ltd.* (1986), 29 C.C.C. (3d) 35, 32 D.L.R. (4th) 321, 53 C.R. (3d) 289 (Ont. C.A.), leave to appeal refused 29 C.C.C. (3d) 35n, 32 D.L.R. (4th) 321n, [1986] 2 S.C.R. viii, for a similar proposition that (at pp. 54-5):

> … [t]he minimum and necessary mental element required for criminal liability for most crimes is knowledge of the circumstances which make up the *actus reus* of the crime and foresight or intention with respect to any consequence required to constitute the *actus reus* of the crime.

The appellant submits that this authority supports a requirement that the minimum mental element required by s. 7 of the Charter for s. 269 includes an intention to cause bodily harm. …

Lamer C.J.C. stated in *Martineau* (at p. 361) that "[i]f Parliament wishes to deter persons from causing bodily harm during certain offences, then it should punish persons for causing the bodily harm." This is exactly what s. 269 attempts to do. In this particular provision the mental element requirement is composed of both the mental element of the underlying unlawful act and the additional requirement of objective foresight of bodily harm. There is, however, no constitutional requirement that intention, either on an objective or a subjective basis, extend to the consequences of unlawful acts in general.

In *R. v. Hundal* (1993), 79 C.C.C. (3d) 97, set out in a previous section, the Supreme Court of Canada decided that dangerous driving under s. 249 of the Code does not require a subjective awareness of risk.

As discussed above, the court in *R. v. Creighton* (1993), 83 C.C.C. (3d) 346 (S.C.C.) holding that subjective foresight is not required for the unlawful act of manslaughter under s. 222(5)(a). The court was divided on the question whether objective foresight of *death* was required, the majority of the court (per McLachlin J.) holding that the section required only reasonable foreseeability of *bodily harm*.

Most recently, the court in *R. v. Finta* addressed the constitutionalization of fault in the context of crimes against humanity.

### R. v. Finta
Supreme Court of Canada
(1994), 88 C.C.C. (3d) 417

[The accused was charged under s. 7(3.71) of the *Criminal Code* with committing unlawful confinement, robbery, kidnapping, and manslaughter that constitutes a war crime or a crime against humanity as a result of his activities as a senior officer at a concentration camp in Hungary. The trial judge ruled that the jury must determine that the accused was aware of the circumstances that would bring his actions within the definition of war crimes or crimes against humanity; the accused was acquitted. The Crown appealed.]

CORY J. (Lamer C.J., Gonthier, and Major JJ. concurring):  The appellant contends that the deeming mechanism in the *Code* provision presently under consideration is such that an accused charged under s. 7(3.71) may be found guilty *not* of "war crimes" or "crimes against humanity" but of "ordinary" *Code* offences such as manslaughter, confinement or robbery. It is further argued that proof of the *mens rea* with respect to the domestic offences provides the element of personal fault required for offences under s. 7(3.71). Thus, it is submitted, proof of further moral culpability is not required, since once the necessary *mens rea* to confine forcibly, rob or commit manslaughter has been proved, it becomes impossible to maintain that the accused was morally innocent.

I cannot accept that argument. What distinguishes a crime against humanity from any other criminal offence under the Canadian *Criminal Code* is that the cruel and terrible actions which are essential elements of the offence were undertaken in pursuance of a policy of discrimination or persecution of an identifiable group or race. With respect to war crimes, the distinguishing feature is that the terrible actions constituted a violation of the laws of war. Although the term laws of war may appear to be an oxymoron, such laws do exist. War crimes, like crimes against humanity, shock the conscience of all right-thinking people. The offences described in s. 7(3.71) are thus very different from, and far more grievous than, any of the underlying offences.

For example, it cannot be denied that the crimes against humanity alleged in this case, which resulted in the cruel killing of thousands of people, are far more grievous than occasioning the death of a single person by an act which constitutes manslaughter in Canada. To be involved in the confinement, robbing and killing of thousands of people belonging to an identifiable group must, in any view of morality or criminality, be more serious than even the commission of an act which would constitute murder in Canada.

Therefore, while the underlying offences may constitute a base level of moral culpability, Parliament has added a further measure of blameworthiness by requiring that the act or omission constitute a crime against humanity or a war crime. If the jury is not satisfied that this additional element of culpability has been established beyond a reasonable doubt, then the accused cannot be found guilty of a war crime or a crime against humanity.

In *R. v. Vaillancourt*, … this court held that there are certain crimes where, because of the special nature of the unavoidable penalties or of the stigma attached to a conviction, the principles of fundamental justice require a mental blameworthiness or a *mens rea* reflecting the particular nature of that crime. It follows that the question which must be answered is not simply whether the accused is morally innocent, but rather, whether the conduct is sufficiently blameworthy to merit the punishment and stigma that will ensue upon conviction for that particular offence. In the present case there must be taken into account not only the stigma and punishment that will result upon a conviction for the domestic offence, but also the additional stigma and opprobrium that will be suffered by an individual whose conduct has been held to constitute crimes against humanity or war crimes. In reality, upon conviction, the accused will be labelled a war criminal and will suffer the particularly heavy public opprobrium that is reserved for these offences. Further, the sentence which will follow upon conviction will reflect the high degree of moral outrage that society very properly feels toward those convicted of these crimes. ...

It cannot be inferred that someone who robs civilians of their valuables during a war has thereby committed a crime against humanity. To convict someone of an offence when it has not been established beyond a reasonable doubt that he or she was aware of conditions that would bring to his or her actions that requisite added dimension of cruelty and barbarism violates the principles of fundamental justice. The degree of moral turpitude that attaches to crimes against humanity and war crimes must exceed that of the domestic offences of manslaughter or robbery. It follows that the accused must be aware of the conditions which render his or her actions more blameworthy than the domestic offence.

I find support for this position in decisions of this court relating to the constitutional requirements for *mens rea*. In *R. v. Martineau* (1990), 58 C.C.C. (3d) 353, [1990] 2 S.C.R. 633, 79 C.R. (3d) 129, the court struck down s. 213(a) of the *Criminal Code*, R.S.C. 1970, c. C-34. This section provided that the offence of murder would be committed in circumstances where a person caused the death of another while committing or attempting to commit certain named offences, and meant to cause bodily harm for the purpose of committing the underlying offence or to facilitate flight after committing the offence. Murder was deemed to have been committed regardless of whether the person meant to cause death and regardless of whether that person knew that death was likely to result from his or her actions. The majority of the court (*per* Lamer C.J.C.) affirmed that in order to secure a conviction for murder, the principles of fundamental justice required subjective foresight of the consequences of death. As was noted in *R. v. DeSousa* (1992), 76 C.C.C. (3d) 124, 95 D.L.R. (4th) 595, [1992] 2 S.C.R. 944, while it is not a principle of fundamental justice that fault or *mens rea* must be proved as to each separate element of the offence, there must be a meaningful mental element demonstrated relating to a *culpable aspect* of the *actus reus*: see also *R. v. Nguyen* (1990), 59 C.C.C. (3d) 161, [1990] 2 S.C.R. 906, 79 C.R. (3d) 332.

These cases make it clear that in order to constitute a crime against humanity or a war crime, there must be an element of subjective knowledge on the part of the accused of the factual conditions which render the actions a crime against humanity.

Thus, for all the reasons set out earlier, I am in agreement with the majority of the Court of Appeal's assessment that the mental element of a crime against humanity must involve an awareness of the facts or circumstances which would bring the acts within the definition of a crime against humanity. However, I emphasize it is *not* necessary to establish that the accused knew that his or her actions were inhumane. As the majority stated at p. 180 C.C.C., p. 116 D.L.R.:

> ... if the jury accepted the evidence of the various witnesses who described the conditions in the boxcars which transported the Jews away from Szeged, the jury would have no difficulty concluding that the treatment was "inhumane" within the definition of that

word supplied by the trial judge. The jury would then have to determine whether Finta was aware of those conditions. If the jury decided that he was aware of the relevant conditions, the knowledge requirement was established regardless of whether Finta believed those conditions to be inhumane.

Similarly, for war crimes, the Crown would have to establish that the accused knew or was aware of the facts or circumstances that brought his or her actions within the definition of a war crime. That is to say the accused would have to be aware that the facts or circumstances of his or her actions were such that, viewed objectively, they would shock the conscience of all right thinking people.

Alternatively, the *mens rea* requirement of both crimes against humanity and war crimes would be met if it were established that the accused was wilfully blind to the facts or circumstances that would bring his or her actions within the provisions of these offences.

La FOREST J. (L'Heureux-Dubé and McLachlin JJ. concurring): A *mens rea* need only be found in relation to the individually blameworthy elements of a war crime or crime against humanity, not every single circumstance surrounding it. This approach receives support in Canadian domestic law. In *R. v. DeSousa* (1992), 76 C.C.C. (3d) 124 at pp. 139-40, 95 D.L.R. (4th) 595 at pp. 610-2, [1992] 2 S.C.R. 944, this court held that reading in such a requirement for every element of an offence misconstrues and overgeneralizes earlier decisions of this court. Rather, the proper approach, it noted, was that "there must be an element of personal *fault in regard to a culpable aspect* of the *actus reus*, but not necessarily in regard to each and every element of the *actus reus*" (emphasis added). ...

I would add that any stigma attached to being convicted under war crimes legislation does not come from the nature of the offence, but more from the surrounding circumstances of most war crimes. Often it is a question of the scale of the acts in terms of numbers, but that is reflected in the domestic offence; for example, a charge of the kidnapping or manslaughter of a hundred people in the domestic context itself raises a stigma because of the scale, but one that s. 7 is not concerned about. Similarly, the jurisprudence does not allow for stigma that may also result from being convicted of an offence in which the surrounding circumstances are legally irrelevant but public disapproval strong. Thus, one convicted of a planned and deliberate murder can face additional stigma because his or her actions were particularly repulsive or violent, but our system does not make any additional allowance for that.

*Appeal dismissed.*

---

See *Crimes Against Humanity and War Crimes Act*, S.C. 2000, c. 24, ss. 4 and 6, which incorporates the definitions of "genocide," "war crimes," and "crimes against humanity" from the Rome Statute establishing the International Criminal Court. See generally, A. Cassese, *International Criminal Law* (Oxford: Oxford University Press, 2003).

ADDITIONAL READING

- K. Roach, *Criminal Law*, 3rd ed. (Toronto: Irwin Law, 2004), chapter 4;
- A. Mewett and M. Manning, *Criminal Law*, 3rd ed. (Toronto: Butterworths, 1994), at 184 *et seq.*;
- D. Stuart, *Canadian Criminal Law*, 3rd ed. (Toronto: Carswell, 1995), at 139 *et seq.*;
- J.C. Smith and B. Hogan, *Criminal Law*, 6th ed. (London: Butterworths, 1988), at 55 *et seq.*;
- G. Williams, *The Mental Element in Crime* (Jerusalem: Magnes Press, 1965);
- G. Williams, *Criminal Law*, 2nd ed. (London: Stevens and Sons, 1961), at 30 *et seq.*;
- G. Williams, *Textbook of Criminal Law*, 2nd ed. (London: Stevens and Sons, 1983), at 70 *et seq.*;
- W.R. LaFave and A.W. Scott, *Criminal Law*, 2nd ed. (St. Paul, MN: West, 1986), at 212 *et seq.*;
- E. Colvin, *Principles of Criminal Law*, 2nd ed. (Toronto: Carswell, 1991), at 105-27.

# PART THREE

# Extensions of Criminal Liability

# CHAPTER EIGHT

# Participation

Criminal offences are not committed only by people who act alone. Where more than one person is involved, each might be involved in a different way or to a different degree. Thus a central topic among the general principles of criminal liability is the matter of participation. On what basis is a person's involvement in the commission of a criminal offence sufficient for him or her to be held liable as a party to the offence? Between the actual perpetrator of the offence and an innocent bystander lies a broad margin of connection or involvement in the commission of an offence. The law relating to participation defines the principles on which the involvement of someone other than the actual perpetrator is accountable as a party to that offence.

There are four modes of participation identified in ss. 21 and 22 of the Code.

21(1) Parties to offence
    (1) Every one is a party to an offence who
        (a) actually commits it;
        (b) does or omits to do anything for the purpose of aiding any person to commit it; or
        (c) abets any person in committing it.

21(2) Common intention
    (2) Where two or more persons form an intention in common to carry out an unlawful purpose and to assist each other therein and any one of them, in carrying out the common purpose, commits an offence, each of them who knew or ought to have known that the commission of the offence would be a probable consequence of carrying out the common purpose is a party to that offence.

22(1) Person counselling offence
    (1) Where a person counsels another person to be a party to an offence and that other person is afterwards a party to that offence, the person who counselled is a party to that offence, notwithstanding that the offence was committed in a way different from that which was counselled.

22(2) Idem
Every one who counsels another person to be a party to an offence is a party to every offence that the other commits in consequence of the counselling that the person who counselled knew or ought to have known was likely to be committed in consequence of the counselling.

22(3)  Definition of "counsel"

    (3)  For the purposes of this Act, "counsel" includes procure, solicit or incite.

This chapter looks at actual commission, aiding and abetting, common intention, and counselling. These are all distinct modes of participation in a criminal offence and a person found guilty by any one of them is a party to the substantive offence. By contrast, an accessory after the fact is not a party to the offence but is nonetheless liable for facilitating a party's escape. Although an accessory is not a party, the principles relating to accessoryship are considered in the last section of this chapter.

Before beginning with principals (actual commission), it is appropriate to note here that Parliament has recently created a new type of offence with regard to organized crime and terrorism. These are offences in which the element of conduct is defined as "facilitating." On its face, this might appear to be a form of aiding or abetting but it is not. Facilitating in these offences does not necessarily mean furthering the commission of a substantive offence. In itself, it *is* a substantive offence and the facilitator is guilty as a principal. Similarly, offences of facilitation cannot be construed as inchoate offences in the nature of attempt or incitement. They are complete offences in and of themselves, not preliminary offences that contemplate the completion of a substantive offence.

## I. PRINCIPALS

Section 21(1)(a) refers to the participation of the person who "actually commits" the offence. Subject to proof of identification, this rarely poses challenges of great difficulty. It is possible, however, for a person to be found guilty as a principal party to the offence when he or she commits that offence through the agency of another.

**R. v. Thatcher**
Supreme Court of Canada
[1987] 1 S.C.R. 652

DICKSON C.J.C. (Beetz, Estey, Wilson, and Le Dain JJ. concurring):

    [1]  On 7th May 1984 Colin Thatcher was arrested and charged with causing the death of his ex-wife, JoAnn Kay Wilson. After a 14-day trial before judge and jury, he was convicted of first degree murder and sentenced to life imprisonment without eligibility for parole for 25 years. An appeal to the Saskatchewan Court of Appeal was dismissed (Vancise J.A. dissenting). Colin Thatcher now appears before this court requesting that the jury's guilty verdict be set aside.

    [2]  The position of the Crown throughout the trial was that Mr. Thatcher had murdered Mrs. Wilson or alternatively that he caused someone else to do so and was therefore guilty as a party to the offence pursuant to s. 21 of the Criminal Code. Mr. Gerald N. Allbright, counsel for Mr. Thatcher, advances a number of grounds of appeal in his factum: (i) that there existed no evidentiary basis for a direction pursuant to s. 21 of the Code; (ii) that the trial judge erred in failing to direct the jury on the application of the legal principles of parties to an offence to the evidence of the case;

(iii) that the trial judge failed to summarize fairly and adequately the evidence and the theory of the defence; (iv) that the trial judge erred in directing the jury to weigh the evidence of Mr. Thatcher against the evidence of other witnesses and to choose which they accepted, thereby reducing the burden of proof; (v) and that the Saskatchewan Court of Appeal erred in ruling that the curative provision found in s. 613(1)(b)(iii) of the Code could be resorted to in the circumstances of the case. These were all grounds in respect of which there was dissent in the Court of Appeal of Saskatchewan, thereby giving rise to an appeal to this court as of right, pursuant to s. 618(1)(a) of the Criminal Code.

[3] Another ground of appeal, in my view of more substance than those just described, was also argued by counsel for Mr. Thatcher. It was not the subject of a dissent in the Court of Appeal and was unanimously dismissed by that court. Leave to argue this ground was sought from this court and was granted. Counsel contended that the trial judge erred in failing to instruct the jury that a verdict of guilty must be unanimous in relation to one or other of the alternative means of committing the offence of murder. The effect of the argument, in the circumstances of this case, was that in order to find Mr. Thatcher guilty of murder the jury had to be unanimous that he intentionally killed his former wife or, alternatively, that he aided or abetted another person or persons in her killing; it was simply not sufficient that some members of the jury would hold to one theory and other members would hold to the other theory. That, as I see it, is the principal issue in this appeal.

## The Facts

### (i) Introductory

[4] Having met as students at the University of Iowa, Colin Thatcher and his former wife JoAnn were married on 12th August 1962. After their marriage they returned to Saskatchewan. They took up residence in Moose Jaw. Mr. Thatcher, the son of a one-time Member of Parliament and Premier of Saskatchewan, developed over the years an active and successful career as rancher, farmer and politician, serving for a time as Minister of Energy and Mines in a Progressive Conservative Government of Saskatchewan. Three children, Greg, Regan and Stephanie, were born of the marriage. Thatcher admitted to infidelity during the course of the marriage. The couple separated in August 1979. JoAnn, taking the two youngest children with her, left Moose Jaw with Mr. Thatcher's best friend, Ron Graham. Relations between the estranged spouses became increasingly bitter and acrimonious as they fought a long, hotly contested series of custody, access and matrimonial property battles. Colin Thatcher became obsessed. At one juncture he spirited Regan out of the country, and was found in contempt and ordered to pay a substantial fine. JoAnn's matrimonial property entitlement was initially held to amount to $820,000 but the judgment was immediately appealed. In 1980 the Thatchers were divorced. In January 1981 JoAnn married Mr. Tony Wilson and moved into a house located across the street from the Legislative Buildings in Regina.

*(ii)  The Spring of 1981*

[5]  On the evening of Sunday, 17th May 1981, JoAnn Wilson was shot and wounded while in the kitchen of her home. A bullet fired from a high powered rifle passed through a triple glaze glass window and struck her in the shoulder. She was hospitalized for about three weeks. The evidence was that JoAnn Wilson was terrified by this attempt on her life. After the shooting she gave up her right to custody of Regan and, a year later, agreed to accept approximately one half of the original court award, spread over five years. No one was charged with the 17th May 1981 incident.

*(iii)  21st January 1983*

[6]  At about six o'clock in the evening of 21st January 1983 JoAnn Wilson came home, drove into the garage of her home and was ferociously beaten and then shot to death. Twenty-seven wounds were inflicted on her head, neck, hands and lower legs. The injuries included a broken arm, a fracture of the wrist and a severed little left finger. A single bullet entered her skull causing death.

[7]  Mr. Craig Dotson testified as to the finding of the body. He stated that he left work at the Legislative Buildings shortly before 6:00 p.m. on 21st January 1983 and was walking home when he noted a green car with a female driver turn into the garage at the Wilson residence. He continued walking for about a block. He heard loud shrill screams behind him. He turned back to investigate. He heard a single loud sharp noise and then silence. As he approached a lane near the Wilson garage he saw a man emerge from the garage. He did not pay any particular attention. It was dark. He was 30 to 40 feet from the individual. He walked a little further and saw a body in a pool of blood on the floor of the garage.

[8]  Mr. Dotson told the police he thought the man he momentarily observed had a beard, was about 30 years old, 5 foot 9 inches to 5 foot 11 inches in height and of medium build. A composite sketch prepared by the police with Mr. Dotson's aid did not fit Colin Thatcher, whom Mr. Dotson knew as a member of the Saskatchewan Legislative Assembly. ...

### The Charge and the Verdict

[58]  In his charge to the jury, despite objection from counsel for the defence, the trial judge indicated to the jury the following direction on potential culpability:

> At the outset I should explain to you that there are two ways in which the offence of murder could have been committed by this accused. If you find on the evidence and are satisfied beyond a reasonable doubt that Colin Thatcher did that act or actions himself that caused the death of JoAnn Wilson, it is open to you to find him guilty of murder. Alternatively, if you find that acts done or performed by the accused resulted in the death of JoAnn Wilson and were done with the intent that they cause her death, even though the actual killing was done by another or others, it is open to you to find this accused guilty of murder.

[59] The trial judge also referred the jury to s. 21(1) of the Criminal Code and further commented:

> Colin Thatcher is charged with committing the offence of murder. If you do not find that he did the act of murder himself, he is equally guilty if you find and are satisfied that he either aided or abetted another or others in its commission.

During the charge the trial judge alluded to the argument of defence counsel that if the jury accepted the evidence of even one of the witnesses who said he was in Moose Jaw at the time of the murder, Thatcher could not have committed the murder. Counsel also told the jury that as the Crown had not produced any evidence that anyone else killed JoAnn Wilson it was the duty of the jury to find him not guilty. The trial judge said:

> With respect, I am unable to agree with this argument. I tell you as a matter of law that the fact that the Crown cannot adduce evidence that another individual or individuals actually did the act does not preclude you from finding that the killing was done on behalf of Colin Thatcher and it is still open to you to return a finding of guilty of murder if you so find.

The judge left the jury with three possible verdicts: not guilty, guilty of first degree murder or guilty of second degree murder. The jury deliberated from Friday, 2nd November 1984, through until Tuesday, 6th November 1984, before returning the verdict of guilty of the offence of first degree murder contrary to s. 218 of the Criminal Code. ...

*(ii) Failure To Relate the Law to the Facts Regarding the Crown's Alternative Theory*

[76] The trial judge read the contents of s. 21(1) to the jury and referred, correctly, to what was meant by the term "aiding" or "abetting": "intentional encouragement or assistance in the commission of the offence." As stated, he pointed out that the actual perpetrator need not be identified. He thus accurately stated the law as to s. 21(1).

[77] Instead of carving his jury charge into discrete sections in which he reviewed the evidence consistent with Thatcher having personally committed the murder, Thatcher having committed the murder by means of s. 21(1) and, finally, Thatcher not having committed the murder at all, the trial judge simply went through the evidence of each witness in turn. I do not think he was wrong in this. Much of the Crown evidence was consistent with *either* Crown theory, and much of the defence evidence was consistent with either Thatcher's innocence or his guilt under s. 21(1). It is not incumbent on a trial judge to go through the evidence in a repetitive fashion which could only have bored the jury. Nor do I think we should assume jurors are so unintelligent that they will fail to see the obvious; the presence of a government car at the home of the victim, when combined with evidence suggesting that the man in the car was not Thatcher, may point to Thatcher's having aided and abetted; and surely

they can discern that the alibi evidence, if believed, when combined with the murder weapon evidence, may point to a similar conclusion.

[78] Furthermore, it is obvious that the two Crown theories are not *legally* different views of what happened. The whole point of s. 21(1) is to put an aider or abetter on the same footing as the principal. To stress the difference between the Crown theories might leave a jury with the erroneous impression that it is vital for the jurors to decide individually and collectively which way the victim was killed. But the correctness of this point hinges on issue (iii), below, and I will pursue it in that context.

*(iii)  Jury Unanimity as to the Material Facts*

[79] This is the most difficult issue presented by the case. I have noted that, as there was no dissent on the point in the Court of Appeal, leave of this court was required and was granted.

[80] I begin my analysis of this issue by quoting s. 21(1) of the Criminal Code:

> 21.(1)  Every one is a party to an offence who
> > (a)  actually commits it,
> > (b)  does or omits to do anything for the purpose of aiding any person to commit
> it, or
> > (c)  abets any person in committing it.

This provision is designed to make the difference between aiding and abetting and personally committing an offence legally irrelevant. It provides that either mode of committing an offence is equally culpable and, indeed, that whether a person personally commits or only aids and abets, he is guilty of *that* offence, in this case causing the death of JoAnn Wilson, and not some separate distinct offence. This is in contrast with the provisions of the Code relating to accessories after the fact or conspirators (ss. 421 and 423), which create distinct offences for involvement falling short of personal commission. ...

[84] Thus, s. 21 has been designed to alleviate the necessity for the Crown choosing between two different forms of participation in a criminal offence. The law stipulates that both forms of participation are not only equally culpable, but should be treated as one single mode of incurring criminal liability. The Crown is not under a duty to separate the different forms of participation in a criminal offence into different counts. Obviously, if the charge against Thatcher had been separated into different counts, he might well have been acquitted on each count notwithstanding that each and every juror was certain beyond a reasonable doubt either that Thatcher personally killed his ex-wife or that he aided and abetted someone else who killed his ex-wife. This is precisely what s. 21 is designed to prevent. ...

[89] The appellant, relying on a recent article by Mark A. Gelowitz entitled "The *Thatcher* Appeal: A Question of Unanimity" (1986), 49 C.R. (3d) 129, argues that, just as in *Brown* where the English Court of Appeal held that "Each ingredient of the offence must be proved to the satisfaction of each and every member of the jury," this court ought to hold that the nature of Thatcher's participation must be proved to each and every juror before he can be convicted of "unlawfully causing" JoAnn Wilson's death.

[90] The appellant accepts, as any reasonable person must, that the jurors need not be unanimous with respect to their acceptance or rejection of each individual piece of evidence. In a long, complicated trial it is absurd to suppose that 12 people could form the same opinion of each item of evidence, and it is absurd to suppose that the Crown could ever prove or explain beyond a reasonable doubt every detail of a murder. A defendant at a murder trial should obviously not be acquitted if some jurors think a .38 calibre bullet was used and others think that a .357 calibre bullet was used. The appellant submits, however, that the jurors ought to be unanimous as to the "material facts" making out the offence. He does not provide a definition of "material facts," except to rely on Mr. Gelowitz for the proposition that jurors must be "in substantial agreement as to just what an accused has done" [p. 136]. This argument, however, overlooks the whole point of s. 21, as I have said, which makes the distinction between principals and aiders and abetters legally irrelevant.

[91] … In the present case, Thatcher was charged that he did "unlawfully cause the death of JoAnn Kay Wilson and did thereby commit first degree murder." The charge was carefully worded, and there is no injustice in his conviction on the indictment irrespective of whether the jurors shared the same view as to the most likely manner in which Thatcher committed the murder. When one considers the implications of the appellant's submission, it becomes even clearer that it is without merit. In the present case there were doubtless three alternatives in the minds of each of the jurors:

(a)  Thatcher personally killed his ex-wife;

(b)  he aided and abetted someone else to do so;

(c)  he is innocent of the crime.

The jurors were told that if any of them had a reasonable doubt regarding (c), Thatcher should be acquitted. Every single juror was, evidently, solidly convinced that (c) was simply not what occurred. Each one was certain that the true statement of affairs was (a) or (b). Even if we suppose, as the appellant would have us do, that the jurors individually went beyond thinking in terms of (a) or (b) and specifically opted for one theory, and that some jurors thought only (a) could have occurred and others thought only (b) could have occurred, I am far from convinced that there would have been any injustice from convicting Thatcher. As stated, there is no legal difference between the two. Much is made of the fact that (a) and (b) are *factually* inconsistent theories, in the sense that evidence proving (a) tends to disprove (b). But this is really only true of one category of evidence, namely identification and alibi evidence. The overwhelming mass of evidence against Thatcher was consistent with *either* theory. In particular, the evidence tracing the murder weapon to Thatcher was highly probative, as were his statements to various witnesses (prior to the murder) of his intention to kill JoAnn Wilson, and his statement to Lynn Mendell (after the murder) that he had "blown away" his wife.

[92] The appellant's suggestion would fail to achieve justice in a significant number of cases. Suppose the evidence in a case is absolutely crystal clear that when X and Y entered Z's house, Z was alive, and when X and Y left, Z was dead. Suppose

that in their evidence each of X and Y says that the other of them murdered Z but each admits to having aided and abetted. Are X and Y each to be acquitted if some of the jurors differ as to which of X and Y actually committed the offence? I can see absolutely no reason in policy or law to uphold such an egregious conclusion. The appellant's submission ignores the very reason why Parliament abolished the old common law distinctions: namely, they permitted guilty persons to go free. As Professor Peter MacKinnon points out in "Jury Unanimity: A Reply to Gelowitz and Stuart" (1986), 51 C.R. (3d) 134, at p. 135, if an accused is to be acquitted in situations when every juror is convinced that the accused committed a murder in one of two ways, merely because the jury cannot agree on *which* of the two ways, "it is difficult to image a situation more likely to bring the administration of justice into disrepute—and deservedly so."

**R. v. H. (L.I.)**

Manitoba Court of Appeal

(2004), 17 C.R. (6th) 338

FREEDMAN J.A.: …

*The Evidence*

[31] It is, therefore, necessary to outline certain parts of the evidence to determine the accused's role. None of the three men who pleaded guilty to or were found guilty of manslaughter testified at this trial, and the accused did not testify.

[32] The evidence which the Crown says shows the accused's participation in the crime resulting in the victim's death, and which in the Crown's submission forms the basis upon which to give a s. 21 charge, is found mainly in the direct examination of Bernadette Young.

[33] She testified that she, her sister Josephine Young, her brothers Adrian and Curtis Young, the accused, John, Austin Hall and the victim, were in the house, drinking on the evening in question. Hudson was also there.

[34] She said her brother Adrian called the victim into the bedroom and 30 seconds later the accused, Hudson and John followed. Adrian told the victim to give him money and then she saw Adrian punch him in the head. He fell down and then all four (the accused, Adrian, John and Hudson) started "kicking him and punching him," on his body and head.

[35] She said that after the accused kicked the victim "quite a few times" he looked in his pockets. Adrian and John were also checking his socks and pockets.

[36] Back in the living room, the accused gave her the victim's car keys. At this point the victim's nose was bleeding and "his face was kind of puffing out."

[37] The accused, John, Adrian and Hudson then all went outside with the victim. She looked through a window and saw John punch the victim, who fell to the ground, and then the four young men who were outside "started beating him up again, … kicking him and punching him … on his body. On his head." They kicked and punched

him all over his body and his head while he lay on the ground. The force of the kicks was "hard."

[38] She testified that she saw the accused kick the victim "4 or 5 times probably," hard, while he lay on the ground. She then went outside because she thought they were overdoing it. She then saw the accused jump on the victim twice in the area of his stomach and chest, and then blood came out of the victim's mouth. She told the accused to stop, and they all did.

[39] The testimony of Bernadette Young described above, in the accused's view, was "but one of many versions" she offered, and in her charge the judge identified a number of inconsistencies in her evidence. Another witness, Maria Courchene, had said that any references to the assault by Bernadette Young were that her "brothers" had beaten the victim. Bernadette Young had made a statement to the police in which she mentioned a fight in which the accused participated, and described him having kicked and punched the victim in the stomach and punched him in the head.

[40] Bernadette Young gave a second interview to the police (soon after the first one) with some inconsistencies, e.g., that the victim arrived at the home at 5:00 a.m., already beaten up. Then the accused and the other three took the victim into a room and the accused closed the door. She could hear banging but did not see what happened. Then the door opened and she saw the victim laying on the floor bleeding badly, and she saw the accused checking the victim's pockets. John dragged the victim by his feet and the accused pulled on his arms, taking him out of the bedroom.

[41] There were other inconsistencies, some of which arose out of her testimony at the preliminary inquiry.

[42] She also gave the police a videotaped statement. She said she saw the accused, in the bedroom, jump on the victim's stomach twice, but later that he jumped on his face twice.

[43] Bernadette Young had consumed considerable alcohol and smoked marihuana on the evening of November 4, and she said that she was drunk during that night and the next morning. She testified she was drunk during her interviews with the police and it was difficult for her to remember details. She said it would be impossible for her to say with any accuracy what happened that night and that what she told the police might be a version of the truth but that she could not say so with 100% accuracy.

[44] Josephine Young's testimony was that all four young men were in the bedroom with the victim. She said that she did not see or know what they did, but the victim was laying on the floor. Then she said Adrian, John and the accused had the victim down and she saw all three of them punch the victim on his upper body. She saw the accused (among others) hit the victim "a couple of times," but then she said she could not say.

### The Charge to the Jury

[45] As mentioned earlier, the charge is silent on s. 21 (other than the direction to ignore certain comments of Crown counsel), but there were several earlier discussions about it, in the absence of the jury. In the result they are immaterial, since the judge formed the view that nothing should be said to the jury in relation to possible liability by virtue of s. 21.

[46]  In the charge the judge did say this:

For you to find [L.H.] guilty of second degree murder, the Crown must prove each of
the following essential elements beyond a reasonable doubt.

First, that [L.H.] caused the death of [the victim]. ...

For an act or omission to cause someone's death it must be at least a contributing
cause, that is beyond something trifling or minor in nature. You do not have to find that
the conduct of the accused was the sole or principal cause of death. It is sufficient if you
are convinced beyond a reasonable doubt that the conduct of [L.H.] was at least a contributing cause of death that was beyond something trivial or insignificant.

There must not be anything that somebody else did later that resulted in [L.H.]'s act
or omission no longer being a contributing cause of the deceased's death.

One way to approach this question is to ask yourself whether the victim's death
would have occurred anyway even if [L.H.] did not assault the victim as he is alleged to
have done. The fact that the victim died and the accused assaulted him does not necessarily mean that his conduct was the cause of death.

[47]  She again pointed out inconsistencies in the evidence of Bernadette Young.
She then asked:

Is it possible that what [L.] did was so insignificant or trivial compared to what the
others did later, that his conduct did not cause the victim's death? ...

[W]as [L.H.]'s conduct at least a contributing cause of death beyond something
minor or trifling? ...

### Decision on the Charge

[48]  There was no charge on s. 21 essentially because the judge believed that the
case largely turned on the evidence of Bernadette Young. Her view seems to have
been that if Bernadette Young was believed the accused would be found guilty, and if
she was not believed he would be acquitted. That view, I have concluded, is an over-
simplification of the case, and led the judge astray.

[49]  The judge focussed on causation and whether the accused's conduct was a
contributing cause of death. This was the wrong focus. The issue was not whether his
actions were a contributing cause of death, which usually implies an intervening act.
The issue was whether the accused caused the victim's death, and importantly, that
could have occurred if he acted as a principal, an aider or an abettor. It was legally
irrelevant which role he played, and neither was it relevant whose blow or blows
killed the victim. If the four young men acted "in concert" (see *McMaster*) and there
was certainly evidence that they did, the accused, like the others, would be guilty.

[50]  Charging the jury with respect to sole, contributing and intervening causes is
problematic in this case, where a considerable part of the evidence indicates that the
accused participated in concert with others in beating the victim, and that the victim
died as a result of injuries from that beating. In such "participation" cases, once the
jury is properly directed to consider s. 21 of the *Criminal Code*, it would not be
necessary to determine if the accused's actions were the sole or contributing cause of

the victim's death. Causation would be proved if the jury was satisfied that the victim died as a result of the assault upon him and that the accused participated or assisted or abetted in that assault. See *R. v. Cribbin* (1994), 89 C.C.C. (3d) 67 (Ont. C.A.), where Arbour J.A. (as she then was) stated (at p. 80):

> Had the trial judge properly distinguished between Cribbin's potential liability for the homicide as a principal offender, on the basis of his own assault on the deceased, and his potential liability as an accessory to Reid's murder, it would have been unnecessary to burden the jury with distinctions between intervening and supervening causes capable or not, in law, of interrupting the chain of causation. The question of intervening cause would only arise if the jury were to conclude that the appellant and Reid were truly independent actors, which was a somewhat remote possibility. ... On any realistic view of the facts, Reid and Cribbin were either co-perpetrators or accomplices.

[51]  See also *R. v. Nette*, [2001] 3 S.C.R. 488, 2001 SCC 78 (S.C.C.) where Arbour J., for the majority, said (at para. 63):

> As ... *Cribbin* and the present case illustrate, causation issues tend to arise in homicides involving multiple parties. Absent s. 21 of the *Criminal Code*, the attribution of criminal responsibility to an individual who aided or abetted another in the commission of the offence would indeed be problematic. However, the law of parties provides that individuals may bear criminal responsibility for the acts of another, and in that way speaks conclusively on some issues of causation.

She then stated (at para. 77):

> In a homicide trial, the question is not what caused the death or who caused the death of the victim but rather did the accused cause the victim's death. The fact that other persons or factors may have contributed to the result may or may not be legally significant in the trial of the one accused charged with the offence. It will be significant, and exculpatory, if independent factors, occurring before or after the acts or omissions of the accused, legally sever the link that ties him to the prohibited result.

She then concluded (at para. 82):

> In my view, it was unnecessary in this case to instruct the jury on the law of causation for homicide, beyond stating the need to find that the accused caused the death of the victim. ... There was no evidence that anything other than the actions of the appellant and his accomplice caused Mrs. Loski's death. Mrs. Loski's death resulted from being left alone hog-tied in her bedroom with a ligature around her neck. Nothing that occurred following the actions of the appellant and his accomplice in tying her up and leaving her alone can be said to have broken the chain of causation linking them with her death.

[52]  *Cribbin* and *Nette* held that where the accused is legally considered to have caused the victim's death by virtue of s. 21, then causation is conclusively established unless there is evidence of an intervening event which breaks the chain of causation linking the accused to the victim's death. In the absence of such evidence, if the accused has either factually (and thus legally) caused the victim's death, or is

legally determined to have caused the victim's death by virtue of s. 21, then there is no need to examine causation any further and no need to consider whether the accused's contribution was a significant "contributing cause."

[53]  When the critical evidence in this case is reviewed and the principles outlined above are applied, it is apparent that the jury should have been directed with respect to the provisions of s. 21(1).

[54]  There was clearly evidence before the jury which, if accepted, would have constituted the accused a co-principal under s. 21(1)(a) to the crime of murder or, depending on intent, manslaughter. The case is in principle indistinguishable from such group assault cases as *Isaac*, *Wood*, *McMaster*, *Biniaris* and others.

[55]  The accused was seen, along with others, kicking and punching the victim, and he was seen jumping on the victim twice. As a result of the beating, the victim died. The evidence was unclear as to which member of the group struck the fatal blow(s). The judge properly warned the jury about the frailties in the evidence. Having done so, it was necessary for the judge, at a minimum, to charge the jury with respect to s. 21(1)(a) and advise the jury that in these circumstances, it was not necessary that the Crown prove that the accused personally struck the fatal blow. As long as the jury was satisfied that the accused participated in the beating with others and had the requisite intent for murder, then he would be guilty of second degree murder, even if he did not personally strike the fatal blow. If the jury was satisfied that he participated in the beating with others but did not have the requisite intent for murder, then he would be guilty of manslaughter if a reasonable person in the circumstances would have appreciated that participation in the assault would likely lead to a risk of harm to another person.

[56]  The evidence, if accepted by the jury, could alternatively have constituted the accused an aider under s. 21(1)(b) if the jury did not think it proved he was a co-principal. A charge on s. 21(1)(b) should therefore also have been given.

[57]  I see no basis in the evidence for a separate charge in respect of s. 21(1)(c). If the evidence described above was accepted, it would be sufficient to impose liability on the accused as either a co-principal or an aider. If the evidence described above was not accepted, he would be acquitted.

[58]  It is apparent to me that the evidence of Bernadette Young, so central to the Crown's case, was not totally disbelieved by the jury. The question the jury asked, discussed in the next section of this decision, could only have arisen if Bernadette Young's evidence, in some respects at least, was regarded as worthy of some credibility.

[59]  Without a charge on the principles and application of s. 21, the jury could be left in doubt or confusion, as I think they were, as demonstrated by the question they asked, about the role that the accused would have had to have played, and particularly whether he had to strike the killing blow, in order to be found guilty. Under s. 21 it is clear that the precise nature of the role, so long as it is either that of a principal or an aider (or if applicable on the evidence, an abettor), is irrelevant, and that should have been explained to the jury. It was not, and for that reason I conclude that the charge was fundamentally flawed.

[60]  An appropriate charge in this case would have included a direction that the jury could find that the accused caused the victim's death in either of two ways:

1)  if the accused personally struck the killing blow, or

2)  if the accused participated or assisted in a joint assault on the victim, and that assault led to the victim's death, regardless of whether the accused struck the killing blow or not.

[61]  In this case, as in the cases of *Cribbin* and *Nette*, there was no evidence regarding a true intervening cause. Thus, there was no need to further instruct the jury to consider whether the accused's actions were a significant contributing cause to the victim's death.

[62]  The accused argued that even if the charge was in error, the onus was on the Crown to satisfy this court that the verdict would not necessarily have been the same. See *R. v. Vézeau* (1976), [1977] 2 S.C.R. 277 (S.C.C.). The Crown has met that burden. The accused also argued that with the unreliability of the Young sisters, it would be unsafe for any jury to convict the accused. In my opinion, the evidence of the Young sisters was appropriately left for the jury to consider, and whether either or both of the Young sisters was credible, wholly, partially or not at all, was for the jury to determine.

### Decision on the Jury's Question

[63]  At the conclusion of her charge the judge gave the jury a "Decision Tree," the first question in which is "Did [L. H.] *cause* the death of the deceased?" [original emphasis]

[64]  The jury retired and at some point sent a question to the judge. The question was:

> With regards to question 1 in the Decision Tree and the cause of death we are asking the following: Are we deciding if [L.] directly caused the death or are we looking at him as a participant that caused the death?

[65]  In the context of the charge the jury's question was unclear and this was apparent to the judge. When the question was received she said to counsel (in the absence of the jury):

> I'm unclear from the question whether the confusion arises about any comments with respect to aiding, abetting or encouraging, or it, it may result from talking about conduct which is at least a contributing cause, and I suspect it's probably the latter.

And then, after considerable discussion with counsel, she said:

> ... we're trying to, trying to figure out the answer by reading the minds of 12 people and, and we can't know what they're thinking. ...
>
>   See it's the word ... directly that's troublesome because I don't know what they mean by that, whether they're saying, you know, does it—we have to know that there

was a direct assault or whether—because they're also getting at the whole issue of the
participant ... and, and I don't know exactly what they mean.

She then responded to the jury's question in these terms, which are essentially an
abbreviated version of part of the main charge:

> ... [Y]ou must be satisfied beyond a reasonable doubt that [L.H.]'s conduct caused the
> death in the sense that his conduct was at least a contributing cause of death beyond
> something minor or trifling.

[66] There is authority for the view that where the jury's question is enigmatic
and the judge and counsel are unclear exactly what is concerning the jury, the judge
should request clarification from the jury. This viewpoint and the jurisprudence on
which it is based is discussed by O'Neill J.A., at paras. 108-18, in *R. v. Allen* (2002),
93 C.R.R. (2d) 55, 2002 NFCA 2 (Nfld. C.A.). Although O'Neill J.A. spoke in dissent, the Supreme Court of Canada overturned the majority decision in *Allen* in favour of the reasons given by O'Neill J.A. While the Supreme Court did not discuss
the issue of whether a judge can or should request clarification when a jury's question is enigmatic, neither did it indicate that O'Neill J.A. and the case law relied upon
are wrong on this point. For the court, Iacobucci J. said that "the trial judge did not
answer the jury's question with the clarity and comprehensiveness required by the
applicable jurisprudence" ([2003] S.C.J. No. 16 (S.C.C.) at para. 3).

[67] In *Allen*, O'Neill J.A. stated (at para. 108):

> It is essential that a trial judge before re-instructing the jury know exactly what the
> jury's concerns are. Here he didn't. In my view, it was incumbent on the trial judge to
> question the foreman of the jury to ascertain clearly what the jury's concern was.

[68] In *R. v. Fleiner* (1985), 23 C.C.C. (3d) 415 (Ont. C.A.), Finlayson J.A. for
the court stated (at p. 420):

> The problem is that the question is not altogether clear and no counsel before us could
> state with assurance what was bothering the jury, although a number of suggestions
> were made. ...
>
> In my respectful view, the learned trial judge should have requested clarification of
> the question before dealing with it. It is very difficult to understand the question and
> answer as recorded ... it is my opinion that the court should not be obliged to speculate
> as to what was concerning the jury. ...

[69] In *R. v. Mohamed* (1991), 64 C.C.C. (3d) 1 (B.C. C.A.), Wood J.A. for the
court stated (at pp. 11-12):

> [T]he trial judge has the ultimate responsibility to see to it that the jury receives the assist-
> ance it requires. It was impossible to discharge that responsibility in this case without first
> determining what the problem was. In my respectful view the trial judge ought to have
> clarified the question with the foreman before embarking on a repetition of an instruc-
> tion which twice previously had failed to clarify the issues of law for the jury.
>
> Before us it was argued that there is an inherent risk of inappropriate disclosure in
> any dialogue with the jury, but that risk can be minimized or even eliminated if the

judge takes the initiative by asking leading questions and cautioning the foreman not to disclose any views which the members of the jury may have on the evidence while answering those questions. I do not think that the risk of improper disclosure by the foreman was much of a real, as opposed to a theoretical, concern. It certainly was not a proper reason to refrain from any attempt to clarify the question in this case.

[70] Also see *R. v. Hall* (1995), 64 B.C.A.C. 200 (B.C. C.A.), where Cumming J.A. for the court approved of the trial judge's decision to send the jury back into the deliberation room in order to further clarify their question.

[71] This approach is consistent with the Supreme Court of Canada's emphasis in several judgments on the importance of a jury being fully instructed after it has submitted a question or aired a concern. In *R. v. S. (W.D.)*, [1994] 3 S.C.R. 521 (S.C.C.), for example, Cory J. stated (at p. 528):

[I]t cannot ever be forgotten that questions from the jury require careful consideration and must be clearly, correctly and comprehensively answered. This is true for any number of reasons which have been expressed by this Court on other occasions. A question presented by a jury gives the clearest possible indication of the particular problem that the jury is confronting and upon which it seeks further instructions. ... The jury must be given a full and proper response to their question. The jury is entitled to no less. It is the obligation of the trial judge assisted by counsel to make certain that the question is fully and properly answered.

[72] In order for a jury's question to give "the clearest possible indication of the particular problem that the jury is confronting," the question itself must be clear. Similarly, in order for the trial judge to "clearly, correctly and comprehensively" answer the jury's question, the judge must be certain what the jury is asking. If the jury's question is unclear, it follows that the trial judge should clarify the question by whatever method is best in the circumstances in order to gain "the clearest possible indication of the particular problem that the jury is confronting," and in order to be able to give a clear, correct and comprehensive answer.

[73] The judge here should have sought and obtained clarification of the question. Only then should it have been answered.

[74] As suggested above, I think the question from the jury demonstrates that the jury did not totally disbelieve Bernadette Young, a considerable part of whose evidence identified the accused as playing a significant role in the assault on the victim. Had the jury been prepared to disbelieve her entirely, the question would not have been asked. If the jury was not prepared to give some credence to her evidence as it related to the accused's involvement in the events leading directly to the death of the victim, there would have been no question attempting to understand the distinction between the accused being the direct cause of, or a participant in causing, the death. The judge had not used the word "participant" in her charge. It is a word that is applicable in a group assault case. The question is a pretty clear signal that the jury's mind was focusing on the issue that the judge had, in fact, incorrectly not put before them to consider.

[75]  I cannot say whether the answer to the jury was adequate or inadequate, or correct or incorrect, because I, like the trial judge, do not fully understand the question.

*Separate Evidentiary Base for S. 21(1)*

[76]  The accused argued that the judge was correct in not charging on s. 21(1) in part because, in his submission, there had to be an evidentiary base for s. 21(1) liability which was separate from an evidentiary base leading to liability as a principal. He argued that if the jury found that he "was involved, he was involved as a principal in the attack." The judge, in comments to counsel after their closing submissions, prior to her charge and in the absence of the jury, seemed to agree with this approach, when she said:

> [I]n our earlier pre-charge discussions, I had, … indicated at that stage that I was strongly disinclined not [*sic*] to charge on parties to an offence or party to an offence unless there was other significant evidence, because at that stage there wasn't any.

[77]  The only authority provided to us by the accused on this issue is the decision of the Ontario Court of Appeal in *R. v. Vermeylen* (1993), 87 C.C.C. (3d) 132 (Ont. C.A.). This was a case dealing mainly with whether there should have been a charge on aiding and abetting as distinct from a charge on liability as a principal.

[78]  In *Vermeylen*, the defence argued that there was a lack of evidence of aiding or abetting, but a charge to the jury on s. 21(1) proceeded. The Court of Appeal considered the appropriateness of charging under s. 21(1), and stated (at p. 140):

> In this court, Crown counsel was requested to refer the court to evidence which would support a charge of aiding or abetting as opposed to a charge of being a principal. Crown counsel pointed to the evidence of Kimber to the effect that Vermeylen had told him that he and Hanson planned to rob and beat Galipeau and to split the money, the evidence of Kimber that Vermeylen had told him they did rob Galipeau and the evidence of Podworny as to the blood stains on the back of Hanson's left leg, suggesting that someone else had struck Galipeau. In my view, nothing was suggested which would provide the factual underpinning for a charge under s. 21(1)(b) or (c) as opposed to a charge against a principal. In my view, therefore, the separate charge under s. 21(1) was ill-conceived and, in the result, served only to confuse.
>
> The court later mentioned again that there was an "absence of any factual foundation for a separate charge under s. 21(1)" (at p. 142).

[79]  In order to convict an accused under s. 21(1)(b) or (c), it is imperative that there is *some* evidence indicating that the accused intentionally assisted or encouraged another person to commit the crime. If there is no such evidence, the jury should not be charged on s. 21(1)(b) or (c): *Dunlop, R. v. Sparrow* (1979), 51 C.C.C. (2d) 443 at 458 (Ont. C.A.). In *Vermeylen*, however, it was suggested that a jury should not be charged with respect to s. 21(1)(b) or (c) where the evidence indicating that the accused assisted or encouraged another to commit the crime is that very evidence indicating that the accused committed the offence as a principal. In other words, *Vermeylen* seems to suggest that the Crown cannot rely on the same actions of

the accused to support a conviction for aiding or abetting as it could for acting as a principal.

[80] *Vermeylen* stands alone on this issue, and other authority does not support the viewpoint expressed in *Vermeylen*. In several cases, it has been accepted that an accused can be convicted either as an aider or abettor, or as a principal, where the evidence indicating that the accused aided and abetted another to commit the crime was the same as the evidence indicating that the accused committed the offence as a principal.

[81] In *Biniaris*, the accused was found guilty by a jury of second degree murder in circumstances where he and another accused, S., had participated together in a violent beating which had left the victim dead. The Crown's expert changed her position and eventually agreed with the defence's expert that the victim's death resulted from the blow that occurred when the victim's head hit the pavement, as a result of being thrown to the ground by S. The implications of this change of position were explained by Arbour J. for the Supreme Court as follows (at para. 44):

> At the outset of the respondent Biniaris' trial and until the change in Dr. Carlyle's opinion, the Crown's position was that Biniaris alone had caused the fatal injuries suffered by Niven and was guilty of second degree murder as a principal. The shift in Dr. Carlyle's evidence led Crown counsel, at the end of the trial, to advance a modified, three-part theory of liability—liability as a principal, liability as a co-perpetrator or liability as an aider or abettor. Boyd J. dealt adequately with the implications of the reversal of Dr. Carlyle's position and the Crown's modified theory in her charge to the jury. The trial judge explained the Crown's position that it was open to the jury to reject the medical evidence offered by Drs. Rice and Carlyle on the issue of causation in favour of their own common sense and, if they were satisfied beyond a reasonable doubt that Biniaris had acted with the requisite intent, to conclude that Biniaris was guilty of second degree murder as the perpetrator of Niven's fatal injuries. However, Boyd J. quite properly urged the jury to be very careful, characterizing the choice to ignore the unanimous expert evidence on causation as a "dangerous venture." The trial judge then explained the circumstances under which it was open to the jury, applying the relevant principles of party liability set out in s. 21(1) of the *Criminal Code*, to convict the accused of second degree murder: …

[82] She then reproduced the trial judge's charge to the jury on the principles of party liability which were available to the jury to apply and specifically noted the "availability of two alternative routes to a second degree murder conviction" (at para. 45), stated that the trial judge had "directed the jury accordingly" with respect to the application of s. 21 (at para. 45), and indicated that the jury had been properly instructed (at para. 51).

[83] It is clear that Arbour J., speaking for the rest of the court, was satisfied that it was open for a jury to find Biniaris guilty as a party, either as a co-perpetrator or as an aider or abettor, despite the fact that the evidence implicating him was the same in either event—in either case, he ran up to the prone victim and stomped on his forehead. Thus, *Biniaris*, in my view, stands for the proposition that the same actions of an accused can support liability as a principal or as an aider or abettor.

[84] See also *R. v. McQuaid*, [1998] 1 S.C.R. 244 (S.C.C.), where, as later in *Biniaris*, the Supreme Court did not require that separate evidentiary bases exist to convict a person as a principal or as an aider or abettor. This is consistent with the rationale underlying s. 21, as explained in *Thatcher*. Whether a person is found guilty of an offence as a principal or as an aider or abettor is legally irrelevant (and the basis of the finding is, of course, not identified by a jury) and so the same evidentiary base can apply to each category.

[85] Holding that the same evidence can be used to ground an accused's liability either as a principal or as an aider or abettor is also consistent with these further comments (of Dickson C.J.C.) in *Thatcher* (at p. 694):

> [I]f there is evidence before a jury that points to an accused either committing a crime personally or, alternatively, aiding and abetting another to commit the offence, provided the jury is satisfied beyond a reasonable doubt that the accused did one or the other, it is "a matter of indifference" which alternative actually occurred: *Chow Bew* [[1956] S.C.R. 124]. It follows, in my view, that s. 21 precludes a requirement of jury unanimity as to the particular nature of the accused's participation in the offence. Why should the juror be compelled to make a choice on a subject which is a matter of legal indifference?

[86] See also the decisions of the Ontario Court of Appeal in *Wood* (at p. 220):

> Where evidence of concerted action in the commission of the offence exists, as in the present case, then it is open to a jury to convict all of the accused either as principals, under s. 229(a), or as aiders or abettors, pursuant to s. 21 of the *Code*, even though the extent of the individual participation in the violence is unclear.

and in *R. v. Suzack* (2000), 141 C.C.C. (3d) 449 (Ont. C.A.), leave to appeal dismissed [2000] S.C.C.A. No. 583 (S.C.C.), where Doherty J.A. stated (at paras. 152 and 155):

> It is beyond question that where two persons, each with the requisite intent, act in concert in the commission of a crime, they are both guilty of that crime. Their liability may fall under one or more of the provisions of s. 21(1) of the *Criminal Code*: *R. v. Sparrow* (1979), 51 C.C.C. (2d) 443 (Ont. C.A.) at 457-58. Trainor J. told the jury that if Suzack and Pennett jointly participated in the murder with the necessary intent, they were "liable as principals." This is potentially a mischaracterization of their liability. They may have been principals or they may have been aiders or abettors depending on what each did in the course of the common design: ...
>
> [Section] 21(1) is structured so as to avoid distinctions based on modes of participation in the crime.

[87] The view that the same evidence can be used to ground an accused's liability either as a principal or as an aider or abettor was expressed very recently in the case of *R. v. Pangowish* (2003), 171 C.C.C. (3d) 506, 2003 BCCA 62 (B.C. C.A.). In that case, Pangowish and Walker brutally assaulted the victim over the course of several hours and left him "hog-tied" in a basement. The victim later died, with blunt head trauma and lack of oxygen being the causes of death. In her charge to the jury, the trial judge read the jury s. 21(1)(b). The accused argued that the trial judge did not

specify that in order to be guilty of aiding, the Crown had to prove that the accused had meant to aid someone else to commit the offence. The Court of Appeal agreed that the trial judge had failed to specify this but stated (at para. 47):

> On the evidence in this case, I think the jury would have understood through the wording of s. 21(1)(b) that an intent to aid was required. This is not a case in which an accused has done something that has the effect of aiding the commission of an offence but may not realize the effect of his actions. Here, the actions of one appellant which might have aided or encouraged the other appellant were all immediate and done in the presence of each other as part of the brutal beating. On the evidence, the purpose of the beating arose from Walker's objections as a resident of the house to the thefts. If the jurors thought there were acts of assistance or encouragement by Pangowish (most of which on the evidence would have to have been the acts of assaults in themselves, affording primary liability under s. 21(1)(a)), they would inevitably have concluded that his intent was to further the beating.

[88]  As long as there is evidence before the jury which indicates that the accused actively participated in the crime with the requisite intent, it will not matter whether the jury finds the accused's participation to be that of a principal, or that of an aider or abettor, as long as the jury is satisfied beyond a reasonable doubt that the accused did actively participate in the crime with another person.

[89]  In my respectful opinion, the clear weight of authority is that a separate evidentiary base distinct from the evidentiary base required to find liability as a principal is not required to find liability as an aider or abettor and to the extent that *Vermeylen* holds otherwise, I would decline to follow it. The evidence in this case warranted a charge, with suitable cautions about the inconsistencies in the evidence, on s. 21(1)(a) and s. 21(1)(b).

[90]  For the foregoing reasons the appeal must be allowed, and a new trial is ordered.

## R. v. Berryman
### British Columbia Court of Appeal
### (1990), 57 C.C.C. (3d) 375

WOOD J.A. (for the Court):

*I*

[1]  This is an appeal by the Crown from the acquittal of the respondent on two counts of forging a passport contrary to s. 57(1)(a) of the Criminal Code. At trial the respondent was convicted of making a written statement on a passport application form, which she knew to be false, for the purpose of procuring a passport, contrary to s. 57(2) of the Code.

[2]  The issue to be resolved is whether a person can be convicted of forgery, when the actus reus of that offence, i.e., the actual making of the false document, is performed by an innocent agent. ...

*III*

[8] There is no doubt that two forged passports were made in the Victoria Regional Passport Office of the Department of External Affairs in July of 1987, and that the respondent, who worked in that office as a passport application examiner, was knowingly and intentionally instrumental in their production. On each of two separate occasions she accepted the applications on which the passports were issued, knowing that the person from whom they were received was not the applicant. She falsely stated in writing, on the face of each application, that the applicant had produced proof of citizenship and identification. She marked the applications with a notation, which ensured that no check would be made of the guarantors, knowing that all of the information on the face of each application, including the declaration of the purported guarantors, was false. Finally, when the passports were completed, she forged the signatures of the purported applicants on the receipt form used by the regional office to record the fact that they had been personally picked up by the persons to whom they were supposedly issued.

[9] The evidence, however, did not go so far as to establish that it was the respondent who actually "made" the false documents. In fact, it seems most likely that the forgeries were unwittingly produced by another employee of the same office, a Miss Venturin, who had no knowledge that the information contained in the applications on which they were based was completely false.

[10] The learned trial judge had no difficulty concluding that the respondent had deliberately made false statements on the two passport applications in order to bring about the production and issuance of two passports, and that as a consequence the two passports were in fact produced and issued. Thus he found her guilty as charged on count three of the indictment. However, he was of the view that counts one and two raised "a difficult legal problem." I refer to his reasons for judgment in which that problem is described and his conclusion is set out:

> There is no question that the two passports were both false, and Miss Berryman knew them to be false. The issue remains as to whether she made those false documents. The applications were both false documents, and Miss Berryman helped in their completion to procure the passports. That is why she is guilty of count 3. But, can it be said she made the false passports? I think the answer to that question is "no."
>
> It seems to me that s. 57(1) contemplates the making of a false passport by somebody outside the passport office. That is not to say that a person cannot make a false passport within that government office, but the word "makes" in s. 366(1) must be interpreted strictly to mean the act of manufacturing or physically producing. The Shorter Oxford Dictionary definition of the word "make" is this:
>
>> To produce by combination of parts, or by giving a certain form to a portion of matter; to construct, frame, fashion, bring into existence.
>
> I do not think the word "makes" in s. 366(1) can be interpreted to mean "causes to be made." Nor do I think it can be said that the making of the false passport commenced when the applications were brought by Miss Berryman into the passport office.

Either of those two approaches would do violence to the principle of strict construction of penal statutes.

I cannot find that Miss Berryman was a party to the offence of forging under Code s. 21 as an aider or abettor. Miss Venturin committed no forgery, and was not therefore a principal offender. There was nobody for Miss Berryman to aid or abet in the commission of the forgery offence.

Miss Berryman did bring about the production of the false passports. She caused another person to make them with that person not knowing they were false, but I find that Miss Berryman did not make the false documents as contemplated by s. 366(1) and by s. 57(1)(a).

*IV*

[11] In English common law, the person who caused a felony to be committed by means of the act of an innocent agent, was considered to be a principal in the first degree. The most common examples of such cases were in connection with the crimes of forgery and false pretences. Thus, for example, in *R. v. Palmer & Hudson* (1804), 2 Leach 978, 168 E.R. 586, Palmer was convicted of uttering a forged bank note on evidence which demonstrated that he had given the note to Hudson who had then followed his instructions and made some small purchase with it in a shop. Although the judges, for whose opinion the conviction was reserved, doubted the jury's conclusion that Hudson was an innocent agent, and thus expressed no view on the conviction for uttering, they took the opportunity, as noted at p. 588 of E.R., to reaffirm:

> ... the doctrine of Mr. Justice Foster (Foster's Crown Law, 349; 1 Hale, 616), that when an innocent person is employed for a criminal purpose, the employer must be answerable. ...

[12] In *R. v. Mazeau* (1840), 9 Car. & P. 676, 173 E.R. 1006, two of the accused were convicted of feloniously engraving and making two plates from which a promissory note for 25 Russian rubles could be printed. The plates were in fact engraved by an Englishman, who is said in the report to have been an innocent agent hired by the accused for that very purpose. Similar results were recorded in *R. v. Bannen* (1844), 2 Mood. 309, 169 E.R. 123; *R. v. Valler, Eurico & Harrison* (1844), 1 Cox C.C. 84; and *R. v. Bull & Schmidt* (1845), 1 Cox C.C. 281.

[13] In *R. v. Bleasdale* (1848), 2 Car. & K. 765, 175 E.R. 321, the accused was convicted of stealing coal which had actually been mined and removed by his employees, Erle J. having instructed the jury that:

> ... if a man does, by means of an innocent agent, an act which amounts to a felony, the employer, and not the innocent agent, is the person accountable for that act.

[14] In *R. v. Dowey* (1868), 11 Cox C.C. 115, the prisoner was indicted on six counts of obtaining money and goods by false pretences. In each case he had sent an innocent agent to purchase goods with notes issued by a bank which was no longer in business. His convictions were affirmed even though the false pretence alleged in

each count was the tendering of the note, by the innocent agent, as though it were the note of a valid and subsisting bank.

[15]  In *R. v. Butt* (1884), 15 Cox C.C. 564, the issue of innocent agency arose in a context which was very similar to that in this case. There the accused was charged with making a false entry in the cash book of his employer. In fact the notation, which was false, was made by another employee, who acted upon a note given to him by the accused in which the amount of money collected from one Sheppard, a customer of his employer, had been deliberately misstated. In affirming the conviction recorded, Lord Coleridge C.J. summarized the argument raised on appeal and the unanimous conclusion of the Court of Crown Cases Reserved at p. 567 of the report:

> It is admitted that in the ordinary sense of the word that was a false entry, and it is equally clear that with the making of that false entry the prisoner had something to do. It is contended, however, that the statute is not broken, because the person who made the entry did not know it was false, and the person who did know it was false did not make the entry. ... This is clearly a false entry as far as Sheppard is concerned. It purports to represent receipts from the persons who have been entered as making payment of such receipts, and it seems to me clear that the prisoner either made it with the innocent hands of Elford, or concurred in the innocent hands of Elford making it. I am of the opinion that this conviction was perfectly right, and must be upheld.

[16]  For these authorities to have application in this country, a hundred years later, it must be demonstrated that the doctrine of innocent agency survived the codification of our criminal law. It is therefore necessary to review the history of those Canadian statutes which have defined who are parties to criminal offences, but before doing so it is useful to remember the common law which those statutes were intended to reflect.

[17]  The common law recognized four categories of felonious offender. They were:

(a)  principals in the first degree,

(b)  principals in the second degree,

(c)  accessories before the fact, and

(d)  accessories after the fact.

[18]  Those who actually committed the offence, or who were deemed to have actually committed it by virtue of the doctrine of innocent agency, were principals in the first degree. Principals in the second degree were those who aided or abetted the commission of the offence by the principal(s) in the first degree. In Taschereau, The Criminal Code of Canada, 1893, reprinted (Toronto: The Carswell Company Limited, 1980), the learned author described either actual or constructive presence at the commission of the crime as an essential prerequisite to aiding or abetting. However, Glanville Williams, in Criminal Law: The General Part, 2nd ed. (London: Stevens & Sons Limited, 1961), suggests that the timing of the act or omission designed to aid, or of the abetting, was the important distinguishing feature of conduct which resulted in a person being characterized as a principal in the second degree.

[19] Accessories before the fact were those who counselled or procured the commission of a felony by another, but who were neither present nor active at the time of its commission. An accessory after the fact was one who, knowing that a felony had been committed by another, received, relieved, comforted, or assisted that person.

[20] Because the law required accessories to be indicted as such, and the punishments mandated for them were often different than those prescribed for principal offenders, much time was spent by lawyers, judges and juries alike, focusing on the often subtle distinctions of fact which, in any given case, separated the aider and abettor from the accessory before the fact. In England, Parliament moved to eliminate the distinction in (1861, 24 & 25 Vict., c. 94), by providing that an accessory before the fact was to be indicted, tried, convicted, and punished in all respects as if he were a principal felon. A similar enactment was passed in this country in 1868: see An Act respecting Accessories to and Abettors of Indictable Offences, 1868 (31 Vict., c. 72).

[21] The next significant development in Canada was the Criminal Code, 1892. Part III of that Code was entitled "Parties to the Commission of Offences." Section 61 provided, in part, as follows:

> 61. Every one is a party to and guilty of an offence who—
>
> (a) actually commits it; or
>
> (b) does or omits an act for the purpose of aiding any person to commit the offence; or
>
> (c) abets any person in commission of the offence; or
>
> (d) counsels or procures any person to commit the offence.

[22] It can be seen that, as a consequence of this enactment, those who formerly were known to the law as principals in the second degree became parties as described in paras. (b) and (c), and those who would previously have been accessories before the fact became parties under para. (d). Whether or not all those who would have been principals in the first degree, including those who committed an offence by means of an innocent agent, must be taken to have been described in para. (a) depends on the construction to be given to the words "actually commits it." Strangely enough, with the exception of one case, the question does not seem to have arisen in the almost 98 years since s. 61, the forerunner to the present s. 21, was enacted.

[23] The sole authority in which the doctrine of innocent agency has been applied in Canada is the decision of the New Brunswick Supreme Court (Appeal Division) in *R. v. MacFadden* (1971), 16 C.R.N.S. 251, 5 C.C.C. (2d) 204, 4 N.B.R. (2d) 59. There the court held that he who employs an innocent agent for the purposes of transporting narcotics is himself guilty of the resulting trafficking. A number of the ancient authorities discussed above were referred to and relied upon in reaching that decision, how ever, the effect of codification of the criminal law in this country does not appear to have been considered by the court.

[24] As a penal statute, and in particular as a section which not only defined who are parties, but also created substantive offences, s. 61 must be strictly construed. At first blush, the plain meaning that would seem to attach to the language in para. (a) suggests that in order to be guilty of an offence, in the capacity formerly known as a

principal in the first degree, a person would have to be the one who actually committed it. If that is the correct construction of the words used, then it would seem that the codification of our criminal law in 1892 spelled the demise of the doctrine of innocent agency.

[25] However, I do not think that the rules of construction require that the language of the section be read without regard for the law as it had evolved prior to 1892. As I read the authorities, the doctrine of innocent agency was predicated on the notion that a person who committed an offence by means of an innocent agent was deemed to be the actual perpetrator. This seems to flow from the language used in a number of the old cases on the subject. For example, in *R. v. Giles* (1827), 1 Mood. 166, 168 E.R. 1227, a case in which one count on the indictment charged the accused with offering a forged bank note, the evidence established that the note in question had in fact been offered to Newton by Burr, who was acting on the instructions of the accused. Vaughan B. instructed the jury that:

> … if they should be of the opinion that Burr knew when he offered the note to Newton that it was a forged note, the prisoner could not be considered as principal; but that if Burr was employed by the prisoner as an innocent instrument, being ignorant that the note was a forged one, *it would then be the act of the prisoner*, and he might properly be convicted. … [Emphasis added.]

[26] Similarly, in *R. v. Clifford* (1845), 2 Car. & K. 202, 175 E.R. 84, in which the prisoner, by a complicated scheme of letters to one James Bartlett, had the latter forge the name of the payee on a postal note and cash it. During the course of the trial, after conferring with Pollock C.B., Platt B. stated at p. 85 of E.R.:

> We agree in thinking, that, as Bartlett was an innocent agent, the signing the name William Smart by him *is just the same as if it had been signed by the prisoner himself*, and it is therefore a forgery. [Emphasis added.]

[27] In *R. v. Michael* (1840), 9 Car. & P. 356, 173 E.R. 867, the prisoner was charged with the murder of her infant child. The evidence was that she had sent a poison solution to a Mrs. Stevens, who was looking after the child, with instructions that it should be administered as a medicine, one teaspoon each evening. Mrs. Stevens declined to follow those instructions and put the bottle on the mantelpiece. Several days later another child found the bottle and administered part of its contents to the prisoner's child who then died. When passing sentence, Alderson B. noted that the judges:

> … were of the opinion that the administering of the poison by the child of Mrs. Stevens, was, under the circumstances of the case, *as much, in point of law, an administering by the prisoner as if the prisoner had actually administered it with her own hand*. [Emphasis added.]

[28] In each of these cases the point is made that where the agent is truly innocent of any complicity in the crime which has undoubtedly been committed, the act of such agent becomes, or is deemed to be, the act of the perpetrator. This approach is reflected by what Glanville Williams has to say at the beginning of para. 120 of Criminal Law: The General Part, which is entitled "Innocent agents":

> The principal in the first degree need not commit the crime with his own hands; he may commit it by a mechanical device, or through an innocent agent, or in any other manner, otherwise than through a guilty agent. An innocent agent is one who is clear of responsibility because of infancy, insanity, lack of *mens rea* and the like. *In law he is a mere machine whose movements are regulated by the offender*. [Emphasis added.]

[29] It is my view, supported by the authorities just referred to, that a person who commits an offence by means of an instrument "whose movements are regulated" by him, actually commits the offence himself. Thus there is no variance between the doctrine of innocent agency and the plain meaning that would seem to attach to s. 61(a) of the Criminal Code, 1892. While there have been substantial changes to that section over the years, none has affected the language used which is relevant to this issue, and I therefore conclude that what is today s. 21(1)(a) of the Criminal Code can and should be construed so as to give effect to the doctrine of innocent agency.

[30] It follows that while the learned trial judge was right in his conclusion that the respondent could not be convicted as an aider or an abettor, because Miss Venturin committed no forgery, it was nonetheless open to him to convict the respondent as a principal in the first degree, under s. 21(1)(a) of the Code. Thus, in concluding that the respondent could not be convicted of forging the passports, because those passports were made by an innocent agent, the learned trial judge was in error.

[31] During the course of argument, counsel's attention was directed to s. 23.1 of the Criminal Code, enacted R.S.C. 1985, c. 24 (2nd Supp.), s. 45, and proclaimed effective 1st September 1986, and which was therefore in effect at the time of the events which gave rise to the charges in this case. It was my impression then that the purpose of that provision might well be to give effect to the doctrine of innocent agency. Counsel were unable to provide any authorities in which this comparatively new section has been discussed, and were not prepared to offer much argument on its meaning.

[32] While I would not want to reach any final decision on the proper construction to be given to s. 23.1, without having the benefit of full argument on the question, it does not appear that it was intended to encompass the doctrine of innocent agency. I say that because by its very language it is restricted to cases where the accused either aids or abets, under s. 21(1)(b) or (c), or counsels or procures, under s. 22(1) or (2), or is an accessory after the fact under s. 23(1). As noted above, the result of the doctrine of innocent agency is to render an accused guilty as a principal in the first degree under s. 21(1)(a). In reaching my conclusion in this case, I have not been influenced by any interpretation which might properly be given to s. 23.1.

*Appeal allowed; conviction entered.*

---

Occasionally cases arise in which the evidence leaves open the possibilities either that the accused actually committed the offence or was a party to it in some other way. In *Thatcher*, [1987] 1 S.C.R. 652, for example, the prosecution's case was either that the accused killed his wife or arranged for her to be killed by another. In such cases, the judge must instruct the jury on alternative modes of participation that are supported by the evidence, even where the identity of other parties or their degree of participation is not known.

## II. AIDING AND ABETTING

### R. v. Kulbacki
Manitoba Court of Appeal
[1966] 1 C.C.C. 167

MILLER C.J.M. (for the Court): This is an appeal by way of stated case from B.P. McDonald, P.M., under the provisions of s. 734 [now s. 830] of the *Criminal Code*.

The accused was charged with driving a motor vehicle in a manner dangerous to the public contrary to s. 221(4) [enacted 1960-61, c. 43, s. 3] [now s. 249(4)] of the *Criminal Code*, and the learned Magistrate, after hearing the evidence, convicted the accused.

The accused, a young man 20 years of age, was not actually driving the motor vehicle himself but was the owner of it and had permitted a female infant, 16 years of age, although duly licensed to drive, to take the wheel of the car and drive the motor vehicle over an unimproved municipal highway in excess of 90 m.p.h. The accused, who was sitting in the front seat beside the driver, was charged with the substantive offence. According to the stated case, the accused did or said nothing to stop, prevent, or attempt to stop or prevent the driver of the car from driving in the manner in which she did.

The Crown contended that the conviction was proper in that the accused had aided and abetted the commission of the offence and, as such, under s. 21(1) of the *Code*, was liable to the same extent as if he had been driving the vehicle.

The defence was strictly one of law that the accused, although present, did nothing to encourage the commission of the offence and did not omit to do anything that [would have] contributed to its commission. The defence maintained that, although the accused was present, he did not participate in the commission of the crime but was merely a passive observer, and, at the most, guilty of mere passive acquiescence. Accused argued that he did not have any duty and was not under any liability to do anything as long as he did not in some way encourage the commission of the offence. Defence counsel cited *R. v. Dutchak*, 43 C.C.C. 74, [1924] 4 D.L.R. 973; *R. v. Hendrie* (1905), 10 C.C.C. 298, 11 O.L.R. 202; *R. v. Dumont* (1921), 37 C.C.C. 166, 64 D.L.R. 128, 49 O.L.R. 222; and *R. v. Dick*, 87 C.C.C. 101, 2 C.R. 417, [1947] 2 D.L.R. 213.

Each of the above-cited cases was decided on its own special facts and the only principles of application to the instant case are that the accused, in order to have been convicted, must have done something to encourage the commission of the offence or omitted to do something which assisted in its commission. It appears to me that when the accused, the owner of car, sat in the front seat on the passenger's side and permitted this young lady to increase the speed to such a dangerous rate, he did, by his lack of action, encourage her to violate the law. Certainly it would not have been wise for him to have grabbed the wheel at this dangerous speed, nor at any time when the car was being driven in excess of 60 m.p.h., as to do so would probably have been catastrophic. To turn off the ignition, as was suggested to us by the Crown, might not have been the best course either. In no uncertain terms he should have told this young lady, the minute she started to speed on this municipal road, to desist and slow down. In my opinion, the failure to even protest is equivalent to encouragement and is fatal to his defence.

The Crown cited to us two very pertinent cases with which I will deal briefly:

The first was *Du Cros v. Lambourne*, [1907] 1 K.B. 40, 21 Cox C.C. 311. The facts of that case are very similar to the facts in the instant case. There, the accused, who had permitted a young lady to drive his car, was charged with the substantive offence when she drove it in an improper manner, and was convicted on the ground that he was an aider and abettor. In 21 Cox C.C. at p. 315, Lord Alverstone C.J., said:

> If Miss Godwin was then driving, she was doing so with consent and approval of the appellant, who was the owner and in control of the car, and was sitting by her side, and he could and ought to have prevented her driving at such excessive and dangerous speed, but instead thereof he allowed her to do so, and did not interfere in any way.

The Court of Appeal held that on that finding of fact it was justified in convicting the accused as if he were the driver, as he was an aider, abettor, etc.

The other case is *R. v. Halmo*, 76 C.C.C. 116, [1941] 3 D.L.R. 6, [1941] O.R. 99, a decision of the Ontario Court of Appeal. In that case the owner of the vehicle was found guilty of the offence of reckless driving committed by his chauffeur.

It is true that in the *Halmo* case, *supra*, the accused, owner of the car, had full knowledge that his chauffeur was intoxicated; in fact, they became intoxicated together. Perhaps in the *Halmo* case circumstances are stronger than in the instant case but, nevertheless, it is an authority in support of the Crown's position. The *Halmo* and the *Du Cros* cases were discussed with apparent approval by the Manitoba Court of Appeal in *R. v. Harder*, 88 C.C.C. 21, 3 C.R. 49, [1947] 2 D.L.R. 593. The *Halmo* case was referred to by the Supreme Court of Canada in another *R. v. Harder* case reported (1956), 114 C.C.C. 129, 23 C.R. 295, 4 D.L.R. (2d) 150, and apparently approved. The following quotation from the *Halmo* case has some application to the instant case (At p. 127 [C.C.C.]):

> Three facts combine to make the accused a person who had in his charge and under his control the motor vehicle in question: (a) He was the owner of the motor vehicle; (b) He was the master of Mayville, his hired servant, who was driving the car; (c) He was personally present at all material times both before and at the time when the motor vehicle was being driven in a manner dangerous to the public.
>
> Being personally present and having in his charge and under his control the motor vehicle, he is a principal party to the offence of a breach of s. 285(6)(a) of the *Code*. *Reg. v. Brown* (1878), 14 Cox C.C. 144. He was guilty of negligence in that being so in charge and control of a dangerous machine he failed and omitted to control his drunken chauffeur and to prevent him from driving the car to the danger of the public.

Every passenger in an unlawfully driven motor vehicle is not necessarily subject to conviction as an aider and abettor, as it is conceivable that a passenger might not have any authority over the car or any right to control the driver, but that is not the situation in the instant case. As above stated, he failed to make any effort to stop or prevent the commission of the offence when he was in a position to do so and when he had the authority to do so.

Therefore, as intimated, I am of the opinion that the learned Magistrate was right in convicting the accused of the substantive offence on the ground that he was an aider and abettor and liable to conviction by virtue of s. 21(1) of the *Criminal Code*. The learned Magistrate's question ought to be answered in the affirmative. The appeal should be dismissed and the conviction affirmed.

*Appeal dismissed.*

---

*Kulbacki* is an example of aiding and abetting by omission rather than by some positive act of assistance or encouragement. Aiding or abetting by way of inaction is comparatively rare, not least because it rests either on a premise of passive encouragement or on a failure to discharge a duty. In this case, the court favours the latter view and, to support it, lays great emphasis on the facts that the accused was the owner of the car and present in it while it was being driven. Of central importance to the Court of Appeal was the position of control occupied by the accused, which gave him the opportunity to prevent or stop any dangerous driving.

To say that Kulbacki is guilty of dangerous driving by aiding and abetting the driver by omission must be close to the outer limits of participation by such means, not least because there is little indication that the accused did not act "for the purpose" of aiding or abetting the driver. As noted, the court's conclusion appears to rest on a faintly articulated premise that an adult person so situated is under a legal duty to ensure the safe operation of the vehicle. This means that a failure to prevent or stop the commission of an offence is tantamount to participation in the offence by aiding or abetting. This is not radically removed from the idea that a person might become a party to an offence actually committed by another by passive observation or acquiescence in the conduct of another. In circumstances such as these, it is also not radically removed from a concept of vicarious liability. Vicarious liability exists where B is held liable for the actions of A by virtue of some special feature in the relationship between them. Although there are some limited exceptions (e.g., corporate criminal liability), the criminal law has traditionally been hostile to vicarious liability because it is inimical to elementary principles of responsibility for individual agency. It is quite plausible to argue that the decision of the Court of Appeal in *Kulbacki* mistakenly substitutes vicarious liability for aiding and abetting under s. 21. The only argument to save the decision from this criticism would be the existence of legal duty to prevent or stop dangerous driving, provided that the person is the owner of the car and present in it under conditions that afford an opportunity to control the actions of the driver. This is problematic enough because it would involve the judicial creation of a duty to support a stretched theory of participation by aiding or abetting.

Apart from the problems raised on these facts, the result in *Kulbacki* is troublesome for another reason. What are the limits of its logic? Does a passenger in a taxi become a party to dangerous driving by the chauffeur by failing to prevent the dangerous driving?

### Dunlop and Sylvester v. The Queen
Supreme Court of Canada
(1979), 47 C.C.C. (2d) 93

[The appellants were tried and convicted by a judge and jury of rape for their part in a mass rape of a 16-year-old complainant by members of a motorcycle gang at an abandoned dump. The complainant testified that the two appellants had raped her. The appellants denied this. One of the appellants testified he had met with the motorcycle gang earlier in the night at the dump and was with the complainant at a bar before the rape. The appellants also testified that they arrived at the dump site, saw a woman having intercourse with a gang member, delivered four cases of beer, and left after three minutes.]

DICKSON J. (Laskin C.J.C., Estey, and Spence JJ. concurring) stated: ... A person is not guilty merely because he is present at the scene of a crime and does nothing to prevent it: Smith & Hogan, *Criminal Law*, 4th ed. (1978), p. 117. If there is no evidence of encouragement by him, a man's presence at the scene of the crime will not suffice to render him liable as aider and abettor. A person who, aware of a rape taking place in his presence, looks on and does nothing is not, as a matter of law, an accomplice. The classic case is the hardened urbanite who stands around in a subway station when an individual is murdered.

In the case at bar I have great difficulty in finding any evidence of anything more than mere presence and passive acquiescence. Presence at the commission of an offence can be evidence of aiding and abetting if accompanied by other factors, such as prior knowledge of the principal offender's intention to commit the offence or attendance for the purpose of encouragement. There was no evidence that while the crime was being committed either of the accused rendered aid, assistance or encouragement to the rape of Brenda Ross. There was no evidence of any positive act or omission to facilitate the unlawful purpose. One can infer that the two accused knew that a party was to be held, and that their presence at the dump was not accidental or in the nature of casual passers-by, but that is not sufficient. A person cannot properly be convicted of aiding or abetting in the commission of acts which he does not know may be or are intended: *per* Viscount Dilhorne in *Director of Public Prosecutions for Northern Ireland v. Maxwell*, [1978] 3 All E.R. 1140 at p. 1144 (H.L.). One must be able to infer that the accused had prior knowledge that an offence of the type committed was planned i.e., that their presence was with knowledge of the intended rape. On this issue, the Crown elicited no evidence.

[Dickson J. also held that the trial judge erred in not responding to the jury's question: "If the accused were aware of a rape taking place in their presence and did nothing to prevent or persuade the discontinuance of the act, are they considered as an accomplice to the act under law?" with an unequivocal "no."

The appeals were allowed and the appellants were acquitted on the ground that the verdict would not necessarily have been the same in the absence of the trial judge's error. Dickson J. stated that the jury's question indicated that they had not accepted evidence of the appellants' direct participation and it was in the interest of justice to acquit the appellants who had already been subjected to two trials.]

MARTLAND J. (Ritchie and Pigeon JJ. concurring) dissented and stated: ... It is not disputed that mere presence at the scene of a crime is not, in itself, sufficient to establish aiding and abetting the commission of an offence, but the trial Judge did not instruct the jury that it was. He charged the jury that "it is only necessary to show that he understood what was being done and by some act on his part assisted or encouraged the attainment of the act." ... In my opinion, there was evidence on which the jury could conclude that the appellants had aided and abetted the offence.

*Appeal allowed and acquittal entered.*

---

In the Supreme Court of Canada case of *Kirkness v. The Queen* (1990), 60 C.C.C. (3d) 97, Wilson J. stated:

> Perhaps the most troubling case on this issue to date is the decision of the Ontario Court of Appeal in *R. v. Salajko* (1970), 9 C.R.N.S. 145, in which the accused was held to have no criminal responsibility in a gang rape at which he was present. The accused had stood by and witnessed the rape take place with his pants down. ... I find it difficult to view such behaviour as "passive acquiescence." In my view, the decision in *Salajko* is anomalous and should not be followed.

Why? Wilson J. asserts that the accused "stood by" but that his presence was not passive acquiescence. What is the principle that would allow Salajko's standing-by to be described as participation in the offence?

In *R. v. Popen* (1981), 60 C.C.C. (2d) 232, the accused was charged with manslaughter of his infant daughter as a result of mistreatment on a number of occasions by his wife. The jury convicted after the trial judge directed the jury that the accused could be convicted as a party to the wife's offence pursuant to s. 21(1)(b). The Ontario Court of Appeal sent the case back for a new trial. Martin J.A. stated as follows:

> After giving this matter our most careful consideration, we are of the view that there was no evidence that the appellant had done or omitted to do anything *for the purpose of* aiding his wife inflict the injuries to the child. Even if the appellant's omission to take action to prevent his wife mistreating the child had the effect of assisting the wife, we are all of the view that there was no evidence upon which a jury could reasonably find that the appellant's inaction was for the purpose of assisting his wife and there was, consequently, no basis for the application of s. 21(1)(b).

Although as previously mentioned, the trial Judge did not leave s. 21(1)(c) with the jury we think that he did not err in this respect and that there is no basis for the application of s. 21(1)(c). In some circumstances, a person who is present at the commission by another of an illegal act, which he has a duty to prevent, may by mere inactivity encourage the illegal act. The law, in our view, is correctly stated in Smith and Hogan, *Criminal Law*, 4th ed. (1978), at pp. 118-9:

> Where D has a right to control the actions of another and he deliberately refrains from exercising it, his inactivity may be a positive encouragement to the other to perform an illegal act, and, therefore, an aiding and abetting.

He then set out a number of cases and then continued:

> In the above cases, the person having a right and a duty to control the actions of another, was present when the illegal acts occurred.
>
> As previously mentioned, the appellant was not shown to have been present on any occasion when his wife mistreated the child and we do not think the authorities referred to by Smith and Hogan in the passage previously quoted, or by Robertson C.J.O. in *R. v. Halmo* (1941), 76 C.C.C. 116 can be applied to the present case in these circumstances.
>
> We think, however, that it would have been open to a jury, properly charged, to find that the appellant was criminally negligent in failing to protect his child from his wife's mis-treatment, when under a duty to do so, and that such failure contributed to the child's death. If the jury reached the conclusion that the appellant was criminally negligent in failing to take proper steps to protect the child, and that his criminal negligence contributed to her death, he would, of course, be independently guilty of manslaughter, as distinct from being a party to his wife's offence.
>
> We are disposed to think that the words "necessaries of life" in s. 197 may be wide enough to include not only food, shelter, care and medical attention necessary to sustain life, but also necessary protection of a child from harm. It is, however, not necessary to decide that question since, in any event, a parent is under a legal duty at common law to take reasonable steps to protect his or her child from illegal violence used by the other parent or by a third person towards the child which the parent foresees or ought to foresee. In our opinion such parent is criminally liable under the *Code* for failing to discharge that duty in circumstances which show a wanton or reckless disregard for the child's safety, where the failure to discharge the legal duty has contributed to the death of the child or has resulted in bodily harm to the child.

---

In *R. v. Nixon* (1990), 57 C.C.C. (3d) 97, the accused was the senior officer in charge of the Vancouver police lock up. He was convicted of aggravated assault of a prisoner, Jacobsen, who was beaten after giving a false name. His appeal was dismissed by the British Columbia Court of Appeal with Legg J.A. stating:

> After concluding that she was satisfied beyond a reasonable doubt that the appellant was present at the time of the assault and knew what happened, the trial judge reasoned that under the *Police Act*, R.S.B.C. 1979, c. 331, and ss. 27 and 37 of the *Criminal Code* of Canada, the appellant had a duty to protect Jacobsen. By failing to act to prevent the assault

on Jacobsen the appellant failed to discharge this duty and, on the basis of this omission, was guilty of aiding and abetting the commission of the assault.

With reference to *Dunlop and Sylvester* she stated:

> This case indicates something more than mere presence was needed. In the circumstances of the case at bar there was more than mere presence. But assuming there was only mere presence, this case has one very important aspect that was not present in either the *R. v. Black* case or the *Dunlop and Sylvester v. The Queen* case. That is the fact that Nixon is a police officer and has the obligation to protect his charges. He has that duty by legislation. He cannot say he was not involved. He was there, he had a duty to involve himself.

A similar result was reached in *R. v. Popen* (1981), 60 C.C.C. (2d) 232 (Ont. C.A.). In that case a child died after being beaten by her mother. There was evidence of a long history of mistreatment by the mother and, while there was no evidence of mistreatment by the father, the court held that it was open to the jury to infer that the father was aware of the mother's actions and that, in the circumstances, the father could be convicted as a principal of criminal negligence causing death. Martin J.A. stated, at p. 240:

> ... a parent is under a legal duty at common law to take reasonable steps to protect his or her child from illegal violence used by the other parent or by a third person towards the child which the parent foresees or ought to foresee.
>
> In our opinion such parent is criminally liable under the *Code* for failing to discharge that duty in circumstances which show a wanton or reckless disregard for the child's safety, where the failure to discharge the legal duty has contributed to the death of the child or has resulted in bodily harm to the child.

I am unable to accept an argument advanced by the appellant that the appellant cannot be convicted of an assault by reason of a failure to act because assault requires the intentional application of force. The appellant was not convicted of assault as a principal but as a party under s. 21 of the *Criminal Code* on the ground that he aided and abetted the commission of the assault by others. ...

The question is whether the appellant aided or abetted the commission of the assault by reason of his failure to protect Jacobsen who was under his care.

The appellant relied on the judgment of Mr. Justice Dickson in *Dunlop and Sylvester v. The Queen, supra,* and submitted that something more than mere presence was needed.

Counsel for the appellant argued that the presence of the appellant at the scene of the assault, without any active steps on his part to aid or encourage its commission, must be interpreted as no more than "mere presence" and is thus not capable of making the appellant a party to the offence.

I am unable to accept that submission. An accused who is present at the scene of an offence and who carries out no overt acts to aid or encourage the commission of the offence may none the less be convicted as a party if his purpose in failing to act was to aid in the commission of the offence. Section 21(1)(b) extends by its very terms to such an omission in that it makes a person a party to an offence who "omits to do anything for the purpose of aiding [in the commission of the offence]." A failure to act in accordance with a duty to act may be an omission to do something for the purpose of aiding or abetting.

In some circumstances the presence of an accused will, in itself, be held to have encouraged the commission of the offence. In this situation there will be more than "mere presence" on the part of the accused and the accused will be liable as a party.

## III. COMMON INTENTION

### R. v. Kirkness
Supreme Court of Canada
[1990] 3 S.C.R. 74

WILSON J. (dissenting): ...

[72] The first step in establishing liability under s. 21(2) is to show that the accused formed an intention in common with others to carry out an unlawful purpose and to assist them in achieving that purpose. This common intention need not be pre-planned in any way. It is sufficient, and the case law supports this proposition, that such intention arise just prior to or at the time of the commission of the offence. Indeed, the common design is usually implied from the facts. For example, in *R. v. Rice* (1902), 4 O.L.R. 223, 5 C.C.C. 509 (C.A.), leave to appeal refused (1902), 32 S.C.R. 480, 5 C.C.C. 529, the accused were being transported by cab from the courthouse to the jail during the course of their trial on charges of burglary. An unknown person threw a package into the cab which contained at least two revolvers. A struggle ensued and one of the prisoners shot a police officer, killing him. In upholding the jury's finding that the accused was guilty of the murder as a party, Osler J.A. remarked at p. 523 [C.C.C.]:

> The common design might certainly be formed as soon as the prisoners found that weapons suitable as means of effecting an escape were in their possession; and the evidence, as reported in the case, supports the inference that there was a common design to effect an unlawful purpose by violent means.

[73] In my opinion, there is no question that a common purpose was shared by Snowbird and Kirkness in this case. Where one has aided or abetted in the commission of an offence, there can be little doubt that a shared intention to effect an unlawful purpose existed. In this case Kirkness was a principal in the break and enter. By his own admission Snowbird asked him to come along in the plan to rob the house. He agreed. Moreover, it was he who effected the break and enter by prying open a window at the back of the house with a handle off a garden tool. It was he who first entered and let Snowbird in through the back door. There is not a scintilla of evidence to suggest that the accused did not share an intention in common with Snowbird. ...

[78] Section 21(2) of the Code deems a party criminally liable for the acts of the principal offender when the accused knew or ought to have known of the probable commission of the acts which constitute the offence. There are two elements to this last branch of s. 21(2): (i) the commission of the ultimate offence has to be probable; and (ii) the accused must know or ought to have known of this probability.

[79]  The first question to be asked is whether the killing of the victim was a probable consequence of the unlawful purpose. If the jury determined that the unlawful purpose encompassed only the breaking and entering, it would be hard to justify a finding that the death of the occupant was a probable consequence of that purpose. If, however, the jury determined that the unlawful purpose encompassed also acts of physical violence against the occupant, then the route to party liability on the part of Kirkness is much clearer. Apart from the particular circumstances surrounding this series of events, it seems to me that violence so often accompanies sexual crimes that it is implicit in the very nature of the offence that some harm short of death is probable. This is so, in my opinion, whenever the common unlawful purpose contemplates physical interference with a person. There may, of course, be situations where the level of physical violence contemplated is so minimal that serious bodily harm is merely a possibility rather than a probability. And it may indeed be the case that this observation would hold true even in some situations where the unlawful purpose is an assault of a sexual nature. While I personally would not have thought that what occurred in this case is one of those instances, the question whether the causing of bodily harm short of death was a probable consequence of the sexual offence committed against Elizabeth Johnson was for the jury to decide. ...

### 5.  Abandonment

[81]  As with other criminal offences, an accused whose liability is established under the provisions applicable to parties will still have open to him a number of defences. In the context of accomplice liability, however, the defence of abandonment is particularly crucial. According to this defence, an accused may absolve himself of criminal liability for the acts of the principal if he can show that he abandoned his purpose to assist in the commission of a criminal offence. Because of my conclusion respecting the appropriate disposition of this appeal, I include here a discussion of the elements of this defence.

[82]  While the defence of abandonment is available to an accused charged under either subs. (1) or (2), the defence has usually been applied in Canada to the common intent provision. For instance, this Court considered the availability of this defence in *Henderson v. R.*, [1948] S.C.R. 226, 5 C.R. 112, 91 C.C.C. 97. In that case, the trial Judge had not adequately put the accused's defence of abandonment to the jury, and a new trial on a charge of murder was ordered. In the course of his reasons, Taschereau J. referred to the test of abandonment as stated by Sloan J.A. in *R. v. Whitehouse (Savage)* (1940), [1941] 1 W.W.R. 112, 55 B.C.R. 420 at 425, [1941] 1 D.L.R. 683 (C.A.):

> After a crime has been committed and before a prior abandonment of the common enterprise may be found by a jury there must be, in my view, in the absence of exceptional circumstances, something more than a mere mental change of intention and physical change of place by those associates who wish to disassociate [*sic*] themselves from the consequences attendant upon their willing assistance up to the moment of the actual commission of that crime. I would not attempt to define too closely what must be done in criminal matters involving participation in a common unlawful purpose to break the

chain of causation and responsibility. That must depend on the circumstances of each case but it seems to me that one essential element ought to be established in a case of this kind: where practicable and reasonable there must be timely communication of the intention to abandon the common purpose from those who wish to dissociate themselves from the contemplated crime to those who desire to continue in it. What is "timely communication" must be determined by the facts of each case but where practicable and reasonable it ought to be such communication verbal or otherwise, that will serve unequivocal notice upon the other party to the common unlawful cause that if he proceeds upon it he does so without the further aid and assistance of those who withdraw. The unlawful purpose of him who continues alone is then his own and not one in common with those who are no longer parties to it nor liable to its full and final consequences.

[83] In that case, three young men arranged to hold up one Ingram, a local merchant. One of the men approached Ingram with an iron pipe which was covered with a piece of hose. Just as he got near him the other two young men ran away. The pipe was later found with human blood on it. Ingram died some time later. At the trial, the Judge instructed the jury that they must consider only two elements in order to find abandonment: (1) a change of mental intention; and (2) quitting the scene before the crime was finally consummated. Sloan J.A. held that the trial Judge erred for the reasons I have quoted above.

[84] *Whitehouse*, supra, was followed by this Court in *Miller v. R.*, [1977] 2 S.C.R. 680, in which two accused were charged with the murder of a police officer. They had been out drinking and were discussing their animosity towards the police. They talked of shooting a police officer. They then left the tavern with a loaded rifle and proceeded to drive around in an erratic manner so as to attract the attention of the police. Miller was at the wheel. Cockriell threw a beer bottle at the local courthouse. The pair were subsequently stopped by the police. As the officer approached the car, Cockriell pulled the trigger on the rifle which had been sitting in Miller's lap.

[85] The Court found that there was no evidence to support a defence of abandonment. Ritchie J. followed the words of Sloan J.A. in *Whitehouse* and held that there was no clear evidence that the intention to abandon the common purpose had been communicated. Ritchie J. also referred with approval to the decision of the Court of Criminal Appeal in *R. v. Becerra* (1975), 62 Cr. App. R. 212 (C.A.), in which the appellant had broken into a house with two other men. When they entered the house Becerra was carrying a knife. Cooper, one of the other accused, knew that Becerra was in possession of this weapon. He had asked to borrow it to cut the telephone wires leading to the house. The three men entered by the window. The occupant of the house, an elderly lady, began switching the bedroom light on and off, presumably to attract attention so that help might arrive. Cooper punched her and covered her head with a pillow. Becerra cut the wires of the telephone at the bedside.

[86] Cooper then took the knife and went into the kitchen. Mr. Lewis, a neighbour, upon hearing the commotion below came downstairs. Becerra and the third man heard him, climbed out the window, and ran away. A struggle between Cooper and Lewis ensued. Lewis was stabbed four times and died as a consequence. Becerra was indicted for the murder of Lewis and convicted. He appealed his conviction on

the ground that the trial Judge erred in failing to properly put the defence of abandon-ment to the jury. The gist of his complaint was that the trial Judge instructed the jury that the defence was not available to an accused who, in providing a weapon which he knows is for the purpose of at least occasioning bodily harm, merely quits the scene. The trial Judge in fact went further and suggested that there was some obligation on Becerra to physically intervene in order to dissociate himself from Cooper's act.

[87] The Court of Appeal unanimously upheld Becerra's conviction. Drawing upon the words of Sloan J.A. in *Whitehouse*, the Court found that Becerra was legally responsible for the acts of Cooper. The Court of Appeal did not find it necessary to decide whether the accused needed to physically intervene. Roskill L.J. said at p. 219:

> On the facts of this case, in the circumstances then prevailing, the knife having already been used and being contemplated for further use when it was handed over by Becerra to Cooper for the purpose of avoiding (if necessary) by violent means the hazards of identification, if Becerra wanted to withdraw at that stage, he would have to "counter-mand," to use the word that is used in some of the cases or "repent" to use another word so used, in some manner vastly different and vastly more effective than merely to say "Come on, let's go" and go out through the window.

[88] Commentators on the defence of abandonment appear to agree that a defend-ant will be held to a different standard depending upon the degree of his participation in the crime. Glanville Williams has suggested that where a defendant has acted posi-tively to assist a crime beyond merely inciting or encouraging it, he must do his best to prevent its commission in order to escape liability. He says that the defendant must warn the victim or do something short, perhaps, of going to the police. This restriction upon the right of withdrawal, is, he contends, an exception to the usual requirement that mens rea and actus reus be contemporaneous. "In effect the defendant is made liable for negligence in failing to prevent the crime": *Textbook of Criminal Law*, 2d ed. (London: Stevens & Sons, 1983), at p. 364. This distinction has also been recognized by Profes-sor Lanham ("Accomplices and Withdrawal" (1981) 97 L.Q. Rev. 575). He too states as a principle that "[w]here the act [of] participation goes beyond encouragement, mere countermand may not be sufficient to exculpate the accused" (at p. 591).

[89] Certain factors have been recognized as relevant to the determination of whether an accused's intention has been legally abandoned. Professor Lanham lists the questions to be considered by the Court as follows at p. 575:

1. Must withdrawal be voluntary?
2. Is countermand necessary?
3. Is countermand sufficient?
4. Must countermand be express?
5. Must withdrawal be timely?
6. Is attempted withdrawal sufficient?
7. Must countermand be communicated to all principals?

Put more succinctly, the issue is, as Professor Manson says, the quality of the with-drawal. In "Re-codifying Attempts, Parties, and Abandoned Intentions" (1989) 14 *Queen's Law J.* 85, he put the matter this way at p. 95:

> Looking at the defence of abandoned intention in respect of parties, the key issues relate to the quality of withdrawal from the original plan and whether more is required to exculpate. These questions take on different significance depending on the form of accomplice liability in issue and the particular circumstances of a given case.

[90]  I agree that it would not only be impossible but also inadvisable for the Court to attempt to set down precisely what should be required of an accused in order to demonstrate that he or she has withdrawn as an accomplice to an offence. I agree with Professor Manson that the issue is the quality of the withdrawal in relation to both the offence and the type of criminal participation in which the party has engaged. Of course, attempts to stop or prevent the commission of a crime which are insufficient to exculpate an accused may always be taken into consideration on sentencing: see Martin Wasik, "Abandoning Criminal Intent" [1980] *Crim. L. Rev.* 785.

[91]  In this case it was open to the jury to find that the participation of Kirkness went beyond mere encouragement. He had physically placed a chair in front of the door to prevent their activities in the house from being discovered. What evidence could the jury have relied upon to support a conclusion that he had effectively withdrawn himself? Kirkness took no steps to remove the chair or to otherwise intervene in Snowbird's domination of the victim. The only action upon which the accused relies to demonstrate his withdrawal is his act of saying to Snowbird, "stop that, you'll kill her." The question for the jury is whether this statement, if believed, is sufficient to negate Kirkness's participation in the crime.

### 6.  Distinguishing Subs. 21(1) from Subs. 21(2)

…

[93]  According to Peter Gillies on *Criminal Law* (Sydney: Law Book, 1985), at p. 140, the common-intender rule was developed to simplify the rules of accessorial liability for juries and was not created as an additional basis upon which to ground criminal liability. On the other hand, this Court has stated that subss. (1) and (2) of s. 21 are conceptually distinct. The essential difference between them was explained by McIntyre J., writing for the Court, in *R. v. Simpson*, [1988] 1 S.C.R. 3, 62 C.R. (3d) 137, 23 B.C.L.R. (2d) 145, [1988] 2 W.W.R. 385, 46 D.L.R. (4th) 466, 81 N.R. 267, 38 C.C.C. (3d) 481. He said at p. 14 [S.C.R., p. 146 C.R.]:

> The two subsections of s. 21 deal with different circumstances. Subsection (1) applies to make everyone a party to an offence who commits it or who aids and abets in its commission. Subsection (2) covers the case where, in the absence of aiding and abetting, a person may become a party to an offence committed by another which he knew or ought to have known was a probable consequence of carrying out an unlawful purpose in common with the actual perpetrator.

[94]  Rose put the matter similarly at p. 65:

> [Section 22(2)] is quite plainly intended to provide liability in the case of *consequential* offences which were not committed nor aided or abetted by the accused, but which *resulted* from the prosecution of the *original* offence.

[Emphasis original.] It is my view that since aiders and abettors have been treated differently from common intenders by Parliament, some difference between these two subsections must be recognized.

[95] On the other hand, circumstances may undoubtedly arise in which it will be difficult to distinguish the applicability of the two subsections. Where an accused has aided or abetted the commission of some crime, party liability under subs. (1) follows where the crime which is ultimately committed is of the same type as the one in which the accused has assisted. Under subs. (2), on the other hand, party liability follows upon a finding that the offence actually committed was one which the accused knew or ought to have known would be a probable consequence of the commission of the contemplated offence in which he assisted. The difficult task for the jury in such cases is to distinguish between when the crime actually committed is of a similar type to that contemplated, and when the crime actually committed is a probable consequence of the crime contemplated.

[96] In my view, the difference between the two is that the doctrine of similarity was not intended to include situations where the principal committed another offence, even a probable one, in order to cover up his crime or to facilitate his escape. I believe that, in order to be an offence "of the type" within the meaning of s. 21(1), the committed offence must not only be similar but must be sufficiently contemporaneous with the contemplated offence. Section 21(2) is, in my view, reserved for those instances where there has been a break in time between the two offences, and the offence actually committed follows after, but as a consequence of the offence originally planned.

### R. v. Maier and Clark
Saskatchewan Court of Appeal
[1968] 2 C.C.C. 328

CULLITON C.J.S. (for the Court): ... I have carefully read both the evidence and the judgment of the learned trial Judge. I am satisfied that the learned trial Judge did not direct his mind to a consideration of this requirement of s. 21(2). The failure of the learned trial Judge to do so, in my opinion, constitutes an error on his part in the interpretation and application of s. 21(2). As a result, the learned trial Judge made no finding of fact that the possession offence was one which Clark should have known was a probable consequence of carrying out their unlawful purpose, nor, in my opinion, was there any evidence upon which such a finding could be made. The prosecution therefore failed to establish one of the essential ingredients necessary to convict Clark of the possession charge through the application of s. 21(2).

Clark's appeal against his conviction on count 1 will be allowed and the conviction quashed.

*Appeal by one accused on one count allowed.*

# R. v. Logan
Supreme Court of Canada
(1990), 58 C.C.C. (3d) 391

[The accused were charged with a number of offences relating to the robbery of a Becker's store and the serious wounding of the cashier, Barbara Turnbull. Two of the accused were convicted of attempted murder and appealed to the Ontario Court of Appeal (1988), 46 C.C.C. (3d) 354. The Court of Appeal held that the objective test in s. 21(2) of the Code is inoperative in relation to attempted murder, stating:

> As previously noted, on a charge of attempted murder, the necessary *mens rea* must be that of an intention to kill. In our opinion, in so far as s. 21(2) permits a conviction of a party for the offence of attempted murder on the basis of objective foreseeability, a lesser degree of *mens rea* than is required for the principal, it is contrary to the principles of fundamental justice. Nor do we think that this departure from the principles of fundamental justice can be saved by s. 1 of the Charter … .
>
> Consistent with what was stated by Lamer J., it is unnecessary, in order to deter others, to convict of attempted murder a person who did not know but ought to have known that the principal would shoot with intent to kill. Under such circumstances, a person who forms an intention with one or more other persons to carry out an armed robbery while armed with a firearm and to assist each other therein would be guilty of armed robbery and of using a firearm in the commission of such an indictable offence.
>
> Severe sentences are imposed for armed robbery where all aggravating factors, such as a severe injury to the person who was robbed, are entitled to be considered. Such a severe sentence should sufficiently deter others from engaging in such criminal conduct.
>
> Thus, on a charge of attempted murder, where s. 21(2) is invoked to determine the liability of a party to the offence, the words of s. 21(2), "ought to have known," must be held to be inoperative and cannot be resorted to by the trier of fact to determine the guilt of such an accused person.
>
> It follows that the conviction of Sutcliffe Logan and Warren Johnson for the attempted murder of Barbara Turnbull cannot stand.
>
> Sutcliffe Logan and Warren Johnson were, however, also found guilty of the armed robbery of Barbara Turnbull (count 10) and of using a firearm while committing that indictable offence (count 11).
>
> Because the jury had also convicted them of the attempted murder of Barbara Turnbull, the learned trial judge stayed the robbery count. With respect, we think that he erred in so doing since the count for attempted murder was a separate and distinct delict from that of the robbery, including separate and additional factors, and there was no reason why both convictions could not stand. In any event, since the conviction for attempted murder cannot stand, there is now no basis for the stay. …
>
> The matter should be remitted to the learned trial judge to sentence both of them for the offence of armed robbery, and in doing so he will, of course, take into consideration the very serious aggravating factors which relate to that offence.
>
> In summary, all of the appeals before us are dismissed save, with respect to the appeals by Sutcliffe Logan and Warren Johnson from their convictions for attempted

murder, convictions for the robbery of Barbara Turnbull are substituted. The matter of
the sentence on these convictions is remitted to the trial judge.

The Supreme Court of Canada dismissed a further appeal (1990), 58 C.C.C. (3d)
391. The issue of the *mens rea* for attempted murder is dealt with in chapter 7.]

LAMER C.J. stated for the Court (with Sopinka and L'Heureux-Dubé JJ. concurring
in the result):  The appellant is challenging the constitutionality of s. 21(2) in general
and, in particular, of the objective component of the section ("ought to have known").
However, the Court of Appeal, quite correctly, did not declare the objective component of s. 21(2) inoperative for all offences. They dealt specifically with the operation of the provision in relation to the offence of attempted murder and the possibility
that a party to an attempted murder could be convicted upon proof of objective intent,
whereas a conviction of the principal would require proof of subjective intent. More
generally, as a basis for their decision, the court determined that it is a principle of
fundamental justice that a party to *any* offence cannot be found guilty of the offence
based on a lower standard of requisite *mens rea* than that required for convicting the
principal.

For this proposition, the court relied on our judgment in *Vaillancourt*. In that case,
this Court held that for a few offences the principles of fundamental justice require
that a conviction cannot stand unless there is proof beyond a reasonable doubt of a
minimum degree of *mens rea*, and that legislation providing for any lesser degree
violates the *Charter* and is inoperative. Murder was one of those offences.

With respect, I cannot construe *Vaillancourt* as saying that, as a general proposition, Parliament cannot ever enact provisions requiring different levels of guilt for
principal offenders and parties. Although I readily admit that, as a matter of policy,
the proposition seems more equitable than not, I am not ready to characterize it as a
principle of fundamental justice. It must be remembered that within many offences
there are varying degrees of guilt and it remains the function of the sentencing process to adjust the punishment for each individual offender accordingly. The argument
that the principles of fundamental justice prohibit the conviction of a party to an
offence on the basis of a lesser degree of *mens rea* than that required to convict the
principal could only be supported, if at all, in a situation where the sentence for a
particular offence is fixed. However, currently in Canada, the sentencing scheme is
flexible enough to accommodate the varying degrees of culpability resulting from
the operation of ss. 21 and 22.

That said, however, there are a few offences with respect to which the operation of
the objective component of s. 21(2) will restrict the rights of an accused under s. 7. If
an offence is one of the few for which s. 7 requires a minimum degree of *mens rea*,
*Vaillancourt* does preclude Parliament from providing for the conviction of a party to
that offence on the basis of a degree of *mens rea* below the constitutionally required
minimum … .

Having completed the initial step of the inquiry, one can proceed to the second
step in determining the requisite *mens rea* for the conviction of a party pursuant to s.
21(2) on a charge of attempted murder. When the principles of fundamental justice

require *subjective* foresight in order to convict a principal of attempted murder, that same minimum degree of *mens rea* is constitutionally required to convict a party to the offence of attempted murder. Any conviction for attempted murder, whether of the principal directly or of a party pursuant to s. 21(2), will carry enough stigma to trigger the constitutional requirement. To the extent that s. 21(2) would allow for the conviction of a party to the offence of attempted murder on the basis of objective foresight, its operation restricts s. 7 of the Charter. ...

The objective of [s. 21(2)] is to deter joint criminal enterprises and to encourage persons who do participate to ensure that their accomplices do not commit offences beyond the planned unlawful purpose. This is a legislative objective of sufficient importance to justify overriding the rights of an accused under s. 7 of the Charter.

The objective component of s. 21(2) unduly impairs rights under s. 7 of the Charter when it operates with respect to an offence for which a conviction carries severe stigma and for which, therefore, there is a constitutionally required minimum degree of *mens rea*. The words "ought to know" allow for the possibility that while a party may not have considered and accepted the risk that an accomplice may do something with the intent to kill in furtherance of the common purpose, the party, through this negligence, could still be found guilty of attempted murder. In other words, parties could be held to be criminally negligent with respect to the behaviour of someone else. For most offences under the *Criminal Code*, a person is only convicted for criminal negligence if consequences have ensued from their actions. While a person may be convicted, absent consequences, for criminal negligence (*e.g.*, dangerous operation of a motor vehicle), none of these forms of criminal negligence carry with them the stigma of being labelled a "killer." In a situation where s. 21(2) is operating in relation to the offence of attempted murder, no consequences have resulted from the actions of the party and yet the party could be convicted of this offence and suffer severe accompanying stigma and penalty.

Because of the importance of the legislative purpose, the objective component of s. 21(2) can be justified with respect to most offences. However, with respect to the few offences for which the Constitution requires subjective intent, the stigma renders the infringement too serious and outweighs the legislative objective which, therefore, cannot be justified under s. 1.

I would, therefore, as did the Court of Appeal, declare inoperative the words "or ought to have known" when considering under s. 21(2) whether a person is a party to any offence where it is a constitutional requirement for a conviction that foresight of the consequences be subjective, which is the case for attempted murder. Once these words are deleted, the remaining section requires, in the context of attempted murder, that the party to the common venture know that it is probable that his accomplice would do something with the intent to kill in carrying out the common purpose.

*Appeal dismissed.*

---

In *R. v. Davy* (1993), 86 C.C.C. (3d) 385, the Supreme Court of Canada dealt with the combination of s. 21(2) and manslaughter. McLachlin J. stated for the Court:

This leaves the question of the *mens rea* required to sustain a conviction for manslaughter under s. 21(2) of the *Criminal Code*. The Court of Appeal held that to be convicted of manslaughter under s. 21(2) of the *Code*, the Crown must establish that the accused knew or ought to have known that *killing* short of murder was a probable consequence of the pursuit of the common unlawful purpose. However, as was previously noted, since the date of the Court of Appeal's decision, this court has held that manslaughter does not require that a risk of death be foreseeable; foreseeability of the risk of harm is sufficient: *Creighton, supra*. This court's decision in *R. v. Trinneer*, [1970] 3 C.C.C. 289, 10 D.L.R. (3d) 568, [1970] S.C.R. 638 (S.C.C.), suggests that there is nothing inherent in s. 21(2) which requires a higher *mens rea* than would otherwise be required for a conviction for manslaughter. There the court held unanimously that an accused could be convicted of constructive murder as a party to that offence under the combination of ss. 21(2) and 230 (then s. 202) of the *Criminal Code*, without the Crown proving that the accused knew or ought to have known that it was probable death would ensue from the execution of the common unlawful purpose. While it would no longer be possible to convict for murder under s. 21(2) without proof of subjective awareness of the risk of death (*R. v. Logan* (1990), 58 C.C.C. (3d) 391, 73 D.L.R. (4th) 40, [1990] 2 S.C.R. 731 (S.C.C.)), the reasoning in *Trinneer*, coupled with *Creighton, supra*, suggests that the appropriate *mens rea* for manslaughter under s. 21(2) is objective awareness of the risk of harm. It must follow that a conviction for manslaughter under s. 21(2) does not require foreseeability of death, but only foreseeability of harm, which in fact results in death.

## IV.  COUNSELLING

### R. v. Lacoursière
Quebec Court of Appeal
(2002), 7 C.R. (6th) 117

PROULX J.C.A.: ...

[5] Ce pourvoi requiert l'examen de trois notions fondamentales en matière de responsabilité pénale, soit *l'incitation* (ou le fait de conseiller un crime), le *complot* et le *retrait* du complot.

*Les faits saillants et le contexte procédural*

[6] L'intimé est inculpé de trois chefs d'accusation reliés à une introduction par effraction commise à la résidence de sa grand-mère et à des infractions de vol qualifié et de séquestration qui en ont découlé.

[7] Au procès, les parties déposent devant le premier juge des admissions de fait contenant notamment des déclarations écrites de l'intimé et de l'un des auteurs des crimes, Nicolas Companozzi. Pour une juste compréhension du litige, il est essentiel de reproduire intégralement certaines de ces admissions:

### 1. La déclaration de l'intimé

En avril dernier, ma grand-mère Jeanne-d'Arc m'a payé un voyage à Cuba. Lorsque je suis revenu de voyage, j'ai rencontré mes amis pour parler de mon voyage. ... Je disais que ma grand-mère avait de l'argent pour me payer ce voyage et d'autres cadeaux qu'elle m'a faits. ... Au début de cette semaine, j'ai été rencontrer Nicolas chez lui. Il m'a parlé qu'il avait vraiment besoin d'argent. Moi aussi j'avais besoin d'argent. Je lui ai dit que j'aimerais voler l'argent de ma grand-mère, mais comme c'est ma grand-mère, je ne pouvais pas faire ça. Nicolas m'a offert d'aller lui voler et qu'il me donnerait un quotte. On parlait ici qui y aurait à peu près 7-8 mille dollars. Ma quotte aurait été de la moitié. Je lui ai cependant dit d'attendre, que je lui dirais quand y aller, parce que je ne voulais pas que ma grand-mère soit là.

### 2. La déclaration de Nicolas Campanozzi

Éric est venu chez moi et on a parlé. Éric m'a parlé que sa grand-mère avait une grosse somme d'argent chez elle. Il disait qu'elle avait plus ou moins 15 000$ dans sa chambre. Il m'a dit qu'il aimerait faire la « piole » à sa grand-mère, en faisant référence de voler l'argent à sa grand-mère. Je lui ai dit qu'il ne pouvait faire ça car c'est sa grand-mère. Par contre si ça se fait, tu pourrais avoir une « cotte ». Il m'a dit d'attendre son O.K. mais il était d'accord.

### 3. Autre admission

Il est admis que, au cours d'une conversation téléphonique entre Nicolas Campanozzi, le 11 août 1999, et Éric Lacoursière, ce dernier a mentionné qu'il ne voulait plus que le vol chez sa grand-mère ait lieu.

[8] Or, c'est le 12 août que les crimes ont été commis par quatre personnes, dont Nicolas Campanozzi.

*Le jugement de première instance*

[9] En substance, le premier juge conclut à la preuve d'un *complot* entre l'intimé et Campanozzi sans toutefois pouvoir déclarer l'intimé coupable de ce complot puisque l'acte d'accusation se limite à des chefs d'introduction par effraction, de vol qualifié et de séquestration.

[10] Par ailleurs, en raison du fait que l'intimé s'est « complètement retiré du complot » le 11 août, soit la veille des délits, le premier juge conclut que ce retrait dégage l'intimé de toute participation dans les crimes commis subséquemment.

[11] Enfin, répondant à la thèse du Ministère public qui plaidait qu'il ne s'agissait pas d'un *complot* mais plutôt d'une *incitation* au sens de l'art. 22 du Code criminel, le juge d'instance a distingué ces deux concepts et retenu qu'en l'espèce il ne s'agissait pas d'une incitation au crime mais bien d'un complot:

> Il faut faire une distinction entre complot et conseil. Parce que autrement toute la juris-prudence établie en matière de complot, que quelqu'un qui se retire du complot ne peut être déclaré coupable des infractions subséquentes mais quelqu'un qui participe à un complot conseille toujours à quelqu'un de commettre une infraction. Quand on conseille

à quelqu'un de commettre une infraction, ça veut pas nécessairement dire qu'on est dans un complot. Si par exemple monsieur Campanozzi avait été voir monsieur Lacoursière en lui disant: J'ai besoin d'argent, moi, je cherche une place où aller, et monsieur Lacoursière lui aurait conseillé d'aller commettre le vol chez sa grand-mère, là la jurisprudence dit que, même si lui change d'idée, si il a conseillé à quelqu'un de commettre un crime ou quoi que ce soit, là il aurait pu être déclaré coupable. C'est la situation inverse qui s'est passée.

Je suis d'avis qu'en l'espèce, lorsqu'il dit qu'il ne veut plus procéder au vol chez sa grand-mère, il ne peut être déclaré coupable d'avoir conseillé à monsieur Campanozzi de commettre cet acte criminel-là. On peut conseiller à une personne, comme je le disais, de commettre un acte criminel, sans être membre du complot. C'est pas le cas en espèce. Il s'agit d'un complot et non d'un conseil. Je ne crois pas qu'il serait juridiquement logique, dans l'espèce, de se retirer d'un complot et de ne pas être capable d'être déclaré coupable de l'acte substantif si on se rabattait toujours sur le conseil. Alors, il s'agit de notions juridiques qui sont totalement indépendantes l'une de l'autre.

### Les questions en litige

[12] C'est la qualification et non l'existence de la participation de l'intimé qui constitue la principale question en litige.

[13] S'il s'agit d'un complot, alors se pose la question subsidiaire de déterminer si le retrait signifié par l'intimé est valide et si ce retrait peut lui éviter d'être partie aux infractions qui ont été commises subséquemment.

[14] Par contre, s'il s'est agi d'une incitation à commettre l'introduction par effraction, comme il est loin d'être sûr tant en doctrine qu'en jurisprudence que le *retrait* peut être invoqué comme dans le cas d'un *complot*, l'intimé n'aurait pas échappé à une condamnation pour les infractions commises subséquemment.

[15] Étant d'avis, comme le premier juge, qu'il s'agit d'un *complot* et non d'une *incitation*, il ne sera donc pas nécessaire de décider des effets juridiques du *retrait* en cas d'incitation: il suffit en l'espèce d'examiner les conditions du *retrait* et ses effets pour les infractions commises dans la réalisation du *complot*.

### Discussion

#### A—Le complot

[16] Le Code criminel traite du complot comme (1) une infraction en soi que prévoit l'art. 465 et (2) un mode de participation criminelle aux conditions prévues par l'art. 21(2).

#### a) L'infraction de complot

[17] La jurisprudence définit un complot comme (1) une entente entre au moins deux personnes (2) qui ont l'intention de participer ensemble (3) à la poursuite d'une fin illégale.

[18] L'entente devient significative dans la mesure où les participants ont l'intention de s'entraider ou de prendre ensemble des moyens pour réaliser la fin

illégale qui leur est commune. Dès lors, si dans leur tractations ou leurs rencontres, les parties se limitent à considérer un projet ou la possibilité de réaliser une fin illégale, elles n'ont pas nécessairement exprimé une entente de même que l'intention de s'entraider dans la poursuite de la fin illégale: le complot ne s'est pas formé.

[19] Il n'est pas cependant requis que la fin illégale se réalise pour que le complot soit consommé.

### b) Mode de participation

[20] L'examen de la responsabilité pénale des parties au complot dans la réalisation du but commun se fait à partir de la norme qu'expose le par. 21(2) du Code criminel.

### B—*Le retrait du complot*

[21] À l'aide de cette distinction entre le complot en tant qu'infraction et comme mode de participation, on comprendra que le complot consommé, le refus d'y donner suite et le retrait n'absout pas le conspirateur pour son adhésion au complot: un crime selon l'art. 465 a été commis et les parties à ce complot peuvent en être inculpées.

[22] En sanctionnant cette conduite, le législateur veut éviter que soit réalisée la fin illégale: « The law punishes comspiracy so that the unlawful object is not attained ».

[23] Par ailleurs, c'est en considérant maintenant le complot comme mode de participation criminelle selon le par. 21(2) C.cr. en regard des infractions commises dans la réalisation de la fin illégale, que le retrait ou le désistement d'un des conspirateurs peut lui éviter d'être partie à ces infractions. Ceux et celles qui poursuivent la mise en oeuvre de la fin illégale encourront une responsabilité pour les infractions commises.

[24] Le retrait du complot signifie que la personne se dissocie du but commun, avec la conséquence que dans l'application de l'art. 21(2) on ne saurait lui imputer une responsabilité pour les actes qu'elle a renoncé à poser. L'article 21(2) entre en jeu quand l'un des conspirateurs commet une infraction dans la réalisation de la *fin commune*: le retrait supprime donc la fin commune quant à celui-là. Dans une certaine mesure, les parties au complot sont encouragées à s'en désister pour éviter parfois le pire: le principe est bien ancré dans la jurisprudence.

[25] Déjà dans l'arrêt *R. v. Henderson* (1948), 91 C.C.C. 97 (S.C.C.), la Cour suprême du Canada affirmait qu'« it is settled law that a person who has been a party to prosecute a common illegal purpose, may dissociate himself with his original co-conspirators » (p. 107); voir également *R. v. Miller* (1976), [1977] 2 S.C.R. 680 (S.C.C.) et *R. v. Kirkness*, [1990] 3 S.C.R. 74 (S.C.C.).

[26] Le principe étant admis, reste à déterminer les conditions de recevabilité du retrait.

[27] À ce sujet, dans les arrêts *Henderson* et *Miller*, la Cour suprême du Canada a adopté les propos du juge Sloan dans *R. v. Whitehouse* (1940), 75 C.C.C. 65 (B.C. C.A.), p. 67-68, qui, en résumé, a formulé les propositions suivantes. Le retrait demeure une question de fait: ce doit être (1) « more than a mere mental change of

intention » (2) « where practicable and reasonable there must be *timely communica-*
*tion* of the intention to abandon the common purpose … », le but étant « to break the
chain of causation and responsibility ».

[28]  En doctrine, les auteurs Fortin et Viau, « Traité de droit pénal général »
(1982), Les Éditions Thémis Inc., résument ainsi les conditions de recevabilité du
retrait:

> Il consiste dans l'abandon de la part du co-conspirateur de la poursuite de l'objet du
> complot. Les tribunaux exigent, en pratique, que celui qui se désiste manifeste son
> désistement par ses paroles ou sa conduite et signifie d'une façon non équivoque à ses
> co-conspirateurs qu'ils ne peuvent plus compter sur son aide dans la perpétration de
> l'objet du complot. (p. 366)

[29]  En résumé, le retrait doit (1) survenir *en temps utile*, soit avant la réalisation
de l'objet du complot, (2) être *définitif* et *non équivoque*, et (3) être *communiqué*
lorsque cela est possible et raisonnable (Côté-Harper, Rainville et Turgeon, « Traité
de droit pénal canadien », 4e éd. (1998) Éditions Yvon Blais, p. 864 à 869).

## B—L'incitation

[30]  Comme dans le cas du complot, l'incitation (ou le fait de conseiller) à un
crime constitue une infraction en soi et de plus un mode de participation criminelle.

[31]  L'article 464 C.cr. prohibe l'incitation au crime dans la mesure où elle est
infructueuse: l'infraction consiste dans le fait de conseiller un crime qui n'est pas
commis. Cela se distingue du complot qui demeure un délit même si le but est atteint.

[32]  Si l'incitation au crime a donné lieu à la commission d'une infraction, c'est
l'incitation comme mode de participation criminelle qui s'applique en accord avec
l'article 22 du Code criminel: …

[33]  En l'espèce, c'est l'article 22 qui s'appliquerait dans l'hypothèse où on aurait
conclu à une incitation.

### L'actus reus de l'incitation

[34]  Au par. (3) de l'art. 22, le législateur définit l'incitation ou le *fait de conseiller*
un crime.

[35]  On remarquera la distinction entre les versions anglaise et française du par.
(3) qui dispose des définitions: le texte français réfère à la fois au mot « conseil » et
au verbe « conseiller » tandis que seul le verbe « counsel » est défini dans la version
anglaise.

[36]  La majorité des auteurs, tant anglais que français, utilisent de préférence le
mot « incitation » ou « incitement » (ou « inciting ») pour désigner l'infraction de
conseiller un crime de même que le fait de conseiller comme mode de participation
criminelle.

[37]  « Amener » ou « inciter » une personne à commettre un crime, ou encore un
« encouragement visant à amener ou inciter », pour reprendre ici les mots choisis par
le législateur au par. (3), signifie plus que recommander: comme la Cour suprême l'a
affirmé récemment, en droit pénal il convient de donner à ces mots « conseiller » ou

« inciter » le sens plus fort d'« encourager activement » (*R. v. Sharpe*, [2001] 1 S.C.R. 45 (S.C.C.), p. 83).

[38] Pour Côté-Harper, Rainville et Turgeon, supra, les gestes ou les paroles du prévenu doivent avoir pour objet de « convaincre » ou doivent dénoter une *volonté d'influencer autrui*, sans pour autant devoir être une incitation « pressante » de sa part (Fortin et Viau, supra, p. 314): selon ces derniers auteurs, c'est l'élément de *persuasion* propre à l'incitation qui permet de distinguer celle-ci de la complicité par aide au sens de l'art. 21(1) du Code criminel.

[39] Par analogie avec le complot, il ne suffit pas de confier à autrui son désir ou son intention de voir une infraction se réaliser; de simples pourparlers s'avéreront insuffisants s'ils ne révèlent pas une volonté de convaincre son interlocuteur de franchir le pas de la criminalité (Côté-Harper, Rainville et Turgeon, supra, p. 803).

### Application à l'espèce

[40] À l'examen des faits pertinents dans le cas à l'étude, faits non contestés et qui se retrouvent dans les admissions des parties, il s'en dégage ce qui suit. Dès le début de leur rencontre, Campanozzi et l'intimé expriment leur « besoin d'argent ». L'intimé, en quête d'une solution, confie à son ami l'idée de « voler l'argent de sa grand-mère » mais qu'il doit y renoncer « comme c'est ma grand-mère ». C'est alors que Campanozzi propose de faire ce vol et qu'en retour il lui donnerait « une quotte », soit la moitié du montant estimé (7-8 mille dollars). L'intimé se montre d'accord mais demande à son ami d'attendre qu'il lui indique le moment propice, soit quand sa grand-mère ne serait pas à sa résidence.

[41] Dès le lendemain, l'intimé s'empresse de communiquer avec Campanozzi pour l'aviser « qu'il ne voulait plus que le vol chez sa grand-mère ait lieu ».

[42] Malheureusement, Campanozzi passe outre et avec trois autres copains, s'introduit par effraction chez la grand-mère de l'intimé pour y commettre un vol avec violence et séquestrer la victime pour quelque temps.

[43] Comme l'a souligné le premier juge, l'intimé n'a en aucun temps conseillé ou incité Campanozzi à commettre ce vol. Il a exprimé une idée, une intention provoquant l'intérêt de l'autre qui a pris l'initiative de lui proposer de faire le coup et même partager avec lui le fruit du vol. Dans ce contexte, c'est Campanozzi et non l'intimé qui propose et l'entente qui en résulte cristallise le *complot*. Ce n'est pas le cas où l'intimé, en réponse au besoin exprimé par Campanozzi, lui aurait proposé le vol comme solution et aurait « tenté de le convaincre » ou encore l'aurait « encouragé activement ». Par contre, la rapacité de l'intimé a abouti à un complot.

[44] En résumé, le premier juge a correctement conclu qu'il s'agissait d'un complot et non d'une incitation: l'intimé n'étant pas inculpé du complot, il ne pouvait en être déclaré coupable.

[45] Par ailleurs, l'intimé a opposé son *retrait* à la responsabilité qui aurait pu lui incomber pour les crimes commis dans la réalisation du complot. Le retrait, selon la preuve, présente toutes les conditions de recevabilité; il fut exprimé dès le lendemain à la bonne personne et en des termes non équivoques. C'est donc à bon droit que le premier juge a conclu au retrait valable de l'intimé.

*Conclusion*

[46] C'est pour ces motifs qu'à l'audition, je fus d'avis, avec l'accord de mes collègues, de rejeter le pourvoi. Je signale qu'au cours de l'audition, l'avocat de l'appelante a finalement reconnu le bien-fondé du jugement de première instance.

*Pourvoi rejeté.*

## V. ACCESSORY AFTER THE FACT

The modes of participation reviewed previously are all concerned with ways in which a person might be considered a party to an offence. The criminal liability of an accessory after the fact is defined in ss. 23, 23.1, and 463 of the Code.

As with modes of participation, accessoryship contemplates some relation between the conduct of the accessory after the fact and the commission of a criminal offence. The accessory is not a party to the offence, however, but a principal party in a distinct offence that consists of facilitating the escape of another person who was a party to the offence.

### R. v. Camponi
British Columbia Court of Appeal
(1993), 82 C.C.C. (3d) 506

WOOD J.A.:

*I*

[1] Donna Marie Camponi appeals her conviction by a jury upon the following charge:

> Count 1: That she, on or about the 28th day of April, A.D. 1990, at or near the District of Burnaby, Province of British Columbia, knowing that James Ervin Gee had murdered Gerald Anthony May, did assist James Ervin Gee for the purpose of enabling James Ervin Gee to escape contrary to s. 240 of the *Criminal Code* of Canada. ...

[2] The sole issue raised on appeal is whether an accessory after the fact to an offence, in this case murder, may be tried and convicted even though the principal offender has not been convicted.

*II*

[3] At the time of his death the deceased, Gerald Anthony May, was the manager of the Inter-City Motel on Kingsway Street in Burnaby. As such, he resided in the manager's suite on the motel premises. The appellant Camponi and James Ervin Gee resided together in Suite 3.

[4] Early on the morning of April 28, 1990, May's body was found in his suite by police who attended in response to a call for an ambulance. Camponi, who had called for the ambulance, told the dispatcher that she had found May either dead or dying

when she went to his suite at about 6:00 a.m. because the toilet in her unit was flooding. An autopsy determined that May, in fact, died sometime between 4:00 and 6:00 a.m. as a result of three stab wounds to the chest and multiple blunt force injuries to the head.

[5]  Over the course of the next few days, Camponi was befriended by Const. Iwanowich who was investigating May's murder in an undercover capacity. During their conversations Camponi acknowledged that she was present when Gee killed May by hitting him numerous times over the head with a bottle, and then "stomping" on his head after she noticed, and pointed out to Gee, that he appeared still to be alive. Camponi also told Const. Iwanowich that she had cleaned the blood off Gee's knife, and the blood and fingerprints off the bottle used to beat May. She had then put everything into a bag which she threw into a garbage container. The bag was never recovered by police. Camponi also disclosed that after the initial police investigation she had washed Gee's clothing "over and over again" to remove all traces of splattered blood.

[6]  During the course of their discussions, Camponi revealed to Const. Iwanowich that robbery was the motive for the killing. Apparently, there was a rumour that May carried "5 to 8 grand" on his person, but when Gee searched the deceased's pockets he found less than $200 which he took.

[7]  Gee was arrested and charged with the second degree murder of May. However, on February 11, 1991, the Crown entered a stay of proceedings on that charge following a voir dire in which the trial judge ruled his inculpatory statements inadmissible as a result of the breach, by the arresting police officers, of his right to counsel guaranteed under s. 10(b) of the *Charter of Rights and Freedoms*.

[8]  When Camponi's trial commenced, her counsel moved in the absence of the jury for an order that she could not be proceeded against as long as Gee had not been convicted of May's murder. The trial judge rejected that argument and ruled that Camponi could be proceeded against notwithstanding the disposition of the charge against Gee. If that ruling is correct, Camponi's conviction must stand, since it is not alleged that there was any error of law in the conduct of the trial itself, or any evidentiary lacunae that would vitiate the verdict of the jury.

*III*

[9]  Camponi was charged and convicted under s. 240 of the *Criminal Code*:

> 240. Every one who is an accessory after the fact to murder is guilty of an indictable offence and liable to imprisonment for life.

This section creates a separate and distinct offence for the charge of accessory after the fact to murder, with the result that the general "accessory" offence provisions found in s. 463, which under para. (a) would otherwise mandate a maximum sentence of 14 years' imprisonment upon conviction, do not apply when the offence alleged against the principal is murder.

[10]  The external and fault elements of the offence of being an accessory after the fact, whether the charge is laid under s. 240 or s. 463, are defined in s. 23.

· · ·

The external elements which the Crown must prove are: (a) conduct on the part of the accused which had the effect of receiving, comforting or assisting a person; and, (b) the circumstance that such person had been a party to the offence with respect to which the accessoryship is alleged. The corresponding fault elements are: (a) intention with respect to the conduct alleged; and (b) knowledge by the accused of the circumstance that the person was a party to the offence with respect to which the accessoryship is alleged. In addition, there is a free standing fault element which is the ulterior intention or desire (purpose) that the person assisted "escape" as a consequence of the conduct alleged. Before anyone can be convicted of being an accessory after the fact, under either s. 240 or s. 463 of the *Criminal Code*, the Crown must prove each of these separate external and fault elements beyond a reasonable doubt.

[11]  It is worth remarking again that the appellant does not allege either an error of law, in the form of any misdirection to the jury by the trial judge, or an evidentiary shortfall, with respect to any of the external or fault elements of the offence charged. Rather, it is argued that there is a policy based statutory prohibition, found in s. 592 of the *Criminal Code*, against trying and convicting an alleged accessory until another "party" has first been convicted of the offence in question:

> 592.  Any one who is charged with being an accessory after the fact to any offence may be indicted, whether or not the principal or any other party to the offence has been indicted or convicted or is or is not amenable to justice.

[12]  The appellant argues that this provision was intended by Parliament to give effect to the common law rule that an accessory could not be convicted if the principal offender had not first been convicted. In fact, the common law rule, simply put was that:

> ... no accessory can be convicted or suffer any punishment where the principal is not attained or hath the benefit of his clergy.

[13]  The rule was much criticized. Its early justification was that it ameliorated the severity of another common law rule, which was that an accessory was punishable in the same manner as the principal felon, i.e. by death. In *Criminal Law: The General Part*, 2nd ed. (London: Stevens & Sons, 1961), at 407, n. 24, Glanville Williams describes the rule as "absurd." Referring to its Latin incarnation, Stephen remarked:

> It is strange to observe how, even in our times, a commonplace which is not even true may be made to look plausible by putting it in Latin.

[14]  In England the common law rule was replaced in 1848 with a statutory provision which permitted the conviction of an accessory notwithstanding that the principal had not been convicted or was not amenable to justice. This statute was in effect in 1858, and thus became part of the law of British Columbia. In Canada, s. 4 of *An Act Respecting Accessories to, and Abettors of, Indictable Offences*, S.C. 1868, c. 72, provided:

> 4. Whosoever becomes an accessory after the fact to any felony, whether the same be a felony at common law or by virtue of any Act passed or to be passed, may be indicted *and convicted*, either as an accessory after the fact to the principal felony, together with the principal felon, or after the conviction of the principal felon, or may be indicted and convicted of a substantive felony, whether the principal felon has or has not been previously convicted, or is or is not amenable to justice, and may thereupon be punished in like manner as any accessory after the fact to the same felony, if convicted as an accessory, may be punished. [Emphasis added]

[15] Thus it can be seen that even before our criminal law was codified in 1892, Canada had rejected the very common law principle which the appellant asserts is preserved by s. 592 of our present *Criminal Code*.

[16] Support for the construction which the appellant would place on s. 592 is said to come from the fact that when *The Criminal Code, 1892* was enacted in 1892, s. 627 thereof replicated s. 4 of the 1868 *Act Respecting Accessories to, and Abettors of, Indictable Offences*, but dropped the words "and convicted," as emphasized above. This, it is argued, reflects the intention of Parliament, at that time, to change the law as stated in the 1868 statute, and to reinstate the common law rule by providing that an accessory after the fact could only be indicted, but not proceeded against further, so long as the principal offender or any other party had not been convicted of the offence alleged.

[17] The margin notes opposite s. 627 of *The Criminal Code, 1892*, S.C. 1892, c. 29, are: *Accessories after the fact, and receivers*. I set the section out, complete with its noted legislative antecedents, as they appear in the original enactment:

> 627. Every one charged with being an accessory after the fact to any offence, or with receiving any property knowing it to have been stolen, may be indicted, whether the principal offender or other party to the offence or person by whom such property was so obtained has or has not been indicted or convicted, or is or is not amenable to justice, and such accessory may be indicted either alone as for a substantive offence or jointly with such principal or other offender or person.
>
> 2. When any property has been stolen any number of receivers at different times of such property, or of any part or parts thereof, may be charged with substantive offences in the same indictment, and may be tried together, whether the person by whom the property was so obtained is or is not indicted with them, or is or is not in custody or amenable to justice.

[18] If one traces the referenced legislative antecedents, it immediately becomes apparent that s. 627 was not, in fact, a replication of s. 4 of 1868 (Can.), c. 72. As can be seen, it claims its origins to be ss. 133, 136 and 138 of c. 174 of the 1886 Consolidation; *The Criminal Procedure Act*. Of those sections, ss. 133 and 138 owed their existence to s. 7 of 1868 (Can.), c. 72:

> 7. Any number of accessories at different times to any felony and any number of receivers at different times of property stolen at one time, may be charged with substantive felonies, in the same indictment, and may be tried together, notwithstanding

the principal felon is not included in the same indictment, or is not in custody or amenable to justice.

Section 136, on the other hand, was said to replicate part of s. 100 of *An Act respecting Larceny and other similar offences*, S.C. 1869, c. 21:

> 100. Whosoever receives any chattel, money, valuable security, or other property whatsoever, the stealing, taking, extorting, obtaining, embezzling, and otherwise disposing whereof, amounts to a felony, either at common law or by virtue of this Act, knowing the same to have been feloniously stolen, taken, extorted, obtained, embezzled or disposed of, is guilty of felony, and may be indicted and convicted either as an accessory after the fact or for a substantive felony, and in the latter case whether the principal felon shall or shall not have been previously convicted, or shall or shall not be amenable to justice; and every such receiver, howsoever convicted, shall be liable to. ...

[19] In his Commentaries, Annotations and Precedents to the 1892 *Criminal Code*, Mr. Justice Taschereau also attributes the origin of s. 627 to ss. 6, 91 and 93 of [the *Larceny Act* (U.K.)] 24 & 25 Vict., c. 96, an Imperial Statute also much concerned with larceny, and receiving stolen property.

[20] Whether one is attempting to trace the origins of s. 627 of the 1892 *Criminal Code*, or alternatively searching for the fate of s. 4 of [*An Act Respecting Accessories to, and Abettors of, Indictable Offences*] S.C. 1868, c. 72, neither exercise could be considered complete without an extensive and careful study of each of the many substantive and procedural criminal statutes that existed in Canada, often with contradictory provisions, from the time of Confederation until all were replaced by the 1892 *Criminal Code*. Such a fascinating journey through history would be out of place in the context of the task at hand. It is in any event unnecessary, for the point which has emerged so far, and which can be stated without completing that journey, is that there is no direct link between the two sections, and thus no legitimate inference can be drawn about the intention of Parliament from the apparent absence of the phrase "and convicted" immediately after the word "indicted" in that portion of the latter which describes the proceedings the Crown may bring against an accessory after the fact.

[21] In fact, the wording which most closely parallels that of s. 627 of the 1892 *Criminal Code*, is to be found in s. 427 of the *Draft Code* proposed by the Criminal Code Bill Commissioners in England in 1879:

> 497. Every one charged with being an accessory after the fact to any offence, or with receiving any property knowing it to have been dishonestly obtained may be indicted, whether the principal offender or other party to the offence or person by whom such property was so obtained has or has not been indicted or convicted, or is or is not amenable to justice, and may be indicted *and tried* either alone as for a substantive offence or jointly with such principal or other offender or person by whom such property was dishonestly obtained. [Emphasis added]

[22] The *Draft Code* was the principal blueprint for our *Criminal Code*. By 1892 it had been 44 years since English law had turned its back on the common law rule

relating to accessories after the fact. It seems likely that the apparently deliberate decision by Canadian legislative drafters, not to adopt the precise wording of s. 497, was more the result of an attempt to combine too many substantive and procedural enactments into a single provision, than it was the product of a deliberate decision to permit accessories after the fact to be indicted before, but not tried until, the principal offender had been convicted.

[23]  In his argument, counsel for the appellant referred to "Accessoryship After the Fact: Substantive, Procedural and Evidentiary Considerations," (1981) 21 C.R. (3d) 307, where, at pp. 321-2, David Watt, as he then was, noted the following:

> A plain reading of the unambiguous words of present s. 521 [592] of the Criminal Code would seem logically to lead to the conclusion that Parliament sought to permit the Crown to indict an accessory even though the principal had not been found, let alone indicted or convicted for his offence. There is much force in the argument that, where the legislation specifically provides for the indictment of A, it by necessary implication permits his conviction independently of the principal offender assisted by him, particularly where A is viewed as committing a substantive crime. *On the other hand, Parliament has apparently viewed the matters of "indictment" and "conviction" as different stages in the criminal process in the latter portion of the same section, and to read "indicted" in the opening part as if it were "indicted and convicted" would mean ascribing to it a meaning different than that which it plainly bears in the latter portion of the same section, absent any good reason for so doing.* [Emphasis added]

The highlighted portion of this comment was offered by counsel as signalling the proper approach to the construction of s. 592.

[24]  That may, indeed, be one approach to take. But, in my view, it is necessary to construe the section in such a way as to give it a meaning consistent both with the historical development of the law relating to accessories after the fact, and with other relevant provisions of the *Criminal Code* relating to accessories after the fact. That brings me to s. 23.1, which was not in existence at the time Mr. Justice Watt wrote his learned article on the subject, and which does not appear to have been brought to the attention of the judge below:

> 23.1  For greater certainty, sections 21 to 23 apply in respect of an accused notwithstanding the fact that the person whom the accused aids or abets, counsels or procures or receives, comforts or assists cannot be convicted of the offence.

[25]  This section was enacted in 1986, c. 32, s. 46. With what must be regarded as an unusually confident legislative tone, it announces an intention to bring greater certainty to the law relating to ss. 21-23 of the Code. Whether it has achieved that lofty goal will be for history to decide. Suffice it to say that in the context of the present discussion its intent seems to have been to put the quietus to any lingering notion that s. 592 preserved, or was intended to preserve, the essence of the common law rule relating to accessories after the fact.

[26]  The appellant also relies on the following dicta of Pigeon J. in *R. v. Vinette*, [1975] 2 S.C.R. 222, at 228-29:

The situation is quite different when a charge of having been an accessory after the fact is involved. In such a case the principal and the accessory are not charged with the same offence, the charge against the accessory being that of having assisted the other party to escape justice. This offence is therefore subsequent to the principal crime. By its very nature it is subject to special rules. Whereas in the case of several persons accused of the same offence, each may be tried before or after the others, plead guilty before or after any of the others, or be convicted regardless of the decision against any of the others, *an accessory after the fact may not be tried or tender a valid plea of guilty until the principal is convicted*, so that if the latter is acquitted the accessory must of necessity be discharged. [Emphasis added]

[27]  In *Vinette* the accused was charged with being an accessory after the fact to manslaughter, the allegation being that he had helped the principal dispose of the body by putting it in a weighted trunk and then dumping the trunk into a water filled quarry. The issue was whether the principal's plea of guilty was admissible against Vinette. The Quebec Court of Appeal held that it was not, and quashed his conviction. In doing so, the majority in that court relied upon several cases in which it was held that a plea of guilty by one of two or more jointly indicted accused is not admissible against the others. It was in that context that Pigeon J., for the majority in the Supreme Court of Canada, found it necessary to draw a distinction between the evidentiary rules applicable as between co-accused, and those applicable to accessories after the fact who are separately indicted and tried.

[28]  In *R. v. Anderson* (1980), 57 C.C.C. (2d) 255 (Alta. C.A.), Moir J.A. concluded that the dicta of Pigeon J. in *Vinette* has been misconstrued. In *R. v. McAvoy* (1981), 60 C.C.C. (2d) 95 (Ont. C.A.), Jessup J.A. concluded that it should not be followed because Pigeon J. apparently did not consider what is now s. 592 of the *Criminal Code*.

[29]  In light of the passage of s. 23.1 of the *Criminal Code*, it is no longer necessary to decide what was meant by Pigeon J. in the *Vinette* case. In my view, that section has put to rest any notion that an accessory after the fact can only be tried and convicted after the principal, or another party to the alleged offence, has been convicted. In this case, because of the inadmissibility of his confession, Gee *cannot* be convicted, at least not until some new and admissible evidence, conclusive of guilt, comes to light. This seems to me to be precisely the contingency that s. 23.1 was meant to address.

[30]  Before concluding, I must note that it is not necessary to consider whether an accessory after the fact can be indicted and convicted, if the principal offender has been acquitted, after a trial on the merits, of the offence with respect to which the accessoryship is alleged. That is a difficult question which raises issues not addressed in the argument before us. In the result, it must await another day and another case for consideration. It does not arise in this case because Gee was not acquitted on the charge of second degree murder. Under the provisions of s. 579(2) the proceedings against him may be recommenced within one year, without the need to lay a new indictment, failing which they shall be deemed never to have been brought in the first place.

*IV*

[31] It follows that I would dismiss the appeal.

*Appeal dismissed.*

### ADDITIONAL READING

- K. Roach, *Criminal Law*, 3rd ed. (Toronto: Irwin Law, 2004), chapter 3;
- D. Stuart, *Canadian Criminal Law*, 4th ed. (Toronto: Carswell, 2001), chapter 9;
- A. Mewett and M. Manning, *Criminal Law*, 3rd ed. (Toronto: Butterworths, 1994), chapter 8;
- E. Colvin, *Principles of Criminal Law*, 2nd ed. (Toronto: Carswell, 1991), chapter 10.

# CHAPTER NINE

# Inchoate Offences

Just as people do not always act alone in the commission of criminal offences, they do not always succeed. This chapter is concerned with criminal liability for incomplete offences. There are three such offences of general application in Canadian criminal law: attempt, incitement (also called counselling), and conspiracy. Each of these offences represents an extension of criminal liability in the sense that each has as its object the completion of an offence that is not actually committed. These offences are typically described as forms of "inchoate" liability precisely because the substantive offences are not completed. Apart from this particular characteristic, inchoate offences define criminal conduct by reference to specific forms of conduct accompanied by specific forms of fault. In other words, inchoate offences recognize criminal liability for culpable conduct and fault that lies between innocent behaviour and the successful completion of a substantive offence.

There is an overarching question of principle that is concerned with the outer limits of inchoate liability. How does the law mark the boundary between innocent behaviour and preliminary conduct that attracts the legitimate imposition of the criminal sanction? The premise for this use of the criminal sanction is that criminality does not lie solely in the completion of an offence. There is a demonstrable and sufficient harm, once the commission of a criminal offence has been set in motion, to sanction the commencement of the offence as criminal conduct on its own. If the bud can be nipped, the poisonous flower cannot grow. Such arguments can draw strength from many quarters but the extent of liability for inchoate offences remains difficult.

There are also many other questions that arise concerning inchoate liability, some of which conjure up entertaining logic puzzles that rarely surface in practice. How do the forms of inchoate liability relate among themselves and to the modes of participation? Can there be an attempted conspiracy or, conversely, a conspiracy to attempt? Can there be incitement to attempt or conspiracy? Under what conditions could a person be a secondary party to an inchoate offence? Can a person be guilty of an inchoate offence if for some reason completion of the substantive offence is impossible?

This chapter focuses on the major principles relating to the inchoate offences of attempt, incitement, and conspiracy. Two preliminary points should be noted.

First, apart from these general inchoate offences, there are various specific offences that sanction inchoate liability. With respect to attempts, see, e.g., ss. 71, 119, 123, 139, 239, and 368 and many of the offences relating to terrorism is part II.1 of the *Criminal Code*. There are also offences that create liability for attempts without describing the conduct as

539

such—see, e.g., ss. 46(2)(d) and 449 "begins to make counterfeit money." With respect to incitement, see, e.g., s. 318. With respect to conspiracy, see, e.g., ss. 46, 59, 466, and 467.

Second, note that inchoate liability contemplates the commission of a substantive offence. This type of liability must be distinguished from a substantive offence that sanctions attempt or incitement where the object is not a criminal offence. For example, s. 319 is concerned with the wilful incitement of hatred. Hatred of an identifiable group is not in itself a crime but public incitement of such hatred is.

## I. ATTEMPT

A person who tries to commit a criminal offence but does not succeed can nevertheless be found guilty of attempting the offence if his or her conduct falls within the terms of s. 24:

24(1) Attempts

(1) Every one who, having an intent to commit an offence, does or omits to do anything for the purpose of carrying out his intention is guilty of an attempt to commit the offence whether or not it was possible under the circumstances to commit the offence.

24(2) Question of law

(2) The question whether an act or omission by a person who has an intent to commit an offence is or is not mere preparation to commit the offence, and too remote to constitute an attempt to commit the offence, is a question of law.

### Actus Reus

It is clear that there must be some act that goes beyond preparation but what that is has often raised difficulty.

### R. v. Cline
#### Ontario Court of Appeal
#### (1956), 115 C.C.C. 18

LAIDLAW J.A.: ... [T]heories and tests have been formulated with a view to finding an answer to the question whether or not an act is sufficient in law to constitute an *actus reus*. It is my respectful opinion that there is no theory or test applicable in all cases, and I doubt whether a satisfactory one can be formulated. Each case must be determined on its own facts, having due regard to the nature of the offence and the particular acts in question. Much of the difficulty and confusion is attributable, in my humble opinion, to an insufficient understanding of the nature and gist of the crime of criminal attempt; and arises also in respect of the vexed question whether a particular act is an act of preparation only, or is an attempt. Perhaps, therefore, it will be helpful to observe carefully certain features of a criminal attempt as the doctrine of that offence was developed and established in the common law. ...

The consummation of a crime usually comprises a series of acts which have their genesis in an idea to do a criminal act; the idea develops to a decision to do that act; a plan may be made for putting that decision into effect; the next step may be preparation only for carrying out the intention and plan; but when that preparation is in fact fully completed, the next step in the series of acts done by the accused for the purpose and with the intention of committing the crime as planned cannot, in my opinion, be regarded as remote in its connection with that crime. The connection is in fact proximate.

After considering the nature of a criminal attempt and the principles as they were developed and established in the common law, together with the cases to which I have referred, and others, I state these propositions in my own words to guide me in the instant case: (1) There must be *mens rea* and also an *actus reus* to constitute a criminal attempt, but the criminality of misconduct lies mainly in the intention of the accused. (2) Evidence of similar acts done by the accused before the offence with which he is charged, and also afterwards if such acts are not too remote in time, is admissible to establish a pattern of conduct from which the Court may properly find *mens rea*. (3) Such evidence may be advanced in the case for the prosecution without waiting for the defence to raise a specific issue. (4) It is not essential that the *actus reus* be a crime or a tort or even a moral wrong or social mischief. (5) The *actus reus* must be more than mere preparation to commit a crime. But (6) when the preparation to commit a crime is in fact fully complete and ended, the next step done by the accused for the purpose and with the intention of committing a specific crime constitutes an *actus reus* sufficient in law to establish a criminal attempt to commit that crime.

## Deutsch v. The Queen
### Supreme Court of Canada
### (1986), 27 C.C.C. (3d) 385

[The accused was charged with attempting to procure female persons to have illicit sexual intercourse with another person contrary to s. 195(1)(a) (see now s. 212(1)(a)) of the *Criminal Code*. The accused had placed an advertisement in a newspaper for a secretary/sales assistant and the evidence of three women who responded to the advertisement, and of a policewoman, was that during each job interview the accused indicated that as part of the job the woman would be required to have sexual intercourse with clients or potential clients of the company where that appeared to be necessary to conclude a contract. He also mentioned that the women could earn up to $100,000 a year.

The trial judge acquitted the accused on the basis that his acts had not gone beyond mere preparation because he had not offered the job to the women. An appeal by the Crown to the Ontario Court of Appeal from the acquittal was allowed. The Supreme Court dismissed the accused's subsequent appeal.]

Le DAIN J. (for the Court): It has been frequently observed that no satisfactory general criterion has been, or can be, formulated for drawing the line between preparation and attempt, and that the application of this distinction to the facts of a particular case must be left to common sense judgment. ... Despite academic appeals for greater clarity and certainty in this area of the law I find myself in essential agreement with this conclusion.

In my opinion the distinction between preparation and attempt is essentially a qualitative one, involving the relationship between the nature and quality of the act in question and the nature of the complete offence, although consideration must necessarily be given, in making that qualitative distinction, to the relative proximity of the act in question to what would have been the completed offence, in terms of time, location and acts under the control of the accused remaining to be accomplished.

I agree with the Court of Appeal that if the appellant had the necessary intent to induce or persuade the women to seek employment that would require them to have sexual intercourse with prospective clients, then the holding out of the large financial rewards in the course of the interviews, in which the necessity of having sexual intercourse with prospective clients was disclosed, could constitute the *actus reus* of an attempt to procure. It would clearly be a step, and an important step, in the commission of the offence. Before an offer of employment could be made in such circumstances an applicant would have to seek the position, despite its special requirement. Thus such inducement or persuasion would be the decisive act in the procuring. There would be little else that the appellant would be required to do towards the completion of the offence other than to make the formal offer of employment. I am further of the opinion that the holding out of the large financial rewards in the course of the interviews would not lose its quality as a step in the commission of the offence, and thus as an *actus reus* of attempt, because a considerable period of time might elapse before a person engaged for the position had sexual intercourse with prospective clients or because of the otherwise contingent nature of such sexual intercourse.

For these reasons I would dismiss the appeal. I agree with the Court of Appeal that because the trial judge did not make a finding as to whether or not there was the necessary intent to procure there must be a new trial.

*Appeal dismissed.*

## Mens Rea

Is the *mens rea* for an attempt the intent to commit the substantive offence or could it be something less?

### R. v. Ancio
Supreme Court of Canada
(1984), 10 C.C.C. (3d) 385

[Ancio, who wanted to speak with his estranged wife, broke into an apartment building with a loaded sawed-off shotgun. Kurely, the man with whom Ancio's wife had been living, went to investigate the sound of breaking glass and threw the chair he was carrying at Ancio when he saw him climbing the stairs. The gun discharged, missing Kurely, and a struggle followed. The trial judge found that Ancio had broken into the apartment building with the intent to use the weapon to force his wife to leave and convicted him of attempted murder by combining ss. 24 and 213(d) (now s. 230(d)). The Court of Appeal overturned the conviction and ordered a new trial. The Crown appealed to the Supreme Court of Canada.]

McINTYRE J. (for the Court): The common law recognition of the fundamental importance of intent in the crime of attempt is carried forward into the *Criminal Code*. A reading of s. 24 of the *Code* and all its predecessors since the enactment of the first *Code* in 1892 confirms that the intent to commit the desired offence is a basic element of the offence of attempt. Indeed, because the crime of attempt may be complete without the actual commission of any other offence and even without the performance of any act unlawful in itself, it is abundantly clear that the criminal element of the offence of attempt may lie solely in the intent. As noted by Glanville Williams, *Criminal Law: The General Part*, 2nd ed. (1961), §207, p. 642, in discussing attempts: "An *actus reus* … need not be a crime apart from the state of mind. It need not even be a tort, or a moral wrong, or a social mischief." The question now arises: What is the intent required for an attempt to commit murder? As has been indicated earlier, the Crown's position is that the intent required for a conviction on a charge of attempt to murder is the intent to do that which will, if death is caused, constitute the commission of murder as defined in ss. 212 [now s. 229] and 213 of the *Code*, so that a combination of ss. 24 and 213(d) can form the basis for a conviction of attempted murder. The respondent, on the other hand, argues that although the authorities presently limit the intent to that which would constitute murder as defined in s. 212 of the *Code*, logic and principle dictate that the intent should be limited to the specific intent to kill described in s. 212(a)(i) … .

The completed offence of murder involves a killing. The intention to commit the complete offence of murder must therefore include an intention to kill. I find it impossible to conclude that a person may intend to commit the unintentional killings described in ss. 212 and 213 of the *Code*. I am then of the view that the *mens rea* for an attempted murder cannot be less than the specific intent to kill.

As I have said earlier, there is a division of opinion upon this point and strong arguments have been raised in favour of the Crown's position that a "lesser intent," such as that provided in s. 212(a)(ii) or even no intent at all relating to the causing of death as provided in s. 213(d), may suffice to found a conviction for attempted murder. This view is supported in *Lajoie*. In my view, with the utmost respect for those who differ, the sections of the *Criminal Code* relied on in that case do not support that position.

As noted above, Martland J.'s analysis of the intent required to found a conviction for attempted murder is based primarily on the change in wording of s. 222 [now s. 239]. In my opinion, emphasis on the amendment of this section is unwarranted for two reasons. First, s. 222 does not define or create the offence of attempted murder. The scheme of the *Criminal Code* in relation to attempts has been the same from its inception. One section defines the offence of attempts generally (s. 72) [now s. 24]. Another sets out the penalties for attempts (s. 57) [now s. 463], and a third creates a separate penalty for attempted murder (s. 264, s. 210 in *Lajoie*) [now s. 239]. Rather than defining or creating an offence, s. 222 merely fixes a penalty for a specific attempt. Despite the categorization of the various means of committing murder set out in the old s. 264, there is no essential difference between the old and the new sections in this respect.

Secondly, the elimination of the words "with intent to commit murder" from s. 264 is not significant. Section 24 defines an attempt as "having an intent to commit an offence." Because s. 24 is a general section it is necessary to "read in" the offence in question. The offence of attempted murder then is defined as "having an intent to commit murder." This does not differ from the old s. 264 reference to "with intent to commit murder," which Martland J. acknowledged was interpreted, in *R. v. Flannery*, to require the specific intent to kill.

Martland J. placed further emphasis on s. 222 of the *Criminal Code* by relying on the words "attempts by any means" to support his conclusion that murder may be attempted in any of the "ways" set out in ss. 212 and 213. In my view, the reference to "any means" in s. 222 refers to ways in which a murder could be accomplished, such as by poisoning, shooting, or stabbing. The earlier version of s. 222 (s. 232 in 1892, s. 264 in 1906) listed the various methods by which a killing could be effected, but the illustrations were replaced in the 1953-54 revision with a general reference to murder "by any means." In any event, ss. 212 and 213 have nothing to do with the means of killing. They are concerned solely with describing the mental elements which will suffice to make a completed killing murder. The fact that certain mental elements, other than an intent to kill, may lead to a conviction for murder where there has been a killing does not mean that anything less than an intent to kill will suffice for an attempt at murder.

It was argued, and it has been suggested in some of the cases and academic writings on the question, that it is illogical to insist upon a higher degree of *mens rea* for attempted murder, while accepting a lower degree amounting to recklessness for murder. I see no merit in this argument. The intent to kill is the highest intent in murder and there is no reason in logic why an attempt to murder, aimed at the completion of the full crime of murder, should have any lesser intent. If there is any illogic in this matter, it is in the statutory characterization of unintentional killing as murder. The *mens rea* for attempted murder is, in my view, the specific intent to kill. A mental state falling short of that level may well lead to conviction for other offences, for example, one or other of the various aggravated assaults, but not a conviction for an attempt at murder. For these reasons, it is my view that *Lajoie* should no longer be followed.

I would accordingly dismiss the Crown's appeal and confirm the Court of Appeal's order for a new trial.

RITCHIE J. (dissenting): I am unable to distinguish this case from that of *Lajoie v. The Queen* (1973), 10 C.C.C. (2d) 313, 33 D.L.R. (3d) 618, [1974] S.C.R. 399, which is a unanimous judgment of this Court and by which I feel bound.

I would therefore allow this appeal.

**R. v. Logan**
Supreme Court of Canada
(1990), 58 C.C.C. (3d) 391

[The accused were charged with a number of offences relating to the robbery of a Becker's store and the serious wounding of the cashier, Barbara Turnbull. Two of the accused were convicted of attempted murder and appealed to the Ontario Court of Appeal (1988), 46 C.C.C. (3d) 354, which set aside the conviction. The Supreme Court of Canada dealt as follows with the issue of the *mens rea* for attempted murder. Other aspects of the case are set out in chapter 8 of this casebook.]

LAMER C.J. (for the Court, Sopinka and L'Heureux-Dubé JJ. concurring in the result): ... With respect to the case at bar, then, the first question which must be answered is whether the principles of fundamental justice require a minimum degree of *mens rea* in order to convict an accused of attempted murder. *Ancio* established that a specific intent to kill is the *mens rea* required for a principal on the charge of attempted murder. However, as the constitutional question was not raised or argued in that case, it did not decide whether that requisite *mens rea* was a *constitutional* requirement. The case simply interpreted the offence as currently legislated.

In *R. v. Martineau* (1990), 58 C.C.C. (3d) 353, a judgment handed down this day, this court has decided, as a constitutional requirement, that no one can be convicted of murder unless the Crown proves beyond a reasonable doubt that the person had *subjective* foresight of that fact that the death of the victim was likely to ensue. Because of both the stigma and the severe penal consequences which result from a conviction for murder, the *Constitution Act, 1982* requires at least that degree of intent.

As defined in *Ancio*, the elements of *mens rea* for attempted murder are identical to those for the most severe form of murder, murder under s. 212(a)(i). For each, the accused must have had the specific intent to kill. All that differs is the "consequences" component of the *actus reus*. Quite simply, an attempted murderer is, if caught and convicted, a "lucky murderer." Therefore, it would seem logical that the requisite *mens rea* for a murder conviction, as described in *Martineau*, must be the same for a conviction of attempted murder. However, logic is not sufficient reason to label something a "constitutional requirement." As I have stated in *Vaillancourt*, the principles of fundamental justice require a minimum degree of *mens rea* for only a very few offences. The criteria by which these offences can be identified are, primarily, the stigma associated with a conviction and, as a secondary consideration, the penalties available.

The stigma associated with a conviction for attempted murder is the same as it is for murder. Such a conviction reveals that although no death ensued from the actions of the accused, the intent to kill was still present in his or her mind. The attempted murderer is no less a killer than a murderer: he may be lucky—the ambulance arrived early, or some other fortuitous circumstance—but he still has the same killer instinct. Secondly, while a conviction for attempted murder does not automatically result in a life sentence, the offence is punishable by life and the usual penalty is very severe.

... The sentencing range available to the judge is not conclusive of the level of *mens rea* constitutionally required. Instead, the crucial consideration is whether there is a continuing serious social stigma which will be imposed on the accused upon conviction ... .

For these reasons, the *mens rea* for attempted murder cannot, without restricting s. 7 of the *Charter*, require of the accused less of a mental element than that required of a murderer under s. 212(a)(i) [now s. 229(a)(i)], that is, *subjective* foresight of the consequences. While Parliament, as I have already implied, could well extend our definition of attempted murder in *Ancio* to include the unsuccessful murderers of s. 212(a)(ii), it cannot go further and include objective foresight as being sufficient for a conviction without restricting s. 7 of the *Charter*.

*Appeal dismissed.*

---

In *R. v. Sorrell and Bondett* (1978), 41 C.C.C. (2d) 9 (Ont. C.A.), the accused were charged with attempted robbery of the manager of a take-out food store in Kingston ("Aunt Lucy's Fried Chicken") and were tried by a judge without a jury. They were acquitted and the Crown appealed. On the night of the incident the manager had closed the store 15 minutes early. Several minutes after this, the accused came to the door of the store and knocked on it. The manager said "Sorry we are closed" and returned to his work. The accused then left. At this time the accused had balaclavas over their heads and another store employee noticed that one of the accused had a gun in his hand. The police were called and arrested the accused a short distance from the store. By this time, they had thrown away the balaclavas but one accused was found in possession of a loaded revolver.

The Court of Appeal dismissed the appeal, stating:

In our view, the trial Judge's reasons are more consistent with a finding that the necessary intent to commit robbery was not proved beyond a reasonable doubt, than with a finding that such intent was established by the evidence. In any event, the Crown has not satisfied us that the trial Judge found the existence of an intent to rob.

If the trial Judge had found that the respondents intended to rob the store, the acts done by them clearly had advanced beyond mere preparation, and were sufficiently proximate to constitute an attempt ... . If the trial Judge had found that the respondents had the necessary intent his finding that the acts done by the respondents did not go beyond mere preparation and did not constitute attempted robbery, would constitute an error of law that would not only warrant, but require our intervention.

The prosecution in this case was forced to rely exclusively upon the acts of the accused, not only to constitute the *actus reus*, but to supply the evidence of the necessary *mens rea*. This Court in *R. v. Cline* rejected the so-called "unequivocal act" test for determining when the stage of attempt has been reached. That test excludes resort to evidence *aliunde*, such as admissions, and holds that the stage of attempt has been reached only when the acts of the accused show unequivocally on their face the criminal intent with which the acts were performed. We are of the view that where the accused's intention is otherwise proved, acts which on their face are equivocal, may none the less, be sufficiently proximate to constitute an attempt. Where, however, there is no extrinsic evidence of the intent with which accused's acts were done, acts of the accused, which on their face are equivocal, may be insufficient to show that the acts were done with the intent to commit the crime that the accused is alleged to have attempted to commit, and hence insufficient to establish the offence of attempt.

## Impossibility

Can a person be guilty of an attempt when completion of the offence is for some reason impossible?

### United States v. Dynar
Supreme Court of Canada
[1997] 2 S.C.R. 462

CORY and IACOBUCCI JJ. (Lamer C.J.C., La Forest, L'Heureux-Dubé, and Gonthier JJ. concurring):

[1] The issue in this appeal is whether the respondent's conduct in the United States would constitute a crime if carried out in this country, thereby meeting the requirement of "double criminality" which is the pre-condition for the surrender of a Canadian fugitive for trial in a foreign jurisdiction. This issue requires the Court to consider the scope of the liability for attempted offences and conspiracy under Canadian criminal law, specifically, whether impossibility constitutes a defence to a charge of attempt or conspiracy in Canada. …

[3] Arye Dynar, a Canadian citizen, was the subject of a failed "sting" operation attempted by the Federal Bureau of Investigation in the United States. Mr. Dynar was indicted together with Maurice Cohen, who is also a Canadian citizen, in the United States District Court of Nevada. The United States indictment charged both Mr. Dynar and Mr. Cohen with one count of attempting to launder money in violation of Title 18, *United States Code*, §1956(a)(3), and one count of conspiracy to violate Title 18, *United States Code*, §1956(a)(3), contrary to Title 18, *United States Code*, §371. The Government of the United States requested their extradition by Diplomatic Note dated November 30, 1992. This appeal relates to the request for the extradition of Mr. Dynar.

[4] The events that formed the basis of the indictment began with a telephone call placed on January 2, 1990, from Canada, by Mr. Dynar to a former associate, Lucky Simone, who was living in Nevada. The call was apparently made to seek investors for a business operation in the United States. Lucky Simone had, unbeknownst to Mr. Dynar, become a confidential informant working for FBI agent William Matthews. He informed Agent Matthews of Mr. Dynar's call, and Agent Matthews requested that Mr. Simone return the call. Mr. Simone gave his consent for Agent Matthews to record the conversation.

[5] Affidavit evidence filed by the Requesting State indicates that, during the 1980s, Mr. Dynar was the subject of investigations in the United States pertaining to the laundering of substantial amounts of money originating in the State of Nevada.

Agent Matthews' involvement in the investigation of Mr. Dynar's activities began in 1988. When Mr. Dynar made contact with Lucky Simone in 1990, Agent Matthews deposed that he decided to determine whether or not Mr. Dynar was still involved in laundering money which was the proceeds of crime. He had Mr. Simone introduce a second confidential informant, known as "Anthony," to Mr. Dynar. Anthony was instructed to ask if Mr. Dynar would be willing to launder large sums obtained as a result of illegal trafficking. When asked, Mr. Dynar agreed with alacrity to launder money for Anthony.

[6] A great many conversations between the two men were recorded over the course of some months. On all of these occasions, Anthony was in Las Vegas, Nevada and Mr. Dynar was in Canada. Eventually, Mr. Dynar and Anthony arranged an initial meeting. The meeting was purportedly to allow Anthony to give money to Mr. Dynar for laundering as a first step towards developing a relationship in which Mr. Dynar would regularly launder money for him. During several of the conversations, it was made clear that the money to be laundered was "drug money." Mr. Dynar insisted more than once that the amounts had to be large in order to make his efforts worthwhile. The conversations also disclosed that Mr. Dynar had an associate named" Moe," who was subsequently identified as Maurice Cohen. Agent Matthews recorded all of the conversations in Las Vegas pursuant to the applicable law of the United States, which only requires the consent of one party for the lawful interception of the conversation. Special Agent Charles Pine of the Internal Revenue Service (IRS) was able to identify the voice of Maurice Cohen in the background of several of the conversations.

[7] The initial plan of the American authorities was to set up the transfer of funds to Mr. Dynar in the United States. However, Mr. Dynar believed that he was the subject of a sealed indictment in the United States charging him with laundering very large sums of money and that if he travelled to that country, he would be arrested. It was accordingly agreed that Mr. Dynar's associate, Maurice Cohen, would meet Anthony's associate in Buffalo. Mr. Cohen was to take the money to Toronto where it would be laundered by Mr. Dynar. It would then be taken back to Buffalo by Mr. Cohen on the following day, after a commission for Mr. Dynar had been deducted.

[8] In Buffalo, Mr. Cohen met with Special Agent Dennis McCarthy of the IRS, who was posing as Anthony's associate. The conversations that took place between them in preparation for the transfer of funds were recorded by Agent McCarthy. They contain several statements to the effect that Mr. Cohen was working for Mr. Dynar, as well as some explanations of the logistics of the laundering scheme. In the end, however, the money was not transferred to Mr. Cohen. The FBI aborted the operation by pretending to arrest Agent McCarthy just prior to the transfer of the money. Mr. Cohen was allowed to return to Canada. ...

[49] The *Criminal Code* creates the crime of attempt to commit an offence:

> 24.(1) Every one who, having an intent to commit an offence, does or omits to
> do anything for the purpose of carrying out the intention is guilty of an attempt to
> commit the offence *whether or not it was possible under the circumstances to commit
> the offence*. [Emphasis added.]

On its face, the statute is indifferent about whether or not the attempt might possibly have succeeded. Therefore it would seem, at first blush, not to matter that Mr. Dynar could not possibly have succeeded in laundering money known to be the proceeds of crime. So long as he attempted to do so, he is guilty of a crime.

[50] In our view, s. 24(1) is clear: the crime of attempt consists of an intent to commit the completed offence together with some act more than merely preparatory taken in furtherance of the attempt. This proposition finds support in a long line of authority. See, e.g., *R. v. Cline* (1956), 115 C.C.C. 18 (Ont. C.A.), at p. 29; *R. v. Ancio*, [1984] 1 S.C.R. 225 (S.C.C.), at p. 247; *R. v. Deutsch*, [1986] 2 S.C.R. 2 (S.C.C.), at pp. 19-26; *R. v. Gladstone*, [1996] 2 S.C.R. 723 (S.C.C.), at para. 19. In this case, sufficient evidence was produced to show that Mr. Dynar intended to commit the money-laundering offences, and that he took steps more than merely preparatory in order to realize his intention. That is enough to establish that he attempted to launder money contrary to s. 24(1) of the *Criminal Code*.

[51] However, the respondent argues that Parliament did not intend by s. 24(1) to criminalize all attempts to do the impossible, but only those attempts that the common law has classified as "factually impossible." An attempt to do the factually impossible, according to the respondent, is an attempt that runs up against some intervening obstacle and for that reason cannot be completed. The classic example involves a pick-pocket who puts his hand into a man's pocket intending to remove the wallet, only to find that there is no wallet to remove.

[52] Traditionally, this sort of impossibility has been contrasted with "legal impossibility." An attempt to do the legally impossible is, according to those who draw the distinction, an attempt that must fail because, even if it were completed, no crime would have been committed. See Eric Colvin, *Principles of Criminal Law* (2nd ed. 1991), at pp. 355-56.

[53] According to the respondent, the *Criminal Code* criminalizes only attempts to do the factually impossible. An attempt to do the legally impossible, in the absence of an express legislative reference to that variety of impossibility, is not a crime.

[54] As support for this interpretation, the respondent offers two arguments. The first is that Parliament based s. 24(1) on an English provision whose purpose was to overrule a decision of the House of Lords that had made factual impossibility a defence. See Barry Brown, "'The attempt, and not the deed, Confounds us': Section 24 and Impossible Attempts" (1981), 19 *U.W.O. L. Rev.* 225, at pp. 228-29. On the strength of this argument, the New Zealand Court of Appeal accepted that New Zealand's equivalent to s. 24(1) criminalizes attempts whose completion is factually impossible but not those whose completion is legally impossible. See *R. v. Donnelly*, [1970] N.Z.L.R. 980 (New Zealand C.A.), at pp. 984, 988.

[55] The respondent's second argument is that Parliament, had it intended to criminalize attempts to do the legally impossible, would have used the words "whether or not it was factually or legally impossible" in s. 24(1). As examples of statutes that were intended to criminalize attempts to do the legally impossible, the respondent cites provisions of statutes from the United Kingdom and from the United States:

*1*—(1) If, with intent to commit an offence to which this section applies, a person does an act which is more than merely preparatory to the commission of the offence, he is guilty of attempting to commit the offence.

(2) A person may be guilty of attempting to commit an offence to which this section applies even though the facts are such that the commission of the offence is impossible.

(3) In any case where—

(a) apart from this subsection a person's intention would not be regarded as having amounted to an intent to commit an offence; but

(b) if the facts of the case had been as he believed them to be, his intention would be so regarded,

then, for the purposes of subsection (1) above, he shall be regarded as having had an intent to commit that offence. (*Criminal Attempts Act 1981* (U.K.), 1981, c. 47.)

If the conduct in which a person engages otherwise constitutes an attempt to commit a crime pursuant to section 110.00, it is no defense to a prosecution for such attempt that the crime charged to have been attempted was, under the attendant circumstances, factually or legally impossible of commission, if such crime could have been committed had the attendant circumstances been as such person believed them to be. (*N.Y. Penal Law* §110.10 (Consol. 1984).)

[56] A third argument, which the respondent does not advance, is that the words "under the circumstances" restrict the scope of s. 24(1) to attempts to do the factually impossible. An attempt that is not possible "under the circumstances," according to this argument, is by implication possible under some other set of circumstances. Otherwise, there would be no need to mention circumstances—the mere mention of impossibility would suffice. President North of the New Zealand Court of Appeal made this very argument in *Donnelly, supra,* at p. 988:

In my opinion the significant words in s. 72(1) [New Zealand's equivalent to s. 24(1) of the *Criminal Code*] are "in the circumstances," which seem to me to imply that in other circumstances it might be possible to commit the offence. This I think points to the conclusion that s. 72(1) went no further than to ensure that a person who had the necessary criminal intent and did an act for the purpose of accomplishing his object was guilty of an attempt even although it so happened that it was not possible to commit the full offence.

[57] In addition there is another way of turning the same language to the respondent's advantage. "Circumstances," in ordinary parlance, are facts. Laws, by contrast, are not circumstances. Accordingly, applying the rule that *expressio unius est exclusio alterius*, the mention in s. 24(1) of attempts that are circumstantially or factually impossible may be taken to exclude attempts that are legally impossible. The question, as one Canadian writer has framed it, is whether "'the circumstances' referred to in [s. 24(1)] include the legal status of the actor's conduct." Brown, *supra,* at p. 229.

[58] Still another argument in favour of the respondent's position, though one that reflects judicial policy rather than the strict ascertainment of legislative intent, is that penal statutes, if ambiguous, should be construed narrowly, in favour of the rights

of the accused. "[T]he overriding principle governing the interpretation of penal provisions is that ambiguity should be resolved in a manner most favourable to accused persons." *R. v. McIntosh*, [1995] 1 S.C.R. 686 (S.C.C.), at p. 705.

[59] Although some of these arguments have a certain force, what force they have is greatly attenuated when it is realized that the conventional distinction between factual and legal impossibility is not tenable. The only relevant distinction for purposes of s. 24(1) of the *Criminal Code* is between imaginary crimes and attempts to do the factually impossible. The criminal law of Canada recognizes no middle category called "legal impossibility." Because Mr. Dynar attempted to do the impossible but did not attempt to commit an imaginary crime, he can only have attempted to do the "factually impossible." For this reason, Mr. Dynar's proposal that s. 24(1) criminalizes only attempts to do the factually impossible does not help him.

[60] As we have already indicated, an attempt to do the factually impossible is considered to be one whose completion is thwarted by mere happenstance. In theory at least, an accused who attempts to do the factually impossible could succeed but for the intervention of some fortuity. A legally impossible attempt, by contrast, is considered to be one which, even if it were completed, still would not be a crime. One scholar has described impossible attempts in these terms:

> Three main forms of impossibility have set the framework for contemporary debate. First, there is impossibility due to inadequate means (Type I). For example, A tries to kill B by shooting at him from too great a distance or by administering too small a dose of poison; C tries to break into a house without the equipment which would be necessary to force the windows or doors. ...
>
> The second form of impossibility arises where an actor is prevented from completing the offence because some element of its *actus reus* cannot be brought within the criminal design (Type II). For example, A tries to kill B by shooting him when he is asleep in bed, but in fact B has already died of natural causes; C tries to steal money from a safe which is empty. ...
>
> The third form of impossibility arises where the actor's design is completed but the offence is still not committed because some element of the *actus reus* is missing (Type III). For example, A may take possession of property believing it to have been stolen when it has not been; B may smuggle a substance for reward believing it to be a narcotic when it is sugar. ...

Colvin, *supra*, at pp. 355-56.

[61] According to Professor Colvin, factually impossible attempts are those that fall into either of the first two categories. Legally impossible attempts are those that fall into the third category.

[62] Colvin's schema appears attractive. But in fact it draws distinctions that do not stand up on closer inspection. There is no legally relevant difference between the pick-pocket who reaches into the empty pocket and the man who takes his own umbrella from a stand believing it to be some other person's umbrella. Both have the *mens rea* of a thief. The first intends to take a wallet that he believes is not his own. The second intends to take an umbrella that he believes is not his own. Each takes some steps in the direction of consummating his design. And each is thwarted by a

defect in the attendant circumstances, by an objective reality over which he has no control: the first by the absence of a wallet, the second by the accident of owning the thing that he seeks to steal. It is true that the latter seems to consummate his design and still not to complete an offence; but the semblance is misleading. The truth is that the second man does not consummate his design, because his intention is not simply to take the particular umbrella that he takes, but to take an umbrella that is not his own. That this man's design is premised on a mistaken understanding of the facts does not make it any less his design. A mistaken belief cannot be eliminated from the description of a person's mental state simply because it is mistaken.

[63]  If it were otherwise, the effect would be to eliminate from our criminal law the defence of mistaken belief. If mistaken beliefs did not form part of an actor's intent—if an actor's intent were merely to do what he in fact does—then a man who honestly but mistakenly believed that a woman had consented to have sexual relations with him and who on that basis actually had sexual relations with that woman, would have no defence to the crime of sexual assault. His intention, on this limited understanding of intention, would have been to sleep with the particular woman with whom he slept; and that particular woman, by hypothesis, is one who did not consent to sleep with him. Substituting the one description ("a woman who did not consent to sleep with him") for the other ("the particular woman with whom he slept"), it would follow that his intention was to sleep with a woman who had not consented to sleep with him. But of course, and as we have already strenuously urged, intention is one thing and the truth is another. Intention has to do with how one sees the world and not necessarily with the reality of the world.

[64]  Accordingly, there is no difference between an act thwarted by a "physical impossibility" and one thwarted "following completion." Both are thwarted by an attendant circumstance, by a fact: for example, by the fact of there being no wallet to steal or by the fact of there being no umbrella to steal. The distinction between them is a distinction without a difference. Professor Colvin himself agrees that" [t]he better view is that impossibility of execution is never a defence to inchoate liability in Canada" (p. 358).

[65]  There is, however, a relevant difference between a failed attempt to do something that is a crime and an imaginary crime. See Pierre Rainville, "La gradation de la culpabilité morale et des formes de risque de préjudice dans le cadre de la répression de la tentative" (1996), 37 *C. de D.* 909, at pp. 954-55. It is one thing to attempt to steal a wallet, believing such thievery to be a crime, and quite another thing to bring sugar into Canada, believing the importation of sugar to be a crime. In the former case, the would-be thief has the *mens rea* associated with thievery. In the latter case, the would-be smuggler has no *mens rea* known to law. Because s. 24(1) clearly provides that it is an element of the offence of attempt to have" an intent to commit an offence," the latter sort of attempt is not a crime.

[66]  Nor should it be. A major purpose of the law of attempt is to discourage the commission of subsequent offences. See Williams' *Textbook of Criminal Law*, *supra*, at pp. 404-5. See also Brown, *supra*, at p. 232; Eugene Meehan, "Attempt—Some Rational Thoughts on Its Rationale" (1976-77), 19 *Crim. L.Q.* 215, at p. 238; Don Stuart, *Canadian Criminal Law* (3rd ed. 1995), at p. 594. But one who attempts to do

something that is not a crime or even one who actually does something that is not a crime, believing that what he has done or has attempted to do is a crime, has not displayed any propensity to commit crimes in the future, unless perhaps he has betrayed a vague willingness to break the law. Probably all he has shown is that he might be inclined to do the same sort of thing in the future; and from a societal point of view, that is not a very worrisome prospect, because by hypothesis what he attempted to do is perfectly legal.

[67] Therefore, we conclude that s. 24(1) draws no distinction between attempts to do the possible but by inadequate means, attempts to do the physically impossible, and attempts to do something that turns out to be impossible "following completion." All are varieties of attempts to do the "factually impossible" and all are crimes. Only attempts to commit imaginary crimes fall outside the scope of the provision. Because what Mr. Dynar attempted to do falls squarely into the category of the factually impossible—he attempted to commit crimes known to law and was thwarted only by chance—it was a criminal attempt within the meaning of s. 24(1). The evidence suggests that Mr. Dynar is a criminal within the contemplation of the Canadian law and so the double criminality rule should be no bar to his extradition to the United States.

[68] Notwithstanding the difficulties associated with the conventional distinction between factual and legal impossibility, a certain reluctance to embrace our conclusion persists in some quarters. It seems to us that this is in part due to a misunderstanding of the elements of the money-laundering offences. Both s. 462.31(1) of the *Criminal Code* and s. 19.2(1) of the *Narcotic Control Act* require knowledge that the property being laundered is the proceeds of crime. It is tempting to think that knowledge is therefore the *mens rea* of these offences. But "*mens rea*" denotes a mental state. *Mens rea* is the subjective element of a crime. See Williams' *Textbook of Criminal Law*, supra, at p. 71. Knowledge is not subjective, or, more accurately, it is not entirely subjective.

[69] As we have already said, knowledge, for legal purposes, is true belief. Knowledge therefore has two components—truth and belief—and of these, only belief is mental or subjective. Truth is objective, or at least consists in the correspondence of a proposition or mental state to objective reality. Accordingly, truth, which is a state of affairs in the external world that does not vary with the intention of the accused, cannot be a part of *mens rea*. As one Canadian academic has said, [translation] "[t]he truth of the accused's belief is not part of the *mens rea* of s. 24(1) Cr.C." See Rainville, *supra*, at p. 963. Knowledge as such is not then the *mens rea* of the money-laundering offences. Belief is.

[70] The truth of an actor's belief that certain monies are the proceeds of crime is something different from the belief itself. That the belief be true is one of the attendant circumstances that is required if the *actus reus* is to be completed. In other words, the act of converting the proceeds of crime presupposes the existence of some money that is in truth the proceeds of crime.

[71] In this, the money-laundering offences are no different from other offences. Murder is the intentional killing of a person. Because a person cannot be killed who is not alive, and because a killing, if is to be murder, must be intentional, it follows

that a successful murderer must believe that his victim is alive. An insane man who kills another believing that the one he kills is a manikin does not have the *mens rea* needed for murder. Thus, the successful commission of the offence of murder presupposes both a belief that the victim is alive just before the deadly act occurs and the actual vitality of the victim at that moment. Both truth and belief are required. Therefore, knowledge is required. But this does not mean that the vitality of the victim is part of the *mens rea* of the offence of murder. Instead, it is an attendant circumstance that makes possible the completion of the *actus reus*, which is the killing of a person.

[72] In general, the successful commission of any offence presupposes a certain coincidence of circumstances. But these circumstances do not enter into the *mens rea* of the offence. As one author observes, it is important "to keep separate the intention of the accused and the circumstances as they really were" (Brown, *supra*, at p. 232).

[73] The absence of an attendant circumstance is irrelevant from the point of view of the law of attempt. An accused is guilty of an attempt if he intends to commit a crime and takes legally sufficient steps towards its commission. Because an attempt is in its very nature an incomplete substantive offence, it will always be the case that the *actus reus* of the completed offence will be deficient, and sometimes this will be because an attendant circumstance is lacking. In *Ancio, supra*, at pp. 247-48, McIntyre J. said:

> As with any other crime, the Crown must prove a *mens rea*, that is, the intent to commit the offence in question and the *actus reus*, that is, some step towards the commission of the offence attempted going beyond mere acts of preparation. Of the two elements the more significant is the *mens rea*. ...
>
> Indeed, because the crime of attempt may be complete without the actual commission of any other offence and even without the performance of any act unlawful in itself, it is abundantly clear that the criminal element of the offence of attempt may lie solely in the intent.

[74] So it should not be troubling that what Mr. Dynar did does not constitute the *actus reus* of the money-laundering offences. If his actions did constitute the *actus reus*, then he would be guilty of the completed offences described in s. 462.31 of the *Criminal Code* and s. 19.2 of the *Narcotic Control Act*. There would be no need even to consider the law of attempt. The law of attempt is engaged only when, as in this case, the *mens rea* of the completed offence is present entirely and the *actus reus* of it is present in an incomplete but more-than-merely-preparatory way.

[75] The respondent argues that, even accepting that the truth of a belief is not a part of the *mens rea*, nevertheless he did not have the requisite *mens rea*. In particular, the respondent suggests that, in determining whether an accused has the requisite *mens rea* for attempt, a court should consider only those mental states that supply the accused's motivation to act.

[76] This proposal is a way of overlooking an accused's mistaken beliefs. Thus, the respondent argues that he did not have the requisite *mens rea* because he desired only to make money by doing a service to Anthony, the undercover agent. It did not matter to Mr. Dynar whether the money was the proceeds of crime or not. He would

have been just as happy to convert funds for the United States Government as for some drug kingpin. Mr. Dynar's only concern was that he should receive a commission for his services.

[77]   The theoretical basis for this thinking appears in Professor George Fletcher's attempted defence of the distinction between factual impossibility and legal impossibility (in *Rethinking Criminal Law* (1978)). Fletcher, on whom the respondent relies, says that an accused's legally relevant intention comprises only those mental states that move the accused to act as he does (at p. 161):

> [M]istaken beliefs are relevant to what the actor is trying to do if they affect his incentive in acting. They affect his incentive if knowing of the mistake would give him a good reason for changing his course of conduct.
>
>    Because most facts are, from the accused's point of view, of no consequence, what the accused thinks about most facts is legally irrelevant.

[78]   Thus, to take one of Fletcher's examples, it does not matter what day a criminal thought it was when he committed a crime, because whatever he might have thought the day was, he would still have acted as he did. In Fletcher's view, similar reasoning explains why it is not a crime to deal with "legitimate" property thinking that one is dealing with the proceeds of crime (at p. 162):

> [I]t seems fairly clear that the fact that the [goods were] stolen does not affect the actor's incentive in paying the price at which [they were] offered to him by the police. If he were told that the goods were not stolen, that would not have provided him with a reason for turning down the offer. If they were not stolen, so much the better. It follows, therefore, that it is inappropriate to describe his conduct as attempting to receive stolen [goods].

[79]   But this view confounds motivation and intention. If attention were paid only to the former, then the number of crimes would be greatly, if not very satisfactorily, reduced, because what moves many criminals to crime is some desire relatively more benign than the desire to commit a crime. We suspect that only the most hardened criminals commit crimes just for the sake of breaking the law. To at least many malefactors, it must be a matter of indifference whether their actions constitute crimes. Probably most thieves would not turn up their noses at the opportunity to loot a house simply because it has been abandoned and so is the property of no one. The goal is the making of a quick dollar, not the flouting of the law. In this, we again agree completely with Glanville Williams, who said:

> Normally, motivation is irrelevant for intention. Every receiver of stolen goods would prefer to have non-stolen goods at the same price, if given the choice; but if he knows or believes the goods are stolen, he intends to receive stolen goods. We have to say that a person intends his act in the circumstances that he knows or believes to exist. This being the rule for consummated crimes, no good reason can be suggested why it should differ for attempts. ("The Lords and Impossible Attempts, or *Quis Custodiet Ipsos Custodes?*," [1986] *Cambridge L.J.* 33, at p. 78.)

[80]  In this case, it is almost certainly true that Mr. Dynar would have been content to convert the United States Government's money even if he had known that it had nothing to do with the sale of drugs. Presumably his only concern was to collect his percentage. The provenance of the money must have been, for him, largely irrelevant. But, from the point of view of the criminal law, what is important is not what moved Mr. Dynar, but what Mr. Dynar believed he was doing. "We have to say that a person intends his act in the circumstances that he knows or believes to exist." And the evidence is clear that Mr. Dynar believed that he was embarked upon a scheme to convert "drug money" from New York City.

[81]  Looking to intent rather than motive accords with the purpose of the criminal law in general and of the law of attempt in particular. Society imposes criminal sanctions in order to punish and deter undesirable conduct. It does not matter to society, in its efforts to secure social peace and order, what an accused's motive was, but only what the accused intended to do. It is no consolation to one whose car has been stolen that the thief stole the car intending to sell it to purchase food for a food bank. Similarly, the purpose of the law of attempt is universally acknowledged to be the deterrence of subsequent attempts. A person who has intended to do something that the law forbids and who has actually taken steps towards the completion of an offence is apt to try the same sort of thing in the future; and there is no assurance that next time his attempt will fail.

[82]  Applying this rationale to impossible attempts, we conclude that such attempts are no less menacing than are other attempts. After all, the only difference between an attempt to do the possible and an attempt to do the impossible is chance. A person who enters a bedroom and stabs a corpse thinking that he is stabbing a living person has the same intention as a person who enters a bedroom and stabs someone who is alive. In the former instance, by some chance, the intended victim expired in his sleep perhaps only moments before the would-be assassin acted. It is difficult to see why this circumstance, of which the tardy killer has no knowledge and over which he has no control, should in any way mitigate his culpability. Next time, the intended victim might be alive. Similarly, even if Mr. Dynar could not actually have laundered the proceeds of crime this time around, there is hardly any guarantee that his next customer might not be someone other than an agent of the United States Government.

[83]  The import of all of this is that Mr. Dynar committed the crime of attempt; and for having done so he should be extradited to the United States. The facts disclose an intent to launder money and acts taken in furtherance of that design. Section 24(1) of the *Criminal Code* requires no more.

[The dissenting opinion of Major J. (Sopinka and McLachlin JJ. concurring) has been omitted.]

## II. INCITEMENT

Criminal liability for incitement, or counselling, exists in two forms in Canadian law. The first is incitement of an offence that is actually committed (s. 22) and the second is incitement of an offence that is not committed (s. 464). The first is a mode of participation in the commission of the offence because the inciter, in effect, causes the commission of an offence through another person. This form of incitement is considered in the previous chapter. The second is an independent offence of inchoate liability and it is considered here.

Section 22 of the Code says that counselling *includes* soliciting, procuring, and inciting. This mode of participation in crime requires not only completion of an offence but completion that is the consequence of the inciter's action. Under s. 464 incitement of an offence that is not completed is criminalized on the theory that by inciting another the inciter has already taken affirmative steps toward the completion of an offence. At what point is this offence complete? Does it matter that the person incited had no intention at any point of completing the offence that he or she was incited to commit?

### Ford v. The Queen
Ontario Court of Appeal
(2000), 145 C.C.C. (3d) 336

MacPHERSON J.A. (for the Court):

### *Introduction*

[1] The appellant, Hugh Ford, was convicted, following a trial with a jury presided over by Lederman J., of the offence of counselling murder. However, he was acquitted of the offences of conspiracy to commit murder and attempted murder. Mr. Ford appeals his conviction from counselling murder. His principal ground of appeal is that the jury's guilty verdict on the charge of counselling murder is inconsistent with its acquittal on the other charges.

### A.  *Factual Background*

[2] On May 13, 1991, the principal Crown witness and alleged co-conspirator, John Doe, shot Martin Bidwell in the face from close range and nearly killed him. It was the theory of the Crown that the appellant headed a band of break and enter artists of which Doe was a member. The Crown contended that the appellant had contracted Doe to kill Bidwell in order to prevent Bidwell from giving testimony against the appellant in a trial on charges of break and enter and possession of stolen property.

[3] The evidence in support of this theory emanated almost entirely from Doe. He testified that he was a member of the break and enter group headed by Ford. According to Doe, about a month prior to the shooting Ford mentioned that he had a problem connected with Martin Bidwell. Ford told Doe that he had been caught with some

stolen property, that the case was going to court, and that Bidwell was going to testify against him. This caused Ford great concern. About a week or a week and a half before the shooting, while they were at The Tavern in the Albion Mall, Ford brought up the topic of killing Bidwell and said that he wanted Doe to do it.

[4] The discussion of the killing extended over several meetings. According to Doe, Ford offered him $1,000 cash, about $500 for lawyer's fees "for whatever happened later on" and a newer weapon. Ford supplied him with a handgun, ammunition, a police scanner and a balaclava and gave him advice about what other equipment he would need.

[5] Doe testified that Ford took him downtown to show him where Bidwell lived and the places he frequented. While they were there, Ford videotaped and photographed Bidwell's apartment and showed Doe possible escape routes. At some point, Ford suggested various scenarios of how to carry out the killing but left the final decision up to Doe.

[6] After "constant goading" from Ford, on May 13, 1991, Doe loaded up his equipment. By coincidence, he met Ford near the Eaton Centre. Doe told Ford that he had come downtown to kill Bidwell "as per his plans." Doe and Ford spent a few hours together. Then Doe went off on his own to kill Bidwell.

[7] Doe proceeded to Bidwell's apartment and gained entry by breaking a window in the front door. He waited inside. Bidwell's roommate, Bert Trapman, arrived at about 4:30 p.m. Doe tackled him but could tell, based on Ford's description, that this was not Bidwell. He bound Trapman with tape and fishing line and waited.

[8] Bidwell arrived home at about 6:10 p.m. Doe jumped out and shot him in the face. Bidwell headed for the stairs. He and Doe fell down the stairs together. Bidwell struggled with the lock on the door and pleaded to be left alone. His assailant replied something like "Calm down" or "Relax." Bidwell managed to get out the door and ran across the courtyard to the front of the building where he saw the building superintendent. He asked the superintendent to call an ambulance for him and then sat down in the open and waited for the ambulance to arrive.

[9] Trapman, still bound inside the apartment, heard Doe come back into the apartment. He thought he was "done for" but all he heard was Doe closing some zippers on a satchel or backpack and then leave.

[10] Bidwell received a gunshot wound to the face which resulted in trauma to his head region. Dr. Edward McDougall testified that the wound could have been fatal. The handgun used in the shooting was identified as a .32 calibre Smith& Wesson manufactured sometime between 1890 and 1930. Testing determined that the weapon was in poor condition and would misfire intermittently.

[11] The case for the defence was presented primarily through the appellant. Ford denied playing any role in, or having any prior knowledge of, Doe's attempt to kill Bidwell. While Ford did discuss his legal problems with Doe and told him about Bidwell's unwillingness to help out, he denied ever suggesting that Bidwell should be killed, contracting Doe to perform the deed, or supplying Doe with the handgun or other paraphernalia to commit murder. Doe was aware of the status of the court proceedings because he asked Ford about it from time to time.

[12] According to Ford, Doe had his own motives to harm Bidwell since it was Bidwell who had fouled up the fencing of the equipment Doe had stolen. Ford testified that Doe felt that Bidwell had betrayed them and he was upset that he would not be getting paid for the stolen computers. Doe would have known Bidwell's address because it was on a list of client contacts that Ford had once prepared and shared with Doe.

[13] It was the position of the defence that Doe was a wholly unreliable witness who acted alone and then tried to shift the blame onto the appellant.

[14] The trial before Lederman J. was the appellant's second trial on the charges relating to the shooting of Martin Bidwell. At his first trial, the jury returned a verdict of guilty on all counts in the indictment. The appellant was sentenced to terms of 20 years imprisonment on the charges of conspiracy and attempted murder and to six years on the charge of attempting to obstruct justice. The charge of counselling murder was stayed pursuant to the rule against multiple convictions for the same wrongful act: see *R. v. Kienapple* (1974), 15 C.C.C. (2d) 524 (S.C.C.). On November 24, 1994, this court allowed Ford's appeal against conviction: see *R. v. Ford* (1994), 77 O.A.C. 246 (Ont. C.A.).

[15] Upon his arraignment at the second trial, the appellant entered a plea of guilty to the charge of attempting to obstruct justice and pleas of not guilty to the other charges. The jury returned verdicts of not guilty on the charges of attempted murder and conspiracy to commit murder and a verdict of guilty on the charge of counselling murder. Lederman J. sentenced the appellant to four years imprisonment on the charge of counselling murder and to 18 months concurrent on the charge of attempting to obstruct justice.

[16] The appellant now appeals the conviction for counselling murder.

*B. Issues*

[17] The issues that need to be considered on this appeal are:

(1) Should the jury's verdict of guilty on the charge of counselling murder be set aside because it is inconsistent with the jury's verdicts of not guilty on the charges of conspiracy to commit murder and attempted murder?

(2) Did the trial judge err in his instructions to the jury on the offence of counselling murder? ...

*C. Analysis*

(1) Inconsistent verdicts

[18] The appellant faces a high hurdle in trying to set aside a jury's verdict of guilty on one charge on the basis that it is inconsistent with the jury's verdict of not guilty on a second charge. In the leading Ontario case dealing with inconsistent verdicts, *R. v. McLaughlin* (1974), 15 C.C.C. (2d) 562 (Ont. C.A.), at 567, Evans J.A. framed the test in this fashion:

The fact that verdicts may be inconsistent does not mean that in all cases the Court of Appeal *ex necessitate* must quash the conviction or grant a new trial. If the verdicts are violently at odds and the same basic ingredients are common to both charges then the conviction will be quashed but the onus is on the appellant to show that no reasonable jury who had applied their minds to the evidence could have arrived at that conclusion.

See also: *R. v. McShannock* (1980), 55 C.C.C. (2d) 53 (Ont. C.A.); *R. v. Ertel* (1987), 35 C.C.C. (3d) 398 (Ont. C.A.); *R. v. Peterson* (1996), 106 C.C.C. (3d) 64 (Ont. C.A.); and *R. v. Tillekaratna* (1998), 124 C.C.C. (3d) 549 (Ont. C.A.).

[19]  The appellant submits that the guilty verdict for counselling to commit murder is "violently at odds" with the not guilty verdicts for conspiracy to commit murder and attempted murder, such that "no reasonable jury who had applied their minds to the evidence could have arrived at that conclusion." In support of this submission, Mr. Norris, in a very able and reflective argument, referred to overlapping between the *Criminal Code* provisions relating to the three offences and to an alleged lack of logic in the jury's verdicts in light of the factual circumstances of the case.

[20]  There is, in my view, some force to Mr. Norris' submissions on this issue, especially with respect to the potential overlap between the offences of attempted murder and counselling to commit murder. Since John Doe admitted that he shot Bidwell, Ford could only be convicted of attempted murder if the jury was convinced beyond a reasonable doubt that Ford aided or abetted Doe in the commission of the offence. The Supreme Court of Canada has defined "abet" for purposes of party liability as including "encouraging, instigating, promoting or procuring the crime to be committed": see *R. v. Greyeyes* (1997), 116 C.C.C. (3d) 334 (S.C.C.), at 344. Section 22(3) of the *Criminal Code* defines "counsel" as including "procure, solicit or incite." There is no doubt that these are similar definitions.

[21]  However, they are not identical definitions. In my view, it is important, as submitted by Ms. Reid for the Crown, to examine closely what the trial judge actually said to the jury about each offence.

[22]  Early in his charge, the trial judge instructed the jury as follows:

You must consider each count of the indictment separately, and when considering a particular count you are only to consider the evidence that is directly relevant to that count. If you come to a verdict in one count, that fact must not influence your decision or any other count.

[23]  The trial judge then provided the jury with definitions of conspiracy, attempted murder (including aiding and abetting) and counselling. There is, without question, some overlap in these definitions. However, in my view, there are sufficient differences in the definitions provided by the trial judge to justify the three verdicts reached by the jury.

[24]  I have no serious problem with a comparison of the jury's guilty verdict for conspiracy to commit murder and its not guilty verdict for counselling to commit murder. The trial judge provided separate definitions of these offences. He then went on and provided the jury with a direct comparison of the two offences:

One person may counsel or procure another person to commit the offence as a result of a long course of persuasion and bargaining. On the other hand, procurement may also occur if there is no more than brief acceptance of an offer to commit an offence with the promise of reward for doing so. There is no necessity that the person who procures another to commit an offence and the person who actually does it form a conspiracy or real agreement as to how it will be done. Therefore, you must remember, too, that conspiracy to commit murder and counselling murder are separate offences. If you find that the Crown has proven beyond a reasonable doubt that Hugh Ford counselled John to commit murder it doesn't mean that you must also find that Hugh Ford committed the offence of conspiracy to commit murder.

[25]  In this passage, the trial judge points out a fundamental distinction between the conspiracy and counselling offences: conspiracy involves an agreement between two persons to do something; counselling involves one person urging another to do something. Agreement is the anchor of conspiracy. Agreement is unconnected to counselling.

[26]  The relationship between the attempted murder (grounded in party liability) and counselling offences is, in my view, a closer and more problematic one. Indeed, in its factum the Crown acknowledges that the jury's verdicts on these offences are "somewhat curious." Nevertheless, in my view, once again the trial judge's charge established that these were different charges involving different conduct by the appellant.

[27]  Concerning "aiding" and "abetting," the trial judge said:

[T]he word "aiding" means help or assist a person. A person can aid a person in the committing of an offence without being present when the crime is committed. The second way in which a person can be a party to an offence is by abetting and the word "abetting" means support or encourage. As with the case with aiding, a person can be an abettor without being present when a crime is committed.

To be guilty of aiding or abetting there must be some actual participation or assistance rendered. A person must associate himself with the criminal venture by participating in it and trying to make it succeed, or actively encouraging that to occur.

[28]  Concerning "counselling," the trial judge said:

The word "counselling" includes procuring, soliciting or inciting. I will explain what each of these words means. To "counsel" means to advise or recommend. To "procure" means to instigate, encourage or persuade. A person can encourage or persuade without having instigated the offence. A person "solicits" another when he or she entreats or urges another to do something. To "incite" has a similar meaning. It means to urge or stir up or stimulate.

[29]  In these passages there is some overlap in the definitions. The word "encourage" appears in the definitions of both abetting and counselling. Nevertheless, there is a clear difference in the definitions. The offence of counselling is limited to oral encouragement by the accused. However, the activity of abetting requires" actual participation or assistance rendered." It may be that the trial judge's definition of

abetting was *narrower* than the definition enunciated in *R. v. Greyeyes*, *supra*. However, that may well have inured to the appellant's benefit in that he was acquitted of the charge of attempted murder, the offence grounded in abetting on the facts of this case. In any event, there was nothing wrong with the trial judge's definition of counselling. Moreover, his definition of counselling was different than his definition of both aiding and abetting.

[30] For these reasons, I do not agree with the appellant's submission that the jury's verdicts in this case meet the high standard set out in *R. v. McLaughlin*, *supra*, and the cases which have followed it. The jury's three verdicts are not violently at odds with each other.

(2)  Instructions about counselling murder

[31]  The appellant was charged with an offence under s. 464 of the *Criminal Code*, counselling an offence that is not committed. That is because the offence counselled was murder, whereas the offence ultimately committed by John Doe was attempted murder. The trial judge correctly instructed the jury on this offence. However, he injected into his charge a brief reference to s. 22 of the *Code* which deals with the circumstances in which a person counselling an offence becomes a party to that offence or other offences which the person counselling knew or ought to have known were likely to be committed in consequence of the counselling. The appellant contends that this reference to s. 22 may have confused the jury or even created in their minds a larger scope of liability for the counselling offence than is warranted on the facts of this case.

[32]  I disagree with this submission. It is true that s. 22(1) was inapplicable in this case. Section 22(2) was either inapplicable or unnecessary. However, viewing the trial judge's instructions on the counselling charge as a whole, the jury could not have been misled about the *only* basis on which it could convict the appellant of counselling—namely, counselling John Doe to commit *murder*. On about a dozen occasions the trial judge instructed the jury that the counselling offence required proof beyond a reasonable doubt of counselling the commission of the offence of murder. No other offence was mentioned. Moreover, on the facts of this case, no other possible offence was in issue. Accordingly, it is not realistic, in my view, to think that the jury could have picked up on the trial judge's brief reference to s. 22(2) and, without more, used it to find the accused guilty of counselling on an entirely different basis than that which the trial judge had placed squarely before it.

*Appeal dismissed.*

---

In *R. v. Dungey* (1979), 51 C.C.C. (2d) 86, the accused, a lawyer, had been charged with unlawfully conspiring with a client to defraud the Law Society of Upper Canada by agreeing with his client that the client would apply for full legal aid and also pay the lawyer a certain amount from his own funds. The trial judge was of the view that the lawyer requested the client to enter into the agreement but acquitted Dungey as he was not satisfied that the client ever entered into the alleged agreement. On appeal from the acquittal, the Crown urged that the trial judge, although not requested to do so, should have convicted the accused of attempting to conspire to defraud the Law Society. Dubin J.A. stated for the Ontario Court of Appeal:

> In the absence of an agreement, there was no offence, and a conviction for attempt to conspire to defraud would be punishment for a guilty intention alone. Notwithstanding that the charge was one of conspiracy, the conduct of the respondent should be viewed as a step preparatory to committing the substantive offence of fraud and, in that sense, what he did would be too remote to constitute an attempt.
>
> I have noted the specific offence in our *Criminal Code* of "incitement." It would be inappropriate here to consider whether that section could have been invoked to meet the circumstances of this case, but where the evidence warrants it, a more fitting charge would be that of inciting to commit the substantive offence of fraud. If conduct falls short of such an offence, it is neither necessary nor desirable to extend the law so that a person could be convicted of an attempt to conspire to commit the substantive offence of fraud.

### R. v. Gonzague
Ontario Court of Appeal
(1983), 4 C.C.C. (3d) 505

MARTIN J.A. (orally, for the Court):

[1] The appellant appeals from his conviction by the verdict of a general sessions jury on an indictment alleging that he:

> ... between the 30th day of May, 1982, and the 1st day of June, 1982, at the City of Timmins, in the District of Cochrane, did procure Charles Charbonneau to commit an indictable offence of first degree murder, which offence was not committed, contrary to the Criminal Code of Canada [R.S.C. 1970, c. C-34], section 422.

[2] The facts are these. The appellant operated a window cleaning business in the town of Timmins. Neil Roy had formerly been employed by him and, after Roy had ceased to be employed by the appellant, he established his own window cleaning business and became a competitor of the appellant.

[3] The Crown called a number of witnesses for the purpose of showing that the appellant was angry with Roy and had made threats against him.

[4] On Sunday, 30th May 1982, the appellant, in the early afternoon, went to a bootlegging establishment in the city of Timmins. There were a number of other persons present, including one Charbonneau. The appellant knew Charbonneau by sight but was not otherwise acquainted with him. The appellant spoke to Charbonneau and offered to buy him a beer. According to Charbonneau, the appellant stated that he nearly went bankrupt because Roy was cutting prices and he wanted him "wiped off the map." The appellant, so Charbonneau said, stated that he had a "couple of guys"

coming from Montreal to do the job. Charbonneau testified that he did not want his friend Roy to be hurt and he said "I'll do it for you."

[5] The appellant left the bootleggers' about mid-afternoon, and Charbonneau went to the home of Roy. The police were subsequently notified. Charbonneau testified that in the early evening of that day he went to the appellant's place of business and asked for $500 on account and that the appellant gave him a cheque for $200 after discussing various ways in which Roy might be disposed of. Charbonneau gave the cheque to the police and it was ultimately cashed and the money retained by them.

[6] On 1st June 1982 Charbonneau was fitted with a body pack recorder by the police and he went back to the appellant's place of business. Charbonneau testified that on this occasion the appellant told him to forget about the matter and that Charbonneau could keep the $200.

[7] The appellant's version of what occurred was this. He testified that at the bootlegger's Charbonneau asked him if he knew Neil Roy and asked the appellant if he could give Charbonneau a job. He also asked the appellant for an advance of $1,000. The appellant said he asked Charbonneau if he had worked for Roy and Charbonneau replied that he had and that Roy owed him $800. The appellant, so he said, told Charbonneau "that he could forget the $800," because Roy could not pay. Charbonneau said he had a gun and would "fix" Roy. The appellant testified that he told Charbonneau to forget about the gun. He said he left the bootlegger's around mid-afternoon, and Charbonneau came to his place around 6:00 p.m. and asked for a cheque. He said that he gave Charbonneau a cheque for $200, and told Charbonneau that when he went to work for the appellant he could pay him back. The appellant's explanation for the conversation with Charbonneau on 1st June 1982, which, unknown to him, had been recorded, was that in the conversation he was telling Charbonneau to forget the gun that Charbonneau had mentioned, and that the appellant was telling Charbonneau that he did not want to hear any more of the talk that had emanated from Charbonneau at the bootlegger's.

[8] The charge was laid under s. 422 [now s. 464] of the Criminal Code, which reads as follows:

> 422. Except where otherwise expressly provided by law, the following provisions apply in respect of persons who counsel, procure or incite other persons to commit offences, namely,
>
> (a) every one who counsels, procures or incites another person to commit an indictable offence is, if the offence is not committed, guilty of an indictable offence and is liable to the same punishment to which a person who attempts to commit that offence is liable; and
>
> (b) every one who counsels, procures or incites another person to commit an offence punishable on summary conviction is, if the offence is not committed, guilty of an offence punishable on summary conviction.

[9] It was an offence at common law to solicit or incite another person to commit either a felony or a misdemeanour and s. 422(a) merely codifies the common law

rule. The word "procure" in the context in which it is used in s. 422 means to instigate, persuade or solicit.

[10] Glanville Williams, in his work Textbook of Criminal Law (1978), states at p. 384:

> The common law offence of incitement (or solicitation) is committed when one person "counsels, procures or commands" another to commit a crime whether or not the other actually commits it. (If he commits it the inciter will, of course, be an accessory and will normally be charged as such; but on a charge of incitement it is no defence to show that the crime was actually committed.)
>
> Any persuasion or encouragement (including a threat) is sufficient; so probably, is a mere suggestion.

[11] The word "procure," which I have indicated is equivalent to incite, does not necessarily mean that the inciter must originate or initiate the transaction and a person may be convicted of incitement although the plan originated with the party alleged to have been incited: see Glanville Williams, Criminal Law (The General Part), 2nd ed. (1961), at p. 612, para. 195. He also states in his Textbook of Criminal Law, at p. 310:

> A person who has incited a crime can still (in general) escape complicity in it if he expressly and clearly countermands the crime or withdraws his assent before it is committed, but he will remain liable for any previous incitement, as an inchoate offence.

[12] Counsel for the appellant advanced as one of the grounds of appeal, in his statement of law and fact, that the learned trial judge erred in failing to instruct the jury that a renunciation by the appellant of the previous act of incitement constituted a defence. The offence of procuring under s. 422 is complete when the solicitation or incitement occurs even though it is immediately rejected by the person solicited, or even though the person solicited merely pretends assent and has no intention of committing the offence. There is no authority in either the Canadian or Commonwealth decisions in support of the view that renunciation of the criminal purpose constitutes a defence to a charge of "counselling, procuring or inciting" under s. 422, although renunciation is an affirmative defence under s. 5.02(3) of the American Model Penal Code to a charge of criminal solicitation: see "Abandoning Criminal Intent" by Martin Wasik, [1980] Crim. L. Rev. 785. This ground of appeal was not argued by Mr. Girones in this court. ...

[27] Mr. Girones, although abandoning any argument that the appellant's renunciation constituted a defence, argued that it should nonetheless have been brought to the jury's attention as bearing on the issue whether the appellant ever had the intention of inciting Charbonneau to kill Roy. There would be much force in this argument if the appellant had testified that, on hearing statements which he had allegedly made that he wanted Roy killed, he had retracted them when he sobered up. That is, however, not the defence advanced. The appellant's evidence was that he never made the statements attributed to him and the trial judge's charge is not open to criticism for

failing to place a view of the facts before the jury which the appellant repudiated, and which might have been damaging to the defence advanced by the appellant.

*Appeal allowed; new trial ordered.*

---

What is the mental element required for proof of incitement under s. 464?

## R. v. Janeteas
### Ontario Court of Appeal
### (2003), 172 C.C.C. (3d) 97

MOLDAVER J.A. (for the Court):

[1]  On October 6, 1999, after trial by judge and jury, the appellant was convicted under s. 464(a) of the *Criminal Code*, R.S.C. 1985, c. C-46, of one count of counselling the indictable offence of murder and two counts of counselling the indictable offence of unlawfully causing bodily harm. On December 12, 1999, the appellant was sentenced to an eighteen-month conditional sentence. He appeals only from his convictions.

[2]  At issue in this appeal is the requisite mental state for the crime of counselling an indictable offence that is not committed. The trial judge instructed the jury that the requisite mental state would be made out if the jury was satisfied beyond a reasonable doubt that the appellant "spoke the words with the intent that his advice or counselling [that the proposed victim be maimed or killed] be accepted" by the recipients of the advice.

[3]  The appellant takes issue with that instruction. He submits that it defines the mental state required for the crime of counselling too narrowly. In his view, the jury should have been told that to convict, they also had to be satisfied that the appellant intended the commission of the offences counselled (in this case murder and/or unlawfully causing bodily harm). The appellant further submits that if he has accurately identified the requisite mental state, he should be acquitted because the Crown has never taken the position that he intended the commission of the substantive offences.

[4]  For reasons that follow, I am of the view that the appellant is correct and that the jury should have been instructed as he contends. In view of this and the Crown's concession that on this record, there is no basis for concluding that the appellant intended that the substantive offences be committed, I am satisfied that the convictions cannot stand and verdicts of acquittal must be substituted. ...

### *Trial Judge's Ruling on the Requisite Mental State for the Offence of Counselling Under S. 464(A) of the Code*

[12]  After the evidence was completed, the trial judge heard submissions from counsel on the mental state required for the crime of counselling an uncommitted

indictable offence. In his ruling, the trial judge accurately summarized the position of the parties as follows:

> Counsel disagree upon what mental element or *mens rea* must be proved by the Crown if a conviction is to be obtained.
>
> The position of the Crown is that considering the external circumstances that existed to the knowledge of accused, the necessary mental element is that the accused intended to speak the words [that] constituted counselling of murder and that his words be taken seriously.
>
> The position of the defence is that the Crown must prove in addition to that, that the accused intended the act counselled to take place.

[13] The trial judge then reviewed a number of authorities and an article from a leading text on criminal law. After noting that he had not been referred to any binding authority "directly on point," he continued as follows:

> Firstly, I will consider the purpose of Section 464. It seems to me to be obvious that the evil it addresses is to prevent the incitement to crime of those who might otherwise not so act. The fact that the crime is not carried out is fortunate but irrelevant. The evil is that one would attempt to persuade another to commit a crime. That is so because it does not matter that the person being incited agrees or is persuaded to act criminally.
>
> Can it be as counsel suggested in response to a question from me, that the law refuses to punish under this section *someone who counsels another to commit murder knowing that his advice has been taken seriously, because unbeknownst to the person being counselled, the counsellor is not serious or has motives other than that the act counselled be carried out* [emphasis in original].
>
> By analogy of Section 264 of the *Criminal Code*, threatening. That is another section where words spoken constitute the *actus reus*. Once the threat is spoken, the external circumstances are complete. If it is proved that the speaker intends that his words be taken seriously, the mental element is made out. It is no defence for the speaker to say later that he never would have carried out the threat conveyed.
>
> Section 22(2) of the *Code* makes the counsellor a party to an offence committed in consequence of the counselling if the counsellor knew or ought to have known the offence was likely to have been committed because of the counselling.
>
> It is difficult for me to accept that parliament intended a higher standard of actual intention for the lesser offence under Section 464.
>
> In this case, there is evidence upon which the jury could find: One, the accused knew both women were emotionally fragile; two, he knew they were very angry at the proposed victim and, according to the accused, had prior thoughts of harming him; three, he intended that his suggestions to them that the proposed victim be killed or maimed be taken seriously. *Under those external circumstances I propose to instruct the jury that the Crown must prove beyond a reasonable doubt that the accused spoke the words with the intent that his advice or counselling that Dr. Bazos be maimed or killed be accepted by Mrs. Bazos and Mrs. Goldie* [emphasis added]. …

[18] To the extent that there is any debate about the mental state required for the offence of counselling, it tends to centre primarily, although not exclusively, on

whether the counsellor must intend the commission of the offence counselled or whether recklessness in that regard will suffice. Apart from the present case and one other (*R. v. Balaban* (1984), 13 W.C.B. 212 (Ont. Gen. Div.)), I know of no other authority or writing that holds that the mental state of the counsellor as to whether the offence counselled is or is not to be committed is irrelevant. Other Canadian authorities, scholarly writings, the U.S. Model Penal Code, and studies conducted by Law Reform Commissions in Canada and Great Britain point not only in the opposite direction but indicate overwhelmingly that the offence of counselling can only be made out upon proof that the counsellor intended the commission of the offence(s) counselled.

[19]  A good discussion of the issue is found in *R. v. Hamilton, supra*, where the accused was charged under s. 464(a) of the *Code* with counselling various indictable offences that were not committed. In rejecting the submission of the Crown that "the *mens rea* required for counselling is simply the intent to counsel," Smith J. reviewed a number of Canadian authorities, including *R. v. Grossman, supra* and *R. c. Dionne* (1987), 38 C.C.C. (3d) 171 (N.B. C.A.); leave to appeal to the S.C.C. refused *R. c. Dionne* (1987), 38 C.C.C. (3d) vi (S.C.C.), and at paras. 35-39, he concluded:

> In my view, the law is correctly set out in *R. v. Grossman* (*mens rea*) and *R. v. Dionne* (*actus reus*). This conclusion is consistent with the elements necessary for a finding of guilt in secondary liability. The *actus reus* ought to be a *substantial act in the furtherance of the offence, and the mens rea an intent to further the offence. Put another way, no one should be found guilty of furthering an offence without intending that the offence be committed.*
>
> Section 22 of the *Criminal Code* sets out the offence of counselling an offence where an offence is subsequently committed. Under s. 22(1), both the counsellor and the offender who commits the predicate offence are parties to the offence. The essential elements of s. 22(1) are that the offender committed the counselled offence (the element absent from s. 464), the counsellor advised, recommended, instigated, or encouraged the offender to commit the counselled offence (the *actus reus*), the offender committed the counselled offence because the counsellor counselled him to commit that offence (causation), and the counsellor knew or intended that his or her conduct would cause the offender to actually commit the offence counselled (the *mens rea* of intent that the actual offence would be committed). In other words, *it is not sufficient that the counsellor counsel the offence and intend his own actions. The counsellor must also intend that his conduct will result in the offender actually committing the offence counselled.*
>
> Thus, counselling under s. 22(1) is a dual *mens rea* offence. The first *mens rea*, the intent to counsel the offence, may be difficult to distinguish from the *actus reus*. In many cases the *actus reus* will lead to the making of an inference of *mens rea*. In my view, the *McLeod* [*R. v. McLeod* (1970), 1 C.C.C. (2d) 5 (B.C.C.A.)] case falls into this category.
>
> *The second mens rea requirement is the intention that the offender actually carry out the offence.*
>
> I conclude *that the mens rea requirement for counselling a specific offence is the same whether or not the offence counselled is actually committed. Where the offence is*

*not committed, the counsellor must both intend his own actions, i.e. to counsel the offence, and must also intend that the offence be carried out* [emphasis added].

[20] The view taken by Smith J. in *R. v. Hamilton* is shared by the learned authors in Smith and Hogan's *Criminal Law, supra.* At p. 276 of that text, the requisite mental state for the crime of incitement is explained as follows:

**Mens rea**

As in the case of counselling and abetting, it must be proved that D knew of (or deliberately closed his eyes to) all the circumstances of the act incited which are elements of the crime in question. *As with attempts, he must intend the consequences in the actus reus.* If D incites E to inflict grievous bodily harm upon P, D is not guilty of incitement to murder, though both D and E will be guilty of murder if death should result from the infliction of the intended harm. *An intention to bring about the criminal result is of the essence of incitement* [footnote omitted] [emphasis added].

[21] Likewise, in LaFave and Scott, *Substantive Criminal Law, supra,* at Ch. 6, §6.1, pp. 3 and 8-9, under the headings "Solicitation" and "Required Mental State and Act," the learned authors explain the offence of soliciting and the required mental state:

**Solicitation**

Assume that *A* wishes to have his enemy *B* killed, and thus—perhaps because he lacks the nerve to do the deed himself—*A* asks *C* to kill *B*. If *C* acts upon *A*'s request and fatally shoots *B*, then both *A* and *C* are guilty of murder. If, again, *C* proceeds with the plan to kill *B*, but he is unsuccessful, then both *A* and *C* are guilty of attempted murder. If C agrees to *A*'s plan to kill *B* but the killing is not accomplished or even attempted, *A* and *C* are nonetheless guilty of the crime of conspiracy. But what if *C* immediately rejects *A*'s homicidal scheme, so that there is never even any agreement between *A* and *C* with respect to the intended crime. Quite obviously, *C* has committed no crime at all. *A, however, because of his bad state of mind in intending that B be killed and his bad conduct in importuning C to do the killing, is guilty of the crime of solicitation. For the crime of solicitation to be completed, it is only necessary that the actor with intent that another person commit a crime, have enticed, advised, incited, ordered or otherwise encouraged that person to commit a crime. The crime solicited need not be committed.*

**Required Mental State and Act**

Although the crime of solicitation might be defined quite simply as asking another person to commit an offense, this does not adequately reflect either the mental element or act which must exist in order for the crime to be completed.

As to the required mental state, none is explicitly stated in the usual common law definition of solicitation, and likewise none is expressly set forth in several solicitation statutes. *However, the acts of commanding or requesting another to engage in conduct which is criminal would seem of necessity to require an accompanying intent that such conduct occur, and there is nothing in the decided cases suggesting otherwise. Virtually all of the more recently enacted solicitation statutes avoid any doubt by setting forth in specific terms the intent requirement. Some state the solicitor must intend that an offense be committed, some that he must intend to promote or facilitate its commission, and some others that he must intend that the person solicited engage in criminal conduct.*

Thus, as to those crimes which are defined in terms of certain prohibited results, *it is necessary that the solicitor intend to achieve that result through the participation of another. If he does not intend such a result, then the crime has not been solicited, and this is true even though the person solicited will have committed the crime if he proceeds with the requested conduct and thereby causes the prohibited result* [footnotes omitted] [emphasis added].

[22] In their discussion, LaFave and Scott refer to §5.02(I) of the U.S. Model Penal Code. That provision reads as follows:

(1) A person is guilty of solicitation to commit a crime *if with the purpose of promoting or facilitating its commission* he commands, encourages or requests another person to engage in specific conduct that would constitute such crime or an attempt to commit such crime or would establish his complicity in its commission or attempted commission [emphasis added].

As the emphasized words make clear, to be guilty of the offence of solicitation, the solicitor must intend that the crime solicited be carried out. Nothing less will suffice.

[23] In *Secondary Liability: Participation in Crime and Inchoate Offences, supra,* the Law Reform Commission of Canada undertook a thorough and comprehensive review of the inchoate crimes of attempt, counselling and conspiracy. With respect to the mental element required for such crimes, which the Commission broadly described as "furthering" offences, the Commission rejected the notion that recklessness as to the consequences should suffice. Rather, for reasons explained in part below, the Commission concluded that criminal responsibility should only attach to those who intend the consequences of their act:

*All this suggests that in a furthering offence mens rea should be restricted to intent (direct or indirect). Criminal liability should only apply to acts intended to further crimes or known as certain to do so. It should not be incurred for acts which are merely very likely to do so.*

Would this be too restrictive? Suppose D lends X his gun knowing that X will probably use it to murder Y. Should D not be liable for such recklessness? Surely, the graver the probable offence, the more reprehensible the act of helping.

To this there can be various answers. *First, the graver the probable offence, the smaller the likelihood that assistance will be given without intent to see the crime committed*—people do not usually lend guns to known potential killers without intending them to use them. ...

*Third, there is the ordinary meaning of words such as "attempting," "counselling" and "inciting." Such words imply an intent that the crime attempted and so forth be committed.* One who attempts to do something must aim at it, therefore to do it has to be his purpose. *One who incites another to do it must urge him on purpose, the purpose being to get him to do it.*

Law, of course, can use words in a special sense. For reasons of convenience it may restrict the vague meaning of a word in popular usage. "Night," for example, has been defined by common law and subsequently by *Criminal Code* section 2 as "the period between nine o'clock in the afternoon and six o'clock in the forenoon of the following day."

With "incitement" and so forth, this has not happened [the word "incitement" has not been given a special legal meaning]. *In law, as well as outside the law, incitement involves an intention by the inciter to get the "incitee" to commit the offence incited.* Attempt involves intent by the attempter to complete the crime (pp. 30-31) [footnotes omitted] [emphasis added].

[24] In the end, the Commission identified five principles that it felt should "govern the mental element of secondary liability." The first of those principles, found at p. 36 under the heading "Conclusion," is directly on point and reads as follows:

(1) No one should be liable for furthering an offence without intending that the offence be committed.

[25] The Law Reform Commission in Great Britain arrived at a similar conclusion in its consultation paper *Assisting and Encouraging Crime, supra.* The Commission made the following observation at p. 66 about the mental element required for the offence of incitement:

The books are clear, however, that in addition to knowledge of the circumstances and elements of the principal crime, the inciter must have as his purpose the commission of the principal crime: "An intention to bring about the criminal result is of the essence of incitement." [footnotes omitted]

[26] Later, at p. 129, under the heading "The mental element of the offence," the Commission stated:

The general policy issue, much debated in connection with *assisting*, as to whether the defendant must have the commission of the principal crime as his purpose, should be much easier to resolve in the case of encouraging crime. That is because the whole notion of encouraging, inciting or exhorting the commission of a crime presupposes that the encourager wishes that crime to be committed. As Ashworth puts it, in connection with the present offence of incitement:

"The fault element in incitement is that D should intend the substantive offence to be committed and should know the facts and circumstances specified by that offence. This is unlikely to cause a problem in most cases, since someone who either encourages or exerts pressure on another person to commit an offence will usually, by definition, intend that offence to be committed." [Andrew Ashworth, *Principles of Criminal Law* (Oxford: Oxford University Press, 1991) at p. 417.]

[27] Notably, in its provisional proposal urging the creation of a new crime identified as the offence of "encouraging crime," the Commission made the following recommendations at p. 133:

We therefore suggest, for critical comment,
(1) A person commits the offence of encouraging crime if he

(a) solicits, commands or encourages another ("the principal") to do or cause to be done an act or acts which, if done, will involve the commission of an offence by the principal; and

(b) *intends that that act or those acts should be done by the principal*; and

(c) knows or believes that the principal, in so acting, will do so with the fault required for the offence in question [footnotes omitted] [emphasis added].

[28]  As indicated, these and other authorities stand for the proposition that the crime of counselling will only be made out upon proof that the counsellor intended the commission of the crime counselled. Various reasons are cited for rejecting recklessness as the standard. Chief among them is ensuring that criminal liability does not attach to instances of counselling that may be casual or accidental. The Great Britain Law Reform Commission expresses this concern as follows "… there should be no danger of conduct that merely happens to fortify P in his criminal inclinations, without that being D's intention or purpose …" (p. 129) A second rationale for rejecting mental element of recklessness recognizes that this lowered standard may catch some legitimate undercover crime investigation techniques that involve encouragement of crime, with no intention that the crime counselled actually be carried out. (LaFave and Scott, *Substantive Criminal Law* at Ch. 6 §6.11, p.14; Glanville Williams, *Textbook of Criminal Law*, 1st Ed. (London: Steven & Sons, 1978 at p. 386).

[29]  Apart from those considerations, which I believe are sound, I can think of no compelling reason why the requisite mental state for the inchoate crime of counselling should be different from the mental state required for the inchoate crimes of attempt and conspiracy.

[30]  With respect to "attempted" crimes, under s. 24(1) of the *Code*, the offender must intend to commit the desired offence (see *R. v. Ancio* (1984), 10 C.C.C. (3d) 385 (S.C.C.), at 401). As for the crime of conspiracy, it is settled law that to be guilty, the offender must intend to commit the offence that forms the subject of the agreement (see *R. v. O'Brien*, [1954] S.C.R. 666 (S.C.C.)). Accordingly, the question that must be asked is whether, as a matter of principle, there is any basis for lowering the mental state required for the inchoate offence of counselling. If such a basis exists, in my view, it can only be that the rationale for criminalizing "counselling" differs from the rationale for criminalizing "attempts" and "conspiracies." And yet, the Law Reform Commission of Canada draws no such distinction. On the contrary, in its report at p. 6, the Commission explains the rationale for inchoate offences in general as follows:

> The same arguments hold for inchoate crimes. Again, if the primary act (for example, killing), is harmful, society will want people not to do it. Equally, it would not want them even to try to do it, or to counsel or incite others to do it. For while the act itself causes actual harm, attempting to do it, or counselling, inciting or procuring someone else to do it, are sources of potential harm—they increase the likelihood of that particular harm's occurrence. Accordingly, society is justified in taking certain measures in respect of them: outlawing them with sanctions, and authorizing intervention to prevent the harm from materializing.

[31] There are some who maintain that the mental element for the crime of counselling should be less onerous than that required for other inchoate crimes because the crime of counselling is inherently more dangerous. The reasoning is that in the case of counselling, even though the counsellor may not intend the commission of a crime, the counsellor may nevertheless lose control of the situation once the seed is planted in the recipient's mind. The point is made by Alexander and Kessler at p. 1156 of their article "Mens Rea and Inchoate Crimes" (1997), 87 J. of Crim. L. and Criminology 1138, as follows:

> There is one further complication. In many cases, defendant will not have complete control over whether he can withdraw his support from the criminal enterprise. Therefore, he is not in an exactly parallel position to the defendant who is planning to commit a crime himself but who can always prevent the crime by changing his mind. Encouragement of another always creates a risk that one will fail in an attempt to withdraw one's support, or that one will be rendered incapable of withdrawing support. There is no analogue to this problem when dealing with incomplete attempts or bare conspiracies.

[32] Alexander and Kessler rely heavily on this distinction in support of their thesis that recklessness should suffice as the mental element for solicitation. At pp. 1175-76 of their article, they write:

> In solicitation and conspiracy, then, we have crimes in which defendant's conduct is dangerous apart from his mental state. That point in turn suggests that we rethink the *mens rea* requirements for these crimes. Although the Model Penal Code requires a purpose that the crime be committed as the *mens rea* for both solicitation and conspiracy, this requirement makes no sense where the danger stems from the encouragement of others to commit the crime. Recklessness should suffice as the *mens rea* for solicitation. Recklessness with its notion of conscious disregard of *unjustified* (and substantial) risk, takes into consideration all legitimate reasons one might have for conduct that one realizes might be taken by someone else as encouragement to commit a crime when the conduct's purpose is not such an encouragement. ...
>
> Although an actor is not culpable for forming a criminal intention or for taking an otherwise harmless step toward realizing that intention, he *is* culpable for encouraging others to commit criminal acts, even if his purpose is innocent, at least if he is reckless regarding the likelihood that they will commit those acts [footnotes omitted] [emphasis in original].

[33] The trial judge appears to have been influenced by this distinction in arriving at his conclusion that the requisite mental state for counselling will be met if the counsellor's advice is "accepted" by the recipients. For convenience, the relevant passage from his ruling is repeated below:

> Can it be as counsel suggested in response to a question from me, that the law refuses to punish under this section *someone who counsels another to commit murder knowing that his advice has been taken seriously, because unbeknownst to the person being counselled, the counsellor is not serious or has motives other than that the act counselled be carried out* [emphasis in original].

[34]  Manifestly, the trial judge was not prepared to accept that someone who encourages the commission of a serious crime, knowing that his advice has been taken
seriously, should go free. Although he did not say so expressly, implicit in his reasoning is the notion that such conduct is inherently dangerous and should be punished.
Indeed, as I understand his reasons, it is this concern that led the trial judge to lower
the bar on the mental state required for the offence of counselling even below that
contemplated by Alexander and Kessler. As indicated earlier, the test fashioned by
the trial judge—did the counsellor speak the words with the intent that his advice be
accepted by the recipients—renders the mental state of the counsellor as to whether
the offence counselled is or is not committed irrelevant.

[35]  The trial judge found support for his thinking in what he considered to be a
ready-made analogy in s. 264.1 (uttering threats) and in his interpretation of s. 22(2)
(offences committed in consequence of counselling) of the *Code*. For convenience, I
repeat those aspects of his ruling:

> By analogy of Section 264 of the *Criminal Code*, threatening. That is another section
> where words spoken constitute the *actus reus*. Once the threat is spoken, the external
> circumstances are complete. If it is proved that the speaker intends that his words be
> taken seriously, the mental element is made out. It is no defence for the speaker to say
> later that he never would have carried out the threat conveyed. …
>
> Section 22(2) of the *Code* makes the counsellor a party to an offence committed in
> consequence of the counselling if the counsellor knew or ought to have known the
> offence was likely to have been committed because of the counselling.
>
> It is difficult for me to accept that parliament intended a higher standard of actual
> intention for the lesser offence under Section 464.

[36]  With respect, I cannot agree with the trial judge's analysis for several reasons.

[37]  First, the s. 264.1 analogy is inexact. Manifestly, s. 264.1 is not an inchoate
offence. As a matter of policy, Parliament has chosen to criminalize conduct that is
meant to instill fear in others. Given that that is the harm which the provision seeks to
prevent, it matters not whether the offender actually intended to follow through with
the threat.

[38]  Second, as I read s. 22(2) of the *Code*, it is of no assistance in resolving the
issue at hand because it only comes into play if the counsellor is otherwise guilty of
counselling the original offence. That, in turn, depends on whether the mental state
for the crime of counselling requires that the counsellor intend the commission of the
original offence.

[39]  Third, to the extent that the trial judge relied upon the "degree of dangerousness" distinction identified by Alexander and Kessler to set a lower bar for the mental
state required for the offence of counselling, I am of the view that the distinction
breaks down when the inchoate offence of counselling is compared with the inchoate
offence of conspiracy. Specifically, I do not accept that a person who counsels another to commit an offence (with no intent that the offence be committed), is somehow more dangerous or engaged in more dangerous activity than a person who conspires with another to commit an offence (with no intent that the offence be
committed). Neither wishes to see an offence committed but both may embolden the

second party to commit the offence and both may lose control over the situation. In my view, this comparison undermines the argument that the mental state for the inchoate crime of counselling should be lowered because counselling is a more dangerous crime than conspiracy.

[40]  Although the "degree of dangerousness" distinction may be somewhat more persuasive in the case of attempts, even there, the issue is not free from controversy. Thus, in contrast to the position taken by Alexander and Kessler (see para. 33, above), LaFave and Scott make the following observations at Ch. 6, §6.1, of their article:

> Similarly, it is claimed that the solicitor does not constitute a menace in view of the fact that he has manifested an unwillingness to carry out the criminal scheme himself. There is not *the dangerous proximity to success which exists when the crime is actually attempted, for, "despite the earnestness of the solicitation, the actor is merely engaging in talk which may never be taken seriously"* [footnotes omitted] [emphasis added].

[41]  In sum, I am not persuaded that the "degree of dangerousness" distinction warrants a reduction in the mental state required for the offence of counselling.

[42]  Fourth, even if I were satisfied that the mental state for the inchoate crime of counselling should be lower than that required for other inchoate crimes, I would not adopt a model that renders the mental state of the counsellor as to whether the offence counselled is or is not to be committed irrelevant. On the contrary, at a minimum, I would require that the offender act in reckless disregard of the consequences. However, for reasons already stated, I find the orthodox view (actual intent) more compelling and I see no reason to depart from it.

[43]  In this regard, as Ashworth notes (see paragraph 27 above), it should not be overlooked that in most cases, a person who counsels another to commit an offence, intending that the advice be taken seriously, "will usually, by definition, intend that offence to be committed." The present case is one of those rare instances where, despite the appellant's intention that his words be taken seriously, the Crown does not maintain that he intended the commission of the crimes counselled. While the appellant's actions were reprehensible, I am not convinced that the reach of the criminal law should be extended, at the expense of established principle, to ensnare the likes of the appellant.

[44]  Even if I am wrong and recklessness as to consequences is sufficient for the offence of counselling unlawful bodily harm, if not murder, the convictions cannot stand because the trial judge did not leave recklessness to the jury. Rather, as I have pointed out, the case was left to the jury on the basis that it need not consider the mental state of the appellant as to whether the crimes counselled were or were not to be committed.

[45]  In the circumstances, had I concluded that recklessness as to consequences was sufficient (at least with respect to the offence of counselling unlawful bodily harm), I would nonetheless have quashed the convictions and substituted verdicts of acquittal because on this record, it cannot be said that the appellant was reckless as to whether the crimes counselled were or were not to be committed. On the contrary, by warning Dr. Bazos immediately after the February 26 phone calls, he demonstrated just the opposite.

*Conclusion*

[46]  The requisite mental element for the offence of counselling requires, among other things, that the counsellor intend the commission of the offence(s) counselled. Crown counsel on appeal concedes that the trial judge's instruction did not convey that information to the jury. He further concedes that on this record, the evidence does not support such a finding. Accordingly, I would allow the appeal, quash the convictions and in their place, substitute verdicts of acquittal.

*Appeal allowed; verdicts of acquittal substituted.*

**R. v. Hamilton**
Alberta Court of Appeal
(2003), 178 C.C.C. (3d) 434

CONRAD J.A. (for the Court):

*I. Introduction*

[1]  This appeal concerns the appropriate *mens rea* for the offence of counselling a criminal offence not committed, in section 464 of the *Criminal Code of Canada* ("the *Code*").

[2]  The respondent sold a package of files to 20 people over the internet. About 5 of the 200 files purchased, or 13 of the 2,000 pages of hard copy producible from these files, contained material relating to constructing bombs, breaking and entering, and "visa hacking." Another file contained information on a credit card number generator.

[3]  The respondent was charged with counselling four indictable offences which were not committed: making explosive substances with intent; doing anything with intent to cause an explosion; break and enter with intent; and fraud through dissemination of a credit card number generator. The trial judge concluded the respondent lacked the requisite *mens rea* on all counts and entered acquittals. The Crown appeals.

*II. Issues*

[4]  The Crown advances two grounds of appeal:

1. The learned trial judge erred in law in her interpretation of the *mens rea* required for the offence of counselling an offence that is not committed.

2. The learned trial judge erred in law in concluding that the respondent was neither reckless nor wilfully blind in counselling the commission of offences.

*III. Decision*

[5]  In discussing the *mens rea* required by section 464, the trial judge held that an accused must both intend to counsel a criminal act and also intend that the counselled

crime be committed. In my view, this is the correct legal test. Furthermore, the trial judge properly applied this test. However, even if recklessness or wilful blindness was the applicable *mens rea*, there is nothing on these subjects in the trial judge's decision that amounts to an error of law justifying appellate intervention. The appeal is dismissed.

## *IV. Background*

### A. *The Facts*

[6] At the time of trial, the respondent was 23 years old with a grade 10 education. He had worked in restaurants and as a graphic designer. Prior to marketing the e-mail files, he and a friend had operated a business under the name of H & H Enterprises. H & H Enterprises had entered into a number of money-losing ventures, including selling dream interpretation and marketing a diet cookie.

[7] The respondent received an e-mail promoting some "Top Secret Reports" advertised using a teaser. He purchased the Top Secret Reports and received a hard copy and a disc containing the information in two "ZIP" files. The ZIP files contained about 200 other files which had been compressed to facilitate transmission. Counsel agreed that the hard copy of the ZIP files printed out would consist of approximately 2,000 pages of printed material. The pages included documents entitled: "visa hacking," "bombs," "bombs2," "bombs3," "Fire Bombs, Napalm etc." and "How to Break In to a House."

[8] The respondent copied the web page used by those who sold the materials to him and duplicated it on his own website, substituting the name and address of H & H Enterprises for the purposes of resale. He copied the spam e-mail, including the teaser that had advertised the files, and also substituted H & H Enterprises for the originator. He did not change the text of the e-mail or the web page appropriated. The teaser did not contain any reference to the files called "bombs," "bomb2," "bombs3," or "How to Break In to a House," although the respondent saw a computer-generated list of the contents of the two ZIP files that included those names.

[9] The visa hacking program, also found on the respondent's computer, was capable of generating working credit card numbers. All the recipes contained in the bomb material, with the exception of the smoke bomb, were capable of producing an effective bomb. The information in the housebreaking file would be of assistance to someone in committing a break and enter.

[10] In an attempt to sell the files, the respondent sent an e-mail advertisement to some 300-500 people whose addresses were obtained from an unknown source on the internet. The advertisement contained the original "teaser," which promoted the sale of both the Top Secret Reports and the credit card number generator. In the end, the respondent sold the advertised files to about 20 people.

[11] The respondent testified that he did not read all the files, particularly the files relating to housebreaking and making bombs. He also testified that he had no interest in encouraging customers to commit crimes of any kind, nor did he intend to encourage them to do so. The trial judge accepted this testimony.

[12] No one who received the files committed an offence as a result of receiving the information, nor did the respondent commit any of the underlying offences. The respondent had used the credit card number generator to produce some credit card numbers for himself, but he never used them. He thought they could not be used without a proper expiry date.

[13] Some recipients of the teaser complained to the Edmonton Police Service who ran a brief undercover operation, during which Detective George purchased the Top Secret Reports from the respondent. Charges were then laid.

## B. *The Trial Decision*

[14] The trial judge looked first at whether the Crown had proven beyond a reasonable doubt that the respondent had committed the *actus reus*. She relied upon the following statement of McLachlin C.J.C. in *R. v. Sharpe*, [2001] 1 S.C.R. 45 (S.C.C.), at para. 56, as a description of the required *actus reus* for counselling:

> "Counsel" is dealt with only in connection with the counseling of an offence: s. 22 of the *Criminal Code*, where it is stated to include "procure, solicit or incite." "Counsel" can mean simply to advise; however in criminal law it has been given the stronger meaning of actively inducing: see *R. v. Dionne* (1987), 38 C.C.C. (3d) 171 (N.B.C.A.), at p. 180, *per* Ayles J.A. While s. 22 refers to a person's actions and s. 163.1(1)(b) refers to material, it seems reasonable to conclude that in order to meet the requirement of "advocates" or "counsels," the material, viewed objectively, must be seen as "actively inducing" or encouraging the described offences with children.

[15] The trial judge concluded she had to review the teaser and the documents sent out by the respondent to determine if the objective test of active encouragement or inducement had been met. The teaser contained, among others, the following statement (para. 19): "PRODUCE … CREDIT CARD NUMBERS!! ALL VALID AND FULLY FUNCTIONAL!!" "WITH ONE STROKE OF THE KEY!!! IT'S THAT EASY!! … IMAGINE THE THINGS THAT YOU COULD DO WITH THIS PROGRAM AND THE VALID CREDIT CARD NUMBERS IT GENERATES!!" The trial judge concluded that this language, viewed objectively, actively promoted the use of the credit card generator.

[16] The other documents contained instructions on how to assemble and detonate bombs. The trial judge concluded that they actively promoted or encouraged the actions described in them. No issue is taken with her findings about the *actus reus*.

[17] The trial judge then turned to the issue of *mens rea*. After reviewing the relevant authorities, she concluded that the appropriate mental element was an intention that the counselled offence be committed. She held at paras. 35 and 39:

> In my view, the law is correctly set out in *R. v. Grossman* (*mens rea*) and *R. v. Dionne* (*actus reus*). This conclusion is consistent with the elements necessary for a finding of guilt in secondary liability. The *actus reus* ought to be a substantial act in the furtherance of the offence, and the *mens rea* an intent to further the offence. Put another way, no one should be found guilty of furthering an offence without intending that the offence be committed. …

Where the offence is not committed, the counsellor must both intend his own actions, i.e. to counsel the offence, and must also intend that the offence be carried out.

[18] Applying this principle, the trial judge concluded the respondent did not intend that the crimes described in the secret files, or the fraud implicit in the credit card number generator scheme, be committed. She also found the accused was neither reckless nor wilfully blind, even though her decision that section 464 required intention made the former findings unnecessary. The trial judge acquitted the respondent.

## V. Analysis

### A. Standard of Review

[19] Since the respondent was acquitted, section 676(1)(a) of the Code permits a Crown appeal only on a matter of law. The standard of review for errors of law is correctness.

### B. Ground One—Did the Learned Justice Err in Determining the Applicable Mens Rea?

[20] The Crown submits in its factum (at para. 17) that the "only *mens rea* required under section 464 is that the counselling be intentional." Thus, according to the Crown, the trial judge erred by requiring that the *mens rea* include an intention that the counselled crime be committed. The Crown also alleges that the trial judge made four specific errors: she misunderstood previous case law, confused intention with the concepts of motive and desire, came to an absurd interpretation, and misinterpreted and misapplied section 22 of the *Code*.

[21] I deal first with the issue of the applicable *mens rea*, then with the allegations of specific error.

#### 1. The Mens Rea Required by Section 464

[22] Section 464 of the *Code* provides:

464. Except where otherwise expressly provided by law, the following provisions apply in respect of persons who counsel other persons to commit offences, namely,

(a) every one who counsels another person to commit an indictable offence is, if the offence is not committed, guilty of an indictable offence and liable to the same punishment to which a person who attempts to commit that offence is liable; and

(b) every one who counsels another person to commit an offence punishable on summary conviction is, if the offence is not committed, guilty of an offence punishable on summary conviction.

[23] It is clear Parliament has not set out the applicable *mens rea* in its description of the offence. In the absence of legislative direction, it is presumed that some form of subjective *mens rea* is required: see *R. v. Lucas*, [1998] 1 S.C.R. 439, 123 C.C.C. (3d) 97 (S.C.C.) at para. 64. When courts refer to subjective *mens rea*, they are usually

talking about three concepts: intention, recklessness or wilful blindness. Dickson J. (as he then was) noted in *R. v. Sault Ste. Marie (City)*, [1978] 2 S.C.R. 1299, 40 C.C.C. (2d) 353 (S.C.C.), at 1309:

> Where the offence is criminal, the Crown must establish a mental element, namely, that the accused who committed the prohibited act did so intentionally or recklessly, with knowledge of the facts constituting the offence, or with wilful blindness toward them.

[24] Of these three, intention is the strictest test. Courts have not defined intention consistently, nor is it necessary to define it precisely here. Prof. D. Stuart, *Canadian Criminal Law*, 4th ed. (Toronto: Carswell, 2001) at 213 notes:

> The Code provides no general definition of intent and our courts have not found it necessary to fill the gap. "Intent" seems to have been construed in a loose colloquial sense of actual desire, end, purpose, aim, objective or design and knowledge to mean actual knowledge, for example, of the contents of the package possessed. It seems futile for criminal law to enter into the unfathomable depths of the philosophical debate as to the meaning of "intent."

[25] It is sufficient to note that intent usually involves an actor's aim or purpose, and is often fulfilled by knowledge of the consequences of performing the *actus reus*. Recklessness, on the other hand, involves knowledge of the *likely* consequences of an act. McLachlin J. (as she then was) described it this way in *R. v. Théroux*, [1993] 2 S.C.R. 5, 79 C.C.C. (3d) 449 (S.C.C.), at 460:

> Recklessness presupposes knowledge of the likelihood of the prohibited consequences. It is established when it is shown that the accused, with such knowledge, commits acts which may bring about these prohibited consequences, while being reckless as to whether or not they ensue.

[26] Wilful blindness is a more inclusive concept than either intention or recklessness. In *R. v. Sansregret*, [1985] 1 S.C.R. 570, 45 C.R. (3d) 193 (S.C.C.), the court held that wilful blindness, while still subjective, dealt with the situation where "a person who has become aware of the need for some inquiry declines to make the inquiry because he does not wish to know the truth" (584 S.C.R.).

[27] In my view, the *mens rea* for counselling under section 464 should be confined to the concept of intention. Section 464 is designed to discourage the devious from inducing others to commit crimes. Its application, therefore, should not result in the conviction of the morally innocent. In coming to a similar conclusion, the Ontario Court of Appeal observed that there are situations where the counselling of an offence can take place in innocent circumstances. The court noted in *R. v. Janeteas* (2003), 172 C.C.C. (3d) 97, [2003] O.J. No. 348 (Ont. C.A.) at para. 28:

> Various reasons are cited for rejecting recklessness as the standard. *Chief among them is ensuring that criminal liability does not attach to instances of counselling that may be casual or accidental. The Great Britain Law Reform Commission expresses this concern as follows "... there should be no danger of conduct that merely happens to fortify P in his criminal inclinations, without that being D's intention or purpose ..."*

*(p. 129). A second rationale for rejecting mental element of recklessness recognizes
that this lowered standard may catch some legitimate undercover crime investigation
techniques that involve encouragement of crime, with no intention that the crime counselled actually be carried out.* (LaFave and Scott, *Substantive Criminal Law* at Ch. 6
§. 6.11, p. 14; Glanville Williams, *Textbook of Criminal Law*, 1st ed. (London: Steven
& Sons, 1978 at p. 386)). [emphasis added]

[28]  The danger in using a lesser standard of subjective *mens rea* (such as recklessness or wilful blindness) to support a conviction under section 464 lies in the
nature of the section. The conduct it prohibits is counselling a crime that is *not* committed. There is no detrimental consequence from the performance of the *actus reus*.
This means that the counsellor's state of mind is the sole factor that determines
whether his or her conduct is criminal. In such a situation, the most demanding standard of subjective *mens rea* should apply.

[29]  This position has the support of others in the legal community. Prof. Stuart
states, at 227 of *Canadian Criminal Law*, *supra*:

> There would appear to be one broad category of *mens rea* offences where there *is* a case
> for restricting to intent and not extending to recklessness: the incomplete crimes of
> attempting, conspiring and counselling an offence which is not committed. The *actus
> reus* requirement is substantially attenuated. The common law wanted to intervene at
> an early stage in the interest of crime prevention. However, since culpability is here
> dependent primarily on *mens rea*, there might well be a need to move with caution and
> restrict to intent. [emphasis original]

[30]  This echoes the view of the Law Reform Commission of Canada. In *R. v.
Janeteas*, *supra*, the Ontario Court of Appeal noted at para. 23:

> In *Secondary Liability: Participation in Crime and Inchoate Offences*, *supra*, the Law
> Reform Commission of Canada undertook a thorough and comprehensive review of
> the inchoate crimes of attempt, counselling and conspiracy. With respect to the mental
> element required for such crimes, which the Commission broadly described as "fur-
> thering" offences, the Commission rejected the notion that recklessness as to the conse-
> quences should suffice. Rather, for reasons explained in part below, the Commission
> concluded that criminal responsibility should only attach to those who intend the con-
> sequences of their act:
>
> > *All this suggests that in a furthering offence* mens rea *should be restricted to intent
> > (direct or indirect). Criminal liability should only apply to acts intended to further
> > crimes or known as certain to do so. It should not be incurred for acts which are merely
> > very likely to do so.* [emphasis original]

[31]  The Supreme Court of Canada came to a similar conclusion in *R. v. Ancio*,
[1984] 1 S.C.R. 225, 10 C.C.C. (3d) 385 (S.C.C.), when discussing the *mens rea* for
the inchoate crime of attempt. The court held that in the absence of a criminal outcome, it was the perpetrator's intention that was actually being proscribed. Speaking
for the majority, McIntyre J. observed at 401-02 (C.C.C.):

A reading of s. 24 of the *Code* and all its predecessors since the enactment of the first *Code* in 1892 confirms that the intent to commit the desired offence is a basic element of the offence of attempt. *Indeed, because the crime of attempt may be complete without the actual commission of any other offence and even without the performance of any act unlawful in itself, it is abundantly clear that the criminal element of the offence of attempt may lie solely in the intent.* As noted by Glanville Williams, *Criminal Law: The General Part*, 2nd ed. (1961), §207, p. 642, in discussing attempts: "An *actus reus* ... need not be a crime apart from the state of mind. It need not even be a tort, or a moral wrong, or a social mischief." [emphasis added]

[32] The similarity between the inchoate crime of counselling a crime not committed, and the inchoate crime of attempt, is underscored by the wording of section 464(a) of the Code:

> (a) every one who counsels another person to commit an indictable offence is, if the offence is not committed, guilty of an indictable offence and liable to the same punishment to which a person who attempts to commit that offence is liable ... .

[33] In summary, intention is the appropriate level of *mens rea* for counselling under section 464 because it is the strictest standard. This section was never intended to catch within its net a professor teaching a class how to make bombs or an RCMP instructor teaching students how criminals create credit cards. Rather, it is aimed at those who encourage others to actually commit crimes.

[34] This does not end the matter, however, because the trial decision, and the Crown's position on appeal, raise the further question of *what* must be intended under section 464. The trial judge held that an accused must intend to counsel the offence, and intend that the counselled offence be committed. The Crown says only the first of these two mental states is required.

[35] To determine what an accused must intend, it is necessary to look at the *actus reus* of the offence. The trial judge found, and the parties concede, that the law on the *actus reus* of counselling was set out by the Supreme Court of Canada in *R. v. Sharpe, supra*. Applied to the crime of counselling under section 464, this means that the accused must pass on material or make statements that, when viewed objectively, "actively" induces or encourages a criminal offence. In *Dionne, supra*, relied on in *Sharpe, supra*, the New Brunswick Court of Appeal stated at 180:

> [T]he offence of counselling involves more serious acts than communicating his intention to have injuries inflicted on someone with a view to having that person inflict those injuries. The acts or words must be such as to induce a person to commit the offences that one desires. ...

In my view, if the acts of counselling must be sufficient to induce a person to commit a crime, and the accused must intend to commit these acts of inducement, it follows that the counsellor must intend that the counselled crime be committed. What other possible consequence could follow from actively inducing someone to commit an offence? As Moldaver J.A. observed in *Janeteas*, at para. 43:

> [I]t should not be overlooked that in most cases, a person who counsels anoth r to commit an offence, intending that the advice be taken seriously, "will usually, by definition, intend that offence to be committed."

Any uncertainty about the propriety of such an interpretation is resolved by a review of the case law. In *R. v. Balaban*, [1984] 13 W.C.B. 212 (Ont. Gen. Div.) [(December 12, 1984), Whealy J. (Ont. Gen. Div.)], W.C.B.J. 452782, the court held that counselling an offence not committed was a crime requiring intention, and that the accused had to intend to "counsel, procure or incite a particular act" (see para. 10). While the court added that section 464 did not require the "intent that the act be committed," in my view, for the reasons already stated, there is no effective difference between an intention "to ... incite a particular act" and to intend the commission of the counselled offence.

[36] In *Dionne*, the accused tried unsuccessfully to convince an undercover police officer to commit an assault. The trial judge found that the mental element for counselling this crime required intention rather than recklessness. He held, however, that the accused had to have the intention "to have another person cause the injuries or make the threats over the telephone, depending on the charge" (see 179). The Court of Appeal upheld this finding. While the decision turned on the *actus reus* of the offence, it confirmed that the requisite mental element was intention, rather than a lesser standard, and that the counsellor had to intend that the person counselled would commit the suggested criminal act.

[37] Both *Balaban* and *Dionne* were considered by MacKinnon J. of the Ontario Court of Justice in *R. v. Grossman*, [1994] O.J. No. 4078 (Ont. Gen. Div.). The accused was alleged to have counselled a kidnapping which was not committed. MacKinnon J. followed *Dionne*, holding at para. 7:

> The *Dionne* case held that for a conviction, it must be shown that the accused intended the substantive act to be committed. I feel constrained to follow the reasoning of the Court of Appeal in New Brunswick in *Dionne* by virtue of *stare decisis* and I do so follow.

The Ontario Court of Appeal discussed the *mens rea* for counselling an offence not committed in *Janeteas*. In following similar logic to that found in *Dionne* and *Grossman*, as well as the trial decision in this case, the court noted that an overwhelming body of opinion supported the position that the *mens rea* for counselling, under section 464 of the *Criminal Code*, required the intention that the counselled offence be committed. Moldaver J.A. held at para. 18:

> Apart from the present case and one other (*R. v. Balaban* ...), I know of no other authority or writing that holds that the mental state of the counsellor as to whether the offence counselled is or is not to be committed is irrelevant. Other Canadian authorities, scholarly writings, the *U.S. Model Penal Code*, and studies conducted by the Law Reform Commission in Canada and Great Britain point not only in the opposite direction but indicate overwhelmingly that the offence of counselling can only be made out upon proof that the counsellor intended the commission of the offence(s) counselled.

[38]  In conclusion, the trial judge did not err by finding that the appropriate *mens rea* in section 464 includes the intention to have the counselled crime committed.

## 2.  The Other Errors Alleged by the Crown

[39]  Along with the general error of misinterpreting the *mens rea* required under section 464, the Crown alleges the trial judge made a number of specific errors. While my concurrence with the trial judge's conclusion disposes of any possible analytical errors she made along the way, I will touch briefly on the alleged errors.

[40]  First, the Crown submits the trial judge erred by relying on the decision of MacKinnon J. in *Grossman* because MacKinnon J. relied upon the New Brunswick Court of Appeal decision in *Dionne*. According to the Crown, this reliance on *Dionne* was misguided as the court there was only dealing with the *actus reus* of counselling.

[41]  I disagree. The explicit error corrected by the Court of Appeal in *Dionne* concerned the trial judge's charge on the issue of the *actus reus*. But the Court of Appeal did not disagree with the trial judge's view that the *mens rea* of the offence of counselling required an intention that the crime actually be committed. Rather, the court confirmed the need for such intent. This is revealed in the following passage from the decision of Ayles J.A. at 179-80:

> Finally, when he [the trial judge] listed the two essential elements of the offence, he said the following: …
>
>> Taking each charge individually, *the crime is complete when, first, the accused had the intention to have another person cause the injuries or make the threats over the telephone*, depending on the charge, and second, when the accused has communicated his intention to another person with a view to having him inflict these injuries or make these threats over the telephone. …
>>
>> In my view these instructions are erroneous since the offence of counselling involves *more serious acts* than communicating his intention to have injuries inflicted on someone with a view to having that person inflict those injuries. [emphasis added]

It is clear from the emphasized passage that the Court of Appeal was questioning the trial judge's reasoning on the *actus reus* of the offence, while agreeing with the trial judge's conclusion regarding the required *mens rea*. Thus, the trial judge did not err in relying on MacKinnon J.'s reasoning in *R. v. Grossman*.

[42]  The second alleged error in the trial judge's reasoning is that she failed to apply the decision in *R. v. Hibbert*, [1995] 2 S.C.R. 973, 99 C.C.C. (3d) 193 (S.C.C.). According to the Crown, that case confirmed that desire and/or motive are not part of the mental element of criminal offences unless Parliament so decrees, and the section has passed *Charter* scrutiny. The Crown argues that by referring to the respondent's motive in her decision, the trial judge confused the concept of intention with notions of motive and desire.

[43]  The trial judge did not err as alleged by the Crown. As she was entitled to do, the trial judge considered motive as part of her fact findings. But her decision was based on other facts relating to the respondent's knowledge. She found, for example,

that the respondent had not read most of the "Top Secret" files. She also found that he was not interested in their contents and that he was, overall, "naive, lazy or ignorant." Dealing with the credit card number generator, the trial judge accepted the respondent's testimony that he did not think any generated numbers could be used because they lacked an expiry date. On the basis of these facts, she found the respondent lacked sufficient knowledge of the consequences of his actions to satisfy the *mens rea* requirement. It is clear that she understood the nature of the test she was bound to apply and did not err in law.

[44]  In addition, the Crown overstates the reach of *Hibbert, supra*. In *Hibbert*, the Supreme Court was interpreting the phrase "for the purpose of" in section 21(1)(b) of the *Code* to determine whether a person accused of being a "party" under that provision could rely on the statutory defence of duress. The court held that section 21(1)(b) of the *Code* did not require "the accused [to] actively view the commission of the offence he or she is aiding as desirable in and of itself" as part of the required *mens rea* (*Hibbert* at para. 39). It applied similar logic in interpreting section 21(2). The court also held, however, that its decision was confined to those sections alone, and that it was necessary to examine each offence found in the *Code* separately to determine its particular *mens rea*.

[45]  The Crown's third submission is that it would be "perverse" or "absurd" if, in some situations, the *mens rea* for counselling an offence which is not committed were more stringent than the mental element required for being convicted of the counselled offence. The Crown points to the crime of fraud as an example, suggesting that an accused can be convicted of fraud upon proof of either recklessness or wilful blindness. Applying this to the trial judge's decision, the Crown submits at para. 22 of its factum:

> It is respectfully submitted that this defies logic. If recklessness or wilful blindness are sufficient thresholds of *mens rea* to convict someone of having committed the offence of fraud then they should be sufficient thresholds to convict someone of counselling the commission of that offence.

[46]  Leaving aside the question of whether the Crown has correctly described the *mens rea* for fraud, its position does not withstand scrutiny. Section 464 is a stand-alone offence, with its own *mens rea*, and culpability does not depend on the nature of the counselled crime. The logical outcome of the Crown's position is that whenever an accused is charged under section 464, the *mens rea* must be determined by referring to the *mens rea* of the crime counselled. This would mean that those accused of counselling under section 464 would have their culpability adjudged on a variable scale even though they had committed the same prohibited act, namely, counselling an offence not committed.

[47]  In my view, this is not what Parliament intended when it enacted section 464. It may be that a court can take into account the different nature of the counselled crimes in sentencing. But those who counsel murder will breach section 464 just as those who counsel robbery.

[48]  The Crown's fourth submission is that the trial judge erred by relying on her own interpretation of section 22(1) of the *Code*. Whatever her reasoning, I need not

deal with this issue as I have found she arrived at the correct interpretation in any event.

[49] In summary, there is no merit to the Crown's allegations of specific error on the trial judge's part.

### C. Ground Two—The Application of Recklessness or Wilful Blindness

[50] The Crown submits the trial judge erred in her application of the principles of recklessness and wilful blindness. This ground of appeal is rendered nugatory by my finding that intention is the proper *mens rea* for this offence. But even if I am wrong in that conclusion, the trial judge's reasons and findings with respect to the respondent's knowledge of the likely consequences of his acts preclude the possible application of either recklessness or wilful blindness to secure a conviction.

[51] There is nothing in the trial judge's reasoning on this subject, therefore, that amounts to an error of law allowing this court to overturn the respondent's acquittal.

*Appeal dismissed.*

## III. CONSPIRACY

A conspiracy exists when two or more people agree to commit a criminal offence and the offence of conspiracy is complete upon their agreement. Difficulties can arise on several points. Was there an agreement and, if so, on what?

### United States v. Dynar
Supreme Court of Canada
[1997] 2 S.C.R. 462

CORY and IACOBUCCI JJ.: …

(a)  What Is a Criminal Conspiracy?

[86]  In *R. v. O'Brien*, [1954] S.C.R. 666 (S.C.C.), at pp. 668-69, this Court adopted the definition of conspiracy from the English case of *Mulcahy v. R.* (1868), L.R. 3 H.L. 306 (U.K. H.L.), at p. 317:

> A conspiracy consists not merely in the intention of two or more, but in the agreement of two or more to do an unlawful act, or to do a lawful act by unlawful means. So long as such a design rests in intention only, it is not indictable. When two agree to carry it into effect, the very plot is an act in itself, and the act of each of the parties … punishable if for a criminal object. …

There must be an intention to agree, the completion of an agreement, and a common design. Taschereau J., in *O'Brien*, *supra*, at p. 668, added that:

> Although it is not necessary that there should be an overt act in furtherance of the conspiracy, to complete the crime, I have no doubt that there must exist *an intention to*

*put the common design into effect*. A common design necessarily involves an intention. Both are synonymous. The intention cannot be anything else but the will to attain the object of the agreement. [Emphasis in original.]

[87] In *R. v. Cotroni*, [1979] 2 S.C.R. 256 (S.C.C.), at p. 276, Dickson J. (as he then was) described the offence of conspiracy as "an inchoate or preliminary crime." In setting out the necessary elements of the offence, he noted at pp. 276-77 that:

> The word "conspire" derives from two Latin words, "con" and "spirare," meaning "to breathe together." To conspire is to agree. The essence of criminal conspiracy is proof of agreement. On a charge of conspiracy the agreement itself is the gist of the offence: *Paradis v. R.*, at p. 168. The *actus reus* is the fact of agreement: *D.P.P. v. Nock*, at p. 66. The agreement reached by the co-conspirators may contemplate a number of acts or offences. Any number of persons may be privy to it. Additional persons may join the ongoing scheme while others may drop out. So long as there is a continuing overall, dominant plan there may be changes in methods of operation, personnel, or victims, without bringing the conspiracy to an end. *The important inquiry is not as to the acts done in pursuance of the agreement, but whether there was, in fact, a common agreement to which the acts are referable and to which all of the alleged offenders were privy.* [Emphasis added.]
>
> Conspiracy is in fact a more "preliminary" crime than attempt, since the offence is considered to be complete before any acts are taken that go beyond mere preparation to put the common design into effect. The Crown is simply required to prove a meeting of the minds with regard to a common design to do something unlawful, specifically the commission of an indictable offence. See s. 465(1)(c) of the *Criminal Code*.

[88] A conspiracy must involve more than one person, even though all the conspirators may not either be identified, or be capable of being convicted. See for example *O'Brien, supra*; *R. v. Guimond*, [1979] 1 S.C.R. 960 (S.C.C.). Further, each of the conspirators must have a genuine intention to participate in the agreement. A person cannot be a conspirator if he or she merely pretends to agree. In *O'Brien*, Rand J. held at p. 670 that

> a conspiracy requires an actual intention in both parties at the moment of exchanging the words of agreement to participate in the act proposed; mere words purporting agreement without an assenting mind to the act proposed are not sufficient.

Where one member of a so-called conspiracy is a police informant who never intends to carry out the common design, there can be no conspiracy involving that person. Nonetheless, a conspiracy can still exist between other parties to the same agreement. It is for this reason that the conspiracy in this case is alleged to involve Mr. Dynar and Mr. Cohen, and not the confidential informant "Anthony."

[89] There can be no doubt that a criminal conspiracy constitutes a serious offence that is properly extraditable. Indeed, it was so recognized in the 1976 treaty between Canada and the U.S. in force at the time of the sting operation. The crime has a long and malevolent history. Conspirators have plotted to overthrow monarchs from biblical times through the time of the Plantaganets and Tudors. Guy Fawkes

conspired with others to blow up the parliament buildings. Today conspirators plot to carry out terrorist acts, to commit murders or to import forbidden drugs. Society is properly concerned with conspiracies since two or more persons working together can achieve evil results that would be impossible for an individual working alone. For example, it usually takes two or more conspirators to manufacture and secrete explosives or to arrange for the purchase, importation and sale of heroin. The very fact that several persons in combination agree to do something has for many years been considered to constitute "a menace to society": *O'Brien*, *supra*, at p. 669. In fact, the scale of injury that might be caused to the fabric of society can be far greater when two or more persons conspire to commit a crime than when an individual sets out alone to do an unlawful act.

[90] As a result, it is obvious that the reason for punishing conspiracy before any steps are taken towards attaining the object of the agreement is to prevent the unlawful object from being attained, and therefore to prevent this serious harm from occurring. See Glanville Williams, *Criminal Law: The General Part* (2nd ed. 1961), at p. 710. It is also desirable to deter similar conduct in the future. Those who conspire to do something that turns out to be impossible betray by their actions a propensity and aptitude to commit criminal acts; and there is no reason to believe that schemers who are thwarted on one occasion will not be successful on the next. Thus, the rationale for punishing conspirators coincides with the rationale for punishing persons for attempted crimes. Not only is the offence itself seen to be harmful to society, but it is clearly in society's best interests to make it possible for law enforcement officials to intervene before the harm occurs that would be occasioned by a successful conspiracy or, if the conspiracy is incapable of completion, by a subsequent and more successful conspiracy to commit a similar offence.

(b)  Is Impossibility a Defence to Conspiracy?

[91] By virtue of the "preliminary" nature of the offence of criminal conspiracy, the mere fact that money was not transferred to Mr. Cohen for laundering by Mr. Dynar would not preclude a finding that a conspiracy existed between them. Criminal liability will still ensue, as long as the agreement and the common intention can be proved. Does it make any difference to the potential liability of the conspirators that they could not have committed the substantive offence even if they had done everything that they set out to do? Put another way, should conspirators escape liability because, owing to matters entirely outside their control, they are mistaken with regard to an attendant circumstance that must exist for their plan to be successful? Such a result would defy logic and could not be justified.

[92] Impossibility as a defence to a charge of criminal conspiracy has received comparatively little attention by courts or academic writers. *Director of Public Prosecutions v. Nock*, [1978] 2 All E.R. 654 (U.K. H.L.), is the leading English case which considered the applicability of the defence of impossibility in a charge of conspiracy. In that case, the conspiracy was found to consist of an agreement to produce cocaine on a particular occasion from a specific substance. The agreement was impossible to carry out because the substance chosen was incapable of producing cocaine. The

impossibility of carrying out this agreement was the basis for the conclusion that the same distinction between factual and legal impossibility that we have criticized in the law of attempt ought to apply to the law of conspiracy. The respondent relies upon *Nock*, and urges the adoption of legal impossibility as a defence to criminal conspiracy in Canada. This submission cannot be accepted.

[93]  In England, *Nock* has been specifically overtaken by the *Criminal Attempts Act 1981*, s. 5, which now makes criminal liability for conspiracy possible where the accused are mistaken as to an attendant circumstance that is necessary to prove the full offence. Effectively, this precludes the defence of legal impossibility as understood in *Nock*, *supra*, but preserves the defence for "imaginary crimes." As we have seen, the latter term encompasses situations where individuals do something they believe contravenes the law when it does not. Thus, for example, in England it is not a crime to conspire to purchase Scotch whisky, because the purchase of that whisky is not a crime known to English law.

[94]  Section 465(1)(c) of the Canadian *Criminal Code* does not specifically state that criminal liability for conspiracy can ensue where the substantive offence is impossible to commit. However, even in the absence of such an explicit legislative direction, the analysis of the House of Lords in *Nock* should not be accepted. The case has been rightly subjected to both academic and judicial criticism, and to the extent that it is based on the same distinction between factual and legal impossibility that has been applied in the law of attempt, it too is conceptually untenable.

[95]  In England, the acceptance of legal impossibility as a defence to conspiracy in *Nock* was predicated on the adoption by the House of Lords of the same position regarding the law of attempt: see *Haughton v. Smith*, [1973] 3 All E.R. 1109 (Eng. C.A.). The House of Lords has now expressly overruled the *Haughton* decision in *R. v. Shivpuri*, [1986] 2 All E.R. 334 (U.K. H.L.). They did so on the basis that quite apart from the provisions of the *Criminal Attempts Act*, the distinction between factual and legal impossibility is untenable in the law of attempt. The application of the distinction in *Nock* must now be questioned as well, even in the absence of legislative amendment. Accordingly, the desirability of using the *Nock* principles in Canada has been appropriately doubted by Cadsby Prov. Ct. J. in *R. v. Atkinson*, (April 13, 1987), Cadsby Prov. J. (Ont. Prov. Ct.). The New Zealand Court of Appeal has also rejected *Nock*, except perhaps in the case of "imaginary crimes": *R. v. Sew Hoy*, [1994] 1 N.Z.L.R. 257 (New Zealand C.A.).

[96]  A number of Canadian academic authorities have also been justly critical of the use of the distinction between factual and legal impossibility in the law of conspiracy, and in particular, have criticized the *Nock* case for this reason. Most writers take the position that if the distinction between factual and legal impossibility is rejected in the case of attempt, it should *a fortiori* be rejected for conspiracy. Thus, for example, Colvin in *Principles of Criminal Law*, *supra*, at p. 358, indicates, in a discussion that deals primarily with the law of attempt, that he prefers the view that "impossibility of execution is never a defence to inchoate liability in Canada." Since this position is clear in the *Criminal Code* with regard to attempt," there is no good reason to treat conspiracy and other forms of inchoate liability any differently."

[97]   Professor Stuart in *Canadian Criminal Law*, *supra*, at pp. 644-45, convincingly contends that the same rationale for rejecting the distinction between factual and legal impossibility in the law of attempt should apply to the law of conspiracy. He puts his position in this way (at p. 644):

> If conspiracy is considered, as it has been suggested that it should, as a preventive crime owing its existence to the fact that it is a step, even though a limited one, towards the commission of a full offence, it is difficult to see why the approach to impossibility should differ.

[98]   According to Professor Alan Mewett and Morris Manning in *Mewett & Manning on Criminal Law* (3rd ed. 1994), at p. 341, if it were not for the decision in *Nock*, the question as to whether impossibility should constitute a defence to the offence of conspiracy ought not to arise at all. In *Nock*, the House of Lords held that because the offence can never materialize, "[t]here was no *actus reus* because there was no act of agreeing to commit an offence." Mewett and Manning criticize this reasoning as unsound because "[i]t is wrong to think that there is something that can, in the abstract, be called an *actus reus*." It is the agreement that is the *actus*, and the intention to do the act that is unlawful (the *mens rea*) that turns the agreement into an *actus reus*, or a "guilty act." These authors would restrict the availability of the defence of impossibility to situations of "true" legal impossibility (which we have referred to as imaginary crimes), where persons conspire to do something that is not a crime known to law regardless of whether the facts are as the accused believe them to be.

[99]   Canadian courts have only rarely considered this issue. In *R. v. Wah*, [1964] 1 C.C.C. 313 (Ont. C.A.), the Ontario Court of Appeal, in a case involving conspiracy to commit forgery, held at p. 315 that "[i]n a prosecution for conspiracy a conviction may not be registered if the operation for the commission of which the accused allegedly conspired would, if accomplished, not have made the accused guilty of the substantive offence." The respondent obviously finds comfort in this case.

[100]   Although some of the language in *Wah* suggests a more general acceptance of the defence of legal impossibility in a case of conspiracy, the case was decided on a much narrower basis. There the substantive offence was defined as involving the making of a false document, knowing it to be false. The resolution of the case turned on the definition of "false document." Kelly J.A. held that the photograph of the false document was not itself a false document. Therefore, the crime could not be committed regardless of the intention of the accused. There was no issue as to mistaken belief regarding particular circumstances. The accused simply intended to do something which was not prohibited by law. In addition, Kelly J.A. found that the Crown had not established that the photograph was intended to be used to induce anyone to believe that the reproduced document was genuine.

[101]   *Wah* should only be accepted as authority for the proposition that impossibility can be a defence to a charge of conspiracy where the conspirators intend to commit an "imaginary crime." This approach to impossibility and conspiracy has also been taken in older cases dealing with economic conspiracies: see for example *R. v. Howard Smith Paper Mills Ltd.*, [1957] S.C.R. 403 (S.C.C.), at p. 406, citing *R. v. Whitchurch* (1890), 24 Q.B.D. 420 (Eng. Q.B.).

[102] None of these authorities stands in the way of a conclusion that, from a purely conceptual perspective, the distinction between factual and legal impossibility is as unsound in the law of conspiracy as it is in the law of attempt. As we concluded in discussing impossible attempts, cases of so-called "legal" impossibility turn out to be cases of factual impossibility and the distinction collapses, except in cases of "imaginary crimes." Conspiracy to commit such fanciful offences of course cannot give rise to criminal liability.

[103] Furthermore, like attempt, conspiracy is a crime of intention. The factual element—or *actus reus*—of the offence is satisfied by the establishment of the agreement to commit the predicate offence. This factual element does not have to correspond with the factual elements of the substantive offence. The goal of the agreement, namely the commission of the substantive offence, is part of the mental element—or *mens rea*—of the offence of conspiracy.

[104] The conspiracy alleged in the case at bar involves the commission of an offence that requires knowledge of a circumstance as one of its essential elements. When a substantive offence requires knowledge of a particular circumstance, the Crown is required to prove a subjective element, which is best described as belief that the particular circumstance exists. The Crown is also required to prove an objective element, namely the truth of the circumstance. It is the presence of the objective circumstance that translates the subjective belief into knowledge or "true belief."

[105] However, since the offence of conspiracy only requires an *intention* to commit the substantive offence, and not the commission of the offence itself, it does not matter that, from an objective point of view, commission of the offence may be impossible. It is the subjective point of view that is important, and from a subjective perspective, conspirators who intend to commit an indictable offence intend to do everything necessary to satisfy the conditions of the offence. The fact that they cannot do so because an objective circumstance is not as they believe it to be does not in any way affect this intention. The intention of the conspirators remains the same, regardless of the absence of the circumstance that would make the realization of that intention possible. It is only in retrospect that the impossibility of accomplishing the common design becomes apparent.

[106] If the failure of a conspiracy as a result of some defect in the attendant circumstances were to be considered to constitute "legal" impossibility and as such a defence to a charge of conspiracy, the fact that the conspirators are not culpable becomes a matter of pure luck, divorced from their true intentions. This result is unacceptable. Rather it would be consistent with the law of conspiracy to hold that the absence of the attendant circumstance has no bearing on the intention of the parties, and therefore no bearing on their liability.

[107] It has long been accepted that conspirators can be punished for their agreement (*actus reus*) and their intention to commit the offence (*mens rea*). This is true even though the police intervene to prevent the conspirators from committing the substantive offence which was the aim of the conspiracy. By the same token, it should make no difference to the culpability of the conspirators if the police intervene in a way that makes the offence impossible to commit because, for example, the money to be laundered is not derived from crime. The conspirators could still be properly

convicted on the basis that the agreement to do the unlawful object is considered dangerous to society and reprehensible in itself.

[108]  This approach does not substitute a different mental element for the offence of conspiracy from that required for the substantive offence of money laundering. In those offences that require knowledge, the mental element is belief. Therefore, the subjective state of mind of a money launderer is the belief that the money is derived from an illicit source. Similarly, the subjective state of mind of the person who conspires with others to launder money is also the belief that the money is derived from an illicit source. For the substantive offence to be committed, the objective circumstance—the existence of actual proceeds of crime—must also exist. But this is *not* the objective element of the offence of conspiracy. The essential element of conspiracy is the existence of the agreement to put the intention of the conspirators into effect.

[109]  It follows from all that has been said above that a conspiracy to commit a crime which cannot be carried out because an objective circumstance is not as the conspirators believed it to be is still capable of giving rise to criminal liability in Canada. Legal impossibility cannot be invoked as a defence to the charge.

## ADDITIONAL READING

- D. Stuart, *Criminal Law*, 4th ed. (Toronto: Carswell, 2001), chapter 10;
- K. Roach, *Criminal Law*, 3rd ed. (Toronto: Irwin Law, 2004), chapter 3;
- E. Meehan and J. Currie, *The Law of Criminal Attempt*, 2nd ed. (Toronto: Carswell, 2000);
- M. Goode, *Criminal Conspiracy in Canada* (Toronto: Carswell, 1975).

CHAPTER TEN

# Corporate Liability

Late in 2003, the law concerning corporate liability under the *Criminal Code* was fundamentally changed by the statutory amendments found in ss. 2, 22.1, and 22.2 of the *Criminal Code*. To understand these changes, it is necessary to understand the common law that existed before these amendments were passed. The first part of this chapter examines the common law concept of the directing minds in the corporations whose fault could be attributed to the corporation on the basis of their authority to direct the corporation and, in particular, to set its policies. The second part of this chapter explores the new statutory regime and, in particular, how it has replaced the common law concept of "directing minds" with a new and broader statutory concept of "senior officer." It also examines how s. 22.1 of the *Criminal Code* provides for organizational liability for criminal offences of negligence and how s. 22.2 provides for organizational liability for criminal offences of subjective intent.

## I. THE OLD COMMON LAW OF DIRECTING MINDS

**R. v. Waterloo Mercury Sales Ltd.**
Alberta District Ct.
(1974), 18 C.C.C. (2d) 248

LEGG D.C.J.:  Waterloo Mercury Sales Ltd. is charged with two counts of fraud under s. 338(1) of the *Criminal Code*.

The accused corporation through its used-car sales manager, Walter Golinowski, purchased some 26 automobiles in Ontario and shipped them to Alberta. After the vehicles were unloaded, but before being placed on the used-car sales lot, the odometers of some of these vehicles were turned back so that the odometer reading showed that the vehicle had been driven a substantially smaller number of miles than it had in fact been driven.

The vehicles which are the subject-matter of the two counts of fraud in the indictment were two of the vehicles purchased in Ontario on which the odometers were turned back.

The odometers were altered by a third party on the instructions of the used car sales manager, Golinowski, and when the vehicles were offered for sale the odometer reading was incorrect.

The main issue in this trial is whether the accused corporation can be held criminally liable for the act of its used-car sales manager if such act is done within the scope of his authority.

In the case at bar the used-car sales manager, Golinowski, was not an officer or director of the accused company. He operated two used car lots for the accused, which was situated close to, but did not form part of the main offices of the accused. His responsibilities were to buy used cars, clean them up, do minor reconditioning on them, fix the sales price, arrange advertising and promotion, demonstrate them to and makes sales to the public. In these duties he was assisted by a sales and other staff consisting of 12 people. He approved all sales made by the salesmen.

In my opinion, Golinowski was not a lesser employee. I find that it was the policy of the accused corporation to delegate to him "the sole active and directing will" of the corporation in all matters relating to the used car operation of the company, and as such he was its directing mind and will. His actions and intent were those of the accused itself and his conduct renders the company criminally liable.

I am mindful of the fact that the findings I have arrived at may be a further extension of the criminal liability of a corporation. None the less, having regard to the facts of this particular case I am of the opinion that it is in line with the judgments of Ford J.A. in *R. v. Fane Robinson Ltd., supra,* and that of Jessup J. in *R. v. J.J. Beamish Construction Co. Ltd.,* [1967] 1 C.C.C. 301.

I accept the evidence of Mr. Purvis [the president of the company] that he had no personal knowledge of the circumstances which led to these charges being laid and that he had circulated written instructions to all segments of his company not to alter odometers on the vehicles. However, this is not, in my opinion, a defence in light of the findings I have made.

Waterloo Mercury Sales Ltd. is guilty on both counts in the indictment.

*Accused convicted.*

### Canadian Dredge and Dock Co., Ltd. et al. v. The Queen
Supreme Court of Canada
(1985), 19 C.C.C. (3d) 1

ESTEY J. for the court:

The position of the corporation in criminal law must first be examined. Inasmuch as all criminal and *quasi*-criminal offences are creatures of statute the amenability of the corporation to prosecution necessarily depends in part upon the terminology employed in the statute. In recent years there has developed a system of classification which segregates the offences according to the degree of intent, if any, required to create culpability.

### (a) Absolute Liability Offences

Where the Legislature by the clearest intendment establishes an offence where liability arises instantly upon the breach of the statutory prohibition, no particular state of mind is a prerequisite to guilt. Corporations and individual persons stand on the same footing in the face of such a statutory offence. It is a case of automatic primary responsibility. Accordingly, there is no need to establish a rule for corporate liability nor a *rationale* therefor. The corporation is treated as a natural person.

### (b) Offences of Strict Liability

Where the terminology employed by the Legislature is such as to reveal an intent that guilt shall not be predicated upon the automatic breach of the statute but rather upon the establishment of the *actus reus*, subject to the defence of due diligence, an offence of strict liability arises: see *R. v. City of Sault Ste. Marie* (1978), 40 C.C.C. (2d) 353, 85 D.L.R. (3d) 161, [1978] 2 S.C.R. 1299. As in the case of an absolute liability offence, it matters not whether the accused is corporate or unincorporate, because the liability is primary and arises in the accused according to the terms of the statute in the same way as in the case of absolute offences. It is not dependent upon the attribution to the accused of the misconduct of others. This is so when the statute, properly construed, shows a clear contemplation by the Legislature that a breach of the statute itself leads to guilt, subject to the limited defence above noted. In this category, the corporation and the natural defendant are in the same position. In both cases liability is not vicarious but primary.

### (c) Offences Requiring Mens Rea

These are the traditional criminal offences for which an accused may be convicted only if the requisite *mens rea* is demonstrated by the prosecution. …

The route which was taken in this country and in the United Kingdom is not that which has been followed by the federal courts of the United States. Criminal responsibility in the corporation has for many years, in those courts, been placed upon the basis of the doctrine of *respondeat superior*. The resultant vicarious liability seems to arise in the corporation out of the criminal acts of any employee, supervisory, menial or otherwise. The United States Supreme Court expounded this principle as far back as *New York Central and Hudson R. v. U.S.* (1909), 212 U.S. 481. Although the statute there before the court specifically imposed liability in the corporation for the acts of its employees (without limitation), the courts have construed the case as establishing vicarious criminal liability in a corporation for the wrongful acts of its employees of all grades and classes. The rule was restated by the Court of Appeal of the 8th Circuit in *Egan v. U.S.* (1943), 137 F. 2d 369 at p. 379, *per* Thomas J.:

> The test of corporate responsibility for the acts of its officers and agents, whether such acts be criminal or tortious, is whether the agent or officer in doing the thing complained of was engaged in "employing the corporate powers actually authorized" for the benefit of the corporation "while acting within the scope of his employment in the business of the principal." If the act was so done it will be imputed to the corporation

whether covered by the agent or officer's instructions, whether contrary to his instructions, and whether lawful or unlawful. Such acts under such circumstances are not ultra vires even though unlawful. There is no longer any distinction in essence between the civil and criminal liability of corporations, based upon the element of intent or wrongful purpose. Malfeasance of their agents is not ultra vires.

These principles have been restated as recently as the judgment in *U.S. v. Basic Construction et al.* (1983), 711 F. 2d 570 (5th C.C.A.).

The state courts have not as consistently pursued the course of vicarious liability of corporations in the criminal law. In *People v. Canadian Fur Trappers Corp.* (1928), 248 N.Y. 159, the New York Court of Appeals, Crane J., speaking for a court that included Chief Justice Cardozo, rejected vicarious liability as a basis for corporate criminal responsibility and seemed to adopt, at pp. 163 and 169, something akin to the identification theory. To the same effect is *State of Idaho v. Adjustment Department Credit Bureau Inc.* (1971), 483 P. 2d 687 at p. 691, where corporate liability was found only if:

> ... the commission of the offense was authorized, requested, commanded or performed (i) by the board of directors, or (ii) by an agent having responsibility for formation of corporate policy or (iii) by a "high managerial agent" having supervisory responsibility over the subject matter of the offense and acting within the scope of his employment in behalf of the corporation.

*State of Louisiana v. Chapman Dodge Center Inc.* (1983), 428 S. 2d 413 at pp. 419-20, is to the same general effect. For a position midway between the *Canadian Fur Trappers, supra*, and these cases, see *Commonwealth of Massachusetts v. Beneficial Finance Co., et al.* (1917), 275 N.E. 2d 33.

At the present time, therefore, the common law in the United States seems to be based, in the federal courts on the doctrine of vicarious liability, and in many of the state courts on something akin to the identification doctrine. Court decisions are not a complete guide to the state law on this matter, however, as some states have adopted the American Law Institute Model Penal Code, which at para. 2.07 attributes criminal liability to the corporation on much the same basis as did the court in *State of Idaho v. Adjustment Department Credit Bureau Inc., supra*. On the other hand, at least one state has by statute applied the doctrine of vicarious liability without a limitation as to the level of responsibility of the employee or agent: see State of Maine, Rev. Stats. Anns. 17-A, s. 60. ...

[The Model Penal Code provides:

> 2.07(1)  A corporation may be convicted of the commission of an offense if: ...
>
> (c)  the commission of the offense was authorized, requested, commanded, or performed by the board of directors or by a high managerial agent acting on behalf of the corporation within the scope of his employment.

Section 2.07(4)(c) defines "high managerial agent" to mean an officer of a corporation, or any other agent of a corporation "having duties of such responsibility that his conduct may fairly be assumed to represent the policy of the corporation or association."]

In summary, therefore, the courts in this country can be said to this date to have declined generally to apply the principle of *respondeat superior* in the determination of corporate criminal responsibility. Criminal responsibility in our courts thus far has been achieved in the *mens rea* offences by the attribution of the corporation of the acts of its employees and agents on the more limited basis of the doctrine of the directing mind or identification. Corporate responsibility in both strict and absolute liability offences has been found to arise on the direct imposition of a primary duty in the corporation in the statute in question, as construed by the court. By what appears to be the same purely pragmatic reasoning, the courts of the United Kingdom find criminal liability in a corporation only by the attribution to it of the conduct of its employees and agents where those natural persons represent the core, mind and spirit of the corporation. The United States federal courts are inclined, as we have seen, to find criminal liability in the corporation by vicarious liability where any employee-agent commits, in the course of his employment, the criminal act.

The criticisms of the United States federal court doctrine are manifold. The net is flung too widely, it is said. Corporations are punished in instances where there is neither moral turpitude nor negligence. No public policy is served by punishing share-holders where the corporate governing body has been guilty of no unlawful act. The disparity between the treatment of the corporate employer and the natural employer is wide and wholly without a basis in justice or political science. The test as applied in the United States federal courts may be on the broad basis above indicated because so many of the federal statutory crimes are regulatory in nature: see Leigh, p. 267, footnote 134.

In the criminal law, a natural person is responsible only for those crimes in which he is the primary actor either actually or by express or implied authorization. There is no vicarious liability in the pure sense in the case of the natural person. That is to say that the doctrine of *respondeat superior* is unknown in the criminal law where the defendant is an individual. Lord Diplock, in *Tesco Supermarkets Ltd. v. Nattras*, [1972] A.C. 153 at p. 199, stated:

> Save in cases of strict liability where a criminal statute, exceptionally, makes the doing of an act a crime irrespective of the state of mind in which it is done, criminal law regards a person as responsible for his own crimes only. It does not recognise the liability of a principal for the criminal acts of his agent: because it does not ascribe to him his agent's state of mind. *Qui peccat per alium peccat* per se is not a maxim of criminal law.

On the other hand, the corporate vehicle now occupies such a large portion of the industrial, commercial and sociological sectors that amenability of the corporation to our criminal law is as essential in the case of the corporation as in the case of the natural person.

Thus where the defendant is corporate the common law has become pragmatic, as we have seen, and a modified and limited "vicarious liability" through the identification doctrine has emerged. ...

The identity doctrine merges the board of directors, the managing director, the superintendent, the manager or anyone else delegated by the board of directors to whom is delegated the governing executive authority of the corporation, and the conduct of any of the merged entities is thereby attributed to the corporation. In *R. v. St. Lawrence Corp. Ltd. and nineteen other corporations*, [1969] 3 C.C.C. 263, 5 D.L.R. (3d) 263, [1969] 2 O.R. 305 (Ont. C.A.), and other authorities, a corporation may, by this means, have more than one directing mind. This must be particularly so in a country such as Canada where corporate operations are frequently geographically widespread. The transportation companies, for example, must of necessity operate by the delegation and subdelegation of authority from the corporate centre; by the division and subdivision of the corporate brain, and by decentralizing by delegation the guiding forces in the corporate undertaking. The application of the identification rule in *Tesco, supra*, may not accord with the realities of life in our country, however appropriate we may find to be the enunciation of the abstract principles of law there made. ...

The identification theory was inspired in the common law in order to find some pragmatic, acceptable middle ground which would see a corporation under the umbrella of the criminal law of the community but which would not saddle the corporation with the criminal wrongs of all of its employees and agents. If there were to be no outer limit on the reach of the doctrine, the common law would have established criminal corporate liability by the doctrine of *respondeat superior*. What then is the appropriate outer limit of the attribution of criminal conduct of a directing mind when he undertakes activities in fraud of the corporation or for his own benefit? ...

Were the charge in question a charge of fraud, there would clearly be no benefit to the corporation, and indeed the design of the dishonest employee was aimed squarely at reducing the financial stature of the employer. It can hardly be said with any reality that a person designing and executing such a scheme could be, while doing so, the directing mind and the *ego* of the company itself. That being so, no longer would we be faced with the logical conundrum that a person however dishonest cannot defraud himself. Once the *ego* is split into its original two parts that problem disappears. The employee would be guilty of fraud and the victim of that fraud would be the company. The victim would, in all logic, have a defence against a charge that it too had committed fraud in its own right. Were the criminal law otherwise, it would not provide protection of any interest in the community. Punishment of the corporation for such acts of its employee would not advantage society by advancing law and order. It is otherwise, however, where there is benefit to the corporation, in whole or in part, from the unlawful acts of its directing mind. ...

In my view, the outer limit of the delegation doctrine is reached and exceeded when the directing mind ceases completely to act, in fact or in substance, in the interests of the corporation. Where this entails fraudulent action, nothing is gained from speaking of fraud in whole or in part because fraud is fraud. What I take to be the distinction raised by the question is where all of the activities of the directing mind are directed against the interests of the corporation with a view to damaging that corporation, whether or not the result is beneficial economically to the directing mind, that may be said to be fraud on the corporation. Similarly, but not so importantly, a benefit to the directing mind in single transactions or in a minor part of the activities of the directing mind is in reality quite different from benefit in the sense that the directing mind intended that the corporation should not benefit from any of its activities in its undertaking. A benefit of course can, unlike fraud, be in whole or in part, but the better standard, in my view, is established when benefit is associated with fraud. The same test then applies. Where the directing mind conceives and designs a plan and then executes it whereby the corporation is intentionally defrauded, and when this is the substantial part of the regular activities of the directing mind in his office, then it is unrealistic in the extreme to consider that the manager is the directing mind of the corporation. His entire energies are, in such a case, directed to the destruction of the undertaking of the corporation. When he crosses that line he ceases to be the directing mind and the doctrine of identification ceases to operate. The same reasoning and terminology can be applied to the concept of benefits.

Where the criminal act is totally in fraud of the corporate employer and where the act is intended to and does result in benefit exclusively to the employee-manager, the employee-directing mind, from the outset of the design and execution of the criminal plan, ceases to be a directing mind of the corporation and consequently his acts could not be attributed to the corporation under the identification doctrine. This might be true as well on the American approach through *respondeat superior*. Whether this is so or not, in my view, the identification doctrine only operates where the Crown demonstrates that the action taken by the directing mind (a) was within the field of operation assigned to him; (b) was not totally in fraud of the corporation, and (c) was by design or result partly for the benefit of the company. ...

I therefore would answer both questions as they relate to the defences of "acting wholly or partly in fraud of the corporation," and "in whole or in part for the benefit of the directing mind," as follows:

1. On the evidence in these records, the respective directing minds of the appellants did not act wholly in fraud of their respective corporate employers.

2. Neither did the four directing minds act wholly for their own benefit in the sense that no benefit from their actions would accrue to the appellants, and in any event the record clearly reveals an intention on their part to benefit their respective corporations.

3. Express or implied instructions prohibiting the unlawful acts specifically, or unlawful conduct generally, are not a defence whether the corporate liability springs from authorization of the acts of an agent or the unlawful acts of a directing mind. In any case, only in the record relating to CD is there any evidence of any such prohibition. ...

I would therefore dismiss all four appeals.

*Appeals dismissed.*

## R. v. Safety-Kleen Canada Inc.
### Ontario Court of Appeal
### (1997), 114 C.C.C. (3d) 214

[The corporate accused was convicted of knowingly giving false information to a provincial officer contrary to s. 145 of the *Environmental Protection Act*, R.S.O. 1980, c. C-141. It appealed on the basis that the individual driver who made the false statement was not the directing mind of the corporation.]

DOHERTY J.A.: ... This appeal concerns the liability of the appellant, a corporate employer, for the misconduct of Mr. Howard, its employee. The appeal from the conviction on count 2 involves a consideration of the scope of corporate responsibility for offences which require proof of a culpable state of mind. ...

Count 2 alleged that the appellant knowingly gave false information in a return to a provincial officer. Section 145 of the Act provided:

> 145.  No person shall knowingly give false information in any application, return or statement made to the Minister, a provincial officer or any employee of the Ministry in respect of any matter under this Act or the regulations.

Assuming that the manifest was a return, it is clear that the offence was made out against Mr. Howard. The manifest was false and Mr. Howard knew it was false. In determining the appellant's liability it is necessary to begin by placing the offence created by s. 145 into one of the three categories identified in *R. v. Sault Ste. Marie (City)*, [1978] 2 S.C.R. 1299, 40 C.C.C. (2d) 353. The parties agree that this offence falls into the first category (*mens rea* offences) as it is an offence which requires proof of a culpable state of mind. Specifically, the prosecution had to prove that Mr. Howard knew the document was false.

Corporations can be convicted of crimes involving a culpable mental state. Absent a statutory basis for that liability, corporate liability for such crimes is determined by the application of the identification theory set down in *R. v. Canadian Dredge & Dock Co. Ltd.*, [1985] 1 S.C.R. 662, 19 C.C.C. (3d) 1, and developed in *"Rhône" (The) v. "Peter A.B. Widener" (The)*, [1993] 1 S.C.R. 497. In *Rhône*, Iacobucci J. succinctly summarized the inquiry demanded by the identification theory at pp. 520-21:

> ... the focus of [the] inquiry must be whether the impugned individual has been delegated the "governing executive authority" of the company within the scope of his or her authority. I interpret this to mean that one must determine whether the discretion conferred on an employee amounts to an express or implied delegation of executive authority to design and supervise the implementation of corporate policy rather than simply to carry out such policy. In other words, the Courts must consider who has been left with the decision-making power in a relevant sphere of corporate activity.

The inquiry described by Iacobucci J. is a fact-driven one which looks beyond titles and job descriptions to the reality of any given situation. Mr. Howard was a truck driver for the appellant. He was also the appellant's sole representative in a very large geographical area. He was responsible for collecting waste, completing necessary documentation, maintaining the appellant's property in the region, billing, and responding to calls from customers and regulators. When Mr. Howard was on holidays, the appellant did not do business in the region. Mr. Howard did not, however, have any managerial or supervisory function. He took no role in shaping any aspect of the appellant's corporate policies.

Unlike the judge at the first level of appeal, I do not read the trial judge's reasons as including a finding that Mr. Howard was a directing mind of the appellant for the relevant purpose. The trial judge clearly rejected the characterization of Mr. Howard as a "low level employee" and found that he had wide authority in his region. Beyond this, she made no finding. Rather, she based her conviction on this count on a finding that the company did not take all reasonable steps to avoid the event. In my view, since the offence alleged in count 2 requires proof of a culpable mental state, a finding of a lack of due diligence is irrelevant. The determinative question of whether Mr. Howard's actual authority was sufficient to justify attributing his culpable mind to the appellant was never addressed. Consequently, no finding on the crucial question of whether Mr. Howard was the directing mind of the appellant for the relevant purpose exists.

There is no doubt that Mr. Howard had many responsibilities and was given wide discretion in the exercise of those responsibilities. It is equally clear that those, like Mr. Corcoran, who dealt with the appellant in the area, equated Mr. Howard with the appellant corporation. Neither of these facts establish the kind of governing executive authority which must exist before the identification theory will impose liability on the corporation. Mr. Howard had authority over matters arising out of the performance of the task he was employed to do. It was his job to collect and transport waste to its eventual destination in Breslau. His authority extended over all matters, like the preparation of necessary documentation, arising out of the performance of those functions. I find no evidence, however, that he had authority to devise or develop corporate policy or make corporate decisions which went beyond those arising out of the transfer and transportation of waste. In my opinion, Mr. Howard's position is much like that of the tugboat captain in The *Rhône*, *supra*. Both had extensive responsibilities and discretion, but neither had the power to design and supervise the implementation of corporate policy. The majority of the Supreme Court of Canada concluded that the captain was not a directing mind of his corporate employer. I reach the same conclusion with respect to Mr. Howard.

## A NOTE ON VICARIOUS LIABILITY AND THE CHARTER

Vicarious liability occurs when the acts and fault of one person are attributed to another. Although widely used in tort law, it is disfavoured under the criminal law and required a clear statement by Parliament before the enactment of the Charter. The Saskatchewan Court of Appeal in *R. v. Burt* (1987), 38 C.C.C. (3d) 299, at 311 held that "the principles of fundamental justice simply do not recognize the ascribing to one person of another's state of mind. Accordingly, where a statute purports to make one person vicariously liable for another's *mens rea* offence the statute may be said to offend ... the principles of fundamental justice." Note, however, that a statute that applies only to corporations may be immune from challenge under s. 7 of the Charter because corporations are not protected under s. 7 as persons that enjoy the right to life, liberty, and security of the person and the right not to be deprived of those rights except in accordance with the principles of fundamental justice.

## II. THE NEW STATUTORY PROVISIONS FOR ORGANIZATIONAL LIABILITY

Three key definitions are now contained in s. 2 of the *Criminal Code*:

"organization" means
    (a) a public body, body corporate, society, company, firm, partnership, trade union or municipality, or
    (b) an association of persons that
        (i) is created for a common purpose
        (ii) has an operational structure, and
        (iii) holds itself out to the public as an association of persons;

"representative," in respect of an organization, means a director, partner, employee, member, agent or contractor of the organization;

"senior officer" means a representative who plays an important role in the establishment of the organization's policies or is responsible for managing an important aspect of the organization's activities and, in the case of a body corporate, includes a director, its chief executive officer and its chief financial officer.

Section 22.1 of the *Criminal Code* provides for organizational liability for negligence-based offences:

In respect of an offence that requires the prosecution to prove negligence, an organization is a party to the offence if:
    (a) acting within the scope of their authority
        (i) one of its representatives is a party to the offence, or
        (ii) two or more of its representatives engage in conduct, whether by act or omission, such that, if it had been the conduct of only one representative, that representative would have been a party to the offence; and
    (b) the senior officer who is responsible for the aspect of the organization's activities that is relevant to the offence departs—or the senior officers, collectively, depart—markedly from the standard of care that, in the circumstances, could reasonably be expected to prevent a representative of the organization from being a party to the offence.

Section 22.2 of the *Criminal Code* provides for organizational liability for subjective intent offences:

In respect of an offence that requires the prosecution to prove fault—other than negligence—an organization is a party to the offence if, with the intent at least in part to benefit the organization, one of its senior officers

(a) acting within the scope of their authority, is a party to the offence;

(b) having the mental state required to be a party to the offence and acting within the scope of their authority, directs the work of other representatives of the organization so that they do the act or make the omission specified in the offences; or

(c) knowing that a representative of the organization is or is about to be a party to the offence, does not take all reasonable measures to stop them from being a party to the offence.

Note that s. 718.21 sets out sentencing principles for organizations and s. 732.1(3.1) provides for probation orders against organizations.

The following article provides a preliminary overview and assessment of the new law concerning organizational liability.

### T. Archibald, K. Jull, and K. Roach, "The Changed Face of Corporate Criminal Liability"
(2004), 48 *Crim. L.Q.* 367

In the dying days of the last Parliamentary session of 2003, Parliament enacted Bill C-45 amending the *Criminal Code* with respect to the liability of corporations and other organizations. The bill had all party approval. It was also supported by the families of 26 miners who died in the Westray mine explosion in 1992, a disaster that might have been prevented by corporate compliance with health and safety regulations. In that case, manslaughter charges were laid against two Westray managers, but were dropped after especially protracted legal proceedings. Bill C-45 was held out by the government as a response to Westray—a response that seems even more pressing after subsequent disasters such as the poisoning of water in Walkerton and the Enron scandal. The wide support for the bill was cited by the *Halifax Herald* as

> witness to the rightness of the cause. ... Holding corporations responsible for their decisions may not be the kind of redress Westray family members had in mind when they began their journey for justice, but they can take comfort in the fact that the measure should be a strong deterrent to the recurrence of such a tragedy in workplaces across the nation. It is only too bad it took so long to bring justice to Westray families.

Bill C-45 constitutes a fundamental change, if not a revolution, in corporate criminal liability. It creates a new regime of criminal liability that applies not only to corporations, but unions, municipalities, partnerships and other associations of persons. It replaces the traditional legal concept of corporate liability based on the fault of the corporation's "directing mind(s)," the board of directors and those with the power to set corporate policy, with liability tied to the fault of all of the corporation's "senior officers." That definition includes all those employees, agents or contractors who play "an important role in the establishment of an organization's policies" or who have responsibility "for managing an important aspect of the organization's activities." It will no longer be necessary for prosecutors to prove fault in the boardrooms or at the highest levels of corporation: the fault of even middle managers may suffice.

It also provides that the conduct of the organization's "representatives" will be attributed to the organization and defines a representative to include not only directors, employees and partners but also agents and contractors. In a word, Bill C-45 significantly expands the net of corporate and organizational liability.

In many ways, the expansion of the corporate liability is overdue. The legal concept of the "directing mind" within the corporate boardroom has become outdated by new forms of organic management. In addition, organizations should not escape responsibility for work that they contract out to those who are not their employees. The new sentencing provisions of Bill C-45 also allow a judge to place a corporation on probation and to take steps to repair harms that it has caused and to prevent similar harms in the future. It is also sensible that the new law sets a lower standard for corporate criminal liability based on crimes of negligence as opposed to crimes of subjective fault. To this extent, the law preserves important gradations of liability.

There are, however, some aspects of Bill C-45 that are more troubling. The new law blurs the traditional and important distinction between regulatory and criminal liability. A corporation could be found guilty of a subjective intent offence because its senior officers (including some managers) knew that a representative of a corporation was or was about to become a party to the offence, but did not take all reasonable measures to stop that representative—an employee, agent or contractor—from being a party to the offence. The distinction between criminal and regulatory liability is also blurred with respect to criminal offences based on negligence. To be sure, prosecutors who bring criminal charges based on negligence will still bear the onus of proving both the *actus reus* and fault beyond a reasonable doubt. The new law also acknowledges that the standard of negligence in criminal law requires proof of not simple negligence but of a marked departure from the reasonable standard of care. In contrast, regulatory offences will only require the prosecutor to prove the commission of the prohibited act or *actus reus* beyond a reasonable doubt, while requiring the corporation to establish due diligence on a balance of probabilities to escape liability. Although these differences are important in a court of law, they may not seem so significant in the wake of some tragedy.

Lawyers will likely advise corporate officers, including middle managers, that their explanations for tragedies may be used against the corporation for both regulatory or criminal charges. A criminal charge—even one based on negligence—may expose corporations and their shareholders to significant publicity and stigma. A manslaughter or criminal negligence charge against a corporation, let alone a murder or a fraud charge, will often be front page news. The expansion of corporate criminal liability in Bill C-45 is bound to make relations between corporations and regulatory investigators far more adversarial than at present.

Greater reliance on criminal liability might be worth it if the result was genuine deterrence and reparation for the harms caused. But there is some reason to doubt that this will be the case. Some corporations facing serious criminal charges may simply declare bankruptcy, ending the promise of Bill C-45 that the criminal law can be used to reform their practice and achieve some reparation for the victims. Moreover, there is reason to be concerned that the threat of criminal liability will lead those in regulated industries to more frequently invoke their right to silence and other

*Charter* protections that are routinely available for those facing criminal changes, and less likely to apply to regulatory charges. Finally, the difficulties of securing criminal convictions even under the enhanced law should not be underestimated and the advantages of a regulatory prosecution which requires the corporation to establish due diligence should not be forgotten. The exact consequences of expanded criminal liability can only be determined by empirical research, but the blurring of criminal and regulatory liability should be carefully monitored. ...

## II.  The New Law of Expanded Organizational Criminal Liability

### (1)  Expanded Definition of "Organization"

One of the more important yet neglected changes in the new law is that it extends far beyond the corporate world to include all "organizations." An organization is now defined in s. 2 of the *Criminal Code* to include a "public body, body corporate, society, company, firm, partnership, trade union or municipality." An organization also includes less formal associations of persons that are "created for a common purpose, has an operational structure and hold itself out to the public as an association of persons." By this definition, some organized criminal gangs could be prosecuted under these provisions, and if convicted, fined and/or placed on probation. The intent appears to widen criminal liability beyond mere structure to include various types of collective organizations. In principle, this makes some sense. In the short term, it will require organizations, such as partnerships, to reconsider their executive structure and to acquire insurance coverage with respect to a much wider potential criminal liability.

The real effect of these changes, if implemented, will be felt in circles outside of the corporation (which was already subject to criminal charges under the common law of *Canadian Dredge*). Governmental institutions may be faced with criminal (and not just regulatory) prosecutions. Charitable organizations, or trade unions, may face criminal prosecutions. While it may have been previously possible under the common law to charge such organizations, the explicit reference to them in this legislation sends a green light to policing bodies and private complainants that they may now become potential targets.

### (2)  Expanded Definition of "Representative"

Under the new law, organizations are held responsible not only for the actions of their senior officers, but also of their "representatives." Representatives are defined broadly to include not only directors, partners, employees and members, but also agents or contractors. In principle, this approach also makes sense given that modern organizations frequently contract out work in order to achieve efficiencies. In some cases, the actions of agents or contractors might have been attributed to the corporation under the common law. Nevertheless, the clarity of the new statutory definition makes it more likely that organizations could be charged on the basis of actions taken on their behalf by "agents" or "contractors." This reality may require organizations to re-think issues such as insurance and the supervision of the activities of agents and contractors.

### (3)  New Definition of "Senior Officer"

The Department of Justice was critical of the doctrine that restricted the concept of directing mind to policy making functions at the highest level. The new law now requires the prosecution to prove only that those who controlled the operation of the organization were criminally liable, and not those who set policy in head office either on the board of directors or as senior executives. The linchpin to the new legislative framework is the concept of a "senior officer." It is the mind of the senior officer that will bind the corporation. "Senior officer" is now defined in s. 2 of the *Criminal Code* as follows:

> "Senior officer" means a representative who plays an important role in the establishment of the organization's policies *or* is responsible for managing an important aspect of the organization's activities and, in the case of a body corporate, includes a director, its chief executive officer and its chief financial officer.

The key distinction in the above definition is the disjunctive test that is established by the use of the word "or." A senior officer may play an important role in the framing of policies *or* is responsible for managing an important aspect of the organization's activities. This new test clearly overrules *The Rhone* [[1993] 1 S.C.R. 497], as it widens the liability of the corporation beyond the boardroom to encompass activities that are operational in nature, at the managerial level. The corporation can be liable if senior managers either created policies or managed an important aspect of the organization's activities that resulted in violations of the law. The policy/operational distinction has been eliminated, as far as organizational liability is concerned.

As to the resolution of what an "important role" will mean, this will be the subject of intense litigation in the future. The test will require the court to inquire into the organizational structure of a particular defendant. It may require either inside testimony from a whistleblower or expert evidence with respect to comparative positions in other companies or industries.

It might be argued that the words "important role" are unconstitutionally vague under s. 7 of the Charter. A threshold problem with such an argument will be whether a corporation charged with a new offence even has standing to challenge a law that applies only to corporations that are not entitled to rights to life, liberty and security of the person under s. 7 of the Charter. [See *Irwin Toy Ltd. v. Quebec*, [1989] 1 S.C.R. 927.] Although corporations have been able to defend criminal and even civil cases on the basis that the law might violate the right of natural persons, the definition of "senior officer" in s. 2 of the *Criminal Code* can only be applied in prosecutions of corporations that are not entitled to s. 7 rights of the Charter.

Some commentators have observed that "a legislature that wanted to insulate a law from section 7 review would thus have to make that law only applicable to corporations, something that is not commonly done." [See R.J. Sharpe, K. Swinton, and K. Roach, *The Canadian Charter of Rights and Freedoms*, 2nd ed. (Toronto: Irwin Law: 2002), at 182.] The new definition of "senior officer" in Bill C-45 is one of those rare laws that applies only to corporations. Even if a corporation has standing to challenge the definition of "senior officer" as unduly vague, the jurisprudence has been characterized by judicial deference. In other words, courts will consider that vague statutory language such as "an important role" is subject to subsequent interpretation by the courts that will make its meaning more precise.

Although the definition of "senior officer" is undoubtedly broader than the old common law definition of "directing mind," the onus remains on the Crown to prove beyond a reasonable doubt that a senior officer had an "important role" either in establishing an organization's policies or managing an important aspect of its activities. Consistent with the principles of strict and purposive construction of the criminal law, courts may give the new concept a narrower reading in cases in which it is not fair and does not make sense to attribute the fault of an employee, low level manager, agent or contractor back to the corporation. The Crown's burden of proof, as well as the uncertainty as to the exact meaning of senior officer, highlights the continued advantage of a regulatory offence prosecution.

In regulatory offences, all the Crown must prove beyond a reasonable doubt is the commission of the prohibited act. The defence must show, as part of due diligence, that it designed and implemented systems to prevent the particular problem without the need to define either the corporation's directing mind or, now, its senior officer. …

In the *Westray* example, the prosecution would be required to prove only that those who controlled the operation of the mine were criminally negligent. Again, this is logical. Why should the entire organization be excused from criminal liability (as is presently the case) because senior policy-makers were insulated from the negligence of operational managers? Modern corporate management no longer resembles the old pyramid, and the organization should not be exempt as a result of the evolution of corporate structures.

The impact of the new definition of "senior officer" varies between subjective intent offences and negligence offences, and as a result these require separate treatment in our analysis.

### (4) Subjective Intent Offences

The case of *Canadian Dredge* dealt with the subjective intent offence of bid-rigging. This offence can be classified as a type of fraud. In Canada, charges against corporations for subjective intent offences are relatively rare. Post-Enron, it is perhaps easier to envisage a corporation being charged with such a crime. This scenario is reflected in the language used by the government in describing its reform initiative:

> The most obvious way for an organization to be criminally responsible is if the senior officer actually committed the crime for the direct benefit of the organization. For example, if the CEO fudges financial reports and records, leading others to provide funds to the organization, both the organization and the CEO will be guilty of fraud.
>
> However, senior officers may direct others to undertake such dishonest work. The Bill therefore makes it clear that the organization is guilty if the senior officer has the necessary intent, but subordinates carry out the actual physical act. For example, a senior officer may be benefiting the organization by instructing employees to deal in goods that are stolen. The senior officer may instruct employees to buy from the supplier offering the lowest price, knowing that the person who offers to sell the goods at the

lowest price can only make such an offer because the goods are stolen. The employees themselves have no criminal intent but the senior officer and the organization could be found guilty.

The newly enacted s. 22.2 of the *Criminal Code* sets out three separate ways in which the organization can be found to have committed a crime requiring fault other than negligence:

> 22.2 In respect of an offence that requires the prosecution to prove fault—other than negligence—an organization is a party to the offence if, with the intent at least in part to benefit the organization, one of its senior officers
>
>   (a)  acting within the scope of their authority, is a party to the offence;
>
>   (b)  having the mental state required to be a party to the offence and acting within the scope of their authority, directs the work of other representatives of the organization so that they do the act or make the omission specified in the offences; or
>
>   (c)  knowing that a representative of the organization is or is about to be a party to the offence, does not take all reasonable measures to stop them from being a party to the offence.

The above definition preserves the common law to the extent that it allows the fault of a senior officer who is the directing mind and acting within the scope of his authority to be attributed to the organization. The evolution in the law is that senior officers who are not directing minds can also have their conduct attributed to the corporation. Section 22.2 requires however that the senior officers act "with intent at least in part to benefit the organization." This means that the fault of a senior officer who has absolutely no intent to benefit the organization will not be attributed to the organization even though his or her actions may have unintentionally benefited the organization. This language may be an important protection for organizations when senior officers act in a rogue fashion for their own gain and with no intent to even partially benefit the organization.

Crimes such as fraud or money laundering have high levels of stigma. It is for this reason that subjective intent is generally a requirement for crimes with high stigma. In the area of fraud, the Supreme Court of Canada [in *Zlatic v. The Queen*, [1993] 2 S.C.R. 29] has maintained the requirement of subjective awareness of the risk to others, although this principle does not require a subjective appreciation of each element:

> Fraud by "other fraudulent means" does not require that the accused subjectively appreciate the dishonesty of his acts. The accused must knowingly, i.e. subjectively, undertake the conduct which constitutes the dishonest act, and must subjectively appreciate that the consequences of such conduct could be deprivation, in the sense of causing another to lose his pecuniary interest in certain property or in placing that interest at risk.

The government's legislation has spread the stigma of a conviction to the entire corporation, even if only one part of the corporation was at fault. This approach is consistent with the new organic corporate structures that have extended decision-making powers beyond the boardroom to diverse sectors. There is, however, something about the application of this approach to subjective criminal law intent offences that is troublesome. Subjective intent offences are more blameworthy and ought to be punished as such. The new law could dilute this notion.

Our Supreme Court has always restricted the notion of a corporation's mind to a policy-making function while appreciating that there could be more than one mind that exercises this function. The new provisions extend the corporation's mind to important aspects of the corporation's activities outside of the boardroom. (Recall that the definition of "senior officer" includes someone who is responsible for managing an important aspect of the organization's activities.) To extend the notion to management at the operational level intuitively seems better suited to crimes of criminal negligence than subjective intent crimes that require some element of "thinking." The corporate mind will now encompass policy and important operational decisions. The following law school exam example shows the difficulty with this doctrine when pushed to the extreme limits, particularly, where the crime is one of the most serious.

Suppose the captain of *The Rhone* is a malevolent person who dislikes the competition so much that he purposely decides to ram another boat with the intent of sinking it, and then decides to run over the stricken sailors who are in the water. If several sailors died, then the Captain could be properly charged with the subjective intent offence of murder. Under the old definition, the company that employed the captain could not be charged with murder, unless there was evidence that it was board policy to ram competitors' ships or harm their workers. Under the new definition, the company could conceivably be charged with murder, since the Captain would qualify as a "senior officer" who was responsible for managing an important aspect of the organization's activities and because his actions were committed with the "intent in part to benefit the organization." The company could become a party to the offence of murder, as the criminal act was done with intent in part to benefit the corporation.

What is troubling in this example is the stigma specifically related to the crime of murder, a subjective intent offence. The company's real fault lies in the domain of negligence in failing to perform the appropriate background checks on the captain (perhaps he has a criminal record for acts of violence). The legislation elevates corporate liability from negligence to the subjective crime of murder by virtue of the result. While this is not pure vicarious liability (as it only applies to senior officers), it borders on that principle. ...

Section 22.2(b) makes the organization liable if the senior officer "having the mental state required to be party to the offence and acting within the scope of their authority, directs the work of other representatives of the organization so that they do the act or make the omission specified in the offence." The requirement that the senior officer has the mental state required under the parties provision of s. 21 of the *Criminal Code* will generally ensure some degree of subjective fault in relation to the crime. Section 21(2) does contemplate liability on the basis that the senior officer ought to have known that the commission of the offence would be a probable consequence of carrying out an unlawful purpose that he or she formed with some person. In such a case, a corporation could be convicted of a subjective fault offence in part on the basis of objective foresight of that particular offence by the senior officer. It should also be recalled that although the senior officer must be at fault under s. 22.2(b), the actual offence could be committed by any "representative" of the organization. That is a broad term encompassing not only all employees but also all agents and contractors of the organization.

Section 22.2(c) even more directly than 22.2(b) makes it possible for an organization to be convicted of a subjective fault offence in part because of a failure of its senior officer to act in a reasonable fashion. Section 22.2(c) is a curious combination of a *mens rea* standard of knowingly being aware that a representative is or is about to be party to the offence, with the objective standard that the corporation is at fault if the senior officer "does not take all reasonable measures to stop [the representatives] from being a party to the offence." The rationale for this preventative section is described by the Department of Justice as follows:

> Finally, an organization would be guilty of a crime if a senior officer knows employees are going to commit an offence but does not stop them because he wants the organization to benefit from the crime. Using the stolen goods example, the senior officer may become aware that an employee is going to get a kickback from the thieves for getting the organization to buy the stolen goods. The senior officer has done nothing to set up the transaction. But, if he does nothing to stop it because the organization will benefit from the lower price, the organization would be responsible.

As an intuitive sentiment, it makes sense that managers ought not to condone illegal conduct of their employees, and if they do, the corporation ought to be responsible. Yet the requirement to take remedial action, and the attachment of criminal liability for the omission to do so, is anomalous for a subjective fault offence. The result is that the corporation may be punished for a subjective fault offence in large part because its senior officer, knowing that a representative of the corporation is or is about to become a party to an offence, did not take all reasonable steps to prevent the offence.

In the case of *Wholesale Travel* [[1991] 3 S.C.R. 154], the court upheld the provision placing the legal onus on the defendant to show that he took all reasonable precautions and exercised due diligence in the context of a regulatory offence. Bill C-45 does not shift the legal onus: the prosecution would still have to prove that the accused did not take all reasonable measures. A parallel can be drawn to recent legislation in the area of sexual assault requiring the accused to take reasonable steps, in the circumstances known to the accused at the time, to ascertain that the complainant was consenting. This legislation has been upheld as meeting minimum constitutional standards in the context that sexual assault is an offence requiring proof of subjective *mens rea*. The courts have pointed out in this context that the accused is not under an obligation to determine all relevant circumstances and is not required to have taken all reasonable steps. [See *R. v. Darrach* (1998), 122 C.C.C. (3d) 225, aff'd. on other grounds [2000] 2 S.C.R. 443.] The issue is what the accused actually knew, not what he or she ought to have known. In contrast, s. 22.2(c) requires senior officers not only to stop themselves, but also to take all reasonable measures to actively stop someone else from acting. The assumption seems to be that senior officers, including managers, will have enough legal knowledge and business acumen to recognize that conduct of lower level officials is criminal. There is a further assumption that they will have sufficient control over their employees, as well as contractors, to stop the conduct. The intent is to require senior officers and managers who know there is a problem in a mine or a problem with fraudulent records to do all that can reasonably be expected to stop the commission of offences. This is a laudable requirement, but one that has traditionally been placed on those charged with regulatory offences and required to prove that they exercised due diligence to prevent the commission of the prohibited act. In contrast, the "all reasonable steps" requirement of s. 22.2(c) applies to a wide range of fault offences, ranging from murder to fraud. In the end, the corporation could be convicted of the most serious offences because of a senior officer's failure to take all reasonable steps to stop or prevent an offence that he or she knows is being committed.

With respect to offences recognized by the courts to have sufficient stigma to require proof of subjective fault in relation to all elements of the prohibited act, there are parts of s. 22.2(b) and (c) that may violate ss. 7 and 11(d) of the Charter. As discussed, a corporation may not have standing to raise a s. 7 challenge given that s. 22.2 only applies to corporations. With respect to s. 11(d) of the Charter it could, however, be argued that the legislative substitution of an "all reasonable steps" requirement for subjective fault in relation to the commission of the prohibited act may violate the presumption of innocence. At the same time, the Crown can argue that the corporation will only be convicted of a subjective fault offence if one of its senior officers has subjective and guilty knowledge that a representative of the organization is or is about to be a party to the offence.

How will courts determine what senior officers should do to satisfy the new and onerous "all reasonable steps" requirement in s. 22.2(c)? Here the blurring of lines between regulatory offences and criminal offences of subjective fault becomes obvious. Courts will look to industry standards, risk management techniques and other factors that have traditionally been relevant to the determination of the due diligence defence. Many of the same factors and evidence of corporate conduct that determines the due diligence defence now will be relevant when the corporation is charged with a serious criminal offence of subjective fault.

### (5) Negligence Offences

Section 22.1 of the *Criminal Code* holds organizations liable for crimes of negligence where the acts and omissions of its representatives, taken as a whole, constitute an offence and the responsible senior officer or manager departs "markedly from the standard of care that, in the circumstances, could reasonably be expected to prevent a representative of the organization from being a party to the offence." As with s. 22.2, this new section brings issues normally associated with the due diligence defence for regulatory offences, into the centre of the determination of the criminal liability of a corporation or other organization. The intent of s. 22.2 to extend corporate criminal liability is clear from the government's explanation of the section:

> With respect to the physical element of the crime, Bill C-45 (proposed s. 22.1 of the *Criminal Code*) provides that an organization is responsible for the negligent acts or omissions of its representative. The Bill provides that the conduct of two or more

representatives can be combined to constitute the offence. It is not therefore necessary that a single representative commit the entire act.

For example, in a factory, an employee who turned off three separate safety systems would probably be prosecuted for causing death by criminal negligence if employees were killed as a result of an accident that the safety systems would have prevented. The employee acted negligently. On the other hand, if three employees each turned off one of the safety systems each thinking that it was not a problem because the other two systems would still be in place, they would probably not be subject to criminal prosecution because each one alone might not have shown reckless disregard for the lives of other employees. However, the fact that the individual employees might escape prosecution should not mean that their employer necessarily would not be prosecuted. After all, the organization, through its three employees, turned off the three systems.

The legislation implements the cumulative concept by permitting collective action to ground corporate liability provided that senior officers have departed markedly from the standards reasonably expected to police and prevent such action. Section 22.1 provides:

> 22.1 In respect of an offence that requires the prosecution to prove negligence, an organization is a party to the offence if:
>
> (a) acting within the scope of their authority
>
>   (i) one of its representatives is a party to the offence, or
>
>   (ii) two or more of its representatives engage in conduct, whether by act or omission, such that, if it had been the conduct of only one representative, that representative would have been a party to the offence; and
>
> (b) the senior officer who is responsible for the aspect of the organization's activities that is relevant to the offence departs—or the senior officers, collectively, depart—markedly from the standard of care that, in the circumstances, could reasonably be expected to prevent a representative of the organization from being a party to the offence.

As a first point, the cumulative or collective concept in s. 22.1(a)(ii) makes good sense in the context of negligence offences. It should not make a difference to corporate criminal liability if the conduct of one, two or ten representatives of the corporation must combine to produce the prohibited act. The heart of these offences relates to a failure of the organization as a whole to properly implement risk management systems to prevent negligence. The new definition recognizes the organic structure of modern corporations.

Some crimes, such as unlawful act manslaughter, have been interpreted by the Supreme Court of Canada as having stigma sufficient only to require the Crown to prove a marked departure from the norm. This standard nonetheless exceeds mere notions of negligence as found in the regulatory defence of due diligence. In fact, for true crimes, regardless of language employed in the Code that is suggestive of the standard of *mere* negligence, the application of the Charter forces these offences to be "read up" to require a marked departure from the norm. [See *R. v. Creighton*, [1993] 3 S.C.R. 3.]

The wording that will be the subject of heated litigation is "could reasonably be expected to prevent." This wording could blur the line between the standard of due diligence in regulatory offences and the new criminal offences. The only difference would be the onus of proof. The Crown would still have the legal onus in the criminal case of proving beyond a reasonable doubt that the corporation departed from reasonable diligence. The practical result would likely be an evidentiary onus on the corporate accused to show that the violation could not have been reasonably prevented in light of industry standards.

In determining what could reasonably be expected to prevent the offence, there is a risk that hindsight bias will be a factor. In other words, what might have been done to prevent the commission of the offence may only emerge with the clarity of hindsight after the commission of the offence. At the same time, a finding that the senior officer did not do all that could reasonably have been expected to have prevented the offence will not be enough for liability under s. 22.1. The Crown will still have to prove beyond a reasonable doubt that the senior officer was criminally negligent in the form of a marked departure from the standard of care that could reasonably have been expected to have prevented the crime. Unlike a regulatory prosecution, the Crown will have to prove both the negligence fault elements of marked departure and breach of a reasonable standard of care beyond a reasonable doubt. Although there is a convergence, especially in evidential and practical terms, between criminal liability under s. 22.1 and regulatory liability, some legal distinctions remain.

## ADDITIONAL READING

(Note that the readings in the following list apply to the old common law and not the new statutory provisions of ss. 22.1 and 22.2 in the *Criminal Code*.)

- K. Roach, *Criminal Law*, 3rd ed. (Toronto: Irwin Law: 2004), chapter 5;
- A. Mewett and M. Manning, *Criminal Law*, 3rd ed. (Toronto: Butterworths, 1994), at 253-66;
- D. Stuart, *Canadian Criminal Law*, 4th ed. (Toronto: Carswell, 2001), at 629-46;
- E. Colvin, *Principles of Criminal Law*, 2nd ed. (Toronto: Carswell, 1991), at 65-68;
- D. Stuart, "Punishing Corporate Criminals with Restraint" (1995), 6 *Criminal Law Forum* 219;
- D. Hanna, "Corporate Criminal Law" (1988-89), 31 *Crim. L.Q.* 452;
- C. Wells, "Corporate Manslaughter: A Cultural and Legal Form" (1995), 6 *Criminal Law Forum* 45;
- "Note, Developments in the Law—Corporate Crime: Regulating Corporate Behavior Through Criminal Sanctions" (1979), 92 *Harv. L. Rev.* 1227;
- V.S. Khanna, "Corporate Criminal Liability: What Purpose Does It Serve?" (1996), 109 *Harv. L. Rev.* 1477;
- C. Tollefson, "Corporate Constitutional Rights and the Supreme Court of Canada" (1993), 19 *Queens L.J.* 309.

# CHAPTER ELEVEN

# Ignorance of the Law

Section 19 of the *Criminal Code* provides: "Ignorance of the law by a person who commits an offence is not an excuse for committing that offence." This can be a harsh rule. Recall as discussed in chapter 1, the courts have been reluctant to hold that laws violate s. 7 of the Charter because of excessive vagueness.

Although the principle that ignorance (or mistake) of law is not an excuse appears simple and absolute, there are a number of complications. The first section of this chapter examines the relevance of the accused's belief about the legality of his or her actions to proof of the particular fault elements for particular offences. The next section examines the related and sometimes illusive distinction between the accused's mistaken belief about the facts—a factor that is relevant to the proof of fault—and the accused's mistaken belief about the law—a factor that under s. 19 of the Code is not an excuse for committing the offence. The next section examines a developing exception to the ignorance of the law is not an excuse principle—namely, the defence of officially induced error. The next section examines the possible direct and indirect effects of the Charter on s. 19, while the final section looks at possible statutory reforms of s. 19.

## I. MISTAKEN BELIEFS ABOUT THE LAW AND PARTICULAR FAULT ELEMENTS

### R. v. Howson
Ontario Court of Appeal
[1966] 3 C.C.C. 348

[An employee of a towing service was charged with theft of a car when he refused to give a towed car back to its owner until the owner paid certain expenses. He was convicted at trial and appealed.]

PORTER C.J.O. (with whom Evans J.A. concurred): ... The relevant sections of the *Criminal Code* [s. 269 is now s. 322] read as follows:

> 269(1) Every one commits theft who fraudulently and without colour of right takes, or fraudulently and without colour of right converts to his use or to the use of another person, anything whether animate or inanimate, with intent,

> (a)  to deprive, temporarily or absolutely, the owner of it or a person who has a
> special property or interest in it, of the thing or of his property or interest in it …
>
> (3)  A taking or conversion of anything may be fraudulent notwithstanding that it is
> effected without secrecy or attempt at concealment.
>
> (4)  For the purposes of this Act the question whether anything that is converted is
> taken for the purpose of conversion, or whether it is, at the time it is converted, in the
> lawful possession of the person who converts it is not material.

In my view the word "right" should be construed broadly. The use of the word cannot be said to exclude a legal right. The word is in its ordinary sense charged with legal implications. I do not think that s. 19 affects s. 269. Section 19 only applies when there is an offence. There is no offence if there is colour of right. If upon all the evidence it may fairly be inferred that the accused acted under a genuine misconception of fact or law, there would be no offence of theft committed. The trial tribunal must satisfy itself that the accused has acted upon an honest, but mistaken belief that the right is based upon either fact or law, or mixed fact and law.

The learned trial Judge held that the removal of the vehicle to Merton St. was not an unreasonable thing to do. Under the circumstances, I would agree with this finding. The real question here is whether the accused had, under the circumstances, a colour of right sufficient to justify his refusal to release the vehicle. If not, upon the facts of this case, he would be guilty of theft.

The accused was an employee of his brother, Walter Howson, who was the owner of the towing company. The evidence indicates that the accused acted upon instructions from his brother. He stated that he believed he had a right to retain the car until the towing charges were paid. He produced a letter from the building superintendent which ostensibly gave him the right to retain the car. Because the accused was asked to give up the car and refused to do so without payment, the Magistrate said that he was wrongfully withholding the car, the company having no lien upon it. He thereupon convicted the accused. However, the Magistrate then proceeded to make certain comments. He said that the accused was not trying to steal a car or intending to steal one. He then said that the type of business was not one that he would encourage.

I think it is clear from this evidence that the Magistrate misdirected himself by failing to consider the question of colour of right. From what he said after the conviction, it was obvious that he did not believe that the accused was trying or intending to steal the car. Under these circumstances he should, I think, have acquitted the accused. There were other points raised in the argument, but since, upon the grounds stated, I would acquit, I do not think it necessary to deal with them.

I would, therefore, allow the appeal, quash the conviction, and direct that a verdict of acquittal be entered.

[For similar and other reasons Laskin J.A. also allowed the appeal.]

*Appeal allowed; conviction quashed.*

---

In *R. v. Docherty* (1989), 51 C.C.C. (3d) 1 (S.C.C.) the accused was charged with wilfully failing to comply with a probation order in the following circumstances. The accused was charged with and pleaded guilty to the offence of having care or control of a motor vehicle when his blood alcohol level exceeded 80 mg of alcohol in 100 ml of blood. At the time of the commission of the offence, the accused was bound by a probation order that required that he "keep the peace and be of good behaviour." It was the allegation of the Crown that the commission of the offence constituted the offence of wilful breach of a probation order. The accused testified that at the time he committed the offence of "over 80" he was unaware that he was breaking the law. The accused had been found in a parked vehicle in an intoxicated state and he testified that he did not think he was breaking the law because the car could not be started. The trial judge accepted the evidence of the accused and acquitted him of the offence. An appeal by the Crown by way of stated case to the Newfoundland Court of Appeal was dismissed as was the Crown's further appeal to the Supreme Court of Canada. Wilson J. stated for the Court:

> I believe, in other words, [that the offence of wilful breach of a probation order] constitutes an exception to the general rule expressed in s. 19 in a case where the commission of a criminal offence is relied on as the *actus reus* under the section. An accused cannot have wilfully breached his probation order through the commission of a criminal offence unless he knew that what he did constituted a criminal offence. However, the conviction is evidence of the *mens rea* only to the extent that wilfulness can be inferred from the *actus reus* as indicated above. Such *mens rea* must be proved and s. 19 of the *Code* does not preclude the respondent from relying on his honest belief that he was not doing anything wrong to negate its presence. Where knowledge is itself a component of the requisite *mens rea*, the absence of knowledge provides a good defence.
>
> I would dismiss the appeal.

Note that subsequent to this case, Parliament amended the offence of breach of a probation order to delete the requirement that the breach be wilful. See s. 733.1 of the *Criminal Code*. Is *Docherty* still good law?

## II. MISTAKE OF FACT AND MISTAKE OF LAW

In *R. v. Prue and Baril* (1979), 46 C.C.C. (2d) 257 the majority of the Supreme Court of Canada held that an accused's lack of knowledge that his licence had been automatically suspended under provincial law after a driving offence was a "question of fact" and not of law when the accused was charged under s. 238 with driving while his licence was suspended (see now s. 259(4)). Laskin C.J. (with whom Spence, Dickson, and Estey JJ. concurred) stated:

> So far as the operation of s. 238(3) is concerned, the existence of a suspension from driving is a question of fact underlying the invocation of that provision, and so too is proof that an accused charged thereunder drove while his licence to do so was under suspension. ... I do not see how this position is affected by whether the provincial legislation operates to make a suspension automatic or whether it arises only upon some notice or other action to be taken

thereunder. For the purpose of the *Criminal Code*, whether there has been an effective suspension is simply a question of fact.

Ritchie J. (with whom Pigeon J. concurred), dissenting, stated:

> ... These cases turn on the finding that the failure to give notice or to take such other administrative step as is required is a question of fact and that the accused's failure to know of the suspension is not a mistake of law.
>
> In the present case the respondent's lack of knowledge of the suspension of their licences was not occasioned by any mistake of fact but rather by ignorance of the law attendant upon failure to be aware of the automatic suspension for which provision is made in s. 86D of the *Motor-vehicle Act*. ...
>
> I am satisfied that the mistake made by the accused in the present cases is nothing more than a mistake as to the legal consequences of a conviction under s. 236 of the *Criminal Code* involving as they do the automatic suspension of the operator's licence under s. 86D of the *Motor-Vehicle Act*.

In *R. v. MacDougall* (1982), 1 C.C.C. (3d) 65 (S.C.C.), the accused was charged with driving a motor vehicle while his licence to do so was cancelled contrary to s. 258(2) of the *Motor Vehicle Act*, R.S.N.S. 1967, c. 191, in the following circumstances. Following his conviction of the offence contrary to s. 233(2) of the *Criminal Code*, the accused was sent an "Order of Revocation of Licence" by the registrar of motor vehicles but when he appealed this conviction he was sent a "Notice of Reinstatement" by the registrar. Subsequently, the accused's appeal was dismissed and he was so informed by his lawyer. Some time later, the registrar sent out another "Order of Revocation of Licence," which, however, the accused did not receive until after he was charged with the offence contrary to s. 258(2). The accused testified that he believed he could drive until he was notified by the registrar that his licence had been revoked and this evidence was accepted by the trial judge. Section 250(3) of the *Motor Vehicle Act* provides that where an appeal is dismissed the driver's licence "shall be thereupon and hereby revoked and shall remain revoked." The accused was acquitted at trial and an appeal by the Crown to the county court was dismissed as was a further appeal by the Crown to the Appeal Division of the Supreme Court of Nova Scotia.

Ritchie J. gave the unanimous judgment of the seven members of the Supreme Court of Canada (which included Laskin C.J.):

> His Honour Judge Sullivan and the majority of the Court of Appeal affirmed these findings and held that they disclosed a defence to the charge here laid on the ground that they disclosed a mistake of fact on the part of the accused within the meaning of *R. v. Sault Ste. Marie*, ... whereas I am unable to treat the respondent's mistake otherwise than as a mistake of law in relation to his right, because of s. 250(3), to drive after his appeal had been dismissed. This was a mistake of law which does not afford the respondent a defence having regard to s. 19 of the *Criminal Code* which provides that:
>
> > 19. Ignorance of the law by a person who commits an offence is not an excuse for committing that offence.

Before concluding, I should make mention of *R. v. Prue; R. v. Baril* (1979), 46 C.C.C. (2d) 257, 96 D.L.R. (3d) 577, [1979] 2 S.C.R. 547, in which the majority of the court held that for the purposes of the *Criminal Code*, whether there has been an effective suspension is simply a question of fact. The case arose under s. 238(3) of the *Criminal Code* and the majority decision, delivered by the Chief Justice at p. 260 C.C.C, p. 580 D.L.R., p. 552 S.C.R., makes it clear that distinction may be drawn between enforcement of a driving offence under the *Criminal Code* and one for the enforcement of a provincial enactment:

> In my opinion, the issue of ignorance of fact or ignorance of law is properly applicable to the enforcement of the provincial enactment under which the suspension from driving is made and not to the enforcement of s. 238(3) of the *Criminal Code*.

> I am of the opinion that nothing in the foregoing reasons runs counter to the decision of the court in *Prue* and *Baril*.

> For all these reasons I would allow this appeal and order a new trial.

Note that the majority of the Supreme Court in *R. v. Pontes* (1995), 100 C.C.C. (3d) 353 (see also chapters 6 and 11), disapproved of *MacDougall*, stressing that it was decided before the Charter. The distinction between a mistake of law and mistake of fact remains difficult to determine and will be discussed again in the chapter on sexual assault.

## III. THE EMERGING DEFENCE OF OFFICIALLY INDUCED ERROR

In *Molis v. The Queen* (1980), 55 C.C.C. (2d) 558 (S.C.C.), the accused was charged with trafficking in a restricted drug, M.D.M.A., contrary to the federal *Food and Drugs Act*. When the accused first began manufacturing the drug it was not restricted, but was added to the Act by a regulation, which was properly published in the *Canada Gazette*. At his trial, the accused argued that he did not know it was illegal to manufacture the drug and that he had exercised due diligence in ascertaining the state of the law. The trial judge refused to leave this defence to the jury and he was convicted. The Supreme Court of Canada upheld the trial judge's decision, stating, *per* Lamer J., that "the defence of due diligence that was referred to in *Sault Ste. Marie* is that of due diligence in the relation to the fulfilment of a duty imposed by law and not in relation to the ascertainment of the existence of a prohibition or its interpretation."

Should the court now decide a case like *Molis* differently under the Charter? Would it matter what precise steps Molis had taken to ascertain the state of the law? Whether he relied upon the his own reading of the law or the advice of a lawyer or the advice of an official responsible for administering the law?

Note that in *Forster v. The Queen* (1992), 70 C.C.C. (3d) 59 (S.C.C.), Lamer C.J.C. reaffirmed *Molis*, stating for the court:

> It is a principle of our criminal law that an honest but mistaken belief in respect of the legal consequences of one's deliberate actions does not furnish a defence to a criminal charge, even when the mistake cannot be attributed to the negligence of the accused: *R. v. Molis* (1980), 55 C.C.C. (2d) 558, 116 D.L.R. (3d) 291, [1980] 2 S.C.R. 356. This court recently

reaffirmed in *R. v. Docherty* (1989), 51 C.C.C. (3d) 1 at p. 15, [1989] 2 S.C.R. 941, 72 C.R. (3d) 1, the principle that knowledge that one's actions are contrary to the law is not a component of the *mens rea* for an offence, and consequently does not operate as a defence.

In *R. v. Cancoil Thermal Corporation and Parkinson* (1986), 27 C.C.C. (3d) 295 (Ont. C.A.), a safety inspector had examined, with apparent approval, a piece of new but unsafe machinery in a plant. The Ontario Court of Appeal permitted the defence of "officially induced error," Lacourcière J.A. stating for the court:

> An article by Professor P.G. Barton, "Officially Induced Error as a Criminal Defence: A Preliminary Look," 22 C.L.Q. 314 (1979-80), contains a helpful consideration of this defence.
>
> In *R. v. MacDougall* (1981), 60 C.C.C. (2d) 137 at p. 160, 46 N.S.R. (2d) 47, 10 M.V.R. 236, the Nova Scotia Court of Appeal, *per* Macdonald J.A., recognized the defence in the following words:
>
>> The defence of officially induced error has not been sanctioned, to my knowledge, by any appellate Court in this country. The law, however, is ever-changing and ideally adapts to meet the changing mores and needs of society. In this day of intense involvement in a complex society by all levels of Government with a corresponding reliance by people on officials of such Government, there is, in my opinion, a place and need for the defence of officially induced error, at least so long as a mistake of law, regardless how reasonable, cannot be raised as a defence to a criminal charge.
>
> On further appeal to the Supreme Court of Canada, Ritchie J. appeared to give approval to the defence [1 C.C.C. (3d) 65 at p. 71, 142 D.L.R. (3d) 216, [1982] 2 S.C.R. 605]:
>
>> It is not difficult to envisage a situation in which an offence could be committed under mistake of law arising because of, and therefore induced by, "officially in-duced error" and if there was evidence in the present case to support such a situation existing it might well be an appropriate vehicle for applying the reasoning adopted by Mr. Justice Macdonald. In the present case, however, there is no evidence that the accused was misled by an error on the part of the registrar.
>
> The defence of "officially induced error" is available as a defence to an alleged violation of a regulatory statute where an accused has reasonably relied upon the erroneous legal opinion or advice of an official who is responsible for the administration or enforcement of the particular law. In order for the accused to successfully raise this defence, he must show that he relied on the erroneous legal opinion of the official and that his reliance was reasonable. The reasonableness will depend upon several factors including the efforts he made to ascertain the proper law, the complexity or obscurity of the law, the position of the official who gave the advice, and the clarity, definitiveness and reasonableness of the advice given.
>
> I agree with the following statement made by Professor Barton in the article referred to *op. cit.* at p. 331:

Where the advice is given by an official who has the job of administering the particular statute, and where the actor relies on this advice and commits what is in fact an offence, even if the agency cannot be estopped does it follow that the actor should not be excused? To do so is not to condone an illegality or say that the agency is estopped into a position of illegality, but to recognize that the advice was illegal but excuse the actor because he acted reasonably and does not deserve punishment.

In the present case, it will be for the trier of fact to decide whether the accused has proved, by a preponderance of evidence, that he was misled by the inspector into thinking that the removal of the manufacturer's guard would not be in contravention of the law. The record makes it clear that the inspector was an official involved in the administration of the relevant law, presumably familiar with the Act and regulations and having the expertise to determine whether a machine was equipped with the prescribed safety devices. Ordinarily, mistake of law cannot be successfully raised as a defence to a criminal or *quasi*-criminal charge or regulatory offence, but an officially induced error of law may, in some circumstances, constitute a valid defence. This will, of course, depend on whether the opinion of the official was reasonable in the circumstances and whether it was reasonable for the accused to follow it.

**R. v. Jorgensen**
Supreme Court of Canada
[1995] 4 S.C.R. 55

LAMER C.J.C.:

[1]  This appeal from a conviction under s. 163(2) of the *Criminal Code*, R.S.C. 1985, c. C-46, raises two issues for our consideration because of the wording of the section: (i) did the accused "knowingly" sell obscene material? and (ii) did he do so "without lawful justification or excuse"? Regarding the first issue, the question of the requisite *mens rea* for this offence, I agree with the reasons of my colleague Justice Sopinka [La Forest, L'Heureux-Dubé, Gonthier, Cory, McLachlin, Iacobucci, and Major JJ. concurring]. In particular, I concur in his conclusion that the law requires the Crown to prove that an accused retailer knew of the specific acts or set of facts which led the court to the conclusion that the material in question is obscene. The Crown is not, of course, required to prove that the accused knew the material was obscene in law, nor is the Crown required to prove that an accused actually viewed the obscene material. As my colleague has pointed out, there are other ways to acquire knowledge of the obscene character of a film. In addition, I concur in Justice Sopinka's conclusion that approval of a film by the Ontario Film Review Board ("OFRB") cannot negative the *mens rea* of this offence. Accordingly, I concur in Justice Sopinka's disposition of the appeal; the accused are entitled to be acquitted.

[2]  On the second issue raised by this appeal, the question of whether the accused acted without lawful justification or excuse, I disagree with Justice Sopinka's conclusion. In my view, the circumstances of this case permit the accused to be excused from conviction on the basis of an officially induced error of law by virtue of

the OFRB's approval of the films in question. While I do not believe film board approval negatives *mens rea* or justifies the accused's criminal actions, I believe that reasonable reliance on this type of official advice is sufficient basis for a judicial stay of proceedings to be entered. Requiring that a stay be entered only in the clearest of officially induced error of law cases does not offend the maxim that ignorance of the law does not excuse. Rather, it provides an exception from this provision, in line with the existing exceptions, which ensures that the morally blameless are not made criminally responsible for their actions. ...

## II. Analysis

### A. Ignorance of the Law Does Not Excuse

[4] While mistakes of fact relevant to the commission of a criminal offence excuse an accused from criminal responsibility, mistakes regarding the law do not. There is no significant difference between a mistake of law and ignorance of the law: see *R. v. Molis* (1980), 55 C.C.C. (2d) 558, 116 D.L.R. (3d) 291, [1980] 2 S.C.R. 356. The common law rule that ignorance of the law does not excuse the commission of a criminal offence is codified in s. 19 of the *Criminal Code*:

> 19. Ignorance of the law by a person who commits an offence is not an excuse for committing that offence.

This principle is a significant barrier to the appellants here because the question of whether or not a film is obscene is a question of law, specifically a question of the interpretation and application of the definition of obscenity contained in s. 163(8) of the *Criminal Code*.

[5] Don Stuart identifies four aspects of the rationale for the rule against accepting ignorance of the law as an excuse:

> 1. Allowing a defence of ignorance of the law would involve the courts in insuperable evidential problems.
> 2. It would encourage ignorance where knowledge is socially desirable.
> 3. Otherwise every person would be a law unto himself, infringing the principle of legality and contradicting the moral principles underlying the law.
> 4. Ignorance of the law is blameworthy in itself.

(*Canadian Criminal Law: A Treatise*, 3rd ed. (Scarborough, Ont.: Carswell, 1995), at pp. 295-8.) While Stuart finds the rule against ignorance of the law crude, and these principles unconvincing in the present era, this maxim is an orienting principle of our criminal law which should not be lightly disturbed. I have concluded that certain types of officially induced errors of law should be permitted to excuse an individual from criminal sanction for his actions, in part because I find that this does not infringe any of the four rationales for the ignorance of the law rule set out above.

[6] Despite the importance of this rule, some exceptions to it are already well established in our law. An accused is excused when the law she was charged under was impossible to gain knowledge of because it had not been published. In addition, a certain number of our *Criminal Code* offences provide an excuse for an accused

who acted with colour of right. The existence of these exceptions demonstrates that the *ignorantia juris* rule is not to be applied when it would render a conviction manifestly unjust. ...

[22] [Some commentators] have interpreted this court's decision in *Molis, supra,* as foreclosing the opportunity for developing an officially induced error of law defence. In light of these interpretations, I will clarify the extent of the decision in *Molis.* In that case, writing for a unanimous court, I asserted that no defence of ignorance of a regulation exists (at p. 562 C.C.C., ), and I concluded (at p. 564 C.C.C.):

> ... the defence of due diligence that was referred to in *Sault Ste. Marie* is that of due diligence in relation to the fulfilment of a duty imposed by law and not in relation to the ascertainment of the existence of a prohibition or its interpretation.

As the Ontario Court of Appeal in *Cancoil Thermal* noted, the defence of due diligence is separate from officially induced error. While due diligence in ascertaining the law does not excuse, reasonable reliance on official advice which is erroneous will excuse an accused but will not, in my view, negative culpability. There are two important distinctions between these related provisions. First, due diligence, in appropriate circumstances, is a full defence. If successfully raised, the elements of the offence are not completed. Officially induced error, on the other hand, does not negative culpability. Rather it functions like entrapment, as an excuse for an accused whom the Crown has proven to have committed an offence. Second, diligence may be necessary to obtain the advice which grounds an officially induced error. This is so because an accused who seeks to rely on this excuse must have weighed the potential illegality of her actions and made reasonable inquiries. This standard, however, does not convert officially induced error into due diligence. ...

[24] Several themes run through the Canadian jurisprudence to date on this defence and raise issues which must be determined to outline the scope of the defence. Most of the cases to date have dealt with regulatory offences only, raising the question of when this defence is applicable. A second group of questions revolves around who is an official and what constitutes "official advice." Finally, officially induced error has sometimes functioned as a full defence, a development which should be discouraged. I turn next to these issues.

## C. Officially Induced Error of Law

[25] Officially induced error of law exists as an exception to the rule that ignorance of the law does not excuse. As several of the cases where this rule has been discussed note, the complexity of contemporary regulation makes the assumption that a responsible citizen will have a comprehensive knowledge of the law unreasonable. This complexity, however, does not justify rejecting a rule which encourages a responsible citizenry, encourages government to publicize enactments, and is an essential foundation to the rule of law. Rather, extensive regulation is one motive for creating a limited exception to the rule that *ignorantia juris neminem excusat.*

[26] As complexity of regulation is linked to the justification for this excuse, it is predictable that it will arise most often in the realm of regulatory offences. None the

less, this excuse is equally valid for "true crimes" with a full *mens rea* component. As
the involvement of the state in our day-to-day lives expands, and the number of officials from whom advice can potentially be sought increases, the chance that an official may give advice about an enactment which would not be classified as "regulatory" multiplies. Officially induced error is distinct from a defence of due diligence,
and there is no reason to confine it to the regulatory offence context, though it is
obvious that for certain crimes, such as those involving moral turpitude, the chances
of success of such an excuse will be nearly nil.

[27]  Furthermore, although the section of the Criminal Code under which the appellants here were charged contains the phrase "without lawful justification or excuse," there is no particular link between those words and officially induced error of
law. Where an accused can raise this argument on the evidence presented, the trial
judge must assess whether the excuse is made out in law, regardless of the wording of
the offence.

[28]  The first step in raising an officially induced error of law argument will be to
determine that the error was in fact one of law or of mixed law and fact. Of course, if
the error is purely one of fact, this argument will be unnecessary. Unlike Professor
Barton, I do not agree that officially induced error should be used to eradicate the
distinction between mistakes of fact and mistakes of law. This distinction is important for all the reasons that I believe the principle that ignorance of the law does not
excuse must stand firm. Distinguishing between mistakes of fact and those of law
remains conceptually important. Mistakes of law will only be exculpatory in narrowly defined circumstances.

[29]  Once it is determined that the error was one of law, the next step is to demonstrate that the accused considered the legal consequences of her actions. By requiring
that an accused must have considered whether her conduct might be illegal and sought
advice as a consequence, we ensure that the incentive for a responsible and informed
citizenry is not undermined. It is insufficient for an accused who wishes to benefit
from this excuse to simply have assumed that her conduct was permissible.

[30]  The next step in arguing for this excuse will be to demonstrate that the advice obtained came from an appropriate official. One primary objective of this doctrine is to prevent the obvious injustice … [of] the state approving conduct with one
hand and seeking to bring criminal sanction for that conduct with the other. In general, therefore, government officials who are involved in the administration of the
law in question will be considered appropriate officials. I do not wish to establish a
closed list of officials whose erroneous advice may be considered exculpatory. The
measure proposed by O'Hearn Co. Ct. J. is persuasive. That is, the official must be
one whom a reasonable individual in the position of the accused would normally consider responsible for advice about the particular law in question. Therefore, the Motor
Vehicle Registrar will be an appropriate person to give advice about driving offences,
both federal and provincial. The determination of whether the official was an appropriate one to seek advice from is to be determined in the circumstances of each case.

[31]  My colleague Sopinka J. argues that, in this case, allowing OFRB approval
to constitute an excuse is an impermissible delegation of power from one level of

government to another. In my view, this argument does not bar officially induced error from constituting an excuse which is considered after culpability has been proven. There is no issue of the action of a provincial board precluding criminal prosecutions. Indeed, we must recall that it is the provincial Attorney General who makes the decision to prosecute offences, even when the offence charged is in the *Criminal Code*. The advice of officials of any level of government may induce an error of law and trigger this provision provided that a reasonable person would consider that particular government organ to be responsible for the law in question. The determination relies on common sense rather than constitutional permutations.

[32] Several other types of advice have been considered in the cases dealing with this excuse, for example advice from private lawyers and reliance on judicial pronouncements. As these examples are beyond the scope of this case, I make no comment at this time on whether these types of advice may provide the basis for officially induced error of law.

[33] Once an accused has established that he sought advice from an appropriate official, he must demonstrate that the advice was reasonable in the circumstances. In most instances, this criterion will not be difficult to meet. As an individual relying on advice has less knowledge of the law than the official in question, the individual must not be required to assess reasonableness at a high threshold. It is sufficient, therefore, to say that if an appropriate official is consulted, the advice obtained will be presumed to be reasonable unless it appears on its face to be utterly unreasonable.

[34] The advice obtained must also have been erroneous. This fact, however, does not need to be demonstrated by the accused. In proving the elements of the offence, the Crown will have already established what the correct law is, from which the existence of error can be deduced. None the less, it is important to note that when no erroneous advice has been given, as in MacDougall, supra, this excuse cannot operate.

[35] Finally, to benefit from this excuse, the accused must demonstrate reliance on the official advice. This can be shown, for example, by proving that the advice was obtained before the actions in question were commenced and by showing that the questions posed to the official were specifically tailored to the accused's situation.

[36] In summary, officially induced error of law functions as an excuse rather than a full defence. It can only be raised after the Crown has proven all elements of the offence. In order for an accused to rely on this excuse, she must show, after establishing she made an error of law, that she considered her legal position, consulted an appropriate official, obtained reasonable advice and relied on that advice in her actions. Accordingly, none of the four justifications for the rule that ignorance of the law does not excuse which Stuart outlined is undermined by this defence. There is no evidentiary problem. The accused, who is the only one capable of bringing this evidence, is solely responsible for it. Ignorance of the law is not encouraged because informing oneself about the law is a necessary element of the excuse. Each person is not a law unto himself because this excuse does not affect culpability. Ignorance of the law remains blameworthy in and of itself. In these specific instances, however, the blame is, in a sense, shared with the state official who gave the erroneous advice.

## D. Procedural Considerations

[37]  As this excuse does not affect a determination of culpability, it is procedurally similar to entrapment. Both function as excuses rather than justifications in that they concede the wrongfulness of the action but assert that under the circumstances it should not be attributed to the actor: see *R. v. Mack* (1988), 44 C.C.C. (3d) 513 at pp. 543-4 [see chapter 3]. As in the case of entrapment, the accused has done nothing to entitle him to an acquittal, but the state has done something which disentitles it to a conviction (*Mack*, at p. 567). Like entrapment, the successful application of an officially induced error of law argument will lead to a judicial stay of proceedings rather than an acquittal. Consequently, as a stay can only be entered in the clearest of cases, an officially induced error of law argument will only be successful in the clearest of cases.

[38]  The question of whether officially induced error constitutes an excuse in law is a question of law or of mixed law and fact. While a jury may determine whether the accused is culpable, and hence whether this argument is necessary, it is for a judge to determine whether the precise conditions for this legal excuse are made out. Only the trial judge is in a position to determine if a stay should be entered. The elements of the officially induced error excuse are to be proven on a balance of probabilities by the accused.

## III. Application to This Case

[41]  The difficult issue in this case is whether the OFRB is an appropriate official body to consult when seeking a determination about whether certain films are legally obscene, that is, whether they infringe community standards of tolerance. ... [T]he OFRB is charged with determining which films may be shown in Ontario and with classifying those films. The Act also provides for an appeal of the board's decision first to a differently constituted panel of the board and then to the Divisional Court. ... While clearly the OFRB is not legally responsible for deciding whether a film infringes the *Criminal Code* provisions, it could presumably itself attract criminal responsibility for approving for distribution a criminally obscene film.

[42]  Most importantly, in my view, the OFRB is understood by the general public as the body which approves films for play in Ontario. When a film is rejected as obscene by the OFRB, the headlines proclaim the film's obscenity. When someone refers to the "censor board," the OFRB is the board Ontarians think of. There is no other public body which would be the logical choice for someone to consult if seeking advice about whether a film can be legally retailed in Ontario. In these circumstances, therefore, I would conclude that had appellants had the requisite *mens rea* for this offence, they would be entitled to a judicial stay of proceedings as a result of officially induced error of law.

SOPINKA J. [stated for the rest of the court]: ...

[123]  ... I have not considered the issue of officially induced error of law as an excuse in this appeal because the matter was not raised either here or in the courts below. Nothing in these reasons should be taken as agreeing or disagreeing with the

reasons of the Chief Justice but I would prefer to address the issue of officially induced error in a case in which it is properly raised and argued.

## IV. MISTAKE OF LAW AND CONSTITUTIONAL CONSIDERATIONS

**Jones and Pamajewon v. The Queen**
Supreme Court of Canada
(1991), 66 C.C.C. (3d) 512

[The accused were charged with operating an unlawful bingo contrary to s. 206 of
the *Criminal Code*. The accused were members of an Indian band and were operating
a bingo on an Indian reserve. The accused had been informed by the police that the
*Criminal Code* prohibits lottery schemes unless operated under the auspices of a provincial licence. The accused, however, purported to renounce the jurisdiction of the
federal and provincial governments in relation to gaming on reserves and to issue
their own licences for operating bingos. The accused were convicted at trial and their
appeal to the Ontario Court of Appeal was dismissed. They appealed to the Supreme
Court of Canada.]

STEVENSON J. stated for the Court:  The appellants must be taken, for the purpose of
this appeal, to acknowledge that they were mistaken in their belief that the *Criminal
Code* did not apply to their activities on the reserve. They have not taken any proceedings to challenge the authority of Canada to enact laws applicable to those activities and have not made any such challenge here. In their factum, the appellants
not only disclaim asking for such a determination, they ask the court not to make
statements that may adversely affect legal issues concerning Indian self-government.
That request will be respected.

There are, in my view, two clear barriers to this alleged defence. First, it is not a
defence to this crime, secondly, any mistake is a mistake of law.

The appellants cited no authority for the proposition that colour of right is relevant
to any crime which does not embrace the concept within its definition. They cited *R.
v. Laybourn* (1987), 33 C.C.C. (3d) 385, 39 D.L.R. (4th) 641, [1987] 1 S.C.R. 782; *R.
v. DeMarco* (1973), 13 C.C.C. (2d) 369, 22 C.R.N.S. 258 (Ont. C.A.); *R. v. Howson*,
[1966] 3 C.C.C. 348, 55 D.L.R. (2d) 582, [1966] O.R. 63 (C.A.); *R. v. Johnson* (1904),
7 O.L.R. 525 (Div. Ct.). *Laybourn* is a case of mistake of fact as an issue in sexual
assault. In the other cases the offences, such as theft, required the absence of a colour
of right.

They argued that mistake of fact is a constitutionally mandated defence to criminal charges. Even assuming that proposition is correct, it can only apply to the *facts*
which constitute the offence. There is no suggestion of any mistake relating to those
facts here; the mistake is in believing that the law does not apply because it is inoperative on reserves.

Section 19 of the *Code* expresses the long-recognized principle that a mistake about the law is no defence to a charge of breaching it. No attack was made on the validity of that section. The argument here is that this legal mistake should be characterized as a mistake of fact and I find it impossible to characterize the mistaken belief put forward here as embracing any mistake of fact.

## R. v. Pontes
Supreme Court of Canada
(1995), 100 C.C.C. (3d) 353

[After *B.C. Motor Vehicle Act* discussed in chapter 6, the British Columbia legislature deleted s. 94(2) of the *Motor Vehicle Act*, which had provided that the offence of driving with a suspended licence was an absolute liability offence. As discussed in the extract in chapter 6, the majority of the court in this case held that the offence remained one of absolute liability. The focus in this extract is on the implications of the decision for the ignorance of the law is no excuse principle.]

CORY J. (Lamer C.J., Sopinka, Iacobucci, and Major JJ. concurring): ... Section 94(1)(a) still refers to s. 92 which, in turn, provides that a driver will "automatically and without notice" be prohibited from driving for a period of 12 months. ... Because the prohibition to drive in s. 92 is automatic and without notice, s. 94 effectively prevents an accused who is unaware of the prohibition from raising a defence of due diligence.

In determining whether either facet of the defence of due diligence is available in this case, it is important to remember the well-established principle, incorporated in s. 19 of the *Criminal Code*, R.S.C. 1985, c. C-46, that a mistake of law is no excuse. In other words, a mistake as to what the law is does not operate as a defence.

The application of this principle leads to the conclusion that an accused cannot put forward as a defence that he made diligent inquiries as to the legality of his actions or status. The submission of such a defence was specifically rejected in *R. v. Molis* (1980), 55 C.C.C. (2d) 558, 116 D.L.R. (3d) 291, [1980] 2 S.C.R. 356. In that case, the accused was charged with trafficking in a drug restricted under the *Food and Drugs Act*. The drug which the accused had begun manufacturing had been unrestricted but later became restricted. At trial, the accused testified that he had exercised due diligence to ascertain the state of the law. This defence was rejected. At p. 564 Lamer J. wrote:

> It is clear to me that we are dealing here with an offence that is not to be considered as one of absolute liability and, hence, a defence of due diligence is available to an accused. But I hasten to add that the defence of due diligence that was referred to in *Sault Ste. Marie* is that of due diligence in relation to the fulfilment of a duty imposed by law and not in relation to the ascertainment of the existence of a prohibition or its interpretation.

These principles must be kept in mind in the assessment of the Crown's contention that the decision of this court in *MacDougall, supra*, constitutes a complete answer to the characterization of the offence. In that case, following a conviction for failing to remain at the scene of an accident, the accused was prohibited from driving by the operation of s. 250(1) of the Nova Scotia *Motor Vehicle Act*. The accused subsequently drove while prohibited and was charged with that offence. At trial, he testified that he did not know of the prohibition. Ritchie J., on behalf of the court, held that the offence was one of strict liability, but that the defence of lack of knowledge of the prohibition was tantamount to a defence of ignorance of the law which, in light of the provision of s. 19 of the *Criminal Code*, could not provide a defence. ...

Two difficulties arise from the *MacDougall* decision. The first difficulty lies in its irreconcilability with the earlier decision of *R. v. Prue; R. v. Baril* (1979), 46 C.C.C. (2d) 257, 96 D.L.R. (3d) 577, [1979] 2 S.C.R. 547. The second lies in the fact that *MacDougall* was rendered prior to the Charter, and that the jurisprudence on the minimal fault requirement has evolved since then.

In *Prue, supra*, the accused were convicted of an offence under the *Criminal Code*. As a result, their licences were automatically suspended under the provisions of the B.C. *Motor Vehicle Act*. They nonetheless drove their vehicles and were charged, not for a violation of the provincial statute under which the suspension was made, but rather under s. 238 of the *Criminal Code*. ... Laskin C.J.C. stated that as a result of the inclusion of the offence in the *Criminal Code*, it was necessary to import *mens rea*. He then considered the submission of the Crown that ignorance of the suspension was ignorance of the law, not a mistake of fact, and therefore could not be put forward as a defence. He then stated at p. 260:

> The effect, if this is a correct appraisal, is to make s. 238(3) an offence of absolute liability where the provincial suspension of a driving licence is automatic under the provincial enactment ... but not if the provincial suspension does not take effect without a requirement of notice.

Laskin C.J.C. thus implied that an offence which was automatic and without notice constituted an absolute liability offence. However, he went on to find that ignorance of the suspension of a licence, in that case, was a mistake of fact.

With respect to the ignorance of the suspension, these reasons simply cannot be reconciled with *MacDougall, supra*. It cannot be that a mistake as to the law under the *Criminal Code* constitutes a mistake of fact, whereas a mistake as to the provisions of the provincial statute constitutes a mistake of law. ...

It must be remembered that the *MacDougall* decision was rendered prior to the Charter. It thus did not consider the constitutionally required minimal fault component outlined by this court in cases such as *Reference re: Section 94(2) of the Motor Vehicle Act, supra*, and *Vaillancourt, supra*. The defence of due diligence must be available to defend a strict liability offence. If that defence is removed, the offence can no longer be classified as one of strict liability. When, as a result of the wording of the section, the only possible defence an accused can put forward is his ignorance of the fact that his licence had been suspended by the provisions of the provincial statute, which constitutes a mistake of law and therefore is not available as a defence, the accused is effectively denied the defence of due diligence. In those circumstances, the offence ought to be characterized as one of absolute liability.

It seems to be clear that the defence of due diligence is not available to an accused charged under ss. 92 and 94 of the B.C. *Motor Vehicle Act*. There are a number of examples which can illustrate this situation. First, take the situation of an accused charged with failure to give a sample of breath. After trial he is found guilty, fined and his licence suspended for three months. Apparently, in British Columbia, he would be given no notice of the automatic suspension of one year provided by the B.C. *Motor Vehicle Act*. Yet, he would be liable to conviction despite his honest and reasonable belief as a lay person that the total sentence imposed by the court was a fine and a suspension of his licence for a period of three months. Certainly, to most people "a court" is a court wherever it may be located and the sentence of that court is what is binding upon them. Even if an accused asked the court to confirm that this was the total extent of his sentence, this would not amount to a defence of due diligence since his error was as to the provisions of the B.C. *Motor Vehicle Act*, and this constitutes an error of law.

Similarly, if an accused is charged and convicted of impaired driving and sentenced to six months' prohibition from driving, he would leave the courtroom believing that this sentence constituted the entire penalty. However, by virtue of s. 92 of the Act, he is also, without any notice to him, automatically prohibited from driving for a period of 12 months from the date of conviction. If he drives after six months have expired and is stopped by the police, he would be charged with "driving while prohibited," despite the fact that he honestly and reasonably believed that he was no longer prohibited from driving. He would not be able to put this forward as a defence since ignorance of the law cannot be invoked as a defence, even if he took steps at his original trial to confirm before the convicting judge that this was the total extent of his penalty. Quite simply, the statute effectively deprives the accused of the defence of due diligence.

*Significance of Notice*

The legislature could readily convert this offence to one of strict liability by permitting the defence of due diligence to be raised. If there was any concern that those accused of the offence would defend on the basis that they had no knowledge of its effect, a provision requiring that notice be given of its consequences could be added. Notice could be given in many ways. The following are a few examples.

Upon the issuance or a renewal of a licence, notice could be given that upon conviction of the listed enumerated offences, there will be an automatic suspension of the licence for a 12-month period. Alternatively, notice of the consequences could be given with the serving of the summons or charge for the underlying offence. In still another manner, the notice could be given as a matter of course upon conviction for the underlying offence, and would thus form part of the record of the court proceedings. There is something so fundamentally fair about the giving of notice that I find it commendable. It must be remembered that regulatory offences number in the tens of thousands. There are federal regulations and provincial regulations that will vary in their terms and provisions from coast to coast. Surely it is not asking too much that the accused be given some form of notice.

GONTHIER J. (with whom La Forest, L'Heureux-Dubé, and McLachlin JJ. concurred) (in dissent): I do not believe that the "principles of fundamental justice" under s. 7 of the Charter require that an accused who is charged with a regulatory offence be entitled to claim due diligence in relation to the existence of the relevant statutory prohibition or its interpretation—that is, to avail himself of the defence of ignorance of the law. The defence of due diligence does not need to be expanded to meet the exigencies of the Charter. Indeed, to do so would eviscerate the ignorance of the law rule and render many of our laws unenforceable. To date, our court has refused to find that ignorance of the law is an excuse for breaking the law. Nor have we ever held that ignorance of the law should be viewed differently in the regulatory and criminal contexts. I respectfully suggest we refrain from doing so henceforth.

I would add that if the defence of due diligence has been expanded in light of s. 7 of the Charter to comprehend a defence of ignorance of the law, then it also appears that this court's ruling in *Molis* (1980), 55 C.C.C. (2d) 558, has been overturned. As already indicated, in *Molis*, Lamer J. stated unambiguously that the defence of due diligence refers to "due diligence in relation to the fulfilment of a duty imposed by law and not in relation to the ascertainment of the existence of a prohibition or its interpretation" (p. 564). To my mind, *Molis* should remain good law and is indistinguishable from the case at bar. It is no more necessary, as a principle of "fundamental justice," to allow the respondent to avail himself of his ignorance of a prohibition from driving by virtue of provincial legislation of general application, than it was to allow the accused drug traffickers in *Molis* to avail themselves of their ignorance that 3-4 methylenedioxy-N-methylamphetamine had been added as a prohibited substance to Sch. H of the *Food and Drugs Act.* ...

It is evident, then, that I disagree with Cory J.'s conclusion that a defence of due diligence is not available in relation to the impugned offence. Cory J. comes to this conclusion because he finds that the only defence effectively available to an accused who has been charged with driving while under a statutory prohibition is his ignorance of the fact that his licence has been suspended by the provisions of a provincial statute; but since this is mistake or ignorance of the law, it is not an available excuse. Furthermore, Cory J. suggests two examples to illustrate his claim that a due diligence defence is unavailable. In both examples, he suggests that an accused who is prohibited under a court order from driving for any period less than 12 months for having committed one of the underlying offences may be misled into believing that he is entitled to drive after the expiry of that prohibition, since he has had no notice of the continuing automatic prohibition effective by virtue of ss. 92 and 94(1). He suggests that such a person would be liable to conviction "despite his honest and reasonable belief as a lay person that the total sentence imposed by the court was a fine and a suspension of his licence for a period of" less than 12 months (at para. 43).

I agree that Cory J.'s examples are within the realm of possibility, and also that there may be a sense in which they can be considered as giving rise to some unfairness. But if this is so, it is an unfairness which our legal system has long countenanced in refusing to allow ignorance of the law to serve as a valid excuse. As a matter of principle, it is no more unfair to convict the accused in this case than it was in *Molis*, *supra*, for the trafficking of a substance he honestly and reasonably believed was not prohibited, or to disallow the accused in *Forster*, *supra*, from relying on her letter of resignation to demonstrate that she lacked the intent for being absent without leave.

Of course, this is not to say that ignorance of the law cannot be successfully pleaded as a factor in mitigation of sentence (Clayton Ruby, *Sentencing*, 4th ed. (Toronto: Butterworths, 1994), at p. 196. In such a case, it may well be appropriate to sentence an offender to the minimum fine of $300 and to seven days' imprisonment under s. 92(1)(c) of the *Motor Vehicle Act*.

Finally, I note that the appellant raised the possibility that a driver whose licence is suspended and who is prohibited from driving by operation of law may also be able to avail himself of the defence of "officially induced error." This defence was not raised here and has yet to be formally recognized by this court, though it was referred to in obiter by Ritchie J. in *R. v. MacDougall, supra*. ... Assuming without deciding that such a defence would be available if an accused were misled by the Superintendent of Motor Vehicles or by some other official responsible for the administration of the *Motor Vehicle Act*, such a defence would not demonstrate absence of negligence in relation to the *actus reus* of driving while under a statutory prohibition, but rather would be an additional defence thereto, operating as an exception to the rule that ignorance of the law does not excuse. As a result, the potential availability of such a defence does not assist in the characterization of the impugned provisions as being of strict liability.

*Appeal dismissed.*

## V. STATUTORY REFORM

Law Reform Commission of Canada, Report 31 (1987), *Recodifying Criminal Law*, at 34-35, provides:

> 3(7) Mistake or Ignorance of Law. No one is liable for a crime committed by reason of mistake or ignorance of law:
>> (a) concerning private rights relevant to that crime; or
>> (b) reasonably resulting from
>>> (i) non-publication of the law in question,
>>> (ii) reliance on a decision of a court of appeal in the province having jurisdiction over the crime charged, or
>>> (iii) reliance on competent administrative authority.

*Comment*

Mistake of law in general is no defence. This is the position at common law, under section 19 of the *Criminal Code* and under clause 3(7) of this Code. It is up to the citizen to find out what the law is and comply with it.

On the other hand no one can fairly be punished for breaking a law which he has no reasonable chance of ascertaining. For this reason present law has created two exceptions to the general rule. Ignorance of law owing to non-publication of regulations is a defence. Mistake of law resulting from officially induced error may also be a defence.

Clause 3(7)(b) codifies these two exceptions, extending one of them and adding another. It extends the first exception to non-publication of any law. It adds an exception in the case of mistake resulting from reliance on the law as stated by the court of appeal in the province where the charge is tried. No one can reasonably be expected to be wiser than the highest court in his jurisdiction; rather he is entitled to assume the law is what that court says it is until the Supreme Court of Canada states otherwise.

In addition there are certain crimes, such as theft and fraud, where honest but erroneous belief in a claim of right negatives criminal liability. Insofar as such belief is based on error of law, mistake of law will operate as a defence. This is the position under present law and also under clause 3(7)(a) of this Code.

Clause 3(7)(b) then provides three exceptions to the general rule, but all three relate solely to mistakes *reasonably* resulting from the factors specified.

The June 1993 *Federal Proposals To Amend the General Principles of the Criminal Code* provides that s. 19 should be repealed and the following section be added to the *Criminal Code*:

34.(1) Neither ignorance of the law nor mistake of law is a defence to an offence unless

(a) the description of the offence provides a defence of claim of right or colour of right, or otherwise provides a defence of ignorance of the law or mistake of law, and the ignorance or mistake relates to that defence;

(b) the description of the offence includes an element that concerns a matter of private rights, and the ignorance or mistake relates to that matter of private rights; or

(c) the offence was committed under an officially induced mistake of law.

(2) For the purpose of paragraph (1)(b), ignorance or mistake relating to the existence or interpretation of an Act or of regulations made thereunder does not constitute ignorance or mistake that relates to a matter of private rights.

(3) For the purpose of paragraph (1)(c), an officially induced mistake of law is a defence only if

(a) the mistake is in respect of the existence or interpretation of a law and results from information or advice given by an official responsible for the administration or enforcement of that law,

(b) the person relied in good faith on that information or advice, and

(c) it was reasonable for the person to have relied on that information or advice,
but information or advice given by an official mentioned in paragraph (a) to the effect that the law will not be enforced in a particular case or in particular circumstances does not provide a basis for the defence of officially induced mistake of law.

(4) Nothing in this section affects the defence of non-publication of regulations that is provided by subsection 11(2) of the *Statutory Instruments Act*.

ADDITIONAL READING

- K. Roach, *Criminal Law*, 3rd ed. (Toronto: Irwin Law, 2004), chapter 2;
- A. Mewett and M. Manning, *Criminal Law*, 3rd ed. (Toronto: Butterworths, 1994), at 380-402;
- D. Stuart, *Canadian Criminal Law*, 4th ed. (Toronto: Carswell, 2001), at 323-56;
- E. Colvin, *Principles of Criminal Law*, 2nd ed. (Toronto: Carswell, 1991), at 159-70, 261-71;
- B.R. Grace, "Notes: Ignorance of the Law as an Excuse" (1986), 86 *Columbia L. Rev.* 1392;
- G. Williams, "The Draft Code and Reliance Upon Official Statements" (1989), 9 *Legal Studies* 177;
- N. Kastner, "Mistake of Law and the Defence of Officially Induced Error" (1986), 28 *Crim. L.Q.* 308;
- H. Stewart, "Mistake of Law Under the Charter" (1998), 40 *Crim. L.Q.* 476;
- A.-M. Boisvert, "Innocence Morale, Diligence Raisonable and Erreur de Droit" (1995), 41 C.R. (4th) 243.

# PART FOUR

# The Special Part: Sexual Assault and Homicide

# CHAPTER TWELVE

# Sexual Assault

Few subjects in the criminal law are as sensitive and difficult as sexual assault and related matters. There are many offences in the Code that are concerned with aspects of sexual behaviour and not all of them are clustered together among offences against the person. In part V, entitled "Sexual Offences, Public Morals and Disorderly Conduct," there is a sequence of offences that deal with sexual misconduct against children and some other matters. In the same part, there are also offences dealing with pornography and obscene material. Part VII contains offences relating to prostitution and disorderly houses.

Apart from these, the principal offences involving sexual violence are found among offences against the person in part VIII of the Code. These offences were substantially reformed in 1983. The old offences of rape, attempted rape, sexual intercourse with the feeble-minded, and indecent assault were all repealed and replaced by offences of sexual assault, sexual assault with a weapon, and aggravated sexual assault. This part of the Code was also amended to reform other aspects of substantive law, procedure, and evidence in the prosecution of sexual offences. In particular, Parliament has attempted on several occasions to clarify the law relating to consent and mistaken belief in consent. It has twice attempted to control the admissibility of evidence concerning the complainant's previous sexual conduct, and it has enacted measures to regulate the extent to which private records relating to the complainant can be disclosed.

The abolition of the old and antiquated offences, especially rape, provided Parliament with an opportunity to rid the law of anachronisms and to address the incidence of sexual violence more effectively. One of the shibboleths that was rejected was the idea that a man could not rape his wife. Another was the doctrine of recent complaint and the requirement of corroboration. Another was the requirement for proof of penetration in cases of rape. All of these and other ideas were abandoned in favour of a more direct and forthright approach. At the core of this new approach was that sexual violence is a form of assault and should be approached as such. This approach accommodates within the notion of assault a range of conduct that can extend from an unwanted kiss or touching to forcible intercourse without consent. The offences of sexual assault with a weapon and aggravated sexual assault specifically allow for other forms of sexual violence to be addressed directly.

There are recurring difficulties in the law relating to sexual assault. How is sexual assault distinguished from assault? What is a valid consent to sexual activity? What is the element of fault in sexual assault and in particular what is the element of fault that will suffice with regard to the absence of consent? Can the accused claim a defence of mistaken belief in consent and, if so, under what restrictions? These and other questions are addressed in the cases that follow.

First, what is a *sexual* assault?

## I. SEXUAL ASSAULT

### R. v. Chase
Supreme Court of Canada
[1987] 2 S.C.R. 293

McINTYRE J.: ... The facts may be briefly described. The respondent, Chase, was a neighbour of the complainant, a 15-year-old girl. They lived in a small hamlet near Fredericton, New Brunswick. On 22nd October 1983 Chase entered the home of the complainant without invitation. The complainant and her 11-year-old brother were in the downstairs portion of the house, playing pool. Their 83-year-old grandfather was upstairs sleeping. Their parents were absent. The respondent seized the complainant around the shoulders and arms and grabbed her breasts. When she fought back, he said: "Come on, dear, don't hit me, I know you want it." The complainant said at trial that: "He tried to grab for my private, but he didn't succeed because my hands were too fast." Eventually, the complainant and her brother were able to make a telephone call to a neighbour and the respondent left. Prior to leaving, he said that he was going to tell everybody that she had raped him. The whole episode lasted little more than half an hour. The respondent was charged with the offence of sexual assault and was found guilty after trial in the Provincial Court. He appealed to the Court of Appeal for New Brunswick, where his appeal was dismissed, a verdict of guilty of the included offence of common assault under s. 245(1) of the Criminal Code was substituted, and a sentence of six months' imprisonment was imposed. ...

Sexual assault is an assault, within any one of the definitions of that concept in s. 244(1) of the Criminal Code, which is committed in circumstances of a sexual nature, such that the sexual integrity of the victim is violated. The test to be applied in determining whether the impugned conduct has the requisite sexual nature is an objective one: "Viewed in the light of all the circumstances, is the sexual or carnal context of the assault visible to a reasonable observer?": *Taylor*, ... per Laycraft C.J.A., at p. 269. The part of the body touched, the nature of the contact, the situation in which it occurred, the words and gestures accompanying the act, and all other circumstances surrounding the conduct, including threats, which may or may not be accompanied by force, will be relevant: see S.J. Usprich, "A New Crime in Old Battles: Definitional Problems with Sexual Assault" (1987), 29 Cr. L.Q. 200, at p. 204. The intent or purpose of the person committing the act, to the extent that this may appear from the evidence, may also be a factor in considering whether the conduct is sexual. If the motive of the accused is sexual gratification, to the extent that this may appear from the evidence it may be a factor in determining whether the conduct is sexual. It must be emphasized, however, that the existence of such a motive is simply one of many factors to be considered, the importance of which will vary depending on the circumstances. ...

Turning to the case at bar, I have no difficulty in concluding, on the basis of the principles I have discussed above, that there was ample evidence before the trial judge upon which he could find that sexual assault was committed. Viewed objectively, in the light of all the circumstances, it is clear that the conduct of the respondent in grabbing the complainant's breasts constituted an assault of a sexual nature. I would therefore allow the appeal, set aside the conviction of common assault recorded by the Court of Appeal and restore the conviction of sexual assault made at trial. The sentence of six months should stand.

*Appeal allowed; conviction restored.*

---

The prosecution of sexual assault can be fraught with evidentiary difficulties because the alleged activity is often not observed by others. The following case deals with two matters. One is an important issue of substantive law: can the accused raise a defence of mistaken belief in consent if that belief, though honest, was unreasonable? The second question concerns the evidentiary threshold that must be met before a matter of defence may be considered by the trier of fact. On the first issue the court was agreed but on the second it was divided.

### Pappajohn v. The Queen
Supreme Court of Canada
(1980), 52 C.C.C. (2d) 481

[The accused, a businessman, met with the complainant, a real estate agent, to discuss the pending sale of his house. After a three-hour lunch during which much liquor was consumed, the accused took the complainant to his house. Some three hours later the complainant ran naked out of the house with a bow-tie round her neck and her hands tied tightly behind her back. At trial the complainant denied any form of consent, testifying that she had physically and mentally resisted throughout. Pappajohn's testimony was the opposite: according to him, there had been preliminary sexual activity with her consent and acts of intercourse, again with her consent; the gagging and binding was done to stimulate sexual activity, and it was only then that she suddenly became hysterical and screamed.

The trial judge refused to instruct the jury that if the accused honestly believed that the complainant consented, whether or not she did in fact consent, then he should be acquitted. The sole issue left with the jury was whether she did in fact consent. An appeal by the accused from his conviction to the British Columbia Court of Appeal was dismissed. Lambert J.A., dissenting (holding that the defence of honest and reasonable mistake of fact should have been left to the jury).]

DICKSON J., with whom Estey J. concurred, dissenting:  Is the accused's perception of consent relevant to a charge under s. 143 of the *Criminal Code*? The argument against the application of *Director of Public Prosecutions v. Morgan*, [1976] A.C. 182, in Canada, is that the *Code* creates a statutory offence of rape which does not expressly advert to, or require, that there be a state of mind or intent to proceed in the absence of consent.

[A number of cases are then examined.]

Counsel for the Crown in the instant appeal reviewed and compared s. 143 of the *Code* with other Part IV *Code* offences, to make the point that the subjective belief of an accused is no part of the case to be proved by the Crown. It was contended that, since reference to intention to proceed in the absence of consent is lacking in s. 143, the statutory wording prevails over case authorities which consider the mental element in terms of the common law definition. Section 148 of the *Code* was cited in comparison. This section specifies as an ingredient of the offence, knowledge or reason for belief that the female person is, by reason of her mental condition, incapable of giving a reasonable consent. Knowledge of the existence of a blood-relationship is a constituent element of the crime of incest, spelled out in s. 150 of the *Code*.

One cannot assume, on the strength of these two sections, that there is no *mens rea* element relating to consent, for crimes of rape. Parliament does not consistently employ wording which indicates express levels of intention (such as knowingly, intentionally, wilfully) for all offences which undoubtedly import a mental element. Even within Part IV, there is no consistency in the wording of the offences. I do not think the determination of the mental element for rape turns, in any way, on a comparative analysis of the wording for Part IV offences.

In summary, intention or recklessness must be proved in relation to all elements of the offence, including absence of consent. This simply extends to rape the same general order of intention as in other crimes. ...

Mistake is a defence, then, where it prevents an accused from having the *mens rea* which the law requires for the very crime with which he is charged. Mistake of fact is more accurately seen as a negation of guilty intention than as the affirmation of a positive defence. It avails an accused who acts innocently, pursuant to a flawed perception of the facts, and none the less commits the *actus reus* of an offence. Mistake is a defence though, in the sense that it is raised as an issue by an accused. The Crown is rarely possessed of knowledge of the subjective factors which may have caused an accused to entertain a belief in a fallacious set of facts.

If I am correct that: (i) s. 143 of the *Criminal Code* imports a *mens rea* requirement, and (ii) the *mens rea* of rape includes intention, or recklessness as to nonconsent of the complainant, a mistake that negatives intention or recklessness entitles the accused to an acquittal. Glanville Williams notes (*Criminal Law, The General Part*, 2nd ed. (1961), p. 173, para. 65):

> It is impossible to assert that a crime requiring intention or recklessness can be committed although the accused laboured under a mistake negativing the requisite intention or recklessness. Such an assertion carries its own refutation.

I do not think the defence of mistaken belief can be restricted to those situations in which the belief has been induced by information received from a third party. That was the situation in the *Morgan* case. In *Morgan*, the belief in consent was induced by information related by the complainant's husband, who spoke of his wife's sexual propensities. The foundation for the defence, incredible as it turned out to be, in view of the violence, was the misinformation of the husband. Had the defendants believed that information, and had the wife's overt conduct been relatively consistent with it, the defendants would have had a defence. That is the effect of the *dicta* of the House of Lords in the *Morgan* case.

In principle, the defence should avail when there is an honest belief in consent, or an absence of knowledge that consent has been withheld. Whether the mistake is rooted in an accused's mistaken perception, or is based upon objective, but incorrect, facts confided to him by another, should be of no consequence. The kind of mistaken fact pleaded by the *Morgan* defendants, however, is more likely to be believed than a bald assertion of mistaken belief during a face-to-face encounter. In any event, it is clear that the defence is available only where there is sufficient evidence presented by an accused, by his testimony or by the circumstances in which the act occurred, to found the plea.

The next question which must be broached is whether a defence of honest, though mistaken, belief in consent must be based on reasonable grounds. A majority of the House of Lords in *Morgan* answered the question in the negative, and that view was affirmed by the Heilbron Committee. There can be no doubt this answer is consonant with principle.

[A number of cases and authorities in other jurisdictions are then set out.]

In Canada, the *Tolson* rule has already been rejected by this Court in favour of the honest belief standard. Unless this Court wishes to overrule *Beaver v. The Queen* (1957), 118 C.C.C. 129, [1957] S.C.R. 531, 26 C.R. 193, it is difficult to see how the minority in *Morgan* can decide this appeal.

It is not clear how one can properly relate reasonableness (an element in offences of negligence) to rape (a "true crime" and not an offence of negligence). To do so, one must, I think, take the view that the *mens rea* goes only to the physical act of intercourse and not to non-consent, and acquittal comes only if the mistake is reasonable. This, upon the authorities, is not a correct view, the intent in rape being not merely to have intercourse, but to have it with a nonconsenting woman. If the jury finds that mistake, whether reasonable or unreasonable, there should be no conviction. If, upon the entire record, there is evidence of mistake to cast a reasonable doubt upon the existence of a criminal mind, then the prosecution has failed to make its case. In an article by Professor Colin Howard, "The Reasonableness of Mistake in the Criminal Law," 4 *U. Queensland L.J.* 45 (1961-64), the following is offered (p. 47):

> To crimes of *mens rea* or elements of a crime which requires *mens rea*, mistake of fact *simpliciter* is a defence; to crimes of negligence, or elements of an offence which requires only negligence, mistake of fact is a defence only if the mistake was in all the circumstances a reasonable one to make.

I am not unaware of the policy considerations advanced in support of the view that if mistake is to afford a defence to a charge of rape, it should, at the very least, be one a reasonable man might make in the circumstances. There is justifiable concern over the position of the woman who alleges she has been subjected to a non-consensual sexual act; fear is expressed that subjective orthodoxy should not enable her alleged assailant to escape accountability by advancing some cock-and-bull story. The usual response of persons accused of rape is—"she consented." Are such persons now to be acquitted, simply by saying: "even if she did not consent, I believed she consented"? The concern is legitimate and real. It must, however, be placed in the balance with other relevant considerations. First, cases in which mistake can be advanced in answer to a charge of rape must be few in number. People do not normally commit rape *per incuriam*. An evidential case must exist to support the plea. Secondly, if the woman in her own mind withholds consent, but her conduct and other circumstances lend credence to belief on the part of the accused that she was consenting, it may be that it is unjust to convict. I do not think it will do to say that in those circumstances she, in fact, consented. If fact, she did not, and it would be open to a jury to so find. Thirdly, it is unfair to the jury, and to the accused, to speak in terms of two beliefs, one entertained by the accused, the other by a reasonable man, and to ask the jury to ignore an actual belief in favour of an attributed belief. The mind with which the jury is concerned is that of the accused. By importing a standard external to the accused, there is created an incompatible mix of subjective and objective factors. If an honest lack of knowledge is shown, then the subjective element of the offence is not proved.

Perpetuation of fictions does little for the jury system or the integrity of criminal justice. The ongoing debate in the Courts and learned journals as to whether mistake must be reasonable is conceptually important in the orderly development of the criminal law, but in my view, practically unimportant because the accused's statement that he was mistaken is not likely to be believed unless the mistake is, to the jury, reasonable. The jury will be concerned to consider the reasonableness of any grounds found, or asserted to be available, to support the defence of mistake. Although "reasonable grounds" is not a precondition to the availability of a plea of honest belief in consent, those grounds determine the weight to be given the defence. The reasonableness, or otherwise, of the accused's belief is only evidence for, or against, the view that the belief was actually held and the intent was, therefore, lacking.

Canadian juries, in my experience, display a high degree of common sense, and an uncanny ability to distinguish between the genuine and the specious.

I come now to what is perhaps the most difficult part of this case, namely, whether there was an evidential base sufficient to require the trial Judge to place before the jury the defence of mistaken belief in consent. The trial Judge and two Judges of the Court of Appeal concluded no such base existed. Chief Justice Farris, in dismissing the appeal, was strongly influenced by the fact that "at no time did the appellant suggest in his evidence that while there was resistance on the part of the complainant none the less he honestly believed that she was in fact consenting. He did testify that there was resistance after acts of bondage but from then on there was no intercourse." With respect, it is not necessary that an accused specifically plead mistake. The issue to which an accused's state of mind is relevant is *mens rea* and that issue is always before the jury, the onus being on the prosecution. Nor is a defence of honest belief necessarily inconsistent with a defence of consent. In raising the latter, an accused is challenging the factual aspect of the offence. Did the complainant or did she not consent? If she did, the *actus reus* was not committed. The defence of honest belief is different in nature, for it rests upon an accused's subjective perception of that factual situation.

If there was "some" evidence to "convey a sense of reality" to a defence of mistake as to consent, then the jury ought to have been instructed to consider that plea.

There is circumstantial evidence supportive of a plea of belief in consent: (1) Her necklace and car keys were found in the living-room. (2) She confirmed his testimony that her blouse was neatly hung in the clothes closet. (3) Other items of folded clothing were found at the foot of the bed. (4) None of her clothes were damaged in the slightest way. (5) She was in the house for a number of hours. (6) By her version, when she entered the house, the appellant said he was going to break her. She made no attempt to leave. (7) She did not leave while he undressed. (8) There was no evidence of struggle, and (9) she suffered no physical injuries, aside from three scratches.

The possibility of a mistaken belief in consent in the pre-bondage phase was an issue that should have been placed before the jury: the Judge's failure to do so makes it imperative, in my opinion, in the interests of justice, that there be a new trial. It was open to the jury to find only token resistance prior to the "bondage" incident, which the appellant may not have perceived as a withholding of consent. The accused was convicted of that which, perhaps, he did not intend to do had he known of no consent. It does not follow that, by simply disbelieving the appellant on consent, in fact, the jury thereby found that there was no belief in consent, and that the appellant could not reasonably have believed in consent.

I would allow the appeal, set aside the judgment of the British Columbia Court of Appeal and direct a new trial.

McINTYRE J., with whom Pigeon, Beetz, and Chouinard JJ. concurred:  In a dissenting judgment, Lambert J.A. was of the opinion that there was sufficient evidence to put the defence to the jury. He would have directed the jury that the accused was entitled to an acquittal if the jury found that he entertained an honest and reasonably held mistaken belief in the existence of consent. This is a view which I cannot share in view of the pronouncement in this Court in *Beaver v. The Queen* (1957), 118 C.C.C. 129 at pp. 136-7, [1957] S.C.R. 531 at p. 538, 26 C.R. 193.

Before any obligation arises to put defences, there must be in the evidence some basis upon which the defence can rest and it is only where such an evidentiary basis is present that a trial Judge must put a defence. Indeed, where it is not present he should not put a defence for to do so would only be to confuse.

In relating the law to the facts of any case, we must keep in mind what it is that the trial Judge must look for in the evidence in deciding whether there is, in the words of Fauteux J., "some evidence or matter apt to convey a sense of reality in the argument, and in the grievance." In this case, to convey such a sense of reality, there must be some evidence which if believed would support the existence of a mistaken but honest belief that the complainant was in fact consenting to the acts of intercourse which admittedly occurred. This requires a more detailed recital of the evidence than would ordinarily be necessary.

[The facts are then examined.]

With that thought in mind and, bearing in mind that the object of the judicial search must be evidence of a mistaken but honest belief in the consent of the complainant, one must first ask the question "Where is this evidence to be found?" It cannot be found in the evidence of the complainant. She denies actual consent and her evidence cannot provide any support for a mistaken belief in consent. Her conduct, according to her description, is that of a terrified, hysterical, non-consenting woman who resisted the appellant's advances, albeit unsuccessfully, and when able fled from his house in search of assistance. Turning then to the evidence of the appellant, it immediately becomes apparent that his evidence speaks of actual consent, even co-operation, and leaves little if any room for the suggestion that she may not have been consenting but he thought she was. The two stories are, as has been noted before, diametrically opposed on this vital issue. It is not for the trial Judge to weigh them and prefer one to the other. It is for him in this situation, however, to recognize the issue which arises on the evidence for the purpose of deciding what defences are open. In this situation the only realistic issue which can arise is the simple issue of consent or no consent. In my opinion, the trial Judge was correct in concluding that there simply was not sufficient evidence to justify the putting of the defence of mistake of fact to the jury. He left the issue of consent and that was the only one arising on the evidence.

In reaching this conclusion, I am not unmindful of the evidence of surrounding circumstances which were said to support the appellant's contention. I refer to the absence of serious injury suffered by the complainant and the absence of damage to clothing, as well as to the long period of time during which the parties remained in the bedroom. These matters may indeed be cogent on the issue of actual consent but, in my view, they cannot by themselves advance a suggestion of a mistaken belief. The finding of the clothes at the foot of the bed, the necklace and the keys in the living-room, are equally relevant on the issue of actual consent and, in my view, cannot affect the issue which was clearly framed by the opposing assertions of consent and non-consent.

It would seem to me that if it is considered necessary in this case to charge the jury on the defence of mistake of fact, it would be necessary to do so in all cases where the complainant denies consent and an accused asserts it. To require the putting of the alternative defence of mistaken belief in consent, there must be, in my opinion, some evidence beyond the mere assertion of belief in consent by counsel for the appellant. This evidence must appear from or be supported by sources other than the appellant in order to give it any air of reality. In *R. v. Plummer and Brown* (1975), 24 C.C.C. (2d) 497, Evans J.A. (as he then was), speaking for the Ontario Court of Appeal, considered that there was such evidence as far as Brown was concerned and directed a new trial because the defence had not been put. In that case, the complainant had gone to Plummer's "pad" where she had been raped by Plummer. Brown entered the room where the rape occurred after Plummer had gone. Apparently, he had arrived at the house separately from Plummer. It was open on the evidence to find that he was unaware then that Plummer had threatened the complainant and terrorized her into submission. He had intercourse with her and she said that because of continuing fear from Plummer's threats, she submitted without protest. In these special circumstances, the defence was required. The facts clearly established at least an air of reality to Brown's defence. In *Morgan*, there was evidence of an invitation by the complainant's husband to have intercourse with his wife and his assurance that her show of resistance would be a sham. In other words, there was evidence explaining, however preposterous the explanation might be, a basis for the mistaken belief. In the case at bar, there is no such evidence.

Where the complainant says rape and the accused says consent, and where on the whole of the evidence, including that of the complainant, the accused, and the surrounding circumstances, there is a clear issue on this point, and where as here the accused makes no assertion of a belief in consent as opposed to an actual consent, it is unrealistic in the absence of some other circumstance or circumstances, such as are found in the *Plummer and Brown* and *Morgan* cases, to consider the Judge bound to put the mistake of fact defence. In my opinion, the trial Judge was correct in refusing to put the defence on the evidence before him.

I might add that I have had the advantage of reading the reasons of my brother Dickson J. and, while it is apparent that I am unable to accept his view on the evidentiary question, I am in agreement with that part of his judgment dealing with the availability as a defence to a charge of rape in Canada of what is generally termed the defence of mistake of fact.

I would dismiss the appeal.

[Martland J. agreed with McIntyre J., but would leave undecided the question whether the accused's belief need be "honest" or "honest and reasonable."]

*Appeal dismissed.*

## II. CONSENT

Section 265(4) of the Code, which came into force in 1983, provides:

> Where an accused alleges that he believed that the complainant consented to the conduct
> that is the subject-matter of the charge, a judge, if satisfied that there is sufficient evidence
> and that, if believed by the jury, the evidence would constitute a defence, shall instruct the
> jury, when reviewing all the evidence relating to the determination of the honesty of the
> accused's belief, to consider the presence or absence of reasonable grounds for that belief.

Does this change the law as stated by the Court in *Pappajohn*?

---

Judges continue to be divided on what constitutes an "air of reality" in a particular case.
See, for example, *Reddick v. The Queen* (1991), 64 C.C.C. (3d) 257 (S.C.C.). In *Laybourn,
Bulmer and Illingworth v. The Queen* (1987), 33 C.C.C. (3d) 385, McIntyre J. stated for
the court: "The statement of the accused alleging a mistaken belief will be a factor but
will not by itself be decisive, and even in its total absence, other circumstances might
dictate the putting of the defence." Lamer J. added: "If this means that the trial judge is
not required to put the defence to the jury merely because the accused's lawyer has
referred to the defence in argument, then I agree ... However, I must respectfully take
issue with the 'air of reality' norm if it is to be understood as going so far as enabling the
trial judge to choose not to leave the defence of honest belief with the jury even in a case
where the accused has taken the stand and asserted under oath that he or she honestly
believed in consent."

---

In *Osolin v. The Queen*, [1993] 4 S.C.R. 595, the issue was, *inter alia*, whether s. 265(4)
infringed s. 11(d) (presumption of innocence) or s. 11(f) (right to trial by jury) of the
Charter. The Supreme Court unanimously held that it did not. All judges agreed with
Cory J.'s analysis of the constitutionality of the provision. Cory J. stated:

> Section 265(4) of the *Criminal Code* is applicable to all assaults, not just sexual assaults. It
> appears to be no more than the codification of the common law defence of mistake of fact.
>
>     It is trite law that a trial judge must instruct the jury only upon those defences for which
> there is a real factual basis. A defence for which there is no evidentiary foundation should
> not be put to the jury. This rule extends well beyond the defence of mistaken belief in
> consent and is of long standing. In *Kelsey v. The Queen*, [1953] 1 S.C.R. 220, at p. 226,
> Fauteux J., writing for the majority, held:
>
> > The allotment of any substance to an argument or of any value to a grievance resting
> > on the omission of the trial Judge from mentioning such argument must be condi-
> > tioned on the existence in the record of some evidence or matter apt to convey *a
> > sense of reality* in the argument and in the grievance. [Emphasis added.]
>
>     In the realm of sexual assault cases the requirement of sufficient evidence has caused
> some confusion. Yet in my view these words require no more than the application of the
> principles that have been set out above. In *Pappajohn, supra*, it was held that the defence of

mistaken belief in consent should only be put to the jury if there was an adequate and evidentiary foundation found for it.

The question that arises is whether this means that in order for the defence to be put to the jury there must be some evidence of mistaken belief in consent emanating from a source other than the accused. In my view, this proposition cannot be correct. There is no requirement that there be evidence independent of the accused in order to have the defence put to the jury. However, the mere assertion by the accused that "I believed she was consenting" will not be sufficient. What is required is that the defence of mistaken belief be supported by evidence beyond the mere assertion of a mistaken belief.

The distinction between a burden of proof with regard to an offence or an element of the offence, and an evidentiary burden is critical. It must be remembered that the accused only bears the evidentiary burden of raising the issue of mistake, and in fact, only bears that burden if sufficient evidence has not already been raised by the prosecution's case.

Section 265(4) does not create a statutory presumption. The accused seeking to raise the defence of mistaken belief only bears a tactical evidentiary burden.

Section 265(4) leaves the burden on the Crown in regard to all the essential elements of the offence. The prosecution must prove both the *mens rea* and the *actus reus* beyond a reasonable doubt: that the accused engaged in sexual intercourse with a woman who was not consenting, and that he intended to engage in sexual intercourse without the consent of the woman.

Cory J. added with respect to the trial by jury issue:

The appellant was provided with a trial by jury. The only elements of the trial that were decided by the trial judge were those things properly within his realm, namely those issues pertaining to trial process and questions of law. There is consequently no violation of the appellant's right to a trial by jury.

Five members of the Court, however, did not agree with Cory J. on the question whether there can be an "air of reality" when the complainant and the accused have given "diametrically opposed" versions of the facts. Three other members of the Court (L'Heureux-Dubé, Iacobucci, and Major JJ.) agreed with Cory J.'s view that in such circumstances there cannot be an "air of reality." Cory J. stated:

In what circumstances will it be appropriate to consider a defence of mistaken belief in consent? It is the position of the intervener, the Attorney General for Ontario, that the defence cannot arise in situations where the evidence of the complainant and the accused are diametrically opposed. For example, if the accused states that there was willing consent and the complainant denies any consent then the defence simply cannot arise. In such circumstances for a jury to accept the defence of mistaken belief in consent it would have to reject all the evidence given at the trial including that tendered by both the complainant (no consent) and that of the accused (willing consent). Indeed in order to give effect to the defence a jury would have to speculate upon and give effect to a third version of events which was not in evidence.

I agree with this position. The defence of mistake may arise when the accused and the complainant tell essentially the same story and then argue that they interpreted it differently. Realistically it can only arise when the facts described by the complainant and the accused generally correspond but the interpretation of those facts leads to a different state of mind for each of the parties. In a situation where the evidence given is directly opposed as to whether there was consent, the defence of mistake as to consent simply cannot exist. However, even in the absence of that defence, the jury will nonetheless be bound to acquit if it has a reasonable doubt as to whether there was consent in light of the conflicting evidence on the issue. Lack of consent is an integral element of the offence. In cases where there is conflicting evidence on the issue the trial judge will always direct the jury that they must be satisfied beyond a reasonable doubt that consent was lacking.

The majority of the court, however, took the same position as McLachlin J. who stated:

> Before leaving this question, I should comment on two points. The first is the argument that the divergent stories of the complainant and the accused on consent, as a matter of law, necessarily preclude a third alternative, the defence of honest but mistaken belief. I am not so convinced as my colleagues that where the evidence consists of two diametrically opposed stories, one alleging lack of consent and the other consent, it is logically impossible to conceive of the defence of honest but mistaken belief arising. While it may rarely occur, it seems to me possible for a jury to accept parts of the testimonies of both the complainant and the accused, concluding that notwithstanding lack of actual consent, the accused honestly believed in consent. As A.W. Bryant states:
>
> > ... the removal of this alternative plea on the basis that the testimony of the complainant and the accused are diametrically opposed, and that there is a lack of common ground for the defence is based, in part, on the premise that the complainant's version is complete—a questionable assumption in some cases. Moreover, a requirement for corroboration may wrongly encourage an accused to dovetail partially his testimony with that of the complainant in order to supply the necessary common ground for the defence.

The test for an "air of reality" applies with respect to any matter of defence that is raised by the evidence and that does not carry a legal burden with it. It means that no matter of defence can be considered by the trier of fact unless it meets this standard. In *R. v. Cinous* (2002), 49 C.R. (5th) 209, the Supreme Court of Canada again reviewed this standard and repeated that the test is whether "a properly instructed jury acting reasonably could acquit." This is a question of law for the trial judge and, in effect, it asks whether the trier of fact, acting reasonably, could find a reasonable doubt. The court also repeated that this is a principle of general application.

The following case turns on the findings of fact made by the trial judge. The Supreme Court nevertheless concludes that the trial judge made an error of law in her disposition of the case. What are the essential findings of fact by the trial and what, according to the Supreme Court, was the mistake of law in her disposition? Can these be reconciled?

## III. MISTAKE

### Sansregret v. The Queen
Supreme Court of Canada
(1985), 18 C.C.C. (3d) 223

McINTYRE J.: ... In this case the accused had been acquitted of rape because the trial judge found that the accused had an honest belief that the complainant was consenting. The trial judge also found that the complainant was absolutely terrified and that her consent was given solely to protect herself from further violence or death. The accused had lived with the appellant for a year before the complainant told the accused to leave in September, 1982. On September 23, 1982 the accused broke into the appellant's house at 4:30 a.m. and terrorized her with a file-like instrument. She was fearful and held out some hope of reconciliation. Sexual intercourse took place. Afterwards the complainant reported the incident to the police stating that she was raped. The complaint was not pursued, in part because, after intervention by the accused's probation officer, the complainant decided not to press the matter.

On October 15, 1982, again at about 4:30 a.m., the appellant broke into the complainant's house through a basement window. She was alone, and, awakened by the entry, she seized the bedroom telephone in an effort to call the police. The appellant picked up a butcher knife in the kitchen and came into the bedroom. He was furious and violent. He accused her of having another boy-friend; pulled the cord of the telephone out of the jack and threw it into the living-room; threatened her with the knife and ordered her to take off her night-dress and made her stand in the kitchen doorway, naked save for a jacket over her shoulders, so he could be sure where she was while he repaired the window to conceal his entry from the police, should they arrive. He struck her on the mouth with sufficient force to draw blood, and on three occasions rammed the knife-blade into the wall with great force, once very close to her. He told her that if the police came he would put the knife through her, and added that if he had found her with a boy-friend he would have killed them both. At one point he tied her hands behind her back with a scarf. The complainant said she was in fear for her life and sanity.

By about 5:30 a.m., after an hour of such behaviour by the appellant, she tried to calm him down. She pretended again that there was some hope of a reconciliation if the appellant would settle down and get a job. This had the desired effect. He calmed down and after some conversation he joined her on the bed and they had intercourse. The complainant swore that her consent to the intercourse was solely for the purpose of calming him down, to protect herself from further violence. This, she said, was something she had learned from earlier experience with him. In her evidence she said:

> I didn't consent at any time.
>
> I was very afraid. My whole body was trembling. I was sure I would have a nervous breakdown. I came very, very close to losing my mind. All I knew was I had to keep this man calm or he would kill me.

The trial judge made the following findings:

> As I said, no rational person could have been under any honest mistake of fact. How-
> ever, people have an uncanny ability to blind themselves to much that they don't want
> to see, and to believe in the existence of facts as they would wish them to be. The
> accused says that, notwithstanding the reign of terror which preceded their chat, not-
> withstanding that he held a knife while they talked, notwithstanding that he did most of
> the talking and that the complainant's answers were clearly equivocal, he presumed
> and believed that everything between them was peachy. This, notwithstanding that three
> weeks earlier, on a replay of the same sort of evening, his probation officer became
> involved and the complainant moved out of her house. Very honestly, despite my confi-
> dence in the ability of people to blind themselves to reality, and even if the accused had
> not lied about other parts of his testimony, I would have been hard pressed to credit the
> honesty of his belief.
>
> However, his honest belief finds support in the testimony of the complainant. She
> knows him and in her opinion, notwithstanding all the objective facts to the contrary,
> he did believe that everything was back to normal between them by the time of the
> sexual encounter. His subsequent behaviour as well, attests to that fact.
>
> I do not like the conclusion which this leads me to. There was no real consent. There
> was submission as a result of a very real and justifiable fear. No one in his right mind
> could have believed that the complainant's dramatic about-face stemmed from any-
> thing other than fear. But the accused did. He saw what he wanted to see, heard what he
> wanted to hear, believed what he wanted to believe.
>
> The facts in *R. v. Pappajohn* (1977) 38 C.C.C. (2d) 106, are quite dissimilar to those
> in this case. The dictum of the Supreme Court of Canada, however, is clear and broad
> and in no way seems to limit itself to the peculiar circumstances of that case. Perhaps
> the Crown will appeal this decision to obtain some direction from the Supreme Court
> on whether it was that court's intention to cover situations where an accused, who dem-
> onstrates the clarity and shrewdness this accused showed in securing his own safety at
> the outset can turn around and because it does not suit his wishes, can go wilfully blind
> to the obvious shortly thereafter. In any event, the ratio of *Pappajohn* is clear and it
> leaves me no alternative but to acquit.

The Manitoba Court of Appeal entered a conviction and the Supreme Court of
Canada dismissed the accused's appeal, McIntyre J. (Dickson C.J.C., Estey,
Chouinard, Lamer, Wilson, and Le Dain JJ.) stating for the court:

> It is evident that the trial judge would have convicted the appellant of rape had it not
> been for the defence of mistake of fact. She considered that the belief in the consent
> expressed by the appellant was an honest one and therefore on the basis of *Pappajohn
> v. The Queen* (1980), 52 C.C.C. (2d) 481, 111 D.L.R. (3d) 1, [1980] 2 S.C.R. 120, even
> if it were unreasonably held, as it is clear she thought it was, he was entitled to his
> acquittal. This application of the defence of mistake of fact would be supportable were
> it not for the fact that the trial judge found in addition that the appellant had been wil-
> fully blind to reality in his behaviour on October 15th. Such a finding would preclude
> the application of the defence and lead to a different result. It is my opinion then that

the trial judge erred in this matter in that though she made the requisite findings of fact that the appellant was wilfully blind to the consequences of his acts she did not apply them according to law. ...

Wilful blindness is distinct from recklessness because, while recklessness involves knowledge of a danger or risk and persistence in a course of conduct which creates a risk that the prohibited result will occur, wilful blindness arises where a person who has become aware of the need for some inquiry declines to make the inquiry because he does not wish to know the truth. He would prefer to remain ignorant. The culpability in recklessness is justified by consciousness of the risk and by proceeding in the face of it, while in wilful blindness it is justified by the accused's fault in deliberately failing to inquire when he knows there is reason for inquiry. ...

This case reveals, in my view, an appropriate set of circumstances for the application of the "wilful blindness" rule. I have outlined the circumstances which form the background. I have referred to the findings of the trial judge that the appellant blinded himself to the obvious and made no inquiry as to the nature of the consent which was given. If the evidence before the court was limited to the events of October 15th, it would be difficult indeed to infer wilful blindness. To attribute criminal liability on the basis of this one incident would come close to applying a constructive test to the effect that he should have known she was consenting out of fear. The position, however, is changed when the evidence reveals the earlier episode and the complaint of rape which it caused, knowledge of which, as I have said, had clearly reached the accused. Considering the whole of the evidence then, no constructive test of knowledge is required. The appellant was aware of the likelihood of the complainant's reaction to his threats. To proceed with intercourse in such circumstances constitutes, in my view, self-deception to the point of wilful blindness.

In my view, it was error on the part of the trial judge to give effect to the "mistake of fact" defence in these circumstances where she had found that the complainant consented out of fear and the appellant was wilfully blind to the existing circumstances, seeing only what he wished to see. Where the accused is deliberately ignorant as a result of blinding himself to reality the law presumes knowledge, in this case knowledge of the nature of the consent. There was therefore no room for the operation of this defence.

This is not to be taken as a retreat from the position taken in *Pappajohn* that the honest belief need not be reasonable. It is not to be thought that any time an accused forms an honest though unreasonable belief he will be deprived of the defence of mistake of fact. This case rests on a different proposition. Having wilfully blinded himself to the facts before him, the fact that an accused may be enabled to preserve what could be called an honest belief, in the sense that he has no specific knowledge to the contrary, will not afford a defence because, where the accused becomes deliberately blind to the existing facts, he is fixed by law with actual knowledge and his belief in another state of facts is irrelevant.

I would dismiss the appeal.

---

An important feature of the reforms of 1983 was an amendment of the Code that would exclude evidence of the complainant's previous sexual conduct. In the past, the law had allowed for the admission of this evidence on the basis that it had probative value on the issue of consent and on the credibility of the complainant as a witness. Parliament rejected these ideas but the provision was challenged on the basis that the new exclusionary could prejudice the accused.

### R. v. Seaboyer
Supreme Court of Canada
(1992), 66 C.C.C. (3d) 321

[In this case, the Supreme Court held that the "rape-shield" provisions of s. 276 of the *Criminal Code* violated ss. 7 and 11(d) of the Charter and were not justified under s. 1. Section 276 provided that in sexual assault trials, evidence concerning the sexual activity of the complainant with any person other than the accused could only be admitted if it (1) rebutted evidence of the complainant's sexual activity or absence thereof adduced by the prosecution; (2) tended to establish the identity of the person who had sexual contact with the complainant on the occasion set out in the charge; and (3) was evidence of sexual activity that took place on the same occasion as the sexual activity in the charge and relates to the consent that the accused alleges he believed was given by the complainant.

The court also unanimously held that s. 277 prohibiting the use of evidence of sexual reputation to challenge the credibility of the complainant was constitutional.

This case will be studied in the course on evidence law. For our purposes, the focus will be on how the impugned evidentiary provisions relate to the defence of honest but not necessarily reasonable belief in the complainant's consent.]

McLACHLIN J. (Lamer C.J.C., La Forest, Sopinka, Cory, Stevenson, and Iacobucci JJ. concurring): The goals of the legislation—the avoidance of unprobative and misleading evidence, the encouraging of reporting and the protection of the security and privacy of the witnesses—conform to our fundamental conceptions of justice. The concern with the legislation is not as to its purpose, which is laudable, but with its effect. The reasons for these concerns emerge from a consideration of the appellant's position, to which I now turn. ...

The appellants contend that the legislation, however laudable its goals, in fact infringes their right to present evidence relevant to their defence and hence violates their right to a fair trial, one of the most important of the principles of fundamental justice.

The precept that the innocent must not be convicted is basic to our concept of justice. One has only to think of the public revulsion felt at the improper conviction of Donald Marshall in this country or the Birmingham Six in the United Kingdom to appreciate how deeply held is this tenet of justice. ...

Section 277 excludes evidence of sexual reputation for the purpose of challenging or supporting the credibility of the plaintiff. The idea that a complainant's credibility might be affected by whether she has had other sexual experience is today universally discredited. There is no logical or practical link between a woman's sexual reputation and whether she is a truthful witness. It follows that the evidence excluded by s. 277 can serve no legitimate purpose in the trial. Section 277, by limiting the exclusion to a purpose which is clearly illegitimate, does not touch evidence which may be tendered for valid purposes, and hence does not infringe the right to a fair trial.

I turn then to s. 276. Section 276, unlike s. 277, does not condition exclusion on use of the evidence for an illegitimate purpose. Rather, it constitutes a blanket exclusion, subject to three exceptions—rebuttal evidence, evidence going to identity, and evidence relating to consent to sexual activity on the same occasion as the trial incident. The question is whether this may exclude evidence which is relevant to the defence and the probative value of which is not substantially outweighed by the potential prejudice to the trial process. To put the matter another way, can it be said *a priori*, as the Attorney-General for Ontario contends, that any and all evidence excluded by s. 276 will necessarily be of such trifling weight in relation to the prejudicial effect of the evidence that it may fairly be excluded?

In my view, the answer to this question must be negative. ...

Consider the defence of honest belief. It rests on the concept that the accused may honestly but mistakenly (and not necessarily reasonably) have believed that the complainant was consenting to the sexual act. If the accused can raise a reasonable doubt as to his intention on the basis that he honestly held such a belief, he is not guilty under our law and is entitled to an acquittal. The basis of the accused's honest belief in the complainant's consent may be sexual acts performed by the complainant at some other time or place. Yet s. 276 would preclude the accused leading such evidence.

I conclude that the operation of s. 276 of the *Criminal Code* permits the infringement of the rights enshrined in ss. 7 and 11(d) of the Charter. In achieving its purpose—the abolition of the outmoded, sexist-based use of sexual conduct evidence— it overshoots the mark and renders inadmissible evidence which may be essential to the presentation of legitimate defences and hence to a fair trial. In exchange for the elimination of the possibility that the judge and jury may draw illegitimate inferences from the evidence, it exacts as a price the real risk that an innocent person may be convicted. The price is too great in relation to the benefit secured, and cannot be tolerated in a society that does not countenance in any form the conviction of the innocent.

L'HEUREUX-DUBÉ J. (Gonthier J. concurring) (in dissent): Sexual assault is not like any other crime. In the vast majority of cases the target is a woman and the perpetrator is a man. (98.7% of those charged with sexual assault are men: *Crime Statistics 1986*, quoted in T. Dawson, "Sexual Assault Law and Past Sexual Conduct of the Primary Witness: The Construction of Relevance," 2 C.J.W.L. 310 (1988), at p. 326, note 72.) Unlike other crimes of a violent nature, it is for the most part unreported. Yet, by all accounts, women are victimized at an alarming rate and there is some evidence that an already frighteningly high rate of sexual assault is on the increase. The prosecution and conviction rates for sexual assault are among the lowest for all violent crimes. Perhaps more than any other crime, the fear and constant reality of sexual assault affects how women conduct their lives and how they define their relationship with the larger society. Sexual assault is not like any other crime.

Conservative estimates inform us that, in Canada, at least one woman in five will be sexually assaulted during her lifetime: see J. Brickman and J. Briere, "Incidence of Rape and Sexual Assault in an Urban Canadian Population," 7 Int'l J. of Women's Stud. 195 (1985). The report of the Committee on Sexual Offences Against Children and Youths warns that one in two females will be the victim of unwanted sexual acts (Sexual Offences Against Children (1984)). ...

The literature and case-law in this area abound with examples of the supposed relevant evidence that is excluded by s. 276. For the most part, however, the "relevant" evidence provided in these examples is, on a principled inquiry, irrelevant; any semblance of relevance depends in large measure upon acceptance of stereotype about women and rape. Much of the remainder is admissible under the provision. One hesitates, however, to construct an argument around the speculative scenarios offered. Many of the scenarios are pure fantasy and have absolutely no grounding in life or experience. Speculating in this manner depends, to some degree, upon the acceptance of stereotypes about women and sexual assault and the will to propagate them.

I am of the firm opinion that no relevant evidence regarding the defence of honest but mistaken belief in consent is excluded by the provision under attack here.

Although, in Canada, the defence is one of honest belief and not one of reasonable belief, the exception in s-s. (1)(c) amply provides for this defence. In *R. v. Laybourn* (1987), 33 C.C.C. (3d) 385, 39 D.L.R. (4th) 641, [1987] 1 S.C.R. 782, this court discussed the effect of s. 244(4) (now s. 265(4)), which codifies this defence, on the defence of honest but mistaken belief in consent articulated by this court in *Pappajohn v. The Queen* (1980), 52 C.C.C. (2d) 481, 111 D.L.R. (3d) 1, [1980] 2 S.C.R. 120. For clarity I will reproduce this section.

> 265(4) Where an accused alleges that he believed that the complainant consented to the conduct that is the subject-matter of the charge, a judge, if satisfied that there is sufficient evidence and that, if believed by the jury, the evidence would constitute a defence, shall instruct the jury, when reviewing all the evidence relating to the determination of the honesty of the accused's belief, to consider the presence or absence of reasonable grounds for that belief.

This court concluded that the *"Pappajohn"* defence had not been legislatively altered. While one may then wonder why Parliament included the codification of this defence in its package of reforms, the decision of this court in *Laybourn, supra,* does not force the conclusion that s-s. (1)(c) of s. 276 excludes relevant evidence. McIntyre J., for the majority in *Laybourn, supra,* held at pp. 391-2 that before the defence of honest but mistaken belief can be put to the jury, the trial judge must conclude that there is an "air of reality" to the defence:

> There will not be an air of reality about a mere statement that "I thought she was consenting" not supported to some degree by other evidence or circumstances arising in the case ... The question he [the trial judge] must answer is this. In all the circumstances of this case, is there any reality in the defence? ...

When the defence of mistake of fact—or for that matter any other defence—is raised, two distinct steps are involved. The first step for the trial judge is to decide if the defence should be put to the jury. It is on this question, as I have said, that the "air of reality" test is applied.

Further, when the trier of fact turns his or her mind to the issue of whether the belief was honestly held, McIntyre J. stated at p. 392:

> This section [s. 244(4), now s. 265(4)], in my view, does not change the law as applied in *Pappajohn*. It does not require that the mistaken belief be reasonable or reasonably held. It simply makes it clear that in determining the issue of the honesty of the asserted belief, the presence or absence of reasonable grounds for the belief are relevant factors for the jury's consideration.

It is my view that, assuming that both the trier of fact and the trier of law are operating in an intellectual environment that is free of rape myth and stereotype about women, any evidence excluded by this subsection would not satisfy the "air of reality" that must accompany this defence nor would it provide reasonable grounds for the jury to consider in assessing whether the belief was honestly held. The structure of the exception provided for in s. 276(1)(c) is, thus, not offensive to such a defence.

---

Parliament responded to *Seaboyer* in Bill C-49 to deal with substantive and evidentiary matters. As enacted, it provides as follows:

An Act to amend the Criminal Code (sexual assault)

> WHEREAS the Parliament of Canada is gravely concerned about the incidence of sexual violence and abuse in Canadian society and, in particular, the prevalence of sexual assault against women and children;
>
> WHEREAS the Parliament of Canada recognizes the unique character of the offence of sexual assault and how sexual assault and, more particularly, the fear of sexual assault affects the lives of the people of Canada;
>
> WHEREAS the Parliament of Canada intends to promote and help to ensure the full protection of the rights guaranteed under sections 7 and 15 of the *Canadian Charter of Rights and Freedoms*;
>
> WHEREAS the Parliament of Canada wishes to encourage the reporting of incidents of sexual violence or abuse, and to provide for the prosecution of offences within a framework of laws that are consistent with the principles of fundamental justice and that are fair to complainants as well as to accused persons;
>
> WHEREAS the Supreme Court of Canada has declared the existing section 276 of the *Criminal Code* to be of no force and effect;
>
> AND WHEREAS the Parliament of Canada believes that at trials of sexual offences, evidence of the complainant's sexual history is rarely relevant and that its admission should be subject to particular scrutiny, bearing in mind the inherently prejudicial character of such evidence;
>
> 1. The *Criminal Code* is amended by adding thereto, immediately after section 273 thereof, the following sections:

273.1(1)  Subject to subsection (2) and subsection 265(3), "consent" means, for the purposes of sections 271, 272 and 273, the voluntary agreement of the complainant to engage in the sexual activity in question.

(2)  No consent is obtained, for the purposes of sections 271, 272 and 273, where

(a)  the agreement is expressed by the words or conduct of a person other than the complainant;

(b)  the complainant is incapable of consenting to the activity;

(c)  the accused induces the complainant to engage in the activity by abusing a position of trust, power or authority;

(d)  the complainant expresses, by words or conduct, a lack of agreement to engage in the activity; or

(e)  the complainant, having consented to engage in sexual activity, expresses, by words or conduct, a lack of agreement to continue to engage in the activity.

(3)  Nothing in subsection (2) shall be construed as limiting the circumstances in which no consent is obtained.

273.2  It is not a defence to a charge under section 271, 272 or 273 that the accused believed that the complainant consented to the activity that forms the subject-matter of the charge, where

(a)  the accused's belief arose from the accused's

(i)  self-induced intoxication, or

(ii)  recklessness or wilful blindness; or

(b)  the accused did not take reasonable steps, in the circumstances known to the accused at the time, to ascertain that the complainant was consenting.

2. Section 276 of the said Act is repealed and the following substituted therefor:

276.(1)  In proceedings in respect of an offence under section 151, 152, 153, 155 or 159, subsection 160(2) or (3) or section 170, 171, 172, 173, 271, 272 or 273, evidence that the complainant has engaged in sexual activity, whether with the accused or with any other person, is not admissible to support an inference that, by reason of the sexual nature of that activity, the complainant

(a)  is more likely to have consented to the sexual activity that forms the subject-matter of the charge; or

(b)  is less worthy of belief.

(2)  In proceedings in respect of an offence referred to in subsection (1), no evidence shall be adduced by or on behalf of the accused that the complainant has engaged in sexual activity other than the sexual activity that forms the subject-matter of the charge, whether with the accused or with any other person, unless the judge, provincial court judge or justice determines, in accordance with the procedures set out in sections 276.1 and 276.2, that the evidence

(a)  is of specific instances of sexual activity;

(b)  is relevant to an issue at trial; and

(c)  has significant probative value that is not substantially outweighed by the danger of prejudice to the proper administration of justice.

(3)  In determining whether evidence is admissible under subsection (2), the judge, provincial court judge or justice shall take into account

(a) the interests of justice, including the right of the accused to make a full answer and defence;

(b) society's interest in encouraging the reporting of sexual assault offences;

(c) whether there is a reasonable prospect that the evidence will assist in arriving at a just determination in the case;

(d) the need to remove from the fact-finding process any discriminatory belief or bias;

(e) the risk that the evidence may unduly arouse sentiments of prejudice, sympathy or hostility in the jury;

(f) the potential prejudice to the complainant's personal dignity and right of privacy;

(g) the right of the complainant and of every individual to personal security and to the full protection and benefit of the law; and

(h) any other factor that the judge, provincial court judge or justice considers relevant.

Perhaps not surprisingly, these amendments were also challenged and so the dialogue continued between the Supreme Court and Parliament. At issue was whether Bill C-49 provided sufficient constitutional protection for both the accused and the complainant.

---

In *R. v. Darrach* (1998), 122 C.C.C. (3d) 225 (Ont. C.A.) the above bill was upheld from Charter challenge. The accused argued that s. 273.2 violated ss. 7 and 11(c) of the Charter by employing objective forms of *mens rea* and requiring the accused to demonstrate that he took reasonable steps to ascertain whether the complainant consented. Morden A.C.J.O. stated:

[85] With respect to the challenge based on s. 7, I am far from satisfied that sexual assault is one of those "very few" offences (*R. v. Vaillancourt*, [1987] 2 S.C.R. 636 at 653, 39 C.C.C. (3d) 118), which carries such a stigma that its *mens rea* component must be one of subjectivity. See Hogg, *Constitutional Law of Canada* (1992), looseleaf ed., vol. 2 at pp. 44-34 to 44-35. I say this because: it is an offence of general intent; it can be prosecuted by way of summary conviction; it is a generic offence which covers a broad range of conduct, some of which may be very minor compared to other offences; there is no minimum penalty, the maximum penalty is 10 years, and within this range the sentence can be tailored to reflect the moral opprobrium of both the offence and the offender. See *R. v. Creighton*, [1993] 3 S.C.R. 3, 83 C.C.C. (3d) 346, particulary at pp. 48-49, with respect to the offence of manslaughter.

[86] Further, I accept that the stigma characterization has been fairly criticized as being a most unstable one for making important constitutional decisions on the applicability of s. 7 of the *Charter* to the substantive elements of offences. See, for example, Hogg, *Constitutional Law of Canada* (1992) loose-leaf ed., at p. 44-35 and Stuart, *Charter Justice in Canadian Criminal Law*, 2nd ed. (Scarborough, ON: Carswell, 1996) at p. 74.

[87] Notwithstanding the foregoing reservations, I am prepared to decide this issue on the basis that the offence of sexual assault carries with it a sufficient social stigma as to require a subjective fault requirement on the part of the accused person. In my view,

notwithstanding s. 273.2(b), the offence is still largely one based on subjective fault—at least to a level that would satisfy constitutional requirements.

[88] No doubt, the provision can be regarded as introducing an objective component into the mental element of the offence but it is one which, in itself, is a modified one. It is personalized according to the subjective awareness of the accused at the time. The accused is to "take reasonable steps, *in the circumstances known to the accused at the time*, to ascertain that the complainant was consenting." In other words, the accused is not under an obligation to determine all the relevant circumstances—the issue is what he actually knew, not what he ought to have known.

[89] In addition, while the provision requires reasonable steps, it does not require that *all* reasonable steps be taken, as it did in the first version of the bill (Bill C-49, s. 1) that resulted in s. 273.2 and as does s. 150.1(4) of the *Criminal Code*, which is referred to in the judgment of the Supreme Court of Canada in *R. v. Hess; R. v. Nguyen*, [1990] 2 S.C.R. 906 at 922 and 925. Clearly, "all reasonable steps" imposes a more onerous burden than that in s. 273.2(b). I, of course, do not intend to express any view on the constitutionality of s. 150.1(4).

[90] The subjective *mens rea* component of the offence remains largely intact. The provision does not require that a mistaken belief in consent must be reasonable in order to exculpate. The provision merely requires that a person about to engage in sexual activity take "reasonable steps ... to ascertain that the complainant was consenting." Were a person to take reasonable steps, and nonetheless make an unreasonable mistake about the presence of consent, he or she would be entitled to ask the trier of fact to acquit on this basis.

[91] The extent to which the provision alters principles of liability underlying the offence of sexual assault is indicated in the reasons of McLachlin J. in *R. v. Esau* (1997), 116 C.C.C. (3d) 289 (S.C.C.) at 314. Although the statement is in a dissenting judgment I do not think that there is any proposition in the majority judgment of Major J. at variance with it. McLachlin J. said:

> A person is not entitled to take ambiguity as the equivalent of consent. If a person, acting honestly and without wilful blindness, perceives his companion's conduct as ambiguous or unclear, his duty is to abstain or obtain clarification on the issue of consent. This appears to be the rule at common law. In this situation, to use the words of Lord Cross of Chelsea in *Morgan, supra,* [[1976] A.C. 182] at p. 203, "it is only fair to the woman and not in the least unfair to the man that he should be under a duty to take reasonable care to ascertain that she is consenting to the intercourse and be at risk of a prosecution if he fails to take such care." As Glanville Williams, *Textbook of Criminal Law* (London: Stevens & Sons, 1978), at p. 101, put it: "the defendant is guilty if he realized the woman might not be consenting and took no steps to find out."

[92] Following this quotation, she said at pp. 314-15:

> I note that Parliament has affirmed this common sense proposition in enacting s. 273.2 of the *Criminal Code* of Canada which states that "[i]t is not a defence to a charge [of sexual assault] that the accused believed that the complainant consented to the activity that forms the subject-matter of the charge, where ... the accused did not take reasonable steps, in the circumstances known to the accused at the time, to

ascertain that the complainant was consenting." See also *R. v. Darrach* (1994), 17 O.R. (3d) 481 (Prov. Div.) [the judgment under appeal before this court]. The question is whether the defendant at bar, properly attentive to the issue of consent (i.e., not wilfully blind), could have, in light of the ambiguity, honestly concluded that the complainant had the capacity and was consenting to the sexual activity.

[93] Finally, having regard to the basic rationale underlying constitutionally mandated fault requirements that it is wrong to punish a person who is "morally innocent" (*Reference re Section 94(2) of the Motor Vehicle Act* (1985), 23 C.C.C. (3d) 289 (S.C.C.) at 311), it is difficult to contemplate that a man who has sexual intercourse with a woman who has not consented is morally innocent if he has not taken reasonable steps to ascertain that she was consenting.

## R. v. Darrach
### Supreme Court of Canada
### [2000] 2 S.C.R. 443

GONTHIER J.:

### *I. Introduction*

[1] The proper use of a complainant's sexual history in sexual offence prosecutions was last before this Court in *R. v. Seaboyer*, [1991] 2 S.C.R. 577 (S.C.C.). There the Court struck down an earlier version of s. 276 of the *Criminal Code*, R.S.C. 1985, c. C-46, because it excluded all evidence about a complainant's sexual history from the judicial process, subject to three exceptions. The majority found that s. 276 could potentially exclude evidence of critical relevance (at p. 616). Parliament then enacted the current s. 276 in Bill C-49 in 1992 (now S.C. 1992, c. 38). It essentially codifies the decision in *Seaboyer* and provides a mechanism for the trial judge to determine the admissibility of evidence of prior sexual activity.

[2] The current s. 276 categorically prohibits evidence of a complainant's sexual history only when it is used to support one of two general inferences. These are that a person is more likely to have consented to the alleged assault and that she is less credible as a witness by virtue of her prior sexual experience. Evidence of sexual activity may be admissible, however, to substantiate other inferences. Sections 276.1 and 276.2 provide a procedure to determine the admissibility of such evidence. In brief, the defence must file a written affidavit; if the judge finds that it discloses relevant evidence capable of being admissible under s. 276(2), the judge will hold a *voir dire* to determine the admissibility of the evidence the defence seeks to adduce.

[3] The accused challenges the constitutionality of parts of s. 276 under the *Canadian Charter of Rights and Freedoms* and the way in which they were interpreted by the trial judge. In my view, his challenge fails. The current version of s. 276 is carefully crafted to comport with the principles of fundamental justice. It protects the integrity of the judicial process while at the same time respecting the rights of the people involved. The complainant's privacy and dignity are protected by a procedure that also vindicates the accused's right to make full answer and defence. The procedure

does not violate the accused's s. 7 *Charter* right to a fair trial nor his s. 11(c) right not to testify against himself or his s. 11(d) right to a fair hearing. For the reasons below, I find that the impugned sections of the law are constitutional and that their application by the trial judge was beyond reproach.

## II. Facts

[4]  The accused met the complainant in October 1991, when she began working at the retail store where he worked as a supervisor. They became friends and began a sexual relationship. After their sexual relationship ended, they saw each other casually, largely because they lived two doors apart on the same street. At some point, the accused lent the complainant $20. On November 6, 1992, he called her at work (he no longer worked there) and asked to be repaid. The complainant met him that night and later that evening, they walked home together. The accused asked her to come into his apartment. Once inside, the accused sexually assaulted the complainant.

[5]  The trial judge accepted the complainant's testimony about the assault as "clear, she was consistent and straightforward." It was uncontradicted and unshaken by cross-examination. The accused called no evidence and made no submissions. [The trial judge refused to admit the evidence of previous sexual activity.] All the elements of the offence were proven by the Crown and the accused was convicted of sexual assault under s. 271 of the *Criminal Code*. He was sentenced to nine months' imprisonment. …

[20]  The current version of s. 276 is in essence a codification by Parliament of the Court's guidelines in *Seaboyer*. It contains substantive sections that prevent evidence of a complainant's past sexual activity from being used for improper purposes and procedural sections that enforce this rule. The constitutional challenge in the case at bar focuses on four aspects of s. 276; two of them are substantive and two are procedural. The ultimate justification for all four is that they are found in some form in the *Seaboyer* guidelines (at p. 635). At a general level, the constitutionality of both the rule and the procedure has already been established. The procedure in particular was not discussed in any detail in *Seaboyer*, however, so I shall review why these rules, in the form in which they were ultimately enacted by Parliament, are constitutional.

[21]  The accused challenges the constitutionality of s. 276 on two grounds. He claims that the substantive sections that exclude evidence violate his s. 7 right to make full answer and defence and his s. 11(d) right to a fair trial and the presumption of innocence. As I show below, his argument fails because the legislation enhances the fairness of the hearing by excluding misleading evidence from trials of sexual offences. It preserves the accused's right to adduce relevant evidence that meets certain criteria and so to make full answer and defence.

[22]  The accused's second challenge is that the procedural sections violate his right not to be compelled to be a witness in proceedings against him, as guaranteed by ss. 7 and 11(c). The arguments relating to self-incrimination fail because s. 276 does not create a legal compulsion to testify. The accused participates voluntarily in order to exculpate himself. Because he seeks to introduce evidence about the complainant's sexual activity, it is up to him to show how it is relevant. The presumption of

innocence is preserved because the Crown still bears the burden of proving all the elements of the offence. His constitutional rights are not infringed by either the substantive or the procedural parts of s. 276. The balance struck in *Seaboyer* among the interests of justice, the accused and the complainant is preserved in the current legislation.

### A. *The Approach to Sections 7, 11(c) and 11(d) of the Charter*

[23]  The accused claims that his right not to be compelled to testify against himself as protected by s. 11(c) and his right to a fair trial with the presumption of innocence as protected by s. 11(d) are infringed by s. 276. He therefore claims that he is deprived of his liberty in a way that is not in accordance with the principles of fundamental justice, contrary to s. 7 of the *Charter*. In *R. v. Mills*, [1999] 3 S.C.R. 668 (S.C.C.), the Court dealt with a claim that s. 11(d) was violated in combination with s. 7, and the Court analysed the issues under the rubric of s. 7 on the grounds that the fair trial specifically protected by s. 11(d) was itself a principle of fundamental justice under s. 7. In *R. v. White*, [1999] 2 S.C.R. 417 (S.C.C.), at paras. 40 and 44, Iacobucci J. described s. 11(c) as a procedural protection that underlies the principle against self-incrimination, which is also a principle of fundamental justice under s. 7. In both cases, the Court analysed the rights involved in the context of s. 7.

[24]  These cases are part of the Court's jurisprudence that has consistently held that the principles of fundamental justice enshrined in s. 7 protect more than the rights of the accused. As McLachlin J. wrote in *Seaboyer*, *supra*, at p. 603:

> the principles of fundamental justice reflect a spectrum of interests, from the rights of the accused to broader societal concerns. ... The ultimate question is whether the legislation, viewed in a purposive way, conforms to the fundamental precepts which underlie our system of justice.

One of the implications of this analysis is that while the right to make full answer and defence and the principle against self-incrimination are certainly core principles of fundamental justice, they can be respected without the accused being entitled to "the most favourable procedures that could possibly be imagined" (*R. v. L. (T.P.)*, [1987] 2 S.C.R. 309 (S.C.C.), at p. 362; cited in *Mills*, *supra*, at para. 72). Nor is the accused entitled to have procedures crafted that take only his interests into account. Still less is he entitled to procedures that would distort the truth-seeking function of a trial by permitting irrelevant and prejudicial material at trial.

[25]  In *Seaboyer*, the Court found that the principles of fundamental justice include the three purposes of s. 276 identified above: protecting the integrity of the trial by excluding evidence that is misleading, protecting the rights of the accused, as well as encouraging the reporting of sexual violence and protecting "the security and privacy of the witnesses" (p. 606). This was affirmed in *Mills*, *supra*, at para. 72. The Court crafted its guidelines in *Seaboyer* in accordance with these principles, and it is in relation to these principles that the effects of s. 276 on the accused must be evaluated.

[26]  The Court in *Mills* upheld the constitutionality of the provisions in the *Criminal Code* that control the use of personal and in therapeutic records in trials of sexual

offences. The use of these records in evidence is analogous many ways to the use of evidence of prior sexual activity, and the protections in the *Criminal Code* surrounding the use of records at trial are motivated by similar policy considerations. L'Heureux-Dubé J. has warned that therapeutic records should not become a tool for circumventing s. 276: "[w]e must not allow the defence to do indirectly what it cannot do directly" (*R. v. O'Connor*, [1995] 4 S.C.R. 411 (S.C.C.), at para. 122, and *R. v. Osolin*, [1993] 4 S.C.R. 595 (S.C.C.), at p. 624). Academic commentators have observed that the use of therapeutic records increased with the enactment of s. 276 nonetheless (see K. Kelly, "'You must be crazy if you think you were raped': Reflections on the Use of Complainants' Personal and Therapy Records in Sexual Assault Trials" (1997), 9 *C.J.W.L.* 178, at p. 181).

[27] The provisions that control the use of personal records contain a two-step procedure like that in s. 276. The defence must first apply in writing under s. 278.3 with grounds to establish that the record is "likely relevant." On a *voir dire*, the judge may order the holder of the record to produce it if the defence can demonstrate that the record is "likely relevant" and "is necessary in the interests of justice." The judge then reviews the material and decides whether or not to produce it to the accused. The *Code* contains a list of factors to help the judge determine the relevance of the record, much like the list in s. 276 to help the trial judge exercise her discretion to admit evidence of prior sexual activity.

[28] The constitutional issue in *Mills* was analogous to that in the present case because the therapeutic records provisions can potentially exclude relevant evidence from a trial. Although this is less likely under s. 276, in the sense that the accused is better able to establish the relevance of sexual activity in which he participated than he can describe therapeutic records not in his possession, it is still possible. This is because the test for admissibility in s. 276(2) requires not only that the evidence be relevant but also that it be more probative than prejudicial. *Mills* dealt with a conflict among the same three *Charter* principles that are in issue in the case at bar: full answer and defence, privacy and equality (at para. 61). The Court defined these rights relationally: "the scope of the right to make full answer and defence must be determined in light of privacy and equality rights of complainants and witnesses" (paras. 62-66 and 94). The exclusionary rule was upheld. The privacy and equality concerns involved in protecting the records justified interpreting the right to make full answer and defence in a way that did not include a right to all relevant evidence. ...

[30] In *Mills* ... the Court defined the scope of the accused's rights in a contextual way that reconciled the principles of fundamental justice. In *Mills*, legislation that excludes evidence was upheld as constitutional, to the benefit of the Crown; in *White*, evidence was excluded to the benefit of the accused, on the grounds that it was unfairly obtained through compulsion. In *Seaboyer*, a blanket exclusionary rule about evidence of prior sexual activity was struck down as unconstitutional in favour of vesting discretionary power to admit evidence in the trial judge. The old s. 276 was held to violate ss. 7 and 11(d) and could not be justified under s. 1. The Court's substitute guidelines were fully constitutional and did not require a s. 1 justification, much like in *Mills*.

[31] In the case at bar, I affirm the reasons in *Seaboyer* and find that none of the accused's rights are infringed by s. 276 as he alleges. *Seaboyer* provides a basic justification for the legislative scheme in s. 276, including the determination of relevance as well as the prejudicial and probative value of the evidence. *Mills* and *White* show how the impact of s. 276 on the principles of fundamental justice relied on by the accused should be assessed in light of the other principles of fundamental justice that s. 276 was designed to protect. The reasons in *Mills* are apposite because they demonstrate how the same principles of equality, privacy and fairness can be reconciled. I shall show below how the procedure created by s. 276 to protect the trial process from distortion and to protect complainants is consistent with the principles of fundamental justice. It is fair to the accused and properly reconciles the divergent interests at play, as the Court suggested in *Seaboyer*.

## B. *The Substantive Sections*

### (1) Section 276(1)—The Exclusionary Rule

[32] The accused objects to the exclusionary rule itself in s. 276(1) on the grounds that it is a "blanket exclusion" that prevents him from adducing evidence necessary to make full answer and defence, as guaranteed by ss. 7 and 11(d) of the *Charter*. He is mistaken in his characterization of the rule. Far from being a "blanket exclusion," s. 276(1) only prohibits the use of evidence of past sexual activity when it is offered to support two specific, illegitimate inferences. These are known as the "twin myths," namely that a complainant is more likely to have consented or that she is less worthy of belief "by reason of the sexual nature of the activity" she once engaged in.

[33] This section gives effect to McLachlin J.'s finding in *Seaboyer* that the "twin myths" are simply not relevant at trial. They are not probative of consent or credibility and can severely distort the trial process. Section 276(1) also clarifies *Seaboyer* in several respects. Section 276 applies to all sexual activity, whether with the accused or with someone else. It also applies to non-consensual as well as consensual sexual activity, as this Court found implicitly in *R. v. Crosby*, [1995] 2 S.C.R. 912 (S.C.C.), at p. 924. Although the *Seaboyer* guidelines referred to "consensual sexual conduct" (pp. 634-35), Parliament enacted the new version of s. 276 without the word "consensual." Evidence of non-consensual sexual acts can equally defeat the purposes of s. 276 by distorting the trial process when it is used to evoke stereotypes such as that women who have been assaulted must have deserved it and that they are unreliable witnesses, as well as by deterring people from reporting assault by humiliating them in court. The admissibility of evidence of non-consensual sexual activity is determined by the procedures in s. 276. Section 276 also settles any ambiguity about whether the "twin myths" are limited to inferences about "unchaste" women in particular; they are not (as discussed by C. Boyle and M. MacCrimmon, "The Constitutionality of Bill C-49: Analyzing Sexual Assault As If Equality Really Mattered" (1998), 41 *Crim. L.Q.* 198, at pp. 231-32).

[34] The *Criminal Code* excludes all discriminatory generalizations about a complainant's disposition to consent or about her credibility based on the *sexual nature* of her past sexual activity on the grounds that these are improper lines of reasoning.

This was the import of the Court's findings in *Seaboyer* about how sexist beliefs about women distort the trial process. The text of the exclusionary rule in s. 276(1) diverges very little from the guidelines in *Seaboyer*. The mere fact that the wording differs between the Court's guidelines and Parliament's enactment is itself immaterial. In *Mills, supra*, the Court affirmed that "[t]o insist on slavish conformity" by Parliament to judicial pronouncements "would belie the mutual respect that underpins the relationship" between the two institutions (para. 55). In this case, the legislation follows the Court's suggestions very closely.

[35] The phrase "by reason of the sexual nature of the activity" in s. 276 is a clarification by Parliament that it is inferences from the *sexual nature* of the activity, as opposed to inferences from other potentially relevant features of the activity, that are prohibited. If evidence of sexual activity is proffered for its non-sexual features, such as to show a pattern of conduct or a prior inconsistent statement, it may be permitted. The phrase "by reason of the sexual nature of the activity" has the same effect as the qualification "solely to support the inference" in *Seaboyer* in that it limits the exclusion of evidence to that used to invoke the "twin myths" (p. 635).

[36] This Court has already had occasion to admit evidence of prior sexual activity under the current version of s. 276. In *Crosby, supra*, such evidence was admissible because it was inextricably linked to a prior inconsistent statement that was relevant to the complainant's credibility (at para. 14). This case itself demonstrates that s. 276 does not function in practice as a blanket exclusion, as alleged by the accused. On the contrary, s. 276 controls the admissibility of evidence of sexual activity by providing judges with criteria and procedures to help them exercise their discretion to admit it. I explain below why the procedure to assess relevance is constitutional. Suffice it here to say that it is this procedure that makes the *Seaboyer* guidelines and the current version of s. 276 constitutional where the earlier version of s. 276 was not.

[37] An accused has never had a right to adduce irrelevant evidence. Nor does he have the right to adduce misleading evidence to support illegitimate inferences: "the accused is not permitted to distort the truth-seeking function of the trial process" (*Mills, supra*, at para. 74). Because s. 276(1) is an evidentiary rule that only excludes material that is not relevant, it cannot infringe the accused's right to make full answer and defence. Section 276(2) is more complicated, and I turn to it now.

(2) Section 276(2)(c)—"Significant Probative Value"

[38] If evidence is not barred by s. 276(1) because it is tendered to support a permitted inference, the judge must still weigh its probative value against its prejudicial effect to determine its admissibility. This essentially mirrors the common law guidelines in *Seaboyer* which contained this balancing test (at p. 635). The accused takes issue with the fact that s. 276(2)(c) specifically requires that the evidence have "significant probative value." The word "significant" was added by Parliament but it does not render the provision unconstitutional by raising the threshold for the admissibility of evidence to the point that it is unfair to the accused.

[39] It may be noted that the word "significant" is not found in the French text; the law speaks simply of "*valeur probante*." The rule of equal authenticity and the rule against unconstitutional interpretation require that the two versions be recon-

ciled where possible. The interpretation of "significant" by the Ontario Court of Appeal satisfies this requirement: Morden A.C.J.O. found that "the evidence is not to be so trifling as to be incapable, in the context of all the evidence, of raising a reasonable doubt" (p. 16). At the same time, Morden A.C.J.O. agrees with *R. v. Santocono* (1996), 91 O.A.C. 26 (Ont. C.A.), at p. 29, where s. 276(2)(c) was interpreted to mean that "it was not necessary for the appellant to demonstrate 'strong and compelling' reasons for admission of the evidence." This standard is not a departure from the conventional rules of evidence. I agree with the Court of Appeal that the word "significant," on a textual level, is reasonably capable of being read in accordance with ss. 7 and 11(d) and the fair trial they protect.

[40] The context of the word "significant" in the provision in which it occurs substantiates this interpretation. Section 276(2)(c) allows a judge to admit evidence of "*significant* probative value that is not *substantially* outweighed by the danger of prejudice to the proper administration of justice" (emphasis added). The adverb "substantially" serves to protect the accused by raising the standard for the judge to exclude evidence once the accused has shown it to have significant probative value. In a sense, both sides of the equation are heightened in this test, which serves to direct judges to the serious ramifications of the use of evidence of prior sexual activity all parties in these cases.

[41] In light of the purposes of s. 276, the use of the word "significant" is consistent with both the majority and the minority reasons in *Seaboyer*. Section 276 is designed to prevent the use of evidence of prior sexual activity for improper purposes. The requirement of "significant probative value" serves to exclude evidence of trifling relevance that, even though not used to support the two forbidden inferences, would still endanger the "proper administration of justice." The Court has recognized that there are inherent "damages and disadvantages presented by the admission of such evidence" (*Seaboyer*, *supra*, at p. 634). As Morden A.C.J.O. puts it, evidence of sexual activity must be significantly probative if it is to overcome its prejudicial effect. The *Criminal Code* codifies this reality.

[42] By excluding misleading evidence while allowing the accused to adduce evidence that meets the criteria of s. 276(2), s. 276 enhances the fairness of trials of sexual offences. Section 11(d) guarantees a fair trial. Fairness under s. 11(d) is determined in the context of the trial process as a whole (*R. v. S. (J.R.)* (1987), 37 C.C.C. (3d) 351 (Ont. C.A.), at pp. 365-66). As L'Heureux-Dubé J. wrote in *Crosby*, *supra*, at para. 11, "[s]ection 276 cannot be interpreted so as to deprive a person of a fair defence." At the same time, the accused's right to make full answer and defence, as was held in *Mills*, *supra*, at para. 75, is not "automatically breached where he or she is deprived of relevant information." Nor is it necessarily breached when the accused is not permitted to adduce relevant information that is not "significantly" probative, under a rule of evidence that protects the trial from the distorting effects of evidence of prior sexual activity.

[43] When the trial judge determines the admissibility of evidence under s. 276(2), she is to take into account the multiple factors in s. 276(3), which include "the right of the accused to make a full answer and defence" in s. 276(3)(a). Section 276 is designed to exclude irrelevant information and only that relevant information that is

more prejudicial to the administration of justice than it is probative. The accused's right to a fair trial is, of course, of fundamental concern to the administration of justice. In a similar situation in *Mills*, the Court preserved the right to make full answer and defence in the following commonsensical way, at para. 94:

> It is clear that the right to full answer and defence is not engaged where the accused seeks information that will only serve to distort the truth-seeking purpose of a trial, and in such a situation, privacy and equality rights are paramount. On the other hand, where the information contained in a record directly bears on the right to make full answer and defence, privacy rights must yield to the need to avoid convicting the innocent.

Thus the threshold criteria that evidence be of "significant" probative value does not prevent an accused from making full answer and defence to the charges against him. Consequently his *Charter* rights under ss. 7 and 11(d) are not infringed by s. 276(2)(c). ...

[52] Nothing in s. 276 obviates the Crown's basic duty to establish all the elements of a sexual offence beyond a reasonable doubt. This burden of proof on the Crown and the fact that the trial must be fair are the essence of the presumption of innocence, as the Court found in *R. v. Oakes*, [1986] 1 S.C.R. 103 (S.C.C.), at p. 121, and *R. v. Whyte*, [1988] 2 S.C.R. 3 (S.C.C.), at p. 15. A fair trial includes the right to make full answer and defence, but as I explained above, the admissibility criteria in ss. 276(2) and 276(3) respect this right. In *Osolin, supra*, at pp. 688-89, the "evidentiary burden" borne by the accused in a sexual offence trial to substantiate a claim of honest but mistaken belief in consent was held not to offend the presumption of innocence because it did not relieve the Crown of the burden of proof of the elements of the offence. The tactical burden under s. 276 is even less onerous on the accused because it relates only to establishing relevance on a *voir dire*; it does not impose any burden on the accused at trial. ...

[58] It is common for the defence in sexual offence cases to deny that the assault occurred, to challenge the identity of the assailant, to allege consent or to claim an honest but mistaken belief in consent. Evidence of prior sexual activity will rarely be relevant to support a denial that sexual activity took place or to establish consent ... . As the Court affirmed in *R. v. Ewanchuk*, [1999] 1 S.C.R. 330 (S.C.C.), at para. 27, the determination of consent is "only concerned with the complainant's perspective. The approach is purely subjective." Actual consent must be given for each instance of sexual activity.

[59] Section 276 is most often used in attempts to substantiate claims of an honest but mistaken belief in consent. To make out the defence, the accused must show that "he believed that the complainant *communicated consent to engage in the sexual activity in question*" (*Ewanchuk, supra*, at para. 46 (emphasis in the original)). To establish that the complainant's prior sexual activity is relevant to his mistaken belief during the alleged assault, the accused must provide some evidence of what he believed at the time of the alleged assault. This is necessary for the trial judge to be able to assess the relevance of the evidence in accordance with the statute. It is an essential part of the legislative scheme which provides a means by which the accused may establish the relevance of the evidence he chooses to put forward. ...

[68] The complainant is not compellable at the *voir dire* pursuant to s. 276.2(2). This provision is both constitutional and an important aspect of s. 276. The accused argues that he is *de facto* compellable *because* the complainant is non-compellable at the *voir dire*. I have already established that he is not compellable nor being compelled at law. His desire to have the complainant testify flows, as would his need to testify himself, from his tactical decision to present evidence and the ensuing need to show its relevance. As we have seen, there is no legal compulsion nor violation of the accused's constitutional rights. Furthermore, the complainant's non-compellability is based on sound legislative goals. To compel the complainant to be examined on her sexual history before the subject has been found to be relevant to the trial would defeat two of the three purposes of the law, as articulated and upheld in *Seaboyer* (at p. 606). It is an invasion of the complainant's privacy and discourages the reporting of crimes of sexual violence. As the Ontario Court of Appeal points out, the accused must know what evidence he wants to introduce on his own; the *voir dire* is not to be a "fishing expedition" (p. 21). The evidence is tested at the *voir dire* and if it meets the criteria in s. 276(2), it may be introduced at trial. The complainant can then be compelled to testify or if the Crown, as it is most likely to do, calls her as a witness, be cross-examined on it.

[69] The right to make full answer and defence, moreover, does not provide a right to cross-examine an accuser. This was explicitly held in *R. v. Cook*, [1997] 1 S.C.R. 1113 (S.C.C.), where the Court affirmed the broad discretion of the Crown to conduct its case. The Crown is free from any requirement to call particular witnesses, and this applies even to the victim of the crime for which the accused faces conviction (at para. 19).

[70] The fair trial protected by s. 11(d) is one that does justice to all the parties. As Cory J. wrote of sexual assault trials in *Osolin*, *supra*, at p. 669:

> The provisions of ss. 15 and 28 of the *Charter* guaranteeing equality to men and women, although not determinative, should be taken into account in determining the reasonable limitations that should be placed upon the cross-examination of a complainant.

## VII. Conclusion

[71] On the basis of this Court's decision in *Seaboyer*, Parliament gave the trial judge the role of deciding whether a complainant's sexual history is relevant in the trial of a sexual offence. She is to exercise her discretion within the structure of a procedure created by s. 276. The legislation lists factors to take into account, similar to those upheld by this Court's decision in *Mills*, *supra*, which prominently include the accused's right to make full answer and defence in s. 276(3)(a). This discretion, of course, cannot be exercised in an unconstitutional manner. The accused's constitutional rights are protected by this legislation. …

*Appeal dismissed.*

In the following case, the Supreme Court was called upon again to review several issues concerning the prosecution of sexual assault. The reasons for judgment clarify some points but at the same time underscore how volatile the issues are in this area of the law.

### R. v. Ewanchuk
Supreme Court of Canada
[1999] 1 S.C.R. 330

MAJOR J. (Lamer C.J.C., Cory, Iacobucci, Bastarache, and Binnie JJ. concurring):

[1] In the present appeal the accused was acquitted of sexual assault. The trial judge relied on the defence of implied consent. This was a mistake of law as no such defence is available in assault cases in Canada. This mistake of law is reviewable by appellate courts, and for the reasons that follow the appeal is allowed.

### I. Facts

[2] The complainant was a 17-year-old woman living in the city of Edmonton. She met the accused respondent Ewanchuk on the afternoon of June 2, 1994, while walking through the parking lot of the Heritage Shopping Mall with her roommate. The accused, driving a red van towing a trailer, approached the two young women. He struck up a conversation with them. He related that he was in the custom woodworking business and explained that he displayed his work at retail booths in several shopping malls. He said that he was looking for staff to attend his displays, and asked whether the young women were looking for work. The complainant's friend answered that they were, at which point the accused asked to interview her friend privately. She declined, but spoke with the accused beside his van for some period of time about the sort of work he required, and eventually exchanged telephone numbers with the accused.

[3] The following morning the accused telephoned the apartment where the complainant and her friend resided with their boyfriends. The complainant answered the phone. She told the accused that her friend was still asleep. When he learned this, the accused asked the complainant if she was interested in a job. She indicated that she was, and they met a short time later, again in the Heritage Mall parking lot. At the accused's suggestion, the interview took place in his van. In the words of the complainant, a "very business-like, polite" conversation took place. Some time later, the complainant asked if she could smoke a cigarette, and the accused suggested that they move outside since he was allergic to cigarette smoke. Once outside the van, he asked the complainant if she would like to see some of his work, which was kept inside the trailer attached to his van, and she indicated that she would.

[4] The complainant entered the trailer, purposely leaving the door open behind her. The accused followed her in, and closed the door in a way which made the complainant think that he had locked it. There is no evidence whether the door was actually locked, but the complainant stated that she became frightened at this point. Once inside the trailer, the complainant and the accused sat down side-by-side on the floor

of the trailer. They spoke and looked through a portfolio of his work. This lasted 10 to 15 minutes, after which the conversation turned to more personal matters.

[5] During the time in the trailer the accused was quite tactile with the complainant, touching her hand, arms and shoulder as he spoke. At some point the accused said that he was feeling tense and asked the complainant to give him a massage. The complainant complied, massaging the accused's shoulders for a few minutes. After she stopped, he asked her to move in front of him so that he could massage her, which she did. The accused then massaged the complainant's shoulders and arms while they continued talking. During this mutual massaging the accused repeatedly told the complainant to relax, and that she should not be afraid. As the massage progressed, the accused attempted to initiate more intimate contact. The complainant stated that, "he started to try to massage around my stomach, and he brought his hands up around— or underneath my breasts, and he started to get quite close up there, so I used my elbows to push in between, and I said, No."

[6] The accused stopped immediately, but shortly thereafter resumed non-sexual massaging, to which the complainant also said, "No." The accused again stopped, and said, "See, I'm a nice guy. It's okay."

[7] The accused then asked the complainant to turn and face him. She did so, and he began massaging her feet. His touching progressed from her feet up to her inner thigh and pelvic area. The complainant did not want the accused to touch her in this way, but said nothing as she said she was afraid that any resistance would prompt the accused to become violent. Although the accused never used or threatened any force, the complainant testified that she did not want to "egg [him] on." As the contact progressed, the accused laid himself heavily on top of the complainant and began grinding his pelvic area against hers. The complainant testified that the accused asserted, "that he could get me so horny so that I would want it so bad, and he wouldn't give it to me because he had self-control."

[8] The complainant did not move or reciprocate the contact. The accused asked her to put her hands across his back, but she did not; instead she lay "bone straight." After less than a minute of this the complainant asked the accused to stop. "I said, Just please stop. And so he stopped." The accused again told the complainant not to be afraid, and asked her if she trusted that he wouldn't hurt her. In her words, the complainant said, "Yes, I trust that you won't hurt me." On the stand she stated that she was afraid throughout, and only responded to the accused in this way because she was fearful that a negative answer would provoke him to use force.

[9] After this brief exchange, the accused went to hug the complainant and, as he did so, he laid on top of her again, continuing the pelvic grinding. He also began moving his hands on the complainant's inner thigh, inside her shorts, for a short time. While still on top of her the accused began to fumble with his shorts and took out his penis. At this point the complainant again asked the accused to desist, saying, "No, stop."

[10] Again, the accused stopped immediately, got off the complainant, smiled at her and said something to the effect of, "It's okay. See, I'm a nice guy, I stopped." At this point the accused again hugged the complainant lightly before opening up his wallet and removing a $100 bill, which he gave to the complainant. She testified that the accused said that the $100 was for the massage and that he told her not to tell

anyone about it. He made some reference to another female employee with whom he also had a very close and friendly relationship, and said that he hoped to get together with the complainant again.

[11] Shortly after the exchange of the money the complainant said that she had to go. The accused opened the door and the complainant stepped out. Some further conversation ensued outside the trailer before the complainant finally left and walked home. On her return home the complainant was emotionally distraught and contacted the police.

[12] At some point during the encounter the accused provided the complainant with a brochure describing his woodwork and gave her his name and address, which she wrote on the brochure. The investigating officer used this information to locate the accused at his home, where he was arrested. He was subsequently charged with sexual assault and tried before a judge sitting alone.

[13] The accused did not testify, leaving only the complainant's evidence as to what took place between them. The trial judge found her to be a credible witness and her version of events was not contradicted or disputed. In cross-examination the complainant testified that, although she was extremely afraid throughout the encounter, she had done everything possible to project a confident demeanour, in the belief that this would improve her chances of avoiding a violent assault. The following passage is illustrative of her evidence:

Q You didn't want to show any discomfort, right?

A No.

Q Okay. In fact, you wanted to project the picture that you were quite happy to be with him and everything was fine, right?

A Not that I was happy, but that I was comfortable.

Q Comfortable, all right. And relaxed?

A Yes.

Q And you did your best to do that, right?

A Yes.

[14] Later in cross-examination, counsel for the accused again asked the complainant about the image she sought to convey to the complainant by her behaviour:

Q And you wanted to make sure that he didn't sense any fear on your part, right?

A Yes.

## II.  Judicial History

### A.  Court of Queen's Bench

[15] The trial judge made a number of findings of fact in his oral judgement. He found that the complainant was a credible witness. He found as facts: that in her mind she had not consented to any of the sexual touching which took place; that she had

been fearful throughout the encounter; that she didn't want the accused to know she was afraid; and that she had actively projected a relaxed and unafraid visage. He concluded that the failure of the complainant to communicate her fear, including her active efforts to the contrary, rendered her subjective feelings irrelevant.

[16] The trial judge then considered the question of whether the accused had raised the defence of honest but mistaken belief in consent, and concluded that he had not. The trial judge characterized the defence position as being a failure by the Crown to discharge its onus of proving "beyond a reasonable doubt that there was an absence of consent." That is, he took the defence to be asserting that the Crown had failed to prove one of the components of the *actus reus* of the offence. This led the trial judge to characterize the defence as one of *"implied consent."* In so doing he concluded that the complainant's conduct was such that it could be *objectively* construed as constituting consent to sexual touching of the type performed by the accused.

[17] The trial judge treated consent as a question of the complainant's behaviour in the encounter. As a result of that conclusion he found that the defence of honest but mistaken belief in consent had no application since the accused made no claims as to his mental state. On the totality of the evidence, provided solely by the Crown's witnesses, the trial judge concluded that the Crown had not proven the absence of consent beyond a reasonable doubt and acquitted the accused.

### B. *Alberta Court of Appeal (1998), 57 Alta. L.R. (3d) 235 (Alta. C.A.)*

[18] Each of the three justices of the Court of Appeal issued separate reasons. McClung and Foisy JJ.A. both dismissed the appeal on the basis that it was a fact-driven acquittal from which the Crown could not properly appeal. In addition, McClung J.A. concluded that the Crown had failed to prove that the accused possessed the requisite criminal intent. He found that the Crown had failed to prove beyond a reasonable doubt that the accused had intended to commit an assault upon the complainant.

[19] Fraser C.J. dissented. She found that the trial judge erred in a number of ways. Specifically, she found that:

- The trial judge erred in his interpretation of the term "consent" as that term is applied to the offence of sexual assault.
- There is no defence of "implied consent," independent of the provisions of ss. 273.1 and 273.2 of the *Criminal Code.*
- It was an error to employ an objective test to determine whether a complainant's "consent" was induced by fear.
- The trial judge erred in the legal effect he ascribed:
  - to the complainant's silence when subjected to sexual contact by the respondent;
  - to the complainant's non-disclosure of her fear when subjected to sexual contact by the respondent;
  - to the complainant's expressed lack of agreement to sexual contact;
  - to the fact that there was no basis for a defence of "implied consent" or "consent by conduct";

- to the fact that there was no consent to sexual activity.

- The defence of mistake of fact had no application to the issue of "consent" in this case.
- The trial judge erred when he failed to consider whether the respondent had been wilfully blind or reckless as to whether the complainant consented.

[20] Fraser C.J. held that the only defence available to the accused was that of honest but mistaken belief in consent, and concluded that this defence could not be sustained on the facts as found. Accordingly, she would have allowed the appeal and substituted a verdict of guilty.

*III. Analysis*

*A. Appealable Questions of Law*

[21] The majority of the Court of Appeal dismissed the appeal on the ground that the Crown raised no question of law but sought to overturn the trial judge's finding of fact that reasonable doubt existed as to the presence or absence of consent. If the trial judge misdirected himself as to the legal meaning or definition of consent, then his conclusion is one of law, and is reviewable. See *R. v. Singer*, [1932] S.C.R. 279 (S.C.C.), *per* Anglin C.J., at p. 296:

> The right of appeal by the Attorney-General, conferred by [the *Criminal Code*] is, no doubt, confined to "questions of law." ... But we cannot regard that provision as excluding the right of the Appellate Divisional Court, where a conclusion of mixed law and fact, such as is the guilt or innocence of the accused, depends as it does here, upon the *legal effect of certain findings of fact* made by the judge or the jury ... to enquire into the soundness of that conclusion, since we cannot regard it as anything else but a question of law—especially where, as here, it is a clear result of misdirection of himself in law by the learned trial judge. [Emphasis added.]

[22] It properly falls to this Court to determine whether the trial judge erred in his understanding of consent in sexual assault, and to determine whether his conclusion that the defence of "implied consent" exists in Canadian law was correct.

*B. The Components of Sexual Assault*

[23] A conviction for sexual assault requires proof beyond reasonable doubt of two basic elements, that the accused committed the *actus reus* and that he had the necessary *mens rea*. The *actus reus* of assault is unwanted sexual touching. The *mens rea* is the intention to touch, knowing of, or being reckless of or wilfully blind to, a lack of consent, either by words or actions, from the person being touched.

(1) Actus Reus

[24] The crime of sexual assault is only indirectly defined in the *Criminal Code*, R.S.C. 1985, c. C-46. The offence is comprised of an assault within any one of the definitions in s. 265(1) of the *Code*, which is committed in circumstances of a sexual

nature, such that the sexual integrity of the victim is violated: see *R. v. S. (P.L.)*, [1991] 1 S.C.R. 909 (S.C.C.). [Sections 265(1) and (2) are then reproduced.]

[25]  The *actus reus* of sexual assault is established by the proof of three elements: (i) touching, (ii) the sexual nature of the contact, and (iii) the absence of consent. The first two of these elements are objective. It is sufficient for the Crown to prove that the accused's actions were voluntary. The sexual nature of the assault is determined objectively; the Crown need not prove that the accused had any *mens rea* with respect to the sexual nature of his or her behaviour: see *R. v. Litchfield*, [1993] 4 S.C.R. 333 (S.C.C.), and *R. v. Chase*, [1987] 2 S.C.R. 293 (S.C.C.).

[26]  The absence of consent, however, is subjective and determined by reference to the complainant's subjective internal state of mind towards the touching, at the time it occurred: see *R. v. Jensen* (1996), 106 C.C.C. (3d) 430 (Ont. C.A.), at pp. 437-38; aff'd [1997] 1 S.C.R. 304 (S.C.C.), *R. v. Park*, [1995] 2 S.C.R. 836 (S.C.C.), at p. 850, *per* L'Heureux-Dubé J., and D. Stuart, *Canadian Criminal Law* (3rd ed. 1995), at p. 513.

[27]  Confusion has arisen from time to time on the meaning of consent as an element of the *actus reus* of sexual assault. Some of this confusion has been caused by the word "consent" itself. A number of commentators have observed that the notion of consent connotes active behaviour: see, for example, N. Brett, "Sexual Offenses and Consent" (1998), 11 *Can. J. Law & Jur.* 69, at p. 73. While this may be true in the general use of the word, for the purposes of determining the absence of consent as an element of the *actus reus*, the actual state of mind of the complainant is determinative. At this point, the trier of fact is only concerned with the complainant's perspective. The approach is purely subjective.

[28]  The rationale underlying the criminalization of assault explains this. Society is committed to protecting the personal integrity, both physical and psychological, of every individual. Having control over who touches one's body, and how, lies at the core of human dignity and autonomy. The inclusion of assault and sexual assault in the *Code* expresses society's determination to protect the security of the person from any non-consensual contact or threats of force. The common law has recognized for centuries that the individual's right to physical integrity is a fundamental principle, "every man's person being sacred, and no other having a right to meddle with it in any the slightest manner": see Blackstone's *Commentaries on the Laws of England* (4th ed. 1770), Book III, at p. 120. It follows that any intentional but unwanted touching is criminal.

[29]  While the complainant's testimony is the only source of direct evidence as to her state of mind, credibility must still be assessed by the trial judge, or jury, in light of all the evidence. It is open to the accused to claim that the complainant's words and actions, before and during the incident, raise a reasonable doubt against her assertion that she, in her mind, did not want the sexual touching to take place. If, however, as occurred in this case, the trial judge believes the complainant that she subjectively did not consent, the Crown has discharged its obligation to prove the absence of consent.

[30]  The complainant's statement that she did not consent is a matter of credibility to be weighed in light of all the evidence including any ambiguous conduct. The

question at this stage is purely one of credibility, and whether the totality of the complainant's conduct is consistent with her claim of non-consent. The accused's perception of the complainant's state of mind is not relevant. That perception only arises when a defence of honest but mistaken belief in consent is raised in the *mens rea* stage of the inquiry.

### (a) "Implied Consent"

[31] Counsel for the respondent submitted that the trier of fact may believe the complainant when she says she did not consent, but still acquit the accused on the basis that her conduct raised a reasonable doubt. Both he and the trial judge refer to this as "implied consent." It follows from the foregoing, however, that the trier of fact may only come to one of two conclusions: the complainant either consented or not. There is no third option. If the trier of fact accepts the complainant's testimony that she did not consent, no matter how strongly her conduct may contradict that claim, the absence of consent is established and the third component of the *actus reus* of sexual assault is proven. The doctrine of implied consent has been recognized in our common law jurisprudence in a variety of contexts but sexual assault is not one of them. There is no defence of implied consent to sexual assault in Canadian law.

### (b) Application to the Present Case

[32] In this case, the trial judge accepted the evidence of the complainant that she did not consent. That being so, he then misdirected himself when he considered the actions of the complainant, and not her subjective mental state, in determining the question of consent. As a result, he disregarded his previous finding that all the accused's sexual touching was unwanted. Instead he treated what he perceived as her ambiguous conduct as a failure by the Crown to prove the absence of consent.

[33] As previously mentioned, the trial judge accepted the complainant's testimony that she did not want the accused to touch her, but then treated her conduct as raising a reasonable doubt about consent, described by him as "implied consent." This conclusion was an error. See D. Stuart, Annotation on *R. v. Ewanchuk* (1998), 13 C.R. (5th) 330 (Alta. C.A.), where the author points out that consent is a matter of the state of mind of the complainant while belief in consent is, subject to s. 273.2 of the *Code*, a matter of the state of mind of the accused and may raise the defence of honest but mistaken belief in consent.

[34] The finding that the complainant did not want or consent to the sexual touching cannot co-exist with a finding that reasonable doubt exists on the question of consent. The trial judge's acceptance of the complainant's testimony regarding her own state of mind was the end of the matter on this point.

[35] This error was compounded somewhat by the trial judge's holding that the complainant's subjective and self-contained fear would not have changed his mind as to whether she consented. Although he needn't have considered this question, having already found that she did not in fact consent, any residual doubt raised by her ambiguous conduct was accounted for by what he accepted as an honest and pervasive fear held by the complainant.

(c)  Effect of the Complainant's Fear

[36]  To be legally effective, consent must be freely given. Therefore, even if the complainant consented, or her conduct raises a reasonable doubt about her non-consent, circumstances may arise which call into question what factors prompted her apparent consent. The *Code* defines a series of conditions under which the law will deem an absence of consent in cases of assault, notwithstanding the complainant's ostensible consent or participation. As enumerated in s. 265(3), these include submission by reason of force, fear, threats, fraud or the exercise of authority, and codify the longstanding common law rule that consent given under fear or duress is ineffective: see G. Williams, *Textbook of Criminal Law* (2nd ed. 1983), at pp. 551-61. [Section 265(3) is then reproduced.]

[37]  The words of Fish J.A. in *St-Laurent c. Québec (Juge de Cour du Québec)* (1993), [1994] R.J.Q. 69 (Que. C.A.), at p. 82, aptly describe the concern which the trier of fact must bear in mind when evaluating the actions of a complainant who claims to have been under fear, fraud or duress:

> "Consent" is ... stripped of its defining characteristics when it is applied to the submission, non-resistance, non-objection, or even the apparent agreement, of a deceived, unconscious or compelled will.

[38]  In these instances the law is interested in a complainant's reasons for choosing to participate in, or ostensibly consent to, the touching in question. In practice, this translates into an examination of the choice the complainant believed she faced. The courts' concern is whether she *freely* made up her mind about the conduct in question. The relevant section of the *Code* is s. 265(3)(b), which states that there is no consent as a matter of law where the complainant believed that she was choosing between permitting herself to be touched sexually or risking being subject to the application of force.

[39]  The question is not whether the complainant would have preferred not to engage in the sexual activity, but whether she believed herself to have only two choices: to comply or to be harmed. If a complainant agrees to sexual activity solely because she honestly believes that she will otherwise suffer physical violence, the law deems an absence of consent, and the third component of the *actus reus* of sexual assault is established. The trier of fact has to find that the complainant did not want to be touched sexually and made her decision to permit or participate in sexual activity as a result of an honestly held fear. The complainant's fear need not be reasonable, nor must it be communicated to the accused in order for consent to be vitiated. While the plausibility of the alleged fear, and any overt expressions of it, are obviously relevant to assessing the credibility of the complainant's claim that she consented out of fear, the approach is subjective.

[40]  Section 265(3) identifies an additional set of circumstances in which the accused's conduct will be culpable. The trial judge only has to consult s. 265(3) in those cases where the complainant has actually chosen to participate in sexual activity, or her ambiguous conduct or submission has given rise to doubt as to the absence of consent. If, as in this case, the complainant's testimony establishes the absence of consent beyond a reasonable doubt, the *actus reus* analysis is complete, and the trial

judge should have turned his attention to the accused's perception of the encounter and the question of whether the accused possessed the requisite *mens rea*.

(2) Mens Rea

[41] Sexual assault is a crime of general intent. Therefore, the Crown need only prove that the accused intended to touch the complainant in order to satisfy the basic *mens rea* requirement. See *R. c. Daviault*, [1994] 3 S.C.R. 63 (S.C.C.).

[42] However, since sexual assault only becomes a crime in the absence of the complainant's consent, the common law recognizes a defence of mistake of fact which removes culpability for those who honestly but mistakenly believed that they had consent to touch the complainant. To do otherwise would result in the injustice of convicting individuals who are morally innocent: see *R. v. Creighton*, [1993] 3 S.C.R. 3 (S.C.C.). As such, the *mens rea* of sexual assault contains two elements: intention to touch and knowing of, or being reckless of or wilfully blind to, a lack of consent on the part of the person touched. See *Park, supra*, at para. 39.

[43] The accused may challenge the Crown's evidence of *mens rea* by asserting an honest but mistaken belief in consent. The nature of this defence was described in *R. v. Pappajohn*, [1980] 2 S.C.R. 120 (S.C.C.), at p. 148, by Dickson J. (as he then was) (dissenting in the result):

> Mistake is a defence … where it prevents an accused from having the *mens rea* which the law requires for the very crime with which he is charged. Mistake of fact is more accurately seen as a negation of guilty intention than as the affirmation of a positive defence. It avails an accused who acts innocently, pursuant to a flawed perception of the facts, and nonetheless commits the *actus reus* of the offence. Mistake is a defence though, in the sense that it is raised as an issue by an accused. The Crown is rarely possessed of knowledge of the subjective factors which may have caused an accused to entertain a belief in a fallacious set of facts.

[44] The defence of mistake is simply a denial of *mens rea*. It does not impose any burden of proof upon the accused (see *R. v. R. (J.D.)*, [1987] 1 S.C.R. 918 (S.C.C.), at p. 936) and it is not necessary for the accused to testify in order to raise the issue. Support for the defence may stem from any of the evidence before the court, including, the Crown's case-in-chief and the testimony of the complainant. However, as a practical matter, this defence will usually arise in the evidence called by the accused.

(a) Meaning of "Consent" in the Context of an Honest but Mistaken Belief in Consent

[45] As with the *actus reus* of the offence, consent is an integral component of the *mens rea*, only this time it is considered from the perspective of the accused. Speaking of the *mens rea* of sexual assault in *Park, supra*, at para. 30, L'Heureux-Dubé J. (in her concurring reasons) stated that:

> … the *mens rea* of sexual assault is not only satisfied when it is shown that the accused knew that the complainant was essentially saying "no," but is also satisfied when it is shown that the accused knew that the complainant was essentially not saying "yes."

[46]  In order to cloak the accused's actions in moral innocence, the evidence must show that he believed that the complainant *communicated consent to engage in the sexual activity in question*. A belief by the accused that the complainant, in her own mind wanted him to touch her but did not express that desire, is not a defence. The accused's speculation as to what was going on in the complainant's mind provides no defence.

[47]  For the purposes of the *mens rea* analysis, the question is whether the accused believed that he had obtained consent. What matters is whether the accused believed that the complainant effectively said "yes" through her words and/or actions. The statutory definition added to the *Code* by Parliament in 1992 is consistent with the common law:

> 273.1(1)  Subject to subsection (2) and subsection 265(3), "consent" means, for the purposes of sections 271, 272 and 273, the voluntary agreement of the complainant to engage in the sexual activity in question.

[48]  There is a difference in the concept of "consent" as it relates to the state of mind of the complainant *vis-à-vis* the *actus reus* of the offence and the state of mind of the accused in respect of the *mens rea*. For the purposes of the *actus reus*, "consent" means that the complainant in her mind wanted the sexual touching to take place.

[49]  In the context of *mens rea*—specifically for the purposes of the honest but mistaken belief in consent—"consent" means that the complainant had affirmatively communicated by words or conduct her agreement to engage in sexual activity with the accused. This distinction should always be borne in mind and the two parts of the analysis kept separate.

(b)  Limits on Honest but Mistaken Belief in Consent

[50]  Not all beliefs upon which an accused might rely will exculpate him. Consent in relation to the *mens rea* of the accused is limited by both the common law and the provisions of ss. 273.1(2) and 273.2 of the *Code*. ... [These sections are then reproduced.]

[51]  For instance, a belief that silence, passivity or ambiguous conduct constitutes consent is a mistake of law, and provides no defence: see *R. v. M. (M.L.)*, [1994] 2 S.C.R. 3 (S.C.C.). Similarly, an accused cannot rely upon his purported belief that the complainant's expressed lack of agreement to sexual touching in fact constituted an invitation to more persistent or aggressive contact. An accused cannot say that he thought "no meant yes." As Fraser C.J. stated at p. 272 of her dissenting reasons below:

> One "No" will do to put the other person on notice that there is then a problem with "consent." *Once a woman says "No" during the course of sexual activity, the person intent on continued sexual activity with her must then obtain a clear and unequivocal "Yes" before he again touches her in a sexual manner.* [Emphasis in original.]

I take the reasons of Fraser C.J. to mean that an unequivocal "yes" may be given by either the spoken word or by conduct.

[52] Common sense should dictate that, once the complainant has expressed her unwillingness to engage in sexual contact, the accused should make certain that she has truly changed her mind before proceeding with further intimacies. The accused cannot rely on the mere lapse of time or the complainant's silence or equivocal conduct to indicate that there has been a change of heart and that consent now exists, nor can he engage in further sexual touching to "test the waters." Continuing sexual contact after someone has said "No" is, at a minimum, reckless conduct which is not excusable. In *R. v. Esau*, [1997] 2 S.C.R. 777 (S.C.C.), at para. 79, the Court stated:

> An accused who, due to wilful blindness or recklessness, believes that a complainant ... in fact consented to the sexual activity at issue is precluded from relying on a defence of honest but mistaken belief in consent, a fact that Parliament has codified: *Criminal Code*, s. 273.2(a)(ii).

(c) Application to the Facts

[53] In this appeal the accused does not submit that the complainant's clearly articulated "No's" were ambiguous or carried some other meaning. In fact, the accused places great reliance on his having stopped immediately each time the complainant said "no" in order to show that he had no intention to force himself upon her. He therefore knew that the complainant was not consenting on four separate occasions during their encounter.

[54] The question which the trial judge ought to have considered was whether anything occurred between the communication of non-consent and the subsequent sexual touching which the accused could honestly have believed constituted consent.

[55] The trial judge explicitly chose not to consider whether the accused had the defence of honest but mistaken belief in consent, and concluded that the defence was probably not available unless the accused testified. This conclusion ignores the right of the accused to have this defence considered solely on the Crown's case. The trial judge paid only passing interest to this defence undoubtedly because he had concluded that the defence of implied consent exonerated the accused. The accused is entitled to have all available defences founded on a proper basis considered by the court, whether he raises them or not: see *R. v. B. (E.H.)*, [1987] 1 S.C.R. 782 (S.C.C.), at p. 789.

[56] In *Esau, supra*, at para. 15, the Court stated that, "before a court should consider honest but mistaken belief or instruct a jury on it there must be some plausible evidence in support so as to give an air of reality to the defence." See also *R. v. Osolin*, [1993] 4 S.C.R. 595 (S.C.C.). All that is required is for the accused to adduce some evidence, or refer to evidence already adduced, upon which a properly instructed trier of fact could form a reasonable doubt as to his *mens rea*: see *Osolin, supra*, at pp. 653-54, and p. 687.

[57] The analysis in this appeal makes no attempt to weigh the evidence. At this point we are concerned only with the facial plausibility of the defence of honest but mistaken belief and should avoid the risk of turning the air of reality test into a substantive evaluation of the merits of the defence.

[58]  As the accused did not testify, the only evidence before the Court was that of the complainant. She stated that she immediately said "NO" every time the accused touched her sexually, and that she did nothing to encourage him. Her evidence was accepted by the trial judge as credible and sincere. Indeed, the accused relies on the fact that he momentarily stopped his advances each time the complainant said "NO" as evidence of his good intentions. This demonstrates that he understood the complainant's "NO's" to mean precisely that. Therefore, there is nothing on the record to support the accused's claim that he continued to believe her to be consenting, or that he re-established consent before resuming physical contact. The accused did not raise nor does the evidence disclose an air of reality to the defence of honest but mistaken belief in consent to this sexual touching.

[59]  The trial record conclusively establishes that the accused's persistent and increasingly serious advances constituted a sexual assault for which he had no defence. But for his errors of law, the trial judge would necessarily have found the accused guilty. In this case, a new trial would not be in the interests of justice. Therefore, it is proper for this Court to exercise its discretion under s. 686(4) of the *Code* and enter a conviction: see *R. v. Cassidy*, [1989] 2 S.C.R. 345 (S.C.C.), at pp. 354-55.

[60]  In her reasons, Justice L'Heureux-Dubé makes reference to s. 273.2(b) of the *Code*. Whether the accused took reasonable steps is a question of fact to be determined by the trier of fact only after the air of reality test has been met. In view of the way the trial and appeal were argued, s. 273.2 (b) did not have to be considered.

## IV.  Summary

[61]  In sexual assault cases which centre on differing interpretations of essentially similar events, trial judges should first consider whether the complainant, in her mind, wanted the sexual touching in question to occur. Once the complainant has asserted that she did not consent, the question is then one of credibility. In making this assessment the trier of fact must take into account the totality of the evidence, including any ambiguous or contradictory conduct by the complainant. If the trier of fact is satisfied beyond a reasonable doubt that the complainant did not in fact consent, the *actus reus* of sexual assault is established and the inquiry must shift to the accused's state of mind.

[62]  If there is reasonable doubt as to consent, or if it is established that the complainant actively participated in the sexual activity, the trier of fact must still consider whether the complainant consented because of fear, fraud or the exercise of authority as enumerated in s. 265(3). The complainant's state of mind in respect of these factors need not be reasonable. If her decision to consent was motivated by any of these factors so as to vitiate her freedom of choice the law deems an absence of consent and the *actus reus* of sexual assault is again established.

[63]  Turning to the question of *mens rea*, it is artificial to require as a further step that the accused separately assert an honest but mistaken belief in consent once he acknowledges that the encounter between him and the complainant unfolded more or less as she describes it, but disputes that any crime took place: see *Park*, *supra*, at p. 851, *per* L'Heureux-Dubé J. In those cases, the accused can only make one claim:

that on the basis of the complainant's words and conduct he believed her to be consenting. This claim both contests the complainant's assertions that in her mind she
did not consent, and posits that, even if he were mistaken in his assessment of her
wishes, he was nonetheless operating under a morally innocent state of mind. It is for
the trier of fact to determine whether the evidence raises a reasonable doubt over
either her state of mind or his.

[64]  In cases such as this, the accused's putting consent into issue is synonymous
with an assertion of an honest belief in consent. If his belief is found to be mistaken,
then honesty of that belief must be considered. As an initial step the trial judge must
determine whether any evidence exists to lend an air of reality to the defence. If so,
then the question which must be answered by the trier of fact is whether the accused
honestly believed *that the complainant had communicated consent*. Any other belief,
however honestly held, is not a defence.

[65]  Moreover, to be honest the accused's belief cannot be reckless, willfully blind
or tainted by an awareness of any of the factors enumerated in ss. 273.1(2) and 273.2.
If at any point the complainant has expressed a lack of agreement to engage in sexual
activity, then it is incumbent upon the accused to point to some evidence from which
he could honestly believe consent to have been re-established *before* he resumed his
advances. If this evidence raises a reasonable doubt as to the accused's *mens rea*, the
charge is not proven.

[66]  Cases involving a true misunderstanding between parties to a sexual encounter infrequently arise but are of profound importance to the community's sense of
safety and justice. The law must afford women and men alike the peace of mind of
knowing that their bodily integrity and autonomy in deciding when and whether to
participate in sexual activity will be respected. At the same time, it must protect those
who have not been proven guilty from the social stigma attached to sexual offenders.

## *V. Disposition*

[67]  The appeal is allowed, a conviction is entered and the matter is remanded to
the trial judge for sentencing.

L'HEUREUX-DUBÉ J. (Gonthier J. concurring):

[68]  Violence against women takes many forms: sexual assault is one of them. In
Canada, one-half of all women are said to have experienced at least one incident of
physical or sexual violence since the age of 16 (Statistics Canada, "The Violence
Against Women Survey," *The Daily*, November 18, 1993). The statistics demonstrate
that 99 percent of the offenders in sexual assault cases are men and 90 percent of the
victims are women (*Gender Equality in the Canadian Justice System: Summary Document and Proposals for Action* (April 1992), at p. 13, also cited in *R. v. Osolin*, [1993]
4 S.C.R. 595 (S.C.C.), at p. 669).

[69]  Violence against women is as much a matter of equality as it is an offence
against human dignity and a violation of human rights. As Cory J. wrote in *Osolin*,
*supra*, at p. 669, sexual assault "is an assault upon human dignity and constitutes a
denial of any concept of equality for women." These human rights are protected by

ss. 7 and 15 of the *Canadian Charter of Rights and Freedoms* and their violation constitutes an offence under the assault provisions of s. 265 and under the more specific sexual assault provisions of ss. 271, 272 and 273 of the *Criminal Code*, R.S.C. 1985, c. C-46.

[70] So pervasive is violence against women throughout the world that the international community adopted in December 18, 1979 (Res. 34/180), in addition to all other human rights instruments, the *Convention on the Elimination of All Forms of Discrimination Against Women*, Can. T.S. 1982 No. 31, entered into force on September 3, 1981, to which Canada is a party, which has been described as "the definitive international legal instrument requiring respect for and observance of the human rights of women." (R. Cook, "Reservations to the Convention on the Elimination of All Forms of Discrimination Against Women" (1990), 30 *Va. J. Int'l L.* 643, at p. 643.) Articles 1 and 2 of the Convention read:

Article 1

For the purposes of the present Convention, the term "discrimination against women" shall mean any distinction, exclusion or restriction made on the basis of sex which has the effect or purpose of impairing or nullifying the recognition, enjoyment or exercise by women, irrespective of their marital status, on a basis of equality of men and women, of human rights and fundamental freedoms in the political, economic, social, cultural, civil or any other field.

Article 2

States Parties condemn discrimination against women in all its forms, agree to pursue by all appropriate means and without delay a policy of eliminating discrimination against women and, to this end, undertake:

(a) To embody the principle of the equality of men and women in their national constitutions or other appropriate legislation if not yet incorporated therein and to ensure, through law and other approprite means, the practical realization of this principle;

(b) *To adopt appropriate legislative and other measures*, including sanctions where appropriate, prohibiting all discrimination against women;

(c) To establish legal protection of the rights of women on an equal basis with men and to ensure through competent national tribunals and other public institutions the effective protection of women against any act of discrimination;

(d) To refrain from engaging in any act or practice of discrimination against women and to ensure that public authorities and institutions shall act in conformity with this obligation;

(e) To take all appropriate measures to eliminate discrimination against women by any person, organization or enterprise;

(f) *To take all appropriate measures, including legislation, to modify or abolish existing laws, regulations, customs and practices which constitute discrimination against women*;

(g) To repeal all national penal provisions which constitute discrimination against women. [Emphasis added.]

[71]  The Committee on the Elimination of Discrimination Against Women, G.A. Res. 34/180, U.N. Doc. A/47/48 (1979), established under Article 17 of the Convention, adopted General Recommendation No. 19 (Eleventh session, 1992) on the interpretation of discrimination as it relates to violence against women:

> 6. The Convention in article 1 defines discrimination against women. *The definition of discrimination includes* gender-based violence, that is, violence that is directed against a woman because she is a woman or that affects women disproportionately. It includes *acts that inflict physical, mental or sexual harm* or suffering, threats of such acts, coercion and other deprivations of liberty. Gender-based violence may breach specific provisions of the Convention, regardless of whether those provisions expressly mention violence.

> 24. In light of these comments, the Committee on the Elimination of Discrimination Against Women recommends:

> (b) States parties should ensure that laws against family violence and abuse, rape, *sexual assault and other gender-biased violence give adequate protection to all women, and respect their integrity and dignity. Appropriate protective and support services should be provided for victims. Gender-sensitive training of judicial and law enforcement officers and other public officials is essential for the effective implementation of the Convention.* [Emphasis added.]

[72]  On February 23, 1994, the U.N. General Assembly adopted the *Declaration on the Elimination of Violence Against Women*, G.A. Res. 48/104, U.N. Doc. A/48/49 (1993). Although not a treaty binding states, it sets out a common international standard that U.N. members states are invited to follow. Article 4 of the Declaration provides:

> Article 4

> States should condemn violence against women and should not invoke any custom, tradition or religious consideration to avoid their obligations with respect to its elimination. States should pursue by all appropriate means and without delay a policy of eliminating violence against women and, to this end, should:

> (i) *Take measures to ensure that law enforcement officers and public officials responsible for implementing policies to prevent,* investigate and punish violence against women *receive training to sensitize them to the needs of women*;

> (j) *Adopt all appropriate measures,* especially in the field of education, to modify the social and cultural patterns of conduct of men and women and *to eliminate prejudices,* customary practices and all other practices *based on* the idea of the inferiority or superiority of either of the sexes and on *stereotyped roles for men and women.* ... [Emphasis added.]

[73]  Our *Charter* is the primary vehicle through which international human rights achieve a domestic effect (see *Slaight Communications Inc. v. Davidson*, [1989] 1 S.C.R. 1038 (S.C.C.); *R. v. Keegstra*, [1990] 3 S.C.R. 697 (S.C.C.)). In particular, s. 15 (the equality provision) and s. 7 (which guarantees the right to life, security and liberty of the person) embody the notion of respect of human dignity and integrity.

[74] It is within that larger framework that, in 1983, Canada revamped the sexual assault provisions of the *Code* (S.C. 1980-81-82-83, c. 125), formerly ss. 143, 149 and 244 (R.S.C. 1970, c. C-34) which are now contained in the general assault provisions of s. 265. Together with the 1992 amendments of the *Code* (*An Act to amend the Criminal Code (sexual assault)*, S.C. 1992, c. 38), mainly ss. 273.1 and 273.2, they govern the issue of consent in the context of sexual assault. In the preamble to the 1992 Act, Parliament expressed its concern about the "prevalence of sexual assault against women and children" and stated its intention to "promote and help to ensure the full protection of the rights guaranteed under sections 7 and 15 of the *Canadian Charter of Rights and Freedoms*."

[75] Fraser C.J., in her dissenting reasons in this case, has set out the legislative history of those provisions. In *R. v. Cuerrier*, [1998] 2 S.C.R. 371 (S.C.C.), Cory J. and I both noted the significant reform of sexual assault provisions undertaken by Parliament. (See C. Boyle, *Sexual Assault* (1984), at pp. 27-29.) I observed in *R. v. Park*, [1995] 2 S.C.R. 836 (S.C.C.), at para. 42, that:

> ... the primary concern animating and underlying the present offence of sexual assault is the belief that women have an inherent right to exercise full control over their own bodies, and to engage only in sexual activity that they wish to engage in. If this is the case, then our approach to consent must evolve accordingly, for it may be out of phase with that conceptualization of the law.

See also *R. v. Seaboyer*, [1991] 2 S.C.R. 577 (S.C.C.).

[76] In the present case, the respondent was charged with sexual assault under s. 271 of the *Criminal Code*. The applicable notions of "assault" and "consent" are defined in ss. 265, 273.1 and 273.2 of the *Criminal Code*. ... [The sections are then reproduced.]

[77] Briefly stated, the accused is charged with sexually assaulting a 17-year-old girl. The accused was acquitted at trial and the acquittal was upheld on appeal, by a majority of the Alberta Court of Appeal, Fraser C.J. dissenting ((1998), 57 Alta. L.R. (3d) 235 (Alta. C.A.)). The appellant alleges that the acquittal and the subsequent decision of the Court of Appeal are based on an error of law in the interpretation of the notion of consent contained in ss. 265(3), 273.1 and 273.2 of the *Code* and invites this Court to enter a conviction.

[78] I have had the benefit of the reasons of Justice Major in this appeal and I agree generally with his reasons on most issues and with the result that he reaches. However, I wish to add some comments and discuss some of the reasoning of the trial judge and of the majority of the Court of Appeal.

[79] Although my colleague has recounted the facts, there are some significant nuances that need to be stated. When the complainant and the accused met in the parking lot of a shopping mall to discuss the job offer, the complainant suggested that the interview be held in the mall. The accused expressed his preference for more privacy and proposed instead that the interview take place in his van to which a trailer was attached. The complainant agreed to sit in the van, but she left the door of the van open since she was still hesitant about discussing the job offer in his vehicle.

[80]  The accused then proposed that they proceed to his trailer. Shortly after entering the trailer, the complainant agreed to massage lightly the accused. However,
she testified that she did not want to give him a massage but was afraid at this point,
considering that she saw and heard the accused lock the door of the trailer and that
the accused was almost twice her size. The accused then asked the complainant to
come in front of him so that he could return the favour. He started massaging the
complainant and brought his hands close to her breasts. The complainant pushed him
away with her elbows and said "no." He then told the complainant to turn around in
order to massage her feet. Again out of fear, she complied. When he began massaging
her feet, the touching progressed to her inner thigh and pelvic area up to a point
where he laid heavily on top of the complainant and started grinding his pelvic area
against hers while telling her, as she testified, that: "he could get me so horny so that I
would want it so bad, and he wouldn't give it to me because he had self-control and
because he wouldn't want to give it to me." The accused stopped after the complainant asked him to "Just please stop" and at one point he said: "I had you worried,
didn't I? You were scared, weren't you? She answered: "Yes, I was very scared."
This is particularly revealing of the accused's knowledge that she was afraid and
certainly not a willing participant. The accused resumed his pelvic grinding, only this
time he tried to touch her vaginal area, exposed his penis and placed it on the complainant's clothed pelvic area under her shorts. He stopped after the complainant said
"No, stop."

[81]  After this ordeal, the accused opened the door at her request and the complainant finally exited the trailer. When the complainant arrived home, she was crying and told her roommate, Ms. Tait, what had occurred. Shortly after, the accused
called the complainant's apartment to ask her if she was fine. She answered that she
was and called the police. This evidence is uncontradicted and the trial judge found
the complainant to be an articulate and intelligent young woman and a credible
witness.

[82]  This case is not about consent, since none was given. It is about myths and
stereotypes, which have been identified by many authors and succinctly described by
D. Archard, *Sexual Consent* (1998), at p. 131:

> Myths of rape include the view that women fantasise about being rape victims; that
> women mean "yes" even when they say "no"; that any woman could successfully resist
> a rapist if she really wished to; that the sexually experienced do not suffer harms when
> raped (or at least suffer lesser harms than the sexually "innocent"); that women often
> deserve to be raped on account of their conduct, dress, and demeanour; that rape by a
> stranger is worse than one by an acquaintance. Stereotypes of sexuality include the
> view of women as passive, disposed submissively to surrender to the sexual advances
> of active men, the view that sexual love consists in the "possession" by a man of a
> woman, and that heterosexual sexual activity is paradigmatically penetrative coitus.

(For example see *Seaboyer*, *supra*, at p. 651, *per* L'Heureux-Dubé J.; M. Burt, "Rape
Myths and Acquaintance Rape," in A. Parrot and L. Bechhofer, eds., *Acquaintance
Rape: The Hidden Crime* (1991); N. Naffine, "Possession: Erotic Love in the Law of

Rape" (1994), 57 *Mod. L. Rev.* 10; R.T. Andrias, "Rape Myths: A persistent problem in defining and prosecuting rape" (1992), 7:2 *Criminal Justice* 2; *Gender Equality in the Canadian Justice System: Summary Document and Proposals for Action*, *supra*; C.A. MacKinnon, *Toward a Feminist Theory of the State* (1989); E.A. Sheehy, "Canadian Judges and the Law of Rape: Should the *Charter* Insulate Bias?" (1989), 21 *Ott. L. Rev.* 741.)

[83]  The trial judge believed the complainant and accepted her testimony that she was afraid and he acknowledged her unwillingness to engage in any sexual activity. In addition, there is no doubt that the respondent was aware that the complainant was afraid since he told her repeatedly not to be afraid. The complainant clearly articulated her absence of consent: she said no. Not only did the accused not stop, but after a brief pause, as Fraser C.J. puts it, he went on to an "increased level of sexual activity" to which twice the complainant said no. What could be clearer?

[84]  The trial judge gave no legal effect to his conclusion that the complainant submitted to sexual activity out of fear that the accused would apply force to her. Section 265(3)(b) states that no consent is obtained where the complainant submits by reason of threats or fear of the application of force. Therefore, s. 265(3)(b) applies and operates to further establish the lack of consent: see *Cuerrier*, *supra*.

[85]  I agree with Major J. that the application of s. 265(3) requires an entirely subjective test. In my opinion, as irrational as a complainant's motive might be, if she subjectively felt fear, it must lead to a legal finding of absence of consent. Accordingly, I agree with Fraser C.J. that any objective factor should be considered under the defence of honest but mistaken belief.

[86]  However, in my view, Major J. unduly restricts the application of s. 265(3) to instances where the complainant chooses "to participate in, or ostensibly consent to, the touching in question" (at para. 38; see also para. 36). Section 265(3) applies to cases where the "complainant submits or *does not resist*" (emphasis added) by reason of the application of force, threats or fear of the application of force, fraud or the exercise of authority. Therefore, that section should also apply to cases where the complainant is silent or passive in response to such situations.

[87]  In the circumstances of this case, it is difficult to understand how the question of implied consent even arose. Although he found the complainant credible, and accepted her evidence that she said "no" on three occasions and was afraid, the trial judge nonetheless did not take "no" to mean that the complainant did not consent. Rather, he concluded that she implicitly consented and that the Crown had failed to prove lack of consent. This was a fundamental error. As noted by Professor Stuart in Annotation on *R. v. Ewanchuk* (1998), 13 C.R. (5th) 330 (Alta. C.A.), at p. 330:

> Both the trial judgment and that of Justice McClung do not make the basic distinction that consent is a matter of the state of mind of the complainant and belief in consent is, subject to s. 273.2 of the *Criminal Code*, a matter of the state of mind of the accused.
>
> This error does not derive from the findings of fact but from mythical assumptions that when a woman says "no" she is really saying "yes," "try again," or "persuade me." To paraphrase Fraser C.J. at p. 263, it denies women's sexual autonomy and implies that women are "walking around this country in a state of constant consent to sexual activity."

[88]  In the Court of Appeal, McClung J.A. compounded the error made by the trial judge. At the outset of his opinion, he stated at p. 245 that "it must be pointed out that the complainant did not present herself to Ewanchuk or enter his trailer in a bonnet and crinolines." He noted, at pp. 245-46, that "she was the mother of a six-month-old baby and that, along with her boyfriend, she shared an apartment with another couple."

[89]  Even though McClung J.A. asserted that he had no intention of denigrating the complainant, one might wonder why he felt necessary to point out these aspects of the trial record. Could it be to express that the complainant is not a virgin? Or that she is a person of questionable moral character because she is not married and lives with her boyfriend and another couple? These comments made by an appellate judge help reinforce the myth that under such circumstances, either the complainant is less worthy of belief, she invited the sexual assault, or her sexual experience signals probable consent to further sexual activity. Based on those attributed assumptions, the implication is that if the complainant articulates her lack of consent by saying "no," she really does not mean it and even if she does, her refusal cannot be taken as seriously as if she were a girl of "good" moral character. "Inviting" sexual assault, according to those myths, lessens the guilt of the accused as Archard, *supra*, notes at p. 139:

> ... the more that a person contributes by her behaviour or negligence to bringing about the circumstances in which she is a victim of a crime, the less responsible is the criminal for the crime he commits. A crime is no less unwelcome or serious in its effects, or need it be any the less deliberate or malicious in its commission, for occurring in circumstances which the victim helped to realise. Yet judges who spoke of women "inviting" or "provoking" a rape would go on to cite such contributory behaviour as a reason for regarding the rape as less grave or the rapist as less culpable. It adds judicial insult to criminal injury to be told that one is the part author of a crime one did not seek and which in consequence is supposed to be a lesser one.

[90]  McClung J.A. writes, at p. 247:

> There is no room to suggest that Ewanchuk knew, yet disregarded, her underlying state of mind as he furthered his *romantic intentions*. He was not aware of her true state of mind. Indeed, his ignorance about that was what she wanted. The facts, set forth by the trial judge, provide support for the overriding trial finding, couched in terms of consent by implication, that the accused had no proven preparedness to assault the complainant to get what he wanted. [Emphasis added.]

On the contrary, both the fact that Ewanchuk was aware of the complainant's state of mind, as he did indeed stop each time she expressly stated "no," and the trial judge's findings reinforce the obvious conclusion that the accused knew there was no consent. These were two strangers, a young 17-year-old woman attracted by a job offer who found herself trapped in a trailer and a man approximately twice her age and size. This is hardly a scenario one would characterize as reflective of "romantic intentions." It was nothing more than an effort by Ewanchuk to engage the complainant sexually, not romantically.

[91] The expressions used by McClung J.A. to describe the accused's sexual assault, such as "clumsy passes" (p. 246) or "would hardly raise Ewanchuk's stature in the pantheon of chivalric behaviour" (p. 248), are plainly inappropriate in that context as they minimize the importance of the accused's conduct and the reality of sexual aggression against women.

[92] McClung J.A. also concluded that "the sum of the evidence indicates that Ewanchuk's advances to the complainant were far less criminal than hormonal" (p. 250) having found earlier that "every advance he made to her stopped when she spoke against it" and that "[t]here was no evidence of an assault or even its threat" (p. 249). According to this analysis, a man would be free from criminal responsibility for having non-consensual sexual activity whenever he cannot control his hormonal urges. Furthermore, the fact that the accused ignored the complainant's verbal objections to any sexual activity and persisted in escalated sexual contact, grinding his pelvis against hers repeatedly, is more evidence than needed to determine that there was an assault.

[93] Finally, McClung J.A. made this point: "In a less litigious age going too far in the boyfriend's car was better dealt with on site—a well-chosen expletive, a slap in the face or, if necessary, a well directed knee" (p. 250). According to this stereotype, women should use physical force, not resort to courts to "deal with" sexual assaults and it is not the perpetrator's responsibility to ascertain consent, as required by s. 273.2(b), but the women's not only to express an unequivocal "no," but also to fight her way out of such a situation. In that sense, Susan Estrich has noted that "rape is most assuredly not the only crime in which consent is a defense; but it is the only crime that has required the victim to resist physically in order to establish nonconsent" ("Rape" (1986), *Yale L.J.* 1087, at p. 1090).

[94] Cory J. referred to the inappropriate use of rape myths by courts in *Osolin*, *supra*, at p. 670:

> A number of rape myths have in the past improperly formed the background for considering evidentiary issues in sexual assault trials. These include the false concepts that: women cannot be raped against their will; only "bad girls" are raped; anyone not clearly of "good character" is more likely to have consented.

In *Seaboyer*, *supra*, I alluded to this issue as follows, at pp. 707-9:

> Parliament exhibited a marked, and justifiedly so, distrust of the ability of the courts to promote and achieve a non-discriminatory application of the law in this area. In view of the history of government attempts, the harm done when discretion is posited in trial judges and the demonstrated inability of the judiciary to change its discriminatory ways, Parliament was justified in so choosing. My attempt to illustrate the tenacity of these discriminatory beliefs and their acceptance at all levels of society clearly demonstrates that discretion in judges is antithetical to the goals of Parliament.
>
> History demonstrates that it was discretion in trial judges that saturated the law in this area with stereotype. My earlier discussion shows that we are not, all of a sudden, a society rid of such beliefs, and hence, discretionary decision making in this realm is absolutely antithetical to the achievement of government's pressing and substantial objective.

[95] This case has not dispelled any of the fears I expressed in *Seaboyer*, *supra*, about the use of myths and stereotypes in dealing with sexual assault complaints (see also Bertha Wilson, "Will Women Judges Really Make a Difference?" (1990), 28 *Osgoode Hall L.J.* 507). Complainants should be able to rely on a system free from myths and stereotypes, and on a judiciary whose impartiality is not compromised by these biased assumptions. The *Code* was amended in 1983 and in 1992 to eradicate reliance on those assumptions; they should not be permitted to resurface through the stereotypes reflected in the reasons of the majority of the Court of Appeal. It is part of the role of this Court to denounce this kind of language, unfortunately still used today, which not only perpetuates archaic myths and stereotypes about the nature of sexual assaults but also ignores the law.

[96] In "The Standard of Social Justice as a Research Process" (1997), 38 *Can. Psychology* 91, K.E. Renner, C. Alksnis and L. Park make a strong indictment of the current criminal justice process, at p. 100:

> The more general indictment of the current criminal justice process is that the law and legal doctrines concerning sexual assault have acted as the principle [*sic*] systemic mechanisms for invalidating the experiences of women and children. *Given this state of affairs, the traditional view of the legal system as neutral, objective and gender-blind is not defensible.* Since the system is ineffective in protecting the rights of women and children, it is necessary to re-examine the existing doctrines which reflect the cultural and social limitations that have preserved dominant male interests at the expense of women and children. [Emphasis added.]

[97] This being said, turning to the facts of the present case, I agree with Major J. that the findings necessary to support a verdict of guilty on the charge of sexual assault have been made. In particular, there is, on the record, no evidence that would give an air of reality to an honest belief in consent for any of the sexual activity which took place in this case. One cannot imply that once the complainant does not object to the massage in the context of a job interview, there is "sufficient evidence" to support that the accused could honestly believe he had permission to initiate sexual contact. This would mean that complying to receive a massage is consent to sexual touching. It would reflect the myth that women are presumptively sexually accessible until they resist. McLachlin J. has recognized in *R. v. Esau*, [1997] 2 S.C.R. 777 (S.C.C.), at para. 82, that reliance on rape myths cannot ground a defence of mistaken belief in consent:

> Care must be taken to avoid the false assumptions or "myths" that may mislead us in determining whether the conduct of the complainant affords a sufficient basis for putting the defence of honest mistake on consent to the jury. One of these is the stereotypical notion that women who resist or say no may in fact be consenting.

Furthermore, I agree with Fraser C.J. at p. 278 that there is no air of reality to a defence of mistaken belief in consent "in the face of the complainant's clearly stated verbal objections."

[98] Moreover, s. 273.2(b) precludes the accused from raising the defence of belief in consent if he did not take "reasonable steps" in the circumstances known to

him at the time to ascertain that the complainant was consenting. This provision and the defence of honest but mistaken belief were before the trial judge and it should have been given full effect. The trial judge erred in law by not applying s. 273.2(b) which was the law of the land at the time of the trial, irrespective of whether the case proceeded on that basis. As stated by McLachlin J. in *Esau*, *supra*, at para. 50, with whom I concurred:

> Major J. [for the majority] does not consider s. 273.2. This may be because it was not argued on the appeal or in the proceedings below. With respect, I do not believe that the force of s. 273.2 may be avoided on that ground. Parliament has spoken. It has set out minimum conditions for the defence of mistaken belief in consent. If those conditions are not met, the defence does not lie.

[99] I agree entirely with Chief Justice Fraser that, unless and until an accused first takes reasonable steps to assure that there is consent, the defence of honest but mistaken belief does not arise (see *R. c. D. (S.)*, [1998] 1 S.C.R. 1220 (S.C.C.); *Esau*, *supra*, *per* McLachlin J. dissenting; and J. McInnes and C. Boyle, "Judging Sexual Assault Law against a Standard of Equality" (1995), 25 *U.B.C. L. Rev.* 341). In this case, the accused proceeded from massaging to sexual contact without making any inquiry as to whether the complainant consented. Obviously, interpreting the fact that the complainant did not refuse the massage to mean that the accused could further his sexual intentions is not a reasonable step. The accused cannot rely on the complainant's silence or ambiguous conduct to initiate sexual contact. Moreover, where a complainant expresses non-consent, the accused has a corresponding escalating obligation to take additional steps to ascertain consent. Here, despite the complainant's repeated verbal objections, the accused did not take any step to ascertain consent, let alone reasonable ones. Instead, he increased the level of his sexual activity. Therefore, pursuant to s. 273.2(b) Ewanchuk was barred from relying on a belief in consent.

[100] Major J., at para. 43, relies on this Court's decision in *R. v. Pappajohn*, [1980] 2 S.C.R. 120 (S.C.C.), to describe the nature of the defence of honest but mistaken belief. In *Pappajohn*, the majority held that this defence does not need to be based on reasonable grounds as long as it is honestly held. That approach has been modified by the enactment of s. 273.2(b) which introduced the "reasonable steps" requirement. Therefore, that decision no longer states the law on the question of honest but mistaken belief in consent.

[101] I wish to point out that, on the facts as found at trial, s. 273.1(2) also applies to this case. Coupled with the reasonable steps requirement of s. 273.2(b), s. 273.1(2) restricts the circumstances in which an accused could claim that he had a mistaken belief in the complainant's agreement to engage in the impugned sexual activity. Particularly relevant to this case, s. 273.1(2)(d) states that no consent is obtained where "the complainant expresses, by words or conduct, a lack of agreement … ." Here, the complainant clearly expressed her lack of consent by saying "no" three times. The application of that provision acknowledges that when a woman says "no" she is communicating her non-agreement, regardless of what the accused thought it meant, and that her expression has an enforceable legal effect. It precludes the accused from

claiming that he thought there was an agreement. That provision was in force at the time of trial and could not be ignored by the trial judge.

*Disposition*

[102] Like my colleague Major J., I would allow the appeal, enter a conviction and send the matter back to the trial judge for sentencing.

McLACHLIN J.:

[103] I agree with the reasons of Justice Major. I also agree with Justice L'Heureux-Dubé that stereotypical assumptions lie at the heart of what went wrong in this case. The specious defence of implied consent (consent implied by law), as applied in this case, rests on the assumption that unless a woman protests or resists, she should be "deemed" to consent (see L'Heureux-Dubé J.). On appeal, the idea also surfaced that if a woman is not modestly dressed, she is deemed to consent. Such stereotypical assumptions find their roots in many cultures, including our own. They no longer, however, find a place in Canadian law.

[104] I join my colleagues in rejecting them.

*Appeal allowed.*

### ADDITIONAL READING

- K. Roach, *Criminal Law*, 3rd ed. (Toronto: Irwin Law, 2004), chapter 4;
- D. Stuart, *Canadian Criminal Law*, 4th ed. (Toronto: Carswell, 2001), chapter 4.

Many additional readings are cited by Stuart in his treatise.

See also:

- J.V. Roberts and R.M. Mohr, *Confronting Sexual Assault: A Decade of Legal and Social Change* (Toronto: U. of T. Press, 1994);
- C. Boyle and M. MacCrimmon, "The Constitutionality of Bill C-49: Analyzing Sexual Assault as if Equality Really Mattered" (1998), 41 *Crim. L.Q.* 198;
- Forum (1993), 42 *U.N.B.L.J.* 319-85;
- L. Vandervort, "Mistake of Law and Sexual Assault: Consent and Mens Rea" (1988), 2 *C.J.W.L.* 233.

# CHAPTER THIRTEEN

# Homicide

This chapter gives special attention to homicide offences. Some forms of homicide, murder in particular, are regarded as the most serious of offences in Canada, and in most other countries. In Canada, special penalties attach to the offences of first- and second-degree murder (see chapter 21, as well as A. Manson, P. Healy, and G. Trotter, *Sentencing and Penal Policy in Canada: Cases, Materials and Commentary* (Toronto: Emond Montgomery, 2000), chapter 14—"Sentencing for Murder"). For historical reasons associated with the social and cultural status of murder, and due to the enhanced sanctions that accompanied a conviction for murder (including the death penalty), the provisions in the *Criminal Code* that concern murder are unique and somewhat complicated. Moreover, the application of the *Charter* to this area of the law has had a dramatic impact on the formal requirements for murder.

Section 222 of the *Criminal Code* defines, in broad terms, the parameters of homicide:

s. 222(1) A person commits homicide when, directly or indirectly, by any means, he causes the death of a human being.

(2) Homicide is culpable or not culpable.

(3) Homicide that is not culpable is not an offence.

(4) Culpable homicide is murder or manslaughter or infanticide.

(5) A person commits homicide when he causes the death of a human being,

(a) by means of an unlawful act,

(b) by criminal negligence,

(c) by causing that human being, by threats or fear of violence or by deception, to do anything that causes his death, or

(d) by wilfully frightening that human being, in the case of a child or sick person.

Read in conjunction with s. 229, which defines murder, all homicides that are not murder, are infanticide or manslaughter. Infanticide, defined in s. 233 of the *Criminal Code*, is a rather obscure and antiquated offence that is rarely charged anymore in Canada. Consequently, the fault requirements for infanticide will not be addressed in this chapter.

In the next section of this chapter, we address the requirements of murder in s. 229 of the *Criminal Code*, including the impact of the *Charter* on this offence. Section II deals with first-degree murder and the various ways in which it can be committed. Section III deals with the residual category of culpable homicide not absorbed by murder (or infanticide)—manslaughter.

## I. SECOND-DEGREE MURDER

Section 229 of the Criminal Code is at the heart of the offence of murder. It sets out three basic ways in which a homicide can be classified as murder. Section 229 states:

> s. 229  Culpable homicide is murder
>> (a)  where the person who causes the death of a human being
>>> (i)  means to cause his death, or
>>> (ii)  means to cause him bodily harm that he knows is likely to cause his death, and is reckless whether death ensues or not;
>>
>> (b)  where a person, meaning to cause death to a human being or meaning to cause him bodily harm that he knows is likely to cause his death, and being reckless whether death ensues or not, by accident or mistake causes death to another human being, notwithstanding that he does not mean to cause death or bodily harm to that human being; or
>>
>> (c)  where a person, for an unlawful object, does anything that he knows or ought to know is likely to cause death, and thereby causes death to a human being, notwithstanding that he desires to effect his object without causing death or bodily harm to any human being.

The fault requirements under each of these sections is dealt with below.

### Section 229(a): Intentional or Reckless Killing

### R. v. Simpson
Ontario Court of Appeal
(1981), 58 C.C.C. (2d) 122

[This case involved two counts of attempted murder. The accused met one victim in a bar and had sex with her in his apartment, following which he strangled her to the point of unconsciousness. The accused attacked the other victim after she left the same bar where the accused met the first victim. The appeal concerned the accuracy of the trial judge's instructions to the jury on the definition of murder in the context of trying to explain the offence of attempted murder.]

MARTIN J.A.: ...

*Misdirection as to Intent Required To Constitute Attempted Murder*

Following the argument of the appeal, and while the decision of the Court was under reserve, the Court requested counsel to submit argument with respect to the effect of a passage in the Judge's charge defining the intent requisite for attempted murder, to which no objection was taken at the trial, and which was not a ground of appeal. The Court reconvened on February 12, 1981, and heard argument with respect to the passage in question.

The learned trial Judge charged the jury as follows:

> Under the *Criminal Code*, anyone who attempts by any means to commit murder is guilty of an indictable offence. In this case neither victim died, most fortunately. So the charge isn't murder but attempted murder. What is murder? It is defined in Section 212 of the *Criminal Code*, in part, as follows:
>
> > "Culpable homicide is murder
> >
> > (a) where the person who causes the death of a human being (1) means to cause his death, or (2) means to cause him bodily harm that he knows is likely to cause his death and is reckless whether death ensues or not."
>
> Now culpable means blameworthy. Culpable homicide is death of a human being for which some person may be blamed in law. The definition that I have just read to you then is one of murder; and the charge we are dealing with here is attempt to murder. I have earlier told you that proof of the intention of the accused is an essential element in the offence of attempt to murder. The Crown must satisfy you beyond a reasonable doubt that the accused stabbed the victim and that he did so intending to cause the death, or intending to cause the victim bodily harm that he knew or ought to have known was likely to cause death and was reckless whether death ensued or not. I repeat the second part of that definition: If the Crown has, on the evidence, satisfied you beyond a reasonable doubt that the accused was the stabber and that in stabbing he intended so cause bodily harm that he knew or ought to have known was likely to cause death and was reckless whether death ensued or not, then the offence of attempted murder has been proved.

It has now been authoritatively decided that either of the intents specified in s. 212(a)(i) and (ii) suffices to constitute the intent required for the offence of attempted murder; see *Lajoie v. The Queen* (1973), 10 C.C.C. (2d) 313; *R. v. Ritchie*, [1970] 5 C.C.C. 336. Unfortunately, the learned trial Judge, in paraphrasing the intent specified in s. 212(a)(ii) namely, an intention to cause bodily harm that the offender knows is likely to cause death—substituted for the requisite intent an intention to cause bodily harm that offender knows or ought to know is likely to cause death. This incorrect summary of the provision of s. 212(a)(ii) constituted a serious error. Liability under s. 212(a)(ii) is subjective and the requisite knowledge that the intended injury is likely to cause death must be brought home to the accused subjectively. To substitute for that state of mind an intention to cause bodily harm that the accused knows or ought to know is likely to cause death is to impose liability on an objective basis. An intention to cause bodily harm that the offender ought to have known was likely to cause death is merely evidence from which, along with all the other circumstances, the jury may infer that the accused actually had the requisite intention and knowledge required by s. 212(a)(ii). It does not, however, constitute the requisite state of mind. ...

The error was never corrected by the learned trial Judge. It is true that in putting the case for the Crown he said:

> The Crown suggests to you that if you are satisfied that Simpson was the attacker, you should in the circumstances have no doubt that he intended to kill or cause bodily harm knowing that it might result in death and being reckless as to whether death ensued or not.

It is to be observed that even this passage is not entirely correct as it refers to an intention to cause bodily harm knowing that it might result in death, as distinct from an intention to inflict bodily harm that the offender knows is likely to cause bodily harm. In any event, the jury would rely on the Judge's instruction, as they had previously been told they must, with respect to the elements of the offence of attempted murder.

In my view, the seriousness of the error requires a new trial unless it is proper to invoke the curative provisions of s. 613(1)(b)(iii). ... I have not been persuaded, even by Mr. Watt's able argument, that it is appropriate to invoke the provisions of s. 613(1)(b)(iii) in relation to the conviction of the appellant on count 2 relating to Cathy Wagenaar. I am not satisfied that a reasonable jury properly instructed, having found that the appellant was Cathy Wagenaar's assailant, would inevitably have found that he intended to kill her or intended to inflict an injury upon her that he knew was likely to kill her. Although it would be open to a properly-instructed jury to conclude that the requisite intent to constitute attempted murder had been established, the accompanying circumstances and the assailant's utterances are not such as to inevitably require a reasonable jury to reach that conclusion. ...

*Appeal allowed.*

## R. v. Cooper
Supreme Court of Canada
(1993), 78 C.C.C. (3d) 289

[The accused was charged with murdering his female acquaintance. He had been drinking with her and they got into an argument. The accused said that the victim had hit him. He testified to remembering strangling the victim, but had no recollection after that until he awoke to find the victim dead. The medical evidence confirmed that the victim had been strangled to death and that the pressure to her throat would have been between 30 seconds to two minutes, and probably closer to two minutes. The trial judge instructed the jury that, once the accused had formed the intent to cause the victim bodily harm, which he knew would likely cause her death, he need not be aware of what he was doing at the moment she actually died. The accused was convicted, but the Court of Appeal found that this instruction was erroneous.]

CORY J.: ...

*The Nature of the Intent Required To Secure a Conviction Under s. 212(a)(ii)*

Section 212(a)(ii) [now s. 229(a)(ii)] provides:

> s. 212  Culpable homicide is murder
>> (a)  where the person who causes the death of a human being ...
>>> (ii)  means to cause him bodily harm that he knows is likely to cause his death, and is reckless whether death ensues or not.

This section was considered in *R. v. Nygaard* (1989), 51 C.C.C. (3d) 417 (S.C.C.). On the issue of the requisite intent the court was unanimous. At p. 435, it was said:

> The essential element is that of intending to cause bodily harm of such a grave and serious nature that the accused knew that it was likely to result in the death of the victim. The aspect of recklessness is almost an afterthought … .

The aspect of recklessness can be considered an afterthought since to secure a conviction under this section it must be established that the accused had the intent to cause such grievous bodily harm that he knew it was likely to cause death. One who causes bodily harm that he knows is likely to cause death must, in those circumstances, have a deliberate disregard for the fatal consequences which are known to be likely to occur. That is to say he must, of necessity, be reckless whether death ensues or not.

The concept of recklessness was considered by this court in *R. v. Sansregret* (1985), 18 C.C.C. (3d) 223. At p. 233 it was said:

> [Recklessness] is found in the attitude of one who, aware that there is danger that his conduct could bring about the result prohibited by the criminal law, nevertheless persists, despite the risk. It is, in other words, the conduct of one who sees the risk and who takes the chance.

The same words can apply to s. 212(a)(ii) with this important addition: it is not sufficient that the accused foresee simply a danger of death; the accused must foresee a likelihood of death flowing from the bodily harm that he is occasioning the victim.

It is for this reason that it was said in *Nygaard* that there is only a "slight relaxation" in the *mens rea* required for a conviction for murder under s. 212(a)(ii) as compared to s. 212(a)(i). The position was put in this way at p. 1089:

> … [where] two accused form the intent to repeatedly and viciously strike a person in the head with a baseball bat realizing full well that the victim will probably die as a result. None the less they continue with the bone-splintering, skull-shattering assault. The accused … must have committed as grave a crime as the accused who specifically intends to kill. … I would conclude that the crime defined in s. 212(a)(ii) [now s. 229(a)(ii)] can properly be described as murder and on a "culpability scale" it varies so little from s. 212(a)(i) as to be indistinguishable.

The intent that must be demonstrated in order to convict under s. 212(a)(ii) has two aspects. There must be (a) subjective intent to cause bodily harm; (b) subjective knowledge that the bodily harm is of such a nature that it is likely to result in death. It is only when those two elements of intent are established that a conviction can properly follow.

### What Degree of Concurrency Is Required Between the Wrongful Act and the Requisite Mens Rea?

There can be no doubt that under the classical approach to criminal law it is the intent of the accused that makes the wrongful act illegal. It is that intent which brings the accused within the sphere of blameworthiness and justifies the penalty or punishment which is imposed upon him for the infraction of the criminal law. The essential aspect of *mens rea* and the absolute necessity that it be present in the case of murder was emphasized by Lamer J. (as he then was) in *R. v. Vaillancourt* (1987), 39 C.C.C. (3d) 118. At p. 133, he stated:

> It may well be that, as a general rule, the principles of fundamental justice require proof of a subjective *mens rea* with respect to the prohibited act, in order to avoid punishing the "morally innocent."

The essential element of a subjectively guilty mind in order to convict a person of murder was again emphasized in *R. v. Martineau* (1990), 58 C.C.C. (3d) 353.

However, not only must the guilty mind, intent or *mens rea* be present, it must also be concurrent with the impugned act. Professor D. Stuart has referred to this as "the simultaneous principle": see *Canadian Criminal Law*, 2nd ed. (1987), p. 305. The principle has been stressed in a number of cases. For example in *R. v. Droste* (1979), 49 C.C.C. (2d) 52 (Ont. C.A.), the accused had intended to murder his wife by pouring gasoline over the interior of the car and setting fire to it while she was within it. Before he could light the gasoline the car crashed into a bridge and ignited prematurely. As a result both his children were killed rather than his wife. He was charged with their murder and convicted. On appeal Arnup J.A., speaking for the Court of Appeal in directing a new trial, stated at pp. 53-54:

> ... the trial Judge did not instruct the jury of the necessity of the Crown showing that at the time of the occurrence at the bridge, the appellant, intending to kill his wife, had done an act with that intention, and in the course of doing so his children were killed. *In short, he did not tell them that the mens rea and the actus reus must be concurrent.* ... (Emphasis added.)

Yet, it is not always necessary for the guilty act and the intent to be completely concurrent: see, for example, *Fagan v. Metropolitan Police Commissioner*, [1968] 3 All E.R. 442 (Q.B.). ... James J., concurring in the result, stated at p. 445:

> It is not necessary that *mens rea* should be present at the inception of the *actus reus*; it can be superimposed on an existing act.

There is, then, the classic rule that at some point the *actus reus* and the *mens reas* or intent must coincide. Further, I would agree with the conclusion of James J. that an act (*actus reus*) which may be innocent or no more than careless at the outset can become criminal at a later stage when the accused acquires knowledge of the nature of the act and still refuses to change his course of action.

The determination of whether the guilty mind or *mens rea* coincides with the wrongful act will depend to a large extent upon the nature of the act. For example, if the accused shot the victim in the head or stabbed the victim in the chest with death ensuing a few minutes after the shooting or stabbing, then it would be relatively easy to infer that the requisite intent or *mens rea* coincided with the wrongful act (*actus reus*) of shooting or stabbing. As well, a series of acts may form part of the same transaction. For example the repeated blows of the baseball bat continuing over several minutes are all part of the same transaction. In those circumstances if the requisite intent coincides at any time with the sequence of blows then that could be sufficient to found a conviction.

An example of a series of acts that might be termed a continuous transaction appears in *Meli v. The Queen*, [1954] 1 W.L.R. 228 (P.C.). There the accused intended to kill the deceased, and to this end struck a number of blows. The effect of the blows was such that the accused thought the victim was dead and threw the body over a cliff. However, it was not the blows but rather the exposure suffered by the victim while he lay at the base of the cliff that resulted in the death. It was argued on behalf of the accused that when there was the requisite *mens rea* (during the beating) death did not ensue and when death did ensue there was no longer any intention to kill. The judicial committee of the Privy Council concluded that the entire episode was one continuing transaction that could not be subdivided in that way. At some point, the requisite *mens rea* coincided with the continuing series of wrongful acts that constituted the transaction. As a result, the conviction for murder was sustained. I agree with that conclusion.

### Application of the "Contemporaneous" Principles to This Case

… There is no question that in order to obtain a conviction the Crown must demonstrate that the accused intended to cause bodily harm that he knew was ultimately so dangerous and serious that it was likely to result in the death of the victim. But that intent need not persist throughout the entire act of strangulation. When Cooper testified that he seized the victim by the neck, it was open to the jury to infer that by those actions he intended to cause her bodily harm that he knew that was likely to cause her death. Since breathing is essential to life, it would be reasonable to infer the accused knew that strangulation was likely to result in death. I would stress that the jury was, of course, not required to make such an inference but, on the evidence presented, it was open to them to do so.

Did the accused possess such a mental state after he started strangling the victim? Here death occurred between 30 seconds and two minutes after he grabbed her by the neck. It could be reasonably inferred by the jury, that when the accused grabbed the victim by the neck and shook her that there was, at that moment, the necessary coincidence of the wrongful act of strangulation and the requisite intent to do bodily harm that the accused knew was likely to cause her death. Cooper was aware of these acts before he "blacked out." Thus although the jury was under no compulsion to do so, it was none the less open to them to infer that he knew that he was causing bodily harm and knew that it was so dangerous to the victim that it was likely to cause her death. It was sufficient that the intent and the act of strangulation coincided at some point. It was not necessary that the requisite intent continue throughout the entire two minutes required to cause the death of the victim. …

The Court of Appeal asked … whether "continuing awareness on his part of what he was doing and its probable result [was] established." The accused argued that in using this expression the Court of Appeal was not going so far as to require the presence of a continuous intent up to the moment of death. Rather, he contended that the court was merely stating that in order for there to be a conviction under this section the *mens rea* must be present at or after the point at which it becomes likely the death will ensue. It was his position that if the intent to cause bodily harm that the accused knew was likely to cause death should disappear before the point was reached at which death became likely then the accused could not be found guilty. He stated that it was only at this point that the *mens reas* and *actus reus* could coalesce into the crime described in s. 212(a)(ii).

This argument should not be accepted. It would require the Crown to provide expert evidence as to the moment at which death physiologically became a likelihood. It would be impossible to fix the time of the "likelihood" of death and difficult to provide evidence as to the duration of the requisite intent of the accused. That cannot be the meaning of this section. Neither the plain wording of this section nor any concept of fairness require the Crown to demonstrate such a complex chronological sequence. In order to obtain a conviction under s. 212(a)(ii), the Crown must prove that the accused caused and intended to cause bodily harm that he knew was likely to cause the death of the victim. If death results from a series of wrongful acts that are part of a single transaction then it must be established that the requisite intent coincided at some point with the wrongful acts. ...

*Appeal allowed; conviction restored.*

### Section 229(b): Transferred Intent

### R. v. Fontaine
Manitoba Court of Appeal
(2002), 168 C.C.C. (3d) 263

[The accused was convicted of one count of first-degree murder, two counts of attempted murder, one count of criminal negligence causing death, and one count of criminal negligence causing bodily harm. The accused was intent on committing suicide and during the course of a high-speed chase, deliberately drove his car into a parked semi-trailer in the oncoming lane. At the time of the collision, there were three individuals in the vehicle being driven by the accused. The accused survived the collision, but one passenger in his car was killed.]

STEEL J.A.: ...

*Section 229(b) of the Criminal Code*

[10] Murder is a crime of specific intent. By virtue of s. 229(b) of the *Criminal Code*, a person will be deemed to have that specific intent when, intending to kill one person, he mistakenly kills another person. Section 229(b) of the *Criminal Code* states:

> 229. Culpable homicide is murder ...
>
> (b) where a person, meaning to cause death to a human being or meaning to cause him bodily harm that he knows is likely to cause his death, and being reckless whether death ensues or not, by accident or mistake causes death to another human being, notwithstanding that he does not mean to cause death or bodily harm to that human being; or ...

[11] The question in the case at bar is whether the above section transfers the specific intent necessary for a charge of murder when, instead of the accused attempting to murder someone else, he attempts to commit suicide and kills another in the process.

[12] The only reported case which raises this issue is that of *R. v. Brown* (1983), 4 C.C.C. (3d) 571 (Ont. H.C.) interpreted the words "cause death to a human being" in s. 229(b) of the *Criminal Code* to read "cause death to any human being (himself included)." This is the interpretation urged upon us by the Crown.

[13] The accused, on the other hand, argues that the decision in Brown and the charge of the trial judge in this case are in error in their interpretation of s. 229(b) of the *Criminal Code*. For example, it is argued that such a reading of s. 229(b) in conjunction with s. 24(1) of the *Criminal Code* could result in a person being convicted of attempted murder for trying to commit suicide. Yet, Parliament has removed attempted suicide from the *Criminal Code*.

[14] Additionally, it is submitted by the accused that the common law definition of transferred intent is of assistance when interpreting s. 229(b) of the *Criminal Code* in terms of the underlying principles justifying punishment based on transferred intent. In both the cases of *R. v. Deakin* (1974), 16 C.C.C. (2d) 1 (Man. C.A.), and *Droste v. The Queen*, [1984] 1 S.C.R. 208, the courts refer to legal texts with approval on the issue that transferred intent only applies within the same crime. That is, it only applies where the harm that follows is of the same legal kind as that intended.

[15] In order to determine whether an intent to commit suicide is properly transferred pursuant to s. 229(b) of the *Criminal Code*, it will be necessary to examine the nature of suicide and how it differs, conceptually, from murder.

[16] Although there are some comments to the contrary, the majority of early English jurisprudence discusses suicide as something different than murder in that murder requires the killing of another person. ...

[19] There are many cases which distinguish between suicide and murder. So, again for example, in the case of *R. v. Burgess* (1862), Le. & Ca. 258, 169 E.R. 1387, it was held that an attempt to commit suicide is not an attempt to commit murder within the meaning of the statute. ...

[20] At the present time, suicide is no longer a crime in England (see the *Suicide Act, 1961* (U.K.), 9 & 10 Eliz. II, c. 60, s. 1). Although suicide is no longer an offence in itself, it is an indictable offence, punishable by 14 years' imprisonment, for any person to aid, abet, counsel, or procure the suicide of another or an attempt by another to commit suicide. (See s. 2(1) of the *Suicide Act, 1961*.)

[21]  It is also interesting to note that the United Kingdom Parliament has retained statutory language which speaks to the killing of "another." Section 1(1) of the *Homicide Act, 1957* (U.K.), 5 & 6 Eliz. II, c. 11, reads:

> 1(1)  Where a person kills another in the course or furtherance of some other offence, the killing shall not amount to murder unless done with the same malice aforethought (express or implied) as is required for a killing to amount to murder when not done in the course or furtherance of another offence.
>
> ...

[24]  With respect to Canadian jurisprudence, this case is very much one of first impression. Counsel has referred our court to a single decision, that being the decision of the Ontario High Court of Justice in Brown. In that case, without reference to any history or case law, O'Brien J. accepted the argument of the Crown that the words "cause death to a human being" in s. 229(b) of the *Criminal Code* (then s. 212(b)) "should be read and construed in their ordinary meaning, and that being so those words would include the accused himself."

[25]  While the above decision appears to be the only one that purports to directly consider the issue of transferred intent in suicide, there are several other cases which may offer us some guidance. ...

[27]  Several cases have referred to murder as the intentional killing of "another." One well-known example is *R. v. Creighton*, [1993] 3 S.C.R. 3. McLachlin J., as she then was, wrote (at pp. 41-42):

> The *Criminal Code* defines three general types of culpable homicide. There is murder, the intentional killing of *another* human being. There is infanticide, the intentional killing of a child. All other culpable homicides fall into the residual category of manslaughter. ... [Emphasis in original.]

[28]  A review of the principles of statutory interpretation as they relate to penal statutes is also instructive in our attempt to interpret s. 229(b) in the context of these facts.

[29]  The original definition of "homicide" in the *Criminal Code*, 1892, 55-56 Vict., c. 29, stated as follows:

> 218.  Homicide is the killing of a human being by another, directly or indirectly, by any means whatsoever.

[30]  In the *Criminal Code*, S.C. 1953-54, c. 51, the above section (then numbered s. 250) was combined and re-enacted as s. 194. Subsection (1) of s. 194 then read:

> (1)  A person commits homicide when, directly or indirectly, by any means, he causes the death of a human being.

Thus, the 1954 amendment deleted the reference to the killing of a human being by another.

[31]  A well-known principle of statutory interpretation is the presumption that change is purposeful. Ruth Sullivan, *Driedger on the Construction of Statutes*, 3rd ed. (Toronto: Butterworths, 1994), writes on this principle (at p. 450):

It is presumed that amendments to the wording of a legislative provision are made for some intelligible purpose: to clarify the meaning, to correct a mistake, to change the law.

...

[33] In our case, language polishing may indeed have been intended as s. 250 [R.S.C. 1927, c. 36] (the former s. 218) was not amended by itself. Rather, s. 250 was combined and re-enacted with ss. 252 (which defined culpable homicide) and 253. A study of this process of amendment leads me to the conclusion that the legislature did not turn its mind to the fact that the definition of "homicide" changed from the killing of a human being "by another" to "causes the death of a human being." They were merely combining three sections and the result, at the end of the day, spoke of the death of a human being.

[34] Moreover, another principle of statutory interpretation, that of the strict construction rule in penal legislation, mitigates in favour of the accused. Penal legislation that create offences punishable by fines, loss of freedom, or curtailment of a privilege or right are strictly construed. Section 229(b) is ambiguous in its interpretation as to whether it is intended to be limited to the killing of another or to include the killing of oneself. Where ambiguity is present in a piece of penal legislation, the statutory interpretation rule of strict construction should be applied because of the potential for serious interference with individual rights. ...

[36] I am aware that there is now one overriding principle of statutory interpretation. All other principles are subservient to the contextual and purposeful interpretation of statutes, where the words of an Act are read in their entire context and in their grammatical and ordinary sense harmoniously with the scheme of the Act, the object of the Act, and the intention of Parliament. See *R. v. Loscerbo (A.)* (1994), 89 C.C.C. (3d) 203 (C.A.), at para. 18, per Scott C.J.M. Most recently, the Supreme Court of Canada had occasion to confirm this one overarching approach to statutory interpretation in *Bell ExpressVu Ltd. Partnership v. Rex*, [2002] 5 W.W.R. 1, at para. 26, per Iacobucci J.

[37] I also agree that this is true, even when struggling with the interpretation of penal statutes. The first step is always to attempt to determine the real intention of the legislature and the meaning of the statute compatible with its goals. However, when attempts at interpretation still leave doubt as to the meaning or scope of the text of the statute, the rule of strict construction of penal statutes can become applicable. See *R. v. Hasselwander*, [1993] 2 S.C.R. 398.

[38] In *Bell ExpressVu*, Iacobucci J., writing for a unanimous court, recognized the exception for penal statutes (at paras. 28-29):

Other principles of interpretation—such as the strict construction of penal statutes and the "Charter values" presumption—only receive application where there is ambiguity as to the meaning of a provision. ...

What, then, in law is an ambiguity? To answer, an ambiguity must be "real" (*Marcotte*, ..., at p. 115). The words of the provision must be "reasonably capable of more than one meaning" (*Westminster Bank Ltd. v. Zang* (1965), [1966] A.C. 182

(U.K.H.L.), at p. 222, per Lord Reid). By necessity, however, one must consider the "entire context" of a provision before one can determine if it is reasonably capable of multiple interpretations. In this regard, Major J.'s statement in *Canadian Oxy Chemicals Ltd. v. Canada (Attorney General)*, [1999] 1 S.C.R. 743 (S.C.C.), at para. 14, is apposite: "It is only when genuine ambiguity arises between two or more plausible readings, *each equally in accordance with the intentions of the statute*, that the courts need to resort to external interpretive aids" [emphasis in original], to which I would add, "including other principles of interpretation."

[39]  Furthermore, the resolution of the ambiguity in favour of the accused in this case is reinforced when one considers the present differing social attitudes toward murder as opposed to suicide.

[40]  In *Creighton*, the Supreme Court of Canada reaffirmed the legal principles relevant to determining the constitutionality of a *mens rea* requirement. Three of those principles are (at p. 46):

1. The stigma attached to the offence, and the available penalties requiring a *mens rea* reflecting the particular nature of the crime;
2. Whether the punishment is proportionate to the moral blameworthiness of the offender; and
3. The idea that those causing harm intentionally must be punished more severely than those causing harm unintentionally.

[41]  Thus, the guiding principle underlying the constitutional analysis of fault in criminal law is that the state cannot punish a person as morally blameworthy unless such blameworthiness has been established. The gravity of the conduct itself, as well as the moral blameworthiness of the offender, must be analyzed in order to determine the extent of the social stigma to be attached to the crime.

[42]  First degree murder is perhaps the most stigmatizing offence known to law. It carries with it the most draconian minimum sentence of life imprisonment with no parole for 25 years. It is normally associated with the act of one who plans and deliberates to take the life of another person. Society as a whole condemns this crime.

[43]  Suicide on the other hand is normally seen as an act of desperation, often impulsive, and the act of a person who is ill and in need of treatment. By removing the crime of attempted suicide from the *Criminal Code*, Parliament recognized society's desire to see individuals who attempt suicide treated instead of criminalized.

[44]  To accept the definition proposed by Brown and equate the *mens rea* for suicide with murder would offend all three principles enumerated by the Supreme Court of Canada. It is not consistent with the stigma and available penalties, and it is not proportionate to the moral blameworthiness of the offender.

[45]  Given the early English treatment of murder and suicide as different crimes, the fact that suicide in Canada is no longer a crime, and the high moral culpability attached to the crime of murder, I conclude that the words of the provision in s. 229(b) of the *Criminal Code* are reasonably capable of more than one meaning. Given that ambiguity, the statutory interpretation rule of strictly construing penal legislation in favour of the accused would result in a conclusion that s. 229(b) refers to the killing of another and not the killing of oneself. ...

*Summary*

[84]  Section 229(b) is ambiguous in its interpretation. A review of English, American, and Canadian jurisprudence leads me to the conclusion that suicide and murder are two different conceptual entities. They have been treated differently historically. Moreover, where one act is legal and the other act is illegal, the transfer of intent from one to another should not necessarily follow.

[85]  There are good policy reasons to differentiate between the two in terms of culpability. Suicide is not currently an offence pursuant to the *Criminal Code*. We can contrast this with murder, which is recognized as the most serious crime in our *Criminal Code* and a crime that requires specific intent. ...

*Appeal allowed.*

### Section 229(c): Unlawful Object

For reasons that will become clear after reading the cases under the heading "Constitutional Considerations" below, s. 229(c) is controversial because it rests liability on the objective standard of "ought to have known." *Tennant and Naccarato* and *Vasil* were decided before the Supreme Court's major cases on the constitutional requirements of fault, which, as will be seen, have the effect of striking down the objective arm of s. 229(c).

### R. v. Tennant and Naccarato
Ontario Court of Appeal
(1975), 23 C.C.C. (2d) 80

BY THE COURT: ... As is well known, s. 212(c) is derived from s. 174(d) of the English Draft Code. Section 212(c) grounds liability for murder upon an objective test, inasmuch as it holds the offender guilty of murder if for an unlawful object he does anything that he *knows or ought to know* is likely to cause death and thereby causes death.

Where the provisions of s. 212(c) are applicable, the words "ought to know" impose liability for murder where death is unlawfully caused by conduct which a reasonable person, with knowledge of the surrounding circumstances which make such conduct dangerous to life, should have foreseen was likely to cause death.

At the time the English Draft Code was prepared and when s. 227, the counterpart of s. 212 in the *Criminal Code* of 1892, was enacted, the accused could not give evidence and his state of mind could *only* be inferred by drawing comparisons from what would have been in the mind of a reasonable man if he had acted as the accused did. Viewed in its historical context, the imposition of liability for murder on an objective basis thus did not constitute the anomaly that it represents in modern times, when, in general, and subject to important exceptions, criminal liability for murder under the *Criminal Code* depends upon proof of subjective states of mind. We have already pointed out, however, that even under s. 212(c), the offender's liability for murder depends upon his knowledge of the surrounding circumstances which make the conduct in question dangerous to life, for example, his knowledge that a pistol which he is brandishing is loaded, or his knowledge of the presence or probable presence of persons in a house to which he sets fire. (Holmes, *The Common Law*, pp. 52-7; *Molleur v. The King* (1948), 93 C.C.C. 36, 6 C.R. 375, [1948] Que. K.B. 406*n.*)

Where liability is imposed on a subjective basis, what a reasonable man ought to have anticipated is merely evidence from which a conclusion may be drawn that the accused anticipated the same consequences. On the other hand, where the test is objective, what a reasonable man should have anticipated constitutes the basis of liability.

The distinction between the imposition of liability on an objective basis rather than on a subjective basis assumes particular importance under s. 212(c), where the accused by reason of intoxication or even stupidity did not in fact foresee the likelihood that his conduct would cause death.

If the accused had the capacity to form the intent necessary for the unlawful object and had knowledge of the relevant facts which made his conduct such as to be likely to cause death, he is guilty of murder if a reasonable man should have anticipated that such conduct was likely to cause death. What the accused ought to have foreseen is judged under s. 212(c) by the standard of the reasonable man.

It follows that the defence of drunkenness is only relevant under s. 212(c) in relation to whether the accused had the intent necessary to constitute the unlawful purpose alleged and had knowledge of the relevant circumstances.

We observe that the *New Zealand Crimes Act* of 1908, like our *Criminal Code*, was derived from the English Draft Code and s. 182 of that Act was the counterpart of s. 227(d) in the *Canadian Criminal Code* of 1892, the predecessor of s. 212(c) in the present *Code*. However, in the 1961 *New Zealand Crimes Act* the words "ought to have known" were deleted from the present s. 167(d). Whether a similar change in the wording of s. 212(c) is desirable is, of course, for Parliament to decide. The Courts must endeavour to give effect to the language of the *Code* as it now reads. We ought not, however, to construe the subsection more widely than its language requires.

Section 212(c) contemplates some act or conduct by the offender done in order to bring about some *further* unlawful object or purpose which he has in mind. A person may strike, or stab or shoot another with no purpose other than to inflict the injury which he, in fact, inflicts.

We are of the view that s. 212(c) ought not to be given an interpretation which permits foreseeability under s. 212(c) to be substituted for the intent required under s. 212(a)(i) and (ii) in cases where personal injury is not inflicted for a *further* unlawful object. To hold otherwise would largely nullify the provisions of the section with respect to the necessity for proof of the requisite intent to kill or to inflict bodily harm which the offender knows is likely to cause death in order to constitute murder (apart from the limited class of case falling within a more stringent definition of murder). Accordingly, s. 212(c) is not applicable where death is caused by an assault which is not shown to have been committed for the purpose of achieving some other unlawful object. It is, however, applicable where death is caused by a separate act which the accused ought to have anticipated was likely to result in death, and which was committed to achieve some further unlawful object; that unlawful object may be an assault.

In the case at bar, the conduct of the accused Naccarato in procuring the loaded pistol after the initial confrontation with the deceased, and his use of it in the circumstances, brought him within the ambit of s. 212(c) in the event that the jury was satisfied beyond a reasonable doubt that the procuring and use of the pistol was for the unlawful purpose of assaulting the deceased and that Naccarato knew or ought to have known that his conduct was likely to bring about a situation in which someone might be killed. The conduct of Naccarato in procuring and using the pistol is sufficiently separated from the unlawful object, that is, the assault, to constitute such conduct a separate act done for an unlawful purpose within the meaning of s. 212(c), in the event that the jury chose to take that view of the evidence.

## R. v. Vasil
Supreme Court of Canada
(1981), 58 C.C.C. (2d) 97

[The accused was convicted of the murder of two children as a result of their death in a fire at the house where they lived. The deceased were the children of the woman with whom the accused was living. Following an argument at a party with this woman, the accused went to the house, took the baby-sitter to her home, and then returned and spread lighter fluid in various parts of the house. He then allegedly set the fire and left the house. The accused was an alcoholic and had been drinking at the party. He testified that he spread the lighter fluid to ruin various items in the house in preparation of leaving the woman. He gave several statements to the police in one of which he stated that he did not realize the children were in the house. The trial judge directed the jury with respect to s. 212(a) and (c) of the *Criminal Code*. The Ontario Court of Appeal allowed the accused's appeal from conviction and ordered a new trial because of, *inter alia*, a failure to properly relate the defence of drunkenness to s. 212(c). The trial judge had limited drunkenness to the intent to have an unlawful object. As to the unlawful object this was said to be "to seek revenge and destroy property." On appeal by the Crown to the Supreme Court of Canada, the accused also argued that s. 212(c) should not have been left to the jury.]

LAMER J. (for the Court): Though s. 212(c) of the *Criminal Code*, R.S.C. 1970, c. C-34, has been with us since codification in 1892 (it was then s. 227(d)), the more serious questions as to its meaning and scope have, save a few exceptions, been raised in the Courts below only recently. We have been told that this may well be explained by the fact that, on an indictment for murder, counsel for the Crown are more frequently than in the past, and quite properly so, requesting, when the factual basis of the case so justifies, that the Judge instruct the jury as to the application of this section in lieu of or subsidiarily to the other murder sections.

Only two cases are to be found in the law reports where this Court has dealt with the meaning and purview of s. 212(c) of the *Criminal Code*: over 65 years ago, in the case of *Graves v. The King (No. 4)* (1913), 21 C.C.C. 44, 9 D.L.R. 589, 47 S.C.R. 568, and almost 40 years ago in the case of *R. v. Hughes, Petryk, Billamy and Berrigan* (1942), 78 C.C.C. 257, [1943] 1 D.L.R. 1, [1942] S.C.R. 517.

The three issues raised in this appeal not only afford but, in my respectful opinion, strongly suggest a reconsideration of how this Court dealt with those issues in the *Graves* case.

The first issue in this appeal turns upon the determination of the nature, and thereby the delimitation, of what may constitute an "unlawful object" within the meaning of s. 212(c).

The other two issues are whether drunkenness may be a defence in relation to an accused's knowledge of the surrounding circumstances at the time he did the act in furtherance of the unlawful object and, if so, the onus and degree of proof of such a defence. In fact, drunkenness raises the more fundamental issue as to whether the test applicable to the knowledge of the surrounding circumstances is objective (that of the reasonable man) or subjective.

It is argued that the trial Judge left the jury with the impression that "seeking revenge" could be an "unlawful object," or part thereof, as that expression is meant at s. 212(c). True, he did not directly tell them so; but not having clearly told them what he thought could be an unlawful object, he then said that, according to the Crown, seeking revenge and destroying property could be such an unlawful object.

Let it be said right now that, in my opinion, the "unlawful object" contemplated by Parliament in that section is that which, if prosecuted fully, would amount to an indictable offence requiring *mens rea.*

Reference to Hansard is not usually advisable. However, as Canada has, at the time of codification, subject to few changes, adopted the English Draft Code of 1878, it is relevant to know whether Canada did so in relation to the various sections for the reasons advanced by the English Commissioners or for reasons of its own.

Indeed, a reading of Sir John Thompson's comments in Hansard of April 12, 1892 (Debates House of Commons, Dominion of Canada, Session 1892, vol. I, pp. 1378-85), very clearly confirms that all that relates to murder was taken directly from the English Draft Code of 1878. Sir John Thompson explained the proposed murder sections by frequently quoting verbatim the reasons given by the Royal Commissioners in Great Britain, and it is evident that Canada adopted not only the British Commissioners' proposed sections but also their reasons.

Some have suggested that the meaning of "unlawful object" should be determined in the light of the following passage of what the Commissioners said in their report:

> For practical purposes we can make no distinction between a man who shoots another through the head expressly meaning to kill him, a man who strikes another a violent blow with a sword, careless whether he dies of it or not, and a man who, intending for some object of his own, to stop the passage of a railway train, contrives an explosion of gunpowder or dynamite under the engine, hoping indeed that death may not be caused, but determined to effect his purpose whether it is so caused or not.

(This passage can be found in Crankshaw's 1st ed. of 1894, *Criminal Code of Canada*, at p. 139). Some might find in that passage of the report an indication that the Commissioners intended to include as being an unlawful object for their proposed murder section endeavours such as those that would qualify as unlawful when considering conspiracy for an unlawful purpose (s. 423(2)) (those words have been recently interpreted in *Re Regina and Gralewicz et al.*, October 7, 1980 [reported 54 C.C.C. (2d) 289, 116 D.L.R. (3d) 276, 33 N.R. 242], where a majority of this Court decided that "unlawful purpose" means contrary to law, that is prohibited by federal or provincial legislation), or, if not to that extent, at least as an indication that the unlawful conduct need not be a crime.

Under the circumstances, I think it not unreasonable to recognize that the intent of Parliament at s. 212(c) is best respected by circumscribing *the words "unlawful object" when used in that murder section as meaning the object of conduct which, if prosecuted fully, would amount to a serious crime, that is an indictable offence requiring mens rea.*

Applying this interpretation of s. 212(c) to the present case, the jury had to be told that, if they believed beyond a reasonable doubt that the accused intended to damage the food and furniture, such an object was an unlawful object; indeed, the fact that Mrs. Gilchrist was sharing in the cost of the furniture is not contested and as a result the wilful destruction, damaging, obstruction, interference with that property is mischief, an indictable *mens rea* offence. As for the dangerous act, it would have been sufficient that they be told that it could be the resorting to the use of fire as a means of prosecuting the unlawful object (the destruction of the furniture), without any need to refer to the fact that setting the fire under those circumstances was also in itself an unlawful act.

The fact that the Judge did not relate drunkenness to the accused's knowledge of the surrounding circumstances is not in dispute. ...

A mere reading of s. 212(c) is of little help in determining whether Parliament intended, once a person is prosecuting an unlawful object, that all of that person's behaviour be measured by a purely objective standard or whether that objective standard be restricted to measuring, when *considering murder*, his morality in relation to a factual situation of which he is conscious. Faced with the problem in the case at bar, the Court of Appeal for Ontario followed one of its previous decisions, that in the case of *R. v. Tennant and Naccarato* (1975), 23 C.C.C. (2d) 80, 7 O.R. (2d) 687, 31 C.R.N.S. 1.

Holmes J., in *The Common Law*, at pp. 53-4 and 56, defined "foresight of consequences" as being:

> ... a picture of a future state of things called up *by knowledge of the present state of things*, the future being viewed as standing to the present in the relation of effect to cause. Again, we must seek a reduction to lower terms. *If the known present state of things is such* that the act done will very certainly cause death, and the probability is a matter of common knowledge, one who does the act, *knowing the present state of things, is guilty of murder*, and the law will not inquire whether he did actually foresee the consequences or not. The test of foresight is not what this very criminal foresaw, but what a man of reasonable prudence would have foreseen. ... But furthermore, on the same principle, the danger which in fact exists under the known circumstances ought to

be of a class which a man of reasonable prudence could foresee. Ignorance of a fact and
inability to foresee a consequence have the same effect on blameworthiness. If a consequence cannot be foreseen, it cannot be avoided. But there is this practical difference,
that whereas, in most cases, the question of knowledge is a question of the actual condition of the defendant's consciousness, the question of what he might have foreseen is
determined by the standard of the prudent man, that is, by general experience. (Emphasis added.)

With this, and with what the Court of Appeal for Ontario said, I agree.

Faced with a text that lends itself to two interpretations one must search for Parliament's intent at the time of its enactment. I take the liberty of repeating that this text
is that of a murder section, essentially a crime of intent, of malice aforethought, the
result of "wickedness" and "heinous conduct" (Kenny's *Outlines of Criminal Law*,
*supra*). In deciding what would be the more appropriate of the two possible interpretations this I think should be borne in mind. To interpret the section of the *Code* as is
suggested by the Crown could result in a conviction for murder of him whose sole
malice would be that of the "unlawful object" coupled to that of getting drunk.

When s. 212(c) includes amongst the guilty even one who "desires to effect his
object without causing death or bodily harm to any human being," reference is being
made to one who consciously takes *a chance* with the life of others by choosing a
dangerous means to an unlawful end; but Parliament could not, in my opinion, have
intended to include one who could not even realize he was taking such a chance with
the life of others because he *could* not, given his ignorance of the surrounding circumstances, even foresee the dangerousness of those means.

A passage from Anglin J.'s opinion in *Graves* (whether in the jury's "opinion the
accused knew or ought to have known that the gun in the hands of the deceased was
loaded") suggests that this Court decided in *Graves* that knowledge of the surrounding circumstances is to be determined by an application of the objective standard,
and that, applying this finding to the present case, there would as a result be no place
for considering drunkenness in appreciating that knowledge.

If that be the decision, then, with the greatest of deference, and after having given
the matter very careful consideration, I would feel compelled not to follow that determination in *Graves*. Whilst it is impossible to know with any degree of certainty
what opinion one would have advanced as correct had one had to deal with these
questions at the time(1913) they were put to this Court, it is likewise and to the same
extent impossible to know what the Judges of this Court in the *Graves* case would
today decide, offered the same opportunity to interpret s. 212(c). Indeed, over 65
years have since elapsed, and the law, specially the criminal law, and even more so
the attitudes of all of those administering it, have greatly evolved. As an illustration
one need but consider the concept of "technical guilt," which having over the years
been gradually limited by a series of decisions was finally drastically so by this Court's
decision in *R. v. City of Sault Ste. Marie* (1978), 40 C.C.C. (2d) 353, 85 D.L.R. (3d)
161, [1978] 2 S.C.R. 1299; or again consider the evolution of the defence of duress
from what this Court decided in *Dunbar v. The King* (1936), 67 C.C.C. 20, [1936] 4

D.L.R. 737, to its ruling in *R. v. Paquette* (1976), 30 C.C.C. (2d) 417, 70 D.L.R. (3d) 129, [1977] 2 S.C.R. 189.

For these reasons, I feel that the interpretation of s. 212(c) as it relates to drunkenness adopted by the Court of Appeal for Ontario in this case and in that of *R. v. Tennant and Naccarato, supra*, is much more in harmony with the current attitudes of this Court in relation to criminal liability than that adopted by this Court in *Graves, supra*. The order of the Court of Appeal directing a new trial should stand.

*Appeal dismissed.*

## Constitutional Considerations

After the Charter came into force, the Supreme Court decided a number of cases that measured statutory fault requirements against the principles of fundamental justice in s. 7 of the Charter. As discussed in chapter 6, the case of *Reference re Section 94(2) of the B.C. Motor Vehicle Act*, [1985] 2 S.C.R. 486 established that the deprivation of liberty predicated upon moral blameworthiness violated the principles of fundamental justice on the basis that it resulted in the punishment of the morally blameworthy. The court built upon and extend its constitutionalization of fault requirements in the context of murder. The prime target was s. 213 of the *Criminal Code*, the "constructive murder" or "felony murder" provision, which imposed fault for murder in the absence of a meaningful fault requirement with respect to the death of the victim. Indeed, with respect to s. 213(d), which was at issue in *Vaillancourt*, the Crown was under no obligation to establish any fault requirement in relation to death.

### Vaillancourt v. The Queen
Supreme Court of Canada
(1987), 39 C.C.C. (3d) 118

LAMER J. (with whom Dickson C.J.C., Estey, and Wilson JJ. concurred): Vaillancourt was convicted of second degree murder following a trial before a Sessions Court judge and jury in Montreal. He appealed to the Quebec Court of Appeal, arguing that the judge's charge to the jury on the combined operation of ss. 213(d) and 21(2) of the *Criminal Code*, R.S.C. 1970, c. C-34, was incorrect. His appeal was dismissed and the conviction was affirmed: (1984), 31 C.C.C. (3d) 75. Before this court, he has challenged the constitutional validity of s. 213(d) alone and in combination with s. 21(2) under the *Canadian Charter of Rights and Freedoms*.

The appellant and his accomplice committed an armed robbery in a pool-hall. The appellant was armed with a knife and his accomplice with a gun. During the robbery, the appellant remained near the front of the hall while the accomplice went to the back. There was a struggle between the accomplice and a client. A shot was fired and the client was killed. The accomplice managed to escape and has never been found. The appellant was arrested at the scene.

In the course of his testimony, the appellant said that he and his accomplice had agreed to commit this robbery armed only with knives. On the night of the robbery, however, the accomplice arrived at their meeting place with a gun. The appellant said that he objected because, on a previous armed robbery, his gun had discharged accidentally, and he did not want that to happen again. He insisted that the gun be unloaded. The accomplice removed three bullets from the gun and gave them to the appellant. The appellant then went to the bathroom and placed the bullets in his glove. The glove was recovered by the police at the scene of the crime and was found at trial to contain three bullets. The appellant testified that, at the time of the robbery, he was certain that the gun was unloaded.

Before this court, the following constitutional questions were formulated:

1.  Is s. 213(d) of the *Criminal Code* inconsistent with the provisions of either s. 7 or s. 11(d) of the *Canadian Charter of Rights and Freedoms*, and, therefore, of no force or effect?

2.  If not, is the combination of s. 21 and s. 213(d) of the *Criminal Code* inconsistent with the provisions of either s. 7 or s. 11(d) of the *Canadian Charter of Rights and Freedoms* and is s. 21 of the *Criminal Code* therefore of no force or effect in the case of a charge under s. 213(d) of the *Criminal Code*?

The appellant has framed his attack on s. 213(d) of the Code in very wide terms. He has argued that the principles of fundamental justice require that, before Parliament can impose any criminal liability for causing a particular result, there must be some degree of subjective *mens rea* in respect of that result. This is a fundamental question with far-reaching consequences. If this case were decided on that basis, doubt would be cast on the constitutional validity of many provisions throughout our *Criminal Code*, in particular s. 205(5)(a), whereby causing death by means of an unlawful act is culpable homicide, and s. 212(c) whereby objective foreseeability of the likelihood of death is sufficient for a murder conviction in certain circumstances.

However, the appellant was convicted under s. 213(d) and the constitutional question is limited to this provision. In my opinion, the validity of s. 213(d) can be decided on somewhat narrower grounds. In addition, the Attorney-General of Canada has seen fit not to intervene to support the constitutionality of s. 213(d), which is clearly in jeopardy in this case, though he may have intervened to support ss. 205(5)(a) and 212(c) and other similar provisions. I will thus endeavour not to make pronouncements the effect of which will be to predispose in *obiter* of other issues more properly dealt with if and when the constitutionality of the other provisions is in issue. I do, however, find it virtually impossible to make comments as regards s. 213(d) that will not have some effect on the validity of the rest of s. 213 or that will not reveal to some extent my views as regards s. 212(c). However, the validity of those sections and of paras. (a) to (c) of s. 213 is not in issue here and I will attempt to limit my comments to s. 213(d).

The appellant has also challenged the combined operation of ss. 21(2) and 213(d). Given my decision on the validity of s. 213(d) and in view of the importance of s. 21(2) and the absence of the Attorney-General of Canada, I do not find it necessary or advisable to deal with s. 21(2) in this appeal.

It is first necessary to analyze s. 213(d) in the context of the other murder provisions in the Code in order to determine its true nature and scope. Murder is defined as a culpable homicide committed in the circumstances set out at ss. 212 and 213 of the Code. There is a very interesting progression through s. 212 to s. 213 with respect to the mental state that must be proven.

The starting point is s. 212(a)(i), which provides:

> 212. Culpable homicide is murder
>> (a) where the person who causes the death of a human being
>>> (i) means to cause his death …

This clearly requires that the accused have actual subjective foresight of the likelihood of causing the death coupled with the intention to cause that death. This is the most morally blameworthy state of mind in our system.

There is a slight relaxation of this requirement in s. 212(a)(ii), which provides:

> 212. Culpable homicide is murder
>> (a) Where the person who causes the death of a human being …
>>> (ii) means to cause him bodily harm that he knows is likely to cause his death, and is reckless whether death ensues or not;

Here again the accused must have actual subjective foresight of the likelihood of death. However, the Crown need no longer prove that he intended to cause the death but only that he was reckless whether death ensued or not. It should also be noted that s. 212(a)(ii) is limited to cases where the accused intended to cause bodily harm to the victim.

Section 212(c) provides:

> 212. Culpable homicide is murder …
>> (c) where a person, for an unlawful object, does anything that he knows or ought to know is likely to cause death, and thereby causes death to a human being, notwithstanding that he desires to effect his object without causing death or bodily harm to any human being.

In part, this is simply a more general form of recklessness and thus the logical extension of s. 212(a)(ii), in that it applies when the accused "does *anything* … he knows … is likely to cause death" (emphasis added). However, there is also a further relaxation of the mental element required for murder in that it is also murder where the accused "does *anything that he … ought to know* is likely to cause death" (emphasis added). This eliminates the requirement of actual subjective foresight and replaces it with objective foreseeability or negligence.

Although the concept of felony murder has a long history at common law, a brief review of the historical development of s. 213 indicates that its legitimacy is questionable. …

Finally, the Law Reform Commission of Canada criticized s. 213 in *Homicide* (1984), Working Paper 33, at pp. 47-51, and excluded the notion of constructive murder from its Draft Criminal Code (*Recodifying Criminal Law* (1986), Report 30, cl. 6(3), p. 54).

Prior to the enactment of the Charter, Parliament had full legislative power with respect to "The Criminal Law" (*Constitution Act*, 1867, s. 91(27)), including the determination of the essential elements of any given crime.

However, federal and provincial legislatures have chosen to restrict through the Charter this power with respect to criminal law. Under s. 7, if a conviction, given either the stigma attached to the offence or the available penalties, will result in a deprivation of the life, liberty or security of the person of the accused, then Parliament must respect the principles of fundamental justice. It has been argued that the principles of fundamental justice in s. 7 are only procedural guarantees. However, in *Reference re s. 94(2) of Motor Vehicle Act* (1985), 23 C.C.C. (3d) 289, 24 D.L.R. (4th) 536, [1985] 2 S.C.R. 486, this court rejected that argument and used s. 7 to review the substance of the legislation. As a result, while Parliament retains the power to define the elements of a crime, the courts now have the jurisdiction and, more important, the duty, when called upon to do so, to review that definition to ensure that it is in accordance with the principles of fundamental justice. ...

It may well be that as, a general rule, the principles of fundamental justice require proof of a subjective *mens rea* with respect to the prohibited act, in order to avoid punishing the "morally innocent." ...

There are many provisions in the Code requiring only objective foreseeability of the result or even only a causal link between the act and the result. As I would prefer not to cast doubt on the validity of such provisions *in this case*, I will assume, but only for the purposes of this appeal, that something less than subjective foresight of the result may, sometimes, suffice for the imposition of criminal liability for causing that result through intentional criminal conduct.

But, whatever the minimum *mens rea* for the act or the result may be, there are, though very few in number, certain crimes where, because of the special nature of the stigma attached to a conviction therefor or the available penalties, the principles of fundamental justice require a *mens rea* reflecting the particular nature of that crime. Such is theft, where, in my view, a conviction requires proof of some dishonesty. Murder is another such offence. The punishment for murder is the most severe in our society and the stigma that attaches to a conviction for murder is similarly extreme. In addition, murder is distinguished from manslaughter only by the mental element with respect to the death. It is thus clear that there must be some special mental element with respect to the death before a culpable homicide can be treated as a murder. That special mental element gives rise to the moral blameworthiness which justifies the stigma and sentence attached to a murder conviction. I am presently of the view that it is a principle of fundamental justice that a conviction for murder cannot rest on anything less than proof beyond a reasonable doubt of subjective foresight. Given the effect of this view on part of s. 212(c), for the reasons I have already given for deciding this case more narrowly, I need not and will not rest my finding that s. 213(d) violates the Charter on this view, because s. 213(d) does not, for reasons I will set out hereinafter, even meet the lower threshold test of objective foreseeability. I will therefore, for the sole purpose of this appeal, go no further than say that it is a principle of fundamental justice that, absent proof beyond a reasonable doubt of at least objective foreseeability, there surely cannot be a murder conviction.

[Lamer J. then discussed s. 11(d) of the Charter and stated, *inter alia*:]

What offends the presumption of innocence is the fact that an accused may be convicted despite the existence of a reasonable doubt on an essential element of the offence, and I do not think that it matters whether this results from the existence of a reverse onus provision or from the elimination of the need to prove an essential element.

The *mens rea* required for s. 213 consists of the *mens rea* for the underlying offence and the intent to commit one of the acts set forth in paras. (a) to (d) (*Swietlinski v. The Queen* (1980), 55 C.C.C. (2d) 481, 117 D.L.R. (3d) 285, [1980] 2 S.C.R. 956). Section 213 does not impose on the accused the burden of disproving objective foreseeability. Further, it does not completely exclude the need to prove any objective foreseeability. Rather, s. 213 has substituted for proof beyond a reasonable doubt of objective foreseeability, if that is the essential element, proof beyond a reasonable doubt of certain forms of intentional dangerous conduct causing death.

The question is, therefore, can Parliament make this substitution without violating ss. 7 and 11(d)? As I have discussed earlier, if Parliament frames the section so that, upon proof of the conduct, it would be unreasonable for a jury not to conclude beyond a reasonable doubt that the accused ought to have known that death was likely to ensue, then I think that Parliament has enacted a crime which is tantamount to one which has objective foreseeability as an essential element, and, if objective foreseeability is sufficient, then it would not be in violation of s. 7 or s. 11(d) in doing so in that way. The acid test of the constitutionality of s. 213 is this ultimate question: *Would it be possible for a conviction for murder to occur under s. 213 despite the jury having a reasonable doubt as to whether the accused ought to have known that death was likely to ensue?* If the answer is yes, then the section is *prima facie* in violation of ss. 7 and 11(d). I should add in passing that if the answer is no, then it would be necessary to decide whether objective foreseeability is sufficient for a murder conviction. However, because in my view the answer is yes and because I do not want to pass upon the constitutionality of s. 212(c) in this case, I will not address that issue. ...

Notwithstanding proof beyond a reasonable doubt of the matters set forth in paras. (a) to (d) a jury could reasonably be left in doubt as regards objective foreseeability of the likelihood that death be caused. In other words, s. 213 will catch an accused who performs one of the acts in paras. (a) to (d) and thereby causes a death but who otherwise would have been acquitted of murder because he did not foresee and could not reasonably have foreseen that death would be likely to result. For that reason, s. 213 *prima facie* violates ss. 7 and 11(d). It is thus not necessary to decide whether objective foreseeability is sufficient for murder as s. 213 does not even meet that standard. This takes us to s. 1 for the second phase of the constitutional inquiry.

Finding that s. 213 of the *Criminal Code* infringes ss. 7 and 11(d) of the Charter does not end the inquiry on the constitutional validity of s. 213. Any or all of paras. (a) to (d) of s. 213 can still be upheld as a reasonable limit "demonstrably justified in a free and democratic society" under s. 1 of the Charter.

In this case and at this stage of the inquiry, we need only consider para. (d) of s. 213. The criteria to be assessed under s. 1 have been set out by this court in several

cases, particularly *R. v. Big M Drug Mart Ltd.* (1985), 18 C.C.C. (3d) 385, 18 D.L.R.
(4th) 321, [1985] 1 S.C.R. 295, and *R. v. Oakes* (1986), 24 C.C.C. (3d) 321, 26 D.L.R.
(4th) 200, [1986] 1 S.C.R. 103. First, the objective which the measures are designed
to serve must be "of sufficient importance to warrant overriding a constitutionally
protected right or freedom" (*Big M Drug Mart, supra,* at p. 430 C.C.C., p. 366 D.L.R.,
p. 352 S.C.R.). Through s. 213(d) of the Code, Parliament intended to deter the use or
carrying of a weapon in the commission of certain offences, because of the increased
risk of death. In my view, it is clear that this objective is sufficiently important.

In addition, the measures adopted must be reasonable and demonstrably justified.
The measures adopted appear to be rationally connected to the objective: indiscriminately punishing for murder all those who cause a death by using or carrying a weapon,
whether the death was intentional or accidental, might well be thought to discourage
the use and the carrying of weapons. I believe, however, that the measures adopted
would unduly impair the rights and freedoms in question (see *Big M Drug Mart,
supra,* at p. 430 C.C.C., p. 366 D.L.R., p. 352 S.C.R.). It is not necessary to convict
of murder persons who did not intend or foresee the death and who could not even
have foreseen the death in order to deter others from using or carrying weapons. If
Parliament wishes to deter the use or carrying of weapons, it should punish the use or
carrying of weapons. A good example of this is the minimum imprisonment for using
a firearm in the commission of an indictable offence under s. 83 of the *Criminal
Code.* In any event, the conviction for manslaughter which would result instead of a
conviction for murder is punishable by, from a day in jail, to confinement for life in a
penitentiary. Very stiff sentences when weapons are involved in the commission of
the crime of manslaughter would sufficiently deter the use or carrying of weapons in
the commission of crimes. But stigmatizing the crime as murder unnecessarily impairs the Charter right.

In my view, therefore, s. 213(d) is not saved by s. 1.

La FOREST J.: I have had the advantage of reading the judgment of Lamer J. and
would dispose of the appeal in the manner proposed by him. I am in agreement with
him that because of the stigma attached to a conviction for murder, the principles of
fundamental justice require a *mens rea* reflecting the particular nature of that crime,
namely, one referable to causing death. In addition to the intention to cause death,
this can include a closely related intention such as intention to cause bodily harm
likely to result in death combined with recklessness as to that result. Whether and
how much further the intention can be extended it is not necessary to explore for the
purposes of this case. It is sufficient to say that the mental element required by
s. 213(d) of the *Criminal Code* is so remote from the intention specific to murder
(which intention is what gives rise to the stigma attached to a conviction for that
crime) that a conviction under that paragraph violates fundamental justice. All the
provision requires is an intention to commit another crime and to possess a weapon
while carrying out this intention or in fleeing afterwards. The provision is so broad
that under it a person may be found guilty of murder even though the death was the
result of an accident. This occurred in *Rowe v. The King* (1951), 100 C.C.C. 97, [1951]
4 D.L.R. 238, [1951] S.C.R. 713, and more extreme examples can easily be imag-

ined. The section is thus not only remote from the *mens rea* specific to murder, but even removes its *actus reus* as traditionally defined: see Isabel Grant and A. Wayne MacKay, "Constructive Murder and the Charter: In Search of Principle," 25 Alta. L. Rev. 129 (1987).

As my colleague notes, the objective of discouraging the use of weapons in the commission of crimes can be achieved by means other than attaching the stigma of a conviction for murder to a person who has caused death in the circumstances like those described in the provision.

BEETZ J. (with whom Le Dain J. concurred): For the reasons given by Mr. Justice Lamer and Mr. Justice La Forest, I agree that s. 213(d) of the *Criminal Code* does not conform to the principles of fundamental justice entrenched in the *Canadian Charter of Rights and Freedoms* and cannot be saved under s. 1. I also agree with Mr. Justice Lamer that s. 213(d) of the *Criminal Code* violates s. 11(d) of the Charter and cannot be justified under s. 1 of the Charter.

Given these conclusions, I do not find it necessary to decide whether there exists a principle of fundamental justice that a conviction for murder cannot rest on anything less than proof beyond a reasonable doubt of subjective foresight.

McINTYRE J. (dissenting): I am not prepared to accept the proposition that s. 213(d) of the *Criminal Code* admits of a conviction for murder without proof of objective foreseeability of death or the likelihood of death, but in the view I take of this case it is not necessary to reach a firm conclusion on that point. The Crown sought the conviction of Vaillancourt on the basis of the interaction of s. 21(2) and s. 213(d) of the Code. For the Crown to succeed in such a prosecution, it would be required to prove that the accused and another had formed an intention in common to carry out an unlawful purpose and to assist each other therein. In addition, in the circumstances of this case, the Crown would be required to prove that the appellant knew or ought to have known that his associate was armed with a pistol and would, if necessary, use it during the commission of the offence or the attempt to commit the offence, or during his flight after committing or attempting to commit the offence, and that as a consequence a death occurred: see *R. v. Munro and Munro* (1983), 8 C.C.C. (3d) 260, 36 C.R. (3d) 193 (*per* Martin J.A.), at p. 301, and the pre-Charter case in this court in *R. v. Trinneer*, [1970] 3 C.C.C. 289, 10 D.L.R. (3d) 568, [1970] S.C.R. 638.

It must be recognized at the outset that Parliament has decided that the possession and use of weapons, particularly firearms, in the course of the commission of offences is a gravely aggravating factor. Experience has shown that the presence of firearms leads to personal injury and loss of life. Parliament has chosen to term a killing arising in the circumstances described here as "murder." In *R. v. Munro and Munro*, *supra*, Martin J.A. speaking for the Ontario Court of Appeal (Arnup, Martin and Houlden JJ.A.), said this, at p. 293:

> Under the provisions of s. 213(d) liability for murder attaches if death ensues as a consequence of the use of the weapon or as a consequence of the possession of a weapon which he has on his person. Manifestly, s. 213(d) is very stringent, but it is equally

obvious that Parliament intended to create a stringent basis of liability where death
ensued as a consequence of the use or possession of a weapon which the offender has
upon his person during the commission or attempted commission of certain offences or
the offender's flight after the commission or attempted commission of the offence. It is
clear that Parliament intended to provide a strong deterrent to the carrying of weapons
in the commission of certain crimes because of the high risk to life which experience
has shown attends such conduct.

The principal complaint in this case is not that the accused should not have been
convicted of a serious crime deserving of severe punishment, but simply that Parliament should not have chosen to call that crime "murder." No objection could be taken
if Parliament classified the offence as manslaughter or a killing during the commission of an offence, or in some other manner. As I have observed before (see *R. v.
Ancio* (1984), 10 C.C.C. (3d) 385 at p. 404, 6 D.L.R. (4th) 577 at p. 596, [1984] 1
S.C.R. 225 at p. 251), while it may be illogical to characterize an unintentional killing as murder, no principle of fundamental justice is offended only because serious
criminal conduct, involving the commission of a crime of violence resulting in the
killing of a human being, is classified as murder and not in some other manner. As
Martin J.A. said in *R. v. Munro and Munro*, *supra*, at p. 301: "This legislation has
frequently been criticized as being harsh, but that is a matter for Parliament and not
for the courts."

As has been noted, the appellant's conviction is based on a combination of s. 21(2)
and s. 213(d) of the *Criminal Code*. There was in this case evidence of active participation in the commission of the robbery, the underlying offence, and the terms of
s. 21(2) were fully met. It must be accepted that the section gives expression to a
principle of joint criminal liability long accepted and applied in the criminal law. I
am unable to say upon what basis one could exempt conduct which attracts criminal
liability, under s. 213 of the *Criminal Code*, from the application of that principle. In
*R. v. Munro and Munro*, *supra*, Martin J.A. said, at p. 301:

> Patently, Parliament has decided that the carrying of weapons during the commission
> of certain crimes, such as robbery, so manifestly endangers the lives of others, that one
> who joins a common purpose to commit one of the specified offences and who knows
> or ought to know that his accomplice has upon his person a weapon which he will use if
> needed, must bear the risk if death, in fact, ensues as a consequence of the use or pos-
> session of the weapon during the commission of one of the specified offences or during
> the flight of the offender after the commission or attempted commission of the underly-
> ing offence. ...

In my view, Martin J.A. has stated the policy considerations which have motivated Parliament in this connection and I would not interfere with the Parliamentary
decision. I would, therefore, dismiss the appeal and answer the two constitutional
questions in the negative.

## R. v. Martineau
Supreme Court of Canada
(1990), 58 C.C.C. (3d) 353

[In this case, the court struck down s. 213(a) (now s. 230(a)). The deceased were deliberately shot by Martineau's accomplice during a robbery.]

LAMER C.J. (at the time of the judgment) stated (concurred in by Dickson C.J. (at the time of hearing), Wilson, Gonthier, and Cory JJ.): ... Thirty witnesses gave evidence including the accused. The evidence revealed that Martineau and his friend, Tremblay, had set out one evening armed with a pellet pistol and rifle respectively. Martineau testified that he knew that they were going to commit a crime, but that he thought it would only be a "b and e." After robbing the trailer and its occupants, Martineau's friend Tremblay shot and killed the McLeans. As they left the trailer, Martineau asked Tremblay why he killed them and Tremblay answered, "they saw our faces." Martineau responded, "But they couldn't see mine 'cause I had a mask on." ...

Parliament, of course, decides what a crime is to be, and has the power to define the elements of a crime. With the advent of the Charter in 1982, Parliament also has, however, directed the courts to review those definitions to ensure that they are in accordance with the principles of fundamental justice. We, as a court, would be remiss not to heed this command of Parliament. This is an unassailable proposition since the decision of Parliament to entrench into our constitutional framework a Charter of Rights and Freedoms and also the principle that the Constitution is the supreme law of the land. Since 1982, this court has consistently assumed its duty to measure the content of legislation against the guarantees in our Charter designed to protect individual rights and freedoms: see for example *Singh v. Canada (Minister of Employment and Immigration)* (1985), 17 D.L.R. (4th) 422, [1985] 1 S.C.R. 177, 14 C.R.R. 13; *Reference re s. 94(2) of Motor Vehicle Act* (1985), 23 C.C.C. (3d) 289, 24 D.L.R. (4th) 536, [1985] 2 S.C.R. 486, and *R. v. Oakes* (1986), 24 C.C.C. (3d) 321, 26 D.L.R. (4th) 200, [1986] 1 S.C.R. 103.

Section 213(a) of the *Code* defines culpable homicide as murder where a person causes the death of a human being while committing or attempting to commit a range of listed offences, whether or not the person means to cause death or whether or not he or she knows that death is likely to ensue if that person means to cause bodily harm for the purpose of facilitating the commission of the offence or flight after committing or attempting to commit the offence. The introductory paragraph of the section, therefore, expressly removes from the Crown the burden of proving beyond a reasonable doubt that the accused had subjective foresight of death. This section stands as an anomaly as regards the other murder provisions, especially in light of the common law presumption against convicting a person of a true crime without proof of intent or recklessness.

A conviction for murder carries with it the most severe stigma and punishment of any crime in our society. The principles of fundamental justice require, because of the special nature of the stigma attached to a conviction for murder, and the available penalties, a *mens rea* reflecting the particular nature of that crime. The effect of s. 213

is to violate the principle that punishment must be proportionate to the moral blame-worthiness of the offender, or as Professor Hart puts it in *Punishment and Responsi-bility* (1968), at p. 162, the fundamental principle of a morally based system of law that those causing harm intentionally be punished more severely than those causing harm unintentionally. The rationale underlying the principle that subjective foresight of death is required before a person is labelled and punished as a murderer is linked to the more general principle that criminal liability for a particular result is not justi-fied except where the actor possesses a culpable mental state in respect of that result.

In my view, in a free and democratic society that values the autonomy and free will of the individual, the stigma and punishment attaching to the most serious of crimes, murder, should be reserved for those who choose to intentionally cause death or who choose to inflict bodily harm that they know is likely to cause death. The essential role of requiring subjective foresight of death in the context of murder is to maintain a proportionality between the stigma and punishment attached to a murder conviction and the moral blameworthiness of the offender. Murder has long been recognized as the "worst" and most heinous of peace time crimes. It is, therefore, essential that to satisfy the principles of fundamental justice, the stigma and punishment attaching to a murder conviction must be reserved for those who either intend to cause death or who intend to cause bodily harm that they know will likely cause death. ...

As regards s. 1 of the Charter, there is no doubt that the objective of deterring the infliction of bodily harm during the commission of certain offences because of the increased risk of death is of sufficient importance to warrant overriding a Charter right. Further, indiscriminately punishing for murder all those who cause death irre-spective of whether they intended to cause death might well be thought to discourage the infliction of bodily harm during the commission of certain offences because of the increased risk of death. But it is not necessary in order to achieve this objective to convict of murder persons who do not intend or foresee the death. In this regard the section unduly impairs the Charter rights. If Parliament wishes to deter persons from causing bodily harm during certain offences, then it should punish persons for caus-ing the bodily harm. Indeed, the conviction for manslaughter that would result in-stead of a conviction for murder is punishable by, from a day in jail, to confinement for life. Very stiff sentences for the infliction of bodily harm leading to death in ap-propriate cases would sufficiently meet any deterrence objective that Parliament might have in mind. The more flexible sentencing scheme under a conviction for manslaugh-ter is in accord with the principle that punishment be meted out with regard to the level of moral blameworthiness of the offender. To label and punish a person as a murderer who did not intend or foresee death unnecessarily stigmatizes and punishes those whose moral blameworthiness is not that of a murderer, and thereby unneces-sarily impairs the rights guaranteed by ss. 7 and 11(d) of the Charter. In my view then, s. 213(a), indeed all of s. 213, cannot be saved by s. 1 of the Charter.

L'HEUREUX-DUBÉ J. dissented: ... This notion of "subjective mental element" from the reasons of Lamer J. in *Vaillancourt* is neither constitutionally mandated nor ne-cessitated by elemental principles of the criminal law. The insistence on a subjective foresight requirement was not germane to the decision in *Vaillancourt*. The *obiter* statements were endorsed by only four of the eight justices who participated in *Vaillancourt*. ...

It should be noted that in the present case the underlying offence was committed, and the intent to inflict bodily harm was clear. Moreover, this amalgamation of indispensable prerequisites establishes that this crime, as phrased by Lamer J. in *Vaillancourt* [at p. 136] is "tantamount to one which has objective foreseeability as an essential element, and, if objective foreseeability is sufficient, then it would not be in violation of s. 7 or s. 11(d) in doing so in that way." I am of the view that in light of these requirements, the test of objective foreseeability is sufficient, and that if that test has been met, then no Charter violation has taken place. The above list requires that the accused specifically intend to, and actually commit the underlying offence, and specifically intend to, and actually inflict bodily harm. In my view, the inexorable conclusion is that the resulting death is objectively foreseeable.

Those who are critical of all forms of the "felony-murder" rule base their denunciation on the premise that *mens rea* is the exclusive determinant of the level of "stigma" that is properly applied to an offender. This appears to me to confuse some very fundamental principles of criminal law and ignores the pivotal contribution of *actus reus* to the definition and appropriate response to proscribed criminal offences. If both components, *actus reus* as well as *mens rea*, are not considered when assessing the level of fault attributable to an offender, we would see manslaughter and assault causing bodily harm as no more worthy of condemnation than an assault. Mere attempts would become as serious as full offences. The whole correlation between the consequences of a criminal act and its retributive repercussions would become obscured by a stringent and exclusive examination of the accused's own asserted intentions.

In the United States the common law notion of felony-murder continues to exist in a modified form in all but three states. Gilbert, "Degrees of Felony Murder" (1983), 40 *Wash. and Lee L. Rev.* 1601. While a number of jurisdictions have limited the rule by requiring the felony to be inherently violent or by requiring violent means to be used during the course of the felony, the rule still contains no requirement of subjective foresight of death. Apart from certain limits *when combined with the death penalty*, the United States Supreme Court has consistently upheld the constitutional validity of the felony-murder rule. *Tison v. Arizona*, 107 S.Ct. 1676 (1987); *Gregg v. Georgia*, 428 U.S. 153 (1976). ...

I find this concentration on social "stigma" to be over-emphasized, and, in the great majority of cases, completely inapplicable. The facts in the present appeals reveal the truly heinous nature of the criminal acts at issue. The concern that these offenders not endure the mark of Cain is, in my view, an egregious example of misplaced compassion. If the apprehension is that the offenders in question will suffer from their "murderer" label, I suspect they will fare little better tagged as "manslaughterers." Accidental killings cannot, after *Vaillancourt*, result in murder prosecutions. Only killings resulting from circumstances in which death is, at a minimum, objectively foreseeable will be prosecuted under s. 213(a). Furthermore, the duration of imprisonment, if at all different, will not attenuate the "stigma." To the extent that any such "stigma" can be said to exist, it is at least as palpable upon release to the outside world as it is within the prison environment itself.

Section 213(a) does not deal with accidental killings, but rather with killings that are objectively foreseeable as a result of the abominable nature of the predicate crimes, committed with specific intent, coupled with the intentional infliction of bodily harm. Given the dual subjective requirement already in place, the deterrence factor is most cogent in these circumstances. Whatever the competing arguments may be with respect to deterring the merely negligent, here we are dealing with those who have already expressly acted with the intent to commit at least two underlying serious crimes. If deterrence is to ever have any application to the criminal law, and in my view it should, this is the place.

Policy considerations in Canada as well as in other jurisdictions have inspired legislation that considers objective foreseeability sufficient as the minimum *mens rea* requirement for murder. While it may not be the very best test for all cases, it is certainly a constitutionally valid one. Parliament did not have to enact s. 213(a), but that is not the question before this Court. The issue is whether it could. In my view, the answer rests on what level of foreseeability will be required before a conviction for murder can be returned. Based on this Court's precedents, and the principles of fundamental justice, I believe that the objective foreseeability of death test for the crime of murder is constitutionally valid. The additional mandatory elements demanded by s. 213(a) lend even greater force to this conclusion.

Striking down the legislation simply because some other scheme may be preferable would be an unwarranted intrusion into Parliament's prerogative, and would undermine the means it has chosen to protect its citizens. The Charter is not designed to allow this Court to substitute preferable provisions for those already in place in the absence of a clear constitutional violation. Such a task should be reserved for the Law Reform Commission or other advisory bodies. This Court's province is to pronounce upon the constitutionality of those provisions properly before it. The Charter does not infuse the courts with the power to declare legislation to be of no force or effect on the basis that they believe the statute to be undesirable as a matter of criminal law policy. For the aforementioned reasons, I do not believe that s. 213(a) offends the *Canadian Charter of Rights and Freedoms*.

[Sopinka J. also struck down the section but did so on the basis that the section does not require even an objective foreseeability of death and would have limited the court's decision to this narrower holding: "Overbroad statements of principle are inimical to the tradition of incremental development of the common law. Likewise, the development of law under the *Canadian Charter of Rights and Freedoms* is best served by deciding cases before the courts, not by anticipating the results of future cases."]

See also *Sit v. The Queen* (1991), 66 C.C.C. 449 dealing with the constitutional validity of s. 213(c) (now s. 230(c)) of the Code. The cause of death was strangulation by one of the accused's accomplices. Lamer C.J.C. stated for the court:

> The respondent argued before this court that the finding of the majority in *Martineau* that subjective foreseeability of death is the minimum constitutional *mens rea* requirement for murder is *obiter dictum*. The respondent emphasized that, under s. 213(a) of the *Code*, an accused could be convicted of murder in the absence of proof that he had *objective* foresight of the death of his victim. Section 213(a), therefore, could have been found to violate ss. 7 and 11(d) of the Charter on the basis that the provision did not require objective foresight of death as an essential element of the offence. In this light, our findings regarding subjective foresight of death were arguably unnecessary to the resolution of the case.
>
> In my opinion, a correct reading of *Martineau* does not support the respondent's submission. In *Martineau*, as I noted above, this court was asked to pronounce on the constitutional validity of s. 213(a) of the *Criminal Code*. To answer this question, it was necessary to determine the minimum degree of *mens rea* required by the Charter for the offence of murder. The determination of this minimum constitutional *mens rea* requirement was, therefore, the live issue before this court. Consequently, our finding in *Martineau* that proof of subjective foresight of death is necessary in order to sustain a conviction for murder and that s. 213(a) of the *Criminal Code* violated the Charter since it did not embrace this requirement, was not *obiter dictum*. This finding was the *ratio decidendi* of the decision.

Note that, while none of the judgments in this line of authority addresses directly the constitutionality of s. 229(c), that section's validity is seriously in doubt. In *Martineau*, above, Lamer C.J. said the following:

> The fact that I have based my reasons on the principle of subjective foresight casts serious doubt on the constitutionality of part of s. 212(c) of the Code, specifically the words "ought to know is likely to cause death." The validity of s. 212(c) of the Code had not been directly attacked in this appeal, but the Court has had the benefit of hearing argument from [a number of Attorneys General] who chose to intervene, on the issue of whether subjective foresight or objective foreseeability of death is the constitutionally required minimum *mens rea* for murder. In my view, subjective foresight of death must be proven beyond a reasonable doubt before a conviction for murder can be sustained, and as result, it is obvious the part of s. 212(c) of the Code allowing for a conviction upon proof that the accused ought to have known that death was the likely result violates ss. 7 and 11(d) of the Charter.

This passage, which must fairly be characterized as *obiter dicta*, has essentially meant an end to the use of this provision. However, it was not formally struck down and is technically operative: see *R. v. Meiler* (1999), 25 C.R. (5th) 161 (S.C.C.).

To a certain extent, Parliament has responded to the court's decisions in this area by enacting a number of mandatory minimum sentencing provisions. In particular, s. 236, reproduced in section III below, establishes a minimum sentence of four years' imprisonment (and a maximum of life imprisonment) for a manslaughter committed with the use of a firearm. In *R. v. Morrrisey* (2000), 148 C.C.C. (3d) 1 (S.C.C.), the court upheld the constitutional validity of a related provision that mandates a four-year minimum sentence for criminal negligence causing death when a firearm is used in the commission of the offence.

## II. FIRST-DEGREE MURDER

In 1976, when the law of murder was vastly reformed, Parliament made a distinction between first-degree murder and second-degree murder. While both categories of murder carry a mandatory sentence of life imprisonment, with second-degree murder the trial judge may set parole ineligibility between 15 to 25 years, whereas with first-degree murder parole ineligibility must be set at 25 years. Thus, the consequences of a conviction for first-degree, as opposed to second-degree, murder are dramatic.

Section 231 of the *Criminal Code* establish the categories of first-degree murder as follows:

231.(1)  Murder is first degree murder or second degree murder.

(2)  Murder is first degree murder when it is planned and deliberate.

(3)  Without limiting the generality of subsection (2), murder is planned and deliberate when it is committed pursuant to an arrangement under which money or anything of value passes or is intended to pass from one person to another, or is promised by one person to another, as consideration for that other's causing or assisting in causing the death of anyone or counselling another person to do any act causing or assisting in causing that death.

(4)  Irrespective of whether a murder is planned and deliberate on the part of any person, murder is first degree murder when the victim is

(a)  a police officer, police constable, constable, sheriff, deputy sheriff, sheriff's officer or other person employed for the preservation and maintenance of the public peace, acting in the course of his duties;

(b)  a warden, deputy warden, instructor, keeper, jailer, guard or other officer or a permanent employee of a prison, acting in the course of his duties; or

(c)  a person working in a prison with the permission of the prison authorities and acting in the course of his work therein.

(5)  Irrespective of whether a murder is planned and deliberate on the part of any person, murder is first degree murder in respect of a person when the death is caused by that person while committing or attempting to commit an offence under one of the following sections:

(a)  section 76 (hijacking an aircraft);

(b)  section 271 (sexual assault);

(c)  section 272 (sexual assault with a weapon, threats to a third party or causing bodily harm);

(d)  section 273 (aggravated sexual assault);

(e)  section 279 (kidnapping and forcible confinement); or

(f)  section 279.1 (hostage taking).

(6)  Irrespective of whether a murder is planned and deliberate on the part of any person, murder is first degree murder when the death is caused by that person while committing or attempting to commit an offence under section 264 and the person committing that offence intended to cause the person murdered to fear for the safety of the person murdered or the safety of anyone known to the person murdered.

(6.01)  Irrespective of whether a murder is planned and deliberate on the part of a person, murder is first degree murder when the death is caused while committing or attempting to commit an indictable offence under this or any other Act of Parliament where the act or omission constituting the offence also constitutes a terrorist activity.

(6.1) Irrespective of whether a murder is planned and deliberate on the part of a person, murder is first degree murder when the death is caused while committing or attempting to commit an offence under section 81 for the benefit of, at the direction of or in association with a criminal organization.

(6.2) Irrespective of whether a murder is planned and deliberate on the part of a person, murder is first degree murder when the death is caused while committing or attempting to commit an offence under section 423.1.

(7) All murder that is not first degree murder is second degree murder.

We examine the formal requirements of some of these categories of first-degree murder in the cases below.

## Section 231(2): "Planned and Deliberate"

### R. v. More
Supreme Court of Canada
[1963] 3 C.C.C. 289

[The accused was depressed over his financial affairs. Fearful that their disclosure would be upsetting to his wife, he planned to kill her and then kill himself. The accused succeeded in killing his wife, but failed at his attempted suicide and was charged with capital murder under previous *Criminal Code* provisions, which required proof that the murder was "planned and deliberate." The accused led psychiatric evidence in an attempt to raise a reasonable doubt as to whether he meant to kill his wife and whether the murder was planned and deliberate. The case turned on the trial judge's directions to the jury on the use that could be made of psychiatric evidence. The court also expressed an opinion on the meaning of planned and deliberate murder.]

CARTWRIGHT J.: … In the circumstances of this case, the defence of insanity having been expressly disclaimed, there were really only two questions for the jury. The first was whether the appellant meant to cause the death of his wife; if this was answered in the affirmative he was guilty of murder. The second, which arises under s. 202A(2) (a) [enacted 1960-61, c. 44, s. 1] of the *Criminal Code*, 1953-54 (Can.), c. 51, was whether this murder was planned and deliberate on his part; if this was answered in the affirmative he was guilty of capital murder.

The evidence that the murder was planned was very strong, but, as was properly pointed out to the jury by the learned trial Judge, they could not find the accused guilty of capital murder unless they were satisfied beyond a reasonable doubt nor only that the murder was planned but also that it was deliberate. The learned trial Judge also rightly instructed the jury that the word "deliberate," as used in s. 202A(2)(a), means "considered, not impulsive."

Other meanings of the adjective given in the *Oxford Dictionary* are "not hasty in decision," "slow in deciding" and "intentional." The word as used in the subsection cannot have simply the meaning "intentional" because it is only if the accused's act was intentional that he can be guilty of murder and the subsection is creating an additional ingredient to be proved as a condition of an accused being convicted of capital murder.

The recital of the facts and the evidence of the appellant as to what occurred at the moment of the discharge of the rifle, set out in the reasons of my brother Judson, show that it was open to the jury to take the view that the act of the appellant in pulling the trigger was impulsive rather than considered and therefore was not deliberate. The evidence of the two doctors and particularly that of Dr. Adamson, also quoted by my brother Judson, that, in his opinion, at the critical moment the appellant was suffering from a depressive psychosis resulting in "impairment of ability to decide even inconsequential things, inability to make a decision in a normal kind of a way" would have a direct bearing on the question whether the appellant's act was deliberate in the sense defined above; its weight was a matter for the jury.

----

The case of *R. v. Widdifield* (1961), 6 Crim. L.Q. 152 (Ont. S.C.) has stood the test of time as an authoritative pronouncement on the content of the expression "planned and deliberate." The following is the reported excerpt from the charge to the jury by Gale J. (later Gale C.J.O.):

> I think that in the Code "planned" is to be assigned, I think, its natural meaning of a calculated scheme or design which has been carefully thought out, and the nature and consequences of which have been considered and weighed. But that does not mean, of course, to say that the plan need be a complicated one. It may be a very simple one, and the simpler it is perhaps the easier it is to formulate.
>
> The important element, it seems to me, so far as time is concerned, is the time involved in developing the plan, not the time between the development of the plan and the doing of the act. One can carefully prepare and plan and immediately it is prepared set out to do the planned act, or, alternatively, you can wait an appreciable time to do it once it has been formed.
>
> As far as the word "deliberate" is concerned, I think that the Code means that it should also carry its natural meaning of "considered," "not impulsive," "slow in deciding," "cautious," implying that the accused must take time to weigh the advantages and disadvantages of his intended action.

In *R. v. Nygaard* (1989), 51 C.C.C. (3d) 417 (S.C.C.), the court held that it was possible for a murder to be classified as first-degree murder on the basis of the secondary intent in s. 229(a)(ii)—a reckless killing. The case involved two accused who planned to beat the victim with baseball bats in relation to a relatively minor dispute over money and property. The victim died. Writing for the majority, Cory J. held in part:

> In my view, the vital element of the requisite intent is that of causing such bodily harm that the perpetrator knows that it is likely to cause death and yet persists in the assault. There can be no doubt that a person can plan and deliberate to cause terrible bodily harm that he knows is likely to result in death. Nothing is added to the aspect of planning and deliberation by the requirement that the fatal assault be carried out in a reckless manner, that is to say by heedlessly proceeding with the deadly assault in the face of the knowledge of the

obvious risks. The planning and deliberation to cause the bodily harm which is likely to be fatal must of necessity include the planning and deliberating to continue and to persist in that conduct despite the knowledge of the risk. The element of recklessness does not exist in a vacuum as a sole *mens rea* requirement, but rather it must act in conjunction with the intentional infliction of terrible bodily harm. I, therefore, conclude that planning and deliberation may well be coupled with the *mens rea* requirement of s. 212(a)(ii) and that a first degree murder conviction can be sustained by virtue of the combined operation of s. 214(2) and s. 212(a)(ii).

As well, the appellant argued it was wrong to label an offence under s. 212(a)(ii) as murder. It was said that the requisite *mens rea* is such that it is not as grave a crime as that defined in s. 212(a)(i) where the requisite intent is to cause the death of someone. I cannot accept that contention. The variation in the degree of culpability is too slight to take into account. Let us consider the gravity of the crime described by s. 212(a)(ii) in the light of three examples which, pursuant to the section, would be murder. First, an accused forms the intent to inflict multiple stab wounds in the abdomen and chest of a person knowing that the wounds are likely to kill the victim and, heedless of the known probable result, proceeds with the stabbing. Secondly, an accused forms the intent to shoot a former associate in the chest knowing that death is likely to ensue and, uncaring of the result, shoots the victim in the chest. Thirdly, two accused form the intent to repeatedly and viciously strike a person in the head with a baseball bat realizing full well that the victim will probably die as a result. None the less they continue with the bone-splintering, skull-shattering assault. The accused in all these examples must have committed as grave a crime as the accused who specifically intends to kill. Society would, I think, find the drawing of any differentiation in the degree of culpability an exercise in futility. The difference in the calibration on the scale of culpability is too minute to merit a distinction. I would conclude that the crime defined in s. 212(a)(ii) can properly be described as murder and on a "culpability scale" it varies so little from s. 212(a)(i) as to be indistinguishable.

## Section 231(4): Murder of Police Officer, etc.

### R. v. Collins
Ontario Court of Appeal
(1989), 48 C.C.C. (3d) 343

[The accused was charged with first-degree murder as the result for killing a police officer. At the time he was killed the officer was on duty and in uniform. He was shot by the accused at very close range. The accused was convicted of first-degree murder on the basis of s. 214(4)(a) (now s. 231(4)(a)) of the *Criminal Code*, which provides that irrespective of whether a murder is planned and deliberate, murder is first-degree murder when the victim is "(a) a police officer, police constable, constable, sheriff, deputy sheriff, sheriff's officer or other person employed for the preservation and maintenance of the public peace, acting in the course of his duties." The accused argued that s. 214(4)(a) was unconstitutional as it infringed s. 7 of the Charter because

an accused could be convicted of first-degree murder without the need to prove planning and deliberation.]

GOODMAN J.A.: … Is s. 214(4)(a) of the *Criminal Code* of Canada (now R.S.C.
1985 c. C-46, s. 231(4)(a)) constitutionally invalid because it is contrary to the provisions of s. 7 of the Charter?

Section 214(4)(a) of the Code (now s. 231(4)(a)) reads as follows:

> 214(4) Irrespective of whether a murder is planned and deliberate on the part of
> any person, murder is first degree murder when the victim is
>     (a) a police officer, police constable, constable, sheriff, deputy sheriff, sheriff's
> officer or other person employed for the preservation and maintenance of the public
> peace, acting in the course of his duties;

Section 7 of the Charter reads:

> 7. Everyone has the right to life, liberty and security of the person and the right not
> to be deprived thereof except in accordance with the principles of fundamental justice.

The constitutionality of s. 214(4) (now s. 231(4)) was not argued at trial. On this
appeal, counsel for the appellant took the position that the stigma associated with
first degree murder and the stricter penalty (mandatory non-eligibility for parole for a
period of twenty-five years as opposed to a possible ten-year minimum non-eligibility for parole period for second degree murder) for such offence can only be justified
on the basis of a higher degree of moral blameworthiness. It was his submission that
only the provisions of s. 214(2) (now s. 231(2)) satisfies this requirement. Section
214(1) and (2) (now s. 231(1) and (2)) read as follows:

> 214(1) Murder is first degree murder or second degree murder.
> (2) Murder is first degree murder when it is planned and deliberate.

The added degree of blameworthiness required for first degree murder under
s-s. (2) consists of the planning and deliberation of a killing. Under s. 214(4)(a) there
is no need to prove planning and deliberation. It is sufficient for the Crown to prove
that the victim is one of the persons designated in s-s. (4)(a) acting in the course of
his duties.

He relied on the decision of the Supreme Court of Canada in *R. v. Vaillancourt* 60
C.R. (3d) 289 and on a decision of this Court in *R. v. Munro and Munro* (1983), 8
C.C.C. (3d) 260. In *Vaillancourt* it was held that it is a principle of fundamental justice that, absent proof beyond a reasonable doubt of at least objective foreseeability
of death this cannot be a murder conviction. The court held that s. 213(d) of the Code
[now s. 230(d)] had substituted for proof beyond a reasonable doubt of objective
foreseeability proof beyond a reasonable doubt of certain forms of intentional dangerous conduct causing death. A person could be convicted under s. 213(d) although
the jury had a reasonable doubt as to whether the accused ought to have known that
death was likely to ensue. An accused in such circumstances, who might otherwise
be convicted of a lesser offence, would bear the stigma of a murder notwithstanding

his lack of intention to kill or objective foreseeability. Accordingly the cour found s. 213(d) to be in violation of ss. 7 and 11(d) of the Charter.

In the case at bar the argument with respect to stigma is much less relevant. Before an accused can be convicted of first degree murder the Crown must prove all of the elements required for a conviction of second degree murder. The stigma of a murder conviction carrying with it a mandatory sentence of life imprisonment attaches to such an accused even if the Crown failed to prove the additional ingredients required for a conviction of first degree murder.

The Supreme Court of Canada has ruled that s. 214 of the Code (now s. 231) does not set out the element of the offence of murder. That was done in ss. 212 and 213 (now ss. 229 and 230). It held that the effect of s. 214 was to classify the offence of murder once it has been found. This was held in *R. v. Farrant* (1983), 4 C.C.C. (3d) 354. In that case Dickson J., as he then was, in delivering the majority judgment of the court said at pp. 365-6:

> Section 214, however, is not the section which sets out the elements of the offence of murder. This is done in ss. 212 and 213. Section 214 does not create a distinct and independent substantive offence of first degree constructive murder pursuant to forcible confinement. The section is subservient to ss. 212 and 213; it classifies for sentencing purposes the offences in ss. 212 and 213 as either first or second degree murder. The importance of the distinction between first and second degree murder is that first degree murder carries with it a mandatory life sentence without eligibility for parole for 25 years (ss. 218, 669(a)). A conviction for second degree murder also carries with it a mandatory life sentence, but parole may be granted after 10 years of imprisonment unless the jury recommends a greater number of years.
>
> There is no distinction between ss. 214(5)(a) and 212 based upon intent. The presence or absence of intent is the distinction between ss. 212 and 213, no s. 214. Intent is an element of the offence of murder under s. 212, be it first or second degree. The distinction between first and second degree murder in s. 214 is not based upon intent; it is based upon (1) the presence of planning and deliberation (s. 212(2)); (2) the identity of the victim (s. 214(4)), or (3) the nature of the offence being committed at the time of the murder (s. 214(5)). The primary and essential determination for a jury to make is whether murder has been committed, either under s. 212 or, where the evidence warrants it, under s. 213. Considerations of the distinctions between first and second degree murder are irrelevant in making this preliminary determination. Once the offence has been found, it is then classified.

In *R. v. Paré*, [1987] 2 S.C.R. 618 Wilson J. had occasion to consider the provisions of ss. 212, 213 and 214 and in delivering the judgment of the court said at p. 625:

> It is clear from a reading of these provisions that s. 214 serves a different function from ss. 212 and 213. Sections 212 and 213 create the substantive offence of murder. Section 214 is simply concerned with classifying for sentencing purposes the offences created by ss. 212 and 213. It tells us whether the murder is first degree or second degree. This view of s. 214 was expressly adopted by this Court in *R. v. Farrant*, [1983] 1 S.C.R. 124 (per Dickson J. (as he then was) at p. 140) and in *Droste v. The Queen*, [1984] 1

S.C.R. 208 (per Dickson J. as he then was) at 218). In this case it is established that the respondent murdered Steeve Duranleau. The issue is whether s. 214(5)(b) makes the murder first degree.

None of the above-mentioned cases involved a charge under s. 214(4)(a).

In *Droste* Dickson J. said at p. 222 under the heading Policy Considerations:

> The rationale behind s. 214(2) is that there is an added moral culpability to a murder that is planned and deliberate which justifies a harsher sentence. This added culpability is present by virtue of the planning and deliberation with relation to the taking of a human life, not with relation to the identity of the intended victim. A mistake or accident as to the victim is not a mitigating factor.

In that case the accused who planned and intended to kill his wife accidentally killed his two children.

Subsection 5 of s. 214, like subsection 4, provides that irrespective of whether the murder is planned or deliberate, it is classified as first degree murder when the death is caused by an accused while committing or attempting to commit certain offences as set forth in s-s.(5). The rationale behind s. 214(5) would appear to be that Parliament regards the offences therein enumerated, which involves an accused exercising dominion and control over other persons of so serious a nature as to require a heavier sentence by way of additional deterrent. It must be noted, however, that in addition to the element of added moral culpability being present, the offender would have full knowledge of the existence of the state of facts which render him liable to the heavier penalty for the commission of a murder in those circumstances.

There can be little doubt that the rationale behind the provisions of s. 214(4) is to provide additional protection to the persons designated in s. 214(4)(a) while acting in the course of their duties. Their occupations are extremely dangerous having regard to the persons with whom they are in frequent contact by reason of the nature of their occupations. The classification of the murder of such persons as first degree murder with the heavier penalty consequent thereon is obviously designed as an additional deterrent to potential murderers. It might be rationalized that the murder of a person whose obligation it is to maintain law and order carries with it an added moral culpability and requires a heavier deterrent to protect the public interest.

It was the position of counsel for the appellant that s. 214(4)(a) does not require the Crown to prove that accused had knowledge of the identity of the victim as one of the persons designated in s-s.(4) and that he was acting in the course of his duties. His submission was that in those circumstances there was no additional moral culpability justifying a heavier penalty upon a conviction for murder and accordingly subsection (4) is constitutionally invalid. He further submitted that if the conviction for first degree murder, as opposed to second degree murder, was registered on the basis of the provisions of subsection 4(a), it cannot stand even though the trial judge charged the jury that it was incumbent on the Crown to prove that the appellant knew the victim was a police constable acting in the course of his duty and there was evidence upon which the jury could so find.

Counsel for the Attorney-General for Canada who appeared on the appeal as an intervener took the position that in s. 214(4)(a) Parliament had identified an aggravating element which would justify the classification of a murder as a first degree murder. It was his submission that the element of *mens rea* is a matter relevant only to the determination whether murder had been committed under ss. 212 and 213 of the Code and that there is no *mens rea* element associated with the inquiry contemplated by s. 214. He submitted that once the Crown has satisfied the jury beyond a reasonable doubt that the accused was guilty of murder under ss. 212 or 213, then the offence of murder will be properly characterized as first degree murder upon proof beyond a reasonable doubt of the aggravating elements set forth in s. 214(4)(a) and no element of *mens rea* is involved in such determination.

In *R. v. Shand* (1971), 3 C.C.C. (2d) 8, the Manitoba Court of Appeal stated by way of obiter that under s. 202A (since repealed) of the Code knowledge on the part of the accused that the person he killed was a police officer or other person mentioned in the section was requisite for a conviction for capital murder. The relevant part of s. 202A read:

> 202A(2) Murder is capital murder, in respect of any person, where such person by his own act caused or assisted in causing the death of
> (a) a police officer ... acting in the course of his duties ...

This court had occasion to deal with s. 214(4)(a) in *R. v. Munro and Munro* 8 C.C.C. (3d) 260. In that case Martin J.A. in delivering judgment for the court noted at p. 295 that the Manitoba Court of Appeal in holding that knowledge by the accused that the person killed was a police officer was requisite to a conviction for capital murder based its decision on the ground that there was a presumption that *mens rea* is an essential ingredient in all criminal cases. The trial judge in *Shand* had charged the jury that knowledge by the accused that the person he killed was a police officer was an essential element of capital murder. On further appeal Fauteux C.J.C. said in dismissing the appeal from the decision of the Manitoba Court of Appeal,

> ... it is unnecessary to express any view on the obiter dictum in the Court below that proof of knowledge is an essential ingredient of the offence of capital murder; 4 C.C.C. (2d) 173n.

In *Munro and Munro*, Martin J.A. said at p. 296:

> I find some difficulty in reconciling the reasoning of the Manitoba Court of Appeal with the analysis of s. 214 by Mr. Justice Dickson, delivering the majority judgment of the Supreme Court of Canada in *R. v. Farrant* (1983), 4 C.C.C. (3d) 354.

He then said at p. 297:

> Even if *mens rea* with respect to the identity of the victim is a requisite element of first degree murder under s. 214(4)(a), the ordinary *mens rea* which suffices where no mental element is specified in the definition of the offence is supplied by either intention or recklessness with respect to the material elements of he *actus reus*.

In *R. v. Chabot* (1985) 16 C.C.C. (3d) 483 Howland C.J.O. said at p. 488 in delivering judgment for the Court:

> Murder is the substantive offence and it is the elements of the offence of murder, the *mens rea* and *actus reus*, which must be established. Once these elements have been established, the accused is guilty of murder.
>
> Once the primary determination has been made that the offence of murder has been committed, there is then a secondary determination under s. 214 of the Code whether the murder should be classified as first degree murder or second degree murder. Section 214 is a classification section for the purpose of sentencing. It is subservient to ss. 212 and 213. First degree murder and second degree murder are not independent substantive offences. The substantive offence is murder. The distinction between first degree murder and second degree murder is not based upon intent.

There can be no doubt that the onus was on the Crown to establish beyond a reasonable doubt the *actus reus* and *mens rea* of the substantive offence of murder under s. 212. I am of the view, however, that under s. 214(4)(a) there is an onus on the Crown to establish beyond a reasonable doubt that the victim was a person who falls within the designation of the occupations set forth in that subsection acting in the course of his duties to the knowledge of the accused or with recklessness on his part as to whether the victim was such a person so acting.

In my opinion there is no binding authority to the contrary. It seems clear to me that the object of the classification of first degree murder in s. 214 is to require a more severe punishment for the offence of murder in circumstances that involve an added degree of moral culpability or to act as a more effective deterrent in the prevention of the murder of persons engaged in the preservation, prevention of infringement and enforcement of the law or of persons who have fallen under the domination of an offender.

It is my view that s. 214(4)(a) should be interpreted in such a manner that requires proof of the facts which give rise to the added moral culpability or which would act as an additional deterrent. It is clear to me that to fulfill such interpretation it is necessary that the Crown prove that the murderer had knowledge of the identity of the victim as one of the persons designated in the subsection and that such person was acting in the course of his duties or was reckless as to such identity and acts of the victim.

The section could, of course, be interpreted to simply require that the Crown prove that the occupation of the victim was one of those set forth in the subsection and that the person was acting in the course of his duties without proof of knowledge thereof on the part of the murderer. The subsection does not refer to proof of such knowledge.

I am satisfied that if the latter interpretation is adopted, it would offend s. 7 of the Charter. If, for example, a gunman sees two persons on the street dressed in plain clothes of whom one is a merchant walking home and the other is a detective on his way to investigate or in the process of investigating a break-in and if the gunman decides without planning and deliberation to shoot and kill one of them and does so he would be guilty of murder no matter which person he killed. In the case of the killing of the ordinary citizen he would be guilty of second degree murder with a sentence of life imprisonment with a possibility of parole eligibility after ten years but in the case of the killing of the detective he would be guilty of first degree murder with a sentence of life imprisonment with a possibility of parole in no less than twenty-five years being the minimum period before parole eligibility (subject of course to the provisions of s. 745 of the Code (formerly s. 672).

Although the crime of murder is deserving of the heavy sentence involved, it seems to me that there would be no difference in moral culpability in the example set forth above no matter which person was the victim nor would there be any additional deterrent provided under s. 214(4)(a) in those circumstances if proof of knowledge that the detective was indeed a detective acting in the course of his duty were not required. There would then be no rational or logical reason for imposing a heavier penalty in the case where the murderer killed the person who he did not know and had no reason to know was a police officer acting in the course of his duties.

On the other hand, if s. 214(4)(a) is interpreted to require proof of such knowledge before the murder can be classified as first degree murder then a heavier sentence can be justified on the basis of added moral culpability or as additional deterrent on the grounds of public policy. In such event, it is my opinion that the subsection would not contravene the provisions of s. 7 of the Charter.

I am of the opinion that where a statutory provision is open to two interpretations, one of which will contravene the Charter and the other of which will not, the provision should be interpreted in such a manner as will not contravene the Charter (see *R. v. Corbett* 64 C.R. (3d) 1 per Beetz J. at p. 23).

I conclude that the onus is on the Crown to prove that the appellant knew that the victim was a police officer who was acting in the course of his duty and I find, accordingly, that the provisions of s. 214(4)(a) do not contravene s. 7 of the Charter. In the present case the trial judge charged the jury in accordance with this conclusion. There was evidence to support a finding of knowledge on the part of the appellant.

*Appeal dismissed.*

## Section 231(5): "While Committing"

The leading case on the requirements of s. 231(5) is the case of *R. v. Paré* (1987), 38 C.C.C. (3d) 97 (S.C.C.). In that case, the court faced the question of what the phrase "while committing" means in the context of the identical predecessor s. 214(5), in a case where the accused killed a young boy shortly after having indecently assaulted him. Paré is substantially reproduced in chapter 1.

### R. v. Russell
Supreme Court of Canada
(2001), 157 C.C.C. (3d) 1

[The accused was charged with first-degree murder on the basis that he caused the death of the victim while forcibly confining another individual, contrary to s. 231(5)(d). It was alleged that the accused tied and gagged his girlfriend in her bed, forced her to have sexual intercourse, left her tied in the bedroom, and then went to the basement and beat and stabbed the deceased to death. The preliminary inquiry judge concluded that the deceased did not have to be the victim of the underlying offence of forcible confinement in order to sustain a charge of first-degree murder under s. 231(5). The Superior Court judge quashed the committal for first-degree murder and substituted a committal for second-degree murder, on the theory that s. 231(5) requires the victim of the murder and the enumerated offence to be the same person. The Court of Appeal reversed, holding that, even if the preliminary inquiry judge erred in his interpretation of s. 231(5)(d), the error constituted an error within his jurisdiction and was not reviewable.]

McLACHLIN C.J.C.: ...

### 2. Section 231(5)

I turn now to the question of whether the preliminary inquiry judge erred in holding that s. 231(5) may apply even if the victim of the murder and the victim of the enumerated offence are not the same.

The question is first and foremost one of statutory interpretation. As such, the governing principles are well-settled: the words in question should be considered in the context in which they are used, and read in a manner consistent with the purpose of the provision and the intention of the legislature: see *R. v. Heywood*, [1994] 3 S.C.R. 761 (citing Elmer A. Driedger, *Construction of Statutes* (2nd ed. 1983), at p. 87; *R. v. Hasselwander*, [1993] 2 S.C.R. 398). "If the ordinary meaning of the words is consistent with the context in which the words are used and with the object of the act, then that is the interpretation which should govern": *Heywood*, supra, at p. 784.

The language of s. 231(5) is clear. The provision does not state that the victim of the murder and the victim of the enumerated offence must be one and the same. It requires only that the accused have killed "while committing or attempting to commit" one of the enumerated offences. Nothing in that phrase suggests that the provision's application is limited to cases in which the victim of the murder and the victim of the enumerated offence are the same. An interpretation of the provision that recognized such a limitation would effectively read into the provision a restriction that is not stated.

Other provisions of the *Criminal Code* indicate that, where Parliament intends to limit the phrase "while committing or attempting to commit," it does so in express language. Section 231(6), for example, provides that "Irrespective of whether a murder is planned and deliberate on the part of any person, murder is first degree murder when the death is caused by that person while committing or attempting to commit an offence under section 264 [Criminal Harassment] and the person committing that offence intended to cause the person murdered to fear for the safety of the person murdered or the safety of anyone known to the person murdered."

Without the limitation, s. 231(6) would apply to a person who had murdered one person while criminally harassing another. The limitation restricts the application of the provision to those who murder the person they are criminally harassing. No analogous limitation is stated in s. 231(5).

Still other provisions of the *Criminal Code* suggest that Parliament's use of the phrase "while committing or attempting to commit" does not in itself reflect an intention to create a same-victim requirement. Section 231(6.1), for example, provides that "[M]urder is first degree murder when the death is caused while committing or attempting to commit an offence under section 81 [using explosives] for the benefit of ... a criminal organization."

Section 81 proscribes conduct that includes using explosives against property: see s. 81(1)(c) ("Every one commits an offence who ... with intent to destroy or damage property without lawful excuse, places or throws an explosive substance anywhere ..."). Parliament must have contemplated, therefore, that s. 231(6.1) might be applied even where there is no "victim" at all to the underlying crime. It would be senseless to say that the victim of the murder and the explosives offence must be one and the same where the latter crime might have no victim at all. Section 231(6.1) suggests that the use of the phrase "while committing or attempting to commit" does not itself create a same-victim requirement.

If Parliament had intended to restrict the scope of s. 231(5), it could have done so explicitly, as it did in s. 231(6). That Parliament did not incorporate such a restriction suggests that it intended "while committing or attempting to commit" to apply even where the victim of the murder and the victim of the enumerated offence are not the same. Indeed, several of the offences enumerated in s. 231(5) quite clearly raise the possibility that the person murdered will not be the same as the victim of the enumerated crime, and it would be difficult to conclude that this possibility did not occur to the drafters of the provision. A hijacker might kill a person on the runway; a kidnapper might kill the parent of the child he means to kidnap; a hostage-taker might kill an innocent bystander or a would-be rescuer. It is difficult to conclude that Parliament did not envision such possibilities.

The fact that s. 231(5) reaches not only successfully executed offences but also attempts raises similar concerns. Many attempt charges stem from crimes that were thwarted or aborted, often because of the intervention of a third party. Parliament surely envisioned such scenarios when it drafted the provision. Had Parliament not wanted the provision to reach these circumstances, it could easily have attached an explicit restriction to the provision's language.

In arguing that s. 231(5) applies only where the victim of the murder and the victim of the enumerated offence are the same, the appellant relies principally on this Court's judgment in *Paré* (1987), 38 C.C.C. (3d) 97 (S.C.C.). In *Paré*, the accused had murdered a boy two minutes after indecently assaulting him. The question was whether the accused had committed the murder "while committing" the indecent assault. Wilson J. quoting Martin J.A. answered the question in the affirmative, holding that a death is caused "while committing" an offence enumerated under s. 231(5) "where the act causing death and the acts constituting the [enumerated offence] all form part of one continuous sequence of events forming a single transaction": *Paré*, supra, at p. 632. Wilson J. reasoned that this understanding of the provision best reflects the underlying policy concerns, which she characterized as follows at p. 633: "The offences listed in s. 214(5) [now s. 231(5)] are all offences involving the unlawful domination of people by other people. Thus an organizing principle for s. 214(5) can be found. This principle is that where a murder is committed by someone already abusing his power by illegally dominating another, the murder should be treated as an exceptionally serious crime."

While that passage does not in itself suggest that s. 231(5) applies only where the victim of the murder and the enumerated offence are the same, Wilson J. went on to write: "it is the continuing illegal domination of the victim which gives continuity to the sequence of events culminating in the murder. The murder represents an exploitation of the position of power created by the underlying crime and makes the entire course of conduct a 'single transaction'": *Paré*, supra, at p. 633. The appellant's argument is that Parliament "never intended that the existence of unlawful domination, in and of itself, [would be] sufficient to warrant classifying a murder as first degree murder." Rather, as Wilson J. recognized, "it is the unlawful domination of the victim that justified this classification."

There is some support for the appellant's interpretation of s. 231(5) in this Court's other judgments dealing with s. 231(5). In *R. v. Arkell*, [1990] 2 S.C.R. 695, we considered whether s. 214(5) (now s. 231(5)) violates s. 7 of the Charter because it results in punishment that is not proportionate to the seriousness of the offences. In rejecting that contention, Lamer C.J. wrote: "Parliament's decision to treat more seriously murders that have been committed while the offender is exploiting a position of power through illegal domination of the victim accords with the principle that there must be proportionality between a sentence and the moral blameworthiness of the offender and other considerations such as deterrence and societal condemnation of the acts of the offender": *Arkell*, supra, at p. 704.

In *Luxton*, ... we addressed the related question of whether the combined effect of s. 214(5) and s. 669(a) infringes s. 7 of the Charter by foreclosing individualized sentences and thereby violating the principle that the severity of a sentence should reflect the degree of moral blameworthiness associated with the crime. Section 669(a) (now s. 745(a)) provides that an accused convicted of first degree murder must be sentenced to life in prison without the possibility of parole until he has served 25 years of his sentence. In finding that the impugned provisions did not infringe s. 7, Lamer C.J. wrote: "Murders that are done while committing offences which involve the illegal domination of the victim by the offender have been classified as first degree murder": *Luxton*.

I am not persuaded, however, that this Court intended in *Paré*, *Arkell*, or *Luxton*, ... to foreclose the application of s. 231(5) to multiple-victim scenarios. None of those cases involved multiple-victim scenarios, and the issue was simply not addressed by the Court. In my view, the references to the "victim" simply reflect the facts of those cases. The essential thrust of Wilson J.'s reasoning in *Paré*, supra, was that the offences enumerated in s. 231(5) are singled out because they are crimes involving the domination of one person by another. The essence of the reasoning was that s. 231(5) reflects Parliament's determination that murders committed in connection with crimes of domination are particularly blameworthy and deserving of more severe punishment. In many cases, such murders will be committed as the culmination of the accused's domination of the victim of the enumerated offence. This was the case in *Paré*, supra, *Arkell*, supra, and *Luxton* ... . In other cases, however, the accused will have murdered one person in connection with the domination of another. I cannot conclude that Wilson J.' s judgment in *Paré*, or Lamer C.J.'s judgments in *Arkell* or *Luxton* foreclose the application of s. 231(5) in such cases.

In my view the appellant states the organizing principle of s. 231(5) too narrowly. The provision reflects Parliament's determination that murders committed in connection with crimes of domination are particularly blameworthy and deserving of more severe punishment. "While committing or attempting to commit" requires the killing to be closely connected, temporally and causally, with an enumerated offence. As long as that connection exists, however, it is immaterial that the victim of the killing and the victim of the enumerated offence are not the same.

In oral argument, the appellant relied heavily on the fact that murder is not itself an offence enumerated under s. 231(5). On the appellant's theory, if Parliament had contemplated that the provision might be applied to multiple-victim scenarios, it would surely have included murder on the list of offences, because murder committed to facilitate another, or other, murder is obviously as morally blameworthy as murder committed to facilitate any of the enumerated offences. In the appellant's view, the absence of murder from the list of offences can only be explained by the fact that Parliament did not contemplate that the provision might be applied to situations in which the victim of the murder and the victim of the enumerated offence are not the same.

I think the more likely explanation for the exclusion of murder from the list of enumerated offences under s. 231(5) is simply that, in most situations in which an accused has killed two or more people and there is a temporal and causal nexus between the killings, s. 231(2) will apply. That provision states that "[m]urder is first degree murder when it is planned and deliberate." While one can imagine situations in which an accused might have killed two or more people spontaneously, without planning or deliberation, such scenarios are surely the exception rather than the rule. In all likelihood, the reason that Parliament did not include murder as an enumerated offence under s. 231(5) is that it concluded that most multiple murders would engage s. 231(2).

The appellant rightly points out that s. 231(5) imposes a severe penalty—indeed, the most severe penalty imposed under our *Criminal Code*—and accordingly it is particularly important that the provision be strictly construed. While this principle is unimpeachable, it cannot in itself justify restricting the ordinary meaning of the provision's words. The cases of this Court dealing with s. 231(5) make clear that an accused commits a murder "while committing or attempting to commit" an enumerated offence only if there is a close temporal and causal connection between the murder and the enumerated offence: see, e.g., *Paré*, supra, at p. 632 (stating that a murder is committed "while committing" an enumerated offence only "where the act causing death and the acts constituting [the enumerated offence] all form part of one continuous sequence of events forming a single transaction"); *R. v. Kirkness*, [1990] 3 S.C.R. 74. In my view this requirement appropriately restricts the application of s. 231(5) to contexts within the intended scope of the provision.

*Appeal dismissed.*

## Constitutional Considerations

Section 231(5) was challenged under the Charter in the following two cases.

### R. v. Arkell
Suprem⸗ Court of Canada
(1990), 59 C.C.C. (3d) 65

[The accused killed the victim during the course of a sexual assault and was convicted of first-degree murder under s. 214(5) (now s. 231(5)) of the *Criminal Code*.]

LAMER C.J.C.: ... For the reasons I have stated in *R. v. Martineau* (1990), 58 C.C.C. (3d) 353 (S.C.C.), released concurrently, s. 213(a) of the *Criminal Code* is of no force or effect, and the first two constitutional questions should, therefore, be answered accordingly. The third and fourth constitutional questions require an analysis of s. 214(5) of the *Criminal Code*. The main argument of the appellant, as regards his constitutional challenge of the section, is that it is arbitrary and irrational and thereby offends s. 7 of the Charter. In my view, this submission is answered by this court's judgment in *Paré*.

In that case a unanimous seven-person panel affirmed that s. 214 is a classification section concerned with sentencing and does not create a substantive offence. Wilson J., speaking for the court, put it this way at pp. 102-3 C.C.C., p. 552 D.L.R.: It is clear from a reading of these provisions that s. 214 serves a different function from ss. 212 and 213. Sections 212 and 213 create the substantive offence of murder. Section 214 is simply concerned with classifying for sentencing purposes the offences created by ss. 212 and 213. It tells us whether the murder is first degree or second degree. This view of s. 214 was expressly adopted by this court in *R. v. Farrant* (1983), 4 C.C.C. (3d) 354 (per Dickson J.) and in *Droste v. The Queen* (1984) 10 C.C.C. (3d) 404 (per Dickson J.). Indeed, the appellant concedes that s. 214(5) is a sentencing classification provision.

The argument of the appellant suggests that the sentencing scheme is flawed and in violation of s. 7 of the Charter because it results in the punishment of individuals that is not proportionate to the seriousness of the offences giving rise to the sentences. First, I must note that as a result of this court's decision in *Martineau*, released concurrently, it can no longer be said that s. 214(5) has the potential to classify unintentional killings as first degree murder. A conviction for murder requires proof beyond a reasonable doubt of subjective foresight of death. Therefore, when we reach the stage of classifying murders as either first or second degree, we are dealing with individuals who have committed the most serious crime in our *Criminal Code*, and who have been proven to have done so with the highest level of moral culpability, that of subjective foresight. Section 214(5) represents a decision by Parliament to impose a more serious punishment on those found guilty of murder while committing certain listed offences.

This leads me to a second point, namely, a consideration of the underlying rationale of s. 214(5). Again, I refer to the decision of this court in *Paré*: All murders are serious crimes. Some murders, however, are so threatening to the public that Parliament has chosen to impose exceptional penalties on the perpetrators. One such class of murders is that found in s. 214(5), murders done while committing a hijacking, a kidnapping and forcible confinement, a rape, or an indecent assault.

The offences listed in s. 214(5) are all offences involving the unlawful domination of people by other people. Thus an organizing principle for s. 214(5) can be found. This principle is that where a murder is committed by someone already abusing his power by illegally dominating another, the murder should be treated as an exceptionally serious crime. Parliament has chosen to treat these murders as murders in the first degree. I can find no principle of fundamental justice that prevents Parliament, guided by the organizing principle identified by this court in *Paré*, from classifying murders done while committing certain underlying offences as more serious, and thereby attaching more serious penalties to them. In the case of the distinction between first and second degree murder, the difference is a maximum extra 15 years that must be served before one is eligible for parole. This distinction is neither arbitrary nor irrational. The section is based on an organizing principle that treats murders committed while the perpetrator is illegally dominating another person as more serious than other murders. Further, the relationship between the classification and the moral blameworthiness of the offender clearly exists. Section 214 only comes into play when murder has been proven beyond a reasonable doubt. In light of *Martineau*, this means that the offender has been proven to have had subjective foresight of death. Parliament's decision to treat more seriously murders that have been committed while the offender is exploiting a position of power through illegal domination of the victim accords with the principle that there must be a proportionality between a sentence and the moral blameworthiness of the offender and other considerations such as deterrence and societal condemnation of the acts of the offender. Therefore, I conclude that, in so far as s. 214(5) is neither arbitrary nor irrational, it does not infringe upon s. 7 of the Charter. I note that in this appeal there was no argument made as regards s. 12 of the Charter, although that issue was raised in a case heard and disposed of concurrently, *R. v. Luxton* [since reported 58 C.C.C. (3d) 449]. ...

I would, accordingly, dismiss the appeal and answer the constitutional questions as follows:

1. Does s. 213(a) of the *Criminal Code* (as it read in November 1984) contravene the rights and freedoms guaranteed by s. 7 and/or s. 11(d) of the *Canadian Charter of Rights and Freedoms*?

A. Yes.

2. If the answer to question 1 is affirmative, is s. 213(a) of the *Criminal Code* (as it read in November 1984) justified by s. 1 of the Charter and therefore not inconsistent with the *Constitution Act, 1982*?

A. No.

3. Does s. 214(5) of the *Criminal Code* (as it read in November 1984) contravene the rights and freedoms guaranteed by s. 7 of the *Canadian Charter of Rights and Freedoms*?

A. No.

4. If the answer to question 3 is affirmative, is s. 214(5) of the *Criminal Code* (as it read in November 1984) justified by s. 1 of the Charter and therefore not inconsistent with the *Constitution Act, 1982*?

A. In light of the answer to question 3, this question does not have to be answered.

*The appeal is dismissed.*

### R. v. Luxton
Supreme Court of Canada
(1990), 58 C.C.C. (3d) 449

[The accused was convicted of first-degree murder on the basis that he forcibly confined the victim, a taxi driver. The accused forced the victim to drive him to a field, where she was repeatedly stabbed in the head and neck.]

LAMER C.J.C.: ... The remaining questions require an examination of the combined effect of ss. 214(5)(e) and 669 of the Code on the rights guaranteed by ss. 7, 9 and 12 of the Charter, and s. 2(e) of the *Canadian Bill of Rights*. The appellant combines his argument in respect of s. 7 of the Charter and s. 2(e) of the *Canadian Bill of Rights*. He submits that the principles of fundamental justice require that differing degrees of moral blameworthiness in different offences be reflected in differential sentences, and that sentencing be individualized. The appellant cites the following judgments as support for the view that the combined effect of ss. 214(5)(e) and 669 offends the principles that a just sentencing system contains a gradation of punishments differentiated according to the malignity of offences and that sentencing be individualized: *Reference re s. 94(2) of Motor Vehicle Act* (1985), 23 C.C.C. (3d) 289, per Wilson J.; *R. v. Smith*, (1987), 34 C.C.C. (3d) 97, per Lamer and Wilson JJ., and *R. v. Lyons* (1987), 37 C.C.C. (3d) 1, per La Forest J. In my view, assuming that s. 7 incorporates the propositions cited by the appellant as principles of fundamental justice, the combined effect of ss. 214(5)(e) and 669 is in accordance with them. Section 214(5) of the *Criminal Code* isolates a particular group of murderers, namely, those who have murdered while committing certain offences involving the illegal domination of the victim, and classifies them for sentencing purposes as murderers in the first degree. As a result of s. 669 the murderer is sentenced to life imprisonment without parole eligibility for 25 years. It is of some note that even in cases of first degree murder, s. 672 of the Code provides that after serving 15 years the offender can apply to the Chief Justice in the province for a reduction in the number of years of imprisonment without eligibility for parole having regard for the character of the applicant, his conduct while serving the sentence, the nature of the offence for which he was convicted and any other matters that are relevant in the circumstances. This indicates that even in the cases of our most serious offenders, Parliament has provided for some sensitivity to the individual circumstances of each case when it comes to sentencing.

I must also reiterate that what we are speaking of here is a classification scheme for the purposes of sentencing. The distinction between first and second degree murder only comes into play when it has first been proven beyond a reasonable doubt that the offender is guilty of murder, that is, that he or she had subjective foresight of death: *R. v. Martineau*, handed down this day. There is no doubt that a sentencing scheme must exhibit a proportionality to the seriousness of the offence, or to put it another way, there must be a gradation of punishments according to the malignity of the offences. However, a sentencing scheme also must take into account other factors that are of significance for the societal interest in punishing wrongdoers. In *Lyons*, supra, at p. 22, La Forest J. considered the dangerous offender designation in the Code and said the following in respect of the relationship between sentencing and its objectives: I accordingly agree with the respondent's submission that it cannot be considered a violation of fundamental justice for Parliament to identify those offenders who, in the interests of protecting the public, ought to be sentenced according to considerations which are not entirely reactive or based on a "just deserts" rationale. The imposition of a sentence which "is partly punitive but is mainly imposed for the protection of the public" ... seems to me to accord with the fundamental purpose of the criminal law generally, and of sentencing in particular, namely, the protection of society. In a rational system of sentencing, the respective importance of prevention, deterrence, retribution and rehabilitation will vary according to the nature of the crime and the circumstances of the offender. In my view the combination of ss. 214(5)(e) and 669 clearly demonstrates a proportionality between the moral turpitude of the offender and the malignity of the offence, and moreover it is in accord with the other objectives of a system of sentencing identified by La Forest J. in *Lyons*. As I have stated, we are dealing with individuals that have committed murder and have done so with the now constitutionally mandated *mens rea* of subjective foresight of death. Parliament has chosen, once it has been proven that an offender has committed murder, to classify certain of those murders as first degree. Murders that are done while committing offences which involve the illegal domination of the victim by the offender have been classified as first degree murder. Forcible confinement is one of those offences involving illegal domination. The added element of forcible confinement, in the context of the commission of a murder, markedly enhances the moral blameworthiness of an offender. Indeed, forcible confinement is punishable by up to 10 years in prison. The decision of Parliament to elevate murders done while the offender commits forcible confinement to the level of first degree murder is consonant with the principle of proportionality between the blameworthiness of the offender and the punishment. Further, it is consistent with the individualization of sentencing especially since only those who have killed with subjective foresight of death while also committing the offence of forcible confinement are subjected to that punishment. I, therefore, can find no principle of fundamental justice that has been violated by the combination of ss. 214(5)(e) and 669 of

the *Criminal Code*. Equally, for these same reasons, I conclude that there is no violation of s. 2(e) of the *Canadian Bill of Rights*.

The appellant also submits in a separate argument that the combination of
ss. 214(5)(e) and 669 contravenes s. 9 of the Charter because of the imposition of a
mandatory term of imprisonment by statute for an offence that encompasses a range
of moral turpitude. This argument overlaps a great deal with the appellant's s. 7
argument and I would only add the following comments to those I have already
made above. The combined effect of the impugned sections does not demonstrate
arbitrariness on the part of Parliament. Indeed, as I noted above, Parliament has
narrowly defined a class of murderers under an organizing principle of illegal domination and has specifically defined the conditions under which the offender can be
found guilty of first degree murder. In order to be found guilty of first degree murder under s. 214(5)(e), the offender must have committed murder with subjective
foresight of death and must have committed the murder "while committing or attempting to commit ... forcible confinement." Where the act causing death and the
acts constituting the forcible confinement all form part of one continuous sequence
of events forming a single transaction, the death is caused "while committing" an
offence for the purposes of s. 214(5): see *Paré* ... , at p. 107. To commit the underlying offence of forcible confinement, the offender must use "physical restraint,
contrary to the wishes of the person restrained, but to which the victim submits
unwillingly, thereby depriving the person of his or her liberty to move from one
place to another": quote from *R. v. Dollan and Newstead* (1980), 53 C.C.C. (2d)
146 (Ont. H.C.J.) at p. 154, as cited with approval in *R. v. Gratton* (1985), 18 C.C.C.
(3d) 462, 13 W.C.B. 368 (C.A.). It is true that the definition of forcible confinement adopted by the courts allows for varying circumstances in each individual
case. But this alone is not a sign of arbitrariness. The offence of forcible confinement
as defined falls clearly under the rubric of the organizing principle enunciated by
Wilson J. in *Paré*, namely, that of the illegal domination of one person by another.
The decision of Parliament to attach a minimum 25-year sentence without eligibility
for parole in cases of first degree murder, having regard to all these circumstances,
cannot be said to be arbitrary within the meaning of s. 9 of the Charter. The incarceration is statutorily authorized, it narrowly defines a class of offenders with respect to
whom the punishment will be invoked and it prescribes quite specifically the conditions under which an offender may be found guilty of first degree murder. Further,
the policy decision of Parliament to classify these murders as first degree murders
accords with the broader objectives of a sentencing scheme. The elevation of murder
while committing a forcible confinement to first degree reflects a societal denunciation of those offenders who choose to exploit their position of dominance and power
to the point of murder.

The appellant's final argument is that the combined effect of ss. 214(5)(e) and 669
contravenes s. 12 of the Charter. Section 12 of the Charter protects individuals against
cruel and unusual punishment. The phrase "cruel and unusual punishment" has been
considered by this court in *R. v. Smith* ... . That case held that the criterion to be
applied in order to determine whether a punishment is cruel and unusual is whether
the punishment is so excessive as to outrage standards of decency. At p. 139 I stated

that: The test for review under s. 12 of the Charter is one of gross disproportionality, because it is aimed at punishments that are more than merely excessive. We should be careful not to stigmatize every disproportionate or excessive sentence as being a constitutional violation, and should leave to the usual sentencing appeal process the task of reviewing the fitness of a sentence. Section 12 will only be infringed where the sentence is so unfit having regard to the offence and the offender as to be grossly disproportionate.

In assessing whether a sentence is grossly disproportionate, the court must first consider the gravity of the offence, the personal characteristics of the offender and the particular circumstances of the case in order to determine what range of sentences would have been appropriate to punish, rehabilitate or deter this particular offender or to protect the public from this particular offender. In *Lyons*, supra, La Forest J. addressed the meaning of the word "grossly" at p. 33: The word "grossly" [as in "grossly disproportionate"] it seems to me, reflects this Court's concern not to hold Parliament to a standard so exacting, at least in the context of s. 12, as to require punishments to be perfectly suited to accommodate the moral nuances of every crime and every offender.

In my view, the combination of ss. 214(5)(e) and 669 does not constitute cruel and unusual punishment. These sections provide for punishment of the most serious crime in our criminal law, that of first degree murder. This is a crime that carries with it the most serious level of moral blameworthiness, namely, subjective foresight of death. The penalty is severe and deservedly so. The minimum 25 years to be served before eligibility for parole reflects society's condemnation of a person who has exploited a position of power and dominance to the gravest extent possible by murdering the person that he or she is forcibly confining. The punishment is not excessive and clearly does not outrage our standards of decency. In my view, it is within the purview of Parliament, in order to meet the objectives of a rational system of sentencing, to treat our most serious crime with an appropriate degree of certainty and severity. I reiterate that, even in the case of first degree murder, Parliament has been sensitive to the particular circumstances of each offender through various provisions allowing for the royal prerogative of mercy, the availability of escorted absences from custody for humanitarian and rehabilitative purposes and for early parole: see ss. 672 (now s. 745), 674 (now s. 747) and 686 (now s. 751) of the *Criminal Code*. In *Smith*, ... at p. 137, I quoted with approval the following statement by Borins D.C.J. in *R. v. Guiller* (1985), 48 C.R. (3d) 226 (Ont. Dist. Ct.):

> It is not for the court to pass on the wisdom of Parliament with respect to the gravity of various offences and the range of penalties which may be imposed upon those found guilty of committing the offences. Parliament has broad discretion in proscribing conduct as criminal and in determining proper punishment. While the final judgment as to whether a punishment exceeds constitutional limits set by the Charter is properly a judicial function the court should be reluctant to interfere with the considered views of Parliament and then only in the clearest of cases where the punishment prescribed is so excessive when compared with the punishment prescribed for other offences as to outrage standards of decency.

Therefore, I conclude that in the case at bar the impugned provisions in combination do not represent cruel and unusual punishment within the meaning of s. 12 of the Charter.

---

See also *R. v. Sand* (2003), 172 Man. R. (2d) 274 (Q.B.), in which *Arkell*, *Luxton*, and *Collins* were followed in a case involving a challenge to s. 231(4)(a) of the *Criminal Code*, where the victim was a police officer.

## III. MANSLAUGHTER

In many ways, manslaughter is a residual category of homicide. As s. 234 of the *Criminal Code* provides:

> Culpable homicide that is not murder or infanticide is manslaughter.

There are many ways in which a verdict of manslaughter can be reached. Many cases start out as a charge of manslaughter, with the Crown alleging a killing that was the product of criminal negligence or, more usually, by an unlawful act, such as assaultive behaviour. These types of manslaughter are captured by in the definition of homicide in s. 222(5) of the *Criminal Code*, reproduced at the beginning of this chapter.

Many manslaughter verdicts are reached more indirectly. The typical case involves the accused who is charged with murder and the Crown is unable to establish the formal requirements for liability, such as a subjective intent to kill. Indeed, this is what most contested murder trials are about—determining whether the accused is guilty of murder or manslaughter. The distinction is hugely important because the punishment for manslaughter is greatly reduced when compared with murder. Section 236 provides:

> s. 236 Every person who commits manslaughter is guilty of an indictable offence and liable
>
> (a) where a firearm is used in the commission of the offence, to imprisonment for life and to a minimum punishment of imprisonment for a term of four years; and
>
> (b) in any other case, to imprisonment for life.

Note that life imprisonment is merely available as an option upon a conviction for manslaughter, it is not mandatory, as it is in the case of murder.

The murder/manslaughter issue will arise in a number of ways in the following chapters that deal with the defences. The issue comes up often in the context of the intoxication, where the accused alleges that he or she did not have the specific intent for murder, due to the distorting influence of alcohol. Manslaughter may also emerge as a final verdict by virtue of provocation in s. 232 of the *Criminal Code*, addressed in chapter 14.

The fault requirements with respect to manslaughter were addressed in chapter 7. In *R. v. Creighton* (1993), 83 C.C.C. (3d) 346 (S.C.C.) the Supreme Court held that the fault requirement for unlawful act manslaughter is objective foreseeability of bodily harm (as opposed to death) that is not transitory or trivial. This was held to meet with the requirements of s. 7 of the Charter, as developed through previous cases like *Vaillancourt* and *Martineau*, reproduced above. We conclude this chapter with the comments of Justice McLachlin (as she then was) about the nature of the offence of manslaughter:

> Before venturing on analysis, I think it appropriate to introduce a note of caution. We are here concerned with a common law offence virtually as old as our system of criminal law. It has been applied in innumerable cases around the world. And it has been honed and refined over the centuries. Because of its residual nature, it may lack the logical symmetry of more modern statutory offences, but it has stood the practical test of time. Could all this be the case, one asks, if the law violates our fundamental notions of justice, themselves grounded in the history of the common law? Perhaps. Nevertheless, it must be with considerable caution that a twentieth century court approaches the invitation which has been put before us: to strike out, or alternatively, rewrite, the offence of manslaughter on the ground that this is necessary to bring the law into conformity with the principles of fundamental justice. ...
>
> To the extent that stigma is relied on as requiring foreseeability of the risk of death in the offence of manslaughter, I find it unconvincing. The most important feature of the stigma of manslaughter is the stigma which is not attached to it. The *Criminal Code* confines manslaughter to non-intentional homicide. A person convicted of manslaughter is not a murderer. He or she did not intend to kill someone. A person has been killed through the fault of another, and that is always serious. But by the very act of calling the killing manslaughter the law indicates that the killing is less blameworthy than murder. It may arise from negligence, or it may arise as the unintended result of a lesser unlawful act. The conduct is blameworthy and must be punished, but its stigma does not approach that of murder.
>
> To put it another way, the stigma attached to manslaughter is an appropriate stigma. Manslaughter is not like constructive murder, where one could say that a person who did not in fact commit murder might be inappropriately branded with the stigma of murder. The stigma associated with manslaughter is arguably exactly what it should be for an unintentional killing in circumstances where risk of bodily harm was foreseeable. There is much common sense in the following observation: The offender has killed, and it does not seem wrong in principle that, when he is far from blameless, he should be convicted of an offence of homicide. To some extent it must be an intuitive conclusion, but it does not seem too difficult to argue that those who kill, and who are going to be convicted of something, should be convicted of homicide. That, after all, is what they have done. (Adrian Briggs, "In Defence of Manslaughter," [1983] *Crim. L.R.* 764 at p. 765.)
>
> It would shock the public's conscience to think that a person could be convicted of manslaughter absent any moral fault based on foreseeability of harm. Conversely, it might well shock the public's conscience to convict a person who has killed another only of aggravated assault—the result of requiring foreseeability of death—on the sole basis that the risk of death was not reasonably foreseeable. The terrible consequence of death demands more. In short, the *mens rea* requirement which the common law has adopted— foreseeability of harm—is entirely appropriate to the stigma associated with the offence of manslaughter. To change the *mens rea* requirement would be to risk the very disparity between *mens rea* and stigma of which the appellant complains.
>
> I come then to the second factor mentioned in *Martineau*, the relationship between the punishment for the offence and the *mens rea* requirement. Here again, the offence of

manslaughter stands in sharp contrast to the offence of murder. Murder entails a mandatory life sentence; manslaughter carries with it no minimum sentence. This is appropriate. Because manslaughter can occur in a wide variety of circumstances, the penalties must be flexible. An unintentional killing while committing a minor offence, for example, properly attracts a much lighter sentence than an unintentional killing where the circumstances indicate an awareness of risk of death just short of what would be required to infer the intent required for murder. The point is, the sentence can be and is tailored to suit the degree of moral fault of the offender. This court acknowledged this in *Martineau*, at p. 362: "The more flexible sentencing scheme under a conviction for manslaughter is in accord with the principle that punishment be meted out with regard to the level of moral blameworthiness of the offender." It follows that the sentence attached to manslaughter does not require elevation of the degree of *mens rea* for the offence.

This brings me to the third factor relating to the gravity of the offence set out in *Martineau*, the principle that those causing harm intentionally must be punished more severely than those causing harm unintentionally. As noted, this principle is strictly observed in the case of manslaughter. It is by definition an unintentional crime. Accordingly, the penalties imposed are typically less than for its intentional counterpart, murder.

I conclude that the standard of *mens rea* required for manslaughter is appropriately tailored to the seriousness of the offence. ...

I have suggested that jurisprudential and historic considerations confirm a test for the *mens rea* of manslaughter based on foreseeability of the risk of bodily injury, rather than death. I have also argued that the considerations of the gravity of the offence and symmetry between the *mens rea* of the offence and its consequences do not entail the conclusion that the offence of manslaughter as it has been historically defined in terms of foreseeability of the risk of bodily harm is unconstitutional. It is my view that policy considerations support the same conclusion. In looking at whether a long-standing offence violates the principles of fundamental justice, it is not amiss, in my view, to look at such considerations.

First, the need to deter dangerous conduct which may injure others and in fact may kill the peculiarly vulnerable supports the view that death need not be objectively foreseeable, only bodily injury. To tell people that if they embark on dangerous conduct which foreseeably may cause bodily harm which is neither trivial nor transient, and which in fact results in death, that they will not be held responsible for the death but only for aggravated assault, is less likely to deter such conduct than a message that they will be held responsible for the death, albeit under manslaughter not murder. Given the finality of death and the absolute unacceptability of killing another human being, it is not amiss to preserve the test which promises the greatest measure of deterrence, provided the penal consequences of the offence are not disproportionate. This is achieved by retaining the test of foreseeability of bodily harm in the offence of manslaughter.

Secondly, retention of the test based on foreseeability of bodily harm accords best with our sense of justice. I have earlier alluded to the view, attested to by the history of the offence of manslaughter, that causing the death of another through negligence or a dangerous unlawful act should be met by a special sanction reflecting the fact that a death occurred, even though death was not objectively foreseeable. This is supported by the sentiment that a person who engages in dangerous conduct that breaches the bodily integrity of another and puts that person at risk may properly be held responsible for an unforeseen death attributable to that person's peculiar vulnerability; the aggressor takes the victim as he finds him. The criminal law must reflect not only the concerns of the accused, but the concerns of the victim and, where the victim is killed, the concerns of society for the victim's fate. Both go into the equation of justice.

Finally, the traditional test founded on foreseeability of the risk of bodily harm provides, in my belief, a workable test which avoids troubling judges and juries about the fine distinction between foreseeability of the risk of bodily injury and foreseeability of the risk of death—a distinction which, as argued earlier, reduces to a formalistic technicality when put in the context of the thin-skull rule and the fact that death has in fact been inflicted by the accused's dangerous act. The traditional common law test permits a principled approach to the offence which meets the concerns of society, provides fairness to the accused, and facilitates a just and workable trial process.

The dissenting reasons of former Chief Justice Lamer are reproduced in chapter 7.

## ADDITIONAL READING

- D. Stuart, *Canadian Criminal Law*, 4th ed. (Toronto: Carswell, 2001), chapter 3;
- K. Roach, *Criminal Law*, 3rd ed. (Toronto: Irwin Law, 2004 ), chapter 4;
- A. Mewett and M. Manning, *Criminal Law*, 3rd ed. (Toronto: Butterworths, 1994), chapter 20;
- I. Grant, D. Chunn, and C. Boyle, *The Law of Homicide* (Toronto: Carswell, 1994) (supplemented);
- B. Archibald, "The Constitutionalization of the General Part of the Criminal Code" (1988), 67 *Can. Bar Rev.* 403;
- D. Stuart, "Further Progress on the Constitutional Requirement of Fault, But Stigma Is Not Enough" (1990), 79 C.R. (3d) 247;
- A. Brudner, "Proportionality, Stigma and Discretion" (1996), 38 *Crim. L.Q.* 302;
- I. Grant, "Rethinking the Sentencing Regime for Murder" (2001), 39 *O.H.L.J.* 655;
- A. Mewett, "First Degree Murder" (1978-1979), 21 *Crim. L.Q.* 82.

# PART FIVE

# Principles of Exculpation

# CHAPTER FOURTEEN

# Provocation

Provocation is a partial defence to the offence of murder only. If this defence is successful, it has the effect of reducing murder to manslaughter, but cannot result in a complete acquittal. Provocation is codified in s. 232 of the *Criminal Code*:

> s. 232(1)  Culpable homicide that otherwise would be murder may be reduced to manslaughter if the person who committed it did so in the heat of passion caused by sudden provocation.
>
> (2)  A wrongful act or insult that is of such a nature as to be sufficient to deprive the ordinary person of the power of self-control is provocation for the purposes of this section if the accused acted on it on the sudden and before there was time for his passion to cool.
>
> (3)  For the purposes of this section, the questions
>
>     (a)  whether a particular wrongful act or insult amounted to provocation, and
>
>     (b)  whether the accused was deprived of the power of self-control by the provocation that he alleges he received,
>
> are questions of fact, but no one shall be deemed to have given provocation to another by doing anything that he had a legal right to do, or by doing anything that the accused incited him to do in order to provide the accused with an excuse to cause death or bodily harm to any human being.
>
> (4)  Culpable homicide that otherwise would be murder is not necessarily manslaughter by reason only that it was committed by a person who was being arrested illegally, but the fact that the illegality of the arrest was known to the accused may be evidence of provocation for the purpose of this section.

As with all defences, before the matter is left to the jury, there must be an air of reality to the claim that the accused acted with provocation: see *R. v. Thibert*, [1996] 1 S.C.R. 37. If an air of reality is established and the matter is left with the jury, the Crown must disprove the existence of provocation beyond a reasonable doubt.

The defence of provocation has been part of the common law for centuries: see Jeremy Horder, *Provocation and Responsibility* (Oxford: Oxford University Press, 1992). It continues to be a controversial defence by virtue of the fact that it privileges the emotion of anger for the purposes of homicide, while not recognizing others (such as compassion or mercy). Moreover, the perceived overuse of the defence in the context of spousal homicide has led to calls to abolish the defence.

## I. APPLYING THE PROVISIONS

Section 232 has often proved difficult for the courts to interpret. Among the issues that the courts and juries struggle with are: What acts or words are capable of constituting provocation? What is meant by the term "sudden" in this section? How is the "ordinary person" conceptualized in s. 232(1)? What is the relationship between provocation and intent?

### R. v. Hill
Supreme Court of Canada
[1986] 1 S.C.R. 313

DICKSON C.J.C. (Beetz, Estey, Chouinard, and La Forest JJ., concurring): Gordon James Elmer Hill was charged with committing first degree murder at the City of Belleville, County of Hastings, on the person of Verne Pegg, contrary to s. 218(1) of the *Criminal Code*, R.S.C. 1970, c. C-34. He was found by the jury not guilty of first degree murder but guilty of second degree murder. He was sentenced to imprisonment for life without eligibility for parole until 10 years of his sentence had been served.

Hill appealed his conviction to the Court of Appeal of Ontario. He raised many grounds of appeal, but the Court of Appeal called upon the Crown with respect to one ground only, relating to the charge on the issue of provocation. The ground of appeal was that the trial judge failed to instruct the jury properly as to the "ordinary person" in s. 215(2) [now s. 232(2)] of the *Criminal Code*. ...

These two subsections, given their plain meaning, produce three sequential questions for answer by the tribunal:

1.  Would an ordinary person be deprived of self-control by the act or insult?

2.  Did the accused in fact act in response to those "provocative" acts; in short, was he or she provoked by them whether or not an ordinary person would have been?

3.  Was the accused's response sudden and before there was time for his or her passion to cool? ...

In the answering of these successive questions, the first or "ordinary person" test is clearly determined by objective standards. The second *de facto* test as to the loss of self-control by the accused is determined, like any other question of fact as revealed by the evidence, from the surrounding facts. The third test as to whether the response was sudden and before passions cooled is again a question of fact.

At the time of the killing, Hill was a male, 16 years of age. The narrow question in this appeal is whether the trial judge erred in law in failing to instruct the jury that if they found a wrongful act or insult they should consider whether it was sufficient to deprive an ordinary person "of the age and sex of the appellant" of his power of self-control. Was it incumbent in law on the trial judge to add that gloss to the section? That is the issue.

*The Facts*

At trial both parties agreed that it was the acts of Hill which caused the death of Pegg but disagreed otherwise. The position of the Crown at trial was that Hill and Pegg were homosexual lovers and that Hill had decided to murder Pegg after a falling-out between them. The Crown argued that Hill deliberately struck Pegg in the head while Pegg lay in bed. This did not kill Pegg who immediately ran from the bedroom into the bathroom to try to and stop the flow of blood from his head. Realizing he had been unsuccessful, Hill took two knives from the kitchen and stabbed Pegg to death.

Hill's version of the events was very different. He admitted to causing the death of Pegg but put forward two defences: self-defence and provocation. Hill testified that he had known Pegg for about a year through the latter's involvement with the "Big Brother" organization. Hill stated that on the night in question he had been the subject of unexpected and unwelcome homosexual advances by Pegg while asleep on the couch in Pegg's apartment. Pegg pursued Hill to the bathroom and grabbed him, at which time Hill picked up a nearby hatchet and swung it at Pegg in an attempt to scare him. The hatchet struck Pegg in the head. Hill then ran from the apartment but returned shortly afterward. Upon re-entering the apartment, he was confronted by Pegg who threatened to kill him. At this point, Hill obtained two knives from the kitchen and stabbed Pegg to death. …

*The Charge*

The trial judge instructed the jury on the defence of provocation in the following terms: …

> Provocation may come from actual words or a series of each or a combination of both, and it must be looked at in the light of all the surrounding circumstances.
>
> First, the actual words must be such as would deprive an ordinary person of self-control. In considering this part of the Defence you are not to consider the particular mental make-up of the accused; rather the standard is that of the ordinary person. You will ask yourselves would the words or acts in this case have caused an ordinary person to lose his self-control.

After reviewing the evidence in support of the defence of provocation the judge continued:

> You will consider that evidence and you will decide whether the words and acts were sufficient to cause an ordinary person to lose his self-control.
>
> The acts were rubbing the accused's legs and chest, grabbing him by the shoulder and spinning him around, and later Pegg grabbing his right wrist before the second stab. The words were, "I am going to kill you, you little bastard."
>
> If you find that they were, you will then secondly consider whether the accused acted on the provocation on the sudden before there was time for his passion to cool. In deciding this question you are not restricted to the standard of the ordinary person. You will take into account the mental, the emotional, the physical characteristics and the age of the accused.

The incidents or the words upon which the provocation is based must be contemporaneous words or closely related to the tragedy. The killing must take place immediately after the acts or words constituting the provocation or so soon thereafter that the
accused's passion had no time to cool.

You will also ask yourselves was the provocation such that it would have led a
person with the mental and physical condition and the age of the accused to respond in
this way.

At trial, counsel for Hill objected to the instruction of the trial judge as to the
objective requirement of the defence of provocation, submitting that the "ordinary
person" referred to in s. 215(2) ought to have been defined as an ordinary person of
the age and sex of the accused. Counsel submitted that the objective requirement
would be satisfied if the judge were to recharge the jury by defining "ordinary person" as an "ordinary person in the circumstances of the accused." The judge refused
to recharge the jury in those terms.

### The Court of Appeal

In oral reasons Brooke J.A. (Martin and Morden JJ.A. concurring) noted that counsel
for the defence, relying on *Director of Public Prosecutions v. Camplin*, [1978] A.C.
705 (H.L.), submitted that the judge should have instructed the jury to consider
whether the wrongful act or insult was sufficient to deprive an "ordinary person" of
the age and sex of the accused of his power of self-control. The Court of Appeal held
that because the trial judge declined to do so he erred. In reaching this conclusion,
Brooke J.A. stated:

> The age and sex of the appellant are not "peculiar characteristics" excluded from con-
> sideration of the "ordinary person" in the objective test in s. 215(2) (see Fauteux J. (as
> he then was) in *Wright v. The Queen*, [1969] 3 C.C.C. 258 at pp. 261-2 ... discussing
> *Bedder v. D.P.P.*, [1954] 2 All E.R. 801).

He also added:

> In our respectful opinion, there is nothing in that judgment which precludes charging
> the jury as the defence requested. As the matter was left to the jury, the age of the
> appellant was only a consideration if and when the jury turned to the question of whether
> the wrongful act or insult deprived him of his power of self-control. The effect of the
> charge was that an ordinary person did not include a 16-year-old or youth and may well
> have established as the standard an ordinary person more experienced and mature than
> the ordinary 16-year-old or youth. If this is so, the jury may have rejected the defence
> judging the objective test on that basis.

The appeal was allowed, the conviction set aside and a new trial on the charge of
second degree murder ordered.

## The Issue

The issue in this appeal is whether the Ontario Court of Appeal erred in law in holding that the trial judge erred in law with respect to the elements of the objective test relevant to the defence of provocation in failing to direct the jury that the "ordinary person" within the meaning of that term in s. 215(2) of the *Criminal Code* was an "ordinary person of the same age and sex as the accused."

## The Defence of Provocation

The defence of provocation appears to have first developed in the early 1800's. Tindal C.J. in *R. v. Hayward* (1833), 6 Car. & P. 157 at p. 159, told the jury that the defence of provocation was derived from the law's "compassion to human infirmity." It acknowledged that all human beings are subject to uncontrollable outbursts of passion and anger which may lead them to do violent acts. In such instances, the law would lessen the severity of criminal liability.

Nevertheless, not all acts done in the heat of passion were to be subject to the doctrine of provocation. By the middle of the 19th century, it became clear that the provoking act had to be sufficient to excite an ordinary or reasonable person under the circumstances. As Keating J. stated in *R. v. Welsh* (1869), 11 Cox C.C. 336 at p. 338:

> The law is, that there must exist such an amount of provocation as would be excited by the circumstances in the mind of a reasonable man, and so as to lead the jury to ascribe the act to the influence of that passion.

The *Criminal Code* codified this approach to provocation by including under s. 215 [now s. 232] three general requirements for the defence of provocation. First, the provoking wrongful act or insult must be of such a nature that it would deprive an ordinary person of the power of self-control. That is the initial threshold which must be surmounted. Secondly, the accused must actually have been provoked. As I have earlier indicated, these two elements are often referred to as the objective and subjective tests of provocation respectively. Thirdly, the accused must have acted on the provocation on the sudden and before there was time for his or her passion to cool.

### (a) The Objective Test of Provocation and the Ordinary Person Standard

In considering the precise meaning and application of the ordinary person standard or objective test, it is important to identify its underlying rationale. Lord Simon of Glaisdale has perhaps stated it most succinctly when he suggested in Camplin, at p. 726, that

> the reason for importing into this branch of the law the concept of the reasonable man [was] ... to avoid the injustice of a man being entitled to rely on his exceptional excitability or pugnacity or ill-temper or on his drunkenness.

If there were no objective test to the defence of provocation, anomalous results could occur. A well-tempered, reasonable person would not be entitled to benefit from the provocation defence and would be guilty of culpable homicide amounting to murder, while an ill-tempered or exceptionally excitable person would find his or her culpability mitigated by provocation and would be guilty only of manslaughter. It is society's concern that reasonable and non-violent behaviour be encouraged that prompts the law to endorse the objective standard. The criminal law is concerned among other things with fixing standards for human behaviour. We seek to encourage conduct that complies with certain societal standards of reasonableness and responsibility. In doing this, the law quite logically employs the objective standard of the reasonable person.

With this general purpose in mind, we must ascertain the meaning of the ordinary person standard. What are the characteristics of the "ordinary person"? To what extent should the attributes and circumstances of the accused be ascribed to the ordinary person? To answer these questions, it is helpful to review the English and Canadian jurisprudence. Since Canadian courts have relied heavily on English developments, I shall begin with the English cases.

(i)  English Law of Provocation and the Ordinary Person Standard

In *R. v. Lesbini* (1914), 11 Cr. App. R. 7, the English Court of *Criminal Appeal* refused to take into account the mental deficiency of the accused in assessing the availability of the provocation defence. It confirmed the threshold objective test for provocation whereby there must be sufficient provocation to excite a reasonable person. A reasonable or ordinary person was not one with mental deficiencies. In *Mancini v. Director of Public Prosecutions*, [1942] A.C. 1, the House of Lords endorsed the *Lesbini* case and further elaborated the objective test of provocation. Viscount Simon L.C. stated, at p. 9:

> The test to be applied is that of the effect of the provocation on a reasonable man, as was laid down by the Court of Criminal Appeal in *Rex v. Lesbini*, so that an unusually excitable or pugnacious individual is not entitled to rely on provocation which would not have led an ordinary person to act as he did.

The ordinary or reasonable person, therefore, was one of normal temperament and average mental capacity.

In 1954, the House of Lords was faced with the question of whether, in applying the objective test of provocation, it should take into account certain physical characteristics of the accused. In *Bedder v. Director of Public Prosecutions*, [1954] 1 W.L.R. 1119, a sexually impotent man killed a prostitute after she taunted him about his physical condition. The House of Lords had to determine whether, in applying the objective test of provocation, the sexual impotence of the accused should be taken into account. The test would then have been whether an ordinary person, who was sexually impotent, would have been provoked. The court rejected this approach and held that the peculiar physical characteristics of the accused were not to be ascribed to the ordinary person for the purposes of the objective test.

Despite the House of Lords' conclusion that the physical characteristics of the accused were irrelevant to the determination of whether a reasonable person would have been provoked, it appears that the court was primarily concerned with the difficulty of distinguishing "temperament" from "physical defects." ...

The *Bedder* approach to the ordinary person standard is no longer the law in England. In *Camplin*, the House of Lords expressly rejected the narrow objective test articulated in *Bedder*. The *Camplin* case involved a youth of 15 years of age who maintained that he had been provoked by a homosexual assault. The House of Lords unanimously concluded that the ordinary person, for the purposes of the objective test of provocation, was to be an ordinary person of the same age and sex as the accused. It should be noted that, in *Camplin*, the trial judge had specifically directed the jury to take age and sex into account and the appeal sought to establish that this was wrong. In the present case, there was no such instruction.

In justifying its shift away from the Bedder approach, the House of Lords relied in part on legislative changes in the law of provocation introduced after the *Bedder* opinion. Specifically, in 1957, s. 3 of the *Homicide Act, 1957* (U.K.), c. 11, was passed; it provides:

> 3. Where on a charge of murder there is evidence on which the jury can find that the person charged was provoked (whether by things done or by things said or by both together) to lose his self-control, the question whether the provocation was enough to make a reasonable man do as he did shall be left to be determined by the jury; and in determining that question the jury shall take into account everything both done and said according to the effect which, in their opinion, it would have on a reasonable man.

The phrase, "the jury shall take into account everything" was interpreted to allow a consideration of relevant characteristics in connection with the objective test.

Lord Diplock clarified the underlying rationale for expanding the notion of the ordinary person when he wrote, at p. 717:

> To taunt a person because of his race, his physical infirmities or some shameful incident in his past may well be considered by the jury to be more offensive to the person addressed, however equable his temperament, if the facts on which the taunt is founded are true than it would be if they were not.

On a similar note, Lord Morris of Borth-y-Gest held, at p. 721:

> If the accused is of particular colour or particular ethnic origin and things are said which to him are grossly insulting it would be utterly unreal if the jury had to consider whether the words would have provoked a man of different colour or ethnic origin—or to consider how such a man would have acted or reacted.

Taking these considerations into account, Lord Simon of Glaisdale formulated the objective test as follows, at p. 727:

> I think that the standard of self-control which the law requires before provocation is held to reduce murder to manslaughter is still that of the reasonable person ... but that, in determining whether a person of reasonable self-control would lose it in the circumstances, the entire factual situation, which includes the characteristics of the accused, must be considered.

One conceptual difficulty was acknowledged by Lord Diplock. He recognized that (p. 717)

> In strict logic there is a transition between treating age as a characteristic that may be taken into account in assessing the gravity of the provocation addressed to the accused and treating it as a characteristic to be taken into account in determining what is the degree of self-control to be expected of the ordinary person ...

In most cases, it is appropriate to assume that the level of self-control or degree of reasonableness is the same regardless of certain physical differences. Age, however, in Lord Diplock's view posed a more difficult problem. He resolved this problem with respect to age by appealing to the acknowledged importance of the law's compassion to human infirmity. On a more general level, he rejected the solution of separating out the inquiry into two phases as overly complicated for the jury.

(ii)  Canadian Case Law

The Supreme Court of Canada has also had occasion to provide guidance on the ordinary person standard for provocation. In *Taylor v. The King* (1947), 89 C.C.C. 209, a case in which the accused was drunk at the time of his alleged provocation, Kerwin J. made clear that for the purposes of the objective test of provocation, the "criterion is the effect on an ordinary person ... the jury is not entitled to take into consideration any alleged drunkenness on the part of the accused."

This Court again rejected a consideration of the drunkenness of the accused in connection with the objective test in *Salamon v. The Queen* (1959), 123 C.C.C. 1, Mr. Justice Fauteux endorsed the trial judge's instruction to the jury not to consider "the character, background, temperament, or condition of the accused" in relation to the objective test of provocation. Similarly, Cartwright J. (dissenting on another issue) wrote that the trial judge correctly "made it plain that on this [objective] branch of the inquiry no account should be taken of the idiosyncrasies of the appellant and that the standard to be applied was that of an ordinary person."

Finally, in *Wright v. The Queen*, [1969] 3 C.C.C. 258, a son was charged with the shooting death of his father. The evidence suggested that there had been some difficulties in their relationship. The father was said to have been a bad-tempered and violent man who had mistreated his son on a number of occasions. The accused had not seen his father for a period of about five years until a few days prior to the fatal incident. On the evening of the shooting, the accused had spent most of the day drinking with his friends. In considering the objective test of provocation, the court rejected the relevance of the quality of the accused's relationship with his father, the mentality of the accused or his possible drunkenness. ... The court went on to state, at p. 262 C.C.C., p. 532 D.L.R., p. 340 S.C.R.:

> While the character, background, temperament, idiosyncrasies, or the drunkenness of the accused are matters to be considered in the second branch of the enquiry, they are excluded from the consideration in the first branch. A contrary view would denude of any sense the objective test. ...

What lessons are to be drawn from this review of the case law? I think it is clear that there is widespread agreement that the ordinary or reasonable person has a normal temperament and level of self-control. It follows that the ordinary person is not exceptionally excitable, pugnacious or in a state of drunkenness.

In terms of other characteristics of the ordinary person, it seems to me that the "collective good sense" of the jury will naturally lead it to ascribe to the ordinary person any general characteristics relevant to the provocation in question. For example, if the provocation is a racial slur, the jury will think of an ordinary person with the racial background that forms the substance of the insult. To this extent, particular characteristics will be ascribed to the ordinary person. Indeed, it would be impossible to conceptualize a sexless or ageless ordinary person. Features such as sex, age or race do not detract from a person's characterization as ordinary. Thus particular characteristics that are not peculiar or idiosyncratic can be ascribed to an ordinary person without subverting the logic of the objective test of provocation. ...

It is important to note that, in some instances, certain characteristics will be irrelevant. For example, the race of a person will be irrelevant if the provocation involves an insult regarding a physical disability. Similarly, the sex of an accused will be irrelevant if the provocation relates to a racial insult. Thus the central criterion is the relevance of the particular feature to the provocation in question. With this in mind, I think it is fair to conclude that age will be a relevant consideration when we are dealing with a young accused person. For a jury to assess what an ordinary person would have done if subjected to the same circumstances as the accused, the young age of an accused will be an important contextual consideration.

I should also add that my conclusion that certain attributes can be ascribed to the ordinary person is not meant to suggest that a trial judge must in each case tell the jury what specific attributes it is to ascribe to the ordinary person. The point I wish to emphasize is simply that in applying their common sense to the factual determination of the objective test, jury members will quite naturally and properly ascribe certain characteristics to the "ordinary person."

### (b) The Subjective Test and Actual Provocation

Once a jury has established that the provocation in question was sufficient to deprive an ordinary person of the power of self-control, it must still determine whether the accused was so deprived. It may well be that an ordinary person would have been provoked, but in fact the accused was not. This second test of provocation is called subjective because it involves an assessment of what actually occurred in the mind of the accused. At this stage, the jury must also consider whether the accused reacted to the provocation on the sudden and before there was time for his passion to cool.

In instructing the jury with respect to the subjective test of provocation, the trial judge must make clear to the jury that its task at this point is to ascertain whether the accused was in fact acting as a result of provocation. In this regard, a trial judge may wish to remind the jury members that, in determining whether an accused was actually provoked, they are entitled to take into account his or her mental state and psychological temperament. ...

I have the greatest of confidence in the level of intelligence and plain common sense of the average Canadian jury sitting on a criminal case. Juries are perfectly capable of sizing the matter up. In my experience as a trial judge I cannot recall a single instance in which a jury returned to the court-room to ask for further instructions on the provocation portion of a murder charge. A jury frequently seeks further guidance on the distinction between first degree murder, second degree murder and manslaughter, but rarely, if ever, on provocation. It seems to be common ground that the trial judge would not have been in error if he had simply read s. 215 of the Code and left it at that, without embellishment. I am loath to complicate the task of the trial judge, in cases such as the case at bar, by requiring him or her as a matter of law to point out to the members of the jury that in applying the objective test they must conceptualize an "ordinary person" who is male and young. The accused is before them. He is male and young. I cannot conceive of a Canadian jury conjuring up the concept of an "ordinary person" who would be either female or elderly, or banishing from their minds the possibility that an "ordinary person" might be both young and male. I do not think anything said by the judge in the case at bar would have led the jury to such an absurdity.

### Conclusion

I find that the trial judge's charge to the jury on the ordinary person standard in the defence of provocation was consistent with the requirements of the Criminal Code and correct in law. It was not necessary to direct the jury that the ordinary person means an ordinary person of the same age and sex as the accused. I would, therefore, allow the appeal and restore the conviction. ...

LAMER J. (dissenting):  I agree with the Chief Justice's exposition of the law in its entirety. As regards age, I therefore agree that, when giving content to the ordinary person standard, as said by the Chief Justice, "age will be a relevant consideration when [we are] dealing with a young accused person," and that, "[f]or a jury to assess what an ordinary person would have done if subjected to the same circumstances as the accused, the young age of an accused will be an important contextual consideration."

I am also of his view that it is not mandatory that the judge instruct the jury "that the ordinary person, for the purposes of the objective test of provocation, is to be deemed to be of the same age and sex as the accused." But I should like to add that there will, in my view, be cases where failure to do so, given the particular circumstances of the case, would be unfair and constitute reversible error; but not because of a special rule applicable to charges on provocation, but rather under the general rule that the judge's charge to the jury must always be fair.

Such is not the case here and the trial judge did not err in failing to give such an instruction. But he erred, in my respectful view, when he gave instructions to the jury tantamount to excluding age as a relevant factor in their consideration of the "first leg" of the provocation test. In his charge, he instructed the jury on the law of provocation as follows. ...

Sharing the Chief Justice's confidence in the level of intelligence and plain common sense of the average Canadian juror, I cannot but conclude that, in all likelihood, the jury understood that the objective test excluded consideration of age, while the subjective test no longer restricted them and that they could, indeed should, at that latter stage then consider the accused's age. It is on this narrow ground, the effect of the trial judge's instructions upon the jury, that I disagree with the Chief Justice.

WILSON J. (dissenting): …

(1) In general, particular characteristics of the individual accused and the circumstances in which the accused is found can be taken into account in applying the objective "ordinary person" test at the first stage of the provocation defence only for the purpose of placing the wrongful act or insult in its proper context with a view to assessing its gravity. The underlying principles of equality and individual responsibility cannot be undermined by importing the accused's subjective level of self-control into the "ordinary person" test set out in s. 215(2) of the *Criminal Code*. The jury must be directed to consider any facts which make the wrongful act or insult comprehensible to them in the same way as it was comprehended by the accused and then, having appreciated the factual context in which the wrongful act or insult took place, must measure the accused's response to this insult against the objective standard of the ordinary person similarly situated and similarly insulted.

(2) The Ontario Court of Appeal was correct in identifying the young age of the respondent as a special factor which can be incorporated into the "ordinary person" standard. This reduction in the standard against which young accused are measured merely reflects the fact that the law does not attribute to individuals in the developmental stage of their youth the same degree of responsibility as is attributed to fully adult actors. This developmental process is properly embodied in an incrementally adjusted formulation of the "ordinary person" test in accordance with the age of the accused. In this way the basic principles of equality and individual responsibility are embodied in the test to an extent commensurate with the age and capacities of the accused.

(3) The Court of Appeal was also correct in holding that the sex of the respondent could be considered on the objective test, not because different standards of self-control are attributable to the two sexes, but in order to put the wrongful act or insult into context for purposes of assessing its gravity. In assessing the reaction of the ordinary person to a sexual assault it is the ordinary person who is a male subjected to a homosexual assault which must be considered.

In summary, the appropriate formulation of the objective standard against which the respondent's reaction to the wrongful act must be measured in this case is the standard of the ordinary 16-year-old male subjected to a homosexual assault. The jury may well, on the basis of the judge's charge and having regard to the existing state of the jurisprudence in Canada, have rejected the respondent's defence because they measured his conduct against a higher standard. I agree with the Court of Appeal that in these circumstances the conviction cannot be allowed to stand.

I would dismiss the appeal.

[Further concurring reasons were written by Le Dain J.]

**R. v. Thibert**
Supreme Court of Canada
[1996] 1 S.C.R. 37

[The defence of provocation was the central issue in this controversial case in which the accused killed his wife's lover. A majority of three judges held that the defence of provocation should have been left with the jury in the circumstances. The essential facts of the case are found in the dissenting judgment of Major J., following the judgment of Cory J.]

CORY J. (Sopinka and McLachlin JJ. concurring):

[1] The sole question to be considered on this appeal is whether the trial judge was correct in leaving the defence of provocation with the jury. Put another way, the issue is whether there was any evidence upon which a reasonable jury acting judicially and properly instructed could find that there had been provocation.

[2] If the trial judge was correct in leaving provocation with the jury, then it is conceded that there must be a new trial. This is the result of the failure to instruct the jury that there was no onus resting upon the appellant to establish the defence but rather that it rested upon the Crown to establish beyond a reasonable doubt that there had not been provocation. The necessity of giving these instructions has been emphasized by this court in *Latour v. The King*, [1951] S.C.R. 19, and in *Linney v. The Queen* (1977), [1978] 1 S.C.R. 646. If on the other hand it was inappropriate for the trial judge to leave the defence of provocation to the jury, then the fact that he erred in the instructions pertaining to provocation was immaterial and it would be appropriate to find that no substantial wrong or miscarriage had been occasioned by the error. ...

[4] The section specifies that there is both an objective and a subjective element to the defence. Both must be satisfied if the defence is to be invoked. First, there must be a wrongful act or insult of such a nature that it is sufficient to deprive an ordinary person of the power of self-control as the objective element. Second, the subjective element requires that the accused act upon that insult on the sudden and before there was time for his passion to cool. The objective aspect would at first reading appear to be contradictory for, as legal writers have noted, the "ordinary" person does not kill. Yet, I think the objective element should be taken as an attempt to weigh in the balance those very human frailties which sometimes lead people to act irrationally and impulsively against the need to protect society by discouraging acts of homicidal violence.

*When Should the Defence of Provocation Be Left to the Jury*

[5] In *Parnerkar v. The Queen*, [1974] S.C.R. 449, Fauteux C.J.C., writing for the majority, held that the defence should not be left with the jury for where:

... the record is denuded of any evidence potentially enabling a reasonable jury acting judicially to find a wrongful act or insult of the nature and effect set forth in s. 203(3)(a) and (b), it is then, as a matter of law, within the area exclusively reserved to the trial Judge to so decide and his duty to refrain from putting the defence of provocation to the jury.

[6] That is to say that before the defence of provocation is left to the jury, the trial judge must be satisfied (a) that there is *some* evidence to suggest that the particular wrongful act or insult alleged by the accused would have caused an ordinary person to be deprived of self-control, and (b) that there is some evidence showing that the accused was actually deprived of his or her self-control by that act or insult. This threshold test can be readily met, so long as there is some evidence that the objective and subjective elements may be satisfied. If there is, the defence must then be left with the jury.

[7] The test in *Parnerkar* was followed by this court in *R. v. Faid*, [1983] 1 S.C.R. 265. This test has been criticized by some writers (see, for example, Don Stuart, *Canadian Criminal Law: A Treatise*, 3rd ed. (Toronto: Carswell, 1995), at p. 498) as being contrary to the plain wording of s. 232. Despite my admiration for the work of Professor Stuart, I cannot accept his position. It is true that the objective and subjective requirements mandated by this section are clearly questions of fact which the jury must decide. None the less, the trial judge must still determine if there is *any* evidence upon which a reasonable jury properly instructed and acting judicially could find that there had been provocation. If the trial judge is satisfied that there is such evidence, then the defence must be put to the jury to determine what weight, if any, should be attached to that evidence. Obviously, the trial judge should not weigh the sufficiency of the evidence. This is the function reserved for the jury. A trial judge considering whether the evidence has met the threshold test must also take into account the nature of the wrongful act or insult and how that act or insult should be viewed in the context of the case.

### The Wrongful Act or Insult

[8] *Taylor v. The King*, [1947] S.C.R. 462, adopted the *Oxford English Dictionary* definition of "insult," and found it to mean:

> ... an act, or the action, of attacking or assailing; an open and sudden attack or assault without formal preparations; injuriously contemptuous speech or behaviour; scornful utterance or action intended to wound self-respect; an affront; indignity.

### The Objective Element of the Test: How Ordinary Is the "Ordinary Person" and Would That Person Have Been Provoked by the Wrongful Act or Insult?

...

[15] The problem was considered by this court in *R. v. Hill*, [1986] 1 S.C.R. 313. There a 16-year-old male fought off the homosexual advances of an older man who was his "Big Brother." The narrow "ordinary person" test was rejected and a more contextual one adopted. Dickson C.J.C., writing for the majority of the court, held that the age and sex of the accused are important considerations in the objective branch of the test. At p. 335 C.C.C., p. 201 D.L.R., he noted that "particular characteristics that are not peculiar or idiosyncratic can be ascribed to an ordinary person without subverting the logic of the objective test of provocation." Although it was not

necessary in the circumstances of that case to go beyond a consideration of the age
and sex of the accused, Dickson C.J.C. did state that the jury should "assess what an
ordinary person would have done if subjected to the same circumstances as the accused" (p. 336 C.C.C., p. 201 D.L.R.). Thus, although characteristics such as a propensity to drunken rages or short-tempered violence cannot be taken into account,
other characteristics may properly be considered without in any way demeaning or
subverting the aim of the objective test to encourage responsible behaviour. So too, it
is proper for the jury to consider the background of the relationship between the deceased and the accused, including earlier insults which culminated in the final provocative actions or words. For a jury to take this into account would not adversely
affect the objective aspect of the test.

[16]  The provincial courts of appeal have widened, I believe correctly, the approach to the objective element in order to consider the background relationship
between the deceased and the accused. In *R. v. Daniels* (1983), 7 C.C.C. (3d) 542
(N.W.T.C.A.), Laycraft J.A., for the court, acknowledged that the personal attributes
of an accused should be excluded from the objective test but held that the background events should be taken into consideration. He put his position in these words
(at p. 554):

> The purpose of the objective test … is to consider the actions of the accused in a spe-
> cific case against the standard of the ordinary person. Hypothetically, the ordinary per-
> son is subjected to the same external pressures of insult by acts or words as was the
> accused. Only if those pressures would cause an ordinary person to lose self-control
> does the next question arise whether the accused did, in fact, lose self-control. In my
> view, the objective test lacks validity if the reaction of the hypothetical ordinary person
> is not tested against all of the events which put pressure on the accused.
>
> The requirement for suddenness of insult and reaction does not preclude a consid-
> eration of past events. The incident which finally triggers the reaction must be sudden
> and the reaction must be sudden but the incident itself may well be coloured and given
> meaning only by a consideration of events which preceded it. Indeed, one could imag-
> ine a case in which a given gesture, in itself innocuous, could not be perceived as in-
> sulting unless the jury was aware of previous events. They disclose the nature, depth
> and quality of the insult.

[17]  In *R. v. Conway* (1985), 17 C.C.C. (3d) 481, 14 W.C.B. 7 (Ont. C.A.),
Howland C.J.O. concluded that the history and background of the relationship between the victim and the accused is relevant and pertinent to the "ordinary person"
test. He stated at p. 487:

> [The trial judge] should have told [the jury] present acts or insults, in themselves insuf-
> ficient to cause an ordinary man to lose self-control, may indeed cause such loss of
> self-control when they are connected with past events and external pressures of insult
> by acts or words and accordingly in considering whether an ordinary man would have
> lost self-control they must consider an ordinary man who had experienced the same
> series of acts or insults as experienced by the appellant. …

[18] In my view, so long as the provocation section remains in the *Criminal Code* in its present form, certain characteristics will have to be assigned to the "ordinary person" in assessing the objective element. The "ordinary person" must be of the same age, and sex, and share with the accused such other factors as would give the act or insult in question a special significance and have experienced the same series of acts or insults as those experienced by the accused.

[19] In summary then, the wrongful act or insult must be one which could, in light of the past history of the relationship between the accused and the deceased, deprive an ordinary person, of the same age, and sex, and sharing with the accused such other factors as would give the act or insult in question a special significance, of the power of self-control.

### The Subjective Element

[20] In *R. v. Tripodi*, [1955] S.C.R. 438, Rand J. interpreted "sudden provocation" to mean that "the wrongful act or insult must strike upon a mind unprepared for it, that it must make an unexpected impact that takes the understanding by surprise and sets the passions aflame" (p. 68 C.C.C., p. 447 D.L.R.). To this definition, I would add that the background and history of the relationship between the accused and the deceased should be taken into consideration. This is particularly appropriate if it reveals a long history of insults, levelled at the accused by the deceased. This is so even if the insults might induce a desire for revenge so long as immediately before the last insult, the accused did not intend to kill. Glanville Williams adopts this position in his *Textbook of Criminal Law*, 2nd ed. (London: Stevens & Sons, 1983). At p. 530, he puts it in this way: "affronts over a long period of time inducing the desire for revenge do not preclude the defence of provocation, if immediately before the last affront the defendant did not intend to kill." He adds further that, "the last affront may be comparatively trivial, merely the last straw that makes the worm turn, so to speak."

[21] Further support for the position that the prior history of the relationship may as well be taken into account in assessing the subjective aspect can be found in the dissenting reasons of Foisy J.A. in *R. v. Sheridan* (1990), 55 C.C.C. (3d) 313. There, Foisy J.A. stated:

> The trial judge's finding that the accused appellant had acted in the heat of passion caused by sudden provocation took into account the finding that the appellant, a cocaine addict, was irritable and anxious at the time. Further there was the sudden throwing of the bottle just after the final and absolute death threat uttered by Miller. This, together with the previous history of threats of violence against the appellant and his wife was found by the learned trial judge to have incited the appellant.

These reasons were specifically adopted by this court: see *R. v. Sheridan*, [1991] 2 S.C.R. 205. These then are the considerations which the trial judge must take into account in making assessment as to whether or not there was any evidence upon which a reasonable jury acting judicially and properly instructed could find that the defence of provocation could be applicable in the circumstances of this case.

*Bearing in Mind the Principles Pertaining to Provocation, Was*
*There Any Evidence Adduced in This Case Which Required the*
*Trial Judge To Leave That Defence with the Jury?*

[22]  In this case, there is no doubt that the relationship of the wife of the accused
with the deceased was the dominating factor in the tragic killing. Obviously, events
leading to the breakup of the marriage can never warrant taking the life of another.
Affairs cannot justify murder. Yet the provocation defence section has always been
and is presently a part of the *Criminal Code*. Any recognition of human frailties must
take into account that these very situations may lead to insults that could give rise to
provocation. Some European penal codes recognize "crimes of passion" as falling
within a special category. Indeed, many of the Canadian cases which have considered
the applicability of the defence arise from such situations: see, for example, the cases
of *Daniels* and *Conway*, supra. The defence of provocation does no more than recognize human frailties. Reality and the past experience of the ages recognize that this
sort of situation may lead to acts of provocation. Each case must be considered in the
context of its particular facts to determine if the evidence meets the requisite threshold test necessary to establish provocation.

*The Objective Element of the Test*

[23]  In this case, it is appropriate to take into account the history of the relationship between the accused and the deceased. The accused's wife had, on a prior occasion, planned to leave him for the deceased but he had managed to convince her to
return to him. He hoped to accomplish the same result when his wife left him for the
deceased on this second occasion. At the time of the shooting he was distraught and
had been without sleep for some 34 hours. When he turned into the parking-lot of his
wife's employer he still wished to talk to her in private. Later, when the deceased
held his wife by her shoulders in a proprietary and possessive manner and moved her
back and forth in front of him while he taunted the accused to shoot him, a situation
was created in which the accused could have believed that the deceased was mocking
him and preventing him from his having the private conversation with his wife which
was so vitally important to him.

[24]  Taking into account the past history between the deceased and the accused, a
jury could find the actions of the deceased to be taunting and insulting. It might be
found that, under the same circumstances, an ordinary person who was a married
man, faced with the breakup of his marriage, would have been provoked by the actions of the deceased so as to cause him to lose his power of self-control. There was
some evidence, therefore, that would satisfy the objective element of the test. Next, it
remains to be seen whether there was evidence that could fulfil the subjective element of the test.

*The Subjective Element of the Test*

[25]  It must be determined whether there was evidence that the appellant was
actually provoked. Once again it is necessary to take into account the past history

involving the accused, the deceased and his wife. Further, it cannot be forgotten that the accused had not slept for some 34 hours and that he described himself as being devastated, stressed out and suicidal. He emphasized how important it was to him to talk to his wife in private, away from the deceased. It was in this manner that he successfully persuaded his wife to stay with him on the earlier occasion. When his wife returned to her employer's parking-lot and the deceased came out of the building, he testified that his thoughts were "here is the man that won't give me a half hour alone with my wife after 21 years and he has had her for 24 hours the night before."

[26] It was when the deceased put his arm around his wife's waist and started leading her back towards the building that the appellant removed the rifle from the car. He testified that he did so as a bluff. He hoped it would make them take him more seriously and succeed in convincing his wife to accompany him so that they could talk privately. From this point, the deceased's actions could be construed as a conscious attempt to test the appellant's limits. When he saw that the appellant had a gun, he advanced towards him. The appellant's wife was in front of the deceased and the deceased had his hands on her shoulders. The appellant recalled that the deceased was swinging Mrs. Thibert from side to side like a moving target. While doing this, the deceased was laughing and grinning at the appellant. He also dared the appellant to fire and taunted him by saying: "Come on big fellow, shoot me. You want to shoot me? Go ahead and shoot me." The deceased continued to approach the appellant, proceeding as fast as he could. In turn, the appellant kept backing up and told the deceased to "stay back," but the deceased continued to approach him. The appellant testified that he remembered wanting to scream because the deceased would not stop coming towards him. The appellant's eyes were tightly closed when he fired the gun. The time the appellant held the gun until he fired was not long. The events unfolded very quickly, in a matter of moments, seconds, not minutes.

[27] The respondent submitted that "[r]ejection in the context of a romantic relationship will not constitute a basis for the provocation defence." This is correct. If the appellant had simply brooded over the unhappy situation, put a rifle in his car and gone looking for the deceased, then the history of the deceased's relationship with the wife of the accused could not be used as a basis for a defence of provocation because the necessary final act of provocation was missing. However, in this case, rejection is not the most significant or overriding factor. The appellant sought to avoid the deceased in order to talk privately with his wife. The evidence indicates that the confrontation with the deceased in the parking-lot was unexpected. The appellant had gone to some lengths to avoid meeting the deceased.

[28] In my view, there was evidence upon which a reasonable jury acting judicially and properly instructed could have concluded that the defence of provocation was applicable. Next, it must be considered whether the acts of the deceased were those which he had a legal right to do and thus within the exemption described in s. 232(3).

*Were the Acts of the Deceased Ones Which He Had a Legal*
*Right To Do but Which Were Nevertheless Insulting?*

[29] It will be remembered that s. 232(3) provides that "no one shall be deemed to have given provocation to another by doing anything that he had a legal right to do." In the context of the provocation defence, the phrase "legal right" has been defined as meaning a right which is sanctioned by law as distinct from something which a person may do without incurring legal liability. Thus, the defence of provocation is open to someone who is "insulted." The words or act put forward as provocation need not be words or act which are specifically prohibited by the law. It was put in this way in *R. v. Galgay*, [1972] 2 O.R. 630 (C.A.), by Brooke J.A.:

> The absence of a remedy against doing or saying something or the absence of a specific legal prohibition in that regard does not mean or imply that there is a legal right to so act. There may be no legal remedy for an insult said or done in private but that is not because of legal right. The section distinguishes legal right from wrongful act or insult and the proviso of the section ought not to be interpreted to license insult or wrongful act done or spoken under the cloak of legal right. ...

[30] Thus, while the actions of the deceased in the parking-lot were clearly not prohibited by law, they could none the less be found by a jury to constitute insulting behaviour. In light of the past history, possessive or affectionate behaviour by the deceased towards the appellant's wife coupled with his taunting remarks could be considered to be insulting. Nor can it be said that these actions really constituted self-defence. The deceased was told by the appellant's wife that the gun was unloaded and he may have believed her. In any event, he continued to advance towards the appellant and to goad him to shoot despite the request to stop. In the circumstances, the actions of the deceased could well be found not to be acts of self-defence. A jury could infer that it was the taunting of the appellant by the deceased who was preventing him from talking privately with his wife which was the last straw that led him to fire the rifle suddenly before his passion had cooled. While the deceased's conduct might not have been specifically prohibited nor susceptible to a remedy it was not sanctioned by any legal right.

[31] In summary, there was some evidence upon which a reasonable jury acting judicially and properly instructed could find that the defence of provocation was applicable. It was appropriate for the trial judge to leave this defence with the jury. Once it was determined the defence should be left, then the trial judge was required to correctly relate the principles of reasonable doubt as they applied to that defence. ...

*Disposition*

[35] In the result, I would allow the appeal, set aside the decision of the Court of Appeal and direct a new trial on the charge of second degree murder.

MAJOR J. (Iacobucci J. concurring, dissenting):

[36] This appeal concerns the application of the defence of provocation found in s. 232 of the *Criminal Code*, R.S.C. 1985, c. C-46. Specifically at issue is whether

the trial judge was correct in leaving the defence with the jury, and if so, whether the jury charge can be saved by s. 686(1)(b)(iii).

*I. Facts*

[37]  The appellant Norman Eugene Thibert was charged with first degree murder in the shooting death of his estranged wife's lover, Alan Sherren. Norman Eugene Thibert married his wife, Joan Thibert, in July, 1970. The couple had two children, Michelle, and Catrina, aged 22 and 19 respectively, at the time of the trial.

[38]  The Thiberts' marriage had its share of problems. Early on in the marriage, Mr. Thibert admitted to his wife that he had had three extramarital affairs. In September, 1990, Mrs. Thibert began an intimate relationship with the deceased, a co-worker. She disclosed this relationship to her husband in April, 1991. He was distraught and eventually convinced his wife to remain with him and attempt to make their marriage work.

[39]  On July 2, 1991, Mrs. Thibert decided to leave her husband. She took a hotel room rather than returning home. The appellant drove around the city that evening, unsuccessfully searching for the hotel where his wife was staying. When he returned home, he removed a rifle and a shotgun from the basement of the house to the garage. He testified that he thought about killing the deceased, his wife, or himself. He loaded the rifle, and then left the guns in a corner of the garage, having at that point abandoned his violent thoughts.

[40]  The daughter, Catrina arrived home to find her father very upset. He told her of her mother's affair. At approximately 11:00 p.m., Mrs. Thibert telephoned her husband at home to tell him of her decision to leave him. At his request, she agreed to meet him the next morning, at Smitty's Restaurant in St. Albert, a suburb of Edmonton at 7:00 a.m.

[41]  The next morning Mr. Thibert and Catrina went to the restaurant to meet Mrs. Thibert who arrived at the meeting with the deceased. The appellant attempted to persuade her to return home with him, but she refused. The meeting at Smitty's lasted approximately one hour. At the end of the meeting, Mr. Thibert promised not to bother his wife at work, and in return, she promised to think about coming home that night to again talk to him. Outside the restaurant, while waiting for Mrs. Thibert to finish talking with Catrina, the appellant told the deceased, "I hope you intend on moving back east or living under assumed names … Because as long as I have got breath in my body I am not going to give up trying to get my wife back from you, and I will find you wherever you go."

[42]  The appellant testified that, when he returned home, he thought about killing himself, and so returned to the garage and retrieved the guns. He sawed off the barrel of the shotgun, but then discovered that the gun was inoperable since the firing pin was broken.

[43]  He telephoned his wife at work several times in an effort to persuade her to return to him.

[44]  During one afternoon call, she asked him to stop phoning her and told him that she was leaving work to make a bank deposit. The appellant then drove into

the city, planning to find his wife while she was at the bank, and away from the influence of the deceased, and again attempt to convince her to give the marriage another try.

[45] He put the loaded rifle in the back of his car before departing, thinking that he might have to kill the deceased. He testified that a few miles from home he abandoned that thought, but instead planned to use the rifle as a final bluff to get his wife to come with him. The police later seized a box of shells from the vehicle, although the appellant stated that he did not remember placing the ammunition in the car.

[46] At approximately 2:45 p.m., the appellant parked across the street from his wife's place of work. When he saw Mrs. Thibert depart for the bank, he followed her. She noticed him at a stoplight, at which time he attempted to persuade her to get into his car so they could talk. The appellant followed Mrs. Thibert to the bank, and insisted that they go some place private to talk. Mrs. Thibert agreed to meet him in a vacant lot but instead, out of fear returned to her workplace. The appellant followed her into the parking-lot. The appellant again tried to persuade Mrs. Thibert to go some place with him to talk, but she continued to refuse.

[47] The appellant told Mrs. Thibert that he had a high-powered rifle in his car, but claimed that it was not loaded. He suggested that he would have to go into Mrs. Thibert's workplace and use the gun. At that time, the deceased came out of the building and began to lead Mrs. Thibert back into the office. The appellant then removed the rifle from the car.

[48] The appellant's evidence was that the deceased began walking towards him, with his hands on Mrs. Thibert's shoulders swinging her back and forth, saying, "You want to shoot me? Go ahead and shoot me." and "Come on big fellow, shoot me. You want to shoot me? Go ahead and shoot me." At some point, Mrs. Thibert either moved, or was moved aside. The appellant testified that the deceased kept coming towards him, ignoring the appellant's instructions to stay back. The appellant testified that his eyes were closed as he tried to retreat inward and the gun discharged.

[49] After the shot, Mrs. Thibert ran into the office building. At some point, the appellant put the gun down, entered the office building, and calmly said that he wanted to talk to his wife. He then exited the building, picked up the gun, put more ammunition in it, and said he was not going to hurt anyone. He placed the gun in his car and drove away.

[50] While he was driving, the appellant noticed a police car following him. He pulled off onto a side-road, and surrendered to the police. At the time of his arrest, Constable Baumgartner recorded that the appellant stated: "It's out of me now. He was fooling around with my wife." Constable Turner recorded the appellant's statement as: "For what it's worth, I was just after him. For what it's worth, it's out of me now. He was fooling around with my wife." ...

*IV. Issues*

1.  Was the defence of provocation properly left with the jury?

2.  If so, can the verdict be saved by the application of s. 686(1)(b)(iii) of the *Criminal Code*?

## V. Analysis

### A. Was the Defence of Provocation Properly Left with the Jury?

...

[63] In my opinion, in this case there is no evidence of a wrongful act or insult sufficient to deprive an ordinary person of the power of self-control. That the deceased may have positioned Mrs. Thibert between himself and the appellant cannot constitute a wrongful act or insult. Nor can the statements "You want to shoot me? Go ahead and shoot me" and "Come on big fellow, shoot me" be considered a wrongful act or insult. Those actions are not contemptuous or scornful; they are legitimate reactions to a dangerous situation. It would be improper to require victims to respond in a certain way when faced with armed, threatening individuals. The defence claim that the wrongful act or insult came from the appellant's evidence that the deceased used Joan Thibert as a shield while taunting him to shoot is ironic. The appellant had control of the only true weapon involved in this situation, the rifle.

[64] Further, that the deceased had a personal relationship with Mrs. Thibert is not a wrongful act or insult sufficient to cause an ordinary person to lose the power of self-control. The breakup of a marriage due to an extramarital affair cannot constitute such a wrongful act or insult. I agree with the statement of Freeman J.A. in *R. v. Young* (1993), 78 C.C.C. (3d) 538 at p. 542 that:

> It would set a dangerous precedent to characterize terminating a relationship as an insult or wrong act capable of constituting provocation to kill. The appellant may have been feeling anger, frustration and a sense of loss, particularly if he was in a position of emotional dependency on the victim as his counsel asserts, but that is not provocation of a kind to reduce murder to manslaughter.

[65] Similarly, it would be a dangerous precedent to characterize involvement in an extramarital affair as conduct capable of grounding provocation, even when coupled with the deceased's reactions to the dangerous situation he faced. At law, no one has either an emotional or proprietary right or interest in a spouse that would justify the loss of self-control that the appellant exhibited.

[66] In that connection, Cory J. states that the events leading to the breakup of a relationship are not factors going to provocation but I wonder whether the effect of his reasons is such that these factors have been taken into account in the context of provocation. My colleague emphasizes that the accused still wished to see his wife alone after the end of the relationship. However, in my view, she had made it clear on a number of occasions that she did not wish to be alone with him. This was a choice that Joan Thibert was free to make. The accused had no right or entitlement to speak with his wife in private. The fact that the accused believed that the deceased was preventing him from doing so is not, with respect, a fact that ought to be taken into account when considering the defence of provocation.

[67] If I am wrong and the objective threshold test for provocation is met, the appeal would fail on the subjective element of the test. The appellant had known of his wife's involvement with the deceased for some time. He knew his wife wanted to leave him, and had seen the deceased with his wife earlier that day. It cannot be said

that the appellant's mind was unprepared for the sight of his wife with the deceased such that he was taken by surprise and his passions were set aflame. There was no element of suddenness on the facts of this case.

[68] For these reasons, I am of the opinion that neither the objective branch nor the subjective branch of the threshold test for leaving the defence of provocation with the jury has been met. There is no evidence on which a reasonable jury, acting judicially could find a wrongful act or insult sufficient to deprive the ordinary person of the power of self-control. Neither is there any evidence that the appellant acted on the sudden. The defence should not have been left with the jury. This was an error that did not prejudice the appellant.

*B. The Application of Section 686(1)(b)(iii)*

[69] In view of the conclusion I have reached regarding the applicability of the defence of provocation in this case, it is not necessary to consider the application of s. 686(1)(b)(iii) of the *Criminal Code*.

*VI. Disposition*

[70] I would dismiss the appeal.

## II. PROVOCATION AND INTENT

The cases in this section explore the relationship of the partial defence of provocation and the intent for murder in s. 229(a) of the *Criminal Code* (see chapter 13). The central issue is whether provocation is a defence that vitiates or compromises the intent for murder, or whether it operates outside the scope of the positive fault requirements for murder as an independent excuse. The issue was first probed in the unlikely context of a case of attempted murder in *R. v. Campbell*. While the court concluded that the partial defence of provocation is available only as a defence to murder, Martin J.A.'s comments on the issue of intent and provocation are valuable.

**R. v. Campbell**
Ontario Court of Appeal
(1977), 38 C.C.C. (2d) 6

[The accused was charged with the attempted murder of his wife, Susan Campbell. Among other things, the accused relied on the defence tried to rely on the defence of provocation. The defence was rejected as a defence to attempted murder, but Mr. Justice Martin made some valuable observations about the defence.]

MARTIN J.A.: ... The first ground of appeal advanced was that the trial Judge erred in failing to leave with the jury the defence of provocation. Mr. Gold, in a very attractive argument, contended that provocation is a defence to attempted murder, as well as murder. He put his argument in this way: The intent requisite for attempted murder is an intent to do that which if death ensued would constitute murder. If the accused's intent to do what he did was the result of provocation sufficient to reduce murder to manslaughter, then he did not have the intent to do that which if death ensued would constitute murder (notwithstanding he had the intent to kill or the intent to cause bodily harm which he knew was likely to cause death under *Criminal Code*, s. 212(a)(i)(ii)) [now s. 229(a)(ii)], since if death ensued he would be guilty of manslaughter only. He contended that if the jury found provocation, the proper verdict was guilty of attempted manslaughter.

This argument assumes that absence of provocation is implicit in the definition of murder. The argument, put in a slightly different way, is that the *actus reus* of murder is an unprovoked killing, which is what the accused must intend to bring about in order to be guilty of attempted murder. In support of this contention we were referred to a number of Australian and New Zealand cases: see *R. v. Newman*, [1948] V.L.R. 61; *R. v. Spartels*, [1953] V.L.R. 194; *R. v. Smith*, [1964] N.Z.L.R. 834. See also *Australian Criminal Law*, 2nd ed., by Colin Howard at pp. 148-52.

In support of his submission that the intent required to constitute attempted murder is an intent to do that which if death ensued would constitute murder. Mr. Gold relied on the judgment of the Supreme Court of Canada in *Lajoie v. The Queen*, [1974] 1 S.C.R. 399, and particularly the following passage at p. 406 S.C.R.:

> The word "intent" does not appear in s. 210 [now s. 222]. It appears in the definition of an attempt in s. 24, but the reference there is to "having an intent to commit an offence." For the reasons already given, it is my view that, in the light of the wording of s. 210, there may be an intent to do that which constitutes the commission of the offence of murder without that intent being to kill the victim.

Provocation as a defence to murder is based on a loss of self-control as a result of sudden provocation rather than on its negativing the requisite intent, and the law is now settled beyond question that provocation reduces murder to manslaughter notwithstanding the existence of an intent to kill: see *A.-G. Ceylon v. Perera*, [1953] A.C. 200; *Lee Chun-Chuen v. The Queen*, [1963] A.C. 220.

Mr. Gold's submission was not, however, that provocation negatives an intent to kill or to cause bodily harm known to the offender to be likely to cause death, but that it negatives intent to murder, which is the intent required to constitute attempted murder, and an intent to murder requires an absence of provocation.

Although the argument is attractive, it is, in my view, unsound. Absence of provocation is not part of the *actus reus* of murder in the sense that absence of consent is part of the *actus reus* of rape. The defence of provocation exists with respect to a charge of murder even though all the elements of the definition of murder have been established; it is an allowance made for human frailty which recognizes that a killing, even an intentional one, is extenuated by the loss of self-control caused by adequate provocation, and is less heinous than an intentional killing by a person in possession of his self-control. It is unnecessary to invoke the defence of provocation until all the elements of murder have been proved. ...

I am, moreover, of the view that the language of s. 215 is consistent only with the defence of provocation being limited to reducing murder to manslaughter. In addition, the great weight of authority in the British Commonwealth holds that the defence of provocation is available only where the charge is murder: see *Holmes v. Director of Public Prosecutions*, [1946] A.C. 588 at p. 601; *R. v. Cunningham* (1958), 43 Cr. App. R. 79 at pp. 82-3; *R. v. Falla*, [1964] V.R. 78; *R. v. Laga*, [1969] N.Z.L.R. 417; *R. v. Jack* (1970), 17 C.R.N.S. 38; *R. v. Bruzas*, [1972] Crim. L.R. 367. I am accordingly of the opinion that the trial Judge was right in not putting the limited defence of provocation to the jury, since it did not apply on a charge of attempted murder.

I would, however, make an additional observation. As previously indicated, the defence of provocation, where it applies, is based on the loss of self-control caused by the provocation, and not on its negativing the intent requisite for murder. Provocation may, of course, inspire the intent required to constitute murder. There may, however, be cases where the conduct of the victim amounting to provocation produces in the accused a state of excitement, anger or disturbance, as a result of which he might not contemplate the consequences of his acts and might not, in fact, intend to bring about those consequences. The accused's intent must usually be inferred from his conduct and the surrounding circumstances, and in some cases the provocation afforded by the victim, when considered in relation to the totality of the evidence, might create a reasonable doubt in the mind of the jury whether the accused had the requisite intent. Thus, in some cases, the provocative conduct of the victim might be a relevant item of evidence on the issue of intent whether the charge be murder or attempted murder. This, I take it, was the view of Eveleigh J., in *R. v. Bruzas*, supra, at p. 369. Provocation in that aspect, however, does not operate as a "defence," but rather as a relevant item of evidence on the issue of intent.

In the present case, if the jury believed the appellant's evidence (or if it left them with a reasonable doubt) the conduct of the complainant in throwing gasoline at the appellant after she, while armed with a gun, had said she was going to kill him, was a relevant circumstance to be considered by the jury in deciding whether the appellant intended to shoot his wife or whether he fired instinctively and blindly as he testified. In my view, however, those circumstances were adequately put to the jury by the trial Judge in relation to the issue with respect to the appellant's intent.

**R. v. Cameron**
Ontario Court of Appeal
(1992), 71 C.C.C. (3d) 272

DOHERTY J.A.: The appellant was convicted of second degree murder. He was sentenced to life imprisonment without eligibility for parole for 10 years. He appeals his conviction alleging that the statutory defence of provocation set out in s. 232 of the Criminal Code contravenes ss. 7 and 11(d) of the *Canadian Charter of Rights and Freedoms*. ...

### *1. The Constitutional Challenge*

The appellant contends that the "defence of provocation operates by negativing an essential element of the *mens rea* for murder." He goes on to argue that as provocation is premised in part on an objective standard, the statutory definition of provocation cannot stand in light of the authorities which hold that liability for murder cannot be determined by reference to an objective fault standard: see *R. v. Martineau* (1990), 58 C.C.C. (3d) 353 (S.C.C.).

The argument misconceives the effect of s. 232. The section does not detract from or negative the fault requirement for murder, but serves as a partial excuse for those who commit what would be murder but for the existence of the partial defence created by s. 232. As the opening words of s. 232 plainly indicate, the defence only need be considered where the Crown has proved beyond a reasonable doubt that the accused committed murder: see *R. v. Campbell* (1977), 38 C.C.C. (2d) 6 at p. 15; *R. v. Oickle* (1984), 11 C.C.C (3d) 180 at p. 190 (S.C. App. Div.).

The statutory defence of provocation does not detract from the *mens rea* required to establish murder, but rather, where applicable, serves to reduce homicides committed with the *mens rea* necessary to establish murder to manslaughter.

The appellant also argues that, even if the statutory defence of provocation stands apart from the *mens rea* required for murder, ss. 7 and 11(d) of the Charter render the section inoperative in so far as it imposes an objective standard on the availability of the defence. He argues that for constitutional purposes there could be no distinction between a statutory provision which imposes liability for murder on an objective basis (e.g., s. 230(d)) and a statutory provision like s. 232 which limits the availability of a defence to murder according to an objective criterion.

I disagree. The former imposes liability in the absence of a constitutionally mandated minimum level of fault. The latter provides a partial excuse despite the existence of the constitutionally required level of fault. Section 232 does not impose liability where subjective fault does not exist but reduces the liability even when that fault exists.

The objective component of the statutory defence of provocation serves a valid societal purpose (see *R. v. Hill* (1986), 25 C.C.C. (3d) 322 at pp. 330-1), and cannot be said to be contrary to the principles of fundamental justice.

Resort to s. 11(d) of the Charter does not assist the appellant. Section 232 does not place any burden of proof on an accused to disprove anything essential to the establishing of his culpability. Indeed, the onus is on the Crown to negate provocation beyond a reasonable doubt: *Linney v. The Queen* (1977), 32 C.C.C. (2d) 294 (S.C.C.). Nor, for the reasons set out above, does s. 232 modify the statutory definition of murder so as to eliminate an element of the offence required by s. 7 of the Charter.

The constitutional argument fails.

### R. v. Parent
Supreme Court of Canada
(2001), 154 C.C.C. (3d) 1

McLACHLIN C.J.C.:

[1] On September 24, 1996, the respondent, Réjean Parent, shot and killed his estranged wife. She had initiated divorce proceedings four years earlier and they were involved in litigation over the division of their assets, some of which were held in a corporation. In the meantime, their financial situation deteriorated, to the point that Mr. Parent's shares were seized and put up for sale. The wife attended the sale, allegedly intending to buy the shares. Mr. Parent also attended. He carried a loaded gun with a locked security catch in his pocket. There, she suggested they speak and they retired into a nearby room. Shortly after, shots were heard. Mr. Parent had shot his wife six times. She died from the wounds later that night.

[2] Mr. Parent was charged with first degree murder. At trial, he testified that when they proceeded to the room his wife had said, in effect: "I told you that I would wipe you out completely." He then felt a hot flush rising and shot. He said he "didn't know what [he] was doing any more" and was aiming in front of him. He said he did not intend to kill his wife. After doing so, he left the building and spent the afternoon in a strip club before giving himself up to police that evening.

[3] At trial, Mr. Parent argued that the verdict should be reduced to manslaughter on the basis of lack of criminal intent or provocation. The jury found him guilty of manslaughter. He was sentenced to 16 years' imprisonment, and a lifetime prohibition on possessing firearms, ammunition and explosives. ...

[4] The Crown appealed the verdict of manslaughter, and Parent appealed the sentence. The Quebec Court of Appeal dismissed the appeal from the verdict without reasons, but in separate proceedings ((1999), 142 C.C.C. (3d) 82) reduced the sentence to six years' imprisonment, after giving Mr. Parent credit of two years for time served. In this Court, the appellant raised one point only: that the judge had erred in his instructions to the jury on the effect of anger, creating a "defence of anger" (défense de colère) distinct from the defence of provocation. The respondent, for his part, argued that any difficulties in the judge's directions to the jury were cleared up in his redirection on provocation in answer to jury questions and that the jury properly convicted the accused of manslaughter on the basis of provocation.

[5] Two issues are raised: (1) whether the trial judge erred in his charge to the jury on intention, and (2) if so, whether that error was cured by the redirection. I conclude that the trial judge erred in his direction on intention and that the recharge did not eliminate the possibility that this error led the jury wrongly to find the respondent guilty of manslaughter. Accordingly, the conviction must be set aside and a new trial ordered.

*1. Did the Trial Judge Err in His Charge to the Jury on Intention?*

[6] The jury had three possible offences before it: first degree murder, second degree murder and manslaughter. All three offences require proof of an act of kill-

ing (*actus reus*) and the corresponding criminal intention (*mens rea*). In rela tion to murder, the defence of provocation does not eliminate the need for proof of intention to kill, but operates as an excuse that has the effect of reducing murder to manslaughter.

[7] The Crown argues that the trial judge erred in suggesting that anger is capable of negating the intention to kill and that the jury could reduce the offence to manslaughter on this basis. More particularly, the Crown suggests that the judge's directions wrongly treated anger as a matter that could negate the criminal intent or *mens rea* of the offence; wrongly suggested that negation of intent can reduce the offence to manslaughter; and wrongly left open the suggestion that anger alone can establish provocation, when in fact other requirements must be met pursuant to s. 232 of the *Criminal Code*, R.S.C. 1985, c. C-46. The gravamen of the Crown's submission is that the trial judge's direction on intention was confusing and wrong and left it open to the jury to convict the accused of manslaughter, not on the basis of provocation (which the trial judge correctly defined), but on the erroneous basis that a high degree of anger short of provocation, as defined in law, could negate the criminal intent or *mens rea* of the offence.

[8] The Crown objects to the portions of the jury charge in which the trial judge stated that the jury must take into account [TRANSLATION] "evidence surrounding the defence of provocation raised by the accused" in determining the accused's intent to kill. The Crown also objects to the trial judge's treatment of *mens rea* in the following passages:

> For example, murder may be reduced to manslaughter where a person's state of mind is affected by alcohol consumption, drug consumption or where a person's state of mind is obscured or diminished by an outside force, by an incident like, for example, *a fit of anger*.
>
> You no doubt appreciate that we are not talking about an arbitrary reduction.
>
> In other words, it is not sufficient for a person to simply say "I was drinking" or "I took some drugs" or "I was really angry."
>
> That alone, that's not enough, and all that always depends on the circumstances. It always depends on the nature of the facts at issue, of external influences, or outside influences capable of affecting one's state of mind.
>
> It depends on the nature of the fact at issue, of its importance, its seriousness, its intensity in relation to the action that was taken by the person who committed the crime, all the while taking into account the evidence as a whole and all the circumstances.
>
> So, you must look at the accused's state of mind when he killed Suzanne Bédard, you look at the entire evidence, including the elements surrounding the provocation defence with a view to determining whether he acted with the criminal intention that I defined earlier.
>
> Here, the accused, when he testified, described to you his state of mind when Suzanne Bédard said the words in question.
>
> You must then decide if this incident *was sufficiently serious, important, intense so as to cause him to lose his faculties to the point of reducing the crime of murder to manslaughter.*

You will ask yourselves if his state of mind was affected, diminished, and if so, the intensity, the degree to which, taking into account all the circumstances at the time when he did what he did.

To reduce murder to manslaughter, you must come to the conclusion that the influence of the events that occurred was *strong enough, important enough, intense enough to cause the accused to not know or not want what he was doing by reason of his state of mind, that his faculties were too diminished to fully assess the situation, or that raise a reasonable doubt in his favour, in this respect.* [Emphasis added.]

[9] The Crown argues that this passage creates a halfway house defence of anger, between non-mental disorder automatism and provocation. I agree. This passage suggests that anger, if sufficiently serious or intense, but not amounting to the defence of provocation, may reduce murder to manslaughter. It also suggests that anger, if sufficiently intense, may negate the criminal intention for murder. These connected propositions are not legally correct. Intense anger alone is insufficient to reduce murder to manslaughter.

[10] The passage cited overstates the effect of anger. Anger can play a role in reducing murder to manslaughter in connection with the defence of provocation. Anger is not a stand-alone defence. It may form part of the defence of provocation when all the requirements of that defence are met: (1) a wrongful act or insult that would have caused an ordinary person to be deprived of his or her self-control; (2) which is sudden and unexpected; (3) which in fact caused the accused to act in anger; (4) before having recovered his or her normal control: *R. v. Thibert* (1996), 104 C.C.C. (3d 1 (S.C.C.). Again, anger conceivably could, in extreme circumstances, cause someone to enter a state of automatism in which that person does not know what he or she is doing, thus negating the voluntary component of the *actus reus*: *R. v. Stone* (1999), 134 C.C.C. (3d) 353 (S.C.C.). However, the accused did not assert this defence. In any event, the defence if successful would result in acquittal, not reduction to manslaughter.

[11] So it seems clear that the trial judge misdirected the jury on the effect of anger in relation to manslaughter. His directions left it open to the jury to find the accused guilty of manslaughter, on the basis of the anger felt by the accused, even if they concluded that the conditions required for the defence of provocation were not met. The directions raise the possibility that the jury's verdict of manslaughter may have been based on erroneous legal principles, unless they were corrected in the recharge to the jury. ...

### 3. Conclusion

[18] The trial judge erred in his charge to the jury on the effect of anger on criminal intent or *mens rea* and its relationship to manslaughter. This error was not corrected on the recharge and we cannot infer from the way the trial proceeded that the jury's verdict of manslaughter was not based on the erroneous initial direction. It follows that the conviction for manslaughter must be set aside and a new trial directed.

[19] As indicated earlier, the Crown in this appeal, relied solely on the trial judge's misdirections on anger and criminal intent. It is therefore unnecessary to comment

further on the applicability of the defence of provocation as it may be tendered at the new trial. It will be for the judge on the new trial to determine whether, on the evidence there presented, the defence of provocation should be put to the jury.

[20] I would allow the appeal and direct a new trial on second degree murder.

[For commentaries on this case, see Gary T. Trotter, "Provocation, Anger and the Intent for Murder: A Comment on *R. v. Parent*" (2002), 47 *McGill L.J.* 669 and Joanne Kleinberg, "Anger and Intent for Murder: The Supreme Court Decision in *R. v. Parent*" (2002), *O.H.L.J.* 37.]

### ADDITIONAL READING

- K. Roach, *Criminal Law*, 3rd ed. (Toronto: Irwin Law, 2004), chapter 8;
- A. Mewett and M. Manning, *Criminal Law*, 3rd ed. (Toronto: Butterworths, 1994), at 582-86;
- D. Stuart, *Canadian Criminal Law*, 4th ed. (Toronto: Carswell, 2001), at 533-48;
- E. Colvin, *Principles of Criminal Law*, 2nd ed. (Toronto: Carswell, 1991), at 253-60;
- A. Mewett, "Murder and Intent: Self-Defence and Provocation" (1984-85), 27 *Crim. L.Q.* 433;
- T.L. Archibald and P.K. Tait, "A Postscript to *R. v. Hill*: Whither Goest Provocation?" (1986-87), 29 *Crim. L.Q.* 172;
- J. Dressler, "Provocation: Partial Justification or Partial Excuse?" (1988), 51 *Mod. L. Rev.* 487;
- T. Quigley, "Deciphering the Defence of Provocation" (1989), 38 *U.N.B.L.J.* 11;
- T. Quigley, "Battered Women and the Defence of Provocation" (1991), 55 *Sask. Law Rev.* 223;
- A. Ashworth, *Principles of Criminal Law*, 2nd ed. (Oxford: Oxford University Press, 1995), at 201-4;
- D. Klimchuk, "Outrage, Self-Control and Culpability" (1994), 44 *U.T.L.J.* 441;
- E.M. Hyland, "*R. v. Thibert*: Are There Any Ordinary People Left?" (1996-97), 28 *Ottawa L. Rev.* 145.

# CHAPTER FIFTEEN

# Mental Disorder

Before 1992, the *Criminal Code* provided:

16.(1) No person shall be convicted of an offence in respect of an act or omission on his part while he was insane.

(2) For the purposes of this section a person is insane when he is in a state of natural imbecility or has disease of the mind to an extent that renders him incapable of appreciating the nature and quality of an act or omission or of knowing that an act or omission is wrong.

(3) A person who has specific delusions, but is in other respects sane, shall not be acquitted on the ground of insanity unless the delusions caused him to believe in the existence of a state of things that, if it existed, would have justified or excused his act or omission.

(4) Every one shall, until the contrary is proved, be presumed to be and to have been sane.

In 1992, s. 16 was changed to provide:

16.(1) No person is criminally responsible for an act committed or an omission made while suffering from a mental disorder that rendered the person incapable of appreciating the nature and quality of the act or omission or of knowing that it was wrong.

(2) Every person is presumed not to suffer from a mental disorder so as to be exempt from criminal responsibility by virtue of subsection (1), until the contrary is proved on the balance of probabilities.

(3) The burden of proof that an accused was suffering from a mental disorder so as to be exempt from criminal responsibility is on the party that raises the issue.

Note that mental disorder is defined in s. 2 as a disease of the mind preserving the pre-1992 jurisprudence on this issue.

This chapter first examines the important preliminary procedural matters affecting the mental disorder defence including fitness to stand trial, restrictions on the ability of the Crown to raise the mental disorder issue, the burden of proof placed on the proponent of the mental disorder issue, and the consequences of acceptance of the defence. The rest of the chapter examines the constituent elements of the mental disorder defence—the first element being the threshold requirement that the accused has a mental disorder or disease of the mind. It then examines the two alternative arms of the mental disorder defence—namely, whether the mental disorder renders the person incapable of appreciating the nature and quality of the act or omission, or whether the mental disorder rendered the person incapable of knowing that the act or omission was wrong. The next section examines the interaction of these alternative arms of the mental disorder defence and the final section examines proposals for legislative reform.

## I. PROCEDURAL ELEMENTS OF THE MENTAL DISORDER DEFENCE

### Unfitness To Stand Trial

The mental disorder defence is directed toward the accused's condition at the time that the offence was alleged to have been committed. Nevertheless, a mental disorder may persist or arise and be of such an extent that that the accused will be found unfit to stand trial. Section 2 of the *Criminal Code* provides that:

> "unfit to stand trial" means unable on account of mental disorder to conduct a defence at any stage of the proceedings before a verdict is rendered or to instruct counsel to do so, and, in particular, unable on account of mental disorder to
>
> (a) understand the nature or object of the proceedings,
>
> (b) understand the possible consequences of the proceedings, or
>
> (c) communicate with counsel;

> 672.22 An accused is presumed fit to stand trial unless the court is satisfied on the balance of probabilities that the accused is unfit to stand trial.

> 672.23(1) Where the court has reasonable grounds, at any stage of the proceedings before a verdict is rendered, to believe that the accused is unfit to stand trial, the court may direct, of its own motion or on application of the accused or the prosecutor, that the issue of fitness of the accused be tried.

> (2) An accused or a prosecutor who makes an application under subsection (1) has the burden of proof that the accused is unfit to stand trial.

> 672.24 Where the court has reasonable grounds to believe that an accused is unfit to stand trial and the accused is not represented by counsel, the court shall order that the accused be represented by counsel. ...

> 672.32(1) A verdict of unfit to stand trial shall not prevent the accused from being tried subsequently where the accused becomes fit to stand trial.

> (2) The burden of proof that the accused has subsequently become fit to stand trial is on the party who asserts it, and is discharged by proof on the balance of probabilities.

### R. v. Whittle
Supreme Court of Canada
[1994] 2 S.C.R. 914

SOPINKA J. observed for the Court: ... By virtue of s. 16 of the *Criminal Code*, persons suffering a disease of the mind in the circumstances defined in that section are exempted from criminal liability and punishment. The section embodies the policy of the law that such persons are sick as opposed to blameworthy and should be treated rather than punished: see *R. v. Chaulk* (1990), 62 C.C.C. (3d) 193 at p. 217. These persons are not, however, exempt from being tried. Part XX.1 of the *Criminal Code* contains detailed provisions providing for mental assessments by physicians and for determination of the fitness of persons suffering from mental disorders to stand trial. Section 672.23 provides that where, at any stage of the proceedings, the court believes on reasonable grounds that the accused is unfit to stand trial, it may direct the trial of that issue. The application can be made on the court's own motion or by the accused or the prosecutor. Many accused persons who are found not guilty by reason of a mental disorder are fit to stand trial. The fact that an accused is not criminally responsible within the meaning of s. 16, does not mean that he or she is unfit to stand trial. If the contrary were true there would be little purpose in providing for the plea authorized by s. 16. Most persons who suffered from the mental disorder defined in the section would be exempted from trial and would not get to plead until they had recovered subsequent to the date of the offence.

The test for fitness to stand trial is quite different from the definition of mental disorder in s. 16. It is predicated on the existence of a mental disorder and focuses on the ability to instruct counsel and conduct a defence. That test which was developed under the common law is now codified in s. 2 of the Code. ... It requires limited cognitive capacity to understand the process and to communicate with counsel. In *R. v. Taylor* (1992), 77 C.C.C. (3d) 551, 17 C.R. (4th) 371, the Ontario Court of Appeal, after reviewing the authorities, held that the trial judge erred in concluding that the accused must be capable of making rational decisions beneficial to him. At p. 567, Lacourcière J.A., on behalf of the court, stated:

> The "limited cognitive capacity" test strikes an effective balance between the objectives of the fitness rules and the constitutional right of the accused to choose his own defence and to have a trial within a reasonable time.

Accordingly, provided the accused possesses this limited capacity, it is not a prerequisite that he or she be capable of exercising analytical reasoning in making a choice to accept the advice of counsel or in coming to a decision that best serves her interests.

### Who Can Raise the Mental Disorder Issue?

**R. v. Swain**
Supreme Court of Canada
(1991), 63 C.C.C. (3d) 481

LAMER C.J. (Sopinka and Cory JJ. concurring) stated: ... I agree that it would be "manifestly" wrong if evidence of insanity were to influence the jury's decision on the issue of whether the accused committed the alleged act, but, with respect, I fail to see how the discretion of the trial judge to refuse to allow the Crown to raise insanity unless there is "convincing evidence" that the accused committed the alleged act will prevent this from happening. In my opinion, while the Ontario Court of Appeal [in *Simpson*] has recognized the prejudicial effect of allowing the Crown to raise evidence of insanity, it has not formulated a mechanism which adequately safeguards the right of the accused to control his or her defence.

In my view, the ability of the Crown to raise evidence of insanity over and above the accused's wishes, under the existing common law rule, does interfere with the accused's control over the conduct of his or her defence. However, this is not to say that if an accused chooses to raise evidence which tends to put his or her mental capacity for criminal intent into question but falls short of raising the defence of insanity (within s. 16), the Crown will be unable to raise its own evidence of insanity. In circumstances where the accused's own evidence tends to put his or her mental capacity for criminal intent into question, the Crown will be entitled to put forward its own evidence of insanity and the trial judge will be entitled to charge the jury on s. 16. ...

In my view, the objective of the common law rule which allows the Crown, in some cases, to raise evidence of insanity over and above the accused's wishes is twofold. One of the objectives was identified by Martin J.A. in *Simpson*, [35 C.C.C. (2d) 337, 77 D.L.R. (3d) 507, 16 O.R. (2d) 129 (Ont. C.A.)], at p. 362:

> ... to avoid the conviction of an accused who may not be responsible on account of insanity, but who refuses to adduce cogent evidence that he was insane.

The common law rule is aimed not only at avoiding the unfair treatment of the accused but also at maintaining the integrity of the criminal justice system itself. The accused is not the only person who has an interest in the outcome of the trial; society itself has an interest in ensuring that the system does not incorrectly label insane people as criminals.

The second objective was aptly characterized by the appellant as the protection of the public from presently dangerous persons requiring hospitalization. This objective arises from the fact that the Crown's option to simply discontinue the prosecution of an accused, whom it suspects was insane at the time of the offence, does not address the concern that such a person may well be presently dangerous and may therefore bring him or herself into contact with the criminal justice system once again. ...

The dual objectives discussed above could be met without unnecessarily limiting Charter rights if the existing common law rule were replaced with a rule which would allow the Crown to raise independently the issue of insanity only after the trier of fact had concluded that the accused was otherwise guilty of the offence charged. Under this scheme, the issue of insanity would be tried after a verdict of guilty had been reached, but prior to a conviction being entered. If the trier of fact then subsequently found that the accused was insane at the time of the offence, the verdict of not guilty by reason of insanity would be entered. Conversely, if the trier of fact found that the accused was not insane, within the meaning of s. 16, at the time of the offence a conviction would then be entered.

Such a rule would safeguard an accused's right to control his or her defence and would achieve both the objective of avoiding the conviction of a person who was insane at the time of the offence and the objective of protecting the public from a person who may be presently dangerous. Of course, an accused would also be entitled, under this scheme, to raise his s. 7 right not to be found guilty if he was insane at the time of the offence. An accused would, if he chooses not to do so earlier, raise the issue of insanity after the trier of fact has concluded that he or she was guilty of the offence charged, but before a verdict of guilty was entered. This is consistent with the accused's right, under our criminal justice system, to force the Crown to discharge its full burden of proof on the elements of *actus reus* and *mens rea* before raising other matters. However, this does not mean that the accused can raise insanity only after both *actus reus* and *mens rea* have been proven. While the Crown would be limited to raising evidence of insanity only after the trier of fact was satisfied that the full burden of proof on *actus reus* and *mens rea* had been discharged or after the accused's own defence has somehow put his or her mental capacity for criminal intent in issue, the accused would have the option of raising evidence of insanity at any time during the trial. ...

In my view, the new common law rule achieves the dual objectives enunciated above without limiting an accused's rights under s. 7 of the Charter. Under the new common law rule, there will only be two instances in which the Crown will be entitled to lead evidence of insanity. First, the Crown may raise evidence of insanity after the trier of fact has concluded that the accused is otherwise guilty of the offence charged. In these circumstances the Crown's ability to raise evidence of insanity cannot interfere with the conduct of the accused's defence because the Crown's ability to do so will not be triggered until after the accused has concluded his or her defence. Second, the Crown may raise evidence of insanity if the accused's own defence has (in the view of the trial judge) put the accused's capacity for criminal intent in issue. In these circumstances the Crown's ability to raise evidence of insanity is not inconsistent with the accused's right to control the conduct of his or her defence because the very issue has been raised by the accused's conduct of his or her defence. Furthermore, as was stated above, the Crown's ability to raise evidence of insanity only after an accused has put his or her mental capacity for criminal intent in issue does not raise the problem of the Crown's being able to place an accused in a position where inconsistent defences must be advanced.

[La Forest J. (Gonthier J. concurring) wrote an opinion substantially concurring with Lamer C.J. WILSON J. concurred in the result but disagreed with Lamer C.J. as to the "second instance" where the Crown can introduce evidence of insanity. She stated:]

While I agree with the Chief Justice that modifying the existing common law rule so as to give the prosecution only a conditional right to introduce evidence of insanity during the course of the trial, i.e., in circumstances where the accused has himself put his mental capacity in issue, is a less intrusive means of achieving the government objective, I am not sure that such modified common law rule can itself survive full Charter scrutiny. In my view, permitting the Crown to raise insanity during the course of the trial, even if that permission is conditional, still infringes upon the accused's right to control his defences. ... Nor can it satisfy the minimal impairment branch of the *Oakes* test because, although it is a less intrusive means of accomplishing the government's objective, it is not the least intrusive means of doing so.

I believe, moreover, that conferring on the prosecution a conditional right to raise the issue of insanity during the course of the trial infringes upon the equality rights of the mentally disabled under s. 15 of the Charter. It denies the mentally disabled, a group in our society which has been negatively stereotyped and historically disadvantaged, the control over their defences reposed in other accused persons and does so in a way which is discriminatory. In denying the mentally disabled personal autonomy in decision-making it reinforces the stereotype that they are incapable of rational thought and the ability to look after their own interests. In a word, it denies them equality with other accused persons under the guise, putting it at its best, of a benign paternalism. The prosecution's conditional right will only pass constitutional muster, in my view, if it can be shown that there exists no alternative that achieves the same objective without limiting the accused's s. 7 or s. 15 rights or at least limiting them to a significantly lesser degree.

It seems to me that the principle advanced in support of the prosecution's right to introduce evidence of insanity can be effectively implemented by having the issue of the accused's insanity raised at the conclusion of the trial in cases where the defences put forward by the accused have been rejected and the essential elements of the offence have been established by the prosecution beyond a reasonable doubt. At that point I think either party should be free to raise the issue of the accused's insanity. I realize, of course, that there is an element of circularity involved in this approach in that insanity has a direct bearing on proof of *mens rea*. However, I prefer this approach since it both respects the accused's right to waive the defence of insanity and ensures that any resultant prejudice he suffers in the finding of guilt flows from his own decision not to avail himself of the defence and not as a consequence of the prosecution's having raised the issue in the middle of the trial process.

## Burden of Proof

### R. v. Chaulk and Morrissette
Supreme Court of Canada
(1990), 62 C.C.C. (3d) 193

[In this case, the majority of the court held that the former s. 16(4) of the *Criminal Code*, which provides that "Everyone shall, until the contrary is proven, be presumed to be and to have been sane," violated s. 11(d) of the Charter, but was a "reasonable limit" under s. 1.]

LAMER C.J. (Dickson C.J., La Forest, Sopinka, and Cory JJ. concurring):  In my view, the principles enunciated in *Whyte* [*supra*, chapter 4] are applicable to this case and establish that the presumption of sanity embodied in s. 16(4) violates the presumption of innocence. If an accused is found to have been insane at the time of the offence, he will not be found guilty; thus the "fact" of insanity precludes a verdict of guilty. Whether the claim of insanity is characterized as a denial of *mens rea*, an excusing defence or, more generally, as an exemption based on criminal incapacity, the fact remains that sanity is essential for guilt. Section 16(4) allows a factor which is essential for guilt to be presumed, rather than proven by the Crown beyond a reasonable doubt. Moreover, it requires an accused to disprove sanity (or prove insanity) on a balance of probabilities; it therefore violates the presumption of innocence because it permits a conviction in spite of a reasonable doubt in the mind of the trier of fact as to the guilt of the accused. …

Accordingly, the objective of s. 16(4) is to avoid placing an impossible burden of proof on the Crown and to thereby secure the conviction of the guilty. In my view, this objective is sufficiently important to warrant limiting constitutionally protected rights and s. 16(4) passes the first branch of the *Oakes* test. …

It is not the role of this Court to second-guess the wisdom of policy choices made by Parliament. In enacting s. 16(4), Parliament may not have chosen the absolutely least intrusive means of meeting its objective, but it has chosen from a range of means which impair s. 11(d) as little as is reasonably possible. Within this range of means it is virtually impossible to know, let alone be sure, which means violate Charter rights the least. …

As I have mentioned above, the Charter does not require Parliament to "roll the dice" in its effort to achieve "pressing and substantial" objectives in order to adopt the absolutely least intrusive legislative provision.

While the effect of s. 16(4) on the presumption of innocence is clearly detrimental, given the importance of the objective that the Crown not be encumbered with an unworkable burden and given that I have concluded above that s. 16(4) limits s. 11(d) as little as is reasonably possible, it is my view that there is proportionality between the effects of the measure and the objective.

Accordingly, s. 16(4) is a reasonable limit on the presumption of innocence which can be upheld under s. 1 of the Charter.

[McLACHLIN J. (L'Heureux-Dubé and Gonthier JJ. concurring) held that s. 16(4) did not violate s. 11(d) of the Charter:]

I arrive then at this conclusion. To conceive the insanity provisions of the *Criminal Code* narrowly in terms of the essential elements of criminal offences or exculpatory defences ignores the historical and philosophical origins of the fundamental precept that sanity is a pre-condition of criminal responsibility. It violates the language of s. 16 of the Code, which refers to capacity for criminal responsibility rather than actual states of mind. It is at odds with the fact that insanity in s. 16 can be raised by the Crown in circumstances where neither the elements of the offence nor a defence are at issue. And it confuses true acquittal, the result of the absence of an essential element of an offence or the presence of a defence to it, with formal acquittal coupled with alternative coercive measures because mental impairment renders the imposition of true penal responsibility inappropriate. Rather than straining to confine the insanity provisions in the dual strait-jacket of the "elements" of or "exculpatory defences" to an offence, I prefer to view s. 16 as referring to a more basic precept of the criminal law system—the notion that the attribution of criminal responsibility and punishment is morally and legally justifiable only for those who have the capacity to reason and thus to choose right from wrong.

The next question is whether the presumption of sanity, viewed as the fundamental pre-condition of criminal responsibility, offends the presumption of innocence embodied in s. 11(d) of the Charter. The answer to this question must be negative. The presumption of innocence found in s. 11(d) of the Charter is merely another way of expressing the principle that the Crown must prove an accused's guilt beyond a reasonable doubt. That being the purpose of the presumption of innocence, it follows that the presumption of sanity cannot be contrary to s. 11(d) because, as Professor Mewett observed in the passage set out earlier, the issue of insanity "does not affect the prosecution's burden to prove beyond a reasonable doubt everything that constitutes guilt." The presumption of sanity in s. 16(4) of the *Criminal Code* merely relieves the Crown from establishing that the accused has the capacity for rational choice which makes attribution of criminal responsibility and punishment morally justifiable. The Crown must still prove the guilt of the accused—i.e., the *actus reus*, the *mens rea*, and the absence of exculpatory defences raised on the evidence—beyond a reasonable doubt.

[WILSON J., dissenting on this issue, held that the provision violated s. 11(d) and could not be justified under s. 1.]

I start from the premise that the government must have been of the view that it was necessary to impose a persuasive burden on the accused to prove his insanity on a balance of probabilities in order to prevent perfectly sane persons who had committed crimes from escaping criminal liability on tenuous insanity pleas. In other words, the government must have concluded that the imposition of a purely evidentiary burden on the accused, i.e., the burden of adducing sufficient evidence to raise a reasonable doubt in the minds of the jury as to his sanity was not enough. Hence the presumption of sanity and the reverse onus on the accused to prove insanity, bringing s. 16(4) into conflict with s. 11(d) of the Charter as explained in *Whyte*.

If I am correct in my starting premise, then it would appear that under the first branch of *Oakes* the government would have to adduce evidence under s. 1 to show that this was a real social problem, that perfectly sane persons who had committed crimes were in significant numbers escaping criminal liability on tenuous insanity pleas and that something had to be done about it.

There is, however, a difficulty here because s. 16(4) merely reflects what, as we have seen, was already the common law and had been the common law for some time prior even to the enactment of the original section in Canada's first *Criminal Code*. There is therefore no historic experience in our jurisdiction with a purely evidentiary burden in order to show that such a burden was not adequate to achieve the government's objective. ...

It would appear that in the United States the evidentiary burden has not resulted in a flood of accused persons being found not guilty by reason of insanity. Nor have the

Americans witnessed a great rush of insanity pleas. As the American Psychiatric Association notes in *Statement on the Insanity Defence* (1982):

> Successful invocation of the (insanity) defence is rare (probably involving a fraction of 1% of all felony cases). While philosophically important for the criminal law, the insanity defence is empirically unimportant.

The respondent, for the reasons discussed above, has not been able to establish that s. 16(4) of the *Criminal Code* was aimed at an existing pressing and substantial concern and, while it may be that the legislature need not necessarily wait until such a concern has arisen, I do not believe that the respondent has succeeded in establishing even a likelihood of its arising. I would conclude therefore that the first requirement of the *Oakes* test has not been met.

## Consequences of Mental Disorder as a Defence

### Winko v. British Columbia (Forensic Psychiatric Institute)
Supreme Court of Canada
[1999] 2 S.C.R. 625

McLACHLIN J. (Lamer C.J.C., Cory, Iacobucci, Major, Bastarache, and Binnie JJ. concurring):

[1] In every society there are those who commit criminal acts because of mental illness. The criminal law must find a way to deal with these people fairly, while protecting the public against further harms. The task is not an easy one.

[2] In 1991 Parliament provided its answer to this challenge: Part XX.1 of the *Criminal Code*, R.S.C. 1985, c. C-46. The appellant Winko submits that Part XX.1 violates his rights to liberty, security of the person and equality under the *Canadian Charter of Rights and Freedoms*. …

[3] I conclude that Part XX.1 of the *Criminal Code* protects the liberty, security of the person, and equality interests of those accused who are not criminally responsible ("NCR") on account of a mental disorder by requiring that an absolute discharge be granted unless the court or Review Board is able to conclude that they pose a significant risk to the safety of the public. It follows that Part XX.1 does not deprive mentally ill accused of their liberty or security of the person in a manner contrary to the principles of fundamental justice. Nor does it violate their right to equal treatment under the law. …

[17] Historically at common law, those who committed criminal acts while mentally ill were charged and required to stand trial like other offenders. At the end of the trial, they were either acquitted or convicted and sentenced accordingly. The common law permitted no special verdict or disposition. The only concession made to the illness that induced the offence was the accused's right to raise the defence that he or she was unable to understand the nature and quality of the act, the *M'Naghten Rules*: see *M'Naghten's Case* (1843), 10 Cl. & Fin. 200, 8 E.R. 718 (H.L.). The law held that

such incapacity deprived the mentally ill accused person of the criminal intent or *mens rea* required for the offence. Sanity, however, was presumed; it was up to the accused to demonstrate the contrary.

[18] Until 1990, the provisions of the *Criminal Code* dealing with criminal acts committed as a result of mental illness reflected the common law approach of treating those offences like any others, subject to the special defence of not understanding the nature and quality of the act. The only verdicts available under the *Criminal Code* were conviction or acquittal. However, even where the accused was acquitted on the basis of mental illness, he or she was not released, but was automatically detained at the pleasure of the Lieutenant Governor in Council: *Criminal Code*, s. 614(2) (formerly s. 542(2)) (repealed S.C. 1991, c. 43, s. 3).

[19] The first *Charter* challenge against this system came in *R. v. Chaulk*, [1990] 3 S.C.R. 1303, 62 C.C.C. (3d) 193, where a majority of this Court ruled that the requirement that the accused prove an inability to understand the nature and quality of his or her act violated the accused's right to be presumed innocent, but that the burden was constitutionally saved under s. 1. A second *Charter* challenge came in *R. v. Swain*, [1991] 1 S.C.R. 933, 63 C.C.C. (3d) 481, where this Court struck down the provision for automatic, indefinite detention of an NCR accused on the basis that it violated the accused's s. 7 liberty rights.

[20] In response to *Swain*, Parliament introduced sweeping changes by enacting Part XX.1 of the *Criminal Code* in 1991. … Part XX.1 reflected an entirely new approach to the problem of the mentally ill offender, based on a growing appreciation that treating mentally ill offenders like other offenders failed to address properly the interests of either the offenders or the public. The mentally ill offender who is imprisoned and denied treatment is ill-served by being punished for an offence for which he or she should not in fairness be held morally responsible. At the same time, the public facing the unconditional release of the untreated mentally ill offender was equally ill-served. To achieve the twin goals of fair treatment and public safety, a new approach was required.

[21] Part XX.1 rejects the notion that the only alternatives for mentally ill people charged with an offence are conviction or acquittal; it proposes a third alternative. Under the new scheme, once an accused person is found to have committed a crime while suffering from a mental disorder that deprived him or her of the ability to understand the nature of the act or that it was wrong, that individual is diverted into a special stream. Thereafter, the court or a Review Board conducts a hearing to decide whether the person should be kept in a secure institution, released on conditions, or unconditionally discharged. The emphasis is on achieving the twin goals of protecting the public and treating the mentally ill offender fairly and appropriately. …

[27] Any disposition regarding an NCR accused must be made in accordance with s. 672.54. The court or Review Board may order that the NCR accused be discharged absolutely, that he or she be discharged on conditions, or that he or she be detained in a hospital and subject to the conditions the court or Review Board considers appropriate. Although the court or Review Board has a wide latitude in determining the appropriate conditions to be imposed, it can only order that psychiatric or other treat-

ment be carried out if the NCR accused consents to that condition, and the court or Review Board considers it to be reasonable and necessary: s. 672.55(1).

[28] The Review Board must hold a further hearing within 12 months of making any disposition other than an absolute discharge and further reviews must be conducted at least every 12 months thereafter: s. 672.81(1). A further hearing also must be held as soon as practicable when the restrictions on the liberty of the NCR accused are increased significantly, or upon the request of the person in charge of the place where the accused is detained or directed to attend: s. 672.81(2). Apart from these mandatory reviews, the Review Board may review any of its dispositions at any time, on the request of the accused or any other party: s. 672.82(1). Any party may appeal against a disposition by a court or the Review Board to the Court of Appeal on a question of law or fact or a question of mixed law and fact: s. 672.72(1). ...

[35] If the NCR verdict is not a verdict of guilt or an acquittal, neither is it a verdict that the NCR accused poses a significant threat to society. Part XX.1 does not presume the NCR accused to pose such a threat. Rather, it requires the court or the Review Board to assess whether such a threat exists in each case. Part XX.1 thus recognizes that, contrary to the stereotypical notions that some may still harbour, the mentally ill are not inherently dangerous. The mentally ill have long been subject to negative stereotyping and social prejudice in our society based on an assumption of dangerousness. ...

[38] In *Swain*, *supra*, at p. 1015, this Court, *per* Lamer C.J.C., recognized that the NCR accused cannot be presumed to be dangerous:

> ... [W]hile the assumption that persons found not guilty by reason of insanity pose a threat to society may well be *rational*, I hasten to add that I recognize that it is not *always* valid. While past violent conduct and previous mental disorder may indicate a greater possibility of future dangerous conduct, this will not necessarily be so. Furthermore, not every individual found not guilty by reason of insanity will have such a personal history. (Emphasis in original.)

[39] In the spirit of supplanting the old stereotypes about mentally ill offenders, Part XX.1 supplements the traditional guilt-innocence dichotomy of the criminal law with a new alternative for NCR accused—an alternative of assessment to determine whether the person poses a continuing threat to society coupled with an emphasis on providing opportunities to receive appropriate treatment. The twin branches of the new system—assessment and treatment—are intimately related. Treatment, not incarceration, is necessary to stabilize the mental condition of a dangerous NCR accused and reduce the threat to public safety created by that condition. As Macfarlane J.A. stated regarding the predecessor scheme in *Re Rebic and The Queen* (1986), 28 C.C.C. (3d) 154 (B.C.C.A.) at p. 171, quoted with approval by Lamer C.J.C. in *Swain*, at p. 1004:

> The *objective* of the legislation is to protect society and the accused until the mental health of the latter has been restored. The objective *is to be achieved by treatment* of the patient in a hospital, rather than in a prison environment. [Emphasis added by Lamer C.J.C.]

[40]  Part XX.1 protects society. If society is to be protected on a long-term basis, it must address the cause of the offending behaviour—the mental illness. It cannot content itself with locking the ill offender up for a term of imprisonment and then releasing him or her into society, without having provided any opportunities for psychiatric or other treatment. Public safety will only be ensured by stabilizing the mental condition of dangerous NCR accused.

[41]  Part XX.1 also protects the NCR offender. The assessment-treatment model introduced by Part XX.1 of the *Criminal Code* is fairer to the NCR offender than the traditional common law model. The NCR offender is not criminally responsible, but ill. Providing opportunities to receive treatment, not imposing punishment, is the just and appropriate response.

[McLachlin J. went on to conclude that the new regime did not violate ss. 7 or 15 of the Charter. Section 672.54 did not create a burden or presumption of dangerousness on the accused, its reference to a significant threat to the safety of the public was not vague, and it was not based on stereotypes about mentally disordered offenders but rather required an "individualized process" that was "the antithesis of the logic of the stereotype."]

## II. MENTAL DISORDER AS A DEFENCE

### Mental Disorder or Disease of the Mind

**R. v. Simpson**
Ontario Court of Appeal
(1977), 35 C.C.C. (2d) 337

MARTIN J.A.: … The threshold question is whether the personality disorder from which it is said that the appellant suffers is a "disease of the mind" within s. 16 of the *Code*, notwithstanding the psychiatric evidence to that effect, since it is a question of law what the words "disease of the mind" mean.

The term "disease of the mind" is a legal concept, although it includes a medical component, and what is meant by that term is a question of law for the judge: see *Regina v. Kemp*, [1957] 1 Q.B. 399 at 403; *Bratty v. The Attorney General For Northern Ireland*, [1963] A.C. 386 at 412; *The Queen v. Cottle*, [1958] N.Z.L.R. 999 at 1028-9; *Regina v. O'Brien*, [1966] 3 C.C.C. 288 at 292-3. It is the function of the psychiatrist to describe the accused's mental condition and how it is considered from the medical point of view. It is for the judge to decide whether the condition described is comprehended by the term "disease of the mind." In practice, however, it is often convenient, where there is no issue whether the accused's mental condition constitutes a disease of the mind, for medical witnesses to be asked directly whether the accused suffers from a disease of the mind, and it is, of course, within the discretion of the trial judge to permit the question to be put in that way.

There has been considerable controversy whether the personality disorders—psychopathic personality, ordinarily, constitute a disease of the mind. See the report of *The Royal Commission on Capital Punishment 1949-53* at pp. 73 and 139; *Regina v. Wilkinson*, [1954] Crim. L.R. 22, 144; Glanville Williams, *Criminal Law (The General Part)* (2nd ed.) pp. 534-5. Whether the psychopathic personality constitutes a mental disease has been the subject of considerable discussion in decisions in the United States. See, for example, *United States v. Brawner*, 471 F. 2d 969, 992-94 (1972); *United States v. Currens*, 290 F. 2d 751, 761-3 (1961); *Blocker v. United States*, 288 F. 2d 853, per Burger J., as he then was, at 857-62 (1961).

In my view, however, it has been implicitly recognized by both the Supreme Court of Canada and the House of Lords that the personality disorders or psychopathic personality are capable of constituting a "disease of the mind." See *The Queen v. Borg*, [1969] S.C.R. 551 at 560; *Chartrand v. The Queen* (1976), 26 C.C.C. (2d) 417 at 420; *Attorney-General for Northern Ireland v. Gallagher*, [1963] A.C. 349, particularly Lord Denning at 382.

Obviously, mental disorders comprehended by the term "disease of the mind" are not confined to those mental disorders that were recognized as such at the time M'Naghten's case was decided. The concept "disease of the mind" is capable of evolving with the advance of medical knowledge...

While the existence of disease of the mind is a necessary condition of insanity under s. 16 of the *Code*, its existence alone does not constitute insanity unless it exists to an extent that renders the accused incapable of appreciating the nature and quality of the act or that it is wrong.

### Cooper v. The Queen
Supreme Court of Canada
(1980), 51 C.C.C. (2d) 129

DICKSON J.: ... Let me say by way of commencement that, to date, the phrase "disease of the mind" has proven intractable, and has eluded satisfactory definition by both medical and legal disciplines. It is not a term of art in either law or psychiatry, Indeed, Glanville Williams, *Textbook of Criminal Law* (1978), p. 592, says that the phrase is no longer in medical use: "It is a mere working concept, a mere abstraction, like sin."

In *R. v. Kemp*, [1957] 1 Q.B. 399, an oft-cited decision, the primary issue was whether arteriosclerosis came within the meaning of "disease of the mind." Devlin J. agreed that there was an absence of medical opinion as to the categories of malfunction properly to be termed "diseases of the mind," and rejected the idea that for legal purposes, a distinction should be made between diseases physical and mental in origin. In his view, arteriosclerosis is a disease of the mind and can provide a defence to a criminal charge. He reviewed the relationship between medical evidence and the legal conclusions to be drawn therefrom (p. 406):

> Doctors' personal views, of course, are not binding upon me. I have to interpret the rules according to the ordinary principles of interpretation, but I derive help from their

interpretations inasmuch as they illustrate the nature of the disease and the matters which from the medical point of view have to be considered in determining whether or not it is a disease of the mind.

In *Bratty v. A.-G. Northern Ireland*, [1963] A.C. 386, Lord Denning agreed that the question of whether an accused suffers from a disease of the mind is properly resolved by the Judge. He acknowledged that "the major mental diseases, which the doctors call psychoses ... are clearly diseases of the mind," and that "any mental disorder which has manifested itself in violence and is prone to recur is a disease of the mind" (p. 412).

In the *Report of the Royal Commission on Capital Punishment* (Eng.) (1949-1953), one finds a useful contribution to the discussion of what is meant by the phrases "mental disease" and "disease of the mind." The Report reads at p. 73:

> ... For us, therefore, mental disease is only one part of mental disorders of all kinds, and broadly corresponds to what are often called major diseases of the mind, or psychoses; although it may also arise in cases, such as those of epilepsy and cerebral tumour, which are not ordinarily regarded by doctors as psychotic. Among the psychoses are the conditions known as schizophrenia, manic-depressive psychoses, and organic disease of the brain. Other conditions, not included under this term, are the minor forms of mental disorder—the neurotic reactions, such as neurasthenia, anxiety states and hysteria—and the disorders of development of the personality—psychopathic personality. We are aware that this classification will not be unconditionally endorsed by all psychiatrists, and that some would prefer to include under the term "disease of the mind" even the minor abnormalities we have referred to. We believe, however, that the nature of the distinction we have drawn will be clear to them, and will be acceptable to them as the basis for a discussion of criminal responsibility.

The classification advanced was arbitrary and recognized as being one which would not be acceptable to all psychiatrists. The passage cited makes it abundantly clear that "disease of the mind" can mean different things to different psychiatrists. To some, for example, it may include such things as neurasthenia, anxiety states, hysteria, and psychopathic personality. Others would exclude such disorders from the definition. It is equally manifest that in law some mental states may be recognized as possibly being within the definition, although, medically speaking, a psychiatrist might not so regard them. Hardening of the arteries is one example (*R. v. Kemp, supra*); psychomotor epilepsy (*R. v. O'Brien*, [1966] 3 C.C.C. 288, 56 D.L.R. (2d) 65) is another. Thus to pose to a psychiatrist the bald question "Is D suffering from a disease of the mind?" and require a bald "yes" or "no" response really tells nothing because one is left in the dark as to the legal criteria applied.

Support for a broad and liberal legal construction of the words "disease of the mind" will be found in the writings of the renowned jurist, formerly Chief Justice of Australia, Sir Owen Dixon, who wrote:

> The reason why it is required that the defect of reason should be "from disease of the mind," in the classic phrase used by Sir Nicholas Tindal, seems to me no more than to exclude drunkenness, conditions of intense passion and other transient states attribut-

able either to the fault or to the nature of man. In the advice delivered by Sir Nicholas Tindal no doubt the words "disease of the mind" were chosen because it was considered that they had the widest possible meaning. He would hardly have supposed it possible that the expression would be treated as one containing words of the law to be weighed like diamonds. I have taken it to include, as well as all forms of physical or material change or deterioration, every recognizable disorder or derangement of the understanding whether or not its nature, in our present state of knowledge, is capable of explanation or determination. (A Legacy of Hadfield, M'Naghten and Maclean, 31 A.L.J. 255 at 260 (1957-58).)

Recently, in Canada, the Ontario Court of Appeal contributed judicial direction in this area of the law, in the cases of *R. v. Rabey* (1977), 37 C.C.C. (2d) 461, 79 D.L.R. (3d) 414, 17 O.R. (2d) 1, and *R. v. Simpson* (1977), 35 C.C.C. (2d) 337, 77 D.L.R. (3d) 507, 16 O.R. (2d) 129, both of which were decided subsequent to the trial of the appellant. Judgment in *Rabey* post dates the decision of the Court of Appeal in the case at bar and is presently on appeal to this Court on an issue unrelated to those raised herein. Mr. Justice Martin, who wrote for the Court in both *Rabey* and *Simpson*, was not among the members of the Court who heard the *Cooper* appeal.

*Simpson* has greater significance for the present appeal. There, the accused appealed the finding of not guilty—by reason of insanity on two charges of attempted murder. The facts, which indicate two incidents of stabbing, are not remarkable. As framed by Martin J.A., the issue was whether a personality disorder is a disease of the mind within the meaning of s. 16 of the Code. He held that, notwithstanding the psychiatric evidence, the question raised must be resolved as a question of law. But the legal position, as I understand it, is properly expressed in the following passage (at pp. 349-50):

> The term "disease of the mind" is a legal concept, although it includes a medical component, and what is meant by that term is a question of law for the judge. ... It is the function of the psychiatrist to describe the accused's mental condition and how it is considered from the medical point of view. It is for the Judge to decide whether the condition described is comprehended by the term "disease of the mind."

As a matter of practice, the trial Judge can permit the psychiatrist to be asked directly whether or not the condition in question constitutes a disease of the mind. Concerning the controversy over the classification of a "psychopathic personality," Martin J.A. found implicit recognition in Canadian and British authorities for the proposition that such a disorder can constitute a disease.

The general principles, not in issue on the further appeal to this Court, were reiterated by Mr. Justice Martin in *R. v. Rabey, supra*. Disease of the mind is a legal term. It is within the Province of the Judge to determine what mental conditions are within the meaning of that phrase and whether there is any evidence that an accused suffers from an abnormal mental condition comprehended by that term. More importantly, he held that if there is any evidence the accused did suffer such a disease in legal terms, the question of fact must be left with the jury.

I think Mr. Justice Dubin correctly characterizes the decision in *Simpson, supra*, as holding that "personality disorder" has been recognized as "being capable of constituting a 'disease of the mind.' " I share his view that "there is no reason to give a narrow or limited interpretation to the term 'disease of the mind.' " Admittedly, in *Simpson*, both of the psychiatrists stated that the personality disorder there in question did or could constitute a disease of the mind. While Martin J.A. in that case had little difficulty finding evidence that the appellant suffered from a "disease of the mind," the case foundered upon the second segment of s. 16(2). It should also be kept in mind that *Simpson* presented an odd situation in which the Crown successfully raised the insanity defence against the wishes of the accused, who appealed the verdict of not guilty by reason of insanity.

What is interesting in these two cases for our purposes is the maintenance of a clear distinction between the weight to be given medical opinions expressed in evidence, however relevant, and the task of the trial Judge to form an independent conclusion as to whether the mental condition falls within the legal concept.

In summary, one might say that in a legal sense "disease of the mind" embraces any illness, disorder or abnormal condition which impairs the human mind and its functioning, excluding however, self-induced states caused by alcohol or drugs, as well as transitory mental states such as hysteria or concussion. In order to support a defence of insanity the disease must, of course, be of such intensity as to render the accused incapable of appreciating the nature and quality of the violent act or of knowing that it is wrong.

---

Note that the concept of mental disorder or disease of the mind is also discussed in the next chapter on automatism. The determination of whether the legal concept of a mental disorder applies is often crucial in cases of automatism or involuntary conduct because an accused who acts in an involuntary manner will satisfy one or both of the arms of the mental disorder defence—namely, he or she will be incapable of (1) appreciating the nature and quality of the act or (2) knowing that the act is wrong. These next two arms of the mental disorder defence will now be explored.

### Appreciating the Nature and Quality of the Act

### Cooper v. The Queen
Supreme Court of Canada
(1980), 51 C.C.C. (2d) 129

DICKSON J.: ... In contrast to the position in England under the M'Naghten rules, where the words used are "knows the nature and quality of his act," s. 16 of the *Code* uses the phrase "appreciating the nature and quality of an act or omission." The two are not synonymous. The draftsman of the *Code*, as originally enacted, made a deliberate change in language from the common law rule in order to broaden the legal and medical considerations bearing upon the mental state of the accused and to make it clear that cognition was not to be the sole criterion. Emotional, as well as intellectual, awareness of the significance of the conduct, is in issue.

The *Report of the Royal Commission on the Law of Insanity as a Defence in Criminal Cases* (McRuer Report) (Canada, Queen's Printer (1956)), contains a useful discussion on the point (p. 12):

> An examination of the civil law of England and Canada shows that there is an important difference between "know" or "knowledge" on the one hand and "appreciate" or "appreciation" on the other when used and applied to a given set of circumstances. This is best illustrated by the principles of law underlying those cases in which the maxim *volenti non fit injuria* is involved. There is a clear distinction between mere knowledge of the risk and appreciation of both the risk and the danger.

To "know" the nature and quality of an act may mean merely to be aware of the physical act, while to "appreciate" may involve estimation and understanding of the consequences of that act. In the case of the appellant, as an example, in using his hands to choke the deceased, he may well have known the nature and quality of that physical act of choking. It is entirely different to suggest, however, that in performing the physical act of choking, he was able to appreciate its nature and quality in the sense of being aware that it could lead to or result in her death. In the opinion of the medical expert who testified at the trial, the appellant could have been capable of intending bodily harm and of choking the girl, but not of having intended her death.

Our *Code* postulates an independent test, requiring a level of understanding of the act which is more than mere knowledge that it is taking place; in short, a capacity to apprehend the nature of the act and its consequences. The position in law is well expressed in the McRuer Report at p. 12:

> Under the Canadian statute law a disease of the mind that renders the accused person incapable of an appreciation of the nature and quality of the act must necessarily involve more than mere knowledge that the act is being committed, there must be an appreciation of the factors involved in the act and a mental capacity to measure and foresee the consequences of the violent conduct.

It should be noted that the issue of appreciation of the nature and quality of the act was not before this Court in *Schwartz v. The Queen, supra*. The sole issue was the meaning of the word "wrong." The decision in *Schwartz* should not be taken as authority for the proposition that "appreciating" the nature and quality of an act is synonymous with "knowing" the physical character of that act.

The test proposed in the McRuer Report, which I would adopt (save for deletion of the word "fully" in the fourth line), is this (p. 13):

> The true test necessarily is, was the accused person at the very time of the offence—not before or after, but at the moment of the offence—by reason of disease of the mind, unable fully to appreciate not only the nature of the act but the natural consequences that would flow from it? In other words was the accused person, by reason of disease of

the mind, deprived of the mental capacity to foresee and measure the consequences of the act?

The legally relevant time is the time when the act was committed.

In the *Simpson* decision, Martin J.A. offered the view that s. 16(2) exempts from liability an accused who, due to a disease of the mind, has no real understanding of the nature, character and consequences of the act at the time of its commission. I agree. With respect, I accept the view that the first branch of the test, in employing the word "appreciates," imports an additional requirement to mere knowledge of the physical quality of the act. The requirement, unique to Canada, is that of perception, an ability to perceive the consequences, impact, and results of a physical act. An accused may be aware of the physical character of his action (*i.e.*, in choking) without necessarily having the capacity to appreciate that, in nature and quality, that act will result in the death of a human being. This is simply a restatement, specific to the defence of insanity, of the principle that *mens rea*, or intention as to the consequences of an act, is a requisite element in the commission of a crime.

---

See also, to the same effect, the unanimous judgments of the Supreme Court of Canada in *Regina v. Barnier* (1980), 51 C.C.C. (2d) 193, *per* Estey J., and *Kjeldsen v. The Queen* (1981), 64 C.C.C. (2d) 161, *per* McIntyre J. In *Kjeldsen*, the court stated:

> To be capable of "appreciating" the nature and quality of his acts, an accused person must have the capacity to know what he is doing; in the case at bar, for example, to know that he was hitting the woman on the head with the rock, with great force, and in addition he must have the capacity to estimate and to understand the physical consequences which would flow from his act, in this case that he was causing physical injury which could result in death.

The court adopted the reasoning in the following statement by Martin J.A. in *Simpson* (1977), 35 C.C.C. (2d) 337 (Ont. C.A.):

> While I am of the view that s. 16(2) exempts from liability an accused who by reason of disease of the mind has no real understanding of the nature, character and consequences of the act at the time of its commission, I do not think the exemption provided by the section extends to one who has the necessary understanding of the nature, character and consequences of the act, but merely lacks appropriate feelings for the victim or lacks feelings of remorse or guilt for what he has done, even though such lack of feeling stems from "disease of the mind." Appreciation of the nature and quality of the act does not import a requirement that the act be accompanied by appropriate feeling about the effect of the act on other people: see *Willgoss v. The Queen* (1960), 105 C.L.R. 295; *R. v. Leech* (1972), 10 C.C.C. (2d) 149, 21 C.R.N.S. 1, [1973] 1 W.W.R. 744; *R. v. Craig* (1974), 22 C.C.C. (2d) 212, [1975] 2 W.W.R. 314 [affirmed 28 C.C.C. (2d) 311.] No doubt the absence of such feelings is a common characteristic of many persons who engage in repeated and serious criminal conduct.

### R. v. Abbey
Supreme Court of Canada
(1982), 68 C.C.C. (2d) 394

[The accused was charged with importing cocaine and possession of cocaine for the purpose of trafficking contrary to ss. 5 and 4(2) of the *Narcotic Control Act*, R.S.C. 1970, c. N-1, and at a trial before a judge without a jury relied on the defence of insanity. The accused had agreed to buy cocaine in Peru for himself and some friends and upon his return the drug was located in a cursory check by customs officials. At the time that he went through customs and in the following period when he was arrested the accused appeared normal. The accused did not testify and the only defence evidence called was that of a psychiatrist who based his opinion on interviews he had with the accused and with the accused's mother and on other psychiatric reports. Both the defence psychiatrist and the Crown psychiatrist who was called in reply agreed that the accused suffered from a disease of the mind known as hypomania, but they differed as to whether he was incapable of appreciating the nature and quality of his acts. They did agree, however, that he knew what he was doing and that it was wrong. In giving effect to the defence, the trial judge found that the accused had a delusion that he was in receipt of power from a source external to himself and that he was protected from punishment by the mysterious external force. The trial judge found that the accused's ability to appreciate the nature and quality of the act was incapacitated to the degree required by s. 16 of the *Criminal Code* in that he failed to appreciate the consequences of punishment for his acts. The trial judge also referred to a closely related delusion that the accused was irrevocably committed to importing the cocaine by reason of a force acting upon him. An appeal by the Crown from the finding of not guilty by reason of insanity was dismissed by the British Columbia Court of Appeal.]

DICKSON J. (for the Court): Dr. Vallance's opinion was that Abbey, at all material times, was suffering from a disease of the mind, a manic illness, known as hypomania. While Abbey appreciated that he was bringing cocaine into Canada and knew that what he was doing was wrong, he believed that, if caught, he would not be punished. Dr. Vallance said:

> He had a considerable disturbance of mood. He had delusional ideas. He had hallucinatory experiences. It's difficult under circumstances like that to fully appreciate what you are doing, particularly when the feelings and delusional ideas are tangled up with what you are doing. If you feel that you are for some delusional idea inordinately powerful or safe, then that impairs good judgment. I am sure he had some appreciation of what he was doing.

Dr. Vallance further testified that, while Abbey was not rendered totally incapable of appreciating the nature and quality of his acts by reason of the disease of mind from which he suffered, there was a degree of impairment of judgment. He had the feeling that he was being looked after by some outside force that was feeding him strength and that no harm would come to him and even if he did get caught it did not matter because somehow he would be looked after. Dr. Vallance made reference to Abbey's delusional belief that he was committed to a particular path of action which he could not change and his further delusional idea, while in Lima, Peru, that he had "astro-travelled" back to Vancouver already and that in getting on the plane in Lima to fly home he was simply having the body follow where the "rest" had already gone.

In finding Abbey not guilty by reason of insanity the judge concluded that "one, who like Abbey suffers from the delusion that he is protected from punishment by some mysterious external force which comes to him as described in the evidence of Dr. Vallance, has his ability to appreciate the nature and quality of his acts incapacitated to the degree required to meet the test of s. 16(2). He is, by disease of the mind, deprived of the ability to assess an important consequence of his act. He is deprived of the effect of the penal sanction. ..."

Taggart J.A., speaking for the Court of Appeal, said that *Cooper v. The Queen, supra,* and *R. v. Barnier* (1980), 51 C.C.C. (2d) 193, 109 D.L.R. (3d) 257, [1980] 1 S.C.R. 1124, made it clear that there is a distinction between "know" and "appreciate" and that the words "appreciate the nature and quality of his acts" connote more than a mere knowledge of the physical nature of the acts being committed. With respect, I agree. The British Columbia Court of Appeal failed, however, to deal with the question of what it is an accused must fail to "appreciate" before he can be found legally insane. The court simply accepted the trial judge's conclusion that somebody who, because of a disease of the mind, has the delusion that he is protected from punishment by some mysterious external force, is incapacitated from appreciating the nature and quality of his acts.

... "Consequences" in *Cooper v. The Queen*; *R. v. Barnier* and *Kjeldsen v. The Queen* refer to the physical consequences of the act. All three cases were murder cases, violent crimes in which there was a victim who suffered the "consequences" of the accused's actions (*Cooper v. The Queen* at p. 147 C.C.C., p. 64 D.L.R., pp. 1162-3 S.C.R.).

Although there is some controversy in academic circles, I adopt the more traditional view espoused by Glanville Williams, *Criminal Law, The General Part,* 2nd ed. (1961), para. 166, p. 525, that a delusion falling under the "first arm" of the insanity defence negatives an element of the crime, the *mens rea.*

A delusion which renders an accused "incapable of appreciating the nature and quality of his act" goes to the *mens rea* of the offence and brings into operation the "first arm" of s. 16(2): he is not guilty by reason of insanity. A delusion which renders an accused incapable of appreciating that the penal sanctions attaching to the commission of the crime are applicable to him does not go to the *mens rea* of the offence, does not render him incapable of appreciating the nature and quality of the act, and does not bring into operation the "first arm" of the insanity defence.

This court having decided in *Schwartz v. The Queen, supra,* that "wrong" means according to law, and it being established that Abbey knew his act was "wrong," his inability to "appreciate" the penal consequences is really irrelevant to the question of legal insanity. There seems to be no doubt on the evidence, and on the judge's findings, that Abbey knew that he was doing an act forbidden by law.

I am of the view that the trial judge erred in law in holding that a person who by reason of disease of the mind does not "appreciate" the penal consequences of his actions is insane within the meaning of s. 16(2) of the *Criminal Code*.

The second ground of appeal is the submission that the trial judge erred in giving effect to a defence of "irresistible impulse." The submission rests upon the following passage from the judgment at trial, and in particular the words "he believed himself irrevocably committed":

> I must also note a second question closely connected with the delusion I have already discussed. It involves the delusion which I find existed with Abbey and which also satisfies the test of s. 16(2) that while he was in Peru he thought he should not go through with the importing and possession of cocaine, but he believed himself irrevocably committed to it. That was not in the sense that having arranged with his friends he was bound to honour the arrangement, but in the sense that he was committed to a path of action which he was, by reason of a force acting upon him, powerless to change.

The Crown maintains that the trial judge found that this "second delusion" independently, of any other delusions, rendered Abbey legally insane. Such a finding, the Crown contends, gives effect to a defence not recognized in Canadian law, that of irresistible impulse. What was said by Cartwright C.J.C. in *R. v. Borg*, [1969] 4 C.C.C. 262, 6 D.L.R. (3d) 1, [1969] S.C.R. 551, is cited in support of this proposition.

There is no issue here at all. Both the majority and minority opinions in *R. v. Borg* deny the existence of a defence, as such, of irresistible impulse. Both the majority and minority opinions in *Borg*, however, recognize that irresistible impulse may be a symptom or manifestation of a disease of the mind which may give rise to a defence of insanity (*per* Hall J. at pp. 281-2 C.C.C., p. 18 D.L.R., 570 S.C.R.):

> When an accused pleads insanity there is a sense in which it is true to say that irresistible impulse of itself is not a defence. However, there are two senses in which it is not true to say that irresistible impulse of itself is not a defence.
>
> There is no legal presumption of insanity merely from the existence of an irresistible impulse. If an accused presents no medical evidence of disease of the mind but merely pleads that he was acting under an irresistible impulse, a jury is not entitled to infer that the man was insane. In that sense irresistible impulse is not of itself a defence. However, if there is medical evidence of disease of the mind as there was here and yet the only symptoms of that disease of the mind are irresistible impulses, the jury may conclude that the accused is insane.

There is no error in the trial judgment in this respect. The trial judge did not give effect to an independent defence of irresistible impulse. His comments with respect to the "second delusion" were made in the context of his consideration of the insanity defence. He specifically rejected the existence of a defence of diminished responsibility in Canada.

I agree with the British Columbia Court of Appeal that the reasons of the trial judge should be understood in the sense that Abbey suffered from a disease of the mind which resulted in two delusions; the first was that some mysterious external force would protect him from punishment; the second that he believed himself irrevocably committed to the course of action of importing cocaine; and that these delusions taken together rendered him incapable of appreciating the nature and quality of his acts. The trial judge did not equate the "delusion" with a defence of irresistible impulse and, that being the case, such authorities as *R. v. Borg, supra, R. v. Creighton* (1908), 14 C.C.C. 349, and other authorities to a similar effect cited by Crown counsel have no application to the case at bar.

*Appeal allowed; new trial ordered.*

## Knowing That the Act Is Wrong

### R. v. Chaulk and Morrissette
Supreme Court of Canada
(1990), 62 C.C.C. (3d) 193

[The accused appealed from the judgment of the Manitoba Court of Appeal, which had dismissed their appeals from convictions for first-degree murder. The Supreme Court's decision upholding the reverse onus provision under s. 1 of the Charter was set out earlier in this chapter.]

LAMER C.J. (Dickson C.J., Wilson, La Forest, Gonthier, and Cory JJ. concurring): ... This Court has also been asked to revisit its interpretation of the meaning of the word "wrong" found in s. 16(2). There are other issues specific to the appeal which are set out further on in these reasons.

On September 3, 1985, the appellants Chaulk and Morrissette entered a home in Winnipeg, plundered it for valuables and then stabbed and bludgeoned its sole occupant to death. A week later they turned themselves in, making full confessions.

After a transfer proceeding in the Youth Court (Chaulk and Morrissette were 15 and 16 years of age, respectively), the appellants were tried and convicted of first degree murder by a jury in the Manitoba Court of Queen's Bench. The only defence raised was insanity within the meaning of s. 16 of the Code. Expert evidence was given at trial that the appellants suffered from a paranoid psychosis which made them believe that they had the power to rule the world and that the killing was a necessary means to that end. They knew the laws of Canada existed, but believed that they were above the ordinary law; they thought the law was irrelevant to them. They thought they had a right to kill the victim because he was "a loser." ...

In his directions to the jury, Ferg J. clearly stated the meaning that was to be given to the term "wrong" for the purposes of s. 16(2). He directed:

> Next as an alternative even if the accused did appreciate the nature and quality of what
> he was doing and it's for you to decide, as I've said, is also insanity if the accused was
> laboring under a disease of the mind that rendered him incapable of knowing that his
> act was wrong. [sic] By wrong I mean that it was a criminal act or legally wrong.

[The trial judge repeated these instructions when the jury, after deliberating for some time, asked the following:

> Re: Knowledge of the laws of Canada:
>     (a)  does this refer to simple knowledge of the rules as evidenced by recognition of the consequences, i.e.: police and jail term or;
>     (b)  does it refer to their awareness of whether the laws apply to them at the time of the murder ...]

Ferg J. answered their question by repeating substantially what he had stated in his original direction. He summarized:

> This part is the alternative, the second part, and this has to do with knowledge capable of knowing his act was wrong. As an alternative even if the accused did—if you find that it's for you to decide—did appreciate the nature and quality of what he was doing, and it's for you to decide as I just said, it is also insanity if the accused was laboring under a disease of the mind that rendered him incapable of knowing that his act was wrong and by the word wrong I mean that it was a criminal act or illegally wrong, if you will, the laws of Canada.

The Court of Appeal found no error on the part of the trial judge in directing the jury, stating that it was clear that the appellants "knew and fully appreciated the nature and consequences of their acts and they knew that what they were doing was legally wrong."

The appellants submit that the term "wrong" for the purposes of s. 16(2) should be interpreted to mean "morally" wrong and not "legally" wrong. The respondent made no submission with respect to this issue in its factum, but argued orally that, regardless of the meaning that is to be given to the word "wrong" in this case, the difference between morally wrong and legally wrong where a very serious offence such as murder is involved "is so narrow as to be hardly worth the effort of deciding between them." It was further argued in oral pleadings that the meaning of "wrong" in s. 16(2), having its source in the seminal judgment of the House of Lords in *M'Naghten's Case* (1843), 10 Cl. & Fin. 200, 8 E.R. 718, incorporates not only a moral but also a legal dimension in such a way that the two cannot be divorced, with the result that a person who knows that an act is legally wrong must also comprehend that the act is morally wrong.

The meaning of the term "wrong" for the purposes of s. 16(2) was determined by this court in *Schwartz v. The Queen* (1976), 29 C.C.C. (2d) 1, 67 D.L.R. (3d) 716, [1977] 1 S.C.R. 673. Speaking for the majority, Martland J. held that the capacity to know that an act is wrong in this context means no more than the capacity to know that what one is doing is against the law of the land. ...

Dickson J., as he then was, dissented in *Schwartz*. He noted that the word "wrong" as used in s. 16(2) is ambiguous and is capable of meaning either "legally" or "morally" wrong. He also noted that the issue had given rise to conflicting lines of authority in England, Australia and Canada.

In order to resolve this question, Dickson J. first examined the internal structure of the Code in order to determine the meaning that Parliament intended to give the term.

It would have been internally coherent, he submitted, for Parliament to use the word "unlawful" if it had intended "wrong" to mean "contrary to law." Furthermore, the use of the word "mauvais" in the French version of s. 16(2) suggests that Parliament intended the term to have a meaning broader than merely "unlawful." Lastly, s. 13 formerly provided that no child between seven and 13 years of age could be convicted of a criminal offence "unless he was competent to know the nature and consequences of his conduct and to appreciate that it was wrong"; it would be insupportable, in this context, to equate knowledge that an act is wrong with the knowledge that the act is contrary to law.

Dickson J. then considered jurisprudential and doctrinal authorities antedating *M'Naghten's Case* and concluded that the historical common law test to determine the criminal responsibility of insane persons was whether the particular accused had the capacity to distinguish between conduct that was good or evil, right or wrong. *M'Naghten's Case*, in his view, did not depart from this standard. In fact, the case drew a clear line between knowledge that an act is illegal and knowledge that the act is one that a person ought not do; this distinction is revealed in the following passage in *M'Naghten's Case*, at p. 210, p. 723 E.R.: "If the accused was conscious that the act was one which he ought not to do, and if that act was at the same time contrary to the law of the land, he is punishable." This passage indicates clearly that an accused will only be convicted if he commits an act which he knows he ought not do and which, at the same time, is contrary to law. ...

More fundamentally, Dickson J. concluded that a reading of s. 16(2) as a whole leads to the conclusion that "wrong" must mean contrary to the ordinary moral standards of reasonable men and women. The object of s. 16(2) is to protect individuals who do not have the capacity to judge whether an act is wrong; the inquiry as to the capacity of an accused to reason must not end simply because it is determined that the accused knew that the act was a crime. He argued that this would not serve to protect amoral persons since any incapacity must result from a disease of the mind (at p. 22):

> Section 16(2) must be read in toto. One looks at capacity to reason and to reach rational decisions as to whether the act is morally wrong. If wrong simply means "illegal" this virtually forecloses any inquiry as to capacity. The question for the jury is whether mental illness so obstructed the thought processes of the accused as to make him incapable of knowing that his acts were morally wrong. The argument is sometimes advanced that a moral test favours the amoral offender and that the most favoured will be he who had rid himself of all moral compunction. This argument overlooks the factor of disease of the mind. If, as a result of disease of the mind, the offender has lost completely the ability to make moral distinctions and acts under an insane delusion, it can well be said that he should not be criminally accountable.

The interpretation of "wrong" as meaning "morally wrong" would not, in his opinion, have the effect of opening up the insanity defence to a far greater number of accused persons. First, what is illegal and what breaches society's moral standards does not often differ. Secondly, "'[m]oral wrong' is not to be judged by the personal standards of the offender but by his awareness that society regards the act as wrong" (p. 13). He concluded that an accused is not therefore free, as a result of such interpretation, to substitute at will his own sense of morality for that of society, but is to be acquitted by reason of insanity if, by reason of disease of the mind, he is incapable of knowing that society generally considers a particular act to be immoral.

With respect for contrary views, it is my opinion that *Schwartz* was wrongly decided by this Court and that the dissenting opinion of Dickson J. (concurred in by Laskin C.J., Spence and Beetz JJ.) is to be preferred. The majority judgment fails, in my respectful view, to appreciate the manner in which insanity renders our normal principles of criminal responsibility inapplicable to an individual as well as the particular objectives of s. 16 of the Code. ...

In my view, *Schwartz* had the effect of expanding the scope of criminal responsibility unacceptably to include persons who, by reason of disease of the mind, were incapable of knowing that an act was wrong according to the normal and reasonable standards of society even though they were aware that the act was formally a crime. It is now necessary for this Court to reconsider its decision in *Schwartz* in order to redefine the scope of criminal liability in a manner that will bring it into accordance with the basic principles of our criminal law.

The rationale underlying the defence of insanity in Canada, as discussed above under the rubric "The Nature of the Insanity Provisions," rests on the belief that persons suffering from insanity should not be subject to standard criminal culpability with its resulting punishment and stigmatization. This belief, in turn, flows from the principle that individuals are held responsible for the commission of criminal offences because they possess the capacity to distinguish between what is right and what is wrong.

Section 16(2) of the Code embodies this conception of criminal responsibility by providing that no person shall be convicted of an offence who, at the time of committing the act in question, is in a state of "natural imbecility" or has disease of the mind to such a degree as to render him incapable of "knowing that an act or omission is wrong." The principal issue in this regard is the capacity of the accused person to know that a particular act or omission is wrong. As such, to ask simply what is the meaning of the word "wrong" for the purposes of s. 16(2) is to frame the question too narrowly. To paraphrase the words of the House of Lords in *M'Naghten's Case*, the courts must determine in any particular case *whether an accused was rendered incapable, by the fact of his mental disorder, of knowing that the act committed was one that he ought not have done.*

Viewed from this perspective, it is plain to me that the term "wrong" as used in s. 16(2) must mean more than simply legally wrong. In considering the capacity of a person to know whether an act is one that he ought or ought not to do, the inquiry cannot terminate with the discovery that the accused knew that the act was contrary to the formal law. A person may well be aware that an act is contrary to law but, by reason of "natural imbecility" or disease of the mind, is at the same time incapable of knowing that the act is morally wrong in the circumstances according to the moral standards of society. This would be the case, for example, if the person suffered from a disease of the mind to such a degree as to know that it is legally wrong to kill but, as described by Dickson J. in *Schwartz*, kills "in the belief that it is in response to a divine order and therefore not morally wrong" (p. 678).

In applying s. 16(2) to a particular set of facts, it may be established that the accused who attempts to invoke the insanity defence is capable of knowing that he ought not do the act because he knows, first, that the act is contrary to the formal law or, secondly, that the act breaches the standard of moral conduct that society expects of its members. ...

An interpretation of s. 16(2) that makes the defence available to an accused who knew that he or she was committing a crime but was unable to comprehend that the act was a moral wrong will not open the floodgates to amoral offenders or to offenders who relieve themselves of all moral considerations. First, the incapacity to make moral judgments must be causally linked to a disease of the mind; if the presence of a serious mental disorder is not established, criminal responsibility cannot be avoided. Secondly, as was pointed out by Dickson J. in *Schwartz*, *supra*, " '[m]oral wrong' is not to be judged by the personal standards of the offender but by his awareness that society regards the act as wrong" (p. 678). The accused will not benefit from substituting his own moral code for that of society. Instead, he will be protected by s. 16(2) if he is incapable of understanding that the act is wrong according to the ordinary moral standards of reasonable members of society.

In the case at bar, the trial judge directed the jury that the insanity defence was not available to the appellants pursuant to the second branch of the test set out in s. 16(2) if it reached the conclusion that the appellants knew, at the time of committing the offence, that the act was contrary to the laws of Canada. Of course, he cannot be faulted for having followed the decision of this Court in *Schwartz*. Nevertheless, for the reasons discussed above, our interpretation of s. 16(2) in *Schwartz* was not correct. As a result, I would order a new trial. ...

McLACHLIN J., with whom L'Heureux-Dubé and Sopinka JJ. concurred, dissenting:  Lamer C.J. has accepted the appellants' invitation to reconsider this Court's earlier conclusion that the capacity to know the act or omission was legally wrong suffices. In his view, an accused who is capable of knowing an act or omission is legally wrong is not subject to the criminal process if mental illness rendered him or her incapable of knowing the act or omission was morally wrong. I, on the other hand, take the view that it does not matter whether the capacity relates to legal wrongness or moral wrongness—all that is required is that the accused be capable of knowing that the act was in some sense "wrong." If the accused has this capacity, then it is neither unfair nor unjust to submit the accused to criminal responsibility and penal sanction.

The latter position is supported in my view by: (a) the plain language of s. 16(2); (b) an historical view of our insanity provisions; (c) the purpose and theory underlying our insanity provisions; and (d) by practical difficulties related to the problem of determining what is "morally wrong." I will consider each of these arguments in turn. ...

... I turn now to the purpose and theory underlying the insanity provisions. In my view, they too support the view that "wrong" in s. 16(2) of the Code means simply that which one "ought not to do." The rationale behind the insanity provisions, as discussed earlier in these reasons, is that it is unfair and unjust to make a person who is not capable of conscious choice between right or wrong criminally responsible. Penal sanctions are appropriate only for those who have the ability to reason right from wrong, people capable of appreciating what they ought and ought not to do. A person may conclude that he or she ought not to do an act for a variety of reasons. One may be that it is illegal. Another may be that it is immoral. The reasons for which one concludes that one ought not to do an act are collateral to the fundamental rationale behind the insanity provisions—that criminal conviction is appropriate only where the person is capable of understanding that he or she ought not to do the act in question.

The wider rationale underlying the criminal law generally supports the same view. While other factors may figure, two main mechanisms function to keep people's conduct within the appropriate legal parameters: (1) a sense of morality, and (2) a desire to obey the law. In most cases, law and morality are coextensive, but exceptionally they are different. Where morality fails, the legal sanction should not be removed as well. To do so is to open the door to arguments that absence of moral discernment should excuse a person from the sanction of the criminal law, and thus remove one of the factors which deters inappropriate and destructive conduct. That should not be done lightly. The fact that such arguments could not be entertained without establishing a "disease of the mind" is small comfort when one takes account of the difficulty of defining or diagnosing "disease of the mind." Recent research seems to suggest that the vast majority of forensic psychiatrists and psychologists, including those who have given evidence with respect to legal insanity in a large number of cases, have no effective understanding of the legal test about which they are expressing an opinion: R. Rogers and R.E. Turner, "Understanding of Insanity: A National Survey of Forensic Psychiatrists and Psychologists" (1987), 7 *Health L. Can.* 71. See also J. Ziskin, D. Faust, *Coping with Psychiatric and Psychological Testimony* (4th ed. 1988), vol. I, at pp. 389-408.

To hold that absence of moral discernment due to mental illnesses should exempt a person who knows that legally he or she ought not do to a certain act is, moreover, to introduce a lack of parallelism into the criminal law; generally absence of moral appreciation is no excuse for criminal conduct. When the moral mechanism breaks down in the case of an individual who is sane, we do not treat that as an excuse for disobeying the law; for example, in the case of a psychopath. The rationale is that an individual either knows or is presumed to know the law, and the fact that his or her moral standards are at variance with those of society is not an excuse. Why, if the moral mechanism breaks down because of disease of the mind, should it exempt the accused from criminal responsibility where he or she knows, or was capable of knowing, that the act was illegal and hence one which he or she "ought not to do." Why should deficiency of moral appreciation due to mental illness have a different consequence than deficiency of moral appreciation due to a morally-impoverished upbringing, for example? I see no reason why the policy of the law should differ in the two cases. ...

The problem with making capacity to appreciate moral wrong the test for criminal responsibility where the incapacity is caused by mental illness is that of determining what society's moral judgment will be in every situation. What result is to obtain on those occasions where an accused claims an incapacity to know that his or her unlawful act was morally wrong and, objectively, the act was one for which the moral wrongfulness can be disputed? Certainly a court is in no position to make determinations on questions of morality, nor is it fair to expect a jury to be able to agree on what is morally right or morally wrong. The prospect of greater certainty, and the avoidance of metaphysical arguments on right and wrong is the chief advantage of adhering to the traditional M'Naghten test for criminal responsibility where causative disease of the mind exists—whether the accused, for whatever reason, was capable of appreciating that his or her act is wrong.

*Appeal allowed; new trial ordered.*


### R. v. Oommen
Supreme Court of Canada
(1994), 91 C.C.C. (3d) 8

[The accused suffered from a paranoid delusion and believed that the woman he repeatedly shot was part of a conspiracy that was coming into his house to kill him. The trial judge held that the accused was not entitled to the mental disorder defence because he had the capacity to know that society in general would regard his acts as wrong even though "subjectively the accused did not believe his act to be wrong" and "he believed that he had no choice to do anything but what he did."

The Supreme Court reversed his murder conviction and ordered a new trial in which the accused could raise the mental disorder defence.]

McLACHLIN J. (for the Court): … In the early morning hours of March 24, 1991, Mathew Oommen killed Gina Lynn Beaton as she lay sleeping on a mattress in his apartment by firing nine to 13 shots at her from a .22 calibre rimfire semi-automatic repeating rifle. On February 26, 1992, he was convicted of second degree murder before a judge alone and sentenced to life imprisonment without eligibility for parole for 10 years. The Alberta Court of Appeal set aside the conviction and ordered a new trial on the ground that the trial judge had erred in his interpretation of the insanity provision of s. 16(1) of the *Criminal Code*, R.S.C., 1985, c. C-46. The Crown appeals to this court against that order, seeking reinstatement of the conviction for murder.

### The Evidence

The evidence disclosed no rational motive for the killing. To understand it, we must delve into the disordered workings of Mr. Oommen's mind.

For a number of years Mr. Oommen had been suffering from a mental disorder described as a psychosis of a paranoid delusional type. As a result, he harboured false and fixed beliefs that he was the butt of conspiracies and situations that endangered him. Mr. Oommen's disorder had led to hospitalization in 1984, 1988 and in February, 1991, shortly before he killed Ms. Beaton.

At the time of the killing, Mr. Oommen's paranoia was fixed on a belief that the members of a local union were conspiring to destroy him. In November, 1986, he had been struck on the head and robbed while driving a taxi-cab. Mr. Oommen attributed this incident to the fact that he had transported certain individuals during labour disputes at one of the local plants. His friends and doctors testified that he became paranoid that there would be further attacks on his life.

At this point, Gina Lynn Beaton came into Mr. Oommen's life and tragically became part of his delusion. The two met prior to Christmas, 1990. Ms. Beaton needed a place to stay. Mr. Oommen let her stay in his apartment for a period of time, in return for some cooking and cleaning. Mr. Oommen sought the advice of both friends and a local police officer as to the propriety of his sheltering Ms. Beaton. He seemed to be concerned that the relationship might be misapprehended as sexual. After a while, Ms. Beaton left the apartment and moved to Edmonton. Shortly before her death, she returned to Fort McMurray and Mr. Oommen's apartment.

Mr. Oommen became fixated with the notion that his assailants and enemies had incorporated Ms. Beaton and commissioned her to kill him. On the evening of the killing he became convinced that members of the conspiracy had surrounded his apartment building with the intention of moving in on him and killing him. This delusion, combined with his belief that Ms. Beaton was one of the conspirators, convinced him that he was obliged to kill her to prevent her from killing him. So he shot her while she lay sleeping on the floor.

It was established that about the time of the killing, Mr. Oommen called a taxi dispatcher several times to request the police. It was also established that someone had rung the buzzers or doorbells of all the apartments. Mr. Oommen said that this was the signal from the conspirators outside to Ms. Beaton to kill him. A tenant, awakened by the doorbell, saw Mr. Oommen outside the building twice soon afterward, apparently putting liquor containers in the garbage. Another tenant, similarly awakened, went out into the hall and met Mr. Oommen, who asked him to call the police because he had just killed someone who had come at him with a knife. When the police arrived Mr. Oommen told the officer: "I called the caretaker. I shot and killed a girl inside. She thought I was sleeping. She came with a knife. I had no other choice, so I shot her, okay." Mr. Oommen repeated this story to the lawyer a friend found for him, Mr. George. He explained that he had shot and killed the girl who had been staying with him. Mr. George asked why. Mr. Oommen replied that she had tried to come with a knife and kill him. He said he saw something, a shiny object, in her hand and "instead [of] she killing me, I went and lowered the gun and killed her."

Mr. Oommen repeated this story at 5:27 a.m. in his statement to the police. Constable Bazowski observed that during the interview, Mr. Oommen vacillated between quiet and animated behaviour. Sometimes his voice would drop to a whisper; sometimes he would pound his fist on the table to emphasize his points. He seemed eager to offer an explanation of what had happened. He explained that he had seen the deceased pass his bedroom door with a knife in her hand as she went to the washroom on more than one occasion during the night. He knew that she was going to kill him, he thought on the instructions of others, and he "opened fire" on her as she lay pretending to be asleep. He had no choice or he would have been killed. Constable

Bazowski gained the impression that Mr. Oommen believed the constable was investigating or ought to investigate why the girl was trying to kill him.

There was no question at trial that Mr. Oommen had killed Ms. Beaton. Nor was there much doubt that Mr. Oommen's insane delusions provoked the killing. As Dr. Trichard testified:

> He, on that very night of the assault, was convinced that there were people outside the building that had staked out the building and were coming to attack him. He had, in fact, heard the buzzers being rung throughout the building and had incorporated this into the idea that he was being pursued.
>
> On the night in question, he also became convinced that his assailants had incorporated the unfortunate deceased and had given her the commission that she was to kill him. So that on that night, it was him alone with her in this apartment, and it was either she was going to kill him, or he had to stop her. I believe that he was therefore acting under a delusion at the time that he committed this offence.

The only issue was whether this delusion exempted Mr. Oommen from criminal responsibility under s. 16(1) of the *Criminal Code* on the ground that he lacked the capacity at the relevant time to know the difference between right and wrong. Dr. Trichard testified that a person suffering from this mental disorder would not lose the intellectual capacity to understand right from wrong and would know that to kill a person is wrong. However, the person's delusions would affect the person's interpretation of events so that the individual would honestly believe killing to be justified under the circumstances. In the abstract, the person would know killing was wrong. But his delusion would cause him to believe that killing was justified under the circumstances as he perceived them. In Crown cross-examination Dr. Trichard stated:

> Q. You have a person suffering from the disease that you have described. He kills someone and does not believe he has done wrong, or does not at the time he is doing the killing believe he is doing wrong. In this disorder as opposed to others, that cannot be because he thinks killing is not wrong in any abstract sense, but because he has some particular delusion or belief, or maybe some actual information—maybe his killing really is justified in a particular situation—but he has some believe [sic] that justifies it to him.
>
> A. I believe that would be so, yes.

And again:

> Q. Dr. Trichard, if you could address yourself then to the account you received of Mr. Oommen's case and the killing that he did, it would be your belief that he, in his own mind at the time of doing it, would, because of his delusions and his fear, feel he was justified in doing what he was doing?
>
> A. Yes, I do believe that.

In other words, Mr. Oommen possessed the general capacity to distinguish right from wrong. However, on the night of the killing, his delusions deprived him of the capacity to know that killing Ms. Beaton was wrong. On the contrary, those delusions led him to believe that killing was necessary and justified. ...

The trial judge found that the accused was acting under the influence of a paranoid delusion at the time of the killing and that this was the cause of the killing: "When I consider what caused the murder, I find that I have very little doubt that it was caused and, indeed, compelled by the mental disorder suffered by [Mr. Oommen] and described by the psychiatrists as a psychosis of a delusional paranoid type." The trial judge found that on a balance of probabilities Mr. Oommen "was capable of knowing that what he was doing was wrong according to moral standards of society. ... [H]e was capable of knowing that society in general would regard it as wrong."

Despite this general capacity to distinguish right from wrong, the trial judge found as a fact that "subjectively the accused did not believe his act to be wrong." Whether because of this subjective belief in the rightness of his act or confusion engendered by the delusion, the trial judge found that Mr. Oommen was unable to apply his general ability to distinguish right from wrong to the act of killing Ms. Beaton: "I must say that I'm certain that the fact of that knowledge could not have in any way assisted the accused in refraining from committing the act because in his own mind he believed he had no choice to do anything but what he did." The trial judge concluded that in view of the accused's general capacity to know right from wrong, he was not relieved from criminal responsibility under s. 16(1), notwithstanding his subjective belief that what he did was right and his inability to apply his general knowledge of right and wrong. ...

Section 16(1) affirms that a person who lacks the capacity to know that the act he is committing is wrong is exempt from criminal responsibility.

This appeal poses the following legal issue. What is meant by the phrase "knowing that [the act] was wrong" in s. 16(1)? Does it refer only to abstract knowledge that the act of killing would be viewed as wrong by society? Or does it extend to the inability to rationally apply knowledge of right and wrong and hence to conclude that the act in question is one which one ought not to do?

A review of the history of our insanity provision and the cases indicates that the inquiry focuses not on general capacity to know right from wrong, but rather on the ability to know that a particular act was wrong in the circumstances. The accused must possess the intellectual ability to know right from wrong in an abstract sense. But he or she must also possess the ability to apply that knowledge in a rational way to the alleged criminal act.

The wording of s. 16(1) suggests this result. It proclaims that the focus is not a general capacity to understand that the act, say of killing, is wrong, but rather the act "committed" or omission "made," i.e., the particular act or omission at issue in the criminal proceedings.

The history of s. 16(1) confirms this. The provision finds its origin in the "*M'Naghten Rules*": *M'Naghten's Case* (1843), 10 Cl. & Fin. 200, 8 E.R. 718. The House of Lords put the following questions, inter alia, to the judges (at p. 203 Cl. & Fin., p. 720 E.R.):

2d. What are the proper questions to be submitted to the jury, when a person alleged to be afflicted with insane delusion respecting one or more particular subjects or persons, is charged with the commission of a crime (murder, for example), and insanity is set up as a defence?

3d. In what terms ought the question to be left to the jury, as to the prisoner's state of mind at the time when the act was committed?

Lord Chief Justice Tindal replied (at p. 210 Cl. & Fin., p. 722 E.R.), that the judges thought that these two questions could be answered together:

> [W]e have to submit our opinion to be, that the jurors ought to be told in all cases that every man is to be presumed to be sane, and to possess a sufficient degree of reason to be responsible for his crimes, until the contrary be proved to their satisfaction; and that to establish a defence on the ground of insanity, it must be clearly proved that, *at the time of the committing of the act, the party accused was labouring under such a defect of* reason, from disease of the mind, as not to know the nature and quality of the act he was doing; or, if he did know it, *that he did not know he was doing what was wrong.*

(Emphasis added.) Both the question and answer demonstrate that the rule focuses not on a general capacity to understand right and wrong in some abstract sense, but on the particular capacity of the accused to understand that his or her act was wrong at the time of committing the act. Lord Chief Justice Tindal added an explanation of the word "wrong" (at pp. 210-1 Cl. & Fin., p. 723 E.R.):

> If the accused was conscious that the act was one which he ought not to do, and if that act was at the same time contrary to the law of the land, he is punishable; and the usual course therefore has been to leave the question to the jury, *whether the party accused had a sufficient degree of reason to know that he was doing an act that was wrong.* …

(Emphasis added.) Tollefson and Starkman, *Mental Disorder in Criminal Proceedings* (1993), p. 30, suggest that what the judges were saying was this:

> We agree with you that the meaning to be conveyed to the jury is that the exemption is based on whether the accused is capable of knowing that the act was contrary to the law. But for practical reasons, the jury cannot be told that in so many words. We therefore use the word "wrong," and make it as clear as possible that the jurors must view the act in the context of the specific charge and not in some general sense.

In *Chaulk, supra*, this court affirmed that the focus must be on capacity to know that the act committed was wrong, and not merely on a general capacity to distinguish right from wrong. Lamer C.J.C., writing for the majority, stated (at p. 230):

> The principal issue in this regard is the capacity of the accused person to know that a particular act or omission is wrong. As such, to ask simply what is the meaning of the word "wrong" for the purposes of s. 16(2) is to frame the question too narrowly. To paraphrase the words of the House of Lords in *M'Naghten's Case*, the courts must determine in any particular case whether an accused was rendered incapable, by the fact of his mental disorder, of knowing that the act committed was one that he ought not have done.

The crux of the inquiry is whether the accused lacks the capacity to rationally decide whether the act is right or wrong and hence to make a rational choice about whether to do it or not. The inability to make a rational choice may result from a variety of mental disfunctions; as the following passages indicate, these include at a minimum the states to which the psychiatrists testified in this case—delusions which make the accused perceive an act which is wrong as right or justifiable, and a disordered condition of the mind which deprives the accused of the ability to rationally evaluate what he is doing.

In *R. v. Porter* (1933), 55 C.L.R. 182 at pp. 189-90 (H.C. Aust.), Dixon J. charged a jury in the following oft-cited manner:

> The question is whether [the accused] was able to appreciate the wrongness of the particular act he was doing at the particular time. Could this man be said to know in this sense whether his act was wrong if through a disease or defect or disorder of the mind he could not think rationally of the reasons which to ordinary people make that act right or wrong? *If through the disordered condition of the mind he could not reason about the matter with a moderate degree of sense and composure it may be said that he could not know that what he was doing was wrong.* ... What is meant by wrong is wrong having regard to the everyday standards of reasonable people.

(Emphasis added.)

In *Stapleton v. The Queen* (1952), 86 C.L.R. 358 at p. 367, the High Court of Australia concluded:

> ... it is enough if [the disease, disorder, or defect of reason] so governed the faculties at the time of the commission of the act that the accused was incapable of reasoning with some moderate degree of calmness as to the wrongness of the act or of comprehending the nature or significance of the act of killing.

G. Arthur Martin, Q.C. (later Martin J.A.), put it this way in "Insanity as a Defence," 8 Crim. L.Q. 240 (1965-66), at p. 246:

> In considering whether an accused was, by reason of insanity, incapable of knowing the nature and quality of the act committed by him, or that it was wrong, the legally relevant time is the time when the act was committed. The accused may by a process of reconstruction after committing some harmful act realize that he has committed the act and know that it was wrong. That is not inconsistent with an inability to appreciate the nature and quality of the act or to know that it was wrong at the moment of committing it.
>
> A person may have adequate intelligence to know that the commission of a certain act, e.g., murder, is wrong but at the time of the commission of the act in question he may be so obsessed with delusions or subject to impulses which are the product of insanity that he is incapable of bringing his mind to bear on what he is doing and the considerations which to normal people would make the act right or wrong. In such a situation the accused should be exempt from criminal liability. ...

Finally, it should be noted that we are not here concerned with the psychopath or the person who follows a personal and deviant code of right and wrong. The accused in the case at bar accepted society's views on right and wrong. The suggestion is that, accepting those views, he was unable because of his delusion to perceive that his act of killing was wrong in the particular circumstances of the case. On the contrary, as the psychiatrists testified, he viewed it as right. This is different from the psychopath

or person following a deviant moral code. Such a person is capable of knowing that
his or her acts are wrong in the eyes of society, and despite such knowledge, chooses
to commit them. To quote Herbert Fingarette, *The Meaning of Criminal Insanity*
(1972), pp. 200-1:

> It should be evident that we are not here reverting to the thesis that "knew it was wrong"
> means "judged it wrong in the light of his own conscience." … such a definition could
> never be acceptable in a viable criminal law. As the courts have rightly insisted, it is a
> public standard of wrong that must be used, whether public law or community morality.
>
> What we are saying here is that "knowing the nature and quality of the act or that it
> is wrong" in the context of insanity (and thus, rationality) means "having the capacity
> to rationally assess—define and evaluate—his own particular act in the light of the
> relevant public standards of wrong." …

The preceding comments should not be taken to mean that a person is not responsible if he holds irrational beliefs, for that is not the case. … The point is that if the
person has a mental makeup which is such that he lacks even the capacity for rationality, then responsibility is vitiated. If he has the capacity but simply fails to use it,
responsibility is not precluded.

### Application of the Law to This Appeal

The evidence indicated that the accused was suffering from a mental disorder causing paranoid delusion at the time of the killing. The trial judge found that this mental
disorder "compelled" the killing. The remaining question was whether the disorder
"rendered [the accused] incapable of appreciating the nature and quality of the act or
omission or of knowing that it was wrong."

The evidence was capable of supporting an affirmative answer to the question of
whether the accused was deprived of the capacity to know his act was wrong. First,
there was evidence that the accused honestly felt that he was under imminent danger
of being killed by Ms. Beaton if he did not kill her first, and that for this reason,
believed that the act of killing her was justified. This delusion would have deprived
the accused of the ability to know that his act was wrong; in his eyes, it was right.
Secondly (and this may be to say the same thing), there was evidence capable of
supporting the conclusion that the accused's mental state was so disordered that he
was unable to rationally consider whether his act was right or wrong in the way a
normal person would.

The trial judge found that while the accused was generally capable of knowing
that the act of killing was wrong, he could not apply that capacity for distinguishing
right from wrong at the time of the killing because of his mental disorder. He further
found that because of that disorder, Mr. Oommen was deluded into believing that he
had no choice but to kill. These findings are consistent with the conclusion that Mr.
Oommen's mental disorder deprived him of the capacity to know his act was wrong
by the standards of the ordinary person. As the cases make clear, s. 16(1) of the *Criminal Code* embraces not only the intellectual ability to know right from wrong, but the
capacity to apply that knowledge to the situation at hand.

*Disposition*

I would dismiss the appeal and confirm the order directing a new trial.

*Appeal dismissed.*

## Considering the Two Alternative Arms of the Mental Disorder Defence Together

In *R. v. Landry* (1988), 48 C.C.C. (3d) 552 (Que. C.A.), the accused was charged with first-degree murder as a result of the killing of a person who had formerly been his friend. The evidence established that the accused had the serious mental illness of paranoid schizophrenia and over a number of years had come to believe that his former friend was Satan and that he, the accused, was God. The accused came to believe that it was necessary for him to kill the deceased so as to save the world from destruction. In explaining the defence of insanity under s. 16 of the *Criminal Code*, the trial judge directed the jury to the effect that that defence was available only if the disease of the mind affected the accused to the extent that he was incapable of knowing that he was killing the deceased or incapable of knowing that killing was unlawful.

On appeal by the accused from his conviction for first-degree murder the Quebec Court of Appeal allowed the appeal and substituted a verdict of not guilty by reason of insanity.

Beauregard J.A. stated for the court:

> I see a difference between, on one hand, the accused who, because of a mental disorder, killed believing that he was killing Satan on the orders of God and, on the other hand, the accused who killed because his mental disorder prevented him from having sympathy for his victim or remorse for his act, or the accused who killed because his mental disorder made him believe that he would not be arrested by the police or that, if he were arrested, he would not be charged. In the first case, the accused's mental state directly affects the accused's *mens rea*; in the other two cases, it does not.
>
> If s. 7 of the *Canadian Charter of Rights and Freedoms* prevents Parliament from permitting a person to be stigmatized by a conviction for murder other than under a legal provision which is in conformity with the principles of fundamental justice, and if one must necessarily interpret laws in conformity with our Constitution, I am of the opinion that s. 16 must be interpreted in a sufficiently broad manner in order to offer a defence to the appellant in the present case.
>
> Landry who knew that he was killing Fortin and who knew that it was unlawful, is guilty of murder despite his mental disorder. But, even if Landry knew the nature and the consequences of his act and even if he knew that it was unlawful, he was incapable of appreciating the nature and quality of his act if, at that moment, he thought that he was God and that Fortin was Satan. This is an error in judgment arising from the confusion between Landry and God, and Fortin and Satan.
>
> As the additional instructions given by the judge were in my opinion insufficient in the present case and as the jury most probably relied on these final instructions in rendering its verdict, assuming that they believed the appellant, the verdict cannot stand.

The Crown appealed to the Supreme Court of Canada, which dismissed the appeal. Lamer C.J.C. stated for the majority of the court (1991), 62 C.C.C. (3d) 117:

In *Chaulk*, this court reconsidered its interpretation of the word "wrong" in s. 16(2). In *Schwartz*, ... the majority of this court held that "wrong" for the purposes of s. 16(2) means "legally wrong." The trial judge and the Court of Appeal in the case at bar relied on our decision in *Schwartz* in interpreting the second arm of s. 16(2) and thus applied that test in a restrictive manner that excluded any consideration of the respondent's capacity to know the *moral* wrongfulness of his act. As a result, Nichols J.A. felt compelled to take into account the respondent's inability to know the moral wrongfulness of the act under the first branch of the test, that is, as part of appreciating the "nature or quality" of the act. Furthermore, Beauregard J.A. invoked s. 7 of the Charter in order to extend the scope at s. 16(2) to protect an accused who is incapable of appreciating the moral wrongfulness of an act.

I am unable to support the reasoning that led to the Court of Appeal's conclusion. The Court of Appeal interpreted s. 16(2) in a manner that clearly contradicted prior judgments of this court. In accordance with our decisions in *R. v. Cooper, supra*; *R. v. Kjeldsen* (1981), 64 C.C.C. (2d) 161, 131 D.L.R. (3d) 121, [1981] 2 S.C.R. 617, and *R. v. Abbey* (1982), 68 C.C.C. (2d) 394, 138 D.L.R. (3d) 202, [1982] 2 S.C.R. 24, the first branch of the s. 16(2) test protects an accused who, because of a disease of the mind, was incapable of appreciating the *physical* consequences of his act. The Court of Appeal erred in using s. 7 of the Charter to modify the established interpretation of this statutory provision.

Despite my disagreement with the reasons of the Court of Appeal, I believe that it reached the correct result. It is my opinion that if the Court of Appeal had had the benefit of this court's judgment in *Chaulk*, it would have reached the identical conclusion for different reasons. It was established at trial and accepted by the Court of Appeal that the respondent in this case suffered from a disease of the mind to the extent that he was rendered incapable of knowing that the act was morally wrong in the circumstances. He suffered from the delusion that he was God and that he had a divine mission to kill the victim.

## III. POSSIBLE STATUTORY REFORM

The Law Reform Commission of Canada in Working Paper #29, *Criminal Law, The General Part: Liability and Defences* (1982), has proposed the following draft legislation:

Mental disorder. Alternative (1)

5. Every one is exempt from criminal liability for his conduct if it is proved that as a result of disease or defect of the mind he was incapable of appreciating the nature, consequences or unlawfulness of such conduct.

Mental disorder. Alternative (2)

5. Every one is exempt from criminal liability for his conduct if it is proved that as a result of disease or defect of the mind he lacked substantial capacity either to appreciate the nature, consequences or moral wrongfulness of such conduct or to conform to the requirements of the law.

Law Reform Commission of Canada, Report #31 (1987), *Recodifying Criminal Law*, at p. 33:

3(6) Mental Disorder. No one is liable for his conduct if, through disease or defect of the mind, he was at the time incapable of appreciating the nature, consequences or legal wrongfulness of such conduct [*or believed what he was doing was morally right*].

Comment

Those not in their right mind and therefore not responsible for their actions should not be punished. Insanity, therefore, has long been recognized as a defence at common law. What counted as insanity was spelled out in the *M'Naghten Rules* in 1843. Those rules were largely reproduced in section 16 of the *Criminal Code*.

That section does four things. It provides a general rule against convicting the insane. It gives a definition of insanity. It has a special rule about insane delusions. Finally, it places the burden of proof on the person wishing to prove insanity.

Clause 3(6) largely follows section 16 of the *Criminal Code* except in three aspects. It has nothing corresponding to the insane delusion provision, a provision seldom applied but frequently criticized because as Maudsley pointed out "it compels the lunatic to be reasonable in his unreason, sane in his insanity" and because the idea of partial insanity is not in accordance with modern medical opinion. It says nothing about presumptions of sanity or burden of proof, but leaves this, along with other evidential matters, to evidence provisions. Finally, while keeping the definition of "insanity" contained in section 16, it replaces that word by "mental disorder," a term more in line with modern medical and social attitudes.

A minority of the Commissioners wished to add the words which are in brackets. To them it seemed that although in general a person cannot be allowed to substitute his views of right and wrong for those contained in the law, nevertheless a mentally disordered person who acts as he does because he thinks it morally right to do so, merits treatment rather than punishment. The words in brackets were drafted to allow for this but at the same time to prevent exemption for the psychopath, who acts as he does not because he thinks it right to do so, but rather because he is indifferent to right and wrong.

## ADDITIONAL READING

- K. Roach, *Criminal Law*, 3rd ed. (Toronto: Irwin Law: 2004), chapter 7;
- D. Stuart, *Canadian Criminal Law*, 4th ed. (Toronto: Carswell, 2001), at 370-416;
- G. Ferguson, "A Critique of Proposals To Reform the Insanity Defence" (1989), 14 *Queen's L.J.* 135;
- A.-M. Boisvert, "Psychanalyse d'une défense: réflexions sur l'aliénation mentale" (1990), 69 *Can. Bar Rev.* 46;
- G.A. Martin, "The Insanity Defence" (1989), 10 *Criminal Lawyer's Association Newsletter* 19;
- A. Mewett and M. Manning, *Criminal Law*, 3rd ed. (Toronto: Butterworths, 1994), at 441-92;
- A. Stalker, "The Law Reform Commission of Canada and Insanity" (1982-83), 25 *Crim. L.Q.* 223;
- P. Healy, "*R. v. Chaulk*: Some Answers and Some Questions on Insanity" (1991), 2 *C.R.* (4th) 95.

# CHAPTER SIXTEEN

# Automatism

As discussed in chapter 5, criminal liability requires proof of voluntary conduct. There are many ways in which involuntary conduct might arise, including accidents and incidents in which a person cannot control his or her actions. Automatism is a specific condition of dissociation between mind and body in which a person cannot consciously control his or her conduct. Where it exists, automatism negates the *actus reus* of an offence and also, in most instances, the *mens rea*. This negation describes the effect of automatism with regard to criminal liability.

The cause of automatism is another matter and it is the cause of automatism that is controversial. As with mental disorder and other medical issues, the law and medicine do not always view automatism in the same way or for the same reasons. The law is concerned with normative concepts for the determination of responsibility and liability.

The cases in this chapter follow the development of automatism through several phases in Canadian law. The first phase involved recognition and acceptance of the concept, though it will be noted in *Rabey* that the acceptance of automatism was not without some caution. The second phase involves a fuller acceptance of this defence in *Parks*, and even greater willingness to separate it from mental disorder, but again there remains concern about the extent of this defence outside s. 16 (mental disorder). In *Stone* the perceived need for control, both as a matter of substantive law and evidence, led to a restatement of the defence that is highly restrictive.

In the following case the Supreme Court affirms that automatism is a defence in Canadian criminal law and that in its two forms it may be classified as non-insane or insane. The former would lead to a complete acquittal and the latter to a verdict of not guilty by reason of mental disorder. Of particular importance is the cogency of the distinction.

## I. INSANE AND NON-INSANE AUTOMATISM AND EMOTIONAL BLOWS

### Rabey v. The Queen
Supreme Court of Canada
[1980] 2 S.C.R. 513

RITCHIE J. (Martland, Pigeon, and Beetz JJ. concurring):

[1] This is an appeal from a judgment of the Court of Appeal for Ontario [17 O.R. (2d) 1, 40 C.R.N.S. 46, 37 C.C.C. (2d) 461, 79 D.L.R. (3d) 414] whereby that court

set aside the appellant's acquittal at trial for "causing bodily harm with intent to wound." ...

[2]  The circumstances under which the alleged offences were committed are recounted with accuracy in the reasons for judgment prepared for delivery by my brother Dickson in this case, which I have had the advantage of reading, and also in the judgment delivered by Martin J.A. on behalf of the Court of Appeal for Ontario. An "agreed statement of facts" has also been filed as a part of the record in these proceedings and, when read together with the factual analyses provided by the judges concerned, it becomes plain that there is no dispute as to the behaviour of the appellant on 28th February and 1st March 1974. On the former date he had agreed to help a girlfriend with some work which she was doing for a geology class, of which they were both members, and in the course of the afternoon he had access, while he was alone, to the girl's notebook, in which he found a letter written to one of her friends disclosing that she considered other members of the opposite sex more exciting and desirable than the appellant, to whom she referred somewhat obliquely as "a nothing."

[3]  It appears to me to be important to note at this stage that it is agreed by para. 5 of the agreed statement of facts that "The appellant had never dated any other girl for any length of time and had only a minimal amount of sexual experience. An introvert, he was infatuated with the attractive, outgoing [girl]." In any event, the appellant took the letter out of his friend's notebook and, taking it home with him, he appears to have brooded on it during the evening and underlined certain portions.

[4]  On the following day (1st March) the appellant had arranged to watch a friend play a game of squash at about noon, and on his way to the squash courts "quite by chance" he met his girlfriend and asked her to join him; when they reached the squash court, however, they entered a gallery from which to view the players, but no one was playing. They started downstairs towards the locker area but on reaching the foot of the stairs the appellant asked the girl what she thought of a mutual friend and, upon her replying that he was "just a friend," the appellant asked what she thought of him, and it was when she said that he was a friend too that he hit her on the head with a rock wrapped in cloth which he had brought from the geology laboratory that morning. The next thing the girl knew was that the appellant was kneeling on the floor with his hands around her neck choking her and crying out "You bitch," "You bitch."

[5]  I have found it necessary to recite the facts in skeletal form in order to illustrate the background against which the defence of non-insane automatism was advanced on behalf of the appellant.

[6]  It should be observed also that the appellant was subjected to a number of interviews with psychiatrists, with the result that the courts have found themselves involved in the shadowy area of mental disorders, concerning which it is not surprising to find that there are wide differences in opinion amongst the "experts." The meaning of the word "automatism"—in any event so far as it is employed in the defence of non-insane automatism—has in my opinion been satisfactorily defined by Lacourcière J. (as he then was) of the Ontario High Court of Justice in the case of *R. v. K.*, [1971] 2 O.R. 401, 3 C.C.C. (2d) 84 at 84:

Automatism is a term used to describe unconscious, involuntary behaviour, the state of a person who, though capable of action, is not conscious of what he is doing. It means an unconscious, involuntary act, where the mind does not go with what is being done.

[7] The defence of automatism, as used in the present case, of course involves a consideration of the provisions of s. 16 of the Criminal Code, R.S.C. 1970, c. C-34. ... [Section 16 is then reproduced.]

[8] What is said here is that at the relevant time the appellant was in a state where, though capable of action, he was not conscious of what he was doing, and more particularly that he was not suffering from a disease of the mind and was therefore not insane. The central question in deciding any case involving the defence of automatism is whether or not the accused was suffering from a disease of the mind. The opinions of psychiatrists go no further than characterizing the condition in which the appellant was found as being "a dissociative state," but it is clear, at least since the case of *Bratty v. A.G. Northern Ireland*, [1963] A.C. 386, 46 Cr. App. R. 1, [1961] 3 All E.R. 523 (H.L.), that the question of whether or not such a state amounts to "a disease of the mind" is a question of law for the judge to determine. The general rule is that it is for the judge as a question of law to decide what constitutes a "disease of the mind," but that the question of whether or not the facts in a given case disclose the existence of such a disease is a question to be determined by the trier of fact. I think it would be superfluous for me to retrace the line of authorities in this area, as they have been so exhaustively discussed by my brother Dickson and also by Martin J.A. of the Court of Appeal and by the learned trial judge. I am satisfied in this regard to adopt the following passages from the reasons for judgment of Martin J.A. at pp. 62-63:

In general, the distinction to be drawn is between a malfunctioning of the mind arising from some cause that is primarily internal to the accused, having its source in his psychological or emotional makeup, or in some organic pathology, as opposed to a malfunctioning of the mind, which is the transient effect produced by some specific external factor such as, for example, concussion. Any malfunctioning of the mind or mental disorder having its source primarily in some subjective condition or weakness internal to the accused (whether fully understood or not) may be a "disease of the mind" if it prevents the accused from knowing what he is doing, but transient disturbances of consciousness due to certain specific external factors do not fall within the concept of disease of the mind. (For an interesting and helpful discussion see "The Concept of Mental Disease In Criminal Law Insanity Tests" 33 University of Chicago L. Rev. 229, by Herbert Fingarette.) Particular transient mental disturbances may not, however, be capable of being properly categorized in relation to whether they constitute "disease of the mind" on the basis of a generalized statement and must be decided on a case-by-case basis.

[9] The same learned judge later stated in the same judgment at p. 68:

In my view, the ordinary stresses and disappointments of life which are the common lot of mankind do not constitute an external cause constituting an explanation for a malfunctioning of the mind which takes it out of the category of a "disease of the mind." To hold otherwise would deprive the concept of an external factor of any real meaning. In my view, the emotional stress suffered by the respondent as a result of his disappointment with respect to Miss X cannot be said to be an external factor producing the automatism within the authorities, and the dissociative state must be considered as having its source primarily in the respondent's psychological or emotional makeup. I conclude, therefore, that, in the circumstances of this case, the dissociative state in which the respondent was said to be constituted a "disease of the mind." I leave aside, until it becomes necessary to decide them, cases where a dissociative state has resulted from emotional shock without physical injury, resulting from such causes, for example, as being involved in a serious accident although no physical injury has resulted; being the victim of a murderous attack with an uplifted knife, notwithstanding that the victim has managed to escape physical injury; seeing a loved one murdered or seriously assaulted, and like situations. Such extraordinary external events might reasonably be presumed to affect the average normal person without reference to the subjective makeup of the person exposed to such experience.

For the above reasons I am of the opinion, with deference, that the learned trial judge erred in holding that the so-called "psychological blow," which was said to have caused the dissociative state, was, in the circumstances of this case, an externally originating cause, and she should have held that if the respondent was in a dissociative state at the time he struck Miss X he suffered from "disease of the mind." A new trial must, accordingly, be had on count 2.

[10] In my view a possible key to the cause of the malfunctioning of the appellant's mind at the time of the alleged assault is to be found in para. 5 of the agreed statement of facts, to which I have already referred, and where it is said of him:

> 5. The Appellant had never dated any other girl for any length of time, and had only a minimal amount of sexual experience. An introvert, he was infatuated with the attractive, outgoing ...

[11] It seems to me that his infatuation with this young woman had created an abnormal condition in his mind, under the influence of which he acted unnaturally and violently to an imagined slight to which a normal person would not have reacted in the same manner.

[12] It was contended on behalf of the appellant that a finding of disease of the mind and consequently of insanity in the present case would involve gross unfairness to the appellant, who could be subject to the provisions of s. 545 [re-en. 1972, c. 13, s. 45; am. 1974-75-76, c. 93, s. 69] of the Criminal Code and thus detained at the pleasure of the Lieutenant-Governor of the province. [With regard to Mental Disorder, see chapter 15.] That such a result does not carry with it the hardship contended for is illustrated by the following passage from the reasons for judgment of Martin J.A. at p. 69:

> It would, of course, be unthinkable that a person found not guilty on account of insanity because of a transient mental disorder constituting a disease of the mind, who was not dangerous and who required no further treatment, should continue to be confined. The present provisions of s. 545(1)(b) [re-en. 1972, c. 13, s. 45], however, authorize the

Lieutenant-Governor to make an order if, in his opinion, it would be in the best interest of the accused and not contrary to the interest of the public for the discharge of a person found not guilty on account of insanity, either absolutely or subject to such conditions as he prescribes. In addition to the periodic reviews required to be made by a board of review appointed pursuant to s. 547(1) of the Code, the Lieutenant-Governor under s. 547(6) of the Code may request the board of review to review the case of any person found not guilty on account of insanity, in which case the board of review is required to report forthwith whether such person has recovered and, if so, whether in its opinion it is in the interest of the public and of that person for the Lieutenant-Governor to order that he be discharged absolutely or subject to such conditions as the Lieutenant-Governor may prescribe.

[13] For all these reasons, as well as for those expressed by Martin J.A. in the Court of Appeal for Ontario, I would dismiss the appeal and dispose of the matter in the manner proposed by him.

DICKSON J. (dissenting) (Estey and McIntyre JJ. concurring):

[14] The automatism "defence" has come into considerable prominence in recent years. Although the word "automatism" made its way but lately to the legal state, it is basic principle that absence of volition in respect of the act involved is always a defence to a crime. A defence that the act is involuntary entitles the accused to a complete and unqualified acquittal. That the defence of automatism exists as a middle ground between criminal responsibility and legal insanity is beyond question. Although spoken of as a defence, in the sense that it is raised by the accused, the Crown always bears the burden of proving a voluntary act.

[15] The issue in this appeal is whether automatism resulting from a "psychological blow" is available to an accused in answer to a charge of causing bodily harm with intent to wound. The appellant, Wayne Kenneth Rabey, suddenly and without warning assaulted a fellow student and friend, causing her injury. The theory of the defence was that his behaviour was caused by a psychological blow, an intense emotional shock which induced a "dissociative state," during which, for a time, the appellant was neither conscious of nor able to control his conduct, so that it was involuntary. This is sometimes spoken of as non-insane automatism, to distinguish it from cases in which the state of automatism is attributable to disease of the mind. …

[18] The term "automatism" first appeared in the cases and in the periodical literature about 30 years ago. It is seen with increasing frequency. The defence of automatism is successfully invoked in circumstances of a criminal act committed unconsciously, and, in the past, has generally covered acts done while sleepwalking or under concussional states following head injuries.

[19] The defence of automatism is, in some respects, akin to that of insanity. In both instances, the issue is whether an accused had sufficient control over or knowledge of his criminal act to be held culpable. The two defences are, however, separate and distinct. As Professor J.Ll.J. Edwards observed in "Automatism and Criminal Responsibility" (1958), 21 Mod. L. Rev. 375 at 384:

Both circumstances are concerned to prove mental irresponsibility, the essential difference ... being that in the case of insanity the defect of the understanding must originate
in a disease of the mind, whereas in the defence of automatism *simpliciter* the criminal
law is not concerned with any question of the disease of the mind.

[20]  Although separate, the relationship between the two defences cannot be discounted. Automatism may be subsumed in the defence of insanity in cases in which
the unconscious action of an accused can be traced to, or rooted in, a disease of the
mind. Where that is so, the defence of insanity prevails. This is all felicitously expressed by Gresson P. in *R. v. Cottle*, [1958] N.Z.L.R. 999 at 1007 (C.A.):

It would appear that automatism raised as a defence to a criminal charge may be something quite different and distinct from insanity. In a particular case, it may be that the
automatism relied on is due to some "disease of the mind" but it is not necessarily so.
Automatism, which strictly means action without conscious volition, has been adopted
in criminal law as a term to denote conduct of which the doer is not conscious—in short
doing something without knowledge of it, and without memory afterwards of having
done it—a temporary eclipse of consciousness that nevertheless leaves the person so
affected able to exercise bodily movements. In such a case, the action is one which the
mind in its normal functioning does not control. This may be due to some "disease of
the mind" or it may not; it may happen with a perfectly healthy mind (e.g. in
somnambulism which may be unaccompanied by an abnormality of mind), or it may
occur where the mind is temporarily affected as the result of a blow, or by the influence
of a drug or other intoxication. It may on the other hand be caused by an abnormal
condition of the mind capable of being designated a mental disease. What are known as
the M'Naghten Rules can have no application unless there is some form of "disease of
the mind," which is not necessarily present in all cases of automatism.

*I*

*The Facts*

[21]  At the time of the alleged offence, 1st March 1974, the appellant, 20 years of
age, was a third-year geology student in an honours science course at the University
of Toronto. During the fall of 1973, he had spent some time with the complainant,
also a third-year science student, with whom he shared a number of classes. Along
with two male classmates, the two studied and lunched together. Their social activities extended to walks together, dinner at one another's homes and forays to a local
bar. The appellant was somewhat shy and, though he began to develop strong feelings for the attractive, outgoing complainant, the sentiment was not reciprocated.

[22]  Plans for a ski trip to Quebec were made in November and the two planned
to share a room. The complainant then invited another student to accompany them,
creating a more platonic overtone. The three did in fact go to Quebec. The appellant
testified that his relationship with the complainant deteriorated in early 1974. They
no longer went on walks or visited for dinner. He still saw much of her at school.

[23]  On 28th February 1974 the complainant asked the appellant to assist her
with an assignment. While she was absent a few moments, he flipped through her

books to locate an equation and found a letter she had written to a female friend. He took the letter without her knowledge and read it at home that evening. The letter contains a number of references to sexual activity, both actual and wished-for. Toward the end of the letter, this paragraph appears:

> And for some reason all the guys I know want to go out with me and not be just friends any more so I can't talk to them. I don't want to go out with them and they know it so there is static in the air which is why I want to leave. Hell I can insult Wayne [the appellant] and Rick and they still bug me in class. I want to be alone or with just one good guy, not with a bunch of nothings.

[24] The appellant was hurt and angry as he read the letter. He marked the passages referred to above with a pen.

[25] The following morning, he removed a rock sample of galena from the geology lab. This was not unusual, for he was permitted to take samples home for purposes of study. At about noon, as he left to watch a squash match, he met the complainant. He testified that, "just for about a second, not even that, I felt sort of strange, I can't describe how I felt." He referred to it as "a flash." He suggested she watch the match with him. The two proceeded to the squash court. The game was not in progress, so they left by the far stairwell. The appellant remembered asking her what she though of Gord, a friend of theirs, hearing the reply that he was "just a friend," and "really the next thing I remember was choking her and I remember the face was a funny colour and I remember seeing a lot of blood and I stopped." He realized his hands were around her throat.

[26] The complainant testified that following the question about Gord the appellant then asked, "What do you think of me?" She replied, "You're just a friend too." As she opened a set of fire doors, she heard a crash and a "crumbling sound." The appellant grabbed her around the arms and struck her on the head. She lost consciousness momentarily. When she recovered consciousness, he was choking her.

[27] A student happened along, to whom the appellant said, "There's been a terrible accident." He was pale, sweating and glassy-eyed and had a frightened expression. When the witness looked over the railing and saw the appellant's head, her body being under the stairs, the appellant said, "I've killed her and I am going to kill you too." The appellant had only a partial recollection of his encounter with this witness.

[28] A professor who was summoned testified that the appellant was very pale and bewildered. His description of the appellant was that he was perspiring; very, very nervous; distraught; upset; absolutely pale, no colour in his face; had moisture about the mouth; was shaky, jerky in his speech; absolutely bewildered, "out of it." In reply, he said that although the appellant was halting in his speech he was coherent. According to the nurse who next saw the appellant, he looked very upset. His pulse was very fast and not strong; he had a limp, "clammy" appearance. She was unable to convince him he had not killed the complainant. To the dean, the appellant said, "I don't know why I started or why I stopped" and that, "he liked her better than anyone he had every known." The dean testified that the appellant spoke slowly in a confused sort of way, was very depressed and perhaps dazed.

[29]  To Constable Pollitt, the appellant said, "I did it, I know I did it, I just couldn't stop hitting her." The appellant gave a statement to the police, which reads in part:

> I was asking her about the ballet, then I asked her if she liked this guy Gord. She said something about just as a friend, then I guess I hit her right then on the head, she was bleeding from the head and the next thing I remember—it all happened so fast—she was on the floor and I was sitting on top of her choking her. I thought she was dead; there was blood everywhere; I just don't know what happened.

The statement concluded:

> I don't know why I did it because I wasn't even mad when this happened, and I don't remember parts of what happened and when I realized what I had done I went to the nurse's office and then to phone the police. I actually thought I'd killed somebody.

[30]  A number of character witnesses spoke highly of the appellant. Evidence was led that he had been a well-behaved young man until this incident. He had never lost his temper or displayed signs of anger.

[31]  The complainant made a complete recovery within a short time.

*II*

*The Medical Evidence*

[32]  The appellant was remanded for psychiatric assessment and committed on 5th March 1974 to the Lakeshore Hospital. He was discharged on 1st April 1974. Detailed medical examinations disclosed no evidence of neurological disease. A psychological survey showed no indication of psychotic process. Dr. Slyfield conducted a number of interviews in the preparation of his report, which concludes:

> Psychological testing done by Mr. Wejtko indicates superior intellectual ability, a personality profile within the range of normality, and a tendency to use the psychological defenses of avoidance, repression and blocking. There was no evidence of psychotic disintegration.
>
> If Wayne is telling the truth about his amnesia for most of the incident, then it is probable that his consciousness was dissociated at the time. His somnambulistic episode lends some support to this explanation. However, such a psychological mechanism need not indicate mental illness.

[33]  In the opinion of Dr. Orchard, assistant professor of psychiatry at the University of Toronto and witness for the defence, the appellant entered into a complete dissociative state, a disorder of consciousness which occurs as a result of part of the nervous system "shutting off." A person in a severe dissociative state may be capable of performing physical actions without consciousness of such actions. When the appellant entered the dissociative state near the foot of the stairs his mind "shut off," and the return of consciousness was gradual. In Dr. Orchard's opinion the dissociative state which occurred was comparable to that produced by a physical blow; though caused by a "psychological blow," certain physical effects were produced as observed by the student, the professor, the nurse and the Dean.

[34]  According to Dr. Orchard the appellant was a young man of average health, or better than average health, with no predisposition to dissociate. The severe dissociative state, such as the appellant suffered, usually occurs in persons within the category of normal people. According to Dr. Orchard it is rare for the severe dissociative state not caused by some underlying pathology to recur. In his opinion there was only a very slight possibility that the appellant would suffer a recurrence of this disorder of consciousness. Dr. Orchard could find no indication of any pathological condition, which he defined as a "diseased condition or abnormally sick condition." In his view the dissociative state itself is an "occurrence," not a mental illness and not a disease of the mind.

[35]  Dr. Rowsell, who, like Dr. Orchard, is a psychiatrist of eminence, examined the appellant and testified on behalf of the Crown. In his opinion, the appellant was not in a dissociative state, but rather was a controlled young man who went into an extreme state of rage at the moment and, while in that state, struck the complainant on the head and choked her. Dr. Rowsell felt that if, contrary to his opinion, the appellant was in a dissociative state, he suffered from disease of the mind. According to Dr. Rowsell, consciousness is the distinguishing factor of mental life; the dissociative state is, by definition, a subdivision of hysterical neurosis, which is a definite mental illness. It is by definition a disorder of the mind. Dr. Rowsell did not suggest there was an underlying pathology which induced the alleged dissociative state. His report reads in part:

> He shows no evidence of psychosis. (A psychosis is a disorder of thinking, feeling and behaviour, accompanied by a break with reality. This means that the individual is no longer able to interpret events, both internal and external, as would a person in good mental health.) …
>
>   There is no evidence of any organic brain disorder which would impair his consciousness. Therefore, the issue could be raised as to whether he was in an automatic state at the time of the event. In my opinion he was not. The psychiatric term for such a state would be Dissociative Reaction.

[36]  The evidence of Dr. Rowsell was that Rabey was conscious at the time of the act but suffered hysterical amnesia *after the event*, which Dr. Rowsell categorized as neurosis, a disease of the mind.

[37]  Dr. Rowsell, unlike Dr. Orchard, was of the opinion that the appellant still had a psychiatric problem for which he required treatment to help him face up to what occurred. The treatment would take six months to a year, and could be undertaken on an out-patient basis. The prognosis was excellent.

[38]  Dr. Orchard, on the other hand, was of the view that, inasmuch as the appellant had been a relatively normal person prior to the occurrence, the likelihood of any recurrence was negligible. In Dr. Orchard's words:

> I think he has a pretty healthy personality and he will find a healthy way through all this. So I don't see it [sic] in need of any treatment. I don't see him as sick. I do agree with Dr. Rowsell he is not in any way a criminal type of person.

[39] Dr. Rowsell considered that the appellant was not "in any way a criminal type of person." Dr. Orchard shared that view.

*III*

*At Trial and on Appeal*

[40] The trial judge, Dymond Co. Ct. J., rejected the Crown theory of planned revenge and the medical opinion advanced by Dr. Rowsell of tremendous rage and loss of memory from protective hysterical amnesia. Referring to *R. v. K.*, [1907] 2 O.R. 401, 3 C.C.C. (2d) 84 (H.C.), and *Parnerkar v. R.*, [1974] S.C.R. 449, 21 C.R.N.S. 129, [1973] 4 W.W.R. 298, 10 C.C.C. (2d) 253, 33 D.L.R. (3d) 683, affirming 6 C.R.N.S. 347, [1972] 1 W.W.R. 161, 5 C.C.C. (2d) 11, the judge concluded that a dissociative state brought on by psychological trauma can support a defence of automatism. The ruling in *Parnerkar* flowed from the medical evidence there, distinctly different from the evidence in this case.

[41]  On the issue of automatic behaviour the judge held:

> I am satisfied from the evidence given by Dr. Orchard, by the accused himself, and by the witnesses Pollard, Turner, Houston, Huggett and Dugutis that there was evidence before the court, to paraphrase from Kelly J.A. in *R. v. Sproule* (1975), 30 C.R.N.S. 56 (Ont. C.A.), "upon which a jury properly instructed could have found that at the time of the wounding Rabey had been suffering from a malfunction of mind described as dissociation of the type brought about by an externally originating cause." Such external cause would have been the words about Gord being a friend, which, tied with the knowledge of what the letter had said, constituted an external blow or trauma which resulted in Rabey's being in a dissociative state. It can be compared with the blow to the skull causing a concussion where the skill is thin.

Elsewhere in the judgment, the following passage appears:

> I am therefore of the opinion that a defence of malfunction of the mind described as a dissociative state or a dissociation brought about by an externally operating cause is still open when the external cause is a psychological trauma, provided the other necessary conditions are met.

The "necessary conditions" to which the judge referred were:

1. There must be no disease of the mind: *Bratty v. A.G. Northern Ireland*, [1963] A.C. 386, 46 Cr. App. R. 1, [1961] 3 All E.R. 523 (H.L.). In this case both psychiatrists have given as their opinion that at the time of the event the appellant was not suffering from any disease of the mind, and no evidence was led to indicate that he was so suffering, other than Dr. Rowsell's opinion that if he were in a dissociative state, it would be a disease of the mind.

2. The condition must not arise as a result of some pre-existing pathological condition or disease. Both doctors agreed there was none.

3. The condition must not be attributable to some self-advanced incapacity, such as the consumption of liquor. The only self-advanced incapacity conceivable was the taking of the letter, and I do not believe the consequences thereof could have been foreseen.

4. The condition could not have been reasonably foreseen as the result of a particular act of omission or commission.

5. According to Lord Denning, a disease of the mind is any mental disorder which has manifested itself in violence and is prone to recur. The opinion of Dr. Orchard was that in so far as there can be any certainty in medicine the state will not recur. This is far from "prone to recur," and Dr. Rowsell did not indicate he thought the actions would recur.

The judge concluded:

> I am satisfied that Rabey was not insane within the meaning of s. 16 of the Criminal Code when the acts were committed, and I am in a state of real doubt—and, I believe, reasonable doubt—as to whether the accused acted in a state of automatism so that there was no mind behind the actions and, in effect, the actions were not his, or whether he intended to perform the acts. I must therefore give the benefit of the doubt to the accused, since I have found that a proper foundation was laid for an inference to be reasonably made that the accused acted in a state of automatism brought about by an external cause.

[42] In acquitting the appellant the judge made two findings of particular significance: first, that the appellant was not insane within the meaning of s. 16 of the Criminal Code when the acts were committed; and, second, that the appellant had acted in a state of automatism brought about by an external cause.

[43] It is important to note that the Crown did not challenge the finding of automatism in this court or in the Ontario Court of Appeal. We must therefore accept for the purposes of this appeal that the acts to which I have referred occurred without will, purpose or reasoned intention on the part of the appellant. The only question for decision is whether, having found automatism, the trial judge was bound in law to find that the appellant was a proper subject for indefinite detention as an insane person.

[44] On appeal to the Ontario Court of Appeal, the acquittal on the charge of causing bodily harm was reversed and a new trial directed on that count [17 O.R. (2d) 1, 40 C.R.N.S. 46, 37 C.C.C. (2d) 461, 79 D.L.R. (3d) 414]. The court held that the psychological blow suffered was not an externally originating cause of the dissociative state. The acquittal at trial on a companion charge of possession of a rock for the purpose of wounding was upheld.

[45] Martin J.A. delivered a lengthy judgment on behalf of the court. He held that "disease of the mind" is a legal term, having both medical and legal, or policy, components. The policy component must compromise exemption from responsibility with the need to protect the public. Ultimately the issue as to what constitutes a disease of the mind is a legal one; the concept is broad, embracing mental disorders of organic

and functional origin, whether curable or incurable, temporary or not, recurring or
non-recurring. With respect, I agree with these views, which were confirmed, at least
in part, by this court in *Cooper v. R.* (1979), 13 C.R. (3d) 97, 51 C.C.C. (2d) 129, 31
N.R. 234.

[46]  Martin J.A. went on to hold, however, that the likelihood of recurrence is not
a factor to be taken into account. In this respect he differed from Lord Denning in
*Bratty v. A.G. Northern Ireland*, supra. Martin J.A. noted that it would be unreasonable to hold that a serious mental disorder did not constitute a disease of the mind
simply because it was unlikely to recur. I agree. A test of proneness to recur does not
entail the converse conclusion, that if the mental malady is not prone to recur it cannot be a disease of the mind. A condition, organic in nature, which causes an isolated
act of unconscious violence could well be regarded as a case of temporary insanity. I
question, however, whether Lord Denning intended to exclude temporary insanity as
a disease of the mind. The phrase "prone to recur" is, I should have thought, merely
another manner of connoting a need for treatment which is, after all, one of the principal reasons for confinement of the mentally ill offender.

[47]  The learned justice of appeal held that transient mental states produced by
external causes (i.e., drugs, concussion) are not diseases of the mind. This is accepted
legal doctrine. He held also that the distinction between insanity and automatism
rests upon determining whether the cause of the malfunction is internal to an accused, or is produced by an external factor. As to this, there may be more doubt.
Martin J.A. said [p. 62]:

> In general, the distinction to be drawn is between a malfunctioning of the mind arising
> from some cause that is primarily internal to the accused, having its source in his psy-
> chological or emotional makeup, or in some organic pathology, as opposed to a mal-
> functioning of the mind which is the transient effect produced by some specific exter-
> nal factor such as, for example, concussion. Any malfunctioning of the mind or mental
> disorder having its source in some subjective condition or weakness internal to the
> accused ... may be a "disease of the mind" ... but transient disturbances of conscious-
> ness due to specific external factors do not fall within the concept of disease of the
> mind.

[48]  I will have more to say on this point, as well as upon the opinion of Martin
J.A. that in *Parnerkar*, supra, the view of Culliton C.J.S. was not dependent on the
evidence of the medical witness; rather, the dissociated state, as induced by the psychological blow, was a pathological condition.

[49]  It was the further view of Martin J.A. that the ordinary stresses and disappointments of life which are the common lot of mankind do not constitute an external
cause; the emotional stress suffered by the appellant could not be said to be an external factor producing automatism, within the authorities; the source of the dissociative state was the appellant's psychological or emotional makeup.

[50]  Martin J.A. considered it "unthinkable" that a person found not guilty on
account of insanity because of a transient mental disorder constituting a disease of
the mind, who was not dangerous and who required no further treatment, would continue to be confined.

*IV*

[51] I turn now to the authorities, with the threshold observation that none of them is binding upon this court or particularly helpful in the resolution of this case. ...

*V*

[81] This case raises interesting issues, and the judicial conclusion, in my view, should be guided by general principles of criminal responsibility. Before alluding to those principles, it is useful to recall s. 16(4) of the Criminal Code, which reads:

> (4) Every one shall, until the contrary is proved, be presumed to be and to have been sane.

[82] In the usual case in which an accused pleads insanity, he has the burden of overcoming the presumption of sanity. In the present case the appellant is not seeking to establish that he was insane on 1st March 1974. The Crown is asserting the insanity in answer to the defence of automatism raised by the appellant. The presumption of sanity runs in the appellant's favour.

[83] We turn to s. 16(2): a person is insane when he is in a state of natural imbecility or has a disease of the mind to an extent that renders him incapable of appreciating the nature and quality of an act or omission or of knowing that an act or omission is wrong. The important words, for present purposes, are "disease of the mind."

[84] The first principle, fundamental to our criminal law, which governs this appeal is that no act can be a criminal offence unless it is done voluntarily. Consciousness is a *sine qua non* to criminal liability.

[85] The prosecution must prove every element of the crime charged. One such element is the state of mind of the accused, in the sense that the act was voluntary. The circumstances are normally such as to permit a presumption of volition and mental capacity. That is not so when the accused, as here, has placed before the court, by cross-examination of Crown witnesses or by evidence called on his own behalf, or both, evidence sufficient to raise an issue that he was unconscious of his actions at the time of the alleged offence. No burden of proof is imposed upon an accused raising such defence beyond pointing to facts which indicate the existence of such a condition: *R. v. Berger* (1975), 27 C.C.C. (2d) 357 at 379, leave to appeal to the Supreme Court of Canada refused 27 C.C.C. (2d) 357n. Whether lack of consciousness relates to *mens rea* or to *actus reus* or both may be important in a case in which the offence charged is one of absolute liability, but the conceptual distinction does not concern us in the case at bar.

[86] The second principle is that no person should be committed to a hospital for the criminally insane unless he suffers from disease of the mind in need of treatment or likely to recur.

[87] The Ontario Court of Appeal held that the excusatory factor was insanity. This finding was reached though the appellant exhibited no pathological symptoms indicative of a previously existing, or ongoing, psychiatric disorder. On medical evidence accepted by the trial judge, the prospect of a recurrence of dissociation is extremely remote. There was no finding that the appellant suffered from psychosis,

neurosis or personality disorder. He does not have an organic disease of the brain. This was an isolated event. The appellant has already spent several weeks in a mental institution undergoing psychiatric, neurological and psychological assessment, the result of which did not indicate need for treatment.

[88] There are undoubtedly policy considerations to be considered. Automatism as a defence is easily feigned. It is said the credibility of our criminal justice system will be severely strained if a person who has committed a violent act is allowed an absolute acquittal on a plea of automatism arising from a psychological blow. The argument is made that the success of the defence depends upon the semantic ability of psychiatrists, tracing a narrow path between the twin shoals of criminal responsibility and an insanity verdict. Added to these concerns is the *in terrorem* argument that the floodgates will be raised if psychological blow automatism is recognized in law.

[89] There are competing policy interests. Where the condition is transient rather than persistent, unlikely to recur, not in need of treatment and not the result of self-induced intoxication, the policy objectives in finding such a person insane are not served. Such a person is not a danger to himself or to society generally.

[90] The Ontario Court of Appeal in the present case focused upon "external cause." The "ordinary stresses and disappointments of life" were held not to constitute an external cause. The court considered that the "emotional stress" suffered by the appellant could not be said to be an external factor producing the automatism; the dissociative state had its source primarily in the psychological or emotional makeup of the appellant.

[91] There is no evidence to support Martin J.A.'s statement attributing the dissociated state to the psychological or emotional makeup of the appellant. To exclude the defence of automatism it lay upon the Crown to establish that the appellant suffered from a disease of the mind at the time of the attack. The existence of the mental disease must be demonstrated in evidence. Here there is no such evidence from any of the expert or other witnesses with reference to the crucial period of the assault. Moreover, as earlier noted, s. 16(4) presumes sanity. The Court of Appeal's conclusion was directly contrary to the testimony of Dr. Orchard, accepted by the trial judge, and finds no support in the testimony of Dr. Rowsell.

[92] Martin J.A. left open the question whether it is possible to dissociate as a result of emotional shock rather than physical injury. The effect of the appellate court judgment was to differ with the trial judge's finding that the dissociation was brought about by an externally operating cause. In the circumstances, I do not think it is open to this court to disturb the findings of fact at trial.

[93] If the effect of the appellate court judgment is that, as a matter of law, emotional stress can never constitute an external factor then, with respect, I disagree. Indeed, in the passage quoted below the court seems to concede as much. If the controlling factor is one of degree of emotional stress, and the application of some form of quantitative test, then the question becomes one of fact for the trier of fact and not one of law for an appellate court.

[94] It is not clear to me why, as a matter of law, an emotional blow—which can be devastating—should be regarded as an external cause of automatism in some cir-

cumstances and an internal cause in others, as the Court of Appeal would seem to propose in this passage [p. 68]:

> I leave aside, until it becomes necessary to decide them, cases where a dissociative state has resulted from emotional shock without physical injury, resulting from such causes, for example, as being involved in a serious accident although no physical injury has resulted; being the victim of a murderous attack with an uplifted knife, notwithstanding that the victim has managed to escape physical injury; seeing a loved one murdered or seriously assaulted, and the like situations. Such extraordinary external events might reasonably be presumed to affect the average normal person without reference to the subjective makeup of the person exposed to such experience.

[95] I cannot accept the notion that an extraordinary external event, i.e., an intense emotional shock, can cause a state of dissociation or automatism if and only if all normal persons subjected to that sort of shock would react in that way. If I understood the quoted passage correctly, an objective standard is contemplated for one of the possible causes of automatism, namely, psychological blow, leaving intact the subjective standard for other causes of automatism, such as physical blow or reaction to drugs.

[96] As in all other aspects of the criminal law (except negligence offences) the inquiry is directed to the accused's actual state of mind. It is his subjective mental condition with which the law is concerned. If he has a brittle skull and sustains a concussion which causes him to run amok, he has a valid defence of automatism. If he has an irregular metabolism which induced an unanticipated and violent reaction to a drug, he will not be responsible for his acts. If he is driven into shock and unconsciousness by an emotional blow, and was susceptible to that reaction but has no disease, there is no reason in principle why a plea of automatism should not be available. The fact that other people would not have reacted as he did should not obscure the reality that the external psychological blow did cause a loss of consciousness. A person's subjective reaction, in the absence of any other medical or factual evidence supportive of insanity, should not put him into the category of persons legally insane. Nor am I prepared to accept the proposition, which seems implicit in the passage quoted, that whether an automatic state is an insane reaction or a sane reaction may depend upon the intensity of the shock.

[97] M.E. Schiffer, in his text Mental Disorder and the Criminal Trial Process (1978), states that psychological blow automatism is described as a reaction to a shock (p. 101):

> However, in cases where the psychological stress has taken the form of a sudden jolt or blow to the accused, the court may be more willing to treat a short-lived bout of automatism as sane. Because the automatism, in order to be a defence in itself, must be an "on the sudden" reaction to psychological stress, the defence of "psychological blow automatism" may be seen as somewhat analogous to the defence of provocation.

[98] I agree with the requirement that there be a shock precipitating the state of automatism. Dissociation caused by a low stress threshold and surrender to anxiety cannot fairly be said to result from a psychological blow. In a recent decision of the

British Columbia Court of Appeal, *R. v. MacLeod*, Vancouver No. CA/760128, 10th January 1980 (not yet reported), Craig J.A. adopted the judgment of Martin J.A. in *Rabey*. The facts of *MacLeod* cannot be compared with those in the instant appeal. There, the accused absorbed four double drinks of liquor prior to entering the alleged state of dissociation. His loss of consciousness cannot be traced to an immediate emotional shock. He had been subject to ongoing stress for some time, which was heightened by his wife's recent departure. Though unwilling to classify it a disease of the mind, the accused's medical witness described it as a "neurotic disorder" which could be induced by an "anxiety reaction." The Court of Appeal held that non-insane automatism was not available.

[99]  Dr. Glanville Williams' new book, Textbook of Criminal Law (1978), is helpful in this discussion, in particular c. 27. The author cites, as the main instances of automatism, "sleepwalking, concussion, some cases of epilepsy, hypoglycaemia and dissociative states." Williams says (pp. 608-609) that "automatism" has come to express "any abnormal state of consciousness (whether confusion, delusion or dissociation) that is regarded as incompatible with the existence of *mens rea*, while not amounting to insanity," adding:

> It would better be called "impaired consciousness," but the orthodox expression can be used if we bear in mind that it does not mean what it says.

And in a footnote [on p. 609]:

> Because automatism is a legal concept, a psychiatrist should be asked to testify to the mental condition as psychiatrically recognized, not to "automatism." It is for the judge to make the translation. In most of the conditions referred to legally as automatism the psychiatrist would speak of an altered state of consciousness.

[100]  The *Parnerkar* case is discussed at some length and the following observations made with respect thereto [p. 613]:

> The decision illustrates the difficulty that can be caused to the courts by over-enthusiastic psychiatrists. If such evidence were regularly given and accepted a considerable breach would be made in the law of homicide. A medical witness who proclaims that the defendant, though awake, did not know that he was stabbing a person because of his dissociated state invites incredulity, particularly where it is shown that the defendant immediately afterwards telephoned for an ambulance and the police. Further, to assert that this medical condition amounts to insanity ignores the distinction that has been developed between sane and non-sane automatism. *If Parnerkar was in a state of automatism at all it was of the non-insane variety, since there was no evidence of psychosis or brain damage or continuing danger.* (The italics are mine.)

[101]  At the conclusion of the discussion on *Parnerkar*, Williams makes the following comment, particularly apt in the present case [p. 613]:

> It may also be remarked that commitment to hospital is inappropriate in a case of hysterical dissociation, since once the episode is over the patient does not need to be detained.

[102] Under the heading "Insanity versus Automatism" Williams states that before the decision in *Quick*, supra, Lord Denning's view in *Bratty*, supra, was generally accepted. The test of insanity was the likelihood of recurrence of danger. In *Quick* the Court of Appeal adopted what might seem at first sight to be a different test for insane versus non-insane automatism. But the real question is whether the violence is likely to be repeated. Williams concludes that "on the whole, it would be much better if the courts kept to Lord Denning's plain rule; the rule in *Quick* adds nothing to it" (p. 615).

[103] This view, which the Ontario Court of Appeal appears to have rejected, finds ample support in the legal literature. See S.M. Beck, "Voluntary Conduct: Automatism, Insanity and Drunkenness" (1966-67), 9 Cr. L.Q. 315 at 321: "The cause of the automatic conduct, and the threat of recurrence, are plainly factors that determine the line between sane and insane automatism"; F.A. Whitlock, Criminal Responsibility and Mental Illness (1963), p. 120: "The test of whether or not an episode of automatism is to be judged as sane or insane action seems to rest on the likelihood of its repetition"; Professor J.Ll.J. Edwards, "Automatism and Criminal Responsibility," at p. 385: "Where evidence is available of recurrent attacks of automatism during which the accused resorts to violence ... [this] inevitably leads to consideration of the imposition of some restraint"; S. Prevezer, "Automatism and Involuntary Conduct," [1958] Crim. L.R. 440 at 441: "If ... it can safely be predicted that his conduct is not likely to recur, having regard to the cause of the automatism, there can be no point in finding him insane and detaining him in Broadmoor"; G.A. Martin, "Insanity as a Defence" (1965-66), 8 Cr. L.Q. 240 at 253: "Perhaps the distinction lies in the likelihood of recurrence and whether the person suffering from it is prone to acts of violence when in that state."

[104] In principle, the defence of automatism should be available whenever there is evidence of unconsciousness throughout the commission of the crime that cannot be attributed to fault or negligence on his part. Such evidence should be supported by expert medical opinion that the accused did not feign memory loss and that there is no underlying pathological condition which points to a disease requiring detention and treatment.

[105] I would add only that s. 16 determines the consequences of the finding of "no consciousness" on the basis of a legal conclusion guided by the medical evidence of the day. What is disease of the mind in the medical science of today may not be so tomorrow. The court will establish the meaning of disease of the mind on the basis of scientific evidence as it unfolds from day to day. The court will find as a matter of fact in each case whether a disease of the mind, so defined, is present.

[106] The circumstances in this case are highly unusual, uncomplicated by alcohol or psychiatric history. The real question in the case is whether the appellant should be confined in an institution for the criminally insane. The trial judge negated an act of passion, lack of self-control or impulsiveness. The medical evidence negated a state of disease or disorder or mental disturbance arising from infirmity. Save what was said by Dr. Rowsell, whose evidence as to *ex post facto* hysterical amnesia was rejected by the trial judge, the medical experts gave the appellant a clean mental bill of health. I can see no possible justification for sending the case back for a new trial.

[107] I would allow the appeal, set aside the judgment of the Ontario Court of Appeal and restore the verdict of acquittal.

*Appeal dismissed.*

## II. SLEEPWALKING

The proper approach to the distinction between insane and non-insane automatism lies behind the next case. According to the evidence, s. 16 was not really in issue. This in turn forced the court to consider whether it was prepared, as Dickson C.J. had said in *Rabey*, to allow the evidence of non-insane automatism to lead to its natural conclusion.

### R. v. Parks
Supreme Court of Canada
(1992), 75 C.C.C. 287

LAMER C.J.C. (for the Court):  In the small hours of the morning of May 24, 1987, the respondent, aged 23, attacked his parents-in-law, Barbara Ann and Denis Woods, killing his mother-in-law with a kitchen knife and seriously injuring his father-in-law. The incident occurred at the home of his parents-in-law while they were both asleep in bed. Their residence was 23 km. from that of the respondent, who went there by car. Immediately after the incident, the respondent went to the nearby police station, again driving his own car. He told the police:

> I just killed someone with my bare hands; Oh my God, I just killed someone; I've just killed two people; My God, I've just killed two people with my hands; My God, I've just killed two people. My hands; I just killed two people. I killed them; I just killed two people; I've just killed my mother- and father-in-law. I stabbed and beat them to death. It's all my fault.

At the trial the respondent presented a defence of automatism, stating that at the time the incidents took place he was sleep-walking. The respondent has always slept very deeply and has always had a lot of trouble waking up. The year prior to the events was particularly stressful for the respondent. His job as a project co-ordinator for Revere Electric required him to work 10 hours a day. In addition, during the preceding summer the respondent had placed bets on horse races which caused him financial problems. To obtain money he also stole some $30,000 from his employer. The following March his boss discovered the theft and dismissed him. Court proceedings were brought against him in this regard. His personal life suffered from all of this. However, his parents-in-law, who were aware of the situation, always supported him. He had excellent relations with them: he got on particularly well with his mother-in-law, who referred to him as the "gentle giant." His relations with his father-in-law were more distant, but still very good. In fact, a supper at their home was planned for May 24th to discuss the respondent's problems and the solutions he intended to suggest. Additionally, several members of his family suffer or have suffered from sleep problems such as sleep-walking, adult enuresis, nightmares and sleep-talking.

The respondent was charged with the first degree murder of Barbara Ann Woods and the attempted murder of Denis Woods.

The trial judge chose to put only the defence of automatism to the jury, which first acquitted the respondent of first degree murder and then of second degree murder. The judge also acquitted the respondent of the charge of attempted murder for the same reasons. The Court of Appeal unanimously upheld the acquittal.

[Galligan J.A. stated for the Ontario Court of Appeal: "I do not think, therefore, that it is open to question in this court that sleepwalking is a form of non-insane automatism which, if it succeeds, entitles an accused to an acquittal."]

[Lamer C.J.C. then reviewed the expert evidence.]

Three very important points emerge from this testimony: (1) the respondent was sleep-walking at the time of the incident; (2) sleep-walking is not a neurological, psychiatric or other illness: it is a sleep disorder very common in children and also found in adults; (3) there is no medical treatment as such, apart from good health practices, especially as regards sleep. It is important to note that this expert evidence was not in any way contradicted by the prosecution, which as the trial judge observed did have the advice of experts who were present during the testimony given by the defence experts and whom it chose not to call.

... I am of the view that in the instant case, based on the evidence and the testimony of the expert witnesses heard, the trial judge did not err in leaving the defence of automatism rather than that of insanity with the jury, and that the instant appeal should be dismissed. For a defence of insanity to have been put to the jury, together with or instead of a defence of automatism, as the case may be, there would have had to have been in the record evidence tending to show that sleep-walking was the cause of the respondent's state of mind. As we have just seen, that is not the case here. This is not to say that sleep-walking could never be a disease of the mind, in another case on different evidence.

As I see it, however, that does not end the matter. Although the expert witnesses were unanimous in saying that sleep-walkers are very rarely violent, I am still concerned by the fact that as the result of an acquittal in a situation like this (and I am relieved that such cases are quite rare), the accused is simply set free without any consideration of measures to protect the public, or indeed the accused himself, from the possibility of a repetition of such unfortunate occurrences. In the case of an outright acquittal, should there not be some control? And if so, how should this be done? I am of the view that such control could be exercised by means of the common law power to make an order to keep the peace vested in any judge or magistrate. This power of "preventive justice" has been recognized in England for centuries. ...

Accordingly, such a power exists. The question remains whether it should be exercised in the case of the respondent Parks, or at least whether its exercise should be considered. I am of the view that this approach should be considered. As I have already said, despite the unanimous and uncontradicted evidence that the chances of such an occurrence taking place again are for all practical purposes nil, I feel that all necessary measures should be taken to ensure that such an event does not recur. After all, before this tragic incident occurred, the probability of Mr. Parks' killing someone while in a somnambulistic state was infinitesimal. Yet this is precisely what took place. Furthermore, the evidence at trial was not adduced with a view to determining whether an order would be justified and to determine the appropriate conditions of such an order. Thus, for example, an order might be made requiring Parks to do certain things suggested by a specialist in sleep disorders, for example to report to him periodically. In appropriate cases of outright acquittals on grounds of automatism measures that would reinforce sleep hygiene and thereby provide greater safety for others should always be considered. If the trial judge considers that making such an order would be in the interest of the public, he should so advise the parties and consider whatever evidence and submissions are tendered. In those situations where an order is made, it should be complied with in the same way as any other order of the court.

[All the other members of the court agreed with Lamer C.J.C. that this was a case of non-insane automatism, but (except for Cory J.) disagreed with Lamer C.J.C.'s view that the matter should be sent back to the trial judge for a further hearing under a "preventive justice" power.]

SOPINKA J. stated: … Furthermore, the potential implications of the course of action contemplated by the Chief Justice are significant not only for the respondent, but also in other cases. Consider an individual who is convicted of a violent crime at trial, but on appeal a stay is entered on the basis that his right to be tried within a reasonable time has been violated. Would the court none the less impose restrictions on his liberty in an attempt to ensure that such an event does not recur? Such restrictions would be a significant departure from fundamental principles of criminal law, yet there is nothing in the authorities relied upon by the Chief Justice which limits the consideration of an order to keep the peace to cases such as the one at bar.

I note that there still exists the possibility of an information being laid pursuant to s. 810 of the *Criminal Code*. This, of course, is subject to the evidentiary basis required under that section, "that the informant has reasonable grounds for his fears" (s. 810(3)), and to constitutional challenge. If such a proceeding is to be initiated, it should not be done so by this court acting *proprio motu*.

McLACHLIN J. stated: … In addition to the difficult issues raised by an order restricting a person's liberty on account of an act for which he has been acquitted, I have concerns whether further proceedings are appropriate in the circumstances before us. Mr. Parks has been living in the shadow of these charges since May 24, 1987, over five years. His acquittal is now confirmed. We are told he has been making courageous efforts to re-establish his life. Should he now be embroiled in a further set of proceedings concerned, not with his guilt or innocence, but with the maintenance of his liberty?

Generally, the courts do not grant remedies affecting the liberty of the subject unless they are asked to do so by the Crown, which is charged with instituting such legal processes as it deems appropriate having regard to the public interest and fairness to the individual involved. In the absence of an application by the Crown, I hesitate to remit the case for consideration of further measures against the accused.

I add that the possibility of supervisory orders in this situation may be a matter which Parliament would wish to consider in the near future.

La FOREST J. stated: … It appears, then, that the judiciary is not practically equipped to administer a "keep the peace order" in the circumstances of this case. For this reason, along with the reasons of my colleagues, I would not remit this case back to the trial judge for the consideration of such an order. I would accordingly dismiss the appeal and uphold the acquittal of the respondent.

*Appeal dismissed.*

## III. MENTAL DISORDER AND NON-MENTAL DISORDER AUTOMATISM

Perhaps *Parks* aroused anxiety. Perhaps it expressed an anxiety that was widely held. In *R. v. Stone* five judges of the Supreme Court were moved to impose strict conditions on the defence of automatism. Note that these conditions not only limit the substantive principles relating to automatism, they also impose significant evidentiary challenges.

### R. v. Stone
Supreme Court of Canada
[1999] 2 S.C.R. 290

BINNIE J. (dissenting) (Lamer C.J.C., Iacobucci, and Major JJ. concurring):

[1] A fundamental principle of the criminal law is that no act can be a criminal offence unless it is performed or omitted voluntarily. In this case the appellant acknowledges that he killed his wife. He stabbed her 47 times with his knife in a frenzy. His defence was that he lost consciousness when his mind snapped under the weight of verbal abuse which the defence psychiatrist characterized as" exceptionally cruel" and "psychologically sadistic." The trial judge ruled in favour of the appellant that "there is evidence of unconsciousness throughout the commission of the crime," and the British Columbia Court of Appeal agreed ((1997), 86 B.C.A.C. 169 (B.C. C.A.), at p. 173) that "a properly instructed jury, acting reasonably, could find some form of automatism."

[2] The appellant had elected trial by jury. He says he was entitled to have the issue of voluntariness, thus properly raised, determined by the jury. He says that there was no proper legal basis for the courts in British Columbia to deprive him of the benefit of an evidentiary ruling which put in issue the Crown's ability to prove the *actus reus* of the offence.

[3] The trial judge ruled that the evidence of involuntariness was only relevant (if at all) to a defence of not criminally responsible by reason of mental disorder (NCRMD). This was upheld by the Court of Appeal. When it is appreciated that all of the experts agreed the appellant did not suffer from any condition that medicine would

classify as a disease of the mind, it is perhaps not surprising that the jury found the accused to be sane. He was convicted of manslaughter. The contention of the appellant that the act of killing, while not the product of a mentally disordered mind, was nevertheless involuntary, was never put to the jury.

[4] The appellant argues that the judicial reasoning that effectively took the issue of voluntariness away from the jury violates the presumption of his innocence and his entitlement to the benefit of a jury trial guaranteed by s. 11(d) and (f) and is not saved by s. 1 of the *Canadian Charter of Rights and Freedoms*. ...

[6] In my view, it follows from the concurrent findings in the courts below (that the appellant successfully put in issue his consciousness at the time of the offence) that he was entitled to the jury's verdict on whether or not his conduct, though sane, was involuntary. That issue having been withdrawn from the jury, and the Crown thereby having been relieved of the one real challenge to its proof, the appellant is entitled to a new trial.

### I. Facts

[7] I do not propose to repeat Justice Bastarache's summary of the facts except where necessary to explain our divergence in the result.

[8] The prelude to the knife attack was a day-long drive from the Okanagan Valley to Vancouver, during which, according to the appellant, his wife created an explosive situation by her aggressive verbal attacks. The appellant had planned to take his sons out to dinner and a movie, but abandoned these plans because of his wife's objection. The appellant instead visited briefly with his sons. His wife waited in the truck. According to the appellant, his wife accelerated her attack on him upon his return to the driver's seat. She taunted him that his former wife had been "fucking all my friends" (while the two had been married) and that "my sons weren't my kids at all." As the verbal abuse continued, he said, "I can see she's losing it," so he pulled into a vacant lot and "she's still yelling at me that I'm nothing but a piece of shit." His wife then allegedly said she had told the police that he had been abusing her and that they were about to arrest him, and threatened to get a court order to force him out of their home leaving her in the house, collecting alimony and child support. He says she told him that she felt sick every time he touched her, that he was a "lousy fuck" with a small penis, and that she would never have sex with him again. As stated, a psychological report filed by the defence at trial characterized the comments attributed to Mrs. Stone as "exceptionally cruel, psychologically sadistic, and profoundly rejecting."

[9] The appellant finally pulled off the highway in Burnaby to a vacant lot and described sitting in the truck with his head down, listening to his wife, and thinking that he and his boys did not deserve to be treated this way and "it's just kind of fading away." From there, he said, he remembered only a" whooshing" sensation washing over him, from his feet to his head. According to his account, when subsequently his eyes focussed, he was staring straight ahead and felt something in his hand. He looked down and saw his wife slumped over on the seat. He was holding the hunting knife

that he kept stored in the truck. His wife was dead, having been stabbed 47 times. The appellant says that, at that time, he had no memory of stabbing his wife.

[10] After 10 or 15 minutes, the appellant put his wife's body in a toolbox in the back of the truck and returned home. The next day, he sold some assets, settled some debts, and flew to Mexico. At trial the appellant recounted that one morning (while in Mexico), he awoke with the sensation of having his throat cut. In trying to recall what he had been dreaming about, the appellant remembered his wife's being stabbed in the chest. While the appellant maintained in his evidence-in-chief that he did not remember picking up the knife or taking it from its sheath, he did admit in cross-examination, when confronted with prior statements attributed to him in the psychiatrist's report, to a vague recollection through the dream of stabbing his wife twice in the chest before the" whooshing" sensation. His psychiatrist, Dr. Paul Janke, testified that the appellant had told him that, while in Mexico, he "became aware of a memory of having a knife in his hand and stabbing Donna Stone twice in the chest *before* having the 'whooshing' sensation ... whenever we talked about the stabbing, it would be in the context of stabbing twice and, and then having the whooshing experience" (emphasis added). One of Dr. Janke's tasks was to separate out the effects of amnesia after the event from the alleged unconsciousness during the events themselves, for as noted by Lord Denning in *Bratty v. Attorney-General for Northern Ireland* (1961), [1963] A.C. 386 (U.K. H.L.), at p. 409: "Loss of memory afterwards is never a defence in itself, so long as he was conscious at the time."

[11] Roughly six weeks after the stabbing, the appellant returned to Canada and surrendered to police.

[12] At trial, Dr. Janke testified for the defence that, at the time of the stabbing, the appellant was in a dissociative state caused by "extreme" psychological blows:

> Q But the comments that you reviewed and that are in evidence between Mrs. Stone and Mr. Stone aren't such, are they, of such an extraordinary nature that they might reasonably be presumed to affect the ordinary person?
>
> A We—I would be astonished if somebody told me that being, being informed that they were about to lose their home and all their possessions; that their, what they thought were their children by a former wife were actually the product of affairs that the wife was having; and ultimately being told that you had a small penis and were poor in bed, most men would find that an extraordinary blow. If somebody told me they weren't upset by that, I would be concerned about it.
>
> Q No question—
>
> A Those are extreme—
>
> Q —that he was upset.
>
> A No, those are extreme blows.

[13] The defence was confronted with the decision of this Court in *R. v. Rabey*, [1980] 2 S.C.R. 513 (S.C.C.), which was said to hold that unless a state of automatism

can be attributed on the evidence to some cause external to the mind of the accused, it must be related to a plea of insanity.

[14] The appellant tried to run simultaneously both the non-insane and insane branches of the automatism plea, as well as provocation. He suggested, based on an *obiter dictum* in *Rabey, supra*, that the "psychological shock" inflicted on him was of so great a magnitude that it would have unhinged the ordinary person, thus qualifying as "externally" induced automatism which had nothing to do with a disease of the mind in any organic or other medical sense. He submitted in the alternative that if, contrary to the psychiatric evidence, the courts were to insist on characterizing his condition as a disease of the mind, then a finding of NCRMD would be consistent with Dr. Janke's evidence that the unconscious nature of his conduct excluded an "appreciation" of the consequences.

## II.  Judgments

### A.  The Supreme Court of British Columbia

#### (1)  The Evidential Ruling in the Appellant's Favour

[15] Brenner J. reasoned that the "defence" of automatism is only available where there is evidence of unconsciousness throughout the entire commission of a crime. While recognizing that there was some evidence before the court to the effect that the appellant recalled stabbing his wife twice in the chest, Brenner J. ultimately held that an accused's having some recollection of what has occurred does not preclude the availability of the defence. That decided, he held, seemingly based on the entirety of the defence testimony, that there was evidence of unconsciousness throughout the commission of the offence and the accused had successfully laid a foundation for the plea of automatism. The relevant portion of his ruling is as follows:

> In this case, it is my view that there is evidence of *unconsciousness throughout the commission of the crime*. The only evidence of recall is the recollection that came to the accused following a dream after he had gone to Mexico some days after the event.
>
> That being the case, it seems to me that the defence has met the threshold test pursuant to which I must at least consider whether the defence of automatism of either the insane or non-insane variety should be left to the jury. [Emphasis added.]

#### (2)  The Withdrawal of the Issue of Non-Insane Automatism from the Jury

[16] Brenner J. considered that, in the absence of evidence to the contrary, the cause of the automatism (if it existed) must have been "internal" to the appellant's brain. On this basis, he concluded that he was bound by *R. v. MacLeod* (1980), 52 C.C.C. (2d) 193 (B.C. C.A.), to withhold the defence of "non-insane automatism" from the jury. In *MacLeod* the British Columbia Court of Appeal had applied the *Rabey* analysis to an accused who claimed to have "dissociated" owing to an accumulation of stresses in his family life and, while dissociated, to have sexually assaulted a five-year-old child who suffered from cerebral palsy. The British Columbia

Court of Appeal in *MacLeod* held that the accused was either insane or should be held criminally responsible for his actions notwithstanding the alleged automatism.

(3) The Jury Charge

[17] Brenner J. referred the jury to the specific pieces of evidence particularly relevant to consideration of the automatism defence. In the course of this process, he highlighted the evidence of dissociation:

> Dr. Janke, the forensic psychiatrist who testified for the defence, expressed the opinion that the accused was in a dissociative state when he killed his wife, and Dr. Murphy, the Crown forensic psychiatrist, expressed the opinion that the likelihood of the accused being in a dissociative state was very low.
>
> You will recall that Dr. Janke explained to you what dissociation was. He explained the phenomenon as a situation where an individual's thinking component and his judgment is separated from his body and his actions. He explained to you it was typically associated with some loss of memory, and I took from his evidence that the degree of memory loss will often or frequently depend on how deep the dissociative state. ...
>
> *He says, in his opinion, at the time the accused killed his wife, he did not have control over his actions*, and a person in the accused's state, in Dr. Janke's opinion, would not appreciate the nature and quality of his act. [Emphasis added.]

[18] Brenner J. concluded his instruction on this point by explaining the series of questions the jury should address:

> If you are satisfied on a balance of probabilities that the evidence establishes that the accused was suffering from a disease of the mind, you must then determine whether the disease of the mind rendered him either incapable of appreciating the nature and quality of the act he was doing or incapable of knowing that the act was wrong.
>
> We do not know, of course, on which aspects of these multi-faceted questions the accused failed to satisfy the jury. We only know that at the conclusion of their deliberations the following exchange took place:
>
> MR. REGISTRAR: Members of the jury, have you reached a verdict?
>
> MR. FOREMAN: We have, my lord.
>
> The Court: Mr. Foreman, do you find the accused criminally responsible or not criminally responsible by reason of mental disorder?
>
> THE FOREMAN: We find that the defendant is criminally responsible.
>
> The Court: Proceed with the next question, Madam Registrar.
>
> MR. REGISTRAR: Do you find the accused guilty or not guilty of second degree murder.
>
> THE FOREMAN: Not guilty.
>
> The Court: Thank you, Mr. Foreman.

> Based on that verdict, I will direct that a verdict of guilty of the offence of man-
> slaughter be entered. ...

The jury was *not* told that if they concluded that the accused was not suffering from a disease of the mind they could nevertheless decide that the appellant's actions were not voluntary and that such a finding, if made, would necessitate an acquittal. The jury was told, in effect, that notwithstanding the trial judge's ruling that there was evidence of "unconsciousness throughout the commission of the crime," the minimum verdict was manslaughter. ...

*B. British Columbia Court of Appeal (1997), 86 B.C.A.C. 169 (B.C. C.A.)*

(1)  The Automatism Issue

[21]  McEachern C.J. began by noting at p. 173 that, when considering whether to put a possible defence to a jury, a trial judge must determine whether there is sufficient evidence to lend an "air of reality" to the defence. He held that the trial judge had found that there was an "air of reality" to the appellant's assertion of automatism, but that this conclusion related to the concept in general, and not to a specific form of automatism.

[22]  Despite somewhat inconsistent evidence, both the trial court and the Court of Appeal held that there was evidence of dissociation throughout the length of the appellant's attack on his wife.

[23]  Referring to *Rabey*, *supra*, McEachern C.J. reasoned at p. 173 that the trial judge next had to determine if there was any evidence "from which the jury could reasonably conclude that the dissociated state was *not* caused by a disease of the mind" (emphasis added). In the absence of such evidence, he held that a dissociated state could only result from a disease of the mind.

[24]  McEachern C.J. noted by a process of elimination that the only potential explanation for Stone's behaviour was the impact of his wife's abuse. He considered that such psychological blows are usually insufficient to cause" non-insane automatism." This led to the conclusion that the violent reaction to psychological trauma should be attributed primarily to the individual's internal psychological or emotional weaknesses. He held that Brenner J. had properly applied the *Rabey* test in concluding that the cause of the appellant's dissociative state, if such had occurred, was primarily related to his reaction to verbal abuse "which is more properly characterized as an *internal* as opposed to an *external* cause, and is, accordingly, a disease of the mind." As such, he held that the trial judge had properly refused to put "sane automatism" to the jury.

[25]  McEachern C.J. noted that this Court's decision in *R. v. Parks*, [1992] 2 S.C.R. 871 (S.C.C.) (the sleepwalker case), may justify using something other than an internal/external cause approach to identify a "disease of the mind." He referred specifically to a passage from the majority judgment of La Forest J. which said that the distinction drawn in *Rabey* between internal and external causes is meant only as an analytical tool, and not as an all-encompassing methodology.

[26] Despite this, McEachern C.J. preferred the *Rabey* approach. He thought, at p. 176, that the present case was one where," but for some ill-defined, but readily understood internal component of a person's psychological state, the ordinary processes of a conscious mind would normally prevent such a violent reaction to criticism and insults." Viewing the problem as one of an exceptional frailty of mind, McEachern C.J. held that the trial judge was correct not to charge the jury on "non-insane automatism." ...

### *III. Analysis*

#### *A. The Automatism Issue*

[29] This appeal raises questions about the allocation of issues between the judge and jury in the difficult area of automatism. Part of the difficulty stems from the concern of some judges that juries may be too quick to accept the story of an accused that he or she doesn't remember what happened, or that the conduct was "uncontrollable," or some other feigned version of events. In *R. v. Szymusiak*, [1972] 3 O.R. 602 (Ont. C.A.), at p. 608, Schroeder J.A. observed that automatism is:

> ... a defence which in a true and proper case may be the only one open to an honest man, but it may just as readily be the last refuge of a scoundrel. It is for these reasons that a Judge presiding at a trial has the responsibility cast upon him of separating the wheat from the chaff.

One might also cite to the same effect the scoffing tone of G. Williams in his *Textbook of Criminal Law* (2nd ed. 1983), at pp. 673-74:

> ... where a person who is fully awake flees from the police, or attacks another in jealousy or anger, a defence of dissociation is hard to credit, however many experts are called to give evidence in support of it. How strange, the layman may say, and how very convenient for the defendant, that this alleged state of dissociation descended on him at the very moment when he had reason for evading the police, or when he was face to face with a person whom he had a strong motive for attacking. The more down-to-earth explanation of the defendant's "narrowing of the field of consciousness" is that it resulted merely from an overwhelming passion which led him to pay no attention to ordinary moral or prudential considerations; this is not inconsistent with the supposition that he was perfectly aware of what he was doing, psychiatric evidence to the contrary notwithstanding.

In giving heed to these wise words of scepticism, the courts must nevertheless respect the allocation by Parliament to the jury the tasks of assessing credibility and the making of findings of fact. A concern that the jury may fall into error is no basis for taking away part of its jurisdiction. The central feature of this appeal is the finding of the trial judge, accepted by the British Columbia Court of Appeal, that there was "evidence of unconsciousness throughout the commission of the crime." The appellant says he was entitled to have his case dealt with by the jury on that basis.

(1)  The Evidentiary Ruling

[30]  The trial judge properly instructed himself with respect to the evidential onus. He applied the test set out by Dickson J., as he then was, in *Rabey, supra*, at p. 552:

> In principle, the defence of automatism should be available whenever there is evidence of unconsciousness throughout the commission of the crime, that cannot be attributed to fault or negligence of his part. Such evidence should be supported by expert medical opinion that the accused did not feign memory loss and that there is no underlying pathological condition which points to a disease requiring detention and treatment.

Although given in dissent, Dickson J.'s statement of the evidential burden was subsequently adopted and applied by the majority of this Court in *Parks, supra*.

[31]  The trial judge properly applied the test. There is no suggestion that the appellant's alleged state of unconsciousness, if it existed, came about through his own fault or negligence. The appellant's evidence that he was unconscious" throughout the commission of the crime" was supported by the expert medical opinion of Dr. Janke, who said it was a "necessary component" of doing his forensic assessment to determine whether the appellant was "fabricating." Dr. Janke went further than merely reporting what the appellant had said to him. Dr. Janke's professional opinion was that the appellant was not fabricating his story, that the allegation of unconsciousness was corroborated to some extent by the appellant's psychological make-up, and that it would be very difficult (albeit not impossible) for the appellant to present a story of dissociation" in a sophisticated way that would fool an experienced forensic psychiatrist." Dr. Janke testified that the appellant suffered from no underlying pathological condition which pointed to a disease requiring detention and treatment.

[32]  The evidence on unconsciousness was somewhat equivocal, in my review of it, but I did not have the advantage of seeing and hearing the appellant or Dr. Janke, and I am not in any position to impeach the conclusion of the trial judge that:

> In this case, it is my view that there is evidence of *unconsciousness throughout the commission of the crime*. The only evidence of recall is the recollection that came to the accused following a dream after he had gone to Mexico some days after the event.
>     *That being the case, it seems to me that the defence has met the threshold test. ...*
> [Emphasis added.]

I agree with Bastarache J. in para. 192 of his reasons that it would be preferable to have additional corroborative evidence, such as bystanders to the event or a documented history of automatistic-like dissociative states. However, the absence of such corroboration cannot relieve the court of the duty to consider the defence that is in fact presented, warts and all. Under our system, once the evidential burden is met, the assessment of the credibility of the defence is up to the jury.

(2)  Proof of the Offence

[33]  In *Parks, supra*, a majority of this Court observed that" voluntariness" can be seen as part of the *actus reus* requirement of criminal liability, *per* La Forest J., at p. 896:

Automatism occupies a unique place in our criminal law system. Although spoken of as a "defence," it is conceptually a sub-set of the *voluntariness* requirement, which in turn is part of the *actus reus* component of criminal liability. [Emphasis added.]

[34] The same point was made by Lamer C.J. and La Forest J. in *R. c. Daviault*, [1994] 3 S.C.R. 63 (S.C.C.). See also McLachlin J. in *R. v. Théroux*, [1993] 2 S.C.R. 5 (S.C.C.) (cited by Cory J. in *Daviault*, at p. 74), who observed, at p. 17:

> The term *mens rea*, properly understood, does not encompass all of the mental elements of a crime. *The* actus reus *has its own mental element; the act must be the voluntary act of the accused* for the *actus reus* to exist. *Mens rea*, on the other hand, refers to the guilty mind, the wrongful intention, of the accused. Its function in criminal law is to prevent the conviction of the morally innocent—those who do not understand or intend the consequences of their acts. Typically, *mens rea* is concerned with the consequences of the prohibited *actus reus*. [Emphasis added.]

[35] Cory J. in *Daviault*, at pp. 75 and 102, pointed out that automatism may also relate in some circumstances to *mens rea*. See also *R. v. Chaulk*, [1990] 3 S.C.R. 1303 (S.C.C.). For the purposes of this appeal, however, it is sufficient to note that a claim of automatism puts in issue the Crown's ability to prove all of the elements of the offence beyond a reasonable doubt.

### (3) Relieving the Crown of Part of Its Persuasive Burden of Proof

[36] The Crown supports the ruling of the courts in British Columbia on a number of grounds:

(a)  the presumption of voluntariness;

(b)  the decision of this Court in *Rabey, supra*;

(c)  the contention that the mental disorder provisions of the *Criminal Code* were appropriate to resolve the automatism issue on the facts of this case.

I will address each of these Crown arguments in turn.

### (a) Ground 1: The Presumption of Voluntariness

[37] The criminal law is premised on the responsibility of sane individuals for their voluntary acts or omissions. We infer from common experience that the acts of an apparently conscious person are usually voluntary. The issue here, however, is whether such an inference of voluntariness can be drawn after the trial judge has ruled that there is credible evidence that the accused was *unconscious* throughout the commission of the offence.

[38] Everyday experience for most of us does not teach whether the acts of a person in a severely impaired state of consciousness, such as sleepwalking or an epileptic fit, are voluntary. Dickson J., dissenting, stated in *Rabey, supra*, at p. 545, "Consciousness is a *sine qua non* to criminal liability."

(I)  RELATIONSHIP BETWEEN VOLUNTARINESS AND CONSCIOUSNESS

[39]  The concepts of unconsciousness and involuntariness are linked in the definition of automatism proposed by the Ontario High Court of Justice in *R. v. K.* (1970), 3 C.C.C. (2d) 84 (Ont. H.C.), at p. 84, and adopted by a majority in this Court in *Rabey, supra*, at p. 518:

> Automatism is a term used to describe unconscious, involuntary behaviour, the state of a person who, though capable of action is not conscious of what he is doing. It means an unconscious involuntary act where *the mind does not go with what is being done.* [Emphasis added.]

The relationship between voluntariness and consciousness was also addressed by Mason C.J., Brennan and McHugh JJ. in *R. v. Falconer* (1990), 50 A. Crim. R. 244 (Australia H.C.), at p. 250:

> Although the prosecution bears the ultimate onus of proving beyond reasonable doubt that an act which is an element of an offence charged was a willed act or, at common law, was done voluntarily … , the prosecution may rely on the *inference that an act done by an apparently conscious actor is willed or voluntary* to discharge that onus unless there are grounds for believing that the accused was unable to control that act. [Emphasis added.]

Just as the High Court was prepared to infer voluntariness from consciousness, evidence of lack of consciousness may support a claim of automatism (i.e., that there was a lack of voluntariness). The question is, What is meant in this context by "lack of consciousness"? In the present case, the Crown psychiatrist contended that in medical terms the appellant could not be considered unconscious:

> A  I'm not sure what unconscious means in the legal sense, but—

> Q  In the medical sense.

> A  In the medical sense, he wasn't unconscious. Unconscious means flat out on the floor. He clearly wasn't, from all the information that we have, unconscious in that sense.

[40]  From the legal perspective, "unconsciousness" is used in the sense that the accused, like the sleepwalker, is shown "not to have known what he was doing." (See *Parks, supra*, at p. 871, and *R. v. Tolson* (1889), 23 Q.B.D. 168 (Eng. Q.B.), at p. 187.) This excludes the person who is provoked and says," I couldn't help myself," or who simply professes to be at a loss to explain uncharacteristic conduct: see generally Lord Denning in *Bratty, supra*, at p. 409, who there defined automatism as:

> … an act which is done by the muscles without any control by the mind, such as a spasm, a reflex action or a convulsion; or an act done by *a person who is not conscious of what he is doing*, such as an act done whilst suffering from concussion or whilst sleep-walking. [Emphasis added.]

Voluntary action presupposes a measure of conscious control. Dickson J. in *Rabey* allowed, at p. 550, that, "[a]t common law a person who engaged in what would otherwise have been criminal conduct was not guilty of a crime if he did so in a state of unconsciousness or *semi-consciousness*" (emphasis added). In context, however, the reference to" semi-consciousness" was to a state of diminished awareness that *negated* control. I think Crown counsel's submissions in oral argument were consistent with this approach. He submitted that automatism describes" involuntary behaviour that occurs without the minimum mental element necessary to *will* the act," and "[i]t is the state of a person who, though capable of action, is *incapable* of knowing that the act is taking place" (emphasis added). His definitions encompassed the notions of awareness *and* control. I agree with the Crown's submissions in this regard. Dr. Janke, the defence psychiatrist, used "consciousness" in the sense of awareness or control, as is clear from the following extracts from his evidence:

> [A person] can, as in Mr. Stone's case, have a fragment of memory and, fragmentary memory even before the attack, the actual attack on Donna Stone, and not be in a, *not have any control* over what they are actually doing. [Emphasis added.] …
>
> Based on Mr. Stone's descriptions of the events and my understanding of the circumstances from the other materials, it would be my opinion that he *did not have control* over his actions. [Emphasis added.]

At the same time, the evidence that the appellant recalled some weeks after the killing "stabbing twice and, *then* having the whooshing experience" raised an important problem for the trial judge. If it were contended that the appellant suffered a "blackout" of consciousness, and was incapable of exercising any conscious control over his actions, voluntariness would be put in issue. The appellant would have identified an explanation for his lack of control, namely that he was unconscious at the time. If, however, the appellant was conscious, even for only the initial stab wounds, he would be confronted with the presumption of voluntariness for that period of time. The trial judge dealt with this issue as follows:

> During the submissions by counsel, I indicated that my review of the authorities suggested that the defence of automatism was only available in the event that there is evidence of unconsciousness throughout the entire commission of a crime. That is the language used by Chief Justice Dickson. In this case, there is some evidence that the accused was aware and was not unconscious throughout the commission of the crime. He was able to testify before the court that he recalled stabbing his wife twice in the chest. The question at issue at this stage is whether that evidence takes this case out of the realm of automatism as a matter of law. …
>
> On my reading of the authorities, I conclude that the authorities do not exclude the possibility of the defence of automatism being available because an accused is able to have some recollection of what occurred.
>
> In this case, it is my view that there is evidence of unconsciousness throughout the commission of the crime. The only evidence of recall is the recollection that came to the accused following a dream after he had gone to Mexico some days after the event.
>
> That being the case, it seems to me that the defence has met the threshold test. …

The trial judge thus found, at the conclusion of a careful analysis, that a properly instructed jury, acting reasonably, could find that the appellant was unconscious "throughout the commission of the crime." He found the evidence was capable (if believed) of satisfying the definition of automatism given by Dickson J. in *Rabey*. In these circumstances, "the defence of automatism should be available" (*Rabey* Dickson J., at p. 552). This initial ruling was not disturbed by the British Columbia Court of Appeal. This Court is thus confronted with concurrent findings on this crucial point. The remaining issue is whether there was any legal justification for depriving the appellant of the benefit of that evidentiary ruling, and taking the issue of automatism away from the jury. ...

(III) ONUS OF PROOF

[44] My colleague Bastarache J. proposes, at para. 179, that the Court take this opportunity to add to the evidential burden on the accused a second and more onerous obstacle, namely the persuasive or legal burden on the accused to establish automatism on a balance of probabilities. The onus issue does not truly arise on the facts of the appeal. The issue of non-mental disorder automatism was not put to the jury at all, and it is superfluous to consider what *ought* to have been said about onus had the trial judge done what he didn't do and, as the appeal is to be dismissed, he will never have to do in this case.

[45] More importantly, piling the persuasive burden on top of the evidential burden represents a change in the law as settled by this Court in *Parks, supra*, only seven years ago. In his majority judgment in *Parks*, La Forest J. reproduced with approval, at p. 897, a portion of Dickson J.'s earlier dissent in *Rabey*. In that passage, Dickson J. was careful to emphasize that imposition of an *evidential* burden as a matter of policy to filter out frivolous claims did not in any way indicate that an accused carried any part of the *persuasive* or legal burden, whether on a balance of probabilities or otherwise. See *Rabey*, at p. 545:

> The prosecution must prove every element of the crime charged. One such element is the state of mind of the accused, in the sense that the act was voluntary. The circumstances are normally such as to permit a presumption of volition and mental capacity. That is not so when the accused, as here, has placed before the court, by cross-examination of Crown witnesses or by evidence called on his own behalf, or both, evidence sufficient to raise an issue that he was unconscious of his actions at the time of the alleged offence. *No burden of proof is imposed upon an accused raising such defence beyond pointing to facts which indicate the existence of such a condition. ...* [Emphasis added.]

La Forest J. in *Parks, supra*, added the following explanation at p. 897:

> ... [the judge] must determine whether there is *some* evidence on the record to support leaving the defence with the jury. This is sometimes referred to as laying the proper foundation for the defence; see *Bratty, supra*, at pp. 405 and 413. Thus an *evidential burden* rests with the accused, and the mere assertion of the defence will not suffice; see *Bratty*, at p. 414. [Emphasis added.]

[46] The concept of an evidential burden is "a product of the jury system," *per* J. Sopinka, S. Lederman and A. Bryant, *The Law of Evidence in Canada* (1992), at p. 61. The authors contrast the evidential burden with the legal or persuasive burden as follows, at p. 58:

> The significance of the evidential burden arises when there is a question as to which party has the right or the obligation to begin adducing evidence. It also arises when there is a question as to whether sufficient evidence has been adduced to raise an issue for determination by the trier of fact. The legal burden of proof normally arises after the evidence has been completed and the question is whether the trier of fact has been persuaded with respect to the issue or case to the civil or criminal standard of proof. The legal burden, however, ordinarily arises after a party has first satisfied an evidential burden in relation to that fact or issue.

It is no part of an "evidential burden" to require an accused to go on to satisfy the jury on a balance of probabilities or otherwise about the facts in issue—*per* Dickson C.J. in *R. v. Schwartz*, [1988] 2 S.C.R. 443 (S.C.C.), at p. 467:

> The party with an evidential burden is not required to convince the trier of fact of anything, only to point out evidence which suggests that certain facts existed.

[47] In neither *Rabey* nor *Parks* was it suggested, much less decided, that the accused should shoulder any part of the persuasive or legal burden of proof. On the contrary, the *evidential* burden was put forward in both cases as a safeguard against putting the Crown too quickly or too lightly to the task of discharging the *persuasive* or legal burden of proof.

[48] This allocation of responsibilities is not without its critics. The Minister of Justice, in her 1993 *Proposals to amend the Criminal Code (general principles)*, suggested that the burden of proof in all cases of automatism be on a balance of probabilities by the party that raised the issue. Parliament has not seen fit to act on this recommendation. I do not believe, with respect, that the Court ought to take it upon itself to reverse the persuasive burden to the disadvantage of the accused simply because the Court may find an unenacted policy initiative more attractive than the established law. Parliament made a choice to impose a persuasive burden on a balance of probabilities in the case of mental disorder which includes mental disorder automatism. It did not do so in the case of non-mental disorder automatism. Any such imposition would require a justification under s. 1 of the *Charter*. On this appeal, however, neither the respondent nor any of the Attorneys General who intervened in the appeal (Canada, Ontario and Alberta) suggested that such a change of onus was either desirable or necessary.

[49] In my view, the decisions of this Court in *Chaulk*, *supra*, and *Daviault*, *supra*, do not warrant a reversal of the persuasive burden. Such a reversal would create a potential for injustice where a jury is obliged to convict an accused who properly raised the issue of automatism even though the jury entertains a reasonable doubt about the voluntariness of the accused's conduct. In *Chaulk* the Court dealt with a statutory reverse onus in the context of insanity. Section 16(4) of the *Code* provided

at the time that "Every one shall, until the contrary is proved, be presumed to be and to have been sane." The Court agreed that placing a burden of proof on the accused to persuade the jury of insanity on a balance of probabilities infringed the presumption of innocence guaranteed by s. 11(d) of the *Charter, per* Lamer C.J., at pp. 1330-31:

> Section 16(4) allows a factor which is essential for guilt to be *presumed*, rather than proven by the Crown beyond a reasonable doubt. Moreover, it requires an accused to disprove sanity (or prove insanity) on a balance of probabilities; it therefore violates the presumption of innocence because it permits a conviction in spite of a reasonable doubt in the mind of the trier of fact as to the guilt of the accused. [Emphasis in original.]

A majority of the Court saved the reverse onus under s. 1 based on evidence and submissions (p. 1337) of the "impossibly onerous burden of disproving insanity." There has been no equivalent showing under s. 1 in this case.

[50]  In *Daviault*, on the other hand, a majority of the Court recognized an exception to the existing common law rule established in *R. v. Leary* (1977), [1978] 1 S.C.R. 29 (S.C.C.), that the *mens rea* of a general intent offence could *not* be negated by evidence of even extreme drunkenness. The Court was concerned that the common law rule violated the *Charter*. As Cory J. stated in *Daviault*, at p. 73:

> In my opinion, the principles embodied in our *Canadian Charter of Rights and Freedoms*, and more specifically in ss. 7 and 11(d), mandate *a limited exception to, or some flexibility in, the application of the* Leary *rule*. [Emphasis added.]

The price of the "limited exception to" the *Leary* rule was that the accused, who experienced the steps by which he got himself drunk, was required to show, on a balance of probability, that the drunkenness induced an absence of awareness that was akin to a state of insanity or automatism. At p. 101, Cory J. explained:

> This Court has recognized, in *R. v. Chaulk* ... that although it constituted a violation of the accused's rights under s. 11(d) of the *Charter*, such a burden could be justified under s. 1. In this case, I feel that the burden can be justified. Drunkenness of the extreme degree required in order for it to become relevant will only occur on rare occasions. It is only the accused who can give evidence as to the amount of alcohol consumed and its effect upon him.

The Court thus concluded that a s. 1 justification had been established. Drunkenness is a matter of degree. It is a reasonably common phenomenon in its lesser manifestations. In its extreme form it may produce a potential defence *akin* to automatism to which special rules apply. *Daviault* did not suggest a reversal of the persuasive burden whenever the state of mind of an accused is successfully put in issue, in provocation for example (s. 232, *R. v. Linney* (1977), [1978] 1 S.C.R. 646 (S.C.C.), *R. v. Thibert*, [1996] 1 S.C.R. 37 (S.C.C.)), or self-defence (s. 34, *R. v. Lavallee*, [1990] 1 S.C.R. 852 (S.C.C.), *R. v. M. (M.A.)*, [1998] 1 S.C.R. 123 (S.C.C.)), or an accused's belief as to consent to an assault (s. 265(4), *R. v. Latour* (1950), [1951] S.C.R. 19 (S.C.C.), *R. v. Osolin*, [1993] 4 S.C.R. 595 (S.C.C.), at pp. 682-83); in all such cases (and many others) the Crown carries the persuasive burden to negate a state of mind asserted by the accused, despite the fact that an accused is often in a better position than the Crown to shed light on his or her state of mind at the time of the alleged crime. The accused may be in a better position to shed light on most elements of the offence. The Crown did not ask for a reverse onus where non-insane automatism is in issue and therefore did not put forward a case for the application of s. 1. I do not believe the Court ought to embark on organizing its own s. 1 justification where none of the Attorneys General saw fit even to propose the shift of the persuasive onus much less to try to justify it.

[51] Courts in most other jurisdictions, including the United Kingdom, the United States, Australia and New Zealand, impose only an evidential burden on an accused. The persuasive or legal burden remains on the Crown—the United Kingdom: see *Bratty, supra, per* Viscount Kilmuir L.C., at p. 406, *per* Lord Denning, at p. 413, and *per* Lord Morris of Borth-y-Gest, at p.416, and see *Halsbury's Laws of England* (4th ed. reissue 1990), vol. 11(1), at para. 6; the United States: see *State v. Hinkle*, 489 S.E.2d 257 (W.Va. 1996), and see W. LaFave and A. Scott, *Substantive Criminal Law* (1986), vol. 1, at p. 545:

> Some authority is to be found to the effect that the defendant has the burden of proving the defense of automatism. The prevailing view, however, is that the defendant need only produce evidence raising a doubt as to his consciousness at the time of the alleged crime. If the defense really is concerned with whether the defendant engaged in a voluntary act, an essential element of the crime, then it would seem that the burden of proof must as a constitutional matter be on the prosecution.

See also Australia: *Falconer, supra*, at p. 250, and *Hawkins v. R.* (1994), 72 A. Crim. R. 288 (Australia H.C.), at pp. 292-93; and New Zealand: *R. v. Cottle*, [1958] N.Z.L.R. 999, at pp. 1007-08, and *Police v. Bannin*, [1991] 2 N.Z.L.R. 237 (New Zealand H.C.), at p. 242.

[52] This weight of criminal practice in comparable jurisdictions would make it awkward for an attorney general to argue that a reverse onus in this case is demonstrably justified "in a free and democratic society" within the meaning of s. 1 of the *Charter*, but, as stated, none of the Attorneys General who appeared before us even attempted to make this argument.

[53] I am not persuaded, in any event, that the onus of proof would be decisive on the facts of this case. There were only two witnesses supporting automatism, the accused and his medical expert. If they were disbelieved, the Crown would have had no difficulty discharging its persuasive onus. If they were believed, on the other hand, switching the persuasive onus to the defence would not have saved the prosecution from defeat.

(b)  Ground 2: The Decision of This Court in Rabey, Supra

[54] The Crown's second principal submission is that even if it were to be found that the conduct of the appellant was involuntary, a majority of this Court in *Rabey, supra*, held that automatism which cannot be attributed to any external cause, such as a blow on the head, should be characterized as a disease of the mind. The Crown says that an "ordinary person" could be assumed to have the capacity to shoulder such a "psychological blow" as was here inflicted on the appellant by his wife without

dissociating. The cause of the appellant's "dissociation," if such it was, should therefore be attributed to a disease of the mind. The *Rabey* classification scheme, it was
acknowledged, is not borrowed from medical science, but the Crown says it can be
justified on the notion that" disease of the mind" is a legal not a medical concept. The
result, says the Crown, is that, as the jury refused to accept the NCRMD plea, it was
properly required to convict the accused without considering evidence (which the
Court has found to be reasonably capable of belief) that the conduct was involuntary.

[55] While I have been using, to this point, the traditional terms "insane" and
"non-insane" automatism, it is more convenient from this point onwards to refer to
"mental disorder" automatism and "non-mental disorder" automatism. This is because the amendments to s. 16 of the *Code* made in 1991 (S.C. 1991, c. 43) removed
all references to the term "insanity" from the *Code* and the common law terms should
be correspondingly up-dated to minimize confusion.

[56] It is important to make careful note of the facts in *Rabey*, *supra*. The accused
was an "emotionally immature" male student at the University of Toronto, who had
become smitten by an attractive outgoing female student. She did not reciprocate his
affections. In fact, she wrote a rather contemptuous and demeaning note about him to
a friend. The note was never intended for the eyes of the accused, but it fell into his
possession and he was devastated by what he read. The accused and the woman subsequently found themselves alone in a university building, at which point the accused, suffering what he said was a "psychological blackout," brutally beat the woman
whom he said he loved more than anyone else he had ever met. Expert evidence
called by the defence at trial supported the theory of a" blackout" induced by a psychological blow without any accompanying" disease of the mind." The trial judge
put the issue of non-mental disorder automatism to the jury, who acquitted. The Ontario Court of Appeal reversed that decision ((1977), 17 O.R. (2d) 1 (Ont. C.A.)).
Martin J.A. comprehensively reviewed the precedents and concluded, at p. 22, that
the student had merely suffered one of" the ordinary stresses and disappointments of
life which are the common lot of mankind" and was not entitled to the benefit of non-
mental disorder automatism. Martin J.A. considered that the so-called "blow" would
not have caused an ordinary person to black out. If it blacked out the accused, he
must have been suffering from some mental frailty which the law would regard as a
disease of the mind. In the absence of a disease of the mind, Martin J.A. seemed to
feel, the evidence of a "blackout" from such a minor rebuff was simply not credible.
Martin J.A. was clearly perturbed that the jury had acquitted on such evidence. The
Court of Appeal set aside the acquittal and ordered a new trial at which the accused
would be allowed to run only an insanity defence. The decision and the reasoning of
Martin J.A. were adopted by a majority of this Court.

[57] Critical to the analysis of Martin J.A. was the concept that a "psychological
blackout" could be attributed to one of three sources: (1) an external cause such as a
blow to the head in which case an accused would be entitled to raise non-mental
disorder automatism, (2) an internal cause that would be likely to produce a similar
psychological impact on a person of everyday sensibilities and psychological makeup, such as a person's witnessing the killing of his or her own children, which could

qualify as an "external" cause and which might (the point was left open) entitle an accused to plead non-mental disorder automatism, or (3) an internal cause which was triggered by no more than "the ordinary stresses and disappointments of life." In the absence of any other credible explanation, the cause of the automatism in the third scenario would be deemed to be a "disease of the mind." It was held in *Rabey* that the accused fell into this third scenario since Martin J.A. concluded that an ordinary person would not have become dissociated in such a situation. Therefore, under the three-part model, the only automatism defence open to Rabey was *mental disorder* automatism. A relevant consideration was the sense that "[e]xternal influences on the accused are perceived as less likely than internal ones to present a danger in the future" (I. Grant, D. Chunn and C. Boyle, *The Law of Homicide* (1994, loose-leaf), p. 6-118).

[58] Martin J.A. was clearly unimpressed with the idea that a university student's unrequited love could sustain the theory of a psychological blow causing dissociation leading to a violent assault. Rabey, he thought, was either suffering from a disease of the mind or his description of events was to be disbelieved.

(I) THE CONCEPT OF DISEASE OF THE MIND

[59] The *Rabey* analysis puts the concept of "disease of the mind" at the centre of the automatism analysis. By expanding the definition of "disease of the mind," the courts have expanded the role of NCRMD, and contracted the area of human conduct that potentially leads to an outright acquittal on the basis of the Crown's failure to prove the *actus reus* of the offence. Given this crucial control function, it is not surprising that the courts have insisted that the definition of "disease of the mind" must be a matter of law, and is not to be dictated by medical experts.

[60] Medical input, of course, is nevertheless an essential component. As La Forest J. stated in *Parks*, *supra*, at p. 898, quoting Martin J.A. in *Rabey*, *supra*, at p. 12:

"Disease of the mind" is a legal term, not a medical term of art; although a legal concept, it contains a substantial medical component as well as a legal or policy component.

Martin J.A. described the "policy function" in *Rabey*, at p. 12, as relating to:

... (a) the scope of the exemption from criminal responsibility to be afforded by mental disorder or disturbance, and (b) the protection of the public by the control and treatment of persons who have caused serious harms while in a mentally disordered or disturbed state.

Having regard to the policy component, Martin J.A., at p. 14 went on to demonstrate that the *legal* concept of "disease" of the mind includes disorders which have no organic or physical cause, and includes "purely functional disorders which, so far as is known, have no physical cause," and may be "permanent or temporary, curable or incurable ... [or] recurring or non-recurring." In this case the medical experts differed over whether the appellant had conscious control over his actions at the time of the killing, but they were unanimous that the appellant did not suffer from any condition that medicine would recognize as a "disease of the mind."

(II) THIS COURT'S SUBSEQUENT DECISION IN PARKS

[61]  This Court's decision in *Rabey* must now be read in light of the subsequent attempt to apply its analytical framework to the case of a sleepwalker in *Parks*. La Forest J. in *Parks* appeared to accept many of the policy considerations that preoccupied the Court in *Rabey* while rejecting any mechanical application of the *Rabey* criteria for classifying cases into what we would now call mental disorder automatism or non-mental disorder automatism.

[62]  In *Parks*, the accused, in a state of somnambulism, killed his mother-in-law and severely assaulted his father-in-law. The jury accepted the expert evidence that the conduct of the accused, while asleep, was involuntary. The Crown appealed the acquittal to the Ontario Court of Appeal, which affirmed the verdict, and again to this Court, which unanimously dismissed the appeal.

[63]  The Crown took the position in *Parks*, based on its analysis of *Rabey*, that somnambulism is an "internal" cause of automatism, and the accused sleepwalker would therefore have to prove on a balance of probabilities that he was NCRMD. In the course of rejecting this submission, La Forest J. in *Parks* identified two policy-driven considerations, namely the" continuing danger" and "internal cause" theories, at p. 901:

> The continuing danger theory holds that any condition likely to present a recurring danger to the public should be treated as insanity. The internal cause theory suggests that a condition stemming from the psychological or emotional make-up of the accused, rather than some external factor, should lead to a finding of insanity. The two theories share a common concern for recurrence, the latter holding that an internal weakness is more likely to lead to recurrent violence than automatism brought on by some intervening external cause.

[64]  Sleepwalking did not fit the *Rabey* analysis. While possibly associated with certain external stimuli, sleepwalking springs from the workings of the internal recesses of the brain, and would therefore have to be classified by proponents of the internal cause theory as a "disease of the brain." However, few people would equate sleepwalking with insanity. Martin J.A. sought to qualify his analysis by identifying sleepwalking as a "separate category" (at p. 17), but in *Parks*, La Forest J. saw sleepwalking as undermining the utility of the internal cause theory itself, which he therefore downgraded to an "analytical tool" (at p. 902).

[65]  I believe the Court was correct in *Parks* to dissociate itself from a mechanical application of the *Rabey* analysis. In the first place, an overly rigid application of the" internal cause" theory produces anomalous distinctions. In *R. v. Quick*, [1973] 3 All E.R. 347 (Eng. C.A.), the accused had assaulted his victim under the influence of an insulin injection, and Lawton J.A. utilized the notion of external cause (i.e., the injection) to *negate* the existence of a disease of the mind. On the other hand, in *R. v. Hennessy* (1989), 89 Cr. App. R. 10 (Eng. C.A.) it was held that the involuntary conduct of a diabetic who *failed* to take his insulin was internally caused (by his diabetes) and must thus be considered an expression of insanity. The differing treatment of diabetes, based on factors which have nothing to do with the underlying

nature of the condition, demonstrates the potential artificiality of the analysis, and thus its limitations.

[66] In the second place, the elastic notion of "mental disorder" can be expanded to the point where it ceases to have any utility for classification. The elasticity of use is not confined to the legal profession. E. Tollefson and B. Starkman note in their *Mental Disorder in Criminal Proceedings* (1993), at p. 53, the view of the Canadian Psychiatric Association that *all* causes of automatism are mental disorders, as they see the world. From a legal perspective, however, classification of a problem as a "mental disorder" has to be given some substantive content, or s. 16 and Part XX.1 of the *Code* (and its tests descended from the M'Naghten Rules (*McNaughten's Case, Re* (1843), 10 Cl. & Fin. 200, (8 E.R. 718 (U.K. H.L.))) may be imposed inappropriately. As pointed out by Williams, *supra*, at p. 676:

> The courts should eschew any effort to discourage the defence of dissociation by interpreting it as evidence of insanity, or by withholding psychiatric evidence from the jury. The defence, if supported by medical evidence, should be adjudicated upon by the triers of fact, and if successful should result in an ordinary acquittal. But what is urgently needed is that the psychiatrist who deposes to dissociation in improbable circumstances should be subjected to skilled and deeply sceptical cross-examination, and that the Crown should, where possible, call counter-evidence.

Williams' concern about proper evidence is met, I think, by Dickson J.'s description of the evidential burden in *Rabey*.

[67] Thirdly, the jurisprudential root of the "internal cause" theory is suspect. *Rabey* traced the doctrine to *Quick*, but as was also pointed out by Williams, *supra*, at p. 675:

> To say that the presence of an external cause of mental trouble saves a man from the imputation of madness, as was held in *Quick*, does not imply that the absence of an external cause necessarily means that he is mad.

[68] Fourthly, *Rabey* contemplated that some psychological blows could be classified as internal causes and others as external causes. Thus Ritchie J. adopted in *Rabey*, at p. 520, the following observation of Martin J.A. in the Ontario Court of Appeal at p. 22:

> … the ordinary stresses and disappointments of life which are the common lot of mankind do not constitute an external cause constituting an explanation for a malfunctioning of the mind which takes it out of the category of a "disease of the mind." To hold otherwise would deprive the concept of an external factor of any real meaning.

Nevertheless, a psychological blow sufficient to unhinge the ordinary person could potentially open up a plea of non-mental disorder automatism, *per* Martin J.A. at p. 22, cited by Ritchie J., at p. 520:

> I leave aside until it becomes necessary to decide them, cases where a dissociative state has resulted from emotional shock without physical injury, resulting from such causes, for example, as being involved in a serious accident although no physical injury has

resulted; being the victim of a murderous attack with an uplifted knife, notwithstanding that the victim has managed to escape physical injury; seeing a loved one murdered or seriously assaulted, and the like situations. *Such extraordinary external events might reasonably be presumed to affect the average normal person without reference to the subjective makeup of the person exposed to such experience.* [Emphasis added.]

The introduction of an "average normal person" test would potentially inject an objective fault standard into the Crown's burden of proof of the *actus reus* and *mens rea*, and thereby create *Charter* problems: see *R. v. Martineau*, [1990] 2 S.C.R. 633 (S.C.C.), and *Cameron*, *supra*, at pp. 273-74, *per* Doherty J.A. More pertinent, for present purposes, is the point made in the dissent of Dickson J., in *Rabey*, at p. 548:

> It is not clear to me why, as a matter of law, an emotional blow, which can be devastating, should be regarded as an external cause of automatism in some circumstances and an internal cause in others. ...

In short, the conceptual problems associated with the "internal cause" theory amply justify downgrading its status to an "analytical tool" (*Parks*, p. 902). A judicially created construct such as the "internal cause theory" does not justify taking away from the jury any case of "lack of consciousness throughout the commission of the offence" just because the accused is unable to identify a specific "external cause." Such an accused, who has met the evidential burden of showing that his or her conduct was unconscious and involuntary should not always be absorbed into what would in his or her case be an artificial debate developed in the context of *conscious* conduct about whether the accused lacked the capacity to appreciate "the nature and quality of the act or omission or of knowing that it was wrong."

[69]  The other philosophical root of the *Parks* analysis is the "continuing danger" theory. The law on automatism is correctly concerned with public safety, and one problem is how to assess the likelihood of recurrence of the violent conduct. As mentioned by Devlin J. in *Hill v. Baxter* (1957), [1958] 1 Q.B. 277 (Eng. Q.B.), at pp. 285-86:

> For the purposes of the criminal law there are two categories of mental irresponsibility, one where the disorder is due to disease and the other where it is not. The distinction is not an arbitrary one. If disease is not the cause, if there is some temporary loss of consciousness arising accidentally, it is reasonable to hope that it will not be repeated and that it is safe to let an acquitted man go entirely free. *But if disease is present, the same thing may happen again*, and therefore, since 1800 (Criminal Lunatics Act, 1800), the law has provided that persons acquitted on this ground should be subject to restraint. [Emphasis added.] ...

[71]  Dickson J., in *Rabey*, also sought to relate the public policy concern about insanity to the "continuing danger theory." While neither the M'Naghten Rules nor s. 16 of the *Code* say anything explicitly about the danger of recurrence, the fact is that an isolated act of violent behaviour, however serious, presents different public policy issues than does conduct rooted in imbecility or other organic disease of the mind which has struck once and may prompt a further act of violence in future. The

risk of recurrence is thus legitimately part of the "policy component" of the legal analysis of "disease of the mind."

[72] La Forest J. in *Parks* cited with approval, at pp. 906-07, the English Court of Appeal (Criminal Division) in *R. v. Burgess*, [1991] 2 All E.R. 769 (Eng. C.A.), at p. 774:

> It seems to us that if there is a danger of recurrence that may be an added reason for categorising the condition as a disease of the mind. On the other hand, the absence of the danger of recurrence is not a reason for saying that it cannot be a disease of the mind.

Thus La Forest J. concluded, at p. 905, that the "continuing danger" theory is simply "a factor at the policy stage of the inquiry." In the present case, neither psychiatrist considered recurrence a significant possibility.

[73] In the circumstances, I do not think that the majority decision in *Rabey* justified the courts in British Columbia in depriving the appellant of the benefit of the evidentiary ruling in his favour on the issue of involuntariness. Where, as here, the trial judge concludes that there was evidence reasonably capable of belief that the accused was in *fact* unconscious throughout the commission of the offence, it is not fatal if the accused fails to go on to establish a *cause* of that state of alleged unconsciousness which the courts can describe as "external." As it is rare for an accused to meet even an *evidential* burden in this sort of case, it is not realistic to talk of a "floodgates" problem. The defence psychiatrist, trained to spot feigned symptoms, says that in his opinion the testimony of the appellant is credible, and finds the symptoms described by the appellant to be credibly related to the alleged unconsciousness. An inability to identify the mechanism of the brain that allegedly rendered him unconscious, except in the very general terms offered by Dr. Janke, may of course undermine the credibility of his story that he lost consciousness in the first place. However, the task of the appellant was to demonstrate the *fact* of unconsciousness (in the sense of lack of awareness and control). It was not incumbent upon him to satisfy the court as to the *cause* of his condition or lose the benefit of the evidentiary ruling. In effect, *Rabey* takes the involuntariness defence which the accused seeks to raise and substitutes for it an insanity defence which neither the accused nor the medical experts can plausibly support. At this point, it is worth reminding ourselves what Cory J. said in *Daviault*, at p. 91:

> In my view, the mental element of voluntariness is a fundamental aspect of the crime which cannot be taken away by a judicially developed policy.

[74] It follows, I think, that once the trial judge exercised his gatekeeper function to screen frivolous or feigned claims, it was for the jury to make up its mind on the credibility of the plea of automatism. This jurisdiction should not be removed by "judicially created policy." It is to be expected that the jury will subject the evidence of involuntariness to appropriate scrutiny. There was discussion in *Rabey* about the need to maintain the credibility of the justice system. In my view, the jury is as well placed as anyone in the justice system to uphold its credibility. The bottom line is,

after all, that the task of weighing the credibility of such defences was confined by Parliament to the jury. The Court should respect the allocation of that responsibility.

(c)  Ground 3: The Contention That the Mental Disorder Provisions of the Criminal Code Were Appropriate To Resolve the Automatism Issue on the Facts of This Case

[75]  The third major submission on behalf of the Crown was that quite apart from this Court's decision in *Rabey* the present case was correctly subjected to the NCRMD provisions of s. 16 of the *Code*. The Crown says that here the operating cause of the dissociation was a "disease of the mind," giving that concept its full *legal* scope, and in such situations questions of involuntariness are properly subsumed into the NCRMD analysis. This is despite the fact that in this case all the experts were agreed that the appellant did not suffer from any "disease of the mind" known to medicine. I accept, as stated, that "disease of the mind" is a legal concept, but nevertheless a significant disconnection between law and medicine on this point will often impose a measure of artificiality to create the medical equivalent of trying to pound square pegs into round holes.

[76]  The issue here is not whether the law, as a matter of policy, can expand its concept of "disease of the mind" to include conduct that has traditionally been considered non-insane automatism. It can do so. The question here is quite different. We are asked to say that even if the plea of NCRMD fails, the Court will still, by an act of judicial policy, relieve the Crown of the burden of proving the most contentious element of the *actus reus* by taking the issue of voluntariness away from the jury.

[77]  It is true that if statements relating voluntariness to the *actus reus* are applied mechanically, even a violent accused suffering from a disease of the mind in which "the mind does not go with what is being done" (*Rabey* (S.C.C.), *supra*, at p. 513, quoting *R. v. K.*, *supra*, at p. 84) could demand an absolute acquittal. This was the position at common law, *per* Devlin J. in *R. v. Kemp*, [1956] 3 All E.R. 249 (Eng. Q.B.), at p. 251:

> In the eyes of the common law if a man is not responsible for his actions he is entitled
> to be acquitted by the ordinary form of acquittal, and it matters not whether his lack of
> responsibility was due to insanity or to any other cause.

In response to the public danger posed by such an outcome, and to a developing understanding of mental disorder, the courts started down the path that eventually subsumed the notion of involuntary conduct into the concept of insanity where the involuntary conduct could be identified as the product of a disease of the mind. A successful plea of insanity led to the verdict of "not guilty by reason of insanity," which carried with it the possibility of indefinite detention at the pleasure of the state.

[78]  The problem is that while s. 16 of the *Code* may provide an appropriate structure to resolve cases of medically defined "diseases of the mind," it may not be responsive to the real issues in cases where the" disease of the mind" derives from legal classification, rather than medical classification. The view of the Canadian Psychiatric Association that all causes of automatism are mental disorders was not accompanied by any ringing endorsement that in all such cases s. 16 of the *Code* provides an

appropriate analytical framework. The focus of the NCRMD provisions of the *Code* is clearly different from the focus of automatism. The latter addresses whether the conduct was voluntary. The former looks at one possible cause of automatism, and asks questions about the impact of the disease of the mind on legally relevant aspects of mental capacity.

[79]  The existence of a "disease of the mind" is a threshold issue in s. 16. The real question, to paraphrase Lord Diplock in *R. v. Sullivan* (1983), [1984] A.C. 156 (U.K. H.L.), at p. 172, is whether "the effect of a disease is to impair these [mental] faculties so severely as to have either of the consequences referred to" in s. 16(1), namely whether the disease rendered the accused "incapable of appreciating the nature and quality of the act or omission or knowing that it was wrong."

[80]  It is clear, in other words, that "the consequences referred to" in s. 16 are directed to issues other than voluntariness. There is much to be said for the observation of Professor D. Stuart in *Canadian Criminal Law: A Treatise* (3rd ed. 1995), at p. 108:

> A "disease of the mind" is only one requirement of the legal defence of insanity. If that defence fails *for any reason*, surely justice dictates that the jury may consider sane automatism. *MacLeod* [*R. v. MacLeod* (1980), 52 C.C.C. (2d) 193 (B.C.C.A.)] decides that psychiatric labelling might well prevent the defence of sane automatism from being put although it is *not* the sole barometer of legal insanity. [Emphasis in original.]

[81]  Two further points emerge from a consideration of s. 16 of the *Code*. Firstly, Parliament has not alluded to whether the conduct is voluntary or involuntary. It is sufficient that the acts occurred or omissions were made at a time when the accused suffered from "a mental disorder" (defined in s. 2 as a "disease of the mind"). Secondly, Parliament addressed the *capacity* of the accused, not proof of the existence or absence of a particular *mens rea* on the particular facts. The finding of a mental disorder therefore displaces the ordinary rules governing criminal responsibility, including voluntariness, and places an accused in the grip of the statutory scheme created to deal with the individuals whom the law used to describe as "criminally insane."

[82]  The difficulty of subsuming the issue of voluntariness into the different issue of mental disorder in cases such as the present was noted 40 years ago by Gresson P. of the New Zealand Court of Appeal in *Cottle, supra*, at p. 1009. In a decision much commented upon by members of the House of Lords in *Bratty, supra*, Gresson P., at p. 1009, expressed his concern about the M'Naghten Rules being applied to an accused who simply lacked volition:

> We must accept the position as it is, but we cannot escape the difficulty that the M'Naghten Rules were never intended to apply to a case where the act was done without volition or consciousness of doing it. *The M'Naghten formula takes account only of the cognitive faculties and presupposes that the doer was conscious of his actions.* Nevertheless, it has become the practice to regard a person as "incapable of understanding the nature and quality" of his act when in truth he was not conscious of having acted at all; and to treat the formula as applicable to cases of automatism. ... It is unfortunate that there should have been this too-liberal application of the M'Naghten Rules. [Emphasis added.]

[83] The s. 16 question has an air of artificiality in the case of someone who claims to have been unconscious at the material time. If true, he or she not only failed to appreciate "the nature and quality of the act" but also failed to appreciate that the act was taking place at all. If false, the accused is simply untruthful. Nevertheless, the presence of a "disease of the mind" does trigger the application of s. 16, and an accused whose automatism is a product of a disease of the mind should be found NCRMD instead of being acquitted. The concept of "disease of the mind" is, and should continue to be, controlled by legal considerations rather than purely medical considerations.

[84] At the same time, where as here medical experts for the prosecution and the defence agree that there is no "disease of the mind" known to medicine, and the only justification offered in support of attributing the conduct to mental disorder is the inability of an accused to identify an "external" cause, there is, in my view, an insufficient basis for (i) shifting the persuasive burden of proof from the Crown to the defence under s. 16, and (ii) taking the issue of non-mental disorder automatism away from the jury.

[85] The appellant's point is that the jury's rejection of the plea of mental disorder automatism may have been because they disbelieved his version of events, or it may be because they thought his acts, though involuntary, were not the product of any disease of the mind. Failure to put the issue of non-mental disorder automatism thus deprived him of a potential acquittal on an issue for which the trial judge ruled he had laid a proper evidentiary foundation. It is on that basis that the appellant says the judge-made rule violates the presumption of his innocence under s. 11(d) of the *Charter* and took away an important element of his right under s. 11(f) of the *Charter* to have his fate determined by the jury. The conclusion that the issue of non-mental disorder automatism ought to have been left with the jury in this case is, I think, consistent with the observations of the majority of the members of the Australian High Court in *Falconer*, *supra*, and in particular the views of Deane and Dawson JJ. (p. 266), Toohey J. (p. 273 and p. 281), and Gaudron J. (p. 285) to the effect that evidence which credibly puts in issue the voluntariness of the acts of the accused (i.e., whether the act or omission occurred independently of the exercise of his will) must be put to the jury.

[86] It is open to the Crown or defence to establish on a balance of probabilities a mental disorder. The Crown, of course, must follow the rule in *R. v. Swain*, [1991] 1 S.C.R. 933 (S.C.C.), which prevents the admission of evidence relating to mental disorder by the Crown until the defence puts in issue the mental capacity of the accused for criminal intent, as explained by Lamer C.J., at p. 976:

> Thus, although it is a principle of fundamental justice that an accused has the right to control his or her own defence, this is not an "absolute" right. If an accused chooses to conduct his or her defence in such a way that *that accused's mental capacity for criminal intent is somehow put into question*, then the Crown will be entitled to "complete the picture" by raising its own evidence of insanity and the trial judge will be entitled to charge the jury on s. 16. [Emphasis added.]

The same point was made by La Forest J. in *Parks*, *supra*, at p. 898, in relation to automatism:

> If the accused pleads automatism, the Crown is then entitled to raise the issue of insanity, but the prosecution then bears the burden of proving that the condition in question stems from a disease of the mind; see *Rabey*, *supra*, at pp. 544-45.

If the jury were satisfied that the s. 16 requirements were met, that would end the matter: the appellant would have been found not criminally responsible on account of mental disorder (NCRMD). He or she would not be permitted to ignore NCRMD status and seek a full acquittal on the basis of involuntariness. However, in my view, if the jury rejects NCRMD status, it should still be left with the elementary instruction that the accused is entitled to an acquittal if the Crown fails to establish beyond a reasonable doubt all of the elements of the offence, including voluntariness.

### (4)  Competence of the Jury

[87]  For these reasons, it is my view that, the trial judge having ruled that the appellant had successfully discharged the evidential onus, the appellant was entitled to have the issue of voluntariness put to the jury. In reaching that conclusion I have not forgotten the sceptical observation of Williams noted earlier, at pp. 673-74:

> How strange, *the layman* may say, and how very convenient for the defendant, that this alleged state of dissociation descended on him at the very moment when he had reason for evading the police, or when he was face to face with a person whom he had a strong motive for attacking. [Emphasis added.]

It is significant that the author pointedly refers to "the layman" and suggests that the layman's common sense would make quick work of the legal complexities conjured up by the jurisprudence on the topic of automatism. Nor have I forgotten Dickson J.'s concern about the potential for fake pleas of automatism which he expressed in *Rabey* at p. 546:

> There are undoubtedly policy considerations to be considered. Automatism as a defence is easily feigned. It is said the credibility of our criminal justice system will be severely strained if a person who has committed a violent act is allowed an absolute acquittal on a plea of automatism arising from a psychological blow. The argument is made that the success of the defence depends upon the semantic ability of psychiatrists, tracing a narrow path between the twin shoals of criminal responsibility and an insanity verdict. Added to these concerns is the *in terrorem* argument that the floodgates will be raised if psychological blow automatism is recognized in law.

In part, Dickson J.'s answer to these concerns was to specify the content of the evidential burden resting on an accused, requiring (at p. 552) that the evidence of the accused

> … should be supported by expert medical opinion that the accused did not feign memory loss and that there is no underlying pathological condition which points to a disease requiring detention and treatment.

Under the Dickson approach, the medical expert has to vouch for the credibility of the accused's evidence of unconsciousness, and thus involuntariness.

[88]  More profoundly, however, I think Dickson J.'s response to these concerns was an endorsement of the role of the jury contemplated by Parliament as he expressed, for example, in *R. v. Corbett*, [1988] 1 S.C.R. 670 (S.C.C.), at p. 693:

> It is of course, entirely possible to construct an argument disputing the theory of trial by jury. Juries are capable of egregious mistakes and they may at times seem to be ill-adapted to the exigencies of an increasingly complicated and refined criminal law. But until the paradigm is altered by Parliament, the Court should not be heard to call into question the capacity of juries to do the job assigned to them.

to which he added, at pp. 693-94:

> We should maintain our strong faith in juries which have, in the words of Sir William Holdsworth, "for some hundreds of years been constantly bringing the rules of law to the touchstone of contemporary common sense" (Holdsworth, *A History of English Law* (7th ed. 1956), vol. I, at p. 349).

[89]  The common sense of members of the jury is a fundamental and vital part of our criminal justice system. As Cory J. stated in *Osolin*, *supra*, at p. 683: "The jury system has in general functioned exceptionally well. Its importance has been recognized in s. 11(f) of the *Charter*." More specifically, in the context of intoxication and *mens rea*, Dickson C.J. observed in *R. v. Bernard*, [1988] 2 S.C.R. 833 (S.C.C.), at p. 848, quoting *R. v. Hill* (1985), [1986] 1 S.C.R. 313 (S.C.C.), at p. 334:

> I have the greatest of confidence in the level of intelligence and plain common sense of the average Canadian jury sitting on a criminal case. Juries are perfectly capable of sizing the matter up.

The jury in this case, for example, had before it the testimony of the Crown psychiatrist that the appellant's violent response to his wife's verbal attack was entirely too purposeful and the loss of memory entirely too convenient to be considered "involuntary." The members of the jury could, I think, have been counted on to exhibit powerful scepticism about such evidence. Anyone who thinks a jury of bus drivers, office workers and other practical people will be less sceptical than members of the bench or professors of law has perhaps spent insufficient time in buses or around office coffee machines.

(5)  Conclusion on the Automatism Issue

[90]  In the result, I believe the appellant was entitled to have the plea of non-mental disorder automatism left to the jury in this case in light of the trial judge's evidentiary ruling that there was evidence the appellant was unconscious throughout the commission of the offence, for the following reasons.

[91] Firstly, I do not accept the Crown's argument that a judge-made classification of situations into mental disorder automatism and non-mental disorder automatism can relieve the Crown of the obligation to prove all of the elements of the offence, including voluntariness. As stated, such an interpretation encounters strong objections under s. 7 and s. 11(d) of the *Charter*, and there has been no attempt in this case to provide a s. 1 justification.

[92] Secondly, imposition of a persuasive burden of proof on the appellant to establish "involuntariness" on a balance of probabilities, in substitution for the present evidential burden, runs into the same *Charter* problems, and no attempt has been made in the record to justify it.

[93] Thirdly, the "internal cause" theory, on which the Crown rested its argument, cannot be used to deprive the appellant of the benefit of the jury's consideration of the voluntariness of his action, once he had met the evidential onus, without risking a violation of s. 11(f) of the *Charter*. *Rabey*'s treatment of the internal cause theory has to be looked at in light of the decision of this Court in *Parks*, *supra*, which signalled some serious reservations about the usefulness of the "internal cause" theory, except as an "analytical tool." *Rabey*, as clarified in *Parks*, does not impose a presumption that a lack of voluntariness must be attributed to the existence of a mental disorder any time there is no identification of a convincing external cause. Once the appellant in this case had discharged his evidential onus, he was entitled to have the issue of voluntariness go to the jury.

[94] Fourthly, it was wrong of the courts to require the appellant to substitute for his chosen defence of involuntariness the conceptually quite different plea of insanity. One of the few points of agreement between the defence and Crown experts at trial was that the appellant did not suffer from anything that could be described medically as a disease of the mind. He was either unconscious at the time of the killing or he was not telling the truth at the time of the trial. This was a question for the jury. The statutory inquiry into whether he was "suffering from a mental disorder" that rendered him "incapable of appreciating the nature and quality of the act of omission or knowing that it was wrong" are qualitative questions that are not really responsive to his allegation that he was not conscious of having acted at all.

[95] Finally, the evidence established that there *are* states of automatism where perfectly sane people lose conscious control over their actions. At that point, it was up to the jury, not the judge, to decide if the appellant had brought himself within the physical and mental condition thus identified. As Dickson C.J. observed in *Bernard*, *supra*, at p. 848, the jurors were "perfectly capable of sizing the matter up." ...

### IV. *Disposition*

[100] In the result, I would have allowed the appeal, set aside the order of the British Columbia Court of Appeal and directed a new trial. Had I shared the conclusion of Bastarache J. to dismiss the appeal against conviction, I would also have concurred in the dismissal of the Crown's appeal on sentence for the reasons he gives.

BASTARACHE J. (L'Heureux-Dubé, Gonthier, Cory, and McLachlin JJ. concurring):

[101]  The present case involves automatism, and more specifically, "psychologi-cal blow" automatism. The appellant claims that nothing more than his wife's words caused him to enter an automatistic state in which his actions, which include stabbing his wife 47 times, were involuntary. How can an accused demonstrate that mere words caused him to enter an automatistic state such that his actions were involuntary and thus do not attract criminal law sanction? This is the issue raised in this appeal. ...

## A.  The Nature of Automatism

[155]  The legal term "automatism" has been defined on many occasions by many courts. In *Rabey*, *supra*, Ritchie J., speaking for the majority of this Court, at p. 518, adopted the following definition of the Ontario High Court of Justice in *R. v. K.* (1970), 3 C.C.C. (2d) 84 (Ont. H.C.), at p. 84:

> Automatism is a term used to describe unconscious, involuntary behaviour, the state of a person who, though capable of action is not conscious of what he is doing. It means an unconscious involuntary act where the mind does not go with what is being done.

[156]  The reference to unconsciousness in the definition of automatism has been the source of some criticism. In her article "Automatism and Criminal Responsibil-ity" (1982-83), 25 *Crim. L.Q.* 95, W.H. Holland points out that this reference to un-consciousness reveals that the law assumes that a person is necessarily either con-scious or unconscious. However, the medical literature speaks of different levels of consciousness (p. 96). Indeed, the expert evidence in the present case reveals that medically speaking, unconscious means "flat on the floor," that is, in a comatose-type state. I therefore prefer to define automatism as a state of impaired conscious-ness, rather than unconsciousness, in which an individual, though capable of action, has no voluntary control over that action.

[157]  Two forms of automatism are recognized at law: insane automatism and non-insane automatism. Involuntary action which does not stem from a disease of the mind gives rise to a claim of non-insane automatism. If successful, a claim of non-insane automatism entitles the accused to an acquittal. In *Parks*, *supra*, La Forest J. cited with approval, at p. 896, the following words of Dickson J. speaking in dissent in *Rabey*, *supra*, at p. 522:

> Although the word "automatism" made its way but lately to the legal stage, it is basic principle that absence of volition in respect of the act involved is always a defence to a crime. A defence that the act is involuntary entitles the accused to a complete and un-qualified acquittal. That the defence of automatism exists as a middle ground between criminal responsibility and legal insanity is beyond question.

[158]  On the other hand, involuntary action which is found, at law, to result from a disease of the mind gives rise to a claim of insane automatism. It has long been recognized that insane automatism is subsumed by the defence of mental disorder, formerly referred to as the defence of insanity. For example, in *Rabey*, *supra*, Ritchie

J. adopted the reasoning of Martin J.A. of the Ontario Court of Appeal. In *R. v. Rabey* (1977), 17 O.R. (2d) 1 (Ont. C.A.), Martin J.A. stated, at p. 12:

> Automatism caused by disease of the mind is subsumed under the defence of insanity leading to the special verdict of not guilty on account of insanity, whereas automatism not resulting from disease of the mind leads to an absolute acquittal. ...

[159] Likewise, in dissent in *Rabey* (S.C.C.), Dickson J. noted, at p. 524:

> Automatism may be subsumed in the defence of insanity in cases in which the unconscious action of an accused can be traced to, or rooted in, a disease of the mind. Where that is so, the defence of insanity prevails.

[160] More recently, in *Parks, supra*, La Forest J. confirmed that insane automatism falls within the scope of the defence of mental disorder as set out in s. 16 of the *Code* when he noted that where automatism stems from a disease of the mind, the accused is entitled to a verdict of insanity rather than an acquittal (p. 896). See also *R. v. Chaulk*, [1990] 3 S.C.R. 1303 (S.C.C.), at p. 1321. This classification is consistent with the wording of s. 16, which makes no distinction between voluntary and involuntary acts. Furthermore, the inclusion of mental disorder automatism within the ambit of s. 16 provides courts with an appropriate framework for protecting the public from offenders whose involuntarily criminal acts are rooted in diseases of the mind. Courts in other commonwealth countries have also recognized that insane automatism is subsumed by the defence of mental disorder or insanity. See for example *Bratty v. Attorney-General for Northern Ireland* (1961), [1963] A.C. 386 (U.K. H.L.), at pp. 410 and 414; *R. v. Falconer* (1990), 50 A. Crim. R. 244 (Australia H.C.), at pp. 255-56, 265 and 273-74; *R. v. Cottle*, [1958] N.Z.L.R. 999, at p. 1007.

[161] Accordingly, a successful claim of insane automatism will trigger s. 16 of the *Code* and result in a verdict of not criminally responsible on account of mental disorder. Thus, although courts to date have spoken of insane" automatism" and non-insane "automatism" for purposes of consistency, it is important to recognize that in actuality true" automatism" only includes involuntary behaviour which does not stem from a disease of the mind. Involuntary behaviour which results from a disease of the mind is more correctly labelled a s. 16 mental disorder rather than insane automatism. For purposes of consistency, I will continue to refer to both as "automatism." However, I believe the terms "mental disorder" automatism and "non-mental disorder" automatism rather than "insane" automatism and "non-insane" automatism more accurately reflect the recent changes to s. 16 of the *Code*, and the addition of Part XX.1 of the *Code*.

### B. *Establishing a Single Approach to All Cases Involving Claims of Automatism*

[162] Automatism may arise in different contexts. For example, in *Parks, supra*, this Court dealt with a claim of automatism attributed to a state of somnambulism. In *R. c. Daviault*, [1994] 3 S.C.R. 63 (S.C.C.), this Court addressed extreme intoxication akin to a state of automatism. In the present case, the appellant claims that nothing more than his wife's words caused him to enter an automatistic state. This type of

claim has become known as "psychological blow" automatism. Automatism attributed to a psychological blow was at the centre of this Court's decision in *Rabey*, *supra*.

[163] The application of different legal tests for automatism dependent on the context in which the alleged automatism arose is a problem because there may be cases in which the facts simply are not conducive to such strict categorization. Cases involving disputes over the cause of the alleged automatism come to mind. The solution to this problem is, of course, to develop a general test applicable to all cases involving claims of automatism. This I will do in these reasons. I therefore emphasize that the following analysis is meant to apply to all claims of automatism and not simply to cases of "psychological blow" automatism. In my opinion, the most effective general test will incorporate various elements of this Court's most recent statements on automatistic-like behaviour; see *Daviault*, *Parks* and *Rabey*.

[164] In *Parks*, *supra*, La Forest J. set out two discrete tasks which trial judges must undertake in determining whether automatism should be left with the trier of fact. First, he or she must assess whether a proper foundation for a defence of automatism has been established. As I will explain below, establishing a proper foundation for automatism is the equivalent of satisfying the evidentiary burden for this defence. The mere assertion of involuntariness will not suffice. If a proper evidentiary foundation has been established, the trial judge must next determine whether the condition alleged by the accused is mental disorder or non-mental disorder automatism (p. 897).

[165] In my opinion, the functionality of such a two-step framework is apparent and warrants making such an approach generally applicable to all cases involving claims of automatism. However, this framework only provides a starting point from which to develop a general legal approach to automatism. I will now clarify the particulars of the legal analysis which must be undertaken at each of the framework's two stages.

## C. Step 1: Establishing a Proper Foundation for a Defence of Automatism

[166] A review of the case law reveals that courts, including this Court, have provided little guidance about exactly what an accused must do to establish a proper foundation for a defence of automatism. Frequently, this stage of the judicial two-step analysis consists of nothing more than a remark that there is sufficient evidence on the record. By far the majority of judicial attention has concentrated on the second stage of the automatism analysis, that is, whether the defence of mental disorder or non-mental disorder automatism should be left with the trier of fact. In my opinion, this Court must provide trial judges with more detail about the required elements of a proper foundation for a defence of automatism. First, however, it is necessary to review how the proper foundation requirement fits into the general structure of our criminal law.

[167] As mentioned above, establishing a proper foundation for automatism is the equivalent of satisfying the evidentiary burden for this defence. In *The Law of*

*Evidence in Canada* (1992), J. Sopinka, S. Lederman and A. Bryant distinguish the evidentiary burden from the legal burden as follows, at p. 53:

> The term "burden of proof" is used to describe two distinct concepts relating to the obligation of a party to a proceeding in connection with the proof of a case. In its first sense, the term refers to the obligation imposed on a party to prove or disprove a fact or issue. In the second sense, it refers to a party's obligation to adduce evidence satisfactorily to the judge, in order to raise an issue.

[168] The first sense of the term "burden of proof" suggested by Sopinka, Lederman and Bryant is referred to as the legal or ultimate burden, while the second is known as the evidentiary burden (p. 54). The first, or proper foundation, stage of the automatism analysis sets out what an accused must do to satisfy the evidentiary burden for automatism. As I will discuss below, this burden is directly related to the nature of the legal burden connected with automatism. Whether the accused has satisfied its evidentiary burden is a question of mixed law and fact for the trial judge. It should be noted that, until recently, this determination was considered to be a question of law; see *Canada (Director of Investigation & Research) v. Southam Inc.*, [1997] 1 S.C.R. 748 (S.C.C.), at paras. 35 and 36. In determining whether the evidentiary burden has been satisfied, the trial judge must assess the evidence before the court. According to Viscount Kilmuir in *Bratty, supra*, at p. 406:

> ... for a defence of automatism to be "genuinely raised in a genuine fashion," there must be evidence on which a jury could find that a state of automatism exists. By this I mean that the defence must be able to point to some evidence, whether it emanates from their own or the Crown's witnesses, from which the jury could reasonably infer that the accused acted in a state of automatism. Whether or not there is such evidence is a matter of law for the judge to decide.

### D. Nature and Origin of the Burdens Applied in Cases Involving Claims of Automatism

[169] This Court has stated on many occasions that it is a fundamental principle of criminal law that only voluntary actions will attract findings of guilt. See for example *Daviault, supra*, at pp. 74-75, *per* Cory J.; *Rabey* (S.C.C.), *supra*, at pp. 522 and 545, *per* Dickson J.; *Parks, supra*, at p. 896, *per* La Forest J.; *Rabey* (Ont. C.A.), *supra, per* Martin J.A., at p. 24, adopted by Ritchie J. In *R. v. Théroux*, [1993] 2 S.C.R. 5 (S.C.C.), McLachlin J. classified voluntariness as the mental element of the *actus reus* of a crime (p. 17). In *Daviault*, Cory J. also recognized that voluntariness may be linked to the *actus reus* (p. 102). See also *Chaulk, supra*, at p. 1321, *per* Lamer C.J.

[170] In *Parks, supra*, La Forest J. classified automatism as a sub-set of the voluntariness requirement, which he too recognized as part of the *actus reus* component of criminal responsibility (p. 896). I agree and would add that voluntariness, rather than consciousness, is the key legal element of automatistic behaviour since a defence of automatism amounts to a denial of the voluntariness component of the *actus reus*.

[171]  The law presumes that people act voluntarily. Accordingly, since a defence of automatism amounts to a claim that one's actions were not voluntary, the accused must rebut the presumption of voluntariness. An evidentiary burden is thereby imposed on the accused. The nature of this evidentiary burden stems from the legal burden imposed in cases involving claims of automatism. Generally, the legal burden in such cases has been on the Crown to prove voluntariness, a component of the *actus reus*, beyond a reasonable doubt—hence Dickson J.'s contention in *Rabey* that an accused claiming automatism need only raise evidence sufficient to permit a properly instructed jury to find a reasonable doubt as to voluntariness in order to rebut the presumption of voluntariness. The Crown then has the legal burden of proving voluntariness beyond a reasonable doubt to the trier of fact. If the Crown fails to satisfy this burden, the accused will be acquitted.

[172]  My colleague, Justice Binnie, relies heavily on Dickson J.'s approach to the nature of the burdens in cases involving claims of automatism. I do not agree that the reasons of Dickson J. provide justification for the refusal to review the appropriateness of these burdens on their merits in the present appeal. Furthermore, I must respectfully disagree with my colleague regarding the treatment of Dickson J.'s views on this point by La Forest J. in *Parks*. I note that in *Parks* the appropriateness of the evidentiary burden on the defence at the proper foundation stage was not directly at issue before this Court. As a result, La Forest J. did not find it necessary to assess the precise nature of either of the burdens of proof as set out by Dickson J. in *Rabey*.

*E. What Should the Burdens of Proof Associated with Automatism Be?*

[173]  The relationship between the burdens associated with automatism dictates that any change in the legal burden of automatism will necessarily result in a change to the evidentiary or proper foundation burden associated with this defence. The evidentiary burden will relate either to evidence sufficient to establish voluntariness beyond a reasonable doubt, as suggested by Binnie J., or, as set out below, to evidence sufficient to establish involuntariness on a balance of probabilities. In my opinion, a review of the legal burden applicable in cases involving claims of automatism is in order. My colleague Binnie J. is of the view that this Court ought not review either the legal or the evidentiary burden set out in the dissenting reasons of Dickson J. in *Rabey*. In support of this position, Binnie J. argues that neither the respondent nor any of the intervening Attorneys General requested such a review. With respect, I disagree. In its written submissions, the respondent invited this Court to reconsider the trial judge's finding that there was a proper foundation for automatism. The respondent also requested that this Court make the proper foundation stage of the automatism analysis more stringent. As explained above, an assessment of an evidentiary or proper foundation burden cannot be undertaken without reference to the related legal burden.

[174]  In her 1993 *Proposals to amend the Criminal Code (general principles)*, the Minister of Justice recommended that the legal burden of proof in all cases of automatism be on the party that raises the issue on a balance of probabilities. This is the same legal burden that this Court applied to a claim of extreme intoxication akin

to a state of automatism in *Daviault*, *supra*. It is also the legal burden Parliament assigned to the defence of mental disorder in s. 16 of the *Code*, which, as mentioned above, is equally applicable to voluntary and involuntary actions stemming from a disease of the mind and therefore applies to mental disorder automatism. As I explained above, different legal approaches to claims of automatism, whether based on the context in which the alleged automatism arose or on the distinction between mental disorder and non-mental disorder automatism, is problematic and should be avoided. Indeed, counsel for the appellant in the present case recognized as much in oral argument before this Court:

> No, I think that the—the conflict arises in a slightly different situation, which I'm going to come to in a moment, and that is that, when one deals with insanity, the evidentiary burden is upon the accused to establish that on the balance of probabilities.
>
> When one comes now, pursuant to this Court's decision in *Daviault*, to drunkenness akin to automatism, again, the onus is upon the accused, and the evidentiary burden as well.
>
> Whereas in non-insane automatism, the onus simply is upon the defence to raise it and for the Crown to then disprove it beyond a reasonable doubt in essence.
>
> So that is where I concede that there is a contradiction and that there may be some merit in having the same test and the same process applied to each of the different kinds of mental disorder, to use the term loosely.

[175] An appropriate legal burden applicable to all cases involving claims of automatism must reflect the policy concerns which surround claims of automatism. The words of Schroeder J.A. in *R. v. Szymusiak*, [1972] 3 O.R. 602 (Ont. C.A.), at p. 608, come to mind:

> … a defence which in a true and proper case may be the only one open to an honest man, but it may just as readily be the last refuge of a scoundrel.

[176] The recognition that policy considerations are relevant is nothing new to this area of criminal law. In *Rabey* (Ont. C.A.), *supra*, Martin J.A., whose reasons were adopted by the majority of this Court, recognized that the term "disease of the mind" contains both a medical component and legal or policy component (p. 425). Dickson J., dissenting in *Rabey* (S.C.C.), noted, at p. 546, that specific policy considerations were involved in determining whether a claim of automatism should be categorized as mental disorder or non-mental disorder:

> There are undoubtedly policy considerations to be considered. Automatism as a defence is easily feigned. It is said the credibility of our criminal justice system will be severely strained if a person who has committed a violent act is allowed an absolute acquittal on a plea of automatism arising from a psychological blow. The argument is made that the success of the defence depends upon the semantic ability of psychiatrists, tracing a narrow path between the twin shoals of criminal responsibility and an insanity verdict. Added to these concerns is the *in terrorem* argument that the floodgates will be raised if psychological blow automatism is recognized in law.

[177] Likewise, in *Parks, supra,* La Forest J. considered policy to be a relevant consideration for trial judges in distinguishing between mental disorder and non-mental disorder automatism (p. 896 and pp. 907-908).

[178] In both *Rabey* and *Parks,* policy considerations were relegated to the second stage of the automatism analysis to determine whether the condition alleged by the accused was mental disorder or non-mental disorder automatism. In neither case is there any indication that this Court intended to preclude the consideration of policy in the determination of an appropriate legal burden for cases involving claims of automatism.

[179] The foregoing leads me to the conclusion that the legal burden in cases involving claims of automatism must be on the defence to prove involuntariness on a balance of probabilities to the trier of fact. This is the same burden supported by Lord Goddard, dissenting in *Hill v. Baxter* (1957), [1958] 1 Q.B. 277 (Eng. Q.B.), at pp. 282-83, and imposed in some American jurisdictions; see for example *State v. Caddell,* 215 S.E.2d 348 (N.C. 1975); *Fulcher v. State,* 633 P.2d 142 (Wyo. 1981); *Polston v. State,* 685 P.2d 1 (Wyo. 1984); *State v. Fields,* 376 S.E.2d 740 (N.C. 1989).

[180] In *Chaulk, supra,* and *Daviault, supra,* this Court recognized that although placing a balance of probabilities burden on the defence with respect to an element of the offence constitutes a limitation of an accused person's rights under s. 11(d) of the *Charter,* it can be justified under s. 1. In my opinion, the burden is also justified in the present case. The law presumes that people act voluntarily in order to avoid placing the onerous burden of proving voluntariness beyond a reasonable doubt on the Crown. Like extreme drunkenness akin to automatism, genuine cases of automatism will be extremely rare. However, because automatism is easily feigned and all knowledge of its occurrence rests with the accused, putting a legal burden on the accused to prove involuntariness on a balance of probabilities is necessary to further the objective behind the presumption of voluntariness. In contrast, saddling the Crown with the legal burden of proving voluntariness beyond a reasonable doubt actually defeats the purpose of the presumption of voluntariness. Thus, requiring that an accused bear the legal burden of proving involuntariness on a balance of probabilities is justified under s. 1. There is therefore no violation of the Constitution. On this latter point, I would note the words of Lamer C.J. in *R. v. Swain,* [1991] 1 S.C.R. 933 (S.C.C.), at pp. 996-97:

> I also wish to point out that, throughout my reasons on this issue, I have been careful to speak of the old common law rule as limiting the s. 7 *Charter* right and as violating the Constitution only after having reached the conclusion that the limitation is not justified under s. 1 of the *Charter.* This choice of language is deliberate but does not depend on the fact that this case involves a *Charter* challenge to a common law rule as opposed to a legislative provision. Whether one is speaking of a legislative provision or a common law rule it is not, in my view, correct to speak of a law violating a particular provision of the *Charter* (such as s. 7) prior to having gone through a s. 1 analysis. The *Charter* guarantees the particular rights and freedoms set out in it subject to reasonable limits which can be, under s. 1, demonstrably justified in a free and democratic society. Thus a law which limits a right set out in the *Charter* will only violate the Constitution if it is not justified under s. 1. In this instance, the law will either be struck down (to the extent

of the inconsistency) under s. 52(1) or it will be reinterpreted so as not to violate the Constitution. If a law which limits a right set out in the *Charter* is justified under s. 1, that law does not violate the Constitution.

[181]  One final point on the issue of justification. My colleague Binnie J. distinguishes the s. 1 analysis in the present case from that in *Daviault* on the basis of the state of the law prior to a change established by this Court. With respect, I cannot agree that the issue of whether the previous state of the law was more or less advantageous to the accused is relevant to the justification of subsequent law. In both instances, the relevant matter is whether an *existing* infringement can be justified as a reasonable limit in a free and democratic society. The relevant subject of the s. 1 analysis is therefore the *current* state of the law rather than the comparative nature of previous law.

[182]  As explained above, what an accused must do to satisfy the evidentiary or proper foundation burden in cases involving claims of automatism is directly related to the nature of the legal burden in such cases. Accordingly, a change to the evidentiary burden associated with automatism is in order. To meet this burden, the defence must satisfy the trial judge that there is evidence upon which a properly instructed jury could find that the accused acted involuntarily on a balance of probabilities. In my opinion, this evidentiary burden is consistent with the two-step approach taken by La Forest J. in *Parks, supra*. As noted above, the appropriateness of the evidentiary burden on the defence at the proper foundation stage was not directly at issue before this Court in *Parks*. This explains why La Forest J. did not find it necessary to refine the burdens associated with automatism to the extent that it has been necessary for me to do in the present case. What then is the nature of the evidence which will be required to satisfy this revised proper foundation or evidentiary burden?

[183]  A review of the case law reveals that an accused must claim that he acted involuntarily at the relevant time in order to satisfy the automatism evidentiary burden. As stated earlier, a mere assertion of involuntariness will not suffice. See for example *Bratty, supra*, at pp. 406 and 413-14; *Rabey* (Ont. C.A.), *supra*, at pp. 24-25, *per* Martin J.A. adopted by Ritchie J; *Parks, supra*, at p. 897, *per* La Forest J.; *Falconer, supra*, at pp. 250-51 and 266.

[184]  In addition to an assertion of involuntariness, the defence must present expert psychiatric evidence confirming its claim. See for example *Bratty, supra*, at p. 413; *Falconer, supra*, at pp. 250-57 and 266; *Daviault, supra*, at pp. 101 and 103; *Rabey* (S.C.C.), *supra*, at p. 552, *per* Dickson J. Even the appellant in the present case concedes that in the absence of such psychiatric evidence it is unlikely that he could satisfy his evidentiary or proper foundation burden.

[185]  The law often requires judges to make subtle and sophisticated determinations about scientific methodology and expert evidence. Cases involving claims of automatism are no exception. Yet as Breyer J. of the United States Supreme Court aptly recognized in *General Electric Co. v. Joiner*, 118 S. Ct. 512 (U.S. Ga. 1997), judges are usually not scientists and thus do not have the scientific training which facilitates the making of such decisions. For this reason, when law and science intersect, judges must undertake their duties with special care (p. 520).

[186] Although cases involving claims of automatism do not deal with complex chemical reactions or the like, they do require judges to assess confusing and often contradictory psychiatric evidence. In particular, when determining whether the evidentiary burden for automatism has been satisfied, trial judges must be careful to recognize that the weight to be given to expert evidence may vary from case to case. If the expert testimony establishes a documented history of automatistic-like dissociative states, it must be given more weight than if the expert is simply confirming that the claim of automatism is plausible. In the former case, the expert is actually providing a medical opinion about the accused. In the latter case, however, the expert is simply providing an opinion about the circumstances surrounding the allegation of automatism as they have been told to him or her by the accused. Trial judges must keep in mind that an expert opinion of this latter type is entirely dependent on the accuracy and truthfulness of the account of events given to the expert by the accused. Indeed, in the present case, Dr. Janke, the defence psychiatrist, qualified his opinion by noting that it was based almost exclusively on the accuracy and truthfulness of the appellant's account of events:

> I think that, that when, in offering the [expert psychiatric] opinion, it is, in this circumstance, it's contingent upon the person being accurate in representing what they recall from that event. There are circumstances where you do have other witnesses who can give you some supportive evidence, but in this situation, you have to rely on a person. If they're not telling the truth, then the opinion is worthless.

[187] In order to satisfy the evidentiary or proper foundation burden, all cases will require an assertion of involuntariness and confirming psychiatric evidence. However, this burden will generally require more than an assertion of involuntariness on the part of the accused accompanied by confirming expert evidence that automatism is plausible assuming the account of events given to the expert by the accused was accurate and truthful. The recognition of Sopinka, Lederman and Bryant in *The Law of Evidence in Canada*, *supra*, at p. 129, that "[p]olicy considerations are important in determining the sufficiency of evidence that is required to satisfy [evidential burdens] in both criminal and civil proceedings" supports such an approach. I will now attempt to provide some guidance on what additional evidence is relevant to the determination of whether the defence has raised evidence which would permit a properly instructed jury to find that the accused acted involuntarily on a balance of probabilities. The factors discussed here are given only by way of example and are meant to illustrate the type of reasoning trial judges should employ when evaluating the evidence adduced at trial.

[188] Both the majority and dissent of this Court in *Rabey*, *supra*, recognized that a "shocking" psychological blow was required before non-mental disorder, rather than mental disorder, automatism could be left with the trier of fact. Although *Rabey* dealt specifically with "psychological blow" automatism, I am of the opinion that it is appropriate in all cases for trial judges to consider the nature of the alleged automatism trigger in order to assess whether the defence has raised evidence on which a properly instructed jury could find that the accused acted involuntarily on a balance of probabilities. With reference to psychological blow automatism specifically, I agree

that the defence will generally have to provide evidence of a trigger equivalent to a "shock" in order to satisfy its evidentiary burden.

[189] The existence or non-existence of evidence which corroborates the accused's claim of automatism will also be relevant to the assessment of whether a properly instructed jury could find that the accused acted involuntarily on a balance of probabilities. Such evidence may take different forms. Two examples are worth noting here. First, evidence of a documented medical history of automatistic-like dissociative states would certainly assist the defence in satisfying a trial judge that a properly instructed jury could find that the accused acted involuntarily on a balance of probabilities. Furthermore, the more similar the historical pattern of dissociation is with the current claim of automatism, the more persuasive the evidence will be on the issue of involuntariness. For example, a documented history of dissociation in response to the particular triggering stimuli in question in the case could serve as strong evidence that the same stimuli once again triggered an involuntary response. Although I would not go so far as to make a medical history of dissociation a requirement for the defence to meet its evidentiary burden at the proper foundation stage, I would note that the lack of such evidence is also a relevant factor in determining whether this defence burden has been satisfied.

[190] Corroborating evidence of a bystander which reveals that the accused appeared uncharacteristically glassy-eyed, unresponsive and or distant immediately before, during or after the alleged involuntary act will also be relevant to the assessment of whether the defence has raised evidence on which a properly instructed jury could find that the accused acted involuntarily on a balance of probabilities. This is confirmed by the expert evidence of Dr. Murphy, the Crown psychiatrist in the present case, as set out above. Indeed, the fact that it is common practice for judges to note specifically witness' comments about the appearance of the accused at the relevant time indicates that this may already be a factor weighed in the assessment of whether or not the defence has satisfied its evidentiary burden in cases involving claims of automatism. I would caution, however, that the evidence of bystanders must be approached very carefully since automatism and rage may often be indistinguishable to untrained bystanders.

[191] Another factor which trial judges should consider in assessing whether the defence has raised evidence which would permit a properly instructed jury to find that the accused acted involuntarily on a balance of probabilities is motive. A motiveless act will generally lend plausibility to an accused's claim of involuntariness. Indeed, in the present case, Dr. Murphy, the Crown psychiatrist, testified that since the mind and body of a person in a dissociative state have been split, she would expect that there would usually be no connection between involuntary acts done in a state of automatism and the social context immediately preceding them. Dr. Murphy also noted that if a single person is both the trigger of the alleged automatism and the victim of the automatistic violence, the claim of involuntariness should be considered suspect. I agree that the plausibility of a claim of automatism will be reduced if the accused had a motive to commit the crime in question or if the "trigger" of the alleged automatism is also the victim. On the other hand, if the involuntary act is random and lacks motive, the plausibility of the claim of automatism will be increased.

A question that trial judges should ask in assessing whether the defence has raised evidence which would permit a properly instructed jury to find that the accused acted involuntarily on a balance of probabilities is therefore whether or not the crime in question is explicable without reference to the alleged automatism. If this question can be answered in the negative, the plausibility of the accused's claim of involuntariness will be heightened. Such was the case in *Parks*, *supra*, for example, where there was no explanation for why the accused would attack his" in-laws," with whom he otherwise had a good relationship, except automatism induced by a state of somnambulism. In contrast, if this question invokes a positive response, the plausibility of the claim of involuntariness will be decreased.

[192] To sum up, in order to satisfy the evidentiary or proper foundation burden in cases involving claims of automatism, the defence must make an assertion of involuntariness and call expert psychiatric or psychological evidence confirming that assertion. However, it is an error of law to conclude that this defence burden has been satisfied simply because the defence has met these two requirements. The burden will only be met where the trial judge concludes that there is evidence upon which a properly instructed jury could find that the accused acted involuntarily on a balance of probabilities. In reaching this conclusion, the trial judge will first examine the psychiatric or psychological evidence and inquire into the foundation and nature of the expert opinion. The trial judge will also examine all other available evidence, if any. Relevant factors are not a closed category and may, by way of example, include: the severity of the triggering stimulus, corroborating evidence of bystanders, corroborating medical history of automatistic-like dissociative states, whether there is evidence of a motive for the crime, and whether the alleged trigger of the automatism is also the victim of the automatistic violence. I point out that no single factor is meant to be determinative. Indeed, there may be cases in which the psychiatric or psychological evidence goes beyond simply corroborating the accused's version of events, for example, where it establishes a documented history of automatistic-like dissociative states. Furthermore, the ever advancing state of medical knowledge may lead to a finding that other types of evidence are also indicative of involuntariness. I leave it to the discretion and experience of trial judges to weigh all of the evidence available on a case by case basis and to determine whether a properly instructed jury could find that the accused acted involuntarily on a balance of probabilities.

### F. Step 2: Determining Whether To Leave Mental Disorder or Non-Mental Disorder Automatism with the Trier of Fact

[193] Only if the accused has laid a proper foundation for a defence of automatism will it be necessary for the trial judge to determine whether mental disorder or non-mental disorder automatism should be left with the trier of fact. If the trial judge concludes that a proper foundation has not been established, the presumption of voluntariness will be effective and neither automatism defence will be available to the trier of fact. In such a case, however, the accused may still claim an independent s. 16 defence of mental disorder.

[194] The determination of whether mental disorder or non-mental disorder automatism should be left with the trier of fact must be undertaken very carefully since it will have serious ramifications for both the individual accused and society in general. As mentioned above, mental disorder automatism is subsumed by the defence of mental disorder as set out in the *Code*. Accordingly, a successful defence of mental disorder automatism will result in a verdict of not criminally responsible on account of mental disorder as dictated by s. 672.34 of the *Code*. Under s. 672.54, an accused who receives this qualified acquittal may be discharged absolutely, discharged conditionally or detained in a hospital. In contrast, a successful defence of non-mental disorder automatism will always result in an absolute acquittal.

[195] The assessment of which form of automatism should be left with the trier of fact comes down to the question of whether or not the condition alleged by the accused is a mental disorder. Mental disorder is a legal term. It is defined in s. 2 of the *Code* as "a disease of the mind." In *Parks*, *supra*, at pp. 898-99, the majority of this Court adopted the reasons of Martin J.A. in *Rabey* (Ont. C.A.), *supra*, which included the following explanation of the term "disease of the mind," at pp. 12-13:

> Although the term "disease of the mind" is not capable of precise definition, certain propositions may, I think, be asserted with respect to it. "Disease of the mind" is a legal term, not a medical term of art; although a legal concept, it contains a substantial medical component as well as a legal or policy component. ...
>
> The evidence of medical witnesses with respect to the cause, nature and symptoms of the abnormal mental condition from which the accused is alleged to suffer, and how that condition is viewed and characterized from the medical point of view, is highly relevant to the judicial determination of whether such a condition is capable of constituting a "disease of the mind." The opinions of medical witnesses as to whether an abnormal mental state does or does not constitute a disease of the mind are not, however, determinative, since what is a disease of the mind is a legal question. ...

[196] In *Rabey* (Ont. C.A.), Martin J.A. described the task of the trial judge in determining the disease of the mind issue as follows, at p. 13:

> I take the true principle to be this: It is for the Judge to determine what mental conditions are included within the term "disease of the mind," and whether there is any evidence that the accused suffered from an abnormal mental condition comprehended by that term.

[197] Taken alone, the question of what mental conditions are included in the term disease of the mind is a question of law. However, the trial judge must also determine whether the condition the accused claims to have suffered from satisfies the legal test for disease of the mind. This involves an assessment of the particular evidence in the case rather than a general principle of law and is thus a question of mixed law and fact. See *Southam*, *supra*, at paras. 35 and 36. The question of whether the accused actually suffered from a disease of the mind is a question of fact to be determined by the trier of fact. See *Rabey* (S.C.C.), *supra*, at p. 519, *per* Ritchie J.; *Parks*, *supra*, at p. 897, *per* La Forest J.; and *Bratty*, *supra*, at p.412, *per* Lord Denning.

[198]  In response to the above-mentioned proposed revisions to the *Code* regarding automatism, the Canadian Psychiatric Association submitted a Brief to the House of Commons Standing Committee on Justice and the Solicitor General. In this brief, the Association, on behalf of its 2,400 members nationwide, suggested that from a medical perspective, all automatism necessarily stems from mental disorder. Accordingly, the Association recommended that non-mental disorder automatism be eliminated and all claims of automatism be classified as mental disorders.

[199]  Since mental disorder is a legal term, the opinion of the Canadian Psychiatric Association, while relevant, is not determinative of whether two distinct forms of automatism, mental disorder and non-mental disorder, should continue to be recognized at law. In my opinion, this Court should not go so far as to eliminate the defence of non-mental disorder automatism as the Association suggests. However, I take judicial notice that it will only be in rare cases that automatism is not caused by mental disorder. Indeed, since the trial judge will have already concluded that there is evidence upon which a properly instructed jury could find that the accused acted involuntarily on a balance of probabilities, there is a serious question as to the existence of an operating mind by the time the disease of the mind issue is considered. The foregoing lends itself to a rule that trial judges start from the proposition that the condition the accused claims to have suffered from is a disease of the mind. They must then determine whether the evidence in the particular case takes the condition out of the disease of the mind category. This approach is consistent with this Court's decision in *Rabey, supra.*

[200]  In *Rabey*, this Court adopted the "internal cause theory" of Martin J.A. as the primary test for determining whether automatism resulting from a psychological blow stems from a disease of the mind. The following is a portion of Martin J.A.'s explanation of this approach, which was cited with approval by the majority of this Court, at p. 519:

> In general, the distinction to be drawn is between a malfunctioning of the mind arising from some cause that is primarily internal to the accused, having its source in his psychological or emotional makeup, or in some organic pathology, as opposed to a malfunctioning of the mind, which is the transient effect produced by some specific external factor such as, for example, concussion. Any malfunctioning of the mind, or mental disorder having its source primarily in some subjective condition or weakness internal to the accused (whether fully understood or not) may be a "disease of the mind" if it prevents the accused from knowing what he is doing, but transient disturbances of consciousness due to certain specific external factors do not fall with the concept of disease of the mind.

[201]  It is clear from Martin J.A.'s reasons that the internal cause theory starts from the proposition that the condition the accused claims to have suffered from is a disease of the mind. At pp. 21-22, he states:

> The malfunctioning of the mind which the respondent suffered, although temporary, is a "disease of the mind," *unless it can be considered as a transient state produced by an external cause within the meaning of the authorities.*

In my view, the ordinary stresses and disappointments of life which are the common lot of mankind do not constitute an external cause constituting an explanation for a malfunctioning of the mind *which takes it out of* the category of a "disease of the mind." [Emphasis added.]

[202]  The reasons of La Forest J. in *Parks, supra*, are sometimes read as reversing the *Rabey* notion that the disease of the mind inquiry should begin from the proposition that the condition the accused claims to have suffered from is a disease of the mind. However, La Forest J. clearly stipulated, at p. 898, that "the approach to distinguishing between insane and sane automatism was settled by this Court's judgement in *Rabey*." Furthermore, in applying the second step of the automatism analysis, La Forest J. considered whether policy factors *precluded* a finding of non-mental disorder automatism (p. 908). In the end, given the fact specific approach taken by this Court in *Parks*, I would conclude that *Parks* cannot be interpreted as reversing *Rabey* on this issue.

### G.  Determining Whether the Condition the Accused Claims To Have Suffered from Is a Disease of the Mind

[203]  In *Parks*, La Forest J. recognized that there are two distinct approaches to the disease of the mind inquiry: the internal cause theory and the continuing danger theory. He recognized the internal cause theory as the dominant approach in Canadian jurisprudence but concluded, at p. 902, that this theory "is really meant to be used only as an analytical tool, and not as an all-encompassing methodology." This conclusion stemmed from a finding that somnambulism, the alleged trigger of the automatism in *Parks*, raises unique problems which are not well-suited to analysis under the internal cause theory. I agree that the internal cause theory cannot be regarded as a universal classificatory scheme for "disease of the mind." There will be cases in which the approach is not helpful because, in the words of La Forest J., at p. 903, "the dichotomy between internal and external causes becomes blurred." Accordingly, a new approach to the disease of the mind inquiry is in order. As I will explain below, a more holistic approach, like that developed by La Forest J. in *Parks*, must be available to trial judges in dealing with the disease of the mind question. This approach must be informed by the internal cause theory, the continuing danger theory and the policy concerns raised in this Court's decisions in *Rabey* and *Parks*.

### (1)  The Internal Cause Theory

[204]  The internal cause theory was developed in the context of psychological blow automatism. Under the internal cause theory, the trial judge must compare the accused's automatistic reaction to the psychological blow to the way one would expect a normal person in the same circumstances to react in order to determine whether the condition the accused claims to have suffered from is a disease of the mind. As K.L. Campbell points out, at p. 354 of his article "Psychological Blow Automatism: A Narrow Defence" (1980-81), 23 *Crim. L.Q.* 342, how can abnormality be defined in any other way but by comparison to what is normal. The words of Martin J.A. in

*Rabey* (Ont. C.A.), *supra*, adopted by the majority of this Court, at p. 520, highlight
this comparative approach to the disease of the mind question:

> In my view, the ordinary stresses and disappointments of life which are the common lot
> of mankind do not constitute an external cause constituting an explanation for a mal-
> functioning of the mind which takes it out of the category of a "disease of the mind." ...
> I leave aside, until it becomes necessary to decide them, cases where a dissociative
> state has resulted from emotional shock without physical injury, resulting from such
> causes, for example, as being involved in a serious accident although no physical in-
> jury has resulted; being the victim of a murderous attack with an uplifted knife, not-
> withstanding that the victim has managed to escape physical injury; seeing a loved one
> murdered or seriously assaulted, and like situations. Such extraordinary external events
> might reasonably be presumed to affect the average normal person without reference to
> the subjective makeup of the person exposed to such experience.

[205] The nature of the alleged trigger of the automatism is at the centre of the
comparison the trial judge must undertake. For example, in the context of psychological blow automatism, both the majority and dissent of this Court in *Rabey* recognized that a "shocking" psychological blow was required before non-mental disorder, rather than mental disorder, automatism could be left with the trier of fact. To
this end, the majority adopted the above-quoted words of Martin J.A. In dissent,
Dickson J. made the following comment, at p. 549:

> I agree with the requirement that there be a shock precipitating the state of automatism.
> Dissociation caused by a low stress threshold and surrender to anxiety cannot fairly be
> said to result from a psychological blow.

[206] Accordingly, in *Rabey*, this Court unanimously supported the notion that
there is a comparative element to the disease of the mind inquiry which involves an
assessment of the nature of the trigger of the alleged automatism. In effect, the trial
judge must consider the nature of the trigger and determine whether a normal person
in the same circumstances might have reacted to it by entering an automatistic state
as the accused claims to have done. Although I recognize that this approach will not
be helpful in all cases, I believe that it remains useful in others. As such, the internal
cause approach is a factor for trial judges to consider in cases in which they deem it
useful. It may be helpful to provide some guidance as to how the comparison involved in the internal cause theory should be undertaken. I will do so in the context
of psychological blow automatism, as I believe the internal cause approach will be
most useful in cases involving automatism claims of this nature.

[207] In his article, *supra*, Campbell points out that in assessing triggers of psychological blow automatism in *Rabey*, the majority of this Court drew the line
between stressful situations and extremely shocking events. Under this approach, a
finding that an alleged condition is not a disease of the mind, and consequently can
support a defence of non-mental disorder automatism, is limited to cases involving
triggers that normal people would find extremely shocking. Involuntariness caused
by any less severe shock or mere stress is presumed to be triggered by a factor inter-

nal to the accused and as such constitutes a disease of the mind which can only give rise to a defence of mental disorder automatism (p. 357). Dickson J., in dissent, drew the line between stressful situations and mildly shocking events. Under this approach, the threshold requirement for a finding that a condition is not a disease of the mind is any shock, no matter what its severity. Only events which cannot be classified as a shock of any degree are labelled as internal, and thus diseases of the mind which can only give rise to the defence of mental disorder automatism (p. 358).

[208] Given that the present case involves psychological blow automatism, I believe it is appropriate to express my opinion that the position of the majority in *Rabey* on this issue is preferable. The point of undertaking the comparison is to determine whether a normal person might have reacted to the alleged trigger by entering an automatistic state as the accused claims to have done. In cases involving claims of psychological blow automatism, evidence of an extremely shocking trigger will be required to establish that a normal person might have reacted to the trigger by entering an automatistic state, as the accused claims to have done.

[209] When undertaking a comparison with a normal person, one is immediately faced with the difficulty of determining the importance of the context in which the comparison is made. I agree with the following comments of the High Court of Australia in *Falconer, supra*, on this issue (at p. 264):

> In determining whether the mind of an ordinary person would have malfunctioned in the face of the physical or psychological trauma to which the accused was subjected, the psychotic, neurotic or emotional state of the accused at that time is immaterial. The ordinary person is assumed to be a person of normal temperament and self-control. Consequently, evidence that, in the week preceding the shooting, [the accused] had demonstrated fear, depression, emotional disturbance and an apparently changed personality would not have been relevant in determining the reaction of an ordinary person. Likewise, evidence of the stress that she suffered on discovering that her husband had sexually assaulted their two daughters would not have been relevant in determining the reaction of the ordinary person to the incidents which took place on the day of the shooting. But the evidence of the objective circumstances of the relationship between the parties would have been relevant to that issue, for only by considering the pertinent circumstances of that relationship could the jury determine whether an ordinary person would have succumbed to a state of dissociation similar to that which [the accused] claims overtook her on that day. Speaking generally, the issue for the jury on this aspect of the case would be whether an ordinary woman of [the accused]'s age and circumstances, who had been subjected to the history of violence which she alleged, who had recently discovered that her husband had sexually assaulted their daughters, who knew that criminal charges had been laid against her husband in respect of these matters and who were separated from her husband as a result of his relationship with another woman, would have entered a state of dissociation as the result of the incidents which occurred on the day of the shooting.

[210] The comparison involved in the disease of the mind inquiry is thus a contextual objective test. The accused's automatistic reaction to the alleged trigger must

be assessed from the perspective of a similarly situated individual. This requires that the circumstances of the case be taken into account. However, I emphasize that this is not a subjective test.

[211] The appellant argues that the objective element of the internal cause theory violates ss. 7 and 11(d) of the *Charter*. According to the appellant, the *Charter* requires that the focus of the disease of the mind inquiry be on the actual, subjective response of the accused rather than that of a normal person. With respect, this argument fails to recognize that the objective inquiry into whether the condition claimed by the accused is a disease of the mind is applied only after a subjective inquiry into whether there is evidence upon which a properly instructed jury could find that the accused acted involuntarily on a balance of probabilities has been completed by the trial judge. That is, the objective standard affects only the classification of the defence rather than the assessment of whether the *actus reus* of the offence has been established. A similar objective standard was applied to the defence of provocation in *R. v. Cameron* (1992), 71 C.C.C. (3d) 272 (Ont. C.A.), where the Ontario Court of Appeal held that the objective standard involved in the defence of provocation does not violate ss. 7 and 11(d) because it does not detract from the *mens rea* required to establish murder. The point I wish to make here is that the objective component of the internal cause theory does not affect the burden of proof on the issue of whether the accused voluntarily committed the offence. Moreover, the impact of the objective comparison is limited even with regard to the disease of the mind inquiry. As noted above, I agree with La Forest J. in *Parks* that the internal cause theory is only an analytical tool. It is not being held out as the definitive answer to the disease of the mind question. In each case, the trial judge must determine whether and to what extent the theory is useful given the facts of the case. Indeed, he or she has the discretion to disregard the theory if its application would not accord with the policy concerns which underlie the disease of the mind inquiry. In this way, the internal cause approach attempts to strike an appropriate balance between the objectives of providing an exemption from criminal liability for morally innocent offenders and protecting the public. In these circumstances, the objective component of the internal cause theory does not limit either s. 7 or s. 11(d) of the *Charter*. I would add that consideration of the subjective psychological make-up of the accused in the internal cause theory would frustrate the very purpose of making the comparison, which is of course to determine whether the accused was suffering from a disease of the mind in a legal sense.

(2)  The Continuing Danger Theory

[212]  As mentioned above, both the majority and dissenting judges of this Court in *Rabey*, as well as La Forest J. in *Parks*, recognized that policy considerations are relevant to the determination of whether a claim of automatism is the result of a disease of the mind. One policy factor which is central to the disease of the mind inquiry is the need to ensure public safety. Indeed, as mentioned above, La Forest J. recognized in *Parks* that the second dominant approach to the disease of the mind question is the continuing danger theory. This theory holds that any condition which

is likely to present a recurring danger to the public should be treated as a disease of the mind. In other words, the likelihood of recurrence of violence is a factor to be considered in the disease of the mind inquiry. This approach must be qualified to recognize that while a continuing danger suggests a disease of the mind, a finding of no continuing danger does not preclude a finding of a disease of the mind. See *Rabey*, *supra*, at p. 15 (Ont. C.A.), *per* Martin J.A., and at pp. 533 and 551 (S.C.C.), *per* Dickson J.; *Parks*, *supra*, at p. 907, *per* La Forest J.

[213] In my opinion, trial judges should continue to consider the continuing danger theory as a factor in the determination of whether a condition should be classified as a disease of the mind. However, I emphasize that the continuing danger factor should not be viewed as an alternative or mutually exclusive approach to the internal cause factor. Although different, both of these approaches are relevant factors in the disease of the mind inquiry. As such, in any given case, a trial judge may find one, the other or both of these approaches of assistance. To reflect this unified, holistic approach to the disease of the mind question, it is therefore more appropriate to refer to the internal cause factor and the continuing danger factor, rather than the internal cause theory and the continuing danger theory.

[214] In examining the continuing danger factor, trial judges may consider any of the evidence before them in order to assess the likelihood of recurrence of violence. However, two issues will be particularly relevant to the continuing danger factor: the psychiatric history of the accused and the likelihood that the trigger alleged to have caused the automatistic episode will recur.

[215] As noted above, the defence must present expert psychiatric evidence in order to establish a proper foundation for a defence of automatism. The weight to be given to such evidence at the foundation stage will depend upon whether it establishes a documented history of automatistic-like dissociative states or simply confirms that a claim of automatism is plausible provided that the account of events given to the expert by the accused was accurate and truthful. The same distinction is again relevant when assessing the continuing danger factor in order to determine whether the condition the accused claims to have suffered from is a disease of the mind. Psychiatric evidence which reveals a documented history of automatistic-like dissociative states suggests that the condition alleged by the accused is of a recurring nature and thus increases the likelihood that automatism will recur. The likelihood of recurrence of violence is in turn heightened by the fact that at least one of the accused's automatistic episodes involved violence. In such a case, the continuing danger factor indicates that the condition the accused claims to have suffered from is likely to be classified as a disease of the mind. I would note that the absence of a history of automatistic-like dissociative states in no way indicates that there will be no recurrence of violence. In such a case, the trial judge will have to determine the recurrence of violence issue through other methods, one of which may be an assessment of the likelihood of recurrence of the alleged trigger of the automatism.

[216] In their Case Comment on *R. v. Parks* (1993), 72 *Can. Bar Rev.* 224, I. Grant and L. Spitz point out that in assessing the likelihood of recurrence of violence, courts have been asking the wrong question. Courts have been focussing on whether the accused is likely to exhibit violent behaviour if he or she were again to encounter the

alleged trigger of the current automatistic episode. According to Grant and Spitz, a more appropriate question is simply whether the alleged trigger is likely to recur. Grant and Spitz reason that there is no way of accurately predicting whether actual violence will recur. Indeed the likelihood of the initial automatistic violence would generally have been remote and thus difficult to predict. In contrast, the likelihood of recurrence of the circumstances which are alleged to have given rise to the automatism is more easily predicted (see pp. 235-36).

[217]  The logic of the reasoning of Grant and Spitz is difficult to deny. Indeed, it reveals that an assessment of the likelihood that the particular accused will again encounter the trigger alleged to have caused the current automatistic episode, or a similar one of at least equal severity, may assist a judge in assessing the continuing danger factor. The greater the anticipated frequency of the trigger in the accused's life, the greater the risk posed to the public and, consequently, the more likely it is that the condition alleged by the accused is a disease of the mind.

(3)  Other Policy Factors

[218]  There may be cases in which consideration of the internal cause and continuing danger factors alone does not permit a conclusive answer to the disease of the mind question. Such will be the case, for example, where the internal cause factor is not helpful because it is impossible to classify the alleged cause of the automatism as internal or external, and the continuing danger factor is inconclusive because there is no continuing danger of violence. Accordingly, a holistic approach to disease of the mind must also permit trial judges to consider other policy concerns which underlie this inquiry. As mentioned above, in *Rabey* and *Parks*, this Court outlined some of the policy concerns which surround automatism. I have already referred to those specific policy concerns earlier in these reasons. I repeat that I do not view those policy concerns as a closed category. In any given automatism case, a trial judge may identify a policy factor which this Court has not expressly recognized. Any such valid policy concern can be considered by the trial judge in order to determine whether the condition the accused claims to have suffered from is a disease of the mind. In determining this issue, policy concerns assist trial judges in answering the fundamental question of mixed law and fact which is at the centre of the disease of the mind inquiry: whether society requires protection from the accused and, consequently, whether the accused should be subject to evaluation under the regime contained in Part XX.1 of the *Code*.

*H.  Available Defences Following the Determination of the Disease of the Mind Question*

[219]  If the trial judge concludes that the condition the accused claims to have suffered from is not a disease of the mind, only the defence of non-mental disorder automatism will be left with the trier of fact as the trial judge will have already found that there is evidence upon which a properly instructed jury could find that the accused acted involuntarily on a balance of probabilities. The question for the trier of fact will then be whether the defence has proven that the accused acted involuntarily

on a balance of probabilities. A positive answer to this question by the trier of fact will result in a successful defence of non-mental disorder automatism and, consequently, an absolute acquittal.

[220]  I would note that in his instructions to the jury on the voluntariness issue in cases of non-mental disorder automatism, the trial judge should begin by thoroughly reviewing the serious policy factors which surround automatism, including concerns about feignability and the repute of the administration of justice. It will also be helpful for the trial judge to refer specifically to evidence relevant to the issue of involuntariness, such as: the severity of the triggering stimulus, corroborating evidence of bystanders, corroborating medical history of automatistic-like dissociative states, whether there is evidence of a motive for the crime, and whether the alleged trigger of the automatism is also the victim of the automatistic violence.

[221]  On the other hand, if the trial judge concludes that the alleged condition is a disease of the mind, only mental disorder automatism will be left with the trier of fact. The case will then proceed like any other s. 16 case, leaving for the trier of fact the question of whether the defence has proven, on a balance of probabilities, that the accused suffered from a mental disorder which rendered him or her incapable of appreciating the nature and quality of the act in question. As mentioned earlier, s. 16 provides a framework within which the protection of the public will be assured when mental disorder automatism is established.

[222]  The trier of fact's determination of whether an accused has made out a successful claim of mental disorder automatism will absorb the question of whether the accused in fact acted involuntarily. That is, if the trial judge concludes that the allegation of automatism, if genuine, could only have resulted from a disease of the mind, a finding that the accused was not suffering from a mental disorder by the trier of fact necessarily extinguishes the validity of the accused's claim of involuntariness. Viscount Kilmuir L.C. put it this way in *Bratty, supra*, at p. 403:

> Where the possibility of an unconscious act depends on, and only on, the existence of a defect of reason from disease of the mind within the M'Naughten Rules, a rejection by the jury of this defence of insanity necessarily implies that they reject the possibility.

See also *Bratty, supra*, at pp. 404, 415 and 417-18; and *Rabey* (Ont. C.A.), *supra*, at pp. 24-25, *per* Martin J.A.

## *I. Application to the Present Case*

[223]  At trial, the appellant claimed both mental disorder and non-mental disorder automatism. The learned trial judge concluded that the appellant had established a proper foundation for a defence of automatism, but that only mental disorder automatism should be left with the jury. In coming to these conclusions, the trial judge did not have the benefit of these reasons to guide him. Nevertheless, this does not warrant allowing the appeal because, as I explain below, the approach taken by the trial judge did not impair the appellant's position.

[224]  In determining whether the appellant had established a proper foundation for a defence of automatism, the trial judge stated that there must be evidence of

unconsciousness throughout the commission of the crime. As I have explained above, automatism is more properly defined as impaired consciousness, rather than unconsciousness. Furthermore, lack of voluntariness, rather than consciousness, is the key legal element of automatism. Accordingly, the trial judge should have concerned himself with assessing whether there was evidence that the appellant experienced a state of impaired consciousness in which he had no voluntary control over his actions rather than whether there was evidence that the appellant was unconscious throughout the commission of the crime. Obviously, unconsciousness as defined by the trial judge supposes involuntariness. However, his finding that there was evidence of unconsciousness throughout the commission of the crime may have been based on a misunderstanding of the nature of the evidentiary burden on the accused at the proper foundation stage.

[225] In accordance with much of the jurisprudence at the time, the trial judge may have found that a proper foundation for automatism had been established because the defence had met an evidentiary burden which amounted to no more than the appellant's claim of involuntariness and confirming expert psychiatric evidence. There is no indication that he assessed whether the defence had raised evidence on which a properly instructed jury could find that the appellant acted involuntarily on a balance of probabilities. Likewise, there is no indication that the trial judge recognized the limited weight to be accorded to the psychiatric evidence in this case, which only served to confirm that the appellant's claim of automatism was plausible provided the account of events he provided to Dr. Janke was accurate and truthful. Nor did the trial judge discuss the relevance of motive or corroborating evidence on his conclusion that a proper foundation for automatism had been established.

[226] Turning to the disease of the mind stage of the automatism analysis, I note that the evidence in this case raised *only one alleged cause* of automatism, Donna Stone's words. Based on this evidence, the trial judge found that only mental disorder automatism should be left with the jury. This conclusion was based primarily on a finding that the present case is indistinguishable from *MacLeod*, *supra*. Such reliance on precedent fails to reveal what effect, if any, the internal cause factor, the continuing danger factor and other policy factors had on the decision to leave only mental disorder automatism with the jury. This is not in accordance with the holistic approach to the disease of the mind question set out in these reasons. However, the internal cause factor and the continuing danger factor, as well as the other policy factors set out in this Court's decisions in *Rabey* and *Parks* all support the trial judge's finding that the condition the appellant alleges to have suffered from is a disease of the mind in the legal sense. In particular, the trigger in this case was not, in the words of Martin J.A. quoted in this Court's decision in *Rabey*, at p. 520, "extraordinary external events" that would amount to an extreme shock or psychological blow that would cause a normal person, in the circumstances of the accused, to suffer a dissociation in the absence of a disease of the mind. Accordingly, I find that the trial judge nevertheless reached the correct result on the disease of the mind question. As previously noted, in such a case, only mental disorder automatism must be put to the jury. There is no reason to go beyond the facts of this case in applying the rules discussed above.

[227] In the end, I must conclude that no substantial wrong or miscarriage of justice occurred in the present case. Even if I had found that the trial judge erred in applying the evidentiary burden at the proper foundation stage of the automatism analysis, this error could only have benefitted the appellant. Although the trial judge did not apply the holistic approach to disease of the mind established in these reasons, he reached the correct result on this issue. There is no reasonable possibility that the verdict would have been different had the errors not been made; see *R. v. Bevan*, [1993] 2 S.C.R. 599 (S.C.C.). I would therefore dismiss this ground of appeal. ...

*Appeals dismissed.*

---

In *R. v. Fontaine* (2004), 18 C.R. (6th) 203, the Supreme Court declined the opportunity to review *Stone*. At issue was whether the trial judge should have left the defence of mental-disorder automatism with the jury. The Quebec Court of Appeal ruled that there was a sufficient evidentiary foundation for the defence and, accordingly, ordered a new trial. The Supreme Court upheld that conclusion in a judgment that is concerned chiefly with the facts of the case. Although the court did not modify the views expressed by the majority in *Stone* on the substantive law concerning automatism, it did take the opportunity to restate its views relating to the evidentiary threshold for defences.

Fish J. noted that discharge of an evidential burden with regard to any affirmative defence is a question of law for the trial judge. The judge must leave to the trier of fact any matter of defence that is supported by the evidence. In making this determination the judge is neither entitled nor required to assess the weight of that evidence or the probability of its success. Those are the functions of the trier of fact. The function of the judge is to determine whether there is relevant evidence that, if accepted by the trier of fact, would tend to support an affirmative defence. This test remains the same whether or not the defence is one that carries a reverse onus. *Fontaine* thus eliminates any suggestion in *Stone* that in considering the evidential burden the judge should assess the weight that might be given to the evidence.

## ADDITIONAL READING

For further discussion of automatism, see:

- D. Stuart, *Canadian Criminal Law*, 4th ed. (Toronto: Carswell, 2001), chapter 2;
- K. Roach, *Criminal Law*, 3rd ed. (Toronto: Irwin Law, 2004), chapter 7;
- A. Brudner, "Insane Automatism: A Proposal for Reform" (2000), 45 *McGill L.J.* 65-85;
- P. Healy, "Automatism Confined" (2000), 45 *McGill L.J.* 87;
- D. Paciocco, "Death by *Stone*-ing: The Demise of the Defence of Simple Automatism" (1999), 26 C.R. (5th) 273-85.

# CHAPTER SEVENTEEN

# Intoxication

To what extent should voluntary, self-induced intoxication by alcohol or another drug afford a defence to the prosecution's case in the sense of negating proof of a voluntary *actus reus* or the *mens rea* of the offence? This question has been a matter of controversy for decades and remains so today.

If an intoxicant can negate the mental element required for an offence or the voluntariness of the *actus reus*, the logic of the law seems to compel an acquittal. Conversely, if a person can become irresponsible by self-induced intoxication, there is a compelling argument that, for reasons of policy, the law should deny him or her a defence and even substitute the fault of being intoxicated for the fault element as defined in the particular offence. Apart from the logic or the policy of the law, there is also an important empirical question: what is the effect of particular intoxicants, given the nature and quantity of the drugs consumed, the time of consumption, and the condition of the person who consumed them?

This chapter focuses on the manner in which the law addresses the competing claims of logic and policy. The first section examines the common law decision that is the genesis of the modern intoxication defence. The second section examines whether the focus of the defence should be on the effect of intoxication on the accused's capacity to form the intent or the actual intent. The third section examines a controversial common law distinction between offences of "specific intent," for which evidence of intoxication can raise a reasonable doubt as to the accused's intent, and offences of "general intent" for which the defence of intoxication has generally been excluded. The fourth section examines the controversial case of *Daviault*, which recognized that extreme intoxication proven by the accused on a balance of probabilities and with expert evidence could be a defence to offences of general intent such as sexual assault. It examines s. 33.1 of the *Criminal Code*, which was enacted within a year of *Daviault* and which precludes— subject to Charter challenge—the use of the *Daviault* defence for general intent offences that infringe bodily integrity.

## I. THE COMMON LAW DEFENCE OF INTOXICATION

### D.P.P. v. Beard
House of Lords
[1920] A.C. 479

LORD BIRKENHEAD L.C.: ... Under the law of England as it prevailed until early in the nineteenth century voluntary drunkenness was never an excuse for criminal misconduct; and indeed the classic authorities broadly assert that voluntary drunkenness must be considered rather an aggravation than a defence. This view was in terms based upon the principle that a man who by his own voluntary act debauches and destroys his will power shall be no better situated in regard to criminal acts than a sober man. An early statement of the law is to be found in *Reniger v. Fogossa* (1 Plowd. 1,19). "If a person that is drunk kills another, this shall be felony, and he shall be hanged for it, and yet he did it through ignorance, for when he was drunk he had no understanding nor memory; but inasmuch as that ignorance was occasioned by his own act and folly, and he might have avoided it, he shall not be privileged thereby." In Hale's Pleas of the Crown, vol. i., p. 32, the learned author says:

> This vice (drunkenness) doth deprive men of the use of reason, and puts many men into
> a perfect, but temporary phrenzy; and therefore, according to some civilians, such a
> person committing homicide shall not be punished simply for the crime of homicide,
> but shall suffer for his drunkenness answerable to the nature of the crime occasioned
> thereby; so that yet the formal cause of his punishment is rather the drunkenness than
> the crime committed in it: but by the laws of England such a person shall have no
> privilege by this voluntary contracted madness, but shall have the same judgment as if
> he were in his right senses.

Blackstone, in his Commentaries, Book IV., c. 2, s. III., 25, states: "As to artificial, voluntarily contracted madness, by drunkenness or intoxication, which, depriving men of their reason, puts them in a temporary phrenzy; our law looks upon this as an aggravation of the offence, rather than as an excuse for any criminal misbehaviour."

Judicial decisions extending over a period of nearly one hundred years make it plain that the rigidity of this rule was gradually relaxed in the nineteenth century, though this mitigation cannot for a long time be affiliated upon a single or very intelligible principle.

[A number of cases decided in the 19th century are then examined.]

Notwithstanding the difference in the language used I come to the conclusion that (except in cases where insanity is pleaded) these decisions establish that where a specific intent is an essential element in the offence, evidence of a state of drunkenness rendering the accused incapable of forming such an intent should be taken into consideration in order to determine whether he had in fact formed the intent necessary to constitute the particular crime. If he was so drunk that he was incapable of

forming the intent required he could not be convicted of a crime which was committed only if the intent was proved. This does not mean that the drunkenness in itself is
an excuse for the crime but that the state of drunkenness may be incompatible with
the actual crime charged and may therefore negative the commission of that crime. In
a charge of murder based upon intention to kill or to do grievous bodily harm, if the
jury are satisfied that the accused was, by reason of his drunken condition, incapable
of forming the intent to kill or to do grievous bodily harm, unlawful homicide with
malice aforethought is not established and he cannot be convicted of murder. But
nevertheless unlawful homicide has been committed by the accused, and consequently
he is guilty of unlawful homicide without malice aforethought, and that is manslaughter: per Stephen J. in *Doherty's Case* (16 Cox C.C. 307). This reasoning may be sound
or unsound; but whether the principle be truly expressed in this view, or whether its
origin is traceable to that older view of the law held by some civilians (as expressed
by Hale) that, in truth, it may be that the cause of the punishment is the drunkenness
which has led to the crime, rather than the crime itself; the law is plain beyond all
question that in cases falling short of insanity a condition of drunkenness at the time
of committing an offence causing death can only, when it is available at all, have the
effect of reducing the crime from murder to manslaughter.

The conclusions to be drawn from these cases may be stated under three heads:

1. That insanity, whether produced by drunkenness or otherwise, is a defence to
the crime charged. The distinction between the defence of insanity in the true sense
caused by excessive drinking, and the defence of drunkenness which produces a condition such that the drunken man's mind becomes incapable of forming a specific
intention, has been preserved throughout the cases. The insane person cannot be convicted of a crime: *Felstead v. The King* ([1914] A.C. 534); but, upon a verdict of
insanity, is ordered to be detained during His Majesty's pleasure. The law takes no
note of the cause of the insanity. If actual insanity in fact supervenes, as the result of
alcoholic excess, it furnishes as complete an answer to a criminal charge as insanity
induced by any other cause. In the early cases of *Burrow* (1 Lewin 75) and *Rennie* (1
Lewin 76) Holroyd J. refused to regard drunkenness as an excuse unless it had induced a continuing and lasting condition of insanity. But in *Reg. v. Davis* (14 Cox
C.C. 563), where the prisoner was charged with wounding with intent to murder,
Stephen J. thought (and I agree with him) that insanity, even though temporary, was
an answer. The defence was that the prisoner was of unsound mind at the time of the
commission of the act, and the evidence established that he was suffering from de-
lirium tremens resulting from overindulgence in drink. Stephen J. said:

> But drunkenness is one thing and the diseases to which drunkenness leads are dif-
> ferent things; and if a man by drunkenness brings on a state of disease which causes
> such a degree of madness, even for a time, which would have relieved him from re-
> sponsibility if it had been caused in any other way, then he would not be criminally
> responsible. In my opinion, in such a case the man is a madman, and is to be treated as
> such, although his madness is only temporary .... If you think there was a distinct
> disease caused by drinking, but differing from drunkenness, and that by reason thereof

he did not know that the act was wrong, you will find a verdict of not guilty on the ground of insanity.

2.  That evidence of drunkenness which renders the accused incapable of forming the specific intent essential to constitute the crime should be taken into consideration with the other facts proved in order to determine whether or not he had this intent.

3.  That evidence of drunkenness falling short of a proved incapacity in the accused to form the intent necessary to constitute the crime, and merely establishing that his mind was affected by drink so that he more readily gave way to some violent passion, does not rebut the presumption that a man intends the natural consequences of his acts.

Would a trial judge be correct in adopting the three propositions set out in *Beard*, above? What objections could you make to a judge's charge that did so? *Beard* has been interpreted by some as restricting the intoxication defence to "specific intent" offences. What is the meaning of the term "specific intent" as used in *Beard?* Does *Beard* distinguish "general intent" offences from those of "specific intent"?

## II. THE INTOXICATION DEFENCE: CAPACITY OR INTENT?

There is a difference between "incapacity to form intent" and "absence of intent." *Beard* speaks in terms of whether a person is so intoxicated that he or she does not have the capacity to form the intent. For many years, courts in Canada followed this formulation of the intoxication defence.

In *Young v. The Queen* (1981), 59 C.C.C. (2d) 305 (S.C.C.), the trial judge had stated: "if you have any doubt at all on that evidence—any reasonable doubt as to his capacity to form intent to do these things because of drunkenness, then you give him the benefit of that doubt." All the members of the Supreme Court of Canada agreed that this was not an appropriate case to reconsider the law of drunkenness. Martland J. stated:

> This statement of the law is in accordance with the decisions of this Court in *McAskill v. The King* (1931), 55 C.C.C. 81, [1931] 3 D.L.R. 166, [1931] S.C.R. 330; *Perrault v. The Queen*, [1970] 5 C.C.C. 217, 12 D.L.R. (3d) 480, [1971] S.C.R. 196, and *Mulligan v. The Queen* (1976), 28 C.C.C. (2d) 266, 66 D.L.R. (3d) 627, [1977] 1 S.C.R. 612. This was not seriously challenged by counsel for the appellant whose real submission was that the law as to drunkenness as stated by the House of Lords in *Director of Public Prosecutions v. Beard*, [1920] A.C. 479, and followed in judgments in this Court, should be reconsidered. I agree with my brother Lamer that this is not a proper case in which to undertake that task.

Lamer J. stated:

> The trial Judge's charge to the jury as regards the defence of drunkenness conformed to the law as laid down by the House of Lords in *Director of Public Prosecutions v. Beard*, [1920] A.C. 479, and later clarified and modified by the Court in *McAskill v. The King* (1931), 55 C.C.C. 81, [1931] 3 D.L.R. 166, [1931] S.C.R. 330; *Malanik v. The Queen* (1952), 103 C.C.C.

1, [1952] 2 S.C.R. 335, 14 C.R. 367, and in *Capson v. The Queen* (1952), 105 C.C.C. 1, [1953] 1 S.C.R. 44, 16 C.R. 1.

Whilst acknowledging this, appellant invites us to reconsider this area of the law dealing with drunkenness, and order a new trial because of misdirection as to the proper test as regards the effect of intoxication on *mens rea*. As I am of the opinion that appellant should succeed on another ground, there is here no compelling reason to do so. Furthermore, I do not think that this is the proper case to reconsider that question as we have been invited to reconsider only the test, and, as a result have had the benefit of argument solely on that aspect of the question. Indeed, if and when we do so, it would then be desirable that we consider not only the test set out in *Beard* (capacity) but also, as was done by my brother Dickson in *Leary v. The Queen* (1977), 33 C.C.C. (2d) 473, 74 D.L.R. (3d) 103, [1978] 1 S.C.R. 29, the logic and desirability of categorizing offences as of general or specific intent. A departure from the "capacity test," without reconsideration of the very existence of those categories, could lead to erratic and undesirable results when the defence of intoxication is applied.

## R. v. Robinson
Supreme Court of Canada
[1996] 1 S.C.R. 683

[The accused killed a man but claimed to have acted without intent because he was intoxicated. The evidence revealed that he had been drinking with the victim and some friends and that the killing occurred when the victim said something to offend him. After being instructed on provocation, self-defence, and intoxication, the jury found the accused guilty of second-degree murder. The B.C. Court of Appeal, however, allowed his appeal and ordered a new trial. The Crown appealed to the Supreme Court of Canada.]

LAMER C.J.C. (for a majority of the Court): In March of 1920, Britain's House of Lords handed down judgment in the now famous *Beard* case (*Director of Public Prosecutions v. Beard*, [1920] A.C. 479). The issue before the Court concerned the manner in which a jury should be instructed on the relationship between intoxication and intent. Lord Birkenhead, in speaking for the Court, formulated rules that evidence of intoxication is to be considered by a jury only in those cases where its effect was to render the accused incapable of forming the requisite intent. In *MacAskill v. The King*, [1931] S.C.R. 330, the *Beard* rules were incorporated into our law and they have been, for the most part, applied by this Court ever since.

I am of the view that the time has finally come for this Court to review the adequacy of *MacAskill* in light of earlier opinions expressed by Laskin and Dickson C.JJ., the Canadian Charter of Rights and Freedoms and other relevant developments in this area in our provincial appellate courts and other common law countries.

It is my opinion that the *Beard* rules incorporated in *MacAskill* are inconsistent with our Charter. They violate ss. 7 and 11(d) because they create a form of constructive liability that was outlawed in *R. v. Vaillancourt*, [1987] 2 S.C.R. 636, and its progeny.

The *Beard* rules put an accused in jeopardy of being convicted despite the fact that a reasonable doubt could exist in the minds of the jurors on the issue of actual intent. Under these rules, if the jury is satisfied that the accused's voluntary intoxication did not render the accused incapable of forming the intent, then they would be compelled to convict despite the fact that the evidence of intoxication raised a reasonable doubt as to whether the accused possessed the requisite intent. *MacAskill* precludes the jury from acting on that reasonable doubt and therefore the *Beard* rules violate ss. 7 and 11(d).

Having reached the conclusion that the *Beard* rules are a restriction on an accused's legal rights, we must next assess whether the restriction constitutes a reasonable limit under s. 1 of the Charter. Since we are dealing with a judge made rule rather than with a legislative enactment, I am of the view that a strict application of the *Oakes* test (*R. v. Oakes*, [1986] 1 S.C.R. 103), and in particular of the proportionality prong of that test, is appropriate. While decisions of our legislatures may be entitled to judicial deference under s. 1 as a matter of policy, such deference is not required where we are being asked to review a law that we as judges have established.

There is no question that the protection of the public from intoxicated offenders is of sufficient importance to warrant overriding a constitutionally protected right or freedom. I am also of the view that there is a rational connection between the "capacity" restriction of the defence contained in the impugned common law rule and its objective.

However, in my opinion the restriction fails the proportionality prong because it does not impair an accused's ss. 7 and 11(d) rights as little as is reasonably possible. In the case at bar, there is more than minimal impairment of ss. 7 and 11(d) because the *Beard* rules lead to the result that all accused persons who had the capacity to form the requisite intent will be unable to rely on their state of intoxication despite the fact that that state might create a reasonable doubt in the minds of the triers of fact as to whether the accused actually intended to kill or cause bodily harm with subjective foresight of death. The objective of protecting society can be met by ensuring that only those who have the necessary blameworthy intent be imprisoned rather than through the creation of a rule which threatens to cast the criminal net too far. It is also important to point out in this context, that society is also protected because the defence is one of mitigation rather than of exculpation. In other words, even if the defence is successful, the accused will nonetheless be convicted of manslaughter which carries a maximum sentence of life imprisonment.

I therefore conclude that the common law rule which limits the defence of intoxication to the capacity of an accused to form the specific intent is contrary to ss. 7 and 11(d) of the Charter and not a reasonable limit under s. 1.

Having reached the conclusion that the *Beard* rules are constitutionally infirm and that therefore *MacAskill* should now be overruled, we need to determine what new common law rule should be put in its place.

How then should juries be instructed on the use they can make of evidence of intoxication? I am of the view that before a trial judge is required by law to charge the jury on intoxication, he or she must be satisfied that the effect of the intoxication was such that its effect might have impaired the accused's foresight of consequences sufficient to raise a reasonable doubt. Once a judge is satisfied that this threshold is met, he or she must then make it clear to the jury that the issue before them is whether the Crown has satisfied them beyond a reasonable doubt that the accused had the requisite intent. In the case of murder the issue is whether the accused intended to kill or cause bodily harm with the foresight that the likely consequence was death.

Therefore, a *Canute*-type charge is a useful model for trial judges to follow as it omits any reference to "capacity" or "capability" and focuses the jury on the question of "intent in fact." In most murder cases, the focus for the trier of fact will be on the foreseeability prong of s. 229(a)(ii) of the Criminal Code, R.S.C., 1985, c. C-46, that is, on determining whether the accused foresaw that his or her actions were likely to cause the death of the victim. For example, consider the case where an accused and another individual engage in a fight outside a bar. During the fight, the accused pins the other individual to the ground and delivers a kick to the head, which kills that person. In that type of a case, the jury will likely struggle, assuming they reject any self-defence or provocation claim, with the question of whether that accused foresaw that his or her actions would likely cause the death of the other individual. At this level of inquiry, the need for the jury to consider issues of capacity will rarely arise since a level of impairment falling short of incapacity will often be sufficient to raise a reasonable doubt on the question of foreseeability.

I should not want to be taken as suggesting that reference to "capacity" as part of a two-step procedure will never be appropriate in a charge to the jury. Indeed, in cases where the only question is whether the accused intended to kill the victim (s. 229(a)(i) of the Code), while the accused is entitled to rely on any evidence of intoxication to argue that he or she lacked the requisite intent and is entitled to receive such an instruction from the trial judge (assuming of course that there is an "air of reality" to the defence), it is my opinion that intoxication short of incapacity will in most cases rarely raise a reasonable doubt in the minds of jurors. For example, in a case where an accused points a shotgun within a few inches from someone's head and pulls the trigger, it is difficult to conceive of a successful intoxication defence unless the jury is satisfied that the accused was so drunk that he or she was not capable of forming an intent to kill. It is in these types of cases where it may be appropriate for trial judges to use a two-step *MacKinlay*-type charge. In addition, I suspect that most accused will want the trial judge to refer to capacity since his or her defence will likely be one of incapacity.

It may be of some assistance to summarize my conclusions in the following manner:

1. A *MacAskill* charge which only refers to capacity is constitutionally infirm and constitutes reversible error;

2. A *Canute*-type charge which only asks the jury to consider whether the evidence of intoxication, along with all of the other evidence in the case, impacted on whether the accused possessed the requisite specific intent is to be preferred for the reasons set out at paras. 49-51;

3.  In certain cases, in light of the particular facts of the case and/or in light of the expert evidence called, it may be appropriate to charge both with regard to the capacity to form the requisite intent and with regard to the need to determine in all the circumstances whether the requisite intent was in fact formed by the accused. In these circumstances a jury might be instructed that their overall duty is to determine whether or not the accused possessed the requisite intent for the crime. If on the basis of the expert evidence the jury is left with a reasonable doubt as to whether, as a result of the consumption of alcohol, the accused had the capacity to form the requisite intent then that ends the inquiry and the accused must be acquitted of the offence and consideration must then be given to any included lesser offences. However, if the jury is not left in a reasonable doubt as a result of the expert evidence as to the capacity to form the intent then of course they *must* consider and take into account all the surrounding circumstances and the evidence pertaining to those circumstances in determining whether or not the accused possessed the requisite intent for the offence.

4.  If a two-step charge is used with "capacity" and "capability" type language and the charge is the subject of an appeal, then a determination will have to be made by appellate courts on a case by case basis of whether there is a reasonable possibility that the jury may have been misled into believing that a determination of capacity was the only relevant inquiry. The following factors, not intended to be exhaustive, should be considered:

    (a)  the number of times that reference to capacity is used;

    (b)  the number of times that reference to the real inquiry of actual intent is used;

    (c)  whether there is an additional "incapacity" defence;

    (d)  the nature of the expert evidence (i.e., whether the expert's evidence relates to the issue of capacity rather than on the effect of alcohol on the brain);

    (e)  the extent of the intoxication defence;

    (f)  whether the defence requested that references to "capacity" be used in the charge to the jury;

    (g)  whether during a two-step charge it was made clear that the primary function of the jury was to determine whether they were satisfied beyond a reasonable doubt that the accused possessed the requisite intent to commit the crime. If this is emphasized during the course of the two-step charge, that will often be sufficient to make the charge acceptable and appropriate in this respect.

[Lamer C.J.C. then dealt with the judge's charge to the jury and concluded:] The trial judge began his charge as follows:

> You must first consider whether the mind of the accused was so affected by his consumption of alcohol that he did not have the *ability to form* the specific intent to cause death or bodily harm that he knew was likely to cause death and was reckless. [Emphasis added.] (p. 660E2)

At no time did the trial judge further instruct them that, even if they were satisfied that the appellant had the ability to form the intent, they were then to consider whether he *in fact* had the intent in light of the evidence of drunkenness.

In my opinion, the appeal should be dismissed. I am not satisfied that at the end of the day, the jury would have adequately understood the issues concerning intoxication and intent or the law and evidence relating to those issues.

*Appeal dismissed.*

---

In *Lemky v. The Queen* (1996), 105 C.C.C. (3d) 137, decided the same day as *Robinson*, the issue was how the trial judge should instruct the jury in the light of the *Robinson* decision. McLachlin J. stated for the Court:

> Against this background, I come to the issue which is fundamental to the determination of this appeal—the threshold for when a jury must be directed on drunkenness relating to intent. Under the Beard rules, capacity to form the necessary intent marked the threshold. Only if the evidence of drunkenness was reasonably capable of supporting an inference that the accused lacked the capacity to foresee the natural consequences of his or her act was it necessary to leave it to the jury with the appropriate instruction. The emphasis in modern jurisprudence on actual intent as the ultimate issue argues against perpetuating capacity as the appropriate signpost informing the trial judge when the jury must be instructed on the defence of drunkenness. If the real question is whether the accused was prevented by drunkenness from actually foreseeing the consequences of his or her act, it follows that the threshold for putting the defence to the jury must be evidence sufficient to permit a reasonable inference that the accused did not in fact foresee those consequences. While capacity and actual intent may be related, it is possible to envisage cases where evidence which falls short of establishing that the accused lacked the capacity to form the intent, may still leave the jury with a reasonable doubt that, when the offence was committed, the accused in fact foresaw the likelihood of death. In such a case, the defence must be put to the jury, notwithstanding that the Beard threshold is not met.

In the actual case, however, the Court ruled there was no air of reality to the defence of intoxication as to the accused's intent and upheld the accused's murder conviction for shooting his female partner. McLachlin J. stated:

> In my view, the evidence, considered most favourably for the accused, falls short of supporting such an inference. His blood-alcohol level shortly after the shooting was only slightly over the legal limit for driving an automobile. He carried out purposeful actions both before and after the shooting, actions which ranged from ordering drinks at the dance beforehand to calling his mother and the police immediately afterward. His conduct before and after the shooting demonstrated an awareness of the consequences of what he was

doing. This demonstrates that he in fact foresaw the consequences of what he was doing immediately before and after the shooting. ...

Although not established here, it remains that, in the proper case, evidence of intoxication which fails to demonstrate incapacity may still have an air of reality about it capable of leaving the jury with a reasonable doubt that the accused knew that death was likely to ensue from his or her actions. The defence commonly arises, for example, in the "barroom brawl" situation. A fight breaks out. One inebriated person strikes another. The *actus reus* and the intent to commit the act are established by the deliberate blow. But the knowledge component of the *mens rea* required by s. 229(a)(ii) may be put in doubt by evidence suggesting that the accused did not realize, by reason of his or her drunkenness, that the blow was likely to cause the death of the victim. In such a case, murder might well be reduced to manslaughter because the trier remained doubtful that the accused knew the probable consequences of his or her actions. The same cannot be said in the instant case, where there is nothing in the circumstances or the evidence to support the inference that the accused might have pulled the trigger without realizing, by reason of his drunkenness, that it might cause her death.

## Air of Reality and the Intoxication Defence

In *R. v. Seymour* (1996), 106 C.C.C. (3d) 520, the Supreme Court allowed an appeal and ordered a new trial in a case where the accused killed his wife by stabbing her repeatedly in the neck before stabbing himself. The only issue was whether he was guilty of second-degree murder or manslaughter. Expert evidence was introduced estimating that the accused's blood-alcohol level was between .198 and .218, two and a half times the legal driving limit. The accused requested, but was denied, a charge based on both the accused's capacity and intent. Nevertheless, the trial judge's recharge to the jury did make reference to the accused's capacity but not his intent. Cory J. stated for the Court:

> ... notwithstanding the general preference for a *Canute*-type charge, this appeal provides a good illustration of the type of case where a two-step instruction, including a reference to the appellant's capacity to form the intent, would have been appropriate. The defence called a forensic alcohol specialist to provide the jury with expert evidence as to the manner in which alcohol affects the human body and the physiological effects of alcohol on the brain. The expert testified that alcohol can interfere with information processing and the transmission of impulses in the brain. This, in turn, can cause a person to perceive a situation incorrectly. The witness testified: "At this level the individuals are *unable* to foresee and evaluate the consequences of their behaviour due to alcohol-induced disruption of the information processing in the brain" [emphasis added]. Defence counsel continued his line of questioning by asking whether the research indicates at what range this *inability* starts. Therefore, since the expert testified in "capacity" terms, this is a case where a two-step charge would have been helpful to the jury. ...

After deliberating at some length, the jury returned with the following question: "Intent, clarification please? What is drunken intent? What is intent, defined? ... ." The trial judge repeated his earlier instructions on this issue and then added:

You should consider the effect of intoxication along with the other facts in deciding whether the accused intended to inflict an injury on the victim which he knew was likely to cause death or whether intoxication affected his ability to foresee the consequences of his actions.

Counsel for the appellant argued that this would indicate to the jury that, if they considered that the accused had the *ability* to foresee the consequences of his actions, he must be taken to have in fact foreseen them and thus to have known that his actions were likely to cause death or grievous bodily harm. I agree with this submission. If this direction were accepted as correct it would mean that the accused could be convicted in circumstances where there exists a reasonable doubt as to the proof of an essential element of that offence; in this case, the requisite intent. While the trial judge was correct to include in his recharge the issue of the appellant's ability to measure or foresee the consequences of his act, he erred in failing to remind the jury that the ultimate issue for its determination was whether the appellant actually intended to cause bodily harm which he knew would be likely to cause death.

## III. INTOXICATION AND SPECIFIC INTENT

### R. v. George
Supreme Court of Canada
(1960), 128 C.C.C. 289

RITCHIE J. (with whom Martland J. concurred): This is an appeal from a judgment of the Court of Appeal of British Columbia affirming the acquittal of the respondent by Morrow Co. Ct. J. of the charge that he did "unlawfully and by violence steal from the person of Nicholas Avgeris the sum of Twenty-two Dollars."

The learned trial Judge has found that: "A man of 84, was violently manhandled by an Indian on the date noted in the Indictment ... as a result of which he was in hospital for a month. During this scuffle he was badly injured, dumped into a bathtub and pulled out again when he agreed to give the Indian what money he had, $22," and he has also "reached the conclusion ... without any doubt that it was the accused who committed the offence on the night in question." The learned trial Judge continued: "The first statement perhaps should be considered. It was obviously written in the words of someone who has not had too much education. In his second paragraph after recalling the drinking period, he said: 'Then I came to and I was in house and I remember hitting man and I don't remember where I went after.'"

Notwithstanding these findings, the learned trial Judge acquitted the respondent, saying: "To me it is very much a border line case. That being so it is my duty to give the accused the benefit of the doubt on the defence of drunkenness that has been set up in my mind."

After acquitting him, the learned trial Judge addressed the accused in part as follows: "You are being acquitted not because you didn't do it—there is no doubt in my mind that you did do it—you are being acquitted because I have found that you were so drunk on the night in question that you were unable to form an intent to do it."

From this acquittal the Crown appealed to the Court of Appeal of British Columbia, and in rendering the decision of the majority of that Court Mr. Justice O'Halloran said:

> I am unable with respect to accept Crown counsel's submission that in failing to convict respondent of assault upon this charge of robbery, the learned trial Judge omitted to instruct himself regarding any difference between the intent to commit the robbery and a specific intent to commit assault as one of the essential ingredients of the robbery with which he was charged.
>
> In my judgment, with respect, a sufficient answer thereto is; that having found the respondent so incapacitated by liquor that he could not form an intent to commit the robbery, it follows rationally in the circumstances here, that he must also be deemed to have found that respondent was equally incapable for the same reason of having an intent to commit the assault. If he could not have the intent to commit the robbery, *viz.*, to assault and steal as charged, then he could not have the intent either to assault or to steal when both occurred together as charged; the charge reads "by violence steal."

Leave to appeal to this Court was granted pursuant to an application made on behalf of the Attorney-General of British Columbia. No appeal was taken from the acquittal of the respondent on the charge of robbery and the grounds of appeal are, in large measure, devoted to the question of whether a distinction should be drawn "between the degree of drunkenness required to negative the existence of" that intent which is, under the *Cr. Code*, an essential ingredient of the crime of robbery and the degree of drunkenness which is necessary to negative such intent as is an ingredient of common assault.

Pursuant to s. 569 [now s. 662] of the *Cr. Code*, the learned trial Judge was under a duty to direct his mind to the "included offence" of assault. ...

In my opinion, the duty which rests upon the trial Judge to direct himself with respect to all included offences of which there is evidence can, in no way, be affected by the fact that the Crown Prosecutor has omitted to make reference to such offences. It follows, in my view, that in a case where the trial Judge has wrongly applied the law applicable to such an offence the Crown is not deprived of its statutory right of appeal because of the omission of its agent at the trial to address the Court on the matter.

The fact that the learned trial Judge found, as I think he did, that the respondent had "violently manhandled" an old man but was not guilty of assault because he was drunk at the time raises the question of law posed by the appellant as to whether, under the circumstances as found by the trial Judge, drunkenness is a valid defence to common assault.

In considering the question of *mens rea*, a distinction is to be drawn between "intention" as applied to acts done to achieve an immediate end on the one hand and acts done with the specific and ulterior motive and intention of furthering or achieving an illegal object on the other hand. Illegal acts of the former kind are done "intentionally" in the sense that they are not done by accident or through honest mistake, but acts of the latter kind are the product of preconception and are deliberate steps taken towards an illegal goal. The former acts may be the purely physical products of momentary passion, whereas the latter involve the mental process of formulating a specific intent. A man, far advanced in drink, may intentionally strike his fellow in the former sense at a time when his mind is so befogged with liquor as to be unable to formulate a specific intent in the latter sense. The offence of robbery, as defined by the *Cr. Code*, requires the presence of the kind of intent and purpose specified in ss. 269 [now s. 322] and 288 [now s. 343], but the use of the word "intentionally" in defining "common assault" in s. 230(a) [now s. 265(1)(a)] of the *Cr. Code* is exclusively referable to the physical act of applying force to the person of another.

I would adopt the following passage from Kenny's Outlines of Criminal Law, 17th ed., pp. 58-9, para. 42, as an authoritative statement on this subject. He there says:

> In *Director of Public Prosecutions v. Beard*, [1920] A.C. 479 ... it was laid down that evidence of such drunkenness as "renders the accused incapable of forming the specific intent, essential to constitute the crime, should be taken into consideration, with the other facts proved, in order to determine whether or not he had this intent." In such a case the drunkenness, if it negatives the existence of the indispensable mental element of the crime, "negatives the commission of that crime." Thus a drunken man's inability to form an intention to kill, or to do grievous bodily harm involving the risk of killing, at the time of committing a homicide, may reduce his offence from murder to manslaughter (which latter crime requires no more than a realization that some bodily harm may be caused). Drunkenness may likewise show that a supposed burglar had no intention of stealing, or that wounds were inflicted without any "intent to do grievous bodily harm," or that a false pretense was made with no "intent to defraud." But it must be remembered that a man may be so drunk as not to form an intention to kill or do grievous bodily harm while yet in sufficient control of his senses to be able to contemplate some harm and so to be guilty of manslaughter or of an unlawful wounding.

The decision of the learned trial Judge, in my opinion, constitutes a finding that the respondent violently manhandled a man and knew that he was hitting him. Under these circumstances, evidence that the accused was in a state of voluntary drunkenness cannot be treated as a defence to a charge of common assault because there is no suggestion that the drink which had been consumed had produced permanent or temporary insanity and the respondent's own statement indicates that he knew that he was applying force to the person of another.

In view of the above, I would allow the appeal.

FAUTEUX J. (with whom Taschereau J. concurred): ... In considering the question of *mens rea*, a distinction is to be made between (i) intention as applied to acts considered in relation to their purposes and (ii) intention as applied to acts considered apart from their purposes. A general intent attending the commission of an act is, in some cases, the only intent required to constitute the crime while, in others, there must be, in addition to that general intent, a specific intent attending the purpose for the commission of the act.

Contrary to what is the case in the crime of robbery, where, with respect to theft, a specific intent must be proved by the Crown as one of the constituent elements of the offence, there is no specific intent necessary to constitute the offence of common assault, which is defined as follows in s. 230, *Cr. Code*:

> A person commits an assault when, without the consent of another person or with consent, where it is obtained by fraud,
>
> > (a) he applies force intentionally to the person of the other, directly or indirectly, or
> >
> > (b) he attempts or threatens, by an act or gesture, to apply force to the person of the other, if he has or causes the other to believe upon reasonable grounds that he has present ability to effect his purpose.

The word "intentionally" appearing in s. 230(a) is exclusively related to the application of force or to the manner in which force is applied. This, indeed, is also made clear in the French version, reading:

> 230. Commet des voies de fait, ou se livre à une attaque, quiconque, sans le consentement d'autrui, ou avec son consentement, s'il est obtenu par fraude,
>
> > (a) *d'une manière intentionnelle*, applique, directement ou indirectement, la force ou la violence contre la personne d'autrui, ou
> >
> > (b) tente ou menace, par un acte ou un geste, d'appliquer la force ou la violence contre la personne d'autrui, s'il est en mesure actuelle, ou s'il porte cette personne à croire, pour des motifs raisonnables, qu'il est en mesure actuelle d'accomplir son dessein. [The italics are mine.]

There can be no pretence, in this case, that the manner in which force was applied by the respondent to his victim was accidental or—excluding at the moment, from the consideration, the defence of drunkenness—unintentional.

On this finding of fact, the accused was guilty of common assault unless there was evidence indicating a degree of drunkenness affording, under the law, a valid defence.

The trial Judge entertained a doubt on the question whether the Crown had proved, as part of its case, that the accused had, owing to drunkenness, the capacity to form the *specific intent* required in the offence of robbery, *i.e.*, the intent to steal. ...

Hence, the question is whether, owing to drunkenness, respondent's condition was such that he was incapable of applying force intentionally. I do not know that, short of a degree of drunkenness creating a condition tantamount to insanity, such a situation could be metaphysically conceived in an assault of the kind here involved. It is certain that, on the facts found by the trial Judge, this situation did not exist in this case.

The accused was acquitted of the offence of robbery, not on the ground that he could not have applied force intentionally, but because of the doubt entertained by the trial Judge on the question whether he had the capacity to form the specific intent required as a constituent element for the offence of theft.

In these views, the finding of the trial Judge that the accused had not the capacity to form the specific intent to commit robbery did not justify the conclusion reached in appeal that he could not then have committed the offence of common assault; nor is it shown that, had the trial Judge considered common assault, the verdict would necessarily have been the same.

In these circumstances, the Court of Appeal should have allowed the appeal from the acquittal and should have proceeded to make an order pursuant to its authority under s. 592(4)(b) [now s. 686(4)(b)], to wit, either enter a verdict of guilty with respect to the offence of which, in its opinion, formed in the light of the law applicable in the matter, the accused should have been found guilty but for the error in law, and pass a sentence warranted in law, or order a new trial.

Under s. 600 [now s. 695], *Cr. Code*, this Court is given the authority to make any order that the Court of Appeal might have made. At the hearing before this Court, it was intimated that should the appeal of the Crown be maintained, this case should be finally disposed of, if possible, and that in such event, respondent could appropriately be given a suspended sentence.

Being of opinion that the accused should have been found guilty of common assault, had that offence been considered in the light of the law applicable to the facts of this case, I would maintain the appeal, set aside the verdict of acquittal with respect to common assault and enter a verdict of guilty of that offence. Prior to his acquittal in the Court below, respondent has been incarcerated during a number of weeks. It would appear more consonant with the representations made with respect to sentence, to sentence respondent to the time already spent by him in jail; and this is the sentence that I would pass.

[LOCKE J. dissented on the basis that the Crown had no right to appeal from an acquittal under these circumstances: "Stated bluntly, the contention of the Crown is that where a trial Judge hearing a criminal charge fails not to deal with, but to consider independently, an offence included in the offence specifically charged, and this is done with the approval of counsel for the Crown, the provisions of s. 584 [now s. 676] may be invoked to again place the accused in jeopardy. I do not think that it was ever contemplated when the legislation was enacted that it might be exercised in circumstances such as these."]

*Appeal allowed: verdict of guilty of common assault entered.*

### Bernard v. The Queen
Supreme Court of Canada
(1988), 45 C.C.C. (3d) 1

[At the accused's trial on a charge of sexual assault causing bodily harm contrary to s. 246.2(c) [now s. 272(c)] of the *Criminal Code*, the only issue left by the trial judge to the jury was the question of consent. The evidence indicated that the complainant was beaten about the face by the accused and that intercourse had taken place without her consent. The accused did not testify but in a statement to the police, which was admitted into evidence, the accused stated that he forced the complainant to have intercourse but he did it because he was drunk and when he realized what he was doing he got off the complainant. The trial judge directed the jury that the only evidence of drunkenness was in the accused's statement but that drunkenness was no defence to the charge alleged against the accused. An appeal by the accused from his conviction to the Ontario Court of Appeal was dismissed. On further appeal by the accused to the Supreme Court of Canada, the court was asked to reconsider its decision in *Leary v. The Queen* holding that the former offence of rape was an offence of general intent for which voluntary intoxication was no defence.]

McINTYRE J. (with whom Beetz J. concurred): A distinction has long been recognized in the criminal law between offences which require the proof of a specific intent and those which require only the proof of a general intent. This distinction forms the basis of the defence of drunkenness and it must be understood and kept in mind in approaching this case. ...

The general intent offence is one in which the only intent involved relates solely to the performance of the act in question with no further ulterior intent or purpose. The minimal intent to apply force in the offence of common assault affords an example. A specific intent offence is one which involves the performance of the *actus reus*, coupled with an intent or purpose going beyond the mere performance of the questioned act. Striking a blow or administering poison with the intent to kill, or assault with intent to maim or wound, are examples of such offences.

This distinction is not an artificial one nor does it rest upon any legal fiction. There is a world of difference between the man who in frustration or anger strikes out at his neighbour in a public house with no particular purpose or intent in mind, other than to perform the act of striking, and the man who strikes a similar blow with intent to cause death or injury. ...

It is not necessary for the purposes of this judgment to review in detail the authorities in this court on the question. It will be sufficient to summarize their effect in the following terms. Drunkenness in a general sense is not a true defence to a criminal act. Where, however, in a case which involves a crime of specific intent, the accused is so affected by intoxication that he lacks the capacity to form the specific intent required to commit the crime charged, it may apply. The defence, however, has no application in offences of general intent.

The criticism of the law with respect to the defence of drunkenness is based on two propositions. It is said, first, that the distinction between the general intent and specific intent offences is artificial and is little more than a legal fiction. Secondly, it is said that it is illogical, because it envisages a defence of drunkenness in certain situations and not in others; it is merely a policy decision made by judges and not based on principle or logic. It will be evident from what I have said that I reject the first ground of criticism. As to the second criticism, that it is based upon grounds of policy, I would say that there can be no doubt that considerations of policy are involved in this distinction. Indeed, in some cases, principally *Majewski, supra,* the distinction has been defended on the basis that it is sound social policy. The fact, however, that considerations of policy have influenced the development of the law in the field cannot, in my view, be condemned. In the final analysis, all law should be based upon and consistent with sound social policy. No good law can be inconsistent with or depart from sound policy.

If the policy behind the present law is that society condemns those who, by the voluntary consumption of alcohol, render themselves incapable of self-control so that they will commit acts of violence causing injury to their neighbours, then in my view, no apology for such policy is needed, and the resulting law affords no affront to the well-established principles of the law or to the freedom of the individual … .

In my view, the common law rules on the defence of drunkenness, though frequently the subject of criticism, have a rationality which not only accords with criminal law theory, but has also served society well. It is not questioned in this case that the defence of drunkenness, as it applies to specific intent offences, is supportable. It is submitted, however, that it should be extended to include all criminal charges. It is my view that this proposition is not sustainable … .

The Chief Justice has expressed the view that evidence of self-induced intoxication should be a relevant consideration in determining whether the *mens rea* of any particular offence has been proved by the Crown. As I have indicated, I am unable to agree with this conclusion. The effect of such a conclusion would be that the more drunk a person becomes by his own voluntary consumption of alcohol or drugs, the more extended will be his opportunity for a successful defence against conviction for the offences caused by such drinking, regardless of the nature of the intent required for those offences … .

This court in *Leary* approved the *Majewski* approach which has long been accepted in the law of Canada, and, for the reasons which I have set out, it is my opinion that this court's judgment in *Leary* ought not to be overruled. I must re-emphasize that the *Leary* rule does not relieve the Crown from its obligation to prove the *mens rea* in a general intent offence. The fact that an accused may not rely on voluntary intoxication in such offences does not have that effect because of the nature of the offence and the mental elements which must be shown. The requisite state of mind may be proved in two ways. First, there is the general proposition that triers of fact may infer *mens rea* from the *actus reus* itself: a person is presumed to have intended the natural and probable consequences of his actions. For example, in an offence involving the mere application of force, the minimal intent to apply that force will suffice to constitute the necessary *mens rea* and can be reasonably inferred from the act itself and the other evidence. Secondly, in cases where the accused was so intoxicated as to raise doubt as to the voluntary nature of his conduct, the Crown may meet its evidentiary obligation respecting the necessary blameworthy mental state of the accused by proving the fact of voluntary self-induced intoxication by drugs or alcohol. This was the approach suggested in *Majewski*. In most cases involving intoxication in general intent offences, the trier of fact will be able to apply the first proposition, namely, that the intent is inferable from the *actus reus* itself. As Fauteux J. observed in *George*, *supra*, at p. 302 C.C.C., p. 879 S.C.R., it is almost metaphysically inconceivable for a person to be so drunk as to be incapable of forming the minimal intent to apply force. Hence, only in cases of the most extreme self-intoxication does the trier of fact need to use the second proposition, that is, that evidence of self-induced intoxication is evidence of the guilty mind, the blameworthy mental state.

The result ... is that, for these crimes, accused persons cannot hold up voluntary drunkenness as a defence. They cannot be heard to say: "I was so drunk that I did not know what I was doing." If they managed to get themselves so drunk that they did not know what they were doing, the reckless behaviour in attaining that level of intoxication affords the necessary evidence of culpable mental condition. Hence, it is logically impossible for an accused person to throw up his voluntary drunkenness as a defence to a charge of general intent. Proof of his voluntary drunkenness can be proof of his guilty mind ... .

It was argued by the appellant that the *Leary* rule converts the offence of sexual assault causing bodily harm into a crime of absolute liability in that the Crown need not prove the requisite intention for the completion of the offence. Therefore, it is said that *Leary* violates ss. 7 and 11(d) of the Charter. In *Reference re s. 94(2) of Motor Vehicle Act* (1985), 23 C.C.C. (3d) 289, 24 D.L.R. (4th) 536, [1985] 2 S.C.R. 486 (S.C.C.), and in *R. v. Vaillancourt* (1987), 39 C.C.C.(3d) 118, 47 D.L.R. (4th) 399, [1987] 2 S.C.R. 636 (S.C.C.), it was held that the requirement for a minimum mental state before the attachment of criminal liability is a principle of fundamental justice. Criminal offences, as a general rule, must have as one of their elements the requirement of a blameworthy mental state. The morally innocent ought not to be convicted. It is said that the *Leary* rule violates this fundamental premise. In my opinion, the *Leary* rule clearly does not offend this essential principle of criminal law but rather upholds it. The *Leary* rule recognizes that accused persons who have voluntarily consumed drugs or alcohol, thereby depriving themselves of self-control leading to the commission of a crime, are not morally innocent and are, indeed, criminally blameworthy. While the rule excludes consideration of voluntary intoxication in the approach to general intent offences, it none the less recognizes that it may be a relevant factor in those generally more serious offences where the *mens rea* must involve not only the intentional performance of the *actus reus* but, as well, the formation of further ulterior motives and purposes. It therefore intrudes upon the security of the person only in accordance with sound principle and within the established boundaries of the legal process. For these reasons, I would say that the Charter is not violated ... .

I would not overrule the judgment of this court in *Leary* and I would confirm the law as it presently stands. Parliament at some time in the future may intervene in the matter with such statutory provisions as it may consider appropriate but failing that occurrence I would not enlarge the defence of drunkenness ...

In any event, should it be considered that I am wrong in my approach to the *Leary* case, this is none the less a case in which the provisions of s. 613(1)(b)(iii) [now s. 686(1)(b)(iii)] of the *Criminal Code* should be applied.

WILSON J. (with whom L'Heureux-Dubé J. concurred): I have had the benefit of the reasons of the Chief Justice and of my colleagues McIntyre and La Forest JJ. I agree with McIntyre J. for the reasons given by him that sexual assault causing bodily harm is an offence of general intent requiring only the minimal intent to apply force. I agree with him also that in most cases involving general intent offences and intoxication the Crown will be able to establish the accused's blameworthy mental state by inference from his or her acts. I think that is the case here. The evidence of intoxication withheld from the trier of fact in this case could not possibly have raised a reasonable doubt as to the existence of the minimal intent to apply force. It is, accordingly, not necessary in this case to resort to self-induced intoxication as a substituted form of *mens rea*. And, indeed, I have some real concerns as to whether the imposition of criminal liability on that basis would survive a challenge under the *Canadian Charter of Rights and Freedoms*.

The facts are fully set out in the reasons of the Chief Justice and I refer to them only to underline why I agree with my colleague, McIntyre J., that the rule in *Leary v. The Queen* (1977), 33 C.C.C. (2d) 473, 74 D.L.R. (3d) 103, [1978] 1 S.C.R. 29 (S.C.C.), should be preserved and applied in this case.

Sexual assault is a crime of violence. There is no requirement of an intent or purpose beyond the intentional application of force. It is first and foremost an assault. It is sexual in nature only because, objectively viewed, it is related to sex either on account of the area of the body to which the violence is applied or on account of words accompanying the violence. Indeed, the whole purpose, as I understand it, of the replacement of the offence of rape by the offence of sexual assault was to emphasize the aspect of violence and put paid to the benign concept that rape was simply the act of a man who was "carried away" by his emotions.

The appellant in his statement to the police admitted that he had forced the complainant to have sexual intercourse with him but claimed that because of his drunkenness he did not know *why* he had done this and that when he realized what he was doing he "got off" the complainant. There was evidence that the appellant had punched the complainant twice with his closed fist and had threatened to kill her. The doctor who examined the complainant testified that the complainant's right eye was swollen shut and that three stitches were required to close the wound. It is clear from this that there was intentional and voluntary, as opposed to accidental or involuntary, application of force.

The evidence of the appellant's intoxication consisted of his own statements to the police that he was drunk; the complainant's testimony that, while the appellant was acting out of character in making advances to her, he was able to walk, talk and put albums on the record-player; a friend's testimony that prior to the incident the appellant had been drinking at a bar and had become "very rowdy" although still capable of talking and walking straight. By his own admission, the appellant had sufficient wits about him after the violent assault to hide a bloodied towel and pillowcase from the police. There is no evidence that we are dealing here with extreme intoxication, verging on insanity or automatism, and as such capable of negating the inference that the minimal intent to apply force was present: see *R. v. Swietlinski* (1978), 44 C.C.C. (2d) 267 at p. 294, 94 D.L.R. (3d) 218, 22 O.R. (2d) 604 (Ont. C.A.); affirmed 55 C.C.C. (2d) 481, 117 D.L.R. (3d) 285, [1980] 2 S.C.R. 956 (S.C.C.). The evidence of intoxication in this case was simply not capable of raising a reasonable doubt as to the existence of the minimal intent required. In this I agree with McIntyre J.

I am less confident about the proposition accepted by my colleague that self-induced intoxication may substitute for the mental element required to be present at the time the offence was committed although I realize that there are statements in judgments of this court to that effect. I do not believe, however, that the court has clearly adopted that proposition. The decision of the House of Lords in *D.P.P. v. Majewski*, [1977] A.C. 443, may stand for the rather harsh proposition that even self-induced intoxication producing a state of automatism cannot constitute a defence to an offence of general intent such as assault but I doubt that our Canadian jurisprudence goes that far. ...

I believe that the *Leary* rule is perfectly consistent with an onus resting on the Crown to prove the minimal intent which should accompany the doing of the prohibited act in general intent offences. I view it as preferable to preserve the *Leary* rule in its more flexible form as Pigeon J. applied it, *i.e.*, so as to allow evidence of intoxication to go to the trier of fact in general intent offences only if it is evidence of extreme intoxication involving an absence of awareness akin to a state of insanity or automatism. Only in such a case is the evidence capable of raising a reasonable doubt as to the existence of the minimal intent required for the offence. I would not overrule *Leary*, as the Chief Justice would, and allow evidence of intoxication to go to the trier of fact in every case regardless of its possible relevance to the issue of the existence of the minimal intent required for the offence. ...

It is, in my view, not strictly necessary in this case to address the constitutionality of substituting self-induced intoxication as the *mens rea* for the minimal *mens rea* requirements of general intent offences. The issue would, in my view, only arise in those rare cases in which the intoxication is extreme enough to raise doubts as to the existence of the minimal intent which characterizes conscious and volitional conduct. However, as both the Chief Justice and McIntyre J. have addressed the issue, I will express my own somewhat tentative views upon it.

This court has affirmed as fundamental the proposition that a person should not be exposed to a deprivation of liberty unless the Crown proves the existence of a blameworthy or culpable state of mind: see *Reference re Motor Vehicle Act, supra*, at pp. 310-5 C.C.C., pp. 513-20 S.C.R. It does not follow from this, however, that those who, through the voluntary consumption of alcohol or drugs incapacitate themselves from knowing what they are doing, fall within the category of the "morally innocent" deserving of such protection. This is not to say that such persons do not have a right under s. 7 or s. 12 of the Charter to be protected against punishment that is disproportionate to their crime and degree of culpability: see *Reference re Motor Vehicle Act, supra*, at pp. 324-5 C.C.C., pp. 532-4 S.C.R.; *Smith v. The Queen* (1987), 34 C.C.C. (3d) 97, 40 D.L.R. (4th) 435, [1987] 1 S.C.R. 1045 (S.C.C.). They do, especially if the consequences of their becoming intoxicated were not intended or foreseen.

The real concern over the substituted form of *mens rea* arises, it seems to me, under s. 11(d) of the Charter. While this court has recognized that in some cases proof of an essential element of a criminal offence can be replaced by proof of a different element, it has placed stringent limitations on when this can happen. In *Vaillancourt, supra*, Lamer J. said at p. 136 C.C.C., p. 656 S.C.R.:

> Finally, the legislature, rather than simply eliminating any need to prove the essential element, may substitute proof of a different element. In my view, this will be constitutionally valid only if upon proof beyond reasonable doubt of the substituted element it

would be unreasonable for the trier of fact not to be satisfied beyond reasonable doubt of the existence of the essential element. If the trier of fact may have a reasonable doubt as to the essential element notwithstanding proof beyond a reasonable doubt of the substituted element, then the substitution infringes ss. 7 and 11(d).

In *Whyte, supra*, the Chief Justice approved the above statement at p. 110 C.C.C., pp. 18-9 S.C.R., and added:

> In the passage from *Vaillancourt* quoted earlier, Lamer J. recognized that in some cases substituting proof of one element for proof of an essential element will not infringe the presumption of innocence if, upon proof of the substituted element, it would be unreasonable for the trier of fact not to be satisfied beyond a reasonable doubt of the existence of the essential element. This is another way of saying that a statutory presumption infringes the presumption of innocence if it requires the trier of fact to convict in spite of a reasonable doubt. Only if the existence of the substituted fact leads inexorably to the conclusion that the essential element exists, with no other reasonable possibilities, will the statutory presumption be constitutionally valid.

In my tentative view, it is unlikely that in those cases in which it is necessary to resort to self-induced intoxication as the substituted element for the minimal intent, proof of the substituted element will "inexorably" lead to the conclusion that the essential element of the minimal intent existed at the time the criminal act was committed. But I prefer to leave this question open as it is unnecessary to decide it in order to dispose of this appeal.

DICKSON C.J.C., dissenting (with whom Lamer J. concurred and La Forest J. expressed "general agreement"):  In my view, the only issue the court needs to address may be put as follows: should evidence of self-induced intoxication be considered by the trier of fact, along with all other relevant evidence, in determining whether the prosecution has proved beyond a reasonable doubt the *mens rea* required to constitute the offence? I am of the opinion that the court should answer that question in the affirmative.

I wish to make clear at the outset, however, that nothing in these reasons is intended to apply with respect to the quite distinct issues raised by offences, such as driving while impaired, where intoxication or the consumption of alcohol is itself an ingredient of the offence. The *mens rea* of such offences can be left for consideration another day. ...

In my dissent in *Leary*, I sought to advance the view that respect for basic criminal law principles required that the legal fiction, the artificial "specific" intent threshold requirement, be abandoned. I do not intend in these reasons to repeat what I said in *Leary*. With due regard for *stare decisis*, as to which I will have more to say in a moment, and with the greatest of respect for those of a contrary view, I would only add that nothing I have heard or read since the judgment in *Leary* has caused me to abandon or modify in the slightest degree the views of dissent which I there expressed. ...

The categories of "specific" intent on the one hand and "basic" or "general" intent on the other have evolved as an artificial device whereby evidence, otherwise relevant, is excluded from the jury's consideration. This court, in *Swietlinski*, has recognized that intoxication may as a matter of fact deprive an accused of "basic" or "general" intent. It is said, however, by those who support the classification that as a matter of policy, consideration of evidence of intoxication must be excluded. Indeed, a notable feature to be found in the analysis of many of those who support restricting the jury's use of evidence relating to drunkenness is the concession that while principle and logic lead in an opposite direction, the policy of protection of the public requires that principle and logic should yield: see, *e.g.*, *D.P.P. v. Majewski*, [1976] 2 All E.R. 142 at pp. 167-68, *per* Lord Edmund-Davies, quoted by Pigeon J. in *Leary*, *supra*, at p. 478 C.C.C., pp. 52-3 S.C.R.

In my view, there are two fundamental problems with this approach. First, if the law is to be altered in the name of policy over principle, that is surely a task for Parliament rather than the courts. ...

Secondly, even if it were appropriate for the courts to bend principle in the name of policy, so far as I am aware, there is no evidence that the artificiality of the specific intent requirement is actually required for social protection.

An unrestrained application of basic *mens rea* doctrine would not, in my opinion, open a gaping hole in the criminal law inimical to social protection. There are several reasons for this. To the extent that intoxication merely lowers inhibitions, removes self-restraint or induces unusual self-confidence or aggressiveness, it would be of no avail to an accused, as such effects do not relate to the *mens rea* requirement for volitional and intentional or reckless conduct. Similarly, intoxication would be of no avail to an accused who got drunk in order to gain the courage to commit a crime or to aid in his defence. Thirdly, one can trust in the good sense of the jury and that of our trial judges to weigh all the evidence in a fair and responsible manner, and they are unlikely to acquit too readily those who have committed offences while intoxicated. ...

The real issue in this appeal, it seems to me, is whether the court should now overrule *Leary*. ...

Since *Leary* was decided, the *Canadian Charter of Rights and Freedoms* has come into force. This court has held that legislation which imposes the sanction of imprisonment without proof of a blameworthy state of mind violates the guarantee of fundamental justice contained in s. 7 of the Charter and must be struck down unless it can meet the exacting test of s. 1: see *Reference re s. 94(2) of Motor Vehicle Act* (1985), 23 C.C.C.(3d) 289, 24 D.L.R. (4th) 536, [1985] 2 S.C.R. 486 (S.C.C.); *R. v. Vaillancourt* (1987), 39 C.C.C. (3d) 118, 47 D.L.R. (4th) 399, [1987] 2 S.C.R. 636 (S.C.C.).

The appellant submits that *Leary* runs counter to s. 7 by providing that intoxication is no defence to a crime of general intent. In circumstances where the requisite mental intent is lacking due to an intoxicated condition, a general intent offence is converted into one of absolute liability in which proof of the commission of the *actus reus* by itself mandates conviction. It is also submitted that *Leary* runs counter to the presumption of innocence and the right to a fair hearing as guaranteed by s. 11(d) of the Charter, in so far as wrongful intent is irrebuttably presumed upon the showing of intoxication. …

The effect of the majority holding in *Leary* is to impose a form of absolute liability on intoxicated offenders, which is entirely inconsistent with the basic requirement for a blameworthy state of mind as a prerequisite to the imposition of the penalty of imprisonment mandated by the above-cited authorities. I agree with the observation of Professor Stuart in *Canadian Criminal Law*, 2nd ed. (1987), that s. 7 of the Charter mandates the reversal of *Leary* and the assertion of "the fundamental principles of voluntariness and fault" in relation to intoxication and the criminal law: p. 378. …

The majority holding in *Leary* also runs counter to the s. 11(d) right to be presumed innocent until proven guilty. With respect to crimes of general intent, guilty intent is in effect presumed upon proof of the fact of intoxication. Moreover, the presumption of guilt created by the *Leary* rule is irrebuttable. …

In my view, the *Leary* rule cannot be upheld by reference to s. 1, as it cannot survive the "proportionality" inquiry. While the protection of the public, said to underlie the *Leary* rule, could serve as an important objective, in my view the *Leary* rule does not achieve that objective in a manner consistent with the proportionality test of *Oakes*, *supra*. *Oakes* requires that "the measures adopted must be carefully designed to achieve the objective in question." …

The *Leary* rule in effect treats the deliberate act of becoming intoxicated as culpable in itself, but inflicts punishment measured by the unintended consequences of becoming intoxicated. Punishment acts as a deterrent where the conduct is intended or foreseen. There is no evidence to support the assertion that the *Leary* rule deters the commission of unintended crimes. Hence, there is no warrant for violating fundamental principles and convicting those who would otherwise escape criminal liability. …

Finally, it is my view that there is a disproportionality between the effects of *Leary* on rights protected by the Charter and the objective of public safety. To paraphrase Lamer J. in *Reference re Motor Vehicle Act*, *supra*, at p. 316 C.C.C., p. 521 S.C.R., it has not been demonstrated that risk of imprisonment of a few innocent persons is required to attain the goal of protecting the public from drunken offenders.

As stated in *R. v. Holmes* (1988), 41 C.C.C. (3d) 497 at p. 517, 50 D.L.R. (4th) 680, [1988] 1 S.C.R. 914 at p. 940: "This effect, given the range of alternative legislative devices available to Parliament, is too deleterious to be justified as a reasonable limit under s. 1 of the Charter. Simply put, the provision exacts too high a price to be justified in a free and democratic society." …

The *Leary* rule fits most awkwardly with that enunciated in *Pappajohn*. Lower courts have held that in the light of *Leary*, where intoxication is a factor in inducing a mistaken belief in consent, the jury must be instructed that while an honest but unreasonable belief will negate *mens rea* (*Pappajohn*) they are to disregard the effect that intoxication might have had in inducing that mistake (*Leary*). …

In my view, the *Leary* qualification on the criminal law principle of general application with respect to mistake of fact unnecessarily and unduly complicates the jury's task. Indeed, I find it difficult to imagine how it is humanly possible to follow the jury instruction apparently mandated by the combination of *Leary* and *Pappajohn*.

This confusing and anomalous result is entirely the product of the deviation from basic criminal law principles which occurred in *Leary* and, accordingly, there is much to support the view that it should be overruled. ...

I have already indicated the confusion created by the combination of *Leary* and *Pappajohn*. I suggest that the distinction between "general" and "specific" intent which *Leary* mandates and the notorious difficulty in articulating a clear and work-able definition of specific intent falls squarely within the principle enunciated in *Ranville* and *Vetrovec*. Because that category is based on policy rather than principle, classification of offences as falling within or without the specific intent category is necessarily an *ad hoc*, unpredictable exercise. ...

The trial judge made no reference in his charge to the jury to the requirement that the Crown prove that the accused acted with the requisite intent. In my view, this is fatal to the conviction. Although the Crown presented a strong case against the ac-cused at trial, no request was made by the respondent that this court apply the provi-sion of s. 613(1)(b)(iii) of the *Criminal Code*, and in any event, it is not for this court to speculate as to the likely result had the jury been properly instructed.

It follows that the appeal should be allowed, the conviction set aside, and a new trial ordered.

*Appeal dismissed.*

---

In *R. v. Quinn* (1988), 44 C.C.C. (3d) 570, decided by the Supreme Court of Canada a week after *Bernard*, the majority of the court (McIntyre, Beetz, Wilson, and L'Heureux-Dubé JJ.) held that breaking and entering and committing the indictable offence of assault causing bodily harm contrary to the present s. 348(1)(b) of the Code is an offence of general intent. Wilson and L'Heureux-Dubé JJ. did not find evidence of such extreme intoxication as to negative the minimal intent, as set out in their analysis in *Bernard*. Dickson C.J.C., Lamer and La Forest JJ. dissented and, as in *Bernard*, would abandon the distinction between specific and general intent.

---

The distinction between specific and general intent exists solely for the purpose of determining whether there is or is not a defence of intoxication at common law. It has no other meaningful purpose or content. Intuitively, perhaps, specific intent connotes a more focused or concentrated form of *mens rea* but this idea has never been coherently developed.

## R. v. Penno
Supreme Court of Canada
(1990), 59 C.C.C. (3d) 344

[The court decided that intoxication could not be a defence to an offence in which it is an element. The offence in this case was care and control of a motor vehicle while impaired.]

McLACHLIN J. (Sopinka and Gonthier JJ. concurring) held that such a conclusion did not violate ss. 7 and 11(d). She stated: If the mental element of an offence is compatible with the unavailability of the defence of impairment, then the absence of that defence constitutes no violation of the *Charter*. On the other hand, if the mental element of the offence is one to which the defence of impairment might be relevant, the absence of that defence will constitute a violation of the *Charter*. The question is which of these two categories s. 234(1) falls into.

In *R. v. King*, [1962] S.C.R. 746, it was held that the mental element involved in the offence of impaired driving was voluntary intoxication. It was this that provided the guilty mind fundamental to the offence. On this view, the unavailability of drunkenness as a defence cannot constitute a violation of the accused's right to make full answer and defence. Even if the accused is too drunk to know that he or she is assuming care and control of the motor vehicle, that does not matter, since the mental element of the offence lies in voluntarily becoming intoxicated. This interpretation recognizes that intoxication is excluded as a defence to impaired driving since it is the very gravamen of the offence.

[WILSON J. (L'Heureux-Dubé J. concurring) and La Forest J. wrote separate concurring judgments holding that the offence was one of general intent requiring a minimal *mens rea* and there was, in the circumstances, no violation of ss. 7 and 11(d) of the Charter.]

LAMER J. stated:  The legal implication of classifying an offence as a general intent offence combined with the removal of the defence of intoxication when intoxication is self-induced will, in certain circumstances, leave the trier of fact with no choice but to convict the accused even though there was a reasonable doubt whether, due to intoxication, the accused's act was voluntary. By the same token, the Crown would be relieved from proving beyond a reasonable doubt the *actus reus* of a general intent offence since a reasonable doubt as to voluntariness arising from intoxication would be discarded from consideration from the outset. I am of the view that the fact that a conviction may follow notwithstanding the existence of a reasonable doubt as to voluntariness, an element essential to the commission of the *actus reus*, is a limit to the rights guaranteed to the accused by ss. 7 and 11(d) of the *Charter*.

[Lamer J. upheld the offence under s. 1 on the basis that "[t]he unavailability of the defence of intoxication is a logical and necessary feature to the achievement of suppressing all the effects of intoxication on the road."]

## IV. EXTREME INTOXICATION AND GENERAL INTENT

**R. v. Daviault**
Supreme Court of Canada
(1994), 93 C.C.C. (3d) 21

[The accused was charged with sexual assault of an elderly woman who was an acquaintance of his wife. The accused was a chronic alcoholic. The accused testified that on the day of the offence he consumed seven or eight bottles of beer and at the request of the complainant brought a 40-oz. bottle of brandy to her. The accused testified that he recalled having one glass of brandy. The complainant subsequently discovered that the bottle of brandy was empty. An expert witness testified that assuming the accused had consumed the beers and the bottle of brandy his blood alcohol content would have been between 400 mg and 600 mg per 100 ml of blood. That blood alcohol ratio would cause death or a coma in an ordinary person. The expert testified that an individual with this level of alcohol might suffer a blackout, lose contact with reality, and that his brain would temporarily dissociate from normal functioning. He would have no awareness of his actions and no memory of them the next day. The trial judge acquitted the accused on the basis that he had a reasonable doubt whether the accused by virtue of his extreme intoxication possessed the minimal intent necessary to commit the offence of sexual assault. An appeal by the Crown to the Quebec Court of Appeal was allowed on the basis that the trial judge erred in holding that intoxication is a defence to a general intent offence, such as sexual assault. The Court of Appeal substituted a conviction.]

CORY J. (Lamer C.J., La Forest, L'Heureux-Dubé, McLachlin, and Iacobucci JJ. concurring): Can a state of drunkenness which is so extreme that an accused is in a condition that closely resembles automatism or a disease of the mind as defined in s. 16 of the *Criminal Code*, R.S.C. 1985, c. C-46, constitute a basis for defending a crime which requires not a specific but only a general intent? That is the troubling question that is raised on this appeal.

The facts of this case and the judgments below are set out in the reasons of Justice Sopinka. Although I agree with my colleague on a number of issues, I cannot agree with his conclusion that it is consistent with the principles of fundamental justice and the presumption of innocence for the courts to eliminate the mental element in crimes of general intent. Nor do I agree that self-induced intoxication is a sufficiently blameworthy state of mind to justify culpability, and to substitute it for the mental element that is an essential requirement of those crimes. In my opinion, the principles embodied in our *Canadian Charter of Rights and Freedoms*, and more specifically in ss. 7 and 11(d), mandate a limited exception to, or some flexibility in, the application of the *Leary* rule. This would permit evidence of extreme intoxication akin to automatism or insanity to be considered in determining whether the accused possessed the minimal mental element required for crimes of general intent.

What options are available with regard to the admissibility and significance of evidence of drunkenness as it may pertain to the mental element in general intent offences? One choice would be to continue to apply the *Leary* rule. Yet, as I will attempt to demonstrate in the next section, the rule violates the Charter and cannot be justified. Thus, this choice is unacceptable.

Another route would be to follow the *O'Connor* decision. Evidence relating to drunkenness would then go to the jury along with all other relevant evidence in determining whether the mental element requirement had been met. It is this path that is enthusiastically recommended by the majority of writers in the field. Yet it cannot be followed. It is now well established by this court that there are two categories of offences. Those requiring a specific intent and others which call for nothing more than a general intent. To follow *O'Connor* would mean that all evidence of intoxication of any degree would always go to the jury in general intent offences. This, in my view, is unnecessary. Further, in *Bernard, supra*, the majority of this court rejected this approach.

A third alternative, which I find compelling, is that proposed by Wilson J. in *Bernard*. I will examine the justifications for adopting this position in more detail shortly, but before doing that it may be helpful to review the nature of the Charter violations occasioned by a rigid application of the *Leary* rule. …

In my view, the strict application of the *Leary* rule offends both ss. 7 and 11(d) of the Charter for a number of reasons. The mental aspect of an offence, or *mens rea*, has long been recognized as an integral part of crime. The concept is fundamental to our criminal law. That element may be minimal in general intent offences; none the less, it exists. In this case, the requisite mental element is simply an intention to commit the sexual assault or recklessness as to whether the actions will constitute an assault. The necessary mental element can ordinarily be inferred from the proof that the assault was committed by the accused. However, the substituted *mens rea* of an intention to become drunk cannot establish the *mens rea* to commit the assault. …

In summary, I am of the view that to deny that even a very minimal mental element is required for sexual assault offends the Charter in a manner that is so drastic and so contrary to the principles of fundamental justice that it cannot be justified under s. 1 of the Charter. The experience of other jurisdictions which have completely abandoned the *Leary* rule, coupled with the fact that under the proposed approach, the defence would be available only in the rarest of cases, demonstrate that there is no urgent policy or pressing objective which needs to be addressed. Studies on the relationship between intoxication and crime do not establish any rational link. Finally, as the *Leary* rule applies to all crimes of general intent, it cannot be said to be well tailored to address a particular objective and it would not meet either the proportionality or the minimum impairment requirements. …

As I have said, the position adopted by Wilson J. in *Bernard* has much to commend it and should be adopted. …

There are some who argue that Wilson J.'s suggestion favours the extremely drunk while ignoring those who are less inebriated: see, for example, T. Quigley, in "Bernard on Intoxication: Principle, Policy and Points in Between—Two Comments," *supra*, at pp. 171-3. I cannot agree with that contention. It must be remembered that those who are a "little" drunk can readily form the requisite mental element to commit the offence. The alcohol-induced relaxation of both inhibitions and socially acceptable behaviour has never been accepted as a factor or excuse in determining whether the accused possessed the requisite *mens rea*. Given the minimal nature of the mental element required for crimes of general intent, even those who are significantly drunk will usually be able to form the requisite *mens rea* and will be found to have acted voluntarily. In reality it is only those who can demonstrate that they were in such an extreme degree of intoxication that they were in a state akin to automatism or insanity that might expect to raise a reasonable doubt as to their ability to form the minimal mental element required for a general intent offence. Neither an insane person nor one in a state of automatism is capable of forming the minimum intent required for a general intent offence. Similarly, as the words themselves imply, "drunkenness akin to insanity or automatism" describes a person so severely intoxicated that he is incapable of forming even the minimal intent required of a general intent offence. The phrase refers to a person so drunk that he is an automaton. As such he may be capable of voluntary acts such as moving his arms and legs but is quite incapable of forming the most basic or simple intent required to perform the act prohibited by a general intent offence. I believe that Wilson J.'s modification of the *Leary* rule is a judge-fashioned remedy that can be adopted to remedy a judge-made law which, by eliminating the mental element of a crime, offends the Charter.

It is obvious that it will only be on rare occasions that evidence of such an extreme state of intoxication can be advanced and perhaps only on still rarer occasions is it likely to be successful. None the less, the adoption of this alternative would avoid infringement of the Charter.

I would add that it is always open to Parliament to fashion a remedy which would make it a crime to commit a prohibited act while drunk.

SOPINKA J. (Gonthier and Major JJ. concurring) dissenting:  Sexual assault is a crime of general intent. In *Leary v. The Queen, supra*, a majority of this court held that drunkenness is not a defence to a crime of general intent. While some of the judges of this court have sought to overrule *Leary*, it has not happened. Accordingly, I agree with the Court of Appeal's decision that the trial judge was bound by the decision in *Leary*. Furthermore, I reject the appellant's submission that *Leary* ought to be overruled. ...

As a result, the decision in *Leary* still stands for the proposition that evidence of intoxication can only provide a defence for offences of specific intent but not for offences of general intent. Since sexual assault is a crime of general intent, intoxication is no defence to a charge of sexual assault. This rule is supported by sound policy considerations. One of the main purposes of the criminal law is to protect the public. This purpose would be frustrated if, as Lawton L.J. put it in the Court of Appeal in *Majewski, supra*, at p. 456, "the more drunk a man became, provided he stopped short of making himself insane, the better chance he had of an acquittal." Society is entitled to punish those who of their own free will render themselves so intoxicated as to pose a threat to other members of the community. The fact that an accused has voluntarily consumed intoxicating amounts of drugs or alcohol cannot excuse the commission of a criminal offence unless it gives rise to a mental disorder within the terms of s. 16. Section 16 is not invoked in this case and, therefore, the circumstances in which alcohol or its effects may engage the provisions of that section are not in issue here. ...

Application of the *Leary* rule in circumstances such as those of the case at bar obviously permits the accused to be convicted despite the existence of a reasonable doubt as to whether he intended to perform the *actus reus* of the offence of sexual assault. In my view, this does not violate either ss. 7 or 11(d) of the Charter. None of the relevant principles of fundamental justice require that the intent to perform the *actus reus* of an offence of general intent be an element of the offence. In my opinion, the requirements of the principles of fundamental justice are satisfied by proof that the accused became voluntarily intoxicated.

The premise upon which the alleged breach of fundamental justice is based is that symmetry between the *actus reus*, or some aspect of it, and the *mens rea* is constitutionally required. This, it is said, is a principle of fundamental justice which is of universal application. This issue has been recently thrashed out in relation to whether consequences forming part of the *actus reus* must be foreseen on an objective or subjective basis or some variation thereof. In *R. v. Creighton* (1993), 83 C.C.C. (3d) 346, 105 D.L.R. (4th) 632, [1993] 3 S.C.R. 3 (S.C.C.), this court divided on this issue with respect to the crime of unlawful act manslaughter. In the view of the Chief Justice, concurred in by three other members of the court, including myself, the mental element required was foreseeability of death on a modified objective standard. The majority opinion, however, adopted an objective standard of foreseeability but limited to bodily harm.

The second requirement of the principles of fundamental justice is that punishment must be proportionate to the moral blameworthiness of the offender. This was held to be a principle of fundamental justice in *R. v. Martineau* (1990), 58 C.C.C. (3d) 353,[1990] 2 S.C.R. 633, 79 C.R. (3d) 129 (S.C.C.), and *R. v. Creighton, supra*. There are a few crimes in respect of which a special level of *mens rea* is constitutionally required by reason of the stigma attaching to a conviction and by reason of the severity of the penalty imposed by law. Accordingly, murder and attempted murder require a *mens rea* based on a subjective standard. No exception from the principle of fundamental justice should be made with respect to these offences and, as specific intent offences, drunkenness is a defence.

By contrast, sexual assault does not fall into the category of offences for which either the stigma or the available penalties demand as a constitutional requirement subjective intent to commit the *actus reus*. Sexual assault is a heinous crime of violence. Those found guilty of committing the offence are rightfully submitted to a significant degree of moral opprobrium. That opprobrium is not misplaced in the case of the intoxicated offender. Such individuals deserve to be stigmatized. Their moral blameworthiness is similar to that of anyone else who commits the offence of sexual assault and the effects of their conduct upon both their victims and society as a whole are the same as in any other case of sexual assault. Furthermore, the sentence for sexual assault is not fixed. To the extent that it bears upon his or her level of moral blameworthiness, an offender's degree of intoxication at the time of the offence may be considered during sentencing. Taking all of these factors into account, I cannot see how the stigma and punishment associated with the offence of sexual assault are disproportionate to the moral blameworthiness of a person like the appellant who commits the offence after voluntarily becoming so intoxicated as to be incapable of knowing what he was doing. The fact that the *Leary* rule permits an individual to be convicted despite the absence of symmetry between the *actus reus* and the mental element of blameworthiness does not violate a principle of fundamental justice. ...

For all of these reasons, in my opinion, the best course is for the court to reaffirm the traditional rule that voluntary intoxication does not constitute a defence to an offence of general intent, subject to the comments I have made with respect to improvements in the definition and application of the distinction between offences of specific and general intent. If a different approach is considered desirable because the *Leary* approach does not comport with social policy, Parliament is free to intervene. I note that this observation was made by McIntyre J. in *R. v. Bernard* but Parliament has not intervened. It has been suggested that Parliament should create a new offence of dangerous intoxication. Such a recommendation was made by the Butler Committee in England and by the Law Reform Commission in Canada: see "Butler Committee Report on Mentally Abnormal Offenders" (1975) (Cmnd. 6244, paras. 18.51-18.59), and Law Reform Commission of Canada, "Recodifying Criminal Law," Report 30, vol. 1 at pp. 27-8 (1986). Such legislation could be coupled with amendments to the *Criminal Code* to extend the defence of drunkenness to some or all offences to which it does not apply. Such changes, however, are for Parliament and not for this court to make.

---

Bill C-72 (later Bill C-32) was proposed as a response to *Daviault*. It was proclaimed into force as s. 33.1 of the *Criminal Code* on September 15, 1995. It provides:

**1st Session, 35th Parliament,**
**42-43-44 Elizabeth II, 1994-95**
**The House of Commons of Canada**
**BILL C-72**

An Act to amend the Criminal Code (self-induced intoxication)

**Preamble**

WHEREAS the Parliament of Canada is gravely concerned about the incidence of violence in Canadian society;

WHEREAS the Parliament of Canada recognizes that violence has a particularly disadvantaging impact on the equal participation of women and children in society and on the rights of women and children to security of the person and to the equal protection and benefit of the law as guaranteed by sections 7, 15 and 28 of the *Canadian Charter of Rights and Freedoms*;

WHEREAS the Parliament of Canada recognizes that there is a close association between violence and intoxication and is concerned that self-induced intoxication may be used socially and legally to excuse violence, particularly violence against women and children;

WHEREAS the Parliament of Canada recognizes that the potential effects of alcohol and certain drugs on human behaviour are well known to Canadians and is aware of scientific evidence that many intoxicants, including alcohol, may not cause a person to act involuntarily;

WHEREAS the Parliament of Canada shares with Canadians the moral view that people who, while in a state of self-induced intoxication, violate the physical integrity of others are blameworthy in relation to their harmful conduct and should be held criminally accountable for it;

WHEREAS the Parliament of Canada desires to promote and help to ensure the full protection of the rights guaranteed under sections 7, 11, 15 and 28 of the *Canadian Charter of Rights and Freedoms* for all Canadians, including those who are or may be victims of violence;

WHEREAS the Parliament of Canada considers it necessary to legislate a basis of criminal fault in relation to self-induced intoxication and general intent offences involving violence;

WHEREAS the Parliament of Canada recognizes the continuing existence of a common law principle that intoxication to an extent that is less than that which would cause a person to lack the ability to form the basic intent or to have the voluntariness required to commit a criminal offence of general intent is never a defence at law;

AND WHEREAS the Parliament of Canada considers it necessary and desirable to legislate a standard of care, in order to make it clear that a person who, while in a state of incapacity by reason of self-induced intoxication, commits an offence involving violence against another person, departs markedly from the standard of reasonable care that Canadians owe to each other and is thereby criminally at fault;

NOW, THEREFORE, Her Majesty, by and with the advice and consent of the Senate and House of Commons of Canada, enacts as follows:

1. The *Criminal Code* is amended by adding the following after section 33:

## Self-induced Intoxication
*When defence not available*

33.1(1)  It is not a defence to an offence referred to in subsection (3) that the accused, by reason of self-induced intoxication, lacked the basic intent or the voluntariness required to commit the offence, where the accused departed markedly from the standard of care as described in subsection (2).

*Criminal fault by reason of intoxication*

(2)  For the purposes of this section, a person departs markedly from the standard of reasonable care generally recognized in Canadian society and is thereby criminally at fault where the person, while in a state of self-induced intoxication that renders the person unaware of, or incapable of consciously controlling, their behaviour, voluntarily or involuntarily interferes or threatens to interfere with the bodily integrity of another person.

*Application*

(3) This section applies in respect of an offence under this Act or any other Act of Parliament that includes as an element an assault or any other interference or threat of interference by a person with the bodily integrity of another person.

*Coming into force*

2. This Act shall come into force on a day to be fixed by order of the Governor in Council.

Section 33.1 is drafted in awkward terms, not least because Parliament was faced with the difficult challenge of reversing the practical effect of *Daviault* without contradicting a pronouncement by the Supreme Court on a question of constitutional law.

In some respects, the state of the law is now more confusing than ever. There are three variations on the defence of intoxication. First, the common law rule in cases such as *Bernard* that restricts the defence to offences of specific intent continues to apply. Accordingly, the need to classify an offence as one of general or specific intent remains. Second, the expanded defence of extreme intoxication, as stated in *Daviault*, applies even to offences of general intent. The application of this defence requires expert evidence concerning the nature and effect of the intoxicant and the defence cannot succeed unless it is proved on a balance of probabilities. Third, s. 33.1 of the Code denies the defence of extreme intoxication to any offence of general intent that involves interference or threatened interference with the bodily integrity of another person, provided that, at the relevant time, the act was performed in a state of intoxication that shows a marked departure from the standard of reasonable care. Imagine the difficulty facing a judge who must deal with two or more of these variations in a single case.

All of the difficulties associated with the traditional common law rule remain. These are compounded in the defence of extreme intoxication. One possible consequence of that defence is that, if accepted, it could be applied to negate the voluntariness of an offence, thus leading to a complete acquittal. As applied to offences of specific or general intent, a central question is the severity of the intoxication. The defence contemplated by *Daviault* obviously puts a premium on a strong evidentiary foundation as to the nature, quantity, and effect of the drug in question. This means not only that there will have to be expert evidence on the issue, but there will have to be clear evidence as to the consumption of drugs by the accused at the relevant times. See, for example, *R. v. B. (S.J.)* (2002), 166 C.C.C. (3d) 537 (Alta. C.A.). And, of course, the evidence must come up to prove on a balance of probabilities for the defence to produce an acquittal.

The underlying theory of s. 33.1 rests on the concept of a substitution of one standard of fault for another—that is, the substitution of a standard of marked negligence for the element of fault in the definition of the offence. In *Vaillancourt* (1987), 39 C.C.C. (3d) 118, the Supreme Court held that a substitution of one standard of fault for another that is constitutionally required for the offence would be valid only if the substituted element was functionally equivalent to the required element. There is no objection to a substitution of one standard of fault for another that is not constitutionally required. Because there is no principle of constitutional law that general intent is a minimal requirement for criminal offences, there can be no objection to a substitution of marked neglige ice in any case where general intent would suffice for conviction.

To this extent, the theory of s. 33.1 is probably defensible. There are other aspects of the provision, however, that might be more problematic. In particular, s. 33.1(3) would specifically deny the defence even if the effect of intoxication was to make the conduct of the accused involuntary. This implies the possibility of conviction not only in the absence of fault but in the absence of *actus reus*.

There have been challenges to the constitutional validity of s. 33.1. To date, however, the Supreme Court of Canada has not had to rule on this question and no provincial or territorial court of appeal has declared that it is invalid. At some point, the matter will undoubtedly arise. See, for example, *Vickberg* (1998) 16 C.R. (5th) 164 (B.C.S.C.) and *Brenton*, [2001] 7 W.W.R. 411 (N.W.T.C.A.).

### ADDITIONAL READING

- K. Roach, *Criminal Law*, 3rd ed. (Toronto: Irwin Law: 2004), chapter 6;
- A. Mewett and M. Manning, *Criminal Law*, 3rd ed. (Toronto: Butterworths, 1994), at 403-40;
- D. Stuart, *Canadian Criminal Law*, 4th ed. (Toronto: Carswell, 2001), at 416-50;
- E. Colvin, *Principles of Criminal Law*, 2nd ed. (Toronto: Carswell, 1991), at 303-14;
- T. Quigley, "Notes and Comments: A Shorn Beard" (1986-87), 10 *Dalhousie L.J.* 167;
- T. Quigley, "Reform of the Intoxication Defence" (1987), 33 *McGill L.J.* 1;
- K.L. Campbell, "Intoxicated Mistakes" (1989), 32 *Crim. L.Q.* 110;
- P. Healy, "*R. v. Bernard*: Difficulties with Voluntary Intoxication" (1990), 35 *McGill L.J.* 610;
- P. Healy, "Intoxication in the Codification of Canadian Criminal Law" (1994), 73 *Can. Bar Rev.* 515;
- P. Healy, "Criminal Reports Forum on Daviault" (1995), 33 *C.R.* (4th) 269;
- K. Smith, "Section 33.1: Denial of the *Daviault* Defence Should Be Held Constitutional" (2000), 28 C.R. (5th) 350.

# CHAPTER EIGHTEEN

# Necessity

Necessity is a controversial common law or judge-made defence that has been firmly recognized in Canadian law only since 1984. It is recognized in Canada as an excuse for crimes committed in urgent situations of clear and imminent peril where the accused has no safe avenue of escape or legal way out. The courts have insisted that necessity never justifies the commission of the crime. As with duress and self-defence to be examined in subsequent chapters, there is also an objective or reasonableness requirement to the necessity defence that requires the accused to reasonably resist the pressures that led to the commission of the crime.

The history of necessity as a defence in Canada is tied up with several very controversial cases. In the first part of this chapter we will examine whether necessity should have been a defence when a doctor was charged with violating Canada's old abortion law by performing an abortion outside of a hospital and without the approval of a hospital committee. The second section will consider the leading case of *Perka v. The Queen*, which recognized necessity as a defence but conceptualized it only as an excuse as opposed to a justification to a crime. A separate section will examine the rejection of the necessity defence in the famous *Latimer* case. The final section will examine proposals to codify the common law defence of necessity.

## I. NECESSITY AND ABORTION

### Morgentaler v. The Queen
Supreme Court of Canada
(1975), 20 C.C.C. (2d) 449

[The Supreme Court of Canada held (6 to 3) that the defence of necessity was not applicable on the facts of the case that involved the accused, Dr. Henry Morgentaler, performing an abortion on a 26-year-old single woman in his clinic in contravention of the *Criminal Code*, which at the time allowed abortions to be committed only in a hospital if approved by a hospital committee. Dr. Morgentaler testified that he was afraid that the woman "might do something foolish" if he did not perform the abortion.]

DICKSON J. (with whom five other members of the court concurred): ... In an attempt to escape the discipline of the statute, the appellant seeks to rely on an ill-defined and elusive concept sometimes referred to as the defence of necessity. The defence of necessity is as rare to Canadian jurisprudence as a s. 45 defence. Standard Canadian texts on criminal law either ignore or make scant reference to the subject. Save in the exceptional case of *R. v. Bourne*, [1939] 1 K.B. 687, to which I will later refer, the defence has never been raised successfully, so far as one can ascertain, in a criminal case in this country or in England. It was unavailing in *U.S. v. Holmes* (1842), 26 Fed. Cas. 36, where, following a shipwreck, the sailors threw 14 passengers overboard to lighten a lifeboat that was sinking and in *R. v. Dudley and Stephens* (1884), 14 Q.B.D. 273, where the accused, two seamen, after 18 days adrift in an open boat and starving, killed a youthful companion and fed on his flesh for four days, at the end of which time they were rescued. It was raised in *Gregson v. Gilbert* (1783), 3 Dougl. 232, where 150 slaves were pushed overboard because of water shortage. The defence of necessity has been held to permit encroachment on private property in the case of great and imminent danger: *Mouse's Case* (1609), 12 Co. Rep. 63, where a casket belonging to Mouse and other things were thrown overboard in order to lighten a barge that was in danger of sinking during a storm. Necessity has been said to justify pulling down a house to prevent the spread of a fire, or the escape of prisoners from a burning prison and it has given rise to endless philosophizing on the right of a person in danger of drowning to push another from a floating plank in order to save himself. These are said to be examples of the defence of necessity, but no clear principle can be detected. It has been held that necessity cannot justify killing: *R. v. Dudley and Stephens*, *supra*, or the stealing of food by a starving man, Hale, *Pleas of Crown* i, 54 or the occupancy of empty housing by those in dire need of accommodation, *Southwark London Borough Council v. Williams*, [1971] 1 Ch. 734. The Courts have been reluctant to give recognition to the doctrine of necessity for, as Lord Denning, M.R., said in the *Williams* case, p. 744: "Necessity would open a door which no man could shut" and "The plea would be an excuse for all sorts of wrong-doing," and Lord Justice Edmund-Davies in the same case, p. 746 "... necessity can very easily become simply a mask for anarchy." The defence of necessity finds little support in the cases. Professor Glanville Williams, who has written frequently on abortion and the doctrine of necessity ((1952) 5 C.L.P. 128; (1953) 6 C.L.P. 216; *Sanctity of Life and the Criminal Law* (1957)) introduces the subject "Authorities on the defence of necessity" in his text on *Criminal Law* (2nd ed. 1961) with the qualified statement, p. 724: "Notwithstanding the doubts that have been expressed, it will here be submitted somewhat confidently that the defence is recognized in English Law." Compare, however, "The Necessity Plea in English Common Law" by P.R. Glazebrook, 1972A *Cambridge Law Journal*, 87, and see "The Defence of Necessity in Criminal Law: The Right to Choose the Lesser Evil" by Arnolds and Garland (1974), 65 *The Journal of Criminal Law and Criminology*, 289. On the authorities it is manifestly difficult to be categorical and state that there is a law of necessity, paramount over other laws, relieving obedience from the letter of the law. If it does exist it can go no further than to justify non-compliance in urgent situations of clear and imminent peril when compliance with the law is demonstrably impossible. No system of positive law can recognize any principle which would entitle a person to violate the law because on his view the law conflicted with some higher social value.

*R. v. Bourne*, *supra*, is sometimes quoted in support of the contention that there is a defence of necessity: for myself, I have some considerable reservations on the point. The *Bourne* decision may be regarded as exceptional and in a sense legislative. Although stated to exemplify the doctrine of necessity, the Judge did not specifically rely on necessity. At the time of *Bourne* the law was unclear as to the legal position of a medical practitioner who procured an abortion on a girl whose life or health was endangered by continued pregnancy. The English statute did not then contain, although it now does, any provision for therapeutic abortion akin to s. 251(4) of the *Code*. The trial Judge, through the word "unlawfully," imported such a concept and on the facts of that case it is of no surprise that the jury acquitted. The question of compliance with statutory law permitting therapeutic abortion did not arise. If the proponents of the existence of defence of necessity have to rely on the case of *Bourne*—and the only support in modern jurisprudence would seem to come from that case and one or two which followed it—to support their position, the very uniqueness of *Bourne* both on facts and law may lead one seriously to question whether a defence of necessity can really be said to exist. I do not think the *Bourne* case is of great assistance to the appellant. In *Bourne* the trial Judge imported into the charge the consideration of "preserving the life of the mother." That same concept finds statutory recognition in our abortion legislation but in the somewhat broader phraseology "likely to endanger her life or health." It is, therefore, clear that a medical practitioner who wishes to procure a miscarriage because continued pregnancy may endanger the life or health of his patient may legally do so if he secures the certificate mentioned in s. 251(4)(c). The defence of necessity, whatever that vague phrase may import, does not entitle a medical practitioner, in circumstances of time and place such as those under consideration, to procure an abortion on his own opinion of the danger to life and health.

Assuming the theoretical possibility of such a defence in the present case, it remains to be seen whether there is evidence to support it. Amid the general imprecision and philosophic uncertainty discernible among the authors as to reach and effect of a defence of necessity, the most definite assertion would seem to be that found in Kenny's *Outlines of Criminal Law*, 19th ed. (1966), where the author says, p. 73:

> Probably no such defence can be accepted in any case (1) where the evil averted was a lesser evil than the offence committed to avert it, or (2) where the evil could have been averted by anything short of the commission of that offence, or (3) where more harm was done than was necessary for averting the evil. Hence it is scarcely safe to lay down any more definite rule than that suggested by Sir James Stephen, viz. that "it is just possible to imagine cases in which the expediency of breaking the law is so overwhelmingly great that people may be justified in breaking it; but these cases cannot be defined beforehand."

Kenny says, p. 72:

Yet, though theoretical writers have been willing to accept this ground of defence, there is no English case in which the defence has been actually raised with success.

Turning our attention to Kenny's (2), we must ask whether the evil averted could have been averted by anything short of the commission of the offence. This raises the question of the urgency of the operation performed by the appellant and whether the appellant could have complied with the law. A defence of necessity at the very least must rest upon evidence from which a jury could find (i) that the accused in good faith considered the situation so emergent that failure to terminate the pregnancy immediately could endanger life or health and (ii) that upon any reasonable view of the facts compliance with the law was impossible.

Upon this evidence I think it perfectly clear the Court of Appeal did not err in concluding there was on the record little evidence of real and urgent medical need. More important, in answer to the question: "Was there any legal way out?" I think one must say that evidence from which a jury could conclude it was impossible for appellant to comply with the law is wholly wanting. The plain fact is that appellant made no attempt to bring himself within the bounds of legality in deciding to perform this abortion. Appellant failed to establish the second condition which Kenny says must be satisfied before the defence of necessity can be accepted in any case. I would hold, therefore, that the defence of necessity was not open to the appellant.

LASKIN C.J., with whom Judson and Spence JJ. concurred, dissenting: The appellant was charged with performing an illegal abortion on August 15, 1973, upon a 26-year-old unmarried female who had come to Canada from a foreign country in 1972 on a student visa. She was without family or close friends in Canada, ineligible to take employment and also ineligible for Medicare benefits. On becoming apprehensive of possible pregnancy in July, 1973, she consulted a physician in general practice who referred her to a gynecologist. He confirmed that she was pregnant, but refused assistance to procure an abortion. On her own initiative she canvassed five Montreal hospitals by telephone and learned that if an abortion was to be performed she would have to bear the fees of a surgeon and an anaesthetist, and could envisage two or three days' hospitalization at $140 per day. This was far beyond her means.

Throughout the period following her apprehension and the confirmation of her pregnancy and until the abortion performed by the appellant, she was anxious, unable to eat or sleep properly, prone to vomiting and quite depressed. Her condition had an adverse effect upon her studies and it was aggravated by her being told that the longer she delayed in having an abortion the more dangerous it would be. One hospital offered her an appointment (which would result in her case coming before the therapeutic abortion committee) at the end of August, 1973, when she would be eight to 10 weeks' pregnant. She got in touch with the appellant at the suggestion of a hospital or hospitals that she had contacted. There is some discrepancy between her evidence and that of the appellant as to the scope and nature of the conversation between them when she visited his clinic where the abortion was performed. In this appeal I think it proper to accept the evidence of the appellant who testified that his discussion with her went beyond asking whether she had previously had an abortion, when she realized she was pregnant and what his fee would be. He asserted that the conversation also encompassed reference to her country of origin, her vocation, her marital status and why an abortion was necessary. During the conversation the appellant said that he assessed the necessity of an abortion by reference to her state of anxiety, her inability to eat or sleep properly and the consequent adverse effect on her physical health. He also considered that her determination to have an abortion might lead her to do something foolish. The appellant was aware that his patient had approached a number of hospitals without success, but did not know that she had been offered an appointment at the end of August, 1973.

It appears quite clearly that what the Quebec Court of Appeal saw in the defence of necessity was urgency of such a nature as to make it impossible to obtain a lawful abortion under s. 251(4). The test it would apply parallels that which can rarely be met, if at all, where the charge against the accused is one arising out of homicide. I am not prepared to take the same stringent view of urgency and impossibility as did the Quebec Court of Appeal, and I would observe, moreover, that there is a danger here in usurping the function of the jury on that question according to the way in which it is defined. I do not doubt, of course, that the necessity must arise out of danger to life or health and not merely out of economic circumstances, although the latter may have an effect in producing the danger to life or health.

It was for the jury to say whether in such circumstances the harm sought to be avoided by performing the abortion was an immediate and physical one (to use the words of Williams) and whether there was enough of an emergency in this respect facing the accused as to make it certain that there could be no effective resort to the machinery of s. 251(4) to cope with the emergency.

I need hardly say that the sufficiency of evidence on any issue is a matter for the jury, which alone is charged to accept what it chooses and to weigh what it accepts in the light of the law given to it by the trial Judge.

## R. v. Morgentaler et al.
Ontario Court of Appeal
(1985), 22 C.C.C. (3d) 353

[The accused were charged with conspiracy to procure a miscarriage contrary to ss. 251(1) and 423(1)(d) of the Code. The accused were acquitted and the Crown appealed to the Ontario Court of Appeal, arguing, *inter alia*, that the defence of necessity should not have been left to the jury. The court agreed and ordered a new trial.]

THE COURT:  With respect, we think that the defence of necessity was misconceived. As has previously been noted, before a defence of necessity is available, the conduct of the accused must be truly involuntary in the sense ascribed in that term in the precedents cited. There was nothing involuntary in the agreement entered into in the case by the respondents. As stated by Fletcher, *Rethinking Criminal Law* (1978), pp. 811-2: "Planning, deliberating, relying on legal precedents—all of these are incompatible with the uncalculating response essential to 'involuntary' conduct."

Furthermore, there must be evidence that compliance with the law was demonstrably impossible, and that there was no legal way out.

Not only did the defendants fail to make every reasonable effort to comply with the law, but they consciously agreed to violate it. Their dissatisfaction with the state of the law, although perhaps relevant to the issue of motive, afforded no basis for the defence of necessity.

The constitutional validity of s. 251 having been upheld by the trial judge, it was not an issue for the jury to weigh the merits of the law enacted by Parliament and to be invited to resolve the public debate on abortion. Yet, it was on the basis of the dissatisfaction with the law that the defence sought to rely on the legal defence of necessity. ...

With respect, the defence of necessity is not premised on dissatisfaction with the law. The defence of necessity recognizes that the law must be followed, but there are certain factual situations which arise and which may excuse a person for failure to comply with the law. It is not the law which can create an emergency giving rise to a defence of necessity, but it is the facts of a given situation which may do so.

This was not a case where two or more doctors agreed to procure the miscarriage of a female person who was in immediate need of medical services in order to avoid danger to her life or health, and in which case the defence of necessity would be a live issue. The defence of necessity cannot be resorted to as an excuse for medical practitioners in Canada to agree in the circumstances of this case to procure abortions on their own opinion of the danger to life or health and at a place of their own choosing in complete disregard to the provisions of s. 251 of the *Criminal Code*.

Although it was for the jury to weigh the evidence, it is the function of an appellate court to examine the record with a view to ascertaining whether there is any evidence to support a defence. On the record before us including the evidence tendered by the Crown as well as for the defence, the defence of necessity was not open to the respondents, and the trial judge erred in leaving that defence to the jury.

[The Supreme Court did not decide whether the defence of necessity should have been left to the jury when on further appeal it held that the abortion law violated s. 7 of the Charter. See *R. v. Morgentaler et al.* (1988), 37 C.C.C. (3d) 449.]

## II. THE CONCEPTUALIZATION OF NECESSITY AS
## AN EXCUSE OR JUSTIFICATION


**Perka v. The Queen**
Supreme Court of Canada
(1984), 14 C.C.C. (3d) 385


[The accused were charged with importing a narcotic and possession of a narcotic for the purpose of trafficking contrary to ss. 5 and 4(2), respectively, of the *Narcotic Control Act*, R.S.C. 1970, c. N-1. The evidence led by the Crown indicated that 33.49 tons of marijuana worth 6 or 7 million dollars was seized from a ship found in Canadian waters on the west coast of Vancouver Island. The accused were members of the crew or officers of the ship or otherwise connected with the shipment of the marijuana. During the defence, the accused adduced evidence as to the condition of the ship during poor weather conditions and the efforts that were made to remedy certain mechanical defects.

The defence presented evidence that the drugs were being shipped from Colombia, South America to Alaska, that there were engine breakdowns, overheating generators, and malfunctioning navigation devices, coupled with eight-to-ten-foot swells and a rising wind. The accused therefore (according to the defence evidence) sought refuge on the west coast of Vancouver Island. In rebuttal the Crown sought to adduce evidence as to the mechanical condition of the ship and, in particular, how easily the authorities were able to start the vessel, and as to how it performed subsequently. The Crown argued that the evidence of the ship's distress was a recent fabrication. The trial judge refused the Crown's application on the basis that the defence of necessity was one that could have been anticipated and that the evidence should have been led by the Crown in its case in chief. The accused were acquitted.

The British Columbia Court of Appeal ordered a new trial, holding that the Crown should have been allowed to call rebuttal evidence. The accused appealed to the Supreme Court of Canada. The five-member court agreed with the Court of Appeal that a new trial should be awarded.]


DICKSON J. (as he then was) stated for Ritchie, Chouinard, and Lamer JJ.: Subsequent to *Morgentaler*, the courts appear to have assumed that a defence of necessity does exist in Canada ... .

In *Morgentaler*, *supra*, I characterized necessity as an "ill-defined and elusive concept." Despite the apparently growing consensus as to the existence of a defence of necessity that statement is equally true today. ...

Criminal theory recognizes a distinction between "justifications" and "excuses." A "justification" challenges the wrongfulness of an action which technically constitutes a crime. The police officer who shoots the hostage-taker, the innocent object of an assault who uses force to defend himself against his assailant, the good Samaritan who commandeers a car and breaks the speed laws to rush an accident victim to the hospital, these are all actors whose actions we consider *rightful*, not wrongful. For such actions people are often praised, as motivated by some great or noble object. The concept of punishment often seems incompatible with the social approval bestowed on the doer.

In contrast, an "excuse" concedes the wrongfulness of the action but asserts that the circumstances under which it was done are such that it ought not to be attributed to the actor. The perpetrator who is incapable, owing to a disease of the mind, of appreciating the nature and consequences of his acts, the person who labours under a mistake of fact, the drunkard, the sleepwalker: these are all actors of whose "criminal" actions we disapprove intensely, but whom, in appropriate circumstances, our law will not punish.

It will be seen that the two different approaches to the "defence" of necessity from Blackstone forward correspond, the one to a justification, the other to an excuse. ...

As a "justification" this residual defence ... would exculpate actors whose conduct could reasonably have been viewed as "necessary" in order to prevent a greater evil than that resulting from the violation of the law. As articulated, especially in some of the American cases, it involves a utilitarian balancing of the benefits of obeying the law as opposed to disobeying it, and when the balance is clearly in favour of disobeying, exculpates an actor who contravenes a criminal statute. This is the "greater good" formulation of the necessity defence: in some circumstances, it is alleged, the values of society, indeed of the criminal law itself, are better promoted by disobeying a given statute than by observing it.

With regard to this conceptualization of a residual defence of necessity, I retain the scepticism I expressed in *Morgentaler*, *supra*, at p. 497 C.C.C., p. 209 D.L.R., p. 678 S.C.R. It is still my opinion that, "[n]o system of positive law can recognize any principle which would entitle a person to violate the law because on his view the law conflicted with some higher social value." The *Criminal Code* has specified a number of identifiable situations in which an actor is justified in committing what would otherwise be a criminal offence. To go beyond that and hold that ostensibly illegal acts can be validated on the basis of their expediency, would import an undue subjectivity into the criminal law. It would invite the courts to second-guess the Legislature and to assess the relative merits of social policies underlying criminal prohibitions. Neither is a role which fits well with the judicial function. Such a doctrine could well become the last resort of scoundrels and, in the words of Edmund Davies L.J. in *Southwark London Borough Council v. Williams et al.*, [1971] Ch. 734 [at p. 746], it could "very easily become simply a mask for anarchy."

Conceptualized as an "excuse," however, the residual defence of necessity is, in my view, much less open to criticism. It rests on a realistic assessment of human weakness, recognizing that a liberal and humane criminal law cannot hold people to the strict obedience of laws in emergency situations where normal human instincts, whether of self-preservation or of altruism, overwhelmingly impel disobedience. The objectivity of the criminal law is preserved; such acts are still wrongful, but in the circumstances they are excusable. Praise is indeed not bestowed, but pardon is, when one does a wrongful act under pressure which, in the words of Aristotle in *The Nicomachean Ethics* (translator Rees, p. 49), "overstrains human nature and which no one could withstand" ... .

In *Morgentaler v. The Queen* (1975), 20 C.C.C. (2d) 449 at p. 497, 53 D.L.R. (3d) 161 at p. 209, [1976] 1 S.C.R. 616 at p. 678, I was of the view that any defence of necessity was restricted to instances of non-compliance "in urgent situations of clear and imminent peril when compliance with the law is demonstrably impossible." In my opinion, this restriction focuses directly on the "involuntariness" of the purportedly necessitous behaviour by providing a number of tests for determining whether the wrongful act was truly the only realistic reaction open to the actor or whether he was in fact making what in fairness could be called a choice. If he was making a choice, then the wrongful act cannot have been involuntary in the relevant sense.

The requirement that the situation be urgent and the peril be imminent, tests whether it was indeed unavoidable for the actor to act at all. ... At a minimum the situation must be so emergent and the peril must be so pressing that normal human instincts cry out for action and make a counsel of patience unreasonable.

The requirement that compliance with the law be "demonstrably impossible" takes this assessment one step further. Given that the accused had to act, could he nevertheless realistically have acted to avoid the peril or prevent the harm, without breaking the law? *Was there a legal way out?* I think this is what Bracton means when he lists "necessity" as a defence, providing the wrongful act was not "avoidable." The question to be asked is whether the agent had any real choice: could he have done otherwise? If there is a reasonable legal alternative to disobeying the law, then the decision to disobey becomes a voluntary one, impelled by some consideration beyond the dictates of "necessity" and human instincts.

The importance of this requirement that there be no reasonable legal alternative cannot be overstressed.

Even if the requirements for urgency and "no legal way out" are met, there is clearly a further consideration. There must be some way of assuring proportionality. No rational criminal justice system, no matter how humane or liberal, could excuse the infliction of a greater harm to allow the actor to avert a lesser evil. In such circumstances we expect the individual to bear the harm and refrain from acting illegally. If he cannot control himself we will not excuse him. ...

... If the conduct in which an accused was engaging at the time the peril arose was illegal, then it should clearly be punished, but I fail to see the relevance of its illegal character to the question of whether the accused's subsequent conduct in dealing with this emergent peril ought to be excused on the basis of necessity. At most the illegality—or if one adopts Jones J.A.'s approach, the immorality—of the preceding conduct will colour the subsequent conduct in response to the emergency as also wrongful. But that wrongfulness is never in any doubt. Necessity goes to *excuse* conduct, not to *justify* it. Where it is found to apply it carries with it no implicit vindication of the deed to which it attaches. That cannot be over-emphasized. Were the defence of necessity to succeed in the present case, it would not in any way amount to a vindication of importing controlled substances nor to a critique of the law prohibiting such importation. It would also have nothing to say about the comparative social utility of breaking the law against importing as compared to obeying the law. The question, as I have said, is never whether what the accused has done is wrongful. It is always and by definition, wrongful. The question is whether what he has done is voluntary. ...

It is now possible to summarize a number of conclusions as to the defence of necessity in terms of its nature, basis and limitations:

(1)  the defence of necessity could be conceptualized as either a justification or an excuse;

(2)  it should be recognized in Canada as an excuse, operating by virtue of s. 7(3) of the *Criminal Code*;

(3)  necessity as an excuse implies no vindication of the deeds of the actor;

(4)  the criterion is the moral involuntariness of the wrongful action;

(5)  this involuntariness is measured on the basis of society's expectation of appropriate and normal resistance to pressure;

(6)  negligence or involvement in criminal or immoral activity does not disentitle the actor to the excuse of necessity;

(7)  actions or circumstances which indicate that the wrongful deed was not truly involuntary do disentitle;

(8)  the existence of a reasonable legal alternative similarly disentitles; to be involuntary the act must be inevitable, unavoidable and afford no reasonable opportunity for an alternative course of action that does not involve a breach of the law;

(9)  the defence only applies in circumstances of imminent risk where the action was taken to avoid a direct and immediate peril;

(10) where the accused places before the court sufficient evidence to raise the issue, the onus is on the Crown to meet it beyond a reasonable doubt.

In my view, the trial judge was correct in concluding that on the evidence before him he should instruct the jury with regard to necessity. There was evidence before him from which a jury might conclude that the accused's actions in coming ashore with their cargo of *cannabis* were aimed at self-preservation in response to an overwhelming emergency. I have already indicated that in my view they were not engaged in conduct that was illegal under Canadian criminal law at the time the emergency arose, and that even if they were, that fact alone would not disentitle them to raise the defence. ...

In the course of his charge on the issue of necessity the trial judge instructed the jury, using the specific words that appear in *Morgentaler v. The Queen* (1975), 20 C.C.C. (2d) 449, 53 D.L.R. (3d) 161, [1976] 1 S.C.R. 616, to the effect that they must find facts which amount to "an urgent situation of clear and imminent peril when compliance with the law is demonstrably impossible" in order for the appellants' non-compliance with the law against importation and possession of *cannabis* to be excused. That is the correct test. It is, with respect, however, my view that in explaining the meaning and application of this test, the trial judge fell into error.

The trial judge was obliged, in my opinion, to direct the jury's attention to a number of issues pertinent to the test for necessity. Was the emergency a real one? Did it constitute an immediate threat of the harm purportedly feared? Was the response proportionate? In comparing this response to the danger that motivated it, was the danger one that society would reasonably expect the average person to withstand? Was there any reasonable legal alternative to the illegal response open to the accused? Although the trial judge did not explicitly pose each and every one of these questions in my view his charge was adequate to bring the consideration underlying them to the jury's attention on every issue except the last one, the question of a reasonable alternative.

WILSON J., concurring, stated:  Inasmuch as the Chief Justice's conclusion as to the defence of necessity seems clearly correct on the facts of this case and his disposition of the appeal manifestly just in the circumstances, I am dealing in these reasons only with the proposition very forcefully advanced by the Chief Justice in his reasons that the appropriate jurisprudential basis on which to premise the defence of necessity is exclusively that of excuse. My concern is that the learned Chief Justice appears to be closing the door on justification as an appropriate jurisprudential basis in some cases and I am firmly of the view that this is a door which should be left open by the court. …

It may generally be said that an act is justified on grounds of necessity if the court can say that not only was the act a necessary one but it was rightful rather than wrongful. When grounded on the fundamental principle that a successful defence must characterize an act as one which the accused was within his rights to commit, it becomes immediately apparent that the defence does not depend on the immediacy or "normative involuntariness" of the accused's act unless, of course, the involuntariness is such as to be pertinent to the ordinary analysis of *mens rea*. The fact that one act is done out of a sense of immediacy or urgency and another after some contemplation cannot, in my view, serve to distinguish the quality of the act in terms of right or wrong. Rather, the justification must be premised on the need to fulfil a duty conflicting with the one which the accused is charged with having breached.

… [In] some circumstances defence counsel may be able to point to a conflicting duty which courts can and do recognize. For example, one may break the law in circumstances where it is necessary to rescue someone to whom one owes a positive duty of rescue (see *R. v. Walker* (1979), 48 C.C.C. (2d) 126, 5 M.V.R. 114 (Ont. Co. Ct.)), since failure to act in such a situation may itself constitute a culpable act or omission: see *R. v. Instan*, [1893] 1 Q.B. 450. Similarly, if one subscribes to the viewpoint articulated by Laskin C.J.C. in *Morgentaler*, *supra*, and perceives a doctor's defence to an abortion charge as his legal obligation to treat the mother rather than his alleged ethical duty to perform an unauthorized abortion, then the defence may be invoked without violating the prohibition enunciated by Dickson J. in *Morgentaler* against choosing a non-legal duty over a legal one … .

Accordingly, where necessity is invoked as a justification for violation of the law, the justification must, in my view, be restricted to situations where the accused's act constitutes the discharge of a duty recognized by law. The justification is not, however, established simply by showing a conflict of legal duties. The rule of proportionality is central to the evaluation of a justification premised on two conflicting duties since the defence rests on the rightfulness of the accused's choice of one over the other.

As the facts before the court in the present case do not involve a conflict of legal duties it is unnecessary to discuss in detail how a court should go about assessing the relative extent of two evils. Suffice it to say that any such assessment must respect the notion of right upon which justification is based. The assessment cannot entail a mere utilitarian calculation of, for example, lives saved and deaths avoided in the aggregate but must somehow attempt to come to grips with the nature of the rights and duties being assessed. This would seem to be consistent with Lord Coleridge's conclusion that necessity can provide no justification for the taking of a life, such an act representing the most extreme form of rights violation. As discussed above, if any defence for such a homicidal act is to succeed, it would have to be framed as an excuse grounded on self-preservation. It could not possibly be declared by the court to be rightful. By contrast, the justification analysis would seem to support those cases in which fulfilment of the legal duty to save persons entrusted to one's care is preferred over the lesser offences of trespass or petty theft: see *Mouse's Case* (1608), 12 Co. Rep. 63, 77 E.R. 1341; *Amiens, Ch. corr., April 22, 1898*, S. 1899.2.1 (*Ménard's Case*). The crucial question for the justification defence is whether the accused's act can be said to represent a furtherance of or a detraction from the principle of the universality of rights.

*Appeals dismissed.*

---

While the view of Chief Justice Dickson undoubtedly establishes necessity as an excuse, as opposed to a justification, the view of Justice Wilson that, in the case of conflicting legal duties, necessity might be conceptualized as a justification, was adopted in the case of *Re A (Children) (Conjoined Twins: Surgical Separation)*, [2000] 4 All E.R. 961 (C.A.). In that case, the Court of Appeal decided that an operation to separate conjoined infant twins, absent their parents' consent, was lawful and justified on the basis of the defence of necessity. Because there was no imminent peril, as contemplated in *Perka*, the court found Justice Wilson's justification analysis, which does not necessarily require an emergency, to be more appealing.

## III. NECESSITY AND THE LATIMER CASE

**Latimer v. The Queen**
Supreme Court of Canada
[2001] 1 S.C.R. 3

BY THE COURT:

[1] This appeal arises from the death of Tracy Latimer, a 12-year-old girl who had a severe form of cerebral palsy. Her father, Robert Latimer, took her life some seven years ago. He was found guilty of second degree murder. This appeal deals with three questions of law arising from his trial. First, did the trial judge mishandle the defence of necessity, resulting in an unfair trial? Second, was the trial unfair because the trial judge misled the jury into believing it would have some input into the appropriate sentence? Third, does the imposition of the mandatory minimum sentence for second degree murder constitute "cruel and unusual punishment" in this case, so that Mr. Latimer ("the appellant") should receive a constitutional exemption from the minimum sentence?

[2] We conclude that the answer to all three questions is no. The defence of necessity is narrow and of limited application in criminal law. In this case, there was no air of reality to that defence. The trial judge was correct to conclude that the jury should not consider necessity. While the timing of the removal of this defence from the jury's consideration was later in the trial than usual, it did not render the appellant's trial unfair or violate his constitutional rights. On the second issue, the trial judge did not prejudice the appellant's rights in replying to a question from the jury on whether it could offer input on sentencing. In answer to the third question, we conclude that the mandatory minimum sentence for second degree murder in this case does not amount to cruel and unusual punishment within the meaning of s. 12 of the *Canadian Charter of Rights and Freedoms*. The test for what amounts to "cruel and unusual punishment" is a demanding one, and the appellant has not succeeded in showing that the sentence in his case is "grossly disproportionate" to the punishment required for the most serious crime known to law, murder.

[3] We conclude that Mr. Latimer's conviction and sentence of life in prison with a mandatory minimum of 10 years' imprisonment for second degree murder should be upheld. This means that the appellant will not be eligible for parole consideration for 10 years, unless the executive elects to exercise the power to grant him clemency from this sentence, using the royal prerogative of mercy. The Court's role is to determine the questions of law that arise in this appeal; the matter of executive clemency remains in the realm of the executive, and it is discussed later in these reasons.

[4] The law has a long history of difficult cases. We recognize the questions that arise in Mr. Latimer's case are the sort that have divided Canadians and sparked a national discourse. This judgment will not end that discourse.

[5] Mr. Latimer perceived his daughter and family to be in a difficult and trying situation. It is apparent from the evidence in this case that he faced challenges of the sort most Canadians can only imagine. His care of his daughter for many years was

admirable. His decision to end his daughter's life was an error in judgment. The taking of another life represents the most serious crime in our criminal law.

## I. Facts

[6] The appellant, Robert Latimer, farmed in Wilkie, Saskatchewan. His 12-year-old daughter, Tracy, suffered a severe form of cerebral palsy. She was quadriplegic and her physical condition rendered her immobile. She was bedridden for much of the time. Her condition was a permanent one, caused by neurological damage at the time of her birth. Tracy was said to have the mental capacity of a four-month-old baby, and she could communicate only by means of facial expressions, laughter and crying. She was completely dependent on others for her care. Tracy suffered seizures despite the medication she took. It was thought she experienced a great deal of pain, and the pain could not be reduced by medication since the pain medication conflicted with her anti-epileptic medication and her difficulty in swallowing. Tracy experienced five to six seizures daily. She had to be spoon-fed, and her lack of nutrients caused weight loss.

[7] There was evidence that Tracy could have been fed with a feeding tube into her stomach, an option that would have improved her nutrition and health, and that might also have allowed for more effective pain medication to be administered. The Latimers rejected the feeding-tube option as being intrusive and as representing the first step on a path to preserving Tracy's life artificially.

[8] Tracy had a serious disability, but she was not terminally ill. Her doctors anticipated that she would have to undergo repeated surgeries, her breathing difficulties had increased, but her life was not in its final stages.

[9] Tracy enjoyed music, bonfires, being with her family and the circus. She liked to play music on a radio, which she could use with a special button. Tracy could apparently recognize family members and she would express joy at seeing them. Tracy also loved being rocked gently by her parents.

[10] Tracy underwent numerous surgeries in her short lifetime. In 1990, surgery tried to balance the muscles around her pelvis. In 1992, it was used to reduce the abnormal curvature in her back.

[11] Like the majority of totally involved, quadriparetic children with cerebral palsy, Tracy had developed scoliosis, an abnormal curvature and rotation in the back, necessitating surgery to implant metal rods to support her spine. While it was a successful procedure, further problems developed in Tracy's right hip: it became dislocated and caused her considerable pain.

[12] Tracy was scheduled to undergo further surgery on November 19, 1993. This was to deal with her dislocated hip and, it was hoped, to lessen her constant pain. The procedure involved removing her upper thigh bone, which would leave her lower leg loose without any connecting bone; it would be held in place only by muscle and tissue. The anticipated recovery period for this surgery was one year.

[13] The Latimers were told that this procedure would cause pain, and the doctors involved suggested that further surgery would be required in the future to relieve the pain emanating from various joints in Tracy's body. According to the appellant's

wife, Laura Latimer, further surgery was perceived as mutilation. As a result, Robert Latimer formed the view that his daughter's life was not worth living.

[14] In the weeks leading up to Tracy's death, the Latimers looked into the option of placing Tracy in a group home in North Battleford. She had lived there between July and October of 1993, just prior to her death, while her mother was pregnant. The Latimers applied to place Tracy in the home in October, but later concluded they were not interested in permanently placing her in that home at that time.

[15] On October 12, 1993, after learning that the doctors wished to perform this additional surgery, the appellant decided to take his daughter's life. On Sunday, October 24, 1993, while his wife and Tracy's siblings were at church, Robert Latimer carried Tracy to his pickup truck, seated her in the cab, and inserted a hose from the truck's exhaust pipe into the cab. She died from the carbon monoxide.

[16] The police conducted an autopsy and discovered carbon monoxide in her blood. The appellant at first maintained that Tracy simply passed away in her sleep. He later confessed to having taken her life, and gave a statement to the investigating police and partially re-enacted his actions on videotape. Mr. Latimer also told police that he had considered giving Tracy an overdose of Valium, or "shooting her in the head."

[17] Mr. Latimer has been convicted of murder twice in this case. He was initially charged with first degree murder and convicted by a jury of second degree murder. The Court of Appeal for Saskatchewan upheld his conviction and life sentence with no eligibility for parole for 10 years, with Bayda C.J.S. dissenting on the sentence: *R. v. Latimer* (1995), 99 C.C.C. (3d) 481 ("*Latimer (No. 1)*"). The case was then appealed to this Court: [1997] 1 S.C.R. 217. It turned out that the prosecutor had interfered with the jury selection process. The Crown conceded that a new trial could not be avoided. In the second trial, Mr. Latimer was again convicted of second degree murder, and it is from that conviction that this appeal arises.

[18] During the second trial, two things occurred that, the appellant submits, resulted in an unfair trial. First, as counsel were about to make closing addresses to the jury, defence counsel asked the trial judge for a ruling on whether the jury could consider the defence of necessity. He wanted this ruling in advance of his closing submissions, since he planned to tailor his address to the judge's ruling. The trial judge, however, refused to make any ruling until *after* hearing counsel's closing addresses. Defence counsel made submissions, including some on the necessity defence. When counsel had concluded their addresses, the trial judge ruled that the jury was *not* entitled to consider necessity.

[19] Second, some time after beginning their deliberations, the jury sent a number of written questions to the trial judge, one of which was: "Is there any possible way we can have input to a recommendation for sentencing?" The trial judge told the jury it was not to concern itself with the penalty. He said:

> … the penalty in any of these charges is not the concern of the jury. Your concern is, as I said, the guilt or innocence of the accused, and you must reach—that's your job, you reach that conclusion, and don't concern yourself what the penalty might be. We say that because we don't want you to be influenced one way or the other with what that

*penalty is. So it may be that later on, once you have reached a verdict, you—we will have some discussions about that, but not at this stage of the game.* You must just carry on and answer the question that was put to you, okay.

The appellant highlights the [italicized] passage as misleading the jury.

[20] After the jury returned with a guilty verdict, the trial judge explained the mandatory minimum sentence of life imprisonment, and asked the jury whether it had any recommendation as to whether Mr. Latimer's ineligibility for parole should exceed the minimum period of 10 years. Some jury members appeared upset, according to the trial judge, and later sent a note asking him if they could recommend less than the 10-year minimum. The trial judge explained that the *Criminal Code* provided only for a recommendation over the 10-year minimum, but suggested that the jury could make any recommendation it liked. The jury recommended one year before parole eligibility. The trial judge then granted a constitutional exemption from the mandatory minimum sentence, sentencing the appellant to one year of imprisonment and one year on probation, to be spent confined to his farm.

[21] The Court of Appeal for Saskatchewan affirmed Mr. Latimer's conviction but reversed the sentence. It imposed the mandatory minimum sentence for second degree murder of life imprisonment without eligibility for parole for 10 years. ...

### III. Judicial History

[23] Mr. Latimer was tried by jury, during the course of which the trial judge made two rulings (besides his handling of the jury's inquiry as to sentence) that are at issue in this appeal. First, as previously outlined, he held that the jury was not entitled to consider the defence of necessity. Second, the trial judge granted a constitutional exemption from the mandatory minimum sentence for second degree murder: (1997), 121 C.C.C. (3d) 326 (Sask. Q.B.). The trial judge concluded that the mandatory sentence amounted to cruel and unusual punishment in this case. He reasoned that the exemption was a valid and appropriate remedy, given the particular circumstances of this offender, his motives, the public reaction to the mandatory sentence in Mr. Latimer's first trial, and his reduced level of criminal culpability.

[24] The Court of Appeal for Saskatchewan dismissed the appeal from conviction in a *per curiam* decision: (1998), 131 C.C.C. (3d) 191. The trial judge was correct to remove the defence of necessity from the jury, the Court of Appeal held, and the timing of the trial judge's ruling did not result in an unfair trial. The court reversed the trial judge's remedy of a constitutional exemption, commenting, at p. 216, that "the learned trial judge took too much upon himself in bypassing the judgment of this Court, the direction of Parliament, and the executive power of clemency." The Court of Appeal concluded that Mr. Latimer must serve the mandatory 10-year sentence before parole eligibility. ...

*(1)  The Availability of the Defence of Necessity*

(a)  The Three Requirements for the Defence of Necessity

[26]  We propose to set out the requirements for the defence of necessity first, before applying them to the facts of this appeal. The leading case on the defence of necessity is *Perka v. The Queen*, [1984] 2 S.C.R. 232. Dickson J., later C.J., outlined the rationale for the defence at p. 248:

> It rests on a realistic assessment of human weakness, recognizing that a liberal and humane criminal law cannot hold people to the strict obedience of laws in emergency situations where normal human instincts, whether of self-preservation or of altruism, overwhelmingly impel disobedience. The objectivity of the criminal law is preserved; such acts are still wrongful, but in the circumstances they are excusable. Praise is indeed not bestowed, but pardon is. …

[27]  Dickson J. insisted that the defence of necessity be restricted to those rare cases in which true "involuntariness" is present. The defence, he held, must be "strictly controlled and scrupulously limited" (p. 250). It is well-established that the defence of necessity must be of limited application. Were the criteria for the defence loosened or approached purely subjectively, some fear, as did Edmund Davies L.J., that necessity would "very easily become simply a mask for anarchy": *Southwark London Borough Council v. Williams*, [1971] Ch. 734 (C.A.), at p. 746.

[28]  *Perka* outlined three elements that must be present for the defence of necessity. First, there is the requirement of imminent peril or danger. Second, the accused must have had no reasonable legal alternative to the course of action he or she undertook. Third, there must be proportionality between the harm inflicted and the harm avoided.

[29]  To begin, there must be an urgent situation of "clear and imminent peril": *Morgentaler v. The Queen*, [1976] 1 S.C.R. 616, at p. 678. In short, disaster must be imminent, or harm unavoidable and near. It is not enough that the peril is foreseeable or likely; it must be on the verge of transpiring and virtually certain to occur. In *Perka*, Dickson J. expressed the requirement of imminent peril at p. 251: "At a minimum the situation must be so emergent and the peril must be so pressing that normal human instincts cry out for action and make a counsel of patience unreasonable." The *Perka* case, at p. 251, also offers the rationale for this requirement of immediate peril: "The requirement … tests whether it was indeed unavoidable for the actor to act at all." Where the situation of peril clearly should have been foreseen and avoided, an accused person cannot reasonably claim any immediate peril.

[30]  The second requirement for necessity is that there must be no reasonable legal alternative to disobeying the law. *Perka* proposed these questions, at pp. 251-52: "Given that the accused had to act, could he nevertheless realistically have acted to avoid the peril or prevent the harm, without breaking the law? *Was there a legal way out?*" (emphasis in original). If there was a reasonable legal alternative to breaking the law, there is no necessity. It may be noted that the requirement involves a realistic appreciation of the alternatives open to a person; the accused need not be placed in the last resort imaginable, but he must have no reasonable legal alternative.

If an alternative to breaking the law exists, the defence of necessity on this aspect fails.

[31] The third requirement is that there be proportionality between the harm inflicted and the harm avoided. The harm inflicted must not be disproportionate to the harm the accused sought to avoid. See *Perka, per* Dickson J., at p. 252:

> No rational criminal justice system, no matter how humane or liberal, could excuse the infliction of a greater harm to allow the actor to avert a lesser evil. In such circumstances we expect the individual to bear the harm and refrain from acting illegally. If he cannot control himself we will not excuse him.

Evaluating proportionality can be difficult. It may be easy to conclude that there is no proportionality in some cases, like the example given in *Perka* of the person who blows up a city to avoid breaking a finger. Where proportionality can quickly be dismissed, it makes sense for a trial judge to do so and rule out the defence of necessity before considering the other requirements for necessity. But most situations fall into a grey area that requires a difficult balancing of harms. In this regard, it should be noted that the requirement is not that one harm (the harm avoided) must always clearly outweigh the other (the harm inflicted). Rather, the two harms must, at a minimum, be of a comparable gravity. That is, the harm avoided must be either comparable to, or clearly greater than, the harm inflicted. As the Supreme Court of Victoria in Australia has put it, the harm inflicted "must not be out of proportion to the peril to be avoided": *R. v. Loughnan*, [1981] V.R. 443, at p. 448.

[32] Before applying the three requirements of the necessity defence to the facts of this case, we need to determine what test governs necessity. Is the standard objective or subjective? A subjective test would be met if the person believed he or she was in imminent peril with no reasonable legal alternative to committing the offence. Conversely, an objective test would not assess what the accused believed; it would consider whether in fact the person *was* in peril with no reasonable legal alternative. A modified objective test falls somewhere between the two. It involves an objective evaluation, but one that takes into account the situation and characteristics of the particular accused person. We conclude that, for two of the three requirements for the necessity defence, the test should be the modified objective test.

[33] The first and second requirements—imminent peril and no reasonable legal alternative—must be evaluated on the modified objective standard described above. As expressed in *Perka*, necessity is rooted in an objective standard: "involuntariness is measured on the basis of society's expectation of appropriate and normal resistance to pressure" (p. 259). We would add that it is appropriate, in evaluating the accused's conduct, to take into account personal characteristics that legitimately affect what may be expected of that person. The approach taken in *R. v. Hibbert*, [1995] 2 S.C.R. 973, is instructive. Speaking for the Court, Lamer C.J. held, at para. 59, that:

> it is appropriate to employ an objective standard that takes into account the particular circumstances of the accused, including his or her ability to perceive the existence of alternative courses of action.

While an accused's perceptions of the surrounding facts may be highly relevant in determining whether his conduct should be excused, those perceptions remain relevant only so long as they are reasonable. The accused person must, at the time of the act, honestly believe, on reasonable grounds, that he faces a situation of imminent peril that leaves no reasonable legal alternative open. There must be a reasonable basis for the accused's beliefs and actions, but it would be proper to take into account circumstances that legitimately affect the accused person's ability to evaluate his situation. The test cannot be a subjective one, and the accused who argues that *he* perceived imminent peril without an alternative would only succeed with the defence of necessity if his belief was reasonable given his circumstances and attributes. We leave aside for a case in which it arises the possibility that an honestly held but mistaken belief could ground a "mistake of fact" argument on the separate inquiry into *mens rea*.

[34] The third requirement for the defence of necessity, proportionality, must be measured on an objective standard, as it would violate fundamental principles of the criminal law to do otherwise. Evaluating the nature of an act is fundamentally a determination reflecting society's values as to what is appropriate and what represents a transgression. Some insight into this requirement is provided by George Fletcher, in a passage from *Rethinking Criminal Law* (1978), at p. 804. Fletcher spoke of the comparison between the harm inflicted and the harm avoided, and suggested that there was a threshold at which a person must be expected to suffer the harm rather than break the law. He continued:

> Determining this threshold is patently a matter of moral judgment about what we expect people to be able to resist in trying situations. A valuable aid in making that judgment is comparing the competing interests at stake and assessing the degree to which the actor inflicts harm beyond the benefit that accrues from his action.

The evaluation of the seriousness of the harms must be objective. A subjective evaluation of the competing harms would, by definition, look at the matter from the perspective of the accused person who seeks to avoid harm, usually to himself. The proper perspective, however, is an objective one, since evaluating the gravity of the act is a matter of community standards infused with constitutional considerations (such as, in this case, the s. 15(1) equality rights of the disabled). We conclude that the proportionality requirement must be determined on a purely objective standard.

(b)  The Application of the Requirements for Necessity in This Case

[35] The inquiry here is not whether the defence of necessity should in fact *excuse* Mr. Latimer's actions, but whether the jury should have been left to consider this defence. The correct test on that point is whether there is an air of reality to the defence. In *R. v. Osolin*, [1993] 4 S.C.R. 595, at p. 676, Cory J. stated:

> … a defence should not be put to the jury if a reasonable jury properly instructed would have been unable to acquit on the basis of the evidence tendered in support of that defence. On the other hand, if a reasonable jury properly instructed could acquit on the basis of the evidence tendered with regard to that defence, then it must be put to the

jury. It is for the trial judge to decide whether the evidence is sufficient to warrant putting a defence to a jury as this is a question of law alone.

The question is whether there is sufficient evidence that, if believed, would allow a reasonable jury—properly charged and acting judicially—to conclude that the defence applied and acquit the accused.

[36]  For the necessity defence, the trial judge must be satisfied that there is evidence sufficient to give an air of reality to each of the three requirements. If the trial judge concludes that there is no air of reality to any one of the three requirements, the defence of necessity should not be left to the jury.

[37]  In this case, there was no air of reality to the three requirements of necessity.

[38]  The first requirement is imminent peril. It is not met in this case. The appellant does not suggest he himself faced any peril; instead he identifies a peril to his daughter, stemming from her upcoming surgery which he perceived as a form of mutilation. Acute suffering can constitute imminent peril, but in this case there was nothing to her medical condition that placed Tracy in a dangerous situation where death was an alternative. Tracy was thought to be in pain before the surgery, and that pain was expected to continue, or increase, following the surgery. But that ongoing pain did not constitute an emergency in this case. To borrow the language of Edmund Davies L.J. in *Southwark London Borough Council*, *supra*, at p. 746, we are dealing not with an emergency but with "an obstinate and long-standing state of affairs." Tracy's proposed surgery did not pose an imminent threat to her life, nor did her medical condition. In fact, Tracy's health might have improved had the Latimers not rejected the option of relying on a feeding tube. Tracy's situation was not an emergency. The appellant can be reasonably expected to have understood that reality. There was no evidence of a legitimate psychological condition that rendered him unable to perceive that there was no imminent peril. The appellant argued that, for him, further surgery *did* amount to imminent peril. It was not reasonable for the appellant to form this belief, particularly when better pain management was available.

[39]  The second requirement for the necessity defence is that the accused had no reasonable legal alternative to breaking the law. In this case, there is no air of reality to the proposition that the appellant had no reasonable legal alternative to killing his daughter. He had at least one reasonable legal alternative: he could have struggled on, with what was unquestionably a difficult situation, by helping Tracy to live and by minimizing her pain as much as possible. The appellant might have done so by using a feeding tube to improve her health and allow her to take more effective pain medication, or he might have relied on the group home that Tracy stayed at just before her death. The appellant may well have thought the prospect of struggling on unbearably sad and demanding. It was a human response that this alternative was unappealing. But it was a reasonable legal alternative that the law requires a person to pursue before he can claim the defence of necessity. The appellant was aware of this alternative but rejected it.

[40]  The third requirement for the necessity defence is proportionality; it requires the trial judge to consider, as a question of law rather than fact, whether the harm avoided was proportionate to the harm inflicted. It is difficult, at the conceptual level,

to imagine a circumstance in which the proportionality requirement could be met for a homicide. We leave open, if and until it arises, the question of whether the proportionality requirement could be met in a homicide situation. In England, the defence of necessity is probably not available for homicide: *R. v. Howe*, [1987] 1 A.C. 417 (H.L.), at pp. 453 and 429; Smith and Hogan, *Criminal Law* (9th ed. 1999), at pp. 249-51. The famous case of *R. v. Dudley and Stephens* (1884), 14 Q.B.D. 273, involving cannibalism on the high seas, is often cited as establishing the unavailability of the defence of necessity for homicide, although the case is not conclusive: see Card, Cross and Jones, *Criminal Law* (12th ed. 1992), at p. 352; Smith and Hogan, *supra*, at pp. 249 and 251. The Law Reform Commission of Canada has suggested the defence should not be available for a person who intentionally kills or seriously harms another person: *Report on Recodifying Criminal Law* (1987), at p. 36. American jurisdictions are divided on this question, with a number of them denying the necessity defence for murder: P. H. Robinson, *Criminal Law Defenses* (1984), vol. 2, at pp. 63-65; see also *United States v. Holmes*, 26 F. Cas. 360 (C.C.E.D. Pa. 1842) (No. 15,383). The American *Model Penal Code* proposes that the defence of necessity *would* be available for homicide: American Law Institute, *Model Penal Code and Commentaries* (1985), at §3.02, pp. 14-15; see also W.R. LaFave and A.W. Scott, *Substantive Criminal Law* (1986), vol. 1, at p. 634.

[41] Assuming for the sake of analysis only that necessity could provide a defence to homicide, there would have to be a harm that was seriously comparable in gravity to death (the harm inflicted). In this case, there was no risk of such harm. The "harm avoided" in the appellant's situation was, compared to death, completely disproportionate. The harm inflicted in this case was ending a life; that harm was immeasurably more serious than the pain resulting from Tracy's operation which Mr. Latimer sought to avoid. Killing a person—in order to relieve the suffering produced by a medically manageable physical or mental condition—is not a proportionate response to the harm represented by the non-life-threatening suffering resulting from that condition.

[42] We conclude that there was no air of reality to *any* of the three requirements for necessity. As noted earlier, if the trial judge concludes that even one of the requirements had no air of reality, the defence should not be left to the jury. Here, the trial judge was correct to remove the defence from the jury. In considering the defence of necessity, we must remain aware of the need to respect the life, dignity and equality of all the individuals affected by the act in question. The fact that the victim in this case was disabled rather than able-bodied does not affect our conclusion that the three requirements for the defence of necessity had no air of reality here. ... Mr. Latimer's appeals against conviction and sentence are dismissed.

---

Note that Latimer's sentence appeal and the court's holding that the mandatory minimum sentence of life imprisonment with no eligibility for parole for 10 years did not violate the right against cruel and unusual punishment under s. 12 of the Charter will be discussed in chapter 21.

*Latimer* has attracted much popular and academic attention. For instance, see K. Roach, "Crime and Punishment in the Latimer Case" (2001), 64 *Sask. L. Rev.* 469; G.T. Trotter, "Necessity and Death: Lessons from Latimer and the Case of the Conjoined Twins" (2003), 40 *Alta. L. Rev.* 817; A. Manson, "Motivation, the Supreme Court and Mandatory Sentencing for Murder" (2001), 39 C.R. (5th) 65; B. Sneiderman, "R. v. Latimer: Juries and Mandatory Penalties" (2001), 39 C.R. (5th) 29; and D. Stuart, "A Hard Case Makes for Too Harsh Law" (2001), 39 C.R. (5th) 58.

## IV.  NECESSITY AND CODIFICATION

The A.L.I. Model Penal Code provides in s. 3.02:

(1) Conduct which the actor believes to be necessary to avoid a harm or evil to himself or to another is justifiable, provided that:

(a) the harm or evil sought to be avoided by such conduct is greater than that sought to be prevented by the law defining the offense charged; and

(b) neither the Code nor other law defining the offense provides exceptions or defenses dealing with the specific situation involved; and

(c) a legislative purpose to exclude the justification claimed does not otherwise plainly appear.

(2) When the actor was reckless or negligent in bringing about the situation requiring a choice of harms or evils or in appraising the necessity for his conduct, the justification afforded by this Section is unavailable in a prosecution for any offense for which recklessness or negligence, as the case may be, suffices to establish culpability.

Law Reform Commission of Canada, Report #31 (1987), *Recodifying Criminal Law*, at p. 36:

3(9) Necessity.

(a) General Rule. No one is liable if:

(i) he acted to avoid immediate harm to the person or immediate serious damage to property;

(ii) such harm or damage substantially outweighed the harm or damage resulting from that crime; and

(iii) such harm or damage could not effectively have been avoided by any lesser means.

(b) Exception. This clause does not apply to anyone who himself purposely causes the death of, or seriously harms, another person.

Comment

The duty to obey the law may conflict with pressure stemming from natural forces or from some other source not covered by the more specific defences known to law. Such cases may be covered by the residual defence of necessity. Though not included in the present *Criminal Code*, it is well recognized by case-law and has been clarified by the Supreme Court of Canada. For the sake of comprehensiveness, clause 3(9) incorporates and codifies the rule laid down there.

The application of the defence in any given case involves a judgment call. The trier of fact must consider whether the harm to be avoided was immediate; necessity relates only to emergencies. He must decide whether the harm avoided substantially outweighed the harm done, once again a matter for assessment.

At common law it was clear that necessity was no defence to murder. This Code replaces that restriction with a more general one parallel to that used in duress and based on the same principle. The defence will not therefore avail one who himself purposely causes the death of, or seriously harms, another person.

The Sub-Committee of the Standing Committee on Justice and the Solicitor-General on the General Part of the Criminal Code stated in its Report of February 1993:

> The Law Reform Commission also proposed that the defence not be available to someone who caused bodily harm or death. The Commission reasoned that no one should harm or kill another person in order to save himself or herself. While it is sympathetic to this reasoning, the Sub-Committee would prefer not to put an express limitation on the actions that could be taken in necessitous circumstances. Such a limit may prove to be arbitrary and unjust.

The June 1993 *Federal Proposals to Amend the General Principles of the Criminal Code* provides that s. 17 should be repealed and the following section added to the *Criminal Code*:

> 36.(1) A person is not guilty of an offence, other than murder, to the extent that the person acts under
>> (a) duress of circumstances; or
>> (b) duress by threats.
>
> (2) A person acts under duress of circumstances if, otherwise than under duress by threats as described in subsection (3) or in defence of a person as described in section 37,
>> (a) the person acts to avoid what the person believes to be significant danger of imminent and otherwise unavoidable death or serious bodily harm to that person or another person,
>> (b) the person's acts are proportionate to the harm that the person seeks to avoid, and
>> (c) the person cannot reasonably be expected to act otherwise in response to the danger that the person believes to exist,
>
> but the defence of duress of circumstances is not available if the person, knowingly and without reasonable excuse, exposed themself to the danger.
>
> (3) A person acts under duress by threats if
>> (a) the person acts in compliance with what the person believes to be a threat made to the person, that the person believes will be carried out, of imminent and otherwise unavoidable death or serious bodily harm to that person or another person,
>> (b) the person's acts are proportionate to the harm that the person seeks to avoid, and
>> (c) the person cannot reasonably be expected to resist the threat that the person believes to exist,
>
> but the defence of duress by threats is not available if the person, knowingly and without reasonable excuse, exposed themself to the risk that the threat would be made.

ADDITIONAL READING

- K. Roach, *Criminal Law*, 3rd ed. (Toronto: Irwin Law, 2004), chapter 8;
- D. Stuart, *Canadian Criminal Law*, 4th ed. (Toronto: Carswell, 2001), at 512-33;
- E. Colvin, *Principles of Criminal Law*, 2nd ed. (Toronto: Carswell, 1991), at 238-49;
- P. Schabas, "Justification, Excuse and the Defence of Necessity: A Comment on *Perka v. The Queen*" (1984-85), 27 *Crim. L.Q.* 278;
- A. Brudner, "A Theory of Necessity" (1987), 7 *Oxford J. of Legal Studies* 339;
- E. Morgan, "The Defence of Necessity: Justification or Excuse?" (1984), 42 *U.T. Fac. L. Rev.* 165;
- D.W. Elliot, "Necessity, Duress and Self-Defence," [1989] *Crim. L. Rev.* 611.

# CHAPTER NINETEEN

# Duress

Duress in Canada is an extremely complicated defence. It is codified in s. 17 of the *Criminal Code*.

> 17. A person who commits an offence under compulsion by threats of immediate death or bodily harm from a person who is present when the offence is committed is excused for committing the offence if the person believes that the threats will be carried out and if the person is not a party to a conspiracy or association whereby the person is subject to compulsion, but this section does not apply where the offence that is committed is high treason or treason, murder, piracy, attempted murder, sexual assault, sexual assault with a weapon, threats to a third party or causing bodily harm, aggravated sexual assault, forcible abduction, hostage taking, robbery, assault with a weapon or causing bodily harm, aggravated assault, unlawfully causing bodily harm, arson or an offence under sections 280 to 283 (abduction and detention of young persons).

The Supreme Court in *Paquette v. The Queen* (1976), 30 C.C.C. (2d) 417 held that this restrictive codification of the defence of duress applied only to persons who actually committed the offence as principal offenders and indicated that a common law or judge-made defence of duress applied to those who committed the offence as a party to the offence. In cases where it was not clear whether an accused had acted as a principal offender or was a party to the offence, the trial judge would have to instruct the jury about both the statutory defence of duress in s. 17 of the *Criminal Code* and the common law defence of duress. The jury would have to decide whether the accused committed the offence (apply s. 17) or was a party to the offence (apply the common law). If an air of reality was established for either defence, the Crown must disprove the existence of the defence of duress beyond a reasonable doubt.

Another complicating factor is that circumstances of duress might raise a reasonable doubt about whether the accused had some forms of subjective *mens rea* or fault. The Supreme Court in *R. v. Hibbert* (1995), 99 C.C.C. (3d) 193, however, narrowed the relevance of duress to *mens rea* by holding that duress could not negate the intent required to be a party to a crime under ss. 21(1)(b) and 21(2) of the *Criminal Code*.

To make matters even more complicated, the Supreme Court has recently held in *R. v. Ruzic*, [2001] 1 S.C.R. 687 that parts of the restrictive statutory defence of duress— namely, the requirements of a threat of *immediate* death or bodily harm from a person who is *present* when the offence is committed—violates s. 7 of the Charter. These parts of s. 17 of the *Criminal Code* violated s. 7 of the Charter because they allow the conviction of a person who commits a crime in a morally involuntary manner. Thus the references to *immediate* death or bodily harm and a threat from a person who is *present* when the offence was committed have been declared of no force and effect and severed from s. 17. In *Ruzic*, the Supreme Court left open the constitutionality of the offences that are categorically excluded under s. 17 from the defence of duress.

Although the defence of duress is complicated, its study will serve as a useful review of many different elements of criminal law. The first section of this chapter examines the common law defence of duress that applies to parties to an offence. The second part examines whether duress can raise a reasonable doubt or negate some fault requirements. The third section examines whether the statutory defence of duress in s. 17 violates s. 7 of the Charter. The next section briefly explores offences excluded from the duress defence. The final section outlines some proposals for parliamentary reform of the duress defence.

## I. THE COMMON LAW DEFENCE OF DURESS

### Paquette v. The Queen
Supreme Court of Canada
(1976), 30 C.C.C. (2d) 417

MARTLAND J. (for the Court): The facts which give rise to this appeal are as follows: During the course of a robbery at the Pop Shoppe, in the City of Ottawa, on March 18, 1973, an innocent bystander was killed by a bullet from a rifle fired by one Simard. The robbery was committed by Simard and one Clermont, both of whom, together with the appellant, were jointly charged with non-capital murder. Simard and Clermont pleaded guilty to this charge.

The appellant was not present when the robbery was committed or when the shooting occurred. The charge against him was founded upon s. 21(2) of the *Criminal Code*.

The appellant made a statement to the police, which was admitted in evidence at the trial and which described his involvement in the matter as follows: On the day of the robbery Clermont telephoned the appellant for a ride as his own car was broken. Clermont asked the appellant where he used to work and was told at the Pop Shoppe. Clermont told him to drive to the Pop Shoppe because Clermont wanted to rob it, and, when the appellant refused, Clermont pulled his gun and threatened to kill him. Simard was picked up later and also a rifle. The appellant drove them to the Pop Shoppe. The appellant had been threatened with revenge if he did not wait for Clermont and Simard. The appellant, in his statement, stated he was afraid and drove around the block. After the robbery and homicide Clermont and Simard attempted twice, unsuccessfully, to get into the appellant's car. Three of the Crown's witnesses supported this later statement.

The trial judge charged the jury as follows:

Now, the defence are asserting Paquette participated in this robbery because he was compelled to do so, and in that connection I charge you that if Paquette joined in the common plot to rob the Pop Shoppe under threats of death or grievous bodily harm, that would negative his having a common intention with Simard to rob the Pop Shoppe, and you must find Paquette not guilty.

The appellant was acquitted. The Crown appealed to the Court of Appeal for Ontario. The reasons delivered by that Court make it clear that the appeal would have been dismissed had it not been for the decision of this Court in *Dunbar v. The King* (1936), 67 C.C.C. 20; [1936] 4 D.L.R. 737 [which had held that duress was an issue of motive which does not negate intent under s. 21(2) of the *Criminal Code.*] ...

Counsel for the Crown submits that the principles of law applicable to the excuse or defence of duress or compulsion are exhaustively codified in s. 17 of the *Criminal Code*, and that the appellant is precluded from relying upon this provision because of the exception contained at the end of it.

In my opinion the application of s. 17 is limited to cases in which the person seeking to rely upon it has himself committed an offence. If a person who actually commits the offence does so in the presence of another party who has compelled him to do the act by threats of immediate death or grievous bodily harm, then, if he believes the threats would be carried out, and is not a party to a conspiracy whereby he is subject to such compulsion, he is excused for committing the offence. The protection afforded by this section is not given in respect of the offences listed at the end of the section, which include murder and robbery.

The section uses the specific words "a person who commits an offence." It does not use the words "a person who is a party to an offence." This is significant in the light of the wording of s. 21(1) which, in paragraph (a), makes a person a party to an offence who "actually commits it." Paragraphs (b) and (c) deal with a person who aids or abets a person committing the offence. In my opinion s. 17 codifies the law as to duress as an excuse for the actual commission of a crime, but it does not, by its terms, go beyond that. *R. v. Carker*, [1967] S.C.R. 114, in which reference was made to s. 17 having codified the defence or excuse of duress, dealt with a situation in which the accused had actually committed the offence.

The appellant, in the present case, did not himself commit the offence of robbery or of murder. ...

[T]he appellant is entitled, by virtue of s. 7(3) of the *Code*, to rely upon any excuse or defence available to him at common law. The defence of duress to a charge of murder against a person who did not commit the murder, but who was alleged to have aided and abetted, was recently considered by the House of Lords in *Director of Public Prosecutions for Northern Ireland v. Lynch*, [1975] A.C. 653, in which the decided cases were fully reviewed. The facts in that case were as follows:

The defendant drove a motor car containing a group of the I.R.A. in Northern Ireland on an expedition in which they shot and killed a police officer. On his trial for aiding and abetting the murder there was evidence that he was not a member of the I.R.A. and that he acted unwillingly under the orders of the leader of the group, being convinced that, if he disobeyed, he would himself be shot. The trial judge held that the defence of

duress was not available to him and the jury found him guilty. The Court of Criminal
Appeal in Northern Ireland upheld the conviction.

The House of Lords, by a 3 to 2 majority, held that on a charge of murder the
defence of duress was open to a person accused as a principal in the second degree
(aider and abettor) and ordered a new trial.

The conclusion of Lord Morris of Borth-y-Gest is stated at p. 677, as follows:

> Having regard to the authorities to which I have referred it seems to me to have been
> firmly held by our courts in this country that duress can afford a defence in criminal
> cases. A recent pronouncement was that in the Court of Appeal in 1971 in the case
> above referred to (*Reg. v. Hudson*, [1971] 2 Q.B. 202). The court stated that they had
> been referred to a large number of authorities and to the views of writers of textbooks.
> In the judgment of the court delivered by Lord Parker C.J. and prepared by Widgery
> L.J. the conclusion was expressed, at p. 206, that "… it is clearly established that du-
> ress provides a defence in all offences including perjury (except possibly treason or
> murder as a principal.")
>
> We are only concerned in this case to say whether duress could be a possible de-
> fence open to Lynch who was charged with being an aider and abettor. Relying on the
> help given in the authorities we must decide this as a matter of principle. I consider that
> duress in such a case can be open as a possible defence. Both general reasoning and the
> requirements of justice lead me to this conclusion.

Lord Wilberforce, at p. 682, cited with approval a passage from the dissenting
reasons of Bray C.J., in *R. v. Brown and Morley*, [1968] S.A.S.R. 467 at 494:

> The reasoning generally used to support the proposition that duress is no defence to a
> charge of murder is, to use the words of Blackstone cited above, that "he ought rather to
> die himself, than escape by the murder of an innocent." Generally speaking I am pre-
> pared to accept this proposition. Its force is obviously considerably less where the act
> of the threatened man is not the direct act of killing but only the rendering of some
> minor form of assistance, particularly when it is by no means certain that if he refuses
> the death of the victim will be averted, or conversely when it is by no means certain
> that if he complies the death will be a necessary consequence. It would seem hard, for
> example, if an innocent passer-by seized in the street by a gang of criminals visibly
> engaged in robbery and murder in a shop and compelled at the point of a gun to issue
> misleading comments to the public, or *an innocent driver compelled at the point of a
> gun to convey the murderer to the victim*, were to have no defence. Are there any au-
> thorities which compel us to hold that he would not?

I am in agreement with the conclusion reached by the majority that it was open to
Lynch, in the circumstances of that case, to rely on the defence of duress, which had
not been put to the jury. If the defence of duress can be available to a person who has
aided and abetted in the commission of murder, then clearly it should be available to
a person who is sought to be made a party to the offence by virtue of s. 21(2). …

I would allow the appeal, set aside the judgment of the Court of Appeal, and restore the verdict of acquittal.

*Appeal allowed.*

**R. v. Mena**
Ontario Court of Appeal
(1987), 34 C.C.C. (3d) 304

MARTIN J.A.: ... In *R. v. Paquette* (1976), 30 C.C.C. (2d) 417, 70 D.L.R. (3d) 129, [1977] 2 S.C.R. 189, the Supreme Court of Canada held that the application of s. 17, excluding certain offences from the defence of compulsion by threats, is limited to cases in which the person seeking to rely upon it has himself committed the offence. The court held that s. 17 does not apply where criminal liability as a party falls to be determined under s. 21(2) of the *Code*. I consider it to be clear from the judgment that s. 17 is also inapplicable where the accused's criminal liability falls to be determined under s. 21(1)(b) or (c) of the *Code*. The Supreme Court of Canada in *R. v. Paquette* held that where s. 17 is inapplicable, an accused is entitled to rely upon the common law defence of duress.

The trial judge in the present case held that the appellant had actually committed the offence of robbery and, hence, s. 17 of the *Code*, which excludes compulsion by threats as a defence where the accused has himself committed the offence of robbery, was exclusively applicable. The trial judge instructed the jury as follows:

> I want to tell you that I have made a ruling of law to which you are bound, that Mr. Mena was present at the commission of the robbery and, with Yee, committed the offence and, therefore, he cannot use the excuse of compulsion, coercion or duress. That was determined by me at the end of all the evidence. That is an important aspect that you have to take into account in your deliberation. ...

It was, in my view, open to the jury to conclude that the appellant, as a result of threats, merely aided the prime culprit ... .

... It would, in my view, be strange if the main culprit recruited two people at gunpoint to assist him in perpetrating a robbery, assigned to one the task of destroying the alarm system and to the other the task of carrying out the money, and the first person had available to him or her the defence of duress, whereas the second person did not. In the present case, the appellant had not inflicted any physical injury on the victim and claimed, as previously mentioned, that he had, in effect, made a pretence of securing him and had merely carried out part of the proceeds of the robbery at Yee's command. Assuming, as we are bound to do, that the jury took the most favourable view of the appellant's evidence, it was open to them to find that he had merely aided Yee and had not himself actually committed the offence of robbery and that, consequently, the common law defence of duress, if its requirements were met, was available to him as a secondary party to the robbery. In my view, it was an issue for the jury whether the appellant intended to act in concert with Yee or whether the acts performed by the appellant were the result of duress. If the jury, on a proper direction, found on the facts that the accused was a co-perpetrator of the offence of robbery, then s. 17 would render the defence of duress unavailable to the accused. The withdrawal of this issue from the jury constitutes a fundamental error: see *R. v. Kozak and Moore* (1975), 20 C.C.C. (2d) 175 at p. 180, 30 C.R.N.S. 7 (Ont. C.A.). ...

Section 17 of the *Code* provides that a person who commits an offence under compulsion by threats of immediate death or bodily harm is excused for committing the offence if he believes that the threats will be carried out, if he is not a party to a conspiracy or association whereby he is subject to compulsion, and if the offence is not one of the offences excluded by the section from the defence of duress. As Professor Stuart has pointed out, s. 17 requires a subjective assessment of the accused's belief. The unreasonableness of the accused's belief is an item of evidence going to whether he genuinely believed the threats would be carried out: see Stuart, *Canadian Criminal Law: A Treatise* (1982), p. 388. ...

Thus, speaking generally, where the defence of duress is invoked, whether the accused failed to avail himself or herself of some opportunity to escape or to render the threat ineffective, is a question for the jury. However, I am disposed to think that, where on the facts not in dispute the accused had an obvious safe means of escape and no reasonable jury could come to any other conclusion, the judge is entitled to hold, as a matter of law, that the defence of duress is not available. ...

In my opinion, the common law defence of duress was available to the appellant and should have been left with the jury. It is not for me to speculate what view the jury would have taken with respect to that defence. Because of the view I have taken, it is unnecessary to consider other issues raised by the appellant, namely, the constitutional validity of s. 17 of the *Code* and the relevance of duress to the appellant's purpose under s. 21(1)(b) of the *Code*.

[The conviction was quashed and a new trial ordered.]

## II. DURESS AND MENS REA

In *Hébert v. The Queen* (1989), 49 C.C.C. (3d) 59, the accused, a Quebec notary, was convicted of perjury. He claimed that several tough-looking motorcycle gang members were present in court and harassed him with their threats. The Supreme Court of Canada upheld the Quebec Court of Appeal, which had reversed an acquittal. The Court of Appeal had stated: "A threat of death from which the respondent could have easily escaped and that he could have rendered unenforceable when he gave his evidence does not permit him to invoke the excuse of compulsion found in s. 17." The Supreme Court agreed, but ordered a new trial on the issue of whether Hébert had the requisite intent, stating:

> While appellant Hébert admitted that he deliberately lied in giving testimony, he none the less stated that he had no intent to mislead in so doing but that, quite the contrary, he intended that the way in which he testified would result in his not being believed and was designed solely to attract the judge's attention so he could tell the judge about the threats which had been made against him. ...
>
> For there to be perjury there has to be more than a deliberate false statement. The statement must also have been made with intent to mislead. While it is true that someone who lies generally does so with the intent of being believed, it is not impossible, though it may be exceptional, for a person to deliberately lie without intending to mislead. It is

always open to an accused to seek to establish such an intent by his testimony or otherwise, leaving to the trial judge the task of assessing its weight. The trial judge did not allow the accused to complete his evidence in this regard, probably because he knew he was going to acquit him on other grounds; that acquittal, however, was properly set aside on appeal.

### Hibbert v. The Queen
Supreme Court of Canada
(1995), 99 C.C.C. (3d) 193

[The victim of the offence was the accused's friend. The accused testified that he was forced by the principal offender to accompany him to the victim's apartment building and to lure the victim down to the lobby. The accused stood by while the principal offender then shot the victim. In the charge to the jury, the trial judge instructed the jury that if the accused joined in the common plot to shoot the victim under threats of death or grievous bodily harm, that would negative his having a common intention with the principal offender to shoot the victim and he must be found not guilty. The trial judge also instructed the jury that the accused could not rely on the common law defence of duress if a safe avenue of escape existed. The accused was acquitted of attempted murder, but convicted of the included offence of aggravated assault. The accused's appeal to the Ontario Court of Appeal was dismissed, but his further appeal to the Supreme Court of Canada was allowed and a new trial was ordered.]

LAMER C.J.C. stated for the Court: … *Paquette* stands for the proposition that duress can provide a "defence" in either of two distinct ways—as an excuse, or by "negating" *mens rea*. In the present case, the appellant argues that this is a correct view of the law, and submits that the trial judge erred by not placing both alternatives before the jury. What falls to be considered, therefore, is the validity of the proposition that the *mens rea* for party liability under the *Criminal Code* can be "negated" by threats of death or bodily harm. That is, the court is called upon to reconsider whether the second aspect of our judgment in *Paquette* reflects a correct understanding of the law of duress in Canada.

That threats of death or serious bodily harm can have an effect on a person's state of mind is indisputable. However, it is also readily apparent that a person who carries out the *actus reus* of a criminal offence in response to such threats will not necessarily lack the *mens rea* for that offence. Whether he or she does or not will depend both on what the mental element of the offence in question happens to be, and on the facts of the particular case. As a practical matter, though, situations where duress will operate to "negate" *mens rea* will be exceptional, for the simple reason that the types of mental states that are capable of being "negated" by duress are not often found in the definitions of criminal offences.

In general, a person who performs an action in response to a threat will *know* what he or she is doing, and will be aware of the probable consequences of his or her actions. Whether or not he or she *desires* the occurrence of these consequences will depend on the particular circumstances. For example, a person who is forced at gunpoint to drive a group of armed ruffians to a bank will usually know that the likely result of his or her actions will be that an attempt will be made to rob the bank, but he or she may not desire this result—indeed, he or she may strongly wish that the robbers' plans are ultimately foiled, if this could occur without risk to his or her own safety. In contrast, a person who is told that his or her child is being held hostage at another location and will be killed unless the robbery is successful will almost certainly have an active subjective desire that the robbery succeed. While the existence of threats clearly has a bearing on the *motive* underlying each actor's respective decision to assist in the robbery, only the first actor can be said not to *desire* that the robbery take place, and neither actor can be said not to have knowledge of the consequences of their actions.

[Lamer C.J.C. first dealt with the meaning of the word "purpose" in s. 21(1)(b) of the Code, which creates liability for a person who "does or omits to do anything for the purpose of aiding any person to commit" an offence. He then went on to discuss s. 21(2) "in the interests of avoiding undue confusion in the law that applies to duress cases."]

It is impossible to ascribe a single fixed meaning to the term "purpose." In ordinary usage, the word is employed in two distinct senses. One can speak of an actor doing something "on purpose" (as opposed to by accident), thereby equating purpose with "immediate intention." The term is also used, however, to indicate the ultimate ends an actor seeks to achieve, which imports the idea of "desire" into the definition. This dual sense is apparent in the word's dictionary definition.

... Our task in the present case is to consider the meaning of "purpose" as it is employed in s. 21(1)(b) of the *Code* in light of the parliamentary objective underlying the subsection. It must be emphasized, however, that the word "purpose" is employed in many different sections of the *Criminal Code*, in a number of distinct contexts. My conclusions in the present case on the proper interpretation of the word "purpose" as it is employed in s. 21(1)(b) of the *Code* are thus restricted to this particular subsection. It may well be that in the context of some other statutory provision a different interpretation of the term will prove to be the most appropriate.

The problems associated with the "purpose equals desire" interpretation are several. First, incorporating the accused's feelings about the desirability of the commission of an offence by the principal into the definition of the *mens rea* for "aiding" can result in distinctions being made which appear arbitrary and unreasonable in light of the policy underlying s. 21(1)(b). As Professor Colvin notes, under the "purpose equals desire" interpretation, a person would not be guilty of aiding in the commission of an offence if he or she were "genuinely opposed or indifferent to it" (p. 123). The reason for the aider's indifference or opposition would be immaterial. The perverse consequences that flow from this are clearly illustrated by the following hypothetical situation described by Mewett and Manning:

> If a man is approached by a friend who tells him that he is going to rob a bank and would like to use his car as a getaway vehicle for which he will pay him $100, when

that person is ... charged under s. 21 for doing something for the purpose of aiding his friend to commit the offence, can he say "My purpose was not to aid the robbery but to make $100"? His argument would be that while he knew that he was helping the robbery, his desire was to obtain the $100 and he did not care one way or the other whether the robbery was successful or not.

(*Criminal Law*, *supra*, at p. 112.) I agree with the authors' conclusion that "[t]hat would seem an absurd result" (p. 112).

The leading English case on the issue of whether duress negates the *mens rea* of parties to offences (under the common law governing party liability) is the House of Lords' decision in *Lynch*, *supra*. As Professor G. Williams observes in his *Textbook of Criminal Law*, 2nd ed. (London: Stevens & Sons, 1983), at p. 624: "The view taken by the majority of the House of Lords in *Lynch* was that duress is a defence on its own, and does not negative either the doing of the act charged or the *mens rea*. This is plainly right."

The position at common law, of course, does not in and of itself determine the meaning to be ascribed to the word "purpose" in the context of s. 21(1)(b) of the *Code*. It can, however, provide useful guidance when it comes to choosing between the two interpretations of the term that are available—one that accords with the common law position and the other that contradicts it. In the absence of reason to believe that Parliament intended its enactment of s. 21(1)(b) to radically alter the common law principles governing party liability, the interpretation that accords with the common law would seem to also be the most likely to accurately embody Parliament's intentions. This observation strengthens my conclusion that Parliament's use of the term "purpose" in s. 21(1)(b) should not be seen as incorporating the notion of "desire" into the mental state for party liability, and that the word should instead be understood as being essentially synonymous with "intention" ...

For these reasons, I conclude that the expression "for the purpose of aiding" in s. 21(1)(b), properly understood, does not require that the accused actively view the commission of the offence he or she is aiding as desirable in and of itself. As a result, the *mens rea* for aiding under s. 21(1)(b) is not susceptible of being "negated" by duress.

As was the case with the term "purpose" in s. 21(1)(b), the phrase "intention in common" [in s. 21(2)] is capable of being understood in more than one sense. One possible interpretation is that "intention in common" means no more than that the two persons must have in mind the same unlawful purpose. Alternatively, however, it might be argued that the requirement of "commonality" requires that the two persons' intentions match in greater detail—in particular, that their motives or subjective views as to the desirability of the commission of the "unlawful purpose" match up. If this latter interpretation were adopted, it could be argued that although persons who assist others to commit criminal acts as a result of threats made by the others would "intend" to provide such assistance, their intention would not be "in common" with the intentions of the threatener, due to the different motives and, possibly, views as to the immediate desirability of the criminal activity at issue. In contrast, under the former interpretation a person would fall within the ambit of s. 21(2) if they intended to assist in the commission of the same offence envisioned by the principal, regard-less of the fact that their intention might be due solely to the principal's threats. Of course, it would be open to such a person to avoid criminal liability through the com-mon law defence of duress.

As noted earlier in *Paquette*, *supra*, Martland J. took the position that "intention in common" meant something more than "intention to commit or aid in the same of-fence," arguing (at p. 423) that:

> A person whose actions have been dictated by fear of death or of grievous bodily injury cannot be said to have formed a genuine common intention to carry out an unlawful purpose with the person who has threatened him with those consequences if he fails to co-operate.

The phrase "intention in common" is certainly open to being interpreted in this man-ner. However, notwithstanding the considerable weight I place on and the respect I have for the opinion of Martland J., I have come to the conclusion that, in the context of s. 21(2), the first interpretation discussed above is more consistent both with Par-liament's intention and with the interpretation of s. 21(1)(b) I have adopted in these reasons. Many of the factors I considered earlier in the course of determining the meaning to be ascribed to the term "purpose" in s. 21(1)(b) apply with similar force to the problem of interpreting s. 21(2).

The conclusions that can be extracted from the discussion in the previous sections may be summarized as follows:

1.  The fact that a person who commits a criminal act does so as a result of threats of death or bodily harm can in some instances be relevant to the question of whether he or she possessed the *mens rea* necessary to commit an offence. Whether or not this is so will depend, among other things, on the structure of the particular offence in question—that is, on whether or not the mental state specified by Parliament in its definition of the offence is such that the presence of coercion can, as a matter of logic, have a bearing on the exist-ence of *mens rea*. If the offence is one where the presence of duress is of potential relevance to the existence of *mens rea*, the accused is entitled to point to the presence of threats when arguing that the Crown has not proven beyond a reasonable doubt that he or she possessed the mental state required for liability.

2.  A person who commits a criminal act under threats of death or bodily harm may also be able to invoke an excuse-based defence (either the statutory de-fence set out in s. 17 or the common law defence of duress, depending on whether the accused is charged as a principal or as a party). This is so regard-less of whether or not the offence at issue is one where the presence of coer-cion also has a bearing on the existence of *mens rea*.

3.  The mental states specified in s. 21(1)(b) and (2) of the *Criminal Code* are not susceptible to being "negated" by duress. Consequently, it is not open to persons charged under these sections to argue that because their acts were

coerced by threats they lacked the requisite *mens rea*. Such persons may, however, seek to have their conduct *excused* through the operation of the common law defence of duress.

It should be reiterated, however, that the holding in the present case is based on an interpretation of the particular terms of two specific offence-creating statutory provisions, s. 21(1)(b) and (2) of the *Criminal Code*. The question of whether other offences can be found, either in the *Code* or in some other statute, that are defined in such a way that the presence of coercion *is* relevant to the existence of *mens rea*, remains open.

### IV. The Common Law Defence of Duress and Moral Involuntariness

[Lamer C.J.C. next considered whether the common law defence of duress applied.]

The [further] issues raised by the appellant have to do with the so-called "safe avenue of escape" rule. The court must decide whether such a rule in fact exists, and, if it does, whether the availability of a "safe avenue" is to be determined on an objective or subjective basis.

The defences of self-defence, necessity and duress all arise under circumstances where a person is subjected to an external danger, and commits an act that would otherwise be criminal as a way of avoiding the harm the danger presents. In the case of self-defence and duress, it is the intentional threats of another person that are the source of the danger, while in the case of necessity the danger is due to other causes, such as forces of nature, human conduct other than intentional threats of bodily harm, etc.

The similarities between defences of duress and necessity have been noted on previous occasions by other commentators. As Lord Simon of Glaisdale observed in his dissenting reasons in *Lynch*, *supra*, at p. 692:

> In the circumstances where either "necessity" or duress is relevant, there are both actus reus and mens rea. In both sets of circumstances there is power of choice between two alternatives; but one of those alternatives is so disagreeable that even serious infraction of the criminal law seems preferable. In both the consequence of the act is intended, within any permissible definition of intention. The only difference is that in duress the force constraining the choice is a human threat, whereas in "necessity" it can be any circumstance constituting a threat to life (or, perhaps, limb). Duress is, thus considered, merely a particular application of the doctrine of "necessity" …

As I noted earlier, the common law defences of necessity and duress apply to essentially similar factual situations. Indeed, to repeat Lord Simon Glaisdale's observation, "[d]uress is … merely a particular application of the doctrine of 'necessity.'" In my view, the similarities between the two defences are so great that consistency and logic requires that they be understood as based on the same juristic principles. Indeed, to do otherwise would be to promote incoherence and anomaly in the criminal law. In the case of necessity, the court has already considered the various alternative theoretical positions available (in *Perka*, *supra*), and has expounded a conceptualization of the defence of necessity as an excuse, based on the idea of normative involuntariness. In my opinion, the need for consistency and coherence in the law dictates that the common law defence of duress also be based on this juridical foundation. If the defence is viewed in this light, the answers to the questions posed in the present appeal can be seen to follow readily from the reasons of Dickson J. in *Perka*.

The so-called "safe avenue of escape" requirement in the law of duress is, in my view, simply a specific example of a more general requirement, analogous to that in the defence of necessity identified by Dickson J.—the requirement that compliance with the law be "demonstrably impossible." As Dickson J. explained, this requirement can be derived directly from the underlying concept of normative involuntariness upon which the defence of necessity is based. As I am of the view that the defence of duress must be seen as being based upon this same theoretical foundation, it follows that the defence of duress includes a similar requirement—namely, a requirement that it can only be invoked if, to adopt Dickson J.'s phrase, there is "no legal way out" of the situation of duress the accused faces. The rule that the defence of duress is unavailable if a "safe avenue of escape" was open to the accused is simply a specific instance of this general requirement—if the accused could have escaped without undue danger, the decision to commit an offence becomes, as Dickson J. observed in the context of necessity, "a voluntary one, impelled by some consideration beyond the dictates of necessity and human instincts."

The defences of self-defence, duress and necessity are essentially similar, so much so that consistency demands that each defence's "reasonableness" requirement be assessed on the same basis. Accordingly, I am of the view that while the question of whether a "safe avenue of escape" was open to an accused who pleads duress should be assessed on an objective basis, the appropriate objective standard to be employed is one that takes into account the particular circumstances and human frailties of the accused.

It should be noted that the question of what sort of objective standard is to be used when assessing the "reasonableness" of the conduct of persons raising an excuse-based defence is different in several key respects from the issue that was before the court in *R. v. Creighton* (1993), 83 C.C.C. (3d) 346, 105 D.L.R. (4th) 632, [1993] 3 S.C.R. 3. In that case, in the course of considering the *mens rea* for "unlawful act manslaughter" under s. 222(5)(a) of the *Criminal Code*, a majority of the court was of the view that (at p. 384, *per* McLachlin J.):

> [C]onsiderations of principle and policy dictate the maintenance of a single, uniform legal standard of care for [offences with a *mens rea* of negligence], subject to one exception: incapacity to appreciate the nature of the risk which the activity in question entails.

Although I dissented on this point in *Creighton* (while concurring in the result), I now consider myself bound by the majority judgment. However, I do not believe that *Creighton* is applicable when what is at issue is the standard of reasonableness to be used in establishing the availability of an excuse-based *defence*, as opposed to the determination of liability under an offence that is defined in terms of a mental state of negligence. In my view, the relevant "considerations of policy and principle" in such cases are quite different from those identifiable in the context of negligence-based offences. Offences defined in terms of negligence typically impose criminal liability on an accused person for the consequences that flowed from his or her inherently hazardous activities—activities that he or she voluntarily and willingly chose to engage in. In *Creighton*, *supra*, the majority was of the view that people "may properly be held to [a strict objective standard] as a condition of choosing to engage in activities which may maim or kill other innocent people" (p. 387). Even if a person fails to foresee the probable consequences of their freely chosen actions, these actions remain the product of genuine choice. In contrast, excuse-based defences, such as duress, are predicated precisely on the view that the conduct of the accused is *involuntary*, in a normative sense—that is, that he or she had no realistic alternative course of action available. In my view, in determining whether an accused person was operating under such constrained options, his or her perceptions of the surrounding facts can be highly relevant to the determination of whether his or her conduct was reasonable under the circumstances, and thus whether his or her conduct is properly excusable.

My conclusions on the [duress] issues raised by the appellant can thus be summarized as follows. An accused person cannot rely on the common law defence of duress if he or she had an opportunity to safely extricate himself or herself from the situation of duress. The rationale for this rule is simply that in such circumstances the condition of "normative involuntariness" that provides the theoretical basis for both the defences of duress and necessity is absent—if the accused had the chance to take action that would have allowed him or her to avoid committing an offence, it cannot be said that he or she had no real choice when deciding whether or not to break the law. Furthermore, I believe that the internal logic of the excuse-based defence, which has theoretical underpinnings directly analogous to those that support the defence of necessity (as set out in *Perka*, *supra*), suggests that the question of whether or not a safe avenue of escape existed is to be determined according to an objective standard. When considering the perceptions of a "reasonable person," however, the personal circumstances of the accused are relevant and important, and should be taken into account.

*Appeal allowed; new trial ordered.*

## III. DURESS AND THE CHARTER

### R. v. Ruzic
Supreme Court of Canada
[2001] 1 S.C.R. 687

LEBEL J. for the Court: ...

### *I. Facts*

[2]  The respondent Marijana Ruzic was born in Belgrade in the former Yugoslavia. She was 21 years old when she entered Canada. When heroin was discovered on her, she was charged with three offences, two of which proceeded to trial: possession and use of a false passport contrary to s. 368 of the *Criminal Code*, and unlawful importation of a narcotic contrary to s. 5(1) of the *Narcotic Control Act*, R.S.C. 1985, c. N-1.

[3]  Ms. Ruzic admitted having committed both offences but claimed that she was then acting under duress and should thus be relieved from any criminal liability. She testified that, two months before her arrival in Canada, a man named Mirko Mirkovic approached her while she was walking her dog in the streets of Belgrade, where she lived in an apartment with her mother. She described him as a "warrior" and believed he was paid to kill people in the war. An expert witness testified at trial that, in 1994, large paramilitary groups roamed Belgrade and engaged in criminal and mafia-like activities. The same expert maintained that people living in Belgrade during that period did not feel safe. They believed the police could not be trusted. There was a real sense that the rule of law had broken down.

[4]  From there began a series of encounters between Mirkovic and the respondent while she was walking her dog. Each time he approached her, he knew more about her, although she had shared no details of her life with him. He phoned her at home. He told her he knew her every move. Ms. Ruzic alleged that his behaviour became more and more intimidating, escalating to threats and acts of physical violence. On one occasion, he burned her arm with a lighter. On another, he stuck a syringe into her arm and injected her with a substance that smelled like heroin and made her nauseous. She indicated that these physical assaults were coupled with sexual harassment and finally threats against her mother.

[5]  On April 25, 1994, Mirkovic phoned the respondent and instructed her to pack a bag and meet him at a hotel in central Belgrade. Once there, he allegedly strapped three packages of heroin to her body and indicated that she was to take them to a restaurant in Toronto. He gave her the false passport, a bus ticket from Belgrade to Budapest and some money. He told her to fly from Budapest to Athens, and then from Athens to Toronto. When she protested, he warned her that, if she failed to comply, he would harm her mother.

[6]  Ms. Ruzic arrived in Budapest on April 26. Late that evening, she boarded a plane to Athens, where she arrived early the next day. She then purchased a ticket to

Toronto. She missed that flight, exchanged her ticket for the next available flight, and left for Toronto two days later, on April 29.

[7] During the two months prior to her journey to Canada, Ms. Ruzic testified that she did not tell her mother or anyone else about Mirkovic. She was afraid he would harm whoever she told. She did not seek police protection because she believed the police in Belgrade were corrupt and would do nothing to assist her. She maintained that she followed Mirkovic's instructions out of fear for her mother's safety. She made no attempt while in Budapest or Athens to seek the assistance of police or other government officials. Similarly, before her arrest, she did not ask any Canadian authorities for help. She asserted that she believed the only way she could protect her mother was to obey Mirkovic's orders. ...

## V. Analysis

### A. Are Statutory Defences Owed Special Deference by Reviewing Courts?

[22] Soon after the Charter came into force, Lamer J. (as he then was) pointed out in *Re B.C. Motor Vehicle Act*, *supra*, at pp. 496-97, that courts have not only the power but the duty to evaluate the substantive content of legislation for Charter compliance. In the realm of criminal law, the courts routinely review the definition of criminal offences to ensure conformity with Charter rights. This has included the *mens rea* element of an offence: e.g., *R. v. Vaillancourt*, [1987] 2 S.C.R. 636; *R. v. Wholesale Travel Group*, [1991] 3 S.C.R. 154. These powers and responsibilities extend equally to statutory defences. Courts would be abdicating their constitutional duty by abstaining from such a review. Defences and excuses belong to the legislative corpus that the Charter submits to constitutional review by the courts.

[23] Subject to constitutional review, Parliament retains the power to restrict access to a criminal defence or to remove it altogether. As Cory J. indicated for the majority in *R. v. Finta*, [1994] 1 S.C.R. 701, a withdrawal of a criminal defence will not automatically breach s. 7 of the Charter. Among other things, *Finta* raised the question whether the removal of the defence of obedience to or authority of de facto law for war crimes and crimes against humanity infringed s. 7. Cory J. observed, at p. 865, that restricting the availability of a defence "will not generally violate s. 7 when a defence is inconsistent with the offence prescribed, in that it would excuse the very evil which the offence seeks to prohibit or punish." Likewise, in *R. v. Penno*, [1990] 2 S.C.R. 865, the removal of drunkenness as a defence to a charge of impaired driving was deemed consistent with s. 7.

[24] The circumstances in this appeal are quite different from those in *Finta* and *Penno*. There is no suggestion that the defence of duress is inconsistent with the offences with which Ms. Ruzic was charged. Section 17 would not excuse the "very evil" that those offences seek to punish. In my view, the relevance of *Finta* and *Penno* to the present appeal is that limitations on a criminal defence may very well be consistent with s. 7 of the Charter. Thus, the issue is not whether the legislature may restrict or remove a criminal defence. It certainly can. The question for the courts is whether restricting the defence of duress accords with Charter rights. ...

*B.  Is It a Principle of Fundamental Justice That Only Morally Voluntary Conduct
Can Attract Criminal Liability?*

[27]  Whether it is a principle of fundamental justice under s. 7 of the Charter that
morally involuntary conduct should not be punished is a novel question before this
Court. We are thus called upon to canvass once more the contents of the "principles
of fundamental justice," this time in the context of the defence of duress as framed by
s. 17 of the *Criminal Code*.

[28]  The Court has on numerous occasions confirmed that the principles of fundamental justice "are to be found in the basic tenets of our legal system": *Re B.C. Motor
Vehicle Act, supra*, at pp. 503 and 512. McLachlin J. (as she then was) added in *R. v.
Seaboyer*, [1991] 2 S.C.R. 577, at p. 603, that they may be distilled from "the legal
principles which have historically been reflected in the law of this and other similar
states." Whether a principle qualifies as a principle of fundamental justice depends on
an analysis of its nature, sources, rationale and essential role within our evolving legal
system: *Re B.C. Motor Vehicle Act, supra*, at p. 513. In *Rodriguez v. British Columbia
(Attorney General)*, [1993] 3 S.C.R. 519, at pp. 590-91, Sopinka J. explained that the
principles of fundamental justice must be capable of being articulated with some precision; they must be more than broad generalizations about our ethical or moral beliefs.
He stated that they are the "principles upon which there is some consensus that they are
vital or fundamental to our societal notion of justice" (p. 590).

[29]  The notion of moral voluntariness was first introduced in *Perka v. The Queen*,
[1984] 2 S.C.R. 232, for the purpose of explaining the defence of necessity and classifying it as an excuse. It was borrowed from the American legal theorist George
Fletcher's discussion of excuses in *Rethinking Criminal Law* (1978). A person acts in
a morally involuntary fashion when, faced with perilous circumstances, she is deprived of a realistic choice whether to break the law. By way of illustration in *Perka*,
Dickson J. evoked the situation of a lost alpinist who, on the point of freezing to
death, breaks into a remote mountain cabin. The alpinist confronts a painful dilemma:
freeze to death or commit a criminal offence. Yet as Dickson J. pointed out at p. 249,
the alpinist's choice to break the law "is no true choice at all; it is remorselessly
compelled by normal human instincts," here of self-preservation. The Court in *Perka*
thus conceptualized the defence of necessity as an excuse. An excuse, Dickson J.
maintained, concedes that the act was wrongful, but withholds criminal attribution to
the actor because of the dire circumstances surrounding its commission. He summarized the rationale of necessity in this way, at p. 250:

> At the heart of this defence is the perceived injustice of punishing violations of the law
> in circumstances in which the person had no other viable or reasonable choice avail-
> able; the act was wrong but it is excused because it was unavoidable.

[30]  Extending its reasoning in Perka to the defence of duress, the Court found in
*R. v. Hibbert*, [1995] 2 S.C.R. 973, that it too rests on the notion of moral voluntariness. In the case of the defences of necessity and duress, the accused contends that he
should avoid conviction because he acted in response to a threat of impending harm.
The Court also confirmed in *Hibbert* that duress does not ordinarily negate the *mens*

*rea* element of an offence. Like the defence of necessity, the Court classified the defence of duress as an excuse, like that of necessity. As such, duress operates to relieve a person of criminal liability only after he has been found to have committed the prohibited act with the relevant *mens rea*: see also *Bergstrom v. The Queen*, [1981] 1 S.C.R. 539, at p. 544 (per McIntyre J.).

[31] Thus duress, like necessity, involves the concern that morally involuntary conduct not be subject to criminal liability. Can this notion of "moral voluntariness" be recognized as a principle of fundamental justice under s. 7 of the Charter? …

[38] It should be emphasized that this Court, in cases like *Sault Ste. Marie* and *Re B.C. Motor Vehicle Act*, has referred to moral innocence in the context of the discussion of the mental element of an offence. *Hibbert*, on the other hand, held that the defence of duress does not normally negate *mens rea*. Rather, it operates to excuse a wrongful act once the *actus reus* and *mens rea* components of the offence have been made out. Laskin J.A. conceded this point, but countered that moral blameworthiness is a broader concept, extending beyond the traditional elements of an offence. Both Laskin J.A. and the respondent rely heavily, in this respect, on Professor Martha Shaffer's article "Scrutinizing Duress: The Constitutional Validity of Section 17 of the Criminal Code" (1998), 40 *C.L.Q.* 444, in making this argument.

[39] Professor Shaffer acknowledges in her article, at pp. 453-54, that moral blameworthiness is an ambiguous concept, the meaning of which this Court has not had occasion to discuss in any significant way. I am reluctant to do so here, particularly since, in my opinion, conduct that is morally involuntary is not always intrinsically free of blame. (See also *R. v. Chaulk*, [1990] 3 S.C.R. 1303, at p. 1396-98.) Moral involuntariness is also related to the notion that the defence of duress is an excuse. Dickson J. maintained in *Perka* that an excuse acknowledges the wrongfulness of the accused's conduct. Nevertheless, the law refuses to attach penal consequences to it because an "excuse" has been made out. In using the expression "moral involuntariness," we mean that the accused had no "real" choice but to commit the offence. This recognizes that there was indeed an alternative to breaking the law, although in the case of duress that choice may be even more unpalatable—to be killed or physically harmed.

[40] Let us consider again the situation of the lost alpinist: can we really say he is blameless for breaking into somebody else's cabin? The State refrains from punishing him not because his actions were innocent, but because the circumstances did not leave him with any other realistic choice than to commit the offence. As Fletcher, *supra*, puts it, at p. 798, excuses absolve the accused of personal accountability by focussing, not on the wrongful act, but on the circumstances of the act and the accused's personal capacity to avoid it. Necessity and duress are characterized as concessions to human frailty in this sense. The law is designed for the common man, not for a community of saints or heroes.

[41] To equate moral involuntariness with moral innocence would amount to a significant departure from the reasoning in *Perka* and *Hibbert*. It would be contrary to the Court's conceptualization of duress as an excuse. Morally involuntary conduct is not always inherently blameless. Once the elements of the offence have been established, the accused can no longer be considered blameless. This Court has never

taken the concept of blamelessness any further than this initial finding of guilt, nor should it in this case. The undefinable and potentially far-reaching nature of the concept of moral blamelessness prevents us from recognizing its relevance beyond an initial finding of guilt in the context of s. 7 of the Charter. Holding otherwise would inject an unacceptable degree of uncertainty into the law. It would not be consistent with our duty to consider as "principles of fundamental justice" only those concepts which are constrained and capable of being defined with reasonable precision. I would therefore reject this basis for finding that it is a principle of fundamental justice that morally involuntary acts should not be punished.

## 2  Moral Voluntariness and Voluntariness in the Physical Sense

[42] The respondent's second approach, which relates moral voluntariness back to voluntariness in the physical sense, rests on firmer ground. It draws upon the fundamental principle of criminal law that, in order to attract criminal liability, an act must be voluntary. Voluntariness in this sense has ordinarily referred to the *actus reus* element of an offence. It queries whether the actor had control over the movement of her body or whether the wrongful act was the product of a conscious will. Although duress does not negate ordinarily *actus reus* per se (just as it does not ordinarily negate *mens rea* as we have just seen), the principle of voluntariness, unlike that of "moral blamelessness," can remain relevant in the context of s. 7 even after the basic elements of the offence have been established. Unlike the concept of "moral blamelessness," duress in its "voluntariness" perspective can more easily be constrained and can therefore more justifiably fall within the "principles of fundamental justice," even after the basic elements of the offence have been established.

[43] Let us examine the notion of "voluntariness" and its interplay with duress more closely. As Dickson J. stated in *Rabey v. The Queen*, [1980] 2 S.C.R. 513, at p. 522, "it is a basic principle that absence of volition in respect of the act involved is always a defence to a crime. A defence that the act is involuntary entitles the accused to a complete and unqualified acquittal." Dickson J.'s pronouncement was endorsed by the Court in *R. v. Parks*, [1992] 2 S.C.R. 871. The principle of voluntariness was given constitutional status in *Daviault*, ... at pp. 102-3, where Cory J. held for the majority that it would infringe s. 7 of the Charter to convict an accused who was not acting voluntarily, as a fundamental aspect of the *actus reus* would be absent. More recently, in *R. v. Stone*, [1999] 2 S.C.R. 290, the crucial role of voluntariness as a condition of the attribution of criminal liability was again confirmed (at para. 1, per Binnie J., and paras. 155-58, per Bastarache J.) in an appeal concerning the defence of automatism. ...

[46] Punishing a person whose actions are involuntary in the physical sense is unjust because it conflicts with the assumption in criminal law that individuals are autonomous and freely choosing agents: see Shaffer, *supra*, at pp. 449-50. It is similarly unjust to penalize an individual who acted in a morally involuntary fashion. This is so because his acts cannot realistically be attributed to him, as his will was constrained by some external force. As Dennis Klimchuk states in "Moral Innocence, Normative Involuntariness, and Fundamental Justice" (1998), 18 C.R. (5th) 96, at p. 102, the

accused's agency is not implicated in her doing. In the case of morally involuntary conduct, criminal attribution points not to the accused but to the exigent circumstances facing him, or to the threats of someone else. Klimchuk explains at p. 104:

> In short, normatively involuntary actions share with actions that are involuntary in the sense relevant to negating actus reus the exculpatorily relevant feature that renders the latter immune from criminal censure, namely, that involuntary actions resist imputation to the actor putatively responsible for their commission.

[47] Although moral involuntariness does not negate the *actus reus* or *mens rea* of an offence, it is a principle which, similarly to physical involuntariness, deserves protection under s. 7 of the Charter. It is a principle of fundamental justice that only voluntary conduct—behaviour that is the product of a free will and controlled body, unhindered by external constraints—should attract the penalty and stigma of criminal liability. Depriving a person of liberty and branding her with the stigma of criminal liability would infringe the principles of fundamental justice if the accused did not have any realistic choice. The ensuing deprivation of liberty and stigma would have been imposed in violation of the tenets of fundamental justice and would thus infringe s. 7 of the Charter.

*C. Do the Immediacy and Presence Requirements in Section 17 Infringe the Principle of Involuntariness in the Attribution of Criminal Responsibility?*

…

[50] The plain meaning of s. 17 is quite restrictive in scope. Indeed, the section seems tailor-made for the situation in which a person is compelled to commit an offence at gun point. The phrase "present when the offence is committed," coupled with the immediacy criterion, indicates that the person issuing the threat must be either at the scene of the crime or at whatever other location is necessary to make good on the threat without delay should the accused resist. Practically speaking, a threat of harm will seldom qualify as immediate if the threatener is not physically present at the scene of the crime. …

[53] I agree with the respondent that a threat will seldom meet the immediacy criterion if the threatener is not physically present at or near the scene of the offence. The immediacy and presence requirements, taken together, clearly preclude threats of future harm.

[54] Neither the words of s. 17 nor the Court's reasons in *Carker* and *Paquette* dictate that the target of the threatened harm must be the accused. They simply require that the threat must be made to the accused. Section 17 may thus include threats against third parties. However, as discussed above, the language of s. 17 does not appear capable of supporting a more flexible interpretation of the immediacy and presence requirements. Even if the threatened person, for example, is a family member, and not the accused person, the threatener or his accomplice must be at or near the scene of the crime in order to effect the harm immediately if the accused resists. Thus, while s. 17 may capture threats against third parties, the immediacy and presence criteria continue to impose considerable obstacles to relying on the defence in hostage or other third party situations.

[55] Thus, by the strictness of its conditions, s. 17 breaches s. 7 of the Charter because it allows individuals who acted involuntarily to be declared criminally liable.

*D. The Common Law of Duress*
...

[64] According to Lamer C.J. in *Hibbert*, the defences of duress and necessity share the same juristic principles. Nevertheless, they target two different situations. In the case of necessity, the accused is a victim of circumstances. Duress finds its origin in man's wrongful acts. Moreover, Lamer C.J. drew some distinctions between the conditions of the defences of duress and of necessity. More particularly, Lamer C.J.'s reasons do not seem to have imported into the defence of duress an absolute immediacy requirement that would entirely duplicate the contents of s. 17 of the *Criminal Code*.

[65] The analysis in *Hibbert* remains focused on the concept of a safe avenue of escape. Although the common law defence traditionally covers situations of threats susceptible of "immediate" execution by the person present and uttering threats, this immediacy requirement has been interpreted in a flexible manner by Canadian juris-prudence and also as appears from the development of the common law in other Commonwealth countries, more particularly Great Britain and Australia. In order to cover, for example, threats to a third person, the immediacy test is interpreted as a requirement of a close connection in time, between the threat and its execution in such a manner that the accused loses the ability to act freely. A threat that would not meet those conditions, because, for example, it is too far removed in time, would cast doubt on the seriousness of the threat and, more particularly, on claims of an absence of a safe avenue of escape.

[66] A recent case on the problem of duress is *Langlois* ... . Writing for the Quebec Court of Appeal, Fish J.A. interpreted the defence of duress at common law as excluding the strict requirements of immediacy and presence which form an essential part of s. 17 (at p. 689). Thus, in *Langlois*, the Quebec Court of Appeal upheld an acquittal based on the defence of duress in a drug trafficking case involving a prison guard. Fish J.A. held that the common law defence was more flexible because it was not bound by the strict conditions imposed by s. 17 of the *Criminal Code* on the availability of the defence (at p. 689):

> Notably, at common law, there is no requirement that the threats be made by a person who is present at the scene of the crime. It has been said that the threat must be "imme-diate" or "imminent" and that persons threatened must resort to the protection of the law if they can do so. While the defence is not available to those who have "an obvious safe avenue of escape," I agree with Martin J.A. that the operative test is "whether the accused failed to avail himself or herself of some opportunity to escape or render the threat ineffective."[References omitted.] ...

5  Summary: Rejection of the Immediacy Requirement at Common Law

[86] This review of the common law defence of duress confirms that, although the common law is not unanimous in the United States, a substantial consensus has

grown in Canada, England and Australia to the effect that the strict criterion of immediacy is no longer a generally accepted component of the defence. A requirement that the threat be "imminent" has been interpreted and applied in a more flexible manner. The English Court of Appeal held in *Hudson* that depending on the circumstances, threats of future harm are sufficient to invoke the defence. *Hudson* remains good law in England and has been adopted by the courts in three Australian states and one territory. However, it is clear from the English cases that there must be a close temporal link between the threat of harm and the commission of the offence. The operative test in the English and Australian cases is whether the threat was effective to overbear the accused's will at the moment he committed the crime. Moreover, the safe avenue of escape test and the proportionality principle also appear to be key elements of the defence.

### E.  The Breach of Section 7 of the Charter: Conclusion in the Case at Bar

...

[88] ... s. 17's reliance on proximity as opposed to reasonable options as the measure of moral choice is problematic. It would be contrary to the principles of fundamental justice to punish an accused who is psychologically tortured to the point of seeing no reasonable alternative, or who cannot rely on the authorities for assistance. That individual is not behaving as an autonomous agent acting out of his own free will when he commits an offence under duress.

[89] The appellant's attempts at reading down s. 17, in order to save it, would amount to amending it to bring it in line with the common law rules. This interpretation badly strains the text of the provision and may become one more argument against upholding its validity.

[90] The underinclusiveness of s. 17 infringes s. 7 of the Charter, because the immediacy and presence requirements exclude threats of future harm to the accused or to third parties. It risks jeopardizing the liberty and security interests protected by the Charter, in violation of the basic principles of fundamental justice. It has the potential of convicting persons who have not acted voluntarily.

### F.  Can the Infringement Be Justified Under s. 1?

[91] Having found that the immediacy and presence requirements infringe s. 7 of the Charter, I turn now to consider whether the violation is a demonstrably justifiable limit under s. 1. The government, of course, bears the burden of justifying a Charter infringement. Consistent with its strategy in the courts below, the appellant made no attempt before this Court to justify the immediacy and presence criteria according to the s. 1 analysis. I therefore conclude at the outset that the appellant has failed to satisfy its onus under s. 1.

[92] Moreover, it is well established that violations of s. 7 are not easily saved by s. 1: *New Brunswick (Minister of Health and Community Services) v. G. (J.)*, [1999] 3 S.C.R. 46, at para. 99. Indeed, the Court has indicated that exceptional circumstances, such as the outbreak of war or a national emergency, are necessary before such an infringement may be justified: *R. v. Heywood*, [1994] 3 S.C.R. 761, at p. 802; *Re B.C.*

*Motor Vehicle Act, supra.* No such extraordinary conditions exist in this case. Furthermore, I am inclined to agree with Laskin J.A. that the immediacy and presence criteria would not meet the proportionality branch of the s. 1 analysis. In particular, it seems to me these requirements do not minimally impair the respondent's s. 7 rights. Given the appellant's failure to make any submissions on the issue, the higher standard of justification for a violation of s. 7, and my doubts concerning proportionality, I conclude that the immediacy and presence conditions cannot be saved by s. 1. ...

## H. The Jury Charge

[96] In the future, when the common law defence of duress is raised, the trial judge should instruct the jury clearly on the components of this defence including the need for a close temporal connection between the threat and the harm threatened. The jury's attention should also be drawn to the need for the application of an objective-subjective assessment of the safe avenue of escape test. ...

[100] There was no misdirection either on the burden of proof. The accused must certainly raise the defence and introduce some evidence about it. Once this is done, the burden of proof shifts to the Crown under the general rule of criminal evidence. It must be shown, beyond a reasonable doubt, that the accused did not act under duress. Similarly, in the case of the defence of necessity, the Court refused to shift the burden of proof to the accused (see *Perka, supra,* pp. 257-59), although the defence must have an air of reality, in order to be sent to the jury, as the Court held in *Latimer, supra.*

## VI. Disposition

[101] The appellant's submissions cannot be accepted. The immediacy and presence requirements of s. 17 of the *Criminal Code* infringe s. 7 of the Charter. As the infringement has not been justified under s. 1, the requirements of immediacy and presence must be struck down as unconstitutional. The Court of Appeal and the trial judge were right in allowing the common law defence of duress go to the jury, and the trial judge adequately instructed the jury on the defence.

[102] I would dismiss the appeal and confirm the acquittal of the respondent.

## IV. DURESS AND EXCLUDED OFFENCES

There are two issues with respect to excluded offences. The first issue is the constitutionality of the excluded offences that apply to principal offenders under s. 17 of the Code. This issue was not decided by the Supreme Court in *R. v. Ruzic* because the offence charged was not one excluded under s. 17 of the Code. The ultimate issue would be whether a person who committed one of the offences excluded under s. 17 could be convicted even though he or she acted in a morally involuntary manner. If so, the excluded offences seem to violate s. 7 of the Charter.

The second issue is whether some offences are excluded from the common law defence of duress that still applies to parties to an offence. In *R. v. Paquette, supra,* the Supreme Court held that the common law defence of duress could apply to a party to murder and in *R. v. Hibbert* the court contemplated that the common law defence could apply to attempted murder. In *R. v. Paquette*, the Supreme Court followed *Lynch*, a decision that has subsequently been overruled by the House of Lords in *R. v. Howe*, [1987] 1 All E.R. 771 on the basis that duress should not excuse the commission of either murder or attempted murder as either a principal offender or a party to the offence. Lord Hailsham concluded:

> In general, I must say that I do not at all accept in relation to the defence of duress that it is either good morals, good policy or good law to suggest, as did the majority in *Lynch*'s case … that the ordinary man of reasonable fortitude is not to be supposed to be capable of heroism if he is asked to take an innocent life rather than sacrifice his own. Doubtless in actual practice many will succumb to temptation, as they did in *R. v. Dudley and Stephens*. But many will not, and I do not believe that as a "concession to human frailty" (see Smith and Hogan *Criminal Law* (5th ed., 1983) p. 215) the former should be exempt from liability to criminal sanctions if they do. I have known in my own lifetime of too many acts of heroism by ordinary human beings of no more than ordinary fortitude to regard a law as either "just or humane" which withdraws the protection of the criminal law from the innocent victim and casts the cloak of its protection on the coward and the poltroon in the name of a "concession to human frailty."

Should any offence be excluded from the common law defence?

Does the categorical exclusion of a large number of offences from the statutory defence of duress under s. 17 of the *Criminal Code* violate s. 7 of the Charter?

## V. DURESS AND STATUTORY REFORM

Law Reform Commission of Canada, Report 31 (1987), *Recodifying Criminal Law*, at p. 35:

> 3(8) Duress. No one is liable for committing a crime in reasonable response to threats of immediate serious harm to himself or another person unless he himself purposely causes the death of, or seriously harms, another person.

Comment

One's duty to obey the law may conflict with pressure stemming from the threats of others. Where the pressure is great and the breach of duty relatively small, the breach becomes unfit for punishment. This is the thrust of the criminal law defence of duress.

The defence of duress is presently contained partly in section 17 of the *Criminal Code* and partly in the common law. According to the case-law, the section concerns the position of the actual committer; the common law that of other parties. Section 17 allows the defence only where there is a threat of immediate death or bodily harm from a person present, where the accused is not a party to a conspiracy subjecting him to the duress and where the crime committed is not one of those listed in the section. The common law is less strict and detailed, does not require the threatener to be present, has no rule on conspiracy and excludes duress only in the case of murder by an actual committer.

Clause 3(8) simplifies and modifies the law in four ways. First, it specifies that the accused's response to the threat must be reasonable. Second, it provides the same rule for all parties. Third, it drops the need for the threatener's presence at the crime and the accused's absence from a conspiracy, on the ground that both are factors going ultimately to the reasonableness or otherwise of the accused's response. Finally, it abandons the *ad hoc* list of excluded crimes and replaces it with a general exclusion for an accused who himself purposely kills or seriously harms another person, the principle being that no one may put his own well-being before the life and bodily integrity of another innocent person.

Judicial reform is also possible. For example, the courts might eventually find that s. 17 should be struck down completely on the basis that it allows the conviction of those who acted in a morally involuntary manner. In such an eventuality, the common law defence would apply to all offenders.

## ADDITIONAL READING

- K. Roach, *Criminal Law*, 3rd ed. (Toronto: Irwin Law, 2004), chapter 8;
- A. Mewett and M. Manning, *Criminal Law*, 3rd ed. (Toronto: Butterworths, 1994), at 519-29;
- D. Stuart, *Canadian Criminal Law*, 4th ed. (Toronto: Carswell, 2001), at 461-75;
- E. Colvin, *Principles of Criminal Law*, 2nd ed. (Toronto: Carswell, 1991), at 229-38;
- P. Rosenthal, "Duress in the Criminal Law" (1990), 32 *Crim. L.Q.* 199;
- P. Healy, "Innocence and Defences" (1994), 19 *C.R.* (4th) 121;
- M. Shaffer, "Scutinizing Duress: The Constitutional Validity of Section 17 of the Criminal Code" (1998), 40 *Crim. L.Q.* 444;
- M. Shaffer, "Coerced into Crime: Battered Women and the Defence of Duress" (1999), 4 *Can. Crim. L. Rev.* 272;
- S. Yeo, "Defining Duress" (2002), 46 *Crim. L.Q.* 293.

# CHAPTER TWENTY

# Self-Defence

## I. INTRODUCTION

This chapter is concerned with the question of when it is permissible for an individual to use force to defend and protect him or herself. Almost all systems of criminal justice recognize the right of a person to defend him or herself against the aggression of another person. Self-defence is a statutory defence in Canada and has remained relatively static since 1892. Although the idea that one can use force to avert force is simple at a level of some generality, it has proven to be a challenging defence to codify and apply in clear terms. Courts of Appeal routinely order new trials based on incorrect or inadequate jury charges on self-defence. As Justice Michael Moldaver said in *R. v. Pintar* (1996), 110 C.C.C. (3d) 402 (Ont. C.A.):

> It is no secret that many trial judges consider their instructions on the law of self-defence to be little more than a source of bewilderment and confusion to the jury. Regardless of their efforts to be clear, trial judges often report glazed eyes and blank stares on the faces of the jury in the course of their instructions on self-defence. Disheartening as this may be, most judges tend to believe that juries are extremely adept at assessing legitimate cases of self-defence and are therefore likely to come to the right result in spite of the confusion created by the charge. While this may be true, it provides little comfort to an accused who has been convicted in the face of legal instruction so complex and confusing that it may well have diverted the jury's attention away from the real basis upon which the claim to self-defence rests. More importantly, it cannot serve to excuse a charge of this nature from constituting an error of law.

The Supreme Court expressed similar sentiments in *R. v. McIntosh* (1995), 95 C.C.C. (3d) 481 (S.C.C.), and criticized the complexity of the current self-defence provisions.

In addition to problems of comprehensibility and complexity, self-defence is sometimes asserted in controversial circumstances, as in the case of the battered woman who kills a spouse who, at the moment he is killed, does not pose an *immediate* threat to the accused. Equally controversial is the case of Bernard Goetz, the so-called subway vigilante, who gunned down four youths on a New York City subway, and then claimed self-defence. Apart from the important consideration of context, the case confronts the thorny issue of whether objective or subjective standards (or a blend of both) should be applied to self-defence, which is a preoccupation in Canadian law.

**People v. Goetz**
New York Court of Appeals
497 N.E.2d 41 (1986)

Chief Judge WACHTLER:  A Grand Jury has indicted defendant on attempted murder, assault, and other charges for having shot and wounded four youths on a New York City subway train after one or two of the youths approached him and asked for $5. The lower courts, concluding that the prosecutor's charge to the Grand Jury on the defense of justification was erroneous, have dismissed the attempted murder, assault and weapons possession charges. We now reverse and reinstate all counts of the indictment.

*I.*

The precise circumstances of the incident giving rise to the charges against defendant are disputed, and ultimately it will be for a trial jury to determine what occurred. We feel it necessary, however, to provide some factual background to properly frame the legal issues before us. Accordingly, we have summarized the facts as they appear from the evidence before the Grand Jury. We stress, however, that we do not purport to reach any conclusions or holding as to exactly what transpired or whether defendant is blameworthy. The credibility of witnesses and the reasonableness of defendant's conduct are to be resolved by the trial jury.

On Saturday afternoon, December 22, 1984, Troy Canty, Darryl Cabey, James Ramseur, and Barry Allen boarded an IRT express subway train in The Bronx and headed south toward lower Manhattan. The four youths rode together in the rear portion of the seventh car of the train. Two of the four, Ramseur and Cabey, had screwdrivers inside their coats, which they said were to be used to break into the coin boxes of video machines.

Defendant Bernhard Goetz boarded this subway train at 14th Street in Manhattan and sat down on a bench towards the rear section of the same car occupied by the four youths. Goetz was carrying an unlicensed .38 caliber pistol loaded with five rounds of ammunition in a waistband holster. The train left the 14th Street station and headed towards Chambers Street.

It appears from the evidence before the Grand Jury that Canty approached Goetz, possibly with Allen beside him, and stated "give me five dollars." Neither Canty nor any of the other youths displayed a weapon. Goetz responded by standing up, pulling out his handgun and firing four shots in rapid succession. The first shot hit Canty in the chest; the second struck Allen in the back; the third went through Ramseur's arm and into his left side; the fourth was fired at Cabey, who apparently was then standing in the corner of the car, but missed, deflecting instead off of a wall of the conductor's cab. After Goetz briefly surveyed the scene around him, he fired another shot at Cabey, who then was sitting on the end bench of the car. The bullet entered the rear of Cabey's side and severed his spinal cord. …

Penal Law article 35 recognizes the defense of justification, which "permits the use of force under certain circumstances" (see, *People v. McManus*, 67 N.Y.2d 541, 545, 505 N.Y.S.2d 43, 496 N.E.2d 202). One such set of circumstances pertains to the use of force in defense of a person, encompassing both self-defense and defense of a third person (Penal Law §35.15). Penal Law §35.15(1) sets forth the general principles governing all such uses of force:

> [a] person may ... use physical force upon another person when and to the extent he *reasonably believes* such to be necessary to defend himself or a third person from what he *reasonably believes* to be the use or imminent use of unlawful physical force by such other person (emphasis added).

Section 35.15(2) sets forth further limitations on these general principles with respect to the use of "deadly physical force":

> A person may not use deadly physical force upon another person under circumstances specified in subdivision one unless (a) He *reasonably believes* that such other person is using or about to use deadly physical force ... or (b) He *reasonably believes* that such other person is committing or attempting to commit a kidnapping, forcible rape, forcible sodomy or robbery (emphasis added).

Thus, consistent with most justification provisions, Penal Law §35.15 permits the use of deadly physical force only where requirements as to triggering conditions and the necessity of a particular response are met (see, Robinson, Criminal Law Defenses §121[a], at 2). As to the triggering conditions, the statute requires that the actor "reasonably believes" that another person either is using or about to use deadly physical force or is committing or attempting to commit one of certain enumerated felonies, including robbery. As to the need for the use of deadly physical force as a response, the statute requires that the actor "reasonably believes" that such force is necessary to avert the perceived threat. ...

When the prosecutor had completed his charge, one of the grand jurors asked for clarification of the term "reasonably believes." The prosecutor responded by instructing the grand jurors that they were to consider the circumstances of the incident and determine "whether the defendant's conduct was that of a reasonable man in the defendant's situation." It is this response by the prosecutor—and specifically his use of "a reasonable man"—which is the basis for the dismissal of the charges by the lower courts. As expressed repeatedly in the Appellate Division's plurality opinion, because section 35.15 uses the term "*he* reasonably believes," the appropriate test, according to that court, is whether a defendant's beliefs and reactions were "reasonable to *him*." Under that reading of the statute, a jury which believed a defendant's testimony that he felt that his own actions were warranted and were reasonable would have to acquit him, regardless of what anyone else in defendant's situation might have concluded. Such an interpretation defies the ordinary meaning and significance of the term "reasonably" in a statute, and misconstrues the clear intent of the Legislature, in enacting section 35.15, to retain an objective element as part of any provision authorizing the use of deadly physical force. ...

In 1961 the Legislature established a Commission to undertake a complete revision of the Penal Law and the Criminal Code. The impetus for the decision to update the Penal Law came in part from the drafting of the Model Penal Code by the American Law Institute, as well as from the fact that the existing law was poorly organized and in many aspects antiquated. ...

The provisions of the Model Penal Code with respect to the use of deadly force in self-defense reflect the position of its drafters that any culpability which arises from a mistaken belief in the need to use such force should be no greater than the culpability such a mistake would give rise to if it were made with respect to an element of a crime (see, ALI, Model Penal Code and Commentaries, part I, at 32, 34 [hereafter cited as MPC Commentaries]; Robinson, Criminal Law Defenses, *op. cit.*, at 410). Accordingly, under Model Penal Code §3.04(2)(b), a defendant charged with murder (or attempted murder) need only show that he "*believe[d]* that [the use of deadly force] was necessary to protect himself against death, serious bodily injury, kidnapping or [forcible] sexual intercourse" to prevail on a self-defense claim (emphasis added). If the defendant's belief was wrong, and was recklessly or negligently formed, however, he may be convicted of the type of homicide charge requiring only a reckless or negligent, as the case may be, criminal intent (see, Model Penal Code §3.09[2]; MPC Commentaries, *op. cit.*, part I, at 32, 150). …

New York did not follow the Model Penal Code's equation of a mistake as to the need to use deadly force with a mistake negating an element of a crime. …

… The drafters of the new Penal Law adopted in large part the structure and content of Model Penal Code §3.04, but, crucially, inserted the word "reasonably" before "believes." …

We cannot lightly impute to the Legislature an intent to fundamentally alter the principles of justification to allow the perpetrator of a serious crime to go free simply because that person believed his actions were reasonable and necessary to prevent some perceived harm. To completely exonerate such an individual, no matter how aberrational or bizarre his thought patterns, would allow citizens to set their own standards for the permissible use of force. It would also allow a legally competent defendant suffering from delusions to kill or perform acts of violence with impunity, contrary to fundamental principles of justice and criminal law. …

Goetz also argues that the introduction of an objective element will preclude a jury from considering factors such as the prior experiences of a given actor and thus, require it to make a determination of "reasonableness" without regard to the actual circumstances of a particular incident. This argument, however, falsely presupposes that an objective standard means that the background and other relevant characteristics of a particular actor must be ignored. To the contrary, we have frequently noted that a determination of reasonableness must be based on the "circumstances" facing a defendant or his "situation" (see, e.g., *People v. Ligouri*, 284 N.Y. 309, 316, 31 N.E.2d 37, *supra*; *People v. Lumsden*, 201 N.Y. 264, 268, 94 N.E. 859, *supra*). Such terms encompass more than the physical movements of the potential assailant. As just discussed, these terms include any relevant knowledge the defendant had about that person. They also necessarily bring in the physical attributes of all persons involved, including the defendant. Furthermore, the defendant's circumstances encompass any prior experiences he had which could provide a reasonable basis for a belief that another person's intentions were to injure or rob him or that the use of deadly force was necessary under the circumstances.

Accordingly, a jury should be instructed to consider this type of evidence in weighing the defendant's actions. The jury must first determine whether the defendant had the requisite beliefs under section 35.15, that is, whether he believed deadly force was necessary to avert the imminent use of deadly force or the commission of one of the felonies enumerated therein. If the People do not prove beyond a reasonable doubt that he did not have such beliefs, then the jury must also consider whether these beliefs were reasonable. The jury would have to determine, in light of all the "circumstances," as explicated above, if a reasonable person could have had these beliefs.

---

Despite the New York Court of Appeals affirmation of objective elements in self-defence and Goetz's confession that he wanted to kill the four youths, the jury at the subsequent trial acquitted Goetz of attempted murder on the basis that his subjective belief that he was acting in self-defence was inconsistent with the intent to murder. The deliberations of the jury on this matter are revealed in Professor George Fletcher's book *A Crime of Self-Defense* (1988) at 186-88:

> … The District Attorney's office fought an appellate battle for nearly a year in order to establish the objective standard for assessing claims of self-defense. The fear and violent response of someone defending himself must be judged not solely by his own motives, but by the hypothetical fear and response of a reasonable person under the circumstances. But as the jury considered Goetz's motive to defend himself as a factor bearing on his intent to kill, they placed the entire burden of their analysis on his subjective perceptions and motives. It could only be these subjective motives—not the moral quality of his act as measured against the standard of reasonableness—that could influence the analysis whether he had a bad motive for shooting. Even an unreasonable belief in the necessity of self-defense was a good-faith belief, and if Goetz was acting in good faith, he did not have a criminal motive. …
>
> As a result of admitting a subjective theory of self-defense by the back door, the jury abandoned the task of judgment that the Court of Appeals had laid before it. They were supposed to consider not only whether Goetz had good motives, but whether he overreacted in formulating those motives. Their job was to get behind his intention and judge whether a reasonable person would have found shooting necessary under the circumstances. Yet they brought their common sense and their moral sensibilities to the instructions that Justice Crane gave them, and as a result they fashioned a mode of analysis that no one expected.

## II. APPLYING THE CRIMINAL CODE PROVISIONS

The *Criminal Code* contains numerous self-defence or justified use of force provisions (ss. 25, 26, 27, 34, 35, 37, 38, 39, 40, and 41), which focus on different situations. The applicability of these provisions is determined by some of the following questions: Who was the aggressor in the incident? Did the victim die or suffer grievous bodily harm? If so, did the accused intend to bring about this consequence? Did the accused provoke the incident? Was the accused obliged to retreat? Was the accused attempting to protect a third party? Was the accused defending his or her property? Is the accused a police officer?

For the purposes of the discussion in this chapter, we consider the two sections that are at the core of most self-defence cases in Canada, ss. 34 and 37. Section 34 reads:

s. 34(1) Everyone who is unlawfully assaulted without having provoked the assault is justified in repelling force by force if the force he uses is not intended to cause death or grievous bodily harm and is no more than is necessary to enable him to defend himself.

(2) Everyone who is unlawfully assaulted and who causes death or grievous bodily harm in repelling the assault is justified if

    (a) he causes it under reasonable apprehension of death or grievous bodily harm from the violence which the assault was originally made or with which the assailant pursues his purposes; and

    (b) he believes, on reasonable grounds, that he cannot otherwise preserve himself from death or grievous bodily harm

## R. v. Bogue
### Ontario Court of Appeal
### (1976), 30 C.C.C. (2d) 403

HOWLAND J.A.: The appellant was found guilty of manslaughter on December 9, 1974, following her trial in the Court of General Sessions of the Peace for the Judicial District of Hamilton-Wentworth, before His Honour Judge Scime and a jury and was sentenced to a term of imprisonment for five years. ...

Several weeks before the killing the appellant had rented an apartment in the City of Hamilton in the name of the deceased, John Moran. There was evidence that the appellant and Moran had consumed a considerable quantity of intoxicating liquor on June 21, 1974. Neighbours, Mr. and Mrs. Avalis, gave evidence of hearing noises, like someone fighting, coming from the apartment in the late evening of that day followed by a thud on the floor, and a woman screaming for help. The neighbours went to the apartment and found the appellant in a defensive position on the floor at Moran's feet. The appellant had a black eye and part of her face was discoloured. Moran who was 5' 10" and weighed 210 pounds, had a gash over his left eye which was bleeding. Mrs. Avalis returned to her own apartment on a lower floor twice to call the police. Mr. Avalis attempted to separate the appellant and the deceased. In the scuffle, Moran was hit over the head with an iron by the appellant. Mr. Avalis then returned to his own apartment to call the police again.

Returning to the scene of the argument, Mr. Avalis found the deceased lying on a bed with stab wounds. The appellant later stated to a police officer that she had stabbed Moran with a knife. According to the evidence of the pathologist, Moran's death resulted from the stab wounds which the appellant admitted she had inflicted.

The investigating officer swore that the appellant had been drinking, but did not think that she was intoxicated. Moran's blood was analyzed and found to contain 220 mg. of alcohol per 100 ml. of blood, a high blood-alcohol level.

The appellant did not testify at her trial but in her written statement, ex. 44, she said: "It was self-defence, I did not mean to kill him ... ." She described the drinking bout and her argument with Moran. ...

Secondly, Mr. Kerbel forcefully argued that there was misdirection in dealing with the defence of self-defence.

In my opinion the learned trial Judge misdirected the jury when dealing with the extent to which self-defence is justified under s. 34(2) of the Criminal Code. ... There is a basic distinction between s. 34(1) and s. 34(2). Section 34(1) deals with a situation where the accused repels an unprovoked assault, but does not intend the force that he uses to cause death or grievous bodily harm. Section 34(2) applies where the accused intentionally kills or intentionally causes grievous bodily harm to his assailant. As Martin, J.A., pointed out in delivering the judgment of this Court in *R. v. Baxter* [27 C.C.C. (2d) 96 at p. 110]:

> In my opinion, the words in s. 34(2) "who causes death or grievous bodily harm" mean "even though be intentionally causes death or grievous bodily harm."

Section 34(1) also specifically provides that in repelling force by force, the force which is used must be no more than is necessary for self-defence. Under s. 34(2) there is no specific requirement that the repelling force used by the accused shall be proportionate to the unlawful assault, if the other conditions of the subsection are satisfied.

As Martin, J.A., stated in *R. v. Baxter*, *supra*, at p. 107:

> Under s. 34(2) of the Code the ultimate question for the jury is not whether the accused was actually in danger of death or grievous bodily harm, and whether the causing of death or grievous bodily harm by him was in fact necessary to preserve himself from death or grievous bodily harm, but whether:
>
> (1) He caused death or grievous bodily harm under a reasonable apprehension of death or grievous bodily harm, and
> (2) He believed on reasonable and probable grounds that he could not otherwise preserve himself from death or grievous bodily harm.

He is entitled to be acquitted, if upon all the evidence, there was reasonable doubt whether or not the blow was delivered under reasonable apprehension of death or grievous bodily harm, and if he believed on reasonable grounds that he could not otherwise preserve himself from death or grievous bodily harm. He does not have to prove that it was so delivered: *R. v. Philbrook* (1941), 77 C.C.C. 26.

There are two criteria to be satisfied under s. 34(2). The reasonable apprehension of death or grievous bodily harm in s. 34(2)(a) must satisfy an objective standard. In addition, s. 34(2)(b) imports a subjective element, the belief of the accused that he cannot otherwise preserve himself from death or grievous bodily harm. However, this belief must meet am objective standard that it is based "on reasonable and probable grounds." As Martin, J.A., stated in *R. v. Baxter*, *supra*, at pp. 108-9:

> In deciding whether the accused's belief was based upon reasonable grounds the jury would of necessity draw comparisons with what a reasonable person in the accused's situation might believe with respect to the extent and the imminence of the danger by which he was threatened, and the force necessary to defend himself against the apprehended danger.

In considering whether the degree of force used by the accused was justified, the difference between the criteria under s. 34(1) and (2) must be carefully borne in mind. In neither case is a person defending himself against a reasonably apprehended attack expected to weigh to a nicety the exact measure of necessary defensive action. *R. v. Baxter*, *supra*, at p. 111 ... .

There is, however, a real difference between the test under s. 34(1) that the force be no more than is necessary to enable the accused to defend himself, and that under s. 34(2)(b) that the accused believe on reasonable grounds that he cannot otherwise preserve himself from death or grievous bodily harm. The belief of the accused may be a reasonable one, but it may be mistaken: *R. v. Chisam* (1963), 47 Cr.App.R. 130. If as a result of threats or an assault a person believes that he may momentarily be shot or stabbed, and he in turn instinctively shoots or stabs his assailant, it may properly be concluded that only reasonable defensive action had been taken to save his life. If on the other hand, the test is an objective one requiring that the force be proportionate to the attack, then the accused may not be justified if he shoots or stabs his assailant, when knocking him unconscious would have been all that was required to preserve his life or save him from grievous bodily harm.

Section 34(2)(b) recognizes the fact that when a man's life is in the balance he cannot be expected to make the same decision as he would on sober reflection. As Holmes, J., stated in *Brown v. United States* (1921), 256 U.S. 335 at p. 343: "Detached reflection cannot be demanded in the presence of an uplifted knife." The essential question to be determined under s. 34(2)(b) in considering whether the force is excessive, is the state of mind of the accused at the time the force is applied. *R. v. Preston*, *supra*, is in point. In that case Preston was convicted of manslaughter for having caused the death of Stevenson by striking him in the head with a partly full whiskey bottle during a struggle in which Stevenson was the aggressor. The trial Judge read verbatim to the jury s. 53 of the *Criminal Code*, which was the predecessor of s. 34. He continued:

> You will remember of course the defence of the accused when he went in the box. He said "I struck this blow, and I struck it in self-defence. I was trying to get away"—and he said he just received a severe blow from the deceased, and saw the deceased coming at him again and that he raised his hands, and as the deceased came at him he brought down the whiskey bottle on the head of the deceased with his hand grasping the bottle. As I say, it is for you to decide whether the accused used more force than was reasonably necessary in his own self-defence. If he used no more force than was necessary in defending himself, then he is entitled to be acquitted, but if you find that he used more force than was necessary in defending himself, then you must convict him. ...

In the present case, there was evidence on which the jury, if properly directed, could have concluded that s. 34(2) was applicable ... . The important question is whether the trial Judge properly directed the jury with respect to s. 34(2). There were three passages in particular where the trial Judge dealer with self-defence within the meaning of s. 34(2). ...

In each of these three statements the trial Judge has clearly indicated that in addition to the criteria in s. 34(2)(a) and (b) the force must be proportionate to the original assault by the deceased. Whether the amount of force used against the accused was disproportionate to the nature of the force used by her was proper to be considered by the jury as a circumstance, or an item of evidence, in deciding whether she had a reasonable apprehension of death or grievous bodily harm and whether she had reasonable and probable grounds to believe that she could not otherwise preserve herself from death or grievous bodily harm. If, however, the jury was either satisfied that the accused had such apprehension and belief, or entertained a reasonable doubt with respect to it, she was entitled to be acquitted. No further requirement existed that the force used by the accused be proportionate to the nature of the attack upon her.

The jury might, however, reasonably have understood from the above passages in the charge that, in addition to the requirements specified in s. 34(2), There was, as a matter of law, a further requirement that the force used by the accused must be proportionate to the assault made upon her by the deceased in order for the defence of self-defence to be available. The addition of the criterion of the force being proportionate to the assault led the trial Judge to concentrate on the reasonableness of the force, rather than on the reasonableness of the accused's belief. The state of mind of the accused at the time when the force is applied has to be considered, and not merely the type of weapon and the severity of the blow. At p. 637 of his charge he asked: "Was it necessary for her to inflict the stab wound to protect herself to preserve her own safety? ... Was it necessary for her to stab him twice to protect herself in these circumstances?" He should have asked whether she believed on reasonable and probable grounds that it was necessary to stab him as she did.

In my opinion there was a serious misdirection with respect to s. 34(2). It cannot be said that this misdirection did not result in any substantial wrong or miscarriage of justice. One can only speculate whether the jury if properly directed, would have been satisfied beyond a reasonable doubt that the acts of the accused were not justified as self-defence within s. 34(2) of the Code.

In my opinion the appeal should be allowed, the verdict of guilty set aside, and a new trial should be directed.

---

Consider whether the following judgment in *R. v. Pawliuk* provides a workable methodology for determining whether to leave ss. 34(1), (2), or both with the jury.

### R. v. Pawliuk
British Columbia Court of Appeal
(2001), 151 C.C.C. (3d) 155

[The accused and co-accused were charged with second-degree murder. The accused shot the deceased, and the co-accused was charged as a party. The accused testified that he thought that the deceased was going to shoot him. The accused testified that he was scared and that he accidentally or involuntarily shot the deceased. The trial judge instructed the jury on s. 34(2) of the *Criminal Code* but did not instruct the jury on s. 34(1). Both the accused and the co-accused were convicted.]

RYAN J.A.: …

[64]  Mr. Pawliuk gave evidence that while he was lawfully acting in self-defence he accidentally, or involuntarily, shot Preyser. The appellant Pawliuk testified at trial that Preyser came running towards him on the street. The appellant said that he believed that Preyser was armed with a gun, he had seen it earlier. He said that he saw Preyser reaching behind him. The appellant said that he pulled out his gun and waved it at Preyser to show him that he too had a gun and that the gun accidentally discharged, killing the deceased. The appellant said:

> I recall him [Preyser] reaching and my gun go off. I pulled it out because I was scared when I saw him reach. I do not recall pulling the trigger. I had no intention to shoot Preyser.

and further,

> I had no intention to shoot that man, my gun was not out until he reached for his gun. I thought he was going to kill me.

[65]  If the jury concluded that the appellant pulled out the gun in self-defence and accidentally fired it, the appellant was entitled to an acquittal based on accident. If, reasonably fearing death or grievous bodily harm he intentionally fired the gun, he was entitled to an acquittal, assuming the other elements of s. 34(2) were met.

[66]  The trial judge instructed the jury on s. 34(2) but refused to charge on s. 34(1). The appellant submitted in this Court that the trial judge erred in failing to leave both subsections with the jury.

[67]  Sections 34(1) and (2) provide of the *Criminal Code*:

> 34(1)  Every one who is unlawfully assaulted without having provoked the assault is justified in repelling force by force if the force he uses is not intended to cause death or grievous bodily harm and is no more than is necessary to enable him to defend himself.
>
> (2)  Every one who is unlawfully assaulted and who causes death or grievous bodily harm in repelling the assault is justified if
>
> (a)  he causes it under reasonable apprehension of death or grievous bodily harm from the violence with which the assault was originally made or with which the assailant pursues his purposes; and
>
> (b)  he believes, on reasonable grounds, that he cannot otherwise preserve himself from death or grievous bodily harm.

[68]  The appellant's argument is that s. 34(1) is the applicable self-defence provision when the accused does not intend to cause death or bodily harm. He says that s. 34(2) applies when the accused responds to an attack intending to cause death or grievous bodily harm.

[69]  I have concluded that the trial judge was right not to leave s. 34(1) with the jury. In my view both ss. 34(1) and (2) may apply where the accused, in repelling an attack, did not intend to cause death or grievous bodily harm. Lack of intention alone does not require a trial judge to leave both subsections with the jury. What differentiates the sections is whether the accused reasonably apprehended that the attack on

him or her was likely to cause his or her own death or grievous bodily harm. If the accused reasonably apprehended his own death or grievous bodily harm then he or she is entitled to the more favourable provisions of s. 34(2). In the case at bar the appellant testified that he feared the deceased was going to kill him and that he responded by pulling out the gun. His defence fell within s. 34(2). It did not fall within s. 34(1)—his entire defence was premised on his belief that the deceased was going to kill or seriously injure him.

[70]  I believe my view of the operation of s-ss. 34(1) and (2) is supported by the decision of the Ontario Court of Appeal in *R. v. Pintar* (1996), 110 C.C.C. (3d) 402, which reconsidered, or perhaps reinterpreted, its previous decision in *R. v. Baxter* (1975), 27 C.C.C. (2d) 96. Until the decision in *Pintar*, this Court, and other courts including the Supreme Court of Canada, had interpreted s. 34(2) to apply only in circumstances where the accused intended to cause death or grievous bodily harm to the victim.

[71]  In *R. v. Baxter*, the accused had injured his victims with shotgun pellets when he discharged a shotgun in their direction. The trial judge, holding that s. 34(1) was inapplicable because grievous bodily harm had resulted, charged the jury only on s. 34(2) of the *Criminal Code*. The Ontario Court of Appeal ordered a new trial. It held that the difference in s-ss. 34(1) and 34(2) did not lie in whether the accused's actions resulted in death or grievous bodily harm, but in whether the accused intended to cause death or grievous bodily harm. Writing for the Court, Martin J.A. held that s. 34(1) is not automatically excluded where death or grievous bodily harm has resulted. Referring to the fact that s. 34(2) contains the words "[an accused] who causes death or grievous bodily harm" while s. 34(1) does not, Martin J.A. said this, at p. 110:

> In my opinion, the words in s. 34(2) "who causes death or grievous bodily harm" mean "even though he intentionally causes death or grievous bodily harm." The language of s. 53(2), the predecessor of s. 34(2) was clearer in this respect. I do not think, however, that in rewording the present section, Parliament intended to alter the law. Any other interpretation would leave unprovided for the case of a person who, using no more force than is necessary to defend himself against an unprovoked assault, accidentally kills or causes grievous bodily harm to his assailant without intending to do so, and who does not fall within s. 34(2) because he did not apprehend death or grievous bodily harm, or did not believe that the only way he could defend himself was by killing his assailant or causing him grievous bodily harm.

Martin J.A. concluded, at p. 111:

> Where there is an issue as to whether the accused intended to cause death or grievous bodily harm the trial Judge, notwithstanding death or grievous bodily harm has resulted, should instruct the jury with respect to the provisions of s. 34(1) and then proceed to s. 34(2) as the applicable provision, in the event that the jury is satisfied that the accused intended to cause death or grievous bodily harm.

[72]  Following this analysis other courts have focused on the presence or absence of the intent to cause death or grievous bodily harm as the principle distinction

between ss. 34(1) and (2). This emphasis is seen, for example, in *R. v. Brisson*, 69 C.C.C. (2d) 97. In that case the Supreme Court of Canada was asked to determine whether s. 34 of the *Criminal Code* accommodated the notion of "excessive self-defence" which would reduce murder to manslaughter. In reaching the conclusion that it did not, Dickson J. set out the "reasonable statutory interpretation of s. 34." He said, at p. 258:

> Section 34(1) may only be invoked if there is no intention to cause death or grievous bodily harm and no more force than is necessary is used. Section 34(2) is invoked where death or grievous harm has resulted but (i) the accused reasonably apprehended his own death or grievous harm and (ii) he believed on reasonable grounds that he had no other means of avoiding his own death or grievous harm. *Section 34(1) affords justification in circumstances where the force used was not intended to cause death or grievous harm and is not excessive. Section 34(2) affords justification where there was an intention to cause death but under circumstances where objectively it was reasonable that the person accused believed he was going to be killed and subjectively he did so believe.* Section 34(2) obviously provides for acquittal, despite the fact that the accused means to cause death or bodily harm that he knows is likely to cause death.
>
> On the construction of s. 34 it is difficult to see how the amount of force used will determine that a murder should be reduced to manslaughter. *In such a case one must of necessity be dealing with s. 34(2), i.e. there exists an intention to cause death. Otherwise we fall under s. 34(1) where there is no intention to cause death and thus no question of reducing murder to manslaughter. In s. 34(2) we are concerned primarily with the person who has caused death and intended to cause death.* All of these elements of murder are present.
>
> On a reasonable interpretation of s. 34 it is apparent that a qualified defence of excessive force does not exist. [Emphasis added.]

[73] In *Pintar* the Ontario Court of Appeal extended the analysis in *Baxter*. While Baxter held that s-ss. 34(1) and (2) are not mutually exclusive when death or grievous bodily harm *results* from the accused's actions, *Pintar* went further to hold that s-ss. 34(1) and (2) are not mutually exclusive where there is no *intention* to cause death or grievous bodily harm. In so concluding, the Court, properly in my view, effectively held that the distinction between the subsections lies primarily in the accused's perception of what is happening to him when he acts against the victim, i.e. whether the accused has a reasonable apprehension of death or grievous bodily harm at the hands of his attacker.

[74] In *Pintar*, Mr. Justice Moldaver said this, at p. 431, C.C.C.:

> Unlike s. 34(1) which speaks to the issue of intent, s. 34(2) does not. The plain wording of s. 34(2) reveals that the provision is triggered when a person who has been unlawfully assaulted *causes death or grievous bodily harm in repelling the assault.* On its face, this wording would certainly suggest that the applicability of s. 34(2) is dependent upon a finding that the original assailant either died or suffered grievous bodily harm as a consequence of the responsive measures taken by the person assaulted. To go beyond that and hold that when the charge is murder, accused persons can only take

advantage of s. 34(2) if they intend to kill or cause grievous bodily harm has the effect not only of adding words to the section which are simply not there, but also of creating an additional hurdle which they must overcome when the charge is murder. [Italics in original.]

and later, at pp. 433-34:

As a matter of policy, I am unable to fathom why accused persons charged with murder, who otherwise meet the criteria of s. 34(2), should be precluded from relying upon the provision simply because they did not intend to kill or cause grievous bodily harm. If anything, these accused are potentially less morally blameworthy than those who intentionally kill or cause grievous bodily harm. I fail to see why s. 34(2) should be interpreted in a manner which puts a premium on a higher degree of moral blameworthiness. My concern is particularly heightened in light of [*R. v.*] *McIntosh* [[1995] 1 S.C.R. 686, 95 C.C.C. (3d) 481], which establishes that unlike s. 34(1), s. 34(2) applies regardless of whether an accused provokes the initial unlawful assault. If s. 34(2) contains, as a fourth constituent element, the intent to kill or cause grievous bodily harm in murder cases, this would mean that accused persons who provoke an assault then intentionally kill their assailant are in a better position than those who provoke an assault and kill unintentionally. I see no reason why effect should be given to such an anomalous and inequitable result.

[75] Moldaver J.A. noted that in *Baxter* Martin J.A. had used the phrase "even if he intends to cause death or bodily harm," rather than "only if etc." Thus, Moldaver J.A. concluded, Baxter should not be read as *limiting* s. 34(2) to cases where the accused intends to cause death or grievous bodily harm. Instead, he found that s. 34(2) *included* cases where the accused intends to cause death or grievous bodily harm.

[76] Although it adds little to the analysis, I am of the view that language employed by Ritchie J. in *R. v. Reilly* (1984), 15 C.C.C. (3d) 1, supports the interpretation of Moldaver J.A. in *Pintar*. Rather than intent, Ritchie J. focused on the accused's reasonable apprehension of the attack upon him and the force employed by him in repelling the attack, rather than whether or not the accused in employing the force intended to cause death or bodily harm. He said, at p. 404:

Subsection (2) of s. 34 places in issue the accused's state of mind at the time he caused the death. The subsection can only afford protection to the accused if he apprehended death or grievous bodily harm from the assault he was repelling and if he believed he could not preserve himself from death or grievous bodily harm *otherwise than by the force he used*. Nonetheless, his apprehension must be a reasonable one and his belief must be based upon reasonable and probable grounds. The subsection requires that the jury consider, and be guided by, what they decide on the evidence was the accused's appreciation of the situation and his belief as to the reaction it required, so long as there exists an objectively verifiable basis for his perception.

[77] This interpretation reflects the reality of the situation when a person is called upon to defend himself or herself from an attack. More often the intent of the person attacked is simply to save him or herself by whatever force required. If he or she were

asked, "Were you trying to kill the deceased?" they would answer, "I did not think about that, I was doing what I had to save myself from being seriously hurt or killed."

[78] The result of the *Pintar* case is that if the accused reasonably apprehends that he is under threat of death or grievous bodily harm he may defend himself using as much force as he reasonably believes is required to preserve himself from death or grievous bodily harm which may or may not include an intention by the accused to cause death or grievous bodily harm. If the accused does *not* reasonably believe that he is under threat of death or grievous bodily harm he may rely on s. 34(1), but only if he did not intend to cause death or grievous bodily harm. If, in response to the attack upon him, the accused intends to cause death or grievous bodily harm he is limited to s. 34(2) and thus he must in turn be under a reasonable apprehension of death or grievous bodily harm from his attacker before it can be said his response is justified.

### British Columbia Jurisprudence

[79] Prior to the *Pintar* decision a majority of the Court held in *R. v. Laverty* (1995), 60 B.C.A.C. 280, that there was no specific error in a jury charge which limited s. 34(2) to circumstances where the accused intended to cause death or grievous bodily harm. The matter went to the Supreme Court of Canada on a dissent on a matter of law unrelated to the question of intent in s. 34(2). The appeal was dismissed "substantially for the reasons of the majority."

[80] In *R. v. Eggleston* (1997), 117 C.C.C. (3d) 566, this Court, in dicta, remarked upon the *Pintar* case with some approval but left the decision for another day when the issue was squarely before the Court.

[81] Next, the *Pintar* case was commented upon in *R. v. Bukmeier* (1998), 103 B.C.A.C. 303, 169 W.A.C. 303 (B.C.C.A.). In *Bukmeier* the Crown conceded that the reasoning in *Pintar* was correct and that the trial judge was wrong in limiting s. 34(2) to cases where the accused intended to cause death or grievous bodily harm. Citing *Laverty*, the Court declined to follow *Pintar*, but noted that even if *Pintar* was right s. 686(1)(b)(iii) would apply in the circumstances of that appeal.

[82] Finally, the issue was raised directly in *R. v. Kindt* (1998), 124 C.C.C. (3d) 20 (B.C.C.A.). In that case, the Crown appealed the accused's acquittal on a charge of murder on the basis that the trial judge had erred in instructing the jury that s. 34(2) applied "even though" the accused did not intend to cause death or grievous bodily harm. Noting that Laverty had not directly raised the question of intent as it relates to s. 34(2), the majority approved the analysis in *Pintar* and dismissed the appeal.

[83] In spite of some dicta to the contrary, I am of the view that the *Pintar* analysis of s. 34(2) now constitutes the law in this province.

[84] I am reinforced in this view by the recent decision of the Supreme Court of Canada in *R. v. Trombley*, [1999] 1 S.C.R. 757, an appeal which came to the Court as of right from the Ontario Court of Appeal. The Ontario Court of Appeal had ordered a new trial for *Trombley* after her conviction for manslaughter ((1998), 126 C.C.C. (3d) 495). A majority of the Court of Appeal found that the trial judge had wrongly left the jury with the impression that s. 34(2) was only applicable if the accused intended to cause death or grievous bodily harm. Finlayson J.A., dissenting, held that

the jury would have understood that s. 34(2) applied whether or not the appellant intended to cause death or grievous bodily harm. Lamer C.J.C. dismissed the appeal in the following terms, at p. 757:

> This appeal comes to us as of right. We all agree substantially with the reasons and disposition of the case by the majority of the Court of Appeal of Ontario. Accordingly, the appeal is therefore dismissed and the order for a new trial on the charge of manslaughter is confirmed.

[85] In my view, *Trombley* is definitive of the issue. An accused may resort to the self-defence provisions in s. 34(2) whether or not he or she intends to cause death or grievous bodily harm.

---

See G.T. Trotter, "*R. v. Pawliuk*: Further Efforts To Clarify Self-Defence" (2001), 40 C.R. (5th) 56.

To what extent should a person be expected to withdraw before acting in self-defence? Compare s. 34 of the Code with the following statement quoted with approval by the Supreme Court of the United States in 1895 (*Beard v. U.S.*, 158 U.S. 550, at 561 (1895)): "a true man who is without fault is not obliged to fly from an assailant, who by violence or surprise maliciously seeks to take his life or do him enormous bodily harm." Note that in *R. v. Deegan* (1979), 49 C.C.C. (2d) 417, the Alberta Court of Appeal adopted the statement of Holmes J. in the U.S. Supreme Court case of *Brown v. United States of America*, 256 U.S. 335 (1920):

> Many respectable writers agree that if a man reasonably believes that he is in immediate danger of death or grievous bodily harm from his assailant, he may stand his ground, and that if he kills him, he has not exceeded the bounds of lawful self-defence. That has been the decision of this court. *Beard v. United States*. Detached reflection cannot be demanded in the presence of an uplifted knife. Therefore, in this court, at least, it is not a condition of immunity that one in that situation should pause to consider whether a reasonable man might not think it possible to fly with safety, or to disable his assailant rather than to kill him.

In *Reilly v. The Queen* (1984), 15 C.C.C. (3d) 1 (S.C.C.), Ritchie J., speaking for five members of the court, rejected the accused's appeal that the trial judge erred in not instructing the jury to consider evidence of intoxication in deciding whether they had a reasonable doubt whether the accused acted in self-defence under s. 34(2) of the Code. He stated:

> Section 34(2) places in issue the accused's state of mind at the time he caused death. The subsection can only afford protection to the accused if he apprehended death or grievous bodily harm from the assault he was repelling and if he believed he could not preserve himself from death or grievous bodily harm otherwise than by the force he used. None the less, his apprehension must be a *reasonable* one and his belief must *be based upon reasonable and probable grounds*. The subsection requires that the jury consider, and be guided by, what they decide on the evidence was the accused's appreciation of the situation and his

belief as to the reaction it required, so long as there exists an objectively verifiable basis for his perception.

Since s. 34(2) places in issue the accused's perception of the attack upon him and the response required to meet it, the accused may still be found to have acted in self-defence even if he was mistaken in his perception. Reasonable and probable grounds must still exist for this mistaken perception in the sense that the mistake must have been one which an ordinary man using ordinary care could have made in the same circumstances.

This statutory requirement of reasonableness is what distinguishes the defence provided by s. 34(2) from the general law upon mistake of fact expressed in *Pappajohn v. The Queen* (1980), 52 C.C.C. (2d) 481, 111 D.L.R. (3d) 1, [1980] 2 S.C.R. 120. In the *Pappajohn* case it was held that an honest, but mistaken belief in facts which, if true, would render the accused's act innocent was sufficient to prevent him from forming the *mens rea* essential to all criminal liability; there was no legal necessity that the mistaken belief be based upon reasonable grounds. It was accepted that intoxication could potentially induce such a mistake of fact.

The fatal difficulty with the appellant's argument in this case is that although intoxication can be a factor in inducing an honest mistake, it cannot induce a mistake which must be based upon reasonable and probable grounds. The perspective of the reasonable man which the language of s. 34(2) places in issue here is the objective standard the law commonly adopts to measure a man's conduct. A reasonable man is a man in full possession of his faculties. In contrast, a drunken man is one whose ability to reason and to perceive are diminished by the alcohol he has consumed.

I should not be taken as saying that the defence under s. 34(2) can never be available to a person who is intoxicated. An intoxicated man may hold a reasonable belief, i.e., the same belief a sober man would form viewing the matter before him upon reasonable and probable grounds. Where he does so, however, it is in spite of his intoxication.

The requirement of an objective basis for the accused's perception of the facts, whether it be mistaken or accurate, eliminates any relevance that evidence of the accused's intoxication might have had to self-defence under s. 34(2). Naturally, if the accused is intoxicated, he is not deprived of the defence provided by the subsection so long as the objective test is met by the existence of reasonable and probable grounds for the accused's perception of the nature of the assault upon him and the response required to meet it.

If "excessive force" is used in self-defence, should the accused person who caused the death be guilty of murder or manslaughter? In *R. v. Reilly* (1982), 66 C.C.C. (2d) 146, Arnup J.A., giving the judgment of the Ontario Court of Appeal, stated:

I have reached the conclusion that the doctrine of excessive force in self-defence rendering the accused guilty only of manslaughter instead of murder should be recognized in Ontario. Without deciding that there are no other requisites for its application in particular cases, I conclude also that the conditions stated by Martin J.A. in *Trecroce* (1980), 55 C.C.C. (2d) 202 should be applied …

(a) The accused must have been justified in using some force to defend himself against an attack, real or *reasonably apprehended*.

(b) The accused must have *honestly* believed that he was justified in using the force he did.

(c) The force used was excessive only because it exceeded what the accused could *reasonably* have considered necessary.

In contrast, Dickson J. speaking for four members of the Supreme Court of Canada (the other five members did not feel it was necessary to discuss the issue) concluded his judgment in *Brisson v. The Queen* (1982), 69 C.C.C. (2d) 97, by stating:

> On the construction of s. 34 it is difficult to see how the amount of force used will determine that a murder should be reduced to manslaughter. In such a case one must of necessity be dealing with s. 34(2), i.e. there exists an intention to cause death. Otherwise we fall under s. 34(1) where there is no intention to cause death and thus no question of reducing murder to manslaughter. In s. 34(2) we are concerned primarily with the person who has caused death and intended to cause death. All of these elements of murder are present.
>
> On a reasonable statutory interpretation of s. 34 it is apparent that a qualified defence of excessive force does not exist.
>
> To summarize, I would reject the notion that excessive force in self-defence, unless related to intent under s. 212 of the *Code* or to provocation, reduces what would otherwise be murder to manslaughter.

In *R. v. Faid* (1983), 2 C.C.C. (3d) 513, excessive self-defence was again the issue before the Supreme Court of Canada. Dickson J. gave the judgment for the seven-member court:

> In *Brisson* I sought to explain why, in my opinion, a verdict of manslaughter, except in the circumstances to which I have earlier alluded, is not available where an accused acting in self-defence, as described in s. 34 of the *Code*, causes a death by the use of an excess of force. I am still of that opinion. The position of the Alberta Court of Appeal that there is a "half-way" house outside s. 34 of the *Code* is, in my view, inapplicable to the Canadian codified system of criminal law, it lacks any recognizable basis in principle, would require prolix and complicated jury charges and would encourage juries to reach compromise verdicts to the prejudice of either the accused or the Crown. Where a killing has resulted from the excessive use of force in self-defence the accused loses the justification provided under s. 34. There is no partial justification open under the section. Once the jury reaches the conclusion that excessive force has been used the defence of self-defence has failed. It does not follow automatically, however, that the verdict must be murder. The accused has become responsible for a killing. He has no justification on the basis of self-defence, but unless it is shown that the killing was accompanied by the intent required under s. 212(a) of the *Code*, it remains a killing without intent, in other words manslaughter. If the jury considers that excessive force has been used, and has resulted in a death, they must then ask themselves whether the accused, in causing the killing, possessed the intent described in s. 212(a) of the *Code*, that is, an intent to kill or cause bodily harm likely to cause death. If they are satisfied beyond a reasonable doubt that the intent was present, they should find the accused guilty of murder. However, in the event they found no such intent existed, or had a doubt as to its existence, they should convict of manslaughter. This conviction would rest upon the fact that an unlawful killing had been committed without the intent required to make it murder under s. 212(a).

**R. v. Cinous**
Supreme Court of Canada
(2002), 162 C.C.C. (3d) 129

[The accused was charged with murder. The accused supported himself through criminal acts, especially the theft of computers. The accused was suspicious that the victim had stolen the accused's revolver. The accused tried to avoid the deceased and a
third party who had been with them when the accused's revolver disappeared. The
accused heard rumours that the deceased and the third party intended to kill him.
Several days after the accused's revolver was stolen, the victim and the third party
proposed that the accused join them in a theft. The accused said that the victim and
the third party behaved suspiciously. When the victim put on latex surgical gloves,
which in the accused's mind were worn to avoid getting blood on one's hands, the
accused believed that he was going to be killed. The accused shot the deceased in the
back of the head at a service station where they had stopped to purchase windshield
wiper fluid. The accused was convicted at trial, but the Quebec Court of Appeal allowed his appeal, finding errors in the trial judge's instructions on self-defence. A
majority of the Supreme Court of Canada allowed the appeal.]

McLACHLIN C.J.C. and BASTARACHE J. (L'Heureux-Dubé and LeBel JJ., concurring): …

[38] While we agree with the Court of Appeal that the trial judge made several
errors in the charge to the jury, we do not agree that any of these, viewed individually
or cumulatively, warrant overturning the conviction and ordering a new trial. It is our
view that since the three conditions of self-defence were not all met on the facts of
this case, the defence lacked the "air of reality" required in order to warrant leaving it
with the jury. Since the defence should never have been put to the jury, any errors
made in the charge to the jury relating to it are irrelevant. These errors of law can be
safely set to one side, and s. 686(1)(b)(iii) should be applied in order to uphold the
conviction.

[After a lengthy discussion of the "air of reality" test for putting defences to the
jury, McLachlin C.J.C. applied the law to the facts of the case.]

[92] This brings us to the application of the air of reality test to the facts of this
case. The question to be asked is whether there is evidence on the record upon which
a properly instructed jury acting reasonably could acquit if it believed the evidence to
be true.
[93] In *Pétel* … , at p. 12, Lamer C.J. stated the three constitutive elements of
self-defence under s. 34(2): "(1) the existence of an unlawful assault; (2) a reasonable apprehension of a risk of death or grievous bodily harm; and (3) a reasonable
belief that it is not possible to preserve oneself from harm except by killing the adversary." All three of these elements must be established in order for the defence to
succeed. The air of reality test must therefore be applied to each of the three ele-

ments. If any of these elements lacks an air of reality, the defence should not be put to the jury. See *Hebert* ... ; *Latimer* ... .

[94] Each of the three elements under s. 34(2) has both a subjective and an objective component. The accused's perception of the situation is the "subjective" part of the test. However, the accused's belief must also be reasonable on the basis of the situation he perceives. This is the objective part of the test. Section 34(2) makes the reasonableness requirement explicit in relation to the second and third conditions. *Pétel* held that the same standard applies to the first component of the defence, namely, the existence of an assault. With respect to each of the three elements, the approach is first to inquire about the subjective perceptions of the accused, and then to ask whether those perceptions were objectively reasonable in the circumstances.

[95] The air of reality analysis must be applied to each component of the defence, both subjective and objective. Evidence capable of supporting a particular finding of fact with respect to one component of the defence will not necessarily be capable of supporting other components of the defence. In the case of a defence of self-defence under s. 34(2), the testimony of the accused as to his perceptions does not necessarily constitute evidence reasonably capable of supporting the conclusion that the perception was reasonable.

[96] The difficult issue in this case is whether there is some evidence upon which a properly instructed jury acting reasonably could have concluded that the accused's purported perceptions were *reasonable* under the circumstances. Since reasonableness is inherently incapable of being established by direct evidence, the key question is whether there is evidence on the basis of which reasonableness could reasonably be inferred by a jury. If a jury could not have reasonably come to the conclusion that the accused's perceptions were reasonable, even accepting that his testimonial evidence was true, then the defence should not have been put to the jury.

[97] There is no authority for the proposition that reasonableness is exempt from the air of reality test, or that evidence satisfying the air of reality test as to the subjective component of defence will automatically confer an air of reality upon the whole defence. Moreover, we consider that the introduction of such a requirement would constitute an unwarranted and illogical break with the rationale underlying air of reality analysis. The long-standing requirement is that the *whole defence* must have an air of reality, not just bits and pieces of the defence. See *Hebert* ... , at para. 16, per Cory J., holding that a defence of self-defence lacked an air of reality precisely in that the reasonableness of an accused's purported perception could not be supported by the evidence. See also *Thibert* ..., per Cory J., at paras. 6 and 7.

### (1) The Putative Evidential Basis for the Defence

[98] The evidence relied upon in this case emanates from the accused's own testimony. While this Court has made it clear that a mere assertion by the accused of the elements of a defence will not be sufficient to clear the air of reality hurdle, that principle does not have any application to the present case. The accused's testimony goes beyond merely asserting the elements of the defence, and provides a comprehensive account of his perceptions and his explanation for them. As was stated

above, credibility is not an issue in air of reality analysis. The issue is not whether the accused (or any other witness) should be believed. Rather, the question is whether, if the jury were to accept the construction of the evidence most favourable to the accused's position, the requisite inferences could reasonably be drawn.

[99]  With these considerations in view, we now turn to a review of the relevant evidence.

[100]  In his testimony, the accused pointed to many things that he perceived as indications that he was about to be attacked. The accused testified that he had heard rumors that the victim, Mike, and his companion, Ice, planned to kill him. He claimed to have received a specific warning to that effect by a friend of his.

[101]  He testified that on the night in question, Mike and Ice did not take off their jackets when they came to his home. The accused testified that Ice put his hand under his coat, in what the accused took to be a suspicious gesture. The accused claimed that these facts led him to believe that Mike and Ice were armed, though they denied it when he asked them about it. They whispered to each other throughout the evening, which the accused also found suspicious.

[102]  The accused testified that his suspicions were further aroused when he entered the van. He ascribed significance to the fact that Ice removed the gloves that he had initially been wearing and replaced them with a different pair, putting them on *before getting in the van*. He testified that this was unusual. He also testified that Mike sat behind the accused, on the passenger side, and was wearing latex surgical gloves. The accused testified that he associated wearing gloves of this type with a "burn" (i.e. an attack on a criminal by another criminal). He testified that this was based on limited personal experience of his own, and on movies that he had seen, in which hit men wore such gloves. The accused testified that Mike loudly snapped the gloves at some point during the ride, which he interpreted as an overt threat. The accused testified that the gloves indicated that a plan to kill him existed and would be executed that very night.

[103]  The accused further testified that the sudden change in the routine of the criminal group had meaning. He testified that Ice avoided eye contact with him, and that everyone in the van was uncharacteristically silent. He testified that Ice repeated the suspicious gesture that he had initially made in the apartment, placing his hand under his coat. He said that Ice did this both in the van and in the gas station. The accused testified that in the gang culture to which he belonged, this gesture is meant to communicate to rival gang members that one is armed. When pressed to say whether the purpose of Ice's gesture was to show he had a gun or to signal to the accused that he was going to kill him, the accused was reluctant to say it was a message that he would kill him. He nevertheless indicated that this gesture had added significance to him because there was a rumor that he was about to be killed.

[104]  The accused testified that he felt trapped, and that he was convinced that Ice and the victim, Mike, were just waiting for the right moment to kill him. He testified that he felt that Ice and Mike had set a trap for him. He testified that he thought that Mike, who was sitting behind him, would be the one to kill him. He testified that he knew that Mike had used firearms before.

[105]  When asked why he did not run away or call the police, the accused claimed not to have thought of these options. When pressed on cross-examination about not running away, he indicated that he felt he should not have to leave the van. With respect to calling the police, he also said: "I'm not used to calling the police, you know. I'm just not used to that. I never called the police in my life. People have been calling the police [on] me all my life. You know, I've been running away from the police all my life." He also stated that the police would have arrived too late to save him. He added that asking the police for help would have meant having to work for them as an informant. He said of being an informant: "that's the only way you can get protection, you know? And since I wasn't going to do that, and I never will—you know what I'm saying?—so there was no way the police was going to protect me, no way!"

[106]  It must now be determined whether a properly instructed jury acting reasonably could base an acquittal on the evidence reviewed above, assuming that evidence to be true. In order to make this determination, the evidence must be considered in relation to each of the three elements of self-defence under s. 34(2).

### (2)  The Existence of an Assault

[107]  Lamer C.J. stated in *Pétel* … , that the existence of an actual assault is not a prerequisite for a defence under s. 34(2). Rather, the starting point is the perspective of the accused. Lamer C.J. stated at p. 13:

> The question that the jury must ask itself is therefore not "was the accused unlawfully assaulted?" but rather "did the accused reasonably believe, in the circumstances, that she was being unlawfully assaulted?"

Of course, in applying the air of reality test, the judge should not try to answer the question stated by Lamer C.J. The focus of the trial judge in air of reality analysis is narrower. The question is whether there is evidence upon which a jury acting reasonably *could* conclude that the accused reasonably believed he was about to be attacked, not whether the jury *should* so conclude. Assuming there is an air of reality to the whole defence, it will be up to the jury to decide whether or not the accused actually believed that he was about to be attacked, and whether or not that perception was reasonable.

[108]  There is an air of reality to the subjective component of the defence. There is direct evidence on the accused's beliefs, in the form of the accused's testimony. It is open to the jury to believe this testimony. It is open to the jury to believe that the accused interpreted the various items pointed out in the evidence reviewed above as indicating that the victim and Ice were going to attack him.

[109]  Whether a jury could reasonably infer on the basis of the evidence that the accused's perception of an attack was reasonable in the circumstances presents a more difficult issue. Nevertheless, here again it seems to us that the threshold test is met. A jury acting reasonably could draw an inference from the circumstances described by the accused, including particularly the many threatening indicators to which he testified, to the reasonableness of his perception that he was going to be attacked.

[110]  We conclude that it would be possible for the jury reasonably to conclude that the accused believed that he was going to be attacked, and that this belief was

reasonable in the circumstances. In coming to this conclusion, we do not express any opinion as to the substantive merits of the defence with respect to the first element of self-defence under s. 34(2). That question is reserved for the jury.

[111]  The inquiry does not end here. In order for the defence to be put to the jury, there must also be an "air of reality" to the remaining two elements of self-defence under s. 34(2), namely the accused's reasonable perception of the risk of death or grievous bodily harm and his belief on reasonable grounds that there was no alternative to killing the victim.

### (3) Reasonable Apprehension of Death or Grievous Bodily Harm

[112]  The analysis as it relates to this second prong of self-defence under s. 34(2) follows substantially the same path as for the first prong. In order for this element of self-defence to clear the air of reality hurdle, it must be possible for the jury reasonably to infer from the evidence not only that the accused reasonably believed that he was facing an attack, but that he faced death or grievous bodily harm from that attack.

[113]  The accused's testimony is unambiguously to the effect that he feared a deadly attack. It is open to the jury to accept this testimony, that is, to accept that he did in fact have this perception. There is therefore an air of reality to the subjective component of the defence.

[114]  There is also an air of reality to the objective component of this element of the defence. On the particular facts of this case, this conclusion goes hand in hand with the determination that there is an air of reality to the first element of self-defence. That is, for the same reason that there is an air of reality to the reasonableness of the accused's perception he was going to be attacked, so too is there an air of reality to the accused's perception that the attack would be deadly. The accused's whole story is that he thought Ice and Mike were carrying out a plan to kill him, and that at least one of them was armed. The jury could not reasonably accept the accused's testimony that he believed that he was going to be attacked, but simultaneously disbelieve his claim that he thought the attack would be deadly. Similarly, the evidential basis for inferring the reasonableness of the accused's perception that he was going to be attacked is also the evidential basis for inferring the reasonableness of his perception that the attack would be deadly.

[115]  A jury acting reasonably could draw an inference from the circumstances described by the accused, including particularly the indications that Mike and Ice were armed, the rumors of a plan to assassinate him, the suspicious behaviour, and the wearing of the gloves, to the reasonableness of his perception that he was in mortal danger.

[116]  Once again, we wish to stress that the conclusion that there is an air of reality to the second prong of this defence does not involve an appraisal of the substantive merits of the defence. This conclusion rests upon our assessment that a properly instructed jury acting reasonably *could* infer the reasonableness of the accused's perception that he faced a deadly attack. Whether a jury *should* come to such a conclusion is an entirely different question, which is entirely irrelevant to the air of reality analysis.

### (4) Reasonable Belief in the Absence of Alternatives to Killing

[117]  We now come to the third and final element of self-defence under s. 34(2). This requirement too has both a subjective and an objective component. The inquiry starts with the subjective perceptions of the accused at the relevant time, and then asks whether those perceptions were reasonable. It must be established both that the accused believed that he could not preserve himself except by shooting the victim, and that he held this belief on reasonable grounds.

[118]  The inquiry into the inferences reasonably capable of being drawn by a jury must focus on the following sequence of events leading up to the accused's killing of Mike, the victim. The accused testified that he feared a deadly attack from Ice and, more particularly, from Mike, who was sitting behind him. The accused testified to the following sequence of events. Reasoning that Mike and Ice would be less likely to carry out their murderous plan in public view, the accused pulled into the well-lit parking lot of a service station. He then set about replenishing the van's supply of window washer fluid. He got out of the van, in which Ice and Mike continued to sit. He entered the service station. There, he had an exchange with the cashier, and realized that he did not have enough money to pay for the fluid. He exited the service station, and returned to the van, in which Mike and Ice still waited. He borrowed money from Ice. He then re-entered the service station, and bought the washer fluid. He exited the service station again. He regained the van, popped open the hood, and replenished the supply of fluid. When he was done, he put down the container, walked to the back door of the van, opened the door, and shot Mike in the head.

[119]  The first question is whether there is an air of reality to the accused's claim that, at the time he shot the victim, he actually believed that he had no alternative. We believe that there is. The starting point in air of reality analysis is that the accused's evidence is assumed to be true. The accused's extensive direct testimony regarding his subjective perceptions at the relevant time amounts to more than a "mere assertion" of the element of the defence. Provided there is an air of reality to the whole defence, a jury is entitled to make a determination as to credibility, and to decide whether the accused really did believe that he could not preserve himself from death or grievous bodily harm except by killing the victim.

[120]  A final issue remains. The question is whether there is anything in the testimony of the accused on the basis of which a properly instructed jury acting reasonably could infer the reasonableness of the accused's belief that he had no alternative but to kill the victim, at the end of the sequence of events described above. We conclude that there is no such evidence to be found in the accused's testimony, or in any other source.

[121]  By specifying that an accused must believe *on reasonable grounds* that he had no alternative, Parliament injected an element of objectivity into the defence of self-defence. It is not enough for an accused to establish a subjective conviction that he had no choice but to shoot his way out of a dangerous situation. Nor is it enough for an accused to provide an explanation setting out just why he believed what he did was necessary. The accused must be able to point to a *reasonable ground* for that belief. The requirement is not just that the accused be able to articulate a reason for holding the belief, or point to some considerations that tended, in his mind, to support

that belief. Rather, the requirement is that the belief that he had no other option but to kill must have been objectively *reasonable*.

[122] The accused testified that calling the police from within the service station would have been ineffective, as he believed that they would not have arrived in time to save him. This part of the accused's testimony may provide an evidential basis from which a jury acting reasonably could infer the reasonableness of the accused's belief that he could not have preserved himself from death by calling the police. There may even be an evidential basis from which a jury acting reasonably could infer a reasonable belief by the accused that it was unsafe to return to his apartment. But this is not an evidential foundation capable of supporting the defence of self-defence under s. 34(2).

[123] Section 34(2) does not require that an accused rule out *a few* courses of action other than killing. The requirement is that the accused have believed on reasonable grounds that there was *no alternative course of action* open to him at that time, so that he reasonably thought he was obliged to kill in order to preserve himself from death or grievous bodily harm. In this case, there is absolutely no evidence from which a jury could reasonably infer the reasonableness of a belief in the absence of alternatives. There is nothing in the evidence to explain why the accused did not wait in the service station rather than go back to the van. There is absolutely nothing to explain why he did not flee once he had left the van. Indeed, there is nothing to suggest the reasonableness of his conclusion that he needed to walk back to the van and shoot the victim.

[124] Self-defence under s. 34(2) provides a justification for killing. A person who intentionally takes another human life is entitled to an acquittal if he can make out the elements of the defence. This defence is intended to cover situations of last resort. In order for the defence of self-defence under s. 34(2) to succeed at the end of the day, a jury would have to accept that the accused believed *on reasonable grounds* that his own safety and survival depended on killing the victim at that moment. There is no evidence in the case on the basis of which a properly instructed jury acting reasonably could come to that conclusion. The inferences required for the defence to succeed are simply not capable of being supported by the accused's testimony.

[125] Since there is no evidential foundation for the third element of self-defence under s. 34(2), the defence as a whole lacks an air of reality.

[126] We conclude that the defence of self-defence under s. 34(2) should never have been put to the jury. The appeal should be allowed.

BINNIE J. (Gonthier J. concurring):

[127] I concur with the Chief Justice and Bastarache J., and with the reasons they have given, that the appeal should be allowed. I add these paragraphs on what I think is the decisive point.

[128] My colleagues have mobilized considerable scholarship for and against all aspects of the issues. When the smoke clears, this appeal comes down to a simple proposition. A criminal code that permitted preemptive killings within a criminal organization on the bare assertion by the killer that no course of action was reasonably available to him while standing *outside* a motor vehicle other than to put a shot in the back of the head of another member sitting *inside* the parked vehicle at a well-lit and

populated gas station is a criminal code that would fail in its most basic purpose of promoting public order.

[129] The respondent says he did not consider going to the police, although he was outside the car and in a position to flee the scene. He said "I never called the police in my life." Even if the police unexpectedly got there before a shoot-out, they would ask for some information in return for protection. "That's how it works," he said. Accordingly, there was evidence that *subjectively*, as a self-styled criminal, he felt his only options were to kill or be killed. He wishes the jury to judge the reasonableness of his conduct by the rules of his criminal subculture, which is the antithesis of public order.

[130] A trial judge should be very slow to take a defence away from a jury. We all agree on that. Here, however, the only way the defence *could* succeed is if the jury climbed into the skin of the respondent and accepted as reasonable a sociopathic view of appropriate dispute resolution. There is otherwise no air of reality, however broadly or narrowly defined, to the assertion that on February 3, 1994, in Montreal, the respondent believed *on reasonable grounds* that he could not otherwise preserve himself from death or grievous bodily harm, as required by s. 34(2)(b) of the Criminal Code, R.S.C. 1985, c. C-46. The *objective* reality of his situation would necessarily be altogether ignored, contrary to the intention of Parliament as interpreted in our jurisprudence.

[131] If, in these circumstances, jurors gave effect to the plea of self-defence, the Crown could be expected to successfully attack the judge's erroneous instruction that left self-defence to their consideration. Even the most patient jurors are entitled to expect that if they are asked to consider a defence, and accept it, the verdict will not be reversed on appeal on the ground that as a matter of law there was no *objective* basis in the evidence for the judge to have put self-defence to them in the first place.

[Justice Arbour wrote a dissenting opinion, concurred in by Iacobucci and Major JJ.]

## III. SELF-DEFENCE AND DOMESTIC VIOLENCE

### R. v. Lavallee
Supreme Court of Canada
(1990), 55 C.C.C. (3d) 97

[At trial, the accused was acquitted of murder by a judge and jury. The Manitoba Court of Appeal reversed and ordered a new trial, in part on the ground that expert testimony at trial relating to the reactions of the accused and other battered women should not be admitted in relation to her plea of self-defence.]

WILSON J.: The appellant, who was 22 years old at the time, had been living with Kevin Rust for some three to four years. Their residence was the scene of a boisterous party on August 30, 1986. In the early hours of August 31 after most of the guests had departed the appellant and Rust had an argument in the upstairs bedroom which was used by the appellant. Rust was killed by a single shot in the back of the head from a .303 calibre rifle fired by the appellant as he was leaving the room.

The appellant did not testify but her statement made to police on the night of the shooting was put in evidence. Portions of it read as follows:

> Me and Wendy argued as usual and I ran in the house after Kevin pushed me. I was scared, I was really scared. I locked the door. Herb was downstairs with Joanne and I called for Herb but I was crying when I called him. I said, "Herb come up here please." Herb came up to the top of the stairs and I told him that Kevin was going to hit me actually beat on me again. Herb said he knew and that if I was his old lady things would be different, he gave me a hug. OK, we're friends, there's nothing between us. He said "Yeah, I know" and he went outside to talk to Kevin leaving the door unlocked. I went upstairs and hid in my closet from Kevin. I was so scared … My window was open and I could hear Kevin asking questions about what I was doing and what I was saying. Next thing I know he was coming up the stairs for me. He came into my bedroom and said "Wench, where are you?" And he turned on my light and he said "Your purse is on the floor" and he kicked it. OK then he turned and he saw me in the closet. He wanted me to come out but I didn't want to come out because I was scared. I was so scared. [The officer who took the statement then testified that the appellant started to cry at this point and stopped after a minute or two.] He grabbed me by the arm right there. There's a bruise on my face also where he slapped me. He didn't slap me right then, first he yelled at me then he pushed me and I pushed him back and he hit me twice on the right hand side of my head. I was scared. All I thought about was all the other times he used to beat me, I was scared, I was shaking as usual. The rest is a blank, all I remember is he gave me the gun and a shot was fired through my screen. This is all so fast. And then the guns were in another room and he loaded it the second shot and gave it to me. And I was going to shoot myself. I pointed it to myself, I was so upset. OK and then he went and I was sitting on the bed and he started going like this with his finger [the appellant made a shaking motion with an index finger] and said something like "You're my old lady and you do as you're told" or something like that. He said "wait till everybody leaves, you'll get it then" and he said something to the effect of "either you kill me or I'll get you" that was what it was. He kind of smiled and then he turned around. I shot him but I aimed out. I thought I aimed above him and a piece of his head went that way.

The relationship between the appellant and Rust was volatile and punctuated by frequent arguments and violence. They would apparently fight for two or three days at a time or several times a week. Considerable evidence was led at trial indicating that the appellant was frequently a victim of physical abuse at the hands of Rust. Between 1983 and 1986 the appellant made several trips to hospital for injuries including severe bruises, a fractured nose, multiple contusions and a black eye. …

The need for expert evidence in … areas [of human behaviour] can, however, be obfuscated by the belief that judges and juries are thoroughly knowledgeable about "human nature" and that no more is needed. They are, so to speak, their own experts on human behaviour. This, in effect, was the primary submission of the Crown to this Court. …

Expert evidence on the psychological effect of battering on wives and common law partners must, it seems to me, be both relevant and necessary in the context of the present case. How can the mental state of the appellant be appreciated without it? The average member of the public (or of the jury) can be forgiven for asking: Why would a woman put up with this kind of treatment? Why should she continue to live with such a man? How could she love a partner who beat her to the point of requiring hospitalization? We would expect the woman to pack her bags and go. Where is her self-respect? Why does she not cut loose and make a new life for herself? Such is the reaction of the average person confronted with the so-called "battered wife syndrome." We need help to understand it and help is available from trained professionals. …

Laws do not spring out of a social vacuum. The notion that a man has a right to "discipline" his wife is deeply rooted in the history of our society. …

Fortunately, there has been a growing awareness in recent years that no man has a right to abuse any woman under any circumstances. Legislative initiatives designed to educate police, judicial officers and the public, as well as more aggressive investigation and charging policies all signal a concerted effort by the criminal justice system to take spousal abuse seriously. However, a woman who comes before a judge or jury with the claim that she has been battered and suggests that this may be a relevant factor in evaluating her subsequent actions still faces the prospect of being condemned by popular mythology about domestic violence. Either she was not as badly beaten as she claims or she would have left the man long ago. Or, if she was battered that severely, she must have stayed out of some masochistic enjoyment of it.

Expert testimony on the psychological effects of battering have been admitted in American courts in recent years. In *State v. Kelly*, 478 A.2d 364 at p. 378 (1984), the New Jersey Supreme Court commended the value of expert testimony in these terms:

> It is aimed at an area where the purported common knowledge of the jury may be very much mistaken, an area where jurors' logic, drawn from their own experience, may lead to a wholly incorrect conclusion, an area where expert knowledge would enable the jurors to disregard their prior conclusions as being common myths rather than common knowledge.

The court concludes at p. 379 that the battering relationship is "subject to a large group of myths and stereotypes." As such, it is "beyond the ken of the average juror and thus is suitable for explanation through expert testimony." I share that view. …

The bare facts of this case, which I think are amply supported by the evidence, are that the appellant was repeatedly abused by the deceased but did not leave him (although she twice pointed a gun at him), and ultimately shot him in the back of the head as he was leaving her room. The Crown submits that these facts disclose all the information a jury needs in order to decide whether or not the appellant acted in self-defence. I have no hesitation in rejecting the Crown's submission. …

In my view, there are two elements of the defence under s. 34(2) of the *Code* which merit scrutiny for present purposes. The first is the temporal connection in s. 34(2)(a) between the apprehension of death or grievous bodily harm and the act allegedly taken in self-defence. Was the appellant "under reasonable apprehension of death or grievous bodily harm" from Rust as he was walking out of the room? The second is the assessment in s. 34(2)(b) of the magnitude of the force used by the accused. Was the accused's belief that she could not "otherwise preserve herself from death or grievous bodily harm" except by shooting the deceased based "on reasonable grounds"?

The feature common to both 34(2)(a) and 34(2)(b) is the imposition of an objective standard of reasonableness on the apprehension of death and the need to repel the assault with deadly force. In *Reilly v. The Queen*, [1984] 2 S.C.R. 396, this Court considered the interaction of the objective and subjective components of s. 34(2) at p. 404:

> Subsection (2) of s. 34 places in issue the accused's state of mind at the time he caused death. The subsection can only afford protection to the accused if he apprehended death or grievous bodily harm from the assault he was repelling and if he believed he could not preserve himself from death or grievous bodily harm otherwise than by the force he used. Nonetheless, his apprehension must be a *reasonable* one and his belief must *be based upon reasonable and probable grounds*. The subsection requires that the jury consider, and be guided by, what they decide on the evidence was the accused's appreciation of the situation and his belief as to the reaction it required, so long as there exists an objectively verifiable basis for his perception.
>
> Since s. 34(2) places in issue the accused's perception of the attack upon him and the response required to meet it, the accused may still be found to have acted in self-defence even if he was mistaken in his perception. Reasonable and probable grounds must still exist for this mistaken perception in the sense that the mistake must have been one which an ordinary man using ordinary care could have made in the same circumstances. [Emphasis in original.]

If it strains credulity to imagine what the "ordinary man" would do in the position of a battered spouse, it is probably because men do not typically find themselves in that situation. Some women do, however. The definition of what is reasonable must be adapted to circumstances which are, by and large, foreign to the world inhabited by the hypothetical "reasonable man." ...

### A. Reasonable Apprehension of Death

Section 34(2)(a) requires that an accused who intentionally causes death or grievous bodily harm in repelling an assault is justified if he or she does so "under reasonable apprehension of death or grievous bodily harm." In the present case, the assault precipitating the appellant's alleged defensive act was Rust's threat to kill her when everyone else had gone.

It will be observed that subsection 34(2)(a) does not actually stipulate that the accused apprehend *imminent* danger when he or she acts. Case law has, however, read that requirement into the defence: see *Reilly v. The Queen, supra*; *R. v. Baxter* (1975), 33 C.R.N.S. 22 (Ont. C.A.); *R. v. Bogue* (1976), 30 C.C.C. (2d) 403 (Ont. C.A.). The sense in which "imminent" is used conjures up the image of "an uplifted knife" or a pointed gun. The rationale for the imminence rule seems obvious. The law

of self-defence is designed to ensure that the use of defensive force is really necessary. It justifies the act because the defender reasonably believed that he or she had
no alternative but to take the attacker's life. If there is a significant time interval
between the original unlawful assault and the accused's response, one tends to suspect that the accused was motivated by revenge rather than self-defence. In the paradigmatic case of a one-time barroom brawl between two men of equal size and
strength, this inference makes sense. How can one feel endangered to the point of
firing a gun at an unarmed man who utters a death threat, then turns his back and
walks out of the room? One cannot be certain of the gravity of the threat or his capacity to carry it out. Besides, one can always take the opportunity to flee or to call the
police. If he comes back and raises his fist, one can respond in kind if need be. These
are the tacit assumptions that underlie the imminence rule.

All of these assumptions were brought to bear on the respondent in *R. v. Whynot*
(1983), 9 C.C.C. 449 (N.S. C.A.). The respondent, Jane Stafford, shot her sleeping
common law husband as he lay passed out in his truck. The evidence at trial indicated
that the deceased "dominated the household and exerted his authority by striking and
slapping the various members and from time to time administering beatings to Jane
Stafford and the others" (at p. 452). The respondent testified that the deceased threatened to kill all of the members of her family, one by one, if she tried to leave him. On
the night in question he threatened to kill her son. After he passed out the respondent
got one of the many shotguns kept by her husband and shot him. The Nova Scotia
Court of Appeal held that the trial judge erred in leaving s. 37 (preventing assault
against oneself or anyone under one's protection) with the jury. The Court stated at
p. 464:

> I do not believe that the trial judge was justified in placing s. 37 of the *Code* before the
> jury any more than he would have been justified in giving them s. 34. Under s. 34 the
> assault must have been underway and unprovoked, and under s. 37 the assault must be
> such that it is necessary to defend the person assaulted by the use of force. No more
> force may be used than necessary to prevent the assault or the repetition of it. In my
> opinion, no person has the right in anticipation of an assault that may or may not hap-
> pen, to apply force to prevent the imaginary assault.

The implication of the Court's reasoning is that it is inherently unreasonable to
apprehend death or grievous bodily harm unless and until the physical assault is actually in progress, at which point the victim can presumably gauge the requisite amount
of force needed to repel the attack and act accordingly. In my view, expert testimony
can cast doubt on these assumptions as they are applied in the context of a battered
wife's efforts to repel an assault. …

[Wilson J. then discussed "the Walker Cycle of Violence," named after a pioneer
researcher in the field of the battered-wife syndrome, Dr. Lenore Walker.]

Dr. Walker first describes the cycle in the book, *The Battered Woman* (1979). In
her 1984 book, *The Battered Woman Syndrome*, Dr. Walker reports the results of a
study involving 400 battered women. Her research was designed to test empirically

the theories expounded in her earlier book. At pp. 95-6 of *The Battered Woman Syndrome*, she summarizes the Cycle Theory as follows:

> A second major theory that was tested in this project is the Walker Cycle Theory of Violence (Walker, 1979). This tension reduction theory states that there are three distinct phases associated in a recurring battering cycle: (1) tension building, (2) the acute battering incident, and (3) loving contrition. During the first phase, there is a gradual escalation of tension displayed by discrete acts causing increased friction such as name-calling, other mean intentional behaviors, and/or physical abuse. The batterer expresses dissatisfaction and hostility but not in an extreme or maximally explosive form. The woman attempts to placate the batterer, doing what she thinks might please him, calm him down, or at least, what will not further aggravate him. She tries not to respond to his hostile actions and uses general anger reduction techniques. Often she succeeds for a little while which reinforces her unrealistic belief that she can control this man. ...
>
> The tension continues to escalate and eventually she is unable to continue controlling his angry response pattern. "Exhausted from the constant stress, she usually withdraws from the batterer, fearing she will inadvertently set off an explosion. He begins to move more oppressively toward her as he observes her withdrawal. ... Tension between the two becomes unbearable" (Walker, 1979, p. 59). The second phase, the acute battering incident, becomes inevitable without intervention. Sometimes, she precipitates the inevitable explosion so as to control where and when it occurs, allowing her to take better precautions to minimize her injuries and pain.
>
> "Phase two is characterized by the uncontrollable discharge of the tensions that have built up during phase one" (p. 59). The batterer typically unleashes a barrage of verbal and physical aggression that can leave the woman severely shaken and injured. In fact, when injuries do occur it usually happens during this second phase. It is also the time police become involved, if they are called at all. The acute battering phase is concluded when the batterer stops, usually bringing with its cessation a sharp physiological reduction in tension. This in itself is naturally reinforcing. Violence often succeeds because it does work.
>
> In phase three which follows, the batterer may apologize profusely, try to assist his victim, show kindness and remorse, and shower her with gifts and/or promises. The batterer himself may believe at this point that he will never allow himself to be violent again. The woman wants to believe the batterer and, early in the relationship at least, may renew her hope in his ability to change. This third phase provides the positive reinforcement for remaining in the relationship, for the woman. In fact, our results showed that phase three could also be characterized by an absence of tension or violence, and no observable loving-contrition behaviour, and still be reinforcing for the woman.

Dr. Walker defines a battered woman as a woman who has gone through the battering cycle at least twice. As she explains in her introduction to *The Battered Woman*, at p. xv: "Any woman may find herself in an abusive relationship with a man once. If it occurs a second time, and she remains in the situation, she is defined as a battered woman."

Given the relational context in which the violence occurs, the mental state of an accused at the critical moment she pulls the trigger cannot be understood except in terms of the cumulative effect of months or years of brutality. As Dr. Shane explained in his testimony, the deterioration of the relationship between the appellant and Rust in the period immediately preceding the killing led to feelings of escalating terror on the part of the appellant.:

> But their relationship some weeks to months before was definitely escalating in terms of tension and in terms of the discordant quality about it. They were sleeping in separate bedrooms. Their intimate relationship was lacking and things were building and building and to a point, I think, where it built to that particular point where she couldn't—she felt so threatened and so overwhelmed that she had to—that she reacted in a violent way because of her fear of survival and also because, I think because of her, I guess, final sense that she was—that she had to defend herself and her own sense of violence towards this man who had really desecrated her and damaged her for so long.

Another aspect of the cyclical nature of the abuse is that it begets a degree of predictability to the violence that is absent in an isolated violent encounter between two strangers. This also means that it may in fact be possible for a battered spouse to accurately predict the onset of violence before the first blow is struck, even if an outsider to the relationship cannot. Indeed, it has been suggested that a battered woman's knowledge of her partner's violence is so heightened that she is able to anticipate the nature and extent (though not the onset) of the violence by his conduct beforehand. …

… In her article "Potential Uses for Expert Testimony: Ideas Toward the Representation of Battered Women Who Kill," 9 *Women's Rights Law Reporter* 227 (1986), psychologist Julie Blackman describes this characteristic at p. 229:

> Repeated instances of violence enable battered women to develop a continuum along which they can "rate" the tolerability or survivability of episodes of their partner's violence. Thus, signs of unusual violence are detected. For battered women, this response to the ongoing violence of their situations is a survival skill. Research shows that battered women who kill experience remarkably severe and frequent violence relative to battered women who do not kill. They know what sorts of danger are familiar and which are novel. They have had myriad opportunities to develop and hone their perceptions of their partner's violence. And, importantly, they can say what made the final episode of violence different from the others: they can name the features of the last battering that enabled them to know that this episode would result in life-threatening action by the abuser. …

Of course, as Dr. Blackman points out, it is up to the jury to decide whether the distinction drawn between "typical" violence and the particular events the accused perceived as "life threatening" is compelling. According to the appellant's statement to police, Rust actually handed her a shotgun and warned her that if she did not kill him, he would kill her. I note in passing a remarkable observation made by Dr. Walker in her 1984 study, *The Battered Woman Syndrome*. Writing about the fifty battered women she interviewed who had killed their partners, she comments at p. 40:

Most of the time the women killed the men with a gun; usually one of several that belonged to him. *Many of the men actually dared or demanded the woman use the gun on him first, or else he said he'd kill her with it.* (Emphasis added.)

Where evidence exists that an accused is in a battering relationship, expert testimony can assist the jury in determining whether the accused had a "reasonable" apprehension of death when she acted by explaining the heightened sensitivity of a battered woman to her partner's acts. Without such testimony I am skeptical that the average fact-finder would be capable of appreciating why her subjective fear may have been reasonable in the context of the relationship. After all, the hypothetical "reasonable man" observing only the final incident may have been unlikely to recognize the batterer's threat as potentially lethal. Using the case at bar as an example the "reasonable man" might have thought, as the majority of the Court of Appeal seemed to, that it was unlikely that Rust would make good on his threat to kill the appellant that night because they had guests staying overnight.

The issue is not, however, what an outsider would have reasonably perceived but what the accused reasonably perceived, given her situation and her experience.

Even accepting that a battered woman may be uniquely sensitized to danger from her batterer, it may yet be contended that the law ought to require her to wait until the knife is uplifted, the gun pointed or the fist clenched before her apprehension is deemed reasonable. This would allegedly reduce the risk that the woman is mistaken in her fear, although the law does not require her fear to be correct, only reasonable. In response to this contention, I need only point to the observation made by Huband J.A. that the evidence showed that when the appellant and Rust physically fought the appellant "invariably got the worst of it." I do not think it is an unwarranted generalization to say that due to their size, strength, socialization and lack of training, women are typically no match for men in hand-to-hand combat. The requirement imposed in *Whynot* that a battered woman wait until the physical assault is "underway" before her apprehensions can be validated in law would, in the words of an American court, be tantamount to sentencing her to "murder by installment": *State v. Gallegos*, 719 P.2d 1268 (N.M. 1986, at p. 1271). I share the view expressed by M.J. Willoughby in "Rendering Each Woman Her Due: Can a Battered Woman Claim Self-Defense When She Kills Her Sleeping Batterer" (1989), 38 *Kan. L. Rev.* 169, at p. 184, that "society gains nothing, except perhaps the additional risk that the battered woman will herself be killed, because she must wait until her abusive husband instigates another battering episode before she can justifiably act."

### B.  Lack of Alternatives to Self-Help

Subsection 34(2) requires an accused who pleads self-defence to believe "on reasonable grounds" that it is not possible to otherwise preserve him or herself from death or grievous bodily harm. The obvious question is if the violence was so intolerable, why did the appellant not leave her abuser long ago? This question does not really go to whether she had an alternative to killing the deceased at the critical moment. Rather, it plays on the popular myth already referred to that a woman who says she was battered yet stayed with her batterer was either not as badly beaten as she claimed or

else she liked it. Nevertheless, to the extent that her failure to leave the abusive relationship earlier may be used in support of the proposition that she was free to leave at
the final moment, expert testimony can provide useful insights. ...

The same psychological factors that account for a woman's inability to leave a
battering relationship may also help to explain why she did not attempt to escape at
the moment she perceived her life to be in danger. The following extract from Dr.
Shane's testimony on direct examination elucidates this point:

> Q. Now, we understand from the evidence that on this night she went—I think
> you've already described it in your evidence—and hid in the closet?
>
> A. Yes.
>
> Q. Can you tell the jury why she, for instance, would stay in that house if she had
> this fear? Why wouldn't she so [sic] someplace else? Why would she have to hide in
> the closet in the same house?
>
> A. Well, I think this is a reflection of what I've been talking about, this ongoing
> psychological process, her own psychology and the relationship, that she felt trapped.
> There was no out for her, this learned helplessness, if you will, the fact that she felt
> paralyzed, she felt tyrannized. She felt, although there were obviously no steel fences
> around, keeping her in, there were steel fences in her mind which created for her an
> incredible barrier psychologically that prevented her from moving out. Although she
> had attempted on occasion, she came back in a magnetic sort of a way. And she felt also
> that she couldn't expect anything more. Not only this learned helplessness about being
> beaten, beaten, where her motivation is taken away, but her whole sense of herself. She
> felt this victim mentality, this concentration camp mentality if you will, where she could
> not see herself be in any other situation except being tyrannized, punished and cruci-
> fied physically and psychologically.

Of course, as Dr. Ewing adds, environmental factors may also impair the woman's
ability to leave—lack of job skills, the presence of children to care for, fear of retaliation by the man, etc., may each have a role to play in some cases.

I emphasize at this juncture that it is not for the jury to pass judgment on the fact
that an accused battered woman stayed in the relationship. Still less is it entitled to
conclude that she forfeited her right to self-defence for having done so. I would also
point out that traditional self-defence doctrine does not require a person to retreat
from her home instead of defending herself: *R. v. Antley*, [1964] 2 C.C.C. 142, [1964]
1 O.R. 545, 42 C.R. 384 (C.A.). A man's home may be his castle but it is also the
woman's home even if it seems to her more like a prison in the circumstances.

If, after hearing the evidence (including the expert testimony), the jury is satisfied
that the accused had a reasonable apprehension of death or grievous bodily harm and
felt incapable of escape, it must ask itself what the "reasonable person" would do in
such a situation. The situation of the battered woman as described by Dr. Shane strikes
me as somewhat analogous to that of a hostage. If the captor tells her that he will kill
her in three days time, is it potentially reasonable for her to seize an opportunity
presented on the first day to kill the captor or must she wait until he makes the attempt on the third day? I think the question the jury must ask itself is whether, given
the history, circumstances and perceptions of the appellant, her belief that she could

not preserve herself from being killed by Rust that night except by killing him first was reasonable. To the extent that expert evidence can assist the jury in making that determination, I would find such testimony to be both relevant and necessary. ...

Obviously the fact that the appellant was a battered woman does not entitle her to an acquittal. Battered women may well kill their partners other than in self-defence. The focus is not on who the woman is, but on what she did. In "The Meaning of Equality for Battered Women Who Kill Men in Self-Defence" (1985) 8 *Harv. Women's L.J.* 121, 149, Phyllis Crocker makes the point succinctly:

> The issue in a self-defence trial is not whether the defendant is a battered woman, but whether she justifiably killed her husband. The defendant introduces testimony to offer the jury an explanation of reasonableness that is an alternative to the prosecution's stereotypic explanations. It is not intended to earn her the status of a battered woman, as if that would make her not guilty. ...

Ultimately, it is up to the jury to decide whether, *in fact*, the accused's perceptions and actions were reasonable. Expert evidence does not and cannot usurp that function of the jury. The jury is not compelled to accept the opinions proffered by the expert about the effects of battering on the mental state of victims generally or on the mental state of the accused in particular. But fairness and the integrity of the trial process demand that the jury have the opportunity to hear them.

[The appeal was allowed and the verdict of acquittal restored. Dickson C.J.C., Lamer, L'Heureux-Dubé, Gonthier, and McLachlin JJ. concurred with Wilson J. Sopinka J. wrote a concurring opinion on a separate issue.]

### R. v. Pétel
Supreme Court of Canada
(1994), 87 C.C.C. (3d) 97

[The accused, Collette Pétel, was charged and convicted of second-degree murder in the killing of Alain Raymond on July 21, 1989. Raymond worked with Serge Edsell in the drug trade and since May of 1989, Edsell had lived with the accused, her daughter, and her granddaughter. The accused testified that Edsell threatened her frequently and beat her daughter during this time.

On July 21, 1989 Edsell went to the accused's house, gave her his weapon to hide, forced her to weigh some cocaine, and threatened to kill her, her daughter, and her granddaughter. After consuming a small amount of drugs, the accused shot and wounded Edsell and perceiving Raymond to be lunging at her, shot and killed him. During their deliberations, the jury asked whether threats or acts taking place in the months prior to July were relevant to determining whether the accused acted in self-defence under s. 34(2). The judge replied:

> these earlier acts or threats help you to determine whether Alain Raymond or Serge Edsell attempted or threatened, because according to the evidence, if you believe it,

this was a common plan, whether as I say Alain Raymond or Serge Edsell attempted or threatened on the evening of July 21, by an act or a gesture, to apply force to Mrs. Pétel, to her daughter or to her granddaughter, whether the assailant had or caused the alleged victim to believe on reasonable grounds that he had present ability to effect his purpose.

So the previous facts help you to assess the situation, but the threat or the assault or the threat or the gesture that evening, in the context of a, of the carrying out of an assault, that must be assessed on July 21.]

LAMER C.J.C. (Sopinka, Cory, McLachlin, and Iacobucci JJ. concurring): The accused appealed her conviction to the Court of Appeal. She argued that the charge to the jury on self-defence was erroneous. She submitted that the judge should have said that the previous threats were relevant in determining not only whether the victims threatened the accused and had present ability to effect their purpose, but also, which he failed to do, in determining the accused's state of mind regarding the imminence of the assault and the belief that she could not otherwise preserve herself from death. The accused based her arguments on *R. v. Lavallee*, [1990] 1 S.C.R. 852. ...

It can be seen from the wording of s. 34(2) of the *Code* that there are three constituent elements of self-defence, when as here the victim has died: (1) the existence of an unlawful assault; (2) a reasonable apprehension of a risk of death or grievous bodily harm; and (3) a reasonable belief that it is not possible to preserve oneself from harm except by killing the adversary.

In all three cases the jury must seek to determine how the accused perceived the relevant facts and whether that perception was reasonable. Accordingly, this is an objective determination. With respect to the last two elements, this approach results from the language used in the *Code* and was confirmed by this Court in *Reilly v. The Queen*, [1984] 2 S.C.R. 396, at p. 404:

> The subsection can only afford protection to the accused if he apprehended death or grievous bodily harm from the assault he was repelling and if he believed he could not preserve himself from death or grievous bodily harm otherwise than by the force he used. Nonetheless, his apprehension must be a *reasonable* one and his belief must *be based upon reasonable and probable grounds*. The subsection requires that the jury consider, and be guided by, what they decide on the evidence was the accused's appreciation of the situation and his belief as to the reaction it required, so long as there exists an objectively verifiable basis for his perception. [Emphasis in original.]

Some doubt may still exist as to whether this passage from *Reilly* also applies to the existence of an assault. For my part, I think that the word "situation" refers to the three elements of s. 34(2). An honest but reasonable mistake as to the existence of an assault is therefore permitted. This is also how the Ontario Court of Appeal understood it in *R. v. Nelson* (1992), 71 C.C.C. (3d) 449, at p. 455. The existence of an assault must not be made a kind of prerequisite for the exercise of self-defence to be assessed without regard to the perception of the accused. This would amount in a sense to trying the victim before the accused. In a case involving self-defence, it is the accused's state of mind that must be examined, and it is the accused (and not the victim) who must be given the benefit of a reasonable doubt. The question that the jury must ask itself is therefore not "was the accused unlawfully assaulted?" but rather "did the accused reasonably believe, in the circumstances, that she was being unlawfully assaulted?"

Moreover, *Lavallee*, *supra*, rejected the rule requiring that the apprehended danger be imminent. This alleged rule, which does not appear anywhere in the text of the *Criminal Code*, is in fact only a mere assumption based on common sense. As Wilson J. noted in *Lavallee*, this assumption undoubtedly derives from the paradigmatic case of self-defence, which is an altercation between two persons of equal strength. However, evidence may be presented (in particular expert evidence) to rebut this presumption of fact. There is thus no formal requirement that the danger be imminent. Imminence is only one of the factors which the jury should weigh in determining whether the accused had a reasonable apprehension of danger and a reasonable belief that she could not extricate herself otherwise than by killing the attacker.

[The chief justice found that the trial judge had made the following errors in his reply to the jury.]

First, the judge's answer suggested that the only relevance of the threats prior to July 21 was in enabling the jury to determine whether there had actually been an assault on the evening of July 21, that is, in the present case, death threats, and whether the assailant was in a position to carry out those threats. This in my view diverted the jury from the question it really should have been considering, namely the reasonable belief of the accused in the existence of an assault. Emphasizing the victims' acts rather than the accused's state of mind has the effect of depriving the latter of the benefit of any error, however reasonable. The jury's attention should not be diverted from its proper concern, the guilt of the accused, by an inquiry into the guilt of the victim.

Secondly, and this is the crucial point, the judge's answer might have led the jury to believe that the threats made before July 21 could serve no other purpose than to determine the existence of the assault and the assailant's ability, thus denying their relevance to reasonable apprehension of a danger of death or grievous bodily harm and to the belief that there was no solution but to kill the attacker.

The importance of failing to relate the earlier threats to the elements of self-defence cannot be underestimated. The threats made by Edsell throughout his cohabitation with the respondent are very relevant in determining whether the respondent had a reasonable apprehension of danger and a reasonable belief in the need to kill Edsell and Raymond. The threats prior to July 21 form an integral part of the circumstances on which the perception of the accused might have been based. The judge's answer to this question might thus have led the jury to disregard the entire atmosphere of terror which the respondent said pervaded her house. It is clear that the way in which a reasonable person would have acted cannot be assessed without taking into account these crucial circumstances. As Wilson J. noted in *Lavallee*, at p. 883:

> The issue is not, however, what an outsider would have reasonably perceived but what
> the accused reasonably perceived, given her situation and her experience.

By unduly limiting the relevance of the previous threats the judge in a sense invited the jury to determine what an outsider would have done in the same situation as the respondent.

The undisputed evidence that Edsell, her alleged attacker, handed over his weapon and asked his future victim to hide it, conduct that is odd to say the least for someone intending to kill, must have had a clear effect on the jury, indeed on any jury composed of reasonable individuals. In the Court of Appeal and in this Court, however, counsel for the Crown did not argue that, given the evidence in this case, no substantial wrong or miscarriage of justice occurred, and that s. 686(1)(b)(iii) of the *Criminal Code* should thus be applied. The Crown has the burden of showing that this provision is applicable: *Colpitts v. The Queen*, [1965] S.C.R. 739. This Court cannot apply it *proprio motu*. Having found an error of law in the judge's answer to the question by the jury, I must accordingly dismiss the appeal and affirm the order for a new trial.

GONTHIER J. (La Forest, L'Heureux-Dubé, and Major JJ. concurring) agreed with the Chief Justice's statement of the relevant law, but dissented and would have upheld the conviction. He stated: With all due respect, I cannot conclude that the judge's answer could have been understood by the jury or could have led it to make a finding other than on the basis of a reasonable belief by the accused in a danger of death which she could not avoid except by killing her attacker. In my opinion, the judge's answer contained no error and was adequate.

*Appeal dismissed.*

## R. v. Malott
Supreme Court of Canada
(1998), 121 C.C.C. (3d) 456

[The accused woman had been in an abusive 19-year relationship with the deceased, which included physical, sexual, verbal, emotional, and psychological abuse, and beatings. The accused was required to make dinners for the deceased and his girlfriend. On the day of the killing, the deceased had choked the accused and told her that she had to start listening. When the deceased returned to the car after trying to obtain some pills at a medical centre, the accused shot and killed him. She testified that she thought the accused was going to hurt her because the deceased needed the pills and was unable to get them. The accused then reloaded her gun, hailed a taxi, found the deceased's girlfriend (Sherwood) and shot her. The accused was convicted of second-degree murder for killing the deceased, and attempted murder for shooting his girlfriend. The accused's appeal to the Court of Appeal for Ontario was dismissed,

Abella J.A. dissenting ((1996), 110 C.C.C. (3d) 499). The accused appealed to the
Supreme Court of Canada.]

MAJOR J. (Lamer C.J.C., McLachlin, Cory, and Iacobucci JJ.): ...

### III.  Issue

[12]  The issue is whether the majority of the Ontario Court of Appeal was correct
in concluding that the trial judge's charge to the jury adequately dealt with evidence
of battered woman syndrome as it relates to the defence of self-defence. As stated, it
is only the appellant's conviction for second degree murder of Paul Malott that is at
issue in this appeal. ...

[17]  In the present case, the charge as a whole should be examined to ascertain
whether the jury were given an adequate charge on battered woman syndrome as it
relates to self-defence.

### B.  Principles Relevant to Battered Woman Syndrome and Self-Defence

[18]  Pursuant to s. 34(2) of the Criminal Code, there are three constituent elements of self-defence where the victim has died: (1) the existence of an unlawful
assault; (2) a reasonable apprehension of a risk of death or grievous bodily harm; and
(3) a reasonable belief that it is not possible to preserve oneself from harm except by
killing the adversary: see *R. v. Pétel*, [1994] 1 S.C.R. 3. On the first element, a majority of this Court held in Pétel that an honest but reasonable mistake as to the existence
of an assault is permitted where an accused relies upon self-defence. Accordingly, the
jury must be told that the question is not "was the accused unlawfully assaulted?" but
rather "did the accused reasonably believe, in the circumstances, that she was being
unlawfully assaulted?" To the extent that expert evidence respecting battered woman
syndrome may assist a jury in assessing the reasonableness of an accused's perceptions, it is relevant to the issue of unlawful assault.

[19]  The relevance of evidence on battered woman syndrome to the issue of self-
defence was recognized in *Lavallee*, where the majority of this Court held that expert
evidence on the psychological effect of the battering of spouses was admissible, as it
was relevant and necessary in the context of that case.

[20]  The admissibility of expert evidence respecting battered woman syndrome
was not at issue in the present case. The admissibility of the expert evidence of Dr.
Jaffe on battered woman syndrome was not challenged. However, once that defence
is raised, the jury ought to be made aware of the principles of that defence as dictated
by *Lavallee*. In particular, the jury should be informed of how that evidence may be
of use in understanding the following:

1.  Why an abused woman might remain in an abusive relationship. As discussed
    in *Lavallee*, expert evidence may help to explain some of the reasons and dispel
    some of the misconceptions about why women stay in abusive relationships.

2.  The nature and extent of the violence that may exist in a battering relation-
    ship. In considering the defence of self-defence as it applies to an accused

who has killed her violent partner, the jury should be instructed on the violence that existed in the relationship and its impact on the accused. The latter
will usually but not necessarily be provided by an expert.

3. The accused's ability to perceive danger from her abuser. Section 34(2)(a)
   provides that an accused who intentionally causes death or grievous bodily
   harm in repelling an assault is justified if he or she does so "under reasonable
   apprehension of death or grievous bodily harm." In addressing this issue,
   Wilson J. for the majority in Lavallee rejected the requirement that the accused apprehend imminent danger. She also stated at pp. 882-83:

Where evidence exists that an accused is in a battering relationship, expert testimony
can assist the jury in determining whether the accused had a "reasonable" apprehension
of death when she acted by explaining the heightened sensitivity of a battered woman
to her partner's acts. Without such testimony I am skeptical that the average fact-finder
would be capable of appreciating why her subjective fear may have been reasonable in
the context of the relationship. After all, the hypothetical "reasonable man" observing
only the final incident may have been unlikely to recognize the batterer's threat as
potentially lethal. …

   The issue is not, however, what an outsider would have reasonably perceived but
what the accused reasonably perceived, given her situation and her experience.

4. Whether the accused believed on reasonable grounds that she could not otherwise preserve herself from death or grievous bodily harm. This principle
   was summarized in *Lavallee* as follows (at p. 890):

By providing an explanation as to why an accused did not flee when she perceived her
life to be in danger, expert testimony may also assist the jury in assessing the reasonableness of her belief that killing her batterer was the only way to save her own life.

[21] These principles must be communicated by the trial judge when instructing
the jury in cases involving battered woman syndrome and the issue of self-defence.

## C. *Jury Charge in This Case*

[22] In the present case, I am satisfied that the trial judge properly charged the
jury with respect to the evidence on battered woman syndrome and how such evidence relates to the law of self-defence. At the beginning of the charge on self-defence, the trial judge set out s. 34(2) of the Criminal Code. He then explained the
legal meaning of "unlawful assault" and reviewed the defence and Crown evidence
relevant to the issue of whether or not an unlawful assault occurred.

[23] In her dissent, Abella J.A. states that the trial judge did not tell the jury which
of the facts described by the appellant could, if believed, constitute unlawful assault.
Nor did he explain how having been abused by Mr. Malott could have affected the
reasonableness of the appellant's perception of the extent to which she was in danger
from him. With respect, I disagree. …

[31] My conclusion that the jury charge was adequate does not mean it was flawless. As with most jury charges, there is room for debate. In particular, it could be

argued that it may have been desirable for the trial judge to have instructed the jury to a greater extent in making the connection between the evidence of battered woman syndrome and the legal issue of self-defence. However, in reviewing the trial judge's charge as a whole, I am satisfied that the jury were left with a sufficient understanding of the facts as they related to the relevant legal issues.

[32] Counsel for the appellant submitted that the trial judge in this case was required to repeat verbatim comments made by this Court in *Lavallee*. In my view, such a requirement would impose an unnecessary and non-productive obligation. There is no precise formula that can be followed in instructing a jury. In reviewing a jury charge, an appellate court should not minutely scrutinize the charge but should consider whether the trial judge reviewed the evidence and related it to the relevant legal issues and principles in a manner that would equip the jury to reach its verdict according to applicable law.

[33] I would add that I do not accept the respondent's submission that, in view of the Crown's concession that the abuse took place, it was not necessary for the trial judge in this case to address the first and second principles from *Lavallee*. In my view, regardless of any concessions made by the Crown, it is incumbent upon a trial judge to explain to the jury the purposes for which expert evidence on battered woman syndrome is admitted in cases such as the present one.

## VI. *Disposition*

[34] The appeal is dismissed.

L'HEUREUX-DUBÉ J. (McLachlin J., concurring) (concurring):

[35] I have read the reasons of my colleague Justice Major, and I concur with the result that he reaches. However, given that this Court has not had the opportunity to discuss the value of evidence of "battered woman syndrome" since *R. v. Lavallee*, [1990] 1 S.C.R. 852, and given the evolving discourse on "battered woman syndrome" in the legal community, I will make a few comments on the importance of this kind of evidence to the just adjudication of charges involving battered women.

[36] First, the significance of this Court's decision in *Lavallee*, which first accepted the need for expert evidence on the effects of abusive relationships in order to properly understand the context in which an accused woman had killed her abusive spouse in self-defence, reaches beyond its particular impact on the law of self-defence. A crucial implication of the admissibility of expert evidence in *Lavallee* is the legal recognition that historically both the law and society may have treated women in general, and battered women in particular, unfairly. *Lavallee* accepted that the myths and stereotypes which are the products and the tools of this unfair treatment interfere with the capacity of judges and juries to justly determine a battered woman's claim of self-defence, and can only be dispelled by expert evidence designed to overcome the stereotypical thinking. The expert evidence is admissible, and necessary, in order to understand the reasonableness of a battered woman's perceptions, which in *Lavallee* were the accused's perceptions that she had to act with deadly force in order to preserve herself from death or grievous bodily harm. Accordingly, the utility of such

evidence in criminal cases is not limited to instances where a battered woman is pleading self-defence, but is potentially relevant to other situations where the reasonableness of a battered woman's actions or perceptions is at issue (e.g. provocation, duress or necessity). See *R. v. Hibbert*, [1995] 2 S.C.R. 973, at p. 1021.

[37] It is clear from the foregoing that "battered woman syndrome" is not a legal defence in itself such that an accused woman need only establish that she is suffering from the syndrome in order to gain an acquittal. As Wilson J. commented in *Lavallee*, at p. 890: "Obviously the fact that the appellant was a battered woman does not entitle her to an acquittal. Battered women may well kill their partners other than in self-defence." Rather, "battered woman syndrome" is a psychiatric explanation of the mental state of women who have been subjected to continuous battering by their male intimate partners, which can be relevant to the legal inquiry into a battered woman's state of mind.

[38] Second, the majority of the Court in *Lavallee* also implicitly accepted that women's experiences and perspectives may be different from the experiences and perspectives of men. It accepted that a woman's perception of what is reasonable is influenced by her gender, as well as by her individual experience, and both are relevant to the legal inquiry. This legal development was significant, because it demonstrated a willingness to look at the whole context of a woman's experience in order to inform the analysis of the particular events. But it is wrong to think of this development of the law as merely an example where an objective test—the requirement that an accused claiming self-defence must reasonably apprehend death or grievous bodily harm—has been modified to admit evidence of the subjective perceptions of a battered woman. More important, a majority of the Court accepted that the perspectives of women, which have historically been ignored, must now equally inform the "objective" standard of the reasonable person in relation to self-defence.

[39] When interpreting and applying *Lavallee*, these broader principles should be kept in mind. In particular, they should be kept in mind in order to avoid a too rigid and restrictive approach to the admissibility and legal value of evidence of a battered woman's experiences. Concerns have been expressed that the treatment of expert evidence on battered women syndrome, which is itself admissible in order to combat the myths and stereotypes which society has about battered women, has led to a new stereotype of the "battered woman": see, e.g., Martha Shaffer, "The battered woman syndrome revisited: Some complicating thoughts five years after R. v. Lavallee" (1997), 47 U.T.L.J. 1, at p. 9; Sheila Noonan, "Strategies of Survival: Moving Beyond the Battered Woman Syndrome," in Ellen Adelberg and Claudia Currie, eds., In Conflict with the Law: Women and the Canadian Justice System (1993), 247, at p. 254; Isabel Grant, "The 'syndromization' of women's experience," in Donna Martinson et al., "A Forum on Lavallee v. R.: Women and Self-Defence" (1991), 25 U.B.C. L. Rev. 23, 51, at pp. 53-54; and Martha R. Mahoney, "Legal Images of Battered Women: Redefining the Issue of Separation" (1991), 90 Mich. L. Rev. 1, at p. 42.

[40] It is possible that those women who are unable to fit themselves within the stereotype of a victimized, passive, helpless, dependent, battered woman will not have their claims to self-defence fairly decided. For instance, women who have

demonstrated too much strength or initiative, women of colour, women who are professionals, or women who might have fought back against their abusers on previous occasions, should not be penalized for failing to accord with the stereotypical image of the archetypal battered woman. See, e.g., Julie Stubbs and Julia Tolmie, "Race, Gender, and the Battered Woman Syndrome: An Australia Case Study" (1995), 8 C.J.W.L. 122. Needless to say, women with these characteristics are still entitled to have their claims of self-defence fairly adjudicated, and they are also still entitled to have their experiences as battered women inform the analysis. Professor Grant, supra, at p. 52, warns against allowing the law to develop such that a woman accused of killing her abuser must either have been "reasonable 'like a man' or reasonable 'like a battered woman.'" I agree that this must be avoided. The "reasonable woman" must not be forgotten in the analysis, and deserves to be as much a part of the objective standard of the reasonable person as does the "reasonable man."

[41] How should the courts combat the "syndromization," as Professor Grant refers to it, of battered women who act in self-defence? The legal inquiry into the moral culpability of a woman who is, for instance, claiming self-defence must focus on the reasonableness of her actions in the context of her personal experiences, and her experiences as a woman, not on her status as a battered woman and her entitlement to claim that she is suffering from "battered woman syndrome." This point has been made convincingly by many academics reviewing the relevant cases: see, e.g., Wendy Chan, "A Feminist Critique of Self-Defense and Provocation in Battered Women's Cases in England and Wales" (1994), 6 Women & Crim. Just. 39, at pp. 56-57; Elizabeth M. Schneider, "Describing and Changing: Women's Self-Defense Work and the Problem of Expert Testimony on Battering" (1992), 14 Women's Rts. L. Rep. 213, at pp. 216-17; and Marilyn MacCrimmon, "The social construction of reality and the rules of evidence," in Donna Martinson et al., supra, 36, at pp. 48-49. By emphasizing a woman's "learned helplessness," her dependence, her victimization, and her low self-esteem, in order to establish that she suffers from "battered woman syndrome," the legal debate shifts from the objective rationality of her actions to preserve her own life to those personal inadequacies which apparently explain her failure to flee from her abuser. Such an emphasis comports too well with society's stereotypes about women. Therefore, it should be scrupulously avoided because it only serves to undermine the important advancements achieved by the decision in *Lavallee*.

[42] There are other elements of a woman's social context which help to explain her inability to leave her abuser, and which do not focus on those characteristics most consistent with traditional stereotypes. As Wilson J. herself recognized in *Lavallee*, at p. 887, "environmental factors may also impair the woman's ability to leave—lack of job skills, the presence of children to care for, fear of retaliation by the man, etc. may each have a role to play in some cases." To this list of factors I would add a woman's need to protect her children from abuse, a fear of losing custody of her children, pressures to keep the family together, weaknesses of social and financial support for battered women, and no guarantee that the violence would cease simply because she left. These considerations necessarily inform the reasonableness of a

woman's beliefs or perceptions of, for instance, her lack of an alternative to the use of deadly force to preserve herself from death or grievous bodily harm.

[43]  How should these principles be given practical effect in the context of a jury trial of a woman accused of murdering her abuser? To fully accord with the spirit of *Lavallee*, where the reasonableness of a battered woman's belief is at issue in a criminal case, a judge and jury should be made to appreciate that a battered woman's experiences are both individualized, based on her own history and relationships, as well as shared with other women, within the context of a society and a legal system which has historically undervalued women's experiences. A judge and jury should be told that a battered woman's experiences are generally outside the common understanding of the average judge and juror, and that they should seek to understand the evidence being presented to them in order to overcome the myths and stereotypes which we all share. Finally, all of this should be presented in such a way as to focus on the reasonableness of the woman's actions, without relying on old or new stereotypes about battered women.

[44]  My focus on women as the victims of battering and as the subjects of "battered woman syndrome" is not intended to exclude from consideration those men who find themselves in abusive relationships. However, the reality of our society is that typically, it is women who are the victims of domestic violence, at the hands of their male intimate partners. To assume that men who are victims of spousal abuse are affected by the abuse in the same way, without benefit of the research and expert opinion evidence which has informed the courts of the existence and details of "battered woman syndrome," would be imprudent.

[45]  In the present appeal, it was uncontested that Margaret Ann Malott suffered years of horrible emotional, psychological, physical and sexual abuse at the hands of her husband, Paul Malott. Dr. Peter Jaffe, the psychologist who testified on Mrs. Malott's behalf, described her as having "one of the most severe cases" of battered woman syndrome that he had ever seen. I agree with Abella J.A. that in such circumstances, the trial judge could have more expansively explained and emphasized the relevance of the expert evidence on battered woman syndrome to Mrs. Malott's claim of self-defence. In this connection, the trial judge's charge to the jury was not perfect. But as my colleague Major J. correctly points out at para. 15, it is unrealistic for an appeal court to review a trial judge's charge to a jury based on a standard of perfection. In deference to this well-established principle, I agree with Major J.'s conclusion that the charge was sufficient. For these reasons, I would dismiss the appeal.

———————————

A rich literature has developed on the issue of battered woman syndrome: see Christine Boyle, "The Battered Wife Syndrome and Self-Defence: *Lavallee v. The Queen*" (1990), 9 *Can. J. of Family Law* 171; Celia Wells, "Battered Woman Syndrome and Defences to Homicide: Where Now?" (1994), 14 *Legal Studies* 266; Martha Shaffer, "*R. v. Lavallee*: A Review Essay" (1990), 22 *Ottawa L. Rev.* 607; Isabel Grant, "The 'Syndromization' of Women's Experience" (1991), 25 *U.B.C. L. Rev.* 51; Martha Shaffer, "The Battered Woman Syndrome Revisited: Some Complicating Thoughts Five Years

After *R. v. Lavallee*" (1997), 47 *U.T.L.J.* 1. After years of lobbying by the Canadian Association of Elizabeth Fry Societies, the federal government appointed Judge Lynn Ratushny to conduct an inquiry of women convicted who might have benefited from the development in *Lavallee*. Justice Ratushny delivered her report in 1997, making recommendations about individual cases, and about the law in general: see Justice Lynn Ratushny, *The Self-Defence Review—Final Report* (Ottawa: Department of Justice Canada, 1997). For a discussion of this report, see Elizabeth Sheehy, "Review of the Self-Defence Review" (2000), 12 *C.J.W.L.* 197, and Gary T. Trotter, "Justice, Politics and the Royal Prerogative of Mercy: Examining the Self-Defence Review" (2001), 26 *Queen's L.J.* 339. Finally, the battered woman's syndrome has been recognized in the context of the defence of duress, which is discussed in chapter 19—Duress.

## IV. PROPOSALS FOR REFORM

Law Reform Commission of Canada, Report 31 (1987), *Recodifying Criminal Law*, at pp. 36-37:

> 3(10)  Defence of the Person.
>
> (a)  General Rule. No one is liable if he acted as he did to protect himself or another person against unlawful force by using such force as was reasonably necessary to avoid the harm or hurt apprehended.
>
> (b)  Exception: Law Enforcement. This clause does not apply to anyone who uses force against a person reasonably identifiable as a peace officer executing a warrant of arrest or anyone present acting under his authority.

Comment

The paramount value set on life and bodily integrity underlies both the prohibitions against crimes of violence and many of the defences in this chapter, specially that of defence of the person. The present law is contained in sections 34 to 37 and subsection 215(4) of the *Criminal Code* in somewhat complex fashion. Section 34 rules out force meant to kill or cause bodily harm; sections 35 and 36 restrict the amount of force permissible to an aggressor in self-defence; section 37 states the general rule allowing unlawful force to be repelled by necessary proportionate force; and subsection 215(4) restricts the right of self-defence against illegal arrest.

Clause 3(10) roughly retains the law but sets it out more simply in one rule with one exception. Clause 3(10)(a) articulates the right to use reasonably necessary force against unlawful force. It provides an objective test and restricts the defence to resisting unlawful force. It does not cover, therefore, resisting lawful force such as lawful arrest or justifiable measures of self-defence. It also omits details about force intended to cause death and about self-defence by an aggressor since these relate really to the question whether the force used is reasonably necessary. On the other hand it does cover force used to protect anyone and not just force used to protect the accused himself or those under his protection.

The exception relates to self-defence against unlawful force used in law enforcement. Clause 3(10)(b) excludes force altogether against arrest made in good faith but in fact under a defective warrant by a person who is clearly a peace officer. The policy is to restrict violence, to render it as far as possible a State monopoly and to make the arrestee submit at the time and have the matter sorted out later by authority.

The June 1993 *Federal Proposals to Amend the General Principles of the Criminal Code* provide that ss. 34 to 42 should be repealed and the following sections added to the *Criminal Code*:

37.(1) A person is not guilty of an offence to the extent that the person acts in self-defence or in defence of another person.

(2) A person acts in self-defence or in defence of another person if, in the circumstances as the person believes them to be,

(a) the person's acts are necessary for the defence of that person or the other person, as the case may be, against force or threatened force;

(b) the force is or would be unlawful; and

(c) the person's acts are reasonable and are proportionate to the harm that the person seeks to avoid.

38.(1) A person in peaceable possession of property under a claim of right is not guilty of an offence to the extent that, in the circumstances as the person believes them to be,

(a) the person acts in order to defend that possession against interference;

(b) the interference is

(i) lawful interference, other than lawful interference that is protected by section 25, or

(ii) unlawful interference; and

(c) the person's acts are reasonable and are proportionate to the interference that the person seeks to avoid or terminate.

(2) A person in peaceable possession of property, whether or not under a claim of right, is not guilty of an offence to the extent that, in the circumstances as the person believes them to be,

(a) the person acts in order to defend that possession against interference;

(b) the interference is unlawful; and

(c) the person's acts are reasonable and are proportionate to the interference that the person seeks to avoid or terminate.

(3) The defences provided by subsections (1) and (2) are also available to a person acting under the authority of a person referred to in those subsections or lawfully assisting such a person.

(4) In this section,

"defend that possession" means to protect the property from interference, to retake possession of the property from a person who has removed it or taken possession of it, or to remove from the property a person who has entered or remains on the property;

"interference" includes destruction of or damage to property, removal of property, taking possession of property, or entering or remaining on property, whether occurring or imminent.

ADDITIONAL READING

- K. Roach, *Criminal Law*, 3rd ed. (Toronto: Irwin Law, 2004), chapter 8;
- D. Stuart, *Canadian Criminal Law*, 4th ed. (Toronto: Carswell, 2001), at 475-512;
- G. Ferguson, "Self-Defence: Selecting Applicable Defences" (2000), 5 *Can. Crim. L.R.* 179;
- A. Mewett and M. Manning, *Criminal Law*, 3rd ed. (Toronto: Butterworths, 1994), at 572-96;
- E. Colvin, *Principles of Criminal Law*, 2nd ed. (Toronto: Carswell, 1991), at 195-221.

# PART SIX

# Disposition

# CHAPTER TWENTY-ONE

# Sentencing

This chapter explores the issue of sentencing in Canadian criminal law. For our purposes, we cover this area in a general way, given that sentencing is itself an area worthy of study. For more extensive materials on sentencing, see Allan Manson, Patrick Healy, and Gary Trotter, *Sentencing and Penal Policy in Canada: Cases, Commentary and Materials* (Toronto: Emond Montgomery, 2000).

Section I of this chapter explores the general principles of sentencing, as articulated by the courts, and in newly enacted sentencing legislation. Section II raises certain problems related to the fact-finding function in the sentencing process. Section III considers the impact of the Charter on sentencing, especially in relation to the application of s. 12 of the Charter, which protects against cruel and unusual treatment and punishment. Section IV gives an overview of sentencing options available under the *Criminal Code*. Finally, section V identifies important issues of race and gender in sentencing.

The *Criminal Code* has recently been amended to define the purposes and principles that should guide judges in exercising their sentencing discretion.

## I. PURPOSE AND PRINCIPLES OF SENTENCING

Before amendments to the *Criminal Code* in 1996, the sentencing function was largely an unfettered exercise of discretion. The *Criminal Code* provided little guidance. Thus, it fell to the courts to fashion appropriate goals and principles of sentencing. Typical of this approach, is the following statement of the Supreme Court of Canada in *R. v. Lyons* (1987), 37 C.C.C. (3d) 1, in which La Forest J. said:

> In a rational system of sentencing, the respective importance of prevention, deterrence, retribution and rehabilitation will vary according to the nature of the crime and the circumstances of the offender. No one would suggest that any of these functional considerations should be excluded from the legitimate purview of legislative or judicial decisions regarding sentencing.

After many years of failed reform initiatives, in 1996, Parliament overhauled the sentencing framework in the *Criminal Code* by introducing Bill C-41 (*An Act To Amend the Criminal Code (Sentencing) and Other Acts in Consequence Thereof*, S.C. 1995, c. 22). Key among the reforms contained in this important piece of legislation is the articulation of the purposes and principles of sentencing in ss. 718 to 718.2, which are set out below:

Purpose

718. The fundamental purpose of sentencing is to contribute, along with crime prevention initiatives, to respect for the law and the maintenance of a just, peaceful and safe
society by imposing just sanctions that have one or more of the following objectives:

(a) to denounce unlawful conduct;

(b) to deter the offender and other persons from committing offences;

(c) to separate offenders from society, where necessary;

(d) to assist in rehabilitating offenders;

(e) to provide reparations for harm done to victims or to the community; and

(f) to promote a sense of responsibility in offenders, and acknowledgment of the
harm done to victims and to the community.

Fundamental principle

718.1 A sentence must be proportionate to the gravity of the offence and the degree of
responsibility of the offender.

Other sentencing principles

718.2 A court that imposes a sentence shall also take into consideration the following
principles:

(a) a sentence should be increased or reduced to account for any relevant aggravating or mitigating circumstances relating to the offence or the offender, and, without
limiting the generality of the foregoing,

(i) evidence that the offence was motivated by bias, prejudice or hate based on
race, national or ethnic origin, language, colour, religion, sex, age, mental or physical
disability, sexual orientation, or any other similar factor, or

(ii) evidence that the offender, in committing the offence, abused the offender's
spouse or child, or,

(iii) evidence that the offender, in committing the offence, abused a position of
trust or authority in relation to the victim shall be deemed to be aggravating
circumstances;

(b) a sentence should be similar to sentences imposed on similar offenders for
similar offences committed in similar circumstances;

(c) where consecutive sentences are imposed, the combined sentence should not be
unduly long or harsh;

(d) an offender should not be deprived of liberty, if less restrictive sanctions may be
appropriate in the circumstances; and

(e) all available sanctions other than imprisonment that are reasonable in the circumstances should be considered for all offenders, with particular attention to the circumstances of aboriginal offenders.

The cases below, some decided before Bill C-41, and others decided after, demonstrate how the courts have struggled to make sense of these purposes and principles of
sentencing.

**R. v. M. (C.A.)**
Supreme Court of Canada
(1996), 105 C.C.C. (3d) 327

[The accused was sentenced by the trial judge to 25 years after pleading guilty to numerous counts of sexual assault and sexual offences against children. The B.C. Court of Appeal reduced the sentence to 18 years and 8 months. The Crown appealed.]

LAMER C.J. for the Court: In my view, within the broad statutory maximum and minimum penalties defined for particular offences under the *Code*, trial judges enjoy a wide ambit of discretion under s. 717 in selecting a "just and appropriate" fixed-term sentence which adequately promotes the traditional goals of sentencing, subject only to the fundamental principle that the global sentence imposed reflect the overall culpability of the offender and the circumstances of the offence.

I conclude that the British Columbia Court of Appeal erred in applying as a principle of sentencing that fixed-term sentences under the *Criminal Code* ought to be capped at 20 years, absent special circumstances. ...

However, in the process of determining a just and appropriate fixed-term sentence of imprisonment, the sentencing judge should be mindful of the age of the offender in applying the relevant principles of sentencing. After a certain point, the utilitarian and normative goals of sentencing will eventually begin to exhaust themselves once a contemplated sentence starts to surpass any reasonable estimation of the offender's remaining natural life span. Accordingly, in exercising his or her specialized discretion under the *Code*, a sentencing judge should generally refrain from imposing a fixed-term sentence which so greatly exceeds an offender's expected remaining life span that the traditional goals of sentencing, even general deterrence and denunciation, have all but depleted their functional value. But with that consideration in mind, the governing principle remains the same: Canadian courts enjoy a broad discretion in imposing numerical sentences for single or multiple offences, subject only to the broad statutory parameters of the *Code* and the fundamental principle of our criminal law that global sentences be "just and appropriate." ...

In *Shropshire* (1995), 102 C.C.C. (3d) 193, this court recently articulated the appropriate standard of review that a court of appeal should adopt in reviewing the fitness of sentence under s. 687(1). In the context of reviewing the fitness of an order of parole ineligibility, Iacobucci J. described the standard of review as follows, at para. 46:

> An appellate court should not be given free reign to modify a sentencing order simply because it feels that a different order ought to have been made. The formulation of a sentencing order is a profoundly subjective process; the trial judge has the advantage of having seen and heard all of the witnesses whereas the appellate court can only base itself upon a written record. A variation in the sentence should only be made if the court of appeal is convinced it is not fit. *That is to say, that it has found the sentence to be clearly unreasonable.*

... The determination of a just and appropriate sentence is a delicate art which attempts to balance carefully the societal goals of sentencing against the moral blameworthiness of the offender and the circumstances of the offence, while at all times taking into account the needs and current conditions of and in the community. The discretion of a sentencing judge should thus not be interfered with lightly.

Sentencing is an inherently individualized process, and the search for a single appropriate sentence for a similar offender and a similar crime will frequently be a fruitless exercise of academic abstraction. As well, sentences for a particular offence should be expected to vary to some degree across various communities and regions in this country, as the "just and appropriate" mix of accepted sentencing goals will depend on the needs and current conditions of and in the particular community where the crime occurred. For these reasons, consistent with the general standard of review we articulated in *Shropshire*, I believe that a court of appeal should only intervene to minimize the disparity of sentences where the sentence imposed by the trial judge is in substantial and marked departure from the sentences customarily imposed for similar offenders committing similar crimes.

With the greatest respect, I believe the Court of Appeal erred in this instance by engaging in an overly interventionist mode of appellate review of the "fitness" of sentence which transcended the standard of deference we articulated in *Shropshire*.

As a second and independent ground of appeal, the Crown argues that the Court of Appeal erred in law by relying on the proposition that "retribution is not a legitimate goal of sentencing" (p. 116) in reducing the sentence imposed by Filmer Prov. Ct. J. to 18 years and eight months.

Retribution, as an objective of sentencing, represents nothing less than the hallowed principle that criminal punishment, in addition to advancing utilitarian considerations related to deterrence and rehabilitation, should also be imposed to sanction the moral culpability of the offender. In my view, retribution is integrally woven into the existing principles of sentencing in Canadian law through the fundamental requirement that a sentence imposed be "just and appropriate" under the circumstances. Indeed, it is my profound belief that retribution represents an important unifying principle of our penal law by offering an essential conceptual link between the attribution of *criminal liability* and the imposition of *criminal sanctions*. With regard to the attribution of criminal liability, I have repeatedly held that it is a principle of "fundamental justice" under s. 7 of the Charter that criminal liability may only be imposed if an accused possesses a minimum "culpable mental state" in respect of the ingredients of the alleged offence: see *R. v. Martineau, supra,* at p. 360. See, similarly, *Reference re: Section 94(2) of the Motor Vehicle Act, supra; R. v. Vaillancourt* (1987), 39 C.C.C. (3d) 118, 47 D.L.R. (4th) 399, [1987] 2 S.C.R. 636. It is this mental state which gives rise to the "moral blameworthiness" which justifies the state in imposing the stigma and punishment associated with a criminal sentence: see *Martineau*, at p. 361. I submit that it is this same element of "moral blameworthiness" which animates the determination of the appropriate quantum of punishment for a convicted offender as a "just sanction." As I noted in *Martineau* in discussing the sentencing scheme for manslaughter under the *Code*, it is a recognized principle of our justice system that "punishment be meted out with regard to the level of moral blameworthiness of the offender" (p. 362): see the similar observations of W.E.B. Code in "Proportionate Blameworthiness and the Rule against Constructive Sentencing" (1992), 11 C.R. (4th) 40 at pp. 41-2.

However, the meaning of retribution is deserving of some clarification. The legitimacy of retribution as a principle of sentencing has often been questioned as a result of its unfortunate association with "vengeance" in common parlance: see, *e.g.*, *R. v. Hinch and Salanski, supra*, at pp. 43-4; *R. v. Calder* (1956), 114 C.C.C. 155 at p. 161, 23 C.R. 191, 17 W.W.R. 528 (Man. C.A.). But it should be clear from my foregoing discussion that retribution bears little relation to vengeance, and I attribute much of the criticism of retribution as a principle to this confusion. As both academic and judicial commentators have noted, vengeance has no role to play in a civilized system of sentencing: see Ruby, *Sentencing, supra*, at p. 13. Vengeance, as I understand it, represents an uncalibrated act of harm upon another, frequently motivated by emotion and anger, as a reprisal for harm inflicted upon oneself by that person. Retribution in a criminal context, by contrast, represents an objective, reasoned and measured determination of an appropriate punishment which properly reflects the *moral culpability* of the offender, having regard to the intentional risk-taking of the offender, the consequential harm caused by the offender, and the normative character of the offender's conduct. Furthermore, unlike vengeance, retribution incorporates a principle of restraint; retribution requires the imposition of a just and appropriate punishment, and *nothing more*. As R. Cross has noted in *The English Sentencing System*, 2nd ed. (London: Butterworths, 1975), at p. 121: "The retributivist insists that the punishment must not be disproportionate to the offender's deserts."

Retribution, as well, should be conceptually distinguished from its legitimate sibling, denunciation. Retribution requires that a judicial sentence properly reflect the moral blameworthiness of that particular *offender*. The objective of denunciation mandates that a sentence should also communicate society's condemnation of that particular offender's *conduct*. In short, a sentence with a denunciatory element represents a symbolic, collective statement that the offender's conduct should be punished for encroaching on our society's basic code of values as enshrined within our substantive criminal law. As Lord Justice Lawton stated in *R. v. Sargeant* (1974), 60 Cr. App. R. 74 at p. 77: "society, through the courts, must show its abhorrence of particular types of crime, and the only way in which the courts can show this is by the sentences they pass." The relevance of both retribution and denunciation as goals of sentencing underscores that our criminal justice system is not simply a vast system of negative penalties designed to prevent objectively harmful conduct by increasing the cost the offender must bear in committing an enumerated offence. Our criminal law is also a system of values. A sentence which expresses denunciation is simply the means by which these values are communicated. In short, in addition to attaching negative consequences to undesirable behaviour, judicial sentences should also be imposed in a manner which positively instills the basic set of communal values shared by all Canadians as expressed by the *Criminal Code*.

As a closing note to this discussion, it is important to stress that neither retribution nor denunciation alone provides an exhaustive justification for the imposition of criminal sanctions. Rather, in our system of justice, normative and utilitarian considerations operate in conjunction with one another to provide a coherent justification for criminal punishment. As Gonthier J. emphasized in *Goltz*, *supra*, at p.495, the goals of the penal sanction are both "broad and varied." Accordingly, the meaning of retribution must be considered in conjunction with the other legitimate objectives of sentencing, which include (but are not limited to) deterrence, denunciation, rehabilitation and the protection of society. Indeed, it is difficult to perfectly separate these interrelated principles. And as La Forest J. emphasized in *Lyons*, the relative weight and importance of these multiple factors will frequently vary depending on the nature of the crime and the circumstances of the offender. In the final analysis, the overarching duty of a sentencing judge is to draw upon all the legitimate principles of sentencing to determine a "just and appropriate" sentence which reflects the gravity of the offence committed and the moral blameworthiness of the offender.

*Appeal allowed; sentence of 25 years' imprisonment restored.*

## II. FACT FINDING AND THE SENTENCING PROCESS

An important issue in sentencing is what facts the trial judge relies upon. Consider the following cases.

### R. v. Ebsary
Nova Scotia Supreme Court, Appellate Division
(1986), 73 N.S.R. (2d) 56

[The accused was charged with manslaughter in the stabbing death of Sandy Seale. He pleaded self-defence but was convicted by a judge and jury. The judge sentenced Ebsary to three years' imprisonment.]

MacDONALD J.A.:  The appellant will be seventy-four years of age on June the 2nd of this year. He has a previous criminal record consisting of a conviction in 1970 under what is now s. 85 of the *Criminal Code* (possession of a weapon dangerous to the public peace) and in 1982 of carrying a concealed weapon.

In imposing sentence Mr. Justice Nunn said in part:

> The evidence disclosed that that night you were armed and perhaps ready to take drastic measures if any situation presented itself. Even so, unless you orchestrated a situation, those facts need not be held against you. If you did orchestrate the situation or attack when unprovoked, it would have been murder. In my own mind, I do believe that these events did occur in a marginal self-defence situation, at least in the public perception of self-defence. It may have been that your reaction was too violent, but there was some element of self-defence involved and I am entitled to take that into account in sentencing.

Later the learned trial judge said:

… Taking into account your health circumstances, mental and physical, taking into account your age, taking into account the previous record that has been indicated to me, particularly the offence before this offence for which you stand convicted, and taking into account the circumstances surrounding the incident itself, taking into account the time since you've first been charged, I still am of the view that deterrence is a strong factor here; deterrence for yourself, who is still believed by some to have a violent nature, and for the public. It is repugnant to our system and one just cannot accept that a person can take matters into his own hands and become an executioner in situations such as you encountered.

Also on the rehabilitation side, there are some pretty strong requirements for rehabilitation. Your use of alcohol, drugs, your inclination to violence all require a period of time to correct. As I said, all of the circumstances have to be taken into account and in so doing, it is my view that the protection of the public can best be served by a period of incarceration in a federal institution.

Considering all of the factors that I've indicated, and giving you the benefit of what I suggest may be a public perception of a marginal self-defence situation, I think the Crown's recommendation is too long, and I can't agree with the Defence submission on probation, so I sentence you to confinement in a federal institution for a period of three years.

As pointed out by this Court in *R. v. Myette* (1985), 67 N.S.R. (2d) 154; 155 A.P.R. 154, at 162, 163:

The offence of manslaughter carries a maximum sentence of life imprisonment. The range of sentences imposed in Nova Scotia has been from suspended sentence (e.g., *R. v. Cormier* (1974), 9 N.S.R. (2d) 687 (N.S. C.A.)), to twenty years' imprisonment (*R. v. Julian* (1973), 6 N.S.R. (2d) 504 (N.S. C.A.)). Lenient sentences have been imposed only where very strong mitigating factors exist or where the act, though culpable, was close to being an accident. In the great majority of manslaughter cases sentences range from four to ten years.

[Medical reports were reviewed indicating that Ebsary had chronic degenerative disease of the spine, cancer of the prostate, chronic lung disease, recently had broken his neck in a fall, and had bowel surgery.]

As Mr. Justice Nunn pointed out there may well have been an element of self-defence present at the time Seale was stabbed. I agree entirely, because it appears inconceivable to me that the appellant would stab Mr. Seale for absolutely no reason. Mr. Marshall on other occasions testified under oath that Seale and himself were engaged in attempting to rob Mr. MacNeil and the appellant at the time Seale was stabbed. This to me is the far more likely version of why the stabbing took place.

In light of the post-sentence reports, the circumstances both of the incident itself and of the appellant and bearing in mind that justice must always be tempered with mercy, it is my opinion that a fit and proper sentence for this offence by this offender would be imprisonment for one year in the Cape Breton County Correctional Center. In result I would dismiss the appeal against conviction, but would allow the application for leave to appeal against sentence, allow the appeal and vary the sentence as indicated.

## R. v. Gardiner
Supreme Court of Canada
(1982), 68 C.C.C. (2d) 477

DICKSON J.: The question now to be addressed is this: what burden of proof must the Crown sustain in advancing contested aggravating facts in a sentencing proceeding, for the purpose of supporting a lengthier sentence; is the standard that of the criminal law, proof beyond a reasonable doubt, or that of the civil law, proof on a balance of probabilities?

The Crown argues for the acceptance of a lesser onus of proof at sentencing than the traditional criminal onus of beyond a reasonable doubt which applies at trial to the determination of guilt.

Relying heavily on American authorities the Crown suggests that there is a sharp demarcation between the trial process and the sentencing process. Once a plea or finding of guilty is entered the presumption of innocence no longer operates and the necessity of the full panoply of procedural protection for the accused ceases. Sentencing is a discretionary and highly subjective exercise on the part of the trial judge. The primary concern at a sentencing hearing is the availability of accurate information upon which the trial judge can rely in determining an appropriate sentence in the particular circumstances of the offender. For this reason the strict rules on the admissibility of evidence are relaxed. The trial judge is no longer confined to the narrow issue of guilt but is engaged in the difficult task of fitting the punishment to the person convicted. To require that the Crown prove contested issues beyond a reasonable doubt would be to complicate and extend sentencing hearings and convert the sentencing process into a second trial with a resultant loss of economy.

In the event that the essentially civil onus of preponderance of evidence is rejected, the Crown proposes, in the alternative, an "intermediate" standard of "clear and convincing" evidence to apply to sentencing hearings.

The respondent, on the other hand, argues for the application of the reasonable doubt standard to sentencing hearings. The "bifurcation" between trial and sentencing proposed by the Crown the respondent finds artificial and against the authorities. From the offender's point of view, sentencing is the most critical part of the whole trial process, it is the "gist of the proceeding" and the standard of proof required with respect to controverted facts should not be relaxed at this point. To do so is prejudicial to the accused. Administrative efficiency is insufficient justification for so radical a departure from the traditional criminal onus of beyond a reasonable doubt.

One of the hardest tasks confronting a trial judge is sentencing. The stakes are high for society and for the individual. Sentencing is the critical stage of the criminal justice system, and it is manifest that the judge should not be denied an opportunity to obtain relevant information by the imposition of all the restrictive evidential rules common to a trial. Yet the obtaining and weighing of such evidence should be fair. A substantial liberty interest of the offender is involved and the information obtained should be accurate and reliable.

It is a commonplace that the strict rules which govern at trial do not apply at a sentencing hearing and it would be undesirable to have the formalities and technicalities characteristic of the normal adversary proceeding prevail. The hearsay rule does not govern the sentencing hearing. Hearsay evidence may be accepted where found to be credible and trustworthy. The judge traditionally has had wide latitude as to the sources and types of evidence upon which to base his sentence. He must have the fullest possible information concerning the background of the accused if he is to fit the sentence to the offender rather than to the crime.

It is well to recall in any discussion of sentencing procedures that the vast majority of offenders plead guilty. Canadian figures are not readily available but American statistics suggest that about 85% of the criminal defendants plead guilty or *nolo contendere*. The sentencing judge therefore must get his facts after plea. Sentencing is, in respect of most offenders, the only significant decision the criminal justice system is called upon to make.

It should also be recalled that a plea of guilty, in itself, carries with it an admission of the essential legal ingredients of the offence admitted by the plea, and no more. Beyond that any facts relied upon by the Crown in aggravation must be established by the Crown. If undisputed, the procedure can be very informal. If the facts are contested the issue should be resolved by ordinary legal principles governing criminal proceedings including resolving relevant doubt in favour of the offender.

To my mind, the facts which justify the sanction are no less important than the facts which justify the conviction; both should be subject to the same burden of proof. Crime and punishment are inextricably linked. "It would appear well established that the sentencing process is merely a phase of the trial process" (Olah, *ibid.*, at p. 107). Upon conviction the accused is not abruptly deprived of all procedural rights existing at trial: he has a right to counsel, a right to call evidence and cross-examine prosecution witnesses, a right to give evidence himself and to address the court.

The *rationale* of the argument of the Crown for the acceptance of a lesser standard of proof is administrative efficiency. In my view, however, the administrative efficiency argument is not sufficient to overcome such a basic tenet suffusing our entire criminal justice system as the standard of proof beyond a reasonable doubt. I am by no means convinced that if the standard of proof were lowered, conservation of judicial resources would be enhanced. In the event of a serious dispute as to facts, it would be in the interests of the accused to plead not guilty in order to benefit at trial from the higher standard of reasonable doubt. This would not only be destructive of judicial economy but at the same time prejudicial to whatever mitigating effect might have come from a guilty plea, as evidence of remorse. There would seem in principle no good reason why the sentencing judge in deciding disputed facts should not observe the same evidentiary standards as we demand of juries.

[Martland, Ritchie, and Chouinard JJ. concurred with Dickson J. Laskin C.J.C., Estey, and McIntyre JJ. dissented on a jurisdictional point.]

Bill C-41 also codified issues of proof for sentencing purposes. Section 724 attempts to codify the position in *Gardiner*:

Information accepted

724.(1) In determining a sentence, a court may accept as proved any information disclosed at the trial or at the sentencing proceedings and any facts agreed on by the prosecutor and the offender.

(2) Where the court is composed of a judge and jury, the court

(a) shall accept as proven all facts, express or implied, that are essential to the jury's verdict of guilty; and

(b) may find any other relevant fact that was disclosed by evidence at the trial to be proven, or hear evidence presented by either party with respect to that fact.

(3) Where there is a dispute with respect to any fact that is relevant to the determination of a sentence,

(a) the court shall request that evidence be adduced as to the existence of the fact unless the court is satisfied that sufficient evidence was adduced at the trial;

(b) the party wishing to rely on a relevant fact, including a fact contained in a presentence report, has the burden of proving it;

(c) either party may cross-examine any witness called by the other party;

(d) subject to paragraph (e), the court must be satisfied on a balance of probabilities of the existence of the disputed fact before relying on it in determining the sentence; and

(e) the prosecutor must establish, by proof beyond a reasonable doubt, the existence of any aggravating fact or any previous conviction by the offender.

Is this provision, particularly s. 724(3)(d), faithful to *Gardiner* and the residual presumption of innocence that survives at the sentencing stage of the proceedings?

## III. CONSTITUTIONAL CONSIDERATIONS

The Charter has added a new dimension to sentencing. Section 7 of the Charter has affected the minimal requirements of fault when imprisonment is the sentence, or a potential sentence. Section 12 addresses the question of the permissible limits of certain sanctions, mostly in the context of imprisonment. Consider the following cases.

### Reference re Section 94(2) of the B.C. Motor Vehicle Act
Supreme Court of Canada
(1985), 23 C.C.C. (3d) 289

WILSON J.: It is now generally accepted among penologists that there are five main objectives of a penal system: see Nigel Walker, *Sentencing in a Rational Society* (1969). They are:

(1) to protect offenders and suspected offenders against unofficial retaliation;

(2) to reduce the incidence of crime;

(3)  to ensure that offenders atone for their offences;

(4)  to keep punishment to the minimum necessary to achieve the objectives of the system, and

(5)  to express society's abhorrence of crime.

Apart from death, imprisonment is the most severe sentence imposed by the law and is generally viewed as a last resort, *i.e.*, as appropriate only when it can be shown that no other sanction can achieve the objectives of the system.

The Law Reform Commission of Canada, in its Working paper 11—Imprisonment and Release (*Studies on Imprisonment*, 1976), states at p. 10:

> Justice requires that the sanction of imprisonment not be disproportionate to the offence, and humanity dictates that it must not be heavier than necessary to achieve its objective.

Because of the absolute liability nature of the offence created by s. 94(2) of the *Motor Vehicle Act* a person can be convicted under the section even though he was unaware at the time he was driving that his licence was suspended and was unable to find this out despite the exercise of due diligence. While the Legislature may as a matter of government policy make this an offence, and we cannot question its wisdom in this regard, the question is whether it can make it mandatory for the courts to deprive a person convicted of it of his liberty without violating s. 7. This, in turn, depends on whether attaching a mandatory term of imprisonment to an absolute liability offence such as this violates the principles of fundamental justice. I believe that it does. I think the conscience of the court would be shocked and the administration of justice brought into disrepute by such an unreasonable and extravagant penalty. It is totally disproportionate to the offence and quite incompatible with the objective of a penal system referred to in para. (4) above.

It is basic to any theory of punishment that the sentence imposed bear some relationship to the offence; it must be a "fit" sentence proportionate to the seriousness of the offence. Only if this is so can the public be satisfied that the offender "deserved" the punishment he received and feel a confidence in the fairness and rationality of the system. This is not to say that there is an inherently appropriate relationship between a particular offence and its punishment but rather that there is a scale of offences and punishments into which the particular offence and punishment must fit. Obviously, this cannot be done with mathematical precision and many different factors will go into the assessment of the seriousness of a particular offence for purposes of determining the appropriate punishment but it does provide a workable conventional framework for sentencing. Indeed, judges in the exercise of their sentencing discretion have been employing such a scale for over 100 years.

I believe that a mandatory term of imprisonment for an offence committed unknowingly and unwittingly and after the exercise of due diligence is grossly excessive and inhumane. It is not required to reduce the incidence of the offence. It is beyond anything required to satisfy the need for "atonement." And society, in my opinion, would not find abhorrent an unintentional and unknowing violation of the

section. I believe, therefore, that such a sanction offends the principles of fundamental justice embodied in our penal system. Section 94(2) is accordingly inconsistent
with s. 7 of the Charter and must, to the extent of the inconsistency, be declared of no
force and effect under s. 52.

### R. v. Smith
Supreme Court of Canada
(1987), 34 C.C.C. (3d) 97

[The Supreme Court of Canada held 5 to 1 that s. 5(2) of the *Narcotics Control Act*,
R.S.C. 1985, c. N-1, a sentencing provision mandating a minimum sentence of seven
years' imprisonment for importing narcotics, violated the prohibition of cruel and
unusual punishment under s. 12 of the Charter and was not justified under s. 1 of the
Charter.]

LAMER J. in delivering the judgment for himself and Dickson C.J.C. stated:  Those
who import and market hard drugs for lucre are responsible for the gradual but inexorable degeneration of many of their fellow human beings as a result of their becoming drug addicts. The direct cause of the hardship cast upon their victims and their
families, these importers must also be made to bear their fair share of the guilt for the
innumerable serious crimes of all sorts committed by addicts in order to feed their
demand for drugs. Such persons, with few exceptions (as an example, the guilt of
addicts who import not only to meet but also to finance their needs is not necessarily
the same in degree as that of cold-blooded non-users), should, upon conviction, in
my respectful view, be sentenced to and actually serve long periods of penal servitude. However, a judge who would sentence to seven years in a penitentiary a young
person who, while driving back into Canada from a winter break in the U.S.A., is
caught with only one, indeed, let's postulate, his or her first "joint of grass," would
certainly be considered by most Canadians to be a cruel and, all would hope, a very
unusual judge. ...

   In imposing a sentence of imprisonment the judge will assess the circumstances of
the case in order to arrive at an appropriate sentence. The test for review under s. 12
of the Charter is one of gross disproportionality, because it is aimed at punishments
that are more than merely excessive. We should be careful not to stigmatize every
disproportionate or excessive sentence as being a constitutional violation, and should
leave to the usual sentencing appeal process the task of reviewing the fitness of a
sentence. Section 12 will only be infringed where the sentence is so unfit having
regard to the offence and the offender as to be grossly disproportionate.

   In assessing whether a sentence is grossly disproportionate, the court must first
consider the gravity of the offence, the personal characteristics of the offender and
the particular circumstances of the case in order to determine what range of sentences
would have been appropriate to punish, rehabilitate or deter this particular offender
or to protect the public from this particular offender. The other purposes which may

be pursued by the imposition of punishment, in particular the deterrence of other potential offenders, are thus not relevant at this stage of the inquiry. This does not mean that the judge or the legislator can no longer consider general deterrence or other penological purposes that go beyond the particular offender in determining a sentence, but only that the resulting sentence must not be grossly disproportionate to what the offender deserves. If a grossly disproportionate sentence is "prescribed by law," then the purpose which it seeks to attain will fall to be assessed under s. 1. Section 12 ensures that individual offenders receive punishments that are appropriate, or at least not grossly disproportionate, to their particular circumstances, while s. 1 permits this right to be overridden to achieve some important societal objective.

One must also measure the effect of the sentence actually imposed. If it is grossly disproportionate to what would have been appropriate, then it infringes s. 12. The effect of the sentence is often a composite of many factors and is not limited to the quantum or duration of the sentence but includes its nature and the conditions under which it is applied. Sometimes by its length alone or by its very nature will the sentence be grossly disproportionate to the purpose sought. Sometimes it will be the result of the combination of factors which, when considered in isolation, would not in and of themselves amount to gross disproportionality. For example, 20 years for a first offence against property would be grossly disproportionate, but so would three months of imprisonment if the prison authorities decide it should be served in solitary confinement. Finally, I should add that some punishments or treatments will always be grossly disproportionate and will always outrage our standards of decency: for example, the infliction of corporal punishment, such as the lash, irrespective of the number of lashes imposed, or, to give examples of treatment, the lobotomisation of certain dangerous offenders or the castration of sexual offenders. ...

The minimum seven-year imprisonment fails the proportionality test enunciated above and therefore *prima facie* infringes the guarantees established by s. 12 of the Charter. The simple fact that s. 5(2) provides for a mandatory term of imprisonment does not by itself lead to this conclusion. A minimum mandatory term of imprisonment is obviously not in and of itself cruel and unusual. ...

For example, a long term of penal servitude for he or she who has imported large amounts of heroin for the purpose of trafficking would certainly not contravene s. 12 of the Charter, quite the contrary. However, the seven-year minimum prison term of s. 5(2) is grossly disproportionate when examined in light of the wide net cast by s. 5(1).

... [T]he offence of importing enacted by s. 5(1) of the *Narcotic Control Act* covers numerous substances of varying degrees of dangerousness and totally disregards the quantity of the drug imported. The purpose of a given importation, such as whether it is for personal consumption or for trafficking, and the existence or non-existence of previous convictions for offences of a similar nature or gravity are disregarded as irrelevant. Thus, the law is such that it is inevitable that, in some cases, a verdict of guilt will lead to the imposition of a term of imprisonment which will be grossly disproportionate. ...

[In considering whether the infringement of s. 12 was justified under s. 1, Lamer J. applied the test outlined in *Oakes*, and stated:]

... In my view, the fight against the importing and trafficking of hard drugs is, without a doubt, an objective "of sufficient importance to warrant overriding a constitutionally protected right or freedom." ...

The certainty that all those who contravene the prohibition against importing will be sentenced to at least seven years in prison will surely deter people from importing narcotics. Therefore, rationality, the first prong of the proportionality test, has been met. But the Crown's justification fails the second prong, namely, minimum impairment of the rights protected by s. 12. Clearly there is no need to be indiscriminate. We do not need to sentence the small offenders to seven years in prison in order to deter the serious offender. ...

... The result sought could be achieved by limiting the imposition of a minimum sentence to the importing of certain quantities, to certain specific narcotics of the schedule, to repeat offenders, or even to a combination of these factors. ...

Having written these reasons some time ago, I have not referred to recent decisions of the courts or recent publications. However, I wish to refer to the Report of the Canadian Sentencing Commission entitled *Sentencing Reform: A Canadian Approach* (1987), which gives some support to my conclusion. The commission recommended the abolition of mandatory minimum penalties for all offences except murder and high treason because it was of the view that (p. 188): "... existing mandatory minimum penalties, with the exception of those prescribed for murder and high treason, serve no purpose that can compensate for the disadvantages resulting from their continued existence." ...

McINTYRE J. in dissent stated: Punishment not *per se* cruel and unusual, may become cruel and unusual due to excess or lack of proportionality only where it is so excessive that it is an outrage to standards of decency. ...

... It is true, in general, that when a judge imposes a sentence, he considers the nature and gravity of the offence, the circumstances in which it was committed, and the character and criminal history of the offender, all with an eye to the primary purposes of punishment: rehabilitation, deterrence, incapacitation, and retribution. But ... sentencing is an imprecise procedure and there will always be a wide range of appropriate sentences. ...

... All that Parliament has done is to conclude that the gravity of the offence alone warrants a sentence of at least seven years' imprisonment. While, again, one may question the wisdom of this conclusion, I cannot agree that this makes the sentencing process arbitrary and, therefore, cruel and unusual in violation of s. 12 of the Charter. ...

---

In *R. v. Goltz* (1991), 67 C.C.C. (3d) 481, the Supreme Court of Canada held that a minimal sentence of seven days' imprisonment for driving with a suspended licence did not violate s. 12 of the Charter. The court held that in considering the constitutionality of a sentence, it should consider the actual circumstances of the offender and those of reasonable hypothetical offenders and that they should not invalidate minimum sentencing provisions on the basis of remote or extreme examples. In *R. v. Morrisey* (2000), 148 C.C.C. (3d) 1 (S.C.C.), the court held that the mandatory sentence of four years' imprisonment for criminal negligence causing death, with use of a firearm, contrary to s. 220(a) of the *Criminal Code*, did not offend the principles laid down in *Smith*, and then later applied in *Goltz*.

The Supreme Court revisited the issue of cruel and unusual punishment and treatment in the controversial *Latimer* case.

**R. v. Latimer**

Supreme Court of Canada

(2001), 150 C.C.C. (3d) 129

[Latimer had been convicted of second-degree murder in the death of his severely disabled daughter. The *Criminal Code* provides for a mandatory sentence of life imprisonment for second-degree murder, with parole to be set between 10 to 25 years by the trial judge. In this case, not realizing the constraints imposed by the *Criminal Code*, the jury recommended that Latimer received one year in prison. The trial judge purported to grant the accused a constitutional exemption from the mandatory sentence and imposed a sentence of one year imprisonment and one year probation. The Saskatchewan Court of Appeal affirmed Latimer's conviction, but set aside the sentence and imposed the mandatory sentence required by law. Latimer's appeal against both his conviction and sentence was dismissed by the Supreme Court of Canada. The following excerpt is restricted to the court's reasons on the sentencing issue.]

BY THE COURT: ...

*(2) Application of Section 12 Principles*

[80]  The first factor to consider is the gravity of the offence. Recently, Gonthier J., in *Morrisey, supra*, provided important guidance for the proper assessment of the gravity of an offence for the purposes of a s. 12 analysis. Specifically, Gonthier J. noted, at para. 35, that an assessment of the gravity of the offence requires an understanding of (i) the character of the offender's actions, and (ii) the consequences of those actions.

[81]  Certainly, in this case one cannot escape the conclusion that Mr. Latimer's actions resulted in the most serious of all possible consequences, namely, the death of the victim, Tracy Latimer.

[82]  In considering the character of Mr. Latimer's actions, we are directed to an assessment of the criminal fault requirement or *mens rea* element of the offence rather than the offender's motive or general state of mind (*Morrisey* ...). We attach a greater degree of criminal responsibility or moral blameworthiness to conduct where the accused knowingly broke the law (*Morrisey, supra*; *R. v. Martineau*, [1990] 2 S.C.R.

633, at p. 645). In this case, the *mens rea* requirement for second degree murder is subjective foresight of death: the most serious level of moral blameworthiness (*Luxton, supra* ...).

[83] Parliament has classified murder offences into first and second degree based on its perception of relative levels of moral blameworthiness. Parliament has also provided for differential treatment between them in sentencing, but only in respect of parole eligibility. As noted by Lamer C.J. in *Luxton* ...:

> I must also reiterate that what we are speaking of here is a classification scheme for the purposes of sentencing. The distinction between first and second degree murder only comes into play when it has first been proven beyond a reasonable doubt that the offender is guilty of murder, that is, that he or she had subjective foresight of death: *R. v. Martineau*, handed down this day. There is no doubt that a sentencing scheme must exhibit a proportionality to the seriousness of the offence, or to put it another way, there must be a gradation of punishments according to the malignity of the offences. ...

[84] However, even if the gravity of second degree murder is reduced in comparison to first degree murder, it cannot be denied that second degree murder is an offence accompanied by an extremely high degree of criminal culpability. In this case, therefore, the gravest possible consequences resulted from an act of the most serious and morally blameworthy intentionality. It is against this reality that we must weigh the other contextual factors, including and especially the particular circumstances of the offender and the offence.

[85] Turning to the characteristics of the offender and the particular circumstances of the offence we must consider the existence of any aggravating and mitigating circumstances. ... Specifically, any aggravating circumstances must be weighed against any mitigating circumstances. In this regard, it is possible that prior to gauging the sentence's appropriateness in light of an appreciation of the particular circumstances weighed against the gravity of the offence, the mitigating and aggravating circumstances might well cancel out their ultimate impact. ... Indeed, this is what occurs in this case. On the one hand, we must give due consideration to Mr. Latimer's initial attempts to conceal his actions, his lack of remorse, his position of trust, the significant degree of planning and premeditation, and Tracy's extreme vulnerability. On the other hand, we are mindful of Mr. Latimer's good character and standing in the community, his tortured anxiety about Tracy's well-being, and his laudable perseverance as a caring and involved parent. Considered together we cannot find that the personal characteristics and particular circumstances of this case displace the serious gravity of this offence.

[86] Finally, this sentence is consistent with a number of valid penological goals and sentencing principles. Although we would agree that in this case the sentencing principles of rehabilitation, specific deterrence and protection are not triggered for consideration, we are mindful of the important role that the mandatory minimum sentence plays in denouncing murder. Denunciation of unlawful conduct is one of the objectives of sentencing recognized in s. 718 of the *Criminal Code*. As noted by the Court in *R. v. M. (C.A.)*, [1996] 1 S.C.R. 500, at para. 81:

> The objective of denunciation mandates that a sentence should communicate society's condemnation of that particular offender's *conduct*. In short, a sentence with a denunciatory element represents a symbolic, collective statement that the offender's conduct should be punished for encroaching on our society's basic code of values as enshrined within our substantive criminal law. [Emphasis in original.]

Furthermore, denunciation becomes much more important in the consideration of sentencing in cases where there is a "high degree of planning and premeditation, and where the offence and its consequences are highly publicized, [so that] like-minded individuals may well be deterred by severe sentences": *R. v. Mulvahill and Snelgrove* (1993), 21 B.C.A.C. 296, at p. 300. This is particularly so where the victim is a vulnerable person with respect to age, disability, or other similar factors.

[87] In summary, the minimum mandatory sentence is not grossly disproportionate in this case. We cannot find that any aspect of the particular circumstances of the case or the offender diminishes the degree of criminal responsibility borne by Mr. Latimer. In addition, although not free of debate, the sentence is not out of step with valid penological goals or sentencing principles. The legislative classification and treatment of this offender meets the requisite standard of proportionality. ...Where there is no violation of Mr. Latimer's s. 12 right there is no basis for granting a constitutional exemption.

[88] Having said all this, we wish to point out that this appeal raises a number of issues that are worthy of emphasis. The sentencing provisions for second degree murder include both ss. 235 and 745(c). Applied in combination these provisions result in a sentence that is hybrid in that it provides for both a mandatory life sentence and a minimum term of incarceration. The choice is Parliament's on the use of minimum sentences, though considerable difference of opinion continues on the wisdom of employing minimum sentences from a criminal law policy or penological point of view.

[89] It is also worth referring again to the royal prerogative of mercy that is found in s. 749 of the *Criminal Code*, which provides "[n]othing in this Act in any manner limits or affects Her Majesty's royal prerogative of mercy." As was pointed out by Sopinka J. in *R. v. Sarson*, [1996] 2 S.C.R. 223, at para. 51, albeit in a different context:

> Where the courts are unable to provide an appropriate remedy in cases that the executive sees as unjust imprisonment, the executive is permitted to dispense "mercy," and order the release of the offender. The royal prerogative of mercy is the only potential remedy for persons who have exhausted their rights of appeal and are unable to show that their sentence fails to accord with the *Charter*.

[90] But the prerogative is a matter for the executive, not the courts. The executive will undoubtedly, if it chooses to consider the matter, examine all of the underlying circumstances surrounding the tragedy of Tracy Latimer that took place on October 24, 1993, some seven years ago. Since that time Mr. Latimer has undergone two trials and two appeals to the Court of Appeal for Saskatchewan and this Court, with attendant publicity and consequential agony for him and his family.

*VI. Disposition*

[91] Mr. Latimer's appeals against conviction and sentence are dismissed.

---

In *R. v. Luxton* (1990), 58 C.C.C. (3d) 449 (S.C.C.), it was argued that the mandatory first-degree murder sentence of 25 years' imprisonment without eligibility for parole violated s. 12 of the Charter when the murder was by way of s. 231(5)(e), which provides that a killing while committing a kidnapping and forcible confinement is first-degree murder irrespective of whether it was planned and deliberate. Lamer J. (Dickson C.J., Wilson, Gonthier, and Cory JJ.) stated:

> This is a crime that carries with it the most serious level of moral blameworthiness, namely, subjective foresight of death. The penalty is severe and deservedly so. The minimum 25 years to be served before eligibility for parole reflects society's condemnation of a person who has exploited a position of power and dominance to the gravest extent possible by murdering the person that he or she is forcibly confining. The punishment is not excessive and clearly does not outrage our standards of decency. In my view, it is within the purview of Parliament, in order to meet the objectives of a rational system of sentencing, to treat our most serious crime with an appropriate degree of certainty and severity. I reiterate that, even in the case of first degree murder, Parliament has been sensitive to the particular circumstances of each offender through various provisions allowing for the royal prerogative of mercy, the availability of escorted absences from custody for humanitarian and rehabilitative purposes and for early parole: see ss. 672 (now s. 745), 674 (now s. 747) and 686 (now s. 751) of the *Criminal Code*.

See also *R. v. Arkell* (1990), 59 C.C.C. (3d) 65 (S.C.C.), in which the court also rejected a challenge to the first-degree murder sentencing provision based on s. 7 of the Charter.

There are a couple of issues related to imprisonment that require attention and put the reach of this sanction in its proper perspective.

## IV. SENTENCING OPTIONS OTHER THAN IMPRISONMENT

In discussions of sentencing, it is easy to get side-tracked by thinking of sentencing in terms of the quantum of imprisonment that ought to be imposed. In reality, most individuals who come before the criminal courts in Canada will receive a sanction other than imprisonment. At the centre of much of the sentencing reform movement in Canada has been push to loosen out reliance on imprisonment as a sanction. The important Canadian Sentencing Commission commented as follows on the use of "community sanctions" in its report *Sentencing Reform: A Canadian Approach* (1987):

> As previously mentioned, the Commission recommends that all sanctions other than custody (e.g., those involving community programs or resources, or those that involve compensation to the community such as fines or compensation to the victim) be referred to as community sanctions. They should not be thought of as "alternatives" to imprisonment, but rather as appropriate sanctions in their own right. The Commission recommends greater use

of community sanctions, but that this greater use be accomplished in a principled way. Through the use of guidelines, mechanisms can be put in place to minimize the likelihood that community sanctions would be used inconsistently and as add-ons to an otherwise adequate sentence.

The Commission makes general recommendations on the need to increase the use of all community sanctions. The Commission also makes detailed recommendations on the use of two community sanctions: fines and restitution. It looked at fines because they are imposed frequently. Also there is evidence of disparity in the impact of fine default on identifiable groups (e.g. native offenders and women). Furthermore, those who fail to pay fines contribute significantly to prison populations. The Commission examined restitution because it is an appropriately constructive sanction which helps to meet some of the needs of victims.

The Commission recommends that fines be imposed only in circumstances where an inquiry reveals it is appropriate to do so. There is no point in imposing a fine on someone who cannot pay. Thus the Commission recommended that before a fine is imposed, an inquiry as to the offender's ability to pay be carried out.

The Commission recommends that we abandon the almost automatic use of imprisonment for fine default. An offender could only be incarcerated for wilful default and only after other methods of collection have been exhausted or were determined to be inappropriate by the court. Finally, if a person were to be incarcerated for wilful default, the Commission is recommending a fixed conversion table which translates dollar amounts of fines into custodial terms.

The Commission also recommends that restitution be used more frequently in order to encourage the offender to take responsibility for his acts and, of course, as a way in which victims can be compensated.

In deciding what sanction is appropriate, the judge may require a probation officer to make a pre-sentencing report. The court may also consider a victim impact statement at this time. Both of these must be filed with the court and made available to the prosecutor and the accused.

## Absolute and Conditional Discharges

If an accused is found guilty of an offence for which there is no minimum punishment prescribed by law and is not punishable by 14 years or life imprisonment, then an absolute or conditional discharge can be given. Under s. 730 of the Code the discharge must be in "the best interests of the accused and not contrary to the public interest. …"

## Probation

The making of probation orders is governed by s. 731 of the Code. Probation orders may be made in addition to a fine or a term of imprisonment not exceeding two years or by themselves where the passing of the sentence is suspended. One condition in all probation orders is that the accused "shall keep the peace and be of good behaviour and shall appear when required to do so by the court."

**R. v. Preston**

British Columbia Court of Appeal

(1990), 79 C.R. (3d) 61

[The accused was convicted of three counts of possession of heroin. Since her last release from prison, she had voluntarily and at her own expense enrolled in a methadone treatment program and had been "clean" of heroin from August 1987 to shortly before December of 1988 when she was charged with the three counts.

The trial judge suspended the passing of sentence and placed the accused on probation. Terms of the probation order included that she attend a drug rehabilitation facility and perform 50 hours of community service. The Crown appealed.]

WOOD J.A.: The respondent is now 41 years old. She has been a heroin addict for over 20 years. In that time she has made a number of unsuccessful attempts to overcome her addiction. As a result of her lack of skills and education, her addiction, and poor health brought on by the self-abuse associated with that addiction, she has not worked for most of that time. She has been on social assistance since 1974.

Up to the time of the matters now before the court, she has amassed a total record of 23 convictions, including eight for narcotics offences, four of which were for trafficking in heroin, five soliciting or other prostitution related convictions, and an assortment of escape, unlawfully at large, failing to appear and breach of probation convictions. Apart from concurrent sentences of two years less one day on three counts of trafficking in heroin, imposed in 1976, her longest sentences have been 18 months on a charge of confinement, also in 1976, and 18 months for another heroin trafficking conviction in 1985. All other sentences imposed upon her have been for 90 days or less. ...

The trial judge gave lengthy reasons for making the orders he did. He was clearly aware of the many decisions of this court, which have either upheld or imposed substantial periods of imprisonment for similar offences committed by similar offenders. In the end he took the view that he ought to order a disposition of these charges which would encourage what he saw as a genuine motivation for rehabilitation on the part of the respondent. As I read his reasons, they can be summarized in this way.

The root of the respondent's problem is obviously her addiction to heroin. As long as she is unable to control that addiction, it is pointless to expect that any sentence imposed will have a deterrent effect on her. As long as she is unable to control her addiction she remains a threat to society in the sense that she can only support that addiction by resorting to crime. Thus the only way to protect society from the respondent, and indeed the only way to protect the respondent from herself, is to control her addiction. The only way her addiction can be controlled is if she herself is motivated to overcome it and is ultimately successful in doing so. ...

It is true that the heroin addict must invariably support his or her addiction with some form of criminal activity. Many studies were referred to by counsel which show a dramatic correlation between drug addiction and high levels of offending. Thus the annual cost to society, in terms of the crimes against property, robberies, prostitution and other such offences, required to keep the estimated 3,200 to 4,200 addicts in this province supplied with heroin, is staggering. In that sense the argument that the opportunity to interrupt the cycle, by a sentence of incarceration during which the addict will not be able to commit crimes against society, has a certain superficial attraction.

However, the protection which society derives from a sentence of imprisonment, imposed upon a heroin addict for the purpose just described, is transitory at best. There is no credible basis for expecting that a term of imprisonment will rehabilitate the addict. Drugs of all sorts are readily available in our prisons and penitentiaries. Only the price varies, in kind and amount, from that which is exacted on the street. When the sentence is served, the addict who re-emerges from custody poses the same threat to society as before, and the whole cycle is ready to be repeated.

The role of incarceration in this cycle not only fails to achieve its ultimate goal which is the protection of society, but it also costs society a great deal of money, which might better be spent elsewhere. Statistics Canada reports that during the 1988/1989 fiscal year the cost of maintaining a prisoner in a custodial facility averaged $46,282 in a federal penitentiary and $36,708 in a provincial jail. ...

What then is the proper approach for the court to take when sentencing in a case such as this? When the benefit to be derived to society as a whole, as a result of the successful rehabilitation of a heroin addict, is balanced against the ultimate futility of the short-term protection which the community enjoys from a sentence of incarceration, I believe it is right to conclude that the principle of deterrence should yield to any reasonable chance of rehabilitation which may show itself to the court imposing sentence. To give the offender a chance to successfully overcome his or her addiction, in such circumstances, is to risk little more than the possibility of failure, with the result that the cycle of addiction leading to crime leading to incarceration will resume, something that is inevitable, in any event, if the chance is not taken. On the other hand, as has already been pointed out, if the effort succeeds the result is fundamentally worthwhile to society as a whole.

I am not persuaded that the trial judge erred in principle in this case when he considered the rehabilitation of the respondent to be of greater importance than any deterrent value that a sentence of incarceration might have. Indeed, I am of the view that he was right in the approach that he took. ...

It is also worth noting that the report of the Canadian Sentencing Commission (the "Archambault" Commission), *Sentencing Reform: A Canadian Approach* (1987), recommends that possession of a narcotic carry a maximum sentence of six months, together with an unqualified presumption that such sentence be served in the community, rather than in a custodial facility. While the recommendations of the commission do not have the force of law, and cannot therefore be said, in that sense, to represent the will of either Parliament or the people, they are nonetheless the end product of a process which included over two years of extensive public hearings held all across the country. In making its recommendations the commission recognized and took into account the fact that one of the goals of sentencing is to preserve the authority of, and to promote respect for, the law through the public's perception that the commission of offences will be met by the imposition of just sanctions.

... As things presently stand, and have stood for almost 30 years, there is no statutory minimum penalty which must be imposed on a person convicted of the offence of possession of a prohibited substance, irrespective of whether the proceedings are launched by way of indictment or by summary conviction. Furthermore, nothing was put before us by the Crown to suggest an overwhelming perception on the part of the public that persons who are convicted of such an offence must be sent to jail if the authority and respect for the law is to be maintained.

The notion that rehabilitation is a legitimate goal of the sentencing process is neither new nor experimental. Every Royal Commission, official report and extensive study done on sentencing in this country, and there have been at least 17 such efforts since 1831, has stressed the obvious, namely, that the ultimate protection of the public lies in the successful rehabilitation of those who transgress society's laws. Those same authorities have also unanimously concluded that rehabilitation is unlikely to occur while the offender is incarcerated. ...

Before concluding these reasons it is important to note two fundamental assumptions upon which I have proceeded. The first is that probation orders are backed by a probation service which has the staff and the resources to provide active supervision, guidance and encouragement to the offenders' efforts to rehabilitate. No one for a moment doubts the sincerity or the professionalism of our probation officers. But if the reality is a service which is overloaded with customers, understaffed with experienced personnel and impoverished in "treatment" options, then few enlightened efforts such as that undertaken by the trial judge in this case can succeed. If society is not prepared to commit the resources necessary to make rehabilitation an attainable goal of the criminal justice system, the courts will have little option but to conclude that the protection of society can only be achieved by warehousing offenders in prisons.

The second assumption which I have made is that when a probation order is breached the offender is brought back before the court, so that the breach can be considered in the light of all the prevailing circumstances, and an appropriate decision can be made whether to continue the rehabilitative effort or to impose the sentence which was suspended. If that is not done, the whole premise upon which the trial judge proceeded is robbed of its validity, and probation, as a vehicle of rehabilitation, loses its credibility.

### Conditional Sentence of Imprisonment

One of the most important, and controversial aspects of Bill C-41 was the creation of a new sanction—the conditional sentence of imprisonment. If a judge determines that an accused should be sentenced to a sentence of less than two years' imprisonment, he or she may, if other conditions are also met, order that the sentence be served in the community, instead of in a traditional custodial setting: see *Criminal Code*, ss. 742.1 to 742.7. The parameters of this new sanction and the proper approach to its use is discussed in the following decision in *R. v. Proulx*.

## R. v. Proulx
Supreme Court of Canada
(2000), 140 C.C.C. (3d) 449

[The 18-year-old accused, after driving for only 7 weeks, was convicted of danger-ous driving causing death and dangerous driving causing bodily harm. He had been drinking. The trial judge determined that a sentence of 18 months was appropriate, and despite the fact that the accused would not endanger the community, a condi-tional sentence of imprisonment would not be consistent with the other principles of sentencing in the *Criminal Code*. Accordingly, an 18-month sentence was imposed. The Court of Appeal allowed the appeal and substituted an 18-month conditional sentence. The Supreme Court of Canada restored the sentence of incarceration, but provided important guidance on the application of this sanction.]

LAMER C.J.C.:

[1]  By passing the *Act to amend the Criminal Code (sentencing) and other Acts in consequence thereof*, S.C. 1995, c. 22 ("Bill C-41"), Parliament has sent a clear mes-sage to all Canadian judges that too many people are being sent to prison. In an at-tempt to remedy the problem of overincarceration, Parliament has introduced a new form of sentence, the conditional sentence of imprisonment. ...

[12]  Since it came into force on September 3, 1996, the conditional sentence has generated considerable debate. With the advent of s. 742.1, Parliament has clearly mandated that certain offenders who used to go to prison should now serve their sentences in the community. Section 742.1 makes a conditional sentence available to a subclass of non-dangerous offenders who, prior to the introduction of this new re-gime, would have been sentenced to a term of incarceration of less than two years for offences with no minimum term of imprisonment.

[13]  In my view, to address meaningfully the complex interpretive issues raised by this appeal, it is important to situate this new sentencing tool in the broader con-text of the comprehensive sentencing reforms enacted by Parliament in Bill C-41. I will also consider the nature of the conditional sentence, contrasting it with proba-tionary measures and incarceration. Next, I will address particular interpretive issues posed by s. 742.1. I will first discuss the statutory prerequisites to the imposition of a conditional sentence. Thereafter, I will consider how courts should determine whether a conditional sentence is appropriate, assuming the prerequisites are satisfied. I con-clude with some general comments on the deference to which trial judges are entitled in matters of sentencing and dispose of the case at hand in conformity with the princi-ples outlined in these reasons.

### V. Analysis

#### A. The 1996 Sentencing Reforms (Bill C-41)

[14]  In September 1996, Bill C-41 came into effect. It substantially reformed Part XXIII of the *Code*, and introduced, *inter alia*, an express statement of the purposes

and principles of sentencing, provisions for alternative measures for adult offenders and a new type of sanction, the conditional sentence of imprisonment.

[15] As my colleagues Cory and Iacobucci JJ. explained in *R. v. Gladue*, [1999] 1 S.C.R. 688, at para. 39, "[t]he enactment of the new Part XXIII was a watershed, marking the first codification and significant reform of sentencing principles in the history of Canadian criminal law." They noted two of Parliament's principal objectives in enacting this new legislation: (i) reducing the use of prison as a sanction, and (ii) expanding the use of restorative justice principles in sentencing (at para. 48).

(1)  Reducing the Use of Prison as a Sanction

[16] Bill C-41 is in large part a response to the problem of overincarceration in Canada. It was noted in *Gladue*, at para. 52, that Canada's incarceration rate of approximately 130 inmates per 100,000 population places it second or third highest among industrialized democracies. In their reasons, Cory and Iacobucci JJ. reviewed numerous studies that uniformly concluded that incarceration is costly, frequently unduly harsh and "ineffective, not only in relation to its purported rehabilitative goals, but also in relation to its broader public goals" (para. 54). See also Report of the Canadian Committee on Corrections, *Toward Unity: Criminal Justice and Corrections* (1969); Canadian Sentencing Commission, *Sentencing Reform: A Canadian Approach* (1987), at pp. xxiii-xxiv; Standing Committee on Justice and Solicitor General, *Taking Responsibility* (1988), at p. 75. Prison has been characterized by some as a finishing school for criminals and as ill-preparing them for reintegration into society: see generally Canadian Committee on Corrections, supra, at p. 314; Correctional Service of Canada, *A Summary of Analysis of Some Major Inquiries on Corrections— 1938 to 1977* (1982), at p. iv. ...

[17] Parliament has sought to give increased prominence to the principle of restraint in the use of prison as a sanction through the enactment of s. 718.2(d) and (e). Section 718.2(d) provides that "an offender should not be deprived of liberty, if less restrictive sanctions may be appropriate in the circumstances," while s. 718.2(e) provides that "all available sanctions other than imprisonment that are reasonable in the circumstances should be considered for all offenders, with particular attention to the circumstances of aboriginal offenders." Further evidence of Parliament's desire to lower the rate of incarceration comes from other provisions of Bill C-41: s. 718(c) qualifies the sentencing objective of separating offenders from society with the words "where necessary," thereby indicating that caution be exercised in sentencing offenders to prison; s. 734(2) imposes a duty on judges to undertake a means inquiry before imposing a fine, so as to decrease the number of offenders who are incarcerated for defaulting on payment of their fines; and of course, s. 742.1, which introduces the conditional sentence. In *Gladue*, at para. 40, the Court held that "[t]he creation of the conditional sentence suggests, on its face, a desire to lessen the use of incarceration."

(2)  Expanding the Use of Restorative Justice Principles in Sentencing

[18] Restorative justice is concerned with the restoration of the parties that are affected by the commission of an offence. Crime generally affects at least three par-

ties: the victim, the community, and the offender. A restorative justice approach seeks to remedy the adverse effects of crime in a manner that addresses the needs of all parties involved. This is accomplished, in part, through the rehabilitation of the offender, reparations to the victim and to the community, and the promotion of a sense of responsibility in the offender and acknowledgment of the harm done to victims and to the community.

[19] Canadian sentencing jurisprudence has traditionally focussed on the aims of denunciation, deterrence, separation, and rehabilitation, with rehabilitation a relative late-comer to the sentencing analysis: see *Gladue*, at para. 42. With the introduction of Bill C-41, however, Parliament has placed new emphasis upon the goals of restorative justice. Section 718 sets out the fundamental purpose of sentencing, as well as the various sentencing objectives that should be vindicated when sanctions are imposed … .

[20] Parliament has mandated that expanded use be made of restorative principles in sentencing as a result of the general failure of incarceration to rehabilitate offenders and reintegrate them into society. By placing a new emphasis on restorative principles, Parliament expects both to reduce the rate of incarceration and improve the effectiveness of sentencing. During the second reading of Bill C-41 on September 20, 1994 (*House of Commons Debates*, vol. IV, 1st Sess., 35th Parl., at p. 5873), Minister of Justice Allan Rock made the following statements:

> A general principle that runs throughout Bill C-41 is that jails should be reserved for those who should be there. Alternatives should be put in place for those who commits offences but who do not need or merit incarceration. …
>
> Jails and prisons will be there for those who need them, for those who should be punished in that way or separated from society … . [T]his bill creates an environment which encourages community sanctions and the rehabilitation of offenders together with reparation to victims and promoting in criminals a sense of accountability for what they have done.
>
> It is not simply by being more harsh that we will achieve more effective criminal justice. We must use our scarce resources wisely.

## B. The Nature of the Conditional Sentence

[21] The conditional sentence was specifically enacted as a new sanction designed to achieve both of Parliament's objectives. The conditional sentence is a meaningful alternative to incarceration for less serious and non-dangerous offenders. The offenders who meet the criteria of s. 742.1 will serve a sentence under strict surveillance in the community instead of going to prison. These offenders' liberty will be constrained by conditions to be attached to the sentence, as set out in s. 742.3 of the *Code*. In case of breach of conditions, the offender will be brought back before a judge, pursuant to s. 742.6. If an offender cannot provide a reasonable excuse for breaching the conditions of his or her sentence, the judge may order him or her to serve the remainder of the sentence in jail, as it was intended by Parliament that there be a real threat of incarceration to increase compliance with the conditions of the sentence.

[22]  The conditional sentence incorporates some elements of non-custodial measures and some others of incarceration. Because it is served in the community, it will
generally be more effective than incarceration at achieving the restorative objectives
of rehabilitation, reparations to the victim and community, and the promotion of a
sense of responsibility in the offender. However, *it is also a punitive sanction capable of achieving the objectives of denunciation and deterrence*. It is this punitive aspect that distinguishes the conditional sentence from probation, and it is to this issue
that I now turn.

(1)  Comparing Conditional Sentences with Probation

[23]  There has been some confusion among members of the judiciary and the
public alike about the difference between a conditional sentence and a suspended
sentence with probation. This confusion is understandable, as the statutory provisions regarding conditions to be attached to conditional sentences (s. 742.3) and
probation orders (s. 732.1) are very similar. Notwithstanding these similarities, there
is an important distinction between the two. While a suspended sentence with probation is primarily a rehabilitative sentencing tool, the evidence suggests that Parliament intended a conditional sentence to address both punitive and rehabilitative
objectives. ...

(b)  Conditional Sentences Must Be More Punitive than Probation

[28]  Despite the similarities between the provisions and the fact that the penalty
for breach of probation is potentially more severe than for breach of a conditional
sentence, there are strong indications that Parliament intended the conditional sentence to be more punitive than probation. It is well accepted principle of statutory
interpretation that no legislative provision should be interpreted so as to render it
mere surplusage. It would be absurd if Parliament intended conditional sentences to
amount merely to probation under a different name. While this argument is clearly
not dispositive, it suggests that Parliament intended there to be a meaningful distinction between the two sanctions. I will now consider more specific arguments in support of this position.

[29]  The conditional sentence is defined in the *Code* as a sentence of imprisonment. The heading of s. 742 reads "Conditional Sentence of Imprisonment." Furthermore, s. 742.1(a) requires the court to impose a sentence of imprisonment of less than
two years before considering whether the sentence can be served in the community
subject to the appropriate conditions. Parliament intended imprisonment, in the form
of incarceration, to be more punitive than probation, as it is far more restrictive of the
offender's liberty. Since a conditional sentence is, at least notionally, a sentence of
imprisonment, it follows that it too should be interpreted as more punitive than
probation.

[30]  On a related note, with the enactment of s. 742.1, Parliament has mandated
that certain non-dangerous offenders who would otherwise have gone to jail for up to
two years now serve their sentences in the community. If a conditional sentence is
not distinguished from probation, then these offenders will receive what are effec-

tively considerably less onerous probation orders instead of jail terms. Such lenient sentences would not provide sufficient denunciation and deterrence, nor would they be accepted by the public. Section 718 provides that the fundamental purpose of sentencing is "to contribute ... to respect for the law and the maintenance of a just, peaceful and safe society." Inadequate sanctions undermine respect for the law. Accordingly, it is important to distinguish a conditional sentence from probation by way of the use of punitive conditions.

[31] Earlier I drew attention to a subtle difference between the residual clauses in the provisions governing the imposition of optional conditions of probation orders and conditional sentences. While the difference between the two residual clauses is subtle, it is also significant. In order to appreciate this difference, it is necessary to consider the case law and practice that has developed with respect to probation.

[32] Probation has traditionally been viewed as a rehabilitative sentencing tool. Recently, the rehabilitative nature of the probation order was explained by the Saskatchewan Court of Appeal in *R. v. Taylor* (1997), 122 C.C.C. (3d) 376. Bayda C.J.S. wrote, at p. 394:

> Apart from the wording of the provision, the innate character of a probation order is such that it seeks to influence the future behaviour of the offender. More specifically, it seeks to secure "the good conduct" of the offender and to deter him from committing other offences. *It does not particularly seek to reflect the seriousness of the offence or the offender's degree of culpability. Nor does it particularly seek to fill the need for denunciation of the offence or the general deterrence of others to commit the same or other offences. Depending upon the specific conditions of the order there may well be a punitive aspect to a probation order but punishment is not the dominant or an inherent purpose. It is perhaps not even a secondary purpose but is more in the nature of a consequence of an offender's compliance with one or more of the specific conditions with which he or she may find it hard to comply.* [Emphasis added.]

[33] Many appellate courts have struck out conditions of probation that were imposed to punish rather than rehabilitate the offender: see *R. v. Ziatas* (1973), 13 C.C.C. (2d) 287 (Ont. C.A.), at p. 288; *R. v. Caja* (1977), 36 C.C.C. (2d) 401 (Ont. C.A.), at pp. 402-3; *R. v. Lavender* (1981), 59 C.C.C. (2d) 551 (B.C.C.A.), at pp. 552-53, and *R. v. L.* (1986), 50 C.R. (3d) 398 (Alta. C.A.), at pp. 399-400. The impugned terms of probation in these cases were imposed pursuant to a residual clause in force at the time whose wording was virtually identical to that presently used in s. 742.3(2)(f).

[34] Despite the virtual identity in the wording of s. 742.3(2)(f) and the old residual clause applicable to probation orders, it would be a mistake to conclude that punitive conditions cannot now be imposed under s. 742.3(2)(f). Parliament amended the residual clause for probation, s. 732.1(3)(h), to read "for protecting society and for *facilitating the offender's successful reintegration into the community*" (emphasis added). It did so to make clear the rehabilitative purpose of probation and to distinguish s. 742.3(2)(f) from s. 732.1(3)(h). The wording used in s. 742.3(2)(f) does not focus principally on the rehabilitation and reintegration of the offender. If s. 742.3(2)(f) were interpreted as precluding punitive conditions, it would frustrate

Parliament's intention in distinguishing the two forms of sentence. Parliament would not have distinguished them if it intended both clauses to serve the same purpose.

[35] In light of the foregoing, it is clear that Parliament intended a conditional sentence to be more punitive than a suspended sentence with probation, notwithstanding the similarities between the two sanctions in respect of their rehabilitative purposes. I agree wholeheartedly with Vancise J.A., who, dissenting in *R. v. McDonald* (1997), 113 C.C.C. (3d) 418 (Sask. C.A.), stated, at p. 443, that conditional sentences were designed to "permit the accused to avoid imprisonment but not to avoid punishment."

[36] Accordingly, conditional sentences should generally include punitive conditions that are restrictive of the offender's liberty. Conditions such as house arrest or strict curfews should be the norm, not the exception. As the Minister of Justice said during the second reading of Bill C-41 (*House of Commons Debates*, *supra*, at p. 5873), "[t]his sanction is obviously aimed at offenders who would otherwise be in jail but who could be in the community under *tight* controls" (emphasis added).

[37] There must be a reason for failing to impose punitive conditions when a conditional sentence order is made. Sentencing judges should always be mindful of the fact that conditional sentences are only to be imposed on offenders who would otherwise have been sent to jail. If the judge is of the opinion that punitive conditions are unnecessary, then probation, rather than a conditional sentence, is most likely the appropriate disposition.

[38] The punitive nature of the conditional sentence should also inform the treatment of breaches of conditions. As I have already discussed, the maximum penalty for breach of probation is potentially more severe than that for breach of a conditional sentence. In practice, however, breaches of conditional sentences may be punished more severely than breaches of probation. Without commenting on the constitutionality of these provisions, I note that breaches of conditional sentence need only be proved on a balance of probabilities, pursuant to s. 742.6(9), whereas breaches of probation must be proved beyond a reasonable doubt.

[39] More importantly, where an offender breaches a condition without reasonable excuse, there should be a presumption that the offender serve the remainder of his or her sentence in jail. This constant threat of incarceration will help to ensure that the offender complies with the conditions imposed: see *R. v. Brady* (1998), 121 C.C.C. (3d) 504 (Alta. C.A.); J.V. Roberts, "Conditional Sentencing: Sword of Damocles or Pandora's Box?" (1997), 2 *Can. Crim. L. Rev.* 183. It also assists in distinguishing the conditional sentence from probation by making the consequences of a breach of condition more severe.

(2) Conditional Sentences and Incarceration

[40] Although a conditional sentence is by statutory definition a sentence of imprisonment, this Court, in *R. v. Shropshire*, [1995] 4 S.C.R. 227, at para. 21, recognized that there "is a very significant difference between being behind bars and functioning within society while on conditional release." See also *Cunningham v. Canada*, [1993] 2 S.C.R. 143, at p. 150, *per* McLachlin J. These comments are equally appli-

cable to the conditional sentence. Indeed, offenders serving a conditional sentence in the community are only partially deprived of their freedom. Even if their liberty is restricted by the conditions attached to their sentence, they are not confined to an institution and they can continue to attend to their normal employment or educational endeavours. They are not deprived of their private life to the same extent. Nor are they subject to a regimented schedule or an institutional diet.

[41]  This is not to say that the conditional sentence is a lenient punishment or that it does not provide significant denunciation and deterrence, or that a conditional sentence can never be as harsh as incarceration. As this Court stated in *Gladue*, *supra*, at para. 72:

> ... in our view a sentence focussed on restorative justice is not necessarily a "lighter" punishment. Some proponents of restorative justice argue that when it is combined with probationary conditions it may in some circumstances impose a greater burden on the offender than a custodial sentence.

A conditional sentence may be as onerous as, or perhaps even more onerous than, a jail term, particularly in circumstances where the offender is forced to take responsibility for his or her actions and make reparations to both the victim and the community, all the while living in the community under tight controls.

[42]  Moreover, the conditional sentence is not subject to reduction through parole. This would seem to follow from s. 112(1) of the *Corrections and Conditional Release Act*, S.C. 1992, c. 20, which gives the provincial parole board jurisdiction in respect of the parole of offenders "serving sentences of imprisonment in provincial correctional facilities" (*R. v. Wismayer* (1997), 115 C.C.C. (3d) 18 (Ont. C.A.), at p. 33).

[43]  I would add that the fact that a conditional sentence cannot be reduced through parole does not in itself lead to the conclusion that as a general matter a conditional sentence is as onerous as or even more onerous than a jail term of equivalent duration. There is no parole simply because the offender is never actually incarcerated and he or she does not need to be reintegrated into society. But even when an offender is released from custody on parole, the original sentence continues in force. As I stated in *M. (C.A.)*, *supra*, at para. 62:

> In short, the history, structure and existing practice of the conditional release system collectively indicate that a grant of parole represents a *change in the conditions* under which a judicial sentence must be served, rather than *a reduction* of the judicial sentence itself ... . But even though the conditions of incarceration are subject to change through a grant of parole to the offender's benefit, the offender's sentence continues in full effect. The offender remains under the strict control of the parole system, and the offender's liberty remains significantly curtailed for the full duration of the offender's numerical or life sentence. [Emphasis in original.]

The parolee has to serve the final portion of his or her sentence under conditions similar to those that can be imposed under a conditional sentence, perhaps even under stricter conditions, as the parolee can be assigned to a "community-based residential facility": see s. 133 of the *Corrections and Conditional Release Act* and s. 161 of the *Corrections and Conditional Release Regulations*, SOR/192-620.

[44] In light of these observations, a conditional sentence, even with stringent conditions, will usually be a more lenient sentence than a jail term of equivalent duration: see also *Gagnon v. La Reine*, [1998] R.J.Q. 2636 (C.A.), at p. 2645; *Brady, supra*, at paras. 36 and 48 to 50. The fact that incarceration is a threatened punishment for those who breach their conditions provides further support for this conclusion. In order for incarceration to serve as a punishment for breach of a conditional sentence, logically it must be more onerous than a conditional sentence.

*C. Application of Section 742.1 of the Criminal Code*

...

(1)  The Offender Must Be Convicted of an Offence That Is Not Punishable by a Minimum Term of Imprisonment

[48]  This prerequisite is straightforward. The offence for which the offender was convicted must not be punishable by a minimum term of imprisonment. Offences with a minimum term of imprisonment are the only statutory exclusions from the conditional sentencing regime.

(2)  The Court Must Impose a Term of Imprisonment of Less than Two Years

[49]  Parliament intended that a conditional sentence be considered only for those offenders who would have otherwise received a sentence of imprisonment of less than two years. There is some controversy as to whether this means that the judge must actually impose a term of imprisonment of a *fixed* duration before considering the possibility of a conditional sentence. Far from addressing purely methodological concerns, this question carries implications as to the role of ss. 718 to 718.2 in the determination of the appropriate sentence, the duration of the sentence, its venue and other modalities.

[50]  A literal reading of s. 742.1(a) suggests that the decision to impose a conditional sentence should be made in two distinct stages. In the first stage, the judge would have to decide the appropriate sentence according to the general purposes and principles of sentencing (now set out in ss. 718 to 718.2). Having found that a term of imprisonment of less than two years is warranted, the judge would then, in a second stage, decide whether this same term should be served in the community pursuant to s. 742.1. At first sight, since Parliament said: "and the court (a) imposes a sentence of imprisonment of less than two years," it seems that the sentencing judge must first impose a term of imprisonment of a *fixed* duration before contemplating the possibility that this term be served in the community.

[51]  This two-step approach was endorsed by the Manitoba Court of Appeal in the present appeal. However, this literal reading of s. 742.1 and the two-step approach it implies introduce a rigidity which is both unworkable and undesirable in practice. ...

(3)  The Safety of the Community Would Not Be Endangered by the Offender Serving the Sentence in the Community

[62]  This criterion, set out in s. 742.1(b), has generated wide discussion in courts and among authors. I intend to discuss the following issues:

(a)  Is safety of the community a prerequisite to any conditional sentence?

(b)  Does "safety of the community" refer only to the threat posed by the specific offender?

(c)  How should courts evaluate danger to the community?

(d)  Is risk of economic prejudice to be considered in assessing danger to the community?

(a)  A Prerequisite to Any Conditional Sentence

[63]  As a prerequisite to any conditional sentence, the sentencing judge must be satisfied that having the offender serve the sentence in the community would not endanger its safety: see *Brady, supra*, at para. 58; *R. v. Maheu*, [1997] R.J.Q. 410, 116 C.C.C. (3d) 361 (C.A.), at p. 368 C.C.C.; *Gagnon, supra*, at p. 2641; *Pierce, supra*, at p. 39; *Ursel, supra*, at pp. 284-86 (*per* Ryan J.A.). *If the sentencing judge is not satisfied that the safety of the community can be preserved, a conditional sentence must never be imposed.*

[64]  With respect, the Manitoba Court of Appeal in the case before us erred in concluding that safety of the community was the primary consideration in the decision to impose a conditional sentence. As the Alberta Court of Appeal in *Brady, supra*, at para. 58, stated:

> So to suggest that danger is the primary consideration is tendentious. It wrongly implies that absence of danger trumps or has paramountcy over other sentencing principles. Either the offender meets the no-danger threshold, or he does not. If he does, this consideration is spent and the focus must then properly be on the other sentencing principles and objectives.

[65]  I agree. It is only once the judge is satisfied that the safety of the community would not be endangered, in the sense explained in paras. 66 to 76 below, that he or she can examine whether a conditional sentence "would be consistent with the fundamental purpose and principles of sentencing set out in sections 718 to 718.2." In other words, rather than being an overarching consideration in the process of determining whether a conditional sentence is appropriate, the criterion of safety of the community should be viewed as a condition precedent to the assessment of whether a conditional sentence would be a fit and proper sanction in the circumstances.

(b)  "Safety of the Community" Refers to the Threat Posed by the Specific Offender

[66]  The issue here is whether "safety of the community" refers only to the threat posed by the specific offender or whether it also extends to the broader risk of undermining respect for the law. The proponents of the broader interpretation argue that, in

certain cases where a conditional sentence could be imposed, it would be perceived that wrongdoers are receiving lenient sentences, thereby insufficiently deterring those who may be inclined to engage in similar acts of wrongdoing, and, in turn, endangering the safety of the community.

[67] Leaving aside the fact that a properly crafted conditional sentence can also achieve the objectives of general deterrence and denunciation, I think the debate has been rendered largely academic in light of an amendment to s. 742.1(b) (S.C. 1997, c. 18, s. 107.1) which clarified that courts must take into consideration the fundamental purpose and principles of sentencing set out in ss. 718 to 718.2 in deciding whether to impose a conditional sentence. This ensures that objectives such as denunciation and deterrence will be dealt with in the decision to impose a conditional sentence. Since these factors will be taken into account later in the analysis, there is no need to include them in the consideration of the safety of the community.

[68] In my view, the focus of the analysis at this point should clearly be on the risk posed by the individual offender while serving his sentence in the community. I would note that a majority of appellate courts have adopted an interpretation of the criterion referring only to the threat posed by the specific offender: see *Gagnon*, *supra*, at pp. 2640-41 (*per* Fish J.A.); *R. v. Parker* (1997), 116 C.C.C. (3d) 236 (N.S.C.A.), at pp. 247-48; *Ursel*, *supra*, at p. 260; *R. v. Horvath*, [1997] 8 W.W.R. 357 (Sask. C.A.), at p. 374; *Brady*, *supra*, at paras. 60-61; *Wismayer*, *supra*, at p. 44.

(c)  How Should Courts Evaluate Danger to the Community?

[69] In my opinion, to assess the danger to the community posed by the offender while serving his or her sentence in the community, two factors must be taken into account: (1) the risk of the offender re-offending; and (2) the gravity of the damage that could ensue in the event of re-offence. If the judge finds that there is a real risk of re-offence, incarceration should be imposed. Of course, there is always some risk that an offender may re-offend. If the judge thinks this risk is minimal, the gravity of the damage that could follow were the offender to re-offend should also be taken into consideration. In certain cases, the minimal risk of re-offending will be offset by the possibility of a great prejudice, thereby precluding a conditional sentence. ...

(4)  Consistent with the Fundamental Purpose and Principles of Sentencing Set Out in Sections 718 to 718.2

[77] Once the sentencing judge has found the offender guilty of an offence for which there is no minimum term of imprisonment, has rejected both a probationary sentence and a penitentiary term as inappropriate, and is satisfied that the offender would not endanger the community, the judge must then consider whether a conditional sentence would be consistent with the fundamental purpose and principles of sentencing set out in ss. 718 to 718.2.

[78] A consideration of the principles set out in ss. 718 to 718.2 will determine whether the offender should serve his or her sentence in the community or in jail. The sentencing principles also inform the determination of the duration of these sentences and, if a conditional sentence, the nature of the conditions to be imposed.

(a) Offences Presumptively Excluded from the Conditional Sentencing
Regime?

[79]  Section 742.1 does not exclude any offences from the conditional sentencing
regime except those with a minimum term of imprisonment. Parliament could have
easily excluded specific offences in addition to those with a mandatory minimum
term of imprisonment but chose not to. As Rosenberg J.A. held in *Wismayer*, *supra*,
at p. 31:

> Parliament clearly envisaged that a conditional sentence would be available even in
> cases of crimes of violence that are not punishable by a minimum term of imprison-
> ment. Thus, s. 742.2 requires the court, before imposing a conditional sentence, to con-
> sider whether a firearms prohibition under s. 100 of the *Criminal Code* is applicable.
> Such orders may only be imposed for indictable offences having a maximum sentence
> of ten years or more "in the commission of which violence against a person is used,
> threatened, or attempted" (s. 100(1)) and for certain weapons and drug offences
> (s. 100(2)).

Thus, a conditional sentence is available in principle for *all* offences in which the
statutory prerequisites are satisfied.

[80]  Several parties in the appeals before us argued that the fundamental purpose
and principles of sentencing support a presumption against conditional sentences for
certain offences. The Attorney General of Canada and the Attorney General for Ontario submitted that a conditional sentence would rarely be appropriate for offences
such as: sexual offences against children; aggravated sexual assault; manslaughter;
serious fraud or theft; serious morality offences; impaired or dangerous driving causing death or bodily harm; and trafficking or possession of certain narcotics. They
submitted that this followed from the principle of proportionality as well as from a
consideration of the objectives of denunciation and deterrence. A number of appellate court decisions support this position.

[81]  In my view, while the gravity of such offences is clearly relevant to determining whether a conditional sentence is appropriate in the circumstances, it would
be both unwise and unnecessary to establish judicially created presumptions that conditional sentences are inappropriate for specific offences. Offence-specific presumptions introduce unwarranted rigidity in the determination of whether a conditional
sentence is a just and appropriate sanction. Such presumptions do not accord with the
principle of proportionality set out in s. 718.1 and the value of individualization in
sentencing, nor are they necessary to achieve the important objectives of uniformity
and consistency in the use of conditional sentences.

[82]  This Court has held on a number of occasions that sentencing is an individualized process, in which the trial judge has considerable discretion in fashioning a fit
sentence. The rationale behind this approach stems from the principle of proportionality, the fundamental principle of sentencing, which provides that a sentence must
be proportional to the gravity of the offence and the degree of responsibility of the
offender. Proportionality requires an examination of the specific circumstances of
both the offender and the offence so that the "punishment fits the crime." As a by-

product of such an individualized approach, there will be inevitable variation in sentences imposed for particular crimes. In *M. (C.A.)*, *supra*, I stated, at para. 92:

> It has been repeatedly stressed that there is no such thing as a uniform sentence for a particular crime … . Sentencing is an inherently individualized process, and the search for a single appropriate sentence for a similar offender and a similar crime will frequently be a fruitless exercise of academic abstraction. As well, sentences for a particular offence should be expected to vary to some degree across various communities and regions in this country, as the "just and appropriate" mix of accepted sentencing goals will depend on the needs and current conditions of and in the particular community where the crime occurred.

[83]  My difficulty with the suggestion that the proportionality principle presumptively excludes certain offences from the conditional sentencing regime is that such an approach focuses inordinately on the gravity of the offence and insufficiently on the moral blameworthiness of the offender. This fundamentally misconstrues the nature of the principle. Proportionality requires that *full consideration* be given to both factors. As s. 718.1 provides:

> A sentence must be proportionate to the gravity of the offence *and* the degree of responsibility of the offender. [Emphasis added.]

[84]  Some appellate courts have held that once the statutory prerequisites are satisfied there ought to be a presumption in favour of a conditional sentence. In the instant appeal, Helper J.A. found at p. 112 that:

> Generally (though certainly not in all cases), it will be that, when a sentencing judge has attributed the appropriate weight to each of the relevant principles in determining that a fit sentence would be less than two years and has found that the offender would not be a danger to the community, a decision to allow the offender to serve his sentence in the community will be consistent with ss. 718 to 718.2.

[85]  It is possible to interpret these comments as implying that once the judge has found that the prerequisites to a conditional sentence are met, a conditional sentence would presumably be consistent with the fundamental purpose and principles of sentencing. Assuming that Helper J.A. intended to suggest that there ought to be a presumption in favour of a conditional sentence once the prerequisites are met, I respectfully disagree with her. For the same reasons that I rejected the use of presumptions against conditional sentences, I also reject presumptions in favour of them. The particular circumstances of the offender and the offence must be considered in each case. …

(c)  Principles Militating For and Against a Conditional Sentence

[90]  First, a consideration of ss. 718.2(d) and 718.2(e) leads me to the conclusion that *serious consideration* should be given to the imposition of a conditional sentence in all cases where the first three statutory prerequisites are satisfied. Sections 718.2(d) and 718.2(e) codify the important principle of restraint in sentencing and were specifically enacted, along with s. 742.1, to help reduce the rate of incarceration

in Canada. Accordingly, it would be an error in principle not to consider the possibility of a conditional sentence seriously when the statutory prerequisites are met. Failure to advert to the possibility of a conditional sentence in reasons for sentence where there are reasonable grounds for finding that the first three statutory prerequisites have been met may well constitute reversible error.

[91]  I pause here to consider an interpretive difficulty posed by s. 718.2(e). By its terms, s. 718.2(e) requires judges to consider "all available sanctions *other than imprisonment* that are reasonable in the circumstances" (emphasis added). A conditional sentence, however, is defined as a sentence of imprisonment. As a sentence of imprisonment, it cannot be an alternative to imprisonment. It would therefore appear as though s. 718.2(e) has no bearing on the sentencing judge's decision as to whether a conditional sentence or a jail term should be imposed. Indeed, if interpreted in the technical sense ascribed to imprisonment in Part XXIII of the *Code*, s. 718.2(e) would only be relevant to the judge's preliminary determination as to whether a sentence of imprisonment, as opposed to a probationary measure, should be imposed. Once the sentencing judge rejects a probationary sentence as inappropriate, the legislative force of s. 718.2(e) is arguably spent.

[92]  This interpretation seems to fly in the face of Parliament's intention in enacting s. 718.2(e)—reducing the rate of incarceration. As this Court held in *Gladue*, *supra*, at para. 40:

> The availability of the conditional sentence of imprisonment, in particular, alters the sentencing landscape in a manner which gives an entirely new meaning to the principle that imprisonment should be resorted to only where no other sentencing option is reasonable in the circumstances. *The creation of the conditional sentence suggests, on its face, a desire to lessen the use of incarceration. The general principle expressed in s. 718.2(e) must be construed and applied in this light.* [Emphasis added.]

Moreover, if this interpretation of s. 718.2(e) were adopted, it could lead to absurd results in relation to aboriginal offenders. The particular circumstances of aboriginal offenders would only be relevant in deciding whether to impose probationary sentences, and not in deciding whether a conditional sentence should be preferred to incarceration. This would greatly diminish the remedial purpose animating Parliament's enactment of this provision, which contemplates the greater use of conditional sentences and other alternatives to incarceration in cases of aboriginal offenders. ...

[96]  Both ss. 718.2(d) and 718.2(e) seek to vindicate the important objective of restraint in the use of incarceration. However, neither seeks to do so at all costs. Section 718.2(d) provides that "an offender should not be deprived of liberty, if less restrictive sanctions *may be appropriate in the circumstances*" (emphasis added). Section 718.2(e) provides that "all available sanctions other than imprisonment *that are reasonable in the circumstances* should be considered" (emphasis added). In my view, a determination of when less restrictive sanctions are "appropriate" and alternatives to incarceration "reasonable" in the circumstances requires a consideration of the other principles of sentencing set out in ss. 718 to 718.2.

[97]  In determining which principles favour of a conditional sentence and which favour incarceration, it is necessary to consider again the nature and purpose of the conditional sentence. Through an appreciation of Parliament's intention in enacting this new sanction and the mischief it seeks to redress, trial judges will be better able to make appropriate use of this innovative tool.

[98]  The conditional sentence, as I have already noted, was introduced in the amendments to Part XXIII of the *Code*. Two of the main objectives underlying the reform of Part XXIII were to reduce the use of incarceration as a sanction and to give greater prominence to the principles of restorative justice in sentencing—the objectives of rehabilitation, reparation to the victim and the community, and the promotion of a sense of responsibility in the offender.

[99]  The conditional sentence facilitates the achievement of both of Parliament's objectives. It affords the sentencing judge the opportunity to craft a sentence with appropriate conditions that can lead to the rehabilitation of the offender, reparations to the community, and the promotion of a sense of responsibility in ways that jail cannot. However, it is also a punitive sanction. Indeed, it is the punitive aspect of a conditional sentence that distinguishes it from probation. As discussed above, it was not Parliament's intention that offenders who would otherwise have gone to jail for up to two years less a day now be given probation or some equivalent thereof.

[100]  Thus, a conditional sentence can achieve both punitive and restorative objectives. To the extent that both punitive and restorative objectives can be achieved in a given case, a conditional sentence is likely a better sanction than incarceration. Where the need for punishment is particularly pressing, and there is little opportunity to achieve any restorative objectives, incarceration will likely be the more attractive sanction. However, even where restorative objectives cannot be readily satisfied, a conditional sentence will be preferable to incarceration in cases where a conditional sentence can achieve the objectives of denunciation and deterrence as effectively as incarceration. This follows from the principle of restraint in s. 718.2(d) and (e), which militates in favour of alternatives to incarceration where appropriate in the circumstances. ...

(V)  SUMMARY

[113]  In sum, in determining whether a conditional sentence would be consistent with the fundamental purpose and principles of sentencing, sentencing judges should consider which sentencing objectives figure most prominently in the factual circumstances of the particular case before them. Where a combination of both punitive and restorative objectives may be achieved, a conditional sentence will likely be more appropriate than incarceration. In determining whether restorative objectives can be satisfied in a particular case, the judge should consider the offender's prospects of rehabilitation, including whether the offender has proposed a particular plan of rehabilitation; the availability of appropriate community service and treatment programs; whether the offender has acknowledged his or her wrongdoing and expresses remorse; as well as the victim's wishes as revealed by the victim impact statement (considera-

tion of which is now mandatory pursuant to s. 722 of the *Code*). This list is not exhaustive.

[114]  Where punitive objectives such as denunciation and deterrence are particularly pressing, such as cases in which there are aggravating circumstances, incarceration will generally be the preferable sanction. This may be so notwithstanding the fact that restorative goals might be achieved by a conditional sentence. Conversely, a conditional sentence may provide sufficient denunciation and deterrence, even in cases in which restorative objectives are of diminished importance, depending on the nature of the conditions imposed, the duration of the conditional sentence, and the circumstances of the offender and the community in which the conditional sentence is to be served.

[115]  Finally, it bears pointing out that a conditional sentence may be imposed even in circumstances where there are aggravating circumstances relating to the offence or the offender. Aggravating circumstances will obviously increase the need for denunciation and deterrence. However, it would be a mistake to rule out the possibility of a conditional sentence *ab initio* simply because aggravating factors are present. I repeat that each case must be considered individually.

[116]  Sentencing judges will frequently be confronted with situations in which some objectives militate in favour of a conditional sentence, whereas others favour incarceration. In those cases, the trial judge will be called upon to weigh the various objectives in fashioning a fit sentence. As La Forest J. stated in *R. v. Lyons*, [1987] 2 S.C.R. 309, at p. 329, "[i]n a rational system of sentencing, the respective importance of prevention, deterrence, retribution and rehabilitation will vary according to the nature of the crime and the circumstances of the offender." There is no easy test or formula that the judge can apply in weighing these factors. Much will depend on the good judgment and wisdom of sentencing judges, whom Parliament vested with considerable discretion in making these determinations pursuant to s. 718.3. ...

## *VIII.  Disposition*

[132]  I would allow the appeal. Accordingly, the 18-month sentence of incarceration imposed by the trial judge should be restored. However, given that the respondent has already served the conditional sentence imposed by the Court of Appeal in its entirety, and that the Crown stated in oral argument that it was not seeking any further punishment, I would stay the service of the sentence of incarceration.

## Restitution

Under s. 738 of the *Criminal Code*, an offender who is convicted or subject to an absolute or conditional discharge can be required to make restitution for damage to property and pecuniary losses from bodily harm that result from the commission of the offence or the arrest of the offender. Reasonable moving and temporary housing costs may also be ordered in cases involving bodily harm or the threat of bodily harm to the offender's spouse or child.

## Fines

Under s. 734(2) of the *Criminal Code*, a court may fine an offender only if it is satisfied that the offender is able to pay the fine or work the fine off under a fine option program contemplated under s. 736. A previous provision, examined in the next case, only required the court to consider the ability of offenders between the ages of 16 and 21 to pay their fines.

### R. v. Hebb
Nova Scotia Supreme Court, Trial Division
(1989), 89 N.S.R. (2d) 137

KELLY J.: In August of 1987 Judith Ann Hebb was convicted of the theft of a package of cigarettes and was fined $500.00 and costs or thirty days in default. She was ordered to pay the fine before a specific date but was unable to pay it within that time and was granted two extensions of time by the court. She failed to make any fine payment within the designated time limits. After her last failure, the Provincial Court issued a warrant of committal to the effect that Ms. Hebb was committed to thirty days' imprisonment.

[The trial judge found that the accused's monthly income was approximately $450 to $500 with $300 being paid for rent in a rooming house with the balance being normally insufficient for her other expenses. The accused was 35 years of age.]

I make the following further findings from the evidence:

1. That Judith Ann Hebb is essentially unemployable and that there is no realistic prospect of her earning an income in excess of her most basic needs.

2. That during the relevant period, that is from the date of her conviction and sentence to the time of this hearing, she did not have the financial ability to pay the fine imposed upon her and it is highly probable that she will never have the financial resources with which to pay the fine.

3. That the nature of social assistance available in this province is such that she will not receive additional funding for the purpose of assisting her with the payment of the criminal fine.

4. Current statistics indicate that approximately 40% of people jailed in Nova Scotia provincial institutions were so committed for having defaulted on the payment of a fine. Of these admissions approximately two-thirds pay their fine and gain their release, normally the day of or the day after their committal. The other one-third serve their time in full for their default of payment of fine. The agreed statement of facts also indicates that on a review of two particular days, one in 1986 and one in 1988, 6.5% and 5.5% of all inmates in the province were fine defaulters.

5. There is no fine option program currently in place in Nova Scotia although a pilot project is planned in the near future for the Bridgewater area.

After making these findings of fact, the essential issue for the court to determine is whether a person sentenced to a fine and a period of time in jail in default of payment of that fine should be incarcerated if they do not pay that fine by reason of being impecunious and unable to pay the fine.

There are those in our society who, for reasons of principle or merely because of a stubborn nature, will refuse to pay a fine and accept incarceration in lieu of payment of such a fine. There are those as well who would seek to test or challenge the administrators of our judicial system and who fail to pay fines and hope that the bureaucracy somehow fumbles so that they are forgotten in the process. These are situations where a person can exercise a true choice as to whether they wish to pay the fine or suffer the consequence.

But no such choice exists for those who are unable to pay their fine because of a temporary financial limitation brought on by either misfortune or bad judgment on their part. As well, no such choice exists for those, such as the applicant in this matter, who are the walking wounded of our society, those who cannot now and are unlikely ever to be in a position to pay a fine of any amount in excess of a few dollars. Judith Ann Hebb comes before this court as a person without financial resources or any prospect of having sufficient resources to pay the fine which is assessed against her.

Parliament has accepted the concept, that there should be an alternative method of sentence satisfaction for a person punished by a fine. This is the fine option program provided for in s. 646.1 of the *Criminal Code* [now s. 718.1] and which has been implemented in a number of other jurisdictions in Canada but has yet to be introduced in Nova Scotia. In such a program a person works off a fine by earning credit for work performed, usually community service. It is argued by counsel for Ms. Hebb that the absence of such a program in this province while it is available in other jurisdictions results in her being treated differently than persons in those jurisdictions. They argue that the criminal law in that respect violates Ms. Hebb's rights to equality as guaranteed by s. 15 of the *Charter*.

In general, Ms. Hebb's counsel argue that her position is analogous to that of imprisonment for debt and submit that the courts should strike down any legislative scheme which is similar to the long ago discredited system of imprisonment for debt.

Before determining if any of Ms. Hebb's constitutional rights have been violated or if any legislation restricts her constitutionally protected rights, a review of the existing provisions of the *Criminal Code* which affect this application would be appropriate. ...

Sections 646(10) and 646(11) are of particular relevance in this matter but a full reading of the section is helpful to understand the legislative scheme within which these subsections are applied:

(10) Where a person who has been allowed time for payment of a fine appears to the court to be not less than sixteen nor more than twenty-one years of age, the court shall, before issuing a warrant committing the person to prison for default of payment

of the fine, obtain and consider a report concerning the conduct and means to pay of the accused.

(11)  Where the time has been allowed for payment under subsection (4), the court that imposed the sentence may, on an application by or on behalf of the accused, allow further time for payment, subject to any rules made by the court under section 482.

### The Fine with Imprisonment in Default as a Sentence

As has been held in *R. v. Grady* (1973), 5 N.S.R. (2d) 264 (C.A.), the primary purpose of sentencing is to protect the public. This purpose can be effected either by rehabilitation or deterrence or a combination of the two. The fine does not normally serve to reform or rehabilitate an offender but in some cases may serve to deter an offender or others from criminal activity. This deterrent effect must obviously be related to the financial capacity of the offender. A court, before determining the amount of the fine, should take into consideration the ability of the offender to pay the fine. If this is not done a fine which may be insignificant to a person of great wealth can well be an impossible burden for an impecunious offender. Thus, a fine of some substance is only appropriate when a court concludes that deterrence is an appropriate method of protecting the public under the circumstances of the offence and the individual and secondly, when the offender is capable of paying the fine.

Professor K.B. Jobson in his article *Fines*, (1970), 16 *McGill L.J.* 633, states at page 644:

> … Whether or not imprisonment in default is rationalized on the ground that the imprisonment is not a punishment of the offence, but merely an enforcement device for collection of fines, until the law prohibits imprisonment as a routine alternative to payment of fines, and bars the use of imprisonment as a routine response to failure to pay, the penal law will continue to be used as an instrument of oppression against the poor.

If the allocation of default time is not part of the considered sentence, then poor persons could be routinely fined and imprisoned in default unless there is a possibility of review. It is irrefutable that it is irrational to imprison an offender who does not have the capacity to pay on the basis that imprisonment will force him or her to pay. If the sentencing court chooses a fine as the appropriate sentence, it is obviously discarding imprisonment as being unnecessary under the particular circumstances. However, default provisions may be appropriate in circumstances where the offender may *choose* not to pay, presumably on principle, and would elect to spend time incarcerated rather than make a payment to the state. For the impecunious offenders, however, imprisonment in default of payment of a fine is not an alternative punishment—he or she does not have any real choice in the matter. At least, this is the situation until fine option programs or related programs are in place. In effect, imprisonment of the poor in default of payment of a fine becomes a punishment that wouldn't otherwise be imposed except for the economic limitations of the convicted person.

Section 646(10) of the *Criminal Code*, in directing a review or consideration by the court before the issuing of a warrant (albeit only to those between 16 and 22 years of age), is a clear protection against imprisonment of persons who do not have the means to pay a fine.

Is it discriminatory to afford persons 18 to 22 years of age the protection of a review under s. 646(10) of the *Criminal Code* and not afford the same protection to someone 35 years of age? "Equality under the law" and "equal benefits of the law" requires that no special class of person be chosen for the imposition of special burdens nor for the receipt of special benefits. Here those over 22 are selected to be treated differently by the criminal law from those who are 21 years of age or younger.

Whatever the original purpose behind s. 646(10), its continued existence creates a class of individuals—those between the ages of 16 and 22 years, who are treated differently than those who are older. Although some of this class, those under the age of 18, are presumably not similarly situated to those more than 21 years of age, it is my opinion that those in the age group of 18 to 22 are similarly situate to the older class in relation to the purpose of the law. Under all of these circumstances, the difference in treatment between these two groups is discriminatory in the sense explained by the courts.

To adopt the words of MacDonald, J.A., in *R. v. Hardiman* (1987), 78 N.S.R. (2d) 55, 193 A.P.R. 55 (C.A.), this "… *unequal and unjustified application of substantive criminal law is on its face prima facie discriminatory within the meaning of s. 15 of the Charter.*"

In my view the creation of a special class who are to receive special benefits under the criminal law creates a *prima facie* violation of a right under s. 15(1) to equal benefits of the law and is clearly discriminatory. …

Here the Crown has not satisfactorily provided the court with evidence to support the imposition of a distinction between those under 22 years of age and those older. A rational basis has not been demonstrated for legislating that a 21 year old person should have a "report" or an inquiry into his or her means before incarceration for default and a person over that age should not have the benefit of such an important inquiry. Whether such distinction was justifiable in the past is not relevant to its present operation. Parliament has determined that those persons under the age of 18 years should have special protections of the law because of their age. There is absolutely no evidence to suggest that any such benefits should be extended to include those up to the age of 22.

I therefore find that the age specific phrase s. 646(10) of the *Criminal Code* is in contravention of s. 15(1) of the *Charter* and is not a reasonable limit on *Charter* rights justified in accordance with s. 1 of the *Charter*. …

To sever the age-related phrase provides protection to persons of all ages who are charged with a crime in that they cannot be incarcerated for failure to pay a fine until a judicial review of their situation is held. On the other hand, by severing the complete s. 646(10), this protection is removed for all persons, including the age group which Parliament determined were worthy of that special protection. …

Section 15 of the *Charter* is legislative expression of their respect for equality and for equal benefits of the law and the court is not unjustifiably interfering into the legislative domain when it applies that *Charter* in such a way as to expand the benefits of the principles enunciated in the *Charter*. It would not be "appropriate and just in the circumstances" to deprive 18 to 22 year olds of such an important safeguard as the requirement of judicial review before incarceration.

## *Conclusion*

Some things are so offensive to the rule of common sense and so offend our sense of propriety that there is no need for precedent of law to condemn them or requirement of scholastic constitutional principle to denounce them.

The *Charter* is a fresh but already treasured legacy that demands from our society those principles of fairness and justice which are inherent in the soul of a mature democracy.

Our *Constitution* enshrines a system of justice based upon a belief in the inherent dignity and worth of every individual. (See *R. v. Big M Drug Mart Ltd.*, *supra*, page 47; *R. v. Oakes*, *supra*, at page 333 and *Reference Re Section 94(2) of the Motor Vehicle Act (B.C.)* (1985), 63 N.R. 266; 48 C.R. (3d) 289 (S.C.C.), at page 317). That a person should be imprisoned only because of his or her inability to pay a fine is inconsistent with such a system.

I therefore conclude that the age-limiting phrase should be removed from s. 646(10) so as to make it age-neutral and it would thus be applied as reading as follows:

> 646(10) Where a person has been allowed time for payment of a fine, the court shall, before issuing a warrant committing the person to prison for default of payment of the fine, obtain and consider a report concerning the conduct and means to pay of the accused.

As there is not evidence that the court in the instant case "considered a report concerning the conduct and means to pay" of Ms. Hebb I grant her an order quashing the Warrant of Commitment.

---

See, generally, K. Jobson and A. Atkins, "Imprisonment in Default and Fundamental Justice" (1985-86), 28 *Crim. L.Q.* 251; A. MacDougall, "Are There No Prisons? Hebb: Imprisonment in Default of Fine Payment and Section 7 of the Charter" (1989), 69 C.R. (3d) 23; Ontario Law Reform Commission, *Report on the Basis of Liability for Provincial Offences* (1990).

## V. SENTENCING OF ABORIGINAL OFFENDERS

**R. v. Gladue**
Supreme Court of Canada
(1999), 133 C.C.C. (3d) 385

CORY and IACOBUCCI JJ.:

[1]  On September 3, 1996, the new Part XXIII of the *Criminal Code*, R.S.C., 1985, c. C-46, pertaining to sentencing came into force. These provisions codify for the first time the fundamental purpose and principles of sentencing. This appeal is particularly concerned with the new s. 718.2(e). It provides that all available sanctions other than imprisonment that are reasonable in the circumstances should be considered for all offenders, with particular attention to the circumstances of aboriginal offenders. This appeal must consider how this provision should be interpreted and applied.

*Factual Background*

[2]  The appellant, one of nine children, was born in McLennan, Alberta in 1976. Her mother, Marie Gladue, who was a Cree, left the family home in 1987 and died in a car accident in 1990. After 1987, the appellant and her siblings were raised by their father, Lloyd Chalifoux, a Metis. The appellant and the victim Reuben Beaver started to live together in 1993, when the appellant was 17 years old. Thereafter they had a daughter, Tanita. In August 1995, they moved to Nanaimo. Together with the appellant's father and two of her siblings, Tara and Bianca Chalifoux, they lived in a townhouse complex. By September 1995, the appellant and Beaver were engaged to be married, and the appellant was five months pregnant with their second child, a boy, whom the appellant subsequently named Reuben Ambrose Beaver in honour of his father.

[3]  In the early evening of September 16, 1995, the appellant was celebrating her 19th birthday. She and Reuben Beaver, who was then 20, were drinking beer with some friends and family members in the townhouse complex. The appellant suspected that Beaver was having an affair with her older sister, Tara. ...

[6]  Mr. Gretchin saw the appellant run toward Beaver with a large knife in her hand and, as she approached him, she told him that he had better run. Mr. Gretchin heard Beaver shriek in pain and saw him collapse in a pool of blood. The appellant had stabbed Beaver once in the left chest, and the knife had penetrated his heart. As the appellant went by on her return to her apartment, Mr. Gretchin heard her say, "I got you. I got you, you fucking bastard." The appellant was described as jumping up and down as if she had tagged someone. Mr. Gretchin said she did not appear to realize what she had done. At the time of the stabbing, the appellant had a blood-alcohol content of between 155 and 165 milligrams of alcohol in 100 millilitres of blood.

[7] On June 3, 1996, the appellant was charged with second degree murder. On February 11, 1997, following a preliminary hearing and after a jury had been selected, the appellant entered a plea of guilty to manslaughter.

[8] There was evidence which indicated that the appellant had stabbed Beaver before he fled from the apartment. A paring knife found on the living room floor of their apartment had a small amount of Beaver's blood on it, and a small stab wound was located on Beaver's right upper arm.

[9] There was also evidence that Beaver had subjected the appellant to some physical abuse in June 1994, while the appellant was pregnant with their daughter Tanita. Beaver was convicted of assault, and was given a 15-day intermittent sentence with one year's probation. …

[10] The appellant's sentencing took place 17 months after the stabbing. Pending her trial, she was released on bail and lived with her father. She took counselling for alcohol and drug abuse at Tillicum Haus Native Friendship Centre in Nanaimo, and completed Grade 10 and was about to start Grade 11. After the stabbing, the appellant was diagnosed as suffering from a hyperthyroid condition, which was said to produce an exaggerated reaction to any emotional situation. The appellant underwent radiation therapy to destroy some of her thyroid glands, and at the time of sentencing she was taking thyroid supplements which regulated her condition. During the time she was on bail, the appellant plead guilty to having breached her bail on one occasion by consuming alcohol.

[11] At the sentencing hearing, when asked if she had anything to say, the appellant stated that she was sorry about what happened, that she did not intend to do it, and that she was sorry to Beaver's family.

[12] In his submissions on sentence at trial, the appellant's counsel did not raise the fact that the appellant was an aboriginal offender but, when asked by the trial judge whether in fact the appellant was an aboriginal person, replied that she was Cree. When asked by the trial judge whether the town of McLennan, Alberta, where the appellant grew up, was an aboriginal community, defence counsel responded: "it's just a regular community." No other submissions were made at the sentencing hearing on the issue of the appellant's aboriginal heritage. Defence counsel requested a suspended sentence or a conditional sentence of imprisonment. Crown counsel argued in favour of a sentence of between three and five years' imprisonment.

[13] The appellant was sentenced to three years' imprisonment and to a ten-year weapons prohibition. Her appeal of the sentence to the British Columbia Court of Appeal was dismissed. …

[31] A core issue in this appeal is whether s. 718.2(e) should be understood as being remedial in nature, or whether s. 718.2(e), along with the other provisions of ss. 718 through 718.2, are simply a codification of *existing* sentencing principles. [Emphasis in original.] The respondent, although acknowledging that s. 718.2(e) was likely designed to encourage sentencing judges to experiment to some degree with alternatives to incarceration and to be sensitive to principles of restorative justice, at the same time favours the view that ss. 718-718.2 are largely a restatement of existing law. Alternatively, the appellant argues strongly that s. 718.2(e)'s specific reference to aboriginal offenders can have no purpose unless it effects a change in the law.

The appellant advances the view that s. 718.2(e) is in fact an "affirmative action" provision justified under s. 15(2) of the *Canadian Charter of Rights and Freedoms*. ...

[33] In our view, s. 718.2(e) is *more* than simply a re-affirmation of existing sentencing principles. [Emphasis in original.] The remedial component of the provision consists not only in the fact that it codifies a principle of sentencing, but, far more importantly, in its direction to sentencing judges to undertake the process of sentencing aboriginal offenders differently, in order to endeavour to achieve a truly fit and proper sentence in the particular case. It should be said that the words of s. 718.2(e) do not alter the fundamental duty of the sentencing judge to impose a sentence that is fit for the offence and the offender. For example, as we will discuss below, it will generally be the case as a practical matter that particularly violent and serious offences will result in imprisonment for aboriginal offenders as often as for non-aboriginal offenders. What s. 718.2(e) does alter is the method of analysis which each sentencing judge must use in determining the nature of a fit sentence for an aboriginal offender. In our view, the scheme of Part XXIII of the *Criminal Code*, the context underlying the enactment of s. 718.2(e), and the legislative history of the provision all support an interpretation of s. 718.2(e) as having this important remedial purpose. ...

[38] The wording of s. 718.2(e) on its face, then, requires both consideration of alternatives to the use of imprisonment as a penal sanction generally, which amounts to a restraint in the resort to imprisonment as a sentence, and recognition by the sentencing judge of the unique circumstances of aboriginal offenders. ...

[40] It is true that there is ample jurisprudence supporting the principle that prison should be used as a sanction of last resort. It is equally true, though, that the sentencing amendments which came into force in 1996 as the new Part XXIII have changed the range of available penal sanctions in a significant way. The availability of the conditional sentence of imprisonment, in particular, alters the sentencing landscape in a manner which gives an entirely new meaning to the principle that imprisonment should be resorted to only where no other sentencing option is reasonable in the circumstances. The creation of the conditional sentence suggests, on its face, a desire to lessen the use of incarceration. The general principle expressed in s. 718.2(e) must be construed and applied in this light.

[41] Further support for the view that s. 718.2(e)'s expression of the principle of restraint in sentencing is remedial, rather than simply a codification, is provided by the articulation of the purpose of sentencing in s. 718. ...

[43] Section 718 now sets out the purpose of sentencing in the following terms:

> 718. The fundamental purpose of sentencing is to contribute, along with crime prevention initiatives, to respect for the law and the maintenance of a just, peaceful and safe society by imposing just sanctions that have one or more of the following objectives:
>
>> (a) to denounce unlawful conduct;
>>
>> (b) to deter the offender and other persons from committing offences;
>>
>> (c) to separate offenders from society, where necessary;
>>
>> (d) to assist in rehabilitating offenders;

(e) *to provide reparations for harm done to victims or to the community*; and

(f) *to promote a sense of responsibility in offenders, and acknowledgment of the harm done to victims and to the community.* [Emphasis added.]

Clearly, s. 718 is, in part, a restatement of the basic sentencing aims, which are listed in para. (a) through (d). What are new, though, are paras. (e) and (f), which along with para. (d) focus upon the restorative goals of repairing the harms suffered by individual victims and by the community as a whole, promoting a sense of responsibility and an acknowledgment of the harm caused on the part of the offender, and attempting to rehabilitate or heal the offender. The concept of restorative justice which underpins paras. (d), (e), and (f) is briefly discussed below, but as a general matter restorative justice involves some form of restitution and reintegration into the community. The need for offenders to take responsibility for their actions is central to the sentencing process: D. Kwochka, "Aboriginal Injustice: Making Room for a Restorative Paradigm" (1996), 60 *Sask. L. Rev.* 153, at p. 165. Restorative sentencing goals do not usually correlate with the use of prison as a sanction. In our view, Parliament's choice to include (e) and (f) alongside the traditional sentencing goals must be understood as evidencing an intention to expand the parameters of the sentencing analysis for all offenders. The principle of restraint expressed in s. 718.2(e) will necessarily be informed by this re-orientation.

[44] Just as the context of Part XXIII supports the view that s. 718.2(e) has a remedial purpose for all offenders, the scheme of Part XXIII also supports the view that s. 718.2(e) has a particular remedial role for aboriginal peoples. The respondent is correct to point out that there is jurisprudence which pre-dates the enactment of s. 718.2(e) in which aboriginal offenders have been sentenced differently in light of their unique circumstances. However, the existence of such jurisprudence is not, on its own, especially probative of the issue of whether s. 718.2(e) has a remedial role. There is also sentencing jurisprudence which holds, for example, that a court must consider the unique circumstances of offenders who are battered spouses, or who are mentally disabled. Although the validity of the principles expressed in this latter jurisprudence is unchallenged by the 1996 sentencing reforms, one does not find reference to these principles in Part XXIII. If Part XXIII were indeed a codification of principles regarding the appropriate method of sentencing different categories of offenders, one would expect to find such references. The wording of s. 718.2(e), viewed in light of the absence of similar stipulations in the remainder of Part XXIII, reveals that Parliament has chosen to single out aboriginal offenders for particular attention. ...

### D. The Context of the Enactment of Section 718.2(e)

[49] Further guidance as to the scope and content of Parliament's remedial purpose in enacting s. 718.2(e) may be derived from the social context surrounding the enactment of the provision. On this point, it is worth noting that, although there is quite a wide divergence between the positions of the appellant and the respondent as to how s. 718.2(e) should be applied in practice, there is general agreement between them, and indeed between the parties and all interveners, regarding the mischief in response to which s. 718.2(e) was enacted.

[50] The parties and interveners agree that the purpose of s. 718.2(e) i᠁ ᠁o respond to the problem of overincarceration in Canada, and to respond, in particular, to the more acute problem of the disproportionate incarceration of aboriginal peoples. They also agree that one of the roles of s. 718.2(e), and of various other provisions in Part XXIII, is to encourage sentencing judges to apply principles of restorative justice alongside or in the place of other, more traditional sentencing principles when making sentencing determinations. As the respondent states in its factum before this Court, s. 718.2(e) "provides the necessary flexibility and authority for sentencing judges to resort to the restorative model of justice in sentencing aboriginal offenders and to reduce the imposition of jail sentences where to do so would not sacrifice the traditional goals of sentencing."

[51] The fact that the parties and interveners are in general agreement among themselves regarding the purpose of s. 718.2(e) is not determinative of the issue as a matter of statutory construction. However, as we have suggested, on the above points of agreement the parties and interveners are correct. A review of the problem of overincarceration in Canada, and of its peculiarly devastating impact upon Canada's aboriginal peoples, provides additional insight into the purpose and proper application of this new provision.

(1)  The Problem of Overincarceration in Canada

[52]  Canada is a world leader in many fields, particularly in the areas of progressive social policy and human rights. Unfortunately, our country is also distinguished as being a world leader in putting people in prison. Although the United States has by far the highest rate of incarceration among industrialized democracies, at over 600 inmates per 100,000 population, Canada's rate of approximately 130 inmates per 100,000 population places it second or third highest: see First Report on Progress for Federal/Provincial/Territorial Ministers Responsible for Justice, *Corrections Population Growth* (1997), Annex B, at p. 1; Bulletin of U.S. Bureau of Justice Statistics, "Prison and Jail Inmates at Midyear 1998" (1999); The Sentencing Project, *Americans Behind Bars: U.S. and International Use of Incarceration, 1995* (1997), at p. 1. Moreover, the rate at which Canadian courts have been imprisoning offenders has risen sharply in recent years, although there has been a slight decline of late: see Statistics Canada, *Infomat: A Weekly Review* (February 27, 1998), at p. 5. This record of incarceration rates obviously cannot instil a sense of pride. ...

[57]  ... [A]lthough imprisonment is intended to serve the traditional sentencing goals of separation, deterrence, denunciation, and rehabilitation, there is widespread consensus that imprisonment has not been successful in achieving some of these goals. Overincarceration is a long-standing problem that has been many times publicly acknowledged but never addressed in a systematic manner by Parliament. In recent years, compared to other countries, sentences of imprisonment in Canada have increased at an alarming rate. The 1996 sentencing reforms embodied in Part XXIII, and s. 718.2(e) in particular, must be understood as a reaction to the overuse of prison as a sanction, and must accordingly be given appropriate force as remedial provisions.

(2)  The Overrepresentation of Aboriginal Canadians in Penal Institutions

[58]  If overreliance upon incarceration is a problem with the general population, it is of much greater concern in the sentencing of aboriginal Canadians. In the mid-1980s, aboriginal people were about 2 percent of the population of Canada, yet they made up 10 percent of the penitentiary population. In Manitoba and Saskatchewan, aboriginal people constituted something between 6 and 7 percent of the population, yet in Manitoba they represented 46 percent of the provincial admissions and in Saskatchewan 60 percent: see M. Jackson, *Locking up Natives in Canada* (1988-89), 23 *U.B.C. L. Rev.* 215 (article originally prepared as a report of the Canadian Bar Association Committee on Imprisonment and Release in June 1988), at pp. 215-16. The situation has not improved in recent years. By 1997, aboriginal peoples constituted closer to 3 percent of the population of Canada and amounted to 12 percent of all federal inmates: Solicitor General of Canada, Consolidated Report, *Towards a Just, Peaceful and Safe Society: The Corrections and Conditional Release Act—Five Years Later* (1998), at pp. 142-55. The situation continues to be particularly worrisome in Manitoba, where in 1995-96 they made up 55 percent of admissions to provincial correctional facilities, and in Saskatchewan, where they made up 72 percent of admissions. A similar, albeit less drastic situation prevails in Alberta and British Columbia: Canadian Centre for Justice Statistics, *Adult Correctional Services in Canada, 1995-96* (1997), at p. 30. ...

[61]  Not surprisingly, the excessive imprisonment of aboriginal people is only the tip of the iceberg insofar as the estrangement of the aboriginal peoples from the Canadian criminal justice system is concerned. Aboriginal people are overrepresented in virtually all aspects of the system. As this Court recently noted in *R. v. Williams*, [1998] 1 S.C.R. 1128, at para. 58, there is widespread bias against aboriginal people within Canada, and "[t]here is evidence that this widespread racism has translated into systemic discrimination in the criminal justice system."

[62]  Statements regarding the extent and severity of this problem are disturbingly common. In *Bridging the Cultural Divide*, supra, at p. 309, the Royal Commission on Aboriginal Peoples listed as its first "Major Findings and Conclusions" the following striking yet representative statement:

> The Canadian criminal justice system has failed the Aboriginal peoples of Canada—First Nations, Inuit and Métis people, on-reserve and off-reserve, urban and rural—in all territorial and governmental jurisdictions. The principal reason for this crushing failure is the fundamentally different world views of Aboriginal and non-Aboriginal people with respect to such elemental issues as the substantive content of justice and the process of achieving justice.

[63]  To the same effect, the Aboriginal Justice Inquiry of Manitoba described the justice system in Manitoba as having failed aboriginal people on a "massive scale," referring particularly to the substantially different cultural values and experiences of aboriginal people: *The Justice System and Aboriginal People*, supra, at pp. 1 and 86.

[64]  These findings cry out for recognition of the magnitude and gravity of the problem, and for responses to alleviate it. The figures are stark and reflect what may fairly be termed a crisis in the Canadian criminal justice system. The drastic

overrepresentation of aboriginal peoples within both the Canadian prison population and the criminal justice system reveals a sad and pressing social problem. It is reasonable to assume that Parliament, in singling out aboriginal offenders for distinct sentencing treatment in s. 718.2(e), intended to attempt to redress this social problem to some degree. The provision may properly be seen as Parliament's direction to members of the judiciary to inquire into the causes of the problem and to endeavour to remedy it, to the extent that a remedy is possible through the sentencing process.

[65] It is clear that sentencing innovation by itself cannot remove the causes of aboriginal offending and the greater problem of aboriginal alienation from the criminal justice system. The unbalanced ratio of imprisonment for aboriginal offenders flows from a number of sources, including poverty, substance abuse, lack of education, and the lack of employment opportunities for aboriginal people. It arises also from bias against aboriginal people and from an unfortunate institutional approach that is more inclined to refuse bail and to impose more and longer prison terms for aboriginal offenders. There are many aspects of this sad situation which cannot be addressed in these reasons. What can and must be addressed, though, is the limited role that sentencing judges will play in remedying injustice against aboriginal peoples in Canada. Sentencing judges are among those decision-makers who have the power to influence the treatment of aboriginal offenders in the justice system. They determine most directly whether an aboriginal offender will go to jail, or whether other sentencing options may be employed which will play perhaps a stronger role in restoring a sense of balance to the offender, victim, and community, and in preventing future crime. ...

## VI. Summary

[93] Let us see if a general summary can be made of what has been discussed in these reasons.

1. Part XXIII of the *Criminal Code* codifies the fundamental purpose and principles of sentencing and the factors that should be considered by a judge in striving to determine a sentence that is fit for the offender and the offence.

2. Section 718.2(e) mandatorily requires sentencing judges to consider all available sanctions other than imprisonment and to pay particular attention to the circumstances of aboriginal offenders.

3. Section 718.2(e) is not simply a codification of existing jurisprudence. It is remedial in nature. Its purpose is to ameliorate the serious problem of overrepresentation of aboriginal people in prisons, and to encourage sentencing judges to have recourse to a restorative approach to sentencing. There is a judicial duty to give the provision's remedial purpose real force.

4. Section 718.2(e) must be read and considered in the context of the rest of the factors referred to in that section and in light of all of Part XXIII. All principles and factors set out in Part XXIII must be taken into consideration in determining the fit sentence. Attention should be paid to the fact that Part XXIII,

through ss. 718, 718.2(e), and 742.1, among other provisions, has placed a new emphasis upon decreasing the use of incarceration.

5. Sentencing is an individual process and in each case the consideration must continue to be what is a fit sentence for this accused for this offence in this community. However, the effect of s. 718.2(e) is to alter the method of analysis which sentencing judges must use in determining a fit sentence for aboriginal offenders.

6. Section 718.2(e) directs sentencing judges to undertake the sentencing of aboriginal offenders individually, but also differently, because the circumstances of aboriginal people are unique. In sentencing an aboriginal offender, the judge must consider:

   (A) The unique systemic or background factors which may have played a part in bringing the particular aboriginal offender before the courts; and

   (B) The types of sentencing procedures and sanctions which may be appropriate in the circumstances for the offender because of his or her particular aboriginal heritage or connection.

7. In order to undertake these considerations the trial judge will require information pertaining to the accused. Judges may take judicial notice of the broad systemic and background factors affecting aboriginal people, and of the priority given in aboriginal cultures to a restorative approach to sentencing. In the usual course of events, additional case-specific information will come from counsel and from a pre-sentence report which takes into account the factors set out in #6, which in turn may come from representations of the relevant aboriginal community which will usually be that of the offender. The offender may waive the gathering of that information.

8. If there is no alternative to incarceration the length of the term must be carefully considered.

9. The section is not to be taken as a means of automatically reducing the prison sentence of aboriginal offenders; nor should it be assumed that an offender is receiving a more lenient sentence simply because incarceration is not imposed.

10. The absence of alternative sentencing programs specific to an aboriginal community does not eliminate the ability of a sentencing judge to impose a sanction that takes into account principles of restorative justice and the needs of the parties involved.

11. Section 718.2(e) applies to all aboriginal persons wherever they reside, whether on- or off-reserve, in a large city or a rural area. In defining the relevant aboriginal community for the purpose of achieving an effective sentence, the term "community" must be defined broadly so as to include any network of support and interaction that might be available, including in an urban centre. At the same time, the residence of the aboriginal offender in an

urban centre that lacks any network of support does not relieve the sentencing judge of the obligation to try to find an alternative to imprisonment.

12. Based on the foregoing, the jail term for an aboriginal offender may in some circumstances be less than the term imposed on a non-aboriginal offender for the same offence.

13. It is unreasonable to assume that aboriginal peoples do not believe in the importance of traditional sentencing goals such as deterrence, denunciation, and separation, where warranted. In this context, generally, the more serious and violent the crime, the more likely it will be as a practical matter that the terms of imprisonment will be the same for similar offences and offenders, whether the offender is aboriginal or non-aboriginal.

### *VII. Was There an Error Made in This Case?*

[94] From the foregoing analysis it can be seen that the sentencing judge, who did not have the benefit of these reasons, fell into error. He may have erred in limiting the application of s. 718.2(e) to the circumstances of aboriginal offenders living in rural areas or on-reserve. Moreover, and perhaps as a consequence of the first error, he does not appear to have considered the systemic or background factors which may have influenced the appellant to engage in criminal conduct, or the possibly distinct conception of sentencing held by the appellant, by the victim Beaver's family, and by their community. However it should be emphasized that the sentencing judge did take active steps to obtain at least some information regarding the appellant's aboriginal heritage. In this regard he received little if any assistance from counsel on this issue although they too were acting without the benefit of these reasons. ...

[96] In most cases, errors such as those in the courts below would be sufficient to justify sending the matter back for a new sentencing hearing. It is difficult for this Court to determine a fit sentence for the appellant according to the suggested guidelines set out herein on the basis of the very limited evidence before us regarding the appellant's aboriginal background. However, as both the trial judge and all members of the Court of Appeal acknowledged, the offence in question is a most serious one, properly described by Esson J.A. as a "near murder" (p. 138). Moreover, the offence involved domestic violence and a breach of the trust inherent in a spousal relationship. That aggravating factor must be taken into account in the sentencing of the aboriginal appellant as it would be for any offender. For that offence by this offender a sentence of three years' imprisonment was not unreasonable.

[97] More importantly, the appellant was granted day parole on August 13, 1997, after she had served six months in the Burnaby Correctional Centre for Women. She was directed to reside with her father, to take alcohol and substance abuse counselling and to comply with the requirements of the Electronic Monitoring Program. On February 25, 1998, the appellant was granted full parole with the same conditions as the ones applicable to her original release on day parole.

[98] In this case, the results of the sentence with incarceration for six months and the subsequent controlled release were in the interests of both the appellant and

society. In these circumstances, we do not consider that it would be in the interests of justice to order a new sentencing hearing in order to canvass the appellant's circumstances as an aboriginal offender.

[99]  In the result, the appeal is dismissed.

---

In *R. v. Wells* (2000), 141 C.C.C.(3d) 129, the Supreme Court of Canada dismissed an aboriginal accused's appeal from a sentence of 20 months' imprisonment for sexual assault. Iacobucci J. stated for the court:

> Notwithstanding what may well be different approaches to sentencing as between aboriginal and non-aboriginal conceptions of sentencing, it is reasonable to assume that for some aboriginal offenders, and depending upon the nature of the offence, the goals of denunciation and deterrence are fundamentally relevant to the offender's community. As held in *Gladue*, at para. 79, to the extent that generalizations may be made, the more violent and serious the offence, the more likely as a practical matter that the appropriate sentence will not differ as between aboriginal and non-aboriginal offenders, given that in these circumstances, the goals of denunciation and deterrence are accorded increasing significance.

On the issue of aboriginal offenders and sentencing, see, generally, M. Jackson, "Locking Up Natives in Canada" (1989), 23 *U.B.C.L.R.* 215; B. Archibald, "Sentencing and Visible Minorities: Equality and Affirmative Action in the Criminal Justice System" (1989), 12 *Dalhousie L.J.* 377; F. Sugar and L. Fox, "Nistum Peyako Séht'wawin Iskwewak: Breaking Chains" (1989-90), 3 *C.J.W.L.* 465; P. Stenning and J. Roberts, "Empty Promises: Parliament, the Supreme Court and the Sentencing of Aboriginal Offenders" (2001), 64 *Sask. L. Rev.* 137; and J. Rudin and K. Roach, "Broken Promises: A Response to Stenning and Roberts, 'Empty Promises'" (2002), 65 *Sask. L. Rev.* 3 and other articles in that response forum.

## ADDITIONAL READING

- A. Manson, *The Law of Sentencing* (Toronto: Irwin Law, 2001);
- A. Manson, P. Healy, and G. Trotter, *Sentencing and Penal Policy in Canada: Cases, Materials, and Commentary* (Toronto: Emond Montgomery, 2000);
- J.V. Roberts and D. Cole, eds., *Making Sense of Sentencing* (Toronto: University of Toronto Press, 1999);
- K. Jobson and G. Ferguson, "Towards a Revised Sentencing Structure for Canada" (1987), 66 *Can. Bar Rev.* 1;
- K. Roach, "Smith and the Supreme Court: Implications for Sentencing Policy and Reform" (1989), 11 *Sup. Ct. L. Rev.* 433;
- J. Roberts and A. von Hirsch, "Statute Sentencing Reform: The Purpose and Principles of Sentencing" (1995), 37 *Crim. L.Q.* 220.